NEW ZEALAND CRICKET

2007 N
CR
ALMANACK

60th Edition

Edited by
Francis Payne
&
Ian Smith

Hodder Moa

SKY SPORT

The Editors welcome contributions from readers for inclusion in the *2008 Almanack*

Please correspond directly with the editors:

Francis Payne,
97 Bond Crescent,
Forrest Hill,
AUCKLAND.
Phone/Fax: (09) 410-5259
E-mail: francisp@xtra.co.nz

Ian Smith,
91 Kamahi Street,
Stokes Valley,
WELLINGTON.
Phone: (04) 9766-477
E-mail: ianelizabeth@paradise.net.nz

Front cover: Scott Styris — Photosport

Back cover: Craig Cumming — Photosport

ISBN 978-1-86971-120-7

A Hodder Moa Book

Published in 2007 by Hachette Livre NZ Ltd
4 Whetu Place, Mairangi Bay, Auckland, New Zealand
Printed by Everbest Printing Co. Ltd, China

CONTENTS

New Zealand Cricket Inc. 5
From the Editors 7
Diary of the Season 9
Players of the Year 15
Promising Players 16
Happenings 17
Obituaries 40
New Zealand Squads in Australia 66
Champions Trophy 75
Sri Lanka in New Zealand 82
New Zealand in Australia 94
Australia in New Zealand 103
ICC World Cup 108
MCC in New Zealand 124
International Summary 125
Provincial Summaries 127
State Championship Review and Match Reports 129
First-class Statistics
- Register of Players 155
- Register of Umpires 157
- Averages 158
- Leading Averages 160
- Centuries 161
- Century Partnerships 162
- Wicketkeeping Dismissals 164
- New Zealanders in Overseas Cricket 164
- Bowling Performances 165
- Career Records 166

State Shield 168
- Averages 190
- Career Records 192

State Twenty20 194
- Averages 203
- Career Records 205

Provincial A Team Competition 207
India Under 19 in New Zealand 209
National Under 19 Tournament 215
National Under 17 Tournament 217
Hawke Cup 219

Women's Cricket ... 225
New Zealand First-class Records
- First-class Match Defined ... 286
- Grounds ... 287
- Provincial Career Records ... 290
- Provincial Records ... 295
- Inter-Provincial Records ... 324
- Provincial Competition Winners ... 339
- Team Records ... 340
- Individual Records ... 349
- Career Records ... 379
- Highest Partnerships ... 386
- Families in First-class Cricket ... 392
- Redpath and Winsor Cups ... 397
- Touring Teams in New Zealand ... 401
- New Zealand Touring Teams ... 404

New Zealand Test Records
- Register of Players ... 414
- Register of Umpires ... 422
- Team Records ... 423
- Grounds ... 431
- Individual Records ... 434
- Record Partnerships ... 450
- Career Records ... 455

New Zealand Limited-over Records
- Limited-over Match Defined ... 463
- Team Records ... 465
- Individual Records ... 468
- History of the Limited-over Competition in New Zealand ... 476
- Inter-Provincial Records ... 477
- Record Partnerships ... 479
- Domestic Career Records ... 480

New Zealand One-day International Records
- Team Records ... 482
- Individual Records ... 497
- Walter Hadlee Trophies ... 501
- Record Partnerships ... 501
- Career Records ... 506

Amendments ... 508
Minor Cricket ... 512

NEW ZEALAND CRICKET

Office Bearers

2006/07

Patron
His Excellency The Hon. Anand Satyanand
Governor-General of New Zealand

President
D.O. Neely, M.B.E.

Vice-Presidents
The Presidents of Major Associations

Board
Sir John Anderson, K.B.E. *(chairman),* D.S. Currie Q.S.O, S.L. Boock, A. Urlwin, A.R. Isaac, S.A. Riddell, J.T.C. Vaughan, D. Radford

Chief Executive
M.C. Snedden

Auditors
Ernst and Young, Chartered Accountants

Solicitor
L.M.C. Robinson, Saunders Robinson

Bankers
The National Bank of New Zealand

Life Members
M. Brito, C.F. Collins, O.B.E., W.A. Hadlee, C.B.E. *(deceased)*, J.H. Heslop C.B.E., J.L. Kerr, O.B.E., J. Lamason, T. Macdonald, Q.S.M., P.F. McKelvey, M.B.E. C.N.Z.M., D.O. Neely, M.B.E., Hon. Justice B.J. Paterson, O.B.E. Q.C. C.N.Z.M., J.R. Reid, O.B.E., Y. Taylor, Sir Allan Wright, K.B.E.

Honorary Cricket Members
J.C. Alabaster, F.J. Cameron, M.B.E., R.O. Collinge, B.E. Congdon, O.B.E., R.S. Cunis, A.E. Dick, G.T. Dowling, O.B.E., J.W. Guy, D.R. Hadlee, B.F. Hastings, J.A. Hayes, H.J. Howarth, A.R. MacGibbon, R.C. Motz, V. Pollard, J.R. Reid, O.B.E., B.W. Sinclair, J.T. Sparling, E.W.T. Tindill, O.B.E., W.M. Wallace.

Honorary Member
H.H. Whiting.

National Selectors
Senior: J.G. Bracewell *(convenor),* Sir Richard Hadlee *(manager),* D.J. Nash, G.M. Turner
Age Group: D.R. Hadlee *(convenor)*, B.D. Morrison, B.L. Cairns, K. Patel, D.N. Patel *(co-opted)*
Women: S.J. Jenkin *(convenor),* J.E. Harris, P.D. Kinsella.

National Code of Conduct Commissioner
N.R.W. Davidson Q.C.

Statistician
F. Payne.

FROM THE EDITORS

The 2007 edition of the *New Zealand Cricket Almanack* celebrates two landmarks. It is the 60th edition overall and the 25th under the current editors. This issue contains the details of another full season starting with two New Zealand squads in Australia in July and ending with the World Cup in West Indies, which finished in April.

During this period the BlackCaps took part in the Champions Trophy in India, met Sri Lanka at home, played in the Commonwealth Bank Series in Australia, hosted the Chappell-Hadlee series and competed in the World Cup. The White Ferns had an early season Rose Bowl series in Australia and later took part in a four-nation tournament in India.

In addition, there was a full domestic schedule with the State Championship, State Shield, an enlarged State Twenty20 competition plus the women's State League programme. There were also the Provincial A team competition, the Under 19 and Under 17 tournaments plus the Hawke Cup and the Women's National Development tourney. All in all a very full season to record.

The World Cup and More

Most attention was focused on the World Cup. The BlackCaps went into the tournament as the third-ranked team, were defeated in the semi-final so really finished as per their seeding. They had gone to the West Indies full of optimism after their 3-0 win in the Chappell-Hadlee series, looking to reach the final for the first time, or even better, win the whole thing.

The Australian team which came to New Zealand was certainly without some leading names, although their bowling attack was basically the same as they used in the World Cup. New Zealand's achievement of inflicting the first ever ten wicket defeat on Australia in a one-day international by any country, winning a one-day series against Australia for the first time and successfully chasing two huge targets was still a superb effort.

As far as New Zealand was concerned, the outcome of the Chappell-Hadlee series was just what the game in this country needed. The shortened international season had long finished and rugby had started at an unprecedented early time of the year. The World Cup was in danger of slipping off the sports fans' radar but New Zealand's memorable efforts against Australia brought cricket right back into the spotlight – and rightly so. After all, it was still only February!

The BlackCaps won their World Cup pool by defeating England, Kenya and Canada. They then beat West Indies, Bangladesh and Ireland before losing to Sri Lanka. They recovered to beat South Africa but then lost comprehensively to Australia. In the semi-final Sri Lanka had the better of New Zealand again.

Indeed, that seemed to be the story of New Zealand's season as in the Champions Trophy they had also accounted for South Africa but had lost to both Sri Lanka and Australia. In the Commonwealth Bank Series two wins, both against England, were not enough to progress to the final.

At Home

The National Bank Series against Sri Lanka finished all-square – the tests, the one-day internationals and the Twenty20 games were all shared. Most of the games, particularly the test matches, were played in bitterly cold conditions. The outcome of this was that neither team were seen to their best advantage. The weather made things difficult for the players, umpires, spectators, ground staff, television cameramen and all concerned.

In what seems to be an ever increasing change in New Zealand weather patterns, it would have been possible to play cricket in many parts of the country well into May and in much more pleasant conditions than the matches against Sri Lanka were played in.

The White Ferns

For the White Ferns it was so close yet so far away. They put up a good fight against Australia in the Rose Bowl but couldn't quite achieve a victory. They were the top qualifiers in the Quadrangular Tournament in India and had one of their best ever wins over Australia. However, their worst performance came in the final, so it was second place again.

The next Rose Bowl series will be played even earlier, in Darwin in July. The White Ferns will then travel to England to play three Twenty20 internationals and six one-day internationals in August.

The Domestic Scene

On the domestic front, the first competition was a pre-season Twenty20 tournament organised by the Southland Cricket Association with all six first-class sides competing. Unfortunately, it was ruined by the weather.

Auckland turned their recent form around and became the one-day team of the season, defeating Otago in both the final of the State Shield and Twenty20 competitions. The Twenty20 competition was expanded to a full round-robin and proved very popular.

Northern Districts won the State Championship in a drawn final against second placed Canterbury. Mention must be made of Michael Papps, who scored 1005 runs in just seven Championship games. He made four centuries and also had three scores in the nineties.

Five of the first six State Championship games were played in the Canterbury area in an effort to provide the best weather and playing conditions for early summer. The State League saw Canterbury defeat top qualifier Wellington in the final.

The South African Connection

Three of the players new to first-class cricket this past season were recent arrivals from South Africa while Colin de Grandhomme, former Zimbabwe Under 19 World Cup player, made his debut for Auckland. This continues the trend of recent seasons of players from southern Africa making their mark in New Zealand first-class cricket.

It does not stop there. The New Zealand Under 19 side had two players born in South Africa. Wicketkeeper Bradley Cachopa is the younger brother of Carl, who has already played for Auckland, while their father, Joe, coaches the 1st XI at Westlake Boys' High School (where Willie Watson, Lou Vincent and new NZC chief executive Justin Vaughan played their cricket). The South African and Zimbabwean influence is particularly strong around this area, East Coast Bays on Auckland's North Shore.

This new pool of players can only be good for the game in New Zealand, a welcome addition to the depth of talent available. It is surely a case of when, not if, the first African-born player represents New Zealand at the highest level.

Obituaries

As we have said on many previous occasions, this section is always difficult to keep up to date and we are again most grateful for the assistance of Warwick Larkins, Warren Shirley, John Heikell, Don Neely, Pat Malcon, Brian Adams and Adrian Hill.

This season saw the passing of some major names in New Zealand cricket, among them Walter Hadlee, Jack Kerr and Dick Motz. Full obituaries appear in this edition. We have also included obituaries for several New Zealand women players whose deaths had previously gone unrecorded. Our thanks to Carey Clements for this information.

Changes

Many things have changed during the 25 years that we have edited the *Almanack*. In 1983 only Richard Hadlee, Geoff Howarth and John Wright were playing county cricket compared with the eleven players who appeared in 2006. In 1983 there were no such things as New Zealand player contracts, let alone the provincial contracts that there are today.

Twenty20 cricket had never been thought of and the World Cup comprised just eight teams. There is now also an Under 19 World Cup. Prior to 1983 New Zealand had won 13 tests; they have now won 62. New Zealand had played 148 tests prior to 1983; they have now played 332.

Acknowledgments

We again wish to thank the associations, scorers and officials throughout the country who supplied information to us. In particular we would like to acknowledge the help of Catherine Campbell *(Women's Cricket)* and the rest of the staff at New Zealand Cricket and Chris McQuaid for his help with women's cricket.

Francis Payne & Ian Smith
June 2007

DIARY OF THE SEASON

July

4 Kirsty Flavell is reappointed as coach of the Canterbury women's team after initially announcing she would be stepping down from the position.

5 Canterbury sign South African Kruger van Wyk, a wicketkeeper and middle-order batsman, who is emigrating to New Zealand with the intention of challenging for future national selection. He was previously associated with Canterbury coach Dave Nosworthy at the Eastern Titans.

Andy Moles is appointed coach of Northern Districts. Moles, 45, who is currently coaching the England Under 19 team, played for Warwickshire and had previous spells as national coach of Hong Kong, Kenya and Scotland.

10 Martin Crowe is invited to deliver The Cowdrey Lecture at Lord's, following previous speakers Richie Benaud, Barry Richards, Sunil Gavaskar, Clive Lloyd and Geoffrey Boycott.

12 Central Districts reappoint Graham Barlow as coach for a further two seasons.

13 New Zealand Cricket name the National Junior Selection Panel for 2006/07. Dayle Hadlee is the convener along with Dipak Patel, Kaushik Patel and Lance Cairns. Michael Sharpe is appointed assistant coach to Dipak Patel with the New Zealand Under 19 team.

15 Stephen Cunis declines a contract to play for Canterbury as he has a full-time teaching job at Christchurch South Intermediate School and does not feel he could do justice to both roles if accepts the cricket offer. He remains available for selection, however.

17 The major associations announce their contracted players for the 2006/07 season. Each association can contract an additional player, twelve in all, under an interim player agreement between New Zealand Cricket, the major associations and the New Zealand Cricket Players' Association. Players without first-class experience who win contracts are: Derek de Boorder *(Auckland)*, Leighton Burtt *(Canterbury)* and Chris Cruikshank, Greg Hay and Dominic Rayner *(Central Districs)*. Kruger van Wyk *(Canterbury)* and Alun Evans *(Northern Districts)* are also named after committing themselves to New Zealand. Another feature is the return of Campbell Furlong who had retired in 2004.

Daryl Tuffey says he will head to Sydney in September to play club cricket as part of his comeback from a bicep injury. He plans to turn out for the Cronulla-based Sutherland club, who also have Glenn McGrath on their books.

26 Wellington name former Australian one-day pace bowler Anthony Stuart, 36, as their new coach. Stuart has been a New South Wales junior development officer, was the state's fast bowling coach and coached 2004/05 Sydney first-grade champions University.

August

1 Former New Zealand women's captain Maia Lewis resigns as Cricket Wellington's community cricket coordinator to take up a similar role in Auckland. Lewis, who was honoured as a Member of the New Zealand Order of Merit at Queen's Birthday, said the move was driven by the wish to be closer to her family. Lewis will be the women's cricket coordinator for Auckland Cricket.

2 The New Zealand Government announces it will pay New Zealand Cricket $406,000 compensation for the proposed tour by Zimbabwe in December 2005 which was called off after the Government decided to withhold visas for the Zimbabwe players.

8 Paul Wiseman declines a contract with Canterbury for 2006/07 and subsequently signs for Durham. He is replaced on the Canterbury list by Brent Findlay. Wiseman, who is working in England and playing league cricket, has a British passport. He is expected to return to New Zealand for the forthcoming summer but will now be classified as an overseas player.

Helen Watson announces that she is moving back to Christchurch and is included in the Canterbury women's winter training squad. Watson began her career with Canterbury but moved to Auckland after the 1999/00 season. Watson's return helps offset the loss of left-arm spinner Rebecca Steele who is no longer available for cricket.

10 Carisbrook is likely to be abandoned in favour of a stadium costing up to $180 million in time for the 2011 Rugby World Cup. The University of Otago will be a major financial partner in the multipurpose stadium. The venue is likely to become the new home for the university's School of Physical Education. Capacity of 32,000 and a roof are being considered. Two waterfront sites in the vicinity of Logan Park are being looked at. If the funding cannot be achieved, it is understood that plans for upgrading Carisbrook would be revisited, an option expected to cost $50 million.

17 Canterbury Cricket shows a surplus of $36,840 for the 2005/06 season, compared to a $100,797 loss the previous year. Operating revenue of $2,294,201 increased by $264,000, while expenses rose by $127,000. Among the expenses was $28,278 for "professional services to assist in the process of identifying a new ground". No decision has yet been made on a new home for Canterbury Cricket.

September

2 Cricket Wellington reports an operating surplus of $30,000 for the year, down from $74,000. Operating revenue increased $200,000 and there was an increase in net working capital of almost $80,000. A number of one-off costs such as re-outfitting the men's and women's teams, buying a $25,000 video analysis training tool and replacing the artificial grass at the indoor facility affected the final result.

6 Central Districts announces a surplus of $2266 for the year, down from $13,015. Income was $1,688,245, up by $85,000, of which $1.3 million came from grants from New Zealand Cricket. Chief executive Blair Furlong had budgeted on an $80,000 return from the one-day international against the West Indies at Napier but he banked only $40,000.

7 Michael Mason is diagnosed with a meniscus tear of his lower back, in the bottom disc close to the point of his tailbone. The symptoms extend into his right leg, where he experiences stiffness after bowling. He suspects he sustained the injury while training indoors three times a week in Palmerston North in cold weather.

Don Neely is appointed president of New Zealand Cricket. He replaces John Reid, who had been in the role since 2003 and was made a life member at NZC's annual meeting in Wellington. Neely, who played for Wellington and Auckland, is a notable cricket historian and author, a life member of NZC, a trustee of the New Zealand Cricket Museum and former president of Cricket Wellington. He also spent 14 years as a New Zealand selector, including seven as convener of selectors. NZC board members Anne Urlwin and Stephen Boock are re-elected to the board at the meeting.

8 Craig Ross is appointed as Northern Districts' new high-performance development coach. Ross, a former pace bowler whose first-class career was hampered by injury, eventually wants to coach at first-class level.

New Zealand Cricket announces a surplus of $217,779 for its four year financial cycle ending on 31 May 2006. NZC recorded a surplus for the year of $3.03 million, before distributions to Major and District Associations. This compared to a budgeted pre-distribution surplus of $2.49m. Distributions to Major and District Associations were $7.41m compared to $6.86m the previous financial year.

17 Scott Styris returns two weeks early from his county season to have a back injury assessed in New Zealand to see if he will be available for the Champions Trophy.

24 New Zealand Cricket announces an overhaul to its coaching structures. High performance manager Ric Charlesworth says there is an increasing shift towards specialisation and NZC is setting up a national network of coaches to tend to the individual needs of players.

October

6 Michael Parlane is named as Wellington captain. He replaces Matthew Bell who stood down after six seasons in charge in order to concentrate on his batting.

10 Ross Taylor is named to go to the Champions Trophy as cover for the injured Scott Styris.

November

2 Auckland announce the signing of Lancashire batsman Mal Loye for the 2006/07 season.

Former Northern Districts cricket chief executive John Turkington is named as the head of Force Three, football's equivalent to Northern Districts. His father, Patrick, won a Chatham Cup winner's medal with Wellington Marist in 1932.

6 Michael Papps requires a plaster cast for about a month after breaking his little finger while fielding during Canterbury's warm-up match against Otago, ruling him out of the start of the first-class season. This is another in a string of injuries that have limited his opportunities at international level.

10 New Zealand Cricket's high performance operation manager Ric Charlesworth announces plans for the future of the High Performance Centre at Lincoln. They include discontinuing the Cricket Academy, decentralising the coaching programme which will be undertaken by major associations, contracting players on the verge of Black Caps status and putting more resources into their development, greater emphasis on case management of players and appointing specialist head coaches for the various disciplines such as batting and bowling.

14 Scott Styris is diagnosed as having a small rupture to a disc in his back and is ruled out of the tests against Sri Lanka.

22 New Zealand Cricket, the six Major Associations and the New Zealand Cricket Players Association sign a Memorandum of Understanding for a new players' contract. The new contract, which goes from 1 June 2006 until 31 May 2010, will see 25% of NZC's forecast revenue allocated to the Player Payment Pool. This is an increase from 22.9% in the previous contract. The agreement also sees increases in player retainers and the number of players contracted by Major Associations increase from 11 to 12.

December

19 New Zealand Cricket's Chief Executive Martin Snedden announces that he will take up a position as Rugby New Zealand 2011 Ltd CEO in May, 2007. Snedden had been NZC's CEO since August 2001.

Tama Canning announces his retirement from first-class cricket in New Zealand. He will return to Perth and focus on developing a career outside of the game and playing in England. In 61 first-class games he scored 2141 runs at 27.44 and took 206 wickets at 24.47. He also played in four one-day internationals.

20 Sri Lankan wicketkeeper Prasanna Jayawardene has his appendix removed in a Wellington hospital. He had been due to return to Sri Lanka as he was not required for the one-day section of the tour.

Former Northern Districts coach Bruce Blair is appointed coach adviser for the New Zealand Academy of Sport North, to support the high-performance coaches working with elite athletes.

21 Dayle Hadlee is appointed as NZC's specialist bowling coach after major changes to the high performance programme. He will be responsible for establishing a network of specialist bowling coaches throughout the country. New Zealand women's coach Steve Jenkin is handed the added responsibility of overseeing player development by co-ordinating case management meetings for specifically targeted players.

31 New Zealand umpire Robert Anderson is appointed Officer of the New Zealand Order of Merit for services to science, education and cricket, in the New Year's Honours List.

February

1 Kirsty Flavell stands down as coach of the Canterbury women's team after four seasons in charge to concentrate on her career as a school teacher. Canterbury reached the State League final each year, winning the title three times.

8 Kyle Mills is ruled out of the World Cup after requiring surgery on his left knee. Mills had only recently rejoined the New Zealand team in Australia following injury.

12 Vaughn Johnson is appointed as NZC's specialist pace bowling coach. He will work with selected players throughout the North Island on a part-time basis, reporting to head bowling coach Dayle Hadlee.

20 New Zealand Cricket announces an Under 19 squad for training camps during the winter. All 19 players will be candidates for a place in the team for the 2008 Under 19 World Cup in Malaysia. The team will be selected following the National Under 19 championship to be held at Lincoln in December and January 2007/08.

The squad is: Corey Anderson *(Canterbury)*, Joe Austin-Smellie *(Wellington)*, Nicholas Beard *(Otago)*, Trent Boult *(Northern Districts)*, Michael Bracewell *(Otago)*, Andy Dodd *(Central Districts)*, Jono Hickey *(Northern Districts)*, Greg Morgan *(Auckland)*, Niranjan Naguleswaran *(Wellington)*, Sam Noster *(Canterbury)*, Ajaz Patel *(Auckland)*, Bradley Rodden *(Otago)*, Tim Southee *(Northern Districts)*, Ben Sprott *(Central Districts)*, Lii Tugaga *(Wellington)*, Kane Williamson *(Northern Districts)*, George Worker *(Central Districts)*, Peter Younghusband *(Central Districts)* and Jeet Raval *(Auckland)*.

24 Chris Martin is named to replace Daryl Tuffey in the New Zealand World Cup squad after Tuffey injured his right bicep during the match against Canada.

26 Lou Vincent is ruled out of the remainder of the World Cup after breaking his wrist during a practice session in Antigua. Vincent was hit by Shane Bond while batting in the nets. Hamish Marshall is named as Vincent's replacement.

30 Rebecca Rolls announces her retirement from all cricket. She played in 104 one-day internationals, scoring 2201 runs at 25.01 and making 133 wicketkeeping dismissals.

March

8 Andre Adams receives a one match ban for grabbing the helmet and shaking the grill of Central Districts batsman Bevan Griggs during a State Championship match. NZC asks the National Code of Conduct Commissioner, Nick Davidson QC, for leave to appeal the decision on the grounds that the penalty was too light given the serious nature of the breach of the Code of Conduct. Mr Davidson grants the appeal and a rehearing is held. The original penalty is increased to a fine of $500 and Adams is suspended from all cricket up to and including 31 March 2007.

April

5 The Zealand A team to play in the Emerging Players Tournament in Maroochydore and Brisbane in July is announced. Fourteen players are named and a further player may be added after the World Cup. The tournament will include seven one-day games and two Twenty20 games against Australia, South Africa and India. The team is: James Marshall *(captain)*, Neil Broom, Grant Elliott, Gareth Hopkins, Jamie How, Nathan McCullum, James McMillan, Warren McSkimming, Rob Nicol, Iain O'Brien, Mark Orchard, Michael Papps, Aaron Redmond and Bradley Scott. Craig Cumming and Jesse Ryder were unavailable. Coach, Dave Nosworthy, assistant coaches, Mike Hesson and Vaughn Johnson.

10 New Zealand Cricket Board member Justin Vaughan is appointed to the position of NZC chief executive. He is a qualified medical practitioner and currently the chief executive of a medical technology company.

14 Brendon McCullum is fined 20 percent of his match fee against Sri Lanka for showing dissent after being given out.

New Zealand Cricket names five of its most promising Under 19 players to join the New Zealand A winter training squad in Darwin. The players – Tim Southee, Corey Anderson, Trent Boult, Greg Morgan and Kane Williamson – will spend nearly three weeks in Darwin ahead of the team's departure for the tournament in Queensland.

19 The New Zealand women's selectors name two training squads for the 2007/08 season. The White Ferns will be selected in mid-June for the Rose Bowl series in Darwin in July before their tour of England in August. The two squads will meet at Lincoln University on 9 and 10 June. The White Ferns squad will reconvene on 22 and 23 September, with the A squad following a week later.

The White Ferns squad is: Suzie Bates, Nicola Browne, Sarah Burke, Rachel Candy, Selena Charteris, Sophie Devine, Lucy Doolan, Maria Fahey, Ros Kember, Sara McGlashan, Beth McNeill, Aimee Mason, Rowan Milburn, Louise Milliken, Rachel Priest, Amy Satterthwaite, Haidee Tiffen, Sarah Tsukigawa and Helen Watson.

The New Zealand A squad is: Kendra Cocksedge, Amanda Cooper, Ingrid Cronin-Knight, Maree Hannay, Megan Kane, Zara McWilliams, Katey Martin, Prashilla Mistry, Megan Murphy, Elizabeth Perry and Megan Wakefield.

25 Stephen Fleming stands down as New Zealand's one-day captain after a world record 218 games in charge. He is still available for the one-day team and wants to remain as captain of the test side.

May

8 Gary Stead is appointed as coach of the Canterbury women's team. Stead, 34, is also a coach at New Zealand Cricket's High Performance Centre.

9 Jesse Ryder signs for Ireland as as their second overseas player in county cricket. He had been playing with New Brighton in the Liverpool League.

Stephen Fleming marries Kelly Payne in a top-secret wedding in Wellington. They became engaged in 2004, and have daughter Tayla, 16 months old.

10 Andy Moles has his two-year contract as Northern Districts cricket coach extended by another year after guiding Northern to the State Championship title.

16 Shane Bond is named The National Bank Player of the Year at New Zealand Cricket's awards night. The batting awards go to Michael Papps *(Redpath Cup)* and Scott Styris *(Walter Hadlee Trophy)* while the bowling awards, for the second year in a row, go to Chris Martin *(Winsor Cup)* and Bond *(Walter Hadlee Trophy)*. Maria Fahey and Helen Watson win the Ruth Martin Cup and Phyl Blackler Cup. awarded for outstanding batting and bowling, while the State Medal and State Plate, for outstanding performances in domestic cricket, go to Chris Harris and Sophie Devine. Mike Shrimpton is awarded the Sutcliffe Medal for outstanding services to cricket.

18 The International Cricket Council announces that New Zealand Cricket will receive $US11.47 million ($NZ15.86 million) from the World Cup plus an additional $US450,000 ($NZ622,406) for reaching the semi-final.

28 Durham sign Scott Styris as their overseas professional for two months from 1 June.

31 New Zealand Cricket name their contracted players for the year. They are Shane Bond, Stephen Fleming, James Franklin, Peter Fulton, Mark Gillespie, Gareth Hopkins, Jamie How, Brendon McCullum, Craig McMillan, Hamish Marshall, Chris Martin, Michael Mason, Kyle Mills, Jacob Oram, Michael Papps, Jeetan Patel, Scott Styris, Ross Taylor, Daniel Vettori and Lou Vincent. Hopkins and Gillespie, newcomers to the list, and McMillan replace Mathew Sinclair, Andre Adams and Nathan Astle.

June

3 Nathan Astle is made a member of the New Zealand Order of Merit in the Queen's Birthday Honours List.

5 The dates for the international matches on New Zealand's tour of England in 2008 are confirmed. Tests – Lord's 15-19 May, Manchester 23-27 May, Nottingham 5-9 June, Twenty20 – Manchester 13 June, One-day Internationals – Chester-le-Street 15 June, Birmingham 18 June, Bristol 21 June, The Oval 25 June, Lord's 28 June.

7 The Government announces it will contribute $2.9 million towards the redevelopment of Napier's McLean Park. The redevelopment will include an upgrade of lighting and other facilities to meet criteria for international cricket and the national provincial rugby championship. The upgrade will also include a new stand.

11 The White Ferns squads for the Rose Bowl series and tour to England are announced. The team to play Australia is Haidee Tiffen *(captain)*, Nicola Browne, Sophie Devine, Maria Fahey, Sara McGlashan, Beth McNeill, Aimee Mason, Rowan Milburn, Louise Milliken, Rachel Priest, Amy Satterthwaite, Sarah Tsukigawa and Helen Watson. They will play one Twenty20 international and five one-day internationals.

Suzie Bates is unavailable for the Rose Bowl but will return for the tour of England, which includes three Twenty20 internationals and six ODIs, and will be joined by Rachel Candy, Selena Charteris and Sarah Burke. Fahey and Devine are unavailable. Priest, Satterthwaite and Candy are the uncapped players in the squad.

15 Hamish Marshall declines a New Zealand Cricket contract for the 2007/08 season in favour of playing county cricket. Marshall had been playing for Gloucestershire as an overseas player but qualifies as a local player as he holds an Irish passport. Mathew Sinclair is subsequently named as Marshall's replacement on the list of contracted players.

18 Brendon McCullum announces he is transferring back to Otago after four seasons with Canterbury. He will continue to live in Christchurch and commute to Otago to play.

20 Gareth Hopkins, who moved from Canterbury to Otago when McCullum moved north, confirms he will play in Auckland in 2007/08.

23 Daryl Tuffey annnounces that he will also join Auckland for the 2007/08 season.

The dates for the international matches on New Zealand's tour of South Africa are confirmed. Tests – Johannesburg 8-12 November, Centurion 16-20 November, Twenty20 – Johannesburg 23 November, One-day Internationals – Durban 24 November, Port Elizabeth 30 November, Cape Town 2 December. After the South Africa tour, the Chappell-Hadlee series will be played at Adelaide, Sydney and Hobart from 14-20 December.

PLAYERS OF THE YEAR

Shane Bond is one of our Players of the Year for the second year in succession. In the past season he played in 22 one-day internationals and took 38 wickets and became the second New Zealand bowler to take a one-day international hat-trick. In addition to this he took ten wickets in the two test matches against Sri Lanka and was instrumental in the BlackCaps winning the test in Christchurch.

Bond started the season slowly, missing the first game in the Champions Trophy, but took five wickets in the next three games, including 3-45 against Pakistan. Back home for the domestic season he took 2-37 and 5-37 against Northern Districts in his only appearance for Canterbury. The two tests followed and then the one-day series against Sri Lanka. The selectors decided that Bond should rest for the first two games and then in the two games he played he got a further three wickets.

New Zealand then went to Australia for the Commonwealth Bank Series against Australia and England. Bond immediately hit the headlines with his hat-trick in the first game, when he took 4-61 against the hosts. In his third game he became the twelfth New Zealander to take 100 wickets in one-day internationals. Finishing with 4-46 in the last game he took his tally in the series to 11 wickets.

Back in New Zealand for the Chappell-Hadlee series he took a magnificent 5-23 as Australia were dismissed for 148 at Wellington. In the World Cup he took 13 wickets at an average of 16.38 and had an impressive economy rate of just over three runs per over. He failed to take a wicket in only one game.

As important as anything was the fact that Bond was injury free for the entire season. New Zealand's forthcoming programme has them touring South Africa, hosting Bangladesh and home and away series against England. It is essential for New Zealand's success that Bond does stay injury free as he has shown that he is still one of the most potent fast bowlers in world cricket.

Michael Papps suffered a broken finger in club cricket in early November which caused him to miss Canterbury's first two State Championship games. Consequently he was not able to be considered for the test team which reverted to playing two specialist openers.

In his first outing for Canterbury he scored 21 and 1 against Auckland but then got 121 against the previous season's champions, Central Districts. Then came the State Shield where Papps scored 258 runs, registering two fifties.

Back in the Championship he had a good double of 98 and 93 at the Basin Reserve, before scoring 169 and 0 against Otago. He again got a hundred in the run-fest against Wellington with 188 in his only innings. He made 86 against Central Districts and in the State Championship final he just failed to score a century in both innings, with totals of 132 and 96.

This gave the Canterbury opener 1005 runs in just seven games, thus becoming only the tenth batsman to score 1000 runs in a New Zealand first-class season.

Papps also became the first player to score as many as four centuries in one season for Canterbury and it should be noted that he also had three scores in the nineties. Papps won the Redpath Cup for his season's efforts and should be back in the BlackCaps side for the tour to South Africa.

PROMISING PLAYERS

Neil Broom made the move to Otago for the 2005/06 season in a bid to get more first-class cricket as he was only a fringe player during his time with Canterbury. He scored 354 runs in his debut season for Otago and during the past season he really blossomed.

In first-class play he scored 644 runs, including two centuries, at the outstanding average of 71.55. He also hit four fifties. He failed to reach twenty in only one innings such was his consistency. He scored his hundreds against Auckland (112) and versus Northern Districts (101). In the State Shield he scored 197 runs, including two fifties.

Broom has shown that he has the temperament and hunger for first-class cricket and he was rewarded with a place in the New Zealand A side to Australia in June and July 2007. One hopes that he can continue with this past season's form to challenge for higher honours in the near future.

Grant Elliott made his debut in his homeland South Africa as a 17-year-old in 1996/97 but had only played 18 games before making his debut for Wellington in 2005/06.

In 2006/07 Elliott really bloomed as an all-rounder, scoring centuries in both State Championship and Shield matches. He was also the joint leading wicket-taker in the State Shield with 18 wickets and had 12 victims in first-class cricket.

Elliott was actually omitted for the second game of the season but at Hamilton, after being recalled, he scored 102 not out as Wellington reached 524. An unbeaten 67 helped Wellington against Canterbury at the Basin Reserve and in the return fixture he played a major part when Wellington chased 614, scoring another century.

In the State Shield he got 79 in the first game and then again showed his liking for Canterbury bowlers with an unbeaten 107, with the winning runs coming off the last ball. He had his best bowling figures of 4-29 against Auckland. Elliott was also Wellington's Cricketer of the Year and, like Broom, has been selected for New Zealand A

Bradley Scott had become the mainstay of the Otago bowling attack by 2005/06 and again kept the Otago attack going this past season. He was the only Otago pace bowler not to miss a game through injury.

He started the season slowly with just two wickets from his first three games but was then instrumental in destroying Wellington with 4-13, as they were dismissed for just 71. Eight wickets in the first game after the one-day break saw him reach 100 wickets in first-class play and two more four wicket hauls in the last three games took his total to 27.

He took 12 wickets for Otago in the State Shield passing fifty wickets in the process. His best return for the season was 3-29 in the semi-final.

Scott showed consistency in the past season and was selected as a replacement player in the 30 man squad named for the World Cup. Even though he eventually missed out he has shown he is in the selectors' minds and will be going to Australia with New Zealand A.

Since this section was introduced in 1983, the following have been chosen as Promising Players of the Year: **1983**, P.S. Briasco, M.D. Crowe, T.J. Franklin, **1984**, K.R. Rutherford, D.A. Stirling, P.J. Visser, **1985**, T.E. Blain, T.D. Ritchie, W. Watson, **1986**, S.W. Duff, D.G. Scott, C.J.P. Smith, **1987**, M.J. Greatbatch, D.K. Morrison, B.A. Young, **1988**, J.P. Millmow, M.R. Pringle, S.A. Thomson, **1989**, F. Beyeler, C.L. Cairns, M.W. Douglas, **1990**, C.Z. Harris, C. Pringle, K.A. Wealleans, **1991**, P.W. Dobbs, P.W. O'Rourke, A.C. Parore, **1992**, M.N. Hart, L.G. Howell, J.W. Wilson, **1993**, S.P. Fleming, D.J. Nash, M.B. Owens, **1994**, R.L. Hayes, B.A. Pocock, A.T. Reinholds, **1995**, M.D. Bell, G.R. Jonas, C.D. McMillan, **1996**, C.J. Nevin, M.H. Richardson, P.J. Wiseman, **1997**, M.J. Horne, M.S. Sinclair, D.L. Vettori, **1998**, C.E. Bulfin, C.D. Cumming, S.B. O'Connor, **1999**, J.I. Englefield, C.S. Martin, L. Vincent, **2000**, T.K. Canning, B.P. Martin, J.D.P. Oram, **2001**, J.E.C. Franklin, K.D. Mills, D.R. Tuffey, **2002**, I.G. Butler, W.A. Cornelius, R.J. Nicol, **2003**, T.G. McIntosh, I.E. O'Brien, J.D. Ryder, **2004**, P.G. Fulton, B.B. McCullum, M.H.W. Papps, **2005**, G.W. Aldridge, M.R. Gillespie, J.M. How, **2006**, J.S.Patel, L.R.P.L. Taylor, E.P. Thompson.

Photosport

NEW ZEALAND v SRI LANKA — 2nd Twenty20 International

Back row: J. Durning *(media liaison officer)*, S. Jackson *(trainer)*, L.M. Crocker *(manager)*, M.R. Gillespie, P.D. McGlashan, M.J. Mason, J.E.C. Franklin, P.G. Fulton, L.R.P.L. Taylor, J.G. Bracewell *(coach)*, T. Wilson *(fielding coach)*, R.M. Carter *(assistant coach)*, D.F. Shackel *(physiotherapist)*.

Front row: J.S. Patel, J.A.H. Marshall, B.B. McCullum, A.R. Adams, S.P. Fleming *(captain)*, N.J. Astle.

Standish & Preece

NEW ZEALAND WOMEN IN INDIA — 2006/07

Back row: S.J. Tsukigawa, S.K. Burke, S.W. Bates, N.J. Browne, S.F.M. Devine, S.J. McGlashan.

Second row: M. Smith (*trainer*), C.A. Campbell (*manager*), C.E. Taylor *(assistant coach)*, L.E. Milliken, H.M. Watson, A. Cadogan *(physiotherapist)*, S.J. Jenkin *(coach)*.

Front row: S.E. Charteris, R.C. Milburn, H.M. Tiffen *(captain)*, R.J. Rolls, A.L. Mason, M.F. Fahey.

Photosport

AUCKLAND — 2006/07

Back row: F. Thomas *(manager)*, M.R. O'Donnell *(coach)*, R.M. Hira, K.W.M. Todd, D.W. Houpapa, M.J. Guptill, C. de Grandhomme, P.A. Hitchcock, I. Lambie *(sports psychologist)*, P. Sail *(physiotherapist)*, M. Smith *(fitness trainer)*.

Front row: M.Y. Pasupati, C.S. Martin, R.J. Nicol, R.A. Jones *(captain)*, A.R. Adams, R.A. Young, K.D. Mills.

NDCA

NORTHERN DISTRICTS— 2006/07

Back row: I. MacErlich *(manager)*, M.G. Orchard, G.W. Aldridge, B.S. Wilson, B.J. Arnel, P.D. McGlashan, T.G. Southee, J.A.F. Yovich, A.J. Moles *(coach)*.

Front row: B.P. Martin, B-J. Watling, S.L. Andrews, A.W. Evans, H.J.H. Marshall, J.A.H. Marshall *(captain)*, G.G. Robinson, N.K.W. Horsley.

New Regent

CANTERBURY — 2006/07

Back row: I.A. Robertson, M.P.F. Davidson, W.M. Lonsdale, Amandeep Singh, L.M. Burtt, C.J. Anderson, S.P. Chan, B.J. Rae.

Front row: A.M. Ellis, T.D. Astle, C.F.K. van Wyk, M.H.W. Papps, D.O. Nosworthy *(coach)*, C.Z. Harris *(captain)*, S.L. Stewart, B.C. Hiini, H.K. Bennett.

New Regent

CANTERBURY WOMEN — 2006/07

Back row: A.E. Satterthwaite, B.H. McNeill, M.L. Mitchell, E.M. Bermingham, E.M. Campbell, S.E. Charteris, S.K. Burke, K.E. Minogue, M.C. Godliman, T.L. Anderson *(manager)*.

Front row: M.F. Fahey, R.C. Milburn, H.M. Tiffen *(captain)*, H.M. Watson, K.E. Bond *(coach)*, L.M. Astle *(selector)*.

CDCA

CENTRAL DISTRICTS — 2006/07

Back row: T.I. Weston, A.D. Niblett, R.J. Schaw, G.J.T. Hegglun, D.L. Rayner, B.M.K. Patton, G.R. Hay, B.B.J. Griggs.
Front row: G.D. Barlow *(coach)*, L.J. Hamilton, M.S. Sinclair, J.M. How *(captain)*, B.E. Hefford, P.J. Ingram, D. Kelly *(trainer)*.

CDCA

CENTRAL DISTRICTS WOMEN — 2006/07

Back row: K. Manley *(manager)*, S.L. Norman, R.H. Priest, Z.A. McWilliams, R.H. Candy, K.M. Winkley, A.K. Burrows, K. Strange *(coach)*.
Front row: K.E. Broadmore, K.M. Cocksedge, S.J. McGlashan, A.L. Mason *(captain)*, N.M. Thessman, K.E. Tunnicliffe

Beetle

OTAGO — 2006/07

Back row: D.V. Lobb, C.M. Smith, K. Noema-Barnett, S.B. Haig.
Second row: D.J. Drew *(physiotherapist)*, G.S. Shaw, G.R. Todd, M.J. Harvie, N.M. Turner, J.M. McMillan, M. Hesson *(coach)*.
Front row: N.T. Broom, J.W. Sheed, G.J. Hopkins, C.D. Cumming (*captain*), N.L. McCullum, A.J. Redmond, B.E Scott.

McRobie

OTAGO WOMEN — 2006/07

Back row: A.L. Kane, J.M. Innes, A.M. Te Wake.
Second row: C.E. Taylor *(player/coach)*, A.J. Blackwell, A.S.M. Kitchen, T.J. Morrison, S.M. King, R. Bates *(manager)*.
Front row: K.J. Martin, S.W. Bates, S.J. Tsukigawa *(captain)*, K.M. Spence, M.J. Kane.

Cricket Wellington

WELLINGTON — 2006/07

Back row: N.R. Parlane, S.M. Mills, G.D. Elliott, D.J. Bowden, L.J. Edwards.
Second row: D. Painter *(manager)*, A.M. Stuart *(coach)*, J.D. Ryder, K.A. Forde, S. Rasmussen, M. Burns, C. van Dyk *(assistant coach)*, J. Tout *(fitness trainer)*.
Front row: S.A. Fairley, L.J. Woodcock, M.E. Parlane *(captain)*, C.J. Nevin, I.E. O'Brien, M.D. Bell.

Cricket Wellington

WELLINGTON WOMEN — 2006/07

Back row: M. Borthwick *(coach)*, E.J. Scurr, M.G. Wakefield, S.F.M. Devine, L.R.V.S. Harford, O.R. Bupha-Intr, S.E.A. Ruck, L.R. Doolan, S. Morrison *(manager)*.
Front row: M.J. Hodgson, S.J. Hill, A.E. Cooper, A.M. Dodd *(captain)*, A.M. Smith, S.J. Bradbury.

J. Booker

The Canterbury and Fiji teams at Lancaster Park, March 1948 (see obituary of Jack Booker who is ninth from left in the back row).

NDCA

NORTHERN DISTRICTS 50th ANNIVERSARY

Back row: K.D. Kennedy, C.M. Presland, C.W. Ross, M.G. Orchard, D.R. Tuffey, G.W. Aldridge, P.D. McGlashan, J.A.F. Yovich, J.A.H. Marshall, B-J. Watling, A. Puna.
Third row: H.R. Bastion, B.A. Young, M.J. Child, J.F. Bailey, P.H. Barton, L.S. Mountain, G.V. Giles, P.D. Stone, M.G. Harding.
Second row: G.M. Tarr, D.N. Matthews, B. Dunning, B.J. Bayley, J.D. Smith, J. Freeman, R.W. Anderson, J.W. Guy, R.C. Hooton, E. Hipkiss, C.W. Dickeson.
Front row: M.C. Langdon, B.H. Pairaudeau, D.L. Donald, P.B. McGregor, J.L. Wyatt, N.R. Wilson, D.C. Hoskin, W.P. Bradburn, H.W. Larmer, T.E. Shaw.

HAPPENINGS

Five of New Zealand's oldest surviving first-class cricketers, Jack Kerr, Walter Hadlee, Jack Scandrett, Gordon Whyte and Graham Botting, died during the past twelve months. Their obituaries are included in this edition of the *Almanack*. Eric Tindill remains the oldest and is also the oldest living test cricketer from any country. As far as can be ascertained, the oldest New Zealand players are now:

		Born
E.W.T. Tindill	*Wellington*	18.12.1910
L.A. Mahoney	*Canterbury*	13. 9.1911
C.L.W. Randall	*Wellington*	8. 8.1913
V. James	*Canterbury*	24. 8.1915
J.A. Ell	*Wellington*	15. 9.1915
N.A. McMahon	*Auckland*	24. 5.1916
W.M. Wallace	*Auckland*	19.12.1916
T.L. Pritchard	*Wellington*	10. 3.1917
C.A. Snedden	*Auckland*	7. 1.1918
S.A. McVicar	*Wellington*	15. 7.1918
J.L. Wyatt	*Northern Districts*	7. 3.1919

• • •

Botting had the distinction of being both the oldest living Central Districts and Otago player. The oldest Central Districts player is now R.E. Brown (born 18.4.1924) while Otago's oldest is I.W. Payne (born 18.7.1921).

• • •

Richard Jones, Michael Parlane and Chris Harris led their teams in every match of the three domestic competitions in 2006/07.

Northern Districts again named both James Marshall and Daniel Vettori as captains at the start of the season, with Vettori taking over when his international commitments permitted. Central Districts used three diferent captains in successive games at one stage. Lance Hamilton stood in for Jamie How, who was on national duty, but broke down in his second over and Ross Taylor took over for the next game. The sides were led by:

	Official captain	***Replacement***
Auckland	Richard Jones	–
Canterbury	Chris Harris	–
Central Districts	Jamie How	Lance Hamilton, Ross Taylor
Northern Districts	James Marshall	Daniel Vettori, Hamish Marshall, Peter McGlashan
Otago	Craig Cumming	Gareth Hopkins
Wellington	Michael Parlane	–

• • •

A number of New Zealand players have a high ratio of catches per match over their first-class careers. Stephen Fleming has now taken 306 catches in 228 first-class games while James Marshall, who has taken 89 (one as a wicketkeeper) in 88 matches, Jamie How, 63 in 59, and Neal Parlane, 58 in 58, also average at least one catch per game.

• • •

The highest run scorer in first-class cricket over the past twelve months was Michael Papps who totalled 1078. Hamish Marshall followed with 766 runs. The most first-class wickets were taken by Chris Martin (40) followed by Iain O'Brien (34).

Stephen Fleming became the first player to captain his country in 200 one-day internationals when New Zealand met Australia at Sydney on 21 January. Only thirteen players have captained their side in as many as 100 one-day internationals and they are:

	P	W	L	T	NR	Win%
S.P. Fleming *(NZ)*	218	98	106	1	13	44
A. Ranatunga *(SL)*	193	89	95	1	8	46
A.R. Border *(A)*	178	107	67	1	3	62
M. Azharuddin *(I)*	173	89	76	2	6	51
R.T. Ponting *(A)*	149	116	25	2	6	77
S.C. Ganguly *(I)*	147	76	66	–	5	51
Imran Khan *(P)*	139	75	59	1	4	53
W.J. Cronje *(SA)*	138	99	35	1	3	71
B.C. Lara *(WI)*	125	59	59	–	7	47
S.T. Jayasuriya *(SL)*	118	66	47	2	3	55
Wasim Akram *(P)*	109	66	41	2	–	60
S.R. Waugh *(A)*	106	67	35	3	1	63
I.V.A. Richards *(WI)*	105	67	36	–	2	63

Ponting is now the only currently active captain on the list. New Zealand's next highest is Geoff Howarth who had 60 games as captain (31 wins). Fleming relinquished the one-day captaincy at the end of the World Cup.

• • •

Only Allan Border has captained his country in test cricket more often than Fleming. At the end of the summer the list of most games as captain read:

	P	W	L	D	Win%
A.R. Border *(A)*	93	32	22	39*	34
S.P. Fleming *(NZ)*	80	28	27	25	35
C.H. Lloyd *(WI)*	74	36	12	26	48
S.R. Waugh *(A)*	57	41	9	7	72
A. Ranatunga *(SL)*	56	12	19	25	21
M.A. Atherton *(E)*	54	13	21	20	24
W.J. Cronje *(SA)*	53	27	11	15	50
M.A. Taylor *(A)*	50	26	13	11	52
I.V.A. Richards *(WI)*	50	27	8	15	54

** includes a tie*

Fleming has had 65 consecutive tests as captain, second only to Border (93).

• • •

New Zealand played only two test matches during the past twelve months but took part in 30 one-day internationals (16 wins, 13 losses). Stephen Fleming was the leading scorer with 853 runs while Shane Bond (38) again took the most wickets. Eight centuries were scored, with Fleming and Ross Taylor getting two each.

Bond was also the most economical bowler, conceding 4.18 runs per over.

• • •

A total of 20 players took part in the 30 one-day internationals for New Zealand with Brendon McCullum again being the only one to appear in every game. Daniel Vettori played in 28 and Stephen Fleming in 27. Mark Gillespie was the only player to make his debut.

During the season Otago's Chris Gaffaney became the thirteenth player to make 100 domestic one-day appearances. Chris Harris equalled Robbie Hart's all-time record. The most games in domestic one-day cricket have now been played by:

matches		*matches*	
122	R.G Hart *ND*	107	C.B. Gaffaney *O*
122	C.Z. Harris *C*	105	L.G. Howell *CD, C, A, ND*
121	G.E. Bradburn *ND*	103	M.D. Bailey *ND*
119	M.E. Parlane *ND, W*	102	M.N. Hart *ND*
114	A.C. Barnes *A*	101	M.W. Douglas *CD, W*
112	C.J. Nevin *W*	100	R.G. Petrie *C, W*
109	M.D. Bell *ND, W*		

A total of 91 players have made 50 or more appearances.

• • •

Harris is now close to dominating all domestic one-day records. Apart from equalling the record for most games, he has scored the most runs (3385), has the most catches by a fielder (69) and is just three short of Alex Tait's record for most wickets (128).

• • •

New Zealand has now taken part in 45 one-day tournaments, winning four. A summary of the tournaments is:

	Series	*Seasons*
World Cup	9	1975-2006/07
World Series/C & U/VB/CB Series	9	1980/81-2006/07
World Championship of Cricket	1	1984/85
Sri Lankan Tournaments	3	1985/86-2002/03
Sharjah Tournaments	8	1987/88-2001/02
Rothmans Cup	1	1989/90
Wills World Series	1	1994/95
Mandela Trophy	1	1994/95
Bank of New Zealand Centenary Series	1	1994/95
Independence Cup Tournaments	2	1996/97-1997/98
ICC Tournaments	5	1998/99-2006/07
Singapore Tournament	1	2000/01
TVS Cup	1	2003/04
NatWest Series	1	2004
Videocon Cup	1	2005/06

• • •

The Cornwall Cricket Club in Auckland again organised the limited-overs national club competition which was played from 10-15 April 2007. Teams involved were East Shirley *(Canterbury)*, Taieri *(Otago)*, New Plymouth Marist United *(Central Districts)*, Naenae *(Wellington)* and Howick-Pakuranga *(Auckland)*.

Players with first-class experience who took part were Colin de Grandhomme, Colin Munro and Gareth Hayne *(Howick-Pakuranga)*, Tim Papps, Michael Papps and Scott Pawson *(East Shirley)*, Grant Elliott, Jesse Ryder *(Naenae)* and Marcel McKenzie *(Taieri)*.

In the final **Howick** 232-4 (J. Newth 123*, A.P. de Boorder 39) **defeated Naenae** 126 (R. Bird 41, N. Strom 4-16, G.P. Hayne 4-25) by 106 runs.

Tournament awards were: Batting – Tim Papps *(East Shirley)*, Bowling – Michael Cornish *(Naenae)*, Player of the Tournament – Derek de Boorder *(Howick)*.

Two New Zealand provincial players appeared for Canada in the World Cup. Former Otago, Wellington and Auckland batsman Ian Billcliff scored 104 runs in three innings, including 50 against New Zealand. He had earlier scored 93 against Bangladesh in the ICC Associates Tri-series which was held at Antigua just prior to the World Cup.

He also added one first-class century to his record scoring 126 (the highest score of his career) against Bermuda in an ICC Inter-Continental Cup match at King City in Ontario. Billcliff, who was born in Canada, also represented them in the 2003 World Cup.

• • •

Central Districts opening batsman Geoff Barnett, who was born in Nelson but whose mother is Canadian, made 88 in his three World Cup knocks. He made 40 against New Zealand when he and John Davison put on 76 for the first wicket in 9.4 overs. He had earlier made 77 against Bangladesh in an ICC Associates Tri-series match.

Barnett also played in three ICC Inter-Continental Cup matches, recording his maiden first-class hundred (136) against Kenya at King City.

• • •

Former Canterbury and Otago all-rounder Darron Reekers appeared for the Netherlands in the World Cup, opening both batting and bowling. He had earlier recorded his maiden one-day international century (104) against Ireland in an ICC World Cricket League match in Nairobi in February.

• • •

Peter Borren, a former New Zealand Under 19 representative, was also a member of the Netherlands team. Borren made his one-day international debut against Sri Lanka in July 2006, and also played in two ICC Inter-Continental Cup first-class matches, having a best score of 49 against Canada at Pretoria.

• • •

Amongst the regular bowlers in the State Shield in 2006/07, the Canterbury pair of Brent Findlay and Sunnie Chan were the most expensive, conceding 6.86 and 6.96 runs per over. The most expensive bowlers in domestic one-day cricket (minimum 100 overs) have been:

	Overs	*Mdns*	*Runs*	*Wkts*	*Ave*	*RPO*
J.D. Ryder *(CD, W)*	110	2	628	22	28.54	5.70
C.R. Pryor *(A, O)*	157.4	3	863	23	37.52	5.47
J.A.F. Yovich *(ND)*	422.5	21	2258	89	25.37	5.34
A.J. Redmond *(C, O)*	119	1	617	17	36.29	5.18
I.G. Butler *(ND)*	200	13	1015	32	31.71	5.07
G.D. Elliott *(W)*	109.4	3	551	20	27.55	5.02

• • •

In the first test at Christchurch, Sri Lanka's second innings ended when Muttiah Muralitharan was run out by Brendon McCullum. After completing a single, Muralitharan had come back down the pitch to congratulate Kumar Sangakkara on reaching his century. However, the ball was not dead and McCullum took the bails off to effect the run out.

A very similar occurrence had taken place the season before at Bulawayo. Zimbabwe's number eleven, Chris Mpofu, trotted down the pitch to congratulate Blessing Mahwire on his fifty but had also failed to ascertain whether the ball was deemed dead and was promptly run out by McCullum, bringing the match to an end.

Jacob Oram scored the fastest century for New Zealand in one-day internationals during the Commonwealth Bank Series but the record stood for just 23 days. This list reads:

balls				
67	C.D. McMillan	v Australia	Hamilton	2006/07
71	J.D.P. Oram	v Australia	Perth	2006/07
75	C.L. Cairns	v India	Christchurch	1998/99
75	C.D. McMillan	v Pakistan	Christchurch	2000/01
81	L. Vincent	v Zimbabwe	Bulawayo	2005/06
85	C.L. Cairns	v India	Pune	1995/96
87	A.C. Parore	v South Africa	Centurion	1994/95
90	S.P. Fleming	v Bangladesh	Antigua	2006/07
93	N.J. Astle	v Pakistan	Dunedin	2000/01
94	K.R. Rutherford	v India	Baroda	1994/95
94	S.B. Styris	v Australia	Christchurch	2005/06
96	K.J. Wadsworth	v Australia	Christchurch	1973/74
96	K.R. Rutherford	v Sri Lanka	East London	1994/95
99	C.L. Cairns	v South Africa	Brisbane	2001/02

McMillan and Oram now have the fastest centuries scored against Australia (previously 79 balls by Herschelle Gibbs at Johannesburg in 2005/06).

• • •

Oram hit six sixes at Perth and McMillan five at Hamilton. The most sixes in a one-day international for New Zealand are:

9	L. Vincent (172)	v Zimbabwe	Bulawayo	2005/06
7	C.L. Cairns (115)	v India	Christchurch	1998/99
6	B.L. Cairns (52)	v Australia	Melbourne	1982/83
6	C.L. Cairns (75)	v West Indies	Auckland	1999/00
6	S.B. Styris (141)	v Sri Lanka	Bloemfontein	2002/03
6	C.L. Cairns (84)	v Pakistan	Lahore	2003/04
6	N.J. Astle (145*)	v USA	The Oval	2004
6	J.D.P. Oram (101*)	v Australia	Perth	2006/07
5†	C.D. McMillan (66)	v Zimbabwe	Harare	1997/98
5	C.D. McMillan (104*)	v Pakistan	Christchurch	2000/01
5	N.J. Astle (122*)	v Pakistan	Dunedin	2001/02
5	C.D. McMillan (117)	v Australia	Hamilton	2006/07
5	C.D. McMillan (71)	v Kenya	Gros Islet	2006/07
5	B.B. McCullum (52*)	v Canada	Gros Islet	2006/07

† *no fours*

• • •

McMillan reached his century at Hamilton with sixes off successive balls from Adam Voges. He had also reached three figures with a six against Pakistan at Christchurch in 2000/01. Lou Vincent (172 v Zimbabwe at Bulawayo in 2005/06) is the only other New Zealand batsman to reach a one-day international century with a six.

• • •

There were plenty of other sixes hit in the Chappell-Hadlee Trophy match at Hamilton. A total of 26 sixes were recorded, 16 by Australia and 10 by New Zealand. This equalled the all-time record set at Johannesburg, in March 2006, when South Africa scored 438-9 in reply to Australia's 434-4.

Australia's 16 sixes in an innings (10 hit by Matthew Hayden) equalled the record set by New Zealand against Zimbabwe at Bulawayo in August 2005.

Matthew Hayden's innings of 181 not out at Hamilton was the highest ever for Australia in one-day internationals, surpassing Mark Waugh's 173 against West Indies at Melbourne in 2000/01. Hayden had reached 100 off 127 balls when he was struck on the foot by a ball from Mark Gillespie. The next ball he was struck again and it later turned out he had broken a toe.

Shane Watson came out to act as a runner and watched as Hayden went on to make 181 off only 166 balls, hitting eight sixes after being struck on the foot. At one stage he hit five sixes off twelve deliveries.

• • •

The record for the fastest fifty for New Zealand in one-day internationals was also broken during the last twelve months. Brendon McCullum, who had shared the record of 21 balls with Lance Cairns, took just 20 balls to reach fifty in the World Cup match against Canada at St Lucia.

It was also the fastest fifty in World Cup history, beating Mark Boucher's 21-ball effort for South Africa against Netherlands just six days earlier.

• • •

New Zealand umpire Brent "Billy" Bowden officiated in six tests and 21 one-day internationals during the past 12 months.

He stood in both tests between Sri Lanka and South Africa, two of the Ashes tests in Australia and the final two tests between England and West Indies.

He stood in the first match of the one-day series between Sri Lanka and India at Colombo (the series was abandoned after this game), five matches in the Champions Trophy, one match between New Zealand and Sri Lanka, all four matches between India and West Indies and one Chappell-Hadlee Trophy game. He also officiated in nine matches at the World Cup.

• • •

Tony Hill, who is on the Emirates International Panel of umpires (backups to the Elite Panel), stood in 19 one-day internationals during the same period. He officiated in three matches in the European Cricket Championships, four games in the DLF Cup in Kuala Lumpur, all three games between Kenya and Bermuda and two matches between New Zealand and Sri Lanka. He also stood in one Chappell-Hadlee Trophy match, three World Cup games and all three matches in the Afro-Asia Cup in India.

Gary Baxter, who is also on the International Panel, stood in nine one-day internationals during the past year. He officiated in two matches between New Zealand and Sri Lanka, six matches in the ICC World Cricket League in Kenya and one Chappell-Hadlee Trophy match.

• • •

Former New Zealand captain Jeff Crowe was the ICC Match Referee in seven tests and 23 one-day internationals over the last 12 months. He was involved in India's visit to West Indies, the Ashes series in Australia, four matches in Toronto, seven games in the Champions Trophy and 12 matches at the World Cup, including the final.

• • •

Michael Burns, who made his debut for Wellington against Canterbury, is the sixth first-class cricketer to be born in Balclutha. The others are Tom Freeman, Otago all-rounder of the 1940s, Bob Wilson, Otago batsman in the 1970s, Bill Aldridge (father of Graeme), who played for Canterbury in 1973/74, Otago all-rounder Chris Finch (who also played first-class rugby) and Otago's long-serving medium-pacer Aaron Gale.

Dominic Rayner, who made his debut for Central Districts against Northern Districts, is just the third first-class player to be born in Marton. The other two were Ken Cox, who played one match for Otago in 1933/34, and Paul Gibbs, Central Districts medium-pacer who played three matches in 1990/91.

• • •

Robbie Schaw, who made his debut for Central Districts in the first round game against Northern Districts, is only the second player born in Waipukurau to play first-class cricket. The only other was all-rounder Craig Findlay, who played for Central in the mid-1990s.

• • •

Greg Hay, who scored 98 not out on his first-class debut, for Central Districts against Wellington, is only the fifth first-class cricketer to be born in Rotorua. He follows Ray Hunter, Auckland off-spinner between 1975/76 and 1984/85, left-arm pace bowler Kingsley Smith, who played for Northern Districts in 1993/94, and current Northern players Daniel Flynn and Brad Leonard.

• • •

Chris Martin scored 0, 0 and 4 (all unbeaten) in his three test innings against Sri Lanka. He has now batted 44 times in tests without ever reaching double figures. This places him well ahead of Zimbabwe's Pommie Mbangwa (25) and South Africa's Cuan McCarthy (24) who also never reached ten at any stage.

He also extended his all-time test record of most consecutive single figure scores at any stage of a career. B.S. Chandrasekhar's "best" sequence was 32, while Australian Bruce Reid's last 31 innings failed to produce a double figure score. Chandra also had another sequence of 27 innings without reaching ten.

• • •

When he dismissed Prasanna Jayawardene in the first test at Christchurch, Martin became the eleventh bowler to take 100 test wickets for New Zealand. At that stage Martin had scored just 48 runs in test cricket, the least by any player at the time of capturing their 100th test wicket.

Other players with less than 100 runs to their name when they took their 100th test wicket were Glenn McGrath (67), Alf Valentine (75), Danish Kaneria (81), B.S. Chandrasekhar and Subhash Gupte (82) and Bruce Reid (88).

• • •

The test at Christchurch began on 7 December, the earliest starting date for any test in New Zealand. This was one day earlier than the test against Pakistan in December 1995, also at Christchurch. In 2002/03 the test against India at Wellington began on 12 December and in 1999/00 the match against West Indies at Hamilton began on 16 December.

• • •

Stu Mills caught Prasanna Jayawardene while fielding substitute in the second test against Sri Lanka at Wellington and, at least for the time being, joins the small list of players who have made a catch in a test for New Zealand without ever actually gaining a test cap.

The other players who have taken a catch as substitute but never gained test selection are: Tim Ritchie (v West Indies 1986/87), Mark Hastings (v Pakistan 1993/94), Marcel McKenzie (v England 2001/02) and Carl Cachopa (v West Indies 2005/06).

Daniel Vettori had a match analysis of 10-183 in the second test, the first time a spin bowler had taken ten wickets in a test at the Basin Reserve. Remarkably, however, his record for the best figures by a spinner at Wellington lasted just one day. Muttiah Muralitharan bowled Sri Lanka to victory the next day and ended with match figures of 10-118.

• • •

New Zealand were left to score 504 runs for victory in the second test, only the third time they had been set a target of over 500 runs to win a test. Details are:

target				*result*
550	v England	Christchurch	2001/02	(lost by 98 runs)
511	v England	Nottingham	1983	(lost by 165 runs)
504	v Sri Lanka	Wellington	2006/07	(lost by 217 runs)

• • •

The fifth one-day international between New Zealand and Sri Lanka at Hamilton was abandoned without any play taking place but, because the toss had been made, counts as an official game.

It was only the second time that this had happened and New Zealand were involved each time, the other game being a NatWest Series match against West Indies at Southampton in 2004, shortly after the ICC had brought in this rule. Players involved in both matches were Stephen Fleming, Nathan Astle, Daniel Vettori and Craig McMillan.

The match was also the 100th one-day international for umpire Billy Bowden, whose first one-dayer was in 1994/95, coincidentally also New Zealand v Sri Lanka at Hamilton.

• • •

By the end of the World Cup Shane Bond had taken 125 wickets in 67 one-day internationals, with the best strike rate of any bowler in one-day international history. The leaders in this particular category are *(minimum 1000 balls bowled)*:

	M	*Balls*	*Runs*	*Wkts*	*Ave*	*SR*
S.E. Bond *(NZ)*	67	3446	2416	125	19.32	27.5
A.H. Gray *(WI)*	25	1270	835	44	18.97	28.8
B. Lee *(A)*	150	7729	6048	267	22.65	28.9
G.I. Allott *(NZ)*	31	1528	1207	52	23.21	29.3
N.W. Bracken *(A)*	67	3303	2393	112	21.36	29.4

• • •

Former New Zealand Under 19 representative Jason Donnelly won a place as a rookie member of the South Australian squad for 2007/08 after impressing during a stint in Adelaide. He was named as part of a 29-strong squad which included past or present internationals Shaun Tait, Darren Lehmann, Matthew Elliott and Jason Gillespie.

He played one game for the South Australia 2nd XI in 2005/06. Donnelly had previously played for the Tracy Village club in Darwin during the New Zealand winter and then Adelaide club Tea Tree Valley, coached by former Australian legspinner Peter Sleep.

• • •

When Australia were dismissed for 148 in the first Chappell-Hadlee Trophy match at Wellington, it was their lowest all out total, batting first, for 14 years. Indeed, in their entire one-day international history Australia had only been bowled out for a lower score, when batting first, on four occasions. Their lowest is 101 against England at Melbourne in 1978/79.

New Zealand won the match without losing a wicket, Lou Vincent finishing the match with a six off Mitchell Johnson. This was the first time that Australia had lost a one-day international by ten wickets (in their 646th match). The unbeaten opening partnership of 149 between Vincent and Stephen Fleming was only the second century stand for the first wicket for New Zealand in 106 matches against Australia. Ken Rutherford and Bruce Edgar had put on 125 at Christchurch in 1985/86.

• • •

New Zealand won the next two matches chasing targets of 337 and 347. It was the first time that New Zealand had won a one-day series against Australia, let alone completed a clean sweep. The highest successful run chases in one-day internationals have all been at Australia's expense in recent times. The list is:

438-9	South Africa v Australia	Johannesburg	2005/06
350-9	New Zealand v Australia	Hamilton	2006/07
340-5	New Zealand v Australia	Auckland	2006/07
332-8	New Zealand v Australia	Christchurch	2005/06

• • •

By the end of the season Michael Parlane had scored 5664 runs in first-class cricket. Excluding players who played county cricket, he has now scored more runs than any other player without ever representing New Zealand. His 13 centuries are also more than anyone else has made without playing for New Zealand.

The only players who have scored more runs than Parlane without playing for New Zealand are Ray Hitchcock (12,473), who played just two matches in New Zealand before embarking on a long county career, and Peter Arnold (8013), who played most of his cricket for Northamptonshire.

Next on the list of most runs without playing for New Zealand are Chris Gaffaney (4711), and Scott Briasco (4390).

• • •

When Leighton Burtt made his first-class debut for Canterbury against Otago, it provided just the seventh instance of three generations of one family playing first-class cricket in New Zealand *(see New Zealand First-class Records).*

Burtt is the grandson of Noel Burtt, Canterbury leg-spinner of the 1930s and 40s and nephew of Noel's son Wayne, who played for Canterbury and Central Districts – 54 first-class games in all. Noel's brother was left-arm spinner Tom Burtt, who played ten tests and captured 408 wickets in first-class cricket.

Leighton Burtt's father, Mark, played hockey for New Zealand while his mother, Vicki (nee McGregor), played cricket for New Zealand. Mark and Wayne Burtt are also first cousins of former New Zealand wicketkeeper John Ward.

• • •

When Jacob Oram dismissed Paul Nixon in the Commonwealth Bank Series match at Adelaide in January he became the sixth New Zealand player to complete the double of 1000 runs and 100 wickets in one-day internationals. This group is:

	Runs	*Ave*	*Wkts*	*Ave*
C.L. Cairns	4950	29.46	201	32.80
R.J. Hadlee	1751	21.61	158	21.56
C.Z. Harris	4379	29.00	203	37.50
J.D.P. Oram	1547	22.75	110	30.58
S.B. Styris	3158	31.89	116	32.42
D.L. Vettori	1284	14.39	203	32.95

In the 2006 *Almanack* we listed instances of fathers and sons who had represented New Zealand in different sports. Following on from that theme, here is a list of players who have represented New Zealand at cricket and another sport.

Athletics: L.A. Cuff
Badminton: P.A. Horne
Basketball: J.C. Alabaster, N.S. Harford
Bowls: M.K. Boon
Football: G.P. Bilby, M.G. Burgess, C.C.R. Dacre, K.W. Hough, D.A.N. McRae, V. Pollard, E.V. Sale
Hockey: T.B. Burtt, E.G. McLeod, C.G. Rowe, K. Thomson
Indoor Cricket: A.R. Adams, I.E. O'Brien, M.B. Owens
Rugby League: V.J. Scott
Rugby Union: W.N. Carson, G.R. Dickinson, M.L. Page, B.J. McKechnie, C.J. Oliver, E.W.T. Tindill, J.W. Wilson

(M.P. Donnelly played cricket for New Zealand and rugby union for England.)

• • •

Sanath Jayasuriya became the leading six hitter in one-day internationals when he despatched Michael Mason over the rope in the fourth match of the series at Auckland. This was his 218th six, passing Shahid Afridi's tally, and, for good measure, Jayasuriya hit Mason's next two deliveries over the boundary as well.

Jayasuriya finished with 70 off 44 balls and at one stage hit five sixes in ten deliveries. New Zealand were bowled out for just 73, losing by 189 runs, their biggest ever defeat (although later surpassed when they lost by 215 runs to Australia in the World Cup).

• • •

Stephen Fleming has had a difficult time facing Sri Lanka's opening attack, particularly Chaminda Vaas, in recent matches. He was trapped in front, second ball, by Vaas at Napier in January 2006 and the next time the two teams met, at the Champions Trophy in October, he lasted 11 balls before falling lbw to Vaas again, for another duck, and then he was leg-before to Vaas' fifth ball at Auckland in January, again without scoring.

The run continued in the World Cup, when Fleming was out lbw to Vaas fourth ball in the Super Eights match at St George's for another duck. In the semi-final at Kingston, Fleming finally broke the sequence with an uppish single off Vaas but was lbw to Lasith Malinga in the next over for 1.

• • •

During the season Northland Cricket Association celebrated the opening of the new Cobham Oval, located on Okara Drive, 750 metres from the old ground, now a shopping area. Cobham Oval is a purpose built cricket facility with a nine wicket block, 75 metre boundaries, three-lane artificial pitch nets, with 30 metre run ups, and grass practice pitches.

There is also an indoor centre with three practice lanes with 25 metre run ups and a Lord's inspired pavilion. Northern Districts played Canterbury at the new ground in Twenty20 and State Shield games on 29 and 31 January. The pavilion was officially opened by the President of New Zealand Cricket, Don Neely, on 30 January.

• • •

When New Zealand White met India A at Darwin in July, it was the first time that two neutral teams had played a first-class game on Australian soil. The venue, Gardens Oval in Darwin, was also a new first-class ground. New Zealand White were also scheduled to play Pakistan A in a first-class game at Cairns but the match was abandoned without a ball being bowled. New Zealand umpire Gary Baxter was due to have stood in this match.

While compiling the obituary of Jack Scandrett, who had been Otago's oldest surviving first-class cricketer, an interesting family photograph came to light. The picture shows the Natal team which played MCC at Durban in January 1906. Included in the group is umpire A.J. Scandrett which was of interest as, previously, the identity of the umpires in this match had been unknown. Scandrett, uncle of Jack, also stood in one Currie Cup game in 1904/05.

He was connected with the New Zealand Insurance Company for 44 years. He joined the Invercargill branch in 1891 and when the Boer War started in 1899 he was sent to Durban to take charge of the company's agency there. He was later transferred to Singapore and in 1921 was appointed manager of the Western Australian branch in Perth, where he remained until his retirement.

• • •

During the winter an article in a New Zealand magazine, featuring an interview with Ross Taylor, revealed that his full name was "Luteru Ross Poutoa Taylor" and not "Ross Luteru Taylor" as he had previously advised us.

The item quoted Taylor as saying that he was used to using "Ross Luteru Taylor" and had not realised we required his full name. However, an examination of his passport record, held by New Zealand Cricket, shows his full name as "Luteru Ross Poutoa Lote Taylor" and we have changed our records accordingly.

• • •

During the season Christchurch student Steven Goulding recorded the second highest innings in non-first class cricket in New Zealand, scoring 358 for the St Bedes third eleven. He went in to bat at 2.30pm after Sydenham had scored 209 in their first innings.

When he was bowled at 6 pm he had amassed 358. Goulding and fellow opener Hamish Catherwood (132) produced an opening stand of 293. Goulding's first hundred was made up of ten sixes and six fours and his final score included 39 sixes and 21 fours. St Bedes declared at 575-2.

• • •

George Worker, who played for the New Zealand Under 19 team against India, is the great-grandson of a first cousin of former New Zealand batsman Rupert Worker. Prior to New Zealand gaining test status Rupert Worker played eight matches for New Zealand and, when he died in April 1989 aged 93, he had been the oldest living New Zealand first-class cricketer.

He also has the distinction of being the only person to play for Auckland, Wellington, Canterbury and Otago. In a first-class career spanning 16 seasons, Worker scored 2338 runs in 37 matches, at 34.90.

• • •

Former New Zealand softball captain Travis Wilson was the New Zealand team's fielding coach during the series against Sri Lanka. He also spent eight years on the books of the Atlanta Braves. He was one of five players called on to help New Zealand during an eventful day in the field during the second test against Sri Lanka at Wellington.

Already on were Wellington players Sam Fairley and Stu Mills (who took a catch) while Jamie Tong, Community Cricket Coordinator for Wellington Cricket, and former Central Districts A player Dave Rankin also had a turn.

A New Zealand Cricket spokesman said coach John Bracewell was close to putting the whites on and may have been next cab off the rank.

Jacob Oram had suffered a hamstring injury, Brendon McCullum sustained finger and foot injuries while batting and Shane Bond and James Franklin required spells off the park as well. Mathew Sinclair deputised behind the stumps, taking one catch.

There were a number of unusual happenings in the State Championship match between Otago and Wellington at University Oval. Otago captain Gareth Hopkins was injured after the toss had been made so had to play. Shaun Haig took over as keeper and Nathan McCullum captained the side in the field. Hopkins batted at number ten.

During the second day, after leaving the New Zealand test squad, Iain O'Brien replaced Scott Rasmussen but, as it turned out, he played no part in the game. Wellington were 5-2 at stumps on the first day and next morning were routed for just 71, after being 21-7 at one stage. O'Brien had not arrived by that time and Rasmussen was required to bat. Wellington followed on and batted out the remainder of the game, with no play being possible on the third day. O'Brien thus added to his tally of first-class games without getting on to the field of play.

• • •

David Houpapa, who made his debut for Auckland during the season, hails from Newman in Western Australia, population around 1000. He lived there until he was 16 before moving to Perth where he played for Wanneroo and age grade Western Australia teams. Team mates included Michael and David Hussey while opponents included Michael Clarke, Shane Watson and Mitchell Johnson.

Houpapa came to New Zealand in September 2003 to visit his grandparents and played for Eastern Suburbs in Wellington before coming to Auckland where he joined the Takapuna club. Houpapa's best effort in his first season of representative cricket was an 87-ball hundred, with seven sixes, in a State Shield match against Wellington.

• • •

The New Zealand Kiwis team which took part in the Hong Kong International Sixes tournament in November 2006 was Danny Morrison, Glen Sulzberger, Craig Spearman, Richard Petrie, Mark Bailey, Steve Brown, Steve Wilkins and Michael Hogan *(manager)*.

New Zealand were in a pool with South Africa and England but lost both matches. They then played off in the Cowdrey Group with Australia and Sri Lanka (who they defeated by 16 runs). South Africa defeated Pakistan in the final.

• • •

When New Zealand went into their Commonwealth Bank Series match against England at Adelaide on 23 January three players, Nathan Astle, Jacob Oram and Shane Bond, all had 99 one-day international wickets to their credit.

Oram and then Bond reached the 100 wicket milestone during the match but Astle was not required at the bowling crease as England were bowled out for just 120. As it happened, Astle announced his retirement after this match and remains the only player with 99 one-day wickets to his name.

• • •

Corey Anderson made his first-class debut for Canterbury against Central Districts at Napier aged just 16 years and 89 days. He was the youngest player to appear in a first-class match in New Zealand since Noel McGregor played for Otago against Fiji in 1947/48 aged 16 years and 86 days.

At the time, however, matches played by Fiji on that tour had been ruled as not first-class by the New Zealand Cricket Council and they were not given first-class status until 40 years later when the International Cricket Council overturned the original ruling.

The youngest player since that time had otherwise been Kirti Puna, who was 16 years and 147 days old when he played for the New Zealand Under 23 XI against Otago in 1971/72. Only seven New Zealand players are known to have been younger than Anderson when they made their first-class debuts.

In their State Shield match against Auckland on 24 January, Northern Districts scraped home with just four balls to spare after their chase was made tougher by the most unlikely set of circumstances.

After Northern had restricted Auckland to 216-8 in their fifty overs, fifty minutes' play was lost due to a fire in a lighting tower control box and some light drizzle. That meant eight overs were lost but Northern's target was reduced by only 18 runs under the Duckworth/Lewis system. An unbeaten stand of 68 for the seventh wicket between James Marshall and Daryl Tuffey saw Northern home.

• • •

Northern Districts allrounder Mark Orchard produced an outstanding double when he scored a century and also took four wickets in four balls for Te Rapa against Old Boys in the Hamilton limited overs club competition.

Orchard made 127 not out in Te Rapa's score of 356-4 and, in reply, Old Boys collapsed to be all out for 59. Orchard claimed the scalps of Cameron Weight (caught), Te Ahu Davis (lbw), Jono McNeil (lbw) and Daniel Wilson (bowled) with the first four balls of his third and last over to finish with figures of 4-3.

• • •

Hamish Marshall came close to equalling John Reid's New Zealand record of centuries in five consecutive first-class matches but fell for 70 in the second innings of Gloucestershire's match against Derbyshire in August 2006. Marshall joined Glenn Turner and Martin Crowe in scoring hundreds in four successive first-class matches:

J.R. Reid (5)			
101 & 118*	New Zealand v Orange Free State	Bloemfontein	1961/62
165 & 0	New Zealand v South African Colts XI	East London	1961/62
112	New Zealand v Natal	Pietermaritzburg	1961/62
60 & 142	New Zealand v South Africa	Johannesburg	1961/62
107	New Zealand v Border	East London	1961/62
G.M. Turner (4)			
118 & 18	Worcestershire v Sussex	Worcester	1979
131 & 14	Worcestershire v Surrey	Guildford	1979
120	Worcestershire v Leicestershire	Leicester	1979
56 & 150*	Worcestershire v Nottinghamshire	Worcester	1979
M.D. Crowe (4)			
151	Central Districts v Northern Districts	Morrinsville	1986/87
151 & 144	Central Districts v Canterbury	New Plymouth	1986/87
3 & 119	New Zealand v West Indies	Wellington	1986/87
10 & 104	New Zealand v West Indies	Auckland	1986/87
H.J.H. Marshall (4)			
112 & 20	Gloucestershire v Worcestershire	Worcester	2006
127 & 53	Gloucestershire v Glamorgan	Cheltenham	2006
21 & 168	Gloucestershire v Leicestershire	Cheltenham	2006
1 & 133	Gloucestershire v Northamptonshire	Northampton	2006

The record for all first-class cricket is held by Bill Ponsford with centuries in ten consecutive innings in 1926/27 and 1927/28. Ponsford's sequence included a quadruple century, two triples and two doubles.

The match in which Marshall scored his fourth hundred in successive matches had an unusual conclusion. Gloucestershire had followed on 278 runs behind against Northamptonshire and had reached 596-6 in its second knock when the innings was declared closed. In the 34 minutes of play that remained in the match Northants scored 35-0 but, more significantly, Marshall and Chris Taylor wheeled down 21 overs at an over rate of 37 per hour, saving their team some penalty points in the process.

• • •

Marshall was also involved in another match which contained a notable occurrence. Glamorgan's Michael Powell became just the second player to be dismissed for 299 in first-class cricket, joining Martin Crowe. Two other players have made 299 not out as this short list shows:

299*	D.G. Bradman	Australia v South Africa	Adelaide	1931/32
299*	S.S. Sugwekar	Maharashtra v Madhya Pradesh	Pune	1988/89
299	M.D. Crowe	New Zealand v Sri Lanka	Wellington	1990/91
299	M.J. Powell	Glamorgan v Gloucestershire	Cheltenham	2006

• • •

Former Northern Districts player Neisha Pratt captained the Hong Kong women's team in their first international series, a three-match contest against Pakistan in Lahore. Pratt recorded her team's highest individual score with 52 in the second match at Bagh-e-Jinnah. The other matches were played at Gaddafi Stadium.

In other women's cricket news, former New Zealand off-spinner and New Zealand Cricket's Women's Cricket Manager Catherine Campbell was the match referee for the three-game East Asia-Pacific Women's Cricket Challenge between Papua New Guinea and Japan at Port Moresby in September 2006.

• • •

Lou Vincent took a leaf out of Glenn Turner's book by scoring a century before lunch on the first morning of Worcestershire's county championship game against Essex on 30 August 2006. Vincent reached three figures with eight minutes remaining before the interval, becoming the first Worcestershire batsman to run up a hundred in the morning session of the first day since Turner did so in 1982.

• • •

Brendon McCullum scored 160 for Glamorgan against Leicestershire at Sophia Gardens in July, surpassing Javed Miandad's 140 not out against Essex at Swansea in 1980 as the highest score for the county by an overseas player on debut.

McCullum opened the batting when Glamorgan replied to Leicestershire's 560 and was third man out at 320. Glamorgan totalled 449 and the match was eventually drawn.

• • •

Although he had retired from international cricket, Chris Cairns was still in good form in England in 2006. He scored 144 not out off 111 balls (16 fours and six sixes) for Bacup against Haslingden in a Lancashire League match and a century from 56 balls (four fours and 11 sixes) against Lowerhouse. He also made a 57-ball unbeaten 113 for club side Lashings against a Cambridge University XI.

Cairns scored 953 runs at 63.53 and took 87 wickets at 10.37 in 25 matches for Bacup but suffered an injury on the last day of the season and was unable to bowl more than five overs. Bacup, who had been favourites to take the title, lost this match and Burnley were crowned champions for the first time since 1979.

The Twenty20 match between Northern Districts and Auckland at Seddon Park had an extraordinary finish and one which determined who hosted the final. Auckland needed 161 to win and after 19 overs were 146-5.

With Bruce Martin having finished his spell, a bowling change was required for the last over. Daryl Tuffey, with 0-27 from three overs, had one over remaining but James Marshall decided to give the ball to Graeme Aldridge, whose two overs had cost just four runs.

With a wicket, three singles and a dot ball Auckland were 149-6 with just one delivery remaining and it seemed certain that Otago would host the final. However, what should have been the final delivery of the game turned out to be a waist-high full toss, which was called no-ball, and also went for four. That meant that one ball still remained and just six were needed. Andre Adams, just the man for such a job, duly obliged and it was Auckland who had secured the right to host the final, where they comfortably defeated Otago by 50 runs.

• • •

Auckland were involved in another unusual incident during the Twenty20 round robin matches. Otago had batted first at Eden Park Outer Oval and reached 175-6 after 20 overs. Auckland, however, had not begun their final over by the stipulated time and Otago were awarded six penalty runs, the first time that this had happened in New Zealand. Auckland made 167-8 in reply, losing by 14 runs.

• • •

Former New Zealand fast bowler Andrew Penn took part in the inaugural Chris Cairns-organised Bob and Weave charity fight-night in London in June 2007. Penn won his bout after former England fast bowler David Lawrence was disqualified for landing knockout blows after the referee had stepped in to start a standing eight count.

After arriving back in New Zealand, where he is a senior solicitor in Wellington law firm Buddle Findlay, Penn said he definitely had no plans to come out of retirement, being quite content with his perfect record.

• • •

Auckland had contrasting fortunes during the State Championship competition in two matches played on Eden Park's Outer Oval in December. First they lost to Canterbury by just six runs – their closest loss ever in terms of runs – and a week later went down to Northern Districts by 318 runs. This was Northern's biggest ever win by a runs margin.

Auckland's only bigger losses had all been more than 80 years earlier – 512 runs against Wellington in 1925/26 (when they were set 631 to win), 365 runs against Wellington in 1923/24 (set 669) and 342 runs against Canterbury in 1924/25. They also lost by 318 runs to Canterbury in 1913/14.

• • •

Three of the players new to first-class cricket in 2006/07 were born in South Africa while another newcomer, with first-class experience behind him, was from Zimbabwe. This continues a trend of immigrants from southern Africa making their mark in New Zealand cricket in recent years.

Pieter Erasmus, who played in Auckland's final game of the season, arrived in New Zealand in July 2002. He started by playing rugby for Silverdale Under 21s and a work mate suggested he join the Birkenhead Cricket Club.

Erasmus played cricket throughout his entire school career, ending up in the 1st XI at Andrew Rabie High School. He also played for the local club's first team when only 17. He later moved to Pretoria where he played for Harlequins Cricket Club.

He captured 51 wickets for Birkenhead in 2006/07, his best figures being 7-49 and 8-31 against Takapuna in the same game.

Colin Munro, who also made his debut for Auckland, came to New Zealand in 2002. He started playing cricket at the age of six against nine-year-olds at Maidstone Primary School. He made his first representative team at the age of ten, playing in the Under 12 age group. He captained the Natal Country Districts Under 13 side and was selected in the Natal Under 13 B team to play in the National B Tournament.

Munro then moved to Glenwood High School where he continued to gain representative honours including the Natal PG Bison Under 15 team that played in the National Tournament in East London. He came to New Zealand the following year.

• • •

Andrew Niblett originally came to Auckland in May 2002 but moved to Napier where he was playing for Napier Old Boys Marist when he gained selection for Central Districts this past season.

Niblett had played senior club cricket in Cape Town and played for East Coast Bays and then Takapuna when he came to New Zealand. He has also been involved in coaching in New Zealand.

• • •

Colin de Grandhomme, who came to New Zealand in October 2006, was also a member of the Auckland team. He played representative cricket in Zimbabwe at Under 12, Under 13, Under 16 and Under 19 levels.

He played for Zimbabwe in the Under 19 World Cup in Bangladesh in February 2004, including the match where Zimbabwe defeated New Zealand by 92 runs. He made his first-class debut in October 2005 for Zimbabwe A against Kenya at Harare and also played five games for Zimbabwe Under 23s in the South African Airways Three-Day Challenge, scoring 109 against Eastern Province.

De Grandhomme's father, Laurence, played 16 first-class games between 1979/80 and 1987/88 including a tour of England in 1985 with the Zimbabwe team which included the young Graeme Hick. Laurence's uncle, Hilary Laurence de Grandhomme, played four matches for Rhodesia in the 1940s.

• • •

Just prior to leaving for the Champions Trophy the New Zealand squad members took part in a match at Lincoln on 30 September between the Bears and Tigers. Scores: **Bears** 229 in 48.5 overs (Mark Orchard 88, Ross Taylor 42, Kyle Mills 32, Nathan McCullum 23, Graeme Aldridge 3-32, Chris Martin 2-33, Jeetan Patel 2-45, Mark Gillespie 2-47) **defeated Tigers** 118 in 39.5 overs (Peter McGlashan 35, Nathan McCullum 2-6, Warren McSkimming 2-12, Kyle Mills 2-25, Shane Bond 2-34) by 111 runs.

• • •

The Auckland team which met Otago in the final State Championship game included four players who were born outside of New Zealand. The players involved were Colin de Grandhomme *(Zimbabwe)*, Carl Cachopa *(South Africa)*, Mayu Pasupati *(Sri Lanka)* and Pieter Erasmus *(South Africa)*.

During the season Auckland also fielded Tama Canning, Scott Styris and David Houpapa *(all born in Australia)*, Mal Loye *(England)* and Colin Munro *(South Africa)*.

• • •

Kumar Sangakkara scored 100 not out in Sri Lanka's total of 170 in the first test at Christchurch. In the entire history of test cricket there has only been one lower completed innings total to include a century and that was also at Christchurch and the batsman also scored exactly 100. John Reid made 100 out of New Zealand's 159 against England in 1962/63.

Sangakkara also achieved the rare feat of scoring at least half his side's runs in a completed test innings in successive matches. He was the first to do so in consecutive innings. This short list is:

L. Hutton	(202/344)	E v WI	The Oval	1950
	(62/122)	E v A	Brisbane	1950/51
C.L. Hooper	(73/139)	WI v P	Rawalpindi	1997/98
	(106/212)	WI v P	Karachi	1997/98
B.C. Lara	(196/347)	WI v SA	Port-of-Spain	2004/05
	(176/296)	WI v SA	Bridgetown	2004/05
K.C. Sangakkara	(100*/170)	SL v NZ	Christchurch	2006/07
	(156*/269)	SL v NZ	Wellington	2006/07

• • •

Daniel Vettori and Jeetan Patel put on 47 for the last wicket for New Zealand against Sri Lanka at the Champions Trophy in October 2006. This was the highest partnership of the innings, the fifth time the tenth wicket partnership had been the best for New Zealand in a one-day international. Not surprisingly, all games were lost. This list is:

10th wkt	*total*				
65	181	M.C. Snedden & E.J. Chatfield	NZ v SL	Derby	1983
46*	171-9	D.J. Nash & C Pringle	NZ v WI	Gauhati	1994/95
46	202	S.B. Styris & C.J. Drum	NZ v I	Hyderabad	1999/00
50	132	K.D. Mills & S.E. Bond	NZ v A	Colombo	2002/03
47	165	D.L. Vettori & J.S. Patel	NZ v SL	Bombay	2006/07

• • •

Chamara Silva created test history when he followed his pair on debut at Christchurch with 61 and 152 not out at Wellington. No other player had previously followed a debut pair with a fifty in their next test, let alone a century.

Indeed, only six other players – G.S. Ramchand, Graham Gooch, Ken Rutherford, Marvan Atapattu, Saeed Anwar and James Franklin – have ever recovered sufficiently from such an unfortunate start to post a century at any stage of their test career.

• • •

A number of other players have followed a pair (but not on debut) with a century in their next test. They are Mohinder Amarnath, Mike Atherton, Ian Botham, Grant Flower, Alvin Kallicharran, Derek McGlew, Ricky Ponting, Clifford Roach, Victor Trumper, Dilip Vengsarkar, Wazir Mohammad, Everton Weekes and Yashpal Sharma. Roach and Vengsarkar each had a sequence of century, pair, century.

• • •

Muttiah Muralitharan took ten wickets in the second test at Wellington but also registered a pair – the second time he had achieved that particular double in test cricket. Other players to have done so are George Lohmann, Clarrie Grimmett, Jack Cowie, Alf Valentine, Derek Underwood, B.S. Chandrasekhar, Waqar Younis and Shane Warne.

Two other players were in line to join the list in the last innings of that match. Daniel Vettori came out to bat in the second innings having also taken ten wickets and having been out for a duck in his first innings (he actually went on to top score with 51) while Lasith Malinga had recorded a pair and had taken five wickets in the first innings (but he added just two more in the second).

Vettori's innings of 51 was actually the highest for New Zealand in the entire game. Taking ten wickets in a test match and also top scoring is an extremely rare feat and had been achieved only three times before as the following reveals:

H. Trumble	(64* and 8-65 & 4-108)	A v E	The Oval	1902
I.T. Botham	(114 and 6-58 & 7-48)	E v I	Bombay	1979/80
C.L. Cairns	(72 and 3-73 & 7-27)	NZ v WI	Hamilton	1999/00
D.L. Vettori	(51 and 3-53 & 7-130)	NZ v SL	Wellington	2006/07

Botham scored the only fifty of the entire game and Vettori scored the only fifty of the match for New Zealand. Botham and Cairns ended up on the winning side, Vettori and Trumble on the loser's.

• • •

New Zealand won the second one-day international against Sri Lanka at Queenstown off the final ball of the game. Michael Mason hit Sanath Jayasuriya for four after playing out the first five balls of the final over which had begun with the scores level.

Here is a list of one-day international matches involving New Zealand which were won by the team batting second off the last possible ball of the match.

New Zealand (213-8)	Pakistan (214-9)	Multan	1984/85
Zimbabwe (258-7)	New Zealand (260-5)	Dhaka	1998/99
New Zealand (191)	South Africa (194-8)	Napier	1998/99
New Zealand (256-9)	South Africa (258-7)	Cape Town	2000/01
New Zealand (291-8)	West Indies (292-6)	Arnos Vale	2001/02
Sri Lanka (224-7)	New Zealand (228-9)	Queenstown	2006/07

• • •

At the end of the test series against Sri Lanka Shane Bond had bowled in 28 test innings and had taken at least one wicket in each. This is easily the best effort for any bowler from the start of his test career. Walter Robins *(England)* and Andy Roberts *(West Indies)* took at least one wicket in the first 23 test innings they bowled in. Johnny Hayes (13 innings), Jacob Oram (12) and Gavin Larsen (10) are New Zealand's other leaders in this category.

• • •

Both captains were dismissed without scoring in the fourth one-day international between New Zealand and Sri Lanka at Auckland. This had happened just six times previously as shown on this list (team batting first is listed first):

			captains
Canada v England	Manchester	1979	B.M. Mauricette & J.M. Brearley
Australia v England	Sydney	1982/83	K.J. Hughes & R.G.D. Willis
Australia v Sri Lanka	Adelaide	1998/99	S.K. Warne & A. Ranatunga
Zimbabwe v Kenya	Dhaka	1998/99	A.D.R. Campbell & Asif Karim
Pakistan v South Africa	Sharjah	1999/00	Moin Khan & S.M. Pollock
West Indies v England	Georgetown	2003/04	R.R. Sarwan & M.P. Vaughan
Sri Lanka v New Zealand	Auckland	2006/07	D.P.M.D. Jayawardene & S.P. Fleming

• • •

Michael Papps appeared for Accrington in the Lancashire League in April 2007 and had some success in their home match against East Lancashire. Papps, whose first-class bowling figures read 2-0-6-0, claimed 5-37 bowling first change and hit an unbeaten century in Accrington's chase. Unfortunately, his team still lost.

The three New Zealand defence forces took part in numerous matches over the past 12 months. Details of these games and also those of the previous season (which were not included in the 2006 *Almanack*) are as follows.

Royal New Zealand Air Force Inter-base Cricket

2006
Ohakea 210-9 (G. Burnnand 71, D. Grant 70, N. Hodges 4-35) **defeated Auckland** 124 (D. Croucher 26, N. Hodges 25, P. Hunter 4-27) by 86 runs *(men's final)*

Auckland 169 (A. Walding 60, T. Harrison 3-20) **defeated Ohakea** 96 (S. Macks 26, S. van Deventer 3-18, A. Walding 2-6) by 73 runs *(women's final)*

2007
Woodbourne 131 (A. Julian 23, H. Madsen 2-15, G. Schofield 2-24, T. Chambers 2-16, B. Cunningham 2-28, P. Hunter 2-40) **lost to Ohakea** 132-6 (D. Swanson 24, H. Madsen 21, G. Whitley 30*, D. Grant 2-12) *(men's final)*

Men's Player of the Tournament was Sgt Glen Whitley *(Ohakea)*

Ohakea 91 (K. Waite 26, R. Blucher 3-18, L. White 2-12, A. Walding 2-21) lost to **Woodbourne** 92-2 (B. Pothan 56*) by 8 wickets *(women's final)*

Women's Player of the Tournament was F/S Karen Middlemiss *(Auckland)*

Inter-services Cricket

2006
Royal New Zealand Navy 270-7 (J. Smilie 118, B. Reardon 37, G. Cossey 3-65) **defeated New Zealand Army** 132 (W. Bramley 46, A. McQuillan 31, G. Simpkins 4-22, R. Jackson 4-24) by 138 runs

Royal New Zealand Navy 162 (J. Smilie 57,B. Cunningham 3-34) **lost to Royal New Zealand Air Force** 166-3 (G. Whitley 61*, K. Bevins 59*) by 7 wickets

New Zealand Army 168 (W. Bramley 58, T. Medland 35, T. Chambers 4-35) **lost to Royal New Zealand Air Force** 169-6 (D. Grant 61, M. Beaven 34, N. Hodges 25*, A. McQuillan 3-30) by 4 wickets.

2007
New Zealand Army 227-7 (R. Lorimar 66, R. King 45, T. Horne 25, D. Tapene 3-80, J. Rees 2-32) **defeated Royal New Zealand Navy** 115 (G. Gatley 23, T Horne 4-42, Z. Langford 3-12) by 112 runs.

New Zealand Army 206 (R. King 52, W. Clews 48, K. Hurrell 43, B. Cunningham 3-7, D. Hamilton 3-42) **lost to Royal New Zealand Air Force** 207-3 (D. Grant 66, M. Robinson 61, K. Bevins 32*, G. Burnnand 27*, R. King 2-31) by 7 wickets.

Royal New Zealand Air Force 197 (M. Robinson 81, K. Bevins 28, D. Grant 25, H. Moon 3-33, D. Walker 2-38, J. Rees 2-29) **defeated Royal New Zealand Navy** 127 (M. O'Brien 25, H. Madsen 3-13, B. Cunningham 2-9, D. Hamilton 2-32) by 70 runs.

RNZAF won the Bill Morley Cup for the 7th year in succession.
Player of the tournament was Sgt Mason Robinson *(RNZAF)*

Other representative matches

Manawatu 239 (J. Cunningham 87*, A. Griffin 51, H. Madsen 25, N. Hodges 3-41) **defeated New Zealand Defence Force** 233 (G. Burnnand 65, N. Hodges 53, D. Grant 44, D. White 3-24, J Davies 3-40) by 6 runs

Wanganui Invitation XI 175 (M. Fraser 80, D. Campion 34, D. Hamilton 7-40) **lost to New Zealand Defence Force** 178-6 (W. Bramley 28, J. Smillie 26, G. Burnnand 25*, D. Grant 22) by 4 wickets.

Royal Australian Air Force 237 (P. Collins 72, M. Cooper 71, M. Beaven 3-42) and 410-7d (A. Bosworth 175, S. Binnion 87, P. Collins 46, D. Morris-Brauer 40, G. Burnnand 2-12) **drew with Royal New Zealand Air Force** 274 (D. Hamilton 72, D. Grant 59, K. Bevins 41, A. Bosworth 5-21) and 187-1 (G. Whitley 100*, D. Grant 69*)

Auckland Development XI 235-7 (G. Morgan 59, K. Todd 47, R. Hira 44*, T. Medland 2-29, T. Horne 2-35, M. Tulloch 2-38) **defeated New Zealand Defence Force** 169 (G. Whitley 37, R. King 33, H. Moon 27, G. Morgan 3-11, J. Raval 2-14) by 66 runs).

• • •

Shane Bond achieved New Zealand's second one-day international hat trick (Danny Morrison took the first) in the Commonwealth Bank Series match against Australia at Hobart on 14 January. Australia's total of 289-8 was the highest to include a hat trick as illustrated by the following table:

Australia (289-8) v New Zealand	Hobart	2006/07	S.E. Bond
West Indies (283) v South Africa	Bridgetown	2004/05	C.K. Langveldt
West Indies (239) v Pakistan	Sharjah	1989/90	Wasim Akram
Zimbabwe (238) v Bangladesh	Harare	2006/07	Shahadat Hossain
Australia (230) v Pakistan	Sharjah	1989/90	Wasim Akram
Australia (224-9) v West Indies	Bombay	2006/07	J.E. Taylor
New Zealand (221-9) v India	Nagpur	1987/88	C. Sharma
Sri Lanka (204-9) v India	Calcutta	1990/91	Kapil Dev

• • •

In New Zealand's Super Eights match against Australia at the World Cup, Peter Fulton opened the innings and was last man out. This had happened only twice before in one-day internationals as listed below. The player concerned ended up on the losing side on each occasion.

A.D.R Campbell (102)	Zimbabwe (239) v Australia	Ahmedabad	1997/98
S. Chanderpaul (67)	West Indies (169) v India	Cuttack	2006/07
P.G. Fulton (62)	New Zealand (133) v Australia	Grenada	2006/07

• • •

Elite Panel umpire Aleem Dar played for Takapuna/Birkdale against RNZAF Base Auckland between the first and second Chappell-Hadlee Trophy matches scoring 47 and conceding 15 runs off five overs. Dar, a right-arm leg-spinner, played 17 first-class matches in Pakistan between 1986/87 and 1997/98.

• • •

Jack Booker, whose obituary appears in this edition of the *Almanack*, played in one first-class game, for Canterbury against Fiji in 1947/48. He actually became a first-class cricketer at the age of 72 when the International Cricket Council ruled that matches played by Fiji against the major associations on that tour should be ranked as first-class.

This was despite the original and several subsequent rulings by the New Zealand Cricket Council that the matches were not to be regarded as such.

The Booker family provided us with a splendid photograph of the two teams, taken in front of the Memorial Gates at Lancaster Park, and we have reproduced it for this edition.

Central Districts batsman Greg Hay, who scored 98 not out on debut, finished the season with 593 runs at 45.61. This is the most runs any New Zealand batsman has scored in his first season of first-class cricket in New Zealand.

Only three players had previously scored as many as 500 runs in their debut season – Barry Cooper (520 in 1980/81), Scott Briasco (519 in 1982/83) and Bill Carson (500 in 1936/37). Carson played just four innings, making 12, 290, 194 and 4.

• • •

A pre-season Twenty20 tournament was held at Invercargill from 10-12 November but was completely ruined by the weather. Details were:

Canterbury 152-8 lost to Auckland 153-7
Otago 174-8 lost to Northern Districts 177-6
Auckland 140-7 lost to Central Districts 99-5 *(D/L)*
Northern Districts 185-6 lost to Wellington 113-7 *(D/L)*

No play was possible in the two matches between Canterbury and Wellington, the two between Central Districts and Otago and the final.

Highest individual innings were Michael Parlane 82 (46), James Marshall 72 (34), Geoff Barnett 64 (30), Gareth Hopkins 61 (25), Craig Cumming 54 (34). Matches were played at Southland Boys' High School and Queen's Park.

• • •

During the season we obtained details of a number of former first-class umpires whose deaths had previously gone unrecorded. They are:

Jack William Henry Annan (1920-2005). Eight first-class matches including the Governor-General's XI v West Indies in 1968/69. He was also a rugby referee.

Robert George Condliffe (1923-2004). One first-class game, one one-day game and one women's one-day international.

Ballantyne (Bal) Dennison (1919-2006). Seven first-class games, two one-day matches (both of which were domestic finals) and one women's test.

Frank Fielding (1919-2006). Three first-class games and four one-day matches.

James Errol Fitzgerald (1931-2005). One first-class game and one one-day game.

Leslie Henry George Harmer (1921-2007). Umpired nine first-class games, and two one-day games including one one-day international, the first ever played between New Zealand and Australia, in Dunedin on 30 March, 1974.

Leslie Francis Jones (1939-2007). 17 first-class games, 10 one-day games and one youth test match.

Adrian Thomas Keown (1955-2007). Two first-class games, six one-day matches, one women's one-day international, one youth test and two youth one-day internationals.

John Joseph Loftus (1917-2004). One first-class game in January 1958 (with Eric Tindill).

William George Cyril Sewell (1921-2005). 20 first-class games and one women's test. He was also a rugby league referee.

The seventeenth Gillette Cup limited-overs competition for secondary school boys was played in Palmerston North from 14-17 December 2006. A total of 168 teams entered the competition which is now organised by each major association within their boundaries, with one winner from each progressing to the final.

The runners-up from Central Districts and Northern Districts, the two associations with the most entries, also contested the finals, which were expanded to four days. Christchurch Boys' High School and King's College were declared joint winners after rain led to the abandonment of play on the final day.

The 2006 Gillette Player of the Year was also shared, with Corey Anderson *(Christchurch Boys' High School)* and Tim Southee *(King's College)* taking the Geoffrey Palmer Cup. Results were:

GROUP A

Round 1
Otago Boys' High School 219-6 lost to **Tauranga Boys' College** 223-3 by 7 wickets
Rathkeale College 130 lost to **King's College** 132-4 by 6 wickets

Round 2
Rathkeale College 184 lost to **Tauranga Boys' College** 185-7 by 3 wickets
Otago Boys' High School 77 lost to **King's College** 81-2 by 8 wickets

Round 3
Otago Boys' High School 220-9 **defeated Rathkeale College** 210 by 10 runs
Tauranga Boys' College 89 lost to **King's College** 91-1 by 9 wickets

GROUP B

Round 1
Christchurch Boys' High School 295-4 defeated **Hamilton Boys' High School** 216-4 by 79 runs
St Patrick's College 171-6 lost to **Palmerston North Boys' High School** 173-7 by 3 wickets

Round 2
Palmerston North Boys' High School 153 defeated **Hamilton Boy' High School** 150 by 3 runs
Christchurch Boys' High School 277-6 defeated **St Patrick's College** 77 by 200 runs

Round 3
St Patrick's College 178-8 defeated **Hamilton Boys' High School** 173 by 5 runs
Palmerston North Boys' High School 202-7 lost to **Christchurch Boys' High School** 206-2 by 8 wickets

Finals
All matches abandoned with no play

Final placings: Christchurch Boys' High School and King's College 1st equal, Palmerston North Boys' High School and Tauranga Boys' College 3rd equal, Otago Boys' High School and St Patrick's College 5th equal, Hamilton Boys' High School and Rathkeale College 7th equal.

• • •

The thirteenth national secondary schools girls competition, sponsored by New Zealand Community Trust, was played in Christchurch from 12-15 December, 2006. The tournament was moved from the traditional venue of Palmerston North to coincide with the Women's Development Tournament, with many of the players being involved in both competitions.

A total of 111 schools entered the competition with eight teams represented at the finals. These were the winners from each major association plus the runners-up of the two associations with the most entries. New Plymouth Girls' High School retained their title while Player of the Tournament (Ina Lamason Trophy) was Katie Perkins *(Westlake Girls High School).*

Results were:

GROUP A

Round 1
Marian College 64 lost to **New Plymouth Girls' High School** 65-3 by 7 wickets
Westlake Girls' High School 188-5 defeated **Tauranga Girls' College** 98 by 90 runs

Round 2
New Plymouth Girls' High School 99-6 defeated **Westlake Girls' High School** 76 by 23 runs
Tauranga Girls' College 138 defeated **Marian College** 66 by 72 runs

Round 3
Westlake Girls' High School 205-3 defeated **Marian College** 36 by 171 runs
Tauranga Girls' College 34-8 lost to **New Plymouth Girls' High School** 35-0 by 10 wickets

GROUP B

Round 1
Havelock North High School 124 defeated **Otago Girls' High School** 48 by 76 runs
Whangarei Girls' High School 198-6 defeated **Wellington Girls' College** 82 by 116 runs

Round 2
Otago Girls' High School 143-4 lost to **Whangarei Girls' High School** 144-3 by 7 wickets
Wellington Girls' College 126 defeated **Havelock North High School** 114 by 12 runs

Round 3
Havelock North High School 139-5 defeated **Whangarei Girls' High School** 86 by 53 runs
Wellington Girls' College 97 lost to **Otago Girls' High School** 98-2 by 8 wickets

Finals
Havelock North High School 49 lost to **New Plymouth Girls' High School** 50-5 by 5 wickets
Westlake Girls' High School 145-6 beat **Whangarei Girls' High School** 71 by 78 runs
Tauranga Girls' College 137-9 beat **Otago Girls' High School** 97 by 40 runs
Marian College 86 beat **Wellington Girls' College** 68 by 18 runs

Final placings: New Plymouth Girls' High School 1st, Havelock North High School 2nd, Westlake Girls' High School 3rd, Whangarei Girls High School 4th, Tauranga Girls College 5th, Otago Girls High School 6th, Marian College 7th, Wellington Girls' College 8th.

• • •

There was some very high scoring during the first-class season. There were five totals of 600 or more recorded in domestic cricket, an extraordinary achievement when, in the entire history of New Zealand first-class cricket, there had been only five prior to this past season. Wellington and Otago reached 600 for the first time ever while Wellington and Central Districts also conceded 600 for the first time ever.

A total of 56 centuries were recorded in first-class cricket in 2006/07 compared to only 30 the previous season. This broke the all-time record of 51, set in 1991/92. A total of 36 players scored hundreds, just short of the record of 39 set in 1998/99.

There were 64 century partnerships in 2006/07 compared to 44 the previous season. The record is 73 in 2000/01.

OBITUARIES

Esther Elizabeth BLACKIE

Born: *Dunedin, 29 January, 1916*

Died: *Invercargill, 9 March, 1991*

Right-hand batsman, wicketkeeper

Esther Blackie was the second Otago player to be selected in a New Zealand women's test team when she made her debut against England in March 1949 at Eden Park. A reliable catcher behind the stumps, Blackie took two catches during England's first innings and a further catch, along with a stumping, from the bowling of Grace Gooder, who was to go on and capture eight wickets in her one and only test. It was to be Blackie's only test as well.

Although an accomplished batsman with Otago, Blackie (nee Ferguson) was placed at number ten during both New Zealand innings of this test. She made 8 in the first innings while in the second she added 20 for the last wicket with Gooder (11), remaining unbeaten on 13 to leave her with a Test batting average of 21. This was the last New Zealand women's test match until the 1954 three-test tour of England.

Blackie's highest score for Otago was 91 against Canterbury at the Basin Reserve in 1949/50 during a Hallyburton-Johnston quadrangular tournament. It was in this game that her near namesake, Phyll Blackler, stamped her mark as a quality all-rounder by scoring an unbeaten 182 during Canterbury's first innings before following this by taking 5-25 during Otago's first innings.

Later in the tournament Blackie made 58 against Wellington and 62 against Auckland. She continued to play for Otago for another decade, captaining her province for several years before being succeeded in this job by another former New Zealand player, Betty Sinclair (nee Butler).

Jack Francis BOOKER

Born: *Christchurch, 4 June, 1915*

Died: *Waikanae, 17 April, 2003*

Right-hand batsman, right-arm medium-pace bowler

Jack Booker became a first-class cricketer at the age of 72 when the International Cricket Council ruled that matches played by Fiji against the major associations in New Zealand in 1947/48 should be ranked as first-class. This was despite the original and subsequent rulings of the New Zealand Cricket Council that the matches were not to be regarded as such.

Booker was educated at Shirley Primary and Christchurch Boys' High School. He joined the West Christchurch club and was a member of the Canterbury team which won the Brabin Shield.

He went to England in 1939 and worked in London. He volunteered with the National Fire Service arm of Civil Defence during the blitz and soon after joined the RAF and saw service with Air Sea Rescue in Iceland. He later transferred to the RNZAF.

During the war, he played cricket for London Harlequins and the New Zealand Services team. Returning to New Zealand after the war he continued with West Christchurch and was selected for Canterbury's game against Fiji in March 1948.

Booker batted at number nine in Canterbury's first innings of 421-9 declared, scoring 25 before being stumped. Opening the bowling he took 1-43 from 16 overs in Fiji's first innings, the wicket of prolific opening batsman Harry Apted, and 3-41, off 17 overs, in the second. Left to score 355 in 275 minutes to win the game, Fiji made a gallant effort before being bowled out for 318.

Booker played senior cricket for West Christchurch from 1934/35 to 1952/53 scoring 822 runs and taking 186 wickets. In 1948/49 he took 46 wickets, the highest in senior cricket that season. In 1953 his company, Lane Walker Rudkin, transferred him to Wellington as branch manager. He remained with the firm until his retirement. From 1954 he played for Hutt District Cricket Club and continued playing in various grades into his 60s.

Throughout his life he was an avid, active and competitive sportsman, with interests in cricket, rugby, tennis, golf and, in his later years, bowls. He had something of a reputation at the Waikanae Bowls Club for snatching a win in the eyes of seeming defeat and for this reason was nicknamed "Burglar" Booker for stealing the game. Consequently, he came home with more than his fair share of meat packs!

Graham Stuart BOTTING

***Born:** Dunedin, 27 June, 1915*

***Died:** Turangi, 8 March, 2007*

Right-hand batsman, wicketkeeper

Graham Botting had the distinction of being both the oldest surviving Central Districts player and, following Walter Hadlee's death, also the oldest living Otago first-class cricketer.

Curiously, though, Botting's entry into the first-class game, at the age of 33, was for neither of these sides. In choosing the team to go to England in 1949 the New Zealand selectors cast their net far and wide and every effort was made to provide the opportunity for every candidate to stake their claim.

Never before had such steps been taken. District trials were conducted so that players from every minor association in the country were given a chance (this at the time when there were only four first-class sides in New Zealand).

Botting (a member of the Athletic Cricket Club in Nelson) played for the North Minor Associations in the South Island trial and then for a New Zealand XI against The Rest in the final trial at Lancaster Park, a match which was given first-class status.

The New Zealand XI included two wicketkeepers, Otago's George Mills being the other, while Len Kent kept for The Rest. Ironically, none of the three gained selection for the tour. Frank Mooney, who was given permission to keep as a substitute after Kent was injured, was the one who got the nod.

Botting had played in the annual Plunket Shield trial between Wellington Town and Country without ever getting a call to higher honours but when Central Districts came in to being from the 1950/51 season, Botting was their first choice as keeper and remained so for their first three seasons.

Central Districts made their debut against Wellington at the Basin Reserve in December 1950 but lost by an innings. They did much better in their second game, defeating Canterbury by 144 runs. Although his overall batting record was modest, Botting made a useful 27 not out in this low-scoring match, putting on an invaluable 40 for the last wicket, in just 28 minutes, with Arthur Cresswell.

Having played in all of Central's Plunket Shield matches to date (plus a two-day game against South Africa in 1952/53) Botting moved to Dunedin for the 1953/54 season where he played for the Grange club. In 1953 the *Almanack* had said "Botting, as usual, was a quiet and efficient wicketkeeper."

Botting played in Otago's first three games. In the match against Wellington he and Ewen Cameron added 31 for the last wicket in Otago's second innings, a match they eventually won by just three runs. In the next match Otago needed 180 to defeat Central Districts. Botting came in at 162-9 and hit Rex Challies for six (his last scoring shot in first-class cricket) to take the score to 174 but Harry Cave then bowled Frank Cameron with the first ball of the next over to end the game.

After leaving Otago Boys' High School, Botting had entered Otago University while he was only 16 and was one of their youngest students ever to graduate with an MA. While at university he played cricket and hockey and was also a useful boxer. He represented New Zealand at hockey against India in 1938.

He also had a life-long interest in education. He attended teachers' training college in Auckland and moved to Palmerston North where he later became friends with future Central Districts and New Zealand wicketkeeper Ian Colquhoun, who had a long career at Palmerston North Boys' High School.

Botting taught at Nelson College during the war, where he also coached the cricket and hockey first elevens. He represented Nelson, opening the batting during the 1940s. He then taught at King Edward Technical College in Dunedin for two years before moving north to become head of English at Hawera Technical High School. He turned out for the Taranaki representative team for several more seasons and he was also a Taranaki hockey selector during this time.

After a short stint in central Hawke's Bay he became a post-primary school inspector in the lower North Island and then a senior inspector. He later returned to teaching and also helped mark the School Certificate English exam for several years.

Botting also held a Diploma in Physical Education and was an army PT instructor in Rotorua during the war, having been ruled unfit for active service because of an eyesight problem. This did not seem to impair his wicketkeeping, however. He was noted for standing up to all bowlers, even the fastest.

He was also adept at making leg-side stumpings, especially off the pace bowlers. At the Basin Reserve in December 1951 he made three stumpings in one innings – two off Harry Cave and one off Fen Cresswell. The match report in the *Almanack* made a special mention of "brilliant wicketkeeping by Botting."

Botting's record in first-class cricket is:

Season	***M***	***I***	***NO***	***HS***	***Runs***	***Ave***	***100***	***50***	***ct/st***
1948/49	1	1	0	3	3	3.00	–	–	1
1950/51	4	7	1	27*	65	10.83	–	–	4/2
1951/52	4	7	0	7	28	4.00	–	–	6/4
1952/53	4	4	1	11*	13	4.33	–	–	4/5
1953/54	3	6	3	16	55	18.33	–	–	9/3
TOTAL	**16**	**25**	**5**	**27***	**164**	**8.20**	–	–	**24/14**

For	***M***	***I***	***NO***	***HS***	***Runs***	***Ave***	***100***	***50***	***ct/st***
CD	12	18	2	27*	106	6.62	–	–	14/11
Otago	3	6	3	16	55	18.33	–	–	9/3
NZ XI	1	1	0	3	3	3.00	–	–	1
TOTAL	**16**	**25**	**5**	**27***	**164**	**8.20**	–	–	**24/14**

Hilda Evelyn BUCK

Born: *Palmerston North, 27 December, 1914*

Died: *Wellington, 10 May, 1990*

Right-hand batsman, wicketkeeper

Although she played only one test, Hilda Buck created New Zealand women's test history by being the first Kiwi player to face a delivery, the first player to be dismissed and the first player to be dismissed without scoring, or Buck-a-Duck as she later jovially called it.

Buck was educated at Brooklyn School alongside the future Prime Minister, Jack Marshall, and Wellington Technical College. After leaving secondary school she became one of the founding members of the Wellington Technical College Old Girls' Club alongside her future sister-in-law and New Zealand team-mate, Agnes Ell.

A sound bat who also possessed many strokes, Buck scored 12 and a duck on her Wellington debut against Wanganui at the Wellington Boys' College Ground in 1934. The following year Buck scored 13 and 17 against the touring English side to secure her a place in the one-off test at Lancaster Park.

Besides being selected for her country, the 1935/36 season was also a good one for Buck as an inaugural member of the winning Hallyburton-Johnstone Shield side and as captain of the successful Tech Old Girls, which won the Wellington women's club championship.

Buck was chosen as a specialist batsman in the test, being dismissed without scoring in the first innings and for 16 in the second, sharing a 34-run opening partnership with Margaret Marks. Although not chosen in the New Zealand side as the wicketkeeper, Buck showed her ability behind the stumps the following season by stumping the future New Zealand wicketkeeper Joan Fowler off the Wellington medium-fast bowler Agnes Ell. She had earlier scored 16 during her side's first innings before being stumped in turn by Fowler.

Buck's highest representative score came against Auckland at the Domain in February 1936 when she made an aggressive 74. Superb form at club level, including 105 against the Wellington Club the following season, saw Buck retain her place in the Wellington team. Her form with the bat at representative level, however, diminished and to her disappointment she missed out to Joan Fowler as the first choice New Zealand wicketkeeper for the tour to New South Wales in 1938.

Buck continued to play for Wellington until 1940 and first began signs of returning to form with 28 against Otago at the Oval Ground in Dunedin in January 1939, before scoring 67 against the same opposition the following year at the Basin Reserve.

Her final match for Wellington, in February 1940, saw her bow out on a high note with 25 and 63 against Canterbury, before being bowled by Phyll Blackler at the Wellington Boys' College Ground. She married the former Wellington player Jimmy Ell in 1946 and in doing so became the sister-in-law of her former Wellington and New Zealand team mate Agnes Hurcomb (nee Ell).

Agnes Elizabeth ELL

Born: *Wellington, 17 January, 1917*

Died: *Wellington, 13 July, 2003*

Right-hand batsman, right-arm medium-fast bowler

The younger sister of former Wellington representative Jimmy Ell, Agnes Ell was in the first New Zealand women's test side which played England at Lancaster Park in 1935.

From a young age, Ell played backyard cricket with her older brother in Johnsonville, where she attended Johnsonville School, before going on to the Wellington Technical College. Renowned for a long bowling run-up and a fine control of the ball, Ell tested many opponents both at club and provincial level in the lead-up to the Second World War.

Ell made her Wellington debut at the age of 17 against Wanganui at the Wellington Boys' College ground in March 1934. She gave an excellent all-round display by top scoring for Wellington with 31 at the top of the order out of a team total of 85, before being bowled by her future New Zealand team-mate, Mabel Corby. She then took 4-20 with the ball. During Wanganui's second innings, Ell went one step better with 4-12 to give her match figures of 8-29. The match was one of the first women's representative fixtures in New Zealand.

The following season, Ell regained her place in the Wellington side after coming away from the Probables-Possibles trial match with figures of 7-22. During the Wellington v England match at the Basin Reserve, Ell made an immediate impact with the ball by bowling the English captain, Myrtle Maclagan, with the first ball of the innings. She finished with 4-58 off 20 overs.

Her only test appearance was nothing short of disappointing, making a single run in each innings and going wicketless, while conceding 55 runs. The following season saw Ell score 29 at number eleven against Nelson, adding 92 for the last wicket with Nan Sheridan (66 not out). There was an irony to this innings as just two seasons earlier she had batted at number one for Wellington during her representative debut.

Useful performances for her Wellington Technical College Old Girls' side kept Ell in the Wellington side until 1940. She married the former Institute Club senior opening batsman Jack Hurcomb in 1942 and soon gave away the game for good. In the 1950s, the Hurcombs were living in Tawa where Agnes helped her husband run a grocery shop and they became members of the Tawanui Bowling Club. In 1962 they won the mixed pairs at the club and later were awarded Life Membership.

Ell's success at outdoor bowls saw her switch to the indoor variety and she represented the North Wellington Indoor Bowls Association against Wairarapa, some 64 years after having first played for Wellington at cricket. Her busy lifestyle, helping to run the grocery shop along with playing bowls at every given opportunity, meant that she never returned in any capacity to the first sport in which she had success.

Violet Helen Maude FARRELL

Born: *London, 20 August, 1913*

Died: *Wellington, 22 April, 1989*

Right-hand batsman, wicketkeeper

Vi Farrell (nee Taylor) moved to New Zealand in 1926 with her parents and older brother and. after leaving school, began work as a gifted commercial artist. Although she had played basketball for the South of England before coming to New Zealand, it was not until around 1935 that she began playing cricket after driving past a ground and noticing that women were playing.

After a handful of club games with the Nairn Street Swifts Club, Taylor (as she was until marrying in 1941) was selected in the 1936 Wellington side as a specialist batsman for a one-off match against Auckland at Eden Park, while Hilda Buck kept wickets. This was to be her only match for Wellington until provincial cricket resumed after World War Two.

Farrell was by now a member of the Kilbirnie Club and after coaching encouragement from both Frank Mooney and John Reid, her wicketkeeping ability shone through. Both thought highly of her ability and soon the bespectacled Farrell was chosen for the Wellington side and made her New Zealand debut on a five-match tour of New South Wales in 1947.

She made her test debut in the one-off test against Australia at the Basin Reserve in 1947-48. The following season Esther Blackie was given preference as the New Zealand wicketkeeper in the single test against England at Eden Park. In 1949 Farrell became a double international, playing for the New Zealand women's basketball team where her 5ft 11in frame was put to good use.

Farrell was selected for the 1954 tour to England but lost her place to the deputy wicketkeeper Joyce Clothier for the first test at Headingley. She was chosen for the second at Worcester and she justified her selection with three stumpings and a catch during England's first innings to set a New Zealand women's record.

She also played in the third and final test at the Oval, taking four catches in the England first innings. During the tour, Farrell collected 24 dismissals, 16 catches and eight stumpings.

After returning from the tour, Farrell retired from cricket after medical advice that suggested her eyesight was deteriorating. She remained active in sport with bowls and table tennis and was secretary of the Mt Victoria Bowling Club for many years and a spectator at the cricket at the Basin Reserve.

Walter Arnold HADLEE

Born: *Lincoln, 4 June, 1915*

Died: *Christchurch, 29 September, 2006*

Right-hand batsman, right-arm medium-pace bowler

Walter Hadlee was an outstanding cricketer and test captain who became an astute administrator. He led one of New Zealand's most highly regarded teams, the famous 1949 side which toured England, at a time when New Zealand had yet to win a test. As an administrator, he guided New Zealand cricket in the mid-1970s during years of increasing professionalism, the World Series controversy and the exiling of South Africa. "Perhaps the greatest contributor to the game of cricket in New Zealand," wrote Don Neely.

Hadlee, who had succeeded Jack Scandrett (who had died a month earlier) as Otago's oldest surviving first-class cricketer, fell in love with cricket when he was about ten. The son of a blacksmith at Lincoln, near Christchurch, Hadlee was a slim, serious youngster fond of all sport, especially cricket and rugby.

He read cricket history avidly, kept scorebooks of all the big games at Lancaster Park, and practised assiduously. He developed into a punishing batsman, particularly strong on the drive, and captained the 1st XI at Christchurch Boys' High School.

The first time that Hadlee played on Lancaster Park was for Waltham Primary School, who played the curtain raiser to the 1926 Ranfurly Shield match between Canterbury and Hawke's Bay. He was back at the park when New Zealand played their first ever test match in 1930.

He took his scorebook to the ground and in his neat, meticulous handwriting scored every ball of the test. Two weeks later, he repeated the effort at the Basin Reserve. As the official scorebooks have disappeared, Hadlee's is the only record of these historic occasions.

He was at a school assembly when three New Zealand cricketers selected for the 1931 England tour were also present. Curly Page said there was no reason "why some boy or boys in this assembly should not be in the next New Zealand team to tour England."

From that moment his fondness for cricket became a passion. He was selected for Canterbury at the age of 18, making his debut against Otago at Lancaster Park in December 1933, scoring 42 and 14. He made runs in all the Plunket Shield matches and 97 and 74 not out against Wellington in an extra first-class game, ending his first season with 350 runs at 50.

He was superbly fit, had an elegant style and played shots all round the wicket. Very nimble on his feet, he was not afraid to advance well down the wicket to attack the bowlers. Spectators commented about his speed between the wickets and splendid returns from the deep.

The following season he was dismissed just thee times in seven innings, ending up with an average of 93.66. He made his first century for Canterbury, 103 not out against Wellington at Lancaster Park, and gained selection in the inter-island match. He made 39 and 53 (both not out) being at the wicket with Ian Cromb when South reached their target of 311.

The next season he gained New Zealand honours for the first time, playing in the final match of the series against Errol Holmes' MCC side at Christchurch. He made 47. He averaged almost fifty the following season and was chosen in the team to go to England in 1937.

In 1936/37, after failing against Auckland, he was surprisingly asked to open against Wellington with Curly Page. The pair began with a first wicket stand of 235, passing their opponents' score without losing a wicket. Hadlee went on to make 194 in 255 minutes.

Selection for the 1937 tour proved to be a turning point in his life as he met his future wife, Lilla, on board the ship taking the team to England. Hadlee made 1225 runs at 29.87 in England, playing in all three tests.

At the start of the tour he was overly defensive, but by the second test at Manchester he had rediscovered his attacking instincts and, with his side in trouble at 119-5, he rose to the occasion and attacked the bowling, scoring 93 out of 137 in 135 minutes. It was a skilful and courageous performance. His innings ended "hit wicket" when he slipped and knocked over his off stump after playing a shot to square leg.

After the war Hadlee accepted the position as branch secretary for large retail company DIC in Dunedin and played for Otago for two seasons. An exceptionally strong Australian side visited New Zealand in 1945/46, winning four of their five matches by an innings. Hadlee was the only local batsman to take a hundred off the Australian attack, and he almost made it a double, scoring 198 in Otago's second innings.

With Otago facing a deficit of 252, he opened the batting and was last man out at 347. He took a fearful pounding from Australian speedster Ray Lindwall and had to twice leave the field for attention to his injuries. Hadlee also captained New Zealand in a test for the first time that season, the low scoring affair at the Basin Reserve. Earlier in the season he had made 157 against Auckland.

Hadlee was now running in to some of the best form of his career. In the next two seasons he amassed 1099 runs at 64.64 with six hundreds. In 1946/47 he made another big hundred (166) against Auckland and also made his one and only test century.

After New Zealand had been put in to bat by England at Lancaster Park, Hadlee and Bert Sutcliffe proceeded to put on 133 for the first wicket. Hadlee went on to make 116, his century having taken just 130 minutes. The match was drawn after rain washed out the third day and, even though both teams agreed to add an extra day, no further play was possible. This was Walter Hammond's final test.

Seven months later he accepted a partnership in the accountancy firm of Pickles and Perkins and returned to Christchurch, where he lived for the rest of his life.

There was no international cricket for New Zealand in 1947/48 but Hadlee still managed to register four centuries in just five first-class games. He also made 97 in Canterbury's first match against Auckland. He and Gordon Leggat put on 218 for the first wicket against Wellington and 179 in the next match, against Otago, when Canterbury lost by 12 runs chasing 364 for victory.

The pair also put on 141 for South Island's first wicket in the inter-island match and Hadlee also hit a hundred against Fiji, although this match was not recognised as first-class until many years later.

Hadlee's captaincy of the 1949 New Zealand team to England proved the pinnacle of his playing career. He scored 1439 runs at 35.97 but that was hardly the whole story. Leading English writer John Woodcock noted "Hadlee was a courageous and enterprising batsman, a popular and successful captain who played his cricket in the sporting manner usually associated with his country."

John Arlott called him a "strategic commander of real ability" while R.C. Robertson-Glasgow wrote "Hadlee must rank among the great captains. He has proved himself a tactician, not inferior to the illustrious Bradman and New Zealand cricket has drawn strength from his leadership. Character is his rich gift; but also his brain."

Although they did not win a test, all four matches being drawn, the deeds of the team captivated the heart of the nation. Don Neely wrote, "They lost only one of 32 first-class games and played cricket with the highest standards of sportsmanship and good humour. They captured all the elements of cricket; style, grace, elegance, stamina, courage and kinship. They established the international credibility and acceptance of New Zealand cricket, just as the 1905 All Blacks had done for rugby."

Back in New Zealand, Hadlee began the 1949/50 season with 125 against Auckland. Later in the summer an unbeaten 22 proved invaluable, saving New Zealand from defeat in a one-off international against a touring Australian team. Facing a deficit of 68, New Zealand batted a second time with just three hours left in the match but collapsed and were 41-6 with an hour still remaining.

Hadlee, defending grimly, saw his side slump to 56-8 and then 67-9. When number eleven Fen Cresswell came to the crease only nine minutes remained, meaning Australia could not bat again, but New Zealand still needed one run to avoid an innings defeat. The Australians tried desperately, but to no avail. Hadlee scored the vital single and New Zealand batted out time to finish on 76-9.

The following season Hadlee was available for only one match for Canterbury but still led New Zealand in the two tests against England. He scored 50 in the first game at Christchurch, which was notable for an act of sportsmanship on Hadlee's part.

England opener Cyril Washbrook was given out lbw after an appeal from Frank Mooney behind the stumps. However, after a discussion between Hadlee and the umpire, Washbrook, who had evidently hit the ball, was recalled.

Hadlee played in Canterbury's first two Plunket Shield matches in 1951/52 before making the decision to retire from first-class cricket with immediate effect. He continued playing senior cricket in Christchurch for another 15 years, however, eventually finishing with a record 15,391 club runs. By the time he retired he had been joined in the side by sons Barry, Martin and Dayle.

He was also a national selector and managed the 1965 New Zealand team on its tour of England, India and Pakistan. He was a member of the management committee and Board of Control of New Zealand Cricket from 1950-83. He was chairman from 1973-78 and president from 1981-83. As a player and administrator the only people with a comparable record in world cricket would be Sir George (Gubby) Allen and Sir Donald Bradman.

As chairman of New Zealand Cricket he espoused the merits of professional treatment for New Zealand cricketers, having previously crossed swords with Glenn Turner when the two had different viewpoints on professional rewards.

It was Hadlee who had to diffuse the situation at Lancaster Park in 1980 when the West Indies staged a sit-in after tea during the test. Hadlee advised Willie Rodriguez, the manager, that his players must take the field. Rodriguez said the team were so annoyed by the umpiring that they would not restart the test and would go home.

Hadlee pointed out that this would cost the West Indies board a lot of money. Rodriguez insisted on contacting Jeff Stollmeyer, a senior West Indies official, until Hadlee revealed that he and Stollmeyer were old administrative friends. The test and the tour resumed.

Hadlee, who was a chartered accountant and director of several companies, had a remarkable memory for facts and figures, including itineraries, dates, matches and hotels. The story is told how, on the 1965 tour of England, Hadlee customarily argued the accuracy of the hotels' laundry bills – and received a refund from every hotel.

The meticulously accurate accountant brought his financial skills to bear for New Zealand Cricket, helping balance its books during a time when there was not the money from television revenues there is today and New Zealand was not always accorded top-tier cricketing status.

Hadlee enhanced New Zealand's stature on the world stage, representing it at numerous International Cricket Council meetings during the 1970s, where his wise counsel was widely sought.

In later years he enjoyed imparting his knowledge to promising players and giving teenagers the benefits of his expertise in the forward and backward defensive technique. Even as an octogenarian it would be nothing for Hadlee to demonstrate the execution of the off or cover drive and dance down from the spot where he was talking as if out in the middle.

He maintained an interest in the young which saw him serve as a Trustee of the National Youth Choir, a member of the Salvation Army Christchurch Advisory Board and as Patron in Perpetuity of the Willows Cricket Club, whose objectives are to encourage secondary school cricket.

Hadlee also represented Canterbury at rugby, playing against Otago in a Ranfurly Shield challenge in 1938, and played hockey for both Canterbury and Otago (alongside Bert Sutcliffe in the latter side). In later years he played golf and bowls.

He was awarded the OBE and CBE. Three of his five sons, Dayle, Richard and Barry ,represented New Zealand. He was inducted into the New Zealand Sports Hall of Fame in 1995. Shortly after his 80th birthday in 1995 a new grandstand was opened at the northern end of Lancaster Park, named the Hadlee Stand.

Friend and former cricket commentator Iain Gallaway said Hadlee was "clearly the greatest figure in the history of New Zealand cricket, on and off the field."

Hadlee's record in first-class cricket is:

Season	***M***	***I***	***NO***	***HS***	***Runs***	***Ave***	***100***	***50***	***ct***	***Wkts***	***Runs***	***Ave***	***Best***
1933/34	4	8	1	97	350	50.00	–	3	1				
1934/35	4	7	4	103*	281	93.66	1	1	1				
1935/36	5	9	0	101	294	32.66	1	1	1	0	8	–	–
1936/37	5	8	0	194	399	49.87	1	1	3	0	18	–	–
1937 (E)	24	44	3	106	1225	29.87	1	7	13	0	13	–	–
1937/38 (A)	2	4	0	51	104	26.00	–	1	–	0	10	–	–
1937/38	3	6	0	28	74	12.33	–	–	3				
1938/39	2	4	0	92	113	28.25	–	1	–				
1939/40	3	5	1	58	137	34.25	–	1	–				
1940/41	2	3	0	144	159	53.00	1	–	2	0	7	–	–
1943/44	4	6	2	105	167	41.75	1	–	2	0	16	–	–
1944/45	4	6	0	74	250	41.66	–	3	3				
1945/46	4	7	0	198	449	64.14	2	–	3	4	85	21.25	3-14
1946/47	5	8	0	166	460	57.50	2	–	3	0	25	–	–
1947/48	5	9	0	149	639	71.00	4	1	3	1	61	61.00	1-20
1948/49	4	8	1	110*	324	46.28	1	1	2	1	14	14.00	1-0
1949 (E)	28	44	4	119*	1439	35.97	2	6	24	0	30	–	–
1949/50	4	8	1	125	311	44.42	1	1	1	0	6	–	–
1950/51	3	5	0	83	203	40.60	–	2	1				
1951/52	2	4	0	55	145	36.25	–	1	4				
TOTAL	**117**	**203**	**17**	**198**	**7523**	**40.44**	**18**	**31**	**70**	**6**	**293**	**48.83**	**3-14**

For	*M*	*I*	*NO*	*HS*	*Runs*	*Ave*	*100*	*50*	*ct*	*Wkts*	*Runs*	*Ave*	*Best*
NZ (Tests)	14	24	2	116	768	34.90	1	4	7				
NZ (Other)	47	79	6	119*	2424	33.20	3	13	34	0	53	–	–
NZ XI	1	1	0	10	10	10.00	–	–	–				
Canterbury	44	80	7	194	3183	43.60	10	13	25	1	130	130.00	1-20
Otago	7	12	0	198	784	65.33	3	–	4	4	110	27.50	3-14
Canterbury/Otago	1	1	0	48	48	48.00	–	–	–				
South Island	2	4	2	149	276	138.00	1	1	–				
Rest of NZ	1	2	0	27	30	15.00	–	–	–	1	0	0.00	1-0
TOTAL	**117**	**203**	**17**	**198**	**7523**	**40.44**	**18**	**31**	**70**	**6**	**293**	**48.83**	**3-14**

Joan Constance HATCHER

Born: *Wellington, 4 November, 1923*

Died: *Wellington, 21 September, 2006*

Right-hand batsman, right-arm medium-pace bowler

An accomplished and patient opening batsman, Joan Hatcher and her older sister Dot Bailey (nee Hatcher) became the first set of sisters to represent New Zealand at cricket when Dot made her test debut against England at Eden Park in 1948/49. It was also the first known instance of sisters opening a test innings together. Ten years earlier, Dot (Doris) Hatcher had toured New South Wales with the New Zealand side.

After beginning cricket at Wellington Girls' College, and later with the Old Girls' Club, Joan Hatcher made her Wellington debut in 1944. The next two seasons saw her continue to score well at club level and she was selected for the New Zealand tour to New South Wales and Queensland in March 1947.

The experience gained from this tour produced good results the following season when she made 51 in the Wellington match against the touring Australian side. This assured Hatcher of her test debut against the same side at the Basin Reserve the following month. Hatcher began with a solid 21 in the first innings before being run out. New Zealand followed-on and were dismissed for 87 to lose by an innings, with Hatcher top scoring with 23, which was to remain her highest test score.

She played against England the following season and went on the 1954 tour to England. She did little in the two tests she played but, nevertheless, had a reasonable tour scoring 324 runs at an average of 23.14 with scores of 58 against the North of England at Harrogate and 64 not out against the South of England at Hastings.

In the final match of the tour, Hatcher finished her New Zealand career with 35 in a 91-run opening partnership with Joyce Clothier (57) against the Combined Services team at the RAF Station in Halton, Buckinghamshire.

Her occupation as a staff clerk inside the Government treasury offices was put to good use during the tour as the tour allowance officer for the team, in conjunction with team manage, Hilda Coldham. Hatcher was also a fine hockey player and represented Wellington at right-half in the 1940s. At the time of her death, she was a Vice-President of the Wellington Cricket Association.

Neville Alfred HUXFORD

Born: *Wellington, 27 October, 1937*

Died: *Auckland, 21 November, 2006*

Right-hand batsman, right-arm medium-pace bowler

Neville Huxford was 27 years old when he was finally given a chance at first-class level and he took it with both hands, capturing seven wickets against Pakistan and six in his next match.

He was educated at Houghton Valley Primary School and Wellington Technical College, which had little tradition in cricket. Huxford's main sport while at school, therefore, became hockey.

However, after he left college he joined the Midland Cricket Club and was persuaded to bowl fast by Bob Blair, the club's New Zealand fast bowler. He trained assiduously and in the 1959/60 season captured 37 senior wickets, at an average of 12.13, to lead Midland to the senior championship while he received the Norwood Award for the Most Improved Bowler of the Year.

Huxford formed a close affinity with the Basin Reserve, where he was aided and abetted by the custodian of the day, Harry Wilkins, whose wickets were always hard with a liberal covering of juicy grass, which ensured that the ball lifted disconcertingly and continually deviated on hitting the seam.

He ran in to bowl with quick, short strides and was nearly tireless. There were no easy runs to be made off him as almost every ball zeroed on to the off stump, working on the theory that if the batsmen missed, he would hit.

In the first over he bowled in first-class cricket, that is exactly what he did. Wellington had lost their first two games of the 1964/65 Plunket Shield season but before their next match they met Pakistan, touring New Zealand for the first time, and Huxford was rewarded for his consistent form at club level and brought into the side.

It was an inauspicious start as Wellington were routed for 53 in 98 minutes. Huxford was last man out for a duck, the final victim of Farooq Hamid who finished with 7-16 off 10.4 overs. However, before he end of the day Huxford, coming on as first change, had bowled Naushad Ali in his first over and run out the other opener, Mohammad Ilyas.

The next day belonged completely to Huxford. He captured all six of Pakistan's remaining wickets, including Hanif Mohammad who fell two short of a century. Huxford finished with 7-95 off 35.5 overs. The *Almanack* said that it was a reward for accurate pace bowling, directed at the stumps.

A week later, when Wellington met Auckland, test bowlers Bruce Blair and Bruce Morrison had been dropped and Huxford was now opening the bowling. This also proved to be to his liking as he bowled Wellington to their first points of the season, finishing with figures of 31.3-20-38-6.

He followed this with six wickets in the match against Northern Districts and five against Otago. He ended the season with 26 wickets at 13.73 and topped the first-class bowling averages.

This proved to be a hard act to follow as his figures the next season were a little more modest but still good enough to help Wellington win the Plunket Shield. However, he had more success in 1966/67 taking 20 wickets at 25.90. He took 6-40 against Northern Districts and 6-86 off 40.2 overs against Les Favell's Australian team at the end of the season. Norm O'Neill, Peter Burge and Favell were amongst his victims in that match.

Huxford had moved to Christchurch for the following summer and captured 23 wickets at 25.17 that season. In his first match for Canterbury, bowling first change, he had figures of 23-12-25-5 against Auckland. Later in the season he opened the bowling with Dick Motz.

He also gained selection in the President's XI which met India in the opening match of their first tour to New Zealand. Huxford again proved his liking for international opposition, taking 3-31 and 2-57.

Huxford played two more seasons for Canterbury before retiring, capturing his 100th wicket in first-class cricket in his final game, which was against Sam Trimble's Australian team.

Huxford played for West Christchurch-University and became very involved with the club's administration. He was club captain in 1968/69 and 1969/70. There was much debate in February 1967 on whether the club should move from Hagley Park and become a closed University club based at Ilam. At a meeting in September 1967 the club decided to stay at Hagley Park but agreed there would have to be a major fund raising exercise to restore or rebuild the old Hagley pavilion.

Under Huxford's prompting the club raised $2000 in two years which allowed them to draw up building plans and put them out to tender. However, the committee decided the mortgage would be beyond the resources of the club and eventually decided to relocate to Burnside Park.

When it came to batting Huxford averaged only 8.38 in 31 first-class matches. Improbably, however, he is still the co-holder of the highest eighth wicket partnership in Wellington club cricket (207) of which he contributed 74 not out with Ian Pollard (117) for Midland against Wellington College Old Boys in 1963/64.

Don Neely captained Huxford in most of his first-class games for Wellington and remembers him as "a wonderful team member, honest, loyal and reliable, who always performed to the maximum of his ability. He was a very skilful bowler but his determination and enthusiasm were greater."

Huxford's record in first-class cricket is:

Season	*M*	*I*	*NO*	*HS*	*Runs*	*Ave*	*ct*	*Wkts*	*Runs*	*Ave*	*5W*	*10W*	*Best*
1964/65	4	4	3	6 *	6	6.00	3	26	357	13.73	2	–	7-95
1965/66	5	3	3	7 *	9	–	2	11	322	29.27	–	–	3-24
1966/67	6	8	2	8	19	3.16	4	20	518	25.90	2	–	6-40
1967/68	7	6	3	19	51	17.00	1	23	579	25.17	1	–	5-25
1968/69	5	4	2	11 *	12	6.00	3	8	335	41.87	–	–	2-40
1969/70	4	4	3	8 *	12	12.00	–	13	308	23.69	–	–	4-50
TOTAL	**31**	**29**	**16**	**19**	**109**	**8.38**	**13**	**101**	**2419**	**23.95**	**5**	**–**	**7-95**

For	*M*	*I*	*NO*	*HS*	*Runs*	*Ave*	*ct*	*Wkts*	*Runs*	*Ave*	*5W*	*10W*	*Best*
Wellington	15	15	8	8	34	4.85	9	57	1197	21.00	4	–	7-95
Canterbury	15	13	8	19	66	13.20	4	39	1134	29.07	1	–	5-25
President's XI	1	1	0	9	9	9.00	–	5	88	17.60	–	–	3-31
TOTAL	**31**	**29**	**16**	**19**	**109**	**8.38**	**13**	**101**	**2419**	**23.95**	**5**	**–**	**7-95**

John Lambert KERR

***Born:** Dannevirke, 28 December, 1910*

***Died:** Christchurch, 27 May, 2007*

Right-hand batsman, right-arm medium pace bowler

Jack Kerr, who died at the age of 96, was the second oldest living test cricketer from any country, being just ten days younger than his old New Zealand team mate, Eric Tindill. He was also the oldest living Canterbury representative.

During his time in international cricket Kerr played against Jack Hobbs, Herbert Sutcliffe, Syd Barnes, Walter Hammond, Duleepsinhji, Frank Woolley, Clarrie Grimmett, Bill Ponsford, Archie Jackson and Don Bradman. As some of these great players were playing before the First World War and Kerr retained all his faculties in later life, it could be said that he had seen all the great players of the last century.

Kerr grew up in Marton, the home of the old Rangitikei association. At this time, Rangitikei were strong enough to win the Hawke Cup and their fixtures against neighbours Wanganui were very keenly anticipated. Kerr had just turned 13 when he was chosen to play for Rangitikei against the New Zealand Nomads at Marton in January 1924 and was still short of his fourteenth birthday when he played his first Hawke Cup match the following season.

He attended Wanganui Technical College as a boarder and was given some assistance by New Zealand batsman Stewie Dempster, who had been employed as a coach by the school for one season while working as a traveller for Sargoods. Kerr played for Wanganui while at college and scored 71 against Taranaki, helping his side to win the Hawke Cup. He followed this up with a century in the first defence against Poverty Bay.

At this time there were only four Plunket Shield sides and selectors were reluctant to choose players from country districts so, to further his chances of playing first-class cricket, Kerr decided to move to Christchurch, where he could also attend Canterbury University to study accountancy.

He joined the West Christchurch Cricket Club and at the time of his death had given eight decades of unstinting service to a club that is known today as Burnside-West Christchurch-University Cricket Club, where he was Patron and Life Member.

He was almost immediately selected to play for Canterbury against Auckland at Eden Park in January 1930. Batting at number seven he scored 61 in Canterbury's first innings and in the second innings he opened and made 69. He made 70 against Otago three weeks later, again opening the batting, thus finishing with 200 runs in three innings in his first season.

He only passed fifty once in the three Plunket Shield matches the following season but it was a memorable innings. Canterbury had been set a target of 473 runs by Auckland and fast bowler Don Cleverley was regarded as the danger man. However, in one over Kerr took 16 runs from him and the chase was on. Kerr made 73 and gave Canterbury the base from which it claimed victory with minutes to spare.

He was chosen for the New Zealand tour of England in 1931 but even though he played in two test matches it could not be said that Kerr's tour was a success.

He only just exceeded 800 runs, at an average of 22.97, and he appeared to lose the timing that had seen him succeed in New Zealand. Around this time, he began having trouble with his eyes, and it was not long afterwards that he began wearing glasses. He remembered it was a wet summer and recalled slipping over on every ground the team played on.

His best score on tour was 88 against Hampshire, in just the third match, and he made 34 and 28 in the second test at The Oval.

Kerr registered his maiden first-class hundred in 1932/33 against Wellington at Lancaster Park and he went on to a career best of 196 out of a total of 366 all out. After reaching his hundred Kerr scored his last 94 runs in only 48 minutes. Curly Page (45) helped Kerr put on 176 in a mere 65 minutes. Kerr played in both tests against England that season, making 59 in the first at Christchurch.

The following summer Kerr made 174, again against Wellington, but it was the 1935/36 season which was his most memorable. In the three Plunket Shield matches his six innings had only yielded 156 runs, most of which came in one match, but perhaps the highlight of Kerr's cricketing career occurred when Canterbury met Errol Holmes' MCC side. He scored 146 not out, batting throughout the innings of 243, and made 71 in the second innings.

After Jack Mills was dropped, after making a pair in the first unofficial test, Kerr came into the New Zealand side and reeled off scores of 2 and 105 not out, 39 and 4 and 132. At the end of the tour Holmes said, "Kerr was an outstanding player. He is in world-class, as his 499 runs against us shows. He has shown that he has every stroke, both in front of, and behind the wicket." Kerr was awarded the Redpath Cup that season with a total of 655 runs at an average of 59.54.

The Christchurch *Press* wrote "that with his high straight backlift and broad shoulders he was a commanding figure at the wicket. His aggressive attitude coupled with his wide range of strong, clean strokes made him a heroic figure to the spectators. His driving and hooking, but particularly his fierce square cutting, were magnificent."

Selected for the 1937 tour of England, Kerr scored three centuries and 1205 runs, averaging 31.71, but could not find consistent form. After an unbeaten 130 against Leicestershire in the middle of the tour he could manage no better than 19 runs an innings for the next five weeks. However, in the last seven matches he refound his touch and accumulated nearly 500 runs.

His last first-class appearance was for New Zealand Army against New Zealand Air Force in April 1943, when he made 51 and 62. He retired from first-class play at the young age of 32 but continued to play club cricket. He played senior cricket from 1928/29 to 1955/56 and then continued in President's Grade.

He was West Christchurch club captain in 1930/31 and 1933/34, treasurer in 1932/33 and president from 1957 to 1972. He then became patron and was in that position until his death. He was also President of the Canterbury Cricket Association in 1960/61.

However, that was far from the extent of his involvement in administration. He was treasurer of the New Zealand Cricket Council for 21 years, chairman of their management committee for 13 years and a committee member for another ten years. He was a national selector for eight years, president for two years and managed the New Zealand team to South Africa in 1953/54.

During the tour it was Kerr who had to tell Bob Blair that his fiancee had been killed in the Tangiwai rail disaster. He then stayed with Blair at the team's hotel while the others went to the ground on the most dramatic and poignant of days in all of New Zealand's sporting history.

Kerr also put in countless hours coaching young players, particularly at St Andrew's College. He was made a Life Member of New Zealand Cricket, awarded an OBE for services to cricket and awarded the CNZM for services to the community.

But his continuing love of the game is best summed up in his own words, "I'd be much poorer if I hadn't been a cricketer."

Kerr's record in first-class cricket is:

Season	*M*	*I*	*NO*	*HS*	*Runs*	*Ave*	*100*	*50*	*ct*	*Wkts*	*Runs*	*Ave*	*Best*
1929/30	2	3	0	70	200	66.66	–	3	–				
1930/31	3	6	0	73	158	26.33	–	1	–				
1931 (E)	22	36	1	88	804	22.97	–	4	7	2	32	16-00	2-32
1931/32	4	8	0	89	280	35.00	–	2	1				
1932/33	5	8	1	196	337	48.14	1	1	5				
1933/34	4	8	0	174	362	45.25	1	1	–				
1934/35	3	6	1	59	223	44.60	–	1	2				
1935/36	7	13	2	146*	655	59.54	3	2	–				
1936/37	5	8	0	27	94	11.75	–	–	–				
1937 (E)	23	40	2	160	1205	31.71	3	3	7	0	4	–	–
1937/38 (A)	3	6	0	41	105	17.50	–	–	–	0	10	–	–
1937/38	1	2	0	14	28	14.00	–	–	–				
1938/39	3	6	0	73	230	38.33	–	2	5				
1939/40	3	5	0	28	35	7.00	–	–	1				
1942/43	1	2	0	62	113	56.50	–	2	2				
TOTAL	**89**	**157**	**7**	**196**	**4829**	**32.19**	**8**	**22**	**30**	**2**	**46**	**23.00**	**2-32**

For	*M*	*I*	*NO*	*HS*	*Runs*	*Ave*	*100*	*50*	*ct*	*Wkts*	*Runs*	*Ave*	*Best*
NZ (Tests)	7	12	1	59	212	19.27	–	1	4				
NZ (Other)	48	81	3	160	2258	28.94	5	7	11	2	46	23.00	2-32
Canterbury	32	61	3	196	2228	38.41	3	12	13				
Canterbury/Otago	1	1	0	18	18	18.00	–	–	–				
NZ Army	1	2	0	62	113	56.50	–	2	2	2			
TOTAL	**89**	**157**	**7**	**196**	**4829**	**32.19**	**8**	**22**	**30**	**2**	**46**	**23.00**	**2-32**

Edgar Milton MEULI

Born: *Hawera, 20 February, 1926*

Died: *Auckland, 15 April, 2007*

Right-hand batsman, right-arm leg-break bowler

Ted Meuli played one test for New Zealand against Jack Cheetham's South African side at the Basin Reserve in the 1951/52 summer. His first-class career spanned 15 seasons.

Born in Hawera, but raised in New Plymouth, Meuli captained the Boys' High 1st XI during the latter years of the war. He moved to Auckland to attend teachers' training college and gained selection in the Auckland team which played North Taranaki in March 1945. The following summer he was a member of the Plunket Shield team, the competition having resumed after being suspended during the war.

His first match was against Canterbury at Lancaster Park, when he opened the batting with Herb Pearson, whose obituary also appears in this edition of the *Almanack*. The 19-year-old's best effort that season was 56, sharing an opening stand of 121 with Pearson, against Wellington in an additional first-class game played for the Centennial Cup.

Meuli returned to New Plymouth to take up his life-long career as a school teacher and was a member of the first Central Districts team to take the field when they entered first-class cricket in 1950/51. He had been a Taranaki representative since 1946/47.

Although a regular member of the side, Meuli's returns in his first two seasons with Central were quite modest. In 16 innings his top score was an unbeaten 48 against Wellington in the opening match of the 1951/52 season. Meuli came in at number three and was unbeaten after 159 minutes when Central were dismissed for 114.

In the second innings Central needed to score 214 for victory and Meuli again top scored with 46. With the scoreboard showing 213-9 number eleven Fen Cresswell ran himself out and the players left the field thinking the match had finished in a tie. Subsequently, however, a missing no-ball was discovered and credited to Central, giving them victory by one wicket.

The 1952/53 season proved to be the most successful of Meuli's career. He scored 355 runs at 44.37 and also came to light with one outstanding spell with the ball.

He began with 71 in 195 minutes against Wellington and then made 15 and 45 against Canterbury. In the next match, having only bowled two overs in first-class cricket before the season began, he took 6-67 off 14.5 overs in an Otago total of 462.

The last match of the summer was against Auckland at Palmerston North and Central batted first but were soon 30-2. Meuli, batting at number three, found an ally in Lawrie Miller and the pair added 89. Rain eventually stopped play for the day with the score at 194-5 and Meuli on 95 after 243 minutes at the crease.

The next day Meuli reached his hundred, after a further 68 minutes, and by the end of the second day, also interrupted by rain, Central were 318-9, Meuli 154. Number eleven Don Cleverley should have been run out but Auckland, not wishing to bat before stumps, deliberately chose not to do so.

The innings ended quickly the next morning when Meuli was dismissed after 455 minutes batting. Auckland were subsequently routed before the close, for 138 and 74, with Harry Cave capturing 13 wickets during the day.

Meuli's form saw him chosen for the first test against South Africa six weeks later. One of four new caps, along wth Eric Fisher, Lawrie Miller and Bob Blair, Meuli scored 15 and 23, in the second innings helping Gordon Leggat put on 63 in 66 minutes for the third wicket.

This was not enough for him to retain his position, however. After New Zealand had been crushed by an innings in the first test, the selectors made five changes, including three more new players. One of these was Eric Dempster who had not played any first-class cricket that season due to unavailability.

Meuli did get the chance to face South Africa again when Central played a two-day game against the tourists at Pukekura Park. More than 10,000 attended the match.

Meuli had to wait until the 1956/57 season to reach three-figures again, this time scoring exactly 100 against Northern Districts at New Plymouth. He batted for just over five hours as he helped Central to another innings victory. The previous season he had made 27 and 57 against West Indies, dismissed by Sonny Ramadhin in both innings.

He finished his first-class career with a single match in 1959/60 but continued to play for Taranaki until the 1968/69 season.

Although ill for some time, he followed New Zealand's fortunes until the very end. Released from North Shore Hospital to his son's home, he insisted on being woken early so he could watch New Zealand's game against South Africa. Shortly after the conclusion of the match he complained of feeling tired so went back to bed. He passed away peacefully in his sleep later that morning.

Meuli's record in first-class cricket is:

Season	*M*	*I*	*NO*	*HS*	*Runs*	*Ave*	*100*	*50*	*ct*	*Wkts*	*Runs*	*Ave*	*5W*	*Best*
1945/46	3	5	0	56	109	21.80	–	1	2					
1950/51	4	8	0	44	173	21.62	–	–	2	0	8	–	–	–
1951/52	4	8	1	48*	185	26.42	–	–	–					
1952/53	5	8	0	154	355	44.37	1	1	–	7	116	16.57	1	6-67
1953/54	2	4	1	58*	102	34.00	–	1	–	0	40	–	–	–
1954/55	4	7	0	43	162	23.14	–	–	1	2	68	34.00	–	1-7
1955/56	5	9	0	75	288	32.00	–	2	4	1	15	15.00	–	1-5
1956/57	6	10	1	100	293	32.55	1	–	–	0	49	–	–	–
1957/58	5	9	0	57	184	20.44	–	1	–	1	26	26.00	–	1-19
1958/59	3	6	0	22	54	9.00	–	–	–	0	7	–	–	–
1959/60	1	2	0	5	9	4.50	–	–	–					
TOTAL	**42**	**76**	**3**	**154**	**1914**	**26.21**	**2**	**6**	**9**	**11**	**329**	**29.90**	**1**	**6-67**

For	*M*	*I*	*NO*	*HS*	*Runs*	*Ave*	*100*	*50*	*ct*	*Wkts*	*Runs*	*Ave*	*5W*	*Best*
NZ (Test)	1	2	0	23	38	19.00	–	–	–					
Auckland	3	5	0	56	109	21.80	–	1	2					
CD	38	69	3	154	1767	26.77	2	5	7	11	329	29.90	1	6-67
TOTAL	**42**	**76**	**3**	**154**	**1914**	**26.21**	**2**	**6**	**9**	**11**	**329**	**29.90**	**1**	**6-67**

Richard Charles MOTZ

Born: *Christchurch, 12 January, 1940*

Died: *Christchurch, 29 April, 2007*

Right-hand batsman, right-arm fast-medium bowler

Dick Motz was one of New Zealand's finest bowlers and the first man to take 100 test wickets for New Zealand. Others have gone well past his tally since but Motz will always be remembered as the first to reach the landmark. Capable of working up considerable pace and hostility, he also had formidable stamina which enabled him to serve as both shock and stock bowler.

A lion-hearted bowler and a crowd-pleasing entertainer with the bat, Motz was a hero to countless youngsters (and many not so young). His style of play would have been tailor-made for the limited-over game but his career finished just as one-day cricket arrived.

At North New Brighton primary school Motz won a reputation both for huge hitting and fast bowling. At Linwood High School his achievements began to attract wider attention. He captained the 1st XI for two years and in his last four innings for Linwood scored three centuries and 76 not out.

He also played rugby and tennis for the school, won the Canterbury junior badminton title, and had a low handicap at golf. He continued with his rugby after leaving school, playing two seasons at full-back for New Brighton in the Canterbury senior competition.

Motz made his entry into first-class cricket, against Northern Districts, in December 1957, just before his 18th birthday, replacing test bowler Tony MacGibbon who had broken his thumb in the previous game.

The young fast bowler was an immediate sensation, taking a wicket in his second over and two more in his third, finishing with 4-40. Chasing Northern's 177 Canterbury were 122-8 when Motz came in to bat. He made only 12 but helped Sam Guillen put on 67 in just 49 minutes to give Canterbury first innings points. At the end of the season he was selected in the two trial matches for New Zealand's tour of England, capturing six wickets.

Motz took 33 wickets at 16.63 in the 1960/61 season, earning New Zealand selection for the first time, playing in all three unofficial tests against Dennis Silk's MCC side. In the first match at Dunedin, Motz scored 36 and 60, top score for New Zealand in the second innings. His knock included three sixes in one David Allen over. In the second match he took 5-34 off 22 overs as MCC were bowled out for 111.

The tour to South Africa in 1961/62 really established Motz. He played in 16 matches, including all five tests, and took 81 wickets at 17.76. He began the tour with 5-65 against Rhodesia and took ten wickets in the match against Natal, including a then career best of 7-70.

He made his test debut at Durban, bowling Eddie Barlow with his tenth delivery. South Africa went on to win a close match by just 30 runs. Motz captured six wickets in the drawn second test, nine in the match against Border and 3-33 in the first innings of the last test. New Zealand won by 40 runs to draw the series 2-2, their first test victories overseas.

Motz had struggled with the bat in South Africa, registering five ducks during the test series. He returned to form with 60 in the first test against England the following season when he and Bryan Yuile put on 95 after New Zealand had been 161-7.

At the end of a successful 1964/65 season, when he took 30 wickets at 19.73, Motz set off with the New Zealand team which played seven matches, all tests, in India and Pakistan on their way to England. Motz took 54 wickets in 14 matches in England and his performances earned him the honour of being named one of *Wisden's* five cricketers of the year.

His first impression, however, was made with the bat in the opening match against Worcestershire. New Zealand was 153-9 when Motz was joined by Frank Cameron. The pair added 107 in 117 minutes before Motz was out for 95, trying to reach his century with a six.

England made 435 in the first test with Motz taking 5-108 off 43 overs. His victims included the top three batsmen Boycott, Barber and Dexter. He went on to dismiss Boycott on another five occasions during his career (twice without scoring). In the next match Motz hit 51 not out (five sixes) in 38 minutes against Yorkshire.

New Zealand met England again in 1965/66, with all three tests ending in draws. New Zealand gained a narrow lead in the first match at Christchurch with Motz (58) and Eric Petrie (55) adding 89 for the eighth wicket. Left to score 196 in 140 minutes New Zealand adopted a defensive attitude and had collapsed to 22-7 when Motz came in. He scored just 2 but stayed with Vic Pollard for a valuable 25 minutes. New Zealand eventually finished on 48-8.

New Zealand's batting woes continued in the next test at Dunedin and they were 100-7 before Motz (57) and Petrie again helped restore order. Motz again showed his liking for David Allen's off-spin, helping himself to three sixes and a four in one over.

Motz was now approaching his peak as a fast bowler and, in what turned out to be his final three home seasons, he took 130 wickets at 19.93. In 1966/67 Motz took 37 wickets at 14.59 for Canterbury, including 8-61 against Wellington (when he also made 51).

Even more impressive were figures of 3-72 and 7-56 against Les Favell's Australian team who toured that season. Motz's victims included Favell (twice), Burge (twice), O'Neill, Sheahan and Booth as Canterbury went on to win by four wickets.

New Zealand visited Australia in the early part of the 1967/68 season, Motz playing an extraordinary innings against South Australia. New Zealand needed only 188 to win but collapsed to 88-7 and then 128-9. Motz, who had not bowled or fielded since the first day owing to an ankle injury, almost snatched victory for his team with a magnificent display of controlled hitting.

He eventually went for 94 (with six sixes and ten fours in 94 minutes) trying to hit Neil Hawke out of the Adelaide Oval. Ian Chappell had been given a bowl and started with a maiden over but his next three went for 20, 18 and 24 before he was taken off with figures of 4-1-62-0.

Back in New Zealand Motz captured 30 wickets in the first four Plunket Shield matches and also registered the only century of his first-class career. Canterbury had batted first against Otago and were 289-6 when Motz came in. He added 49 in 27 minutes with Keith Thomson and then a further 72 for the eighth wicket with John McIntyre in just 23 minutes, McIntyre's share being 5.

Motz had reached 96 when McIntyre was run out then hit a seventh six off Ata Matatumua to reach his century. He also hit eight fours in his 55 minutes at the crease. It was then the fastest century scored in New Zealand first-class cricket.

There was still nearly an hour left until stumps on day one and Motz took the new ball and bowled future All Black coach Graham Henry with the first ball of the innings. Motz eventually finished with match figures of 9-98 and Otago were beaten by an innings.

Motz took 5-86 in the first test against India later that season and followed up with 6-63 in the next match at Christchurch when New Zealand gained a rare and welcome test victory. This was the match where Graham Dowling scord 239 in his first test as captain.

When West Indies toured the following season Motz claimed two more five wicket test hauls. He took 6-69 at Wellington, again being instrumental in a New Zealand victory, and 5-113 at Christchurch. His victims in those two innings included Fredericks (twice), Nurse, Butcher (twice), Sobers (twice) and Lloyd.

Another tour to England followed and, in the third test at The Oval, Motz trapped Phil Sharpe lbw to become the first player to capture 100 test wickets for New Zealand. Five further games were scheduled for New Zealand after the final test and Motz played in the first two of them. He failed to take a wicket in his final game, against Lancashire, but signed off with a trademark 73 not out at number nine, with four sixes and seven fours.

During the next game it was announced that a back complaint that Motz had played with for a considerable time had been diagnosed as a displaced vertebra. After that, even he had to accept the inevitability of retirement, although he was still only 29, and he returned home without accompanying the team to India and Pakistan.

After retiring from cricket Motz ran a sports business and then kept a pub in Timaru. He had always had trouble with his weight, tending to bowl himself into fitness over a season. In Timaru, however, his bulk began to cause concern. He returned to Christchurch and continued in the hotel trade, with spells on the west coast of the South Island and in Melbourne. He also managed the Rangiora Town and Country Club in the north of Canterbury.

Motz's death was discovered by his former New Zealand and Canterbury captain Graham Dowling during a weekend visit to his home. Dowling was a regular caller, along with other Canterbury-based New Zealand players of the 1960s and members of the Riccarton club who Motz played for during his career after leaving school.

"He was a great fast bowler who never knew when to stop," remembered Dowling. "Although he had back trouble, he kept on going. Sometimes, after he came off the field at a break, I'd jump on his back, and he'd get going again."

Motz's record in first-class cricket is:

Season	*M*	*I*	*NO*	*HS*	*Runs*	*Ave*	*100*	*50*	*ct*	*Wkts*	*Runs*	*Ave*	*5W*	*10W*	*Best*
1957/58	6	7	3	36	86	21.50	–	–	5	20	427	21.35	–	–	4-40
1958/59	6	11	1	29	108	10.80	–	–	1	14	488	34.85	–	–	3-25
1959/60	7	12	3	57	200	22.22	–	1	2	22	586	26.63	–	–	3-29
1960/61	8	12	0	65	357	29.75	–	2	4	33	549	16.63	2	1	7-48
1961/62 (A)	2	3	0	1	1	0.33	–	–	–	4	126	31.50	–	–	3-53
1961/62 (SA)	16	25	2	34	195	8.47	–	–	5	81	1439	17.76	3	1	7-70
1961/62	1	2	0	12	13	6.50	–	–	–	2	99	49.50	–	–	1-7
1962/63	8	14	2	60	199	16.58	–	1	3	27	742	27.48	–	–	4-14
1963/64	9	17	2	63	244	16.26	–	1	1	25	677	27.08	1	–	6-87
1964/65	8	13	1	36	236	19.66	–	–	4	30	592	19.73	–	–	4-38
1964/65 (I)	3	4	1	21	37	12.33	–	–	–	7	311	44.42	–	–	3-87
1964/65 (P)	1	2	0	2	2	1.00	–	–	–	2	35	17.50	–	–	2-35
1965 (E)	14	21	3	95	355	19.72	–	2	–	54	1241	22.98	4	–	6-63
1965/66	8	16	0	58	281	17.56	–	2	2	31	621	20.03	1	–	5-31
1966/67	10	16	1	51	313	20.86	–	1	3	43	807	18.76	4	2	8-61
1967/68	10	14	1	103*	289	22.23	1	–	5	47	907	19.29	6	–	6-57
1967/68 (A)	4	7	0	94	132	18.85	–	1	–	10	326	32.60	–	–	3-72
1968/69	9	12	0	30	158	13.16	–	–	4	40	878	21.95	3	–	6-69
1969 (E)	12	17	1	73*	288	18.00	–	2	2	26	916	35.23	–	–	4-29
TOTAL	**142**	**225**	**21**	**103***	**3494**	**17.12**	**1**	**13**	**41**	**518**	**11,767**	**22.71**	**24**	**4**	**8-61**

For	*M*	*I*	*NO*	*HS*	*Runs*	*Ave*	*100*	*50*	*ct*	*Wkts*	*Runs*	*Ave*	*5W*	*10W*	*Best*
NZ (tests)	32	56	3	60	612	11.55	–	3	9	100	3148	31.48	5	–	6-63
NZ (other)	45	66	7	95	1139	19.30	–	5	7	157	3366	21.43	7	1	7-70
Canterbury	56	90	10	103*	1535	19.18	1	3	19	239	4587	19.19	12	3	8-61
Robins' XI	1	2	0	53	54	27.00	–	1	–	1	107	107.00	–	–	1-58
NZ XI	5	7	1	63	126	21.00	–	1	1	12	338	28.16	–	–	3-39
South Island	3	4	0	10	28	7.00	–	–	5	9	221	24.55	–	–	3-31
TOTAL	**142**	**225**	**21**	**103***	**3494**	**17.12**	**1**	**13**	**41**	**518**	**11,767**	**22.71**	**24**	**4**	**8-61**

Herbert Taylor PEARSON

Born: *Palmerston North, 5 August, 1910*

Died: *Auckland, 15 June, 2006*

Right-hand batsman

Herb Pearson had been New Zealand's oldest living first-class cricketer. His career spanned 16 seasons and included 30 matches. He was 35 before he hit his first century and his best season was his last, when he was aged 37.

Best remembered as a stubborn opening batsman, Pearson batted as low as number nine when he made his first-class debut at Lancaster Park in 1932, the day before Christmas. There was plenty of competition for places in the Auckland lineup at that time with Jack Mills, Paul Whitelaw, Lindsay Weir, Giff Vivian, Ces Dacre and Mal Matheson all ahead of Pearson. He made a useful 29, however, sharing a fifty run partnership with All Black Ron Bush.

A week later Auckland met Otago at Carisbrook and Pearson was moved up to number six only to fall cheaply in both innings. Auckland's third and final Plunket Shield match for the season was against Wellington at Eden Park and Pearson was back down at number eight, being dismissed for a single in his first innings.

Auckland trailed by 31 on the first innings and were 151-6 in their second knock when Pearson came to the crease. Bush and Matheson soon fell but Pearson found an ally in Raoul Garrard and the pair added 99 for the ninth wicket. Pearson ended with 66 and Garrard, who made 55, then went on to bowl Wellington out to give Auckland victory by just 43 runs.

There were two notable debuts in this match. Eric Tindill, playing as a specialist batsman, scored a century while Doug Freeman, the schoolboy leg-spinner from Nelson College, opened the bowling and took nine wickets in the match. Freeman was immediately picked in the New Zealand side to play Douglas Jardine's very strong England team.

Garrard, 35, also a leg-spinner, had played for New Zealand against Archie MacLaren's MCC side in 1922/23, and, despite taking ten wickets in the match against Wellington, was overlooked in favour of the youngster.

Pearson managed just one appearance over the next four seasons but from 1937/38 became a more regular member of the side. Auckland had won the Plunket Shield the previous season and went on to make it four in a row.

The Auckland batting continued to be exceptionally strong at this stage, with players such as Merv Wallace, Bill Carson, Scott Sale and Verdun Scott coming into prominence, and Pearson was only required to bat twice that season and the next. His best effort during that time was 49 against Otago at Carisbrook in 1938/39, when he shared a 90 run partnership for the third wicket with Alf Postles.

Pearson played in all three Plunket Shield fixtures the following season, the last before the war. By now he was opening the batting and recorded successive fifties against Wellington and Otago, sharing a 114 run opening stand with Paul Whitelaw in the latter game.

Pearson served in both the navy and army during the war. A draper by trade, working in the family business at Otahuhu, he enlisted in February 1942, joined the navy in November and transferred to the army in June 1944. He was finally discharged in September 1948.

During the war years a limited first-class programme was in place and Pearson's best scores in that time were 70 against Wellington in 1940/41, 58 against Canterbury in 1943/44 and 71 against Wellington in 1944/45.

In January 1944 he scored 91 and 38 for the Navy against the Air Force in a two-day match played at the Basin Reserve and in March that year he captained New Zealand Services against a New Zealand XI at the Basin Reserve.

This game, which carried first-class status, was a special match arranged for patriotic purposes. Pearson made 27 and 10, his first innings score being the second highest in the Services' total of 99 all out. Twelve months later he made 9 and 15 opening the batting for North Island against South, at Eden Park, in another low scoring affair which North won by just 34 runs.

Pearson, now aged 35, had his best season to date the following summer, and registered his maiden century against Otago at Carisbrook. He reached his century with a six off former test bowler Cyril Allcott and was finally dismissed for 107, including one other six and eight fours. He and Verdun Scott had put on 165 in 225 minutes for the third wicket. Pearson followed this up with 72 against Wellington in his next innings in a match played for the Centennial Cup, a first-class fixture played in addition to the Plunket Shield.

While Pearson just failed to reach international recognition as a batsman he was still involved in consideration for a world cricketing record. When Auckland met Bill Brown's Australian team in March 1946 Ray Lindwall bowled Pearson, hitting only the off bail, but with such force the bail came to rest very close to the third man boundary. The estimate was that the bail travelled at least 70 yards. Later research found a record of 83 yards 21 inches in Hobart in 1925.

Pearson had one further season at first-class level, captaining Auckland in 1947/48. It turned out to be his best with a tally of 397 runs at 39.70 and a career best 172 against Canterbury at Lancaster Park in the opening match of the season. Pearson was ninth out at 353, his innings including 18 fours. He put on 139 for the first wicket with Ivan Wyatt (67), who was making his first-class debut. Auckland's final total of 355 took more than eight hours to compile and came off 168.4 overs.

In the three Plunket Shield fixtures Pearson totalled 293 runs at 48.83 and his career ended with two games against Fiji, that season's main tourists. Their matches against the major associations were only ruled first-class many years later when the ICC overturned the New Zealand Cricket Council's original ruling, and one which they had confirmed several times thereafter, regarding the status of the games.

Pearson attended King's College in Auckland and played club cricket for King's Old Boys and Middlemore over a period of more than 20 years. He was the first winner of both the Riddolls Cup for the most improved player in first grade, in 1931/32, and the Ridings Cup for the highest score on Eden Park, in 1947/48.

When his playing career ended Pearson became sole selector for Auckland for three seasons from 1950/51 then spent two more as a member of the panel. He also spent seven years as his club's delegate to the Auckland Cricket Association's Management Committee.

Pearson was a member of the Grange Golf Club for many years where he played in the Auckland Cricket Association's inaugural golf day. He remained a popular figure at Eden Park cricket matches as Keeper of the Key, which gave access to liquid refreshments in an unused dressing room behind the old wooden main stand just before lunch and after stumps.

Writing in the ACA's annual report Peter Badley described Pearson as "a forthright but friendly character, a consistent opening bat, an astute captain and a great contributor to Auckland cricket at all levels."

Pearson was also a solid fullback in the Auckland rugby side, playing 14 games from 1932 to 1937. He scored six tries and kicked one conversion, with a best of three tries against West Coast in 1932.

Pearson's record in first-class cricket is:

Season	*M*	*I*	*NO*	*HS*	*Runs*	*Ave*	*100*	*50*	*ct*
1932/33	3	6	0	66	122	20.33	–	1	–
1935/36	1	1	1	27*	27	–	–	–	1
1937/38	2	2	0	14	22	11.00	–	–	1
1938/39	2	2	0	49	54	27.00	–	–	–
1939/40	3	4	0	53	152	38.00	–	2	1
1940/41	2	3	1	70	84	42.00	–	1	1
1941/42	1	1	0	8	8	8.00	–	–	1

Season	*M*	*I*	*NO*	*HS*	*Runs*	*Ave*	*100*	*50*	*ct*
1943/44	3	6	1	58	134	26.80	–	1	1
1944/45	3	6	0	71	155	25.83	–	1	6
1945/46	5	8	0	107	237	29.62	1	1	5
1947/48	5	10	0	172	397	39.70	1	–	1
TOTAL	**30**	**49**	**3**	**172**	**1392**	**30.26**	**2**	**7**	**18**

For	*M*	*I*	*NO*	*HS*	*Runs*	*Ave*	*100*	*50*	*ct*
Auckland	28	45	3	172	1331	31.69	2	7	16
NZ Services	1	2	0	27	37	18.50	–	–	–
North Island	1	2	0	15	24	12.00	–	–	2
TOTAL	**30**	**49**	**3**	**172**	**1392**	**30.26**	**2**	**7**	**18**

Pearson also bowled two overs for Auckland conceding seven runs.

Gerald Alan ROSE

Born: *Palmerston North, 11 April, 1941*

Died: *Sydney, 12 June, 2007*

Left-hand batsman

Opening batsman Gerry Rose had a somewhat unusual first-class career, playing one season for Central Districts in 1958/59, as a 17-year-old, and one season for Northern Districts nine years later.

He attended Palmerston North Boys' High School where he excelled in a variety of sporting pursuits. He was captain of the 1st XI, half-back for the 1st XV, winner of the most scientific boxer award and also a school prefect. In his final year at school he was awarded the Dux Ludorum prize for his efforts.

Rose made his debut for Manawatu in 1956/57, aged just 15, and the following season made 160 and 53, both not out, against Wairarapa.

His first-class career began while still at school when he became the youngest player, at 17 years and 258 days, to appear for Central Districts. Rose was one of two 17-year-olds making their debut (the other being Gary Bartlett) when Central opened their Plunket Shield campaign against Northern Districts at Palmerston North on Christmas Day 1958. Two other Central players, Peter Coutts and Doug Armstrong, were also new to first-class cricket.

After a shortened opening day, Northern were finally dismissed for 217 on the second afternoon and Rose and Coutts walked out to open the innings at 3 pm. Coutts went at 23 but Rose battled on, eventually being bowled by former test spinner Allen Lissette for 33, made in 128 minutes. As it happened, this turned out to be the highest score Rose was destined to make at first-class level.

He scored 23 in the next match against Auckland, top score in Central's 59 all out. Rose again batted for 128 minutes while Auckland sent down 51.3 overs, 23 of which were maidens. Rose retained his place for all five matches but his final tally was just 116 runs at 11.60. However, the youngster had shown determination and sound defence.

He had also done enough to gain a place in Merv Wallace's cricket coaching clinic in Auckland. Contemporaries at the clinic included Graham Dowling, Brian Hastings and Ross Morgan.

On leaving school Rose went to Victoria University in Wellington to study veterinary science and during this time he gained his rugby and cricket blues for the university.

In 1961 he went to Sydney University to complete his veterinary degree. He played half-back for the University in the Sydney competition and had two games for New South Wales in 1963. He also played for the Rest of Australia against the Australian team that had returned from their South African tour.

On completion of his degree he returned to New Zealand to work in Taranaki and later in Tauranga. In November 1967 he showed early season form with 23 and 57 not out for Bay of Plenty against Thames Valley and was subsequently named in the Northern Districts side.

His first match was against Central Districts at Seddon Park where he opened the batting with former England player Martin Horton, who was also the national coach at the time.

Horton top-scored with 30, Rose made a duck and Northern were dismissed for just 98. Rose made 17 in the second innings sharing, in an opening stand of 56. It turned out to be a difficult season for both Northern, who finished in last place with just one point, and Rose, who could muster only 58 runs in eight innings.

In 1969 Rose, along with his Australian-born wife Helen and their children, returned to Sydney where he continued with his veterinary career. He continued playing country cricket until his late thirties.

His passion for the horse racing industry led him into specialising in equine veterinary work. In 1978 he established a company specialising in equine products which went on to become a global success.

From 1974, in partnership with advertising magnate John Singleton, Rose owned and raced thoroughbreds, including Belle du Jour, which won the Golden Slipper. Bob Hawke, ex-Australian prime minister, was also a part owner. At Rosehill racecourse there is now a room named after Belle du Jour.

Other successful horses were Zigalia, sixth in the Melbourne Cup, and Mirror Mirror, winner of the Magic Millions on the Gold Coast. Rose had an innate ability to pick successful horses as his record showed. Speakers at his funeral gave praise to an outstanding Australian – New Zealand born and bred Gerald Rose.

Rose's record in first-class cricket is:

M	*I*	*NO*	*HS*	*Runs*	*Ave*	*ct*
9	18	0	33	174	9.66	4

John Michael RUSTON

Born: *Wellington, 4 March, 1941*

Died: *Brisbane, 30 April, 2006*

Right-hand batsman

John Ruston, a stalwart of the St Albans club in Christchurch, played two matches for Canterbury in the 1962/63 season.

Ruston had joined St Albans in the 1958/59 season after leaving Papanui High School and immediately made an impression with his tough, uncompromising approach. He went on to captain the senior team, displaying innovative leadership and consistent batting which brought him respect from his contemporaries.

He was a thoughtful player who knew the game extremely well. Over the years he also brought many Papanui High School 1st XI players to St Albans and many of those went on to become very successful players and administrators with the club.

In the club's annual report Alan Jamieson wrote that Ruston was a cricketer's cricketer, a colourful character who always played the game as it deserved to be played. He said that Ruston was honest, some would say blunt, but was always encouraging and helpful to his colleagues.

After Canterbury had won its opening two games of the 1962/63 Plunket Shield season, Ruston was called into the team in place of Zin Harris and made his debut against Central Districts at Lancaster Park. Ruston, who batted at number five, made 1 and 16, victim of Bryan Yuile on both occasions.

The highlight of the match was the innings of 150 by Mike Shrimpton, who had been twelfth man in Central's first two games and only got his opportunity because John Guy was unavailable.

Shrimpton only managed a further 24 runs in his other four innings for Central but was subsequently called on to make his test debut against Ted Dexter's England team later that summer.

Canterbury had a three week break before their next game, against Northern Districts at Hamilton. Ruston was made twelfth man while Keith Thomson came into the side. Canterbury's final match, against Auckland at Eden Park, began the day after their previous game ended and Ruston was brought back into the team to bat at number seven, at the expense of off-spinner Bruce Irving.

Ruston made 6 in each innings, falling to John Sparling both times and his career at first-class level was all over, at the age of 21. However, he continued to excel at club level and in the 1968/69 season his aggregate of 533 runs was the best in Christchurch senior cricket. He later went on to play for the Harewood Club in the Christchurch Suburban senior competition and then completed his career with Riccarton.

In 149 games for St Albans Ruston totalled 5784 runs, seventh on the club's all time list. In the field he took 76 catches and made 37 dismissals as a stand-in wicketkeeper. In February 2005 he and his wife, Annette, came from Brisbane to be present for the St Alban's centennial weekend.

Pearl Hannah SAVIN

Born: *Christchurch, 20 June, 1914*

Died: *Auckland, 19 November, 2000*

Right-hand batsman, wicketkeeper

Although she played in only one test, Pearl Savin created several milestones against Betty Archdale's touring England side at Lancaster Park in February 1935. As well as being New Zealand's first woman test wicketkeeper, Savin was also the first wicketkeeper, man or woman, to lead New Zealand in a test.

After New Zealand had been bowled out for 44 in its first innings the Kiwi captain, Ruth Symons, was required to go off during England's massive total of 503 for five, after a ball hit her in the eye as she tried to take a catch while looking into the sun. Savin took over the captaincy.

In a 1994 interview, Savin recalled the problems she faced as captain in the field as Betty Snowball (189), Molly Hide (110) and Mollie Child (86 not out) tore the inexperienced Kiwi bowling to shreds. "We had not been together long enough for me to know what my team-mates were like as bowlers," Savin said. "It was a bit tricky in knowing when to bring what bowlers on and so it was very much of a case of hoping for the best after Ruth had gone off." Prior to the Symons injury, Savin said she did not realise that she was the vice-captain of the team as no official appointment had been made.

New Zealand fared slightly better in their second innings by making 122 but lost by the huge margin of an innings and 337 runs.

Savin left Christchurch at a young age and was educated at Epsom Girls' Grammar in Auckland where she won some cricketing trophies as well as winning the Auckland secondary school tennis championship. She made her debut for Auckland and continued to play for her province until 1936 before going to Auckland Teachers' Training College, where she played hockey. In 1937 she went to Fiji to teach before returning to New Zealand in 1940. As a result she was unavailable for the New Zealand women's tour of New South Wales in 1938.

After returning from Fiji Savin went to Dunedin and trained as a physiotherapist and worked in the profession for some time before taking another career change as a reporter with the *Timaru Herald*. She made her last move to Leigh and then Warkworth in 1968. She was also a keen golfer until she gave the game away around 1990.

Savin said as a batsman she was unorthodox, but also had good hand-eye co-ordination that allowed her to go out and "give the ball a good whack".

John Carruthers SCANDRETT

Born: *Invercargill, 22 February, 1915*

Died: *Nelson, 29 August, 2006*

Left-hand batsman, right-arm off-spin bowler

Jack Scandrett, an elegant left-handed batsman who appeared in four matches over a period of nine seasons during the 1930s and 40s, had been Otago's oldest surviving first-class cricketer. He was the first player from Southland to play Plunket Shield cricket for Otago.

Scandrett was the son of Doug Scandrett, who had also represented Southland and was later a champion bowler, and grandson of a former mayor of Invercargill. He got his first cricketing experience at Waihopai Primary School where he gained selection for the Southland schools side.

He later attended Southland Boys' High School, making the first eleven in his second year. He entered first grade cricket at 17, when the High School was admitted to the Southland Cricket Association's senior competition. He scored a century that season, 134 not out against Appleby, and later linked up with the Old Boys' Club where he went on to become a prolific run scorer. Apart from his prowess with the bat, he was also a first-class slips fieldsman.

He made his debut for Southland in December 1932, aged just 17, in a two-day match against Otago. His first-class debut followed three years later in the opening Plunket Shield match of the 1935/36 season, which began at Eden Park the day before Christmas. At that time Auckland had a very strong side which included seven past or future New Zealand representatives plus all-rounder Les Townsend, a professional coach who had played four tests for England.

After an evenly contested first innings, the home team went on to win by 292 runs with the highlight being Lindsay Weir's 191. Scandrett made 6 and 7, being bowled by Mal Matheson and Giff Vivian.

Scandrett was not selected for Otago's next game (played a month later) but returned for the third and last fixture against Canterbury at Lancaster Park. Otago made only 173 in their first innings, with Bill Merritt taking 6-56, but the home team could only manage a lead of one run.

Otago batted consistently to total 350 in their second innings, with Merritt taking another seven wickets. Despite a Walter Hadlee hundred, Canterbury went down by 119 runs, giving them the wooden spoon for the season. Scandrett made 14 and 18, dismissed by Merritt in both innings.

Next season Scandrett made only one appearance, the opening Shield fixture against Wellington at the Basin Reserve. Two days play were lost because of poor weather and the match was drawn. Scandrett, batting at number nine, had just one innings, being bowled by Jack Lamason for 5. In the second innings Otago were in trouble chasing 233 for victory and Scandrett had an anxious wait as next man in while Ken Uttley and Mac McGregor held out, taking the score from 98-7 to 127-7 at the close.

Scandrett made 149 for Southland in a two-day match against Otago in 1940/41 (out of a total of 261 all out) and his final appearance at first-class level was at Lancaster Park in the 1943/44 season, when a restricted first-class programme was in place because of the war. Scandrett made 22 and 1, with Otago going down to Canterbury by an innings.

The home team batted first and ran up 510 with Walter Hadlee and Frank O'Brien scoring hundreds. Otago made 201 and 242 with Tom Burtt, who was making his first-class debut at the age of 28, taking 6-56 in the first innings. In Otago's second innings Dave Watt scored 105. This was the only first-class match he ever played.

Jim Gill, a former Otago player from Southland and a recent president of the Otago association, said "Scandrett was without doubt the best batsman produced in Southland; a magnificent player."

Sam Richardson, a former Southland team mate of the 1940s, said "In my treasure chest of happy memories, up near its pinnacle, would be at the Southland Boys' High School grounds on a sunny afternoon being enthralled watching an innings of sublime grace unfolding from the bat of Jack Scandrett."

He went on to remember that "defensive play was not in Scandrett's makeup as, irrespective of the quality of the opposing bowlers, the fluency of his stroke making was sheer poetry in motion. I have seen most of the great left-handed batsmen – Martin Donnelly, Bert Sutcliffe, Arthur Morris, David Gower – and not one of them would excel Jack for sheer grace and fluency of stroke making."

Richardson also said "the tragedy was that, due to the parochial attitude of the Otago selection committee, New Zealand cricket was denied the talent of an unbridled one-in-a-lifetime cricketer."

Scandrett is believed to be the only batsman to have made a double century in the Invercargill senior competition. In November 1937 he made 201 for Old Boys against Marist. Only Victor Trumper (211 for Sims' XI v Southland in 1913/14) and Warwick Armstrong (335 for Melbourne C.C. v Southland in 1905/06, after surviving an easy stumping chance first ball) had previously made a double century in any form of cricket in Southland.

Scandrett took two hours to get to his century (reached with a six), had to retire with an injured hand on 174, but returned to complete the double hundred in just over three hours before being run out. When he reached two hundred play in all the matches on the High School ground stopped for a moment as Scandrett was accorded a hearty ovation.

He was a noted figure in the business community, spending his entire working life with Southland Frozen Meat. He joined the company as an office boy in 1932 and retired in 1974, after nine years as general manager.

Scandrett's record in first-class cricket is:

M	*I*	*NO*	*HS*	*Runs*	*Ave*	*ct*	*Wkts*	*Runs*	*Ave*
4	7	0	22	73	10.42	2	0	20	–

Gordon Lindsay WHYTE

Born: *Wellington, 13 August, 1915*

Died: *Wellington, 24 June, 2007*

Left-hand batsman, right-arm leg-break bowler

Gordon Whyte, who played one first-class game for Wellington, had a long career as a cricket and soccer commentator on both television and radio.

Whyte's parents emigrated to New Zealand from Scotland in 1910. At primary school he was drawn to cricket by one of the teachers placing a penny on a single wicket in the playground. Anyone who bowled accurately and hit the wicket got the penny. Whyte went on to take many wickets for the school team and the Brooklyn Club in Boys' League matches.

Although a Wellington primary school representative, he failed to gain a place in a cricket team at Wellington College so continued playing for Brooklyn. He ended his college days without ever playing a summer or winter sport for the school. With any winter sport other than rugby not allowed, Whyte also had to join a club in order to play soccer.

He took up a career in the Public Service which included being assigned to the Hansard Department in Parliament to work as a short-hand typist and reporter. In January 1941 he joined the 2nd Battalion of the Wellington Regiment and then joined the Air Force as a flight rigger. However, his call up was delayed when he was posted to Fiji by the Public Service. An airfield, crucial to the war effort in the Pacific, was being constructed at Nadi. The work became even more urgent when Japan bombed Pearl Harbor two days after Whyte left Auckland for Fiji.

He finally did establish himself in the Air Force and in March 1949 Warrant Officer Whyte was awarded the British Empire Medal for meritorious service. Returning to civilian life, he became one of the original staff of the National Airways Corporation, retiring in 1972.

In 1949 he was asked if he would be interested in doing soccer commentary for 2YA from the Basin Reserve. Their usual commentator was filling in for rugby's Winston McCarthy at Athletic Park (McCarthy being in South Africa with the All Blacks) giving Whyte his first opportunity. He took over as the number one commentator the following season until he retired from broadcasting in 1972.

In 1953, while he was still captaining the Wellington College Old Boys side, he added cricket to his broadcasting repertoire and in 1960 he was asked to make the move to television. Whyte was a commentator at the first sporting fixture to be televised from the capital, the first test against South Africa in February 1964.

Like many other players, Whyte's cricket career was affected by the war. He actually made his debut in the last Plunket Shield match played before the competition was suspended at the end of 1939/40.

Whyte played in three successive Town v Country games, virtual Plunket Shield trial matches, and eventually gained selection for Wellington B in 1939/40. He played against Hawke's Bay and Rangitikei where he came up against Herbie Lambert and Rupert Worker, both New Zealand representatives during the 1920s.

The Wellington selectors chose Whyte for their last Plunket Shield game of the season and the team travelled to Carisbrook. Otago were bowled out for 138 in their first innings and Wellington replied with 220, Whyte scoring 3 at number ten, but the home side were more resolute second time around.

This time Otago amassed 351, with Whyte taking 1-45 off nine overs. Set 269 to win, Wellington were 161-8 when Whyte joined Eric Tindill, who was suffering from lumbago and was using a runner. The pair added 50 in just 49 minutes – Whyte's share being a swashbuckling 42. The last wicket fell immediately, however, and Otago had won by 58 runs.

Whyte played senior cricket for Wellington College Old Boys for 13 seasons, capturing 473 wickets, including a best of 72 in one season. In one match, against Petone in 1941/42, he took 7-9 and 6-10. The next week he left for Fiji. After the war he captained Wellington in matches against Nelson. After joining NAC he also took part in Mercantile League cricket.

In 1955/56 he made a comeback to senior cricket and took 8-27 against Kilbirnie on his return. He played second grade from 1958/59 and had another season in the Mercantile League to round out his career.

Whyte played soccer at representative level for Wellington B and later served on the New Zealand Football Association council, where he became deputy chairman. He also managed the New Zealand team which played in New Caledonia in 1967.

In later years he was also very much involved with community work such as IHC, the local senior citizens' club and police volunteer work and was also a Justice of the Peace. His autobiography, *It's Not All Cricket*, was published in 2005.

John Churchill WILLIAMS

Born: *Gisborne, 9 May, 1941*

Died: *Auckland, 17 March, 2007*

Right-hand batsman, right-arm medium-pace bowler

Jack Williams played six matches for Auckland in the early 1970s, four of those in the 1971/72 season when he was already aged 30. The established opening bowling pairing of Bob Sutton and Bob Cunis had made it difficult for Williams to break into the Auckland lineup earlier in his career.

He attended Mangapapa Primary School, Gisborne Intermediate and Gisborne Boys High School where he excelled at cricket and made the 1st XI for four years from 1956 to 1959. His fast-medium bowling brought him numerous wickets from the outset.

He performed splendidly in local senior cricket and stood out in interschool fixtures. In 1957 he took 4-44 against Napier Boys' High School and in 1958 he took 4-10 against Wanganui Collegiate and 5-40 against the Old Students.

By 1959 he was near unplayable in the interschool game against Napier Boys' High, destroying their top order and returning outstanding figures of 5-5, backed up with 3-17 in the second innings.

Not surprisingly, he came to the notice of the local selectors and was chosen for the Poverty Bay side while at school. In January 1958 he took 5-16 in a pacy and controlled spell against Hawke's Bay and, in December 1958, he had handy figures of 2-18 and 3-70, also against Hawke's Bay.

Other good spells saw him take 2-34 against Bay of Plenty, 2-16 against Thames Valley and 2-30 and 2-62 against the same side in a return match, all in the 1959/60 season. He then moved to Auckland to attend university and linked up with the Grafton club.

He was also a fine rugby player and was in the Gisborne Boys' High School 1st XV for two years, 1958 and 1959, playing on the wing. In 1959 he scored five tries – two each against the Old Students and Sacred Heart College and one against East Coast Combined Schools. He also played senior rugby for Suburbs in Auckland.

Williams finally got his chance at first-class level at the end of the 1970/71 season when Auckland played the New Zealand Under 23 XI. Auckland were missing a number of regulars in John Sparling (their captain), Bob Cunis, Roger Harris, Hedley Howarth and Rex Baddeley.

Apart from Williams, Cam Maingay and Ken Parker (older brother of test batsmen John and Murray) were also making their first-class debuts. For the latter two it turned out to be their only appearance at this level.

The Under 23 side had as many as five players new to first-class cricket, including two eighteen-year-olds named Jeremy Coney and Warren Lees. Williams was used sparingly in the match, however, capturing one wicket in each innings.

The following season was more profitable for Williams. Bob Cunis had gained selection in the World XI team, which toured Australia after the proposed South African tour was cancelled, and was not available for the first four Plunket Shield matches. In his absence, Williams proved to be the most successful of the Auckland pace bowlers, capturing 11 wickets at 22.81.

Auckland won their first game, against Central Districts, by an innings. Williams played a leading role taking 4-52, off 16 overs, in the first innings and 4-49, from 15.6 overs, in the second, after Central had been forced to follow on 306 runs behind.

Auckland, and Williams, had less success in their next games, however. For the last match of the season Williams was one of several players who were replaced. Cunis was now available and Nick Smith, former Otago pace bowler who had been twelfth man in the first four games, joined him in the side.

The following season Williams appeared only for Auckland B, capturing 5-86 against Nelson. He did return for one final game at first-class level against Australia in 1973/74. Williams went wicketless on this occasion but the match was notable for Kerry O'Keeffe being left on 99 not out when the Australian innings ended. Ashley Mallett, who had survived for 36 minutes, was run out when the batsmen attempted an impossible single. O'Keeffe never did score a first-class hundred.

Williams also played in three games for Auckland in the early years of domestic one-day cricket. His figures of 8-3-7-2 (eight-ball overs), against Northern Districts in 1971/72, are still an Auckland record. Williams was later an Auckland selector.

Former Auckland and Grafton team mate John McIntyre described Williams as "a great guy on and off the field and one of the backbones of the club."

Williams' record in first-class cricket is:

M	*I*	*NO*	*HS*	*Runs*	*Ave*	*ct*	*Wkts*	*Runs*	*Ave*	*Best*
6	7	6	9	19	19.00	5	13	346	26.61	4-49

NEW ZEALAND SQUADS IN AUSTRALIA

Two New Zealand sides took part in a series of matches in Australia in July. Both teams played in the Top End Series in Darwin and Cairns which also involved India A and Pakistan A. New Zealand Black also participated in an Emerging Players Tournament in Brisbane along with the Australian Centre of Excellence, the Karnataka State Cricket Association XI and a South African Emerging Players side.

The squads were: New Zealand Black: P.G. Fulton *(captain, Canterbury)*, J.A.H. Marshall *(vice-captain, Northern Districts)*, G.W. Aldridge *(Northern Districts)*, B.J. Diamanti *(Central Districts)*, M.R. Gillespie *(Wellington)*, J.M. How *(Central Districts)*, N.L. McCullum *(Otago)*, P.D. McGlashan *(Northern Districts)*, W.C. McSkimming *(Otago)*, J.D. Ryder *(Wellington)*, B.E. Scott *(Otago)*, S.L. Stewart *(Canterbury)*, L.R.P.L. Taylor *(Central Districts)*, Coach, R.M. Carter; Manager, Sir Richard Hadlee; Assistant Coaches and Video Analysis, A. Ross and M. Hesson.

New Zealand White: C.D. McMillan *(captain, Canterbury)*, M.D. Bell *(vice-captain, Wellington)*, H.K. Bennett *(Canterbury)*, G.J. Hopkins *(Otago)*, B.P. Martin *(Northern Districts)*, C.S. Martin *(Auckland)*, R.J. Nicol *(Auckland)*, M.G. Orchard *(Northern Districts)*, M.H.W. Papps *(Canterbury)*, J.S. Patel *(Wellington)*, M.S. Sinclair *(Central Districts)*, R.R. Sherlock *(Canterbury)*, J.A.F. Yovich *(Northern Districts)*. Coach, M.R. O'Donnell; Manager, D.R. Hadlee; Assistant Coach, V.F. Johnson.

Scott and Yovich replaced M.J. Mason *(Central Districts)* and K.D. Mills *(Auckland)* who withdrew because of injury. L. Vincent *(Auckland)* withdrew from the New Zealand Black team to take up a county contract and was replaced by Stewart. Papps played one game for New Zealand Black, who were depleted through injuries, and Orchard joined New Zealand Black after the White team had finished their programme.

The first-class match between New Zealand White and Pakistan A was abandoned after no play had been possible on the first two days and plans to stage two one-day games instead were also thwarted because of the conditions.

NEW ZEALAND BLACK v NEW ZEALAND WHITE (Twenty20)

At Fretwell Park, Cairns 1 July, 2006

New Zealand Black 129-8 (J.A.H. Marshall 48*) **defeated New Zealand White** 124-6 (M.S. Sinclair 38, R.J. Nicol 33*, N.L. McCullum 4-17) by 5 runs

NEW ZEALAND BLACK v NEW ZEALAND WHITE

At Fretwell Park, Cairns 2 July, 2006

New Zealand Black 179 (P.G. Fulton 51, C.S. Martin 3-27, J.A.F. Yovich 3-32) **lost to New Zealand White** 180-8 (R.J. Nicol 56*, M.H.W. Papps 42, M.S. Sinclair 41) by 2 wickets *(no restriction on bowlers' overs)*

NORTHERN TERRITORY CHIEF MINISTER'S XI v NEW ZEALAND WHITE

At Gardens Oval, Darwin 6 July, 2006

New Zealand White 262-6 (M.D. Bell 102, M.H.W. Papps 72, S.J. Regan 3-41) **defeated Northern Territory Chief Minister's XI** 234-7 (D.K. Richards 58, T. Scollay 57*, R.M. Bowden 37, B.P. Martin 3-23) by 28 runs

NORTHERN TERRITORY CHIEF MINISTER'S XI v NEW ZEALAND BLACK

At Gardens Oval, Darwin 7 July, 2006

New Zealand Black 344 (P.G. Fulton 80, S.L. Stewart 70, J.D. Ryder 65, L.R.P.L. Taylor 43) **defeated Northern Territory Chief Minister's XI** 177 (S.L. Lavers 52, A. Dilley 30, L.R.P.L. Taylor 5-31) by 167 runs

AUSTRALIA A v NEW ZEALAND BLACK — One-day

at Marrara Cricket Ground, Darwin on 5 July, 2006
Toss : Australia A. Umpires : R.L. Parry & R.J. Tucker
New Zealand Black won by 8 wickets.

Gillespie, who took the first three wickets, and McSkimming reduced Australia A to 51-5 before Hodge took charge. He added 175 in 136 minutes with Hopes as the home side got through to 236-7. Gillespie ended with the best figures while McCullum was economical.

New Zealand Black made light work of their target with Papps and How putting on 196 for the opening partnership in just 137 minutes. How reached three figures from 106 balls and was unbeaten at the end. The visitors won with 9.3 overs remaining.

AUSTRALIA A

	Runs	Mins	Balls	6s	4s
P.A.Jaques b Gillespie	3	11	8	-	-
B.J.Haddin*† lbw b Gillespie	8	18	9	-	2
M.J.Cosgrove c Aldridge b Gillespie	11	20	11	1	-
B.J.Hodge b Aldridge	123	173	140	1	16
T.R.Birt c Taylor b McSkimming	6	15	7	-	1
S.R.Watson c Taylor b McSkimming	4	9	5	-	1
J.R.Hopes not out	61	147	115	-	3
B.R.Dorey lbw b Aldridge	0	1	1	-	-
M.G.Johnson not out	5	10	5	-	-
S.W.Tait					
D.J.Cullen					
Extras (lb 2, w 9, nb 4)	15				
TOTAL (50 overs) (7 wkts)	**236**	205			

NEW ZEALAND BLACK

	Runs	Mins	Balls	6s	4s
M.H.W.Papps c Haddin b Watson	64	137	96	-	4
J.M.How not out	123	168	123	1	17
L.R.P.L.Taylor c Dorey b Watson	2	3	2	-	-
P.G.Fulton* not out	27	26	22	-	4
J.A.H.Marshall					
P.D.McGlashan†					
N.L.McCullum					
W.C.McSkimming					
M.R.Gillespie					
G.W.Aldridge					
B.E.Scott					
Extras (b 6, lb 6, w 11)	23				
TOTAL (40.3 overs) (2 wkts)	**239**	168			

Bowling	*O*	*M*	*R*	*W*
NEW ZEALAND BLACK				
McSkimming	9	0	57	2
Gillespie	10	1	49	3
Scott	10	1	40	0
Aldridge	6	0	28	2
McCullum	10	1	37	0
Taylor	5	0	23	0
AUSTRALIA A				
Tait	8	0	36	0
Johnson	7	0	41	0
Dorey	3	0	23	0
Watson	8.3	0	60	2
Cullen	9	1	36	0
Hopes	3	0	21	0
Hodge	2	0	10	0

Fall of Wickets	***AA***	***NZB***
1st	4	196
2nd	19	198
3rd	30	-
4th	47	-
5th	51	-
6th	226	-
7th	226	-
8th	-	-
9th	-	-
10th	-	-

NEW ZEALAND WHITE v PAKISTAN A — Twenty20

at Marrara Cricket Ground, Darwin on 9 July, 2006
Toss : New Zealand White. Umpires : R.L. Parry & R.J. Tucker
Pakistan A won by 61 runs.

PAKISTAN A

	Runs	Mins	Balls	6s	4s
Mohammad Hafeez c Sinclair b Sherlock	1	8	6	-	-
Rafatullah Mohmand c Hopkins b Sherlock	1	6	2	-	-
Mohammad Salman† c Martin B.P. b Yovich	2	19	5	-	-
Misbah-ul-Haq* not out	107	71	76	5	8
Bazid Khan b Patel	12	26	12	-	1
Hasan Raza run out	17	16	14	1	-
Fawad Alam not out	13	9	6	1	1
Mansoor Amjad					
Wasim Khan					
Abdur Rehman					
Mohammad Irshad					
Extras (lb 1, w 8, nb 2)	11				
TOTAL (20 overs) (5 wkts)	**164**	80			

NEW ZEALAND WHITE

	Runs	Mins	Balls	6s	4s
M.H.W.Papps c Mohmand b Khan	14	21	14	-	1
M.S.Sinclair c Amjad b Khan	12	14	9	-	1
C.D.McMillan* c Raza b Irshad	11	13	9	-	1
G.J.Hopkins† run out	14	18	13	-	-
R.J.Nicol c Salman b Alam	7	13	11	-	-
M.G.Orchard lbw b Rehman	24	26	23	2	-
J.A.F.Yovich st Salman b Amjad	3	3	5	-	-
B.P.Martin run out	5	3	4	-	1
J.S.Patel run out	3	4	3	-	-
R.R.Sherlock b Alam	2	2	3	-	-
C.S.Martin not out	4	8	6	-	-
Extras (lb 2, w 2)	4				
TOTAL (16.4 overs)	**103**	67			

Bowling	O	M	R	W
NEW ZEALAND WHITE				
Martin C.S.	3	0	18	0
Sherlock	4	0	47	2
Yovich	2	0	16	1
Martin B.P.	4	0	33	0
Patel	4	0	22	1
Orchard	3	0	27	0
PAKISTAN A				
Khan	3	0	15	2
Irshad	3	0	27	1
Amjad	3	0	20	1
Alam	4	0	13	2
Rehman	2.4	0	17	1
Hafeez	1	0	9	0

Fall of Wickets	*PA*	*NZW*
1st	8	21
2nd	9	31
3rd	32	42
4th	89	61
5th	133	61
6th	-	66
7th	-	73
8th	-	79
9th	-	83
10th	-	103

AUSTRALIA A v NEW ZEALAND WHITE — Twenty20

at Marrara Cricket Ground, Darwin on 9 July, 2006
Toss : Australia A. Umpires : R.L. Parry & R.J. Tucker
Australia A won by 16 runs.

AUSTRALIA A

	Runs	Mins	Balls	6s	4s
M.J.Cosgrove c Patel b Martin C.S.	9	8	8	-	1
P.A.Jaques c Bell b Yovich	17	28	17	-	2
S.R.Watson c Hopkins b Martin C.S.	8	9	8	-	-
B.J.Hodge b Patel	40	38	29	-	3
B.J.Haddin*† c Bennett b Yovich	52	44	34	1	2
J.R.Hopes st Hopkins b Patel	19	20	16	-	1
C.J.L.Rogers c McMillan b Yovich	1	10	3	-	-
M.G.Johnson c Patel b Yovich	5	2	4	-	1
C.B.Bailey run out	1	2	1	-	-
B.R.Dorey not out	0	1	1	-	-
D.J.Cullen					
Extras (lb 2, w 4, nb 2)	7				
TOTAL (20 overs) (9 wkts)	**160**	84			

NEW ZEALAND WHITE

	Runs	Mins	Balls	6s	4s
M.D.Bell c Haddin b Dorey	5	6	9	-	-
M.S.Sinclair c & b Dorey	5	13	6	-	-
C.D.McMillan* c Cosgrove b Hopes	12	33	26	-	1
G.J.Hopkins† c Hodge b Dorey	7	8	5	-	1
R.J.Nicol c Hodge b Cullen	39	47	29	2	4
M.G.Orchard c Rogers b Watson	53	26	28	2	4
J.A.F.Yovich c Hopes b Watson	3	7	6	-	-
B.P.Martin c Haddin b Watson	3	7	5	-	-
J.S.Patel st Haddin b Cullen	2	4	3	-	-
H.K.Bennett c & b Cullen	0	4	1	-	-
C.S.Martin not out	1	2	2	-	-
Extras (b 2, lb 4, w 8)	14				
TOTAL (20 overs)	**144**	83			

Bowling	O	M	R	W
NEW ZEALAND WHITE				
Martin C.S.	4	0	30	2
Bennett	4	0	29	0
Yovich	4	0	36	4
Martin B.P.	4	0	35	0
Patel	4	0	28	2
AUSTRALIA A				
Johnson	4	0	12	0
Dorey	4	0	25	3
Watson	4	0	30	3
Hopes	2	0	27	1
Bailey	2	0	21	0
Cullen	4	0	23	3

Fall of Wickets	*AA*	*NZW*
1st	14	8
2nd	28	13
3rd	46	23
4th	116	47
5th	142	132
6th	154	135
7th	159	139
8th	159	141
9th	160	143
10th	-	144

NEW ZEALAND WHITE v INDIA A — First-class

at Gardens Oval, Darwin on 11, 12, 13, 14 July, 2006
Toss : New Zealand White. Umpires : I.H. Lock & R.L. Parry
Close of play: 1st day: NZ White 257-4, McMillan 62, Orchard 2; 2nd day: India A 209-6, Sharma 51, Singh 41
3rd day: India A 1-0, Pujara 0, Dhawan 1
India A won by 3 wickets.

This was the first time that a first-class game between neutral sides had been played in Australia while Gardens Oval became a new first-class venue.

McMillan was the mainstay of the New Zealand White innings, reaching his century after 302 minutes from 206 balls. India A recovered from 142-6 to reach 257, to trail by 52, and then bowled New Zealand White out for just 153. On the last day Badrinath held the Indian innings together and was unbeaten on 70 when victory was achieved.

NEW ZEALAND WHITE

FIRST INNINGS	Runs	Mins	Balls	6s	4s	SECOND INNINGS	Runs	Mins	Balls	6s	4s
M.D.Bell c Patel b Trivedi	1	6	8	-	-	(2) b Trivedi	0	7	8	-	-
M.H.W.Papps b Chawla	69	190	126	-	8	(1) lbw b Singh R.P.	4	13	1	-	1
M.S.Sinclair lbw b Chawla	76	152	134	1	12	c Uthappa b Chawla	33	83	50	-	3
C.D.McMillan* run out	108	320	239	3	8	c Badrinath b Chawla	15	41	27	-	2
R.J.Nicol run out	36	129	101	-	4	c & b Singh R.P.	55	143	135	1	4
M.G.Orchard c Patel b Singh R.P.	2	40	35	-	2	b Pujara	21	50	5	-	3
G.J.Hopkins† b Chawla	17	96	65	-	-	b Singh R.P.	9	32	28	-	-
B.P.Martin c Patel b Trivedi	7	41	22	-	1	lbw b Pujara	7	35	28	-	1
J.S.Patel c Singh T.P. b Chawla	0	21	16	-	-	run out	1	2	5	-	-
H.K.Bennett lbw b Chawla	2	14	14	-	-	not out	1	45	32	-	-
C.S.Martin not out	0	1	0	-	-	c Uthappa b Singh R.P.	0	3	4	-	-
Extras (b 1, lb 5, w 2, nb 6)	14					(b 2, lb 3, nb 2)	7				
TOTAL (125.4 overs)	**332**	514				(63 overs)	**153**	265			

INDIA A

FIRST INNINGS	Runs	Mins	Balls	6s	4s	SECOND INNINGS	Runs	Mins	Balls	6s	4s
S.Dhawan c Hopkins b Martin C.S.	4	3	2	-	1	(2) lbw b Patel	15	93	64	-	-
C.A.Pujara c Hopkins b Orchard	6	61	34	-	-	(1) run out	2	25	13	-	-
A.R.Uthappa b Bennett	0	4	2	-	-	c Hopkins b Bennett	9	31	16	-	1
P.A.Patel*† c Papps b Patel	35	59	49	-	6	c Papps b Orchard	8	23	15	-	1
S.Badrinath lbw b Martin B.P.	55	105	67	-	9	not out	70	218	145	-	5
R.S.Sodhi c Bennett b Martin B.P.	23	36	20	3	-	(8) c Nicol b Patel	1	13	14	-	-
R.Sharma b Patel	57	172	123	1	4	c Hopkins b Martin C.S.	22	37	30	1	2
T.P.Singh c Hopkins b Orchard	85	163	123	-	11	(6) b Patel	46	106	79	1	4
Piyush Chawla st Hopkins b Patel	8	15	10	-	1	not out	26	37	38	2	1
R.P.Singh c Martin C.S. b Patel	0	9	9	-	-						
S.K.Trivedi not out	0	5	1	-	-						
Extras (lb 5, nb 2)	7					(b 6, lb 3, nb 1)	10				
TOTAL (73 overs)	**280**	325				(68.4 overs) (7 wkts)	**209**	301			

Bowling	*O*	*M*	*R*	*W*	*O*	*M*	*R*	*W*
INDIA A								
Singh R.P.	27	13	53	1	18	6	33	4
Trivedi	26	9	69	2	9	3	18	1
Sodhi	12	0	41	0	3	0	9	0
Chawla	39.4	10	86	5	21	1	51	2
Singh T.P.	16	0	61	0	4	1	14	0
Badrinath	4	0	7	0	2	0	7	0
Sharma	1	0	9	0				
Pujara					6	1	16	2
NEW ZEALAND WHITE								
Martin C.S.	16	3	42	1	19	1	48	1
Bennett	9	0	68	1	7	0	18	1
Orchard	15	2	38	2	10	0	23	1
Patel	17	3	68	4	20	0	46	3
Martin B.P.	16	0	59	2	12.4	0	65	0

Fall of Wickets	***NZW*** *1st*	***IA*** *1st*	***NZW*** *2nd*	***IA*** *2nd*
1st	1	5	6	5
2nd	149	7	6	20
3rd	157	47	38	34
4th	240	47	68	44
5th	257	100	96	138
6th	312	142	115	170
7th	329	257	132	175
8th	330	273	133	-
9th	332	275	153	-
10th	332	280	153	-

NEW ZEALAND WHITE v PAKISTAN A — First-class

at Fretwell Park, Cairns on 17, 18, 19, 20 July, 2006
Match abandoned without a ball being bowled

QUEENSLAND XI v NEW ZEALAND BLACK (Twenty20)

At Cazaly's Stadium, Cairns 23 July, 2006

Queensland XI 138-6 (C.T. Perren 47, N.J. Reardon 34) **lost to New Zealand Black** 139-4 (P.G. Fulton 64, L.R.P.L. Taylor 48*) by 6 wickets

NEW ZEALAND BLACK v INDIA A — One-day

at Cazaly's Stadium, Cairns on 24 July, 2006
Toss : New Zealand Black. Umpires : R.L. Parry & P.R. Reiffel
New Zealand Black won by 7 wickets.

Gambhir and Badrinath provided the bulk of the runs for India A and put on 53 in 45 minutes for the fourth wicket. Gillespie took three wickets with his last eight deliveries to finish with 5-35 and he was well supported by McCullum.

How went without scoring in reply but Ryder was in fine touch racing to his fifty off 40 balls and his hundred just 38 balls later. Fulton helped him add 96 in only 47 minutes as New Zealand Black gained victory with 15.5 overs to spare.

INDIA A

	Runs	Mins	Balls	6s	4s
A.R.Uthappa c Ryder b Gillespie	3	16	10	-	-
G.Gambhir c How b McCullum	64	111	76	-	9
T.P.Singh c McCullum b McSkimming	12	18	18	-	2
Y.Venugopal Rao* run out	8	29	17	-	2
S.Badrinath c Marshall b Gillespie	63	134	97	-	3
P.A.Patel† c How b McCullum	2	14	11	-	-
R.Sharma c Marshall b Gillespie	8	11	12	-	1
R.S.Sodhi c Taylor b Scott	23	44	37	-	2
R.A.Jadeja c Taylor b Gillespie	5	14	10	-	-
Piyush Chawla not out	4	9	4	-	-
R.P.Singh b Gillespie	4	7	8	-	-
Extras (b 6, lb 3, w 7, nb 4)	20				
TOTAL (49.4 overs)	**216**				

NEW ZEALAND BLACK

	Runs	Mins	Balls	6s	4s
J.M.How b Singh R.P.	0	2	2	-	-
J.D.Ryder† st Patel b Singh T.P.	114	124	84	6	10
L.R.P.L.Taylor run out	21	73	52	-	2
P.G.Fulton* not out	54	65	57	2	5
J.A.H.Marshall not out	13	17	13	-	1
S.L.Stewart					
M.G.Orchard					
N.L.McCullum					
W.C.McSkimming					
M.R.Gillespie					
B.E.Scott					
Extras (b 2, lb 6, w 5, nb 3)	16				
TOTAL (34.1 overs) (3 wkts)	**218**	142			

Bowling	O	M	R	W
NEW ZEALAND BLACK				
Gillespie	9.4	2	35	5
McSkimming	10	1	46	1
Orchard	10	0	51	0
Scott	10	1	34	1
McCullum	10	0	41	2
INDIA A				
Singh R.P.	8.1	0	45	1
Sodhi	3	0	33	0
Jadeja	7	0	35	0
Chawla	10	1	47	0
Venugopal Rao	3	0	21	0
Singh T.P.	3	0	29	1

Fall of Wickets	*IA*	*NZB*
1st	11	0
2nd	39	86
3rd	72	182
4th	125	-
5th	134	-
6th	143	-
7th	195	-
8th	208	-
9th	209	-
10th	216	-

NEW ZEALAND BLACK v PAKISTAN A — One-day

at Cazaly's Stadium, Cairns on 27 July, 2006
Toss : Pakistan A. Umpires : P.R. Reiffel & J.D. Ward
New Zealand Black won by 50 runs.

Most of the New Zealand Black batsmen made starts but no one was able to reach fifty. How, who scored a patient 48, was the top scorer being fourth out at 129.

McSkimming took two early wickets when Pakistan A batted and after Fulton had run out Hafeez at 59 New Zealand Black never relinquished control of the game. Misbah was run out to make the score 77-5 and Pakistan A were finally dismissed for 172 in the 48th over.

NEW ZEALAND BLACK

	Runs	Mins	Balls	6s	4s
J.M.How c Bazid b Amjad	48	127	86	-	3
J.D.Ryder c & b Khalil	14	45	23	-	3
L.R.P.L.Taylor c Bazid b Khalil	21	28	23	1	2
P.G.Fulton* c Misbah b Rehman	17	23	22	1	1
J.A.H.Marshall c Mohmand b Amjad	38	53	52	-	-
M.G.Orchard b Hafeez	25	48	46	-	-
P.D.McGlashan† c Hafeez b Amjad	6	13	8	-	-
N.L.McCullum b Hafeez	10	18	10	-	-
B.E.Scott c Mohmand b Hafeez	20	17	17	1	1
W.C.McSkimming st Salman b Rehman	12	13	11	1	-
B.J.Diamanti not out	0	3	2	-	-
Extras (b 2, lb 4, w 2, nb 3)	11				
TOTAL (49.4 overs)	**222**	203			

PAKISTAN A

	Runs	Mins	Balls	6s	4s
Mohammad Hafeez run out	39	60	57	-	6
Rafatullah Mohmand c How b McSkimming	1	25	16	-	-
Shahid Yousuf c Orchard b McSkimming	0	2	3	-	-
Hasan Raza c McGlashan b Orchard	13	39	21	-	1
Bazid Khan run out	19	53	49	-	-
Misbah-ul-Haq* run out	8	17	11	-	-
Mansoor Amjad c Orchard b Taylor	23	40	36	-	1
Mohammad Salman† c Fulton b Orchard	33	56	55	-	2
Abdur Rehman run out	2	16	9	-	-
Mohammad Irshad c Ryder b McCullum	6	6	7	-	1
Mohammad Khalil not out	15	19	21	1	-
Extras (lb 2, w 10, nb 1)	13				
TOTAL (47.2 overs)	**172**	176			

Bowling	*O*	*M*	*R*	*W*
PAKISTAN A				
Irshad	7	0	32	0
Khalil	8	2	23	2
Rehman	9.4	0	58	2
Hafeez	10	0	44	3
Amjad	10	0	40	3
Yousuf	5	0	19	0
NEW ZEALAND BLACK				
McSkimming	6	1	15	2
Scott	7	0	37	0
Orchard	6.2	0	18	2
Diamanti	6	0	24	0
McCullum	10	0	24	1
Taylor	10	0	45	1
How	2	0	7	0

Fall of Wickets	***NZB***	***PA***
1st	35	21
2nd	62	21
3rd	92	59
4th	129	66
5th	157	77
6th	174	104
7th	186	118
8th	197	130
9th	214	141
10th	222	172

EMERGING PLAYERS TOURNAMENT

AUSTRALIAN CENTRE OF EXCELLENCE v KARNATAKA STATE CRICKET ASSOCIATION (Twenty20)
At Trevor Barsby Oval, Brisbane 10 July, 2006

Australian Centre of Excellence 139-7 (A.C. Voges 40) **defeated Karnataka State Cricket Association** 116-6 (C. Raghu 32*) by 23 runs

AUSTRALIAN CENTRE OF EXCELLENCE v SOUTH AFRICA EMERGING PLAYERS (Twenty20)
At Albury Oval, Brisbane 10 July, 2006

South Africa Emerging Players 168-7 (J.A. Morkel 49*, M.N. van Wyk 34) **lost to Australian Centre of Excellence** 172-4 (T.D. Paine 69*, A.C. Voges 41*, S.E. Marsh 38) by 6 wickets

NEW ZEALAND BLACK v KARNATAKA STATE CRICKET ASSN (Twenty20)
At Trevor Barsby Oval, Brisbane 10 July, 2006

New Zealand Black 186-7 (J.D. Ryder 61, J.A.H. Marshall 39*, M.R. Gillespie 30) **defeated Karnataka State Cricket Association** 83 (N.L. McCullum 3-13, W.C. McSkimming 3-19) by 103 runs

NEW ZEALAND BLACK v SOUTH AFRICA EMERGING PLAYERS (Twenty20)
At Albury Oval, Brisbane 10 July, 2006

South Africa Emerging Players 214-2 (A.N. Petersen 137*, N.D.. McKenzie 43*) **defeated New Zealand Black** 193-5 (J.D. Ryder 67, P.D. McGlashan 45*) by 21 runs

AUSTRALIAN CENTRE OF EXCELLENCE v NEW ZEALAND BLACK (Twenty20)
At Albury Oval, Brisbane 11 July, 2006

Australian Centre of Excellence 122-5 (S.E. Marsh 51, C.J. Ferguson 39*) **lost to New Zealand Black** 124-1 (S.L. Stewart 47*, J.D. Ryder 40) by 9 wickets

KARNATAKA STATE CRICKET ASSOCIATION v SOUTH AFRICA EMERGING PLAYERS (Twenty20)
At Trevor Barsby Oval, Brisbane 11 July, 2006

South Africa Emerging Players 183-5 (L.L. Bosman 55, A.N. Petersen 45) **defeated Karnataka State Cricket Association** 152-5 (G. Dhiman 54) by 31 runs

AUSTRALIAN CENTRE OF EXCELLENCE v KARNATAKA STATE CRICKET ASSOCIATION
At Allan Border Field, Brisbane 12 July, 2006

Australian Centre of Excellence 304-7 (D.A. Warner 89, S.E. Marsh 63, A.J. Crosthwaite 50*, A.J. Finch 36) **defeated Karnataka State Cricket Association** 215 (D.T. Patil 63, C. Raghu 33, Amit Verma 33, D.A. Chougule 32, K. Waingankar 3-42) by 89 runs

NEW ZEALAND BLACK v SOUTH AFRICA EMERGING PLAYERS
At Peter Burge Oval, Brisbane 12 July, 2006

South Africa Emerging Players 200-8 (R.J. Peterson 46*, J.A. Morkel 33, M.R. Gillespie 3-51) **lost to New Zealand Black** 201-7 (J.A.H. Marshall 104*, W.C. McSkimming 36, J.J. van der Wath 3-46) by 3 wickets

AUSTRALIAN CENTRE OF EXCELLENCE v SOUTH AFRICA EMERGING PLAYERS

At Allan Border Field, Brisbane 14 July, 2006

South Africa Emerging Players 213 (J.P. Duminy 56, L.L. Bosman 54, A.A. Noffke 3-23) **lost to Australian Centre of Excellence** 217-9 (S.E. Marsh 118*, A.C. Thomas 3-40, M. Zondeki 3-42, J.J. van der Wath 3-51) by 1 wicket

NEW ZEALAND BLACK v KARNATAKA STATE CRICKET ASSOCIATION

At Peter Burge Oval, Brisbane 14 July, 2006

Karnataka State Cricket Association 164-8 (B. Chipli 89*, M.R. Gillespie 5-24) **defeated New Zealand Black** 120 (J.A.H. Marshall 30, C. Raghu 3-8) by 44 runs

AUSTRALIAN CENTRE OF EXCELLENCE v NEW ZEALAND BLACK

At Peter Burge Oval, Brisbane 15 July, 2006

New Zealand Black 205-8 (P.D. McGlashan 52, P.G. Fulton 48) **lost to Australian Centre of Excellence** 175-5 (B. Casson 77, G.J. Bailey 40, B.E. Scott 4-35) by 5 wickets *(D/L)*

KARNATAKA STATE CRICKET ASSN v SOUTH AFRICA EMERGING PLAYERS

At Allan Border Field, Brisbane 15 July, 2006

Karnataka State Cricket Association 189 (B. Chipli 87, D.A. Chougule 40, G.J.P. Kruger 4-24, R.J. Peterson 4-33) **lost to South Africa Emerging Players** 183-2 (A.N. Petersen 110*, N.D. McKenzie 49*) by 8 wickets

AUSTRALIAN CENTRE OF EXCELLENCE v KARNATAKA STATE CRICKET ASSN

At Albury Oval, Sandgate 17 July, 2006

Karnataka State Cricket Association 256-9 (R. Vijay Bharadwaj 82, D.T. Patil 59, P.M. Siddle 3-53, K. Waingankar 3-58) **lost to Australian Centre of Excellence** 258-4 (G.J. Bailey 106, C.J. Ferguson 71*, A.J. Finch 37) by 6 wickets

NEW ZEALAND BLACK v SOUTH AFRICA EMERGING PLAYERS

At Trevor Barsby Oval, Brisbane 17 July, 2006

South Africa Emerging Players 185-8 (N.D. McKenzie 63, J.P. Duminy 43, T.L. Tsolekile 38) **defeated New Zealand Black** 118 (N.L. McCullum 49, G.J.P. Kruger 3-13) by 67 runs

AUSTRALIAN CENTRE OF EXCELLENCE v SOUTH AFRICA EMERGING PLAYERS

At Trevor Barsby Oval, Brisbane 18 July, 2006

Australian Centre of Excellence 241 (G.J. Bailey 88, C.J. Ferguson 56, M. Zondeki 3-34) **tied with South Africa Emerging Players** 241-8 (M.N. van Wyk 57, D.J. Jacobs 47, J.P. Duminy 44, P.M. Siddle 3-55)

NEW ZEALAND BLACK v KARNATAKA STATE CRICKET ASSOCIATION

At Albury Oval, Brisbane 18 July, 2006

Karnataka State Cricket Association 225-9 (D.A. Chougule 55, R.R. Bhatkal 40) **lost to New Zealand Black** 227-1 (J.D. Ryder 144, J.M. How 68*) by 9 wickets

KARNATAKA STATE CRICKET ASSN v SOUTH AFRICA EMERGING PLAYERS

At Peter Burge Oval, Brisbane 20 July, 2006

Karnataka State Cricket Association 164 (D.A. Chougule 86*, G.J.P. Kruger 3-30) **defeated South Africa Emerging Players** 103 (A.N. Petersen 37, R. Vinay Kumar 4-20, C.S. Ragvendra 3-21) by 61 runs

AUSTRALIAN CENTRE OF EXCELLENCE v NEW ZEALAND BLACK
At Allan Border Field, Brisbane 20 July, 2006

New Zealand Black 264 (L.R.P.L. Taylor 66, P.D. McGlashan 47, J.M. How 38, J.D. Ryder 33) **lost to Australian Centre of Excellence** 268-3 (A.C. Voges 124*, G.J. Bailey 105*) by 7 wickets

Points: Australian Centre of Excellence 24, South Africa Emerging Players 12, New Zealand Black 10, Karnataka State Cricket Association 8.

AUSTRALIAN CENTRE OF EXCELLENCE v SOUTH AFRICA EMERGING PLAYERS
At Allan Border Field, Brisbane 21 July, 2006 (final)

Australian Centre of Excellence 266 (A.J. Finch 88, C.J. Ferguson 54, A.J. Crosthwaite 44, J.J. van der Wath 4-36) **lost to South Africa Emerging Players** 268-9 (R.J. Peterson 148*, D.E. Bollinger 3-37) by 1 wicket

NEW ZEALAND BLACK v KARNATAKA STATE CRICKET ASSOCIATION
At Peter Burge Oval, Brisbane 21 July, 2006 (third place playoff)

New Zealand Black 150 (M.R. Gillespie 29, R. Vinay Kumar 3-18, C.S. Ragavendra 3-23) **lost to Karnataka State Cricket Association** 151-3 (G. Dhiman 66, S.N. Amit 31) by 7 wickets

CHAMPIONS TROPHY

The 2006 Champions Trophy was held in India and was won by Australia who defeated West Indies in the final. New Zealand reached the semi-final of the competition but were well beaten byAustralia.

The squad had left New Zealand with Bond and Styris under injury clouds and both players missed games due to these injuries. The team had good victories against South Africa and Pakistan but lost to Sri Lanka to finish in second place in the group on run rate.

The batting, in particular the top order, let New Zealand down. Only four fifties were registered, two by Fleming and one each by Styris and Vettori. Vincent, Marshall and Fulton scored just 55 runs between them and consequently big totals were hard to come by.

Mills was the star bowler taking ten wickets in four games, including 4-38 against Australia. Oram, Bond and Patel took five wickets each. Patel had success in the first two games but when the team played away from Mumbai the extra seamer was preferred.

The squad was: S.P. Fleming *(captain, Wellington)*, N.J. Astle *(Canterbury)*, S.E. Bond *(Canterbury)*, J.E.C. Franklin *(Wellington)*, P.G. Fulton *(Canterbury)*, M.R. Gillespie *(Wellington)*, B.B. McCullum *(Canterbury)*, H.J.H. Marshall *(Northern Districts)*, K.D. Mills *(Auckland)*, J.D.P. Oram *(Central Districts)*, J.S. Patel *(Wellington)*, S.B. Styris *(Auckland)*, D.L. Vettori *(Northern Districts)*, L. Vincent *(Auckland)*. Coach, J.G. Bracewell; Assistant coach/Video analyst, R.M. Carter; Manager, L.M. Crocker; Physiotherapist, D.F. Shackel; Sports psychologist, G.L. Hermansson.

L.R.P.L. Taylor *(Central Districts)* joined the team as cover for Styris but under the rules of the tournament could only be an official member of the squad if he replaced another player. As New Zealand wanted Styris to be available for the final, if required, Taylor was never available for selection.

New Zealand Averages

BATTING	*M*	*I*	*NO*	*HS*	*Agg*	*Ave*	*100s*	*50s*	*Ct*	*St*	*SR*
D.L. Vettori	4	4	2	79	134	67.00	-	1	4	-	80
S.P. Fleming	4	4	0	89	184	46.00	-	2	3	-	71
S.B. Styris	2	2	0	86	89	44.50	-	1	-	-	71
J.D.P. Oram	4	4	0	43	87	21.75	-	-	1	-	69
N.J. Astle	4	4	0	42	71	17.75	-	-	1	-	58
K.D. Mills	4	3	1	21	31	15.50	-	-	2	-	81
B.B. McCullum	4	4	0	27	58	14.50	-	-	4	1	71
J.E.C. Franklin	3	3	1	9*	26	13.00	-	-	1	-	92
S.E. Bond	3	2	1	9*	10	10.00	-	-	1	-	66
L. Vincent	4	4	0	17	34	8.50	-	-	2	-	36
J.S. Patel	2	2	0	10	12	6.00	-	-	1	-	26
P.G. Fulton	3	3	0	7	11	3.66	-	-	1	-	28
H.J.H. Marshall	3	3	0	5	10	3.33	-	-	1	-	40

BOWLING	*O*	*M*	*R*	*W*	*Ave*	*Best*	*R/O*
J.S. Patel	12.1	0	43	5	8.60	3-11	3.53
K.D. Mills	28.3	2	118	10	11.80	4-38	4.14
J.D.P. Oram	30	3	108	5	21.60	3-26	3.60
S.E. Bond	27	0	146	5	29.20	3-45	5.41
D.L. Vettori	37	1	153	3	51.00	1-15	4.14
J.E.C. Franklin	27	1	128	2	64.00	1-47	4.74
N.J. Astle	5	0	24	0	-	-	4.80

NEW ZEALAND v SOUTH AFRICA — Champions Trophy

at Brabourne Stadium, Mumbai on 16 October, 2006 (d/n)
Toss : South Africa. Umpires : Aleem Dar & M.R. Benson
New Zealand won by 87 runs. *Points: New Zealand 2, South Africa 0*

New Zealand omitted Bond, Gillespie and Styris for their opening match of the tournament. After New Zealand had been sent in to bat Fleming played a lone hand and was the only batsman to pass 21. He reached fifty from 64 deliveries. Vincent had earlier become Pollock's 350th wicket in one-day internationals.

With the wicket taking turn and keeping low South Africa were always in trouble after losing their first two wickets very quickly. Smith and Kemp passed twenty but there was precious little else. Kemp reached 1000 runs and Patel had career best bowling figures as the Black Caps had a comfortable 87 run win. South Africa were bowled out with 15.5 overs still remaining.

NEW ZEALAND

	Runs	Mins	Balls	6s	4s
L.Vincent b Pollock	17	29	29	-	3
S.P.Fleming* c Pollock b Kallis	89	193	112	-	11
N.J.Astle b Hall	14	48	26	-	2
H.J.H.Marshall b Nel	1	7	6	-	-
P.G.Fulton c Boucher b Kallis	2	16	11	-	-
J.D.P.Oram c Dippenaar b Peterson	7	19	18	-	1
B.B.McCullum† c & b Peterson	21	29	34	-	2
D.L.Vettori c Boucher b Smith	9	10	10	-	-
J.E.C.Franklin b Kallis	9	18	12	-	1
K.D.Mills not out	4	16	10	-	-
J.S.Patel run out	2	6	7	-	-
Extras (b 4, lb 4, w 11, nb 1)	20				
TOTAL (45.4 overs)	**195**	200			

SOUTH AFRICA

	Runs	Mins	Balls	6s	4s
G.C.Smith* c Vettori b Oram	42	89	57	-	5
H.H.Dippenaar lbw b Mills	0	2	3	-	-
H.H.Gibbs b Mills	0	6	2	-	-
J.H.Kallis c & b Mills	8	24	18	-	1
M.V.Boucher† c McCullum b Oram	8	28	28	-	-
J.M.Kemp not out	26	80	55	-	-
S.M.Pollock c Patel b Oram	1	8	3	-	-
A.J.Hall c Vincent b Patel	13	28	31	-	1
R.J.Peterson c Fleming b Vettori	0	6	4	-	-
A.Nel b Patel	0	5	5	-	-
M.Ntini b Patel	1				
Extras (lb 5, w 1, nb 3)	9				
TOTAL (34.1 overs)	**108**	144			

Bowling	*O*	*M*	*R*	*W*
SOUTH AFRICA				
Pollock	6	1	18	1
Ntini	6	0	35	0
Nel	6	2	15	1
Hall	4	0	25	1
Kallis	7	0	28	3
Peterson	8.4	0	34	2
Smith	8	0	32	1
NEW ZEALAND				
Mills	6	0	18	3
Franklin	10	0	33	0
Oram	8	1	26	3
Vettori	7	1	15	1
Patel	3.1	0	11	3

Fall of Wickets	***NZ***	***SA***
1st	27	1
2nd	74	3
3rd	76	25
4th	86	50
5th	99	69
6th	135	71
7th	156	99
8th	180	100
9th	192	105
10th	195	108

MCA PRESIDENT'S XI v NEW ZEALAND

At Middle Income Group Ground, Mumbai 12 October, 2006

New Zealand 246-8 (L. Vincent 59, S.P. Fleming 52, H.J.H. Marshall 43) **defeated MCA President's XI** 207 (R. Sharma 61, A. Nayyar 43, M.R. Gillespie 3-37, J.S. Patel 3-39) by 39 runs

BARODA v NEW ZEALAND

At Middle Income Group Ground, Mumbai 13 October, 2006

New Zealand 267-8 (S.B. Styris 52 retd, S.E. Bond 43*, H.J.H. Marshall 40, N.J. Astle 36, M.Y. Vahora 3-60) **defeated Baroda** 208-9 (J.J. Martin 45, P.A. Parab 41, M.R. Gillespie 3-19) by 59 runs

NEW ZEALAND v SRI LANKA — Champions Trophy

at Brabourne Stadium, Mumbai on 20 October, 2006 (d/n)
Toss : New Zealand. Umpires : Aleem Dar & R.E. Koertzen
***Sri Lanka won by 7 wickets.** Points: Sri Lanka 2, New Zealand 0*

Styris and Bond replaced Fulton and Franklin in the New Zealand line-up. After problems with the pitch in earlier games, the playing area was sprayed with glue in the hope that it would hold together and last for the entire match.

Only Astle and Vettori were able to to pass 13 for New Zealand in a disappointing batting effort. Muralitharan caused most trouble, taking 4-23 from his ten overs. Sri Lanka had no such problems and started quickly with an opening stand of 45 from 37 balls. Tharanga, who had scored two centuries in the qualifying section, reached fifty off 69 balls. Patel took two late wickets but Sri Lanka won with 14 overs to spare.

NEW ZEALAND

	Runs	Mins	Balls	6s	4s
L.Vincent b Maharoof	13	56	41	-	1
S.P.Fleming* lbw b Vaas	0	23	1	-	-
N.J.Astle c Malinga b Muralitharan	42	107	74	-	6
H.J.H.Marshall c Dilshan b Malinga	4	22	6	-	1
S.B.Styris c Sangakkara b Jayasuriya	3	17	12	-	-
J.D.P.Oram b Muralitharan	6	18	22	-	-
B.B.McCullum† c Jayawardene b Muralitharan	9	30	30	-	-
D.L.Vettori not out	46	81	53	-	5
K.D.Mills lbw b Muralitharan	6	14	11	-	1
S.E.Bond c Sangakkara b Jayasuriya	1	4	4	-	-
J.S.Patel c Jayawardene b Malinga	10	45	39	-	-
Extras (lb 8, w 10, nb 7)	25				
TOTAL (49.2 overs)	**165**	212			

SRI LANKA

	Runs	Mins	Balls	6s	4s
W.U.Tharanga st McCullum b Patel	56	119	77	-	9
S.T.Jayasuriya c McCullum b Mills	20	30	15	1	2
D.P.M.D.Jayawardene* c Vettori b Patel	48	73	85	-	6
K.C.Sangakkara† not out	19	39	32	-	-
M.S.Atapattu not out	10	36	27	-	-
C.K.Kapugedera					
T.M.Dilshan					
M.F.Maharoof					
W.P.U.J.C.Vaas					
M.Muralitharan					
S.L.Malinga					
Extras (lb 1, w 4, nb 8)	13				
TOTAL (36 overs) (3 wkts)	**166**	156			

Bowling	*O*	*M*	*R*	*W*
SRI LANKA				
Vaas	10	1	41	1
Malinga	9.2	1	22	2
Maharoof	8	0	34	1
Jayasuriya	10	0	26	2
Muralitharan	10	1	23	4
Dilshan	2	0	11	0
NEW ZEALAND				
Mills	5	0	24	1
Bond	7	0	46	0
Oram	4	0	14	0
Vettori	10	0	45	0
Patel	9	0	32	2
Astle	1	0	4	0

Fall of Wickets	***NZ***	***SL***
1st	14	45
2nd	37	134
3rd	56	135
4th	66	-
5th	82	-
6th	87	-
7th	101	-
8th	115	-
9th	118	-
10th	165	-

NEW ZEALAND v PAKISTAN — Champions Trophy

at Punjab CA Stadium, Chandigarh on 25 October, 2006 (d/n)
Toss : Pakistan. Umpires : M.R. Benson & R.E. Koertzen
***New Zealand won by 51 runs.** Points: New Zealand 2, Pakistan 0*

Fulton and Franklin replaced Marshall (ill) and Patel. Vincent was bowled in the second over and Astle went soon afterwards. Fleming and Styris added 108 for the fourth wicket with Fleming reaching his fifty off 76 balls, three balls quicker than Styris. Some lusty hitting from Oram and McCullum took the total to a healthy 274-7.

In reply, Yousuf and Shoaib were the only Pakistan batsmen able to reach fifty (Yousuf took 66 balls and Shoaib 64). However, Pakistan were always struggling to reach the New Zealand total and were bowled out in the 47th over. Oram had a good spell and Bond took three wickets to give the Black Caps a 51 run win and a place in the semi-final.

NEW ZEALAND

	Runs	Mins	Balls	6s	4s
L.Vincent b Gul	3	5	8	-	-
S.P.Fleming* c & b Malik	80	165	105	1	8
N.J.Astle c Younis Khan b Naved	15	24	17	-	3
P.G.Fulton lbw b Iftikhar	7	33	14	-	1
S.B.Styris c Iftikhar b Gul	86	143	113	-	10
J.D.P.Oram c Gul b Razzaq	31	28	26	1	4
B.B.McCullum† c Malik b Razzaq	27	26	13	1	3
J.E.C.Franklin not out	9	12	5	-	1
D.L.Vettori not out	0	1	0	-	-
K.D.Mills					
S.E.Bond					
Extras (lb 8, w 7, nb 1)	16				
TOTAL (50 overs) (7 wkts)	**274**	225			

PAKISTAN

	Runs	Mins	Balls	6s	4s
Mohammad Hafeez c McCullum b Oram	43	61	46	-	8
Imran Farhat c Mills b Bond	6	18	11	-	1
Younis Khan* c Vincent b Mills	2	22	12	-	-
Mohammad Yousuf c Fleming b Bond	71	124	92	-	9
Shahid Afridi c Bond b Oram	4	18	16	-	-
Shoaib Malik c Astle b Vettori	52	112	70	-	4
Abdul Razzaq c Franklin b Bond	6	19	15	-	-
Kamran Akmal† c Fleming b Mills	16	30	14	-	1
Naved-ul-Hasan c McCullum b Franklin	1	5	5	-	-
Umar Gul run out	8	14	12	-	-
Iftikhar Anjum not out	0	1	0	-	-
Extras (lb 5, w 5, nb 4)	14				
TOTAL (46.3 overs)	**223**	221			

Bowling	*O*	*M*	*R*	*W*
PAKISTAN				
Naved	8	0	44	1
Gul	9	1	47	2
Iftikhar	8	2	41	1
Razzaq	10	1	60	2
Shahid Afridi	10	0	49	0
Malik	5	0	25	1
NEW ZEALAND				
Mills	7.3	1	38	2
Bond	10	0	45	3
Franklin	9	0	47	1
Oram	8	1	25	2
Vettori	10	0	52	1
Astle	2	0	11	0

Fall of Wickets

	NZ	***P***
1st	3	22
2nd	23	45
3rd	60	65
4th	168	83
5th	220	177
6th	254	195
7th	270	202
8th	-	205
9th	-	223
10th	-	223

NEW ZEALAND v AUSTRALIA Champions Trophy Semi-final

at Punjab CA Stadium, Chandigarh on 1 November, 2006 (d/n)
Toss : New Zealand. Umpires : S.A. Bucknor & R.E. Koertzen
Australia won by 34 runs

Marshall replaced the injured Styris in the New Zealand line-up. Mills dismissed both the Australian openers in his second over but then Ponting and Martyn added 66 for the third wicket. Ponting got fifty from 73 balls and Symonds scored fifty off 46 deliveries to lift Australia to 240-9. Mills bowled superbly finishing with 4-38 (his best performance against Australia).

In the first fifteen overs of the New Zealand innings they lost six wickets for a mere 35 runs before Oram and Vettori mounted a recovery with a record seventh wicket stand for New Zealand against Australia. Vettori got fifty from 74 balls but when he was ninth out, New Zealand's hopes of reaching the final were all but extinguished. Australia won by 34 runs with four overs to spare.

AUSTRALIA

	Runs	Mins	Balls	6s	4s
A.C.Gilchrist† c Oram b Mills	3	13	11	-	-
S.R.Watson c Fulton b Mills	0	10	4	-	-
R.T.Ponting* c Vettori b Mills	58	118	80	-	9
D.R.Martyn lbw b Vettori	26	72	54	-	4
M.E.K.Hussey c Marshall b Franklin	35	94	52	-	2
A.Symonds b Bond	58	74	58	1	3
M.J.Clarke c Vettori b Mills	14	28	2	-	1
B.Lee b Bond	5	8	5	-	-
M.G.Johnson run out	3	11	9	-	-
N.W.Bracken not out	15	10	8	1	1
G.D.McGrath not out	0	1	0	-	-
Extras (lb 6, w 14, nb 3)	23				
TOTAL (50 overs) (9 wkts)	**240**	228			

NEW ZEALAND

	Runs	Mins	Balls	6s	4s
L.Vincent c Ponting b McGrath	1	23	15	-	-
S.P.Fleming* c Ponting b Bracken	15	51	28	-	2
N.J.Astle b Lee	0	3	4	-	-
H.J.H.Marshall c Gilchrist b McGrath	5	14	13	-	-
P.G.Fulton b McGrath	2	18	13	-	-
J.D.P.Oram st Gilchrist b Symonds	43	111	59	-	5
B.B.McCullum† c Martyn b Bracken	1	4	4	-	-
D.L.Vettori b Johnson	79	125	103	-	7
J.E.C.Franklin c Gilchrist b Watson	8	15	11	-	1
K.D.Mills c Gilchrist b Lee	21	18	17	1	2
S.E.Bond not out	9	12	11	-	1
Extras (lb 7, w 13, nb 2)	22				
TOTAL (46 overs)	**206**	211			

Bowling	*O*	*M*	*R*	*W*
NEW ZEALAND				
Mills	10	1	38	4
Bond	10	0	55	2
Franklin	8	1	48	1
Oram	10	1	43	0
Vettori	10	0	41	1
Astle	2	0	9	0
AUSTRALIA				
Lee	8	0	31	2
McGrath	10	2	22	3
Bracken	7	1	36	2
Johnson	7	0	38	1
Watson	7	0	27	1
Symonds	7	0	45	1

Fall of Wickets	***AUS***	***NZ***
1st	3	16
2nd	4	20
3rd	70	30
4th	123	30
5th	188	34
6th	211	35
7th	220	138
8th	223	159
9th	236	180
10th	-	206

Qualifying Round

7th October 2006
Chandigarh: **Sri Lanka beat Bangladesh by 37 runs**
Sri Lanka 302 for 8 (50 overs) (W.U.Tharanga 105, M.S.Atapattu 40, D.P.M.D.Jayawardene 35, S.T.Jayasuriya 31);
Bangladesh 265 for 9 (50 overs) (Saqibul Hasan 67*, Farhad Reza 34, Aftab Ahmed 33, Masrafe bin Mortaza 30, M.F.Maharoof 3-47)

8th October 2006
Ahmedabad: **West Indies beat Zimbabwe by 9 wickets**
Zimbabwe 85 (30.1 overs) (C.H.Gayle 3-3);
West Indies 90 for 1 (14.2 overs) (C.H.Gayle 41)

10th October 2006
Ahmedabad: **Sri Lanka beat Zimbabwe by 144 runs**
Sri Lanka 285 for 7 (50 overs) (W.U.Tharanga 110, K.C.Sangakkara 80, M.S.Atapattu 33*);
Zimbabwe 141 (42.3 overs) (H.Masakadza 30, B.R.M.Taylor 30, S.L.Malinga 3-25)

11th October 2006
Jaipur: **West Indies beat Bangladesh by 10 wickets**
Bangladesh 161 (46.3 overs) (Aftab Ahmed 59, Shahriar Nafees 38, D.J.Bravo 3-14);
West Indies 164 for 0 (36.4 overs) (C.H.Gayle 104*, S.Chanderpaul 52*)

13th October 2006
Jaipur: **Bangladesh beat Zimbabwe by 101 runs**
Bangladesh 231 for 6 (50 overs) (Shahriar Nafees 123*, Saqibul Hasan 36, Habibul Bashar 30);
Zimbabwe 130 (44.4 overs) (B.R.M.Taylor 52, Saqibul Hasan 3-18)

14th October 2006
Mumbai: **Sri Lanka beat West Indies by 9 wickets**
West Indies 80 (30.4 overs) (M.F.Maharoof 6-14);
Sri Lanka 83 for 1 (13.2 overs) (S.T.Jayasuriya 45*, D.P.M.D.Jayawardene 34*)

Points: Sri Lanka 6, West Indies 4, Bangladesh 2, Zimbabwe 0.

15th October 2006
Jaipur: **India beat England by 4 wickets**
England 125 (37 overs) (P.D.Collingwood 38, M.M.Patel 3-18, R.R.Powar 3-24);
India 126 for 6 (29.3 overs) (S.R.Tendulkar 35)

17 October 2006
Jaipur: **Pakistan beat Sri Lanka by 4 wickets**
Sri Lanka 253 (49.2 overs) (S.T.Jayasuriya 48, K.C.Sangakkara 39, W.U.Tharanga 38, M.S.Atapattu 36, D.P.M.D.Jayawardene 31, Abdul Razzaq 4-50);
Pakistan 255 for 6 (48.1 overs) (Imran Farhat 53, Yousuf Youhana 49, Shoaib Malik 46*, Abdul Razzaq 38*)

18th October 2006
Mumbai: **West Indies beat Australia by 10 runs**
West Indies 234 for 6 (50 overs) (R.S.Morton 90*, B.C.Lara 71);
Australia 224 for 9 (50 overs) (A.C.Gilchrist 92, M.J.Clarke 47, J.E.Taylor 4-49)

21st October 2006
Jaipur: **Australia beat England by 6 wickets**
England 169 (45 overs) (A.J.Strauss 56, I.R.Bell 43, S.R.Watson 3-16, M.G.Johnson 3-40);
Australia 170 for 4 (36.5 overs) (D.R.Martyn 78, M.E.K.Hussey 32*)

24th October 2006
Ahmedabad: **South Africa beat Sri Lanka by 78 runs**
South Africa 219 for 9 (50 overs) (A.B.de Villiers 54, J.H.Kallis 43, S.L.Malinga 4-53);
Sri Lanka 141 (39.1 overs) (D.P.M.D.Jayawardene 36, T.M.Dilshan 36, A.Nel 3-41)

26th October 2006
Ahmedabad: **West Indies beat India by 3 wickets**
India 223 for 9 (50 overs) (M.S.Dhoni 51, R.S.Dravid 49, I.D.R.Bradshaw 3-30);
West Indies 224 for 7 (49.4 overs) (R.R.Sarwan 53, S.Chanderpaul 51, R.S.Morton 45, C.H.Gayle 34)

27th October 2006
Chandigarh: **South Africa beat Pakistan by 124 runs**
South Africa 213 for 8 (50 overs) (M.V.Boucher 69, J.M.Kemp 64, Umar Gul 3-36);
Pakistan 89 (25 overs) (M.Ntini 5-21, C.K.Langeveldt 3-20)

28th October 2006
Ahmedabad: **England beat West Indies by 3 wickets**
West Indies 272 for 4 (50 overs) (D.J.Bravo 112*, C.H.Gayle 101);
England 276 for 7 (48.3 overs) (K.P.Pietersen 90*, A.J.Strauss 50, I.R.Bell 50, C.H.Gayle 3-31)

29th October 2006
Chandigarh: **Australia beat India by 6 wickets**
India 249 for 8 (50 overs) (V.Sehwag 65, R.S.Dravid 52, M.Kaif 30);
Australia 252 for 4 (45.4 overs) (D.R.Martyn 73*, R.T.Ponting 58, S.R.Watson 50)

Points
Group A – Australia 4, West Indies 4, India 2, England 2.
Group B – South Africa 4, New Zealand 4, Sri Lanka 2, Pakistan 2.

2nd November 2006 (semi-final)
Jaipur: **West Indies beat South Africa by 6 wickets**
South Africa 258 for 8 (50 overs) (H.H.Gibbs 77, A.B.de Villiers 46, L.L.Bosman 39);
West Indies 262 for 4 (44 overs) (C.H.Gayle 133*, S.Chanderpaul 57*)

5th November 2006 (final)
Mumbai: **Australia beat West Indies by 8 wickets (D/L)**
West Indies 138 (30.4 overs) (C.H.Gayle 37, N.W.Bracken 3-22);
Australia 116 for 2 (28.1 overs) (S.R.Watson 57*, D.R.Martyn 47*)

SRI LANKA IN NEW ZEALAND

Sri Lanka visited New Zealand for the third season in a row. Each of the series were drawn, with the tests and twenty20 matches being shared 1-1 and the one-day series 2-2, with the last game abandoned.

Sri Lanka were well served by Sangakkara, who got two centuries in the tests and two fifties in the one-day games. Silva made his test debut at Christchurch and got a pair but made a fifty and a century at Wellington. Jayasuriya was devastating in the one-day internationals. The captain, Jayawardene, scored runs against Otago but from then on could find no form at all.

Muralitharan was the most impressive bowler throughout the tour. With his unique action Malinga also caused problems and he bowled considerably faster than when he came the previous year. Vaas also had some good figures in the limited overs games.

The touring party was: D.P.M.D. Jayawardene *(captain)*, M.S. Atapattu, C.M. Bandara, T.M. Dilshan, C.R.D. Fernando, W.C.A. Ganegama, S.T. Jayasuriya, H.A.P.W. Jayawardene, C.K. Kapugedera, M.F. Maharoof, S.L. Malinga, M. Muralitharan, P.D.R.L. Perera, K.C. Sangakkara, L.P.C. Silva, W.U. Tharanga, W.P.U.J.C. Vaas. Coach, T.M. Moody; Manager, M.H. Tissera.

Ganegama and Prasanna Jayawardene were replaced for the limited-overs games bv Atapattu, Bandara and Perera. Jaywardene's return to Sri Lanka was delayed after he was admitted to hospital in Wellington with appendicitis.

New Zealand Test Averages

BATTING	***M***	***I***	***NO***	***HS***	***Agg***	***Ave***	***100s***	***50s***	***Ct***	***St***
D.L. Vettori	2	3	0	63	114	38.00	-	2	1	-
C.D. Cumming	2	4	0	43	119	29.75	-	-	-	-
B.B. McCullum	2	4	1	43	74	24.66	-	-	8	1
M.S. Sinclair	2	4	0	37	83	20.75	-	-	4	-
S.P. Fleming	2	4	0	48	75	18.75	-	-	7	-
J.M. How	2	4	0	33	70	17.50	-	-	2	-
J.E.C. Franklin	2	3	0	44	45	15.00	-	-	2	-
N.J. Astle	2	4	0	24	52	13.00	-	-	1	-
J.D.P. Oram	2	4	1	12*	18	6.00	-	-	1	-
S.E. Bond	2	3	0	8	15	5.00	-	-	1	-
C.S. Martin	2	3	3	4*	4	-	-	-	-	-

BOWLING	***O***	***M***	***R***	***W***	***Ave***	***Best***	***5w***	***10w***
J.D.P. Oram	20	6	59	4	14.75	2-30	-	-
D.L. Vettori	58.3	7	193	10	19.30	7-130	1	1
S.E. Bond	67.1	11	258	10	25.80	4-63	-	-
J.E.C. Franklin	62	11	173	6	28.83	3-30	-	-
C.S. Martin	63.4	7	223	7	31.85	3-50	-	-
N.J. Astle	9	2	24	0	-	-	-	-

Sri Lanka Test Averages

BATTING	*M*	*I*	*NO*	*HS*	*Agg*	*Ave*	*100s*	*50s*	*Ct*	*St*
K.C. Sangakkara	2	4	2	156*	268	134.00	2	-	4	-
L.P.C. Silva	2	4	1	152*	213	71.00	1	1	2	-
W.U. Tharanga	2	4	0	33	84	21.00	-	-	-	-
H.A.P.W. Jayawardene	2	4	0	37	80	20.00	-	-	3	-
C.K. Kapugedera	2	4	0	37	70	17.50	-	-	1	-
W.P.J.U.C. Vaas	2	4	0	47	51	12.75	-	-	-	-
S.T. Jayasuriya	2	4	0	31	46	11.50	-	-	-	-
D.P.M.D. Jayawardene	2	4	0	31	39	9.75	-	-	2	-
M.F. Maharoof	2	4	0	15	27	6.75	-	-	-	-
M. Muralitharan	2	4	0	14	22	5.50	-	-	-	-
S.L. Malinga	2	4	1	7*	7	2.33	-	-	-	-

BOWLING	*O*	*M*	*R*	*W*	*Ave*	*Best*	*5w*	*10w*
M. Muralitharan	94.2	24	217	17	12.76	6-87	1	1
S.L. Malinga	57.4	8	208	9	23.11	5-68	1	-
W.P.J.U.C. Vaas	52	9	154	6	25.66	3-49	-	-
M.F. Maharoof	33	6	116	3	38.66	1-10	-	-
S.T. Jayasuriya	6	3	10	0	-	-	-	-

New Zealand One-day International Averages

BATTING	*M*	*I*	*NO*	*HS*	*Agg*	*Ave*	*100s*	*50s*	*Ct*	*St*	*SR*
J.E.C. Franklin	4	3	2	45*	62	62.00	-	-	1	-	75
L.R.P.L. Taylor	5	4	1	128*	143	47.66	1	-	6	-	84
N.J. Astle	3	2	0	83	83	41.50	-	1	-	-	93
C.D. McMillan	3	2	1	29*	31	31.00	-	-	-	-	44
P.G. Fulton	5	4	1	43*	78	26.00	-	-	-	-	72
B.B. McCullum	5	4	0	32	81	20.25	-	-	5	-	117
J.A.H. Marshall	3	3	0	50	55	18.33	-	1	-	-	56
H.J.H. Marshall	4	4	0	29	53	13.25	-	-	1	-	80
D.L. Vettori	4	3	0	19	35	11.66	-	-	1	-	59
J.S. Patel	1	1	0	6	6	6.00	-	-	-	-	41
M.R. Gillespie	5	3	1	11	12	6.00	-	-	-	-	42
M.J. Mason	5	2	1	4*	5	5.00	-	-	3	-	26
A.R. Adams	3	3	0	6	10	3.33	-	-	1	-	37
S.E. Bond	3	1	0	2	2	2.00	-	-	-	-	18
S.P. Fleming	2	1	0	0	0	0.00	-	-	1	-	0

BOWLING	*O*	*M*	*R*	*W*	*Ave*	*Best*	*R/O*
D.L. Vettori	23.2	2	80	4	20.00	2-7	3.42
S.E. Bond	18	3	84	3	28.00	2-47	4.67
M.R. Gillespie	35	4	161	5	32.20	3-39	4.60
M.J. Mason	35	3	196	6	32.66	4-24	5.60
J.E.C. Franklin	27	1	147	4	36.75	2-69	5.44
A.R. Adams	26	2	149	1	149.00	1-53	5.73
C.D. McMillan	2	0	9	0	-	-	4.50
J.S. Patel	9	0	41	0	-	-	4.56

Sri Lanka One-day International Averages

BATTING	*M*	*I*	*NO*	*HS*	*Agg*	*Ave*	*100s*	*50s*	*Ct*	*St*	*SR*
K.C. Sangakkara	5	4	0	89	219	54.75	-	2	5	-	77
S.T. Jayasuriya	5	4	0	111	182	45.50	1	1	-	-	133
M.F. Maharoof	4	3	1	29*	63	31.50	-	-	1	-	76
M.S. Atapattu	5	4	1	34	94	31.33	-	-	-	-	61
W.U. Tharanga	5	4	0	68	124	31.00	-	1	-	-	66
L.P.C. Silva	3	2	0	31	35	17.50	-	-	1	-	58
D.P.M.D. Jayawardene	5	4	1	34*	39	13.00	-	-	2	-	60
T.M. Dilshan	3	2	0	18	26	13.00	-	-	3	-	46
M. Muralitharan	5	1	0	8	8	8.00	-	-	-	-	200
P.D.R.L. Perera	1	1	0	0	0	0.00	-	-	-	-	0
W.P.U.J.C. Vaas	4	2	2	9*	14	-	-	-	-	-	155
C.K. Kapugedera	2	1	1	10*	10	-	-	-	-	-	58
C.R.D. Fernando	4	1	1	8*	8	-	-	-	-	-	42
S.L. Malinga	4	-	-	-	-	-	-	-	1	-	-

BOWLING	*O*	*M*	*R*	*W*	*Ave*	*Best*	*R/O*
M. Muralitharan	31.3	3	104	7	14.85	3-31	3.30
W.P.U.J.C. Vaas	28	3	106	7	15.14	3-10	3.79
P.D.R.L. Perera	5	0	37	2	18.50	2-37	7.40
S.L. Malinga	28	3	133	6	22.16	3-14	4.75
C.R.D. Fernando	15.3	1	90	4	22.50	2-34	5.80
M.F. Maharoof	16	1	80	3	26.66	1-13	5.00
T.M. Dilshan	12	0	57	1	57.00	1-25	4.75
S.T. Jayasuriya	15	0	70	0	-	-	4.67

OTAGO v SRI LANKA — Not first-class

at University Oval, Dunedin on 30 November, 1, 2, 3 December, 2006
Toss : Sri Lanka. Umpires : G.A. Baxter & E.A. Watkin
Close of play: 1st day: Sri Lanka 141-3, Sangakkara 51, Dilshan 14; 2nd day: Otago 140-2, Redmond 20, Todd 5
3rd day: Sri Lanka 240-2, Sangakkara 19, Jaywawardene 16
Match drawn

The four-day game was not classified as a first-class game as both sides used twelve players. After Sri Lanka lost both openers cheaply, the next seven batsmen all got good starts with the lowest score being 34 and the highest 70 as four players reached fifties. The Otago bowlers toiled away with Scott and Redmond being the most successful taking four and three wickets respectively.

Otago had a 109 run stand for the first wicket with Sheed and Cumming getting fifties and then Redmond also reached this mark, but the home team collapsed from 197-2 to be all out for 276. Malinga, with 3-76, was the most successful bowler for the tourists.

With a lead of 137 Sri Lanka opted for more batting practice. Openers Tharanga and Jayasuriya put on 190 for the first wicket with Tharanga getting a century. All batsmen had useful time at the crease and when the declaration came they were 541 ahead. In 85 minutes batting Otago got 46-2 before the game was called off.

SRI LANKA

FIRST INNINGS	*Runs*	*Mins*	*Balls*	*6s*	*4s*	*SECOND INNINGS*	*Runs*	*Mins*	*Balls*	*6s*	*4s*
W.U.Tharanga b Scott	19	41	28	-	3	c & b Scott	108	201	164	-	13
S.T.Jayasuriya b Shaw	0	5	1	-	-	run out	85	163	108	1	6
K.C.Sangakkara c Haig b Scott	65	192	122	-	9	c Broom b Smith	20	64	56	-	7
D.P.M.D.Jayawardene* c Cumming b Smith	48	84	71	-	9	b McCullum	67	105	78	2	9
T.M.Dilshan c Hopkins b Scott	36	62	47	-	6	not out	67	117	98	1	9
C.K.Kapugedera c Hopkins b Harvie	68	179	127	1	9						
L.P.C.Silva c Scott b Redmond	70	116	117	1	7	(6) not out	37	38	24	4	2
H.A.P.W.Jaywardene† b Redmond	34	115	80	2	1						
M.F.Maharoof c & b Redmond	53	71	56	-	10						
S.L.Malinga lbw b Scott	1	7	8	-	-						
W.C.A.Ganegama not out	0	2	0	-	-						
C.R.D.Fernando											
Extras (lb 6, w 3, nb 10)	19					(b 9, lb 4, w 1, nb 6)	20				
TOTAL(108.3 overs)	**413**	441				(87 overs) (4 wkts dec)	**404**	346			

OTAGO

FIRST INNINGS	*Runs*	*Mins*	*Balls*	*6s*	*4s*	*SECOND INNINGS*	*Runs*	*Mins*	*Balls*	*6s*	*4s*
J.W.Sheed c Sangakkara b Jayasuriya	57	109	82	-	10	c Jaywardene b Maharoof	1	8	8	-	-
C.D.Cumming* c Malinga b Fernando	50	95	59	-	9	not out	8	85	51	-	-
A.J.Redmond lbw b Fernando	53	109	90	-	8						
G.R.Todd c Jaywardene b Maharoof	30	147	81	-	4	not out	10	21	19	-	2
N.T.Broom c Ganegama b Maharoof	27	42	29	-	6						
G.J.Hopkins† lbw b Malinga	4	37	19	-	-						
N.L.McCullum c Dilshan b Ganegama	14	34	24	-	2						
S.B.Haig not out	7	36	20	-	-	(3) lbw b Ganegama	18	54	34	-	4
B.E.Scott b Malinga	4	4	3	-	1						
C.M.Smith b Malinga	0	21	18	-	-						
G.S.Shaw b Ganegama	0	4	1	-	-						
M.J.Harvie											
Extras (lb 8, w 2, nb 20)	30					(b 1, nb 8)	9				
TOTAL (67.5 overs)	**276**	323				(17.2 overs) (2 wkts)	**46**	85			

Bowling	*O*	*M*	*R*	*W*	*O*	*M*	*R*	*W*
OTAGO								
Harvie	24	5	101	1	13	1	42	0
Shaw	19	3	89	1	10	0	60	0
Scott	26	10	56	4	21	1	73	1
Smith	16	1	70	1	10	0	43	1
McCullum	14	3	49	0	23	0	105	1
Redmond	8.3	0	41	3	9	1	61	0
Cumming	1	0	1	0				
Broom					1	0	7	0
SRI LANKA								
Malinga	17	1	67	3	4	1	6	0
Maharoof	17	2	61	2	6	3	7	1
Ganegama	16.5	4	50	2	2.2	0	3	1
Fernando	13	0	84	2	5	0	29	0
Jayasuriya	4	1	6	1				

Fall of Wickets

	SL *1st*	***O*** *1st*	***SL*** *2nd*	***O*** *2nd*
1st	4	107	190	1
2nd	32	118	219	33
3rd	116	197	241	-
4th	176	235	327	-
5th	183	238	-	-
6th	288	256	-	-
7th	323	258	-	-
8th	407	266	-	-
9th	412	275	-	-
10th	413	276	-	-

NEW ZEALAND v SRI LANKA — First Test

at Jade Stadium, Christchurch on 7, 8, 9 December, 2006
Toss : Sri Lanka. Umpires : S.J.A. Taufel & B.G. Jerling
Close of play: 1st day: NZ 85-2, Cumming 37, Fleming 7; 2nd day: Sri Lanka 125-8, Sangakkara 63, Malinga 0
New Zealand won by 5 wickets.

Cumming and Sinclair got recalls to the test side after not playing the previous season. Silva made his test debut for Sri Lanka.

Bond got three wickets in his first six overs to give the BlackCaps the early initiative. Tharanga and Kapugedera added 50 for the fourth wicket before Franklin took three quick wickets. When Martin took the wicket of Prasanna Jayawardene he became the eleventh New Zealand bowler to take 100 test wickets. Sri Lanka were eventually dismissed for just 154.

How was dismissed in the second over of New Zealand's reply before Cumming and Sinclair added 70 for the second wicket. New Zealand went from 106-2 to 113-6 but a 75 run stand between Fleming and Vettori ensured a first innings lead of 52 for the home side. The experienced Vaas and Muralitharan had three and four wickets respectively.

Sri Lanka lost five wickets before clearing the deficit. Silva got a pair on debut as Bond once again led the way. Only a determined innings from Sangakkara gave the tourists some hope. He and Malinga broke the Sri Lankan ninth wicket record against New Zealand, adding 44, with Malinga failing to score. The innings ended in controversy when Muralitharan left his ground while the ball was live, to congratulate Sangakkara on his century, and was run out by McCullum.

New Zealand needed 119 for victory and the openers got them on the way with a 58 run stand but jitters crept in as another three wickets fell for 10 runs. Astle held the innings together and New Zealand won by five wickets with over two days to spare.

SRI LANKA

FIRST INNINGS	*Runs*	*Mins*	*Balls*	*6s*	*4s*	*SECOND INNINGS*	*Runs*	*Mins*	*Balls*	*6s*	*4s*
W.U.Tharanga c How b Franklin	33	138	96	1	3	c Fleming b Bond	24	47	40	-	3
S.T.Jayasuriya c Fleming b Bond	5	12	7	-	1	run out	10	13	11	1	-
K.C.Sangakkara c Sinclair b Bond	4	8	7	-	1	not out	100	222	154	1	12
D.P.M.D.Jayawardene* c Franklin b Bond	8	24	16	-	2	c Fleming b Franklin	0	9	6	-	-
C.K.Kapugedera lbw b Franklin	37	115	86	-	7	c Oram b Bond	1	5	6	-	-
L.P.C.Silva b Franklin	0	5	2	-	-	c Vettori b Bond	0	2	3	-	-
H.A.P.W.Jayawardene† c How b Martin	7	61	39	-	1	run out	11	49	35	-	2
W.P.J.U.C.Vaas c McCullum b Oram	4	19	11	-	-	c McCullum b Oram	0	6	3	-	-
M.F.Maharoof c Fleming b Oram	15	38	32	-	1	c McCullum b Bond	7	23	18	-	-
S.L.Malinga not out	7	30	17	-	1	c McCullum b Franklin	0	50	28	-	-
M.Muralitharan c Astle b Martin	14	15	9	-	2	run out	8	37	19	-	2
Extras (lb 13, w 1, nb 6)	20					(lb 5, nb 4)	9				
TOTAL (52.4 overs)	**154**	237				(53.1 overs)	**170**	236			

NEW ZEALAND

FIRST INNINGS	*Runs*	*Mins*	*Balls*	*6s*	*4s*	*SECOND INNINGS*	*Runs*	*Mins*	*Balls*	*6s*	*4s*
C.D.Cumming b Muralitharan	43	186	131	-	5	c Jayawardene H.A.P.W. b Vaas	43	6	57	2	4
J.M.How lbw b Malinga	0	6	4	-	-	lbw b Muralitharan	11	54	31	-	-
M.S.Sinclair c Jayawardene H.A.P.W. b Vaas	36	100	84	-	5	c Sangakkara b Muralitharan	4	22	18	-	-
S.P.Fleming* c Kapugedera b Maharoof	48	210	158	-	6	lbw b Vaas	0	5	3	-	-
N.J.Astle lbw b Muralitharan	2	2	4	-	-	lbw b Muralitharan	24	50	39	-	3
J.D.P.Oram c Silva b Vaas	1	11	3	-	-	not out	12	55	46	-	1
B.B.McCullum† b Vaas	0	3	3	-	-	not out	14	9	8	1	2
D.L.Vettori c Jayawardene D.P.M.D. b Malinga	63	142	114	-	8						
J.E.C.Franklin lbw b Muralitharan	0	6	9	-	-						
S.E.Bond lbw b Muralitharan	1	16	8	-	-						
C.S.Martin not out	0	5	3	-	-	(b 1, lb 1, w 5, nb 4)	11				
Extras (lb 5, nb 7)	12					(33 overs) (5 wkts)	**119**	133			
TOTAL (85.4 overs)	**206**	348									

Bowling	*O*	*M*	*R*	*W*	*O*	*M*	*R*	*W*
NEW ZEALAND								
Bond	13	2	43	3	19.1	5	63	4
Martin	16.4	2	37	2	11	2	38	0
Franklin	12	0	30	3	13	1	34	2
Oram	10	5	30	2	7	1	19	1
Astle	1	0	1	0	1	0	1	0
Vettori					2	0	10	0
SRI LANKA								
Vaas	18	4	49	3	12	3	33	2
Malinga	19.4	2	43	2	4	1	35	0
Maharoof	14	3	44	1	3	0	15	0
Muralitharan	34	7	65	4	14	5	34	3

Fall of Wickets

	SL *1st*	***NZ*** *1st*	***SL*** *2nd*	***NZ*** *2nd*
1st	11	3	18	58
2nd	17	73	44	66
3rd	37	106	45	66
4th	87	108	46	68
5th	87	113	46	103
6th	106	113	74	-
7th	110	188	80	-
8th	121	190	99	-
9th	132	206	143	-
10th	154	206	170	-

NEW ZEALAND v SRI LANKA — Second Test

at Allied Prime Basin Reserve, Wellington on 15, 16, 17, 18 December, 2006
Toss : Sri Lanka. Umpires : S.J.A. Taufel & B.G. Jerling
Close of play: 1st day: NZ 66-4, Sinclair 6; 2nd day: Sri Lanka 225-5, Silva 79, H.A.P.W.Jayawardene 22
3rd day: NZ 75-2, Sinclair 10, Fleming 4
Sri Lanka won by 217 runs.

Both sides were unchanged. Jayasuriya went in the second over and, apart from Sangakkara and Silva who added 121 for the fifth wicket, Sri Lanka struggled. Sangakkara got fifty from 54 balls and went to a second successive century off 113 balls. Silva got fifty from 65 balls. Sangakkara remained defiant being on 156 when he ran out of partners. Only three players had reached double figures in the innings.

The New Zealand batsmen also struggled with only How and McCullum reaching twenty. Malinga caused trouble, taking 5-68, and was ably assisted by Muralitharan with 4-31. Sri Lanka had a lead of 138.

Silva dominated the second innings, coming in at 100-4. He got his second fifty of the match from 84 balls and then went to a maiden test century from 145 deliveries.

He became the first player to score a pair in his first test and then get a century in the next. He went to 150 from 214 balls as the tourists reached 365. Vettori, with 7-130, had the best match and innings figures by a spin bowler at the Basin Reserve. It was his 13th five wicket haul and third ten wicket bag.

New Zealand were set 504 to win and had a 56 run opening stand but none of the top order could play the big innings that was required. The best stand of the innings was 96 for the eighth wicket with Vettori, fifty from 66 balls, and Franklin. Sangakkara kept wicket in the second innings as Jayawardene was unwell. Muralitharan got another five wicket bag and broke Vettori's record for the best match figures by a spinner at the Basin Reserve. Sri Lanka levelled the two match series with a 217 run win.

SRI LANKA

FIRST INNINGS	*Runs*	*Mins*	*Balls*	*6s*	*4s*	*SECOND INNINGS*	*Runs*	*Mins*	*Balls*	*6s*	*4s*
W.U.Tharanga c McCullum b Martin	7	33	23	-	1	lbw b Martin	20	31	28	-	3
S.T.Jayasuriya c Fleming b Martin	0	6	3	-	-	c Fleming b Vettori	31	61	36	-	2
K.C.Sangakkara not out	156	265	192	1	21	c Franklin b Bond	8	22	14	-	-
D.P.M.D.Jayawardene* b Martin	0	11	4	-	-	c Sinclair b Vettori	31	161	121	-	2
C.K.Kapugedera c Sinclair b Oram	5	43	23	-	1	b Vettori	27	59	53	-	4
L.P.C.Silva c Fleming b Franklin	61	104	82	1	7	not out	152	328	219	-	20
H.A.P.W.Jayawardene† lbw b Vettori	25	47	52	1	3	c sub (S.M.Mills) b Martin	37	119	104	-	4
W.P.J.U.C.Vaas c McCullum b Bond	0	3	5	-	-	c McCullum b Vettori	47	92	74	-	4
M.F.Maharoof c McCullum b Vettori	4	11	5	-	-	lbw b Vettori	1	9	9	-	-
S.L.Malinga c Sinclair b Vettori	0	8	5	-	-	lbw b Vettori	0	7	1	-	-
M.Muralitharan c & b Bond	0	5	3	-	-	st McCullum b Vettori	0	3	2	-	-
Extras (b 1, lb 1, nb 8)	10					(lb 7, nb 4)	11				
TOTAL (65 overs)	**268**	272				(109.3 overs)	**365**	450			

NEW ZEALAND

	Runs	*Mins*	*Balls*	*6s*	*4s*		*Runs*	*Mins*	*Balls*	*6s*	*4s*
C.D.Cumming b Maharoof	13	42	39	-	2	c Sangakkara b Muralitharan	20	70	55	-	3
J.M.How lbw b Malinga	26	48	26	1	3	lbw b Malinga	33	63	41	-	6
M.S.Sinclair b Malinga	6	72	43	-	-	c Jayawardene D.P.M.D. b Muralitharan	37	125	87	-	3
S.P.Fleming* c Jayawardene H.A.P.W. b Malinga	0	8	6	-	-	c Sangakkara b Malinga	27	72	63	-	4
N.J.Astle b Malinga	17	41	33	-	3	lbw b Muralitharan	9	60	33	-	-
B.B.McCullum† b Muralitharan	43	81	61	-	5	b Muralitharan	17	37	36	-	3
D.L.Vettori b Malinga	0	8	3	-	-	(8) lbw b Muralitharan	51	101	68	-	7
J.D.P.Oram lbw b Muralitharan	1	7	8	-	-	(7) lbw b Vaas	4	17	15	-	1
J.E.C.Franklin lbw b Muralitharan	1	8	3	-	-	c Silva b Muralitharan	44	133	95	1	4
S.E.Bond lbw b Muralitharan	8	20	12	-	2	c Sangakkara b Maharoof	6	25	18	-	1
C.S.Martin not out	0	17	3	-	-	not out	4	10	7	-	1
Extras (b 7, lb 6, nb 2)	15					(b 9, lb 7, w 11, nb 7)	34				
TOTAL (39.1 overs)	**130**	180				(85.1 overs)	**286**	361			

Bowling	*O*	*M*	*R*	*W*	*O*	*M*	*R*	*W*
NEW ZEALAND								
Bond	16	1	85	2	19	3	67	1
Martin	13	2	50	3	23	1	98	2
Franklin	12	2	46	1	25	8	63	0
Oram	3	0	10	1				
Vettori	14	1	53	3	42.3	6	130	7
Astle	7	2	22	0				
SRI LANKA								
Vaas	4	0	8	0	18	2	64	1
Malinga	18	4	68	5	16	1	62	2
Maharoof	5	2	10	1	11	1	47	1
Muralitharan	12.1	3	31	4	34.1	9	87	6
Jayasuriya					6	3	10	0

Fall of Wickets

	SL *1st*	***NZ*** *1st*	***SL*** *2nd*	***NZ*** *2nd*
1st	0	30	44	56
2nd	27	40	62	60
3rd	41	40	62	115
4th	81	66	100	139
5th	202	75	168	156
6th	239	85	262	161
7th	240	90	350	163
8th	251	98	356	259
9th	259	116	365	278
10th	268	130	365	286

Sinclair kept wicket on the second day and caught D.P.M.D.Jayawardene, after McCullum suffered a minor injury
Sangakkara kept wicket in New Zealand's second innings

NEW ZEALAND v SRI LANKA First Twenty20 International

at Westpac Stadium, Wellington on 22 December, 2006 (d/n)
Toss : New Zealand. Umpires : E.A. Watkin & A.L. Hill
Sri Lanka won by 18 runs.

New Zealand got off to a bright start getting their first fifty from 27 balls and then reached 100 off 58 deliveries, but the loss of wickets in the middle and end of the innings slowed the pace and the BlackCaps had to be content with 162-8.

Sri Lanka got 50 from 33 balls and Jayasuriya scored his half century from just 23 deliveries, the fastest in any Twenty20 international. Drizzle set in and the game was called off with Sri Lanka victorious under the Duckworth/Lewis system.

NEW ZEALAND

	Runs	Mins	Balls	6s	4s
B.B.McCullum c Tharanga b Muralitharan	39	33	22	4	2
S.P.Fleming* b Maharoof	38	29	24	-	6
J.E.C.Franklin lbw b Jayasuriya	18	17	15	1	2
L.R.P.L.Taylor lbw b Muralitharan	21	25	21	-	2
N.J.Astle b Jayasuriya	19	21	13	1	1
J.A.H.Marshall c Silva b Jayasuriya	1	3	4	-	-
P.D.McGlashan† st Sangakkara b Silva	5	11	12	-	-
A.R.Adams not out	6	9	5	-	-
S.E.Bond b Vaas	0	1	2	-	-
M.R.Gillespie not out	3	1	2	-	-
J.S.Patel					
Extras (lb 8, w 4)	12				
TOTAL (20 overs) (8 wkts)	**162**	79			

SRI LANKA

	Runs	Mins	Balls	6s	4s
W.U.Tharanga c Fleming b Bond	6	15	10	-	-
S.T.Jayasuriya not out	51	23	23	1	10
D.P.M.D.Jayawardene* not out	2	7	2	-	-
K.C.Sangakkara†					
M.S.Atapattu					
L.P.C.Silva					
C.K.Kapugedera					
M.F.Maharoof					
W.P.J.U.C.Vaas					
C.R.D.Fernando					
M.Muralitharan					
Extras (lb 1, w 2)	3				
TOTAL (5.5 overs) (1 wkt)	**62**	23			

Bowling	*O*	*M*	*R*	*W*
SRI LANKA				
Vaas	4	0	28	1
Maharoof	3	0	30	1
Fernando	3	0	36	0
Muralitharan	4	0	27	2
Jayasuriya	4	0	21	3
Jayawardene	1	0	8	0
Silva	1	0	4	1
NEW ZEALAND				
Bond	3	0	24	1
Franklin	2	0	19	0
Adams	0.5	0	18	0

Fall of Wickets	***NZ***	***SL***
1st	80	36
2nd	82	-
3rd	106	-
4th	131	-
5th	135	-
6th	150	-
7th	156	-
8th	159	-
9th	-	-
10th	-	-

NEW ZEALAND v SRI LANKA Second Twenty20 International

at Eden Park, Auckland on 26 December, 2006
Toss : New Zealand. Umpires : B.F. Bowden & A.L. Hill
New Zealand won by 5 wickets.

New Zealand put Sri Lanka into bat and the move paid dividends in the first over. Franklin bowled well getting 3-23 and Gillespie, having his first bowl in an international, did well before limping off the field in his fourth over. Only a 44 run stand for the ninth wicket enabled Sri Lanka to reach 100.

The New Zealand openers put on 51 off 35 balls but three wickets fell quickly before an unbeaten 40 from Astle got New Zealand home with nine balls to spare and this series was also levelled at 1-1.

SRI LANKA

	Runs	*Mins*	*Balls*	*6s*	*4s*
W.U.Tharanga b Franklin	0	1	3	-	-
C.K.Kapugedera c Franklin b Mason	12	18	12	1	1
D.P.M.D.Jayawardene* c Patel b Franklin	9	13	7	-	1
K.C.Sangakkara† c McGlashan b Adams	13	23	17	-	2
M.S.Atapattu c Fulton b Franklin	5	1	8	-	-
T.M.Dilshan run out	3	15	10	-	-
L.P.C.Silva c McGlashan b Adams	12	23	19	-	-
C.M.Bandara c Taylor b Gillespie	1	4	2	-	-
S.L.Malinga b Patel	27	25	19	2	2
C.R.D.Fernando c Adams b Astle	21	14	14	-	4
P.D.R.L.Perera not out	0	1	0	-	-
Extras (lb 2, w 9, nb 1)	12				
TOTAL (18.2 overs)	**115**	77			

NEW ZEALAND

	Runs	*Mins*	*Balls*	*6s*	*4s*
B.B.McCullum run out	28	40	28	-	6
S.P.Fleming* c Kapugedera b Fernando	17	27	16	-	4
L.R.P.L.Taylor run out	4	9	7	-	-
N.J.Astle not out	40	42	37	1	4
P.G.Fulton b Fernando	14	13	13	1	1
P.D.McGlashan† c Dilshan b Fernando	2	6	4	-	-
J.E.C.Franklin not out	3	19	6	-	-
A.R.Adams					
M.R.Gillespie					
M.J.Mason					
J.S.Patel					
Extras (b 4, lb 1, w 3)	8				
TOTAL (18.3 overs) (5 wkts)	**116**	80			

Bowling	*O*	*M*	*R*	*W*
NEW ZEALAND				
Franklin	4	0	23	3
Mason	3	0	19	1
Gillespie	3.1	0	13	1
Adams	4	0	20	2
Astle	2.5	0	30	1
Patel	1.2	0	8	1
SRI LANKA				
Malinga	3	0	15	0
Perera	4	0	49	0
Fernando	4	0	19	3
Dilshan	3.3	0	8	0
Bandara	4	0	20	0

Fall of Wickets

	SL	***NZ***
1st	0	51
2nd	24	56
3rd	26	57
4th	44	82
5th	51	86
6th	58	-
7th	61	-
8th	71	-
9th	115	-
10th	115	-

NEW ZEALAND v SRI LANKA — First One-day International

at McLean Park, Napier on 28 December, 2006
Toss : New Zealand. Umpires : S.J. Davis & A.L. Hill
Sri Lanka won by 7 wickets.

New Zealand rested Fleming and Bond while Styris, Oram and Mills were unavailable due to injury. Gillespie made his debut while there were recalls for James Marshall, Adams, Mason and Taylor.

New Zealand lost McCullum early but then Astle and Taylor added 151 for the second wicket. It was New Zealand's highest stand against Sri Lanka in one-day cricket. Astle got fifty from 45 balls, seven balls quicker than Taylor, who reached his maiden fifty. Taylor went to his century from 115 deliveries as New Zealand reached 285-8.

Sri Lanka had an unbelievable start to their innings. The openers put on 201 off only 24.1 overs, a Sri Lanka record against New Zealand. Jayasuriya got fifty from 39 balls and reached his century off 78 balls as the New Zealand bowlers could do nothing to stop him. Only Vettori conceded less than 6.5 runs an over and the tourists won with ten overs to spare.

NEW ZEALAND

	Runs	Mins	Balls	6s	4s
B.B.McCullum† lbw b Vaas	10	20	16	1	1
N.J.Astle run out	83	119	87	2	8
L.R.P.L.Taylor not out	128	191	133	4	12
P.G.Fulton c Sangakkara b Muralitharan	24	31	29	-	1
D.L.Vettori* c Jayawardene b Vaas	5	11	11	-	-
J.A.H.Marshall lbw b Vaas	0	1	1	-	-
H.J.H.Marshall c Sangakkara b Fernando	17	22	17	-	2
J.E.C.Franklin b Malinga	2	4	3	-	-
A.R.Adams b Malinga	3	8	5	-	-
M.R.Gillespie not out	1	5	2	-	-
M.J.Mason					
Extras (lb 4, w 4, nb 4)	12				
TOTAL (50 overs) (8 wkts)	**285**	213			

SRI LANKA

	Runs	Mins	Balls	6s	4s
W.U.Tharanga c McCullum b Franklin	68	107	73	-	9
S.T.Jayasuriya c Mason b Franklin	111	105	82	5	12
D.P.M.D.Jayawardene* not out	34	61	39	-	6
K.C.Sangakkara† c & b Vettori	36	47	41	-	5
M.S.Atapattu not out	10	11	16	-	2
T.M.Dilshan					
L.P.C.Silva					
W.P.U.J.C.Vaas					
S.L.Malinga					
C.R.D.Fernando					
M.Muralitharan					
Extras (b 3, lb 3, w 12, nb 12)	30				
TOTAL (40 overs) (3 wkts)	**289**	168			

Bowling	*O*	*M*	*R*	*W*
SRI LANKA				
Vaas	10	0	50	3
Malinga	10	0	66	2
Fernando	5	0	43	1
Muralitharan	10	0	48	1
Jayasuriya	10	0	42	0
Dilshan	5	0	32	0
NEW ZEALAND				
Franklin	10	0	69	2
Mason	6	0	60	0
Gillespie	9	0	64	0
Adams	7	0	54	0
Vettori	8	0	36	1

Fall of Wickets	***NZ***	***SL***
1st	18	201
2nd	169	201
3rd	222	271
4th	229	-
5th	229	-
6th	257	-
7th	262	-
8th	280	-
9th	-	-
10th	-	-

NEW ZEALAND v SRI LANKA Second One-day International

at Queenstown Events Centre on 31 December, 2006
Toss : New Zealand. Umpires : G.A. Baxter & S.J. Davis
New Zealand won by 1 wicket.

Sri Lanka lost two very quick wickets and it was left to Sangakkara to hold the innings together. He scored fifty from 73 balls as the BlackCap bowlers, in an improved performance, restricted the tourists to 224-7.

James Marshall, opening while Astle was rested, scored his maiden fifty from 79 balls but New Zealand then lost their way. They were 194-8 and were indebted to a 29 run stand between Franklin (highest score) and Gillespie, but the latter was out at 223 with ten balls left.

Some tight bowling kept the scores level with just one ball remaining until Mason hit Jayasuriya to the boundary to give New Zealand a one wicket win to level the series.

SRI LANKA

	Runs	Mins	Balls	6s	4s
W.U.Tharanga c Taylor b Mason	23	51	29	-	3
S.T.Jayasuriya b Mason	1	7	8	-	-
D.P.M.D.Jayawardene† b Gillespie	4	11	8	-	1
K.C.Sangakkara* run out	89	155	122	-	10
M.S.Atapattu b Vettori	22	53	35	-	2
L.P.C.Silva c Marshall H.J.H. b Franklin	31	74	53	-	2
T.M.Dilshan c Taylor b Gillespie	8	22	15	-	-
M.F.Maharoof not out	29	32	24	1	2
W.P.U.J.C.Vaas not out	9	14	7	-	1
S.L.Malinga					
M.Muralitharan					
Extras (lb 3, w 4, nb 1)	8				
TOTAL (50 overs) (7 wkts)	**224**	214			

NEW ZEALAND

	Runs	Mins	Balls	6s	4s
J.A.H.Marshall run out	50	108	80	-	6
B.B.McCullum† lbw b Maharoof	32	40	24	1	5
L.R.P.L.Taylor run out	15	28	26	-	2
P.G.Fulton lbw b Muralitharan	2	9	9	-	-
D.L.Vettori* b Malinga	19	49	33	-	1
C.D.McMillan c Jayawardene b Muralitharan	2	5	5	-	-
H.J.H.Marshall c & b Dilshan	29	43	35	1	-
J.E.C.Franklin not out	45	83	46	-	3
A.R.Adams lbw b Muralitharan	6	16	15	-	-
M.R.Gillespie c Maharoof b Vaas	11	29	23	-	-
M.J.Mason not out	4	7	6	-	1
Extras (lb 5, w 4, nb 4)	13				
TOTAL (50 overs) (9 wkts)	**228**	213			

Bowling	*O*	*M*	*R*	*W*
NEW ZEALAND				
Gillespie	10	0	46	2
Mason	10	1	50	2
Franklin	10	0	46	1
Adams	10	0	42	0
Vettori	10	0	37	1
SRI LANKA				
Vaas	10	0	46	1
Malinga	10	0	53	1
Maharoof	8	0	40	1
Muralitharan	10	1	31	3
Jayasuriya	5	0	28	0
Dilshan	7	0	25	1

Fall of Wickets

	SL	*NZ*
1st	4	57
2nd	14	87
3rd	50	91
4th	102	121
5th	176	126
6th	177	141
7th	192	175
8th	-	194
9th	-	223
10th	-	-

NEW ZEALAND v SRI LANKA — Third One-day International

at Jade Stadium, Christchurch on 2 January, 2007
Toss : New Zealand. Umpires : S.J. Davis & A.L. Hill
New Zealand won by 4 wickets.

Bond returned to the New Zealand side but Fleming was rested for one further game. Sri Lanka struggled against Mason who had career best figures while rain twice interrupted the Sri Lankan innings.

At 32-2 and 68-5 there were stoppages and the game was reduced to 46 overs per side. By dismissing Sri Lanka within its number of overs New Zealand were set a target of 110 to win.

Two wickets fell in the first two overs but Fulton held New Zealand together and saw them through to a comfortable win.

SRI LANKA

	Runs	Mins	Balls	6s	4s
W.U.Tharanga c McCullum b Mason	11	59	34	-	1
S.T.Jayasuriya c McCullum b Bond	0	6	2	-	-
M.S.Atapattu c Taylor b Mason	28	23	26	-	5
K.C.Sangakkara† c Taylor b Mason	15	19	18	-	3
D.P.M.D.Jayawardene* run out	1	32	16	-	-
L.P.C.Silva c & b Mason	4	10	7	-	1
T.M.Dilshan run out	18	57	41	-	2
M.F.Maharoof c McCullum b Vettori	13	65	47	-	1
C.R.D.Fernando not out	8	29	19	-	1
M.Muralitharan c Taylor b Franklin	8	5	4	-	2
P.D.R.L.Perera c Franklin b Vettori	0	2	2	-	-
Extras (w 2, nb 4)	6				
TOTAL (35.2 overs)	**112**	158			

NEW ZEALAND

	Runs	Mins	Balls	6s	4s
B.B.McCullum† c Silva b Perera	22	19	16	2	1
N.J.Astle b Maharoof	0	1	2	-	-
L.R.P.L.Taylor c Dilshan b Perera	0	6	4	-	-
P.G.Fulton not out	43	94	57	2	5
D.L.Vettori* c Sangakkara b Fernando	11	20	15	-	2
J.A.H.Marshall c Dilshan b Muralitharan	5	17	16	-	-
H.J.H.Marshall b Fernando	4	4	4	-	1
J.E.C.Franklin not out	15	38	33	-	3
S.E.Bond					
M.R.Gillespie					
M.J.Mason					
Extras (b 1, lb 7, w 2)	10				
TOTAL (24.3 overs) (6 wkts)	**110**	103			

Bowling	*O*	*M*	*R*	*W*
NEW ZEALAND				
Mason	9	1	24	4
Bond	8	1	37	1
Franklin	7	1	32	1
Gillespie	6	3	12	0
Vettori	5.2	2	7	2
SRI LANKA				
Maharoof	4	1	13	1
Perera	5	0	37	2
Muralitharan	9	2	18	1
Fernando	6.3	0	34	2

Fall of Wickets	***SL***	***NZ***
1st	0	1
2nd	32	8
3rd	50	27
4th	55	51
5th	61	65
6th	68	70
7th	92	-
8th	99	-
9th	112	-
10th	112	-

NEW ZEALAND v SRI LANKA — Fourth One-day International

at Eden Park, Auckland on 6 January, 2007 (d/n)
Toss : Sri Lanka. Umpires : G.A. Baxter & S.J. Davis
Sri Lanka won by 189 runs.

Fleming returned to captain the side. The Sri Lankan openers raced to a century stand off 14.1 overs. Jayasuriya got another fast fifty, this time from 32 balls while Sangakkara scored a half century off 80 deliveries. Gillespie had his best bowling figures.

The New Zealand innings was a disaster. Only two players reached double figures in what was New Zealand's second lowest total in a one-day international. It was also their heaviest defeat in one-day cricket. New Zealand managed only 73 as Vaas and Malinga caused havoc. The Sri Lankan win levelled the series.

SRI LANKA

	Runs	Mins	Balls	6s	4s
W.U.Tharanga b Gillespie	22	80	50	-	2
S.T.Jayasuriya c Mason b Gillespie	70	69	44	5	7
D.P.M.D.Jayawardene* c Fleming b Gillespie	0	2	2	-	-
K.C.Sangakkara† c Taylor b Bond	79	131	103	1	8
M.S.Atapattu c McCullum b Adams	34	99	75	-	2
C.K.Kapugedera not out	10	37	17	-	-
M.F.Maharoof c Adams b Bond	21	10	11	2	1
W.P.U.J.C.Vaas not out	5	2	2	-	1
C.R.D.Fernando					
M.Muralitharan					
S.L.Malinga					
Extras (lb 11, w 6, nb 4)	21				
TOTAL (50 overs) (6 wkts)	**262**	218			

NEW ZEALAND

	Runs	Mins	Balls	6s	4s
B.B.McCullum† c Sangakkara b Maharoof	17	18	13	-	4
S.P.Fleming* lbw b Vaas	0	10	5	-	-
L.R.P.L.Taylor lbw b Vaas	0	11	7	-	-
P.G.Fulton lbw b Malinga	9	33	13	-	2
H.J.H.Marshall lbw b Vaas	3	9	10	-	-
C.D.McMillan not out	29	91	64	-	5
A.R.Adams lbw b Malinga	1	9	7	-	-
S.E.Bond c & b Malinga	2	21	11	-	-
M.R.Gillespie c Sangakkara b Fernando	0	7	4	-	-
J.S.Patel b Muralitharan	6	23	14	-	1
M.J.Mason lbw b Muralitharan	1	7	13	-	-
Extras (lb 2, w 1, nb 2)	5				
TOTAL (26.3 overs)	**73**	124			

Bowling	*O*	*M*	*R*	*W*
NEW ZEALAND				
Mason	10	1	62	0
Bond	10	2	47	2
Gillespie	10	1	39	3
Adams	9	2	53	1
Patel	9	0	41	0
McMillan	2	0	9	0
SRI LANKA				
Vaas	8	3	10	3
Malinga	8	3	14	3
Maharoof	4	0	27	1
Fernando	4	1	13	1
Muralitharan	2.3	0	7	2

Fall of Wickets	***SL***	***NZ***
1st	102	5
2nd	102	17
3rd	103	17
4th	194	25
5th	232	37
6th	256	39
7th	-	49
8th	-	54
9th	-	71
10th	-	73

NEW ZEALAND v SRI LANKA — Fifth One-day International

at Westpac Park, Hamilton on 9 January, 2006 (d/n)
Toss : New Zealand. Umpires : B.F. Bowden & S.J. Davis
No result

No play was possible but as the toss had been made the game counts as an official match and also became the 100th one-day international for umpire Billy Bowden. The series was thus shared at 2-2.

New Zealand: S.P.Fleming*, B.B.McCullum†, N.J.Astle, L.R.P.L.Taylor, P.G.Fulton, C.D.McMillan, D.L.Vettori, J.E.C.Franklin, M.R.Gillespie, S.E.Bond, M.J.Mason

Sri Lanka: W.U.Tharanga, S.T.Jayasuriya, D.P.M.D.Jayawardene*, K.C.Sangakkara†, M.S.Atapattu, C.K.Kapugedera, M.F.Maharoof, W.P.U.J.C.Vaas, C.R.D.Fernando, M.Muralitharan, S.L.Malinga

NEW ZEALAND IN AUSTRALIA

This was a series where New Zealand were so close to qualifying for the final but so far away. In three of the four games against Australia, the games were lost in the last two overs. Against England, the BlackCaps won two and lost two. The two losses were close but fielding let them down, with dropped catches coming at crucial moments.

Fourteen players started the series and replacements were made as players recovered from injury. Nathan Astle retired from international cricket after four games and his replacement, Lou Vincent, made 263 runs in four innings. There was inconsistency in the batting, with only Fleming and Oram able to score centuries. Bond was the leading wicket-taker with 11. He took a hat-trick in New Zealand's first game. Vettori, Franklin and Gillespie all had their moments.

The squad was: S.P. Fleming *(captain, Wellington)*, D.L. Vettori *(vice-captain, Northern Districts)*, A.R. Adams *(Auckland)*, N.J. Astle *(Canterbury)*, S.E. Bond *(Canterbury)*, J.E.C. Franklin *(Wellington)*, P.G. Fulton *(Canterbury)*, M.R. Gillespie *(Wellington)*, B.B. McCullum *(Canterbury)*, C.D. McMillan *(Canterbury)*, H.J.H. Marshall *(Northern Districts)*, M.J. Mason *(Central Districts)*, K.D. Mills *(Auckland)*, J.D.P. Oram *(Central Districts)*, J.S. Patel *(Wellington)*, S.B. Styris *(Auckland)*, L.R.P.L. Taylor *(Central Districts)*, L. Vincent *(Auckland)*. Coach, J.G. Bracewell; Assistant coach/Video analyst, R.M. Carter; Fielding coach, T. Wilson; Manager, L.M. Crocker; Physiotherapist, D.F. Shackel, Trainer, D. Cochran, Sports psychologist, G.L. Hermansson. Oram, Mills, Vincent and Styris replaced Adams, Astle and Marshall.

New Zealand Averages

BATTING	*M*	*I*	*NO*	*HS*	*Agg*	*Ave*	*100s*	*50s*	*Ct*	*St*	*SR*
J.D.P. Oram	5	5	2	101*	261	87.00	1	2	1	-	124
L. Vincent	4	4	0	90	263	65.75	-	3	1	-	77
L.R.P.L Taylor	8	8	0	84	282	35.25	-	2	6	-	77
S.P. Fleming	8	8	0	106	231	28.87	1	-	8	-	63
P.G. Fulton	8	8	0	60	217	27.12	-	1	2	-	65
S.B. Styris	2	2	0	34	50	25.00	-	-	1	-	89
C.D. McMillan	6	6	0	89	131	21.83	-	1	1	-	82
B.B. McCullum	8	8	1	46*	152	21.71	-	-	7	1	80
M.R. Gillespie	7	4	3	10	21	21.00	-	-	1	-	77
J.E.C. Franklin	7	7	2	22*	102	20.40	-	-	2	-	107
S.E. Bond	6	4	2	22*	34	17.00	-	-	-	-	62
N.J. Astle	4	4	0	45	46	11.50	-	-	2	-	58
D.L. Vettori	8	7	2	11*	44	8.80	-	-	-	-	80
M.J. Mason	1	1	0	4	4	4.00	-	-	-	-	57
J.S. Patel	4	1	0	4	4	4.00	-	-	2	-	80
H.J.H. Marshall	1	1	0	0	0	0.00	-	-	1	-	0
K.D. Mills	1	-	-	-	-	-	-	-	-	-	-

BOWLING	*O*	*M*	*R*	*W*	*Ave*	*Best*	*R/O*
M.J. Mason	10	2	46	2	23.00	2-46	4.60
C.D. McMillan	22.5	1	124	5	24.80	2-38	5.43
S.E. Bond	56.5	3	290	11	26.36	4-46	5.10
J.E.C. Franklin	56	6	275	10	27.50	3-17	4.91
D.L. Vettori	75	1	321	10	32.10	4-24	4.28
M.R. Gillespie	59.2	7	322	8	40.25	2-34	5.42
J.S. Patel	40	1	218	5	43.60	2-34	5.45
K.D. Mills	10	1	72	1	72.00	1-72	7.20
S.B. Styris	15	0	76	1	76.00	1-50	5.07
J.D.P. Oram	29	1	170	1	170.00	1-17	5.86
L.R.P.L Taylor	2	0	16	0	-	-	8.00
N.J. Astle	8.4	0	44	0	-	-	5.07

AUSTRALIA v NEW ZEALAND — Commonwealth Bank Series

at Bellerive Oval, Hobart on 14 January, 2007
Toss : Australia. Umpires : Asad Rauf & D.J. Harper
Australia won by 105 runs.

Australia batted after winning the toss and enjoyed an 83 run opening stand before Hayden was first out. Gilchrist got fifty from 54 balls and Symonds got his fifty from 60 deliveries. Bond took a hat-trick getting White, Symonds and Bracken with successive deliveries.

New Zealand lost both openers early and never recovered with only three players reaching double figures. Taylor got fifty off 57 balls but New Zealand were well beaten by 105 runs.

AUSTRALIA

	Runs	Mins	Balls	6s	4s
A.C.Gilchrist† lbw b Patel	61	78	58	2	8
M.L.Hayden c McCullum b Gillespie	27	58	39	-	2
R.T.Ponting* c Fleming b Gillespie	10	41	22	-	2
M.J.Clarke c Astle b Bond	33	58	52	-	3
A.Symonds c McCullum b Bond	69	109	70	-	6
M.E.K.Hussey c sub (H.J.H.Marshall) b McMillan	20	33	32	-	1
C.L.White c McMillan b Bond	45	36	32	3	2
M.G.Johnson not out	2	5	1	-	-
N.W.Bracken b Bond	0	1	1	-	-
S.R.Clark not out	1	1	1	-	-
B.W.Hilfenhaus					
Extras (lb 7, w 6, nb 8)	21				
TOTAL (50 overs) (8 wkts)	**289**	214			

NEW ZEALAND

	Runs	Mins	Balls	6s	4s
B.B.McCullum† lbw b Hilfenhaus	5	15	16	-	1
N.J.Astle c Gilchrist b Bracken	0	8	3	-	-
S.P.Fleming* c Hussey b Johnson	29	73	47	1	1
L.R.P.L.Taylor c Gilchrist b Johnson	84	114	82	3	10
P.G.Fulton c Symonds b Clark	37	59	44	1	1
C.D.McMillan run out	2	6	7	-	-
D.L.Vettori c Hayden b Clark	1	14	5	-	-
J.E.C.Franklin c Clarke b White	6	18	13	-	-
S.E.Bond b Symonds	2	5	5	-	-
M.R.Gillespie not out	4	7	4	-	-
J.S.Patel c Hilfenhaus b Symonds	4	4	5	-	1
Extras (lb 3, w 7)	10				
TOTAL (38.3 overs)	**184**	166			

Bowling	*O*	*M*	*R*	*W*
NEW ZEALAND				
Franklin	4	0	31	0
Bond	10	0	61	4
Gillespie	10	2	50	2
Patel	10	0	64	1
Vettori	10	1	48	0
Astle	4	0	18	0
McMillan	2	0	10	1
AUSTRALIA				
Bracken	7	0	25	1
Hilfenhaus	7	1	26	1
Johnson	7	0	27	2
Clark	8	0	40	2
Symonds	6.3	0	41	2
White	3	0	22	1

Fall of Wickets	***A***	***NZ***
1st	83	5
2nd	104	7
3rd	117	80
4th	164	161
5th	196	165
6th	286	166
7th	286	171
8th	286	175
9th	-	175
10th	-	184

12 January, 2007
Melbourne: **Australia beat England by 8 wickets**
England 242 for 8 (50 overs) (K.P.Pietersen 82, A.Flintoff 47*, P.D.Collingwood 43, N.W.Bracken 3-46);
Australia 246 for 2 (45.2 overs) (R.T.Ponting 82*, A.C.Gilchrist 60, M.J.Clarke 57*)

NEW ZEALAND v ENGLAND — Commonwealth Bank Series

at Bellerive Oval, Hobart on 16 January, 2007
Toss : New Zealand. Umpires : Asad Rauf & S.J. Davis
England won by 3 wickets.

New Zealand batted after winning the toss but were only able to manage a disappointing 205. Nine of the ten batsmen reached double figures but no one was able to reach fifty. Anderson was impressive getting four wickets.

Strauss passed 2000 runs when he was on 25 but it was Flintoff's innings that set England on course to victory, with his fifty coming from 59 balls.

England, however, still made hard work of their task and only won with one ball to spare. The Wellington duo Franklin and Patel were the best of the New Zealand bowlers.

NEW ZEALAND

	Runs	Mins	Balls	6s	4s
B.B.McCullum† c Vaughan b Anderson	16	28	15	1	2
N.J.Astle b Collingwood	45	106	63	1	6
S.P.Fleming* b Anderson	12	39	29	-	1
L.R.P.L.Taylor c Vaughan b Anderson	1	5	7	-	-
P.G.Fulton c Vaughan b Flintoff	27	65	52	-	1
C.D.McMillan c & b Collingwood	22	59	40	-	2
D.L.Vettori lbw b Panesar	11	21	17	-	1
J.E.C.Franklin c Collingwood b Flintoff	20	45	30	-	-
S.E.Bond not out	22	57	37	-	1
M.R.Gillespie b Anderson	10	15	10	-	1
J.S.Patel					
Extras (lb 9, w 10)	19				
TOTAL (50 overs) (9 wkts)	**205**	221			

ENGLAND

	Runs	Mins	Balls	6s	4s
A.J.Strauss lbw b Franklin	28	79	58	-	3
M.P.Vaughan* c Taylor b Franklin	17	49	29	-	3
I.R.Bell lbw b Patel	45	112	72	-	2
E.C.Joyce run out	5	29	19	-	-
P.D.Collingwood c Taylor b Patel	10	22	21	-	-
A.Flintoff not out	72	101	75	-	7
P.A.Nixon† run out	15	57	22	-	-
J.W.M.Dalrymple c Patel b Gillespie	1	3	5	-	-
J.Lewis not out	2	9	6	-	-
M.S.Panesar					
J.M.Anderson					
Extras (b 1, w 2, nb 8)	11				
TOTAL (49.5 overs) (7 wkts)	**206**	224			

Bowling	*O*	*M*	*R*	*W*
ENGLAND				
Lewis	9	0	51	0
Anderson	10	0	42	4
Flintoff	10	1	37	2
Panesar	10	0	36	1
Collingwood	10	1	25	2
Dalrymple	1	0	5	0
NEW ZEALAND				
Franklin	9	1	34	2
Bond	8	0	29	0
Gillespie	6	0	40	1
Astle	2	0	4	0
Patel	10	1	34	2
Vettori	10	0	42	0
McMillan	4.5	0	22	0

Fall of Wickets	***NZ***	***E***
1st	26	39
2nd	61	62
3rd	67	79
4th	97	98
5th	127	138
6th	144	198
7th	146	201
8th	185	-
9th	205	-
10th	-	-

19th January 2007
Brisbane: **Australia beat England by 4 wickets**
England 155 (42 overs) (M.B.Loye 36, J.W.M.Dalrymple 31, G.D.McGrath 3-24, N.W.Bracken 3-24);
Australia 156 for 6 (38.4 overs) (M.E.K.Hussey 46*, M.J.Clarke 36, J.Lewis 4-36)

AUSTRALIA v NEW ZEALAND Commonwealth Bank Series

at Sydney Cricket Ground on 21 January, 2007 (d/n)
Toss : New Zealand. Umpires : Asad Rauf & S.J.A. Taufel
Australia won by 2 wickets.

New Zealand again had a horror start losing two wickets for just 7 runs. Taylor and McMillan were the only players to pass twenty. McMillan got fifty from 64 balls before becoming McGrath's 350th one-day wicket. Clark had his best bowling performance in one-day internationals.

Australia also started badly being 17-3 but Clarke (fifty off 92 balls) and Hussey (fifty off 65 balls) saw them through to a narrow win with eight balls to spare.

NEW ZEALAND

	Runs	Mins	Balls	6s	4s
S.P.Fleming* c Hussey b Clark	12	63	43	-	1
N.J.Astle c Gilchrist b Lee	0	13	4	-	-
H.J.H.Marshall c Gilchrist b Lee	0	7	3	-	-
L.R.P.L.Taylor c Hussey b Clark	26	59	43	-	5
P.G.Fulton c Hayden b Clark	19	59	39	-	1
C.D.McMillan c & b McGrath	89	133	87	3	7
B.B.McCullum† lbw b McGrath	15	32	24	1	-
D.L.Vettori c Ponting b Clark	6	11	10	-	-
J.E.C.Franklin c Hayden b McGrath	18	34	18	-	1
M.R.Gillespie not out	6	20	12	-	1
M.J.Mason b Bracken	4	10	7	-	-
Extras (b 2, lb 12, w 5, nb 4)	23				
TOTAL (47.4 overs)	**218**	219			

AUSTRALIA

	Runs	Mins	Balls	6s	4s
A.C.Gilchrist† c McCullum b Franklin	3	7	3	-	-
M.L.Hayden c Taylor b Mason	0	13	10	-	-
M.J.Clarke c Taylor b Vettori	75	165	111	-	9
R.T.Ponting* lbw b Mason	5	16	15	-	1
A.Symonds b Vettori	38	54	40	-	7
M.E.K.Hussey not out	65	147	73	1	6
C.L.White c Fulton b Gillespie	5	14	15	-	-
B.Lee c Marshall b Gillespie	2	21	12	-	-
N.W.Bracken c Taylor b McMillan	14	14	16	-	1
S.R.Clark not out	1	5	3	-	-
G.D.McGrath					
Extras (lb 6, w 4, nb 6)	16				
TOTAL (48.4 overs) (8 wkts)	**224**	228			

Bowling	*O*	*M*	*R*	*W*
AUSTRALIA				
Lee	10	1	43	2
Bracken	8.4	2	33	1
McGrath	10	1	24	3
Clark	10	1	54	4
Symonds	8	0	44	0
White	1	0	6	0
NEW ZEALAND				
Mason	10	2	46	2
Franklin	10	1	47	1
Gillespie	10	2	34	2
Vettori	10	0	41	2
Astle	2.4	0	22	0
McMillan	6	0	28	1

Fall of Wickets	***NZ***	***A***
1st	5	6
2nd	7	6
3rd	38	17
4th	53	77
5th	84	167
6th	126	175
7th	136	198
8th	193	217
9th	205	-
10th	218	-

NEW ZEALAND v ENGLAND — Commonwealth Bank Series

at Adelaide Oval on 23 January, 2007 (d/n)
Toss : New Zealand. Umpires : D.J. Harper & I.L. Howell
New Zealand won by 90 runs.

The New Zealand batting again looked fragile as they went to 67-5 before Oram and McCullum added 120 for the sixth wicket. It was Oram's highest score with his fifty coming from 66 balls. However, the end of the partnership signalled a collapse and the last five wickets went for just 23.

England fared even worse and struggled with only Joyce passing 20 against a good New Zealand attack. Oram and then Bond reached 100 one-day international wickets. Vettori and Franklin had good performances with the ball as New Zealand won easily by 90 runs.

NEW ZEALAND

	Runs	Mins	Balls	6s	4s
S.P.Fleming* c Nixon b Flintoff	20	52	42	1	2
N.J.Astle c Collingwood b Anderson	1	7	8	-	-
P.G.Fulton c Collingwood b Lewis	24	75	39	1	2
L.R.P.L.Taylor c Collingwood b Panesar	15	58	44	-	1
C.D.McMillan lbw b Collingwood	2	12	7	-	-
J.D.P.Oram c Strauss b Anderson	86	112	89	2	6
B.B.McCullum† b Flintoff	30	88	56	-	-
J.E.C.Franklin run out	14	22	9	1	-
D.L.Vettori c Nixon b Flintoff	2	6	5	-	-
S.E.Bond b Flintoff	2	2	2	-	-
M.R.Gillespie not out	1	6	1	-	-
Extras (b 2, lb 3, w 6, nb 2)	13				
TOTAL (50 overs)	**210**	223			

ENGLAND

	Runs	Mins	Balls	6s	4s
A.J.Strauss lbw b Franklin	19	37	33	-	3
M.B.Loye c Fleming b Franklin	8	26	14	-	1
I.R.Bell c Fleming b Franklin	2	17	15	-	-
E.C.Joyce c Gillespie b Vettori	47	106	70	-	5
P.D.Collingwood lbw b Vettori	10	58	37	-	-
A.Flintoff* c McCullum b Vettori	9	17	17	-	-
P.A.Nixon† c McCullum b Oram	6	17	17	-	-
J.W.M.Dalrymple c Fleming b Vettori	0	7	6	-	-
J.Lewis c Fleming b Bond	5	17	8	-	1
M.S.Panesar c Astle b Bond	6	13	12	-	-
J.M.Anderson not out	0	2	0	-	-
Extras (lb 5, w 1, nb 2)	8				
TOTAL (37.5 overs)	**120**	163			

Bowling	*O*	*M*	*R*	*W*
ENGLAND				
Lewis	10	1	31	1
Anderson	10	2	47	2
Flintoff	10	2	21	4
Collingwood	8	0	40	1
Panesar	9	0	44	1
Dalrymple	3	0	22	0
NEW ZEALAND				
Franklin	7	2	17	3
Bond	9.5	1	32	2
Gillespie	5	2	25	0
Oram	7	1	17	1
Vettori	9	0	24	4

Fall of Wickets	***NZ***	***E***
1st	5	21
2nd	37	30
3rd	55	31
4th	61	76
5th	67	92
6th	187	107
7th	191	107
8th	194	107
9th	196	120
10th	210	120

26th January 2007
Adelaide: **Australia beat England by 9 wickets**
England 110 (34.3 overs) (I.R.Bell 35, M.G.Johnson 4-45);
Australia 111 for 1 (24.3 overs) (R.T.Ponting 51*, M.L.Hayden 30*)

AUSTRALIA v NEW ZEALAND Commonwealth Bank Series

at Western Australia C.A. Ground, Perth on 28 January, 2007 (d/n)
Toss : Australia. Umpires : Asad Rauf & S.J.A. Taufel
Australia won by 8 runs.

After Gilchrist went early, Hayden and Ponting added 200 off 202 balls. Hayden scored his century from 104 balls, nine balls quicker than his captain. The total of 343 was Australia's highest score against New Zealand.

Vincent got New Zealand off to a positive start getting fifty from 56 balls. Oram and McCullum added an unbeaten 137 for the sixth wicket to set a New Zealand record against Australia. Oram got fifty from just 39 balls and reached his maiden century off 71 balls, a New Zealand record. At the end of the game, however, they finished eight runs short of Australia's total

AUSTRALIA

	Runs	Mins	Balls	6s	4s
A.C.Gilchrist† c Patel b Mills	13	26	20	-	2
M.L.Hayden b Vettori	117	171	111	-	15
R.T.Ponting* c Fulton b McMillan	111	170	122	1	8
M.J.Clarke c sub (H.J.H.Marshall) b Patel	7	16	8	-	-
A.Symonds b Gillespie	24	24	13	2	-
M.E.K.Hussey not out	29	33	16	3	-
C.L.White not out	20	22	12	1	1
B.Lee					
M.G.Johnson					
N.W.Bracken					
G.D.McGrath					
Extras (b 2, w 18, nb 2)	22				
TOTAL (50 overs) (5 wkts)	**343**	225			

NEW ZEALAND

	Runs	Mins	Balls	6s	4s
L.Vincent lbw b Clarke	66	105	82	1	8
S.P.Fleming* c Gilchrist b McGrath	28	39	27	-	6
P.G.Fulton c Hayden b Johnson	23	37	26	-	4
L.R.P.L.Taylor b Clarke	39	61	50	-	2
C.D.McMillan run out	5	5	6	-	1
J.D.P.Oram not out	101	130	72	6	4
B.B.McCullum† not out	46	101	39	1	4
D.L.Vettori					
M.R.Gillespie					
K.D.Mills					
J.S.Patel					
Extras (b 2, lb 5, w 18, nb 2)	27				
TOTAL (50 overs) (5 wkts)	**335**	233			

Bowling	*O*	*M*	*R*	*W*
NEW ZEALAND				
Mills	10	1	72	1
Gillespie	10	1	76	1
Oram	5	0	50	0
Vettori	10	0	34	1
Patel	10	0	67	1
McMillan	3	0	26	1
Taylor	2	0	16	0
AUSTRALIA				
Lee	10	0	53	0
Bracken	10	1	75	0
McGrath	10	0	72	1
Johnson	6	0	48	1
Clarke	9	0	48	2
Symonds	5	0	32	0

Fall of Wickets	***A***	***NZ***
1st	28	47
2nd	228	107
3rd	254	142
4th	275	150
5th	293	198
6th	-	-
7th	-	-
8th	-	-
9th	-	-
10th	-	-

NEW ZEALAND v ENGLAND — Commonwealth Bank Series

at Western Australia C.A. Ground, Perth on 30 January, 2007 (d/n)
Toss : New Zealand. Umpires : Asad Rauf & S.J. Davis
New Zealand won by 58 runs.

Vincent and Taylor added 137 for the third wicket after New Zealand had been 53-2. Vincent got fifty off 73 balls and passed 2000 runs in the process. Taylor reached his fifty from 64 balls. Later in the innings Oram continued his good run getting another half-century from 32 balls.

Joyce was promoted to open for England and made his highest score, his fifty came from 60 balls. Bell reached 1000 runs when on 13. Nixon made his highest score but England finished 58 runs short of the New Zealand score and now needed to win their last two games to have any chance of reaching the final.

NEW ZEALAND

	Runs	Mins	Balls	6s	4s
L.Vincent c Dalrymple b Plunkett	76	181	111	-	7
S.P.Fleming* lbw b Plunkett	15	28	14	-	3
P.G.Fulton c Nixon b Plunkett	15	19	19	-	1
L.R.P.L.Taylor c Panesar b Collingwood	71	117	81	1	7
C.D.McMillan st Nixon b Panesar	11	25	12	-	2
J.D.P.Oram not out	54	64	33	4	3
B.B.McCullum† c Strauss b Panesar	19	19	18	1	1
J.E.C.Franklin c Plunkett b Tremlett	9	13	8	-	-
D.L.Vettori not out	11	19	7	-	1
S.E.Bond					
J.S.Patel					
Extras (lb 12, w 22, nb 3)	37				
TOTAL (50 overs) (7 wkts)	**318**	233			

ENGLAND

	Runs	Mins	Balls	6s	4s
E.C.Joyce run out	66	120	82	-	7
M.B.Loye c Fleming b Franklin	15	22	17	1	2
I.R.Bell c Fleming b Patel	31	62	42	1	3
A.J.Strauss st McCullum b Vettori	12	30	20	-	-
P.D.Collingwood c Fleming b McMillan	17	33	30	-	1
A.Flintoff* b Vettori	13	32	22	-	-
J.W.M.Dalrymple c Franklin b McMillan	14	34	21	-	1
P.A.Nixon† c Oram b Bond	49	68	47	2	2
L.E.Plunkett not out	25	44	25	-	2
C.T.Tremlett					
M.S.Panesar					
Extras (b 1, lb 2, w 8, nb 7)	18				
TOTAL (50 overs) (8 wkts)	**260**	212			

Bowling	*O*	*M*	*R*	*W*
ENGLAND				
Plunkett	9	0	54	3
Tremlett	10	0	72	1
Flintoff	10	0	66	0
Panesar	10	2	35	2
Dalrymple	5	0	43	0
Collingwood	6	0	36	1
NEW ZEALAND				
Franklin	8	1	45	1
Bond	10	0	58	1
Oram	5	0	23	0
Patel	10	0	53	1
Vettori	10	0	40	2
McMillan	7	1	38	2

Fall of Wickets	***NZ***	***E***
1st	32	27
2nd	53	99
3rd	190	123
4th	213	136
5th	219	156
6th	246	162
7th	268	184
8th	-	260
9th	-	-
10th	-	-

2nd February 2007
Sydney: **England beat Australia by 92 runs**
England 292 for 7 (50 overs) (E.C.Joyce 107, I.R.Bell 51, J.W.M.Dalrymple 30);
Australia 200 (38.5 overs) (M.L.Hayden 51, A.Symonds 39*, L.E.Plunkett 3-24)

AUSTRALIA v NEW ZEALAND Commonwealth Bank Series

at Melbourne Cricket Ground on 4 February, 2007 (d/n)
Toss : New Zealand. Umpires : Asad Rauf & S.J. Davis
Australia won by 5 wickets.

After Fleming went early, Vincent and Fulton broke the New Zealand second wicket record against Australia adding 151. Their partnership came from 171 balls. Vincent got fifty from 64 balls, four balls faster than Fulton. New Zealand ended with 290-7.

Australia were in some trouble at 112-3 but then Ponting and Hodge added 154 for the fourth wicket. Ponting got fifty from 57 balls and his century came from 105 deliveries. Hodge made his fifty off 58 balls and was left on 99 not out when Australia won with ten balls to spare.

NEW ZEALAND

	Runs	Mins	Balls	6s	4s
L.Vincent b Tait	90	160	113	1	6
S.P.Fleming* c Hussey b Lee	9	14	11	-	1
P.G.Fulton lbw b Clarke	60	134	81	-	4
L.R.P.L.Taylor b Clarke	21	47	31	-	1
S.B.Styris c Hussey b Clark	34	53	36	-	2
J.D.P.Oram c Hodge b Lee	15	13	9	1	1
B.B.McCullum† b Clark	19	27	14	-	1
D.L.Vettori not out	3	9	4	-	-
J.E.C.Franklin not out	13	4	5	1	-
M.R.Gillespie					
S.E.Bond					
Extras (b 2, lb 11, w 9, nb 4)	26				
TOTAL (50 overs) (7 wkts)	**290**	230			

AUSTRALIA

	Runs	Mins	Balls	6s	4s
A.C.Gilchrist† b Franklin	29	46	28	-	4
M.L.Hayden c Taylor b Franklin	28	63	44	-	2
R.T.Ponting* c Vincent b Gillespie	104	171	113	1	6
M.J.Clarke c McCullum b Vettori	9	45	20	-	-
B.J.Hodge not out	99	123	86	1	7
M.E.K.Hussey run out	8	9	5	-	1
C.L.White not out	1	5	1	-	-
B.Lee					
M.G.Johnson					
S.R.Clark					
S.W.Tait					
Extras (lb 1, w 3, nb 9)	13				
TOTAL (48.2 overs) (5 wkts)	**291**	219			

Bowling	*O*	*M*	*R*	*W*
AUSTRALIA				
Lee	10	0	71	2
Tait	10	1	26	1
Clark	10	1	61	2
Johnson	7	0	48	0
Clarke	9	0	45	2
White	4	0	26	0
NEW ZEALAND				
Franklin	10	0	56	2
Bond	9	0	64	0
Gillespie	8.2	0	45	1
Oram	5	0	44	0
Vettori	10	0	55	1
Styris	6	0	26	0

Fall of Wickets	***NZ***	***A***
1st	12	56
2nd	163	65
3rd	188	112
4th	212	266
5th	233	279
6th	269	-
7th	275	-
8th	-	-
9th	-	-
10th	-	-

NEW ZEALAND v ENGLAND — Commonwealth Bank Series

at Woolloongabba, Brisbane on 6 February, 2007 (d/n)
Toss : England. Umpires : D.J. Harper & I.L. Howell
England won by 14 runs.

The winner of this game would play Australia in the final. England lost three early wickets before Strauss and Collingwood put on 103 for the fourth wicket. Strauss got fifty off 51 balls with Collingwood requiring 68 balls. His century came from 118 balls.

New Zealand had a good start with an 81 run opening partnership. Fleming got fifty off 72 balls and his century from 138 balls but the innings lost momentum when Taylor was run out.

New Zealand went from 203-3 to 232-8 and ended up 14 runs short of England who qualified for the final series and went on to beat Australia 2-0.

ENGLAND

	Runs	Mins	Balls	6s	4s
E.C.Joyce c McCullum b Franklin	26	68	40	-	4
M.P.Vaughan* b Bond	0	6	1	-	-
I.R.Bell c Styris b Bond	12	33	28	-	2
A.J.Strauss b Styris	55	120	63	1	3
P.D.Collingwood b Bond	106	164	121	-	8
A.Flintoff c Franklin b Bond	17	31	15	-	2
J.W.M.Dalrymple not out	29	51	26	-	2
P.A.Nixon† b Gillespie	0	3	2	-	-
L.E.Plunkett not out	15	7	7	-	2
S.I.Mahmood					
M.S.Panesar					
Extras (lb 4, w 3, nb 3)	10				
TOTAL (50 overs) (7 wkts)	**270**	241			

NEW ZEALAND

	Runs	Mins	Balls	6s	4s
L.Vincent c Flintoff b Panesar	31	72	32	-	3
S.P.Fleming* c Nixon b Flintoff	106	141	149	-	11
P.G.Fulton c Bell b Plunkett	12	41	30	-	1
L.R.P.L.Taylor run out	25	55	27	-	1
S.B.Styris c Panesar b Collingwood	16	36	20	-	-
J.D.P.Oram c Nixon b Plunkett	5	6	7	-	1
B.B.McCullum† b Plunkett	2	10	6	-	-
D.L.Vettori c Vaughan b Collingwood	10	9	7	-	2
J.E.C.Franklin not out	22	24	12	-	3
S.E.Bond not out	8	18	10	-	-
M.R.Gillespie					
Extras (b 1, lb 3, w 15)	19				
TOTAL (50 overs) (8 wkts)	**256**	214			

Bowling	*O*	*M*	*R*	*W*
NEW ZEALAND				
Franklin	8	1	45	1
Bond	10	2	46	4
Gillespie	10	0	52	1
Oram	7	0	36	0
Vettori	6	0	37	0
Styris	9	0	50	1
ENGLAND				
Plunkett	10	0	60	3
Mahmood	10	0	62	0
Flintoff	10	3	37	1
Collingwood	10	0	46	2
Panesar	8	1	38	1
Dalrymple	2	0	9	0

Fall of Wickets

	E	*NZ*
1st	1	81
2nd	28	107
3rd	52	169
4th	155	203
5th	191	208
6th	250	212
7th	251	224
8th	-	232
9th	-	-
10th	-	-

9th February 2007 (First Final)
Melbourne: **England beat Australia by 4 wickets**
Australia 252 (48.3 overs) (M.L.Hayden 82, R.T.Ponting 75, M.J.Clarke 33, A.Flintoff 3-41);
England 253 for 6 (49.3 overs) (P.D.Collingwood 120*, I.R.Bell 65, A.Flintoff 35, B.Lee 3-41)

11th February 2007 (Second Final)
Sydney: **England beat Australia by 34 runs**
England 246 for 8 (50 overs) (P.D.Collingwood 70, M.B.Loye 45, A.Flintoff 42);
Australia 152 for 8 (27 overs) (B.J.Hodge 49, S.R.Watson 37, L.E.Plunkett 3-43)

AUSTRALIA IN NEW ZEALAND

New Zealand won the Chappell-Hadlee series by defeating Australia 3-0 in one of the most memorable series seen in New Zealand.

The first game in Wellington saw New Zealand dismiss Australia for 148 and then openers Vincent and Fleming hit the runs off with an unbroken record partnership for New Zealand against Australia. In the next two games, New Zealand scored record targets when chasing victories. They surpassed the 332 scored at Christchurch in 2005/06 by getting 340 at Auckland and then 350 at Hamilton. These are the second and third highest winning totals batting second in all one-day internationals.

Four centuries were scored in the series, Michael Hussey scored 105 at Auckland with Ross Taylor getting 117 in the same match, while at Hamilton Matthew Hayden scored an unbeaten 181, the highest score by an Australian in a one-day international. Craig McMillan scored 117 in the New Zealand chase.

Wickets were hard to achieve, but Shane Bond took 5-23 at Wellington, his fourth five wicket bag, for the figures of the series.

Australia rested Ponting and Gilchrist for the series and Symonds was injured. However Clarke had come over under an injury cloud and never played while Lee injured his ankle the day before the Wellington game. Both players returned home to Australia for treatment. Lee was to be ruled unfit for the World Cup.

The Australian party was: M.E.K. Hussey *(captain)*; M.J. Clarke *(vice-captain)*, N.W. Bracken, B.J. Haddin, M.L. Hayden, B.J. Hodge, G.B. Hogg, P.A. Jaques, M.G. Johnson, B. Lee, G.D. McGrath, S.W. Tait, A.C. Voges, S.R. Watson, C.L. White. Coach, J.M. Buchanan; Manager, S.R. Bernard.

Tait replaced Lee while Jaques had travelled to New Zealand as cover for Clarke.

New Zealand Averages

BATTING	*M*	*I*	*NO*	*HS*	*Agg*	*Ave*	*100s*	*50s*	*Ct*	*St*	*SR*
P.G. Fulton	2	2	1	76*	127	127.00	-	2	-	-	120
C.D. McMillan	3	2	0	117	169	84.50	1	1	-	-	134
L.R.P.L. Taylor	3	2	0	117	128	64.00	1	-	2	-	92
L. Vincent	3	3	1	73*	110	55.00	-	1	1	-	86
S.P. Fleming	3	3	1	70*	85	42.50	-	1	3	-	90
M.R. Gillespie	3	1	0	28	28	28.00	-	-	-	-	186
S.B. Styris	3	2	0	17	17	8.50	-	-	1	-	53
D.R. Tuffey	3	1	0	8	8	8.00	-	-	-	-	100
J.E.C. Franklin	1	1	0	2	2	2.00	-	-	-	-	40
B.B. McCullum	3	2	2	86*	108	-	-	1	1	-	104
J.S. Patel	1	1	1	0*	0	-	-	-	-	-	0
D.L. Vettori	2	-	-	-	-	-	-	-	3	-	-
J.D.P. Oram	1	-	-	-	-	-	-	-	1	-	-
S.E. Bond	2	-	-	-	-	-	-	-	2	-	-

BOWLING	*O*	*M*	*R*	*W*	*Ave*	*Best*	*R/O*
S.E. Bond	18.3	6	62	6	10.33	5-23	3.35
D.L. Vettori	19	1	80	3	26.66	2-26	4.21
M.R. Gillespie	29	2	167	5	33.40	2-27	5.76
J.S. Patel	10	0	70	2	35.00	2-70	7.00
C.D. McMillan	9	0	75	2	37.50	1-3	8.33
D.R. Tuffey	28	0	177	1	177.00	1-68	6.32
J.D.P. Oram	10	0	22	0	-	-	2.20
L. Vincent	2	0	22	0	-	-	11.00
J.E.C. Franklin	10	0	43	0	-	-	4.30
S.B. Styris	14	0	101	0	-	-	7.21

Australia Averages

BATTING	*M*	*I*	*NO*	*HS*	*Agg*	*Ave*	*100s*	*50s*	*Ct*	*St*	*SR*
M.L. Hayden	3	3	1	181*	219	109.50	1	-	-	-	90
B.J. Hodge	3	3	1	97*	131	65.50	-	1	2	-	90
M.E.K. Hussey	3	3	0	105	160	53.33	1	-	4	-	85
S.R. Watson	3	2	0	68	76	38.00	-	1	-	-	75
C.L. White	3	3	1	42*	68	34.00	-	-	-	-	151
B.J. Haddin	3	3	0	49	93	31.00	-	-	3	-	95
G.B. Hogg	3	1	0	20	20	20.00	-	-	-	-	86
M.G. Johnson	2	1	0	8	8	8.00	-	-	-	-	44
P.A. Jaques	2	2	0	3	4	2.00	-	-	1	-	16
N.W. Bracken	3	1	0	0	0	0.00	-	-	1	-	0
A.C. Voges	1	1	1	16*	16	-	-	-	1	-	160
G.D. McGrath	2	1	1	5*	5	-	-	-	-	-	85
S.W. Tait	2	-	-	-	-	-	-	-	-	-	

BOWLING	*O*	*M*	*R*	*W*	*Ave*	*Best*	*R/O*
S.R. Watson	24	0	174	5	34.80	3-58	7.25
M.G. Johnson	18	0	130	3	43.33	3-81	7.22
N.W. Bracken	26.3	2	140	3	46.66	2-66	5.28
S.W. Tait	19	0	124	2	62.00	2-60	6.53
C.L. White	3	0	29	0	-	-	9.67
A.C. Voges	3	0	33	0	-	-	11.00
G.D. McGrath	15.4	1	76	0	-	-	4.85
G.B. Hogg	16	0	114	0	-	-	7.13

NEW ZEALAND v AUSTRALIA — First One-day International

at Westpac Stadium, Wellington on 16 February, 2007 (d/n)
Toss : New Zealand. Umpires : Aleem Dar & B.F. Bowden
New Zealand won by 10 wickets.

New Zealand won the toss and decided to bowl first. In the second over Jaques went and worse was to follow for Australia when Haddin was dismissed in the fourth over. Bond had his best spell of the season and troubled all the batsmen, finishing with 5-23. Oram broke his finger taking the catch that dismissed Johnson.

Vincent and Fleming were in no trouble against the Australian bowlers. Vincent got fifty from 61 balls, one ball faster than Fleming. The century partnership came from 130 balls as they broke the first wicket record for New Zealand against Australia in one-day internationals and gave New Zealand a 1-0 lead in the three match series.

AUSTRALIA

	Runs	Mins	Balls	6s	4s
M.L.Hayden c Fleming b Gillespie	14	77	39	-	2
P.A.Jaques c Vettori b Bond	1	7	8	-	-
B.J.Haddin† b Bond	6	8	5	-	1
M.E.K.Hussey* c Taylor b McMillan	42	135	96	-	4
B.J.Hodge c Fleming b Vettori	22	62	49	-	2
C.L.White c & b Bond	13	29	18	-	-
S.R.Watson c Bond b Vettori	8	32	32	-	-
G.B.Hogg b Bond	20	46	23	-	2
M.G.Johnson c Oram b Gillespie	8	16	8	-	1
N.W.Bracken b Bond	0	3	4	-	-
G.D.McGrath not out	5	10	6	-	-
Extras (b 1, lb 2, w 5, nb 1)	9				
TOTAL (49.3 overs)	**148**	217			

NEW ZEALAND

	Runs	Mins	Balls	6s	4s
L.Vincent not out	73	117	87	2	8
S.P.Fleming* not out	70	117	76	2	8
L.R.P.L.Taylor					
S.B.Styris					
J.D.P.Oram					
C.D.McMillan					
B.B.McCullum†					
D.L.Vettori					
S.E.Bond					
M.R.Gillespie					
D.R.Tuffey					
Extras (lb 3, w 2, nb 1)	6				
TOTAL (27 overs) (0 wkts)	**149**	117			

Bowling	*O*	*M*	*R*	*W*
NEW ZEALAND				
Tuffey	8	0	29	0
Bond	9.3	2	23	5
Oram	10	0	22	0
Gillespie	9	0	27	2
Vettori	9	1	26	2
Styris	2	0	15	0
McMillan	2	0	3	1
AUSTRALIA				
McGrath	6	1	23	0
Bracken	7	1	30	0
Johnson	8	0	49	0
Watson	4	0	28	0
Hogg	2	0	16	0

Fall of Wickets

	A	*NZ*
1st	3	-
2nd	16	-
3rd	45	-
4th	86	-
5th	98	-
6th	108	-
7th	120	-
8th	133	-
9th	133	-
10th	148	-

NEW ZEALAND v AUSTRALIA Second One-day International

at Eden Park, Auckland on 18 February, 2007
Toss : New Zealand. Umpires : Aleem Dar & A.L. Hill
New Zealand won by 5 wickets.

Fulton came into the New Zealand squad and replaced the injured Oram. Tait replaced Johnson for Australia.

Fleming again decided to field but the bowlers struggled, despite taking two early wickets. Australia reached the highest one-day score recorded at Eden Park. Hussey and Hodge added 130 for the fourth wicket off 101 balls. Hussey got his fifty from 52 balls and raced to a century from 81 deliveries. Hodge got fifty from 50 balls and was stranded on 97 at the end of the innings.

Fleming went in the third over and Vincent soon followed. Taylor then delighted the big crowd with some lovely shots going to fifty off 53 balls and then getting his second century from 102 deliveries. Fulton scored fifty from 49 balls and McMillan played a cameo, getting a 27 ball half-century. New Zealand won an enthralling game with eight balls to spare and took an unbeatable 2-0 lead in the series.

AUSTRALIA

	Runs	Mins	Balls	6s	4s
M.L.Hayden c Vettori b Gillespie	24	58	36	-	5
P.A.Jaques c Fleming b Bond	3	27	16	-	-
B.J.Haddin† c & b Vettori	49	76	61	2	5
M.E.K.Hussey* c Taylor b McMillan	105	123	84	6	8
B.J.Hodge not out	97	100	86	2	10
C.L.White not out	42	32	19	3	3
S.R.Watson					
G.B.Hogg					
N.W.Bracken					
G.D.McGrath					
S.W.Tait					
Extras (b 1, lb 5, w 8, nb 2)	16				
TOTAL (50 overs) (4 wkts) .	**336**	215			

NEW ZEALAND

	Runs	Mins	Balls	6s	4s
L.Vincent c Jaques b Bracken ..	26	37	27	1	2
S.P.Fleming* c Haddin b Bracken	6	9	7	-	1
L.R.P.L.Taylor c Hussey b Watson	117	157	127	1	16
S.B.Styris c Hussey b Watson ..	17	49	25	-	2
P.G.Fulton not out	76	136	65	2	5
C.D.McMillan c Hussey b Watson	52	40	30	2	7
B.B.McCullum† not out	22	15	12	1	1
D.L.Vettori					
M.R.Gillespie					
S.E.Bond					
D.R.Tuffey					
Extras (b 1, lb 11, w 10, nb 2)	24				
TOTAL (48.4 overs) (5 wkts)	**340**	224			

Bowling	*O*	*M*	*R*	*W*
NEW ZEALAND				
Tuffey	10	0	80	0
Bond	9	4	39	1
Gillespie	10	2	57	1
Vettori	10	0	54	1
Styris	4	0	34	0
McMillan	5	0	44	1
Vincent	2	0	22	0
AUSTRALIA				
Bracken	10	1	66	2
McGrath	9.4	0	53	0
Tait	9	0	64	0
Watson	10	0	58	3
Hogg	7	0	58	0
White	3	0	29	0

Fall of Wickets	***A***	***NZ***
1st	26	9
2nd	52	47
3rd	122	113
4th	252	228
5th	-	313
6th	-	-
7th	-	-
8th	-	-
9th	-	-
10th	-	-

NEW ZEALAND v AUSTRALIA — Third One-day International

at Westpac Park, Hamilton on 20 February, 2007 (d/n)
Toss : Australia. Umpires : Aleem Dar & G.A. Baxter
New Zealand won by 1 wicket.

Vettori and Bond were rested and replaced by Patel and Franklin. Voges made his debut for Australia. Australia won the toss and batted and reached 100 off 124 balls. Then the onslaught started as Hayden got fifty from 82 balls, a century from 127 balls and his 150 from 153 balls.

It was the highest score made by an Australian in one-day internationals. All the New Zealand bowlers suffered as Hayden hit 10 sixes in his innings. He broke a toe when Gillespie hit him on the foot and batted for the latter part of his innings with a runner.

New Zealand were in dire straits at 41-4 but then Fulton got fifty from 38 balls to set the New Zealand innings in motion. McMillan and McCullum set a New Zealand sixth wicket partnership against all countries when they added 165 off 147 balls. McMillan scored fifty from 39 balls and then hit New Zealand's fastest century from just 67 balls. It was his third century and his highest score.

McCullum got fifty from 66 balls and then went to his highest score. Gillespie hit a quick fire 28 and McCullum hit a six and a four in the last over to give the BlackCaps a 3-0 win with three balls to spare. It was the highest match total in New Zealand and the BlackCaps' highest score batting second.

AUSTRALIA

	Runs	Mins	Balls	6s	4s
M.L.Hayden not out	181	227	166	10	1
S.R.Watson lbw b Patel	68	104	69	-	8
B.J.Haddin† c Vincent b Tuffey	38	65	31	1	4
B.J.Hodge b Patel	12	17	10	1	-
M.E.K.Hussey* c McCullum b Gillespie	13	13	8	1	-
C.L.White c Styris b Gillespie	13	8	8	2	-
A.C.Voges not out	16	15	10	1	-
G.B.Hogg					
N.W.Bracken					
M.G.Johnson					
S.W.Tait					
Extras (b 1, lb 1, w 1, nb 2)	5				
TOTAL (50 overs) (5 wkts)	**346**	227			

NEW ZEALAND

	Runs	Mins	Balls	6s	4s
L.Vincent c Hodge b Tait	11	25	13	-	2
S.P.Fleming* c Hodge b Tait	9	15	11	-	2
L.R.P.L.Taylor c & b Bracken	11	15	12	-	1
S.B.Styris c Haddin b Johnson	0	18	7	-	-
P.G.Fulton c Hussey b Watson	51	48	40	3	6
C.D.McMillan b Watson	117	138	96	5	13
B.B.McCullum† not out	86	149	91	2	5
J.E.C.Franklin c Voges b Johnson	2	6	5	-	-
D.R.Tuffey c Haddin b Johnson	8	11	8	-	1
M.R.Gillespie run out	28	20	15	-	3
J.S.Patel not out	0	4	0	-	-
Extras (lb 4, w 22, nb 1)	27				
TOTAL (49.3 overs) (9 wkts)	**350**	230			

Bowling	*O*	*M*	*R*	*W*
NEW ZEALAND				
Tuffey	10	0	68	1
Franklin	10	0	43	0
Gillespie	10	0	83	2
Patel	10	0	70	2
Styris	8	0	52	0
McMillan	2	0	28	0
AUSTRALIA				
Bracken	9.3	0	44	1
Tait	10	0	60	2
Johnson	10	0	81	3
Watson	10	0	88	2
Hogg	7	0	40	0
Voges	3	0	33	0

Fall of Wickets

	A	***NZ***
1st	122	23
2nd	210	34
3rd	251	38
4th	279	41
5th	302	116
6th	-	281
7th	-	285
8th	-	303
9th	-	339
10th	-	-

ICC WORLD CUP

New Zealand went to the World Cup in the West Indies buoyed by their performances in the Chappell-Hadlee series. However, the Australians bounced back to convincingly win the World Cup for an unprecedented third time in a row and their fourth in all.

New Zealand won their pool with wins over England, Kenya and Canada. In the Super Eights they started with wins over West Indies and the two surprise teams, Bangladesh and Ireland. Sri Lanka then defeated the BlackCaps who bounced back to defeat South Africa and guarantee themselves a place in the semi-finals. After losing to Australia by a record 215 runs, New Zealand then lost to Sri Lanka in the semi-final by 81 runs.

The final finished in confusion. After a rain interruption, the umpires recalled the players for three overs despite the minimum twenty having been bowled. The game ended in darkness.

Lou Vincent and Daryl Tuffey were replaced because of injury. Mark Gillespie suffered from a virus and struggled for fitness. Scott Styris was the BlackCaps' player of the tournament, scoring 499 runs and taking nine wickets. Stephen Fleming scored 353 runs and Peter Fulton 297. Daniel Vettori was the leading wicket-taker with 16 followed by Shane Bond 13, and James Franklin and Jacob Oram with 10.

The squad was: S.P. Fleming *(captain, Wellington)*, D.L. Vettori *(vice-captain, Northern Districts)*, S.E. Bond *(Canterbury)*, J.E.C. Franklin *(Wellington)*, P.G. Fulton *(Canterbury)*, M.R. Gillespie *(Wellington)*, B.B. McCullum *(Canterbury)*, C.D. McMillan *(Canterbury)*, H.J.H. Marshall *(Northern Districts)*, C.S. Martin *(Auckland)*, M.J. Mason *(Central Districts)*, J.D.P. Oram *(Central Districts)*, J.S. Patel *(Wellington)*, S.B. Styris *(Auckland)*, L.R.P.L. Taylor *(Central Districts)*, D.R. Tuffey *(Northern Districts)*, L. Vincent *(Auckland)*. Coach, J.G. Bracewell; Assistant coach/Video analyst, R.M. Carter; Bowling coach, D.R. Hadlee; Manager, L.M. Crocker; Physiotherapist, D.F. Shackel, Trainer, W. Frost, Sports psychologist, G.L. Hermansson. Marshall replaced Vincent and Martin replaced Tuffey.

New Zealand Averages

BATTING	*M*	*I*	*NO*	*HS*	*Agg*	*Ave*	*100s*	*50s*	*Ct*	*St*	*SR*
J.E.C Franklin	9	5	4	34*	95	95.00	-	-	2	-	98
S.B. Styris	10	9	3	111*	499	83.16	1	4	5	-	83
H.J.H. Marshall	3	3	1	50*	81	40.50	-	1	-	-	82
S.P. Fleming	10	10	1	102*	353	39.22	1	3	2	-	86
P.G. Fulton	8	8	0	83	297	37.12	-	2	1	-	70
J.S. Patel	6	2	1	34	34	34.00	-	-	1	-	87
L. Vincent	3	3	0	101	101	33.66	1	-	-	-	79
J.D.P. Oram	9	7	2	63*	165	33.00	-	1	5	-	70
C.D. McMillan	10	9	2	71	228	32.57	-	1	-	-	87
B.B. McCullum	10	7	2	52*	117	23.40	-	1	13	1	134
L.R.P.L. Taylor	6	6	0	85	107	17.83	-	1	1	-	67
D.L. Vettori	10	5	1	14*	28	7.00	-	-	2	-	96
S.E. Bond	8	2	1	2	2	2.00	-	-	3	-	50
M.R. Gillespie	2	1	0	2	2	2.00	-	-	1	-	25
M.J. Mason	5	1	0	0	0	0.00	-	-	2	-	0
D.R. Tuffey	1	-	-	-	-	-	-	-	-	-	

BOWLING	*O*	*M*	*R*	*W*	*Ave*	*Best*	*R/O*
S.E. Bond	69.4	9	213	13	16.38	3-31	3.05
J.D.P. Oram	62.3	7	252	10	25.20	3-23	4.03
S.B. Styris	57	3	242	9	26.88	4-43	4.25
D.L. Vettori	97.4	2	447	16	27.93	4-23	4.57
J.E.C. Franklin	65.2	7	331	11	30.09	3-74	5.06
J.S. Patel	54.2	2	245	7	35.00	3-25	4.50
C.D. McMillan	22.3	0	110	3	36.66	3-23	4.88
M.J. Mason	27.3	3	134	3	44.66	2-29	4.87
D.R. Tuffey	6	0	40	0	-	-	6.67
M.R. Gillespie	12.1	1	109	0	-	-	8.96

GROUP A

14th March 2007
Basseterre: **Australia beat Scotland by 203 runs**
Australia 334 for 6 (50 overs) (R.T.Ponting 113, M.L.Hayden 60, A.C.Gilchrist 46, G.B.Hogg 40*);
Scotland 131 (40.1 overs) (C.J.O.Smith 51, G.D.McGrath 3-14)

16th March 2007
Basseterre: **South Africa beat Netherlands by 221 runs**
South Africa 353 for 3 (40 overs) (J.H.Kallis 128*, M.V.Boucher 75*, H.H.Gibbs 72, G.C.Smith 67);
Netherlands 132 for 9 (40 overs) (R.N.ten Doeschate 57)

18th March 2007
Basseterre: **Australia beat Netherlands by 229 runs**
Australia 358 for 5 (50 overs) (B.J.Hodge 123, M.J.Clarke 93*, A.C.Gilchrist 57);
Netherlands 129 (26.5 overs) (D.L.S.van Bunge 33, G.B.Hogg 4-27)

20th March 2007
Basseterre: **South Africa beat Scotland by 7 wickets**
Scotland 186 for 8 (50 overs) (D.R.Brown 45*, R.R.Watson 31, A.J.Hall 3-48);
South Africa 188 for 3 (23.2 overs) (G.C.Smith 91, A.B.de Villiers 62)

22nd March 2007
Basseterre: **Netherlands beat Scotland by 8 wickets**
Scotland 136 (34.1 overs) (W.F.Stelling 3-12);
Netherlands 140 for 2 (23.5 overs) (R.N.ten Doeschate 70*, B.Zuiderent 43*)

24th March 2007
Basseterre: **Australia beat South Africa by 83 runs**
Australia 377 for 6 (50 overs) (M.L.Hayden 101, M.J.Clarke 92, R.T.Ponting 91, A.C.Gilchrist 42);
South Africa 294 (48 overs) (A.B.de Villiers 92, G.C.Smith 74, J.H.Kallis 48, G.B.Hogg 3-61)

Points: Australia 6, South Africa 4, Netherlands 2, Scotland 0.

GROUP B

15th March 2007
Port of Spain: **Sri Lanka beat Bermuda by 243 runs**
Sri Lanka 321 for 6 (50 overs) (D.P.M.D.Jayawardene 85, K.C.Sangakkara 76, L.P.C.Silva 55*, W.U.Tharanga 30);
Bermuda 78 (24.4 overs) (M.F.Maharoof 4-23, S.L.Malinga 3-10)

17th March 2007
Port of Spain: **Bangladesh beat India by 5 wickets**
India 191 (49.3 overs) (S.C.Ganguly 66, Yuvraj Singh 47, Masrafe bin Mortaza 4-38, Mohammad Rafique 3-35, Abdur Razzaq 3-38);
Bangladesh 192 for 5 (48.3 overs) (Mushfiqur Rahim 56*, Saqibul Hasan 53, Tamim Iqbal 51)

19 March, 2007
Port of Spain: **India beat Bermuda by 257 runs**
India 413 for 5 (50 overs) (V.Sehwag 114, S.C.Ganguly 89, Yuvraj Singh 83, S.R.Tendulkar 57*);
Bermuda 156 (43.1 overs) (D.L.Hemp 76*, A.B.Agarkar 3-38, A.R.Kumble 3-38)

21st March 2007
Port of Spain: **Sri Lanka beat Bangladesh by 198 runs (D/L)**
Sri Lanka 318 for 4 (50 overs) (S.T.Jayasuriya 109, K.C.Sangakkara 56, L.P.C.Silva 52*, D.P.M.D.Jayawardene 46);
Bangladesh 112 (37 overs) (Mohammad Ashraful 45*, S.L.Malinga 3-27)

23rd March 2007
Port of Spain: **Sri Lanka beat India by 69 runs**
Sri Lanka 254 for 6 (50 overs) (W.U.Tharanga 64, L.P.C.Silva 59, T.M.Dilshan 38);
India 185 (43.3 overs) (R.S.Dravid 60, V.Sehwag 48, M.Muralitharan 3-41)

25th March 2007
Port of Spain: **Bangladesh beat Bermuda by 7 wickets (D/L)**
Bermuda 94 for 9 (21 overs) (Abdur Razzaq 3-20);
Bangladesh 96 for 3 (17.3 overs) (S.Mukuddem 3-19)

Points: Sri Lanka 6, Bangladesh 4, India 2, Bermuda 0.

GROUP C

14th March 2007
St Lucia: **Kenya beat Canada by 7 wickets**
Canada 199 (50 overs) (G.E.F.Barnett 41, I.S.Billcliff 34, S.Dhaniram 34*);
Kenya 203 for 3 (43.2 overs) (S.O.Tikolo 72*, M.A.Ouma 58, T.Mishra 35*)

18th March 2007
St Lucia: **England beat Canada by 51 runs**
England 279 for 6 (50 overs) (E.C.Joyce 66, P.D.Collingwood 62*, M.P.Vaughan 45, S.Dhaniram 3-41);
Canada 228 for 7 (50 overs) (A.A.Mulla 58, A.M.Samad 36, S.Dhaniram 30)

24th March 2007
St Lucia: **England beat Kenya by 7 wickets**
Kenya 177 (43 overs) (S.O.Tikolo 76);
England 178 for 3 (33 overs) (E.C.Joyce 75, K.P.Pietersen 56*)

Points: New Zealand 6, England 4, Kenya 2, Canada 0.

NEW ZEALAND v ENGLAND — World Cup – Group C

at Beausejour Stadium, Gros Islet, St Lucia on 16 March, 2007
Toss : New Zealand. Umpires : Asad Rauf & R.E. Koertzen
New Zealand won by 6 wickets.

Fulton, Mason, Tuffey and the injured Gillespie were omitted from the New Zealand squad. New Zealand had immediate success with Joyce being dismissed off the first legitimate ball of the innings. At 52-3 England needed a partnership and Pietersen and Collingwood added 81.

Pietersen reached fifty off 73 balls but England collapsed, going from 133-3 to 138-7, before Nixon and Plunkett added 71 for the eighth wicket, an England record against New Zealand.

The BlackCaps started poorly, being 19-3 and then 72-4 before Styris and Oram added an unbeaten 138 for the fifth wicket, a New Zealand record against England. Styris got his fifty from 70 balls, two balls slower than Oram, as New Zealand took the two vital points for their six wicket win.

ENGLAND

	Runs	Mins	Balls	6s	4s
E.C.Joyce c McCullum b Franklin	0	1	2	-	-
M.P.Vaughan* b Franklin	26	69	52	-	3
I.R.Bell c McCullum b Oram	5	38	19	-	-
K.P.Pietersen c Franklin b Bond	60	108	92	1	4
P.D.Collingwood c McCullum b Styris	31	72	54	-	2
A.Flintoff c Styris b Bond	0	8	1	-	-
J.W.M.Dalrymple c McCullum b Styris	3	14	12	-	-
P.A.Nixon† not out	42	57	41	-	5
L.E.Plunkett not out	29	46	34	1	1
J.M.Anderson					
M.S.Panesar					
Extras (lb 2, w 4, nb 7)	13				
TOTAL (50 overs) (7 wkts)	**209**	210			

NEW ZEALAND

	Runs	Mins	Balls	6s	4s
L.Vincent c Nixon b Anderson	0	4	6	-	-
S.P.Fleming* c Joyce b Anderson	7	25	1	-	1
L.R.P.L.Taylor c Flintoff b Plunkett	0	4	1	-	-
S.B.Styris not out	87	127	113	-	9
C.D.McMillan c Dalrymple b Panesar	27	52	34	-	3
J.D.P.Oram not out	63	118	83	1	4
B.B.McCullum†					
D.L.Vettori					
J.E.C.Franklin					
S.E.Bond					
J.S.Patel					
Extras (b 2, lb 11, w 11, nb 2)	26				
TOTAL (41 overs) (4 wkts)	**210**	167			

Bowling	*O*	*M*	*R*	*W*
NEW ZEALAND				
Franklin	9	0	43	2
Bond	10	1	19	2
Oram	6	0	25	1
Patel	8	0	42	0
Vettori	10	0	53	0
Styris	7	0	25	2
ENGLAND				
Anderson	8	0	39	2
Plunkett	7	0	43	1
Flintoff	8	1	17	0
Collingwood	3	0	20	0
Panesar	10	0	47	1
Dalrymple	4	0	29	0
Pietersen	1	0	2	0

Fall of Wickets	***E***	***NZ***
1st	1	1
2nd	30	3
3rd	52	19
4th	133	72
5th	133	-
6th	134	-
7th	138	-
8th	-	-
9th	-	-
10th	-	-

NEW ZEALAND v BANGLADESH

At Three Ws Oval, Bridgetown 6 March, 2007

New Zealand 226 (J.D.P. Oram 88, B.B. McCullum 46, Abdur Razzak 4-26, Masrafe bin Mortaza 4-44) **lost to Bangladesh** 230-8 (Tamim Iqbal 46, Javed Omer 45, Masrafe bin Mortaza 30*, D.L. Vettori 3-38) by 2 wickets

NEW ZEALAND v SRI LANKA

At Three Ws Oval, Bridgetown 9 March, 2007

New Zealand 285 (L. Vincent 70, S.P. Fleming 65, P.G. Fulton 59, L.R.P.L. Taylor 30) **defeated Sri Lanka** 267 (W.U. Tharanga 106, L.P.C. Silva 40, R.P. Arnold 32*) by 18 runs

NEW ZEALAND v KENYA

World Cup – Group C

at Beausejour Stadium, Gros Islet, St Lucia on 20 March, 2007
Toss : Kenya. Umpires : B.R. Doctrove & R.E. Koertzen
New Zealand won by 148 runs.

Mason replaced Patel in the New Zealand line-up. Vincent went to the fourth ball of the innings but then Fleming and Taylor added 105. Their hundred run stand came from 110 balls. Fleming got fifty from 53 balls and Taylor needed 80 deliveries.

Further fifties followed to Styris (56 balls) and McMillan (37 balls). Odoyo got his 100th one day wicket when he dismissed Oram. During the New Zealand innings Taylor injured a hamstring which would cause him to miss the next four games.

Kenya started disastrously being 8-2 in the sixth over and then 29-4. They never recovered, making 183 to give New Zealand a 148 run win

NEW ZEALAND

	Runs	Mins	Balls	6s	4s
L.Vincent c Tikolo b Odoyo	0	3	4	-	-
S.P.Fleming* run out	60	93	61	3	7
L.R.P.L.Taylor c & b Tikolo	85	146	107	1	8
S.B.Styris c Mishra b Onyango	63	92	62	3	3
C.D.McMillan c Tikolo b Ongondo	71	64	48	5	3
J.D.P.Oram b Odoyo	3	5	6	-	-
B.B.McCullum† c Varaiya b Ongondo	6	13	9	-	-
D.L.Vettori not out	14	7	7	-	2
J.E.C.Franklin not out	0	1	0	-	-
S.E.Bond					
M.J.Mason					
Extras (lb 3, w 21, nb 5)	29				
TOTAL (50 overs) (7 wkts)	**331**	216			

KENYA

	Runs	Mins	Balls	6s	4s
M.A.Ouma† run out	4	24	21	-	-
D.O.Obuya lbw b Mason	1	8	5	-	-
R.D.Shah c & b Vettori	71	138	89	2	8
S.O.Tikolo* c Vettori b Mason	7	28	16	-	1
T.Mishra c Fleming b Franklin	2	2	4	-	-
C.O.Obuya run out	21	46	31	-	-
T.M.Odoyo c Oram b Bond	42	94	67	1	4
J.K.Kamande b Vettori	12	21	15	1	-
L.N.Onyango run out	6	19	17	-	-
P.J.Ongondo c & b Franklin	4	27	21	-	-
H.A.Varaiya not out	1	16	16	-	-
Extras (lb 2, w 2, nb 8)	12				
TOTAL (49.2 overs)	**183**	215			

Bowling	*O*	*M*	*R*	*W*
KENYA				
Odoyo	10	0	55	2
Ongondo	10	0	64	2
Onyango	8	0	63	1
Kamande	9	0	61	0
Varaiya	7	0	40	0
Tikolo	6	0	45	1
NEW ZEALAND				
Mason	9	0	29	2
Bond	8	2	19	1
Franklin	7.2	2	20	2
McMillan	10	0	39	0
Vettori	10	0	45	2
Oram	5	0	29	0

Fall of Wickets	***NZ***	***K***
1st	0	4
2nd	105	8
3rd	192	26
4th	274	29
5th	280	76
6th	307	122
7th	321	149
8th	-	167
9th	-	179
10th	-	183

NEW ZEALAND v CANADA

World Cup – Group C

at Beausejour Stadium, Gros Islet, St Lucia on 22 March, 2007
Toss : Canada. Umpires : Asad Rauf & B.R. Doctrove
New Zealand won by 114 runs.

Fulton, Patel and Tuffey replaced Taylor (who was injured), Franklin and Bond. New Zealand had an opening stand of 142, with the hundred coming from 93 balls. Fleming got fifty from 53 balls and Vincent 55 deliveries. Vincent then went to his third one day hundred from 115 balls.

McCullum hit a whirlwind fifty from just 20 balls, a World Cup and New Zealand record, to give his side an imposing 363-5.

Canada started positively with an opening stand of 76 off 58 balls between Davison (fifty from 23 balls) and Central Districts player Barnett. Former New Zealand provincial player Billcliff got fifty from 55 balls but Canada went from 188-2 to 249 all out as Patel and Vettori both took three wickets.

This gave New Zealand a 114 run win and they finished top of Group C. Tuffey suffered a recurrence of the bicep injury which had caused him to miss the previous season. He was replaced by Chris Martin for the balance of the tournament.

NEW ZEALAND

	Runs	Mins	Balls	6s	4s
L.Vincent c & b Davison	101	178	117	1	9
S.P.Fleming* c Billcliff b Sandher	66	96	67	1	8
P.G.Fulton lbw b Sandher	47	50	47	1	4
S.B.Styris c Bagai b Samad	28	12	17	-	6
C.D.McMillan c Samad b Davison	10	4	6	-	1
J.D.P.Oram not out	35	36	27	3	-
B.B.McCullum† not out	52	27	21	5	1
D.L.Vettori					
D.R.Tuffey					
J.S.Patel					
M.J.Mason					
Extras (b 1, lb 5, w 17, nb 1)	24				
TOTAL (50 overs) (5 wkts)	**363**	207			

CANADA

	Runs	Mins	Balls	6s	4s
J.M.Davison* c & b Mason	52	44	31	1	9
G.E.F.Barnett c McCullum b Vettori	40	93	72	-	5
A.Bagai† b Vettori	37	95	64	-	3
I.S.Billcliff b Styris	50	57	56	-	4
A.M.Samad run out	9	18	17	-	1
A.A.Mulla lbw b Vettori	0	2	2	-	-
S.Dhaniram retired hurt	17	21	19	1	1
U.Bhatti b Patel	10	35	28	-	1
A.C.Cummins not out	9	20	8	-	1
K.T.Sandher b Patel	2	5	6	-	-
H.Osinde b Patel	0	1	1	-	-
Extras (b 4, lb 5, w 5, nb 9)	23				
TOTAL (49.2 overs)	**249**	203			

Bowling	*O*	*M*	*R*	*W*
CANADA				
Cummins	10	1	59	0
Bhatti	5.3	1	25	0
Samad	2.3	0	31	1
Osinde	4	0	45	0
Sandher	10	0	58	2
Davison	10	0	67	2
Dhaniram	8	0	72	0
NEW ZEALAND				
Tuffey	6	0	40	0
Mason	8	0	60	1
Oram	7	1	16	0
Patel	9.2	0	25	3
Vettori	10	0	57	3
Styris	6	0	21	1
McMillan	3	0	21	0

Fall of Wickets	***NZ***	***C***
1st	142	76
2nd	222	110
3rd	253	188
4th	266	201
5th	278	206
6th	-	207
7th	-	245
8th	-	249
9th	-	249
10th	-	-

Dhaniram retired hurt at 226-6

GROUP D

13th March 2007
Kingston: **West Indies beat Pakistan by 54 runs**
West Indies 241 for 9 (50 overs) (M.N.Samuels 63, R.R.Sarwan 49, B.C.Lara 37, D.R.Smith 32, Iftikhar Anjum 3-44);
Pakistan 187 (47.2 overs) (Shoaib Malik 62, Mohammad Yousuf 37, Inzamam-ul-Haq 36, D.R.Smith 3-36, D.J.Bravo 3-42)

15th March 2007
Kingston: **Ireland tied with Zimbabwe**
Ireland 221 for 9 (50 overs) (J.P.Bray 115*);
Zimbabwe 221 (50 overs) (S.Matsikenyeri 73*, V.Sibanda 67)

17th March 2007
Kingston: **Ireland beat Pakistan by 3 wickets (D/L)**
Pakistan 132 (45.4 overs) (W.B.Rankin 3-32);
Ireland 133 for 7 (41.4 overs) (N.J.O'Brien 72, Mohammad Sami 3-29)

19th March 2007
Kingston: **West Indies beat Zimbabwe by 6 wickets**
Zimbabwe 202 for 5 (50 overs) (S.C.Williams 70*, B.R.M.Taylor 50, E.Chigumbura 30*);
West Indies 204 for 4 (47.5 overs) (B.C.Lara 44*, C.H.Gayle 40, D.J.Bravo 37*)

21st March 2007
Kingston: **Pakistan beat Zimbabwe by 93 runs (D/L)**
Pakistan 349 (49.5 overs) (Imran Nazir 160, Inzamam-ul-Haq 37, Iftikhar Anjum 32, E.Chigumbura 3-50, G.B.Brent 3-68);
Zimbabwe 99 (19.1 overs) (Shahid Afridi 3-20)

23rd March 2007
Kingston: **West Indies beat Ireland by 8 wickets (D/L)**
Ireland 183 for 8 (48 overs) (J.P.Bray 41);
West Indies 190 for 2 (38.1 overs) (S.Chanderpaul 102*, R.R.Sarwan 36)

Points: West Indies 6, Ireland 3, Pakistan 2, Zimbabwe 1.

SUPER EIGHTS

27th March 2007
Antigua: **Australia beat West Indies by 103 runs**
Australia 322 for 6 (50 overs) (M.L.Hayden 158, M.J.Clarke 41, R.T.Ponting 35, S.R.Watson 33*);
West Indies 219 (45.3 overs) (B.C.Lara 77, D.Ramdin 52, G.D.McGrath 3-31, G.B.Hogg 3-56)

28th March 2007
Guyana: **South Africa beat Sri Lanka by 1 wicket**
Sri Lanka 209 (49.3 overs) (T.M.Dilshan 58, R.P.Arnold 50, C.K.Langeveldt 5-39);
South Africa 212 for 9 (48.2 overs) (J.H.Kallis 86, G.C.Smith 59, H.H.Gibbs 31, S.L.Malinga 4-54, M.Muralitharan 3-34)

30th March 2007
Guyana: **England beat Ireland by 48 runs**
England 266 for 7 (50 overs) (P.D.Collingwood 90, K.P.Pietersen 48, A.Flintoff 43, I.R.Bell 31);
Ireland 218 (48.1 overs) (N.J.O'Brien 63, A.R.White 38, W.T.S.Porterfield 31, A.Flintoff 4-43)

31st March 2007
Antigua: **Australia beat Bangladesh by 10 wickets**
Bangladesh 104 for 6 (25 overs) (G.D.McGrath 3-16);
Australia 106 for 0 (13.5 overs) (A.C.Gilchrist 59*, M.L.Hayden 47*)

1st April 2007
Guyana: **Sri Lanka beat West Indies by 113 runs**
Sri Lanka 303 for 5 (50 overs) (S.T.Jayasuriya 115, D.P.M.D.Jayawardene 82, T.M.Dilshan 39*);
West Indies 190 (44.3 overs) (S.Chanderpaul 76, R.R.Sarwan 44, S.T.Jayasuriya 3-38)

3rd April 2007
Guyana: **South Africa beat Ireland by 7 wickets (D/L)**
Ireland 152 for 8 (35 overs) (A.R.White 30, C.K.Langeveldt 3-41);
South Africa 165 for 3 (31.3 overs) (J.H.Kallis 66*, A.G.Prince 47*, G.C.Smith 41)

4th April 2007
Antigua: **Sri Lanka beat England by 2 runs**
Sri Lanka 235 (50 overs) (W.U.Tharanga 62, D.P.M.D.Jayawardene 56, S.I.Mahmood 4-50, A.Flintoff 3-35);
England 233 for 8 (50 overs) (K.P.Pietersen 58, R.S.Bopara 52, I.R.Bell 47, P.A.Nixon 42, C.R.D.Fernando 3-41)

7th April 2007
Guyana: **Bangladesh beat South Africa by 67 runs**
Bangladesh 251 for 8 (50 overs) (Mohammad Ashraful 87, Tamim Iqbal 38, Aftab Ahmed 35, A.Nel 5-45);
South Africa 184 (48.4 overs) (H.H.Gibbs 56*, J.H.Kallis 32, Abdur Razzaq 3-25)

8th April 2007
Antigua: **Australia beat England by 7 wickets**
England 247 (49.5 overs) (K.P.Pietersen 104, I.R.Bell 77, N.W.Bracken 3-33, S.W.Tait 3-41, G.D.McGrath 3-62);
Australia 248 for 3 (47.2 overs) (R.T.Ponting 86, M.J.Clarke 55*, M.L.Hayden 41)

10th April 2007
Grenada: **South Africa beat West Indies by 67 runs**
South Africa 356 for 4 (50 overs) (A.B.de Villiers 146, J.H.Kallis 81, H.H.Gibbs 61*, M.V.Boucher 52);
West Indies 289 for 9 (50 overs) (R.R.Sarwan 92, D.B.L.Powell 48*, D.S.Smith 33, C.H.Gayle 32)

11th April 2007
Bridgetown: **England beat Bangladesh by 4 wickets**
Bangladesh 143 (37.2 overs) (Saqibul Hasan 57*, M.S.Panesar 3-25, S.I.Mahmood 3-27);
England 147 for 6 (44.5 overs) (M.P.Vaughan 30)

13th April 2007
Bridgetown: **Australia beat Ireland by 9 wickets**
Ireland 91 (30 overs) (G.D.McGrath 3-17, S.W.Tait 3-39);
Australia 92 for 1 (12.2 overs) (A.C.Gilchrist 34, M.E.K.Hussey 30*)

15th April 2007
Bridgetown: **Ireland beat Bangladesh by 74 runs**
Ireland 243 for 7 (50 overs) (W.T.S.Porterfield 85, K.J.O'Brien 48, J.P.Bray 31, D.T.Johnston 30);
Bangladesh 169 (41.2 overs) (Mohammad Ashraful 35, Habibul Bashar 32)

16th April 2007
Grenada: **Australia beat Sri Lanka by 7 wickets**
Sri Lanka 226 (49.4 overs) (D.P.M.D.Jayawardene 72, L.P.C.Silva 64, N.W.Bracken 4-19);
Australia 232 for 3 (42.4 overs) (R.T.Ponting 66*, A.Symonds 63*, M.L.Hayden 41, A.C.Gilchrist 30)

17th April 2007
Bridgetown: **South Africa beat England by 9 wickets**
England 154 (48 overs) (A.J.Strauss 46, P.D.Collingwood 30, A.J.Hall 5-18, A.Nel 3-35);
South Africa 157 for 1 (19.2 overs) (G.C.Smith 89*, A.B.de Villiers 42)

18th April 2007
Grenada: **Sri Lanka beat Ireland by 8 wickets**
Ireland 77 (27.4 overs) (M.Muralitharan 4-19, M.F.Maharoof 4-25);
Sri Lanka 81 for 2 (10 overs) (D.P.M.D.Jayawardene 39*)

19th April 2007
Bridgetown: **West Indies beat Bangladesh by 99 runs**
West Indies 230 for 5 (50 overs) (R.R.Sarwan 91*, S.Chanderpaul 50, B.C.Lara 33, M.N.Samuels 31);
Bangladesh 131 (43.5 overs) (Mushfiqur Rahim 38*, Masrafe bin Mortaza 37, D.B.L.Powell 3-38)

21st April 2007
Bridgetown: **England beat West Indies by 1 wicket**
West Indies 300 (49.5 overs) (C.H.Gayle 79, D.S.Smith 61, M.N.Samuels 51, S.Chanderpaul 34, M.P.Vaughan 3-39);
England 301 for 9 (49.5 overs) (K.P.Pietersen 100, M.P.Vaughan 79, P.A.Nixon 38)

Points: Australia 14, Sri Lanka 10, New Zealand 10, South Africa 8, England 6, West Indies 4, Bangladesh 2, Ireland 2.

WEST INDIES v NEW ZEALAND — World Cup – Super Eights

at Sir Vivian Richards Stadium, Antigua on 29 March, 2007
Toss : New Zealand. Umpires : Asad Rauf & R.E. Koertzen
New Zealand won by 7 wickets.

Vincent had broken a bone in his hand facing Shane Bond at practice and was replaced by Hamish Marshall who was immediately brought into the side. Franklin and Bond replaced Patel and Tuffey.

Chanderpaul went early and, apart from a 52 run stand for the second wicket, there was no real substance to the hosts' batting, and they were dismissed for 177. Bond, Oram and Vettori all bowled well, getting three wickets each.

Replacement opener Fulton went second ball but an unbeaten stand of 102 for the fourth wicket between Styris and McMillan took New Zealand to a comfortable win. Their hundred partnership came from 110 balls with Styris getting his third fifty of the competition off 72 balls.

WEST INDIES

	Runs	Mins	Balls	6s	4s
C.H.Gayle b Oram	44	96	56	-	8
S.Chanderpaul c Styris b Bond	4	31	28	-	-
R.R.Sarwan c McCullum b Oram	19	35	27	-	2
M.N.Samuels c McCullum b Oram	9	16	18	-	1
B.C.Lara* c McCullum b Styris	37	65	49	-	1
D.J.Bravo c McCullum b Bond	18	40	30	-	-
D.Ramdin† c Oram b Vettori	15	32	22	-	2
L.M.P.Simmons not out	14	34	26	-	2
D.R.Smith b Vettori	8	8	6	1	-
D.B.L.Powell lbw b Vettori	0	2	1	-	-
C.D.Collymore b Bond	0	3	5	-	-
Extras (b 1, lb 5, w 3)	9				
TOTAL (44.4 overs)	**177**	190			

NEW ZEALAND

	Runs	Mins	Balls	6s	4s
P.G.Fulton b Powell	0	2	2	-	-
S.P.Fleming* run out	45	96	66	1	6
H.J.H.Marshall c Lara b Powell	15	31	23	-	2
S.B.Styris not out	80	139	90	-	7
C.D.McMillan not out	33	77	57	-	3
J.D.P.Oram					
B.B.McCullum†					
D.L.Vettori					
J.E.C.Franklin					
S.E.Bond					
M.J.Mason					
Extras (lb 1, w 3, nb 2)	6				
TOTAL (39.2 overs) (3 wkts)	**179**	175			

Bowling	*O*	*M*	*R*	*W*
NEW ZEALAND				
Mason	6	2	14	0
Bond	8.4	0	31	3
Franklin	3	0	29	0
Oram	8	2	23	3
Styris	10	1	35	1
Vettori	9	1	39	3
WEST INDIES				
Powell	10	2	39	2
Smith	5	0	24	0
Collymore	9	0	43	0
Bravo	8	0	32	0
Gayle	6.2	0	35	0
Sarwan	1	0	5	0

Fall of Wickets	***WI***	***NZ***
1st	14	0
2nd	66	36
3rd	78	77
4th	81	-
5th	128	-
6th	150	-
7th	158	-
8th	176	-
9th	176	-
10th	177	-

NEW ZEALAND v BANGLADESH World Cup – Super Eights

at Sir Vivian Richards Stadium, Antigua on 2 April, 2007
Toss : New Zealand. Umpires : Aleem Dar & R.E. Koertzen
New Zealand won by 9 wickets.

New Zealand were unchanged for this game. Bangladesh made a steady start but Mason was injured after bowling just nine balls. Bangladesh sufered a collapse, going from 105-2 to 140-9, before a 34 run stand for the last wicket gave them some hope. Styris, with 4-43, and Vettori, who took 3-30, were the best bowlers.

Fulton went at 44 but then Fleming and Marshall put on an unbroken stand of 134 for the second wicket. The New Zealand captain got fifty from 61 balls and reached his eighth hundred from 90 balls. When he reached 100 he had scored 1000 runs in World Cup games. Marshall got his half-century off 54 balls as New Zealand won with 20.4 overs to spare.

BANGLADESH

	Runs	Mins	Balls	6s	4s
Javed Omer c McCullum b Oram	22	79	51	-	3
Tamim Iqbal st McCullum b Oram	29	69	54	-	4
Aftab Ahmed c sub b Styris	27	43	39	-	3
Saqibul Hasan b Bond	25	61	41	-	1
Habibul Bashar* run out	9	16	21	-	-
Mohammad Ashraful b Styris	3	19	8	-	-
Mushfiqur Rahim† b Bond	0	2	5	-	-
Masrafe bin Mortaza b Styris	2	23	16	-	-
Mohammad Rafique not out	30	42	36	2	1
Abdur Razzaq c sub (M.R.Gillespie) b Styris	0	1	2	-	-
Syed Rasel b Oram	10	22	18	-	1
Extras (b 5, lb 10, w 2)	17				
TOTAL (48.3 overs)	**174**	197			

NEW ZEALAND

	Runs	Mins	Balls	6s	4s
P.G.Fulton c Tamim b Rasel	15	41	30	-	2
S.P.Fleming* not out	102	118	92	3	10
H.J.H.Marshall not out	50	76	54	1	2
S.B.Styris					
C.D.McMillan					
J.D.P.Oram					
B.B.McCullum †					
D.L.Vettori					
J.E.C.Franklin					
S.E.Bond					
M.J.Mason					
Extras (w 11)	11				
TOTAL (29.2 overs) (1 wkt)	**178**	118			

Bowling	*O*	*M*	*R*	*W*
NEW ZEALAND				
Mason	1.3	1	4	0
Bond	10	4	15	2
McMillan	1.3	0	6	0
Franklin	6	1	27	0
Oram	9.3	0	30	3
Vettori	10	0	34	0
Styris	10	1	43	4
BANGLADESH				
Mortaza	6	0	41	0
Rasel	7	0	22	1
Razzaq	8	0	38	0
Rafique	5	0	37	0
Saqibul	3	0	33	0
Ashraful	0.2	0	7	0

Fall of Wickets	***B***	***NZ***
1st	55	44
2nd	62	-
3rd	105	-
4th	122	-
5th	127	-
6th	127	-
7th	129	-
8th	140	-
9th	140	-
10th	174	-

NEW ZEALAND v IRELAND

World Cup – Super Eights

at Providence Stadium, Guyana on 9 April, 2007
Toss : New Zealand. Umpires : S.A. Bucknor & S.J.A. Taufel
New Zealand won by 129 runs.

Patel replaced the injured Mason for New Zealand. New Zealand gave a steady batting display, with Fulton reaching fifty off 66 balls. There were two rain interruptions but they did not shorten the innings.

At the end of the innings McCullum and Franklin had added 71 off 43 balls to get the score to a respectable 263-8.

Bond struck early and only the O'Brien brothers made any headway. An unfortunate run out saw Ireland go from 110-3 to 134 all out in the space of nine overs as New Zealand virtually assured themselves of a place in the semi-final.

NEW ZEALAND

	Runs	Mins	Balls	6s	4s
P.G.Fulton lbw b McCallan	83	160	110	-	9
S.P.Fleming* c Porterfield b Rankin	10	26	11	-	1
H.J.H.Marshall c Morgan b Langford-Smith	16	21	21	-	2
S.B.Styris c O'Brien N.J. b Langford-Smith	10	25	15	-	1
C.D.McMillan c Johnston b McCallan	22	29	29	1	1
J.D.P.Oram c Morgan b White	20	78	48	-	-
B.B.McCullum† c Morgan b Johnston	47	49	37	1	2
D.L.Vettori c O'Brien N.J. b White	5	6	7	-	-
J.E.C.Franklin not out	34	31	22	1	3
S.E.Bond not out	0	1	0	-	-
J.S.Patel					
Extras (b 3, lb 1, w 12)	16				
TOTAL (50 overs) (8 wkts)	**263**	217			

IRELAND

	Runs	Mins	Balls	6s	4s
W.T.S.Porterfield c Styris b Bond	11	32	22	-	-
J.P.Bray c McCullum b Bond	1	7	5	-	-
E.J.G.Morgan c McCullum b Oram	15	46	37	-	2
N.J.O'Brien† c Oram b Patel	30	109	75	-	2
K.J.O'Brien run out	49	67	45	6	2
D.T.Johnston* lbw b Patel	13	27	19	-	1
A.R.White lbw b Vettori	0	2	4	-	-
P.G.Gillespie lbw b Vettori	2	8	8	-	-
W.K.McCallan b Vettori	0	9	8	-	-
D.Langford-Smith not out	0	6	4	-	-
W.B.Rankin lbw b Vettori	0	2	1	-	-
Extras (lb 3, w 8, nb 2)	13				
TOTAL (37.4 overs)	**134**	166			

Bowling	*O*	*M*	*R*	*W*
IRELAND				
Langford-Smith	10	1	41	2
Rankin	8	0	55	1
Johnston	10	0	63	1
McCallan	10	0	35	2
White	10	0	45	2
O'Brien K.J.	2	0	20	0
NEW ZEALAND				
Franklin	8	1	27	0
Bond	5	0	18	2
Oram	6	2	15	1
Patel	7	1	32	2
Vettori	8.4	1	23	4
Styris	3	0	16	0

Fall of Wickets	***NZ***	***I***
1st	35	5
2nd	59	22
3rd	83	35
4th	118	110
5th	172	125
6th	181	127
7th	189	133
8th	260	133
9th	-	134
10th	-	134

NEW ZEALAND v SRI LANKA — World Cup – Super Eights

at National Cricket Stadium, Grenada on 12 April, 2007
Toss : New Zealand. Umpires : Asad Rauf & B.R. Doctrove
Sri Lanka won by 6 wickets.

Taylor and Gillespie were now fit and came into the side for Patel and Marshall. There was a disastrous start for New Zealand as they lost two wickets for just four runs to Vaas. This slowed the tempo of the innings considerably.

Styris held the innings together. He got another fifty from 82 balls and reached his fourth one-day hundred after 152 balls. He also reached 3000 one-day runs. He and Franklin added an unbeaten 64 off 55 balls at the close. Vaas and Muralitharan were the pick of the bowlers.

Sri Lanka started positively. Jayasuriya and Sangakkara added 100 off 128 balls for the second wicket. Jayasuriya got fifty from 65 balls, 21 balls faster than Sangakkara. Vettori took his 200th wicket in one-day internationals but the BlackCaps were beaten for the first time in the tournament, with 29 balls to spare.

NEW ZEALAND

	Runs	Mins	Balls	6s	4s
P.G.Fulton c Silva b Vaas	28	92	54	-	4
S.P.Fleming* lbw b Vaas	0	3	4	-	-
L.R.P.L.Taylor c Sangakkara b Vaas	0	7	2	-	-
S.B.Styris not out	111	198	157	-	6
C.D.McMillan c Silva b Muralitharan	1	11	7	-	-
J.D.P.Oram c Maharoof b Dilshan	31	52	45	1	-
B.B.McCullum† lbw b Muralitharan	1	4	2	-	-
D.L.Vettori c Silva b Muralitharan	5	8	7	-	-
J.E.C.Franklin not out	25	37	27	1	-
S.E.Bond					
M.R.Gillespie					
Extras (b 2, lb 2, w 8, nb 5)	17				
TOTAL (50 overs) (7 wkts)	**219**	210			

SRI LANKA

	Runs	Mins	Balls	6s	4s
W.U.Tharanga c Bond b Franklin	11	20	21	-	1
S.T.Jayasuriya c McCullum b Oram	64	111	80	1	5
K.C.Sangakkara† not out	69	184	104	-	3
D.P.M.D.Jayawardene* c sub (H.J.H.Marshall) b Vettori	15	21	16	-	2
L.P.C.Silva c Bond b Vettori	23	33	34	-	4
T.M.Dilshan not out	14	33	24	-	-
R.P.Arnold					
M.F.Maharoof					
W.P.U.J.C.Vaas					
C.R.D.Fernando					
M.Muralitharan					
Extras (b 4, lb 7, w 7, nb 8)	26				
TOTAL (45.1 overs) (4 wkts)	**222**	205			

Bowling	O	M	R	W
SRI LANKA				
Vaas	9	2	33	3
Fernando	7	2	31	0
Maharoof	6	0	31	0
Muralitharan	10	0	32	3
Jayasuriya	10	0	44	0
Dilshan	8	1	44	1
NEW ZEALAND				
Franklin	8	0	49	1
Bond	8	0	26	0
Gillespie	6.1	1	42	0
Vettori	10	0	35	2
Styris	7	1	28	0
Oram	6	0	31	1

Fall of Wickets	***NZ***	***SL***
1st	1	30
2nd	4	130
3rd	71	152
4th	77	180
5th	141	-
6th	145	-
7th	155	-
8th	-	-
9th	-	-
10th	-	-

NEW ZEALAND v SOUTH AFRICA World Cup – Super Eights

at National Cricket Stadium, Grenada on 14 April, 2007
Toss : New Zealand. Umpires : M.R. Benson & D.J. Harper
New Zealand won by 5 wickets.

Patel replaced Gillespie in the New Zealand side. On a wicket giving the bowlers assistance South Africa lost two quick wickets and were never able to score at a quick rate. Gibbs got fifty from 84 balls. McMillan had his best bowling figures getting 3-23.

Fleming and Styris were again the anchors of the New Zealand batting, both getting fifties. Fleming needed 83 balls and Styris 77 as the BlackCaps won with ten balls to spare.

SOUTH AFRICA

	Runs	Mins	Balls	6s	4s
G.C.Smith* c Oram b Bond	1	7	12	-	-
A.B.de Villiers lbw b Franklin	0	10	6	-	-
J.H.Kallis c Bond b Vettori	22	77	54	1	1
H.H.Gibbs b McMillan	60	139	100	1	2
A.G.Prince c Patel b McMillan	37	73	57	-	2
M.V.Boucher† c Fulton b McMillan	16	21	21	-	1
S.M.Pollock not out	21	38	26	1	-
A.J.Hall c Oram b Bond	17	25	17	-	1
R.J.Peterson not out	8	6	8	-	1
A.Nel					
M.Ntini					
Extras (lb 3, w 7, nb 1)	11				
TOTAL (50 overs) (7 wkts)	**193**	205			

NEW ZEALAND

	Runs	Mins	Balls	6s	4s
P.G.Fulton c Hall b Ntini	16	30	32	-	3
S.P.Fleming* c Boucher b Pollock	50	133	84	-	6
L.R.P.L.Taylor lbw b Nel	10	22	17	-	1
S.B.Styris c Gibbs b Peterson	56	141	84	-	4
C.D.McMillan not out	38	84	55	1	2
J.D.P.Oram b Nel	10	22	18	-	1
B.B.McCullum† not out	4	1	1	-	1
D.L.Vettori					
J.E.C.Franklin					
S.E.Bond					
J.S.Patel					
Extras (lb 3, w 8, nb 1)	12				
TOTAL (48.2 overs) (5 wkts)	**196**	217			

Bowling	*O*	*M*	*R*	*W*
NEW ZEALAND				
Franklin	7	2	16	1
Bond	10	1	26	2
Oram	5	2	23	0
Patel	10	1	36	0
Vettori	10	0	50	1
Styris	3	0	16	0
McMillan	5	0	23	3
SOUTH AFRICA				
Pollock	10	0	30	1
Ntini	10	0	42	1
Nel	9.2	0	33	2
Hall	8	0	32	0
Kallis	4	0	17	0
Peterson	7	0	39	1

Fall of Wickets

	SA	***NZ***
1st	3	25
2nd	3	42
3rd	52	120
4th	128	176
5th	143	192
6th	149	-
7th	181	-
8th	-	-
9th	-	-
10th	-	-

NEW ZEALAND v AUSTRALIA World Cup – Super Eights

at National Cricket Stadium, Grenada on 20 April, 2007
Toss : Australia. Umpires : Aleem Dar & Asad Rauf
Australia won by 215 runs.

Oram had a heel injury and Bond was unwell so Gillespie and Mason came into the side. After Gilchrist went to the seventh ball of the innings, the Australian batsmen took control. There was a second wicket stand of 137 at better than a run a ball. Ponting got fifty off 53 balls, the same number as Hayden. The latter went to his hundred after 96 deliveries. Australia added 91 off the last ten overs as Watson scored 65 off 32 balls to enable his side to reach 348-6.

The New Zealand innings was a disastrous affair with only three players reaching double figures. Fulton was the shining light getting fifty from 54 balls. The New Zealand total off 133 meant they suffered their worst losing margin in one-day internationals and ensured Australia of top qualifying spot for the semi-finals.

AUSTRALIA

	Runs	Mins	Balls	6s	4s
A.C.Gilchrist† c Gillespie b Franklin	1	7	2	-	-
M.L.Hayden c & b Styris	103	150	100	2	10
R.T.Ponting* c Taylor b Patel	66	96	70	-	7
M.J.Clarke b Franklin	49	59	46	-	7
M.E.K.Hussey c Styris b Franklin	37	75	44	-	2
A.Symonds c Mason b Patel	11	20	16	-	1
S.R.Watson not out	65	44	32	4	4
G.B.Hogg not out	0	3	0	-	-
N.W.Bracken					
S.W.Tait					
G.D.McGrath					
Extras (lb 1, w 5, nb 10)	16				
TOTAL (50 overs) (6 wkts)	**348**	230			

NEW ZEALAND

	Runs	Mins	Balls	6s	4s
P.G.Fulton b Hogg	62	127	72	-	5
S.P.Fleming* c Ponting b Tait	12	18	9	1	1
L.R.P.L.Taylor c Hussey b McGrath	3	8	6	-	-
S.B.Styris c Hayden b McGrath	27	30	22	-	5
C.D.McMillan lbw b Tait	1	6	5	-	-
J.E.C.Franklin b Watson	6	11	9	-	-
B.B.McCullum† c Hussey b Hogg	7	19	16	-	-
D.L.Vettori c Symonds b Hogg	4	7	4	-	1
M.R.Gillespie c McGrath b Hogg	2	9	8	-	-
M.J.Mason c Gilchrist b Tait	0	6	5	-	-
J.S.Patel not out	0	3	1	-	-
Extras (w 7, nb 2)	9				
TOTAL (25.5 overs)	**133**	127			

Bowling	*O*	*M*	*R*	*W*
NEW ZEALAND				
Mason	3	0	27	0
Franklin	8	0	74	3
Patel	10	0	48	2
Vettori	10	0	60	0
Styris	10	0	50	1
Gillespie	6	0	67	0
McMillan	3	0	21	0
AUSTRALIA				
Bracken	4	0	27	0
Tait	6	0	32	3
McGrath	4	0	25	2
Hogg	6.5	1	29	4
Watson	5	0	20	1

Fall of Wickets	***A***	***NZ***
1st	7	21
2nd	144	29
3rd	216	77
4th	233	80
5th	257	89
6th	334	111
7th	-	117
8th	-	127
9th	-	133
10th	-	133

NEW ZEALAND v SRI LANKA — World Cup Semi-final

at Sabina Park, Kingston, Jamaica on 24 April, 2007
Toss : Sri Lanka. Umpires : R.E. Koertzen & S.J.A. Taufel
Sri Lanka won by 81 runs.

Oram and Bond returned for Gillespie and Mason. Franklin got two early wickets but Tharanga and Jayawardene took control. They added 178 off the last 25 overs with 102 coming off the last ten. Jayawardene was slow for the first part of his innings, getting fifty off 76 balls, but his next fifty needed only 28 balls, as Sri Lanka scored a very competitive 289-5.

Fleming went in the second over but New Zealand recovered to 105-2. At that stage five wickets went for 11 runs, as New Zealand went to 116-7, and the game was as good as over. Only a 59 run stand between Franklin and Patel (highest score) got the BlackCaps past 200.

Sri Lanka deserved their 81 run win and went through to the final.

SRI LANKA

	Runs	Mins	Balls	6s	4s
W.U.Tharanga b Vettori	73	112	74	1	9
S.T.Jayasuriya b Franklin	1	1	6	-	-
K.C.Sangakkara† c Fleming b Franklin	18	50	42	-	2
D.P.M.D.Jayawardene* not out	115	15	109	3	10
L.P.C.Silva lbw b Bond	21	36	33	1	-
T.M.Dilshan lbw b Oram	30	42	27	-	3
R.P.Arnold not out	14	24	14	-	2
W.P.U.J.C.Vaas					
S.L.Malinga					
M.Muralitharan					
C.R.D.Fernando					
Extras (lb 3, w 9, nb 5)	17				
TOTAL (50 overs) (5 wkts)	**289**	218			

NEW ZEALAND

	Runs	Mins	Balls	6s	4s
P.G.Fulton c Silva b Jayasuriya	46	116	77	1	2
S.P.Fleming* lbw b Malinga	1	7	4	-	-
L.R.P.L.Taylor lbw b Vaas	9	43	25	-	1
S.B.Styris c Jayawardene b Dilshan	37	50	38	3	2
J.D.P.Oram c & b Muralitharan	3	8	7	-	-
B.B.McCullum† c Silva b Muralitharan	0	1	1	-	-
C.D.McMillan b Jayasuriya	25	36	20	2	1
D.L.Vettori lbw b Muralitharan	0	5	4	-	-
J.E.C.Franklin not out	30	57	38	-	2
S.E.Bond b Muralitharan	2	6	4	-	-
J.S.Patel c Fernando b Dilshan	34	33	38	1	2
Extras (b 5, lb 2, w 8, nb 6)	21				
TOTAL (41.4 overs)	**208**	181			

Bowling	*O*	*M*	*R*	*W*
NEW ZEALAND				
Franklin	9	1	46	2
Bond	10	1	59	1
Oram	10	0	60	1
Vettori	10	0	51	1
Patel	10	0	62	0
Styris	1	0	8	0
SRI LANKA				
Vaas	8	1	25	1
Malinga	7	2	21	1
Fernando	5	0	45	0
Muralitharan	8	0	31	4
Jayasuriya	9	0	57	2
Dilshan	4.4	0	22	2

Fall of Wickets	***SL***	***NZ***
1st	13	2
2nd	67	32
3rd	111	105
4th	152	114
5th	233	114
6th	-	115
7th	-	116
8th	-	144
9th	-	149
10th	-	208

25th April 2007 (Semi-final)
St Lucia: **Australia beat South Africa by 7 wickets**
South Africa 149 (43.5 overs) (J.M.Kemp 49*, H.H.Gibbs 39, S.W.Tait 4-39, G.D.McGrath 3-18);
Australia 153 for 3 (31.3 overs) (M.J.Clarke 60*, M.L.Hayden 41)

28th April 2007 (Final)
Bridgetown: **Australia beat Sri Lanka by 53 runs (D/L)**
Australia 281 for 4 (38 overs) (A.C.Gilchrist 149, M.L.Hayden 38, R.T.Ponting 37);
Sri Lanka 215 for 8 (36 overs) (S.T.Jayasuriya 63, K.C.Sangakkara 54)

MCC IN NEW ZEALAND

An MCC team played five games in New Zealand following a visit to Papua New Guinea.

The team included England wicketkeeper Geraint Jones, former Central Otago player Ronnie Kotkamp and former Otago and Wellington batsman Scott McHardy. The team was:

L.W. Marshall *(captain)*, B.J. Claypole, D. Evans, M.R.J. Eyles, D.S. Harrison, S.L.J.M. Hawk, G.O. Jones, R. Kotkamp, M.A.K. Lawson, D.S. McHardy. M.J. Powell, J.C. Tredwell, M.A. Wallace. Manager, M.S.L. Rollinson; Player/Physiotherapist, P.A.W. Heseltine; Umpire, B. Leadbeater.

CANTERBURY EMERGING PLAYERS v MCC
At MainPower Oval, Rangiora 7 February, 2007

Canterbury Emerging Players 277-6 (L.J. Vivian 74, B.R. Findlay 49) **defeated MCC** 267 (G.O. Jones 93, J.C. Tredwell 49, B. McCord 3-24, I.C. King 3-46) by 10 runs

CANTERBURY EMERGING PLAYERS v MCC
At MainPower Oval, Rangiora 8 February, 2007

MCC 245 (G.O. Jones 50, L.W. Marshall 40, J.C. Tredwell 39, I.C. King 6-41) **lost to Canterbury Emerging Players** 246-9 (K.R. Ambler 82, L.J. Vivian 36, C.J. Anderson 32*, D.S. Harrison 3-44, D. Evans 3-59) by 1 wicket

OTAGO COUNTRY v MCC
At Queenstown Events Centre 11 March, 2007

Otago Country 203-9 (L. Morgan 50, C. Blair 31, R. Kotkamp 3-35) **lost to MCC** 205-9 (B.J. Claypole 48, M.A.K. Lawson 39*, L.W. Marshall 34, J. Lovelock 3-29, B. Paterson 3-45) by 1 wicket

OTAGO COUNTRY v MCC
At Queenstown Events Centre 13 March, 2007

Otago Country 214-8 (N. Perkins 66, J. Pyle 49, C. Rutherford 32*, J.C. Tredwell 3-29) **lost to MCC** 216-3 (M.J. Powell 101*, S.L.J.M. Hawk 96) by 7 wickets

AUCKLAND XI v MCC
At Eden Park Outer Oval, Auckland 15, 16 March, 2007

MCC 253-8d (M.J. Powell 103*, M.A.K. Lawson 39, D.S. McHardy 34, M.A. Wallace 33, Azhar Abbas 3-87) and 142-2d (S.L.J.M. Hawk 69*, M.A. Wallace 67) **defeated Auckland XI** 117-2d (A.K. Kitchen 66, S.P.L. Singe 46*) and 221 (S.P.L. Singe 55, K.W.M. Todd 49, A.P. de Boorder 49, R. Sharma 35, J.C. Tredwell 4-26) by 57 runs

INTERNATIONAL SUMMARY

2006/07

Test Matches

	Played	*Won*	*Lost*	*Drawn*
Sri Lanka	2	1	1	–
TOTAL	2	1	1	–

New Zealand Test Averages

BATTING	*M*	*I*	*NO*	*HS*	*Agg*	*Ave*	*100s*	*50s*	*Ct*	*St*
D.L. Vettori	2	3	0	63	114	38.00	-	2	1	-
C.D. Cumming	2	4	0	43	119	29.75	-	-	-	-
B.B. McCullum	2	4	1	43	74	24.66	-	-	8	1
M.S. Sinclair	2	4	0	37	83	20.75	-	-	4	-
S.P. Fleming	2	4	0	48	75	18.75	-	-	7	-
J.M. How	2	4	0	33	70	17.50	-	-	2	-
J.E.C. Franklin	2	3	0	44	45	15.00	-	-	2	-
N.J. Astle	2	4	0	24	52	13.00	-	-	1	-
J.D.P. Oram	2	4	1	12*	18	6.00	-	-	1	-
S.E. Bond	2	3	0	8	15	5.00	-	-	1	-
C.S. Martin	2	3	3	4*	4	-	-	-	-	-

BOWLING	*O*	*M*	*R*	*W*	*Ave*	*Best*	*5w*	*10w*
J.D.P. Oram	20	6	59	4	14.75	2-30	-	-
D.L. Vettori	58.3	7	193	10	19.30	7-130	1	1
S.E. Bond	67.1	11	258	10	25.80	4-63	-	-
J.E.C. Franklin	62	11	173	6	28.83	3-30	-	-
C.S. Martin	63.4	7	223	7	31.85	3-50	-	-
N.J. Astle	9	2	24	0	-	-	-	-

One-day Internationals

	Played	Won	Lost	Tied	NR
Australia	9	3	6	–	–
Sri Lanka	8	2	5	–	1
England	5	3	2	–	–
South Africa	2	2	–	–	–
Pakistan	1	1	–	–	–
Kenya	1	1	–	–	–
Canada	1	1	–	–	–
West Indies	1	1	–	–	–
Bangladesh	1	1	–	–	–
Ireland	1	1	–	–	–
TOTAL	**30**	**16**	**13**	**–**	**1**

New Zealand One-day International Averages

BATTING	*M*	*I*	*NO*	*HS*	*Agg*	*Ave*	*100s*	*50s*	*Ct*	*St*	*SR*
S.B. Styris	17	15	3	111*	655	54.58	1	5	7	-	80
J.D.P. Oram	19	16	4	101*	513	42.75	1	3	8	-	90
L. Vincent	14	14	1	101	508	39.07	1	4	4	-	74
S.P. Fleming	27	26	2	106	853	35.54	2	6	17	-	75
C.D. McMillan	22	19	3	117	559	34.93	1	3	1	-	91
L.R.P.L. Taylor	22	20	1	128*	660	34.73	2	3	15	-	79
P.G. Fulton	26	25	2	83	730	31.73	-	5	4	-	72
J.E.C. Franklin	24	19	9	45*	287	28.70	-	-	6	-	93
B.B. McCullum	30	25	5	86*	516	25.80	-	2	30	3	97
N.J. Astle	11	10	0	83	200	20.00	-	1	3	-	69
J.A.H. Marshall	3	3	0	50	55	18.33	-	1	-	-	56
D.L. Vettori	28	19	5	79	241	17.21	-	1	10	-	78
K.D. Mills	5	3	1	21	31	15.50	-	-	2	-	81
H.J.H. Marshall	11	11	1	50*	144	14.40	-	1	3	-	75
M.R. Gillespie	17	9	4	28	63	12.60	-	-	2	-	79
J.S. Patel	14	7	2	34	56	11.20	-	-	4	-	53
S.E. Bond	22	9	4	22*	48	9.60	-	-	6	-	57
D.R. Tuffey	4	1	0	8	8	8.00	-	-	-	-	100
A.R. Adams	3	3	0	6	10	3.33	-	-	1	-	37
M.J. Mason	11	4	1	4*	9	3.00	-	-	5	-	29

BOWLING	*O*	*M*	*R*	*W*	*Ave*	*Best*	*R/O*
K.D. Mills	38.3	3	190	11	17.27	4-38	4.93
S.E. Bond	190	21	795	38	20.92	5-23	4.18
D.L. Vettori	252	7	1081	36	30.02	4-23	4.29
C.D. McMillan	56.2	1	318	10	31.80	3-23	5.64
J.S. Patel	125.3	3	617	19	32.47	3-11	4.91
M.J. Mason	72.3	8	376	11	34.18	4-24	5.18
J.E.C. Franklin	185.2	15	924	27	34.22	3-17	4.98
J.D.P. Oram	1313	11	552	16	34.50	3-23	4.19
S.B. Styris	86	3	419	10	41.90	4-43	4.87
M.R. Gillespie	135.3	14	759	18	42.16	3-39	5.60
A.R. Adams	26	2	149	1	149.00	1-53	5.73
D.R. Tuffey	34	0	217	1	217.00	1-68	6.38
L.R.P.L. Taylor	2	0	16	0	-	-	8.00
L. Vincent	2	0	22	0	-	-	11.00
N.J. Astle	13.4	0	68	0	-	-	4.97

PROVINCIAL SUMMARIES

AUCKLAND CRICKET ASSOCIATION

Formed 1883, affiliated 1894/95.

Selectors: M.R. O'Donnell, R.M.J. Armour, K. Patel and R. Smith.

Auckland proved to be the dominant one-day team by winning the State Shield (their first win in the provincial one-day competition since 1989/90) and the Twenty20 competition. They finished fourth in the State Championship but were still in with a chance of qualifying for the final in the last round.

Captain Richard Jones led the way with the bat scoring 360 in the Shield competition. Chris Martin and Roneel Hira each took 13 wickets. Jones (630) and Rob Nicol (519) were the leading scorers in the State Championship. Jones scored a century in each innings against Central Districts while Tim McIntosh scored a double century in the first game. Andre Adams captured 32 wickets and Chris Martin took 31. Lance Shaw complemented them, getting 20. Reece Young had 24 dismissals, the most by any wicketkeeper.

Mark O'Donnell again coached the side and was reappointed for 2007/08. Contracted players were: Carl Cachopa, Tama Canning, Derek de Boorder, Martin Guptill, Paul Hitchcock, Richard Jones, Tim Lythe, Tim McIntosh, Andy McKay, Rob Nicol, Lance Shaw and Reece Young. During the season Canning retired and moved to Perth.

CANTERBURY CRICKET ASSOCIATION

Formed 1877, affiliated 1894/95.

Selectors: D.O. Nosworthy and G.K. MacDonald

Canterbury had a reversal of fortunes in the various competitions, failing to qualify for either of the one-day finals but finishing runner-up the State Championship.

They introduced several newcomers after losing five players to the BlackCaps. Captain Chris Harris was voted domestic player of the year. He scored the only century in Twenty20 and made 362 runs in the State Shield. During the season he became the highest runscorer in domestic one-day cricket. He was the only Canterbury player to reach 300 runs.

In the State Championship, Michael Papps missed the first two games with a broken finger but still scored 1005 runs with four centuries. Shanan Stewart scored 606 runs while Leighton Burtt was the only player to take 20 wickets. South African Kruger van Wyk kept wicket.

David Nosworthy again coached the side and was selected to coach the New Zealand A side to Australia in June and July 2007. Contracted players were: Todd Astle, Hamish Bennett, Leighton Burtt, Andrew Ellis, Chris Harris, Brandon Hiini, Craig McMillan, Iain Robertson, Richard Sherlock, Shanan Stewart, Kruger van Wyk and Paul Wiseman (who did not play after securing a coaching contract with Durham and was replaced by Brent Findlay).

CENTRAL DISTRICTS CRICKET ASSOCIATION

Formed 1950, affiliated 1954/55.

Selectors: G.D. Barlow and P.S. Briasco

Central Districts had a season to forget. After being the dominant team in 2005/06 they failed to qualify for the State Shield finals and finished in fifth place in the Championship. They struggled after their international players left and had injuries to key players Lance Hamilton and Ewen Thompson.

In the State Shield Peter Ingram was the only player to reach 300 runs (344) while Brendon Diamanti was equal leading wicket taker with 18. Thompson got 13.

Ingram scored 617 runs in the State Championship, with four centuries. He also became the third Central Districts player in the last three seasons to score three centuries in successive innings. Newcomer Greg Hay (593) and Bevan Griggs (580) also passed 500 runs. Michael Mason took 15 wickets. The team was again coached by former England player Graham Barlow. Contracted players were: Geoff Barnett, Chris Cruikshank, Brendon Diamanti, Campbell Furlong, Bevan Griggs, Lance Hamilton, Greg Hay, Brent Hefford, Greg Hegglun, Dominic Rayner, Ewen Thompson and Tim Weston.

NORTHERN DISTRICTS CRICKET ASSOCIATION

Formed 1953, granted Plunket Shield status 1956/57

Selectors: A.J. Moles, P.J. Malcon and C.J. Stevens

Northern Districts won the State Championship this season but failed to finish in the top three of the State Shield. In the State Championship they finished as top qualifier and drew the final with Canterbury.

Peter McGlashan (380), Alun Evans (328) and captain James Marshall (308) were their leading one-day run-scorers. Graeme Aldridge (13) was again their leading wicket-taker.

Three batsmen scored over 500 runs in the State Championship – Hamish Marshall (766), BJ Watling (564) and Evans (535). Aldridge was their leading wicket taker with 33.

McGlashan again kept wickets and when he was injured Watling took his place behind the stumps. Northern Districts had a new coach with former Warwickshire player Andy Moles taking the reins.

Contracted players were: Graeme Aldridge, Ian Butler, Alun Evans, Daniel Flynn, Nick Horsley, Peter McGlashan, James Marshall, Bruce Martin, Mark Orchard, Daryl Tuffey, BJ Watling and Joseph Yovich.

OTAGO CRICKET ASSOCIATION

Formed 1876, affiliated 1894/95.

Selectors: M. Hesson, S.F. Forde and A. Sainsbury

Otago showed a vast improvement in one-day cricket, reaching the final of both the State Shield and Twenty20 competitions. However, they finished last in the State Championship, which was disappointing considering the performances of many of their players.

Captain Craig Cumming was the leading run-scorer in the State Shield getting 445 runs. Aaron Redmond and Greg Todd both scored 314 runs. Matt Harvie was equal leading wicket taker with 18 wickets.

In the State Championship they had four players scoring in excess of 500 runs – Neil Broom (644), Redmond (555), Todd (522) and wicket-keeper Gareth Hopkins (514). Bradley Scott got 27 wickets and was assisted by James McMillan with 23.

Mike Hesson again coached the side and was named assistant coach for New Zealand A in Australia. Contracted players were: Neil Broom, Craig Cumming, Gareth Hopkins, Nathan McCullum, James McMillan, Warren McSkimming, Aaron Redmond, Bradley Scott, Gareth Shaw, Jordan Sheed, Craig Smith and Greg Todd.

WELLINGTON CRICKET ASSOCIATION

Formed 1875, affiliated 1894/95.

Selectors: A.M. Stuart, G.M. Hooper, L.R. Dry and M.R. Heissenbuttel

Wellington finished third in both the State Shield and Championship. In both competitions they had chances to top the tables but fell away near the end.

New captain Michael Parlane was their only batsman to score 300 runs in State Shield, getting 307. Grant Elliott was joint leading wicket taker in the competition with 18.

The Parlane brothers both scored over 500 runs in State Championship games. Michael got 613 and Neal 536. Iain O'Brien was the competition's leading wicket taker with 34 victims. This included 13 wickets in the game against Auckland when he beat the previous best Wellington performance in this fixture.

Chris Nevin started the season as wicket-keeper but was injured and Stu Mills took over the gloves for the rest of the season with Nevin playing as a batsman. Former Australian and New South Wales bowler Anthony Stuart took over as coach.

Contracted players were: Matthew Bell, Dewayne Bowden, Grant Elliott, Sam Fairley, Mark Gillespie, Stu Mills, Chris Nevin, Iain O'Brien, Michael Parlane, Neal Parlane, Jesse Ryder and Luke Woodcock.

STATE CHAMPIONSHIP REVIEW 2006/07

Each side again played eight matches with the two top qualifiers meeting in the final. The top qualifier, Northern Districts, hosted the final while the second placed team, Canterbury, had to win outright to take the title.

As in the previous season, the final went into the fifth day. Canterbury gained a 124 run first innings lead, after being sent in, but Northern had no difficulty batting out the last afternoon before the match was called off.

The competition began three weeks earlier than the previous season, on 15 November. In a new move, five of the first six games were scheduled for the Canterbury region in an effort to utilise better early season pitch and weather conditions.

Four rounds of matches were played prior to Christmas and before the commencement of the State Shield and the expanded State Twenty20 competition. The Championship resumed on 19 February and after each team had played each other once, the remaining three rounds saw the teams placed 1, 2, and 3 in 2005/06 drawn against the sides placed 4, 5, and 6. Points were carried through from the first five rounds.

Only 13 of the the 25 matches ended in an outright decision, the same as the previous season. In round-robin play, Northern Districts had four outright wins, Canterbury and Wellington three, Auckland two and Central Districts one. Canterbury and Wellington each lost only one match outright.

Wellington, who hosted the final in 2005/06, finished third, while Canterbury rose from fourth to second. Central Districts, who won the title the previous season, dropped to fifth place and Otago went from third to last, an exact reversal of their previous summer's form. Auckland went from fifth to fourth while the eventual champions, Northern Districts, had been last in 2005/06, without a single outright victory.

Playing time was again six and a half hours per day, although this was extended if the number of overs to be bowled in the day had not been completed. Teams were required to bowl 100 overs a day with no reduction for change of innings. The only penalties for slow over rates were financial and these were calculated round by round instead of over the whole season.

Points were awarded as follows:

a) six points for an outright win
b) two points for a first innings win
c) three points for a tie
d) one point each for a first innings tie (providing the team did not win outright)
e) one point each for a no result on the first innings

Final points and placings were:

	P	*OW*	*OL*	*1st Inns W*	*1st Inns L*	*NR*	*Total*
Northern Districts	8	4	2	2	—	—	32
Canterbury	8	3	1	2	2	—	28
Wellington	8	3	1	2	2	—	26
Auckland	8	2	3	2	1	—	22
Central Districts	8	1	4	—	3	—	10
Otago	8	—	2	3	3	—	8

Northern Districts defeated Central Districts and Otago outright after trailing on the first innings
Wellington defeated Auckland outright after trailing on the first innings

CANTERBURY v OTAGO State Championship

at Queen Elizabeth II Park, Christchurch on 15, 16, 17, 18 November, 2006
Toss : Otago. Umpires : B.F. Bowden & D.M. Quested
Close of play: 1st day: Otago 352-4, Todd 77; 2nd day: Canterbury 144-4, McMillan 30, Harris 2
3rd day: Canterbury 330-7, Harris 103, Small 8
***First innings win to Otago.** Points: Otago 2, Canterbury 0*

Burtt and Small made their first-class debuts while van Wyk, Amandeep Singh and Hogg played their first games for their provinces.

After Cumming and Sheed began with a century opening partnership Otago went on to amass 601-9 before declaring, just one short of their highest ever total. Todd (highest score) reached his century from 174 balls in 209 minutes.

Despite centuries from McMillan (226 minutes and 179 balls) and Harris (239 minutes and 172 balls) Canterbury were required to follow on. In a good match for the McMillan cousins, James captured five wickets in an innings for the first time.

Todd Astle (who equalled his best score) and Papps put on 111 for the first wicket when Canterbury batted again and there was never any chance that Otago would break through for a win.

OTAGO

FIRST INNINGS	*Runs*	*Mins*	*Balls*	*6s*	*4s*	*SECOND INNINGS*	*Runs*	*Mins*	*Balls*	*6s*	*4s*
C.D.Cumming* c Astle T.D. b Burtt	63	160	151	-	11						
J.W.Sheed c Harris b Astle T.D.	66	221	151	-	13						
A.J.Redmond c Astle T.D. b Burtt	75	160	130	1	13						
G.R.Todd c & b Harris	160	294	244	-	23						
N.T.Broom c van Wyk b Singh	45	67	54	1	7						
G.J.Hopkins† c & b Harris	38	118	90	-	6						
K.W.Hogg lbw b Astle T.D.	0	14	4	-	-						
N.L.McCullum c McCullum b Astle N.J.	19	34	30	-	3						
B.E.Scott not out	52	93	67	3	2						
C.M.Smith c Fulton b McMillan	49	64	64	1	7						
J.M.McMillan											
Extras (b 2, lb 8, w 3, nb 21)	34										
TOTAL (160.4 overs) (9 wkts dec)	**601**	609									

CANTERBURY

	Runs	*Mins*	*Balls*	*6s*	*4s*		*Runs*	*Mins*	*Balls*	*6s*	*4s*
T.D.Astle b McMillan	12	45	38	-	2	lbw b McCullum	56	108	104	-	8
B.B.McCullum c Scott b McMillan	67	123	72	-	13	c Smith b McCullum	60	159	99	2	7
P.G.Fulton c Smith b McCullum	17	63	51	1	2	not out	62	84	82	4	5
C.D.McMillan c Hopkins b McMillan	101	233	183	2	11	not out	20	33	24	2	-
N.J.Astle c Broom b McCullum	6	20	20	-	1						
C.Z.Harris* b McMillan	122	299	210	2	15						
A.M.Ellis c Cumming b McMillan	0	10	7	-	-						
C.F.K.van Wyk† c Hopkins b McMillan	0	1	1	-	-						
C.A.Small not out	17	14	75	-	1						
L.M.Burtt lbw b McMillan	2	9	8	-	-						
A.Singh lbw b Redmond	6	17	17	-	1						
Extras (b 4, lb 11, nb 2)	17					(b 6, lb 6, nb 3)	15				
TOTAL (113.3 overs)	**367**	463				(51 overs) (2 wkts)	**213**	184			

Bowling	*O*	*M*	*R*	*W*	*O*	*M*	*R*	*W*
CANTERBURY								
Singh	22	5	77	1				
Burtt	25	5	100	2				
Ellis	4	1	12	0				
Small	27	8	87	0				
Astle N.J.	17	3	46	1				
Harris	29	6	104	2				
McMillan	17.4	1	61	1				
Astle T.D.	19	2	104	2				
OTAGO								
McMillan	27	8	105	7	3	1	11	0
Hogg	16	3	47	0	8	1	30	0
Scott	10	3	28	0				
Smith	18	4	66	0	4	0	13	0
McCullum	25	3	74	2	20	2	80	2
Redmond	17.3	2	32	1	12	4	43	0
Cumming					3	0	6	0
Broom					1	0	18	0

Fall of Wickets	***O***	***C***	***C***
	1st	*1st*	*2nd*
1st	119	50	111
2nd	156	105	150
3rd	275	110	-
4th	352	133	-
5th	478	295	-
6th	481	305	-
7th	485	305	-
8th	526	351	-
9th	601	353	-
10th	-	367	-

WELLINGTON v CENTRAL DISTRICTS State Championship

at Allied Prime Basin Reserve, Wellington on 21, 22, 23, 24 November, 2006
Toss : Central Districts. Umpires : A.L. Hill & E.A. Watkin
Close of play: 1st day: CD 42-1, Barnett 16, Sinclair 4; 2nd day: Wellington 77-1, M.E.Parlane 35, Patel 3
3rd day: CD 52-2, Barnett 16, Taylor 2
***Central Districts won by 3 wickets.** Points: Central Districts 8, Wellington 0*

Michael Parlane captained a team at first-class level for the first time while Hay made his debut for Central Districts.

The Welington captain and Ryder top-scored for Wellington and shared a 94 run stand for the third wicket. In reply Central lost their ninth wicket at 285 with Hay fourteen runs short of a century on debut. Hamilton held on for 25 minutes while Hay added 12 runs and took Central to a first innings lead. Hay took a single from the first ball of Gillespie's 23rd over, to move to 98, only to see the number eleven caught behind four balls later. Hay and Griggs had put on 102 for the sixth wicket, a record for Central against Wellington.

Michael Parlane scored his second fifty of the match but none of his team mates could offer prolonged resistance and Central were left to make 227 for victory. Barnett, with 74, and Thompson, with a rapid 40, made sure Central reached their target with time to spare, the match ending at 2.29 pm.

WELLINGTON

FIRST INNINGS	*Runs*	*Mins*	*Balls*	*6s*	*4s*	*SECOND INNINGS*	*Runs*	*Mins*	*Balls*	*6s*	*4s*
M.D.Bell lbw b Hamilton	0	16	13	-	-	c Griggs b Hamilton	30	85	67	-	6
M.E.Parlane* c Griggs b Diamanti	68	138	118	-	11	c Griggs b Diamanti	53	188	140	-	7
S.P.Fleming lbw b Thompson	23	40	36	1	2	(4) c Griggs b Hamilton	26	67	47	-	6
J.D.Ryder lbw b Mason	68	175	111	-	11	(5) b Thompson	38	44	33	-	8
N.R.Parlane lbw b Thompson	20	52	37	-	4	(6) lbw b Diamanti	20	92	77	-	2
J.E.C.Franklin b Hamilton	64	128	105	1	8	(7) c Griggs b Diamanti	22	70	59	-	3
C.J.Nevin† b Mason	33	107	92	-	5	(8) not out	13	54	40	-	1
G.D.Elliott b Thompson	8	27	16	-	2	(9) b Mason	5	24	16	-	1
M.R.Gillespie b Mason	0	1	3	-	-	(10) c Griggs b Mason	0	1	1	-	-
J.S.Patel not out	0	5	1	-	-	(3) b Mason	4	39	26	-	-
I.E.O'Brien lbw b Thompson	0	1	1	-	-	c Diamanti b Mason	0	9	6	-	-
Extras (lb 2, w 4, nb 6)	12					(b 2, lb 8, w 1, nb 6)	17				
TOTAL (87.5 overs)	**296**	349				(84.2 overs)	**228**	341			

CENTRAL DISTRICTS

FIRST INNINGS	*Runs*	*Mins*	*Balls*	*6s*	*4s*	*SECOND INNINGS*	*Runs*	*Mins*	*Balls*	*6s*	*4s*
J.M.How* c Parlane M.E. b Franklin	12	25	20	-	3	c Elliott b Gillespie	9	16	15	-	2
G.E.F.Barnett lbw b O'Brien	16	44	42	-	1	b Franklin	78	18	151	-	7
M.S.Sinclair lbw b Franklin	5	26	10	-	-	b Franklin	17	30	24	-	3
L.R.P.L.Taylor lbw b O'Brien	41	34	38	-	8	c Nevin b Franklin	12	46	37	-	1
T.I.Weston b O'Brien	5	53	23	-	-	c Bell b Gillespie	14	18	16	-	1
G.R.Hay not out	98	254	182	-	14	c Bell b Patel	17	92	55	-	2
B.B.J.Griggs† c Parlane M.E. b O'Brien	58	122	103	1	7	not out	19	69	48	-	3
E.P.Thompson c Franklin b Patel	11	42	33	-	2	c Franklin b Gillespie	40	50	43	2	4
B.J.Diamanti b Gillespie	11	21	20	-	1	not out	4	1	1	-	1
M.J.Mason c Nevin b Gillespie	16	22	25	1	1						
L.J.Hamilton c Nevin b Gillespie	0	25	22	-	-						
Extras (b 2, lb 6, w 1, nb 16)	25					(b 6, lb 8, nb 4)	18				
TOTAL (83.5 overs)	**298**	334				(64.2 overs) (7 wkts)	**228**	254			

Bowling	*O*	*M*	*R*	*W*	*O*	*M*	*R*	*W*
CENTRAL DISTRICTS								
Mason	21	9	39	3	18.2	9	44	4
Hamilton	18	4	58	2	16	1	54	2
Thompson	11.5	0	77	4	20	7	30	1
Diamanti	20	2	71	1	14	4	43	3
How	14	3	33	0	16	3	47	0
Taylor	3	0	16	0				
WELLINGTON								
Gillespie	22.5	4	83	3	9.2	2	42	3
Franklin	15	1	69	2	16	2	51	3
Patel	27	7	73	1	13	3	39	1
O'Brien	19	8	65	4	21	2	71	0
Elliott					5	0	11	0

Fall of Wickets	***W***	***CD***	***W***	***CD***
	1st	*1st*	*2nd*	*2nd*
1st	2	27	63	17
2nd	36	42	83	50
3rd	130	53	128	89
4th	170	90	128	111
5th	212	99	178	163
6th	284	201	201	167
7th	292	239	212	224
8th	292	259	224	-
9th	296	285	224	-
10th	296	298	228	-

AUCKLAND v OTAGO — State Championship

at Bert Sutcliffe Oval, Lincoln on 22, 23, 24, 25 November, 2006
Toss : Auckland. Umpires : G.A. Baxter & P.D. Jones
Close of play: 1st day: Auckland 312-3, McIntosh 173, Nicol 86; 2nd day: Otago 52-4, Broom 19, Hopkins 5
3rd day: Auckland 102-1, Jones 53, Loye 36
***First innings win to Auckland.** Points: Auckland 2, Otago 0*

Hira made his first-class debut while Loye, who would later play for England in the Commonwealth Bank Series, made his Auckland debut.

Auckland, and McIntosh, batted throughout the first day. The Auckland opener reached his century from 206 balls in 260 minutes and next day went to his first double century after 451 minutes and 357 balls. Nicol cashed in to register his highest score (century in 279 minutes from 222 balls) and Adams joined in with a hundred from just 87 balls in 113 minutes.

It was Auckland's highest total against Otago and the highest in five first-class games at the ground. McIntosh and Nicol put on 273 for the fourth wicket, an Auckland record against Otago.

Otago made a disastrous start and were 37-4 before Broom and Hopkins combined to add 219 for the fifth wicket. Broom (highest score) reached three figures off 206 balls in 239 minutes while Hopkins faced 199 balls in 244 minutes. With conditions so much in favour of batting there was never any chance of a result.

AUCKLAND

FIRST INNINGS	*Runs*	*Mins*	*Balls*	*6s*	*4s*	*SECOND INNINGS*	*Runs*	*Mins*	*Balls*	*6s*	*4s*
T.G.McIntosh c sub (C.M.Smith) b McCullum	205	465	367	1	26	b Cumming	9	13	6	-	1
R.A.Jones* c Hopkins b Scott	29	97	65	-	4	lbw b Scott	55	54	58	-	10
M.B.Loye lbw b Hogg	11	32	19	-	2	retired hurt	36	39	41	-	7
L.Vincent lbw b Hogg	0	16	9	-	-	not out	25	35	30	1	2
R.J.Nicol c & b Redmond	160	442	350	2	19						
T.K.Canning st Hopkins b McCullum	1	24	16	-	-						
R.A.Young† run out	79	189	144	-	9						
A.R.Adams not out	117	132	94	8	10	(5) not out	18	33	21	1	-
L.J.Shaw not out	1	42	21	-	-						
R.M.Hira											
C.S.Martin											
Extras (b 2, lb 11, w 6, nb 5)	24					(lb 2)	2				
TOTAL (180 overs) (7 wkts dec)	**627**	709				(26 overs) (2 wkts dec)	**145**	88			

OTAGO

FIRST INNINGS	*Runs*	*Mins*	*Balls*	*6s*	*4s*	*SECOND INNINGS*	*Runs*	*Mins*	*Balls*	*6s*	*4s*
C.D.Cumming* c Nicol b Martin	7	22	11	-	-	(2) c sub (M.J.Guptill) b Shaw	41	178	134	-	3
J.W.Sheed c Canning b Adams	1	14	10	-	-	(1) lbw b Adams	86	172	136	-	14
A.J.Redmond b Adams	0	4	4	-	-	not out	22	52	46	-	2
G.R.Todd lbw b Canning	16	44	34	-	2	not out	10	46	26	-	1
N.T.Broom b Martin	112	291	240	-	10						
G.J.Hopkins† not out	139	340	273	-	21						
K.W.Hogg not out	53	90	84	-	8						
N.L.McCullum											
B.E.Scott											
M.J.Harvie											
J.M.McMillan											
Extras (b 1, lb 15, nb 4)	20					(b 5, lb 1)	6				
TOTAL (108.4 overs) (5 wkts dec)	**348**	402				(57 overs) (2 wkts)	**165**	218			

Bowling	*O*	*M*	*R*	*W*	*O*	*M*	*R*	*W*
OTAGO								
McMillan	27	4	96	0				
Harvie	22	2	98	0	4	0	13	0
Hogg	25	3	59	2				
Scott	32	13	78	1	5	0	30	1
Cumming	6	1	18	0	8	0	53	1
McCullum	43	4	149	2				
Redmond	25	2	116	1				
Sheed					9	2	47	0
AUCKLAND								
Martin	23	6	90	2	11	4	23	0
Adams	26	4	79	2	13	2	47	1
Canning	25	12	53	1	12	4	29	0
Shaw	9	0	41	0	8	1	20	1
Hira	19	4	41	0	9	5	25	0
Nicol	6	2	20	0	2	0	11	0
Vincent	0.4	0	8	0	2	1	4	0

Fall of Wickets

	A	***O***	***A***	***O***
	1st	*1st*	*2nd*	*2nd*
1st	74	9	23	132
2nd	98	10	102	132
3rd	104	10	-	-
4th	377	37	-	-
5th	391	256	-	-
6th	465	-	-	-
7th	579	-	-	-
8th	-	-	-	-
9th	-	-	-	-
10th	-	-	-	-

Loye retired hurt at 102-1

CANTERBURY v NORTHERN DISTRICTS State Championship

at MainPower Oval, Rangiora on 22, 23, 24, 25 November, 2006
Toss : Canterbury. Umpires : R.D. Anderson & D.J. Walker
Close of play: 1st day: Canterbury 26-1, McCullum 16, Hiini 1; 2nd day: ND 15-0, Evans 3, Watling 6
3rd day: Canterbury 60-1, T.D.Astle 28
***Canterbury won by 6 wickets.** Points: Canterbury 8, Northern Districts 0*

Having been sent in, Northern lost Evans without a run on the board and were indebted to Watling who made his highest score before being fifth man out, seven short of a maiden hundred.

In reply Canterbury lost wickets at regular intervals and only squeezed out a first innings lead with the last pair at the wicket. Having gained the advantage Canterbury pressed it home, reducing Northern to 81-6. Vettori hit 86 of the final 116 runs scored while he was at the crease. The normally aggressive McGlashan made only 12 out of a partnership of 70 with his captain.

Canterbury needed 196 to win and were untroubled in doing so, with Nathan Astle not out 61 when the end came just after lunch on the last day.

NORTHERN DISTRICTS

FIRST INNINGS	*Runs*	*Mins*	*Balls*	*6s*	*4s*	*SECOND INNINGS*	*Runs*	*Mins*	*Balls*	*6s*	*4s*
B-J.Watling c & b Harris	93	220	191	-	12	(2) c Hiini b McMillan	10	43	40	-	2
A.W.Evans c Astle N.J. b Burtt	0	4	1	-	-	(1) run out	19	93	64	-	2
H.J.H.Marshall c Astle N.J. b Singh	30	75	53	-	4	lbw b Hiini	1	36	19	-	-
J.A.H.Marshall c Astle N.J. b Burtt	39	98	75	-	6	c Harris b Bond	20	93	66	-	-
D.R.Flynn lbw b Burtt	0	2	2	-	-	c McCullum b Bond	18	75	66	-	3
M.G.Orchard c Astle N.J. b Hiini	12	54	30	-	1	c Astle N.J. b Bond	6	32	24	-	1
J.A.F.Yovich c McCullum b McMillan	14	75	72	-	-	c Harris b Bond	1	19	15	-	-
D.L.Vettori* c McMillan b Bond	40	94	66	-	6	c Astle T.D. b Bond	86	153	109	-	11
P.D.McGlashan† c McCullum b Singh	7	67	42	-	1	lbw b McMillan	13	94	65	-	-
D.R.Tuffey c Harris b Bond	2	10	10	-	-	c Astle T.D. b Burtt	9	28	26	-	1
G.W.Aldridge not out	3	20	15	-	-	not out	0	5	4	-	-
Extras (b 6, lb 14, w 1, nb 11)	32					(b 1, lb 6, w 4, nb 3)	14				
TOTAL (91 overs)	**272**	357				(82.3 overs)	**197**	336			

CANTERBURY

	Runs	*Mins*	*Balls*	*6s*	*4s*		*Runs*	*Mins*	*Balls*	*6s*	*4s*
T.D.Astle c Marshall H.J.H. b Tuffey	9	19	19	-	-	c Marshall J.A.H. b Vettori	30	118	93	-	3
B.B.McCullum† c McGlashan b Orchard	30	68	34	-	5	lbw b Vettori	25	83	57	1	1
B.C.Hiini c McGlashan b Orchard	7	37	33	-	1						
P.G.Fulton c McGlashan b Tuffey	37	139	123	1	3	(3) c & b Vettori	20	67	59	-	4
C.D.McMillan b Yovich	42	172	121	-	6						
N.J.Astle b Tuffey	37	136	102	-	7	(5) not out	61	88	74	-	13
C.Z.Harris* b Orchard	38	105	88	1	5	(6) not out	14	36	28	-	3
S.L.Stewart not out	26	83	50	-	3	(4) c Aldridge b Marshall H.J.H.	32	83	70	-	5
S.E.Bond c McGlashan b Orchard	8	26	14	-	1						
L.M.Burtt c Evans b Aldridge	5	36	31	-	1						
A.Singh lbw b Vettori	3	6	7	-	-						
Extras (b 5, lb 9, w 7, nb 11)	32					(lb 12, w 1, nb 3)	16				
TOTAL (101.4 overs)	**274**	413				(63 overs) (4 wkts)	**198**	231			

Bowling	*O*	*M*	*R*	*W*	*O*	*M*	*R*	*W*
CANTERBURY								
Bond	19	8	37	2	19.3	5	37	5
Burtt	15	1	37	3	14	2	41	1
Singh	14	2	74	2	8	2	27	0
Hiini	19	8	53	1	13	10	9	1
Astle N.J.	7	2	19	0	7.5	4	21	0
Harris	10	4	13	1	12	2	25	0
McMillan	7	0	19	1	5.1	1	16	2
Astle T.D.					3	0	14	0
NORTHERN DISTRICTS								
Tuffey	24	8	61	3	5	0	15	0
Aldridge	20	4	68	1	6	1	28	0
Orchard	24	11	33	4	12	3	43	0
Vettori	13.4	1	31	1	18	8	38	3
Yovich	14	2	57	1	16	4	35	0
Marshall H.J.H.	6	3	10	0	6	2	27	1

Fall of Wickets

	ND	***C***	***ND***	***C***
	1st	*1st*	*2nd*	*2nd*
1st	0	16	26	60
2nd	57	41	42	77
3rd	146	46	70	98
4th	146	117	75	151
5th	186	140	80	-
6th	196	218	81	-
7th	229	226	151	-
8th	252	250	169	-
9th	254	267	197	-
10th	272	274	197	-

In Northern Districts' second innings Watling retired hurt at 15-0 on 6 and resumed at 151-7*

AUCKLAND v WELLINGTON — State Championship

at Queen Elizabeth II Park, Christchurch on 29, 30 November, 1, 2 December, 2006
Toss : Auckland. Umpires : A.L. Hill & D.M. Quested
Close of play: 1st day: Wellington 2-0, Bell 2, M.E.Parlane 0; 2nd day: no play
3rd day: Wellington 184-3, Bell 65, N.R.Parlane 18
***First innings win to Wellington.** Points: Wellington 2, Auckland 0*

Auckland were dismissed just before the end of play on the first day. At one stage they were in a comfortable position at 134-3 with Jones and Nicol batting well. However, the loss of the Auckland captain saw wickets fall regularly, with Nicol top scoring with 85. O'Brien took 5-57.

After rain washed out the second day and caused a delay the next morning, Bell and Ryder put on 128 for the third wicket in Wellington's reply. With half-centuries from Neal Parlane and Franklin, Wellington coasted to a 133 run lead.

With so much time lost there was little chance of a result and McIntosh and Jones made sure of that with an unbroken century stand before the match was called off at tea.

AUCKLAND

FIRST INNINGS	Runs	Mins	Balls	6s	4s
T.G.McIntosh c Bell b O'Brien	9	31	24	-	1
R.A.Jones* b Patel	62	184	154	-	7
M.J.Guptill lbw b O'Brien	0	14	14	-	-
L.Vincent c Nevin b Gillespie	29	67	46	-	4
R.J.Nicol b Gillespie	85	198	191	-	13
K.D.Mills c Ryder b O'Brien	16	80	53	-	3
T.K.Canning c Ryder b Gillespie	22	79	50	-	3
R.A.Young† b O'Brien	7	25	13	-	1
L.J.Shaw c Ryder b O'Brien	1	15	8	-	-
R.M.Hira lbw b Patel	4	14	9	-	1
C.S.Martin not out	0	5	4	-	-
Extras (lb 7, nb 3)	10				
TOTAL (93.3 overs)	**245**	360			

SECOND INNINGS	Runs	Mins	Balls	6s	4s
not out	50	91	78	-	9
not out	47	91	69	-	5
b 1, w 1, nb 3)	5				
(24 overs) (0 wkts)	**102**	91			

WELLINGTON

	Runs	Mins	Balls	6s	4s
M.D.Bell c Young b Canning	91	209	219	-	10
M.E.Parlane* b Martin	8	47	35	-	2
S.P.Fleming lbw b Canning	6	18	13	-	1
J.D.Ryder c Young b Vincent	77	106	88	-	14
N.R.Parlane b Shaw	55	101	88	-	8
J.E.C.Franklin c Jones b Canning	54	99	95	-	9
C.J.Nevin† c Vincent b Shaw	45	97	50	-	6
L.J.Woodcock not out	16	34	20	-	4
J.S.Patel not out	11	7	6	1	1
M.R.Gillespie					
I.E.O'Brien					
Extras (b 6, lb 9, nb 10)	25				
TOTAL (101 overs) (7 wkts dec)	**388**	414			

Bowling	*O*	*M*	*R*	*W*	*O*	*M*	*R*	*W*
WELLINGTON								
Gillespie	21	6	43	3	5	0	24	0
Franklin	14	2	45	0	5	1	18	0
O'Brien	23	9	57	5	9	1	43	0
Ryder	3	0	14	0				
Patel	22.3	4	52	2	5	1	16	0
Woodcock	10	1	27	0				
AUCKLAND								
Martin	30	6	111	1				
Mills	9	3	22	0				
Canning	27	7	108	3				
Shaw	15	1	75	2				
Hira	19	6	49	0				
Vincent	1	0	8	1				

Fall of Wickets

	A	***W***	***A***
	1st	*1st*	*2nd*
1st	24	16	-
2nd	28	29	-
3rd	86	157	-
4th	134	246	-
5th	177	279	-
6th	217	332	-
7th	232	371	-
8th	236	-	-
9th	245	-	-
10th	245	-	-

CENTRAL DISTRICTS v NORTHERN DISTRICTS

at Bert Sutcliffe Oval, Lincoln on 29, 30 November, 1, 2 December, 2006
Toss : Central Districts. Umpires : B.G. Frost & P.D. Jones
Close of play: 1st day: CD 366-5, Hay 62, Griggs 15; 2nd day: no play
3rd day: CD 26-0, How 15, Barnett 11
***Northern Districts won by 2 wickets.** Points: Northern Districts 6, Central Districts 2*

Leg-spiner Schaw made his first-class debut for Central Districts in this game and watched his team amass 366-5 by stumps on the first day. After a century stand between How and Barnett, Sinclair reached his century off 189 balls in 272 minutes while Hay continued his impressive start to his first-class career.

After no play on the second day, Central were finally bowled out for 464 on the third. Northern batted for 117 minutes before declaring 402 runs behind and Central faced just eight overs before leaving Northern 429 to win.

Hamish Marshall led the way reaching his century off 134 balls in 152 minutes. He went at 240-5 but Orchard and Vettori added 99 in even time and McGlashan helped his skipper put on 74 in just 68 minutes. Vettori had reached his century from 132 balls in 207 minutes and fittingly struck the winning runs which came at 7.25 pm.

CENTRAL DISTRICTS

FIRST INNINGS	*Runs*	*Mins*	*Balls*	*6s*	*4s*	*SECOND INNINGS*	*Runs*	*Mins*	*Balls*	*6s*	*4s*
J.M.How* c Vettori b Martin	50	103	88	1	8	not out	15	23	20	-	2
G.E.F.Barnett c McGlashan b Martin	59	158	115	-	8	not out	11	23	28	-	2
M.S.Sinclair c Flynn b Arnel	109	246	207	1	13						
L.R.P.L.Taylor c Flynn b Vettori	47	87	83	-	7						
J.D.P.Oram c Marshall J.A.H. b Yovich	0	6	5	-	-						
G.R.Hay lbw b Arnel	74	176	120	-	13						
B.B.J.Griggs† c Vettori b Martin	31	93	70	-	4						
E.P.Thompson lbw b Martin	20	60	40	-	-						
M.J.Mason c Arnel b Yovich	1	5	4	-	-						
R.J.Schaw c McGlashan b Vettori	31	72	69	-	4						
B.E.Hefford not out	15	31	32	-	3						
Extras (b 3, lb 10, nb 14)	27						0				
TOTAL (137.1 overs)	**464**	518				(8 overs) (0 wkts dec)	**26**	23			

NORTHERN DISTRICTS

	Runs	*Mins*	*Balls*	*6s*	*4s*		*Runs*	*Mins*	*Balls*	*6s*	*4s*
J.A.H.Marshall b Mason	3	12	10	-	-	lbw b Schaw	17	100	71	-	-
B.S.Wilson c Barnett b Thompson	4	32	30	-	-	c Griggs b Thompson	8	27	20	-	1
H.J.H.Marshall not out	33	104	66	1	3	b Mason	153	250	206	1	24
A.W.Evans not out	10	84	60	-	1	c Taylor b Thompson	23	75	45	-	3
D.R.Flynn						lbw b Oram	7	53	34	-	-
D.L.Vettori*						not out	120	207	147	-	16
M.G.Orchard						b Mason	0	8	5	-	-
J.A.F.Yovich						b Mason	52	99	86	-	7
P.D.McGlashan†						c & b Thompson	16	68	36	-	2
B.P.Martin						not out	5	18	17	-	1
B.J.Arnel											
Extras (lb 8, nb 4)	12					(b 8, lb 10, w 3, nb 7)	28				
TOTAL (27 overs) (2 wkts dec)	**62**	117				(110.2 overs) (8 wkts)	**429**	465			

Bowling	*O*	*M*	*R*	*W*	*O*	*M*	*R*	*W*
NORTHERN DISTRICTS								
Yovich	25	5	79	2				
Arnel	25	4	102	2				
Orchard	20	5	90	0				
Vettori	27.1	5	63	2				
Martin	40	9	117	4				
Marshall J.A.H.					4	0	10	0
Marshall H.J.H.					4	0	16	0
CENTRAL DISTRICTS								
Mason	6	2	14	1	25.2	5	74	3
Thompson	7	3	7	1	27	5	120	3
Oram	5	3	4	0	22	5	52	1
Hefford	6	2	15	0	21	6	62	0
Schaw	3	0	14	0	11	0	70	1
How					2	0	18	0
Taylor					2	0	15	0

Fall of Wickets

	CD	***ND***	***CD***	***ND***
	1st	*1st*	*2nd*	*2nd*
1st	106	7	-	14
2nd	137	18	-	72
3rd	217	-	-	158
4th	218	-	-	199
5th	339	-	-	240
6th	390	-	-	240
7th	400	-	-	339
8th	406	-	-	413
9th	434	-	-	-
10th	464	-	-	-

CENTRAL DISTRICTS v OTAGO — State Championship

at McLean Park, Napier on 7, 8, 9, 10 December, 2006
Toss : Central Districts. Umpires : R.D. Anderson & P.D. Jones
Close of play: 1st day: Otago 72-1, Haig 42, Redmond 23; 2nd day: Otago 448-6, Hopkins 43, McCullum 1
3rd day: CD 102-1, Barnett 51, Griggs 9
***First innings win to Otago.** Points: Otago 2, Central Districts 0*

Niblett made his first-class debut as Central enjoyed another good day's batting, being dismissed for 394, although it could have been more as they were 210-2 at one stage. Taylor was the star reaching three figures from 93 balls in 136 minutes and his first double century from 191 balls in 281 minutes. It was the highest innings in a first-class game at McLean Park. Taylor and Schaw put on 113 for the eighth wicket, a Central record against Otago.

In reply Otago piled on the runs reaching the highest total in their history, the highest by any team against Central and the highest at McLean Park. Haig reached his maiden hundred after 155 minutes from 122 balls while Hopkins took 212 minutes and 142 balls.

Central were 230 behind but gave another sound batting display. Barnett reached his first century for Central Districts from 164 balls in 205 minutes and by the time the last wicket fell, Otago needed 166 but only 13 overs remained. Broom reached fifty off just 26 balls but the target was too stiff.

In the absence of How, Hamilton led Central for the first time but broke down in just his second over. McCullum took six catches in the field during the match, a record for Otago, while his four in the first innings equalled the Otago record.

CENTRAL DISTRCTS

FIRST INNINGS	*Runs*	*Mins*	*Balls*	*6s*	*4s*	*SECOND INNINGS*	*Runs*	*Mins*	*Balls*	*6s*	*4s*
G.E.F.Barnett c Hopkins b McMillan	21	34	20	-	2	c sub (C.M.Smith) b Redmond	118	236	193	1	14
P.J.Ingram c McCullum b Harvie	15	29	26	-	2	c Hopkins b McCullum	31	73	47	1	3
B.B.J.Griggs† c Hopkins b McMillan	75	137	101	-	12	lbw b Harvie	83	304	217	-	10
L.R.P.L.Taylor c McCullum b McMillan	217	315	212	2	26	c McCullum b Redmond	3	8	7	-	-
T.I.Weston c Redmond b Hogg	4	17	10	-	-	c Redmond b Hogg	35	91	73	-	2
G.R.Hay c McCullum b McMillan	0	4	3	-	-	run out	54	134	90	-	5
E.P.Thompson c McCullum b Harvie	10	16	15	-	2	c Harvie b McCullum	21	27	35	-	3
A.D.Niblett c Hopkins b McCullum	14	29	25	-	3	b McCullum	0	1	1	-	-
R.J.Schaw c Sheed b McCullum	23	95	74	-	2	c McCullum b Harvie	17	85	95	-	1
B.E.Hefford b Hogg	0	13	8	-	-	not out	13	35	27	-	2
L.J.Hamilton* not out	0	2	0	-	-	b Harvie	0	3	4	-	-
Extras (b 2, lb 6, w 2, nb 5)	15					(b 2, lb 8, w 6, nb 4)	20				
TOTAL (81.3 overs)	**394**	350				(130.5 overs)	**395**	508			

OTAGO

	Runs	*Mins*	*Balls*	*6s*	*4s*		*Runs*	*Mins*	*Balls*	*6s*	*4s*
J.W.Sheed c Barnett b Thompson	0	15	8	-	-	b Thompson	3	6	5	-	-
S.B.Haig c Hefford b Niblett	111	162	126	1	14	lbw b Hefford	5	12	8	-	-
A.J.Redmond c Taylor b Niblett	38	91	69	-	6						
G.R.Todd c Taylor b Thompson	85	210	160	-	8	c Schaw b Thompson	11	12	7	-	1
N.T.Broom c Taylor b Hefford	79	149	137	1	7	(3) not out	63	51	36	4	2
G.J.Hopkins*† not out	126	242	157	2	8						
K.W.Hogg b Niblett	71	101	69	-	10	(5) c & b Thompson	12	17	14	1	-
N.L.McCullum c Griggs b Taylor	48	67	60	-	4	(6) not out	5	14	9	-	-
B.E.Scott run out	29	53	43	-	2						
J.M.McMillan lbw b Schaw	3	6	6	-	-						
M.J.Harvie b Schaw	8	5	7	-	2						
Extras (b 8, lb 13, w 1, nb 4)	26					(nb 1)	1				
TOTAL (139.4 overs)	**624**	555				(13 overs) (4 wkts)	**100**	58			

Bowling	*O*	*M*	*R*	*W*	*O*	*M*	*R*	*W*
OTAGO								
McMillan	15.3	1	82	4	3.1	0	13	0
Harvie	16	1	82	2	26.5	3	106	3
Hogg	17	4	60	2	26	4	78	1
Scott	10	1	57	0	14	4	25	0
Redmond	9	0	58	0	25	6	74	2
McCullum	13	3	42	2	35.5	10	89	3
Broom	1	0	5	0				
CENTRAL DISTRICTS								
Hamilton	1.3	1	8	0				
Thompson	30	6	123	2	6	0	45	3
Hefford	37.3	5	174	1	6	0	51	1
Niblett	27	2	123	3	1	0	4	0
Barnett	3	0	15	0				
Schaw	25.4	4	97	2				
Taylor	15	0	63	1				

Fall of Wickets

	CD	***O***	***CD***	***O***
	1st	*1st*	*2nd*	*2nd*
1st	38	20	68	7
2nd	42	129	204	17
3rd	210	171	208	44
4th	231	332	270	80
5th	236	332	300	-
6th	250	445	338	-
7th	275	530	338	-
8th	388	600	378	-
9th	392	608	395	-
10th	394	624	395	-

NORTHERN DISTRICTS v WELLINGTON State Championship

at Seddon Park, Hamilton on 7, 8, 9, 10 December, 2006
Toss : Wellington. Umpires : B.F. Bowden & D.J. Walker
Close of play: 1st day: Wellington 351-5, N.R.Parlane 66, Elliott 14; 2nd day: ND 83-5, Yovich 3, Orchard 1
3rd day: ND 16-1, Evans 9, H.J.H.Marshall 6
***Wellington won by 10 wickets.** Points: Wellington 8, Northern Districts 0*

Jefferson, who had played age group cricket in the area before he played for Wellington, made his debut for Northern Districts.

Wellington batted all the first day to end at 351-5. Next day Elliott carried on to reach his first century for Wellington after 220 minutes from 173 balls. The innings was declared shortly afterwards at 524-8.

Northern came nowhere near matching this total and, although they did recover from 112-6, were all out 271 runs behind and had to follow on before the close of the third day.

They fared just as badly in the second innings and were 104-7 when James Marshall, who had earlier retired hurt, returned to join Orchard. Marshall went on to reach a hundred from 104 balls in 110 minutes and the pair added 152 for the eighth wicket, equalling the Northern record against all teams.

Arnel then held out for 96 minutes as he and Orchard added a valuable 39 runs for the last wicket. It was not quite enough, however, and Wellington were able to score the required runs off the first ball of the last of the five overs available to them.

WELLINGTON

FIRST INNINGS	*Runs*	*Mins*	*Balls*	*6s*	*4s*	*SECOND INNINGS*	*Runs*	*Mins*	*Balls*	*6s*	*4s*
M.D.Bell b Aldridge	101	231	177	1	14						
L.J.Woodcock c McGlashan b Aldridge	1	5	2	-	-						
M.E.Parlane* c McGlashan b Orchard	61	141	90	2	8	(2) not out	7	25	11	-	-
J.D.Ryder c McGlashan b Jefferson	37	80	62	-	6	(1) not out	26	25	16	2	1
N.R.Parlane c Orchard b Arnel	89	212	173	-	14						
C.J.Nevin† c McGlashan b Arnel	50	99	90	2	3						
G.D.Elliott not out	102	222	175	1	12						
D.J.Bowden run out	42	77	49	-	8						
J.S.Patel c McGlashan b Orchard	15	28	28	1	-						
M.R.Gillespie											
I.E.O'Brien											
Extras (b 3, lb 12, w 2, nb 9)	26					(lb 2, nb 2)	4				
TOTAL (139.4 overs) (8 wkts dec)	**524**	554				(4.1 overs) (0 wkts)	**37**	25			

NORTHERN DISTRICTS

	Runs	Mins	Balls	6s	4s		Runs	Mins	Balls	6s	4s
B-J.Watling c Parlane M.E. b O'Brien	14	38	31	-	3	(2) c Parlane M.E. b Gillespie	0	17	13	-	-
A.W.Evans run out	43	112	73	-	7	(1) c Bell b Bowden	34	126	97	-	6
H.J.H.Marshall c Ryder b O'Brien	4	8	6	-	-	c Nevin b Gillespie	11	16	12	-	2
J.A.H.Marshall* c Parlane M.E. b O'Brien	4	11	8	-	1	c Bowden b Gillespie	128	149	138	1	19
D.R.Flynn b O'Brien	9	17	10	-	2	b Bowden	9	50	28	-	1
J.A.F.Yovich c Bell b Gillespie	31	161	125	-	3	c Bell b Elliott	3	26	20	-	-
M.G.Orchard lbw b Elliott	17	48	41	-	3	not out	74	338	255	1	9
P.D.McGlashan† b Patel	50	164	116	-	7	c Nevin b Gillespie	5	42	28	-	1
M.R.Jefferson c Patel b Woodcock	29	75	59	-	3	c Bell b O'Brien	6	41	34	-	1
G.W.Aldridge b Gillespie	22	36	33	-	3	lbw b O'Brien	7	5	7	-	1
B.J.Arnel not out	6	25	21	-	1	b Gillespie	8	98	67	-	1
Extras (lb 7, w 4, nb 13)	24					(b 1, lb 9, nb 7)	17				
TOTAL (85 overs)	**253**	352				(113.5 overs)	**302**	459			

Bowling	*O*	*M*	*R*	*W*	*O*	*M*	*R*	*W*
NORTHERN DISTRICTS								
Yovich	21	2	107	0				
Aldridge	26	4	97	2				
Orchard	36.4	10	102	2	2.1	0	22	0
Arnel	24	3	73	2	2	0	13	0
Jefferson	22	1	95	1				
Marshall J.A.H.	10	1	35	0				
WELLINGTON								
Gillespie	23	2	91	2	27.5	6	93	5
O'Brien	26	8	69	4	27	9	75	2
Patel	16	3	37	1	21	10	30	0
Elliott	8	3	21	1	22	9	43	1
Woodcock	7	2	18	1	4	1	8	0
Bowden	5	0	10	0	12	2	43	2

Fall of Wickets	***W***	***ND***	***ND***	***W***
	1st	*1st*	*2nd*	*2nd*
1st	3	22	9	-
2nd	137	30	25	-
3rd	210	38	60	-
4th	210	55	67	-
5th	309	80	68	-
6th	399	112	84	-
7th	485	157	104	-
8th	524	219	256	-
9th	-	225	263	-
10th	-	253	302	-

In Northern Districts' second innings J.A.H.Marshall retired hurt at 32-2 on 5 and resumed at 104-7*

AUCKLAND v CANTERBURY

State Championship

at Eden Park Outer Oval, Auckland on 7, 8, 9, 10 December, 2006
Toss : Auckland. Umpires : T.J. Parlane & E.A. Watkin
Close of play: 1st day: Auckland 4-0, McIntosh 4, Jones 0; 2nd day: Canterbury 69-3, Fulton 34, Harris 12
3rd day: Auckland 52-2, Guptill 20, Vincent 26
***Canterbury won by 6 runs.** Points: Canterbury 8, Auckland 0*

Chan and Munro made their first-class debuts in this game which saw Auckland send Canterbury in to bat. It was Chan who helped his side to some respectability with 35 at number eleven. Auckland, however, still found this total too much and were bowled out for just 180. No one reached 30.

The bowlers again dominated when Canterbury batted again and Auckland were left 272 to win. They were 52-2 at stumps. Next day Auckland collapsed to 89-6 before Canning and Young took the score to 162. Adams came in and smashed fifty off just 21 balls in 23 minutes and, although he and Canning adopted a more cautious approach as the target neared, at 263-7 Auckland appeared assured of an unexpected victory.

Harris brought McMillan on to bowl and he soon accounted for Adams, 263-8. Next over Hiini trapped Lythe and it was 264-9. Munro survived the last three balls. Canning took a single off the fifth ball of McMillan's next over but Munro failed to see out the last ball and Canterbury had won by just six runs. It was Auckland's closest ever loss in terms of runs.

CANTERBURY

FIRST INNINGS	*Runs*	*Mins*	*Balls*	*6s*	*4s*	*SECOND INNINGS*	*Runs*	*Mins*	*Balls*	*6s*	*4s*
T.D.Astle b Adams	12	35	42	-	1	c Jones b Canning	4	13	12	-	1
M.H.W.Papps lbw b Munro	21	79	56	-	2	lbw b Adams	1	17	14	-	-
P.G.Fulton c McIntosh b Hitchcock	68	111	99	2	9	c Young b Adams	34	75	61	1	5
C.D.McMillan c Young b Adams	12	77	59	-	2	lbw b Canning	9	17	16	-	2
C.Z.Harris* lbw b Canning	23	96	68	1	1	c Young b Adams	52	157	125	-	8
S.L.Stewart b Lythe	23	98	85	-	2	lbw b Adams	21	68	63	-	3
C.F.K.van Wyk† lbw b Adams	10	64	41	-	-	run out	0	7	2	-	-
B.C.Hiini lbw b Vincent	15	35	35	-	2	not out	39	122	94	-	6
C.A.Small not out	12	81	68	-	2	run out	18	71	50	-	2
L.M.Burtt run out	1	6	7	-	-	(11) lbw b Adams	7	20	16	-	1
S.P.Chan c Young b Munro	35	59	44	-	6	(10) lbw b Vincent	0	1	2	-	-
Extras (b 4, lb 2, w 4, nb 9)	19					(b 1, lb 8, nb 6)	15				
TOTAL (99.3 overs)	**251**	376				(74.5 overs)	**200**	288			

AUCKLAND

	Runs	*Mins*	*Balls*	*6s*	*4s*		*Runs*	*Mins*	*Balls*	*6s*	*4s*
T.G.McIntosh c van Wyk b Chan	14	54	39	-	3	c van Wyk b Chan	2	25	17	-	-
R.A.Jones* c Harris b Small	27	87	65	-	4	lbw b Burtt	1	11	8	-	-
M.J.Guptill c Stewart b Small	6	44	34	-	1	c van Wyk b Hiini	30	71	55	-	4
L.Vincent b Hiini	2	14	6	-	-	c Harris b Hiini	41	54	26	-	9
R.J.Nicol lbw b Small	4	15	7	-	1	c van Wyk b Chan	1	22	14	-	-
P.A.Hitchcock c van Wyk b Burtt	19	55	40	-	3	b Chan	7	32	20	-	1
T.K.Canning c van Wyk b Burtt	4	16	12	-	-	not out	90	162	123	1	12
R.A.Young† lbw b Hiini	26	49	41	-	4	c van Wyk b Astle	25	62	46	-	4
A.R.Adams c Burtt b Small	29	93	67	-	4	c Small b McMillan	65	73	49	3	8
T.I.Lythe c Harris b Astle	18	95	78	-	3	lbw b Hiini	0	5	4	-	-
C.Munro not out	20	26	25	-	3	c van Wyk b McMillan	0	6	4	-	-
Extras (lb 2, w 2, nb 7)	11					(b 1, lb 2)	3				
TOTAL (67.5 overs)	**180**	279				(61 overs)	**265**	266			

Bowling	*O*	*M*	*R*	*W*	*O*	*M*	*R*	*W*
AUCKLAND								
Canning	28	11	64	1	17	9	19	2
Adams	25	7	57	3	24.5	11	58	5
Munro	17.3	2	57	2	12	3	44	0
Hitchcock	16	7	40	1	11	3	27	0
Lythe	12	4	25	1	9	1	42	0
Vincent	1	0	2	1	1	0	1	1
CANTERBURY								
Burtt	12	2	34	2	13	4	66	1
Chan	14	3	41	1	16	1	58	3
Hiini	19	5	40	2	15	2	57	3
Small	12	0	50	4	5	0	40	0
Harris	10	4	13	0	7	3	14	0
Astle	0.5	0	0	1	2	0	23	1
McMillan					3	0	4	2

Fall of Wickets

	C	A	C	A
	1st	*1st*	*2nd*	*2nd*
1st	23	29	10	5
2nd	55	45	10	5
3rd	120	53	29	77
4th	122	53	72	78
5th	165	59	120	80
6th	175	73	125	89
7th	199	92	138	162
8th	203	116	185	263
9th	204	159	185	264
10th	251	180	200	265

CANTERBURY v CENTRAL DISTRICTS State Championship

at Queen Elizabeth II Park, Christchurch on 14, 15, 16, 17 December, 2006
Toss : Canterbury. Umpires : B.F. Bowden & T.J. Parlane
Close of play: 1st day: Canterbury 12-0, Astle 7, Papps 4; 2nd day: Canterbury 305-4, Stewart 2, Hiini 6
3rd day: CD 148-1, Ingram 76, Griggs 37
***First innings win to Canterbury.** Points: Canterbury 2, Central Districts 0*

Central had their third captain in as many games with Taylor doing the job at first-class level for the first time following the injury to Hamilton in the previous match.

Central were sent in and only Ingram showed any resistance. He reached his century of 173 balls in 239 minutes before being seventh out at 233.

Canterbury had no such problems when they batted with three players making hundreds. Papps took 285 balls and 366 minutes, McMillan 141 balls in 180 minutes and nightwatchman Hiini (highest score) took 213 minutes and 182 balls. Papps and McMillan put on 208 for the third wicket, a Canterbury record against Central.

Facing a deficit of 236 Central were untroubled in batting out the remainder of the match. Ingram reached his second century of the game from 297 balls in 378 minutes, beating his previous best in both innings. The match was called off at tea.

CENTRAL DISTRICTS

FIRST INNINGS	*Runs*	*Mins*	*Balls*	*6s*	*4s*	*SECOND INNINGS*	*Runs*	*Mins*	*Balls*	*6s*	*4s*
G.E.F.Barnett run out	16	41	30	-	3	run out	32	46	33	-	6
P.J.Ingram b Astle	119	279	213	-	18	not out	166	413	326	-	26
B.B.J.Griggs† c McMillan b Burtt	6	23	18	-	1	c Harris b Small	72	196	155	-	10
L.R.P.L.Taylor* c van Wyk b Chan	21	41	32	-	2	c van Wyk b Astle	7	14	11	-	1
T.I.Weston run out	3	9	7	-	-	not out	65	154	158	-	10
G.R.Hay lbw b Harris	41	71	54	1	6						
B.J.Diamanti st van Wyk b Astle	18	77	62	-	2						
M.J.Mason lbw b Harris	4	15	17	-	-						
R.J.Schaw not out	25	50	35	-	4						
G.J.T.Hegglun b Burtt	6	33	42	-	1						
B.E.Hefford c Harris b Chan	0	12	5	-	-						
Extras (lb 4, nb 1)	5					(b 9, lb 6, w 1)	16				
TOTAL (85.3 overs)	**264**	330				(114 overs) (3 wkts)	**358**	413			

CANTERBURY

	Runs	Mins	Balls	6s	4s
T.D.Astle c Griggs b Mason	17	86	72	-	1
M.H.W.Papps b Hegglun	121	422	327	-	14
P.G.Fulton c Hay b Hegglun	32	78	64	1	5
C.D.McMillan c Griggs b Hegglun	117	242	180	1	15
S.L.Stewart lbw b Mason	76	186	124	-	8
B.C.Hiini not out	103	234	182	-	14
C.Z.Harris* not out	21	61	46	-	2
C.F.K.van Wyk†					
C.A.Small					
L.M.Burtt					
S.P.Chan					
Extras (b 6, lb 3, w 3, nb 1)	13				
TOTAL (165.3 overs) (5 wkts dec)	**500**	657			

Bowling	*O*	*M*	*R*	*W*	*O*	*M*	*R*	*W*
CANTERBURY								
Burtt	15	2	60	2	5	1	20	0
Chan	15.3	2	60	2	13	0	56	0
Hiini	16	3	46	0	18	6	39	0
Small	5	1	18	0	20	2	65	1
McMillan	10	2	36	0	10	2	36	0
Harris	17	9	21	2	21	7	46	0
Astle	7	0	19	2	24	1	74	1
Stewart					3	0	7	0
CENTRAL DISTRICTS								
Mason	31	9	72	2				
Hefford	33.3	12	89	0				
Hegglun	30	6	94	3				
Diamanti	30	2	107	0				
Schaw	28	6	102	0				
Taylor	13	0	27	0				

Fall of Wickets

	CD *1st*	***C*** *1st*	***CD*** *2nd*
1st	42	29	53
2nd	60	86	230
3rd	98	294	241
4th	101	297	-
5th	164	456	-
6th	226	-	-
7th	233	-	-
8th	233	-	-
9th	259	-	-
10th	264	-	-

AUCKLAND v NORTHERN DISTRICTS State Championship

at Eden Park Outer Oval, Auckland on 14, 15, 16, 17 December, 2006
Toss : Auckland. Umpires : B.G. Frost & E.J. Gray
Close of play: 1st day: ND 278-7, McGlashan 45, Jefferson 0; 2nd day: ND 60-1, Watling 24, H.J.H.Marshall 17
3rd day: Auckland 63-5, Lythe 7, Canning 1
***Northern Districts won by 318 runs.** Points: Northern Districts 8, Auckland 0*

Just four days after their narrow loss to Canterbury Auckland sent Northern in but saw the visitors enjoy a solid day's batting, being 278-7 at stumps. Northern continued into the second day and were eventually all out for 306.

Auckland were 60-0 but then lost all ten wickets for just a further 76 runs. Northern led by 170 and extended this to 435 with a sound second innings display. Hamish Marshall was dismissed one short of a century.

Auckland began their second innings badly, being 13-3, and it did not get any better. At stumps they were 63-5 and by 12.17 pm the next day the match was all over. Aldridge picked up a career best return to help Northern on their way to the biggest winning margin in their history.

NORTHERN DISTRICTS

FIRST INNINGS	*Runs*	*Mins*	*Balls*	*6s*	*4s*	*SECOND INNINGS*	*Runs*	*Mins*	*Balls*	*6s*	*4s*
B-J.Watling b Canning	1	24	22	-	-	(2) b Canning	27	114	95	-	4
A.W.Evans b Shaw	30	130	110	-	2	(1) lbw b Shaw	17	37	32	-	3
H.J.H.Marshall b Adams	22	60	54	-	3	c Adams b Munro	99	263	175	-	11
J.A.H.Marshall* lbw b Adams	56	136	97	-	12	lbw b Shaw	0	13	11	-	-
N.K.W.Horsley c Young b Adams	28	98	80	-	3	c Munro b Shaw	58	136	107	1	8
J.A.F.Yovich lbw b Shaw	10	65	37	-	2	c Shaw b Vincent	4	14	17	-	1
M.G.Orchard c Young b Adams	59	152	128	-	8	c Munro b Adams	13	64	53	-	3
P.D.McGlashan† c Nicol b Canning	48	125	105	-	7	not out	26	76	54	-	2
M.R.Jefferson not out	15	68	58	-	2	st Young b Adams	7	22	26	-	1
G.W.Aldridge lbw b Canning	1	4	3	-	-	lbw b Canning	1	4	2	-	-
B.J.Arnel c Nicol b Canning	6	31	29	-	1	lbw b Canning	1	4	4	-	-
Extras (b 10, lb 15, nb 5)	30					(b 1, lb 2, w 6, nb 3)	12				
TOTAL (119.4 overs)	**306**	451				(95.2 overs)	**265**	378			

AUCKLAND

	Runs	*Mins*	*Balls*	*6s*	*4s*		*Runs*	*Mins*	*Balls*	*6s*	*4s*
T.G.McIntosh lbw b Orchard	20	100	85	-	2	c McGlashan b Orchard	5	30	22	-	1
R.A.Jones* c Jefferson b Yovich	50	142	97	-	6	c McGlashan b Aldridge	0	17	13	-	-
M.B.Loye c McGlashan b Aldridge	0	12	6	-	-	c Evans b Aldridge	4	7	5	-	1
L.Vincent c McGlashan b Yovich	18	40	30	-	4	c McGlashan b Arnel	27	73	49	-	5
R.J.Nicol not out	12	89	49	-	-	c McGlashan b Arnel	9	51	44	-	-
T.K.Canning b Arnel	0	4	4	-	-	(7) c McGlashan b Yovich	1	35	24	-	-
R.A.Young† lbw b Arnel	0	1	1	-	-	(8) c McGlashan b Aldridge	17	48	33	-	3
A.R.Adams b Arnel	20	24	13	-	4	(9) b Aldridge	4	7	6	-	1
T.I.Lythe b Arnel	0	1	1	-	-	(6) b Aldridge	17	129	94	-	2
C.Munro c Watling b Aldridge	6	28	26	-	1	c Aldridge b Arnel	13	24	22	-	2
L.J.Shaw b Orchard	2	14	15	-	-	not out	0	4	0	-	-
Extras (lb 3, nb 5)	8					(b 3, lb 14, nb 3)	20				
TOTAL (53.4 overs)	**136**	232				(51.3 overs)	**117**	217			

Bowling	*O*	*M*	*R*	*W*	*O*	*M*	*R*	*W*
AUCKLAND								
Adams	35	14	57	4	20	5	36	2
Canning	36.4	17	54	4	25.2	9	62	3
Munro	19	4	58	0	16	6	31	1
Shaw	22	6	66	2	19	4	61	3
Lythe	4	0	34	0	6	0	31	0
Nicol	1	0	5	0				
Vincent	2	0	7	0	9	0	41	1
NORTHERN DISTRICTS								
Aldridge	17	4	38	2	12	3	33	5
Orchard	14.4	5	33	2	18	11	16	1
Yovich	10	0	31	2	9	2	25	1
Arnel	12	3	31	4	12.3	5	26	3

Fall of Wickets

	ND *1st*	***A*** *1st*	***ND*** *2nd*	***A*** *2nd*
1st	11	60	28	5
2nd	47	67	71	9
3rd	72	88	72	13
4th	150	95	190	37
5th	161	96	201	62
6th	198	96	224	67
7th	278	119	246	100
8th	288	119	260	104
9th	290	131	263	113
10th	306	136	265	117

OTAGO v WELLINGTON — State Championship

at University Oval, Dunedin on 14, 15, 16, 17 December, 2006
Toss : Wellington. Umpires : G.A. Baxter & D.J. Walker
Close of play: 1st day: Wellington 5-2, Woodcock 3, Ryder 2; 2nd day: Wellington 201-1, Bell 103, M.E.Parlane 85
3rd day: no play
***First innings win to Otago.** Points: Otago 2, Wellington 0*

Hopkins was injured after the toss had been made so had to play. Haig took over as keeper and McCullum captained the side in the field.

Otago were sent in and were soon in trouble but recovered thanks to Redmond, Todd, Broom and Hogg. Wellington lost two wickets before stumps and next morning suffered an astonishing collapse which saw them reeling at 21-7. At one stage Scott had figures of 8-6-2-4.

Wellington staged some sort of a recovery but were still bowled out for 71 and had to follow on. In a vastly improved performance they were 201-1 at stumps and, when the third day was washed out, had no trouble in saving the game. Parlane reached his hundred off 203 balls in 252 minutes while Bell took 212 balls and 259 minutes. The second wicket stand of 279 between the pair was a record for all teams against Otago.

After leaving the New Zealand test squad O'Brien replaced Rasmussen but, as it turned out, he played no part in the game.

OTAGO

FIRST INNINGS	*Runs*	*Mins*	*Balls*	*6s*	*4s*	*SECOND INNINGS*	*Runs*	*Mins*	*Balls*	*6s*	*4s*
J.W.Sheed c Nevin b Gillespie	6	30	24	-	1						
S.B.Haig c Nevin b Rasmussen	0	5	1	-	-						
A.J.Redmond c Nevin b Elliott	32	105	82	-	5						
G.R.Todd c Parlane N.R. b Rasmussen	46	124	97	-	8						
N.T.Broom c Nevin b Patel	67	176	121	-	10						
K.W.Hogg c Woodcock b Patel	34	96	83	-	6						
N.L.McCullum c & b Woodcock	14	31	27	1	1						
B.E.Scott c Parlane M.E. b Rasmussen	24	57	42	2	1						
C.M.Smith c Parlane N.R. b Gillespie	21	64	58	-	2						
G.J.Hopkins*† not out	4	22	14	-	1						
M.J.Harvie b Gillespie	0	10	9	-	-						
Extras (lb 8, w 1, nb 13)	22										
TOTAL (91 overs)	**270**	360									

WELLINGTON

	Runs	*Mins*	*Balls*	*6s*	*4s*		*Runs*	*Mins*	*Balls*	*6s*	*4s*
M.E.Parlane* b Harvie	0	3	4	-	-	(3) c Hogg b Harvie	140	355	279	2	19
L.J.Woodcock lbw b Smith	8	79	54	-	1	c Haig b Scott	6	18	17	-	1
J.S.Patel c Haig b Harvie	0	1	1	-	-						
J.D.Ryder b Scott	3	32	25	-	-	b Scott	23	29	23	2	1
M.D.Bell lbw b Scott	0	25	16	-	-	(1) not out	161	440	327	-	23
N.R.Parlane lbw b Scott	8	22	18	-	1	(5) not out	13	35	39	-	-
C.J.Nevin† c Broom b McCullum	6	42	25	-	-						
G.D.Elliott c Haig b Scott	0	5	2	-	-						
D.J.Bowden run out	25	49	44	-	3						
M.R.Gillespie not out	18	28	21	1	3						
S.Rasmussen lbw b Smith	0	8	5	-	-						
I.E.O'Brien											
Extras (lb 2, nb 1)	3					(b 1, lb 5, nb 3)	9				
TOTAL (35.4 overs)	**71**	148				(114 overs) (3 wkts)	**352**	440			

Bowling	*O*	*M*	*R*	*W*	*O*	*M*	*R*	*W*
WELLINGTON								
Gillespie	24	4	89	3				
Rasmussen	19	7	40	3				
Elliott	14	4	42	1				
Bowden	11	3	38	0				
Patel	15	4	28	2				
Woodcock	8	3	25	1				
OTAGO								
Harvie	12	5	30	2	19	2	86	1
Hogg	2	1	1	0	7	0	38	0
Scott	10	6	13	4	24.2	7	59	2
Smith	6.4	3	7	2	23	11	39	0
McCullum	5	2	18	1	24	4	69	0
Redmond					11	1	35	0
Broom					3.4	0	18	0
Todd					2	1	2	0

Fall of Wickets

	O	*W*	*W*
	1st	*1st*	*2nd*
1st	0	0	12
2nd	9	0	291
3rd	70	6	324
4th	100	12	-
5th	194	21	-
6th	221	21	-
7th	221	21	-
8th	260	45	-
9th	270	66	-
10th	270	71	-

CENTRAL DISTRICTS v AUCKLAND State Championship

at McLean Park, Napier on 19, 20, 21 February, 2007
Toss : Central Districts. Umpires : P.D. Jones & D.J. Walker
Close of play: 1st day: Auckland 137-3, Nicol 36, de Grandhomme 65; 2nd day: CD 114-4, Schaw 1, Weston 0
***Auckland won by 8 wickets.** Points: Auckland 8, Central Districts 0*

Houpapa and Hayne made their first-class debuts while former Zimbabwe Under 19 player de Grandhomme made his Auckland debut. After Central won the toss and batted Ingram registered his third century in successive innings. He reached his hundred after 237 minutes and 179 balls and was eighth out at 179.

Auckland were 137-3 at stumps and went on to amass a lead of 149. Nicol's hundred took 322 minutes and 242 balls. Central progressed to 109-4 by the close but offered little resistance the next day, as Shaw picked up his first five wicket haul.

Auckland needed just 40 to win. McIntosh and Guptill went without scoring before the winning runs came at 2.21 pm.

CENTRAL DISTRICTS

FIRST INNINGS	*Runs*	*Mins*	*Balls*	*6s*	*4s*	*SECOND INNINGS*	*Runs*	*Mins*	*Balls*	*6s*	*4s*
J.M.How* c Adams b Martin	0	3	5	-	-	c de Grandhomme b Shaw	72	101	84	-	12
P.J.Ingram c Young b Martin	105	248	186	1	15	b Martin	2	20	9	-	-
M.S.Sinclair c Hayne b Adams	3	9	6	-	-	c Young b Martin	11	22	14	-	1
G.R.Hay b Adams	7	8	9	-	1	c Guptill b Adams	23	69	63	-	4
T.I.Weston b Martin	8	14	13	-	1	(6) c Guptill b Adams	16	62	41	-	2
B.B.J.Griggs† c Jones b Adams	31	91	69	-	6	(7) c Young b Martin	25	81	73	-	2
A.D.Niblett c Young b Shaw	15	52	37	-	1	(8) c Guptill b Shaw	0	2	2	-	-
R.J.Schaw c Jones b Hayne	3	44	37	-	-	(5) c Jones b Shaw	26	121	93	-	3
M.J.Mason not out	5	29	19	-	-	c de Grandhomme b Shaw	2	6	3	-	-
G.J.T.Hegglun b Martin	0	2	3	-	-	c Adams b Shaw	0	2	2	-	-
B.E.Hefford b Martin	0	5	8	-	-	not out	3	21	18	-	-
Extras (lb 2, w 2)	4					(lb 3, pen 5)	8				
TOTAL (65.2 overs)	**181**	256				(67 overs)	**188**	257			

AUCKLAND

	Runs	*Mins*	*Balls*	*6s*	*4s*		*Runs*	*Mins*	*Balls*	*6s*	*4s*
T.G.McIntosh c Griggs b Hegglun	20	50	40	-	2	b Mason	0	3	6	-	-
R.A.Jones* c Griggs b Hefford	7	12	8	-	1	not out	28	54	40	-	4
M.J.Guptill c How b Mason	4	20	17	-	-	lbw b Hefford	0	10	4	-	-
R.J.Nicol c Griggs b Hegglun	134	377	294	1	17	not out	11	38	31	-	1
C.de Grandhomme c Hefford b Niblett	87	142	14	1	12						
D.W.Houpapa c Schaw b Hefford	1	14	10	-	-						
R.A.Young† c Hay b Hefford	2	6	3	-	-						
A.R.Adams c Hay b Niblett	48	126	109	1	7						
L.J.Shaw c Weston b Hegglun	1	27	13	-	-						
G.P.Hayne c Ingram b Hegglun	0	2	2	-	-						
C.S.Martin not out	4	33	15	-	1						
Extras (lb 17, w 2, nb 3)	22					(nb 1)	1				
TOTAL (103.4 overs)	**330**	411				(13.2 overs) (2 wkts)	**40**	54			

Bowling	*O*	*M*	*R*	*W*	*O*	*M*	*R*	*W*
AUCKLAND								
Martin	18.2	6	48	5	16	6	38	3
Adams	19	5	54	3	19	7	58	2
Shaw	16	4	41	1	15	1	63	5
Houpapa	2	0	7	0				
Hayne	10	1	29	1	17	5	21	0
CENTRAL DISTRICTS								
Mason	22	7	57	1	7	2	18	1
Hefford	27	8	88	3	6.2	1	22	1
Hegglun	24.4	9	52	4				
Niblett	20	5	73	2				
Schaw	10	1	43	0				

Fall of Wickets

	CD	***A***	***CD***	***A***
	1st	*1st*	*2nd*	*2nd*
1st	0	16	19	0
2nd	3	21	51	7
3rd	13	35	113	-
4th	22	173	113	-
5th	89	180	148	-
6th	135	182	173	-
7th	160	285	173	-
8th	179	304	177	-
9th	179	304	177	-
10th	181	330	188	-

OTAGO v NORTHERN DISTRICTS — State Championship

at University Oval, Dunedin on 19, 20, 21, 22 February, 2007
Toss : Northern Districts. Umpires : R.D. Anderson & D.M. Quested
Close of play: 1st day: Otago 366-9, Harvie 13, Turner 10; 2nd day: ND 181-3, Watling 85, Robinson 14
3rd day: Otago 21-0, Cumming 14, Sheed 6
Northern Districts won by 4 wickets. *Points: Northern Districts 6, Otago 2*

Southee and Turner made their first-class debuts in this match which saw Northern send Otago in to bat. The home side was 49-3 but recovered well. Hopkins and McCullum added 146 for the sixth wicket, an Otago record against Northern while Hopkins reached his century after 192 minutes from 147 balls. Otago's total was a record for University Oval.

Northern's reply was built around a maiden hundred from Watling who was fifth man out for 153. His century took 383 minutes and 299 balls as Northern scored at barely two runs an over. Otago declared at 179-4 in their second innings, leaving Northern 247 for victory.

On this occasion the visitors were far more positive with Hamish Marshall and Evans adding 112 in 103 minutes for the second wicket. The later batsmen all played their part and victory was achieved at 6.45 pm. Martin hit McCullum for six to level the scores and a bye off the next ball was the winning run.

OTAGO

FIRST INNINGS	*Runs*	*Mins*	*Balls*	*6s*	*4s*	*SECOND INNINGS*	*Runs*	*Mins*	*Balls*	*6s*	*4s*
C.D.Cumming* lbw b Southee	16	64	50	-	1	c Aldridge b Yovich	55	168	134	2	6
J.W.Sheed lbw b Aldridge	3	19	13	-	-	c Southee b Martin	57	180	133	-	7
A.J.Redmond c & b Yovich	23	54	32	-	5	(4) b Martin	1	2	4	-	-
G.R.Todd c Marshall J.A.H. b Martin	28	108	67	-	2	(3) not out	22	54	33	-	1
N.T.Broom b Yovich	61	91	86	-	9	(6) not out	21	25	21	1	1
G.J.Hopkins† c Marshall H.J.H. b Martin	110	200	153	1	11						
N.L.McCullum c Watling b Horsley	61	131	103	-	7	(5) c Aldridge b Martin	12	13	14	1	1
B.E.Scott lbw b Martin	6	10	8	-	1						
C.M.Smith b Yovich	13	42	32	-	1						
M.J.Harvie b Southee	34	91	65	-	3						
N.M.Turner not out	27	84	80	-	2						
Extras (b 5, lb 8, w 4, nb 5)	22					(b 4, lb 3, w 1, nb 3)	11				
TOTAL (114 overs)	**404**	452				(56 overs) (4 wkts dec)	**179**	233			

NORTHERN DISTRICTS

FIRST INNINGS	*Runs*	*Mins*	*Balls*	*6s*	*4s*	*SECOND INNINGS*	*Runs*	*Mins*	*Balls*	*6s*	*4s*
A.W.Evans lbw b Scott	58	234	185	-	4	(2) lbw b Scott	55	146	118	-	9
B-J.Watling† c & b Redmond	153	520	411	1	18	(1) c Hopkins b Turner	11	42	34	-	1
H.J.H.Marshall b Turner	9	22	19	-	2	lbw b Scott	86	152	98	2	12
J.A.H.Marshall* lbw b Scott	0	13	13	-	-	c Hopkins b Scott	29	59	38	-	5
G.G.Robinson c Hopkins b Scott	37	157	114	-	4	b McCullum	29	63	40	-	2
N.K.W.Horsley c Broom b Redmond	16	113	95	-	2	c McCullum b Turner	1	5	4	-	-
J.A.F.Yovich not out	18	122	92	-	1	not out	19	43	25	-	1
B.P.Martin b Scott	11	38	28	-	2	not out	6	6	3	1	-
G.W.Aldridge b Turner	2	28	16	-	-						
T.G.Southee lbw b Turner	0	9	4	-	-						
B.J.Arnel b Scott	1	21	21	-	-						
Extras (b 6, lb 20, w 2, nb 4)	32					(b 5, lb 5, w 1)	11				
TOTAL (165.4 overs)	**337**	643				(60 overs) (6 wkts)	**247**	266			

Bowling	*O*	*M*	*R*	*W*	*O*	*M*	*R*	*W*
NORTHERN DISTRICTS								
Aldridge	23	1	78	1	10	2	21	0
Arnel	19	3	51	0	7	4	14	0
Southee	16	2	61	2	13	3	42	0
Yovich	17	1	100	3	6	0	26	1
Martin	34	7	86	3	20	3	69	3
Marshall H.J.H.	3	0	10	0				
Horsley	2	0	5	1				
OTAGO								
Harvie	15	2	41	0	5	2	16	0
Scott	33.4	13	50	5	19	5	54	3
Turner	29	12	57	3	12	1	42	2
McCullum	47	16	67	0	10	1	52	1
Smith	14	5	33	0	8	3	20	0
Redmond	26	9	62	2	4	0	37	0
Cumming	1	0	1	0	2	0	16	0

Fall of Wickets

	O *1st*	***ND*** *1st*	***O*** *2nd*	***ND*** *2nd*
1st	6	122	116	23
2nd	44	141	124	135
3rd	49	142	126	187
4th	143	238	142	192
5th	146	287	-	193
6th	292	300	-	240
7th	301	322	-	-
8th	332	331	-	-
9th	347	332	-	-
10th	404	337	-	-

WELLINGTON v CANTERBURY — State Championship

at Allied Prime Basin Reserve, Wellington on 19, 20, 21, 22 February, 2007
Toss : Wellington. Umpires : S. George & E.J. Gray
Close of play: 1st day: Wellington 314-8, Elliott 36, O'Brien 30; 2nd day: Canterbury 204-4, Ellis 14, Burtt 1
3rd day: Wellington 213-7, Woodcock 7
***Wellington won by 123 runs.** Points: Wellington 8, Canterbury 0*

Lonsdale, Rae and Burns all made their first-class debuts in this game which saw Wellington bat after winning the toss. Bell went for a duck but Wellington recovered to post 365 when they were dismissed early on the second day. Michael Parlane's hundred took 253 minutes and 182 balls. Burtt had his first five wicket haul in first-class cricket.

Canterbury had an opening stand of 90 and were 171-2 but fell away and were all out 73 runs behind the home side. Wellington built on their lead and when they declared at 248-8 Canterbury needed 322 for victory. Ryder had scored his hundred off 148 balls in 162 minutes.

Canterbury's second innings was similar to the first. Astle and Papps put on 101 for the first wicket and Papps fell for his second ninety of the match. Apart from that there was very little resistance and Wellington wrapped up a surprisingly comfortable win at 5.16 pm.

WELLINGTON

FIRST INNINGS	*Runs*	*Mins*	*Balls*	*6s*	*4s*	*SECOND INNINGS*	*Runs*	*Mins*	*Balls*	*6s*	*4s*
M.D.Bell b Burtt	0	18	13	-	-	(2) c van Wyk b Bennett	11	43	23	-	2
S.A.Fairley lbw b Lonsdale	10	49	37	-	2	(1) b Lonsdale	9	58	45	-	1
M.E.Parlane* c Burtt b Robertson	116	279	205	2	17	b Harris	31	63	36	-	5
J.D.Ryder lbw b Burtt	38	80	61	-	8	run out	112	194	161	1	15
N.R.Parlane c Papps b Robertson	52	153	135	-	8	b Robertson	24	48	47		3
G.D.Elliott not out	67	173	124	-	10	c Robertson b Harris	17	52	50	-	-
S.M.Mills† c Robertson b Burtt	3	15	15	-	-	c Papps b Harris	0	22	17		-
L.J.Woodcock b Burtt	0	18	12	-	-	not out	18	48	44	-	1
D.J.Bowden lbw b Burtt	0	8	3	-	-	c Lonsdale b Burtt	9	12	9	-	2
I.E.O'Brien lbw b Bennett	44	76	61	-	6	not out	15	15	13	-	1
M.Burns lbw b Harris	5	38	27	-	1						
Extras (b 8, lb 11, w 3, nb 8)	30					(lb 1, nb 1)	2				
TOTAL (114.1 overs)	**365**	458				(74 overs) (8 wkts dec)	**248**	281			

CANTERBURY

FIRST INNINGS	*Runs*	*Mins*	*Balls*	*6s*	*4s*	*SECOND INNINGS*	*Runs*	*Mins*	*Balls*	*6s*	*4s*
T.D.Astle c Parlane N.R. b Burns	27	132	95	-	2	c Mills b Woodcock	42	114	113	-	5
M.H.W.Papps b Ryder	98	245	224	-	16	c Fairley b Woodcock	93	265	198	-	15
S.L.Stewart c Fairley b Woodcock	42	157	130	-	5	c Mills b O'Brien	2	21	16	-	-
A.M.Ellis lbw b Elliott	16	77	42	-	3	lbw b O'Brien	0	3	4	-	-
C.Z.Harris* c Parlane M.E. b Elliott	5	15	13	-	1	b Woodcock	2	11	9	-	-
L.M.Burtt lbw b Elliott	8	40	28	-	1	(9) c Mills b O'Brien	4	34	22	-	-
B.J.Rae run out	23	90	54	-	4	(6) lbw b Elliott	6	24	16	-	1
C.F.K.van Wyk† c Burns b O'Brien	33	108	77	-	4	(7) lbw b Bowden	29	92	72	-	4
I.A.Robertson lbw b Burns	18	25	23	-	3	(8) lbw b Woodcock	0	9	6	-	-
H.K.Bennett b O'Brien	0	7	7	-	-	c Mills b O'Brien	1	11	11	-	-
W.M.Lonsdale not out	0	7	5	-	-	not out	1	17	11	-	-
Extras (b 1, lb 9, w 7, nb 5)	22					(b 6, lb 8, nb 4)	18				
TOTAL (115.1 overs)	**292**	456				(79 overs)	**198**	305			

Bowling	*O*	*M*	*R*	*W*	*O*	*M*	*R*	*W*
CANTERBURY								
Burtt	24	12	45	5	11	2	51	1
Bennett	23	3	91	1	11	1	57	1
Lonsdale	19	3	80	1	5	3	3	1
Ellis	13	4	51	0	5	0	30	0
Harris	19.1	6	26	1	22	5	43	3
Robertson	14	4	37	2	20	1	63	1
Astle	2	0	16	0				
WELLINGTON								
O'Brien	29.1	8	80	2	28	8	67	4
Burns	19	4	48	2	7	2	14	0
Bowden	17	3	35	0	6	1	20	1
Woodcock	17	2	42	1	27	8	55	4
Elliott	23	9	48	3	10	2	22	1
Ryder	10	1	29	1				
Parlane N.R.					1	0	6	0

Fall of Wickets

	W *1st*	***C*** *1st*	***W*** *2nd*	***C*** *2nd*
1st	12	90	20	101
2nd	26	171	28	112
3rd	90	193	79	112
4th	229	198	132	115
5th	250	207	177	128
6th	259	225	197	188
7th	263	268	214	192
8th	264	290	224	192
9th	333	291	-	193
10th	365	292	-	198

CANTERBURY v OTAGO — State Championship

at Queen Elizabeth II Park, Christchurch on 26, 27, 28 February, 1 March, 2007
Toss : Otago. Umpires : B.G. Frost & S. George
Close of play: 1st day: Canterbury 279-5, Papps 143, van Wyk 13; 2nd day: Otago 96-2, Redmond 34, Todd 5
3rd day: Otago 35-0, Cumming 23, Sheed 12
***Canterbury won by 119 runs.** Points: Canterbury 8, Otago 0*

Canterbury introduced another new player with Davidson making his debut. The home team were sent in by Otago and batted all day to be 279-5. Papps continued his run scoring spree and reached a hundred off 188 balls in 254 minutes. Next morning a maiden century from Robertson, batting at number eight, (128 balls and 184 minutes), took Canterbury to 468-9 before they declared.

Otago declared 203 runs behind after Redmond had made his highest score, reaching three figures in 260 minutes from 189 balls. Canterbury ran up 234 in 38 overs against friendly bowling, leaving Otago 438 to win. Astle's fifty took 22 balls and 26 minutes.

Cumming reached his century from 216 balls in 264 minutes and Otago were 214-1 at one stage. However, wickets fell quickly from then on and Canterbury wrapped up the game at 5.37 pm.

CANTERBURY

FIRST INNINGS	*Runs*	*Mins*	*Balls*	*6s*	*4s*	*SECOND INNINGS*	*Runs*	*Mins*	*Balls*	*6s*	*4s*
T.D.Astle b Turner	38	151	126	-	5	b Harvie	55	45	28	1	10
M.H.W.Papps c McMillan b Harvie	169	462	333	-	25	c McCullum b McMillan	0	3	2	-	-
S.L.Stewart lbw b Redmond	15	40	35	-	3	c Todd b Sheed	97	110	98	1	16
A.M.Ellis c Redmond b Harvie	0	13	5	-	-	not out	59	93	85	-	9
C.Z.Harris* b Scott	25	89	79	-	2	not out	17	23	19	-	2
B.J.Rae c McCullum b Scott	19	62	44	-	2						
C.F.K.van Wyk† c Turner b Harvie	20	78	69	-	3						
I.A.Robertson not out	102	185	129	4	8						
M.P.F.Davidson c Todd b Scott	34	85	68	2	4						
H.K.Bennett c Hopkins b Scott	12	19	21	-	2						
W.M.Lonsdale not out	1	55	30	-	-						
Extras (b 4, lb 12, w 1, nb 16)	33					(lb 2, nb 4)	6				
TOTAL (154 overs) (9 wkts dec)	**468**	624				(38 overs) (3 wkts dec)	**234**	138			

OTAGO

	Runs	*Mins*	*Balls*	*6s*	*4s*		*Runs*	*Mins*	*Balls*	*6s*	*4s*
C.D.Cumming* c van Wyk b Davidson	8	20	19	-	1	lbw b Bennett	108	289	228	1	16
J.W.Sheed c Rae b Davidson	46	86	64	-	8	lbw b Harris	37	137	94	-	5
A.J.Redmond not out	135	308	229	1	23	c Rae b Ellis	58	145	107	-	8
G.R.Todd not out	68	242	199	-	9	c Robertson b Ellis	6	20	12	-	1
N.T.Broom						c & b Astle	39	123	94	-	4
G.J.Hopkins†						b Robertson	16	25	22	-	3
N.L.McCullum						run out	4	5	4	-	1
B.E.Scott						c & b Robertson	4	6	7	-	1
M.J.Harvie						c van Wyk b Ellis	18	41	47	-	3
N.M.Turner						lbw b Lonsdale	15	45	38	-	2
J.M.McMillan						not out	0	17	19	-	-
Extras (b 2, lb 1, nb 5)	8					(b 9, lb 3, nb 1)	13				
TOTAL (84.2 overs) (2 wkts dec)	**265**	329				(111.5 overs)	**318**	431			

Bowling	*O*	*M*	*R*	*W*				
OTAGO								
McMillan	25	6	77	0	5	0	19	1
Harvie	28	6	91	3	7	1	59	1
Turner	27	10	47	1				
Scott	36	8	101	4				
Cumming	2	0	18	0	12	2	78	0
McCullum	19	3	63	0				
Redmond	17	3	55	1	5	1	21	0
Sheed					8	0	50	1
Broom					1	0	5	0
CANTERBURY								
Bennett	18	3	73	0	16	3	58	1
Davidson	13.2	4	31	2	7.4	1	31	0
Lonsdale	11	2	45	0	12.5	4	30	1
Ellis	11	4	26	0	14	4	51	3
Harris	22	11	31	0	22.2	12	24	1
Robertson	4	0	24	0	24	3	61	2
Astle	3	0	25	0	15	4	51	1
Stewart	2	0	7	0				

Fall of Wickets

	C	***O***	***C***	***O***
	1st	*1st*	*2nd*	*2nd*
1st	111	19	5	93
2nd	140	85	69	214
3rd	147	-	185	214
4th	204	-	-	222
5th	256	-	-	246
6th	307	-	-	250
7th	320	-	-	257
8th	405	-	-	288
9th	424	-	-	313
10th	-	-	-	318

WELLINGTON v AUCKLAND — State Championship

at Allied Prime Basin Reserve, Wellington on 26, 27, 28 February, 1 March, 2007
Toss : Wellington. Umpires : T.J. Parlane & E.A. Watkin
Close of play: 1st day: Auckland 157-7, Young 51, Shaw 7; 2nd day: Wellington 243-3, N.R.Parlane 87, Elliott 24
3rd day: Auckland 141-5, Houpapa 33, Young 38
***Wellington won by 145 runs.** Points: Wellington 6, Auckland 2*

Wellington won the toss and batted but would have regretted doing so after being bowled out for 103 and losing Bell to injury for the rest of the season. Auckland reached 157-7 at stumps, with sixteen wickets falling on the first day. At one stage Auckland had been 67-5.

The next day Auckland reached 174 with O'Brien finishing with career best figures of 8-55. Wellington gave a much improved display in their second innings, with Neal Parlane reaching his century off 175 balls in 227 minutes.

Auckland needed 319 to win but came nowhere close. They were 62-5 before a fighting innings from Young, who top scored in both innings, gave them some hope. O'Brien was not to denied, however, taking another five wickets to give him his first ten wicket haul and the best ever match figures for a Wellington bowler against Auckland. The match was all over by 11.07 am on the fourth morning.

WELLINGTON

FIRST INNINGS	*Runs*	*Mins*	*Balls*	*6s*	*4s*	*SECOND INNINGS*	*Runs*	*Mins*	*Balls*	*6s*	*4s*
M.D.Bell retired hurt	3	30	22	-	-	absent hurt					
S.A.Fairley lbw b Adams	2	13	7	-	-	(1) lbw b Martin	6	26	27	-	1
M.E.Parlane* c McIntosh b Martin	10	33	24	-	2	lbw b Shaw	55	124	95	-	7
J.D.Ryder c Jones b Martin	6	27	20	-	1	(6) c Houpapa b Hayne	32	60	50	2	1
N.R.Parlane b Shaw	14	67	48	-	2	(4) b Martin	135	329	250	-	18
G.D.Elliott b Shaw	19	65	58	-	2	(5) c Jones b Shaw	29	164	127	-	4
S.M.Mills† b Martin	16	55	44	-	2	lbw b Martin	0	3	1	-	-
L.J.Woodcock c Jones b Adams	4	10	8	-	1	(2) lbw b Martin	59	242	198	-	8
D.J.Bowden c Young b Adams	17	39	33	-	4	(8) not out	33	63	49	1	2
I.E.O'Brien lbw b Martin	1	15	11	-	-	(9) b Hayne	6	17	16	-	-
M.Burns not out	1	12	9	-	-	(10) b Martin	8	36	34	-	-
Extras (b 4, lb 4, nb 2)	10					(b 5, lb 15, w 5, nb 1)	26				
TOTAL (47 overs)	**103**	187				(141 overs)	**389**	536			

AUCKLAND

	Runs	*Mins*	*Balls*	*6s*	*4s*		*Runs*	*Mins*	*Balls*	*6s*	*4s*
T.G.McIntosh c Parlane N.R. b O'Brien	6	24	16	-	1	b O'Brien	27	92	69	-	3
R.A.Jones* c Burns b O'Brien	22	33	29	-	3	c Mills b Burns	6	6	6	-	1
M.J.Guptill b Ryder	40	145	122	-	7	c Ryder b O'Brien	5	11	14	-	-
R.J.Nicol lbw b O'Brien	4	16	9	-	1	c Mills b Bowden	18	84	74	-	-
C.de Grandhomme c Parlane M.E. b O'Brien	17	27	23	1	2	c sub (C.J.Nevin) b O'Brien	4	15	6	-	-
D.W.Houpapa b O'Brien	0	1	2	-	-	lbw b Burns	33	105	88	-	5
R.A.Young† b O'Brien	53	117	94	-	10	c Mills b O'Brien	70	128	103	-	13
A.R.Adams c Mills b O'Brien	1	17	13	-	-	c Mills b Burns	0	2	3	-	-
L.J.Shaw not out	20	31	25	-	3	b Burns	0	1	1	-	-
G.P.Hayne c Mills b Elliott	1	5	7	-	-	b O'Brien	0	11	7	-	-
C.S.Martin b O'Brien	0	15	12	-	-	not out	0	10	2	-	-
Extras (b 2, lb 4, w 1, nb 3)	10					(b 1, lb 8, nb 1)	10				
TOTAL (58.1 overs)	**174**	220				(62 overs)	**173**	237			

Bowling	*O*	*M*	*R*	*W*	*O*	*M*	*R*	*W*
AUCKLAND								
Martin	14	5	29	4	42	10	107	5
Adams	17	5	33	3	12	6	16	0
Shaw	10	7	9	2	25	5	88	2
Houpapa	1	0	9	0				
Hayne	5	0	15	0	37	11	87	2
Nicol					8	0	28	0
de Grandhomme					16	0	43	0
McIntosh					1	1	0	0
WELLINGTON								
O'Brien	21.1	5	55	8	23	7	62	5
Burns	5	0	24	0	10	3	44	4
Bowden	10	3	26	0	10	3	19	1
Elliott	11	4	36	1				
Woodcock	4	2	14	0	10	3	20	0
Ryder	7	3	13	1	9	4	19	0

Fall of Wickets

	W	A	W	A
	1st	*1st*	*2nd*	*2nd*
1st	12	26	8	8
2nd	18	31	83	15
3rd	23	46	166	52
4th	56	65	279	60
5th	63	67	340	62
6th	74	145	340	141
7th	101	150	345	141
8th	101	159	360	141
9th	103	160	389	156
10th	-	174	-	173

Bell retired hurt at 12-1

NORTHERN DISTRICTS v CENTRAL DISTRICTS

at Harry Barker Reserve, Gisborne on 26, 27, 28 February, 1 March, 2007
Toss : Northern Districts. Umpires : G.A. Baxter & D.M. Quested
Close of play: 1st day: ND 10-0, Watling 0, Wilson 9; 2nd day: ND 329-3, J.A.H.Marshall 86, Robinson 43
3rd day: CD 108-3, Hay 52, Griggs 4
***Northern Districts won by 8 wickets.** Points: Northern Districts 8, Central Districts 0*

Rayner made his first-class debut in this game which saw Northern ask Central to bat first. The visitors were dismissed just before stumps, with fifties from Sinclair and Hay being the highlights.

By the end of the second day Northern had secured first innings points and had lost just three wickets. They continued the next day, finally being bowled out for 516, their best score against Central and the highest by anyone at this ground. James Marshall and Watling were both dismissed in the 90s.

Facing a deficit of 211, Central reached 203-3 but once Hay went, after reaching his maiden century (150 balls and 196 minutes), wickets fell quickly. Northern needed just 108 to win and knocked off the runs in quick time, mainly thanks to a 40-ball fifty from Horsley.

CENTRAL DISTRICTS

FIRST INNINGS	*Runs*	*Mins*	*Balls*	*6s*	*4s*	*SECOND INNINGS*	*Runs*	*Mins*	*Balls*	*6s*	*4s*
J.M.How* c Robinson b Aldridge	30	90	68	-	5	b Aldridge	0	3	4	-	-
P.J.Ingram b Aldridge	4	10	7	-	1	c Watling b Southee	4	8	4	-	1
M.S.Sinclair lbw b Aldridge	78	153	110	-	12	lbw b Andrews	44	71	70	-	6
G.R.Hay lbw b Andrews	66	158	112	-	9	c Robinson b Aldridge	106	205	157	-	13
B.B.J.Griggs† b Southee	22	48	51	-	2	c Aldridge b Southee	62	228	184	-	9
T.I.Weston c Watling b Southee	28	59	42	-	5	c Watling b Marshall H.J.H.	25	142	105	-	2
A.D.Niblett c & b Marshall H.J.H.	11	46	45	-	2	c Watling b Southee	4	11	9	-	1
R.J.Schaw b Andrews	24	72	59	-	3	c Watling b Aldridge	20	33	28	-	4
D.L.Rayner c Robinson b Aldridge	5	35	23	-	-	not out	11	96	71	-	-
G.J.T.Hegglun b Martin	11	37	32	-	1	c Watling b Aldridge	6	38	34	-	-
B.E.Hefford not out	12	23	14	-	3	c Watling b Aldridge	7	48	46	-	-
Extras (lb 8, w 2, nb 4)	14					(b 3, lb 15, w 9, nb 2)	29				
TOTAL (93.1 overs)	**305**	370				(118.2 overs)	**318**	437			

NORTHERN DISTRICTS

	Runs	*Mins*	*Balls*	*6s*	*4s*		*Runs*	*Mins*	*Balls*	*6s*	*4s*
B-J.Watling† b Schaw	91	264	217	-	11	(2) c Weston b Sinclair	31	80	42	-	2
B.S.Wilson lbw b Hefford	56	176	152	-	3						
H.J.H.Marshall c Griggs b Rayner	35	50	29	-	5	not out	15	21	14	-	3
J.A.H.Marshall* c Ingram b Niblett	99	203	147	-	11	not out	6	6	8	-	1
G.G.Robinson lbw b Hefford	44	153	103	-	3						
N.K.W.Horsley c Hegglun b How	66	149	104	1	9	(1) st Griggs b How	51	65	41	-	7
S.L.Andrews c How b Niblett	14	75	6	-	2						
J.A.F.Yovich c Ingram b Sinclair	19	52	44	-	2						
B.P.Martin not out	28	56	43	-	3						
G.W.Aldridge c Schaw b Sinclair	13	20	13	-	2						
T.G.Southee lbw b Hegglun	17	27	22	-	1						
Extras (b 12, lb 11, w 5, nb 6)	34					(b 1, lb 2, w 3)	6				
TOTAL (155.4 overs)	**516**	617				(17.3 overs) (2 wkts)	**109**	87			

Bowling	*O*	*M*	*R*	*W*	*O*	*M*	*R*	*W*
NORTHERN DISTRICTS								
Aldridge	21	4	65	4	30.2	8	85	5
Southee	19	5	58	2	27	8	88	3
Yovich	10	1	66	0				
Andrews	20	8	46	2	24	6	66	1
Marshall H.J.H.	5	1	25	1	7	3	6	1
Martin	18.1	7	37	1	28	8	48	0
Horsley					2	0	7	0
CENTRAL DISTRICTS								
Hefford	33	10	71	2	6	0	36	0
Niblett	39	9	121	2	4	0	27	0
Rayner	24	4	90	1				
Hegglun	18.4	4	67	1	3	0	15	0
Schaw	23	4	82	1				
Sinclair	9	1	24	2	1.3	0	13	1
How	9	1	38	1	3	0	15	1

Fall of Wickets

	CD	***ND***	***CD***	***ND***
	1st	*1st*	*2nd*	*2nd*
1st	5	118	0	75
2nd	60	175	6	99
3rd	157	202	90	-
4th	193	334	203	-
5th	228	344	253	-
6th	239	392	260	-
7th	252	443	294	-
8th	280	455	294	-
9th	284	478	304	-
10th	305	516	318	-

NORTHERN DISTRICTS v OTAGO — State Championship

at Seddon Park, Hamilton on 5, 6, 7, 8 March, 2007
Toss : Otago. Umpires : R.D. Anderson & E.A. Watkin
Close of play: 1st day: ND 331-4, H.J.H.Marshall 36, Horsley 23; 2nd day: Otago 209-3, Redmond 86, Broom 95
3rd day: ND 47-3, Wilson 16
***First innings win to Northern Districts.** Points: Northern Districts 2, Otago 0*

Sent in by Otago, Northern piled up their highest total of all time and their second score of over 500 in successive games. Watling (234 balls and 285 minutes) and Hamish Marshall (166 balls and 237 minutes) scored hundreds and Andrews chimed in with a maiden fifty.

Otago's batsmen also found conditions to their liking with Redmond (190 balls and 267 minutes) and Broom (157 balls and 196 minutes) also making centuries.

In their second innings Northern raced to 150-5 off 28 overs before declaring, mainly thanks to two overs from Sheed which cost 19 and 24. Otago needed 266 to win but never looked likely. The ninth wicket fell with two overs remaining but Scott and McMillan held out till the end.

NORTHERN DISTRICTS

FIRST INNINGS	*Runs*	*Mins*	*Balls*	*6s*	*4s*	*SECOND INNINGS*	*Runs*	*Mins*	*Balls*	*6s*	*4s*
B-J.Watling† c Sheed b Turner	104	289	239	-	16	c Harvie b McMillan	8	17	13	-	1
B.S.Wilson lbw b Scott	37	137	95	-	6	c Redmond b Harvie	37	107	77	-	6
A.W.Evans lbw b McMillan	90	195	146	-	16	b McMillan	6	8	6	-	1
H.J.H.Marshall c Scott b Redmond	119	269	186	1	20	lbw b McMillan	10	20	13	-	2
J.A.H.Marshall* lbw b McMillan	2	10	6	-	-	(6) not out	45	67	51	2	6
N.K.W.Horsley c McCullum b Scott	53	136	100	1	8	(7) not out	29	11	10	1	4
S.L.Andrews not out	59	99	104	1	7						
B.P.Martin lbw b McCullum	0	4	2	-	-						
G.W.Aldridge not out	14	15	18	-	1	(5) b Scott	0	2	2	-	-
T.G.Southee											
B.J.Arnel											
Extras (b 1, lb 18, w 2, nb 24)	45					(b 1, lb 4, w 5, nb 5)	15				
TOTAL (146 overs) (7 wkts dec)	**523**	580				(28 overs) (5 wkts dec)	**150**	118			

OTAGO

	Runs	*Mins*	*Balls*	*6s*	*4s*		*Runs*	*Mins*	*Balls*	*6s*	*4s*
C.D.Cumming* lbw b Aldridge	4	18	19	-	-	b Andrews	18	80	68	-	3
J.W.Sheed c Watling b Aldridge	0	10	6	-	-	c Watling b Southee	0	6	3	-	-
A.J.Redmond c Wilson b Aldridge	127	338	247	1	19	c Watling b Aldridge	34	91	59	-	4
G.R.Todd b Aldridge	6	17	15	-	1	lbw b Southee	46	124	97	-	7
N.T.Broom lbw b Arnel	101	204	163	-	17	b Arnel	7	33	22	-	1
G.J.Hopkins† c Watling b Southee	63	153	119	-	11	lbw b Aldridge	9	22	20	-	2
N.L.McCullum c Evans b Aldridge	41	8	63	-	6	b Aldridge	5	15	14	-	1
B.E.Scott lbw b Marshall H.J.H.	1	5	2	-	-	not out	29	146	105	1	4
M.J.Harvie not out	17	62	42	1	2	run out	12	38	28	1	1
N.M.Turner not out	1	24	15	-	-	b Arnel	10	64	46	-	1
J.M.McMillan						not out	0	8	6	-	-
Extras (b 13, lb 16, w 15, nb 3)	47					(b 5, lb 19, w 2, nb 1)	27				
TOTAL (114.4 overs) (8 wkts dec)	**408**	464				(78 overs) (9 wkts)	**197**	318			

Bowling	*O*	*M*	*R*	*W*	*O*	*M*	*R*	*W*
OTAGO								
McMillan	26	4	81	2	11	1	53	3
Harvie	25	4	104	0	5	0	21	1
Scott	33	15	79	2	9	3	14	1
Turner	24	5	95	1				
Cumming	4	1	22	0	1	0	14	0
McCullum	26	4	87	1				
Redmond	8	0	36	1				
Sheed					2	0	43	0
NORTHERN DISTRICTS								
Aldridge	30	10	75	5	22	8	37	3
Arnel	27	11	78	1	19	9	48	2
Andrews	12	1	50	0	16	1	34	1
Southee	24	3	84	1	17	4	45	2
Martin	10.4	0	58	0	4	2	9	0
Marshall H.J.H.	11	4	34	1				

Fall of Wickets

	ND	***O***	***ND***	***O***
	1st	*1st*	*2nd*	*2nd*
1st	94	7	12	0
2nd	240	8	20	58
3rd	285	14	47	66
4th	290	218	50	87
5th	402	305	93	100
6th	487	357	-	114
7th	491	358	-	140
8th	-	394	-	166
9th	-		-	197
10th	-	-	-	-

AUCKLAND v CENTRAL DISTRICTS — State Championship

at Eden Park Outer Oval, Auckland on 5, 6, 7, 8 March, 2007
Toss : Central Districts. Umpires : G.A. Baxter & B.G. Frost
Close of play: 1st day: Auckland 314 all out; 2nd day: Auckland 77-1, Jones 57, Guptill 2
3rd day: Auckland 274-4, Nicol 51, Houpapa 31
***Auckland won by 94 runs.** Points: Auckland 8, Central Districts 0*

Baldwin made his first-class debut for Central who won the toss and sent Auckland in to bat. Jones, who reached his hundred from 128 balls in 165 minutes, put on 127 for the second wicket with Guptill. Once the partnership was broken, however, wickets began to fall and Auckland were dismissed just before stumps.

Central struggled to 132-8 before Schaw and Hegglun (maiden fifty) put on 82, a Central ninth wicket record against Auckland. Jones added another century to his tally (in 196 minutes from 145 balls) and declared early on the last day, leaving Central 375 to win.

By the seventh over the visitors were 10-4, Adams having figures of 3-5, having bowled a first ball wide whch went to the boundary. Weston joined Griggs and the pair added 168, a Central fifth wicket record against Auckland. Weston reached his maiden hundred after 206 minutes and 166 balls before being ninth man out. Hegglun went three balls later and Auckland had the match won by 5.47 pm.

AUCKLAND

FIRST INNINGS	*Runs*	*Mins*	*Balls*	*6s*	*4s*	SECOND INNINGS	Runs	Mins	Balls	6s	4s
T.G.McIntosh b Hefford	15	90	71	-	2	c Hegglun b Hefford	14	87	65	-	1
R.A.Jones* c & b Schaw	143	240	179	1	26	b Baldwin	120	233	164	1	15
M.J.Guptill c Griggs b Hegglun	65	271	227	1	10	c Sinclair b Schaw	24	141	111	-	2
R.J.Nicol run out	0	11	9	-	-	not out	54	143	124	-	4
C.de Grandhomme c Hay b Hefford	0	10	4	-	-	c Hay b Schaw	29	56	45	-	4
D.W.Houpapa c Hegglun b Schaw	8	37	28	-	-	c Griggs b Hegglun	32	70	60	1	3
R.A.Young† c Sinclair b How	19	20	16	1	3	not out	4	11	10	-	1
A.R.Adams c Sinclair b Hegglun	16	30	21	-	3						
L.J.Shaw b Hegglun	8	19	13	-	1						
G.P.Hayne c How b Hegglun	18	21	20	1	2						
C.S.Martin not out	0	10	3	-	-						
Extras (b 5, lb 5, w 7, nb 5)	22					(lb 3, w 1, nb 3)	7				
TOTAL (97.4 overs)	**314**	384				(96 overs) (5 wkts dec)	**284**	373			

CENTRAL DISTRICTS

	Runs	Mins	Balls	6s	4s		Runs	Mins	Balls	6s	4s
J.M.How* c Young b Shaw	22	110	90	-	3	c Young b Adams	3	18	16	-	-
P.J.Ingram c Young b Adams	10	29	19	-	2	lbw b Martin	1	26	15	-	-
M.S.Sinclair c McIntosh b Adams	17	36	32	-	2	lbw b Adams	0	1	2	-	-
G.R.Hay c Young b Martin	40	82	62	-	6	c Guptill b Adams	0	8	3	-	-
B.B.J.Griggs† c Jones b Martin	16	28	21	-	2	lbw b Hayne	69	190	154	-	10
T.I.Weston c McIntosh b Martin	11	27	20	-	1	c Adams b Martin	152	291	226	2	19
S.B.C.Baldwin c Hayne b Adams	0	11	9	-	-	c Jones b Hayne	0	8	2	-	-
A.D.Niblett c Young b Martin	4	21	13	-	1	st Young b Hayne	22	32	26	1	3
R.J.Schaw c McIntosh b Martin	34	96	80	-	2	c McIntosh b Nicol	2	38	39	-	-
G.J.T.Hegglun not out	52	94	71	1	7	c Young b Martin	9	25	23	-	1
B.E.Hefford lbw b Adams	5	14	20	-	1	not out	0	2	0	-	-
Extras (b 4, lb 2, nb 7)	13					(b 7, lb 4, w 8, nb 3)	22				
TOTAL (71.5 overs)	**224**	274				(84 overs)	**280**	321			

Bowling	*O*	*M*	*R*	*W*	*O*	*M*	*R*	*W*
CENTRAL DISTRICTS								
Hefford	20	5	53	2	13	3	32	1
Niblett	22	4	74	0	12	2	34	0
Hegglun	18.4	8	54	4	15	3	50	1
Baldwin	11	3	48	0	13	2	33	1
Schaw	18	5	49	2	31	3	96	2
How	8	2	26	1	11	0	29	0
Sinclair					1	0	7	0
AUCKLAND								
Martin	19	2	52	5	21	4	80	3
Adams	21.5	5	59	4	18	4	47	3
Shaw	12	5	34	1	12	1	49	0
de Grandhomme	2	0	2	0	2	1	3	0
Hayne	15	1	59	0	26	3	80	3
Nicol	2	0	12	0	3	1	5	1
McIntosh					2	1	5	0

Fall of Wickets

	A *1st*	***CD*** *1st*	***A*** *2nd*	***CD*** *2nd*
1st	71	16	59	10
2nd	198	45	163	10
3rd	198	74	163	10
4th	211	104	212	10
5th	234	118	278	178
6th	259	123	-	188
7th	285	123	-	234
8th	293	132	-	267
9th	300	214	-	280
10th	314	224	-	280

CANTERBURY v WELLINGTON State Championship

at Queen Elizabeth II Park, Christchurch on 5, 6, 7, 8 March, 2007
Toss : Wellington. Umpires : P.D. Jones & D.M. Quested
Close of play: 1st day: Canterbury 327-3, Papps 160, Harris 13; 2nd day: Wellington 51-0, Fairley 22, Woodcock 20
3rd day: Wellington 316-5, Elliott 73, Mills 58
***First innings win to Wellington.** Points: Wellington 2, Canterbury 0*

Wellington sent Canterbury in to bat in what turned out to be one of the more extraordinary games of first-class cricket played in New Zealand.

Canterbury began with an opening stand of 201. Astle just missed his maiden hundred while Papps reached three figures from 167 balls in 219 minutes. Rae (maiden fifty), van Wyk and Robertson all hit half centuries as Canterbury batted on till almost the end of the second day. It was the first time that Wellington had ever conceded a total of 600.

Wellington looked headed for a massive deficit when they were 198-5 but Elliott and Mills put on 184 to give them some hope. This was a sixth wicket record for any team against Canterbury. Nevin, only recalled to the side because of the injury to Bell, joined Mills, who was on 90. The Wellington keeper reached his maiden century from 231 balls in 277 minutes and the pair added a further 176, a Wellington record against Canterbury.

At 568-8 Wellington still had some work to do but Bowden and O'Brien were untroubled in adding 46 in 51 minutes to give Wellington the points. Otago's record score at the ground, made in November, had been overhauled twice.

CANTERBURY

FIRST INNINGS	*Runs*	*Mins*	*Balls*	*6s*	*4s*
T.D.Astle c Ryder b Elliott	97	196	168	-	15
M.H.W.Papps c Mills b Woodcock	188	466	373	1	25
S.L.Stewart lbw b Burns	8	28	22	-	1
A.M.Ellis c Mills b Elliott	25	75	59	-	4
C.Z.Harris* c Mills b Ryder	33	159	104	-	3
B.J.Rae run out	58	159	139	-	6
C.F.K.van Wyk† b Burns	64	171	113	-	5
I.A.Robertson not out	65	79	65	-	10
B.C.Hiini not out	45	62	53	-	7
H.K.Bennett					
W.M.Lonsdale					
Extras (b 6, lb 8, w 6, nb 10)	30				
TOTAL (181 overs) (7 wkts dec)	**613**	701			

WELLINGTON

	Runs	*Mins*	*Balls*	*6s*	*4s*
S.A.Fairley c Harris b Bennett	59	298	227	-	5
L.J.Woodcock c Hiini b Bennett	30	104	81	1	4
M.E.Parlane* c Rae b Ellis	31	73	50	-	5
J.D.Ryder c Ellis b Astle	25	31	30	-	5
N.R.Parlane c & b Astle	9	12	12	-	1
G.D.Elliott c van Wyk b Hiini	107	325	267	-	16
S.M.Mills† b Bennett	171	502	391	1	25
C.J.Nevin c Harris b Bennett	98	219	184	1	12
D.J.Bowden not out	31	83	53	1	3
I.E.O'Brien not out	15	51	34	1	1
M.Burns					
Extras (b 8, lb 15, w 4, nb 11)	38				
TOTAL (219.5 overs) (8 wkts)	**614**	853			

Bowling	*O*	*M*	*R*	*W*
WELLINGTON				
O'Brien	15	1	65	0
Burns	32	6	105	2
Bowden	27	4	112	0
Ryder	14	2	63	1
Elliott	43	7	115	2
Woodcock	40	11	100	1
Parlane M.E.	10	2	39	0
CANTERBURY				
Bennett	33	9	99	4
Lonsdale	30	10	83	0
Hiini	28	3	101	1
Robertson	29.5	6	112	0
Harris	31	15	42	0
Ellis	30	7	62	1
Astle	38	9	92	2

Fall of Wickets	***C***	***W***
	1st	*1st*
1st	201	66
2nd	220	111
3rd	276	146
4th	377	162
5th	377	198
6th	492	382
7th	521	558
8th	-	568
9th	-	-
10th	-	-

WELLINGTON v NORTHERN DISTRICTS State Championship

at Allied Prime Basin Reserve, Wellington on 12, 13, 14, 15 March, 2007
Toss : Northern Districts. Umpires : P.D. Jones & D.M. Quested
Close of play: 1st day: Wellington 301-8, Mills 54, Rasmussen 2; 2nd day: ND 8-1, Wilson 2
3rd day: no play
***First innings win to Northern Districts.** Points: Northern Districts 2, Wellington 0*

Northern Districts sent Wellington in to bat and had early success. Neal Parlane came to the rescue with 97 and more runs from Mills and Nevin produced a respectable total of 314.

With little play possible on the second day and none at all on the third the match became a first innings affair. Wellington, because their net run rate was better than Canterbury's, needed only two points to gain a place in the final. When they had Northern 215-8 this outcome seemed a formality.

Southee, however, chose this occasion to register a remarkable maiden fifty, off 37 balls in 48 minutes. He and Aldridge added 104 in an hour with Southee ending the game by hitting Burns for six.

WELLINGTON

FIRST INNINGS	*Runs*	*Mins*	*Balls*	*6s*	*4s*
S.A.Fairley b Aldridge	4	10	13	-	-
L.J.Woodcock c Horsley b Davis	13	32	18	-	2
M.E.Parlane* c Wilson b Southee	33	144	118	-	4
J.D.Ryder c Davis b Aldridge	13	19	14	-	2
N.R.Parlane c McGlashan b Davis	97	162	130	-	18
G.D.Elliott lbw b Martin	7	51	43	-	1
S.M.Mills† not out	58	200	142	-	6
C.J.Nevin b Aldridge	59	134	95	-	11
D.J.Bowden c Martin b Davis	0	7	6	-	-
S.Rasmussen lbw b Martin	3	38	40	-	-
M.Burns c McGlashan b Southee	3	10	10	-	-
Extras (b 8, lb 5, w 2, nb 9)	24				
TOTAL (103.2 overs)	**314**	408			

NORTHERN DISTRICTS

	Runs	Mins	Balls	6s	4s
B-J.Watling c Elliott b Bowden	1	19	19	-	-
B.S.Wilson c Mills b Bowden	16	49	36	-	1
A.W.Evans c Parlane N.R. b Burns	17	69	52	-	1
H.J.H.Marshall c Mills b Elliott	17	74	52	-	2
J.A.H.Marshall* c Rasmussen b Elliott	12	18	17	-	1
N.K.W.Horsley b Ryder	57	182	165	-	6
P.D.McGlashan† c Fairley b Woodcock	63	148	116	-	10
B.P.Martin lbw b Woodcock	6	18	17	-	1
G.W.Aldridge not out	25	63	45	-	3
T.G.Southee not out	75	60	47	5	7
T.T.Davis					
Extras (lb 17, nb 13)	30				
TOTAL (92.2 overs) (8 wkts)	**319**	353			

Bowling	*O*	*M*	*R*	*W*
NORTHERN DISTRICTS				
Aldridge	23	6	59	3
Southee	23.2	8	44	2
Davis	23	5	97	3
Marshall H.J.H.	15	1	36	0
Martin	19	1	65	2
WELLINGTON				
Rasmussen	21	2	71	0
Bowden	14	4	45	2
Burns	11.2	1	45	1
Elliott	15	5	56	2
Woodcock	18	5	58	2
Ryder	13	6	27	1

Fall of Wickets

	W	***ND***
	1st	*1st*
1st	4	8
2nd	21	32
3rd	34	64
4th	112	77
5th	169	82
6th	177	209
7th	286	215
8th	291	215
9th	303	-
10th	314	-

OTAGO v AUCKLAND — State Championship

at University Oval, Dunedin on 12, 13, 14, 15 March, 2007
Toss : Otago. Umpires : G.A. Baxter & E.A. Watkin
Close of play: 1st day: Otago 10-0, Cumming 6, Haig 4; 2nd day: Otago 130-4, Todd 15, Hopkins 1
3rd day: Auckland 15-2, McIntosh 1, Nicol 0
***First innings win to Auckland.** Points: Auckland 2, Otago 0*

Erasmus and Lobb made their first-class debuts in this game. Auckland were sent in and were 129-8 before being rescued by Pasupati who was playing his first first-class game for Auckland, and only his fourth in ten seasons overall. He and Erasmus added 82 for the ninth wicket, an Auckland record against Otago.

Otago also found the going tough and were bowled out 27 short of Auckland's score. Pasupati finished with 4-39 to complete a memorable debut. The final day was washed out.

AUCKLAND

FIRST INNINGS	*Runs*	*Mins*	*Balls*	*6s*	*4s*	*SECOND INNINGS*	*Runs*	*Mins*	*Balls*	*6s*	*4s*
T.G.McIntosh c Scott b McMillan	15	71	54	-	3	not out	1	28	15	-	-
R.A.Jones* c Redmond b Scott	21	29	22	-	4	c Redmond b McMillan	12	23	22	-	2
M.J.Guptill lbw b Scott	0	8	6	-	-	lbw b McMillan	0	2	2	-	-
R.J.Nicol c Hopkins b McMillan	27	50	37	-	4	not out	0	1	3	-	-
C.de Grandhomme lbw b McMillan	30	54	28	-	5						
C.Cachopa lbw b Lobb	17	29	22	-	4						
R.A.Young† c Hopkins b Scott	8	15	8	-	2						
M.Y.Pasupati not out	76	95	73	2	13						
L.J.Shaw c Hopkins b McMillan	3	10	9	-	-						
P.B.Erasmus run out	15	50	27	-	2						
C.S.Martin c McCullum b Scott	8	25	17	-	-						
Extras (b 1, lb 3, w 2)	6					(nb 2)	2				
TOTAL (50.3 overs)	**226**	222				(6.4 overs) (2 wkts)	**15**	28			

OTAGO

	Runs	Mins	Balls	6s	4s
C.D.Cumming* c Young b Shaw	16	43	30	-	3
S.B.Haig c Nicol b Martin	38	52	35	2	6
A.J.Redmond lbw b Pasupati	10	21	13	-	2
G.R.Todd c Young b Martin	18	127	89	-	1
N.T.Broom lbw b Pasupati	49	85	70	-	10
G.J.Hopkins† b Martin	9	19	15	-	2
N.L.McCullum b Pasupati	31	92	52	1	2
B.E.Scott c Young b Pasupati	19	54	38	-	3
M.J.Harvie b Erasmus	1	5	4	-	-
D.V.Lobb c Jones b Erasmus	4	17	19	-	1
J.M.McMillan not out	0	3	1	-	-
Extras (lb 1, nb 3)	4				
TOTAL (60.3 overs)	**199**	263			

Bowling	*O*	*M*	*R*	*W*				
OTAGO								
McMillan	16	4	73	4	3	0	7	2
Scott	16.3	4	42	4	3.4	2	8	0
Harvie	8	0	53	0				
Lobb	7	1	37	1				
Redmond	3	0	17	0				
AUCKLAND								
Martin	23	5	95	3				
Erasmus	9	3	15	2				
Shaw	13	3	46	1				
Pasupati	14.3	3	39	4				
Nicol	1	0	3	0				

Fall of Wickets

	A *1st*	***O*** *1st*	***A*** *2nd*
1st	28	48	14
2nd	28	58	14
3rd	49	64	-
4th	72	127	-
5th	113	140	-
6th	122	141	-
7th	122	186	-
8th	129	189	-
9th	211	199	-
10th	226	199	-

CENTRAL DISTRICTS v CANTERBURY State Championship

at McLean Park, Napier on 12, 13, 14, 15 March, 2007
Toss : Central Districts. Umpires : E.J. Gray & D.J. Walker
Close of play: 1st day: CD 375-6, Weston 34, Schaw 12; 2nd day: Canterbury 208-2, Stewart 56, Ellis 17
3rd day: Canterbury 376-6, van Wyk 13, Robertson 9
***First innings win to Canterbury.** Points: Canterbury 2, Central Districts 0*

Patton and 16-year-old Anderson made their first-class debuts in this game. Central batted throughout the first day with Ingram registering his fourth century of the season from 119 balls in 172 minutes.

The home side were finally all out for 460 and Canterbury knew they had to get first innings points to have any chance of reaching the final. Astle and Papps gave them a good start and Stewart carried on, reaching his hundred from 225 balls in 281 minutes.

Solid batting from Rae, van Wyk, Robertson and young Anderson saw Canterbury gain the lead with eight wickets down. With no result possible, How took the chance to bring up a hundred from 153 balls in 217 minutes when Central batted again.

CENTRAL DISTRICTS

FIRST INNINGS	*Runs*	*Mins*	*Balls*	*6s*	*4s*	*SECOND INNINGS*	*Runs*	*Mins*	*Balls*	*6s*	*4s*
J.M.How* b Anderson	34	88	64	-	7	not out	102	228	167	1	14
P.J.Ingram c van Wyk b Astle	159	282	210	1	18	b Hiini	1	5	3	-	-
M.S.Sinclair c Papps b Hiini	78	143	111	-	13	lbw b Hiini	13	30	20	-	2
G.R.Hay c Harris b Hiini	35	121	112	-	5	c Papps b Astle	32	83	59	-	4
B.B.J.Griggs† lbw b Harris	1	9	9	-	-	lbw b Hiini	10	25	23	-	1
T.I.Weston not out	87	237	159	-	11	not out	26	81	55	-	3
B.M.K.Patton lbw b Bennett	0	5	8	-	-						
R.J.Schaw c Stewart b Harris	17	56	42	-	2						
A.D.Niblett lbw b Hiini	1	7	9	-	-						
G.J.T.Hegglun c van Wyk b Ellis	8	28	28	-	-						
B.E.Hefford c Rae b Robertson	12	80	68	-	-						
Extras (b 1, lb 14, w 9, nb 4)	28					(b 1, lb 9, w 2, nb 1)	13				
TOTAL (136 overs)	**460**	522				(54.2 overs) (4 wkts)	**197**	228			

CANTERBURY

	Runs	Mins	Balls	6s	4s
T.D.Astle c Patton b Niblett	41	84	62	-	6
M.H.W.Papps c Niblett b Hefford	86	208	151	-	14
S.L.Stewart c Ingram b Schaw	146	38	304	-	14
A.M.Ellis run out	21	82	69	-	2
C.Z.Harris* c Griggs b Niblett	7	29	26	-	1
B.J.Rae c How b Schaw	41	153	134	-	5
C.F.K.van Wyk† c Griggs b Niblett	32	97	78	-	3
I.A.Robertson not out	34	147	84	-	5
C.J.Anderson run out	29	31	35	-	6
B.C.Hiini not out	10	21	23	-	2
H.K.Bennett					
Extras (b 1, lb 6, w 2, nb 6)	15				
TOTAL (160 overs) (8 wkts dec)	**462**	620			

Bowling	*O*	*M*	*R*	*W*	*O*	*M*	*R*	*W*
CANTERBURY								
Bennett	23	2	101	1	10	0	50	0
Hiini	26	8	87	3	14.2	5	31	3
Anderson	13	1	59	1	7	2	26	0
Ellis	16	1	48	1	8	3	21	0
Harris	32	9	71	2				
Robertson	4	1	21	1	3	0	8	0
Stewart	4	0	11	0				
Astle	18	0	47	1	12	0	51	1
CENTRAL DISTRICTS								
Hefford	33	8	72	1				
Niblett	33	7	121	3				
Hegglun	29	7	70	0				
Schaw	40	4	140	2				
Sinclair	16	4	32	0				
Patton	1	0	1	0				
How	8	1	19	0				

Fall of Wickets

	CD	*C*	*CD*
	1st	*1st*	*2nd*
1st	79	84	8
2nd	254	183	39
3rd	293	235	101
4th	294	250	130
5th	352	352	-
6th	353	355	-
7th	385	410	-
8th	386	443	-
9th	405	-	-
10th	460	-	-

NORTHERN DISTRICTS v CANTERBURY — Final

at Seddon Park, Hamilton on 22, 23, 24, 25, 26 March, 2007
Toss : Northern Districts. Umpires : B.G. Frost & D.J. Walker
Close of play: 1st day: Canterbury 260-2, Papps 109, Ellis 3; 2nd day: ND 151-4, H.J.H.Marshall 42, Horsley 25
3rd day: Canterbury 19-2, Papps 12, Hiini 5; 4th day: ND 65-1, Wilson 22, Evans 24
Match drawn.

Northern sent Canterbury in and had immediate success when Astle went in the first over. This, however, only paved the way for Papps (century from 257 balls in 344 minutes) and Stewart (219 balls and 280 minutes) to put on 243, a Canterbury second wicket record against all teams.

Harris declared at 443-8 and Northern were not convincing as they went to 151-5. Horsley, Yovich and McGlashan helped take the total to 319 but Canterbury had a good lead.

Requiring an outright win to take the title Canterbury declared again to leave Northern 374 to win or to bat out time. Although Watling went early, Northern had little trouble. Evans reached his century after 292 minutes and 246 balls and the match was soon called off.

Immediately after the game Hamish Marshall left to join the New Zealand team in West Indies following the injury to Lou Vincent.

CANTERBURY

FIRST INNINGS	Runs	Mins	Balls	6s	4s	*SECOND INNINGS*	Runs	Mins	Balls	6s	4s
T.D.Astle lbw b Aldridge	0	3	4	-	-	c McGlashan b Southee	0	14	14	-	-
M.H.W.Papps run out	132	418	310	-	20	b Martin	96	239	174	-	12
S.L.Stewart b Marshall H.J.H.	118	327	250	1	19	b Aldridge	0	6	5	-	-
A.M.Ellis lbw b Southee	28	90	66	-	4	(5) c Wilson b Martin	15	61	45	-	1
C.Z.Harris* c Watling b Southee	15	22	15	1	2	(6) not out	54	92	64	2	4
C.F.K.van Wyk† not out	55	127	86	1	8	(7) run out	24	42	37	1	-
I.A.Robertson c McGlashan b Yovich	21	45	31	-	3	(8) not out	18	13	12	-	2
C.J.Anderson b Southee	3	14	8	-	-						
B.C.Hiini c Marshall J.A.H. b Yovich	14	4	4	-	-	(4) c Horsley b Martin	30	118	91	-	3
L.M.Burtt not out	29	42	35	1	3						
H.K.Bennett											
Extras (b 8, lb 14, w 7, nb 12)	41					(b 2, lb 6, nb 4)	12				
TOTAL (133 overs) (8 wkts dec)	**443**	550				(73 overs) (6 wkts dec)	**249**	295			

NORTHERN DISTRICTS

FIRST INNINGS	Runs	Mins	Balls	6s	4s	*SECOND INNINGS*	Runs	Mins	Balls	6s	4s
B-J.Watling c van Wyk b Burtt	16	72	51	-	3	lbw b Hiini	4	38	26	-	-
B.S.Wilson c Astle b Bennett	7	19	12	-	1	b Ellis	43	176	137	-	2
A.W.Evans b Ellis	29	94	67	-	5	not out	104	298	250	-	14
H.J.H.Marshall c van Wyk b Bennett	42	121	83	-	8	not out	80	160	113	-	14
J.A.H.Marshall* c Harris b Bennett	7	15	12	-	1						
N.K.W.Horsley c Ellis b Robertson	66	160	136	1	8						
J.A.F.Yovich b Burtt	52	274	199	-	6						
P.D.McGlashan† b Bennett	46	163	140	-	6						
B.P.Martin not out	10	48	29	-	1						
T.G.Southee c van Wyk b Burtt	4	10	7	-	1						
G.W.Aldridge b Harris	1	23	13	-	-						
Extras (b 19, lb 4, w 1, nb 15)	39					(b 4, lb 13, w 5, nb 5)	27				
TOTAL (122.3 overs)	**319**	504				(87 overs) (2 wkts)	**258**	337			

Bowling	*O*	*M*	*R*	*W*	*O*	*M*	*R*	*W*
NORTHERN DISTRICTS								
Aldridge	26	4	104	1	21	2	65	1
Southee	30	7	73	3	15	6	40	1
Yovich	24	3	104	2	13	1	51	0
Marshall H.J.H.	28	10	60	1	2	0	12	0
Martin	25	7	80	0	22	1	73	3
CANTERBURY								
Bennett	27	8	46	4	21	2	81	0
Burtt	23.5	8	70	3	12	1	37	0
Hiini	15	5	38	0	10	6	12	1
Harris	20.4	11	35	1	12	1	30	0
Anderson	9	2	27	0	3	0	17	0
Ellis	13	6	34	1	6	1	9	1
Astle	6	0	21	0	18	4	38	0
Robertson	8	2	25	1	5	1	17	0

Fall of Wickets

	C	*ND*	*C*	*ND*
	1st	*1st*	*2nd*	*2nd*
1st	0	15	1	28
2nd	243	59	4	109
3rd	310	87	100	-
4th	311	102	142	-
5th	326	151	166	-
6th	366	213	220	-
7th	383	301	-	-
8th	384	303	-	-
9th	-	307	-	-
10th	-	319	-	-

2006/07 FIRST-CLASS STATISTICS

REGISTER OF PLAYERS

The following players appeared in first-class cricket for New Zealand teams during the 2006/07 season.

		Born	*At*	*Type*			*First-class debut*	
Adams Andre Ryan	A	17. 7.75	Auckland	RHB	RFM		A v O	97/98
Aldridge Graeme William	ND	15.11.77	Christchurch	RHB	RFM		ND v W	98/99
Amandeep **Singh**	C	17. 8.87	Punjab, India	RHB	RFM		ND v CD	05/06
Anderson Corey James	C	13.12.90	Christchurch	LHB	LFM		C v CD	06/07
Andrews Simon Leslie	ND	11. 7.80	Auckland	RHB	RFM		ND v O	00/01
Arnel Brent John	ND	3. 1.79	Hamilton	RHB	RFM		ND v C	05/06
Astle Nathan John	C, NZ	15. 9.71	Christchurch	RHB	RM		C v CD	91/92
Astle Todd Duncan	C	24. 9.86	Palmerston North	RHB	RLB		C v W	05/06
Baldwin Scott Bruce Cameron	CD	19.11.83	Wanganui	RHB	RM		CD v A	06/07
Barnett Geoffrey Edward Fulton	CD	3. 2.84	Nelson	LHB			CD v O	04/05
Bell Matthew David	W	25. 2.77	Dunedin	RHB	ROB	WK	ND v NZA	93/94
Bennett Hamish Kyle	C	22. 2.87	Timaru	LHB	RFM		C v W	05/06
Bond Shane Edward	C, NZ	7. 6.75	Christchurch	RHB	RF		C v CD	96/97
Bowden Dewayne Jamie	W	27. 2.82	Wellington	LHB	LFM		W v ND	05/06
Broom Neil Trevor	O	20.11.83	Christchurch	RHB	RM		C v W	02/03
Burns Michael	W	6. 7.79	Balclutha	RHB	RFM		W v C	06/07
Burtt Leighton McGregor	C	17. 4.84	Christchurch	RHB	RM		C v O	06/07
Cachopa Carl	A	17. 5.86	Bloemfontein, S.Africa	RHB	RM		A v W	04/05
Canning Tamahau Karangatukituki	A	7. 4.77	Adelaide, Australia	RHB	RFM		AA v Mat Inv	98/99
Chan Sunnie Percival	C	4. 2.82	Wellington	RHB	RFM		C v A	06/07
Cumming Craig Derek	O, NZ	31. 8.75	Timaru	RHB	RM		C v CD	95/96
Davis Te Ahu Trevor	ND	9.12.85	Auckland	RHB	RFM		ND v O	04/05
de Grandhomme Colin	A	22. 7.86	Harare	RHB	RM		Zim A v Kenya	05/06
Davidson Michael Philip Forbes	C	24. 9.81	Christchurch	RHB	LFM		C v O	06/07
Diamanti Brendon John	CD	30. 4.81	Blenheim	RHB	RM		CD v W	03/04
Elliott Grant David	W	21. 3.79	Johannesburg, S.Africa	RHB	RFM		Natal B v Trans B	96/97
Ellis Andrew Malcolm	C	24. 3.82	Christchurch	RHB	RFM		C v A	02/03
Erasmus Pieter Bernardus	A	19. 3.83	Ceres, South Africa	RHB	LFM		A v O	06/07
Evans Alun Wyn	ND	20. 8.75	Glanamman, Wales	RHB	RM		Glam v OU	96
Fairley Samuel Anthony	W	19. 9.80	Whakatane	LHB	RM		W v O	01/02
Fleming Stephen Paul	W, NZ	1. 4.73	Christchurch	LHB	RSM		C v ND	91/92
Flynn Daniel Raymond	ND	16. 4.85	Rotorua	LHB	SLA		ND v O	04/05
Franklin James Edward Charles	W, NZ	7.11.80	Wellington	LHB	LFM		W v I	98/99
Fulton Peter Gordon	C, NZ	1. 2.79	Christchurch	RHB	RM		C v A	00/01
Gillespie Mark Raymond	W	17.10.79	Wanganui	RHB	RFM		W v O	99/00
Griggs Bevan Barry John	CD	29. 3.78	Palmerston North	RHB		WK	CD v O	00/01
Guptill Martin James	A	30. 9.86	Auckland	RHB	ROB		A v W	05/06
Haig Shaun Barry	O	19. 3.82	Auckland	RHB	RM	WK	O v CD	05/06
Hamilton Lance John	CD	5. 4.73	Papakura	RHB	LFM		CD v W	96/97
Harris Chris Zinzan	C	20.11.69	Christchurch	LHB	RM		C v O	89/90
Harvie Mathew James	O	6.12.84	Dunedin	RHB	RFM		O v A	03/04
Hay Gregory Robert	CD	14. 7.84	Rotorua	RHB	ROB		CD v W	06/07
Hayne Gareth Peter	A	13. 6.81	Auckland	RHB	ROB		A v CD	06/07
Hefford Brent Edward	CD	8. 5.78	Blenheim	LHB	RM		CD v C	99/00
Hegglun Gregory James Tristran	CD	7. 8.84	Blenheim	RHB	RM		CD v C	04/05
Hiini Brandon Christopher	C	11.12.81	Invercargill	RHB	RM		C v CD	05/06
Hira Roneel Magan	A	23. 1.87	Auckland	LHB	SLA		A v O	06/07
Hitchcock Paul Anthony	A	23. 1.75	Wellington	RHB	RM		W v ND	99/00
Hogg Kyle William	O	2 .7.83	Birmingham, England	LHB	RFM		Lancs v DU	01
Hopkins Gareth James	O	24.11.76	Lower Hutt	RHB	WK		NC v CC	97/98
Horsley Nicholas Keith Woodward	ND	22. 9.80	Hamilton	LHB	ROB		A v CD	01/02
Houpapa David Wiremu	A	14.11.81	Newman, Australia	LHB	RM		A v CD	06/07
How Jamie Michael	CD, NZ	19. 5.81	New Plymouth	RHB	ROB		CD v W	00/01
Ingram Peter John	CD	25.10.78	Hawera	RHB	ROB		CD v O	01/02
Jefferson Mark Robin	ND	28. 6.76	Oamaru	LHB	SLA		W v A	96/97
Jones Richard Andrew	A	22.10.73	Auckland	RHB			A v C	93/94
Lobb Dion Victor	O	3.12.80	Dunedin	RHB	RM		O v A	06/07
Lonsdale William Meehan	C	16. 9.86	Christchurch	RHB	LFM		C v W	06/07
Loye Malachy Bernard	A	27. 9.72	Northampton, England	RHB	ROB		North v Worcs	91
Lythe Timothy Ignatius	A	19. 4.80	Auckland	RHB	ROB		A v CD	05/06

		Born	At	Type			First-class debut	
Marshall Hamish John Hamilton	ND	15. 2.79	Warkworth	RHB	RM		ND v W	98/99
Marshall James Andrew Hamilton	ND	15. 2.79	Warkworth	RHB	RM		ND v W	97/98
Martin Bruce Philip	ND	25. 4.80	Whangarei	RHB	SLA		ND v CD	99/00
Martin Christopher Stewart	A, NZ	10.12.74	Christchurch	RHB	RFM		C v W	97/98
Mason Michael James	CD	27. 8.74	Carterton	RHB	RFM		CD v ND	97/98
McCullum Brendon Barrie	C, NZ	27. 9.81	Dunedin	RHB		WK	O v CD	99/00
McCullum Nathan Leslie	O	1. 9.80	Dunedin	RHB	ROB		O v W	99/00
McGlashan Peter Donald	ND	22. 6.79	Napier	RHB		WK	CD v O	00/01
McIntosh Timothy Gavin	A	4.12.79	Auckland	LHB			A v ND	98/99
McMillan Craig Douglas	C	13. 9.76	Christchurch	RHB	RM		C v O	94/95
McMillan James Michael	O	14. 6.78	Christchurch	RHB	RFM		O v CD	00/01
Mills Kyle David	A	15. 3.79	Auckland	RHB	RFM		A v O	98/99
Mills Stuart Michael	W	22. 6.82	Wellington	RHB		WK	W v CD	03/04
Munro Colin	A	11. 3.87	Durban, South Africa	LHB	RM		A v C	06/07
Nevin Christopher John	W	3. 8.75	Dunedin	RHB		WK	W v ND	95/96
Niblett Andrew Dylan	CD	25. 4.77	Vanderbijl Park, S.Africa	RHB	RFM		CD v O	06/07
Nicol Robert James	A	28. 5.83	Auckland	RHB	ROB		A v CD	01/02
O'Brien Iain Edward	W	10. 7.76	Lower Hutt	RHB	RM		W v O	00/01
Oram Jacob David Philip	CD, NZ	28. 7.78	Palmerston North	LHB	RM		NZA v B	97/98
Orchard Mark Geoffrey	ND	8.11.78	Hamilton	RHB	RM		ND v C	01/02
Papps Michael Hugh William	C	2. 7.79	Christchurch	RHB		WK	C v O	98/99
Parlane Michael Edward	W	22. 7.72	Pukekohe	RHB		WK	ND v A	92/93
Parlane Neal Ronald	W	9. 8.78	Whangarei	RHB			ND v CD	96/97
Pasupati Mayu Yoga	A	5.12.76	Jaffna, Sri Lanka	RHB	RFM		W v CD	97/98
Patel Jeetan Shashi	W	7. 5.80	Wellington	RHB	ROB		W v A	99/00
Patton Bradley Michael King	CD	9.11.79	Hastings	LHB	RM		CD v C	06/07
Rae Benjamin Joseph	C	22.10.86	Christchurch	RHB			C v W	06/07
Rasmussen Scott	W	18.11.78	Wellington	RHB	RFM		W v ND	05/06
Rayner Dominic Leo	CD	26. 8.83	Marton	RHB	RM		CD v ND	06/07
Redmond Aaron James	O	23. 9.79	Perth, Australia	RHB	RLB		SI v NI	99/00
Robertson Iain Anthony	C	9.11.82	Christchurch	RHB	ROB		C v CD	05/06
Robinson Grant Geoffrey	ND	24. 7.79	Gisborne	LHB	LM		ND v A	01/02
Ryder Jesse Daniel	W	6. 8.84	Masterton	LHB	RM		CD v ND	02/03
Schaw Robert James	CD	12. 5.84	Waipukurau	LHB	RLB		CD v ND	06/07
Scott Bradley Esmond	O	16. 9.79	Ashburton	LHB	LFM		O v A	00/01
Shaw Lance Joseph	A	24. 8.83	Auckland	RHB	RFM		A v CD	05/06
Sheed Jordan William	O	24. 9.82	Timaru	RHB	RLB		O v C	01/02
Sinclair Mathew Stuart	CD	9.11.75	Katherine, Australia	RHB	RM	WK	CD v C	95/96
Small Christopher Arran	C	30.11.86	Christchurch	LHB	RM		C v O	06/07
Smith Craig Murray	O	9. 1.85	Oamaru	RHB	LM		O v A	04/05
Southee Timothy Grant	ND	11.12.88	Whangarei	RHB	RFM		ND v O	06/07
Stewart Shanan Luke	C	21. 6.82	Christchurch	RHB	RM		C v ND	01/02
Taylor Luteru Ross Poutoa Lote	CD	8. 3.84	Lower Hutt	RHB	ROB		CD v C	02/03
Thompson Ewen Paul	CD	17.12.79	Warkworth	LHB	LFM		CD v O	00/01
Todd Gregory Rex	O	17. 6.82	Masterton	LHB	RM		CD v O	00/01
Turner Nicholas Mirek	O	3. 8.83	Invercargill	LHB	RM		O v ND	06/07
van Wyk Cornelius Francoius Kruger	C	7. 2.80	Wolmaransstad, S.Africa	RHB		WK	N v GW	00/01
Vettori Daniel Luca	ND, NZ	27. 1.79	Auckland	RHB	SLA		ND v E	96/97
Vincent Lou	A	11.11.78	Warkworth	RHB	ROB	WK	A v O	97/98
Watling Bradley-John	ND	9. 7.85	Durban, S.Africa	RHB		WK	ND v A	04/05
Weston Timothy Ian	CD	6. 6.82	Stratford	RHB		WK	CD v C	05/06
Wilson Bradley Svend	ND	10. 4.85	Auckland	RHB	ROB		ND v O	04/05
Woodcock Luke James	W	19. 3.82	Wellington	LHB	SLA	WK	W v O	01/02
Young Reece Alan	A	15. 9.79	Auckland	RHB		WK	A v C	98/99
Yovich Joseph Adam Frank	ND	15.12.76	Whangarei	LHB	RFM		ND v C	96/97

Key

RHB	right-hand batsman	*SLA*	slow left-arm	*RSM*	right slow-medium
LHB	left-hand batsman	*RLB*	right leg-break	*LFM*	left fast-medium
RM	right medium	*ROB*	right off-break	*LSM*	left slow-medium
LM	left medium	*RFM*	right fast-medium	*WK*	wicketkeeper
NC	Northern Conference	*CC*	Central Conference	*NZA*	New Zealand Academy
AA	Australian Academy	*N*	Northerns	*GW*	Griqualand West

FIRST-CLASS UMPIRES

2006/07

Twenty local umpires officiated in domestic competition matches. Tim Parlane went to South Africa and stood in two first-class games while Shaun George made a reciprocal visit to New Zealand. Brent Bowden was again on the Emirates Elite Panel and Tony Hill and Gary Baxter were on the second tier panel. Bowden and Hill umpired in the World Cup. Evan Watkin was again on the third umpire panel.

Anderson, Robert Donald *(Manawatu)*. Age 59. Debut in 1997/98. Has now stood in 49 first-class games, 33 one-day games and six Twenty20 matches. Awarded NZ Order Of Merit in New Year's Honours List.

Baxter, Gary Arthur *(Canterbury)*. Age 55. Debut in 1998/99. Is on the ICC Second Tier Panel and has stood in 12 one-day internationals, 50 first-class games, 35 one-day matches and two Twenty20 games.

Bowden, Brent Fraser *(Auckland)*. Age 43. Debut in 1992/93. Has now umpired more test matches than any other New Zealand umpire. Has stood in 41 Tests and 101 first-class games. Has also umpired in 114 one-day internationals, 70 one-day games and six Twenty20 games.

Brandon, David Maurice *(Wellington)*. Age 58. Umpired in Australia standing in seven first-class games and two one-day matches. Debut in New Zealand in 2005/06. Has umpired three one-day games and two Twenty20 games.

Busby, Jeremy Martin *(Canterbury)*. Age 45. Debut in 1996/97 and has now stoood in seven first-class games and five one-day matches.

Cross, Kathleen *(Wellington)*. Age 48. Debut in 2003/04 and has now officiated in five one-day games and one Twenty20 game.

Frost, Barry George *(Auckland)*. Age 49. Debut in 1998/99 and has now stood in 40 first-class games and 39 one-day matches. Also stood in three Twenty20 games.

Gasston, Peter Louis *(Auckland)*. Age 46. Debut in 2005/06. Two one-day and one Twenty20 game.

George, Michael Peter *(Horowhenua-Kapiti)*. Age 48. Debut in 1999/00 and has now stood in 24 first-class games and 23 one-day games

Gray, Evan John *(Wellington)*. Age 52. Former New Zealand and Wellington player. Debut in 2005/06 and has now officiated in five first-class and seven one-day games. Also umpired four Twenty20 games.

Hill, Anthony Lloyd *(Counties)*. Age 56. Debut in 1993/94. A member of the ICC Second Tier panel. Has umpired four test matches and 61 first class games. Also stood in 40 one-day internationals, 71 one-day games and eight Twenty20 games.

Jones, Philip David *(Auckland)*. Age 46. Debut in 2002/03 and has now stood in 19 first-class games and 11 one-day matches. Also stood in three Twenty20 games.

Knights, Wayne Roger *(Auckland)*. Age 36. Debut in 2001/02 and has now umpired six one-day and one Twenty20 game

Manley, Kevin Charles *(Auckland)*. Age 56. Debut in 1999/00 and has now stood in three first-class games, three one-day matches and one Twenty20 game

Morris, Craig Justin *(Manawatu)*. Age 43. Debut in 2000/01 and has now umpired six first-class games and eight one-day matches.

Parlane, Tim James *(Northland)*. Age 40. Debut in 2001/02 and has now stood in 16 first-class games and 19 one-day matches. Also stood in two Twenty20 games.

Paterson, David Gordon *(Marlborough)*. Age 45. Debut in 2001/02 and has now umpired seven one-day matches.

Quested, David Murray *(Canterbury)*. Age 60. Debut in 1990/91. Has umpired five Tests and 98 first-class games. Also officiated in 31 one-day internationals, 80 one-day games and two Twenty20 games.

Walker, Derek John *(Otago)*. Age 47. Former Otago player from 1980/81 to 1988/89. Made his umpiring debut in 2004/05 and has now stood in 14 first-class games and 11 one-day matches. Also four Twenty20 games.

Watkin, Evan Allan *(Wellington)*. Age 55. Debut in 1989/90 making him New Zealand's longest serving umpire. Umpired in two tests and 96 first-class games. Also umpired in 21 one-day internationals, 96 one-day games and four Twenty20 games.

COMPLETE AVERAGES

	M	In	NO	HS	Runs	Ave	100	50	Ct	St	O	M	R	W	Ave	5WI	10WM	Best
A.R.Adams	6	10	2	117*	318	39.75	1	1	4	-	250.4	75	601	32	18.78	1	-	5-58
G.W.Aldridge	8	12	4	25*	89	11.12	-	-	5	-	287.2	61	853	33	25.84	3	-	5-33
Amandeep Singh	2	2	0	6	9	4.50	-	-	-	-	44	9	178	3	59.33	-	-	2-74
C.J.Anderson	2	2	0	29	32	16.00	-	-	-	-	32	5	129	1	129.00	-	-	1-59
S.L.Andrews	2	2	1	59*	73	73.00	-	1	-	-	72	16	196	4	49.00	-	-	2-46
B.J.Arnel	5	5	1	8	22	5.50	-	-	1	-	147.3	42	436	14	31.14	-	-	4-31
N.J.Astle	4	7	1	61*	156	26.00	-	1	6	-	40.5	11	110	1	110.00	-	-	1-46
T.D.Astle	9	15	0	97	440	29.33	-	3	7	-	167.5	20	575	12	47.91	-	-	2-19
S.B.C.Baldwin	1	2	0	0	0	0.00	-	-	-	-	24	5	81	1	81.00	-	-	1-33
G.E.F.Barnett	4	8	1	118	351	50.14	1	2	2	-	3	0	15	0	-	-	-	-
M.D.Bell	6	9	2	161*	397	56.71	2	1	7	-								
H.K.Bennett	5	3	0	12	13	4.33	-	-	-	-	182	31	656	12	54.66	-	-	4-46
S.E.Bond	3	4	0	8	23	5.75	-	-	1	-	105.4	24	332	17	19.52	1	-	5-37
D.J.Bowden	6	8	2	42	157	26.16	-	-	1	-	112	23	348	6	58.00	-	-	2-43
N.T.Broom	8	11	2	112	644	71.55	2	4	3	-	6.4	0	46	0	-	-	-	-
M.Burns	4	4	1	8	17	5.66	-	-	2	-	84.2	16	280	9	31.11	-	-	4-44
L.M.Burtt	6	7	1	29*	56	9.33	-	-	2	-	169.5	40	561	20	28.05	1	-	5-45
C.Cachopa	1	1	0	17	17	17.00	-	-	-	-								
T.K.Canning	4	6	1	90*	118	23.60	-	1	1	-	171	69	389	14	27.78	-	-	4-54
S.P.Chan	2	2	0	35	35	17.50	-	-	-	-	58.3	6	215	6	35.83	-	-	3-58
C.D.Cumming	8	14	0	108	455	32.50	1	2	1	-	39	4	226	1	226.00	-	-	1-53
M.P.F.Davidson	1	1	0	34	34	34.00	-	-	-	-	21	5	62	2	31.00	-	-	2-31
T.T.Davis	1	0	0	0	0	-	-	-	1	-	23	5	97	3	32.33	-	-	3-97
C.de Grandhomme	4	6	0	87	167	27.83	-	1	2	-	20	1	48	0	-	-	-	-
B.J.Diamanti	2	3	1	18	33	16.50	-	-	1	-	64	8	221	4	55.25	-	-	3-43
G.D.Elliott	7	10	2	107	361	45.12	2	1	2	-	151	43	394	12	32.83	-	-	3-48
A.M.Ellis	6	9	1	59*	164	20.50	-	1	2	-	120	31	344	7	49.14	-	-	3-51
P.B.Erasmus	1	1	0	15	15	15.00	-	-	-	-	9	3	15	2	7.50	-	-	2-15
A.W.Evans	8	15	2	104*	535	41.15	1	3	3	-								
S.A.Fairley	4	6	0	59	90	15.00	-	1	3	-								
S.P.Fleming	4	7	0	48	130	18.57	-	-	7	-								
D.R.Flynn	3	5	0	18	43	8.60	-	-	2	-								
J.E.C.Franklin	4	6	0	64	185	30.83	-	2	4	-	112	17	356	11	32.36	-	-	3-30
P.G.Fulton	4	7	1	68	270	45.00	-	2	1	-								
M.R.Gillespie	4	3	1	18*	18	9.00	-	-	-	-	133	24	465	19	24.47	1	-	5-93
B.B.J.Griggs	8	15	1	83	580	41.42	-	6	18	1								
M.J.Guptill	6	11	0	65	174	15.81	-	1	4	-								
S.B.Haig	3	4	0	111	154	38.50	1	-	3	-								
L.J.Hamilton	2	3	1	0*	0	0.00	-	-	-	-	35.3	6	120	4	30.00	-	-	2-54
C.Z.Harris	9	14	4	122	428	42.80	1	2	16	-	287.1	105	538	13	41.38	-	-	3-43
M.J.Harvie	7	7	1	34	90	15.00	-	-	2	-	192.5	28	800	13	61.53	-	-	3-91
G.R.Hay	8	14	1	106	593	45.61	1	4	5	-								
G.P.Hayne	3	4	0	18	19	4.75	-	-	2	-	110	21	291	6	48.50	-	-	3-80
B.E.Hefford	7	11	5	15*	67	11.16	-	-	2	-	242.2	60	765	12	63.75	-	-	3-88
G.J.T.Hegglun	5	8	1	52*	92	13.14	-	1	3	-	139	37	402	13	30.92	-	-	4-52
B.C.Hiini	6	8	4	103*	250	62.50	1	-	2	-	193.2	61	513	15	34.20	-	-	3-31
R.M.Hira	2	1	0	4	4	4.00	-	-	-	-	47	15	115	0	-	-	-	-
P.A.Hitchcock	1	2	0	19	26	13.00	-	-	-	-	27	10	67	1	67.00	-	-	1-40
K.W.Hogg	4	5	1	71	170	42.50	-	2	1	-	101	16	313	5	62.60	-	-	2-59
G.J.Hopkins	8	9	3	139*	514	85.66	3	1	14	1								
N.K.W.Horsley	6	10	1	66	425	47.22	-	6	2	-	4	0	12	1	12.00	-	-	1-5
D.W.Houpapa	3	5	0	33	74	14.80	-	-	1	-	3	0	16	0	-	-	-	-
J.M.How	8	16	2	102*	419	29.92	1	2	6	-	71	10	225	3	75.00	-	-	1-15
P.J.Ingram	6	12	1	166*	617	56.09	4	-	4	-								
M.R.Jefferson	2	4	1	29	57	19.00	-	-	1	-	22	1	95	1	95.00	-	-	1-95
R.A.Jones	8	16	2	143	630	45.00	2	3	11	-								
D.V.Lobb	1	1	0	4	4	4.00	-	-	-	-	7	1	37	1	37.00	-	-	1-37
W.M.Lonsdale	3	3	3	1*	2	-	-	-	1	-	77.5	22	241	3	80.33	-	-	1-3
M.B.Loye	2	4	1	36*	51	17.00	-	-	-	-								
T.I.Lythe	2	4	0	18	35	8.75	-	-	-	-	31	5	132	1	132.00	-	-	1-25
H.J.H.Marshall	9	17	3	153	766	54.71	2	3	3	-	87	24	236	5	47.20	-	-	1-6
J.A.H.Marshall	9	16	2	128	467	33.35	1	2	4	-	14	1	45	0	-	-	-	-

	M	In	NO	HS	Runs	Ave	100	50	Ct	St	O	M	R	W	Ave	5WI	10WM	Best
B.P.Martin	6	7	4	28*	66	22.00	-	-	1	-	220.5	45	642	16	40.12	-	-	4-117
C.S.Martin	8	9	7	8	16	8.00	-	-	-	-	281	61	896	38	23.57	3	-	5-48
M.J.Mason	4	5	1	16	28	7.00	-	-	-	-	130.4	43	318	15	21.20	-	-	4-44
B.B.McCullum	4	8	1	67	256	36.57	-	2	12	1								
N.L.McCullum	8	10	1	61	240	26.66	-	1	11	-	267.5	52	790	14	56.42	-	-	3-89
P.D.McGlashan	6	9	1	63	274	34.25	-	2	23	-								
T.G.McIntosh	8	16	2	205	412	29.42	1	1	6	-	3	2	5	0	-	-	-	-
C.D.McMillan	4	6	1	117	301	60.20	2	-	2	-	52.5	6	172	6	28.66	-	-	2-4
J.M.McMillan	6	4	3	3	3	3.00	-	-	1	-	161.4	29	617	23	26.82	1	-	7-105
K.D.Mills	1	1	0	16	16	16.00	-	-	-	-	9	3	22	0	-	-	-	-
S.M.Mills	4	6	1	171	248	49.60	1	1	15	-								
C.Munro	2	4	1	20*	39	13.00	-	-	2	-	64.3	15	190	3	63.33	-	-	2-57
C.J.Nevin	6	7	1	98	304	50.66	-	3	10	-								
A.D.Niblett	5	9	0	22	71	7.88	-	-	1	-	158	29	577	10	57.70	-	-	3-121
R.J.Nicol	8	14	4	160	519	51.90	2	2	4	-	23	3	84	1	84.00	-	-	1-5
I.E.O'Brien	6	7	2	44	81	16.20	-	-	-	-	241.2	66	709	34	20.85	3	1	8-55
J.D.P.Oram	3	5	1	12*	18	4.50	-	-	1	-	47	14	115	5	23.00	-	-	2-30
M.G.Orchard	4	7	1	74*	181	30.16	-	2	1	-	127.3	45	339	9	37.66	-	-	4-33
M.H.W.Papps	7	11	0	188	1005	91.36	4	4	4	-								
M.E.Parlane	8	13	1	140	613	51.08	2	4	8	-	10	2	39	0	-	-	-	-
N.R.Parlane	8	12	1	135	536	48.72	1	4	5	-	1	0	6	0	-	-	-	-
M.Y.Pasupati	1	1	1	76*	76	-	-	1	-	-	14.3	3	39	4	9.75	-	-	4-39
J.S.Patel	4	5	2	15	30	10.00	-	-	1	-	119.3	32	275	7	39.28	-	-	2-28
B.M.K.Patton	1	1	0	0	0	0.00	-	-	1	-	1	0	1	0	-	-	-	-
B.J.Rae	4	5	0	58	147	29.40	-	1	4	-								
S.Rasmussen	2	2	0	3	3	1.50	-	-	1	-	40	9	111	3	37.00	-	-	3-40
D.L.Rayner	1	2	1	11*	16	16.00	-	-	-	-	24	4	90	1	90.00	-	-	1-90
A.J.Redmond	8	12	2	135*	555	55.50	2	2	8	-	162.3	28	586	8	73.25	-	-	2-62
I.A.Robertson	5	7	4	102*	258	86.00	1	1	4	-	111.5	18	368	7	52.57	-	-	2-37
G.G.Robinson	2	3	0	44	110	36.66	-	-	3	-								
J.D.Ryder	8	13	1	112	498	41.50	1	2	6	-	56	16	165	4	41.25	-	-	1-13
R.J.Schaw	7	11	1	34	222	22.20	-	-	4	-	189.4	27	693	10	69.30	-	-	2-49
B.E.Scott	8	8	2	52*	164	27.33	-	1	3	-	256.1	84	638	27	23.62	1	-	5-50
L.J.Shaw	7	9	3	20*	36	6.00	-	-	1	-	176	38	593	20	29.65	1	-	5-63
J.W.Sheed	7	12	0	86	305	25.41	-	3	2	-	19	2	140	1	140.00	-	-	1-50
M.S.Sinclair	8	15	0	109	458	30.53	1	2	7	-	27.3	5	76	3	25.33	-	-	2-24
C.A.Small	3	3	2	18	47	47.00	-	-	1	-	69	11	260	5	52.00	-	-	4-50
C.M.Smith	3	3	0	49	83	27.66	-	-	2	-	73.4	26	178	2	89.00	-	-	2-7
T.G.Southee	5	4	1	75*	96	32.00	-	1	1	-	184.2	46	535	16	33.43	-	-	3-73
S.L.Stewart	8	13	1	146	606	50.50	2	2	2	-	9	0	25	0	-	-	-	-
L.R.P.L.Taylor	4	7	0	217	348	49.71	1	-	4	-	33	0	121	1	121.00	-	-	1-63
E.P.Thompson	3	5	0	40	102	20.40	-	-	2	-	101.5	21	402	14	28.71	-	-	4-77
G.R.Todd	8	13	3	160	522	52.20	1	2	2	-	2	1	2	0	-	-	-	-
D.R.Tuffey	1	2	0	9	11	5.50	-	-	-	-	29	8	76	3	25.33	-	-	3-61
N.M.Turner	3	4	2	27*	53	26.50	-	-	1	-	92	28	241	7	34.42	-	-	3-57
C.F.K.van Wyk	8	10	1	64	267	29.66	-	2	20	1								
D.L.Vettori	4	6	1	120*	360	72.00	1	3	4	-	117.2	21	325	16	20.31	1	1	7-130
L.Vincent	4	7	1	41	142	23.66	-	-	1	-	16.4	1	71	4	17.75	-	-	1-1
B-J.Watling	8	15	0	153	564	37.60	2	2	14	-								
T.I.Weston	7	14	3	152	479	43.54	1	2	2	-								
B.S.Wilson	5	8	0	56	208	26.00	-	1	3	-								
L.J.Woodcock	7	10	2	59	155	19.37	-	1	2	-	145	38	367	10	36.70	-	-	4-55
R.A.Young	8	12	1	79	310	28.18	-	3	22	2								
J.A.F.Yovich	7	11	2	52	223	24.77	-	2	1	-	165	21	681	12	56.75	-	-	3-100

LEADING AVERAGES

BATTING *(top 20, qualification six innings)*

	M	I	NO	HS	Runs	Ave	100s	50s
M.H.W. Papps	7	11	0	188	1005	91.36	4	4
I.A. Robertson	5	7	4	102*	258	86.00	1	1
G.J. Hopkins	8	9	3	139*	514	85.66	3	1
D.L. Vettori	4	6	1	120*	360	72.00	1	3
N.T. Broom	8	11	2	112	644	71.55	2	4
B.C. Hiini	6	8	4	103*	250	62.50	1	-
C.D. McMillan	4	6	1	117	301	60.20	2	-
M.D. Bell	6	9	2	161*	397	56.71	2	1
P.J. Ingram	6	12	1	166*	617	56.09	4	-
A.J. Redmond	8	12	2	135*	555	55.50	2	2
H.J.H. Marshall	9	17	3	153	766	54.71	2	3
G.R. Todd	8	13	3	160	522	52.20	1	2
R.J. Nicol	8	14	4	160	519	51.90	2	2
M.E. Parlane	8	13	1	140	613	51.08	2	4
C.J. Nevin	6	7	1	98	304	50.66	-	3
S.L. Stewart	8	13	1	146	606	50.50	2	2
G.E.F. Barnett	4	8	1	118	351	50.14	1	2
L.R.P.L. Taylor	4	7	0	217	348	49.71	1	-
S.M. Mills	4	6	1	171	248	49.60	1	1
N.R. Parlane	8	12	1	135	536	48.72	1	4

BOWLING *(top 20, qualification 10 wickets)*

	Overs	Mdns	Runs	Wkts	Ave	5WI	10WM	Best
M. Muralitharan	94.2	24	217	17	12.76	1	1	6-87
A.R. Adams	250.4	75	601	32	18.78	1	-	5-58
S.E. Bond	105.4	24	332	17	19.52	1	-	5-37
D.L. Vettori	117.2	21	325	16	20.31	1	1	7-130
I.E. O'Brien	241.2	66	709	34	20.85	3	1	8-55
M.J. Mason	130.4	43	318	15	21.20	-	-	4-44
C.S. Martin	281	61	896	38	23.57	3	-	5-48
B.E. Scott	256.1	84	638	27	23.62	1	-	5-50
M.R. Gillespie	133	24	465	19	24.47	1	-	5-93
G.W. Aldridge	287.2	61	853	33	25.84	3	-	5-33
J.M. McMillan	161.4	29	617	23	26.82	1	-	7-105
T.K. Canning	171	69	389	14	27.78	-	-	4-54
L.M. Burtt	169.5	40	561	20	28.05	1	-	5-45
E.P. Thompson	101.5	21	402	14	28.71	-	-	4-77
L.J. Shaw	176	38	593	20	29.65	1	-	5-63
G.J.T. Hegglun	139	37	402	13	30.92	-	-	4-52
B.J. Arnel	147.3	42	436	14	31.14	-	-	4-31
J.E.C. Franklin	112	17	356	11	32.36	-	-	3-30
G.D. Elliott	151	43	394	12	32.83	-	-	3-48
T.G. Southee	184.2	46	535	16	33.43	-	-	3-73

CENTURIES

There were 56 centuries in first-class cricket in 2006/07 compared to 30 the previous season. This broke the previous record of 51set in 1991/92. A total of 36 players scored hundreds (the record being 39 in 1998/99). M.H.W. Papps and P.J. Ingram each scored four, G.J. Hopkins made three and A.J. Redmond, B-J. Watling, C.D. McMillan, G.D. Elliott, H.J.H. Marshall, M.D. Bell, M.E. Parlane, N.T. Broom, R.A. Jones, R.J. Nicol, S.L. Stewart and K.C. Sangakkara each scored two. The fastest hundred of the season was scored by A.R. Adams who took 87 balls to reach his century for Auckland against Otago at Lincoln.

217	L.R.P.L. Taylor	Central Districts v Otago	Napier
205	T.G. McIntosh	Auckland v Otago	Lincoln
188	M.H.W. Papps	Canterbury v Wellington	Christchurch
†171	S.M. Mills	Wellington v Canterbury	Christchurch
169	M.H.W. Papps	Canterbury v Otago	Christchurch
166*	P.J. Ingram	Central Districts v Canterbury	Christchurch
161*	M.D. Bell	Wellington v Otago	Dunedin
160	G.R. Todd	Otago v Canterbury	Christchurch
160	R.J. Nicol	Auckland v Otago	Lincoln
159	P.J. Ingram	Central Districts v Canterbury	Napier
156*	K.C. Sangakkara	Sri Lanka v New Zealand *(Second Test)*	Wellington
153	H.J.H. Marshall	Northern Districts v Central Districts	Lincoln
†153	B-J. Watling	Northern Districts v Otago	Dunedin
152*	L.P.C. Silva	Sri Lanka v New Zealand *(Second Test)*	Wellington
†152	T.I. Weston	Central Districts v Auckland	Auckland
146	S.L. Stewart	Canterbury v Central Districts	Napier
143	R.A. Jones	Auckland v Central Districts	Auckland
140	M.E. Parlane	Wellington v Otago	Dunedin
139*	G.J. Hopkins	Otago v Auckland	Lincoln
135*	A.J. Redmond	Otago v Canterbury	Christchurch
135	N.R. Parlane	Wellington v Auckland	Wellington
134	R.J. Nicol	Auckland v Central Districts	Napier
132	M.H.W. Papps	Canterbury v Northern Districts	Hamilton
128	J.A.H. Marshall	Northern Districts v Wellington	Hamilton
127	A.J. Redmond	Otago v Northern Districts	Hamilton
126*	G.J. Hopkins	Otago v Central Districts	Napier
122	C.Z. Harris	Canterbury v Otago	Christchurch
121	M.H.W. Papps	Canterbury v Central Districts	Christchurch
120*	D.L. Vettori	Northern Districts v Central Districts	Lincoln
120	R.A. Jones	Auckland v Central Districts	Auckland
119	P.J. Ingram	Central Districts v Canterbury	Christchurch
119	H.J.H. Marshall	Northern Districts v Otago	Hamilton
†118	G.E.F. Barnett	Central Districts v Otago	Napier
118	S.L. Stewart	Canterbury v Northern Districts	Hamilton
117*	A.R. Adams	Auckland v Otago	Lincoln
117	C.D. McMillan	Canterbury v Central Districts	Christchurch
116	M.E. Parlane	Wellington v Canterbury	Wellington
112	N.T. Broom	Otago v Auckland	Lincoln
112	J.D. Ryder	Wellington v Canterbury	Wellington
†111	S.B. Haig	Otago v Central Districts	Napier
110	G.J. Hopkins	Otago v Northern Districts	Dunedin
109	M.S. Sinclair	Central Districts v Northern Districts	Lincoln
108	C.D. Cumming	Otago v Canterbury	Christchurch
107	G.D. Elliott	Wellington v Canterbury	Christchurch
†106	G.R. Hay	Central Districts v Northern Districts	Gisborne

105	P.J. Ingram	Central Districts v Auckland	Napier
104	B-J. Watling	Northern Districts v Otago	Hamilton
104*	A.W. Evans	Northern Districts v Canterbury	Hamilton
103*	B.C. Hiini	Canterbury v Central Districts	Christchurch
102*	G.D. Elliott	Wellington v Northern Districts	Hamilton
†102*	I.A. Robertson	Canterbury v Otago	Christchurch
102*	J.M. How	Central Districts v Canterbury	Napier
101	C.D. McMillan	Canterbury v Otago	Christchurch
101	M.D. Bell	Wellington v Northern Districts	Hamilton
101	N.T. Broom	Otago v Northern Districts	Hamilton
100*	K.C. Sangakkara	Sri Lanka v New Zealand *(First Test)*	Christchurch

† *maiden first-class century*

CENTURY PARTNERSHIPS

There were 64 century partnerships in 2006/07 compared to 44 the previous season. The record is 73 in 2000/01.

FIRST WICKET

201	T.D.Astle & M.H.W.Papps	Canterbury v Wellington	Christchurch
132	C.D.Cumming & J.W.Sheed	Otago v Auckland	Lincoln
122	A.W.Evans & B-J.Watling	Northern Districts v Otago	Dunedin
119	C.D.Cumming & J.W.Sheed	Otago v Canterbury	Christchurch
118	B-J.Watling & B.S.Wilson	Northern Districts v Central Districts	Gisborne
116	C.D.Cumming & J.W.Sheed	Otago v Northern Districts	Dunedin
111	T.D.Astle & B.B.McCulum	Canterbury v Otago	Christchurch
111	T.D.Astle & M.H.W.Papps	Canterbury v Otago	Christchurch
106	J.M.How & G.E.F.Barnett	Central Districts v Northern Districts	Lincoln
102*	T.G.McIntosh & R.A.Jones	Auckland v Wellington	Christchurch
101	T.D.Astle & M.H.W.Papps	Canterbury v Wellington	Wellington

SECOND WICKET

279	M.D. Bell & M.E.Parlane	Wellington v Otago	Dunedin
243	M.H.W.Papps & S.L.Stewart	Canterbury v Northern Districts	Hamilton
177	P.J.Ingram & B.B.J.Griggs	Central Districts v Canterbury	Christchurch
175	P.J.Ingram & M.S.Sinclair	Central Districts v Canterbury	Napier
146	B-J.Watling & A.W.Evans	Northern Districts v Otago	Hamilton
136	G.E.F.Barnett & B.B.J.Griggs	Central Districts v Otago	Napier
134	M.D.Bell & M.E.Parlane	Wellington v Northern Districts	Hamilton
127	R.A.Jones & M.J.Guptill	Auckland v Central Districts	Auckland
121	C.D.Cumming & A.J.Redmond	Otago v Canterbury	Christchurch
112	A.W.Evans & H.J.H.Marshall	Northern Districts v Otago	Dunedin
109	S.B.Haig & A.J.Redmond	Otago v Central Districts	Napier
104	R.A.Jones & M.J.Guptill	Auckland v Central Districts	Auckland

THIRD WICKET

208	M.H.W.Papps & C.D.McMillan	Canterbury v Central Districts	Christchurch
180*	A.J.Redmond & G.R.Todd	Otago v Canterbury	Christchurch
168	B.B.J.Griggs & L.R.P.L.Taylor	Central Districts v Otago	Napier
149*	A.W.Evans & H.J.H.Marshall	Northern Districts v Canterbury	Hamilton
128	M.D.Bell & J.D.Ryder	Wellington v Auckland	Christchurch
119	A.J.Redmond & G.R.Todd	Otago v Canterbury	Christchurch
116	S.L.Stewart & A.M.Ellis	Canterbury v Otago	Christchurch

FOURTH WICKET

273	T.G.McIntosh & R.J.Nicol	Auckland v Otago	Lincoln
204	A.J.Redmond & N.T.Broom	Otago v Northern Districts	Hamilton
161	N.T.Broom & G.J.Hopkins	Otago v Central Districts	Napier
139	M.E.Parlane & N.R.Parlane	Wellington v Canterbury	Wellington
138	R.J.Nicol & C.de Grandhomme	Auckland v Central Districts	Napier
132	J.A.H.Marshall & G.G.Robinson	Northern Districts v Central Districts	Gisborne
118	H.J.H.Marshall & N.K.W.Horsley	Northern Districts v Auckland	Auckland
117*	P.J.Ingram & T.I.Weston	Central Districts v Canterbury	Christchurch
113	N.R.Parlane & G.D.Elliott	Wellington v Auckland	Wellington

113	G.R.Hay & B.B.J.Griggs	Central Districts v Northern Districts	Gisborne
101	M.H.W.Papps & C.Z.Harris	Canterbury v Wellington	Christchurch
FIFTH WICKET			
219	N.T.Broom & G.J.Hopkins	Otago v Auckland	Lincoln
168	B.B.J.Griggs & T.I.Weston	Central Districts v Auckland	Auckland
162	C.D.McMillan & C.Z.Harris	Canterbury v Otago	Christchurch
159	S.L.Stewart & B.C.Hiini	Canterbury v Central Districts	Christchurch
126	G.R.Todd & G.J.Hopkins	Otago v Canterbury	Christchurch
121	K.C.Sangakkara & L.P.C.Silva	Sri Lanka v New Zealand *(Second Test)*	Wellington
121	M.S.Sinclair & G.R.Hay	Central Districts v Northern Districts	Lincoln
112	H.J.H.Marshall & N.K.W.Horsley	Northern Districts v Otago	Hamilton
102	S.L.Stewart & B.J.Rae	Canterbury v Central Districts	Napier
SIXTH WICKET			
184	G.D.Elliott & S.M.Mills	Wellington v Canterbury	Christchurch
146	G.J.Hopkins & N.L.McCullum	Otago v Northern Districts	Dunedin
127	N.K.W.Horsley & P.D.McGlashan	Northern Districts v Wellington	Wellington
115	B.J.Rae & C.F.K.van Wyk	Canterbury v Wellington	Christchurch
113	K.W.Hogg & N.L.McCullum	Otago v Central Districts	Napier
102	G.R.Hay & B.B.J.Griggs	Central Districts v Wellington	Wellington
SEVENTH WICKET			
176	S.M.Mills & C.J.Nevin	Wellington v Canterbury	Christchurch
114	R.A.Young & A.R.Adams	Auckland v Otago	Lincoln
109	S.M.Mills & C.J.Nevin	Wellington v Northern Districts	Wellington
103	R.J.Nicol & A.R.Adams	Auckland v Central Districts	Napier
EIGHTH WICKET			
152	J.A.H.Marshall & M.G.Orchard	Northern Districts v Wellington	Hamilton
113	L.R.P.L.Taylor & R.J.Schaw	Central Districts v Otago	Napier
101	T.K.Canning & A.R.Adams	Auckland v Canterbury	Auckland
NINTH WICKET			
104*	G.W.Aldridge & T.G.Southee	Northern Districts v Wellington	Wellington

WICKETKEEPING DISMISSALS

The following New Zealand players who appeared in 2006/07 have made at least one dismissal in first-class cricket while keeping wicket.

	ct	st	total
G.J.Hopkins	247	18	265
C.J.Nevin	233	8	241
R.A.Young *	206	5	211
C.F.K.van Wyk *	168	9	177
B.B.J.Griggs	142	5	147
B.B.McCullum	128	12	140
P.D.McGlashan *	80	4	84
S.M.Mills *	35	–	35
M.H.W.Papps	30	4	34
L.Vincent	25	–	25
B-J.Watling	21	–	21
M.S.Sinclair	11	1	12
M.D.Bell	4	–	4
L.J.Woodcock	3	–	3
S.B.Haig	3	–	–
C.D.Cumming	1	–	1
J.A.H.Marshall	1	–	1

** no further catches taken as fielder*

NEW ZEALANDERS IN OVERSEAS CRICKET

Andre Adams *(Essex)*, Scott Styris *(Middlesex)*, Stephen Fleming *(Nottinghamshire)*, Craig Spearman *(Gloucestershire)*, Nathan Astle *(Lancashire)*, James Franklin and Brendon McCullum *(Glamorgan)*, Lou Vincent *(Worcestershire)*, Daniel Vettori *(Warwickshire)*, Paul Wiseman *(Durham)* and Hamish Marshall *(Gloucestershire)* all appeared in county cricket in 2006.

At the time of going to print we were not able to include the final figures for players in county cricket in 2007 and the career records do not include performances in any of these matches.

The details for 2006 were:

	M	I	NO	HS	Runs	Ave	100	50	ct
A.R. Adams	8	9	2	75	230	32.85	-	1	4
N.J. Astle	8	12	0	86	429	35.75	-	3	3
S.P. Fleming	13	22	2	192	992	49.60	2	8	17
J.E.C. Franklin	9	15	1	94	346	24.71	-	2	4
B.B. McCullum	3	6	1	160	306	61.20	1	1	3
H.J.H. Marshall	11	21	1	168	1218	60.90	5	7	6
C.M. Spearman	16	31	0	192	1370	44.19	6	2	18
S.B. Styris	10	17	1	133	677	42.31	1	5	14
D.L. Vettori	1	1	0	27	27	27.00	-	-	-
L. Vincent	6	11	1	141	469	46.90	2	1	5
P.J. Wiseman	2	2	1	6*	10	10.00	-	-	-

	O	M	R	W	Ave	5WI	10WM	Best
A.R. Adams	278.1	63	830	21	39.52	-	-	4-72
N.J. Astle	58.3	12	178	4	44.50	-	-	1-9
J.E.C. Franklin	251.4	45	950	31	30.64	1	-	5-68
H.J.H. Marshall	26	7	63	1	63.00	-	-	1-16
S.B. Styris	198.3	37	670	18	37.22	1	-	6-71
D.L. Vettori	31	4	92	0	-	-	-	-
L. Vincent	22	2	76	1	76.00	-	-	1-12
P.J. Wiseman	56	11	230	1	230.00	-	-	1-127

BOWLING PERFORMANCES

There were 19 instances of a bowler taking five wickets or more in an innings. 13 bowlers achieved this feat with C.S. Martin, I.E. O'Brien and G.W. Aldridge achieving the feat three times each.

FIVE WICKETS IN AN INNINGS

8-55	I.E. O'Brien	Wellington v Auckland	Wellington
7-105	J.M. McMillan	Otago v Canterbury	Christchurch
7-130	D.L. Vettori	New Zealand v Sri Lanka *(Second Test)*	Wellington
6-87	M. Muralitharan	Sri Lanka v New Zealand *(Second Test)*	Wellington
5-33	G.W. Aldridge	Northern Districts v Auckland	Auckland
5-37	S.E. Bond	Canterbury v Northern Districts	Rangiora
5-45	L.M. Burtt	Canterbury v Wellington	Wellington
5-48	C.S. Martin	Auckland v Central Districts	Napier
5-50	B.E. Scott	Otago v Northern Districts	Dunedin
5-52	C.S. Martin	Auckland v Central Districts	Auckland
5-57	I.E. O'Brien	Wellington v Auckland	Christchurch
5-58	A.R. Adams	Auckland v Canterbury	Auckland
5-62	I.E. O'Brien	Wellington v Auckland	Wellington
5-63	L.J. Shaw	Auckland v Central Districts	Napier
5-68	S.L. Malinga	Sri Lanka v New Zealand *(Second Test)*	Wellington
5-75	G.W. Aldridge	Northern Districts v Otago	Hamilton
5-85	G.W. Aldridge	Northern Districts v Central Districts	Gisborne
5-93	M.R. Gillespie	Wellington v Northern Districts	Hamilton
5-107	C.S. Martin	Auckland v Wellington	Wellington

TEN WICKETS IN A MATCH

13-117	I.E. O'Brien	Wellington v Auckland	Wellington
10-118	M. Muralitharan	Sri Lanka v New Zealand *(Second Test)*	Wellington
10-183	D.L. Vettori	New Zealand v Sri Lanka *(Second Test)*	Wellington

CAREER AVERAGES

as at 1 April, 2007 for players active during the 2006/07 season

	M	In	NO	HS	Runs	Ave	100	50	Ct	St	Wkts	Runs	Ave	5WI	10WM	Best
A.R.Adams	74	98	8	124	2276	25.28	3	10	48	-	278	7023	25.26	10	1	6-25
G.W.Aldridge	56	71	23	49	847	17.64	-	-	25	-	140	4298	30.70	4	-	5-33
Amandeep Singh	3	3	0	6	9	3.00	-	-	-	-	5	216	43.20	-	-	2-38
C.J.Anderson	2	2	0	29	32	16.00	-	-	-	-	1	129	129.00	-	-	1-59
S.L.Andrews	6	6	2	59*	76	19.00	-	1	2	-	10	471	47.10	-	-	2-22
B.J.Arnel	9	9	2	12	34	4.85		-	-	4	20	683	34.15	-	-	4-31
N.J.Astle	171	272	24	223	9321	37.58	19	50	133	-	150	4897	32.64	2	-	6-22
T.D.Astle	14	22	0	97	605	27.50	-	4	10	-	15	694	46.26	-	-	2-19
S.B.C.Baldwin	1	2	0	0	0	0.00	-	-	-	-	1	81	81.00	-	-	1-33
G.E.F.Barnett	18	34	2	136	960	30.00	2	5	16	-	1	101	101.00	-	-	1-10
M.D.Bell	141	241	16	219	7939	35.28	18	47	111	-	0	23	-	-	-	-
H.K.Bennett	13	13	4	27	73	8.11	-	-	3	-	29	1494	51.51	-	-	4-43
S.E.Bond	51	57	20	100	694	18.75	1	2	22	-	181	4486	24.78	9	1	6-51
D.J.Bowden	10	14	3	79	340	30.90	-	1	1	-	17	634	37.29	-	-	3-53
N.T.Broom	32	50	4	112	1819	39.54	3	10	20	-	3	152	50.66	-	-	1-8
M.Burns	4	4	1	8	18	5.66	-	-	2	-	9	280	31.11	-	-	4-44
L.M.Burtt	6	7	1	29*	56	9.33	-	-	2	-	20	561	28.05	1	-	5-45
C.Cachopa	9	12	0	69	240	20.00	-	1	4	-	0	5	-	-	-	-
T.K.Canning	61	88	10	115	2155	27.62	3	8	29	-	206	5042	24.47	6	-	6-44
S.P.Chan	2	2	0	35	35	17.50	-	-	-	-	6	215	35.83	-	-	3-58
C.D.Cumming	99	180	16	187	5615	34.23	11	26	46	-	27	1472	54.51	-	-	3-31
M.P.F.Davidson	1	1	0	34	34	34.00	-	-	-	-	2	62	31.00	-	-	2-31
T.T.Davis	5	6	1	8	13	2.60	-	-	4	-	10	410	41.00	-	-	3-61
C.de Grandhomme	10	18	0	109	464	25.77	1	2	6	-	5	274	54.80	-	-	3-26
B.J.Diamanti	13	18	3	50	287	19.13	-	1	4	-	35	1228	35.08	2	1	6-73
G.D.Elliott	31	50	2	125	1342	27.95	3	7	22	-	48	1630	33.95	-	-	4-56
A.M.Ellis	26	41	7	78	910	26.76	-	6	16	-	32	1398	43.68	1	-	5-63
P.B.Erasmus	1	1	0	15	15	15.00	-	-	-	-	2	15	7.50	-	-	2-15
A.W.Evans	56	96	11	125	2631	30.95	3	12	34	-	0	91	-	-	-	-
S.A.Fairley	16	25	3	59*	443	20.13	-	2	7	-						
S.P.Fleming	228	375	31	274*	14,889	43.28	31	86	306	-	0	129	-	-	-	-
D.R.Flynn	15	27	2	107	553	22.12	1	2	2	-						
J.E.C.Franklin	89	131	19	208	3106	27.73	3	14	32	-	310	7690	24.80	11	1	7-30
P.G.Fulton	53	87	9	301*	3659	46.91	6	20	38	-	11	399	36.27	-	-	4-49
M.R.Gillespie	43	55	10	81*	838	18.62	-	3	8	-	167	4166	24.94	7	-	6-81
B.B.J.Griggs	55	86	10	100*	2098	27.60	1	12	147	5						
M.J.Guptill	8	15	0	99	351	23.40	-	3	4	-						
S.B.Haig	7	10	0	111	369	36.90	1	2	8	-						
L.J.Hamilton	60	83	28	23	266	4.83	-	-	16	-	212	5391	25.42	8	-	6-32
C.Z.Harris	128	200	42	251*	7228	45.75	14	41	115	-	157	5656	36.03	-	-	4-22
M.J.Harvie	11	10	4	34	95	15.83	-	-	3	-	22	1128	51.27	-	-	3-45
G.R.Hay	8	14	1	106	593	45.61	1	4	5	-						
G.P.Hayne	3	4	0	18	19	4.75	-	-	2	-	6	291	48.50	-	-	3-80
B.E.Hefford	39	53	16	26	319	8.62	-	-	12	-	99	3032	30.62	1	-	5-50
G.J.T.Hegglun	8	11	1	52*	112	11.20	-	1	5	-	21	623	29.66	-	-	4-52
B.C.Hiini	10	14	7	103*	401	57.28	2	-	5	-	28	844	30.14	1	-	5-82
R.M.Hira	2	1	0	4	4	4.00	-	-	-	-	0	115	-	-	-	-
P.A.Hitchcock	10	15	3	51	278	23.16	-	1	1	-	14	747	53.35	-	-	3-27
K.W.Hogg	33	42	3	71	872	22.35	-	7	11	-	59	2350	39.83	-	1	5-48
G.J.Hopkins	94	150	24	175*	3866	30.68	7	14	250	18	0	13	-	-	-	-
D.W.Houpapa	3	5	0	33	74	14.80	-	-	1	-	0	16	-	-	-	-
N.K.W.Horsley	41	67	4	159	2299	36.49	3	17	16	-	2	36	18.00	-	-	1-5
J.M.How	59	100	8	169	3018	32.80	8	14	63	-	19	1014	53.36	-	-	3-57
P.J.Ingram	41	75	5	166*	1766	25.22	5	5	28	-	0	47	-	-	-	-
M.R.Jefferson	48	69	12	114	1399	24.54	2	5	14	-	90	3468	38.53	1	-	5-42
R.A.Jones	96	170	10	188	5367	33.54	12	28	89	-	1	0	0.00	-	-	1-0
D.V.Lobb	1	1	0	4	4	4.00	-	-	-	-	1	37	37.00	-	-	1-37
W.M.Lonsdale	3	3	3	1*	2	-	-	-	1	-	3	241	80.33	-	-	1-3
M.B.Loye	214	340	30	322*	12,890	41.58	38	52	104	-	1	61	61.00	-	-	1-8
T.I.Lythe	9	14	1	66	352	27.07	-	3	4	-	9	537	59.66	-	-	2-46
H.J.H.Marshall	84	142	11	168	4679	35.71	10	22	40	-	8	412	51.50	-	-	1-6
J.A.H.Marshall	88	150	5	235	4130	28.48	6	23	89	-	4	256	64.00	-	-	1-5
B.P.Martin	69	89	28	113*	1235	20.24	1	3	32	-	183	5797	31.67	12	2	7-33

	M	In	NO	HS	Runs	Ave	100	50	Ct	St	Wkts	Runs	Ave	5WI	10WM	Best
C.S.Martin	110	136	64	25	310	4.30	-	-	22	-	343	10,598	30.89	16	1	6-54
M.J.Mason	61	80	22	64*	938	16.17	-	1	18	-	202	4911	24.31	8	1	6-56
B.B.McCullum	59	98	6	160	3071	33.38	6	16	142	12						
N.L.McCullum	29	43	4	93	1041	26.69	-	6	35	-	48	2115	44.06	1	-	5-28
P.D.McGlashan	32	47	7	103*	1121	28.02	1	5	80	4						
T.G.McIntosh	64	108	9	205	3084	31.15	10	11	56	-	0	66	-	-	-	-
C.D.McMillan	137	224	27	168*	7815	39.67	16	42	57	-	88	3148	35.77	1	-	6-71
J.M.McMillan	24	29	14	19	78	5.20	-	-	3	-	66	1951	29.56	-	-	4-32
K.D.Mills	48	68	19	117*	1504	30.69	1	9	18	-	140	3711	26.50	3	1	5-33
S.M.Mills	13	20	4	171	455	28.43	1	2	35	-						
C.Munro	2	4	1	20*	39	13.00	-		2	-	3	190	63.33	-	-	2-57
C.J.Nevin	88	134	20	143*	3890	34.12	3	20	238	8	0	0	-	-	-	-
A.D.Niblett	5	9	0	22	71	7.88	-	-	1	-	10	577	57.70	-	-	3-121
R.J.Nicol	54	84	10	160	2850	38.51	6	16	40	-	14	743	53.07	-	-	2-26
I.E.O'Brien	45	48	15	44	293	8.87	-	-	8	-	170	3960	23.29	8	1	8-55
J.D.P.Oram	64	101	15	155	3147	36.59	6	16	32	-	106	3040	28.62	2	-	6-45
M.G.Orchard	35	60	8	175	1539	29.59	1	10	24	-	58	1937	33.39	1	-	5-10
M.H.W.Papps	82	144	9	192	4919	36.43	12	22	93	4	0	6	-	-	-	-
M.E.Parlane	109	183	8	203	5664	32.36	13	22	63	-	1	56	56.00	-	-	1-14
N.R.Parlane	58	93	9	147	2934	34.92	5	19	58	-	0	27	-	-	-	-
M.Y.Pasupati	4	4	1	76*	88	29.33	-	1	1	-	8	166	20.75	-	-	4-39
J.S.Patel	58	70	29	58*	775	18.90	-	2	18	-	113	4493	39.76	3	-	6-32
B.M.K.Patton	1	1	0	0	0	0.00	-	-	1	-	0	1	-	-	-	-
B.J.Rae	4	5	0	58	147	29.40	-	1	4							
S.Rasmussen	6	6	1	10	14	2.80	-	-	1	-	17	434	25.52	-	-	4-39
D.L.Rayner	1	2	1	11*	16	16.00	-	-	-	-	1	90	90.00	-	-	1-90
A.J.Redmond	58	98	7	101	2732	30.02	3	16	33	-	80	3651	45.63	-	-	4-35
I.A.Robertson	6	9	4	102*	259	51.80	1	1	5	-	7	412	58.85	-	-	2-37
G.G.Robinson	19	31	1	125*	670	22.33	1	2	8	-	0	16	-	-	-	-
J.D.Ryder	36	56	4	236	2334	44.88	5	12	30	-	32	850	26.56	-	-	4-23
R.J.Schaw	7	11	1	34	222	22.20	-	-	4	-	10	693	69.30	-	-	2-49
B.E.Scott	35	44	11	96	678	20.54	-	2	13	-	111	2938	26.46	4	-	6-48
L.J.Shaw	11	15	5	20*	54	5.40	-	-	3	-	36	1022	28.38	1	-	5-63
J.W.Sheed	38	66	4	89	1335	21.53	-	11	21	-	2	196	98.00	-	-	1-30
M.S.Sinclair	131	223	22	268	9327	46.40	22	50	125	1	8	382	47.75	-	-	2-24
C.A.Small	3	3	2	18	47	47.00	-	-	1	-	5	260	52.00	-	-	4-50
C.M.Smith	5	6	1	49	93	18.60	-	-	2	-	6	344	57.33	-	-	2-7
T.G.Southee	5	4	1	75*	96	32.00	-	1	1	-	16	535	33.43	-	-	3-73
S.L.Stewart	40	70	2	149	2256	33.17	3	13	11	-	4	272	68.00	-	-	2-52
S.B.Styris	109	179	18	212*	5181	32.18	9	26	89	-	199	6000	30.18	9	1	6-32
L.R.P.L.Taylor	35	54	2	217	1914	36.80	3	11	30	-	4	298	74.50	-	-	2-34
E.P.Thompson	34	50	7	126	1228	28.55	3	5	11	-	108	3324	30.77	2	1	7-55
G.R.Todd	29	53	11	160	1459	34.73	2	7	11	-	13	732	56.30	-	-	2-26
D.R.Tuffey	70	87	20	89*	899	13.41	-	3	30	-	237	6146	25.93	9	1	7-12
N.M.Turner	3	4	2	27*	53	26.50	-	-	1	-	7	241	34.42	-	-	3-57
C.F.K.van Wyk	56	83	14	104	2018	29.24	1	11	168	9	1	9	9.00	-	-	1-7
D.L.Vettori	119	163	23	137*	3649	26.06	4	20	57	-	381	12,288	32.25	23	3	7-87
L.Vincent	84	135	10	224	4584	36.67	10	27	101	-	10	527	52.70	-	-	2-37
B-J.Watling	24	46	1	153	1222	27.15	2	6	30	-						
T.I.Weston	13	24	6	152	807	44.83	1	5	7	-						
B.S.Wilson	13	23	0	96	540	23.47	-	3	4	-						
L.J.Woodcock	44	72	6	106	1674	25.36	1	8	18	-	38	1427	37.55	-	-	4-3
R.A.Young	68	86	14	101*	1399	19.43	1	7	206	5						
J.A.F.Yovich	80	123	23	144	2848	28.48	2	16	22	-	219	7129	32.55	8	1	7-64

STATE SHIELD

2006/07

Auckland won the State Shield for 2006/07 when they comfortably beat top qualifier Otago in the final at Dunedin. It was Auckland's first win in the one-day final since 1989/90 and it gave them the one-day double as they had earlier beaten Otago in the Twenty20 final.

The competition lead changed hands many times,with Wellington and Otago going into the last round in front and the teams to play each other. Otago won the game to get home advantage. Wellington subsequently lost the semi-final to third placed Auckland. Northern Districts, Central Districts and Canterbury seemed to struggle and finished in the bottom three.

The leading run-scorer was Craig Cumming *(Otago)* with 445 runs who was ahead of Peter McGlashan *(Northern Districts)* (380), Chris Harris *(Canterbury)* (362) and Richard Jones *(Auckland)* (360).

Three bowlers took 18 wickets. They were Matt Harvie *(Otago)*, Brendon Diamanti *(Central Districts)* and Grant Elliott *(Wellington)*. Four bowlers took 13 wickets.

The fastest fifty of the season was scored by Kyle Mills *(Auckland)*, who took 28 balls, while David Houpapa *(Auckland)* scored the fastest century, from 87 balls. James Marshall *(Northern Districts)* had the highest score of the season with 152 not out, only the second time in New Zealand domestic competition that there had been an innings of 150 or more.

The format was the same as that used in 2005/06, with the top qualifier having home advantage in the final. Power plays were again used.

Final points were:

	P	*W*	*L*	*T*	*NR*	*Bonus*	*Points*
Otago	10	7	3	–	–	2	30
Wellington	10	6	3	–	1	2	28
Auckland	10	5	3	–	2	1	25
Northern Districts	10	4	6	–	–	2	18
Central Districts	10	3	5	–	2	1	17
Canterbury	10	2	7	–	1	–	10

First Round

Loye, Houpapa, Munro, Hira *(Auckland)*, Vivian, Hiini, van Dyk *(Canterbury)*, Hay *(Central Districts)*, Mills, Bowden and Burns *(Wellington)* all made their debuts.

Canterbury had a good start, with Robertson getting his highest score and McMillan scoring fifty from 41 balls, and they reached 238-5. Otago lost three quick wickets before Redmond (fifty off 72 balls) and Todd added 88. Harvie had his highest score at the tail end but with Bennett getting his best bowling figures, Canterbury won by 23 runs.

Northern Districts lost two early wickets but fifties to Evans (79 balls) and Marshall (48 balls) helped them reach 239. Vincent went in the first over in reply but good contributions from the balance of the top order saw Auckland through with 15 balls to spare. Jones had scored his fifty from 54 balls while English professional Loye took 50 balls for his half-century.

Wellington took three early wickets before Sinclair and Hay added 117 for the fourth wicket. Sinclair got fifty from 79 balls, one more than Hay. At the end of the innings Thompson reached his maiden fifty from the last ball he faced. Wellington were in dire straits at 63-4 but a 123 run stand by Elliott (50 off 64 balls) and Mills saw them through to a reduced target.

CANTERBURY v OTAGO — State Shield

at MainPower Oval, Rangiora on 23 December, 2006
Toss : Otago. Umpires : J.M. Busby & E.J. Gray
Canterbury won by 23 runs. *Points: Canterbury 4, Otago 0*

CANTERBURY

	Runs	Mins	Balls	6s	4s
I.A.Robertson st Haig b McCullum	37	65	52	-	5
M.H.W.Papps c Gaffaney b Cumming	28	85	58	-	3
C.D.McMillan c Gaffaney b Redmond	69	58	52	1	8
S.L.Stewart b Cumming	21	60	36	-	-
C.Z.Harris* not out	39	55	35	1	2
L.J.Vivian c Broom b Smith	8	12	11	-	1
C.F.K.van Wyk† not out	15	20	15	-	-
B.R.Findlay					
B.C.Hiini					
S.P.Chan					
H.K.Bennett					
Extras (b 4, lb 5, w 11, nb 1)	21				
TOTAL (43 overs) (5 wkts)	**238**	180			

OTAGO

	Runs	Mins	Balls	6s	4s
C.D.Cumming* c Harris b Bennett	1	3	2	-	-
S.B.Haig† b Bennett	17	20	13	-	3
A.J.Redmond c sub (A.M.Ellis) b Chan	53	106	76	-	6
N.T.Broom b Bennett	0	1	1	-	-
G.R.Todd lbw b Harris	43	107	78	-	2
C.B.Gaffaney run out	9	29	16	-	-
N.L.McCullum c sub (A.M.Ellis) b Hiini	17	24	17	-	1
J.W.Sheed not out	35	53	35	-	-
B.E.Scott c Vivian b Findlay	2	6	3	-	-
C.M.Smith lbw b Harris	1	7	3	-	-
M.J.Harvie not out	19	23	15	1	-
Extras (lb 7, w 9, nb 2)	18				
TOTAL (43 overs) (9 wkts)	**215**	194			

Bowling	*O*	*M*	*R*	*W*
OTAGO				
Harvie	5	0	23	0
Smith	9	0	58	1
Scott	9	0	42	0
McCullum	9	0	39	1
Cumming	6	0	27	2
Redmond	3	0	18	1
Todd	2	0	22	0
CANTERBURY				
Bennett	8	0	29	3
Chan	8	0	62	1
Harris	9	0	34	2
Hiini	9	0	39	1
Findlay	5	0	29	1
McMillan	1	0	5	0
Robertson	3	0	10	0

Fall of Wickets	***C***	***O***
1st	70	6
2nd	92	28
3rd	159	28
4th	182	116
5th	197	135
6th	-	144
7th	-	163
8th	-	167
9th	-	176
10th	-	-

AUCKLAND v NORTHERN DISTRICTS

State Shield

at Eden Park Outer Oval, Auckland on 23 December, 2006
Toss : Auckland. Umpires : P.D. Jones & T.J. Parlane
***Auckland won by 5 wickets.** Points: Auckland 4, Northern Districts 0*

NORTHERN DISTRICTS

	Runs	Mins	Balls	6s	4s
N.K.W.Horsley c Pasupati b Shaw	6	20	18	-	1
B-J.Watling† c Jones b Shaw	0	10	2	-	-
A.W.Evans c Young b Hira	70	135	96	1	7
H.J.H.Marshall* c Young b Hitchcock	59	61	54	-	10
D.R.Flynn c Young b Hira	20	37	35	-	2
J.A.F.Yovich run out	11	14	14	-	-
M.G.Orchard c Jones b Shaw	24	44	33	1	-
B.P.Martin run out	3	10	13	-	-
D.R.Tuffey c Houpapa b Nicol	4	3	4	-	1
G.W.Aldridge not out	21	26	22	-	2
B.J.Arnel not out	10	11	11	-	1
Extras (lb 3, w 6, nb 2)	11				
TOTAL (50 overs) (9 wkts)	**239**	190			

AUCKLAND

	Runs	Mins	Balls	6s	4s
L.Vincent c Horsley b Aldridge	0	3	5	-	-
P.A.Hitchcock b Orchard	39	68	41	1	5
R.A.Jones* b Arnel	52	79	62	-	9
M.B.Loye c Orchard b Martin	90	105	79	1	13
R.J.Nicol c Marshall b Aldridge	39	98	74	-	5
D.W.Houpapa not out	7	20	21	-	1
R.A.Young† not out	2	13	6	-	-
M.Y.Pasupati					
C.Munro					
R.M.Hira					
L.J.Shaw					
Extras (b 1, lb 1, w 7, nb 3)	12				
TOTAL (47.3 overs) (5 wkts)	**241**	196			

Bowling	*O*	*M*	*R*	*W*
AUCKLAND				
Shaw	10	1	45	3
Hitchcock	9	2	50	1
Pasupati	8	0	45	0
Munro	4	0	21	0
Hira	10	0	38	2
Nicol	9	0	37	1
NORTHERN DISTRICTS				
Aldridge	9	2	33	2
Tuffey	10	1	50	0
Arnel	9.3	0	47	1
Yovich	1	0	16	0
Orchard	8	0	50	1
Martin	10	0	43	1

Fall of Wickets	***ND***	***A***
1st	10	0
2nd	11	90
3rd	100	113
4th	136	228
5th	155	231
6th	178	-
7th	185	-
8th	191	-
9th	215	-
10th	-	-

CENTRAL DISTRICTS v WELLINGTON

State Shield

at Trafalgar Park, Nelson on 23 December, 2006
Toss : Wellington. Umpires : D.M. Quested & D.J. Walker
***Wellington won by 4 wickets (D/L).** Points: Wellington 4, Central Districts 0*

CENTRAL DISTRICTS

	Runs	Mins	Balls	6s	4s
J.M.How* c Mills b Burns	18	28	24	-	3
G.E.F.Barnett c Mills b Rasmussen	0	9	2	-	-
P.J.Ingram c Parlane N.R. b O'Brien	18	52	44	-	2
M.S.Sinclair c Elliott b O'Brien	67	131	91	-	5
G.R.Hay c O'Brien b Woodcock	55	95	84	-	5
B.B.J.Griggs† not out	20	41	26	-	1
E.P.Thompson not out	50	37	33	1	6
B.J.Diamanti					
C.J.M.Furlong					
M.J.Mason					
G.J.T.Hegglun					
Extras (b 1, lb 6, w 3, nb 3)	13				
TOTAL (50 overs) (5 wkts)	**241**	195			

WELLINGTON

	Runs	Mins	Balls	6s	4s
M.D.Bell b Mason	16	37	32	-	2
M.E.Parlane* lbw b Thompson	3	17	9	-	-
J.D.Ryder c & b Thompson	4	6	4	-	1
N.R.Parlane c Furlong b Diamanti	27	41	39	1	3
G.D.Elliott c sub (B.E.Hefford) b Sinclair	78	104	91	-	7
S.M.Mills† b Furlong	49	85	63	1	3
L.J.Woodcock not out	21	49	23	-	1
D.J.Bowden not out	24	27	16	-	3
I.E.O'Brien					
S.Rasmussen					
M.Burns					
Extras (lb 4, w 7, nb 2)	13				
TOTAL (45.5 overs) (6 wkts)	**235**	192			

Bowling	*O*	*M*	*R*	*W*
WELLINGTON				
Burns	6	0	22	1
Rasmussen	10	0	44	1
O'Brien	10	1	46	2
Elliott	10	0	55	0
Woodcock	10	1	42	1
Bowden	4	0	25	0
CENTRAL DISTRICTS				
Mason	10	1	43	1
Thompson	7	0	35	2
Hegglun	8.5	0	47	0
Diamanti	9	0	54	1
Furlong	9	0	37	1
Sinclair	2	0	15	1

Fall of Wickets	***CD***	***W***
1st	6	13
2nd	23	17
3rd	49	32
4th	166	63
5th	167	186
6th	-	193
7th	-	-
8th	-	-
9th	-	-
10th	-	-

Second Round

Turner *(Otago)* and Forde *(Wellington)* made their debuts.

Wellington completely dominated Canterbury who were dismissed for just 92 runs, their second lowest score. There had been a rain disruption meaning Wellington had a reduced target of 90 off 24 overs which they easily achieved in 17 overs. Parlane had reached fifty from 49 balls.

Northern Districts lost two early wickets but managed to reach 200-8 against a tight Otago attack. Cumming dominated the Otago innings, getting fifty off 67 balls, and reaching his maiden century off 116 deliveries to give Otago a comfortable win with 15.1 overs to spare.

The Central Districts v Auckland game was abandoned without a ball being bowled

CANTERBURY v WELLINGTON — State Shield

at Allied Prime Basin Reserve, Wellington on 27 December, 2006
Toss : Wellington. Umpires : R.D. Anderson & P.D. Jones
Wellington won by 9 wickets (D/L). *Points: Wellington 5, Canterbury 0*

CANTERBURY

	Runs	Mins	Balls	6s	4s
I.A.Robertson c Parlane M.E. b Burns	1	13	10	-	-
M.H.W.Papps c Bell b Burns	10	23	13	-	1
S.L.Stewart b Forde	8	33	25	-	-
C.D.McMillan run out	16	40	30	1	1
C.Z.Harris* b Elliott	12	24	19	-	1
L.J.Vivian b Bowden	4	12	8	-	-
C.F.K.van Wyk† not out	13	29	17	-	-
B.R.Findlay run out	7	8	6	-	1
B.C.Hiini c Bowden b Elliott	0	3	3	-	-
S.P.Chan run out	6	9	10	-	-
H.K.Bennett c Mills b Forde	0	1	1	-	-
Extras (b 1, lb 6, w 5, nb 3)	15				
TOTAL (23.2 overs)	**92**				

WELLINGTON

	Runs	Mins	Balls	6s	4s
M.D.Bell b Hiini	4	33	21	-	-
M.E.Parlane* not out	53	73	52	-	7
J.D.Ryder not out	27	39	30	-	3
N.R.Parlane					
G.D.Elliott					
S.M.Mills†					
L.J.Woodcock					
D.J.Bowden					
K.A.Forde					
M.Burns					
S.Rasmussen					
Extras (w 5, nb 1)	6				
TOTAL (17 overs) (1 wkt)	**90**	73			

Bowling	O	M	R	W
WELLINGTON				
Rasmussen	5	1	17	0
Burns	6	1	15	2
Forde	4.2	1	15	2
Elliott	5	0	22	2
Bowden	2	0	8	1
Ryder	1	0	8	0
CANTERBURY				
Bennett	5	0	30	0
Chan	4	0	25	0
Hiini	3	0	12	1
McMillan	2	0	12	0
Harris	3	0	11	0

Fall of Wickets	C	W
1st	7	32
2nd	14	-
3rd	30	-
4th	48	-
5th	61	-
6th	65	-
7th	77	-
8th	81	-
9th	92	-
10th	92	-

NORTHERN DISTRICTS v OTAGO **State Shield**

at Owen Delany Park, Taupo on 27 December, 2006
Toss : Northern Districts. Umpires : T.J. Parlane & D.J. Walker
***Otago won by 8 wickets.** Points: Otago 5, Northern Districts 0*

NORTHERN DISTRICTS

	Runs	Mins	Balls	6s	4s
N.K.W.Horsley c Redmond b Harvie	8	38	30	-	1
B-J.Watling c McCullum b Harvie	3	20	11	-	-
A.W.Evans b Redmond	33	98	84	-	2
M.G.Orchard c Scott b McCullum	40	74	52	1	5
I.G.Butler c Broom b Cumming	26	70	49	-	4
D.R.Flynn lbw b Cumming	15	32	20	-	1
J.A.F.Yovich c Cumming b Scott	39	45	38	1	3
P.D.McGlashan*† not out	11	22	13	-	-
D.R.Tuffey run out	1	4	3	-	-
G.W.Aldridge not out	3	3	2	-	-
B.J.Arnel					
Extras (b 4, lb 5, w 10, nb 2)	21				
TOTAL (50 overs) (8 wkts)	**200**	207			

OTAGO

	Runs	Mins	Balls	6s	4s
C.D.Cumming* not out	102	152	116	1	16
S.B.Haig† c Tuffey b Aldridge	15	23	17	-	3
A.J.Redmond b Tuffey	32	65	40	-	6
N.T.Broom not out	34	62	40	1	1
J.W.Sheed					
G.R.Todd					
C.B.Gaffaney					
N.L.McCullum					
B.E.Scott					
M.J.Harvie					
N.M.Turner					
Extras (lb 7, w 10, nb 4)	21				
TOTAL (34.5 overs) (2 wkts)	**204**	152			

Bowling	*O*	*M*	*R*	*W*
OTAGO				
Scott	10	3	31	1
Harvie	9	0	30	2
Todd	4	0	11	0
Turner	7	1	30	0
McCullum	10	1	40	1
Redmond	3	0	17	1
Cumming	7	0	32	2
NORTHERN DISTRICTS				
Tuffey	9.5	1	47	1
Aldridge	7	0	38	1
Arnel	5	0	25	0
Orchard	5	0	32	0
Butler	5	0	30	0
Yovich	3	0	25	0

Fall of Wickets

	ND	***O***
1st	8	26
2nd	22	110
3rd	92	-
4th	96	-
5th	125	-
6th	170	-
7th	191	-
8th	193	-
9th	-	-
10th	-	-

CENTRAL DISTRICTS v AUCKLAND **State Shield**

at Pukekura Park, New Plymouth on 27 December, 2006
***Abandoned without a ball being bowled.** Points: Central Districts 2, Auckland 2*

Third Round

Jefferson (previously Wellington) made his debut for Northern Districts.

Otago struggled against a determined Wellington attack with Rasmussen getting career best figures. Rain interruptions gave Wellington a revised target of 90 off 28 overs, which was achieved in just 12.2 overs.

Canterbury batted first and Papps reached fifty off 65 balls, Harris controlled the latter stages of the innings getting fifty from 73 balls. Hitchcock and Jones added 156 for the second wicket for Auckland. Hitchcock, who passed 1000 runs, got fifty from 71 balls, ten more than Jones. Auckland won with 10.3 overs to spare.

McGlashan controlled the Northern innings getting fifty from 75 balls and reaching his highest score. Hefford took his 50th wicket. Central had a 153 run opening stand with Barnett reaching his highest score. Central cruised to an easy win with ten overs to spare.

WELLINGTON v OTAGO — State Shield

at Allied Prime Basin Reserve, Wellington on 30 December, 2006
Toss : Wellington. Umpires : P.D. Jones & T.J. Parlane
***Wellington won by 9 wickets (D/L).** Points: Wellington 5, Otago 0*

OTAGO

	Runs	Mins	Balls	6s	4s
C.D.Cumming* c sub (N.R.Parlane) b Burns	39	60	55	2	4
S.B.Haig† b Rasmussen	0	8	3	-	-
A.J.Redmond c Bowden b Rasmussen	0	13	7	-	-
N.T.Broom b O'Brien	21	47	30	-	4
G.R.Todd run out	5	22	10	-	-
C.B.Gaffaney b Elliott	14	30	24	-	1
N.L.McCullum lbw b Woodcock	2	13	8	-	-
W.C.McSkimming b Woodcock	11	22	19	-	1
B.E.Scott not out	21	45	33	-	3
M.J.Harvie lbw b Rasmussen	4	13	6	-	1
N.M.Turner st Mills b Woodcock	0	12	12	-	-
Extras (lb 1, w 8, nb 2)	11				
TOTAL (34 overs)	**128**	147			

WELLINGTON

	Runs	Mins	Balls	6s	4s
M.D.Bell c McCullum b Scott	7	21	11	-	1
M.E.Parlane* not out	37	60	38	1	3
J.D.Ryder not out	36	38	25	1	4
C.J.Nevin					
G.D.Elliott					
S.M.Mills†					
L.J.Woodcock					
D.J.Bowden					
M.Burns					
I.E.O'Brien					
S.Rasmussen					
Extras (lb 2, w 10)	12				
TOTAL (12.2 overs) (1 wkt)	**92**	60			

Bowling	*O*	*M*	*R*	*W*
WELLINGTON				
Burns	8	1	25	1
Rasmussen	9	1	39	3
O'Brien	6	2	24	1
Elliott	4	1	19	1
Woodcock	7	0	20	3
OTAGO				
McSkimming	4	0	29	0
Scott	4	0	25	1
Harvie	2.2	0	29	0
McCullum	2	0	7	0

Fall of Wickets

	O	**W**
1st	3	22
2nd	11	-
3rd	67	-
4th	73	-
5th	76	-
6th	91	-
7th	91	-
8th	111	-
9th	121	-
10th	128	-

AUCKLAND v CANTERBURY — State Shield

at Eden Park Outer Oval, Auckland on 30 December, 2006
Toss : Auckland. Umpires : B.G. Frost & W.R. Knights
***Auckland won by 5 wickets.** Points: Auckland 5, Canterbury 0*

CANTERBURY

	Runs	Mins	Balls	6s	4s
I.A.Robertson b Pasupati	19	58	45	-	2
M.H.W.Papps run out	56	107	74	-	9
S.L.Stewart c Young b Pasupati .	4	27	17	-	-
A.M.Ellis b Pasupati	2	7	5	-	-
C.Z.Harris* not out	67	98	82	-	8
L.J.Vivian b Nicol	9	17	19	-	1
C.F.K.van Wyk† c Young b Martin	38	55	55	-	2
B.R.Findlay not out	14	11	9	1	1
B.C.Hiini					
S.P.Chan					
H.K.Bennett					
Extras (lb 7, w 11, nb 6)	24				
TOTAL (50 overs) (6 wkts) .	**233**	193			

AUCKLAND

	Runs	Mins	Balls	6s	4s
P.A.Hitchcock c & b Harris	82	158	107	-	12
L.Vincent c Findlay b Hiini	26	27	18	-	6
R.A.Jones* c Harris b Hiini	81	119	92	1	10
S.B.Styris not out	25	25	18	-	3
D.W.Houpapa b Findlay	1	6	6	-	-
R.J.Nicol lbw b Harris	0	2	2	-	-
M.Y.Pasupati not out	1	4	2	-	-
K.D.Mills					
R.A.Young†					
R.M.Hira					
C.S.Martin					
Extras (lb 5, w 6, nb 8)	19				
TOTAL (39.3 overs) (5 wkts)	**235**	173			

Bowling	*O*	*M*	*R*	*W*
AUCKLAND				
Mills	7	0	35	0
Martin	8	0	46	1
Hitchcock	6	1	31	0
Pasupati	9	0	46	3
Nicol	10	0	27	1
Hira	10	0	41	0
CANTERBURY				
Bennett	6	0	47	0
Chan	7	0	46	0
Hiini	10	1	48	2
Harris	9	0	35	2
Findlay	4.3	0	34	1
Robertson	3	0	20	0

Fall of Wickets	***C***	***A***
1st	58	45
2nd	86	201
3rd	97	217
4th	103	220
5th	125	221
6th	206	-
7th	-	-
8th	-	-
9th	-	-
10th	-	-

CENTRAL DISTRICTS v NORTHERN DISTRICTS — State Shield

at Pukekura Park, New Plymouth on 30 December, 2006
Toss : Central Districts. Umpires : C.J. Morris & E.A. Watkin
***Central Districts won by 9 wickets.** Points: Central Districts 5, Northern Districts 0*

NORTHERN DISTRICTS

	Runs	Mins	Balls	6s	4s
N.K.W.Horsley c Griggs b Hefford	19	37	29	-	3
A.W.Evans b Hegglun	18	50	46	-	2
P.D.McGlashan*† not out	86	159	104	1	7
M.G.Orchard c Griggs b Thompson	0	9	5	-	-
D.R.Flynn lbw b Hegglun	8	20	10	-	1
J.A.F.Yovich c Diamanti b Furlong	11	31	34	-	-
I.G.Butler lbw b Furlong	7	11	17	-	1
M.R.Jefferson run out	0	2	3	-	
D.R.Tuffey c Griggs b Thompson	28	52	47	1	1
G.W.Aldridge not out	15	13	8	1	1
B.J.Arnel					
Extras (lb 10, w 8, nb 3)	21				
TOTAL (50 overs) (8 wkts) .	**213**	197			

CENTRAL DISTRICTS

	Runs	Mins	Balls	6s	4s
J.M.How* not out	78	155	108	3	7
G.E.F.Barnett lbw b Jefferson ..	91	113	99	3	10
P.J.Ingram not out	43	40	33	1	6
M.S.Sinclair					
G.R.Hay					
B.B.J.Griggs†					
E.P.Thompson					
B.J.Diamanti					
C.J.M.Furlong					
G.J.T.Hegglun					
B.E.Hefford					
Extras (b 1, lb 2, w 4)	7				
TOTAL (40 overs) (1 wkt) ...	**219**	155			

Bowling	*O*	*M*	*R*	*W*
CENTRAL DISTRICTS				
Thompson	10	1	45	2
Hefford	10	0	37	1
Hegglun	9	0	44	2
Diamanti	4	0	26	0
Furlong	10	2	19	2
How	7	0	32	0
NORTHERN DISTRICTS				
Tuffey	8	0	40	0
Aldridge	9	0	42	0
Arnel	5	0	23	0
Orchard	5	0	43	0
Jefferson	10	2	32	1
Butler	1	0	16	0
Flynn	2	0	20	0

Fall of Wickets	***W***	***CD***
1st	38	153
2nd	42	-
3rd	44	-
4th	72	-
5th	103	-
6th	120	-
7th	120	-
8th	185	-
9th	-	-
10th	-	-

Fourth Round

After Northern lost an early wicket Evans consolidated the innings with a fifty from 64 balls. Butler had his highest score and Northern managed 246. Wellington never recovered from being 11-2. Jefferson had a good return against his former province and Arnel had best bowling figures.

Vincent went to the second ball of the game and only two Auckland batsmen reached 30. Jones had reached 2000 runs and Young got his highest score (fifty off 59 balls). Otago had a good opening stand but a collapse saw them at 186-8 before Gaffaney and Scott saw them through with six balls left. Hira and Vincent had best bowling figures.

Robertson scored his maiden fifty (60 balls) as Canterbury reached 239-8 after being 204-3. Central lost both openers early and only 95 from Ingram (fifty off 61 balls) kept them in the game. They lost regular wickets, however, and finished up 12 runs short of their target.

NORTHERN DISTRICTS v WELLINGTON — State Shield

at Owen Delany Park, Taupo on 2 January, 2007
Toss : Wellington. Umpires : B.G. Frost & E.J. Gray
***Northern Districts won by 113 runs.** Points: Northern Districts 5, Wellington 0*

NORTHERN DISTRICTS

	Runs	Mins	Balls	6s	4s
A.W.Evans run out	79	142	115	-	8
B-J.Watling c Bell b O'Brien	2	13	6	-	-
P.D.McGlashan*† c Patel b Elliott	30	31	25	1	3
M.G.Orchard c Mills b Woodcock	18	43	30	-	2
D.R.Flynn lbw b Patel	15	25	16	-	2
J.A.F.Yovich b Woodcock	2	1	10	-	-
I.G.Butler c Ryder b O'Brien	43	62	59	-	4
M.R.Jefferson run out	17	43	26	-	2
D.R.Tuffey b Elliott	2	9	4	-	-
G.W.Aldridge not out	11	12	8	-	1
B.J.Arnel b O'Brien	2	6	6	-	-
Extras (b 4, lb 5, w 11, nb 5)	25				
TOTAL (50 overs)	**246**	203			

WELLINGTON

	Runs	Mins	Balls	6s	4s
M.D.Bell c McGlashan b Aldridge	16	34	20	-	3
M.E.Parlane* b Tuffey	4	12	7	-	1
J.D.Ryder c Watling b Aldridge	1	4	3	-	-
C.J.Nevin b Yovich	32	59	38	-	5
G.D.Elliott c Tuffey b Aldridge	16	38	28	-	1
S.M.Mills† lbw b Jefferson	23	50	50	-	1
L.J.Woodcock c Evans b Arnel	22	68	41	-	2
D.J.Bowden st McGlashan b Jefferson	5	18	16	-	-
J.S.Patel st McGlashan b Jefferson	1	7	4	-	-
I.E.O'Brien b Arnel	0	8	3	-	-
S.Rasmussen not out	0	3	4	-	-
Extras (lb 1, w 9, nb 3)	13				
TOTAL (35.2 overs)	**133**	155			

Bowling	*O*	*M*	*R*	*W*
WELLINGTON				
Rasmussen	8	0	67	0
O'Brien	10	0	39	3
Elliott	8	0	43	2
Bowden	4	0	18	0
Patel	10	1	41	1
Woodcock	10	2	29	2
NORTHERN DISTRICTS				
Tuffey	6	0	36	1
Aldridge	8	0	32	3
Yovich	8	0	26	1
Arnel	9.2	0	30	2
Jefferson	4	0	8	3

Fall of Wickets	***ND***	***A***
1st	10	10
2nd	71	11
3rd	119	37
4th	151	76
5th	159	80
6th	175	114
7th	229	130
8th	230	130
9th	237	131
10th	246	133

OTAGO v AUCKLAND

State Shield

at Queenstown Events Centre on 2 January, 2007
Toss : Auckland. Umpires : K. Cross & D.J. Walker
***Otago won by 2 wickets.** Points: Otago 4, Auckland 0*

AUCKLAND

	Runs	Mins	Balls	6s	4s
L.Vincent lbw b McSkimming	0	1	2	-	-
P.A.Hitchcock b McSkimming	7	25	15	-	1
R.A.Jones* c Hopkins b Scott	22	41	34	-	4
S.B.Styris lbw b Redmond	34	81	59	-	5
R.J.Nicol lbw b McCullum	23	73	53	-	1
D.W.Houpapa st Hopkins b McSkimming	15	59	42	-	1
R.A.Young† b Cumming	68	83	72	-	7
K.D.Mills c Gaffaney b Harvie	12	23	15	-	1
M.Y.Pasupati c McCullum b Cumming	8	13	7	-	1
R.M.Hira run out	1	2	2	-	-
C.S.Martin not out	0	1	0	-	-
Extras (lb 2, w 8, nb 2)	12				
TOTAL (49.5 overs)	**202**	205			

OTAGO

	Runs	Mins	Balls	6s	4s
C.D.Cumming* c Young b Pasupati	41	57	40	-	8
J.W.Sheed c Mills b Hira	40	88	67	-	6
A.J.Redmond st Young b Hira	20	41	35	-	4
N.T.Broom lbw b Hira	14	47	47	-	1
G.R.Todd c Martin b Hira	37	53	57	-	4
G.J.Hopkins† c Young b Martin	11	29	18	-	1
C.B.Gaffaney not out	10	37	21	-	-
N.L.McCullum lbw b Vincent	0	2	2	-	-
W.C.McSkimming b Vincent	0	2	4	-	-
B.E.Scott not out	12	18	10	-	2
M.J.Harvie					
Extras (lb 6, w 7, nb 7)	20				
TOTAL (49 overs) (8 wkts)	**205**	191			

Bowling	*O*	*M*	*R*	*W*
OTAGO				
McSkimming	10	1	40	3
Harvie	7	2	27	1
Scott	10	1	41	1
McCullum	10	0	32	1
Cumming	6.5	0	33	2
Redmond	6	0	27	1
AUCKLAND				
Mills	7	1	21	0
Martin	10	1	43	1
Hitchcock	4	0	32	0
Pasupati	2	0	21	1
Nicol	10	1	26	0
Hira	10	2	31	4
Vincent	6	0	25	2

Fall of Wickets	***A***	***O***
1st	0	79
2nd	28	101
3rd	33	113
4th	88	150
5th	92	175
6th	147	185
7th	181	186
8th	200	186
9th	202	
10th	202	

CANTERBURY v CENTRAL DISTRICTS

State Shield

at Queen Elizabeth II Park, Christchurch on 2 January, 2007
Toss : Canterbury. Umpires : T.J. Parlane & E.A. Watkin
***Canterbury won by 11 runs.** Points: Canterbury 4, Central Districts 0*

CANTERBURY

	Runs	Mins	Balls	6s	4s
I.A.Robertson c & b How	60	91	66	1	9
M.H.W.Papps c Griggs b Diamanti	37	57	50	-	7
C.D.McMillan c Barnett b Hegglun	31	69	40	-	2
S.L.Stewart c How b Thompson	44	79	73	-	5
C.Z.Harris* c How b Diamanti	25	62	47	-	-
L.J.Vivian c sub (G.R.Hay) b Thompson	7	7	6	-	1
B.R.Findlay b Diamanti	3	12	10	-	-
C.F.K.van Wyk† not out	4	11	6	-	-
S.P.Chan b Hegglun	1	3	2	-	-
B.C.Hiini not out	10	5	4	-	2
H.K.Bennett					
Extras (b 5, lb 4, w 4, nb 4)	17				
TOTAL (50 overs) (8 wkts)	**239**	202			

CENTRAL DISTRICTS

	Runs	Mins	Balls	6s	4s
J.M.How* b Chan	9	8	8	-	1
G.E.F.Barnett b Hiini	2	18	4	-	-
P.J.Ingram st van Wyk b Hiini	95	173	139	2	7
M.S.Sinclair st van Wyk b Harris	22	41	35	-	3
J.D.P.Oram c Chan b Hiini	43	74	58	1	1
B.B.J.Griggs† b Harris	8	19	17	-	-
E.P.Thompson c McMillan b Harris	4	5	8	-	-
C.J.M.Furlong run out	11	25	19	-	-
B.J.Diamanti not out	9	12	9	-	-
G.J.T.Hegglun not out	4	7	5	-	-
B.E.Hefford					
Extras (lb 8, w 10, nb 3)	21				
TOTAL (50 overs) (8 wkts)	**228**	195			

Bowling	*O*	*M*	*R*	*W*
CENTRAL DISTRICTS				
Thompson	10	0	37	2
Hefford	5	0	45	0
Diamanti	10	0	50	3
Furlong	10	0	32	0
How	4	0	28	1
Sinclair	1	0	5	0
Hegglun	10	0	33	2
CANTERBURY				
Bennett	2	0	19	0
Chan	3	0	21	1
Hiini	10	1	38	3
Harris	10	0	38	3
McMillan	10	0	53	0
Findlay	5	0	22	0
Robertson	10	0	29	0

Fall of Wickets	***C***	***CD***
1st	69	15
2nd	116	26
3rd	160	73
4th	204	167
5th	214	187
6th	222	193
7th	222	214
8th	225	216
9th	-	-
10th	-	-

Fifth Round

Astle *(Canterbury)* made his debut.

The Wellington v Auckland game used the new portable pitch at Westpac Stadium. After a slow start, reaching fifty off 63 balls, Houpapa then accelerated and scored his maiden hundred from 87 balls. Elliott had his best bowling figures. Wellington lost an early wicket and tight bowling from Martin and Hitchcock stifled Wellington, despite Bell, Neal Parlane and Elliott all scoring fifties.

Redmond was the shining light in the Otago innings getting fifty from 71 balls as his side reached 208-8. Central lost three early wickets but fifty from Sinclair (67 balls) kept them in the game. After reaching 183-5 they lost four wickets for 20 and failed to reach their target, giving Otago a four run win..

Northern reached their highest ever score thanks to McGlashan (fifty from 58 balls) and Marshall. The Northern captain got fifty from 49 balls and then got his second century after 103 deliveries. He went on to get the highest individual score for Northern. Canterbury were in awful trouble at 67-5 before van Wyk and Harris added 139. The Canterbury keeper reached his highest score. He needed 74 balls for his fifty, nine more than Harris, but Northern had an easy 81 run win.

WELLINGTON v AUCKLAND — State Shield

at Westpac Stadium, Wellington on 5 January, 2007
Toss : Wellington. Umpires : A.L. Hill & T.J. Parlane
***Auckland won by 10 runs.** Points: Auckland 4, Wellington 0*

AUCKLAND

	Runs	Mins	Balls	6s	4s
P.A.Hitchcock c Mills b O'Brien	0	8	7	-	-
L.Vincent c Ryder b Bowden	48	54	41	3	6
R.A.Jones* b Elliott	27	66	37	1	3
S.B.Styris c & b Elliott	7	29	23	-	1
R.J.Nicol c Nevin b Woodcock	12	33	24	-	1
D.W.Houpapa b Ryder	101	102	89	7	9
R.A.Young† c Woodcock b Elliott	15	34	23	-	2
K.D.Mills c Mills b Bowden	11	29	21	-	1
M.Y.Pasupati not out	11	20	15	-	2
R.M.Hira run out	1	5	5	-	-
C.S.Martin b Elliott	0	1	2	-	-
Extras (lb 2, w 10)	12				
TOTAL (47.5 overs)	**245**	195			

WELLINGTON

	Runs	Mins	Balls	6s	4s
M.D.Bell lbw b Nicol	52	128	111	-	5
M.E.Parlane* c Jones b Martin	2	16	9	-	-
J.D.Ryder c Young b Martin	18	26	14	2	-
C.J.Nevin c Young b Hitchcock	0	5	6	-	-
N.R.Parlane c Nicol b Hira	50	97	79	-	6
G.D.Elliott st Young b Hitchcock	53	64	42	2	2
S.M.Mills† b Hira	13	6	11	1	1
D.J.Bowden not out	25	43	32	1	-
L.J.Woodcock not out	2	4	2	-	-
M.Burns					
I.E.O'Brien					
Extras (lb 8, w 6, nb 6)	20				
TOTAL (50 overs) (7 wkts)	**235**	198			

Bowling	*O*	*M*	*R*	*W*
WELLINGTON				
O'Brien	9	2	43	1
Burns	9	1	55	0
Bowden	10	0	37	2
Elliott	8.5	0	29	4
Woodcock	8	0	53	1
Ryder	3	0	26	1
AUCKLAND				
Mills	10	2	56	0
Martin	10	2	33	2
Hitchcock	10	1	31	2
Pasupati	4	0	25	0
Hira	8	0	50	2
Nicol	8	0	32	1

Fall of Wickets	***A***	***W***
1st	5	7
2nd	74	39
3rd	89	40
4th	93	120
5th	117	136
6th	166	152
7th	211	230
8th	238	-
9th	244	-
10th	245	-

OTAGO v CENTRAL DISTRICTS **State Shield**

at Molyneux Park, Alexandra on 5 January, 2007
Toss : Central Districts. Umpires : E.J. Gray & D.M. Quested
Otago won by 4 runs. *Points: Otago 4, Central Districts 0*

OTAGO

	Runs	Mins	Balls	6s	4s
C.D.Cumming* c Thompson b Hegglun	2	14	14	-	-
J.W.Sheed c Thompson b Diamanti	24	85	52	-	3
A.J.Redmond c Oram b Furlong	67	132	93	-	7
N.T.Broom c Griggs b Thompson	31	56	47	-	3
G.J.Hopkins† c & b How	7	18	11	-	-
G.R.Todd b Diamanti	33	62	39	-	1
C.B.Gaffaney run out	9	16	19	-	1
N.L.McCullum c Sinclair b Diamanti	13	25	20	-	1
B.E.Scott not out	3	10	2	-	-
M.J.Harvie not out	2	4	5	-	-
N.M.Turner					
Extras (lb 3, w 11, nb 3)	17				
TOTAL (50 overs) (8 wkts)	**208**	215			

CENTRAL DISTRICTS

	Runs	Mins	Balls	6s	4s
J.M.How* c Cumming b Harvie	39	71	62	-	7
G.E.F.Barnett c Hopkins b Scott	6	27	14	-	-
P.J.Ingram b Harvie	1	24	17	-	-
M.S.Sinclair c Todd b Scott	54	98	69	3	2
J.D.P.Oram c Scott b Harvie	18	67	47	-	1
G.R.Hay not out	28	86	44	-	1
B.B.J.Griggs† lbw b Redmond	25	44	35	-	-
E.P.Thompson b Turner	6	5	6	-	-
C.J.M.Furlong b Scott	0	11	5	-	-
B.J.Diamanti run out	9	4	3	-	2
G.J.T.Hegglun not out	1	2	1	-	-
Extras (lb 3, w 11, nb 3)	17				
TOTAL (50 overs) (9 wkts)	**204**	226			

Bowling	*O*	*M*	*R*	*W*
CENTRAL DISTRICTS				
Thompson	8	2	27	1
Hegglun	9	1	49	1
Oram	6	1	14	0
Diamanti	10	0	51	3
How	7	1	25	1
Furlong	10	0	39	1
OTAGO				
Scott	10	1	38	3
Harvie	10	0	52	3
Turner	10	2	31	1
Cumming	4	0	21	0
McCullum	10	0	25	0
Redmond	6	0	34	1

Fall of Wickets	***O***	***CD***
1st	4	24
2nd	73	38
3rd	134	58
4th	134	127
5th	147	141
6th	165	183
7th	194	192
8th	204	194
9th	-	203
10th	-	-

CANTERBURY v NORTHERN DISTRICTS **State Shield**

at Queen Elizabeth II Park, Christchurch on 6 January, 2007
Toss : Northern Districts. Umpires : D.J. Walker & E.A. Watkin
Northern Districts won by 81 runs. *Points: Northern Districts 5, Canterbury 0*

NORTHERN DISTRICTS

	Runs	Mins	Balls	6s	4s
N.K.W.Horsley c Vivian b Burtt	9	10	6	-	2
A.W.Evans run out	22	38	26	-	3
P.D.McGlashan† c Hiini b Chan	87	134	95	-	9
J.A.H.Marshall* not out	152	161	137	1	15
D.R.Flynn b Burtt	21	23	17	1	3
I.G.Butler b Hiini	10	9	8	1	-
J.A.F.Yovich not out	16	20	12	-	1
M.G.Orchard					
M.R.Jefferson					
D.R.Tuffey					
G.W.Aldridge					
Extras (lb 5, w 9, nb 1)	15				
TOTAL (50 overs) (5 wkts)	**332**	200			

CANTERBURY

	Runs	Mins	Balls	6s	4s
I.A.Robertson c Butler b Aldridge	19	41	33	-	2
M.H.W.Papps c Butler b Aldridge	16	24	15	-	3
S.L.Stewart c Marshall b Orchard	10	28	16	-	1
L.J.Vivian c McGlashan b Orchard	11	19	17	-	2
B.R.Findlay b Orchard	2	20	11	-	-
C.F.K.van Wyk† not out	85	148	103	-	5
C.Z.Harris* b Butler	64	105	85	2	7
T.D.Astle run out	9	22	16	-	-
B.C.Hiini not out	5	6	4	-	-
S.P.Chan					
L.M.Burtt					
Extras (lb 9, w 21)	30				
TOTAL (50 overs) (7 wkts)	**251**	210			

Bowling	*O*	*M*	*R*	*W*
CANTERBURY				
Burtt	9	0	75	2
Chan	6	0	41	1
Hiini	10	1	57	1
Harris	4	1	13	0
Findlay	5	0	43	0
Robertson	10	0	55	0
Astle	6	0	43	0
NORTHERN DISTRICTS				
Tuffey	10	0	60	0
Aldridge	10	1	38	2
Orchard	10	1	36	3
Butler	10	0	51	1
Jefferson	10	1	57	0

Fall of Wickets	***ND***	***C***
1st	21	31
2nd	52	46
3rd	218	53
4th	269	58
5th	287	67
6th	-	206
7th	-	241
8th	-	-
9th	-	-
10th	-	-

Sixth Round

Cumming got fifty from 72 balls and then his second century of the season after 115 deliveries to give Otago a good base. They were able to reach 279-8 aided by a McCullum cameo. The Northern batsmen struggled and only fifty from Yovich (67 balls) helped. Harvie and Turner both had career best bowling figures as Otago won by 61 runs.

The games between Auckland and Wellington and Central Districts and Canterbury were both abandoned.

OTAGO v NORTHERN DISTRICTS — State Shield

at University Oval, Dunedin on 9 January, 2007
Toss : Northern Districts. Umpires : E.J. Gray & W.R. Knights
Otago won by 61 runs. *Points: Otago 5, Northern Districts 0*

OTAGO

	Runs	Mins	Balls	6s	4s
C.D.Cumming* run out	112	181	129	3	9
J.W.Sheed c Evans b Aldridge	0	6	4	-	-
A.J.Redmond c & b Yovich	27	45	38	-	5
N.T.Broom c Butler b Yovich	15	43	30	-	2
G.R.Todd b Jefferson	24	31	27	-	4
G.J.Hopkins† c Yovich b Jefferson	3	7	7	-	-
C.B.Gaffaney run out	27	37	31	1	1
N.L.McCullum not out	45	31	24	3	4
B.E.Scott c McGlashan b Yovich	2	6	3	-	-
M.J.Harvie not out	5	17	9	-	-
N.M.Turner					
Extras (w 17, nb 2)	19				
TOTAL (50 overs) (8 wkts)	**279**	206			

NORTHERN DISTRICTS

	Runs	Mins	Balls	6s	4s
N.K.W.Horsley lbw b Harvie	1	55	39	-	3
A.W.Evans c Hopkins b Harvie	15	8	3	-	-
P.D.McGlashan† c Gaffaney b Harvie	21	53	40	-	2
J.A.H.Marshall* c Todd b Turner	8	21	17	-	2
D.R.Flynn c Hopkins b Turner	4	23	14	-	-
M.G.Orchard c Scott b McCullum	44	58	46	1	4
J.A.F.Yovich c Hopkins b McCullum	50	91	68	1	3
I.G.Butler c Hopkins b Harvie	15	13	18	1	-
M.R.Jefferson lbw b Harvie	0	2	2	-	-
D.R.Tuffey c Todd b Turner	25	47	34	1	2
G.W.Aldridge not out	9	22	17	-	-
Extras (lb 6, w 19, nb 1)	26				
TOTAL (49.3 overs)	**218**	201			

Bowling	*O*	*M*	*R*	*W*
NORTHERN DISTRICTS				
Tuffey	10	2	36	0
Aldridge	10	0	72	1
Orchard	8	0	50	0
Yovich	10	1	43	3
Butler	2	0	22	0
Jefferson	9	1	48	2
Marshall	1	0	8	0
OTAGO				
Scott	10	0	40	0
Harvie	10	2	40	5
Turner	8.3	2	32	3
Cumming	6	1	21	0
McCullum	10	1	49	2
Redmond	5	0	30	0

Fall of Wickets	***O***	***ND***
1st	0	6
2nd	54	49
3rd	101	51
4th	154	63
5th	159	75
6th	216	136
7th	226	155
8th	232	160
9th	-	191
10th	-	218

AUCKLAND v WELLINGTON — State Shield

at Eden Park Outer Oval, Auckland on 9 January, 2007
Abandoned without a ball being bowled. *Points: Auckland 2, Wellington 2*

CENTRAL DISTRICTS v CANTERBURY — State Shield

at Pukekura Park, New Plymouth on 9 January, 2007
Abandoned without a ball being bowled. *Points: Central Districts 2, Canterbury 2*

Seventh Round

Frauenstein *(Canterbury)* and Schaw *(Central Districts)* made their debuts.

Ingram and Sinclair added 143 for the third wicket for Central Districts. Ingram got fifty from 36 balls and his second century from 91 balls. Sinclair needed 71 deliveries for his fifty. Central went from 242-2 to 291-7. McGlashan got another fifty (73 balls) but Northern were behind the rate throughout. Diamanti had career best figures as Central won by 46 runs.

Papps went early but Canterbury recovered with Stewart leading the way. He got fifty from 73 balls as Canterbury made 248-8. Wellington made a disastrous start, being 37-4, but then Elliott dominated the innings. His fifty took 71 balls and he scored his maiden hundred from a further 40 deliveries as Wellington won off the last ball of the match.

Fifties to Redmond and Todd enabled Otago to pass 200. Redmond needed 67 balls compared to Todd's 82 for their fifties. Styris led the way for Auckland reaching fifty from 57 balls. Nicol passed 1000 runs as Auckland cruised to an easy win with seven overs to spare.

NORTHERN DISTRICTS v CENTRAL DISTRICTS State Shield

at Seddon Park, Hamilton on 15 January, 2007 (d/n)
Toss : Central Districts. Umpires : B.G. Frost & A.L. Hill
***Central Districts won by 46 runs.** Points: Central Districts 4, Northern Districts 0*

CENTRAL DISTRICTS

	Runs	Mins	Balls	6s	4s
J.M.How* c Jefferson b Aldridge	22	39	24	-	4
G.E.F.Barnett c Orchard b Yovich	45	73	66	-	9
P.J.Ingram c Aldridge b Orchard	104	132	96	2	10
M.S.Sinclair not out	79	130	91	1	4
J.D.P.Oram c McGlashan b Orchard	0	3	4	-	-
E.P.Thompson c McGlashan b Orchard	2	6	4	-	-
B.J.Diamanti c Devcich b Tuffey	21	11	13	2	1
B.B.J.Griggs† c Tuffey b Arnel	1	4	2	-	-
G.R.Hay not out	2	3	2	-	
C.J.M.Furlong					
R.J.Schaw					
Extras (lb 4, w 9, nb 2)	15				
TOTAL (50 overs) (7 wkts)	**291**	204			

NORTHERN DISTRICTS

	Runs	Mins	Balls	6s	4s
A.W.Evans c Hay b Diamanti	33	63	46	-	3
A.P.Devcich b Diamanti	35	78	50	-	5
P.D.McGlashan† b Oram	56	87	78	-	4
J.A.H.Marshall* b Furlong	6	20	17	-	-
D.R.Flynn c How b Furlong	6	6	6	-	1
J.A.F.Yovich c Griggs b Furlong	21	21	26	-	1
M.G.Orchard lbw b Diamanti	39	48	35	-	5
M.R.Jefferson c Oram b How	4	11	9	-	-
D.R.Tuffey b Diamanti	15	5	6	1	2
G.W.Aldridge not out	12	14	10	-	1
B.J.Arnel b Diamanti	2	6	4	-	-
Extras (b 4, lb 5, w 7)	16				
TOTAL (47.5 overs)	**245**	184			

Bowling	*O*	*M*	*R*	*W*
NORTHERN DISTRICTS				
Tuffey	10	2	41	1
Aldridge	10	0	55	1
Arnel	10	2	61	1
Orchard	6	1	37	3
Yovich	7	0	50	1
Jefferson	3	0	18	0
Devcich	4	0	25	0
CENTRAL DISTRICTS				
Oram	9	2	42	1
Thompson	5	0	27	0
Diamanti	8.5	0	58	5
Furlong	10	0	44	3
Schaw	10	0	37	0
How	5	0	28	1

Fall of Wickets

	CD	***ND***
1st	37	66
2nd	99	82
3rd	242	105
4th	242	117
5th	248	147
6th	273	179
7th	277	197
8th	-	214
9th	-	233
10th	-	245

CANTERBURY v WELLINGTON — State Shield

at Queen Elizabeth II Park, Christchurch on 16 January, 2007
Toss : Wellington. Umpires : G.A. Baxter & B.G. Frost
***Wellington won by 3 wickets.** Points: Wellington 4, Canterbury 0*

CANTERBURY

	Runs	Mins	Balls	6s	4s
S.L.Stewart c Elliott b Ryder	73	131	111	-	7
M.H.W.Papps c Ryder b Burns	4	12	12	-	1
I.A.Robertson b Elliott	39	73	58	-	6
A.M.Ellis run out	46	54	48	-	4
C.Z.Harris* not out	39	55	35	1	1
C.F.K.van Wyk† b Ryder	13	19	21	-	1
C.Frauenstein c Parlane N.R. b Bowden	8	7	7	-	1
B.R.Findlay b Ryder	2	4	3	-	-
B.C.Hiini c Parlane N.R. b Elliott	11	8	7	-	2
L.M.Burtt not out	5	3	2	-	1
H.K.Bennett					
Extras (w 4, nb 4)	8				
TOTAL (50 overs) (8 wkts)	**248**	187			

WELLINGTON

	Runs	Mins	Balls	6s	4s
M.D.Bell c van Wyk b Burtt	0	1	1	-	-
M.E.Parlane* c Harris b Bennett	22	33	27	-	4
J.D.Ryder c van Wyk b Bennett	4	20	14	-	-
C.J.Nevin c Hiini b Frauenstein	43	91	67	-	5
N.R.Parlane c Papps b Burtt	2	14	11	-	-
G.D.Elliott not out	107	152	115	-	11
S.M.Mills† run out	23	41	34	1	-
L.J.Woodcock st van Wyk b Frauenstein	20	18	13	1	1
D.J.Bowden not out	17	26	18	-	-
I.E.O'Brien					
M.Burns					
Extras (lb 8, w 3)	11				
TOTAL (50 overs) (7 wkts)	**249**	201			

Bowling	O	M	R	W
WELLINGTON				
Bowden	10	1	36	1
Burns	4	1	22	1
O'Brien	8	0	30	0
Elliott	9	0	66	2
Woodcock	10	0	38	0
Ryder	9	0	56	3
CANTERBURY				
Burtt	9	1	39	2
Bennett	8	2	32	2
Harris	10	0	43	0
Hiini	10	1	56	0
Robertson	5	0	22	0
Frauenstein	8	0	49	2

Fall of Wickets	*C*	*W*
1st	7	0
2nd	98	22
3rd	164	31
4th	174	37
5th	197	105
6th	207	167
7th	213	206
8th	236	-
9th	-	-
10th	-	-

AUCKLAND v OTAGO — State Shield

at Eden Park Outer Oval, Auckland on 16 January, 2007
Toss : Otago. Umpires : P.D. Jones & E.A. Watkin
***Auckland won by 6 wickets.** Points: Auckland 4, Otago 0*

OTAGO

	Runs	Mins	Balls	6s	4s
C.D.Cumming* c Mills b Hitchcock	17	47	27	-	3
J.W.Sheed c Nicol b Martin	11	35	32	-	1
A.J.Redmond c Styris b Nicol	53	89	72	-	6
N.T.Broom lbw b Hitchcock	10	27	24	-	1
G.R.Todd b Martin	53	137	87	-	1
G.J.Hopkins† c Hitchcock b Styris	37	36	31	2	2
N.L.McCullum c Vincent b Hitchcock	10	21	15	-	-
B.E.Scott c Styris b Martin	0	4	4	-	-
C.B.Gaffaney not out	14	12	1	-	2
W.C.McSkimming not out	7	8	4	-	1
M.J.Harvie					
Extras (b 2, lb 1, w 8, nb 7)	18				
TOTAL (50 overs) (8 wkts)	**230**	211			

AUCKLAND

	Runs	Mins	Balls	6s	4s
M.B.Loye b McSkimming	34	61	34	2	3
L.Vincent c Scott b Harvie	19	31	27	-	4
R.A.Jones* c Broom b McCullum	43	81	64	1	5
S.B.Styris not out	74	112	81	3	6
D.W.Houpapa run out	4	8	6	-	-
R.J.Nicol not out	38	51	46	3	1
P.A.Hitchcock					
K.D.Mills					
R.A.Young†					
R.M.Hira					
C.S.Martin					
Extras (b 4, lb 3, w 13)	20				
TOTAL (43 overs) (4 wkts)	**232**	174			

Bowling	O	M	R	W
AUCKLAND				
Mills	9.4	2	30	0
Martin	8.2	0	41	3
Hitchcock	10	1	43	3
Styris	7	0	36	1
Hira	9	0	44	0
Nicol	6	0	33	1
OTAGO				
McSkimming	10	1	44	1
Harvie	8	0	51	1
Scott	8	0	29	0
Cumming	4	0	22	0
Redmond	5	0	41	0
McCullum	8	0	38	1

Fall of Wickets	*O*	*A*
1st	26	38
2nd	42	77
3rd	64	147
4th	122	158
5th	183	-
6th	205	-
7th	207	-
8th	210	-
9th	-	-
10th	-	-

Eighth Round

Oram and Diamanti both scored fifties for Central after a steady start. Oram needed 59 balls while Diamanti took only 32 as Central reached 275-7. Hopkins had his 100th victim. Broom led the way for Otago reaching fifty off 51 balls as the southern men won with nine balls left.

Vincent struck form as Auckland made an imposing 303-6. He got fifty from 49 balls and reached his third hundred after 114 balls. Mills recorded the fastest fifty of the season, needing just 28 balls. Canterbury were always behind the rate after losing four quick wickets. Fifties from Harris (66 balls) and van Wyk (39) helped. Harris became the leading run scorer in domestic one-day games during this innings.

Bell and Neal Parlane added 147 for Wellington's second wicket. Bell needed 61 balls for fifty, 20 fewer than Parlane. Another fifty from McGlashan was the Northern shining light and there was a cameo from Butler but it wasn't enough as Wellington won by 43 runs.

CENTRAL DISTRICTS v OTAGO — State Shield

at Fitzherbert Park, Palmerston North on 18 January, 2007
Toss : Central Districts. Umpires : T.J. Parlane & E.A. Watkin
Otago won by 5 wickets. *Points: Otago 4, Central Districts 0*

CENTRAL DISTRICTS

	Runs	Mins	Balls	6s	4s
J.M.How* c McMillan b Cumming	19	67	41	-	3
G.E.F.Barnett b McCullum	48	106	78	-	7
P.J.Ingram c Sheed b Cumming	19	31	27	-	3
M.S.Sinclair c Cumming b McMillan	4	16	12	-	-
J.D.P.Oram not out	70	99	69	1	6
G.R.Hay c McSkimming b Scott	28	31	28	-	4
B.B.J.Griggs† st Hopkins b Redmond	6	14	14	-	-
B.J.Diamanti c Broom b Scott	60	41	35	4	3
E.P.Thompson not out	0	1	0	-	-
C.J.M.Furlong					
R.J.Schaw					
Extras (lb 6, w 11, nb 4)	21				
TOTAL (50 overs) (7 wkts)	**275**	206			

OTAGO

	Runs	Mins	Balls	6s	4s
C.D.Cumming* c Ingram b Schaw	46	79	56	2	5
J.W.Sheed c Furlong b Oram	19	18	19	-	4
A.J.Redmond c Diamanti b Schaw	23	49	36	-	4
N.T.Broom c Griggs b Thompson	87	101	84	3	5
G.R.Todd c How b Oram	35	51	45	1	1
G.J.Hopkins† not out	56	57	39	3	4
C.B.Gaffaney not out	11	17	12	-	1
N.L.McCullum					
B.E.Scott					
W.C.McSkimming					
J.M.McMillan					
Extras (b 1, w 1)	2				
TOTAL (48.3 overs) (5 wkts)	**279**	190			

Bowling	O	M	R	W
OTAGO				
McSkimming	9	1	64	0
McMillan	9	1	58	1
Scott	10	1	40	2
Cumming	7	0	39	2
McCullum	10	0	38	1
Redmond	5	0	30	1
CENTRAL DISTRICTS				
Oram	9.3	1	44	2
Thompson	9	0	49	1
Diamanti	8	0	49	0
Schaw	7	0	46	2
Furlong	10	0	51	0
How	3	0	18	0
Sinclair	2	0	21	0

Fall of Wickets	***CD***	***O***
1st	70	23
2nd	99	78
3rd	105	91
4th	116	174
5th	161	246
6th	178	-
7th	267	-
8th	-	-
9th	-	-
10th	-	-

CANTERBURY v AUCKLAND — State Shield

at Queen Elizabeth II Park, Christchurch on 19 January, 2007
Toss : Canterbury. Umpires : G.A. Baxter & A.L. Hill
***Auckland won by 38 runs.** Points: Auckland 4, Canterbury 0*

AUCKLAND

	Runs	Mins	Balls	6s	4s
P.A.Hitchcock c Harris b Burtt	7	50	24	-	1
L.Vincent lbw b Hiini	129	181	141	-	19
R.A.Jones* c Harris b Robertson	69	62	66	2	7
D.W.Houpapa c & b Robertson	0	8	4	-	-
R.J.Nicol c Harris b Robertson	22	33	27	-	1
K.D.Mills c Robertson b Bennett	52	38	29	2	6
R.A.Young† not out	13	15	8	-	1
M.Y.Pasupati not out	1	1	1	-	-
M.J.Guptill					
R.M.Hira					
C.S.Martin					
Extras (lb 3, w 7)	10				
TOTAL (50 overs) (6 wkts)	**303**	197			

CANTERBURY

	Runs	Mins	Balls	6s	4s
S.L.Stewart lbw b Pasupati	38	65	47	-	5
M.H.W.Papps run out	8	22	15	-	1
I.A.Robertson lbw b Martin	5	17	12	-	1
A.M.Ellis b Hira	35	83	57	-	2
C.Frauenstein c Guptill b Hitchcock	0	4	3	-	-
C.Z.Harris* b Hitchcock	71	83	82	1	5
C.F.K.van Wyk† not out	63	72	56	-	7
B.R.Findlay c Jones b Hitchcock	11	21	14	-	-
B.C.Hiini not out	20	20	15	-	2
L.M.Burtt					
H.K.Bennett					
Extras (lb 2, w 7, nb 5)	14				
TOTAL (50 overs) (7 wkts)	**265**	197			

Bowling	*O*	*M*	*R*	*W*
CANTERBURY				
Burtt	7	0	42	1
Bennett	8	0	42	1
Harris	9	0	53	0
Hiini	10	0	59	1
Findlay	3	0	28	0
Frauenstein	3	0	18	0
Robertson	10	0	58	3
AUCKLAND				
Mills	9	0	55	0
Martin	9	0	49	1
Hitchcock	10	0	56	3
Pasupati	6	0	26	1
Nicol	10	0	42	0
Hira	6	1	35	1

Fall of Wickets	***A***	***C***
1st	58	17
2nd	164	38
3rd	170	68
4th	226	69
5th	254	132
6th	302	189
7th	-	231
8th	-	-
9th	-	-
10th	-	-

WELLINGTON v NORTHERN DISTRICTS — State Shield

at Allied Prime Basin Reserve, Wellington on 21 January, 2007
Toss : Wellington. Umpires : D.M. Quested & D.J. Walker
***Wellington won by 43 runs.** Points: Wellington 4, Northern Districts 0*

WELLINGTON

	Runs	Mins	Balls	6s	4s
M.D.Bell lbw b Orchard	81	165	101	-	6
M.E.Parlane* c Butler b Arnel	35	58	45	2	4
N.R.Parlane st McGlashan b Butler	89	125	104	3	6
J.D.Ryder c Flynn b Butler	23	11	11	1	3
C.J.Nevin c Marshall b Arnel	19	20	13	-	2
S.M.Mills† c Orchard b Tuffey	15	19	14	-	1
D.J.Bowden not out	12	10	11	-	-
L.J.Woodcock not out	2	4	1	-	-
G.D.Elliott					
I.E.O'Brien					
S.Rasmussen					
Extras (lb 5, w 10)	15				
TOTAL (50 overs) (6 wkts)	**291**	209			

NORTHERN DISTRICTS

	Runs	Mins	Balls	6s	4s
A.W.Evans c Rasmussen b Bowden	12	18	16	-	1
B-J.Watling c Mills b Rasmussen	5	47	29	-	-
P.D.McGlashan† b Ryder	59	107	92	-	4
J.A.H.Marshall* c Mills b Elliott	30	29	23	-	6
D.R.Flynn c Mills b Elliott	2	2	3	-	-
M.G.Orchard c Mills b Woodcock	27	65	43	-	2
I.G.Butler b O'Brien	47	45	37	3	2
B.P.Martin st Mills b Ryder	5	11	13	-	-
D.R.Tuffey c sub (M.Burns) b Elliott	27	37	28	1	-
G.W.Aldridge b O'Brien	1	4	3	-	-
B.J.Arnel not out	11	15	13	-	1
Extras (lb 11, w 10, nb 1)	22				
TOTAL (49.5 overs)	**248**	193			

Bowling	*O*	*M*	*R*	*W*
NORTHERN DISTRICTS				
Tuffey	10	1	37	1
Aldridge	10	0	58	0
Arnel	9	0	51	2
Martin	5	0	39	0
Orchard	10	0	59	1
Butler	6	0	42	2
WELLINGTON				
Bowden	8	1	32	1
Rasmussen	6	0	25	1
Elliott	8.5	0	48	3
O'Brien	10	2	34	2
Woodcock	9	0	51	1
Ryder	8	0	47	2

Fall of Wickets	***W***	***ND***
1st	65	16
2nd	212	36
3rd	241	79
4th	249	81
5th	275	138
6th	281	165
7th	-	180
8th	-	217
9th	-	222
10th	-	248

Ninth Round

Cruikshank *(Central Districts)* made his debut.

Central lost two early wickets and How, fifty from 67 balls, went at 142-4. Hay and Griggs then added 72 with both getting fifties (Hay needing 62 balls and Griggs 46). Wellington had a century opening stand as Michael Parlane took control. His fifty came from 50 balls and his fourth century needed a further 39 deliveries. Some quick wickets fell but Wellington reached their target with 8.2 overs to spare.

Canterbury scored 232-6 after being sent in. Papps (fifty off 75 balls) was the top scorer. Steady batting from Otago saw them win with 17 balls to spare. Broom got fifty from 80 balls.

Vincent again led the way for Auckland getting fifty from 75 balls. After a disruption that reduced Northern's innings to 42 overs they had a revised target of 199 which they passed with four balls to spare. Marshall had led from the front getting fifty from 63 balls.

WELLINGTON v CENTRAL DISTRICTS — State Shield

at Allied Prime Basin Reserve, Wellington on 24 January, 2007
Toss : Wellington. Umpires : B.G. Frost & E.A. Watkin
Wellington won by 4 wickets. *Points: Wellington 4, Central Districts 0*

CENTRAL DISTRICTS

	Runs	Mins	Balls	6s	4s
J.M.How* c Parlane M.E. b Ryder	93	123	119	-	15
G.E.F.Barnett b Bowden	1	15	13	-	-
P.J.Ingram c Mills b Burns	3	18	13	-	-
M.S.Sinclair run out	24	51	32	1	1
G.R.Hay run out	53	95	65	-	5
B.B.J.Griggs† run out	50	45	47	1	4
B.J.Diamanti not out	23	18	11	1	2
E.P.Thompson c O'Brien b Ryder	0	2	1	-	-
G.J.T.Hegglun not out	0	1	0	-	-
C.J.M.Furlong					
C.P.Cruikshank					
Extras (lb 2, w 3, nb 1)	6				
TOTAL (50 overs) (7 wkts)	**253**	188			

WELLINGTON

	Runs	Mins	Balls	6s	4s
S.A.Fairley c sub (R.J.Schaw) b Diamanti	28	81	64	-	1
M.E.Parlane* c How b Thompson	132	159	116	2	16
N.R.Parlane c Griggs b Thompson	13	31	22	-	2
C.J.Nevin c & b Diamanti	26	28	21	-	5
J.D.Ryder b Diamanti	17	21	13	-	2
G.D.Elliott c Griggs b Diamanti	2	7	5	-	-
S.M.Mills† not out	3	8	6	-	-
D.J.Bowden not out	2	5	5	-	-
L.J.Woodcock					
I.E.O'Brien					
M.Burns					
Extras (b 4, lb 7, w 18, nb 2)	31				
TOTAL (41.4 overs) (6 wkts)	**254**	173			

Bowling	*O*	*M*	*R*	*W*
WELLINGTON				
Bowden	10	1	34	1
Burns	6	0	22	1
O'Brien	9	1	47	0
Elliott	9	0	57	0
Woodcock	8	0	43	0
Ryder	8	0	48	2
CENTRAL DISTRICTS				
Thompson	10	1	51	2
Cruikshank	5	0	35	0
Hegglun	5	1	38	0
Furlong	8	0	47	0
How	3	0	20	0
Diamanti	10	1	51	4
Sinclair	0.4	0	1	0

Fall of Wickets	***CD***	***W***
1st	19	108
2nd	29	161
3rd	95	214
4th	142	246
5th	214	249
6th	246	250
7th	249	-
8th	-	-
9th	-	-
10th	-	-

OTAGO v CANTERBURY

State Shield

at University Oval, Dunedin on 24 January, 2007
Toss : Otago. Umpires : K. Cross & D.M. Quested
***Otago won by 5 wickets.** Points: Otago 4, Canterbury 0*

CANTERBURY

	Runs	Mins	Balls	6s	4s
S.L.Stewart b Turner	14	51	46	-	1
M.H.W.Papps b Redmond	62	124	87	-	8
I.A.Robertson b McMillan	10	31	30	-	1
A.M.Ellis b Redmond	26	51	49	-	1
C.Z.Harris* lbw b McCullum	7	32	25	-	-
C.F.K.van Wyk† not out	29	61	32	-	2
C.Frauenstein lbw b Turner	48	33	29	1	6
B.R.Findlay not out	8	5	5	-	1
B.C.Hiini					
L.M.Burtt					
H.K.Bennett					
Extras (lb 12, w 13, nb 3)	28				
TOTAL (50 overs) (6 wkts)	**232**	197			

OTAGO

	Runs	Mins	Balls	6s	4s
C.D.Cumming* c van Wyk b Hiini	34	65	46	1	5
J.W.Sheed b Hiini	14	56	33	-	2
A.J.Redmond c Harris b Burtt	33	39	34	-	7
N.T.Broom c Harris b Burtt	55	111	84	1	2
G.R.Todd c Frauenstein b Harris	29	50	50	-	1
G.J.Hopkins† not out	46	49	28	2	4
C.B.Gaffaney not out	9	19	10	-	1
N.L.McCullum					
B.E.Scott					
N.M.Turner					
J.M.McMillan					
Extras (lb 9, w 3, nb 2)	14				
TOTAL (47.1 overs) (5 wkts)	**234**	197			

Bowling	*O*	*M*	*R*	*W*
OTAGO				
McMillan	10	2	38	1
Scott	10	2	46	0
Turner	8	1	39	2
Cumming	4	0	17	0
McCullum	9	1	44	1
Redmond	9	0	36	2
CANTERBURY				
Burtt	10	1	34	2
Bennett	10	0	57	0
Hiini	7	1	37	2
Findlay	3.1	1	16	0
Robertson	9	1	46	0
Harris	8	0	35	1

Fall of Wickets	***C***	***O***
1st	49	46
2nd	68	60
3rd	120	90
4th	130	150
5th	142	208
6th	222	-
7th	-	-
8th	-	-
9th	-	-
10th	-	-

NORTHERN DISTRICTS v AUCKLAND

State Shield

at Seddon Park, Hamilton on 24 January, 2007 (d/n)
Toss : Northern Districts. Umpires : M.P. George & D.G Paterson
***Northern Districts won by 4 wickets (D/L).** Points: Northern Districts 4, Auckland 0*

AUCKLAND

	Runs	Mins	Balls	6s	4s
P.A.Hitchcock lbw b Aldridge	11	15	13	-	2
L.Vincent lbw b Orchard	51	111	82	1	8
R.A.Jones* c McGlashan b Aldridge	0	15	9	-	-
S.B.Styris run out	17	25	13	-	3
R.J.Nicol not out	43	148	97	-	2
D.W.Houpapa c Marshall b Butler	22	30	34	-	4
M.J.Guptill c McGlashan b Butler	4	12	9	-	-
R.A.Young† c McGlashan b Butler	22	29	27	-	2
M.Y.Pasupati c Orchard b Aldridge	25	16	14	1	3
R.M.Hira not out	4	3	2	-	1
C.S.Martin					
Extras (lb 5, w 12)	17				
TOTAL (50 overs) (8 wkts)	**216**	206			

NORTHERN DISTRICTS

	Runs	Mins	Balls	6s	4s
A.W.Evans c Styris b Hitchcock	15	24	24	-	2
B-J.Watling c Young b Styris	35	71	50	-	6
P.D.McGlashan† c Young b Styris	30	40	27	-	5
J.A.H.Marshall* not out	61	103	77	-	7
G.G.Robinson c Young b Styris	6	17	11	-	1
M.G.Orchard c Vincent b Pasupati	6	16	11	-	1
I.G.Butler c Nicol b Styris	5	5	7	-	1
D.R.Tuffey not out	32	56	43	-	5
B.P.Martin					
G.W.Aldridge					
B.J.Arnel					
Extras (lb 2, w 7, nb 2)	11				
TOTAL (41.2 overs) (6 wkts)	**201**	169			

Bowling	*O*	*M*	*R*	*W*
NORTHERN DISTRICTS				
Tuffey	10	1	45	0
Aldridge	9	1	41	3
Arnel	5	0	35	0
Orchard	10	4	19	1
Butler	10	0	50	3
Martin	6	0	21	0
AUCKLAND				
Hitchcock	8	0	31	1
Martin	9	0	34	0
Pasupati	7	0	40	1
Styris	9	0	38	4
Vincent	5.2	0	34	0
Hira	1	0	9	0
Nicol	2	0	13	0

Fall of Wickets	***A***	***ND***
1st	18	23
2nd	21	85
3rd	51	88
4th	105	107
5th	129	127
6th	139	133
7th	175	-
8th	211	-
9th	-	-
10th	-	-

Tenth Round

Weston *(Central Districts)* made his debut.

Otago lost two quick wickets but recovered to make 230-9 in the match to decide the top placing. Wellington were in trouble at 100-6 before Mills hit his maiden fifty from 65 balls. Otago, however, won by 18 runs to secure top spot. Scott had taken his 50th wicket.

Harris played his 122nd game, a record for domestic cricket. Stewart got fifty from 92 balls as Canterbury made 228-7 on the new Cobham Oval. With fifty from Marshall (52 balls) and a highest score from Robinson, Northern won with 19 balls left.

Central Districts made 232-9 with Ingram (fifty off 50 balls) being the main contributor. Auckland knew that if they won they would finish in second place but lost two early wickets. Only Young was able to reach fifty (45 balls) and they failed to reach their target.

OTAGO v WELLINGTON

State Shield

at Queen's Park, Invercargill on 30 January, 2007
Toss : Wellington. Umpires : P.D. Jones & D.J. Walker
***Otago won by 18 runs.** Points: Otago 4, Wellington 0*

OTAGO

	Runs	Mins	Balls	6s	4s
C.D.Cumming* c Parlane N.R. b Elliott	40	105	74	1	4
J.W.Sheed c Mills b Rasmussen	0	6	3	-	-
A.J.Redmond c Parlane N.R. b Rasmussen	2	9	12	-	-
N.T.Broom lbw b Woodcock	29	69	52	1	2
G.R.Todd c Bell b Woodcock	5	15	22	-	-
G.J.Hopkins† c O'Brien b Elliott	47	68	48	2	2
C.B.Gaffaney c Bell b Woodcock	4	9	10	-	1
N.L.McCullum c Parlane N.R. b Elliott	31	47	38	-	2
B.E.Scott c Ryder b Rasmussen	35	33	26	3	-
M.J.Harvie not out	11	28	17	-	-
N.M.Turner not out	2	2	2	-	-
Extras (lb 6, w 13, nb 5)	24				
TOTAL (50 overs) (9 wkts)	**230**	200			

WELLINGTON

	Runs	Mins	Balls	6s	4s
M.D.Bell c Hopkins b Harvie	21	23	23	-	5
M.E.Parlane* c McCullum b Scott	4	17	10	-	1
N.R.Parlane c & b Redmond	15	83	46	-	1
C.J.Nevin b Harvie	0	6	6	-	-
J.D.Ryder b Harvie	14	16	14	-	3
G.D.Elliott c Gaffaney b McCullum	30	61	56	-	3
S.M.Mills† c Sheed b Scott	60	86	79	2	4
L.J.Woodcock c Redmond b Scott	47	76	55	-	2
D.J.Bowden not out	2	11	6	-	-
I.E.O'Brien b Broom	0	2	1	-	-
S.Rasmussen run out	1	4	3	-	-
Extras (b 2, lb 4, w 9, nb 3)	18				
TOTAL (49.2 overs)	**212**	198			

Bowling	*O*	*M*	*R*	*W*
WELLINGTON				
Bowden	10	2	22	0
Rasmussen	10	1	59	3
O'Brien	10	0	63	0
Elliott	10	0	32	3
Woodcock	10	0	48	3
OTAGO				
Scott	9.2	2	29	3
Harvie	10	0	47	3
Turner	10	1	47	0
McCullum	10	1	30	1
Cumming	1	0	5	0
Redmond	6	0	35	1
Broom	3	0	13	1

Fall of Wickets

	O	*W*
1st	2	18
2nd	6	26
3rd	83	28
4th	92	42
5th	94	90
6th	103	100
7th	174	207
8th	182	207
9th	227	209
10th	-	212

NORTHERN DISTRICTS v CANTERBURY — State Shield

at Cobham Oval, Whangarei on 31 January, 2007
Toss : Canterbury. Umpires : P.L. Gasston & A.L. Hill
***Northern Districts won by 5 wickets.** Points: Northern Districts 4, Canterbury 0*

CANTERBURY

	Runs	Mins	Balls	6s	4s
I.A.Robertson c Evans b Tuffey ..	0	1	2	-	-
M.H.W.Papps† b Flynn	37	96	67	-	3
C.Frauenstein c Davis b Tuffey	17	26	22	-	2
S.L.Stewart c Marshall b Butler	73	144	116	-	5
C.Z.Harris* c Robinson b Butler	38	66	63	-	2
A.M.Ellis c Aldridge b Butler	16	21	12	-	1
L.J.Vivian not out	18	24	16	-	1
B.R.Findlay c Robinson b Davis .	0	4	1	-	-
B.C.Hiini not out	10	7	7	-	1
L.M.Burtt					
H.K.Bennett					
Extras (lb 13, nb 6)	19				
TOTAL (50 overs) (7 wkts) .	**228**	198			

NORTHERN DISTRICTS

	Runs	Mins	Balls	6s	4s
A.W.Evans c Papps b Harris	31	50	23	-	3
B-J.Watling† c Papps b Bennett	16	42	35	-	1
D.R.Flynn c Ellis b Robertson ..	17	25	27	-	3
J.A.H.Marshall* b Robertson	51	88	55	-	2
G.G.Robinson not out	77	116	109	-	6
M.G.Orchard c Harris b Burtt	17	37	28	-	1
J.A.F.Yovich not out	9	7	5	-	1
I.G.Butler					
D.R.Tuffey					
G.W.Aldridge					
T.T.Davis					
Extras (b 7, lb 1, w 5, nb 1)	14				
TOTAL (46.5 overs) (5 wkts)	**232**	185			

Bowling	*O*	*M*	*R*	*W*
NORTHERN DISTRICTS				
Tuffey	8	1	25	2
Aldridge	7	1	33	0
Davis	7	0	45	1
Orchard	10	0	23	0
Flynn	10	0	49	1
Butler	8	0	40	3
CANTERBURY				
Bennett	7.5	0	53	1
Burtt	9	1	46	1
Harris	10	0	24	1
Hiini	7	0	48	0
Robertson	10	0	27	2
Frauenstein	1	0	8	0
Findlay	2	0	18	0

Fall of Wickets	***C***	***ND***
1st	0	46
2nd	26	59
3rd	92	75
4th	175	176
5th	186	217
6th	209	-
7th	214	-
8th	-	-
9th	-	-
10th	-	-

AUCKLAND v CENTRAL DISTRICTS — State Shield

at Eden Park Outer Oval, Auckland on 31 January, 2007
Toss : Central Districts. Umpires : R.D. Anderson & E.J. Gray
***Central Districts won by 26 runs.** Points: Central Districts 4, Auckland 0*

CENTRAL DISTRICTS

	Runs	Mins	Balls	6s	4s
J.M.How* b Adams	8	16	15	-	2
E.P.Thompson c Guptill b Pasupati	32	52	40	-	7
P.J.Ingram c Jones b Hira	61	93	66	-	10
M.S.Sinclair c Martin b Hira	23	43	42	-	2
G.R.Hay not out	49	83	70	-	4
B.B.J.Griggs† lbw b Nicol	3	9	9	-	-
T.I.Weston c Martin b Hira	11	22	21	-	1
B.J.Diamanti lbw b Hira	4	10	3	-	1
G.J.T.Hegglun c Hira b Nicol	0	3	4	-	-
C.J.M.Furlong run out	33	33	30	1	3
B.E.Hefford					
Extras (b 1, w 7)	8				
TOTAL (50 overs) (9 wkts) .	**232**	190			

AUCKLAND

	Runs	Mins	Balls	6s	4s
P.A.Hitchcock c Furlong b Hefford	34	40	40	-	7
M.J.Guptill b Thompson	0	2	1	-	-
R.A.Jones* c Griggs b Thompson	0	1	2	-	-
K.W.M.Todd lbw b Hefford	8	23	10	-	1
R.J.Nicol c Griggs b Thompson	24	81	50	-	1
D.W.Houpapa b Furlong	39	65	56	1	5
R.A.Young† c Diamanti b Hegglun	54	83	51	4	4
A.R.Adams c How b Diamanti ..	19	28	27	-	3
M.Y.Pasupati c Hefford b Diamanti	7	14	12	1	-
R.M.Hira b Furlong	3	11	11	-	-
C.S.Martin not out	4	23	10	-	1
Extras (lb 7, w 5, nb 2)	14				
TOTAL (44.5 overs).............	**206**	190			

Bowling	*O*	*M*	*R*	*W*
AUCKLAND				
Adams	10	0	60	1
Martin	8	1	36	0
Hitchcock	10	0	52	0
Pasupati	4	0	17	1
Hira	10	1	40	4
Nicol	8	0	26	2
CENTRAL DISTRICTS				
Thompson	10	1	65	3
Hefford	9	1	36	2
Hegglun	8.5	0	34	1
Diamanti	7	0	31	2
Furlong	10	0	33	2

Fall of Wickets	***CD***	***A***
1st	16	1
2nd	63	1
3rd	123	39
4th	137	54
5th	148	115
6th	165	115
7th	172	144
8th	173	163
9th	232	169
10th	-	206

WELLINGTON v AUCKLAND — Semi-final

at Allied Prime Basin Reserve, Wellington on 6 February, 2007
Toss : Auckland. Umpires : B.G. Frost & E.A. Watkin
Auckland won by 71 runs

Zimbabwe Under 19 representative Colin de Grandhomme made his debut for Auckland. Houpapa again showed his liking for the Wellington bowling as he scored fifty from 76 balls. This enabled Auckland to reach 259-9.

Wellington never looked likely to reach the target after slumping to 46-5. Ryder (fifty off 61 balls) and Mills (highest score) gave Wellington some hope but the home team were soundly beaten by 71 runs. Martin had taken his 100th wicket.

AUCKLAND

	Runs	Mins	Balls	6s	4s
P.A.Hitchcock c Mills b Bowden	27	75	43	-	3
M.J.Guptill run out	24	34	28	-	4
R.A.Jones* c Parlane N.R. b Bowden	22	47	37	-	3
C.de Grandhomme c Bell b Ryder	38	84	53	-	2
R.J.Nicol c & b Elliott	4	12	11	-	1
D.W.Houpapa c Woodcock b O'Brien	66	101	91	2	3
R.A.Young† lbw b Ryder	37	31	29	-	5
A.R.Adams c Nevin b Ryder	20	11	10	1	1
M.Y.Pasupati run out	0	3	0	-	-
R.M.Hira not out	1	2	1	-	-
C.S.Martin					
Extras (lb 11, w 6, nb 3)	20				
TOTAL (50 overs) (9 wkts)	**259**	204			

WELLINGTON

	Runs	Mins	Balls	6s	4s
M.D.Bell b Martin	0	2	3	-	-
M.E.Parlane* c de Grandhomme b Hitchcock	15	46	36	-	2
N.R.Parlane c Young b Martin	4	10	9	-	1
C.J.Nevin b Pasupati	8	37	23	-	1
J.D.Ryder c Adams b Nicol	52	68	68	-	7
G.D.Elliott c Young b Pasupati	0	1	2	-	-
S.M.Mills† c Young b Adams	65	111	93	-	9
L.J.Woodcock b Adams	16	39	26	-	-
D.J.Bowden run out	2	1	2	-	-
I.E.O'Brien not out	1	11	6	-	-
S.Rasmussen lbw b Pasupati	1	3	5	-	-
Extras (b 5, lb 6, w 11, nb 2)	24				
TOTAL (45.1 overs)	**188**	169			

Bowling	*O*	*M*	*R*	*W*
WELLINGTON				
O'Brien	10	1	56	1
Bowden	10	1	52	2
Rasmussen	9	0	46	0
Woodcock	8	0	27	0
Elliott	6	0	29	1
Ryder	7	0	38	3
AUCKLAND				
Martin	8	1	30	2
Adams	10	0	28	2
Hitchcock	7	0	28	1
Pasupati	4.1	1	24	3
Hira	6	0	32	0
Nicol	10	0	35	1

Fall of Wickets	***A***	***W***
1st	35	4
2nd	79	19
3rd	80	42
4th	89	46
5th	175	46
6th	237	128
7th	241	181
8th	253	183
9th	259	185
10th	-	188

OTAGO v AUCKLAND — Final

at University Oval, Dunedin on 10 February, 2007
Toss : Auckland. Umpires : A.L. Hill & B.F. Bowden
Auckland won by 5 wickets

Auckland won the toss on a green wicket and in overcast conditions they immediately had Otago on the ropes. The home side were 65-7 with only Todd (fifty off 107 balls) able to reach 20. Martin took 3-7 off eight overs.

Auckland lost an early wicket but forties from Jones and Styris gave them an easy five wicket win, to take the State Shield for the first time. It was the first time that Auckland had won the domestic one-day competition since 1989/90.

OTAGO

	Runs	Mins	Balls	6s	4s
C.D.Cumming* b Martin	11	42	38	-	1
S.B.Haig c Styris b Adams	3	13	8	-	-
A.J.Redmond c Young b Adams	4	9	6	-	1
N.T.Broom b Martin	1	3	4	-	-
G.R.Todd b Nicol	50	130	111	-	5
G.J.Hopkins† lbw b Martin	0	7	4	-	-
C.B.Gaffaney lbw b Hitchcock	2	12	9	-	-
N.L.McCullum c Houpapa b Adams	17	29	26	-	3
B.E.Scott c Young b Pasupati	17	52	35	-	1
M.J.Harvie c Hitchcock b Nicol	2	5	7	-	-
N.M.Turner not out	1	5	2	-	-
Extras (b 1, lb 5, w 5)	11				
TOTAL (41.4 overs)	**119**	158			

AUCKLAND

	Runs	Mins	Balls	6s	4s
P.A.Hitchcock c Hopkins b Scott	8	6	7	-	1
L.Vincent c McCullum b Turner	17	42	22	-	2
R.A.Jones* c Hopkins b Harvie	44	55	43	-	7
S.B.Styris c Turner b Harvie	40	48	40	2	4
R.J.Nicol b Harvie	3	1	10	-	-
D.W.Houpapa not out	6	18	7	-	-
C.de Grandhomme not out	0	2	0	-	-
R.A.Young†					
A.R.Adams					
M.Y.Pasupati					
C.S.Martin					
Extras (lb 1, w 1)	2				
TOTAL (21.3 overs) (5 wkts)	**120**	93			

Bowling	*O*	*M*	*R*	*W*
AUCKLAND				
Martin	8	3	7	3
Adams	8	2	29	3
Hitchcock	8	0	24	1
Styris	6	2	18	0
Pasupati	7	0	26	1
Nicol	4.4	0	9	2
OTAGO				
Harvie	7.3	0	45	3
Scott	9	1	47	1
Turner	5	0	27	1

Fall of Wickets	***O***	***A***
1st	8	9
2nd	17	58
3rd	18	86
4th	31	92
5th	36	119
6th	43	-
7th	65	-
8th	105	-
9th	110	-
10th	119	-

2006/07 STATE SHIELD AVERAGES

	M	In	NO	HS	Runs	Ave	100s	50s	Ct	St	O	M	R	W	Ave	R/O	Best
A.R.Adams	3	2	0	20	39	19.50	-	-	1	-	28	2	117	6	19.50	4.18	3-29
G.W.Aldridge	10	7	6	21*	72	72.00	-	-	2	-	89	5	442	13	34.00	4.97	3-32
B.J.Arnel	7	4	2	11*	25	12.50	-	-	-	-	52.5	2	272	6	45.33	5.14	2-30
T.D.Astle	1	1	0	9	9	9.00	-	-	-	-	6	0	43	0	-	7.17	-
G.E.F.Barnett	7	7	0	91	193	27.57	-	1	1	-							
M.D.Bell	9	9	0	81	197	21.88	-	2	5	-							
H.K.Bennett	8	1	0	0	0	0.00	-	-	-	-	54.5	2	309	7	44.14	5.63	3-29
D.J.Bowden	10	8	6	25*	89	44.50	-	-	2	-	68	6	264	8	33.00	3.88	2-37
N.T.Broom	11	11	1	87	297	29.70	-	2	4	-	3	0	13	1	13.00	4.33	1-13
M.Burns	6	-	-	-	-	-	-	-	-	-	39	4	161	6	26.83	4.13	2-15
L.M.Burtt	5	1	1	5*	5	-	-	-	-	-	44	3	236	8	29.50	5.36	2-34
I.G.Butler	8	7	0	47	153	21.85	-	-	4	-	42	0	251	9	27.88	5.98	3-40
S.P.Chan	5	2	0	6	7	3.50	-	-	1	-	28	0	195	3	65.00	6.96	1-21
C.P.Cruikshank	1	-	-	-	-	-	-	-	-	-	5	0	35	0	-	7.00	-
C.D.Cumming	11	11	1	112	445	44.50	2	-	3	-	45.5	1	217	8	27.12	4.73	2-27
T.T.Davis	1	-	-	-	-	-	-	-	1	-	7	0	45	1	45.00	6.43	1-45
C.de Grandhomme	2	2	1	38	38	38.00	-	-	1	-							
A.P.Devcich	1	1	0	35	35	35.00	-	-	1	-	4	0	25	0	-	6.25	-
B.J.Diamanti	8	6	2	60	126	31.50	-	1	4	-	66.5	1	370	18	20.55	5.53	5-58
G.D.Elliott	10	7	1	107*	286	47.66	1	2	4	-	78.4	1	400	18	22.22	5.08	4-29
A.M.Ellis	5	5	0	46	125	25.00	-	-	1	-							
A.W.Evans	10	10	0	79	328	32.80	-	2	3	-							
S.A.Fairley	1	1	0	28	28	28.00	-	-	-	-							
B.R.Findlay	9	8	2	14*	47	7.83	-	-	1	-	27.4	1	190	2	95.00	6.86	1-29
D.R.Flynn	9	9	0	21	108	12.00	-	-	1	-	12	0	69	1	69.00	5.75	1-49
K.A.Forde	1	-	-	-	-	-	-	-	-	-	4.2	1	15	2	7.50	3.46	2-15
C.Frauenstein	4	4	0	48	73	18.25	-	-	1	-	12	0	75	2	37.50	6.25	2-49
C.J.M.Furlong	8	3	0	33	44	14.66	-	-	3	-	77	2	302	9	33.55	3.92	3-44
C.B.Gaffaney	11	10	4	27	109	18.16	-	-	5	-							
B.B.J.Griggs	8	7	1	50	113	18.83	-	1	11	-							
M.J.Guptill	4	3	0	24	28	9.33	-	-	2	-							
S.B.Haig	4	4	0	17	35	8.75	-	-	-	1							
C.Z.Harris	9	9	3	71	362	60.33	-	3	10	-	72	1	286	9	31.77	3.97	3-38
M.J.Harvie	9	6	4	19*	43	21.50	-	-	-	-	68.5	4	344	18	19.11	4.99	5-40
G.R.Hay	7	6	3	55	215	71.66	-	2	1	-							
B.E.Hefford	3	-	-	-	-	-	-	-	1	-	24	1	118	3	39.33	4.92	2-36
G.J.T.Hegglun	6	4	3	4*	5	5.00	-	-	-	-	50.4	2	245	6	40.83	4.83	2-33
B.C.Hiini	9	6	4	20*	56	28.00	-	-	2	-	76	5	394	11	35.81	5.18	3-38
R.M.Hira	9	5	2	4*	10	3.33	-	-	1	-	70	4	320	13	24.61	4.57	4-31
P.A.Hitchcock	10	9	0	82	215	23.88	-	1	2	-	82	5	378	12	31.50	4.61	3-43
G.J.Hopkins	8	8	2	56*	207	34.50	-	1	9	2							
N.K.W.Horsley	5	5	0	19	43	8.60	-	-	1	-							
D.W.Houpapa	10	10	2	101	261	32.62	1	1	2	-							
J.M.How	8	8	1	93	286	40.85	-	2	8	-	29	1	151	3	50.33	5.21	1-25
P.J.Ingram	8	8	1	104	344	49.14	1	2	1	-							
M.R.Jefferson	5	4	0	17	21	5.25	-	-	1	-	36	4	163	6	27.16	4.53	3-8
R.A.Jones	10	10	0	81	360	36.00	-	3	5	-							
M.B.Loye	2	2	0	90	124	62.00	-	1	-	-							
H.J.H.Marshall	1	1	0	59	59	59.00	-	1	1	-							
J.A.H.Marshall	6	6	2	152*	308	77.00	1	2	4	-	1	0	8	0	-	8.00	-
B.P.Martin	3	2	0	5	8	4.00	-	-	-	-	21	0	103	1	103.00	4.90	1-43
C.S.Martin	9	3	2	4*	4	4.00	-	-	3	-	78.2	8	319	13	24.53	4.07	3-7
M.J.Mason	1	-	-	-	-	-	-	-	-	-	10	1	43	1	43.00	4.30	1-43
N.L.McCullum	11	8	1	45*	135	19.28	-	-	5	-	88	4	342	9	38.00	3.89	2-49
P.D.McGlashan	8	8	2	87	380	63.33	-	4	8	3							
C.D.McMillan	3	3	0	69	116	38.66	-	1	1	-	13	0	70	0	-	5.38	-
J.M.McMillan	2	-	-	-	-	-	-	-	1	-	19	3	96	2	48.00	5.05	1-38
W.C.McSkimming	4	3	1	11	18	9.00	-	-	1	-	33	3	177	4	44.25	5.36	3-40
K.D.Mills	5	3	0	52	75	25.00	-	1	2	-	42.4	5	197	0	-	4.61	-
S.M.Mills	10	8	1	65	251	35.85	-	2	13	2							
C.Munro	1	-	-	-	-	-	-	-	-	-	4	0	21	0	-	5.25	-
C.J.Nevin	8	7	0	43	128	18.28	-	-	2	-							
R.J.Nicol	10	10	2	43*	208	26.00	-	-	3	-	77.4	1	280	9	31.11	3.60	2-9
I.E.O'Brien	9	3	1	1*	1	0.50	-	-	3	-	82	9	382	10	38.20	4.66	3-39
J.D.P.Oram	4	4	1	70*	131	43.66	-	1	2	-	24.3	4	100	3	33.33	4.08	2-44
M.G.Orchard	10	9	0	44	215	23.88	-	-	4	-	72	6	349	9	38.77	4.85	3-36

	M	In	NO	HS	Runs	Ave	100s	50s	Ct	St	O	M	R	W	Ave	R/O	Best
M.H.W.Papps	9	9	0	62	258	28.66	-	2	3	-							
M.E.Parlane	10	10	2	132	307	38.37	1	1	2	-							
N.R.Parlane	8	7	0	89	200	28.57	-	2	7	-							
M.Y.Pasupati	9	7	3	25	53	13.25	-	-	1	-	51.1	1	270	11	24.54	5.27	3-24
J.S.Patel	1	1	0	1	1	1.00	-	-	1	-	10	1	41	1	41.00	4.10	1-41
S.Rasmussen	7	3	1	1	2	1.00	-	-	1	-	57	3	297	8	37.12	5.21	3-39
A.J.Redmond	11	11	0	67	314	28.54	-	3	3	-	48	0	268	8	33.50	5.58	2-36
I.A.Robertson	9	9	0	60	190	21.11	-	1	2	-	60	1	267	5	53.40	4.45	3-58
G.G.Robinson	2	2	1	77*	83	83.00	-	1	2	-							
J.D.Ryder	10	10	2	52	196	24.50	-	1	4	-	36	0	223	11	20.27	6.19	3-38
R.J.Schaw	2	-	-	-	-	-	-	-	-	-	17	0	83	2	41.50	4.88	2-46
B.E.Scott	11	8	3	35	92	18.40	-	-	4	-	99.2	11	408	12	34.00	4.10	3-29
L.J.Shaw	1	-	-	-	-	-	-	-	-	-	10	1	45	3	15.00	4.50	3-45
J.W.Sheed	9	8	1	40	143	20.42	-	-	2	-							
M.S.Sinclair	8	7	1	79*	273	45.50	-	3	1	-	5.4	0	42	1	42.00	7.42	1-15
C.M.Smith	1	1	0	1	1	1.00	-	-	-	-	9	0	58	1	58.00	6.44	1-58
S.L.Stewart	9	9	0	73	285	31.66	-	2	-	-							
S.B.Styris	6	6	2	74*	197	49.25	-	1	4	-	22	2	92	5	18.40	4.18	4-38
E.P.Thompson	8	7	2	50*	94	18.80	-	1	3	-	69	5	336	13	25.84	4.87	3-65
G.R.Todd	11	10	0	53	314	31.40	-	2	3	-	6	0	33	0	-	5.50	-
K.W.M.Todd	1	1	0	8	8	8.00	-	-	-	-							
D.R.Tuffey	10	8	1	32*	134	19.14	-	-	3	-	91.5	9	417	6	69.50	4.54	2-25
N.M.Turner	7	3	2	2*	3	3.00	-	-	1	-	48.3	7	206	7	29.42	4.24	3-32
C.F.K.van Wyk	8	8	6	85*	260	130.00	-	2	3	3							
L.Vincent	8	8	0	129	290	36.25	1	1	2	-	11.2	0	59	2	29.50	5.20	2-25
L.J.Vivian	6	6	1	18*	57	11.40	-	-	2	-							
B-J.Watling	6	6	0	35	61	10.16	-	-	1	-							
T.I.Weston	1	1	0	11	11	11.00	-	-	-	-							
L.J.Woodcock	10	7	3	47	130	32.50	-	-	2	-	80	3	351	11	31.90	4.39	3-20
R.A.Young	10	7	2	68	211	42.20	-	2	17	2							
J.A.F.Yovich	8	8	2	50	159	26.50	-	1	2	-	29	1	160	5	32.00	5.52	3-43

HIGHEST STRIKE RATES *(qualification 150 runs)*

		Runs	Balls	S/R
G.J.Hopkins	*O*	207	186	111
J.D.Ryder	*W*	196	197	99
R.A.Young	*A*	211	216	97
J.A.H.Marshall	*ND*	308	326	94
M.E.Parlane	*W*	307	348	88
L.Vincent	*A*	290	338	85
C.F.K.van Wyk	*C*	260	305	85
G.D.Elliott	*W*	286	339	84
S.B.Styris	*A*	197	234	84
R.A.Jones	*A*	360	446	80

MOST ECONOMICAL BOWLING *(qualification 30 overs)*

		O	M	R	W	Ave	R/O
R.J.Nicol	*A*	77.4	1	280	9	31.11	3.60
D.J.Bowden	*W*	68	6	264	8	33.00	3.88
N.L.McCullum	*O*	88	4	342	9	38.00	3.89
C.J.M.Furlong	*CD*	77	2	302	9	33.55	3.92
C.Z.Harris	*C*	72	1	286	9	31.77	3.97
C.S.Martin	*A*	78.2	8	319	13	24.53	4.07
B.E.Scott	*O*	99.2	11	408	12	34.00	4.10
M.Burns	*W*	39	4	161	6	26.83	4.13
N.M.Turner	*O*	48.3	7	206	7	29.42	4.24
L.J.Woodcock	*W*	80	3	351	11	31.90	4.39

CAREER RECORDS

	M	In	NO	HS	Runs	Ave	100s	50s	Ct	St	O	M	R	W	Ave	R/O	Best
A.R.Adams	43	35	8	47	414	15.33	-	-	10	-	367.5	28	1589	65	24.44	4.31	5-7
G.W.Aldridge	67	37	18	28	277	14.57	-	-	13	-	501	36	2299	98	23.45	4.59	5-34
B.J.Arnel	12	5	3	11*	27	13.50	-	-	2	-	85.5	4	469	11	42.63	5.46	2-30
T.D.Astle	1	1	0	9	9	9.00	-	-	-	-	6	0	43	0	-	7.17	-
G.E.F.Barnett	19	19	1	91	416	23.11	-	3	3	-							
M.D.Bell	109	104	8	121*	2462	25.64	3	12	56	-	0.2	0	4	0	-	-	-
H.K.Bennett	10	1	0	0	0	0.00	-	-	-	-	63.3	2	369	7	52.71	5.81	3-29
D.J.Bowden	10	8	6	25*	89	44.50	-	-	2	-	68	6	264	8	33.00	3.88	2-37
N.T.Broom	27	25	5	93	711	35.55	-	5	8	-	19	0	105	2	52.50	5.53	1-13
M.Burns	6	-	-	-	-	-	-	-	-	-	39	4	161	6	26.83	4.13	2-15
L.M.Burtt	9	2	1	5*	10	10.00	-	-	-	-	64.1	5	355	14	25.35	5.53	5-26
I.G.Butler	28	19	5	47	224	16.00	-	-	4	-	200	13	1015	32	31.71	5.08	3-15
S.P.Chan	6	3	1	6	11	5.50	-	-	1	-	32	0	213	3	71.00	6.66	1-21
C.P.Cruikshank	1	-	-	-	-	-	-	-	-	-	5	0	35	0	-	7.00	-
C.D.Cumming	83	78	1	112	1869	24.27	2	11	34	-	332	12	1506	33	45.63	4.54	2-18
T.T.Davis	4	-	-	-	-	-	-	-	1	-	22.1	0	173	3	57.66	7.80	2-41
C.de Grandhomme	2	2	1	38	38	38.00	-	-	1	-							
A.P.Devcich	3	3	0	35	57	19.00	-	-	2	-	20	0	115	1	115.00	5.75	1-42
B.J.Diamanti	28	17	3	60	213	15.21	-	1	10	-	216.5	17	1002	41	24.43	4.62	5-58
G.D.Elliott	16	11	3	107*	322	40.25	1	2	4	-	109.4	3	551	20	27.55	5.02	4-29
A.M.Ellis	11	8	1	46	157	22.42	-	-	3	-	22	1	122	3	40.66	5.55	2-45
A.W.Evans	23	22	1	89	661	31.47	-	4	9	-	4	0	27	0	-	6.75	-
S.A.Fairley	2	2	1	28	28	28.00	-	-	-	-							
B.R.Findlay	13	10	2	14*	56	7.00	-	-	1	-	44	1	284	5	56.80	6.45	2-35
D.R.Flynn	20	20	2	82	479	26.61	-	4	3	-	12	0	69	1	69.00	5.75	1-49
K.A.Forde	1	-	-	-	-	-	-	-	-	-	4.2	1	15	2	7.50	3.46	2-15
C.Frauenstein	4	4	0	48	73	18.25	-	-	1	-	12	0	75	2	37.50	6.25	2-49
C.J.M.Furlong	68	51	19	62*	720	22.50	-	1	29	-	555.5	37	2248	67	33.55	4.04	4-9
C.B.Gaffaney	107	104	7	101*	2357	24.29	1	11	33	-	6	0	36	1	36.00	6.00	1-4
B.B.J.Griggs	59	43	8	59	619	17.68	-	2	74	3							
M.J.Guptill	9	8	1	36	128	18.28	-	-	3	-							
S.B.Haig	5	5	0	17	37	7.40	-	-	-	1							
C.Z.Harris	122	111	37	107	3385	45.74	1	20	69	-	957.3	65	3473	125	27.78	3.62	4-28
M.J.Harvie	13	9	5	19*	60	15.00	-	-	-	-	96.5	6	500	20	25.00	5.16	5-40
G.R.Hay	7	6	3	55	215	71.66	-	2	1	-							
B.E.Hefford	35	16	6	16*	60	6.00	-	-	6	-	273.3	28	1160	52	22.30	4.24	3-13
G.J.T.Hegglun	14	6	4	5*	11	5.50	-	-	3	-	111.3	10	495	15	33.00	4.43	4-60
B.C.Hiini	9	6	4	20*	56	28.00	-	-	2	-	76	5	394	11	35.81	5.18	3-38
R.M.Hira	9	5	2	4*	10	3.33	-	-	1	-	70	4	320	13	24.61	4.57	4-31
P.A.Hitchcock	73	65	15	108	1133	22.66	2	1	16	-	598.3	37	2779	113	24.59	4.64	5-10
G.J.Hopkins	90	75	12	82	1515	24.04	-	6	87	16							
N.K.W.Horsley	36	36	2	89*	695	20.44	-	3	7	-							
D.W.Houpapa	10	10	2	101	261	32.62	1	1	2	-							
J.M.How	47	46	1	95	1287	28.60	-	11	22	-	48	1	242	5	48.40	5.04	1-17
P.J.Ingram	16	16	1	104	506	33.73	2	2	1	-							
M.R.Jefferson	77	53	18	48*	509	14.54	-	-	17	-	514.3	35	2134	60	35.56	4.14	4-32
R.A.Jones	98	97	6	92	2216	24.35	-	10	25	-							
M.B.Loye	2	2	0	90	124	62.00	-	1	-	-							
H.J.H.Marshall	74	71	6	93	1523	23.43	-	10	31	-	3	0	18	1	18.00	6.00	1-14
J.A.H.Marshall	71	69	7	152*	2184	35.22	2	14	31	-	48.1	1	269	4	67.25	5.58	1-20
B.P.Martin	41	29	7	33	285	12.95	-	-	15	-	333.2	22	1231	45	27.35	3.69	4-28
C.S.Martin	71	25	14	13	53	4.81	-	-	12	-	593.3	55	2688	103	26.09	4.52	5-43
M.J.Mason	66	38	14	20	216	9.00	-	-	14	-	514	60	2101	95	22.11	4.09	6-25
N.L.McCullum	53	44	10	65	550	16.17	-	2	17	-	369	17	1610	41	39.26	4.36	3-23
P.D.McGlashan	44	41	12	87	973	33.55	-	5	46	7							
C.D.McMillan	88	84	12	125	2550	35.41	7	9	36	-	185.2	8	926	35	26.45	4.99	5-38
W.C.McSkimming	62	48	15	59*	469	14.21	-	1	19	-	502.3	45	2261	76	29.75	4.49	5-9
K.D.Mills	51	43	11	55	717	22.40	-	2	14	-	421.1	43	1727	68	25.39	4.10	4-40
S.M.Mills	10	8	1	65	251	35.85	-	2	13	2							
C.Munro	1	-	-	-	-	-	-	-	-	-	4	0	21	0	-	5.25	-
C.J.Nevin	112	106	6	149	2823	28.23	5	13	144	12							
R.J.Nicol	45	45	6	88*	1118	28.66	-	7	17	-	115.4	2	466	14	33.28	4.02	3-39
I.E.O'Brien	19	7	5	1*	3	1.50	-	-	4	-	165	14	744	28	26.57	4.51	5-35
J.D.P.Oram	50	45	4	127	1260	30.73	2	6	16	-	204	20	782	28	27.92	3.83	3-44
M.G.Orchard	36	29	7	79	455	20.68	-	1	11	-	247.4	15	1160	33	35.15	4.68	4-47

	M	In	NO	HS	Runs	Ave	100s	50s	Ct	St	O	M	R	W	Ave	R/O	Best
M.H.W.Papps	53	53	6	137*	1962	41.74	4	11	33	2							
M.E.Parlane	119	119	7	132	3351	29.91	4	20	20	-	0.3	0	5	0	-	-	-
N.R.Parlane	78	72	4	96*	1613	23.72	-	10	37	-							
M.Y.Pasupati	69	53	13	42	681	17.02	-	-	12	-	435.4	15	2163	69	31.34	4.96	4-33
J.S.Patel	22	13	4	22*	76	8.44	-	-	9	-	179.5	5	814	19	42.84	4.52	3-19
S.Rasmussen	12	4	1	1	2	0.66	-	-	1	-	82	4	436	10	43.60	5.32	3-39
A.J.Redmond	49	47	4	72	915	21.27	-	5	13	-	119	1	617	17	36.29	5.18	3-40
I.A.Robertson	13	12	0	60	213	17.75	-	1	2	-	62	1	279	5	55.80	4.50	3-58
S.P.Robertson	17	15	1	42	220	15.71	-	-	5	-	58.1	5	264	13	20.30	4.53	4-51
G.G.Robinson	13	13	3	77*	303	30.30	-	2	7	-							
J.D.Ryder	40	39	2	63	803	21.70	-	5	13	-	110	2	628	22	28.54	5.71	4-39
R.J.Schaw	2	-	-	-	-	-	-	-	-	-	17	0	83	2	41.50	4.88	2-46
B.E.Scott	41	27	12	44	319	21.26	-	-	11	-	346.3	23	1595	52	30.67	4.60	4-63
L.J.Shaw	5	4	0	20	37	9.25	-	-	-	-	26	2	133	4	33.25	5.12	3-45
J.W.Sheed	23	18	2	49	319	19.93	-	-	6	-							
M.S.Sinclair	98	95	12	110	2670	32.16	1	21	48	1	5.4	0	42	1	42.00	7.42	1-15
C.M.Smith	2	1	0	1	1	1.00	-	-	2	-	14	0	89	1	89.00	6.36	1-58
S.L.Stewart	53	52	4	102	1494	31.12	2	5	10	-							
S.B.Styris	80	73	18	123	1957	35.58	1	12	35	-	557	46	2389	98	24.37	4.29	4-19
E.P.Thompson	35	21	4	50*	198	11.64	-	1	9	-	270	25	1152	52	22.15	4.27	4-22
G.R.Todd	31	28	4	54*	570	23.75	-	3	12	-	71.3	2	378	12	31.50	5.28	2-23
K.W.M.Todd	3	3	0	8	18	6.00	-	-	-	-							
D.R.Tuffey	71	38	20	32*	328	18.22	-	-	19	-	561.3	44	2426	75	32.34	4.32	3-11
N.M.Turner	7	3	2	2*	3	3.00	-	-	1	-	48.3	7	206	7	29.42	4.24	3-32
C.F.K.van Wyk	8	8	6	85*	260	130.00	-	2	3	3							
L.Vincent	58	56	3	145	1685	31.79	3	9	55	3	16	0	78	3	26.00	4.88	2-25
L.J.Vivian	6	6	1	18*	57	11.40	-	-	2	-							
B-J.Watling	16	16	1	116*	381	25.40	1	3	5	-							
T.I.Weston	1	1	0	11	11	11.00	-	-	-	-							
L.J.Woodcock	36	28	6	71	501	22.77	-	1	10	-	194.3	4	917	19	48.26	4.71	4-36
R.A.Young	49	39	12	68	624	23.11	-	2	61	12							
J.A.F.Yovich	79	67	14	70	1056	19.92	-	5	25	-	422.5	21	2258	89	25.37	5.34	4-44

STATE TWENTY20

2006/07

The second season of domestic Twenty20 competition saw the six teams play a full round-robin of 15 matches, whereas in 2005/06 they had been split into two groups. Auckland finished at the top of the table and hosted second placed Otago in the final.

In the event of the scores being level at the end of a match, a bowl out was to be used to find the winner. If that was not possible, the toss of a coin would have decided the result. Fielding restrictions remained in place for the first six overs while a foot-fault no-ball cost two runs and was followed by a free hit.

Chris Harris (from 51 balls) scored the only century while the fastest fifty was made by David Houpapa (20 balls).

Final points were:

	P	*W*	*L*	*NR*	*Points*
Auckland	5	4	1	–	16
Otago	5	3	1	1	14
Canterbury	5	3	2	–	12
Wellington	5	2	2	1	10
Central Districts	5	1	4	–	4
Northern Districts	5	1	4	–	4

AUCKLAND v WELLINGTON — State Twenty20

at Eden Park Outer Oval, Auckland on 11 January, 2007
Toss : Auckland. Umpires : R.D. Anderson & B.F. Bowden
***Auckland won by 7 wickets.** Points: Auckland 4, Wellington 0*

WELLINGTON

	Runs	Mins	Balls	6s	4s
M.E.Parlane* c Houpapa b Mills	4	2	3	-	1
M.D.Bell b Mills	2	12	8	-	-
C.J.Nevin c Young b Styris	18	24	13	-	2
N.R.Parlane c Young b Styris	13	12	10	-	3
G.D.Elliott b Hitchcock	6	13	10	-	-
S.M.Mills† not out	53	48	46	1	4
D.J.Bowden c Hira b Pasupati	7	10	5	-	1
L.J.Woodcock not out	36	27	25	2	1
K.A.Forde					
M.Burns					
S.Rasmussen					
Extras (lb 3, w 6)	9				
TOTAL (20 overs) (6 wkts)	**148**	76			

AUCKLAND

	Runs	Mins	Balls	6s	4s
P.A.Hitchcock c Elliott b Forde	36	36	29	-	5
L.Vincent b Elliott	35	56	43	1	2
R.A.Jones* not out	47	30	29	2	4
S.B.Styris c Parlane M.E. b Elliott	18	10	11	2	-
D.W.Houpapa not out	4	1	1	-	1
R.J.Nicol					
K.D.Mills					
R.A.Young†					
M.Y.Pasupati					
R.M.Hira					
C.S.Martin					
Extras (b 1, lb 1, w 4, nb 4)	10				
TOTAL (18.3 overs) (3 wkts)	**150**	69			

Bowling	*O*	*M*	*R*	*W*
AUCKLAND				
Mills	4	0	20	2
Martin	4	0	31	0
Styris	4	0	35	2
Hitchcock	4	0	37	1
Pasupati	2	0	8	1
Hira	2	0	14	0
WELLINGTON				
Bowden	4	0	17	0
Rasmussen	4	0	39	0
Forde	2	0	12	1
Burns	2	0	26	0
Elliott	3.3	0	25	2
Woodcock	3	0	29	0

Fall of Wickets

	W	***A***
1st	4	62
2nd	11	112
3rd	42	146
4th	43	-
5th	64	-
6th	88	-
7th	-	-
8th	-	-
9th	-	-
10th	-	-

CENTRAL DISTRICTS v CANTERBURY — State Twenty20

at Pukekura Park, New Plymouth on 11 January, 2007
Toss : Canterbury. Umpires : D.M. Brandon & D.J. Walker
***Central Districts won by 76 runs.** Points: Central Districts 4, Canterbury 0*

CENTRAL DISTRICTS

	Runs	Mins	Balls	6s	4s
J.M.How* c Chan b Small	11	7	7	-	2
G.E.F.Barnett b Harris	39	28	21	1	6
P.J.Ingram c Harris b Chan	0	1	3	-	-
M.S.Sinclair c Ellis b Small	0	5	3	-	-
J.D.P.Oram b Frauenstein	57	37	28	6	3
G.R.Hay b Hiini	23	30	24	-	2
B.B.J.Griggs† run out	14	13	9	-	2
E.P.Thompson b Harris	2	8	6	-	-1
B.J.Diamanti c Ellis b Frauenstein	12	13	13	-	1
R.J.Schaw not out	8	11	8	-	-
B.E.Hefford					
Extras (b 4, lb 7, w 1, nb 2)	14				
TOTAL (20 overs) (9 wkts)	**180**	80			

CANTERBURY

	Runs	Mins	Balls	6s	4s
S.L.Stewart c Hefford b Thompson	15	23	14	-	2
M.H.W.Papps b Thompson	8	9	8	-	2
I.A.Robertson b Thompson	0	1	1	-	-
C.Z.Harris* lbw b Thompson	2	10	6	-	-
C.Frauenstein b Schaw	22	17	18	-	4
A.M.Ellis c Sinclair b Schaw	12	22	12	-	1
B.R.Findlay c Oram b How	26	21	20	1	2
C.F.K.van Wyk† c Sinclair b Diamanti	4	5	5	-	-
C.A.Small c Sinclair b Diamanti	3	5	5	-	-
S.P.Chan not out	0	5	2	-	-
B.C.Hiini st Griggs b Schaw	0	2	2	-	-
Extras (b 2, lb 1, w 7, nb 2)	12				
TOTAL (15.2 overs)	**104**	66			

Bowling	O	M	R	W
CANTERBURY				
Chan	4	0	30	1
Small	3	0	28	2
Harris	4	0	15	2
Hiini	4	0	34	1
Findlay	1	0	24	0
Robertson	1	0	17	0
Frauenstein	3	0	21	2
CENTRAL DISTRICTS				
Hefford	2	0	19	0
Oram	3	0	19	0
Thompson	2	0	12	4
How	3	0	22	1
Schaw	3.2	0	21	3
Diamanti	2	0	8	2

Fall of Wickets	***CD***	***C***
1st	24	24
2nd	24	24
3rd	30	33
4th	60	38
5th	135	65
6th	145	74
7th	159	81
8th	160	95
9th	180	104
10th	-	104

OTAGO v NORTHERN DISTRICTS — State Twenty20

at University Oval, Dunedin on 11 January, 2007
Toss : Northern Districts. Umpires : E.J. Gray & W.R. Knights
***Otago won by 100 runs.** Points: Otago 4, Northern Districts 0*

OTAGO

	Runs	Mins	Balls	6s	4s
C.B.Gaffaney c Horsley b Arnel	27	21	24	-	5
C.D.Cumming* c Yovich b Aldridge	9	15	8	-	1
S.B.Haig c McGlashan b Aldridge	0	3	1	-	-
N.T.Broom b Yovich	33	29	23	1	4
K.Noema-Barnett run out	30	20	16	2	3
G.R.Todd b Orchard	30	27	24	-	4
G.J.Hopkins† c Arnel b Butler	1	2	2	-	-
N.L.McCullum c Marshall b Orchard	26	15	14	2	2
B.E.Scott not out	16	6	4	1	2
N.Turner not out	1	4	5	-	-
J.M.McMillan					
Extras (lb 6, w 4, nb 2)	12				
TOTAL (20 overs) (8 wkts)	**185**	75			

NORTHERN DISTRICTS

	Runs	Mins	Balls	6s	4s
N.K.W.Horsley run out	1	9	5	-	-
P.D.McGlashan† b McMillan	24	18	15	2	1
D.R.Flynn c Scott b McMillan	2	2	4	-	-
J.A.H.Marshall* b McMillan	4	15	10	-	-
A.P.Devcich c Scott b McCullum	19	20	16	-	2
J.A.F.Yovich b McCullum	14	14	14	-	2
I.G.Butler b McCullum	0	1	1	-	-
M.G.Orchard run out	4	6	7	-	-
A.W.Evans st Hopkins b Broom	6	9	8	-	-
G.W.Aldridge c Todd b McCullum	2	7	4	-	-
B.J.Arnel not out	1	2	4	-	-
Extras (b 1, lb 4, w 3)	8				
TOTAL (14.4 overs)	**85**	56			

Bowling	O	M	R	W
NORTHERN DISTRICTS				
Aldridge	4	0	25	2
Arnel	4	0	37	1
Yovich	4	0	45	1
Orchard	4	0	29	2
Butler	4	0	43	1
OTAGO				
McMillan	4	0	15	3
Scott	2	0	23	0
Turner	2	0	9	0
McCullum	3.4	0	16	4
Broom	3	0	17	1

Fall of Wickets	***O***	***ND***
1st	38	25
2nd	41	27
3rd	41	29
4th	95	44
5th	115	67
6th	120	68
7th	165	69
8th	165	75
9th	-	83
10th	-	85

NORTHERN DISTRICTS v CENTRAL DISTRICTS State Twenty20

at Seddon Park, Hamilton on 13 January, 2007 (d/n)
Toss : Northern Districts. Umpires : R.D. Anderson & A.L. Hill
***Northern Districts won by 1 run.** Points: Northern Districts 4, Central Districts 0*

NORTHERN DISTRICTS

	Runs	Mins	Balls	6s	4s
A.W.Evans c Griggs b Oram	1	4	4	-	-
P.D.McGlashan† c Hay b Thompson	5	10	9	-	-
D.R.Flynn b Furlong	18	18	11	1	2
J.A.H.Marshall* st Griggs b Schaw	54	32	35	1	6
A.P.Devcich run out	0	1	1	-	-
I.G.Butler c Hay b How	9	12	12	1	-
J.A.F.Yovich st Griggs b Diamanti	10	16	14	-	-
M.G.Orchard not out	28	31	22	-	3
T.G.Southee b Thompson	2	5	5	-	-
D.R.Tuffey c How b Diamanti	3	10	5	-	-
B.J.Arnel b Diamanti	1	2	3	-	-
Extras (lb 5, w 6, nb 2)	13				
TOTAL (20 overs)	**144**	75			

CENTRAL DISTRICTS

	Runs	Mins	Balls	6s	4s
G.E.F.Barnett b Tuffey	12	19	16	1	1
J.M.How* c Southee b Tuffey	16	22	14	-	3
P.J.Ingram c Butler b Southee	27	31	24	-	3
M.S.Sinclair c McGlashan b Orchard	11	9	6	1	-
J.D.P.Oram c Arnel b Orchard	19	14	14	-	4
G.R.Hay not out	14	33	18	-	1
B.B.J.Griggs† b Orchard	0	2	2	-	-
B.J.Diamanti run out	4	3	4	-	1
E.P.Thompson b Butler	27	16	20	2	1
R.J.Schaw run out	3	1	2	-	-
C.J.M.Furlong not out	0	2	1	-	-
Extras (lb 6, w 2, nb 2)	10				
TOTAL (20 overs) (9 wkts)	**143**	61			

Bowling	*O*	*M*	*R*	*W*
CENTRAL DISTRICTS				
Thompson	4	0	25	2
Oram	4	0	36	1
Furlong	3	0	18	1
Schaw	4	0	24	1
How	1	0	12	1
Diamanti	4	0	24	3
NORTHERN DISTRICTS				
Tuffey	4	1	33	2
Arnel	3	0	21	0
Yovich	2	0	20	0
Orchard	4	0	26	3
Southee	4	0	25	1
Butler	3	0	12	1

Fall of Wickets

	ND	*CD*
1st	5	34
2nd	13	35
3rd	45	51
4th	45	85
5th	85	96
6th	92	98
7th	110	102
8th	115	138
9th	141	141
10th	144	-

AUCKLAND v OTAGO State Twenty20

at Eden Park Outer Oval, Auckland on 14 January, 2007
Toss : Otago. Umpires : P.D. Jones & E.A. Watkin
***Otago won by 14 runs.** Points: Otago 4, Auckland 0*

OTAGO

	Runs	Mins	Balls	6s	4s
C.B.Gaffaney c Pasupati b Hira	43	35	29	1	5
C.D.Cumming* c Houpapa b Mills	1	11	5	-	-
A.J.Redmond c Jones b Mills	7	11	6	1	-
G.J.Hopkins† c Nicol b Styris	47	45	30	4	2
G.R.Todd run out	30	22	22	1	2
N.T.Broom c Pasupati b Martin	10	18	10	-	1
K.Noema-Barnett b Hitchcock	1	4	3	-	-
N.L.McCullum not out	20	13	12	1	2
B.E.Scott not out	4	8	5	-	-
W.C.McSkimming					
J.M.McMillan					
Extras (lb 7, w 1, nb 4, pen 6)	18				
TOTAL (20 overs) (7 wkts)	**181**	86			

AUCKLAND

	Runs	Mins	Balls	6s	4s
P.A.Hitchcock b McSkimming	0	1	2	-	-
L.Vincent run out	11	18	12	-	2
R.A.Jones* run out	75	75	57	2	7
S.B.Styris b McMillan	2	3	4	-	-
R.J.Nicol run out	1	4	2	-	-
D.W.Houpapa c McSkimming b Cumming	26	21	17	2	2
K.D.Mills c Broom b McCullum	10	13	11	-	1
M.Y.Pasupati c Broom b McCullum	28	15	14	1	3
R.A.Young† not out	1	3	1	-	-
R.M.Hira not out	0	1	1	-	-
C.S.Martin					
Extras (lb 2, w 9, nb 2)	13				
TOTAL (20 overs) (8 wkts)	**167**	81			

Bowling	*O*	*M*	*R*	*W*
AUCKLAND				
Mills	4	0	27	2
Martin	4	0	33	1
Styris	3	0	39	1
Hira	2	0	10	1
Hitchcock	4	0	22	1
Nicol	1	0	15	0
Pasupati	2	0	22	0
OTAGO				
McSkimming	3	0	22	1
McMillan	4	0	27	1
Scott	4	0	28	0
McCullum	4	0	42	2
Broom	3	0	33	0
Cumming	2	0	13	1

Fall of Wickets

	O	*A*
1st	11	0
2nd	26	29
3rd	60	37
4th	116	42
5th	137	97
6th	141	125
7th	149	158
8th	-	166
9th	-	-
10th	-	-

CANTERBURY v WELLINGTON — State Twenty20

at Queen Elizabeth II Park, Christchurch on 14 January, 2007
Toss : Wellington. Umpires : G.A. Baxter & B.G. Frost
***Canterbury won by 9 wickets.** Points: Canterbury 4, Wellington 0*

WELLINGTON

	Runs	Mins	Balls	6s	4s
M.E.Parlane* lbw b Hiini	2	7	3	-	-
J.D.Ryder c Findlay b Harris	19	11	13	1	1
C.J.Nevin c Harris b Robertson	23	27	25	-	2
N.R.Parlane b Hiini	63	41	46	-	6
G.D.Elliott run out	1	3	5	-	-
S.M.Mills† not out	37	24	18	2	3
D.J.Bowden not out	17	10	10	-	2
K.A.Forde					
L.J.Woodcock					
S.Rasmussen					
I.E.O'Brien					
Extras (lb 1, w 6)	7				
TOTAL (20 overs) (5 wkts)	**169**	64			

CANTERBURY

	Runs	Mins	Balls	6s	4s
S.L.Stewart not out	66	64	45	1	7
M.H.W.Papps b Woodcock	66	53	53	-	10
C.Z.Harris* not out	25	10	12	-	4
I.A.Robertson					
C.F.K.van Wyk†					
B.R.Findlay					
B.C.Hiini					
S.P.Chan					
A.M.Ellis					
C.A.Small					
C.Frauenstein					
Extras (lb 5, w 4, nb 4)	13				
TOTAL (18 overs) (1 wkt)	**170**	64			

Bowling	*O*	*M*	*R*	*W*
CANTERBURY				
Hiini	4	0	25	2
Small	1	0	12	0
Harris	4	0	30	1
Frauenstein	3	0	33	0
Robertson	4	0	31	1
Chan	2	0	22	0
Findlay	2	0	15	0
WELLINGTON				
O'Brien	2	0	16	0
Rasmussen	2	0	17	0
Forde	2	0	24	0
Bowden	2	0	16	0
Elliott	3	0	30	0
Woodcock	4	0	31	1
Ryder	3	0	31	0

Fall of Wickets	***W***	***C***
1st	20	136
2nd	22	-
3rd	93	-
4th	96	-
5th	136	-
6th	-	-
7th	-	-
8th	-	-
9th	-	-
10th	-	-

WELLINGTON v NORTHERN DISTRICTS — State Twenty20

at Allied Prime Basin Reserve, Wellington on 19 January, 2007
Toss : Wellington. Umpires : D.M. Quested & D.J. Walker
***Wellington won by 6 wickets.** Points: Wellington 4, Northern Districts 0*

NORTHERN DISTRICTS

	Runs	Mins	Balls	6s	4s
A.W.Evans c Parlane M.E. b Bowden	45	46	37	-	6
A.P.Devcich b Rasmussen	8	9	5	-	2
P.D.McGlashan† b Bowden	5	4	3	-	1
J.A.H.Marshall* b Ryder	27	26	26	-	3
D.R.Flynn c Rasmussen b O'Brien	23	19	18	-	2
I.G.Butler c Parlane M.E. b O'Brien	21	15	12	2	-
M.G.Orchard not out	10	11	8	-	1
J.A.F.Yovich b O'Brien	3	4	4	-	-
B.P.Martin st Mills b Elliott	2	3	5	-	-
D.R.Tuffey not out	2	2	2	-	-
B.J.Arnel					
Extras (lb 4)	4				
TOTAL (20 overs) (8 wkts)	**150**	74			

WELLINGTON

	Runs	Mins	Balls	6s	4s
C.J.Nevin c Evans b Tuffey	1	5	5	-	-
J.D.Ryder b Martin	60	54	39	2	6
M.E.Parlane* c Butler b Arnel	10	5	8	1	-
N.R.Parlane c Tuffey b Yovich	39	32	31	-	5
G.D.Elliott not out	16	20	14	-	2
S.M.Mills† not out	14	20	11	-	3
L.J.Woodcock					
D.J.Bowden					
M.Burns					
I.E.O'Brien					
S.Rasmussen					
Extras (lb 12)	12				
TOTAL (18 overs) (4 wkts)	**152**	65			

Bowling	*O*	*M*	*R*	*W*
WELLINGTON				
Rasmussen	2	0	15	1
Burns	1	0	16	0
Bowden	3	0	13	2
O'Brien	4	0	21	3
Ryder	4	0	33	1
Woodcock	2	0	15	0
Elliott	4	0	33	1
NORTHERN DISTRICTS				
Arnel	3	0	16	1
Tuffey	4	0	35	1
Orchard	3	0	30	0
Yovich	3	0	29	1
Martin	4	0	23	1
Butler	1	0	7	0

Fall of Wickets	***ND***	***W***
1st	25	5
2nd	34	16
3rd	86	108
4th	96	128
5th	133	-
6th	133	-
7th	140	-
8th	143	-
9th	-	-
10th	-	-

CENTRAL DISTRICTS v OTAGO — State Twenty20

at McLean Park, Napier on 20 January, 2007
Toss : Otago. Umpires : T.J. Parlane & E.A. Watkin
***Otago won by 46 runs.** Points: Otago 4, Central Districts 0*

OTAGO

	Runs	Mins	Balls	6s	4s
C.B.Gaffaney c Hay b Thompson	23	17	15	-	4
C.D.Cumming* lbw b Thompson	5	7	5	-	1
A.J.Redmond c Sinclair b Furlong	59	43	34	2	7
N.T.Broom run out	3	10	9	-	-
G.J.Hopkins† b Thompson	24	25	17	-	3
G.R.Todd c Furlong b Thompson	2	5	6	-	-
K.Noema-Barnett c Barnett b Thompson	5	8	5	-	-
N.L.McCullum b Diamanti	0	2	1	-	-
B.E.Scott not out	20	19	19	-	2
M.J.Harvie c Hegglun b Hamilton	10	16	12	-	-
J.M.McMillan					
Extras (b 5, lb 3, w 4, nb 4)	16				
TOTAL (20 overs) (9 wkts)	**167**	79			

CENTRAL DISTRICTS

	Runs	Mins	Balls	6s	4s
G.E.F.Barnett b McMillan	13	12	10	-	1
J.M.How* c McMillan b Broom	45	61	45	1	2
P.J.Ingram c Scott b Harvie	4	3	2	-	1
M.S.Sinclair c Gaffaney b McCullum	13	13	13	-	2
G.R.Hay b Redmond	8	10	6	-	1
B.B.J.Griggs† run out	1	3	3	-	-
B.J.Diamanti c Cumming b Redmond	4	5	5	-	-
E.P.Thompson b Redmond	2	3	4	-	-
C.J.M.Furlong lbw b Redmond	1	1	2	-	-
G.J.T.Hegglun not out	13	17	10	-	2
L.J.Hamilton b McMillan	10	13	14	1	-
Extras (lb 3, w 4)	7				
TOTAL (19 overs)	**121**	75			

Bowling	O	M	R	W
CENTRAL DISTRICTS				
Hamilton	4	0	17	1
Thompson	4	0	32	5
Hegglun	3	0	18	0
Furlong	4	0	40	1
Diamanti	4	0	33	1
How	1	0	19	0
OTAGO				
McMillan	4	0	18	2
Harvie	3	0	24	1
Scott	3	0	20	0
McCullum	4	0	27	1
Redmond	4	0	24	4
Broom	1	0	5	1

Fall of Wickets	***O***	***CD***
1st	10	18
2nd	36	25
3rd	48	50
4th	127	68
5th	130	71
6th	132	84
7th	133	93
8th	137	95
9th	167	98
10th	-	121

CANTERBURY v AUCKLAND — State Twenty20

at Queen Elizabeth II Park, Christchurch on 21 January, 2007
Toss : Auckland. Umpires : B.G. Frost & T.J. Parlane
***Auckland won by 15 runs.** Points: Auckland 4, Canterbury 0*

AUCKLAND

	Runs	Mins	Balls	6s	4s
P.A.Hitchcock run out	77	66	50	3	7
L.Vincent c Burtt b Findlay	47	37	31	3	4
R.A.Jones* c Robertson b Findlay	2	6	7	-	-
R.J.Nicol c Harris b Burtt	41	25	26	-	5
D.W.Houpapa not out	14	6	6	1	-
K.W.M.Todd not out	1	2	1	-	-
R.A.Young†					
M.J.Guptill					
M.Y.Pasupati					
R.M.Hira					
C.S.Martin					
Extras (lb 8, w 6, nb 2)	16				
TOTAL (20 overs) (4 wkts)	**198**	73			

CANTERBURY

	Runs	Mins	Balls	6s	4s
S.L.Stewart b Martin	3	6	6	-	-
M.H.W.Papps c Hira b Pasupati	53	41	34	2	6
I.A.Robertson c Vincent b Pasupati	0	9	9	-	-
C.Z.Harris* b Martin	100	56	52	6	8
A.M.Ellis run out	8	4	3	-	2
C.Frauenstein b Hira	7	16	12	-	-
B.R.Findlay not out	6	1	4	-	1
B.C.Hiini not out	1	1	1	-	-
C.F.K.van Wyk †					
L.M.Burtt					
H.K.Bennett					
Extras (lb 2, w 1, nb 2)	5				
TOTAL (20 overs) (6 wkts)	**183**	75			

Bowling	O	M	R	W
CANTERBURY				
Bennett	2	0	22	0
Burtt	4	0	33	1
Harris	4	0	47	0
Findlay	4	0	18	2
Hiini	2	0	33	0
Robertson	4	0	37	0
AUCKLAND				
Hitchcock	4	0	37	0
Martin	4	0	37	2
Pasupati	4	0	35	2
Nicol	4	0	32	0
Hira	4	0	40	1

Fall of Wickets	***A***	***C***
1st	98	7
2nd	105	22
3rd	174	88
4th	184	100
5th	-	150
6th	-	182
7th	-	-
8th	-	-
9th	-	-
10th	-	-

WELLINGTON v CENTRAL DISTRICTS — State Twenty20

at Allied Prime Basin Reserve, Wellington on 26 January, 2007
Toss : Wellington. Umpires : D.M. Brandon & B.G. Frost
***Wellington won by 6 wickets.** Points: Wellington 4, Central Districts 0*

CENTRAL DISTRICTS

	Runs	Mins	Balls	6s	4s
G.E.F.Barnett lbw b Bowden	19	24	15	-	3
J.M.How* lbw b Houghton	63	41	39	-	3
P.J.Ingram c Burns b Houghton	7	9	10	-	1
M.S.Sinclair c Ryder b Elliott	0	3	3	-	-
G.R.Hay not out	27	31	19	-	3
B.B.J.Griggs† c & b Houghton	22	14	16	1	1
B.J.Diamanti not out	36	15	19	1	3
E.P.Thompson					
R.J.Schaw					
G.J.T.Hegglun					
B.E.Hefford					
Extras (lb 3, w 1, nb 2)	6				
TOTAL (20 overs) (5 wkts)	**180**	70			

WELLINGTON

	Runs	Mins	Balls	6s	4s
C.J.Nevin not out	87	71	53	3	8
J.D.Ryder b Hefford	1	3	2	-	-
M.E.Parlane* lbw b Hefford	0	1	1	-	-
N.R.Parlane lbw b Thompson	6	9	5	-	1
G.D.Elliott c How b Hegglun	57	39	38	1	7
S.M.Mills† not out	22	15	13	-	4
D.J.Bowden					
S.A.Fairley					
M.V.Houghton					
M.Burns					
S.Rasmussen					
Extras (lb 4, w 3, nb 2)	9				
TOTAL (18.3 overs) (4 wkts)	**182**	71			

Bowling	O	M	R	W
WELLINGTON				
Rasmussen	4	0	44	0
Burns	2	0	25	0
Bowden	4	0	20	1
Ryder	3	0	35	0
Houghton	4	0	24	3
Elliott	3	0	29	1
CENTRAL DISTRICTS				
Hefford	3	0	26	2
Thompson	4	0	20	1
Hegglun	4	0	48	1
Schaw	2	0	23	0
Diamanti	3.3	0	40	0
Sinclair	1	0	13	0
How	1	0	8	0

Fall of Wickets

	CD	W
1st	67	4
2nd	78	4
3rd	94	21
4th	96	144
5th	132	-
6th	-	-
7th	-	-
8th	-	-
9th	-	-
10th	-	-

OTAGO v CANTERBURY — State Twenty20

at University Oval, Dunedin on 26 January, 2007
Toss : Canterbury. Umpires : K. Cross & D.M. Quested
***Canterbury won by 4 wickets.** Points: Canterbury 4, Otago 0*

OTAGO

	Runs	Mins	Balls	6s	4s
C.B.Gaffaney c van Wyk b Hiini	17	26	11	-	3
C.D.Cumming* c Harris b Burtt	30	13	21	-	6
A.J.Redmond c Hiini b Burtt	10	7	8	1	-
N.T.Broom c Frauenstein b Hiini	12	16	13	-	1
G.J.Hopkins† c van Wyk b Harris	1	3	4	-	-
G.R.Todd b Findlay	14	18	18	-	1
K.Noema-Barnett st van Wyk b Robertson	5	13	10	-	-
N.L.McCullum c & b Harris	37	22	21	2	2
B.E.Scott b Findlay	3	8	7	-	-
M.J.Harvie c Frauenstein b Harris	2	8	5	-	-
J.M.McMillan not out	0	1	1	-	-
Extras (b 1, lb 6, w 1)	8				
TOTAL (19.5 overs)	**139**	72			

CANTERBURY

	Runs	Mins	Balls	6s	4s
S.L.Stewart c Gaffaney b Scott	19	16	21	-	3
M.H.W.Papps lbw b Scott	2	14	3	-	-
I.A.Robertson c Todd b Harvie	7	13	8	-	1
A.M.Ellis c Hopkins b Harvie	1	2	2	-	-
C.Z.Harris* not out	65	51	45	3	6
C.F.K.van Wyk† c Hopkins b Broom	9	11	11	-	1
C.Frauenstein lbw b McCullum	8	3	6	-	1
B.R.Findlay not out	17	26	19	-	1
B.C.Hiini					
L.M.Burtt					
H.K.Bennett					
Extras (b 1, lb 3, w 5, nb 4)	13				
TOTAL (18.5 overs) (6 wkts)	**141**	71			

Bowling	O	M	R	W
CANTERBURY				
Bennett	3	0	31	0
Burtt	3	0	16	2
Hiini	4	0	36	2
Harris	3.5	0	14	3
Findlay	3	0	10	2
Robertson	3	0	25	1
OTAGO				
McMillan	1.1	0	11	0
Harvie	4	0	28	2
Cumming	0.5	0	4	0
Scott	3.5	0	29	2
McCullum	4	0	14	1
Redmond	1	0	11	0
Broom	4	0	40	1

Fall of Wickets

	O	C
1st	34	30
2nd	46	31
3rd	61	32
4th	66	45
5th	78	68
6th	93	77
7th	97	-
8th	116	-
9th	135	-
10th	139	-

OTAGO v WELLINGTON — State Twenty20

at Queen's Park, Invercargill on 28 January, 2007
Abandoned without a ball being bowled. *Points: Otago 2, Wellington 2*

NORTHERN DISTRICTS v AUCKLAND — State Twenty20

at Seddon Park, Hamilton on 28 January, 2007
Toss : Northern Districts. Umpires : R.D. Anderson & A.L. Hill
Auckland won by 4 wickets. *Points: Auckland 4, Northern Districts 0*

NORTHERN DISTRICTS

	Runs	Mins	Balls	6s	4s
A.W.Evans run out	55	61	50	1	4
D.R.Flynn c Nicol b Adams	8	17	14	-	1
P.D.McGlashan† c Adams b Pasupati	44	34	33	-	5
I.G.Butler b Martin	7	10	8	-	1
J.A.H.Marshall* not out	24	11	9	-	5
M.G.Orchard not out	15	9	8	-	1
J.A.F.Yovich					
B.P.Martin					
D.R.Tuffey					
G.W.Aldridge					
B.J.Arnel					
Extras (b 1, w 2, nb 4)	7				
TOTAL (20 overs) (4 wkts)	**160**	73			

AUCKLAND

	Runs	Mins	Balls	6s	4s
P.A.Hitchcock c Martin b Arnel	16	18	11	-	3
M.J.Guptill b Orchard	38	42	35	2	3
R.A.Jones* b Aldridge	8	1	8	-	1
S.B.Styris st McGlashan b Martin	18	21	20	-	2
R.J.Nicol not out	31	37	25	-	3
D.W.Houpapa c Evans b Orchard	5	3	3	-	1
K.W.M.Todd b Aldridge	29	17	15	1	3
A.R.Adams not out	11	5	4	1	1
R.A.Young†					
M.Y.Pasupati					
C.S.Martin					
Extras (lb 2, w 1, nb 2)	5				
TOTAL (20 overs) (6 wkts)	**161**	80			

Bowling	*O*	*M*	*R*	*W*
AUCKLAND				
Adams	4	0	14	1
Martin	4	0	52	1
Styris	4	0	21	0
Hitchcock	4	0	36	0
Pasupati	2	0	20	1
Nicol	2	0	16	0
NORTHERN DISTRICTS				
Arnel	4	0	24	1
Tuffey	3	0	27	0
Aldridge	3	0	19	2
Orchard	4	0	29	2
Martin	4	0	32	1
Butler	2	0	28	0

Fall of Wickets	***ND***	***A***
1st	28	33
2nd	98	52
3rd	119	70
4th	119	88
5th	-	97
6th	-	147
7th	-	-
8th	-	-
9th	-	-
10th	-	-

AUCKLAND v CENTRAL DISTRICTS — State Twenty20

at Eden Park Outer Oval, Auckland on 29 January, 2007
Toss : Central Districts. Umpires : R.D. Anderson & E.J. Gray
***Auckland won by 19 runs.** Points: Auckland 4, Central Districts 0*

AUCKLAND

	Runs	Mins	Balls	6s	4s
P.A.Hitchcock c Diamanti b Hegglun	38	30	24	1	5
M.J.Guptill lbw b Schaw	33	39	26	-	5
R.A.Jones* b Hegglun	18	26	15	1	1
S.B.Styris b Schaw	25	6	9	4	-
D.W.Houpapa not out	74	35	31	4	8
A.R.Adams c Thompson b Diamanti	13	10	8	1	1
K.W.M.Todd run out	0	1	1	-	-
M.Y.Pasupati not out	6	11	6	-	-
R.J.Nicol					
R.A.Young†					
C.S.Martin					
Extras (lb 2, w 3)	5				
TOTAL (20 overs) (6 wkts)	**212**	82			

CENTRAL DISTRICTS

	Runs	Mins	Balls	6s	4s
E.P.Thompson b Hitchcock	25	36	16	2	1
J.M.How* b Adams	52	27	28	2	8
P.J.Ingram b Adams	0	1	1	-	-
M.S.Sinclair c Martin b Styris	23	19	17	1	2
G.R.Hay not out	38	43	30	1	3
B.B.J.Griggs† b Hitchcock	34	23	22	-	5
B.J.Diamanti not out	9	6	7	-	1
R.J.Schaw					
G.J.T.Hegglun					
B.E.Hefford					
C.P.Cruikshank					
Extras (b 4, lb 1, w 5, nb 2)	12				
TOTAL (20 overs) (5 wkts)	**193**	80			

Bowling	*O*	*M*	*R*	*W*
CENTRAL DISTRICTS				
Thompson	4	0	41	0
Hefford	4	0	45	0
Hegglun	4	0	42	2
Diamanti	4	0	35	1
Schaw	3	0	27	2
Cruikshank	1	0	20	0
AUCKLAND				
Adams	4	0	27	2
Martin	4	0	52	0
Styris	4	0	45	1
Nicol	2	0	19	0
Hitchcock	4	0	31	2
Pasupati	2	0	14	0

Fall of Wickets	***A***	***CD***
1st	64	79
2nd	86	79
3rd	114	92
4th	147	122
5th	181	181
6th	182	-
7th	-	-
8th	-	-
9th	-	-
10th	-	-

NORTHERN DISTRICTS v CANTERBURY — State Twenty20

at Cobham Oval, Whangarei on 29 January, 2007
Toss : Northern Districts. Umpires : P.L. Gasston & A.L. Hill
***Canterbury won by 2 runs.** Points: Canterbury 4, Northern Districts 0*

CANTERBURY

	Runs	Mins	Balls	6s	4s
S.L.Stewart c McGlashan b Aldridge	11	24	20	-	-
M.H.W.Papps† c Butler b Aldridge	21	35	24	-	1
I.A.Robertson b Martin	23	24	27	1	1
C.Z.Harris* not out	45	39	33	2	3
A.M.Ellis c Flynn b Aldridge	14	19	13	-	1
L.J.Vivian not out	2	5	3	-	-
C.Frauenstein					
B.R.Findlay					
B.C.Hiini					
L.M.Burtt					
H.K.Bennett					
Extras (lb 6, w 3)	9				
TOTAL (20 overs) (4 wkts)	**125**	75			

NORTHERN DISTRICTS

	Runs	Mins	Balls	6s	4s
A.W.Evans c Vivian b Hiini	12	18	10	-	2
D.R.Flynn c Papps b Hiini	15	12	13	-	2
P.D.McGlashan† c Hiini b Findlay	0	3	1	-	-
J.A.H.Marshall* c Robertson b Burtt	48	49	47	-	5
M.G.Orchard lbw b Harris	11	18	11	-	1
J.A.F.Yovich not out	21	43	29	-	-
I.G.Butler c Vivian b Hiini	0	2	2	-	-
D.R.Tuffey c & b Burtt	2	5	5	-	-
G.W.Aldridge run out	1	2	1	-	-
B.P.Martin not out	0	2	1	-	-
B.J.Arnel					
Extras (b 2, lb 6, w 5)	13				
TOTAL (20 overs) (8 wkts)	**123**	81			

Bowling	*O*	*M*	*R*	*W*
NORTHERN DISTRICTS				
Tuffey	3	1	10	0
Arnel	4	0	22	0
Aldridge	4	0	30	3
Orchard	4	0	16	0
Martin	3	0	22	1
Butler	2	0	19	0
CANTERBURY				
Burtt	4	0	26	2
Bennett	1	0	13	0
Hiini	4	0	17	3
Findlay	2	0	14	1
Frauenstein	1	0	7	0
Harris	4	0	22	1
Robertson	4	0	16	0

Fall of Wickets	***C***	***ND***
1st	26	27
2nd	44	33
3rd	64	33
4th	104	69
5th	-	114
6th	-	114
7th	-	120
8th	-	122
9th	-	-
10th	-	-

AUCKLAND v OTAGO

State Twenty20 Final

at Eden Park Outer Oval, Auckland on 4 February, 2007
Toss : Auckland. Umpires : A.L. Hill & E.A. Watkin
Auckland won by 60 runs.

After Auckland won the toss and batted, Hitchcock and Guptill were severe on the Otago opening bowlers and had raised the fifty by the end of the fifth over. Hitchcock reached his fifty off 32 balls and Auckland's first Twenty20 hundred partnership arrived in the tenth over.

Adams was promoted in the order and responded with a half-century from 30 balls and Auckland finished with 211 after 20 overs.

In reply, Otago reached fifty in the seventh over but had already lost three wickets and then immediately lost a fourth. Hopkins and Todd added fifty for the fifth wicket but Otago were always behind the required rate and eventually fell well short.

AUCKLAND

	Runs	*Mins*	*Balls*	*6s*	*4s*
P.A.Hitchcock b McCullum	53	40	38	1	7
M.J.Guptill c Gaffaney b McCullum	36	34	25	3	1
A.R.Adams not out	54	39	31	4	2
D.W.Houpapa c Todd b Scott	19	19	12	1	1
R.A.Young† b Turner	26	9	12	1	4
M.Y.Pasupati b Turner	2	1	2	-	-
R.A.Jones* not out	1	1	1	-	-
R.J.Nicol					
K.W.M.Todd					
C.de Grandhomme					
C.S.Martin					
Extras (b 4, lb 3, w 11, nb 2)	20				
TOTAL (20 overs) (5 wkts)	**211**	74			

OTAGO

	Runs	*Mins*	*Balls*	*6s*	*4s*
C.B.Gaffaney run out	6	5	5	-	1
C.D.Cumming* c Martin b Pasupati	18	28	16	-	2
A.J.Redmond c Houpapa b Adams	11	12	13	-	2
N.T.Broom c Guptill b Pasupati	12	4	7	-	3
G.J.Hopkins† lbw b Nicol	26	26	18	1	3
G.R.Todd c Pasupati b Adams	29	26	29	-	3
N.L.McCullum c Pasupati b Hitchcock	4	9	6	-	-
K.Noema-Barnett c Houpapa b Nicol	3	2	4	-	-
B.E.Scott b Hitchcock	12	10	6	1	1
M.J.Harvie not out	14	14	11	-	2
N.Turner lbw b Martin	3	5	6	-	-
Extras (b 4, lb 5, w 2, nb 2)	13				
TOTAL (20 overs)	**151**	75			

Bowling	*O*	*M*	*R*	*W*
OTAGO				
Scott	4	0	38	1
Harvie	4	0	56	0
Turner	4	0	39	2
McCullum	4	0	23	2
Redmond	2	0	19	0
Broom	2	0	29	0
AUCKLAND				
Adams	4	0	38	2
Martin	4	0	23	1
Pasupati	4	0	31	2
Hitchcock	4	0	21	2
Todd	2	0	17	0
Nicol	2	0	12	2

Fall of Wickets	***A***	***O***
1st	100	12
2nd	111	31
3rd	172	44
4th	208	51
5th	210	101
6th	-	113
7th	-	117
8th	-	118
9th	-	146
10th	-	151

2006/07 STATE TWENTY20 AVERAGES

	M	*In*	*NO*	*HS*	*Runs*	*Ave*	*100s*	*50s*	*Ct*	*St*	*O*	*M*	*R*	*W*	*Ave*	*R/O*	*Best*
A.R.Adams	3	3	2	54*	78	78.00	-	1	1	-	12	0	79	5	15.80	6.58	2-27
G.W.Aldridge	3	2	0	2	3	1.50	-	-	-	-	11	0	74	7	10.57	6.73	3-30
B.J.Arnel	5	2	1	1*	2	2.00	-	-	2	-	18	0	120	3	40.00	6.67	1-16
G.E.F.Barnett	4	4	0	39	83	20.75	-	-	1	-							
M.D.Bell	1	1	0	2	2	2.00	-	-	-	-							
H.K.Bennett	3	-	-	-	-	-	-	-	-	-	6	0	66	0	-	11.00	-
D.J.Bowden	4	2	1	17*	24	24.00	-	-	-	-	13	0	66	3	22.00	5.08	2-13
N.T.Broom	5	5	0	33	70	14.00	-	-	2	-	13	0	124	3	41.33	9.54	1-5
M.Burns	3	-	-	-	-	-	-	-	1	-	5	0	67	0	-	13.40	-
L.M.Burtt	3	-	-	-	-	-	-	-	2	-	11	0	75	5	15.00	6.82	2-16
I.G.Butler	5	5	0	21	37	7.40	-	-	3	-	12	0	109	2	54.50	9.08	1-12
S.P.Chan	2	1	1	0*	0	-	-	-	1	-	6	0	52	1	52.00	8.67	1-30
C.P.Cruikshank	1	-	-	-	-	-	-	-	-	-	1	0	20	0	-	20.00	-
C.D.Cumming	5	5	0	30	63	12.60	-	-	1	-	2.5	0	17	1	17.00	6.00	1-13
C.de Grandhomme	1	-	-	-	-	-	-	-	-	-							
A.P.Devcich	3	3	0	19	27	9.00	-	-	-	-							
B.J.Diamanti	5	5	2	36*	65	21.66	-	-	1	-	17.3	0	140	7	20.00	8.00	3-24
G.D.Elliott	4	4	1	57	80	26.66	-	1	1	-	13.3	0	117	4	29.25	8.66	2-25
A.M.Ellis	5	4	0	14	35	8.75	-	-	2	-							
A.W.Evans	5	5	0	55	119	23.80	-	1	2	-							
S.A.Fairley	1	-	-	-	-	-	-	-	-	-							
B.R.Findlay	5	3	2	26	49	49.00	-	-	1	-	12	0	81	5	16.20	6.75	2-10
D.R.Flynn	5	5	0	23	66	13.20	-	-	1	-							
K.A.Forde	2	-	-	-	-	-	-	-	-	-	4	0	36	1	36.00	9.00	1-12
C.Frauenstein	5	3	0	22	37	12.33	-	-	2	-	7	0	61	2	30.50	8.71	2-21
C.J.M.Furlong	2	2	1	1	1	1.00	-	-	1	-	7	0	58	2	29.00	8.29	1-18
C.B.Gaffaney	5	5	0	43	116	23.20	-	-	3	-							
B.B.J.Griggs	5	5	0	34	71	14.20	-	-	1	3							
M.J.Guptill	4	3	0	38	107	35.66	-	-	1	-							
S.B.Haig	1	1	0	0	0	0.00	-	-	-	-							
L.J.Hamilton	1	1	0	10	10	10.00	-	-	-	-	4	0	17	1	17.00	4.25	1-17
C.Z.Harris	5	5	3	100	237	118.50	1	1	5	-	19.5	0	128	7	18.28	6.45	3-14
M.J.Harvie	3	3	1	14*	26	13.00	-	-	-	-	11	0	108	3	36.00	9.82	2-28
G.R.Hay	5	5	3	38*	110	55.00	-	-	3	-							
B.E.Hefford	3	-	-	-	-	-	-	-	1	-	9	0	90	2	45.00	10.00	2-26
G.J.T.Hegglun	3	1	1	13*	13	-	-	-	1	-	11	0	108	3	36.00	9.82	2-42
B.C.Hiini	5	2	1	1*	1	1.00	-	-	2	-	18	0	145	8	18.12	8.06	3-17
R.M.Hira	3	1	1	0*	0	-	-	-	2	-	8	0	64	2	32.00	8.00	1-10
P.A.Hitchcock	6	6	0	77	220	36.66	-	2	-	-	24	0	184	6	30.66	7.67	2-21
G.J.Hopkins	5	5	0	47	99	19.80	-	-	2	1							
N.K.W.Horsley	1	1	0	1	1	1.00	-	-	1	-							
M.V.Houghton	1	-	-	-	-	-	-	-	1	-	4	0	24	3	8.00	6.00	3-24
D.W.Houpapa	6	6	3	74*	142	47.33	-	1	4	-							
J.M.How	5	5	0	63	187	37.40	-	2	2	-	6	0	61	2	30.50	10.17	1-12
P.J.Ingram	5	5	0	27	38	7.60	-	-	-	-							
R.A.Jones	6	6	2	75	151	37.75	-	1	1	-							
J.A.H.Marshall	5	5	1	54	157	39.25	-	1	1	-							
B.P.Martin	3	2	1	2	2	2.00	-	-	1	-	11	0	77	3	25.66	7.00	1-22
C.S.Martin	6	-	-	-	-	-	-	-	2	-	24	0	228	5	45.60	9.50	2-37
N.L.McCullum	5	5	1	37	87	21.75	-	-	-	-	19.4	0	122	10	12.20	6.20	4-16
P.D.McGlashan	5	5	0	44	78	15.60	-	-	3	1							
J.M.McMillan	4	1	1	0*	0	-	-	-	1	-	13.1	0	71	6	11.83	5.39	3-15
W.C.McSkimming	1	-	-	-	-	-	-	-	1	-	3	0	22	1	22.00	7.33	1-22
K.D.Mills	2	1	0	10	10	10.00	-	-	-	-	8	0	47	4	11.75	5.88	2-20
S.M.Mills	4	4	4	53*	126	-	-	1	-	1							
C.J.Nevin	4	4	1	87*	129	43.00	-	1	-	-							
R.J.Nicol	6	3	1	41	73	36.50	-	-	2	-	11	0	94	2	47.00	8.55	2-12
K.Noema-Barnett	5	5	0	30	44	8.80	-	-	-	-							
I.E.O'Brien	2	-	-	-	-	-	-	-	-	-	6	0	37	3	12.33	6.17	3-21
J.D.P.Oram	2	2	0	57	76	38.00	-	1	1	-	7	0	55	1	55.00	7.86	1-36
M.G.Orchard	5	5	3	28*	68	34.00	-	-	-	-	19	0	130	7	18.57	6.84	3-26
M.H.W.Papps	5	5	0	66	150	30.00	-	2	1	-							
M.E.Parlane	4	4	0	10	16	4.00	-	-	3	-							
N.R.Parlane	4	4	0	63	121	30.25	-	1	-	-							
M.Y.Pasupati	6	3	1	28	36	18.00	-	-	4	-	16	0	130	6	21.66	8.13	2-31

	M	In	NO	HS	Runs	Ave	100s	50s	Ct	St	O	M	R	W	Ave	R/O	Best
S.Rasmussen	4	-	-	-	-	-	-	-	1	-	12	0	115	1	115.00	9.58	1-15
A.J.Redmond	4	4	0	59	87	21.75	-	1	-	-	7	0	54	4	13.50	7.71	4-24
I.A.Robertson	5	4	0	23	30	7.50	-	-	2	-	16	0	126	2	63.00	7.88	1-25
J.D.Ryder	3	3	0	60	80	26.66	-	1	1	-	10	0	99	1	99.00	9.90	1-33
R.J.Schaw	4	2	1	8*	11	11.00	-	-	-	-	12.2	0	95	6	15.83	7.70	3-21
B.E.Scott	5	5	3	20*	55	27.50	-	-	3	-	16.5	0	138	3	46.00	8.19	2-29
M.S.Sinclair	5	5	0	23	47	9.40	-	-	4	-	1	0	13	0	-	13.00	-
C.A.Small	2	1	0	3	3	3.00	-	-	-	-	4	0	40	2	20.00	10.00	2-28
T.G.Southee	1	1	0	2	2	2.00	-	-	1	-	4	0	25	1	25.00	6.25	1-25
S.L.Stewart	5	5	1	66*	114	28.50	-	1	-	-							
S.B.Styris	4	4	0	25	63	15.75	-	-	-	-	15	0	140	4	35.00	9.33	2-35
E.P.Thompson	5	4	0	27	56	14.00	-	-	1	-	18	0	130	12	10.83	7.22	5-32
G.R.Todd	5	5	0	30	105	21.00	-	-	3	-							
K.W.M.Todd	4	3	1	29	30	15.00	-	-	-	-	2	0	17	0	-	8.50	-
D.R.Tuffey	4	3	1	3	7	3.50	-	-	1	-	14	2	105	3	35.00	7.50	2-33
N.Turner	2	2	1	3	4	4.00	-	-	-	-	6	0	48	2	24.00	8.00	2-39
C.F.K.van Wyk	4	2	0	9	13	6.50	-	-	2	1							
L.Vincent	3	3	0	47	93	31.00	-	-	1	-							
L.J.Vivian	1	1	1	2*	2	-	-	-	2	-							
L.J.Woodcock	3	1	1	36*	36	-	-	-	-	-	9	0	75	1	75.00	8.33	1-31
R.A.Young	6	2	1	26	27	27.00	-	-	2	-							
J.A.F.Yovich	5	4	1	21*	48	16.00	-	-	1	-	9	0	94	2	47.00	10.44	1-29

CAREER RECORDS

	M	In	NO	HS	Runs	Ave	100s	50s	Ct	St	O	M	R	W	Ave	R/O	Best
A.R.Adams	3	3	2	54*	78	78.00	-	1	1	-	12	0	79	5	15.80	6.58	2-27
G.W.Aldridge	5	3	1	5*	8	4.00	-	-	1	-	17	0	117	11	10.63	6.88	4-19
B.J.Arnel	6	2	1	1*	2	2.00	-	-	2	-	20	0	138	5	27.60	6.90	2-18
G.E.F.Barnett	6	5	0	39	92	18.40	-	-	1	-	1	0	17	0	-	17.00	-
M.D.Bell	3	2	1	13*	15	15.00	-	-	2	-							
H.K.Bennett	3	-	-	-	-	-	-	-	-	-	6	0	66	0	-	11.00	-
D.J.Bowden	6	4	2	17*	29	14.50	-	-	-	-	17	0	110	3	36.66	6.47	2-13
N.T.Broom	7	7	1	33	86	14.33	-	-	2	-	18	0	169	4	42.25	9.39	1-5
M.Burns	3	-	-	-	-	-	-	-	1	-	5	0	67	0	-	13.40	-
L.M.Burtt	4	-	-	-	-	-	-	-	2	-	13	0	89	6	14.83	6.85	2-16
I.G.Butler	5	5	0	21	37	7.40	-	-	3	-	12	0	109	2	54.50	9.08	1-12
S.P.Chan	3	1	1	0*	0	-	-	-	1	-	7	0	66	1	66.00	9.43	1-30
C.P.Cruikshank	1	-	-	-	-	-	-	-	-	-	1	0	20	0	-	20.00	-
C.D.Cumming	7	7	0	30	89	12.71	-	-	1	-	2.5	0	17	1	6.00	6.80	1-13
C.de Grandhomme	1	-	-	-	-	-	-	-	-	-							
A.P.Devcich	5	5	0	28	55	11.00	-	-	-	-	5	0	43	0	-	8.60	-
B.J.Diamanti	7	6	2	36*	69	17.25	-	-	1	-	25.3	0	219	10	21.90	8.58	3-24
G.D.Elliott	5	5	2	57	112	37.33	-	1	1	-	15.3	0	139	5	27.80	8.96	2-25
A.M.Ellis	5	4	0	14	35	8.75	-	-	2	-							
A.W.Evans	6	5	0	55	119	23.80	-	1	2	-							
S.A.Fairley	1	-	-	-	-	-	-	-	-	-							
B.R.Findlay	5	3	2	26	49	49.00	-	-	1	-	12	0	81	5	16.20	6.75	2-10
D.R.Flynn	7	7	1	23	71	11.83	-	-	1	-							
K.A.Forde	2	-	-	-	-	-	-	-	-	-	4	0	36	1	36.00	9.00	1-12
C.Frauenstein	5	3	0	22	37	12.33	-	-	2	-	7	0	61	2	30.50	8.71	2-21
C.J.M.Furlong	2	2	1	1	1	1.00	-	-	1	-	7	0	58	2	29.00	8.29	1-18
C.B.Gaffaney	7	7	0	101	232	33.14	1	-	3	-							
B.B.J.Griggs	7	6	1	34	82	16.40	-	-	3	3							
M.J.Guptill	5	4	1	38	136	45.33	-	-	2	-							
S.B.Haig	1	1	0	0	0	0.00	-	-	-	-							
L.J.Hamilton	2	2	0	10	14	7.00	-	-	-	-	7.4	0	50	2	25.00	6.52	1-17
C.Z.Harris	8	8	6	100	281	140.50	1	1	5	-	28.5	0	201	9	22.33	6.97	3-14
M.J.Harvie	3	3	1	14*	26	13.00	-	-	-	-	11	0	108	3	36.00	9.82	2-28
G.R.Hay	5	5	3	38*	110	55.00	-	-	3	-							
B.E.Hefford	5	1	1	0*	0	-	-	-	1	-	17	0	173	3	57.66	10.18	2-26
G.J.T.Hegglun	3	1	1	13*	13	-	-	-	1	-	11	0	108	3	36.00	9.82	2-42
B.C.Hiini	5	2	1	1*	1	1.00	-	-	2	-	18	0	145	8	18.12	8.06	3-17
R.M.Hira	3	1	1	0*	0	-	-	-	2	-	8	0	64	2	32.00	8.00	1-10
P.A.Hitchcock	9	9	0	77	295	32.77	-	2	3	-	35	0	253	9	28.11	7.23	2-21
G.J.Hopkins	7	6	0	47	106	17.66	-	-	2	1							
N.K.W.Horsley	3	3	0	51	73	24.33	-	1	1	-							
M.V.Houghton	1	-	-	-	-	-	-	-	1	-	4	0	24	3	8.00	6.00	3-24
D.W.Houpapa	6	6	3	74*	142	47.33	-	1	4	-							
J.M.How	7	7	1	74*	302	50.33	-	3	3	-	6	0	61	2	30.50	10.17	1-12
P.J.Ingram	5	5	0	27	38	7.60	-	-	-	-							
R.A.Jones	9	9	3	75	198	33.00	-	1	1	-							
J.A.H.Marshall	7	7	1	54	170	28.33	-	1	2	-	4	0	31	0	-	7.75	-
B.P.Martin	5	3	1	10	12	6.00	-	-	1	-	19	0	139	5	27.80	7.32	1-21
C.S.Martin	9	-	-	-	-	-	-	-	4	-	35	0	326	8	40.75	9.31	2-27
N.L.McCullum	7	7	1	52	141	23.50	-	1	2	-	22.4	0	135	11	12.27	5.95	4-16
P.D.McGlashan	7	7	0	94	177	25.28	-	1	3	2							
J.M.McMillan	4	1	1	0*	0	-	-	-	1	-	13.1	0	71	6	11.83	5.39	3-15
W.C.McSkimming	3	1	1	15*	15	-	-	-	2	-	9	0	95	1	95.00	10.56	1-22
K.D.Mills	3	2	0	10	12	6.00	-	-	-	-	11	0	91	5	18.20	8.27	2-20
S.M.Mills	4	4	4	53*	126	-	-	1	-	1							
C.J.Nevin	6	6	1	87*	187	37.40	-	1	1	-							
R.J.Nicol	9	5	2	78*	170	56.66	-	1	5	-	13	0	118	3	39.33	9.08	2-12
K.Noema-Barnett	5	5	0	30	44	8.80	-	-	-	-							
I.E.O'Brien	2	-	-	-	-	-	-	-	-	-	6	0	37	3	12.33	6.17	3-21
J.D.P.Oram	4	4	0	57	89	22.25	-	1	3	-	7	0	55	1	55.00	7.86	1-36
M.G.Orchard	5	5	3	28*	68	34.00	-	-	-	-	19	0	130	7	18.57	6.84	3-26
M.H.W.Papps	7	5	0	66	150	30.00	-	2	1	-							
M.E.Parlane	5	5	0	11	27	5.40	-	-	3	-							
N.R.Parlane	6	6	0	63	192	32.00	-	1	1	-							
M.Y.Pasupati	9	5	1	28	52	13.00	-	-	5	-	27.2	0	200	8	25.00	7.31	2-16

	M	In	NO	HS	Runs	Ave	100s	50s	Ct	St	O	M	R	W	Ave	R/O	Best
S.Rasmussen	4	-	-	-	-	-	-	-	1	-	12	0	115	1	115.00	9.58	1-15
A.J.Redmond	6	5	0	59	102	20.40	-	1	-	-	11	0	89	5	17.80	8.09	4-24
I.A.Robertson	5	4	0	23	30	7.50	-	-	2	-	16	0	126	2	63.00	7.88	1-25
J.D.Ryder	5	5	0	60	115	23.00	-	1	2	-	18	1	169	1	169.00	9.39	1-33
R.J.Schaw	4	2	1	8*	11	11.00	-	-	-	-	12.2	0	95	6	15.83	7.70	3-21
B.E.Scott	7	6	4	20*	55	27.50	-	-	3	-	22.5	0	210	4	52.50	9.19	2-29
M.S.Sinclair	7	7	0	58	110	15.71	-	1	4	-	1	0	13	0	-	13.00	-
C.A.Small	2	1	0	3	3	3.00	-	-	-	-	4	0	40	2	20.00	10.00	2-28
T.G.Southee	1	1	0	2	2	2.00	-	-	1	-	4	0	25	1	25.00	6.25	1-25
S.L.Stewart	7	5	1	66*	114	28.50	-	1	-	-							
S.B.Styris	6	6	0	62	143	23.83	-	1	-	-	22.1	0	193	7	27.57	8.70	2-35
E.P.Thompson	7	6	1	27	66	13.20	-	-	1	-	26	0	203	13	15.61	7.81	5-32
G.R.Todd	6	6	0	30	133	22.16	-	-	4	-							
K.W.M.Todd	4	3	1	29	30	15.00	-	-	-	-	2	0	17	0	-	8.50	-
D.R.Tuffey	4	3	1	3	7	3.50	-	-	1	-	14	2	105	3	35.00	7.50	2-33
N.Turner	2	2	1	3	4	4.00	-	-	-	-	6	0	48	2	24.00	8.00	2-39
C.F.K.van Wyk	4	2	0	9	13	6.50	-	-	2	1							
L.Vincent	5	5	0	47	148	29.60	-	-	1	-							
L.J.Vivian	1	1	1	2*	2	-	-	-	2	-							
L.J.Woodcock	5	3	1	36*	72	36.00	-	-	-	-	13	0	109	2	54.50	8.38	1-24
R.A.Young	9	3	2	26	40	40.00	-	-	3	1							
J.A.F.Yovich	7	6	2	21*	66	16.50	-	-	1	-	16	0	171	2	85.50	10.69	1-29

PROVINCIAL A TEAM COMPETITION

The Provincial A competition took place from 12 December to 27 January. The first round was played on a nearest neighbour basis and the remainder of the competition at Lincoln and Rangiora. Each team played three three-day games and two one-day matches. Final points were: Otago and Wellington 16, Auckland 15, Canterbury and Northern Districts 10, Central Districts 1.

CANTERBURY v OTAGO *Otago won by 3 wickets*
At Hagley Park, Christchurch 12, 13, 14 December, 2006

Canterbury 417-9 dec (M.P.F. Davidson 140*, C. Frauenstein 96, A. Robertson 88, N.M. Turner 3-44) and 178-5 dec (A.M. Ellis 53, B.R. Findlay 43*)

Otago 288 (K. Noema-Barnett 57, H.K. Bennett 5-72, B. Newton 3-57) and 308-7 (L.J. Morgan 148, M. Peacock 4-81)

AUCKLAND v NORTHERN DISTRICTS *First innings win to Auckland*
At Devonport Domain, Auckland 9, 10, 11 January, 2007

Auckland 227 (T.G. McIntosh 74, T.I. Lythe 43, P. Thomas 4-28)

Northern Districts 220 (B.J. Hatwell 79, A. Thompson 3-23, S.L. Andrews 3-45, B.J. Leonard 3-52)

CENTRAL DISTRICTS v WELLINGTON *No result*
At Trentham Memorial Park, Upper Hutt 9, 10, 11 January, 2007

Central Districts 89-6 (M. Cornish 4-32)

Wellington

OTAGO v NORTHERN DISTRICTS *First innings win to Northern Districts*
At Lincoln No.3 19, 20, 21 January, 2007

Otago 271 (A.J. Harris 59, S.W. Eathorne 54, M. Ellison 45, B.J. Leonard 6-44, T.T. Davis 3-57) and 305-8 (L.J. Morgan 70, S.B. Haig 66, N. Morrison 62, G.G. Robinson 3-48)

Northern Districts 273-7 dec (B-J. Watling 74, B.J. Hatwell 51, N.K.W. Horsley 51*, R.R. Shutte 40, D.V. Lobb 3-55) and 279-9 (G.G. Robinson 103, S.L. Andrews 47, D.V. Lobb 3-61)

AUCKLAND v WELLINGTON *Auckland won by 5 wickets*
At Lincoln Green 19, 20, 21 January, 2007

Wellington 376-6 dec (S.A. Fairley 168, A.T. Newdick 76, G.P. Hayne 3-50) and second innings forfeited

Auckland first innings forfeited and 377-5 (T.G. McIntosh 125, C. Cachopa 80*, S.P.L. Singe 66, A.K. Kitchen 40, B.R. Jansen 3-112)

CANTERBURY v CENTRAL DISTRICTS *Canterbury won by 1 wicket*
At MainPower Oval, Rangiora 19, 20, 21 January, 2007

Central Districts 223 (D.L. Rayner 43*, W.M. Lonsdale 3-37) and 175 (B.M.K. Patton 51, B. Newton 4-55, M.P.F. Davidson 3-61)

Canterbury 229-6 dec (T.J.T. Papps 80, L.J. Vivian 40) and 170-9 (D. Broom 68, C. Cruikshank 4-46)

CANTERBURY v NORTHERN DISTRICTS *Northern Districts won by 16 runs*
At MainPower Oval, Rangiora 22 January, 2007

Northern Districts 277 (R.R. Shutte 73, B.S. Wilson 46)

Canterbury 261 (B.J. Rae 88, T.J.T. Papps, 40, B. Langrope 31*, T.T. Davis 3-48, L. Martin 3-55)

CENTRAL DISTRICTS v AUCKLAND *Auckland won by 7 wickets*
At Lincoln No.3 22 January, 2007

Central Districts 225 (B.M.K. Patton 99*)

Auckland 229-3 (M.J. Guptill 110, T.G. McIntosh 73)

WELLINGTON v OTAGO *Otago won by 27 runs*
At Lincoln Green 22 January, 2007

Otago 327-6 (S. Wells 107, L.J. Morgan 80)

Wellington 300 (S.A. Fairley 83, M.V. Houghton 71, B.R. Jansen 54, G.S. Shaw 3-58, D.V. Lobb 3-59)

OTAGO v CENTRAL DISTRICTS *First innings win to Otago*
At Lincoln Green 24, 25, 26 January, 2007

Central Districts 402 (B.M.K. Patton 166, N. Phelps 79, D.V. Lobb 4-104, H. Finch 3-35, G.S. Shaw 3-70) and 16-0

Otago 403-4 dec (S. Wells 113*, M. Ellison 104, L.J. Morgan 75, N. Morrison 70*)

CANTERBURY v AUCKLAND *First innings win to Auckland*
At MainPower Oval, Rangiora 24, 25, 26 January, 2007

Canterbury 313 (A. Robertson 98*, L.J. Vivian 62, W. Eastgate 61, D. Broom 37, C. Munro 4-96) and 61-1

Auckland 508-5 dec (C. de Grandhomme 130*, S.P.L. Singe 111, A.K. Kitchen 104, T.G. McIntosh 81)

WELLINGTON v NORTHERN DISTRICTS *Wellington won by an inns and 71 runs*
At Lincoln No.3 24, 25, 26 January, 2007

Northern Districts 206 (N.K.W. Horsley 114, L.J. Edwards 4-47) and 160 (D.R. Flynn 45, K.A. Forde 3-28)

Wellington 437 (B.J. Crook 146, L. Chrisp 75, B.R. Jansen 57, S.L. Andrews 5-100)

OTAGO v AUCKLAND *Otago won by 4 wickets*
At Lincoln No.3 27 January, 2007

Auckland 230-9 (T.I. Lythe 45*, C. Munro 41)

Otago 231-6 (M. Ellison 54, H. Finch 43, S. Wells 43*)

NORTHERN DISTRICTS v CENTRAL DISTRICTS *Northern won by 32 runs*
At Lincoln Green 27 January, 2007

Northern Districts 278-9 (N.K.W. Horsley 79, J. Boult 56, S.L. Andrews 45)

Central Districts 246 (T.I. Weston 74*, S.B.C. Baldwin 50)

CANTERBURY v WELLINGTON *Wellington won by 55 runs*
At MainPower Oval, Rangiora 27 January, 2007

Wellington 202 (A.T. Newdick 54)

Canterbury 147 (T.J.T. Papps 80*, L. Chrisp 3-31)

INDIA UNDER 19 IN NEW ZEALAND

The New Zealand Under 19 team played three tests and three one-day internationals against their Indian counterparts. The test series was drawn 1-1 while India won the final one-day game to take the series 2-1.

NEW ZEALAND v INDIA — First Youth Test

at Bert Sutcliffe Oval, Lincoln on 21, 22, 23, 24 January, 2007
Toss : New Zealand. Umpires : G.A. Baxter & A.L. Hill
Close of play: 1st day: India 338-6, Chawla 21, Gurav 0; 2nd day: NZ 179-4, de Boorder 58, Cachopa 26
3rd day: NZ 77-3, Williamson 50, Taiaroa 1
India won by an innings and 50 runs

INDIA

FIRST INNINGS	*Runs*	*Mins*	*Balls*	*6s*	*4s*	*SECOND INNINGS*	*Runs*	*Mins*	*Balls*	*6s*	*4s*
D.B.Ravi Teja c sub (B.P.Rodden) b Worker	105	203	167	-	14						
A.M.Rahane c Williamson b Anderson	49	111	72	-	5						
T.M.Srivastava run out	9	36	18	-	1						
V.Kohli b Morgan	113	159	129	-	18						
B.Sumanth c Anderson b Raval	29	96	84	-	4						
R.A.Jadeja lbw b Southee	9	18	10	-	2						
Piyush Chawla* c Raval b Worker	119	139	90	1	19						
O.D.Gurav† b Southee	2	17	14	-	-						
V.Y.Mahesh not out	61	110	83	1	8						
A.N.Ahmed											
I.Sharma											
Extras (lb 1, w 1, nb 1)	3										
TOTAL (111 overs) (8 wkts dec)	**499**	448									

NEW ZEALAND

	Runs	*Mins*	*Balls*	*6s*	*4s*		*Runs*	*Mins*	*Balls*	*6s*	*4s*
J.A.Raval b Jadeja	24	122	96	-	4	c Gurav b Ahmed	2	9	8	-	-
G.H.Worker c Ravi Teja b Mahesh	24	154	126	-	3	c & b Jadeja	15	61	33	-	2
K.S.Williamson b Ahmed	20	55	51	-	4	b Ahmed	53	119	104	-	4
A.P.de Boorder* b Sharma	87	196	146	-	12	b Chawla	4	16	15	-	-
M.P.Taiaroa lbw b Sharma	4	16	16	-	-	c Gurav b Chawla	42	129	101	-	4
B.Cachopa† lbw b Sharma	60	164	158	-	6	c Sumanth b Ahmed	10	21	15	-	2
C.J.Anderson not out	32	83	66	-	4	b Chawla	1	22	10	-	-
T.R.Muir b Sharma	8	27	16	-	2	lbw b Chawla	0	8	5	-	-
G.J.Morgan c Gurav b Sharma	0	2	1	-	-	c Jadeja b Sharma	3	20	18	-	-
T.G.Southee c Ravi Teja b Chawla	16	40	30	1	2	c Gurav b Chawla	5	11	7	-	1
T.A.Boult c sub (Singh) b Chawla	0	2	1	-	-	not out	0	7	2	-	-
Extras (b 6, lb 14, nb 7)	27					(lb 7, nb 5)	12				
TOTAL (116.4 overs)	**302**	435				(52.1 overs)	**147**	216			

Bowling	*O*	*M*	*R*	*W*	*O*	*M*	*R*	*W*
NEW ZEALAND								
Southee	26	4	93	2				
Boult	24	2	105	0				
Morgan	22	2	91	1				
Anderson	13	1	80	1				
Muir	2	0	14	0				
Worker	15	2	69	2				
Raval	9	1	46	1				
INDIA								
Ahmed	26	6	73	1	16	2	55	3
Sharma	30	9	55	5	15	3	39	1
Mahesh	11	4	39	1				
Chawla	30.4	6	75	2	13.1	4	19	5
Kohli	5	0	13	0	1	0	8	0
Jadeja	14	7	27	1	4	2	3	1
Srivastava					3	0	16	0

Fall of Wickets

	I *1st*	*NZ* *1st*	*NZ* *2nd*
1st	113	51	2
2nd	149	73	55
3rd	204	95	62
4th	306	112	85
5th	308	242	100
6th	322	245	125
7th	340	265	127
8th	499	265	140
9th	-	301	142
10th	-	302	147

NEW ZEALAND v INDIA — Second Youth Test

at Carisbrook, Dunedin on 27, 28, 29, 30 December, 2007
Toss : India. Umpires : D.M. Quested & E.A. Watkin
Close of play: 1st day: India 105-6, S.Sharma 1, Chawla 6; 2nd day: New Zealand 251-6, Taiaroa 65, Morgan 8
3rd day: India 222-9, Kulkarni 19, I.Sharma 19
New Zealand won by 73 runs

NEW ZEALAND

FIRST INNINGS	*Runs*	*Mins*	*Balls*	*6s*	*4s*	*SECOND INNINGS*	*Runs*	*Mins*	*Balls*	*6s*	*4s*
J.A.Raval lbw b Ahmed	2	10	8	-	-	c & b Chawla	16	70	53	-	1
G.H.Worker b Sharma I.	3	14	10	-	-	c Kohli b Kulkarni	24	56	56	-	4
K.S.Williamson b Ahmed	7	24	18	-	1	b Sharma I.	22	95	86	-	1
A.P.de Boorder* c Ahmed b Kulkarni	44	147	115	-	6	c Gurav b Sharma I.	18	51	42	-	2
M.P.Taiaroa b Chawla	7	77	59	-	-	c Chawla b Sharma S.	102	295	245	-	10
B.Cachopa† c Gurav b Kulkarni	5	15	12	-	1	c Gurav b Kulkarni	3	23	18	-	-
C.J.Anderson c Gurav b Chawla	8	38	34	-	-	run out	88	83	79	4	10
G.J.Morgan c Jadeja b Kulkarni	0	8	4	-	-	c Rahane b Ahmed	8	42	35	-	-
T.G.Southee run out	1	9	4	-	-	b Ahmed	6	24	21	-	1
D.J.Bartlett lbw b Jadeja	8	26	19	-	-	c Srivastava b Sharma S.	31	82	69	-	3
T.A.Boult not out	3	19	16	-	-	not out	1	5	3	-	-
Extras (lb 3, w 1, nb 8)	12					(b 1, lb 6, w 6, nb 2)	15				
TOTAL (48.3 overs)	**100**	198				(117.3 overs)	**334**	417			

INDIA

FIRST INNINGS	*Runs*	*Mins*	*Balls*	*6s*	*4s*	*SECOND INNINGS*	*Runs*	*Mins*	*Balls*	*6s*	*4s*
D.B.Ravi Teja b Southee	0	3	5	-	-	c Cachopa b Southee	5	17	16	-	1
A.M.Rahane c Raval b Southee	19	81	61	-	2	c Southee b Anderson	55	137	105	-	6
T.M.Srivastava c Bartlett b Boult	47	81	60	-	7	c Williamson b Southee	37	93	54	-	3
V.Kohli c Raval b Southee	12	58	47	-	2	lbw b Southee	0	9	7	-	-
R.A.Jadeja c Raval b Boult	12	59	37	-	2	c Bartlett b Boult	34	95	62	-	5
D.Kulkarni c Raval b Southee	1	27	13	-	-	(9) c Raval b Southee	24	120	103	1	-
S.Sharma c Cachopa b Southee	1	3	2	-	-	b Morgan	4	18	11	-	1
Piyush Chawla* b Boult	19	57	28	-	2	(6) c Cachopa b Southee	2	13	8	-	-
O.D.Gurav† c Raval b Boult	4	22	26	-	1	(8) b Southee	7	53	36	-	1
A.N.Ahmed c Williamson b Southee	3	11	8	-	-	c Cachopa b Boult	5	12	10	-	1
I.Sharma not out	0	3	5	-	-	not out	28	98	84	-	2
Extras (lb 6, w 1, nb 4)	11					(b 6, lb 13, w 1, nb 11)	31				
TOTAL (48.1 overs)	**129**	207				(80.5 overs)	**232**	336			

Bowling	*O*	*M*	*R*	*W*	*O*	*M*	*R*	*W*
INDIA								
Ahmed	11	4	26	2	25	6	61	2
Sharma I.	16	4	35	1	30	5	103	2
Kulkarni	15	3	33	3	17	6	42	2
Chawla	6	4	2	2	33	11	80	1
Jadeja	0.3	0	1	1				
Sharma S.					12.3	0	41	2
NEW ZEALAND								
Southee	19	7	36	6	24.5	4	56	6
Boult	18.1	5	42	4	18	5	52	2
Morgan	6	1	24	0	17	2	49	1
Bartlett	5	1	21	0	7	0	28	0
Anderson					7	1	17	1
Raval					6	2	11	0
Worker					1	1	0	0

Fall of Wickets

	NZ *1st*	***I*** *1st*	***NZ*** *2nd*	***I*** *2nd*
1st	6	0	35	6
2nd	6	68	42	79
3rd	17	73	77	89
4th	53	97	88	107
5th	61	97	95	118
6th	88	98	222	133
7th	88	106	255	165
8th	88	120	272	165
9th	90	129	331	174
10th	100	129	334	232

NEW ZEALAND v INDIA — Third Youth Test

at Bert Sutcliffe Oval, Lincoln on 2, 3, 4, 5 February, 2007
Toss : New Zealand. Umpires : D.M. Quested & D.J. Walker
Close of play: 1st day: NZ 116-2, Raval 51, de Boorder 35; 2nd day: India 76-0, Rahane 28, Ravi Teja 46
3rd day: India 531-5, Chawla 18, Sumanth 3
Match drawn

INDIA

FIRST INNINGS	Runs	Mins	Balls	6s	4s	SECOND INNINGS	Runs	Mins	Balls	6s	4s
A.M.Rahane c Cachopa b Bartlett	56	189	131	-	7	c Raval b Morgan	179	399	274	5	18
D.B.Ravi Teja c Raval b Southee	1	8	6	-	-	b Anderson	50	123	92	-	9
T.M.Srivastava c Worker b Bartlett	22	59	41	-	4	c Bartlett b Boult	170	218	173	-	23
V.Kohli c Williamson b Bartlett	5	15	12	-	1	b Boult	54	100	83	-	6
B.Sumanth b Southee	7	12	7	-	1	c Morgan b Southee	30	71	41	1	3
S.Sharma c Raval b Morgan	5	21	15	-	1	c Anderson b Boult	35	61	36	-	4
Piyush Chawla* c Raval b Morgan	0	1	1	-	-	b Southee	13	22	24	-	1
Sarabjeet Singh† lbw b Morgan	0	1	1	-	-	not out	6	9	8	-	-
V.Y.Mahesh c Cachopa b Southee	15	84	70	-	1						
I.Sharma c Cachopa b Southee	0	6	4	-	-						
K.P.Appanna not out	0	9	2	-	-						
Extras (b 4, w 1, nb 8)	13					(b 8, lb 9, w 9, nb 3)	29				
TOTAL (47 overs)	**124**	206				(121.2 overs) (7 wkts dec)	**566**	507			

NEW ZEALAND

FIRST INNINGS	Runs	Mins	Balls	6s	4s	SECOND INNINGS	Runs	Mins	Balls	6s	4s
J.A.Raval c Sharma S. b Chawla	70	201	137	-	9	b Appanna	89	224	199	-	12
G.H.Worker c Kohli b Mahesh	8	46	36	-	1	c Sumanth b Appanna	17	78	65	-	2
K.S.Williamson st Singh b Appanna	14	31	23	-	2	b Sharma I.	30	66	64	-	3
A.P.de Boorder* c Singh b Mahesh	109	263	218	-	16	c Singh b Rahane	33	97	83	1	2
M.P.Taiaroa b Chawla	9	38	42	-	1	not out	21	103	107	-	-
B.Cachopa† c Singh b Sharma I.	0	27	17	-	-	c Srivastava b Chawla	7	28	14	-	-
C.J.Anderson b Chawla	14	16	14	-	3	c Kohli b Chawla	8	12	14	-	1
G.J.Morgan c Mahesh b Sharma I.	34	116	88	-	4	not out	6	39	36	-	1
T.G.Southee c Sharma S. b Sharma I.	7	16	14		1						
D.J.Bartlett b Chawla	0	21	16	-	-						
T.A.Boult not out	5	17	5	-	1						
Extras (b 1, lb 5, w 7, nb 17)	30					(b 4, lb 5, w 4, nb 7)	20				
TOTAL (98.5 overs)	**300**	402				(96 overs) (6 wkts)	**231**	328			

Bowling	*O*	*M*	*R*	*W*	*O*	*M*	*R*	*W*
NEW ZEALAND								
Southee	14	2	48	4	30	4	131	2
Boult	13	4	16	0	23.2	0	104	3
Morgan	11	5	23	3	22	0	103	1
Bartlett	9	1	33	3	8	0	30	0
Anderson					17	0	74	1
Raval					7	0	37	0
Worker					12	1	58	0
de Boorder					2	0	12	0
INDIA								
Mahesh	24	4	75	2	9	3	27	0
Sharma I.	29.5	4	104	3	13	5	34	1
Appanna	15	3	41	1	26	10	59	2
Sharma S.	5	0	15	0	12	2	33	0
Chawla	25	3	59	4	30	8	62	2
Ravi Teja					3	2	1	0
Rahane					2	0	3	1
Sumanth					1	0	3	0

Fall of Wickets

	I 1st	*NZ* 1st	*I* 2nd	*NZ* 2nd
1st	3	56	89	59
2nd	50	69	380	123
3rd	63	164	446	169
4th	72	189	477	187
5th	84	202	524	198
6th	84	223	552	206
7th	84	258	566	-
8th	114	269	-	-
9th	117	275	-	-
10th	124	300	-	-

NEW ZEALAND v INDIA First Youth One-day International

at Bert Sutcliffe Oval, Lincoln on 7 February, 2007
Toss : New Zealand. Umpires : P.D. Jones & W.R. Knights
India won by 9 wickets

NEW ZEALAND

	Runs	Mins	Balls	6s	4s
G.H.Worker c Sumanth b Mahesh	0	3	7	-	-
C.J.Anderson b Ahmed	0	5	1	-	-
K.S.Williamson b Mahesh	8	24	18	-	1
A.P.de Boorder* c Sumanth b Chabra	29	40	52	-	4
M.P.Taiaroa c Srivastava b Mahesh	2	9	7	-	-
B.Cachopa† c Ravi Teja b Chawla	16	50	41	-	-
B.P.Rodden c Gurav b Jadeja	10	40	34	-	-
G.J.Morgan run out	10	31	32	-	-
T.G.Southee c Gurav b Sharma	6	10	9	1	-
T.R.Muir c Jadeja b Mahesh	7	30	40	-	1
T.A.Boult not out	2	19	12	-	-
Extras (lb 6, w 5, nb 2)	13				
TOTAL (39.5 overs)	**103**	140			

INDIA

	Runs	Mins	Balls	6s	4s
A.M.Rahane run out	19	29	22	-	3
D.B.Ravi Teja not out	52	59	44	2	6
G.Chabra not out	23	29	18	-	5
T.M.Srivastava					
S.Sharma					
B.Sumanth					
Piyush Chawla*					
O.D.Gurav†					
R.A.Jadeja					
V.Y.Mahesh					
A.N.Ahmed					
Extras (w 9, nb 1)	10				
TOTAL (13.5 overs) (1 wkt)	**104**	59			

Bowling	*O*	*M*	*R*	*W*
INDIA				
Mahesh	7.5	1	17	4
Ahmed	6	1	27	1
Chabra	5	0	28	1
Chawla	10	3	11	1
Jadeja	6	2	11	1
Sharma	5	2	3	1
NEW ZEALAND				
Southee	7	0	44	0
Boult	2.5	0	36	0
Morgan	4	0	24	0

Fall of Wickets	***NZ***	***I***
1st	2	37
2nd	2	-
3rd	23	-
4th	32	-
5th	54	-
6th	76	-
7th	79	-
8th	92	-
9th	95	-
10th	103	-

NEW ZEALAND v INDIA Second Youth One-day International

at Bert Sutcliffe Oval, Lincoln on 8 February, 2007
Toss : New Zealand. Umpires : P.D. Jones & W.R. Knights
New Zealand won by 1 wicket

INDIA

	Runs	Mins	Balls	6s	4s
A.M.Rahane c Anderson b Southee	15	20	16	1	2
D.B.Ravi Teja c Cachopa b Southee	4	8	6	-	-
G.Chabra b Southee	9	20	16	-	2
T.M.Srivastava c Muir b Morgan	57	93	69	1	7
B.Sumanth c Muir b Anderson	9	24	16	-	2
R.A.Jadeja c Cachopa b Morgan	24	67	39	-	3
Piyush Chawla* b Boult	5	17	15	-	-
S.Sharma c Williamson b Rodden	0	14	9	-	-
O.D.Gurav† lbw b Boult	2	21	8	-	-
V.Y.Mahesh not out	13	24	24	-	2
A.N.Ahmed c Cachopa b Southee	0	7	6	-	-
Extras (lb 1, w 11, nb 2)	14				
TOTAL (37 overs)	**152**	167			

NEW ZEALAND

	Runs	Mins	Balls	6s	4s
J.A.Raval b Mahesh	0	2	1	-	-
K.S.Williamson run out	17	76	67	-	1
A.P.de Boorder* b Mahesh	2	9	12	-	-
M.P.Taiaroa run out	12	31	28	-	1
B.Cachopa† c Jadeja b Chawla	24	80	81	3	-
C.J.Anderson c Jadeja b Chawla	34	40	38	-	1
B.P.Rodden c Sharma b Mahesh	13	34	35	-	-
G.J.Morgan run out	9	19	19	1	-
T.G.Southee b Mahesh	5	13	8	-	-
T.R.Muir not out	16	12	11	2	-
T.A.Boult not out	7	4	4	1	-
Extras (lb 6, w 5, nb 4)	15				
TOTAL (50 overs) (9 wkts)	**154**	169			

Bowling	*O*	*M*	*R*	*W*
NEW ZEALAND				
Southee	7	2	29	4
Boult	8	1	28	2
Morgan	8	2	25	2
Anderson	6	0	31	1
Muir	2	0	18	0
Rodden	6	0	20	1
INDIA				
Mahesh	9	1	27	4
Ahmed	6	1	14	0
Chawla	9	1	28	2
Jadeja	10	3	31	0
Sharma	10	0	29	0
Rahane	6	1	19	0

Fall of Wickets

	I	***NZ***
1st	11	3
2nd	22	7
3rd	32	32
4th	58	48
5th	128	97
6th	131	101
7th	134	121
8th	134	124
9th	148	131
10th	152	-

NEW ZEALAND v INDIA Third Youth One-day International

at Bert Sutcliffe Oval, Lincoln on 10 February, 2007
Toss : New Zealand. Umpires : P.D. Jones & W.R. Knights
India won by 76 runs

INDIA

	Runs	Mins	Balls	6s	4s
A.M.Rahane c Cachopa b Rodden	110	151	125	3	11
D.B.Ravi Teja c Cachopa b Southee	16	31	18	-	2
T.M.Srivastava c de Boorder b Southee	110	165	165	1	12
V.Kohli run out	66	52	50	1	7
R.A.Jadeja not out	2	6	2	-	-
S.Sharma					
G.Chabra					
Piyush Chawla*					
Sarabjeet Singh†					
V.Y.Mahesh					
I.Sharma					
Extras (b 1, lb 1, w 7, nb 2)	11				
TOTAL (50 overs) (4 wkts)	**315**	206			

NEW ZEALAND

	Runs	Mins	Balls	6s	4s
J.A.Raval c Chawla b Mahesh	9	35	26	-	-
K.S.Williamson c Chawla b Sharma S.	67	105	90	1	6
A.P.de Boorder* c Chawla b Jadeja	26	43	33	-	3
M.P.Taiaroa c Jadeja b Sharma S.	19	32	33	-	-
C.J.Anderson c Singh b Chawla	28	42	30	1	2
B.Cachopa† run out	42	39	24	1	5
B.P.Rodden c Singh b Jadeja	8	11	9	-	1
T.G.Southee c Kohli b Chawla	9	15	11	-	1
G.J.Morgan not out	8	28	20	-	-
T.R.Muir c Chawla b Sharma S.	14	10	13	1	1
T.A.Boult b Mahesh	2	9	5	-	-
Extras (b 4, w 9, nb 3)	16				
TOTAL (48.3 overs)	**248**	194			

Bowling	*O*	*M*	*R*	*W*
NEW ZEALAND				
Southee	10	1	64	2
Boult	10	0	57	0
Morgan	10	0	57	0
Anderson	2	1	17	0
Rodden	10	1	55	1
de Boorder	6	0	42	0
Muir	1	0	12	0
Raval	1	0	9	0
INDIA				
Mahesh	9.3	1	31	2
Sharma I.	9	0	39	0
Jadeja	9	1	48	2
Chabra	1	0	10	0
Chawla	10	0	58	2
Sharma S.	8	0	44	3
Rahane	2	0	14	0

Fall of Wickets

	I	*NZ*
1st	39	28
2nd	212	88
3rd	307	125
4th	315	130
5th	-	199
6th	-	200
7th	-	217
8th	-	221
9th	-	240
10th	-	248

NATIONAL UNDER 19 TOURNAMENT

The Under 19 tournament was held from 27 December to 9 January. Each team played three three-day games and two-one day matches with points from all matches being combined. The first round featured nearest neighbours while the other four rounds were played at Lincoln. Final placings were: Canterbury, Auckland, Otago, Northern Districts, Central Districts, Wellington.

FIRST ROUND

AUCKLAND v NORTHERN DISTRICTS *First innings win to Northern Districts*

Northern Districts 150 (G. Bell 31, G. Morgan 6-29, Ajaz Patel 4-37) and 264 (M. Dodunski 92*, S. Rae 37, D. Bartlett 3-36, Ajaz Patel 3-36)

Auckland 138 (A. de Boorder 78, T. Southee 4-44, T. Boult 3-38, M. Dodunski 3-29) and 32-0

WELLINGTON v CENTRAL DISTRICTS *Central Districts won by 4 wickets*

Wellington 211 (F. Colson 79, M. Green 35) and 306 (A. Pennell 117, F. Colson 74, G. Worker 3-52)

Central Districts 336 (G. Worker 126, M. Taiaroa 125, R. Karaitiana 4-61) and 182-6 (V. Tosi 53, M. Taiaroa 46*, G. Worker 38)

OTAGO v CANTERBURY *Canterbury won by 221 runs*

Canterbury 186 (R. McCone 44, C. Rutherford 3-22, P. Breen 3-58) and 174-4 dec (S. Noster 89*, C. Bartholomeusz 54, P. Breen 3-26)

Otago 72 (B. Hill 40*, B. Langrope 5-21) and 67 (I. King 7-16)

SECOND ROUND

NORTHERN DISTRICTS v CANTERBURY *Canterbury won by 197 runs*

Canterbury 255 (C. Anderson 121, S. Noster 34, T. Southee 3-75, M. Dodunski 3-80) and 256-9 dec (C. Anderson 55, C. Bartholomeusz 46, H. Fisher 46, J. Trembath 3-50, T. Southee 3-64)

Northern Districts 157 (B. Simpson 42, S. Rae 31*, M. Kain 4-44) and 157 (M. Wilson 47, M. Dodunski 40, H. Fisher 5-46, T. Muir 5-65)

WELLINGTON v AUCKLAND *Auckland won by 46 runs*

Auckland 361-8 dec (A. de Boorder 110, B. Cachopa 67) and 102-1 dec (J. Raval 47*, M. Guptill-Bunce 46*)

Wellington 129-6 dec (J. Evans 41) and 288 (M. Green 117, R. Karaitiana 44, G. Morgan 3-17, Ajaz Patel 3-42)

CENTRAL DISTRICTS v OTAGO *First innings win to Otago*

Otago 484 (B. Rodden 109, B. Hill 84, C. Clark 63)

Central Districts 398 (M. Taiaroa 139, O. Newton 3-56, P. Breen 3-102)

THIRD ROUND

WELLINGTON v NORTHERN DISTRICTS *Northern Districts won by 74 runs*

Northern Districts 200 (A. Sclater 82*, A. Corliss 3-37)

Wellington 126 (A. Corliss 29*)

AUCKLAND v OTAGO *Auckland won by 5 wickets*

Otago 217-8 (G. Dawson 54*, H. Rutherford 43, C. Clark 41)

Auckland 219-5 (J. Raval 62, A. de Boorder 61*, J. Dowd 44)

CENTRAL DISTRICTS v CANTERBURY *Canterbury won by 7 wickets*

Central Districts 190 (B.Grant 43)

Canterbury 193-3 (T. Muir 59*, S. Noster 56)

FOURTH ROUND

AUCKLAND v CENTRAL DISTRICTS *Auckland won by 71 runs*

Auckland 504-3 dec (A. de Boorder 208*, B. Cachopa 137*, B. Schoeman 62, M. Guptill-Bunce 62) and 128-3 (A. de Boorder 59*)

Central Districts 259-8 dec (M. Taiaroa 118, B. Grant 43*, S. Badger 3-35) and 302 (S. Wraight 84, S. Davidson 68, J. Dravitski 50, Ajaz Patel 3-32)

NORTHERN DISTRICTS v OTAGO *Otago won by 11 runs*

Otago 426 (C. Hendry 115, S. Ward 53, T. Boult 4-69, T. Southee 4-88) and 208-8 dec (C. Clark 78)

Northern Districts 278-8 dec (T. Southee 102, G. Bell 79, B. Rodden 3-37) and 345 (K. Williamson 94, A. Sclater 73*, B. Simpson 59, B. Purvis 4-34)

CANTERBURY v WELLINGTON *First innings win to Wellington*

Canterbury 300 (J. O'Gorman 101, T. Muir 86, C. Anderson 46, R. Karaitiana 4-42) and 193 (A. Bruce 58, T. Muir 33*, N. Naguleswaran 5-29)

Wellington 305 (J. Evans 83, N. Naguleswaran 56, J. Austin-Smellie 40, R. McCone 3-41, T. Muir 3-69) and 143-8 (F. Colson 57, B. Langrope 4-21)

FIFTH ROUND

WELLINGTON v OTAGO *Otago won by 7 wickets*

Wellington 218-7 (M. Green 67, C. Tait 49, O. Newton 3-26)

Otago 221-3 (H. Rutherford 102*, B. Rodden 44)

CANTERBURY v AUCKLAND *Canterbury won by 46 runs*

Canterbury 203 (T. Muir 40, C. Anderson 33, Ajaz Patel 4-45, G. Morgan 3-26)

Auckland 157 (R. Khan 33, M. Kain 3-26)

CENTRAL DISTRICTS v NORTHERN DISTRICTS *Northern won by 81 runs*

Northern Districts 321-9 (B. Simpson 86, K. Williamson 76, T. Southee 67, G. Bell 36*)

Central Districts 240 (S. Davidson 88, M. Dodunski 3-42, T. Southee 3-45)

NATIONAL UNDER 17 TOURNAMENT

The National Under 17 tournament was held in Napier from 16 to 24 January. Otago won the title with 16 points followed by Wellington (12), Central Districts (12), Northern Districts (10), Auckland (10) and Canterbury (10).

A tournament team was selected at the completion of the fifth round. It was A. Manning *(Auckland)*, B. Warren *(Auckland)*, A. Dodd *(Central Districts)*, B. Meehan *(Central Districts)*, J. Hickey *(Northern Districts)*, T. Clarke *(Northern Districts)*, N. Beard *(Otago)*, M. Bracewell *(Otago)*, M. Souter *(Otago)*, J. Austin-Smellie *(Wellington)*, T. Friday *(Wellington)*, I. Tugaga *(Wellington)*.

FIRST ROUND

AUCKLAND v NORTHERN DISTRICTS *Auckland won by an innings and 128 runs*

Auckland 380 (J. Neesham 78, V. Davies 54, T. Manning 40, S. Wood 32, J. Hickey 4-77, A. Verma 3-67))

Northern Districts 122 (T. Clarke 51, B. Warren 3-19, V. Davies 3-24) and 130 (J. Neesham 3-19)

WELLINGTON v CENTRAL DISTRICTS *First innings win to Welington*

Wellington 197 (J. Austin-Smellie 40, V. Ward 38, F. Colson 32, D. van Deventer 4-42, D. Bracewell 3-40)

Central Districts 196 (A. Dodd 48, D. Bracewell 33, H. Boam 4-64, I. Tugaga 3-28, T. Friday 3-38)

CANTERBURY v OTAGO *First innings win to Otago*

Canterbury 145 (M. Laffey 33, S. Swain 4-22, M. Souter 3-27) and 32-0

Otago 171 (G. Scott 50, M. Farrant 3-35, M. McEwan 3-45)

SECOND ROUND

NORTHERN DISTRICTS v CANTERBURY *First innings win to Northern Districts*

Northern Districts 176 (T. Clarke 40, A. Verma 41*, M. McEwan 3-35, M. Latham 3-30) and 198-5 (B. O'Connor 68, G. Schwikkard 48, J. Hickey 36)

Canterbury 137 (J. Hickey 6-46)

WELLINGTON v OTAGO *First innings win to Otago*

Otago 222 (M. Bracewell 105) and 48-2

Wellington 202 (J. Austin-Smellie 85, F. Colson 53, N. Beard 4-38, B. Frost 3-43)

AUCKLAND v CENTRAL DISTRICTS *First innings win to Central Districts*

Central Districts 351-7 dec (B. Meehan 151, A. Dodd 68, D. Bracewell 30*, B. Khamal 3-44)

Auckland 314 (J. Rosenberg 58, J. Bassett-Graham 56, S. Huri 44, B. Schmulian 48, J. Neesham 38)

THIRD ROUND

CENTRAL DISTRICTS v CANTERBURY *First innings win to Central Districts*

Canterbury 277 (M. Laffey 63*, J. Reeves 61, L. Barthomeusz 44, B. Walsh 35, P. Younghusband 3-40)

Central Districts 279-9 (A. Dodd 105, D. Bracewell 41, B. Meehan 36, D. Kruger 3-40)

NORTHERN DISTRICTS v OTAGO *Northern Districts won by 162 runs*

Northern Districts 228 (T. Clark 44, G. Schwikkard 33, F. Allen 31, N. Beard 3-28, M. Souter 3-38) and 155-8 dec (T. Clarke 48, J. Simpson 5-73)

Otago 133 (J. Simpson 38, J. Hickey 4-41) and 88 (A. Herwels 3-15)

WELLINGTON v AUCKLAND *First innings win to Wellington*

Wellington 297 (J. Proctor 95, R. Cargill 48*, T. Pere 41, I. Tugaga 33, B. Warren 4-40, T. Horrocks 3-47)

Auckland 204 (T. Manning 76, B. Schmulian 50, I. Tugaga 3-13)

FOURTH ROUND

AUCKLAND v CANTERBURY *Auckland won by 5 wickets*

Canterbury 114 (V. Davies 5-22))

Auckland 115-5 (T. Manning 35*, D. Kruger 3-14)

NORTHERN DISTRICTS v WELLINGTON *Wellington won by 8 wickets*

Northern Districts 80 (T. Friday 4-26, J. Widerstrom 3-18)

Wellington 83-2 (H. Boam 48*)

OTAGO v CENTRAL DISTRICTS *Otago won by 4 wickets*

Central Districts 225-8 (A. Dodd 61, M. Souter 4-30)

Otago 226-6 (G. Scott 62, S. Paulin 47, J. Simpson 42)

FIFTH ROUND

AUCKLAND v OTAGO *Otago won by 62 runs*

Otago 211 (N. Beard 58, M. Bracewell 30, B. Warren 3-18)

Auckland 149 (S. Wood 39, B. Frost 5-36)

WELLINGTON v CANTERBURY *Canterbury won by 14 runs*

Canterbury 250-5 (B. Walsh 78, L. Bartholomeusz 62, M. Latham 35*)

Wellington 236 (J. Austin-Smellie 74, F. Colson 63; D. Kruger 8-44)

NORTHERN DISTRICTS v CENTRAL DISTRICTS *Central won by 24 runs*

Central Districts 182 (A. Dodd 38, B. Meehan 32)

Northern Districts 158 (R. Wilson 42, N. Dodd 4-17)

HAWKE CUP

The major competition for the District (formerly Minor) Associations reverted to the Hawke Cup from 1999/00. The Fuji Xerox Cup since 1995/96, it was renamed the National District Championship in 1998/99. The competition was for the U-Bix Cup from 1985/86 to 1994/95.

Apart from tournaments in 1910/11, 1912/13 and 2000/01, the competition has always been on a challenge basis. To reduce the number of challenges received by the holders it was decided to pair off all the Minor Associations. This scheme commenced in the 1924/25 season, when the first three elimination matches were played. Since then numerous elimination matches have been staged to determine the right to challenge the holders of the cup.

At the end of 1999/00 it was decided to exclude the teams from the four major centres who had taken part in the tournament in recent seasons. As Dunedin Metropolitan held the trophy at the time, a national zonal tournament was held to find a new holder and the challenge format resumed in 2001/02.

Holders

Southland, 1910/11; won the tournament of six matches.
Southland, March 14, 1911, to March 25, 1913; resisted one challenge.
South Auckland, 1912/13; won the tournament of four matches.

	Challenges resisted
Wanganui, December 26, 1913, to March 28, 1919	5
Poverty Bay, March 28, 1919, to February 15, 1921	4
Wairarapa, February 15, 1921, to December 26, 1921	1
Rangitikei, December 26, 1921, to January 3, 1922	—
Nelson, January 3, 1922, to April 1, 1922	2
Wanganui, April 1, 1922, to January 22, 1924	7
Nelson, January 22, 1924, to February 2, 1926	7
Wanganui, February 2, 1926, to December 6, 1926	2
Taranaki, December 6, 1926, to December 20, 1927	3
Wanganui, December 20, 1927, to February 23, 1928	2
Manawatu, February 23, 1928, to March 29, 1930	9
Rangitikei, March 29, 1930, to December 15, 1930	—
Waikato, December 15, 1930, to January 2, 1933	11
Nelson, January 2, 1933, to December 27, 1933	2
Taranaki, December 27, 1933, to December 27, 1934	3
Manawatu, December 27, 1934, to February 14, 1938	15
Waikato, February 14, 1938, to January 30, 1940	7
Manawatu, January 30, 1940, to April 7, 1947	9
Hawke's Bay, April 7, 1947, to February 14, 1948	1
Wanganui, February 14, 1948, to December 13, 1948	1
Hutt Valley, December 13, 1948, to April 11, 1950	7
Hawke's Bay, April 11, 1950, to January 3, 1951	2
Wairarapa, January 3, 1951, to March 12, 1951	1
Waikato, March 12, 1951, to December 10, 1951	—
Nelson, December 10, 1951, to December 30, 1952	6
Wanganui, December 30, 1952, to December 28, 1955	13
Hutt Valley, December 28, 1955, to January 2, 1956	—
Northland, January 2, 1956, to December 8, 1956	2
Waikato, December 8, 1956, to December 8, 1958	9
Nelson, December 8, 1958, to February 1, 1965	28
Manawatu, February 1, 1965, to January 24, 1967	9
North Canterbury, January 24, 1967, to February 27, 1967	—
Nelson, February 27, 1967, to December 17, 1967	—
Hutt Valley, December 17, 1967, to January 7, 1968	1
Marlborough, January 7, 1968, to March 3, 1968	1
Hawke's Bay, March 3, 1968, to February 23, 1969	4

	Challenges resisted
Waikato, February 23, 1969, to February 7, 1970	3
Southland, February 7, 1970, to December 29, 1970	1
Taranaki, December 29, 1970, to March 12, 1973	12
Southland, March 12, 1973, to February 27, 1977	14
Wairarapa, February 27, 1977, to February 5, 1979	6
Nelson, February 5, 1979, to February 21, 1983	14
Northland, February 21, 1983, to March 14, 1983	2
Hawke's Bay, March 14, 1983, to February 20, 1984	2
Northland, February 20, 1984, to February 27, 1984	—
Nelson, February 27, 1984, to February 24, 1986	8
Hawke's Bay, February 24, 1986, to March 18, 1986	1
Bay of Plenty, March 18, 1986, to February 23, 1987	2
Hawke's Bay, February 23, 1987, to March 16, 1987	—
Bay of Plenty, March 16, 1987, to March 23, 1987	—
Southland, March 23, 1987, to March 15, 1988	4
North Canterbury, March 15, 1988, to March 22, 1988	—
Taranaki, March 22, 1988, to February 13, 1989	—
Northland, February 13, 1989, to February 27, 1989	—
Southland, February 27, 1989, to February 24, 1992	15
Northland, February 24, 1992, to March 23, 1992	1
Nelson, March 23, 1992, to March 15, 1993	3
Canterbury Country, March 15, 1993, to March 29, 1993	—
Manawatu, March 29, 1993, to February 28, 1994	2
Marlborough, February 28, 1994 to March 14, 1994	—
Taranaki, March 14, 1994 to January 29, 1995	7
Central Otago, January 29, 1995 to February 12, 1996	—
Nelson, February 12, 1995 to February 26, 1996	—
Hutt Valley, February 26, 1996 to January 20, 1997	2
Nelson, January 20, 1997 to February 17, 1997	1
Auckland-Manukau, February 17, 1997 to March 3, 1997	—
Bay of Plenty, March 3, 1997 to January 26, 1998	1
Wellington City, January 26, 1998 to February 9, 1998	—
Manawatu, February 9, 1998 to February 23, 1998	—
Auckland-Waitakere, February 23, 1998 to March 9, 1998	—
Northland, March 9, 1998 to February 8, 1999	2
Wellington City, February 8, 1999 to February 22, 1999	—
Canterbury Country, February 22, 1999 to January 24, 2000	2
South Canterbury, January 24, 2000 to February 7, 2000	—
Dunedin Metropolitan, February 7, 2000 to March 26, 2001	3
Hamilton, March 26, 2001 to March 25, 2002	4
Manawatu, March 25, 2002 to February 17, 2003	—
Hawke's Bay, February 17, 2003 to 3 March, 2003	—
Northland, 3 March, 2003 to 16 February, 2004	2
Mid-Canterbury, 16 February, 2004 to 7 February, 2005	1
Canterbury Country, 7 February, 2005 to 7 March, 2005	1
Hamilton, 7 March, 2005 to 12 March, 2007	5
Taranaki, 12 March, 2007	—

Career Aggregates

BATTING	M	I	NO	HS	Runs	Ave
Leggat I.B. *(Nelson)*, 1948-68	38	56	1	130	1968	35.78
Reade L.B. *(Nelson)*, 1958-73	35	57	2	117	1951	35.47
Lowans G.E. *(Nelson)*, 1958-73	30	48	1	148	1811	38.53
Anderson R.W. *(Northland and Southland)*, 1970-77	16	31	6	255	1773	70.92
McVicar C.C. *(Manawatu)*, 1935-54	28	44	1	180	1754	40.79
Spence D.V. *(Hawkes Bay and Nelson)*, 1949-67	34	51	8	151	1574	36.60
Hoskin R.N.*(Southland and Central Otago)*, 1978-96	31	35	4	162	1429	46.09
Pierce R.A. *(Nelson)*, 1969-89	24	31	2	150	1426	49.17
Congdon B.E. *(Nelson)*, 1959-65	19	28	2	133	1413	54.34
Gallichan N. *(Manawatu)*, 1925-47	29	48	5	142	1409	32.76
Hampton B.L. *(Nelson)*, 1960-75	21	32	3	236	1391	49.26
Hodgson W.G. *(Nelson)*, 1978-86	24	29	2	265	1348	49.92
Norris W.E. *(Manawatu)*, 1926-47	42	61	6	84	1242	22.58
Orton R.W. *(Rangitikei and Wanganui)*, 1911-26	20	33	1	204	1222	38.18
Hayward R.E. *(Nelson)*, 1979-89	23	26	2	113	1115	46.45
Holland C.A. *(Wanganui)*, 1912-28	24	38	4	111	1060	31.17
Edwards G.N. *(Nelson)*, 1972-86	24	30	2	236	1038	37.07
Toynbee M.H. *(Nelson)*, 1974-81	13	17	3	200*	1031	73.64

BOWLING	M	Runs	Wkts	Ave
Holland C.A. *(Wanganui)*, 1912-28	24	2202	189	11.65
Gallichan N. *(Manawatu)*, 1925-47	29	2053	177	11.59
Leggat I.B. *(Nelson)*, 1948-67	38	2149	134	16.03
Spence D.V. *(Hawkes Bay and Nelson)*, 1949-67	34	1697	110	15.42
Alabaster G.D. *(Thames Valley and Southland)*, 1961-79	20	1508	102	14.78
Newman J. *(Nelson)*, 1922-46	20	1348	97	13.89
Alabaster J.C. *(Southland)*, 1955-74	14	1223	92	13.29
Bernau E.H.L. *(Wanganui and Hawkes Bay)*, 1912-28	14	1009	90	11.21

Highest Individual Innings

272*	Kinzett C.A.	Nelson v Marlborough	Nelson	1933/34
268	Robinson G.G.	Hamilton v Northland	Hamilton	2005/06
265	Hodgson W.G.	Nelson v Taranaki	Nelson	1983/84
264	Everest J.K.	Waikato v Manawatu	Hamilton	1956/57
255	Anderson R.W.	Southland v Ashburton County	Invercargill	1976/77
236	Hampton B.L.	Nelson v Waikato	Nelson	1963/64
236	Edwards G.N.	Nelson v North Canterbury	Nelson	1984/85
229	Douglas M.W.	Nelson v Southland	Nelson	1992/93

Best Bowling in an Innings

10-35	Holland C.A.	Wanganui v South Taranaki	Wanganui	1922/23
9-103	Jordan A.B.	Taranaki v Hutt Valley	New Plymouth	1971/72
8-9	Clough R.	Waikato v Bay of Plenty	Hamilton	1938/39
8-20	Andrews S.L.	Hamilton v Northland	Hamilton	2001/02
8-25	Smith J.D.	Waikato v Horowhenua	Hamilton	1969/70
8-25	Jordan A.B.	Taranaki v Franklin	New Plymouth	1971/72
8-26	Haycock R.S.	Nelson v Marlborough	Nelson	1924/25

Best Bowling in a Match

14-79	Holland C.A.	Wanganui v South Taranaki	Wanganui	1922/23
14-89	Jordan A.B.	Taranaki v Franklin	New Plymouth	1971/72
14-133	Upston I.A.	Hutt Valley v Wanganui	Wanganui	1955/56
14-149	Sulzberger G.P.	Taranaki v Manawatu	New Plymouth	1994/95

HAMILTON v NORTHLAND

Hawke Cup

at Galloway Park, Hamilton on 10, 11, 12 February, 2007
Toss : Hamilton. Umpires : K.C. Manley & E.J. Gray
Close of play: 1st day: Hamilton 287-5, Hatwell 4, Devcich 4; 2nd day: Northland 181 all out
First innings win to Hamilton

HAMILTON

FIRST INNINGS	Runs	Mins	Balls	6s	4s	SECOND INNINGS	Runs	Mins	Balls	6s	4s
B-J.Watling c Hood b Child	89	289	219	-	11	c Lee b Yovich	11	32	26	-	2
G.D.Irwin run out	7	20	17	-	-	c Marshall H.J.H. b Child	32	96	78	1	3
M.G.Orchard c Child b Yovich	5	31	27	-	-						
G.G.Robinson b Schwartfeger	47	92	86	-	4	c Marshall J.A.H. b Child	47	94	87	-	5
N.K.W.Horsley c Knox b Yovich	98	179	151	1	15	c sub (J.Phillips) b Child	29	74	85	-	4
B.J.Hatwell not out	70	222	150	-	3						
A.P.Devcich c Thompson b Marshall H.J.H.	20	64	58	-	2	(6) b Child	21	18	14	2	1
R.R.Shutte lbw b Marshall H.J.H.	0	7	8	-	-	(3) lbw b Marshall H.J.H.	12	29	25	-	1
S.J.M.McLeod lbw b Yovich	7	35	31	-	1	(7) not out	0	4	2	-	-
N.M.Daley*† c Marshall J.A.H. b Thompson	24	68	77	-	1						
T.T.Davis c Marshall J.A.H. b Thompson	6	8	10	1	-						
Extras (b 13, lb 17, w 3, nb 12)	45					(lb 1, nb 2)	3				
TOTAL (137.3 overs)	**418**	512				(51.2 overs) (6 wkts)	**155**	176			

NORTHLAND

	Runs	Mins	Balls	6s	4s
S.T.Knox lbw b Orchard	7	56	50	-	-
B.S.Wilson not out	59	247	181	-	8
A.W.Evans c Devcich b Irwin	52	58	50	-	10
H.J.H.Marshall b Davis	5	25	21	-	-
J.A.H.Marshall* c Robinson b McLeod	19	33	23	-	2
J.B.Lee c Daley b Shutte	8	28	28	-	1
J.A.F.Yovich c Daley b Shutte	6	14	16	-	1
B.L.Hood† c Robinson b Shutte	1	9	6	-	-
A.D.Thompson lbw b Shutte	2	9	10	-	-
J.S.Child lbw b Shutte	0	3	2	-	-
S.Schwartfeger lbw b Shutte	0	3	4	-	-
Extras (lb 2, w 1, nb 19)	22				
TOTAL (62 overs)	**181**	247			

Bowling	*O*	*M*	*R*	*W*	*O*	*M*	*R*	*W*
NORTHLAND								
Yovich	36	10	83	3	7	4	9	1
Schwartfeger	20	4	64	1	5	0	18	0
Child	26	6	55	1	14.2	5	27	4
Marshall H.J.H.	25	5	75	2	6	2	9	1
Thompson	23.3	6	78	2	19	0	91	0
Evans	5	1	16	0				
Wilson	2	0	17	0				
HAMILTON								
Davis	15	1	62	1				
Orchard	10	5	19	1				
Shutte	14	6	53	6				
Irwin	11	2	18	1				
McLeod	12	3	27	1				

Fall of Wickets

	H *1st*	*N* *1st*	*H* *2nd*
1st	15	25	19
2nd	27	97	35
3rd	96	100	68
4th	262	143	125
5th	283	163	152
6th	325	175	155
7th	329	177	-
8th	345	179	-
9th	408	181	-
10th	418	181	-

HAMILTON v CANTERBURY COUNTRY — Hawke Cup

at Galloway Park, Hamilton on 24, 25, 26 February, 2007
Toss : Canterbury Country. Umpires : D.G. Paterson & K. Cross
Close of play: 1st day: Hamilton 26-0, Bettley 5, Irwin 16; 2nd day: Hamilton 310-6, Shutte 34
First innings win to Hamilton

CANTERBURY COUNTRY

FIRST INNINGS	*Runs*	*Mins*	*Balls*	*6s*	*4s*
P.J.Rugg* c Dodunski b Shutte	43	175	25	-	8
R.M.Frew b Verma	1	7	8	-	-
C.G.Bartholomuesz lbw b Verma	4	16	14	-	-
A.W.Robertson† b Irwin	34	59	55	-	6
D.H.Fulton lbw b Shutte	3	18	17	-	-
M.P.Goldstein b Dodunski	36	60	61	-	6
W.D.Bell run out	57	114	89	-	7
S.C.Dunnett lbw b Verma	10	25	21	-	1
S.L.Langrope c Shutte b Irwin	4	13	7	-	1
J.M.Domigan not out	37	103	85	-	5
I.C.King lbw b Dodunski	27	39	41	-	5
Extras (b 3, lb 6, w 3, nb 3)	15				
TOTAL (86.4 overs)	**271**	319			

HAMILTON

	Runs	*Mins*	*Balls*	*6s*	*4s*
K.G.Bettley lbw b King	5	77	73	-	-
G.D.Irwin c Fulton b Goldstein	112	340	289	-	14
S.J.M.McLeod lbw b Goldstein	30	88	80	-	4
A.P.Devcich b Langrope	25	68	48	-	3
B.J.Hatwell b Langrope	5	46	38	-	-
R.R.Shutte c Langrope b Domigan	84	181	155	1	12
L.W.Martin c Rugg b Bell	37	102	101	-	7
G.D.Steele not out	76	143	127	1	7
N.M.Daley*† b Domigan	7	8	9	-	1
M.D.Dodunski lbw b Domigan	4	7	7	-	1
A.Verma run out	43	104	72	-	4
Extras (b 12, lb 12, w 2, nb 5)	31				
TOTAL (169 overs)	**459**	586			

Bowling	*O*	*M*	*R*	*W*
HAMILTON				
Verma	20	6	54	3
Dodunski	22.4	5	60	2
Shutte	19	4	80	2
Irwin	15	4	44	2
McLeod	8	0	19	0
Devcich	2	0	5	0
CANTERBURY COUNTRY				
King	21	12	27	1
Langrope	23	6	73	2
Domigan	30	9	68	3
Bell	24	6	81	1
Dunnett	21	6	29	0
Goldstein	40	8	116	2
Bartholomuesz	10	1	41	0

Fall of Wickets	***CC***	***H***
	1st	*1st*
1st	1	31
2nd	2	95
3rd	54	146
4th	61	173
5th	119	218
6th	131	310
7th	161	323
8th	170	330
9th	220	334
10th	271	459

HAMILTON v TARANAKI — Hawke Cup

at Galloway Park, Hamilton on 10, 11, 12 March, 2007
Toss : Taranaki. Umpires : D.J. Ellwood & D.G. Paterson
Close of play: 1st day: Taranaki 257-7, Watkins 44, Bolstad 11; 2nd day: Hamilton 150-3, McLeod 24, Dodunski 3
First innings win to Taranaki

TARANAKI

FIRST INNINGS	Runs	Mins	Balls	6s	4s
M.Broadmore* c Hatwell b Dodunski	13	35	35	-	2
K.Muller c Daley b Shutte	16	68	43	-	1
K.Tai c Daley b Irwin	55	220	180	1	7
A.Habib lbw b Shutte	17	44	37	-	2
L.Johnston c Daley b Dodunski	35	92	85	-	7
T.Stewart† b Robinson	27	72	60	-	4
J.Watkins c McLeod b Verma	126	259	185	2	17
D.Good c Martin b Verma	12	40	32	-	2
D.Bolstad c Daley b Shutte	11	75	57	-	2
N.Taylor c sub (K.G.Bettley) b Verma	3	14	13	-	-
C.Cruikshank not out	18	104	90	-	-
Extras (b 5, lb 19, w 6, nb 7)	37				
TOTAL (135.1 overs)	**370**	516			

SECOND INNINGS	Runs	Mins	Balls	6s	4s
not out	20	23	16	-	3
not out	5	23	20	-	-
	0				
(6 overs) 0 wkts)	**25**	23			

HAMILTON

	Runs	Mins	Balls	6s	4s
G.D.Steele lbw b Watkins	20	115	97	-	2
G.D.Irwin c Stewart b Taylor	66	165	151	-	10
S.J.M.McLeod c Muller b Bolstad	33	117	93	-	3
G.G.Robinson c Habib b Cruikshank	25	32	33	-	3
M.D.Dodunski not out	64	223	200	-	7
B.J.Hatwell lbw b Bolstad	0	16	16	-	-
R.R.Shutte c Broadmore b Cruikshank	18	50	35	-	2
A.P.Devcich c Stewart b Watkins	20	24	14	-	4
L.W.Martin c Stewart b Taylor	13	22	23	-	3
N.M.Daley*† b Cruikshank	11	21	20	-	2
A.Verma st Stewart b Watkins	5	50	50	-	-
Extras (b 1, lb 4, w 1, nb 9)	15				
TOTAL (115.3 overs)	**290**	422			

Bowling	*O*	*M*	*R*	*W*				
HAMILTON								
Verma	24.1	8	53	3	3	1	13	0
Dodunski	23	6	50	2	1	1	0	0
Shutte	27	8	58	3				
Irwin	26	7	68	1	2	0	12	0
Martin	15	5	31	0				
McLeod	7	1	27	0				
Robinson	13	0	59	1				
TARANAKI								
Cruikshank	30	8	92	3				
Bolstad	21	9	50	2				
Taylor	30	7	65	2				
Watkins	21.3	9	60	3				
Good	13	9	18	0				

Fall of Wickets

	T	*H*	*T*
	1st	*1st*	*2nd*
1st	22	81	-
2nd	38	106	-
3rd	76	139	-
4th	134	161	-
5th	168	161	-
6th	187	193	-
7th	216	228	-
8th	257	250	-
9th	267	265	-
10th	370	290	-

WOMEN'S CRICKET

Compiled by Catherine Campbell

The White Ferns' season started in October with Cricket Australia hosting the Rose Bowl series in Brisbane. The team tied the Twenty20 international, lost the resulting bowl-off then went on to lose the Rose Bowl series 5-0 with the first three matches being decided in the last over. Two players made their international debuts in the series, Ros Kember from the State Auckland Hearts and 17-year-old Sophie Devine from the State Wellington Blaze.

The State League was won by the State Canterbury Magicians. Wellington led for most of the competition and qualified top to host the final with Canterbury being one of four teams who could have made the final going into the last round, such was the evenness of the competition. Canterbury convincingly beat the home team in the final played at the Basin Reserve.

The White Ferns and New Zealand A teams played a series of matches against each other at Lincoln University before New Zealand A hosted the Australian Youth team in a three-match series at Lincoln with the teams winning one match each with one match tied.

The White Ferns headed to India in February to play in a Quadrangular tournament involving the top four countries in the world – Australia, India, New Zealand and England. After qualifying at the top of round robin play with only one loss, the White Ferns lost the final to Australia. During the tournament two players made their international debuts – Rowan Milburn and Selena Charteris, both from Canterbury.

During the tournament Rebecca Rolls became the ninth woman to play 100 one-day internationals and the twelfth to bring up 2000 one-day international runs.

The National Development Tournament was hosted for the first time by New Zealand Cricket at its grounds at Lincoln University but unfortunately the tournament was badly affected by wet weather. The title was won by Wellington.

New Plymouth Girls' High School continued their dominance at secondary schoolgirls level winning the New Zealand Community Trust Cup played at the Ilam Playing Fields. Christchurch and Cobham Intermediate won the Milo Shield, the national intermediate schoolgirls' knockout competition.

PLAYER OF THE YEAR

Maria Fahey is the Player of the Year. Left handed opener Fahey was the White Ferns' leading run scorer in the season amassing 387 runs in 12 innings. She averaged 32.25 and scored five fifties. In the Rose Bowl Series played in Brisbane in October 2006 she scored 202 runs at an average of 40.40.

Returning to play in the State League she scored 380 runs for the State Canterbury Magicians at an average of 42.22. In the Quadrangular Series played in India in February 2007 Fahey scored 185 runs at an average of 26.42.

Fahey has played 40 one-day internationals and has scored 1120 runs at an average of 30.27. A tenacious opening batsman she was the backbone of the White Ferns' batting lineup in 2006/07 and will be looking to build on her impressive performances on the 2007 winter tours. She won the Ruth Martin Cup at the New Zealand Cricket Awards Dinner for the most meritorious batting performance in international cricket in the 2006/07 season.

PROMISING PLAYER

Lucy Doolan from the State Wellington Blaze is the promising player of the year. Doolan captained Wellington in the National Development Tournament and was joint winner of the Trish McKelvey Trophy for the most outstanding player at the tournament.

She then went on to score 172 runs for Wellington in the State League where she also took 11 wickets at an average of 18.72. These performances saw her earn selection in the New Zealand A team for the series against Australia Youth at Lincoln University in February. She scored 126 runs in three innings opening the batting and had a strike rate of 75.

Her all-round skills of top-order batting, off-spin bowling and wicketkeeping make her a very promising player and she has been selected in the White Ferns 2007 winter squad.

ROSE BOWL

Due to the Quadrangular Series being played in India in February, Cricket Australia hosted the Rose Bowl Series in Brisbane in October. Although the series was won by Australia 5-0 it was very evenly contested with the first two matches being decided in the last over. The closeness was not surprising given the Twenty20 international to start the series was tied.

Two players made their debuts for the White Ferns in the series – State Auckland Hearts opening batsman Ros Kember and 17-year-old Sophie Devine from the State Wellington Blaze. Maria Fahey scored 202 runs in the series at an average of 40.40 and a strike rate of 65.

The team was: Haidee Tiffen *(captain)*, Sarah Burke, Maria Fahey, Helen Watson, *(Canterbury)*, Ros Kember, Rebecca Rolls *(Auckland)*, Sophie Devine, Anna Dodd *(Wellington)*, Sara McGlashan, Aimee Mason *(Central Districts)*, Sarah Tsukigawa *(Otago)*, Nicola Browne, Louise Milliken *(Northern Districts)*. Coach, Steve Jenkin; Manager, Catherine Campbell; Assistant Coach, Gary Stead; Physiotherapist, Rachelle Guy; Trainer, Greg Owen.

New Zealand Averages

BATTING	*M*	*I*	*NO*	*HS*	*Agg*	*Ave*	*100s*	*50s*	*Ct*	*St*	*SR*
M.F. Fahey	5	5	0	69	202	40.40	-	2	2	-	65
A.L. Mason	4	4	0	71	122	30.50	-	1	1	-	78
N.J. Browne	5	5	2	35*	90	30.00	-	-	1	-	60
R.J. Rolls	5	5	0	66	133	26.60	-	1	3	1	91
A.M. Dodd	5	5	3	20*	45	22.50	-	-	3	-	83
S.J. McGlashan	5	5	0	45	92	18.40	-	-	-	-	59
S.K. Burke	4	2	1	9	16	16.00	-	-	-	-	84
H.M. Tiffen	5	5	0	30	78	15.60	-	-	1	-	55
H.M. Watson	5	5	0	39	77	15.40	-	-	1	-	74
R.J. Kember	3	3	0	18	42	14.00	-	-	2	-	41
S.J. Tsukigawa	4	4	0	10	29	7.25	-	-	1	-	42
S.F.M. Devine	3	2	1	6*	7	7.00	-	-	1	-	20
L.E. Milliken	2	1	0	0	0	0.00	-	-	-	-	0

BOWLING	*O*	*M*	*R*	*W*	*Ave*	*Best*	*R/O*
L.E. Milliken	18	3	72	4	18.00	3-45	4.00
H.M. Watson	47.4	7	158	6	26.33	2-32	3.31
S.F.M. Devine	21.5	1	92	3	30.66	2-32	4.21
N.J. Browne	28	3	124	4	31.00	2-36	4.43
S.K. Burke	34	6	124	4	31.00	1-19	3.65
A.M. Dodd	36	3	160	4	40.00	2-18	4.44
S.J. Tsukigawa	28	0	135	3	45.00	2-39	4.82
A.L. Mason	34	3	184	1	184.00	1-47	5.41

Australia Averages

BATTING	*M*	*I*	*NO*	*HS*	*Agg*	*Ave*	*100s*	*50s*	*Ct*	*St*	*SR*
K.L. Rolton	2	2	1	44	60	60.00	-	-	-	-	63
S. Nitschke	5	5	3	31	87	43.50	-	-	4	-	83
L.C. Sthalekar	5	5	0	53	210	42.00	-	2	1	-	70
L.J. Poulton	5	5	0	101	197	39.40	1	1	1	-	71
M.A.J. Goszko	4	4	0	40	98	24.50	-	-	-	-	62
J. Hayes	5	5	2	36*	60	20.00	-	-	2	-	72
J.M. Purves	5	5	0	33	80	16.00	-	-	5	-	70
K.A. Blackwell	4	4	0	18	54	13.50	-	-	1	-	41
M.J. Bulow	5	5	0	29	54	10.80	-	-	1	-	40
K.E. Pike	4	2	1	3*	4	4.00	-	-	3	-	66
S.J. Andrews	4	2	0	4	6	3.00	-	-	-	-	85
C.L. Fitzpatrick	3	2	0	2	3	1.50	-	-	-	-	13
S.J. Edwards	1	1	1	45*	45	-	-	-	1	-	93
C.R. Smith	3	1	1	11*	11	-	-	-	-	-	47

BOWLING	*O*	*M*	*R*	*W*	*Ave*	*Best*	*R/O*
K.E. Pike	31	5	97	6	16.16	4-23	3.13
S. Nitschke	42	4	128	7	18.28	3-32	3.05
C.R. Smith	22.3	2	90	4	22.50	2-18	4.00
S.J. Andrews	32	3	147	6	24.50	2-19	4.59
K.L. Rolton	10	2	27	1	27.00	1-27	2.70
J. Hayes	37	6	197	6	32.83	3-37	5.32
C.L. Fitzpatrick	25.4	0	134	4	33.50	2-49	5.22
L.C. Sthalekar	40	3	140	3	46.66	1-17	3.50

QUEENSLAND v NEW ZEALAND — One-day

at Peter Burge Oval, Brisbane on 16 October, 2006
Toss : New Zealand. Umpires : D.L. Orchard & B.N.J. Oxenford
New Zealand won by 45 runs.

Both sides used 13 players in this match, New Zealand's only warm-up match before the Rose Bowl series which was being played very early in the season and well before New Zealand's domestic State League had begun.

McGlashan was easily the best of the visiting batsmen, scoring 50 off 63 balls, with four boundaries. The wickets were shared by the Queensland bowlers.

In reply the home team began badly and wickets fell at regular intervals. Only White and Price could reach double figures. Six New Zealand bowlers had success.

NEW ZEALAND

	Runs	Mins	Balls	6s	4s
R.J.Rolls† run out	2	3	4	-	-
M.F.Fahey b Matheson	22	56	34	-	2
H.M.Tiffen* b RImmington	17	35	27	-	2
S.J.Tsukigawa c Harris b White	8	14	12	-	2
S.J.McGlashan c Matheson b Price	50	89	63	-	4
R.J.Kember c Price b Matheson	4	8	13	-	-
A.L.Mason c Matheson b Broadfoot	9	27	17	-	2
N.J.Browne c Matheson b Broadfoot	2	11	14	-	-
H.M.Watson c Matheson b Bates	4	15	22	-	-
L.E.Milliken c Whittaker b Price	5	30	29	-	-
S.K.Burke not out	0				
S.F.M.Devine					
A.M.Dodd					
Extras (lb 2, w 21, nb 2)	25				
TOTAL (40.1 overs) (8 wkts)	**148**	152			

QUEENSLAND

	Runs	Mins	Balls	6s	4s
B.Matheson* run out	0	5	6	-	-
J.C.Price† b Browne	20	64	37	-	-
D.L.Hollis run out	7	35	27	-	1
C.Reibelt c Rolls b Watson	5	40	36	-	-
L.C.Broadfoot run out	1	28	16	-	-
M.L.White c Kember b Dodd	36	64	41	-	7
K.Short c Tiffen b Devine	1	13	10	-	-
L.Bates b Tsukigawa	1	5	7	-	-
A.Christie st Rolls b Mason	0	24	19	-	-
S.Harris not out	7	12	13	-	1
D.Kimmince st Rolls b Dodd	0	2	4	-	-
R.Rimmington					
F.Whittaker					
Extras (lb 2, w 23)	25				
TOTAL (36 overs)	**103**	151			

Bowling	*O*	*M*	*R*	*W*
QUEENSLAND				
Rimmington	6	1	16	1
Kimmince	6	0	35	0
White	5	0	35	1
Matheson	4	1	6	2
Broadfoot	10	0	35	2
Bates	7	0	17	1
Price	2.1	0	2	2
NEW ZEALAND				
Milliken	5	2	9	0
Burke	5	0	20	0
Browne	5	2	7	1
Watson	5	1	17	1
Devine	5	1	21	1
Tsukigawa	5	1	9	1
Mason	3	1	12	1
Dodd	3	0	6	2

Fall of Wickets	*NZ*	*Q*
1st	2	1
2nd	42	29
3rd	54	39
4th	57	50
5th	62	60
6th	101	66
7th	111	69
8th	124	93
9th	145	102
10th	148	103

AUSTRALIA v NEW ZEALAND — Twenty20 International

at Allan Border Field, Brisbane on 18 October, 2006
Toss : Australia. Umpires : A.R. Curran & N.S. McNamara
Australia won a bowl out after scores finished level.

Australia put New Zealand into bat in the first ever Twenty20 International between the two countries. Rolls and Fahey got the innings underway with a partnership of 80 in 10.1 overs. Rolls, 41 off 30 balls, including six fours and a six, and Fahey, 43 off 39 balls, including six fours, were the backbone of the innings. After twenty overs New Zealand was 141-7.

In reply Rolton scored 71 not out off 59 balls, including 11 fours. Australia needed three off the last ball to win but managed only two and the scores were tied. Australia won the resulting bowl out.

NEW ZEALAND

	Runs	Mins	Balls	6s	4s
R.J.Rolls† lbw b Rolton	41	38	30	1	6
M.F.Fahey c Sthalekar b Hayes	43	45	39	-	6
H.M.Tiffen* st Purves b Hayes	16	20	20	-	-
S.J.Tsukigawa lbw b Sthalekar	6	8	9	-	-
A.L.Mason run out	15	14	11	-	2
S.J.McGlashan c Hayes b Andrews	11	10	8	1	-
N.J.Browne not out	2	2	2	-	-
S.F.M.Devine run out	0	1	0	-	-
H.M.Watson not out	1	1	1	-	-
S.K.Burke					
L.E.Milliken					
Extras (lb 3, w 3)	6				
TOTAL (20 overs) (7 wkts)	**141**	81			

AUSTRALIA

	Runs	Mins	Balls	6s	4s
M.J.Bulow run out	11	26	13	-	1
L.J.Poulton c Rolls b Milliken	10	10	10	-	1
K.L.Rolton* not out	71	65	59	-	11
L.C.Sthalekar c Rolls b Browne	7	7	12	-	1
K.A.Blackwell b Devine	20	23	20	-	2
M.A.J.Goszko run out	9	14	9	-	1
J.M.Purves† not out	2	5	2	-	-
C.L.Fitzpatrick					
J.Hayes					
K.E.Pike					
S.J.Andrews					
Extras (lb 1, w 5, nb 5)	11				
TOTAL (20 overs) (5 wkts)	**141**	81			

Bowling	*O*	*M*	*R*	*W*
AUSTRALIA				
Fitzpatrick	4	0	18	0
Andrews	4	0	42	1
Pike	2	0	22	0
Rolton	2	0	11	1
Sthalekar	4	0	26	1
Hayes	4	0	19	2
NEW ZEALAND				
Milliken	4	0	28	1
Devine	4	0	27	1
Burke	3	0	30	0
Browne	4	0	19	1
Mason	4	0	31	0
Watson	1	0	5	0

Fall of Wickets	***NZ***	***A***
1st	80	19
2nd	94	43
3rd	109	58
4th	113	105
5th	138	133
6th	139	-
7th	140	-
8th	-	-
9th	-	-
10th	-	-

AUSTRALIA v NEW ZEALAND — Rose Bowl

at Allan Border Field, Brisbane on 20 October, 2006
Toss : Australia. Umpires : T.P. Laycock & N.S. McNamara
Australia won by 1 run.

Australia won the toss and elected to bat first. Lisa Sthalekar top scored with 51 off 75 balls, including two fours. At the end of fifty overs Australia had made 201-9 with Dodd taking 2-18 off six overs.

In reply Mason led the New Zealand run chase with 71 off 82 balls, including ten fours and a six. New Zealand required nine runs from the final over and then three off the last ball but Burke was run out going for a second run and Australia had won by one run to lead the series 1–0.

AUSTRALIA

	Runs	Mins	Balls	6s	4s
M.J.Bulow c Browne b Watson	29	69	58	-	5
L.J.Poulton lbw b Burke	0	11	9	-	-
K.L.Rolton* c Dodd b Mason	44	89	64	-	6
L.C.Sthalekar lbw b Milliken	51	89	75	-	2
K.A.Blackwell c Rolls b Dodd	11	28	27	-	-
M.A.J.Goszko c Watson b Dodd	5	12	19	-	-
J.M.Purves† run out	15	26	20	-	2
C.L.Fitzpatrick b Browne	2	5	4	-	-
J.Hayes run out	10	12	7	-	1
S.Nitschke not out	6	16	13	-	-
K.E.Pike not out	3	8	6	-	-
Extras (lb 5, w 13, nb 7)	25				
TOTAL (50 overs) (9 wkts)	**201**	187			

NEW ZEALAND

	Runs	Mins	Balls	6s	4s
R.J.Rolls† run out	1	2	1	-	-
M.F.Fahey run out	21	61	47	-	3
H.M.Tiffen* lbw b Fitzpatrick	14	19	21	-	3
S.J.Tsukigawa lbw b Pike	10	25	24	-	2
S.J.McGlashan c Purves b Sthalekar	21	60	56	-	2
A.L.Mason run out	71	98	82	1	10
N.J.Browne b Fitzpatrick	17	45	41	-	-
H.M.Watson c Purves b Rolton	11	11	8	-	1
A.M.Dodd not out	15	20	10	-	1
S.K.Burke run out	9	13	10	-	-
L.E.Milliken					
Extras (lb 2, w 8)	10				
TOTAL (50 overs) (9 wkts)	**200**	181			

Bowling	*O*	*M*	*R*	*W*
NEW ZEALAND				
Milliken	8	2	27	1
Burke	6	2	19	1
Browne	7	1	33	1
Watson	10	0	31	1
Tsukigawa	4	0	21	0
Mason	9	0	47	1
Dodd	6	1	18	2
AUSTRALIA				
Fitzpatrick	10	0	49	2
Rolton	10	2	27	1
Pike	7	1	17	1
Hayes	7	0	43	0
Sthalekar	9	1	32	1
Nitschke	7	0	30	0

Fall of Wickets	***A***	***NZ***
1st	0	1
2nd	53	21
3rd	93	44
4th	123	49
5th	135	106
6th	166	164
7th	174	166
8th	182	183
9th	189	200
10th	-	-

AUSTRALIA v NEW ZEALAND — Rose Bowl

at Allan Border Field, Brisbane on 22 October, 2006
Toss : New Zealand. Umpires : A.R. Curran & T.P. Laycock
Australia won by 1 wicket.

New Zealand won the toss and chose to bat. Rolls scored an aggressive 66 off only 54 balls, including 12 fours and put on 78 for the first wicket with Fahey who made 29. However, the later batsmen could not capitalise on the good start and New Zealand were all out for 175 in 46.4 overs.

In reply Australia reached victory off the second to last ball, with nine wickets down. Nitschke, with 31 off 36 balls, including four fours and one six, guided the team home. Milliken was the most successful of the New Zealand bowlers with 3-45 off ten overs.

NEW ZEALAND

	Runs	Mins	Balls	6s	4s
R.J.Rolls† c Blackwell b Andrews	66	72	54	-	12
M.F.Fahey b Sthalekar	29	45	39	-	6
H.M.Tiffen* run out	2	5	3	-	-
S.J.McGlashan b Andrews	8	15	10	-	2
A.L.Mason b Hayes	15	29	30	-	2
R.J.Kember run out	9	36	23	-	2
N.J.Browne c Purves b Nitschke	6	22	23	-	1
H.M.Watson b Fitzpatrick	24	54	46	-	3
A.M.Dodd b Hayes	2	10	18	-	-
L.E.Milliken lbw b Hayes	0	5	6	-	-
S.F.M.Devine not out	6	26	29	-	-
Extras (lb 2, w 5, nb 1)	8				
TOTAL (46.4 overs)	**175**	164			

AUSTRALIA

	Runs	Mins	Balls	6s	4s
M.J.Bulow c Dodd b Devine	0	6	3	-	-
L.J.Poulton lbw b Browne	16	34	25	-	3
L.C.Sthalekar run out	53	95	74	-	7
K.A.Blackwell c Rolls b Milliken	18	53	55	-	2
J.M.Purves† c Dodd b Milliken	0	2	1	-	-
C.L.Fitzpatrick b Dodd	1	22	19	-	1
J.Hayes run out	8	34	32	-	-
S.Nitschke lbw b Milliken	31	44	36	1	4
K.L.Rolton* not out	16	50	31	-	-
S.J.Andrews run out	2	2	3	-	-
C.R.Smith not out	11	25	23	-	1
Extras (lb 4, w 13, nb 3)	20				
TOTAL (49.5 overs) (9 wkts)	**176**	188			

Bowling	*O*	*M*	*R*	*W*
AUSTRALIA				
Fitzpatrick	6.4	0	37	1
Smith	7	1	27	0
Sthalekar	9	1	34	1
Hayes	10	4	37	3
Andrews	6	1	32	2
Nitschke	8	4	6	1
NEW ZEALAND				
Milliken	10	1	45	3
Devine	7.5	1	34	1
Browne	2	0	6	1
Watson	10	0	26	0
Mason	10	2	35	0
Dodd	10	2	26	1

Fall of Wickets	***NZ***	***A***
1st	78	11
2nd	82	42
3rd	106	99
4th	107	100
5th	127	105
6th	132	108
7th	149	128
8th	153	152
9th	153	154
10th	175	-

AUSTRALIA v NEW ZEALAND — Rose Bowl

at Allan Border Field, Brisbane on 24 October, 2006
Toss : Australia. Umpires : A.R. Curran & B.N.J. Oxenford
Australia won by 5 runs.

Australia won the toss and decided to bat. Opener Leah Poulton scored 101 off 136 balls, including seven fours and one six, and combined in a 106 run partnership for the third wicket with Sthalekar. After fifty overs Australia had scored 236-6. Devine and Watson each took two wickets.

In reply New Zealand made steady progress. Fahey top scored with 69 off 103 balls, with 11 fours, and Rolls, Tiffen, Brown and Dodd all made useful contributions but New Zealand ended up just short at 231-8 at the end of fifty overs, giving Australia victory by five runs and an unbeatable 3-nil series lead.

AUSTRALIA

	Runs	Mins	Balls	6s	4s
M.J.Bulow c Rolls b Burke	9	15	19	-	2
L.J.Poulton b Watson	101	184	136	1	7
M.A.J.Goszko c Fahey b Devine	24	50	31	-	2
L.C.Sthalekar* c & b Tsukigawa	46	69	66	-	2
K.A.Blackwell lbw b Watson	10	17	15	-	2
J.M.Purves† c & b Devine	10	21	18	-	-
S.Nitschke not out	14	14	12	-	1
J.Hayes not out	4	6	5	-	-
C.L.Fitzpatrick					
S.J.Andrews					
K.E.Pike					
Extras (lb 3, w 13, nb 2)	18				
TOTAL (50 overs) (6 wkts)	**236**	191			

NEW ZEALAND

	Runs	Mins	Balls	6s	4s
R.J.Rolls† c & b Pike	25	37	31	-	3
M.F.Fahey c Purves b Andrews	69	113	103	-	12
H.M.Tiffen* c Pike b Nitschke	23	57	53	-	3
S.J.Tsukigawa run out	10	15	17	-	1
S.J.McGlashan c & b Hayes	18	42	28	-	3
A.L.Mason c Hayes b Andrews	14	23	19	-	-
N.J.Browne not out	35	43	27	-	4
S.F.M.Devine b Fitzpatrick	1	5	6	-	-
H.M.Watson b Hayes	1	4	2	-	-
A.M.Dodd not out	20	16	14	-	2
S.K.Burke					
Extras (lb 8, w 7)	15				
TOTAL (50 overs) (8 wkts)	**231**	181			

Bowling	*O*	*M*	*R*	*W*
NEW ZEALAND				
Browne	8	0	32	0
Burke	10	2	30	1
Devine	7	0	32	2
Mason	7	1	38	0
Watson	9	0	42	2
Dodd	4	0	28	0
Tsukigawa	5	0	31	1
AUSTRALIA				
Fitzpatrick	9	0	48	1
Andrews	10	1	51	2
Pike	7	2	21	1
Sthalekar	5	0	26	0
Hayes	10	2	53	2
Nitschke	9	0	24	1

Fall of Wickets	***A***	***NZ***
1st	12	46
2nd	60	108
3rd	166	135
4th	190	136
5th	214	162
6th	221	181
7th	-	181
8th	-	187
9th	-	-
10th	-	-

AUSTRALIA v NEW ZEALAND — Rose Bowl

at Allan Border Field, Brisbane on 26 October, 2006
Toss : Australia. Umpires : A.R. Curran & T.P. Laycock
Australia won by 85 runs.

Australia won the toss and chose to bat. Poulton held the innings together with 68 off 77 balls, including ten boundaries. Sthalekar scored 43 off 42 balls and Purvis a run-a-ball 33. Watson and Tsukigawa each took two wickets and after fifty overs Australia had made 252-9.

Chasing the biggest score of the series New Zealand never really got underway. Fahey, batting at number four, top scored with 56 off 78 balls, including seven fours but it was in vain as New Zealand were all out for 167 in 43.3 overs.

AUSTRALIA

	Runs	Mins	Balls	6s	4s
M.J.Bulow c Kember b Watson	14	40	37	-	3
L.J.Poulton run out	68	121	77	-	10
M.A.J.Goszko c Kember b Burke	29	55	52	-	4
L.C.Sthalekar* c Mason b Dodd	43	38	42	-	5
K.A.Blackwell c Tiffen b Watson	15	43	33	-	-
J.M.Purvest† lbw b Tsukigawa	33	40	33	-	4
S.Nitschke not out	20	25	20	-	2
J.Hayes b Tsukigawa	2	5	3	-	-
K.E.Pike run out	1	1	1	-	-
S.J.Andrews run out	4	6	4	-	1
C.R.Smith					
Extras (b 4, lb 1, w 16, nb 2)	23				
TOTAL (50 overs) (9 wkts)	**252**	191			

NEW ZEALAND

	Runs	Mins	Balls	6s	4s
R.J.Rolls† lbw b Smith	11	29	26	-	-
R.J.Kember c Poulton b Nitschke	18	50	43	-	3
H.M.Tiffen* b Nitschke	30	28	31	-	4
M.F.Fahey b Andrews	56	91	78	-	7
S.J.McGlashan b Nitschke	0	9	7	-	-
S.J.Tsukigawa c Bulow b Sthalekar	5	14	12	-	1
N.J.Browne retired hurt	6	18	13	-	1
A.L.Mason c Nitschke b Hayes	22	18	25	-	3
H.M.Watson b Andrews	2	12	7	-	-
A.M.Dodd c Sthalekar b Smith	6	13	10	-	-
S.K.Burke not out	7	10	9	-	1
Extras (lb 2, w 2	4				
TOTAL (43.3 overs)	**167**	156			

Bowling	*O*	*M*	*R*	*W*
NEW ZEALAND				
Browne	3	1	17	0
Burke	9	1	42	1
Watson	10	4	32	2
Mason	8	0	64	0
Dodd	10	0	53	1
Tsukigawa	10	0	39	2
AUSTRALIA				
Andrews	7	0	19	2
Smith	6.3	1	18	2
Pike	7	0	36	0
Nitschke	8	0	32	3
Sthalekar	8	0	17	1
Hayes	7	0	43	1

Fall of Wickets	***A***	***NZ***
1st	38	23
2nd	113	54
3rd	157	60
4th	182	67
5th	212	85
6th	238	143
7th	244	154
8th	245	155
9th	252	167
10th	-	-

Browne retired hurt at 102-5

AUSTRALIA v NEW ZEALAND — Rose Bowl

at Allan Border Field, Brisbane on 28 October, 2006
Toss : New Zealand. Umpires : T.P. Laycock & N.S. McNamara
Australia won by 4 wickets.

New Zealand won the toss and batted. McGlashan scored 45 off 54 balls, including seven fours, and put on 65 runs with Watson for the seventh wicket. Watson scored 39 off 41 balls, including three fours and a six. At the end of fifty overs New Zealand had scored 204-8.

Australia lost an early wicket and were in trouble at 18-2 and when they were 108-5 New Zealand were in a good position to gain a win.

However, an unbeaten seventh wicket partnership of 71 between Edwards and Hayes took Australia to victory in 47.4 overs. Browne was the most successful of the New Zealand bowlers with 2-36 off eight overs.

NEW ZEALAND

	Runs	Mins	Balls	6s	4s
R.J.Rolls† c Purves b Pike	30	44	33	-	5
R.J.Kember c Pike b Nitschke	15	33	35	-	3
H.M.Tiffen* c Nitschke b Pike	9	46	32	-	-
M.F.Fahey c Edwards b Pike	27	50	43	-	3
S.J.McGlashan c & b Nitschke	45	56	54	-	7
S.J.Tsukigawa c Nitschke b Pike	4	13	16	-	1
N.J.Browne lbw b Smith	26	68	44	-	2
H.M.Watson b Smith	39	37	41	1	3
A.M.Dodd not out	2	2	2	-	-
S.K.Burke					
S.F.M.Devine					
Extras (b 2, lb 1, w 4)	7				
TOTAL (50 overs) (8 wkts)	**204**	178			

AUSTRALIA

	Runs	Mins	Balls	6s	4s
M.J.Bulow run out	2	17	14	-	-
L.J.Poulton st Rolls b Watson	12	28	31	-	2
M.A.J.Goszko b Browne	40	67	56	1	6
L.C.Sthalekar* run out	17	48	39	-	2
S.Nitschke c Fahey b Burke	16	35	23	-	1
J.M.Purves† b Browne	22	58	41	-	3
S.J.Edwards not out	45	66	48	-	2
J.Hayes not out	36	36	36	-	5
K.E.Pike					
S.J.Andrews					
C.R.Smith					
Extras (lb 4, w 9, nb 2)	15				
TOTAL (47.4 overs) (6 wkts)	**205**	180			

Bowling	*O*	*M*	*R*	*W*
AUSTRALIA				
Andrews	9	1	45	0
Smith	9	0	45	2
Nitschke	10	0	36	2
Pike	10	2	23	4
Hayes	3	0	21	0
Sthalekar	9	1	31	0
NEW ZEALAND				
Burke	9	1	33	1
Watson	8.4	3	27	1
Devine	7	0	26	0
Dodd	6	0	35	0
Tsukigawa	9	0	44	0
Browne	8	1	36	2

Fall of Wickets	***NZ***	***A***
1st	36	9
2nd	49	18
3rd	78	71
4th	105	80
5th	119	108
6th	136	134
7th	201	-
8th	204	-
9th	-	-
10th	-	-

NEW ZEALAND IN INDIA

In February 2007 the BCCI hosted the second women's Quadrangular Tournament, involving New Zealand, Australia, England and India. The tournament was based in Chennai and the teams played each other twice culminating in a final between the top two teams.

The White Ferns went into the tournament ranked number three from the 2005 World Cup but in round-robin play were only defeated once and topped the table. In their opening match they chased down Australia's 260 winning by six wickets with five overs to spare. A feature of the tournament was the White Ferns' aggressive batting. Centuries were scored by Rebecca Rolls (104 not out against Australia) and Suzie Bates (122 against India).

The White Ferns' worst performance was in the final where their batting did not fire and the Australians easily reached the target to win the tournament. England finished third although victory in the play-off for third and fourth was their only win in the tournament.

The next time the four teams meet will be in the 2009 ICC World Cup to be played in Australia. Two players made their debut for the White Ferns in the tournament, State Canterbury Magicians' Selena Charteris and Rowan Milburn. Rebecca Rolls announced her retirement after the tournament.

The team was: Haidee Tiffen *(captain)*, Sarah Burke, Selena Charteris, Maria Fahey, Rowan Milburn, Helen Watson *(Canterbury)*, Rebecca Rolls *(Auckland)*, Sophie Devine *(Wellington)*, Sara McGlashan, Aimee Mason *(Central Districts)*, Suzie Bates, Sarah Tsukigawa *(Otago)*, Nicola Browne, Louise Milliken *(Northern Districts)*. Coach, Steve Jenkin; Manager, Catherine Campbell; Assistant coach, Clare Taylor; Physiotherapist, Angela Cadogan; Trainer, Mike Smith.

New Zealand Averages

BATTING	*M*	*I*	*NO*	*HS*	*Agg*	*Ave*	*100s*	*50s*	*Ct*	*St*	*SR*
S.J. Tsukigawa	5	5	2	78*	214	71.33	-	1	-	-	89
R.J. Rolls	6	6	1	104*	218	43.60	1	1	10	1	103
H.M. Watson	6	4	3	19*	35	35.00	-	-	-	-	81
S.W. Bates	7	7	0	122	241	34.42	1	-	2	-	80
S.J. McGlashan	7	7	1	55	177	29.50	-	1	-	-	73
N.J. Browne	6	5	2	41	86	28.66	-	-	2	-	66
M.F. Fahey	7	7	0	59	185	26.42	-	3	2	-	61
H.M. Tiffen	7	7	0	58	162	23.14	-	1	4	-	61
S.F.M. Devine	3	2	0	30	40	20.00	-	-	1	-	50
R.C. Milburn	2	2	0	25	32	16.00	-	-	2	-	69
A.L. Mason	7	6	0	48	85	14.16	-	-	3	-	80
L.E. Milliken	7	3	1	19*	22	11.00	-	-	2	-	50
S.K. Burke	5	2	1	10*	10	10.00	-	-	1	-	83
S.E. Charteris	2	1	1	20*	20	-	-	-	-	-	133

BOWLING	*O*	*M*	*R*	*W*	*Ave*	*Best*	*R/O*
N.J. Browne	52.2	5	196	8	24.50	2-20	3.74
S.K. Burke	38.2	3	156	6	26.00	3-42	4.06
L.E. Milliken	64	4	316	11	28.72	4-42	4.94
A.L. Mason	37	1	215	7	30.71	3-36	5.81
H.M. Watson	53	14	174	5	34.80	3-30	3.28
S.F.M. Devine	18	0	126	3	42.00	3-38	7.00
H.M. Tiffen	8	0	49	1	49.00	1-29	6.13
S.E. Charteris	8	0	52	1	52.00	1-32	6.50

NEW ZEALAND v AUSTRALIA — Quadrangular Tournament

at ITT-Chemplast Ground, Chennai on 21 February, 2007
Toss : Australia. Umpires : S.M. Raju & K. Srinivasan
New Zealand won by 6 wickets.

Australia won the toss and batted. New Zealand made an early breakthrough when Watson picked up Poulton with the score on 20 then Browne removed the dangerous Rolton with the score just 39.

At 46-4 Australia were in trouble but Sthalekar and Nitschke put on 82 for the fifth wicket and solid partnerships took Australia to 260-9 after 50 overs. Watson took 3-30 and Milliken and Browne both took two wickets each.

New Zealand lost Bates at 45, but solid batting had them well placed at 153-4. Rolls and Tsukigawa then put on an unbroken partnership of 108 for the fifth wicket with Rolls scoring 104 not out off 87 balls, including 18 fours and one six. Tsukigawa ended on 42 off 47 balls, including five fours, as New Zealand won in the 45th over.

AUSTRALIA

	Runs	Mins	Balls	6s	4s
L.J.Poulton c Tiffen b Watson	8	18	21	-	2
A.J.Blackwell c Rolls b Watson	25	46	38	-	5
K.L.Rolton* c Rolls b Browne	4	17	15	-	1
L.C.Sthalekar c Devine b Browne	65	109	76	-	11
S.J.Edwards c Rolls b Watson ...	0	6	6	-	-
S.Nitschke lbw b Milliken	33	58	51	-	6
J.M.Purves† c & b Milliken	33	49	40	-	6
C.L.Fitzpatrick run out	33	43	26	2	2
K.E.Pike b Bates	13	16	14	-	2
E.M.Sampson not out	9	14	12	-	-
C.R.Smith not out	9	4	3	-	2
Extras (lb 2, w 24, nb 2)	28				
TOTAL (50 overs) (9 wkts) .	**260**	194			

NEW ZEALAND

	Runs	Mins	Balls	6s	4s
M.F.Fahey c Purves b Fitzpatrick	53	96	74	-	8
S.W.Bates lbw b Sampson	15	29	21	-	3
H.M.Tiffen* lbw b Pike	14	40	29	-	2
R.J.Rolls† not out	104	106	87	1	18
S.J.McGlashan c Sthalekar b Nitschke	9	20	13	-	2
S.J.Tsukigawa not out	42	60	47	-	5
H.M.Watson					
A.L.Mason					
N.J.Browne					
L.E.Milliken					
S.F.M.Devine					
Extras (b 1, lb 8, w 14, nb 1) ..	24				
TOTAL (45 overs) (4 wkts) .	**261**	177			

Bowling	*O*	*M*	*R*	*W*
NEW ZEALAND				
Milliken	9	1	44	2
Watson	10	5	30	3
Browne	10	0	40	2
Mason	2	0	19	0
Devine	7	0	57	0
Tsukigawa	7	0	30	0
Bates	5	0	38	1
AUSTRALIA				
Fitzpatrick	8	1	48	1
Sampson	9	0	48	1
Smith	8	1	27	0
Pike	9	0	53	1
Sthalekar	4	0	41	0
Nitschke	7	0	35	1

Fall of Wickets	***A***	***NZ***
1st	20	45
2nd	39	80
3rd	42	122
4th	46	153
5th	128	-
6th	176	-
7th	196	-
8th	227	-
9th	248	-
10th	-	-

NEW ZEALAND v AUSTRALIA YOUTH

At Lincoln No.3 11 February, 2007

New Zealand 246-8 (S.J. Tsukigawa 65, A.L. Mason 47, N.J. Browne 37, M.F. Fahey 33, R.J. Rolls 30, E. Perry 3-68) **defeated Australia Youth** 180-9 (E. Perry 50*, R.M. Farrell 46, R.L. Haynes 38, A.L. Mason 3-35) by 66 runs

INDIA B v NEW ZEALAND

At Central Polytechnic Ground. Chennai 19 February, 2007

New Zealand 304-7 (H.M. Tiffen 75, S.W. Bates 55, S.J. McGlashan 43) **defeated India B** 158 (A.L. Mason 4-29) by 146 runs

NEW ZEALAND v ENGLAND — Quadrangular Tournament

at ITT-Chemplast Ground, Chennai on 23 February, 2007
Toss : England. Umpires : S.M. Rajun & K. Srinivasan
New Zealand won by 19 runs.

England won the toss and elected to field. New Zealand scored 291-6 by the end of their fifty overs. Fahey scored 50 off 67 balls, including eight fours, and Tiffen 58 off 85 balls, including seven fours. The best partnership of the innings was for the seventh wicket between Tsukigawa and Browne, who put on an entertaining 104 runs in 9.1 overs.

Tsukigawa scored 78 not out off just 56 balls, including seven fours and two sixes, and Browne 36 not out off 23 balls, including two fours and two sixes.

England was in early trouble at 25-2 but Taylor, with 56 off 58 balls, and Edwards, with 86 off 93 balls, chased well. Burke took three wickets, Milliken and Bates two wickets each and England was all out for 272 in 48.2 overs.

NEW ZEALAND

	Runs	Mins	Balls	6s	4s
M.F.Fahey run out	50	88	67	-	8
S.W.Bates c Taylor S.J. b Rainford-Brent	12	18	13	-	2
H.M.Tiffen* st Taylor S.J. b Colvin	58	111	85	-	7
R.J.Rolls† c Rainford-Brent b Colvin	6	8	6	-	1
S.J.McGlashan b Newton	13	30	27	-	1
S.J.Tsukigawa not out	78	58	56	4	7
A.L.Mason c Morgan b Newton	19	24	23	-	2
N.J.Browne not out	36	29	23	2	2
H.M.Watson					
L.E.Milliken					
S.K.Burke					
Extras (lb 9, w 8, nb 2)	19				
TOTAL (50 overs) (6 wkts)	**291**	185			

ENGLAND

	Runs	Mins	Balls	6s	4s
C.M.G.Atkins c Mason b Milliken	0	1	1	-	-
L.K.Newton c Rolls b Watson	12	14	14	-	3
S.C.Taylor c Rolls b Mason	56	87	58	1	7
S.J.Taylor† run out	41	54	48	-	7
C.M.Edwards* lbw b Milliken	86	106	93	-	13
L.S.Greenway c & b Burke	13	19	14	-	3
B.L.Morgan c Rolls b Bates	20	47	33	-	2
J.L.Gunn c Browne b Burke	15	24	22	-	1
E.J.C.L.R.C.Rainford-Brent c Bates b Burke	7	10	5	-	1
I.T.Guha not out	1	6	1	-	-
H.L.Colvin lbw b Bates	0	2	2	-	-
Extras (lb 8, w 12, nb 1)	21				
TOTAL (48.2 overs)	**272**	189			

Bowling	*O*	*M*	*R*	*W*
ENGLAND				
Gunn	7	0	40	0
Rainford-Brent	5	0	24	1
Guha	8	0	59	0
Morgan	9	0	36	0
Colvin	8	0	40	2
Newton	9	0	51	2
Edwards	4	0	32	0
NEW ZEALAND				
Milliken	10	0	60	2
Watson	6	0	36	1
Burke	7	0	42	3
Browne	6	0	22	0
Mason	8	0	48	1
Tsukigawa	7	0	36	0
Bates	4.2	1	20	2

Fall of Wickets

	NZ	*E*
1st	30	0
2nd	109	25
3rd	116	107
4th	150	127
5th	152	164
6th	187	230
7th	-	256
8th	-	265
9th	-	271
10th	-	272

INDIA v NEW ZEALAND — Quadrangular Tournament

at M.A.Chiddambaram Stadium, Chennai on 25 February, 2007
Toss : India. Umpires : R. Radhakrishnan & S.M. Raju
New Zealand won by 3 wickets.

India won the toss and batted first and were dismissed in 49.2 overs for 201. Kala top scored with 65 off 96 balls, including five fours and one six. Tsukigawa took 3-33 and Bates and Browne each took two wickets.

New Zealand was 30-3 after nine overs but a partnership of 96 for the fourth wicket, between Fahey and McGlashan, set up the victory. Fahey scored 59 off 95 balls, including six fours, and McGlashan 55 off 78 balls, including six fours and a six. Watson ended the match with a cameo 19 runs off 11 balls.

INDIA

	Runs	Mins	Balls	6s	4s
K.V.Jain† b Milliken	0	1	2	-	-
J.Sharma lbw b Browne	24	49	40	-	5
M.Raj* run out	21	60	46	-	3
A.Chopra c Bates b Browne	0	17	13	-	-
M.D.T.Kamini c Rolls b Tsukigawa	37	85	65	-	6
H.Kala st Rolls b Tsukigawa	65	116	96	1	5
R.Dhar run out	10	20	18	-	1
A.Sharma c Tiffen b Bates	14	16	12	-	2
J.Goswami not out	0	7	0	-	-
R.Goel lbw b Bates	0	1	1	-	-
P.Dimri b Tsukigawa	7	6	3	1	-
Extras (lb 3, w 17, nb 3)	23				
TOTAL (49.2 overs)	**201**	192			

NEW ZEALAND

	Runs	Mins	Balls	6s	4s
R.J.Rolls† b Goswami	15	19	17	1	1
S.W.Bates lbw b Goswami	0	2	1	-	-
H.M.Tiffen* c Jain b Goswami	7	35	23	-	1
M.F.Fahey run out	59	147	95	-	6
S.J.McGlashan st Jain b Kamini	55	81	78	1	6
S.J.Tsukigawa b Goswami	14	21	23	-	2
A.L.Mason c Chopra b Dimri	10	14	14	-	2
N.J.Browne not out	4	22	14	-	-
H.M.Watson not out	19	17	11	-	4
L.E.Milliken					
S.E.Charteris					
Extras (b 5, lb 2, w 12)	19				
TOTAL (47.1 overs) (7 wkts)	**202**	179			

Bowling	*O*	*M*	*R*	*W*
NEW ZEALAND				
Milliken	10	0	47	1
Browne	10	3	20	2
Watson	10	4	22	0
Mason	6	0	30	0
Bates	4	0	26	2
Charteris	4	0	20	0
Tsukigawa	5.2	0	33	3
INDIA				
Goswami	10	2	26	4
Dhar	8	1	33	0
Sharma A.	5	0	26	0
Dimri	10	1	44	1
Kamini	10	0	45	1
Goel	4.1	0	21	0

Fall of Wickets	*I*	*NZ*
1st	1	1
2nd	43	21
3rd	52	30
4th	52	134
5th	138	156
6th	162	173
7th	189	181
8th	193	-
9th	193	-
10th	201	-

NEW ZEALAND v AUSTRALIA — Quadrangular Tournament

at ITT-Chemplast Ground, Chennai on 28 February, 2007
Toss : New Zealand. Umpires : G.A. Pratapkumar & S. Ravi
Australia won by 49 runs.

New Zealand won the toss and decided to field. The dangerous Rolton was dismissed early but all the other batsmen made contributions and Australia finished with 232-8 off fifty overs. Mason and Browne both took two wickets each.

In reply New Zealand lost wickets regularly with the best partnership being 52 for the ninth wicket between Devine and Milliken. McGlashan top scored with 35 off 45 balls, including seven fours. New Zealand was all out for 183 in 45 overs, losing by 49 runs.

AUSTRALIA

	Runs	Mins	Balls	6s	4s
A.J.Blackwell c Mason b Browne	18	47	41	-	4
M.J.Bulow run out	17	42	30	-	3
K.L.Rolton* c & b Browne	9	51	39	-	2
L.C.Sthalekar c Rolls b Tiffen	45	81	67	-	7
S.Nitschke lbw b Watson	14	22	19	-	2
K.A.Blackwell b Mason	33	51	44	-	4
C.L.Fitzpatrick c Tiffen b Mason	29	22	21	1	4
J.M.Purves† b Milliken	26	28	27	-	3
S.J.Andrews not out	21	16	13	-	3
K.E.Pike not out	0	4	2	-	-
C.R.Smith					
Extras (lb 7, w 10, nb 3)	20				
TOTAL (50 overs) (8 wkts)	**232**	186			

NEW ZEALAND

	Runs	Mins	Balls	6s	4s
M.F.Fahey c Bulow b Andrews	15	37	25	-	2
S.W.Bates b Andrews	25	28	24	-	5
H.M.Tiffen* run out	3	19	17	-	-
R.J.Rolls† c Purves b Pike	33	47	40	1	5
S.J.McGlashan c Purves b Pike	35	62	45	-	7
A.L.Mason c Blackwell A.J. b Fitzpatrick	5	20	10	-	1
N.J.Browne lbw b Sthalekar	5	22	12	-	1
H.M.Watson c Purves b Pike	0	1	1	-	-
S.F.M.Devine c Fitzpatrick b Nitschke	30	58	57	-	5
L.E.Milliken not out	19	44	36	-	2
S.K.Burke lbw b Nitschke	0	3	2	-	-
Extras (b 2, lb 4, w 7)	13				
TOTAL (45 overs)	**183**	174			

Bowling	*O*	*M*	*R*	*W*
NEW ZEALAND				
Milliken	9	1	39	1
Burke	10	1	32	0
Browne	10	1	30	2
Watson	10	2	44	1
Tiffen	5	0	29	1
Devine	3	0	31	0
Mason	3	0	20	2
AUSTRALIA				
Fitzpatrick	8	1	33	1
Smith	7	2	28	0
Andrews	5	0	27	2
Pike	10	2	31	3
Nitschke	7	0	27	2
Sthalekar	8	0	31	1

Fall of Wickets	***A***	***NZ***
1st	39	36
2nd	39	43
3rd	79	51
4th	107	96
5th	119	121
6th	165	121
7th	197	121
8th	216	130
9th	-	182
10th	-	183

INDIA v NEW ZEALAND — Quadrangular Tournament

at M.A.Chiddambaram Stadium, Madras on 1 March, 2007
Toss : India. Umpires : S. Ravi & K. Srinivasan
New Zealand won by 91 runs.

India won the toss and elected to field. Bates scored her maiden one-day international century with 122 runs off 134 balls, including 12 fours. She put on 104 runs in a third wicket partnership with Rolls who scored 58 off 54 balls, including four fours and a six. New Zealand finished with 272-7 off fifty overs.

In reply India managed only 181-8 after 50 overs. Mason was the most successful of the New Zealand bowlers, with 3-36, and Browne and Burke took two wickets each.

NEW ZEALAND

	Runs	Mins	Balls	6s	4s
M.F.Fahey c Kala b Dhar	4	26	24	-	-
S.W.Bates b Dimri	122	159	134	-	12
H.M.Tiffen* c Goswami b Al Khader	34	72	55	-	3
R.J.Rolls† st Jain b Dimri	58	67	54	1	4
S.J.McGlashan not out	24	33	17	-	1
A.L.Mason c Jain b Goswami	3	4	6	-	-
R.C.Milburn run out	7	16	8	-	-
N.J.Browne b Goswami	0	1	1	-	-
H.M.Watson not out	1	1	1	-	-
L.E.Milliken					
S.K.Burke					
Extras (b 3, lb 3, w 13)	19				
TOTAL (50 overs) (7 wkts)	**272**	194			

INDIA

	Runs	Mins	Balls	6s	4s
K.V.Jain† run out	13	48	29	-	2
J.Sharma lbw b Browne	29	56	53	-	4
M.Raj* c Rolls b Mason	31	78	54	-	2
H.Kala b Mason	7	39	30	-	1
R.Dhar c Mason b Burke	11	18	21	-	1
M.D.T.Kamini b Mason	11	29	30	-	2
S.A.Paranjpe c Rolls b Browne	4	34	19	-	-
A.Sharma lbw b Burke	0	1	1	-	-
J.Goswami not out	27	47	38	-	3
N.Al Khader not out	19	32	26	-	2
P.Dimri					
Extras (b 4, lb 1, w 23, nb 1)	29				
TOTAL (50 overs) (8 wkts)	**181**	195			

Bowling	*O*	*M*	*R*	*W*
INDIA				
Goswami	10	2	43	2
Dhar	10	1	28	1
Sharma A.	3	0	24	0
Dimri	10	0	57	2
Al Khader	10	0	61	1
Kamini	6	0	41	0
Kala	1	0	12	0
NEW ZEALAND				
Milliken	8	0	47	0
Watson	10	3	17	0
Browne	9	1	27	2
Mason	10	1	36	3
Tiffen	3	0	20	0
Burke	8	2	18	2
Bates	2	0	11	0

Fall of Wickets	***NZ***	***I***
1st	10	52
2nd	112	55
3rd	216	83
4th	232	107
5th	235	118
6th	269	125
7th	269	126
8th	-	136
9th	-	-
10th	-	-

NEW ZEALAND v ENGLAND — Quadrangular Tournament

at ITT-Chemplast Ground, Chennai on 3 March, 2007
Toss : England. Umpires : S. Ravi & K. Srinivasan
New Zealand won by 27 runs.

England won the toss and elected to field. Fahey was run out early but steady contributions from most of the team saw New Zealand reach 267-9 off 50 overs. Bates and Mason top scored with 48 apiece.

After a fine opening spell from Milliken, England sunk to 82-6 but the lower order rallied and took the score to 240 before the last wicket fell in the 46th over. Milliken finished with 4-42 off ten overs and Devine took 3-38 off eight overs to give New Zealand a win by 27 runs.

NEW ZEALAND

	Runs	Mins	Balls	6s	4s
M.F.Fahey run out	4	10	7	-	-
S.W.Bates b Colvin	48	86	63	-	6
H.M.Tiffen* c Newton b Askew	13	12	16	-	2
S.J.Tsukigawa lbw b Newton	41	52	45	1	5
A.L.Mason st Taylor S.J. b Colvin	48	70	51	1	5
S.J.McGlashan b Newton	30	43	33	-	5
R.C.Milburn† lbw b Askew	25	41	38	-	1
S.F.M.Devine c Newton b Colvin	10	21	22	-	2
S.K.Burke not out	10	22	9	-	-
L.E.Milliken lbw b Guha	2	4	5	-	-
S.E.Charteris not out	20	14	15	-	2
Extras (lb 2, w 10, nb 4)	16				
TOTAL (50 overs) (9 wkts)	**267**	192			

ENGLAND

	Runs	Mins	Balls	6s	4s
S.J.Taylor† c Fahey b Milliken	22	35	25	-	4
L.K.Newton b Milliken	0	2	1	-	-
S.C.Taylor c Milburn b Milliken	13	22	18	-	2
C.M.Edwards* c Milburn b Charteris	42	100	56	-	6
J.L.Gunn c Fahey b Milliken	0	2	4	-	-
L.S.Greenway b Devine	0	17	10	-	-
B.L.Morgan lbw b Devine	13	23	29	-	2
L.R.F.Askew b Devine	68	86	71	1	11
E.J.C.L.R.C.Rainford-Brent lbw b Mason	7	5	7	-	1
I.T.Guha lbw b Burke	26	54	37	-	3
H.L.Colvin not out	13	19	17	-	2
Extras (lb 7, w 26, nb 3)	36				
TOTAL (45.2 overs)	**240**	177			

Bowling	*O*	*M*	*R*	*W*
ENGLAND				
Rainford-Brent	2	0	16	0
Askew	10	1	55	2
Gunn	7	0	49	0
Guha	6	0	35	1
Newton	10	1	41	2
Colvin	10	0	37	3
Morgan	5	0	32	0
NEW ZEALAND				
Milliken	10	2	42	4
Burke	9.2	0	51	1
Devine	8	0	38	3
Bates	8	1	29	0
Mason	6	0	41	1
Charteris	4	0	32	1

Fall of Wickets	***NZ***	***E***
1st	18	2
2nd	34	37
3rd	114	42
4th	122	42
5th	190	57
6th	208	82
7th	233	131
8th	234	138
9th	239	211
10th	-	240

NEW ZEALAND v AUSTRALIA — Quadrangular Final

at M.A.Chiddambaram Stadium Chennai on 5 March, 2007
Toss : New Zealand. Umpires : G.A. Pratapkumar & S. Ravi
Australia won by 6 wickets.

New Zealand won the toss and decided to bat in the series final. Fahey was dismissed in the first over and the innings never recovered from the initial setback. Tiffen scored 33, Tsukigawa 39 and Browne 41 but progress was slow and after fifty overs New Zealand had reached only 177-9.

Australia were never in trouble chasing the target and openers Bulow and Nitschke put on 120 runs for the first wicket. Australia easily achieved victory in 38.2 overs to win the match by six wickets and to win the Quadrangular Series.

NEW ZEALAND

	Runs	Mins	Balls	6s	4s
M.F.Fahey b Fitzpatrick	0	4	6	-	-
S.W.Bates c Fitzpatrick b Sampson	19	64	45	-	2
H.M.Tiffen* run out	33	46	39	-	4
R.J.Rolls† c Sthalekar b Pike	2	6	4	-	-
S.J.McGlashan c Fitzpatrick b Pike	11	31	29	-	2
S.J.Tsukigawa lbw b Sthalekar	39	86	69	1	4
A.L.Mason c Purves b Pike	0	1	1	-	-
N.J.Browne c Purves b Fitzpatrick	41	87	80	-	6
H.M.Watson not out	15	33	24	-	1
L.E.Milliken run out	1	4	3	-	-
S.K.Burke					
Extras (b 5, lb 4, w 7)	16				
TOTAL (50 overs) (9 wkts)	**177**	185			

AUSTRALIA

	Runs	Mins	Balls	6s	4s
M.J.Bulow c Milliken b Tsukigawa	50	83	72	-	9
S.Nitschke b Milliken	81	114	81	1	12
K.L.Rolton* c Tiffen b Tsukigawa	1	7	3	-	-
L.C.Sthalekar not out	32	54	48	-	5
K.A.Blackwell b Bates	3	14	11	-	-
S.J.Edwards not out	8	16	16	-	1
C.L.Fitzpatrick					
J.M.Purves†					
K.E.Pike					
E.M.Sampson					
C.R.Smith					
Extras (w 5, nb 1)	6				
TOTAL (38.2 overs) (4 wkts)	**181**	147			

Bowling	*O*	*M*	*R*	*W*
AUSTRALIA				
Fitzpatrick	10	0	27	2
Smith	5	0	21	0
Sampson	8	1	29	1
Pike	10	3	21	3
Nitschke	9	1	39	0
Sthalekar	8	1	31	1
NEW ZEALAND				
Milliken	8	0	37	1
Watson	7	0	25	0
Browne	7.2	0	57	0
Mason	2	0	21	0
Tsukigawa	8	1	20	2
Burke	4	0	13	0
Bates	2	0	8	1

Fall of Wickets	***NZ***	***A***
1st	1	120
2nd	54	125
3rd	60	146
4th	64	159
5th	82	-
6th	82	-
7th	140	-
8th	171	-
9th	177	-
10th	-	-

NEW ZEALAND A

A New Zealand A team was selected to play two matches against the White Ferns and a three match series against Australia Youth. All matches were played at NZC's grounds at Lincoln University.

New Zealand comfortably beat New Zealand A in their two matches which served as excellent preparation before they departed for India and the Quadrangular Series. New Zealand A drew the series against Australia Youth with both teams winning one match and one match was tied. The team was: Anna Dodd *(captain)*, Amanda Cooper, Lucy Doolan, Megan Wakefield *(Wellington)*, Ros Kember, Victoria Lind, Prashilla Mistry *(Auckland)*, Beth McNeill, Amy Satterthwaite *(Canterbury)*, Rachel Candy, Zara McWilliams, Rachel Priest *(Central Districts)* and Megan Murphy *(Northern Districts)*. The team was coached by Gary Stead and he was assisted by former White Ferns Kirsty Bond and Katrina Keenan.

NEW ZEALAND A v NEW ZEALAND
At Lincoln No.3   7 February, 2007

New Zealand A 209-7 (R.H. Priest 39, A.E. Satterthwaite 38, M.G. Wakefield 38, L.R. Doolan 31) **lost to New Zealand** 210-3 (R.J. Rolls 90, H.M. Tiffen 59*, S.W. Bates 33) by seven wickets.

NEW ZEALAND A v NEW ZEALAND
At Lincoln No.3   9 February, 2007

New Zealand 281 (H.M. Watson 68*, S.W. Bates 52 retd, M.F. Fahey 48, A.L. Mason 42, L.R. Doolan 4-47) **defeated New Zealand A** 107-9 (M.G. Wakefield 30, S.W. Bates 3-9) by 174 runs

NEW ZEALAND A v AUSTRALIA YOUTH — One-day

at Bert Sutcliffe Oval, Lincoln on 13 February, 2007
Toss : Australia Youth. Umpires : G.A. Baxter & B.F. Bowden
Australia Youth won by 4 runs.

AUSTRALIA YOUTH

	Runs	Mins	Balls	6s	4s
R.L.Haynes b McNeill	10	22	22	-	1
R.M.Farrell b Candy	23	50	45	-	4
K.Owen run out	8	46	31	-	1
S.E.Aley* st Priest b McWilliams	125	132	109	-	15
N.E.Bolton lbw b Doolan	26	58	44	-	2
R.K.Chappell c McWilliams b McNeill	8	18	12	-	1
E.J.Inglis run out	10	13	13	-	-
E.Perry not out	15	28	18	-	1
A.Healy† not out	10	6	7	-	1
J.Cameron					
R.Rimmington					
D.M.Kimmince					
Extras (b 2, lb 9, w 6, nb 1)	18				
TOTAL (50 overs) (7 wkts)	**253**	190			

NEW ZEALAND A

	Runs	Mins	Balls	6s	4s
L.R.Doolan c Aley b Farrell	42	68	62	-	8
R.J.Kember c Haynes b Cameron	43	91	75	-	2
V.J.Lind b Rimmington	82	117	89	-	11
A.E.Satterthwaite c Bolton b Chappell	14	39	28	-	1
M.G.Wakefield b Chappell	1	6	7	-	-
R.H.Priest† b Rimmington	36	36	34	-	6
A.E.Cooper b Rimmington	1	3	2	-	-
R.H.Candy not out	9	11	7	-	-
B.H.McNeill not out	2	4	2	-	-
A.M.Dodd*					
Z.A.McWilliams					
P.Mistry					
Extras (b 1, lb 3, w 9, nb 6)	19				
TOTAL (50 overs) (7 wkts)	**249**	192			

Bowling	O	M	R	W
NEW ZEALAND A				
McNeill	9	2	39	2
Mistry	10	2	28	0
Candy	7	2	32	1
Satterthwaite	5	0	21	0
Dodd	4	0	27	0
Doolan	3	0	18	1
McWilliams	5	0	26	1
Cooper	7	0	51	0
AUSTRALIA YOUTH				
Rimmington	10	2	38	3
Kimmince	5	0	23	0
Farrell	7	1	45	1
Cameron	6	0	37	1
Perry	7	1	23	0
Chappell	9	1	50	2
Aley	6	0	29	0

Fall of Wickets

	AY	*NZA*
1st	23	67
2nd	42	97
3rd	66	147
4th	144	149
5th	179	228
6th	197	231
7th	241	239
8th	-	-
9th	-	-
10th	-	

NEW ZEALAND A v AUSTRALIA YOUTH — One-day

at Bert Sutcliffe Oval, Lincoln on 15 February, 2007
Toss : Australia Youth. Umpires : A.L. Hill & D.M. Quested
Match tied.

AUSTRALIA YOUTH

	Runs	Mins	Balls	6s	4s
A.Healy c Kember b McNeill	41	56	58	-	6
R.M.Farrell c Kember b Candy	13	15	8	-	1
R.K.Chappell b Cooper	57	115	70	1	4
N.E.Bolton lbw b Dodd	6	12	11	-	1
E.J.Inglis† run out	32	26	26	-	4
J.Cameron b Candy	3	10	6	-	-
E.Perry c Dodd b Murphy	10	19	24	-	1
R.L.Haynes not out	10	26	17	-	-
L.A.Shave b Murphy	1	6	6	-	-
D.M.Kimmince lbw b Cooper	1	14	12	-	-
S.E.Aley* lbw b Cooper	0	2	1	-	-
K.Owen					
Extras (b 1, lb 1, w 10, nb 3)	15				
TOTAL (39.2 overs)	**189**	184			

NEW ZEALAND A

	Runs	Mins	Balls	6s	4s
L.R.Doolan b Shave	15	41	34	-	3
R.J.Kember c Inglis b Shave	9	10	8	-	1
V.J.Lind c Inglis b Perry	8	18	13	-	2
M.G.Wakefield b Cameron	13	40	44	-	2
R.H.Priest† b Chappell	6	16	12	-	1
M.P.Murphy run out	40	55	38	1	5
A.E.Cooper b Cameron	0	7	4	-	-
A.M.Dodd* c Aley b Farrell	5	29	24	-	-
B.H.McNeill not out	51	71	68	-	7
Z.A.McWilliams st Inglis b Aley	24	67	50	-	1
R.H.Candy b Aley	0	1	1	-	-
P.Mistry					
Extras (lb 5, w 13)	18				
TOTAL (49.2 overs)	**189**	183			

Bowling	O	M	R	W
NEW ZEALAND A				
Candy	7	1	36	2
Mistry	3	0	19	0
McWilliams	3	0	24	0
McNeill	7	1	22	1
Dodd	10	0	54	1
Doolan	2	0	17	0
Murphy	4	1	8	2
Cooper	3.2	0	7	3
AUSTRALIA YOUTH				
Shave	10	5	24	2
Perry	8	1	39	1
Chappell	8	0	23	1
Kimmince	5	1	5	0
Cameron	4	0	24	2
Haynes	3	1	16	0
Farrell	5	0	17	1
Aley	6.2	0	36	2

Fall of Wickets

	AY	*NZA*
1st	19	13
2nd	78	24
3rd	93	43
4th	151	60
5th	159	65
6th	176	72
7th	176	109
8th	178	111
9th	189	189
10th	189	189

NEW ZEALAND A v AUSTRALIA YOUTH — One-day

at Bert Sutcliffe Oval, Lincoln on 16 February, 2007
Toss : New Zealand A. Umpires : A.L. Hill & D.M. Quested
New Zealand A won by 22 runs.

NEW ZEALAND A

	Runs	Mins	Balls	6s	4s
L.R.Doolan c Inglis b Chappell .	69	85	71	-	10
R.J.Kember st Healy b Cameron	86	155	107	-	9
V.J.Lind run out	4	9	8	-	-
A.E.Satterthwaite c Bolton b Cameron	31	52	41	-	5
M.P.Murphy c Aley b Chappell	7	11	10	-	-
R.H.Priest† run out	2	15	7	-	-
B.H.McNeill c Inglis b Cameron	3	15	17		-
Z.A.McWilliams lbw b Cameron	0	9	7	-	-
A.E.Cooper st Inglis b Cameron .	9	12	14	-	-
A.M.Dodd* not out	2	7	4	-	-
P.Mistry c Owen b Cameron	0	1	2	-	-
R.H.Candy					
Extras (lb 3, w 17, nb 1)	21				
TOTAL (47.5 overs)	**234**	184			

AUSTRALIA YOUTH

	Runs	Mins	Balls	6s	4s
R.L.Haynes b Murphy	6	33	31	-	-
A.Healy† c Cooper b Doolan	63	116	84	-	9
E.Perry b Doolan	18	41	40	-	3
S.E.Aley* c & b Doolan	9	18	20	-	1
E.J.Inglis lbw b Cooper	19	18	20	-	3
N.E.Bolton run out	20	36	30	-	2
R.K.Chappell c Lind b Candy	16	33	20	-	1
K.Owen run out	5	9	5	-	-
R.Rimmington c Priest b Candy .	7	11	10	-	1
J.Cameron c Kember b Candy .	17	21	14	-	2
D.M.Kimmince not out	2	13	5	-	-
L.A.Shave					
Extras (lb 7, w 20, nb 3)	30				
TOTAL (46.1 overs)	**212**	178			

Bowling	*O*	*M*	*R*	*W*
AUSTRALIA YOUTH				
Kimmince	5	0	27	0
Perry	7	0	38	0
Rimmington	6	1	22	0
Shave	4	0	36	0
Bolton	7	0	32	0
Chappell	10	0	48	2
Cameron	8.5	0	28	6
NEW ZEALAND A				
Candy	9.1	1	41	3
Mistry	3	0	12	0
Murphy	4	1	7	1
McNeill	4	0	18	0
Dodd	8	1	33	0
Doolan	10	1	51	3
Cooper	4	0	17	1
Satterthwaite	4	0	26	0

Fall of Wickets	***NZA***	***AY***
1st	130	40
2nd	142	77
3rd	194	105
4th	207	135
5th	210	135
6th	219	179
7th	221	179
8th	228	191
9th	233	193
10th	234	212

STATE LEAGUE

2006/07

State Canterbury Magicians won the 2006/07 State League competition. State Wellington Blaze won seven of their ten State League matches to ensure home advantage with a game to spare whereas Canterbury only sealed second place in their final round robin match. The final was a one sided match with Canterbury winning easily.

Canterbury's White Fern Maria Fahey was the top run scorer in the competition with 380 runs at an average of 42.22 and another White Fern, Sophie Devine, from Wellington was the top wicket taker with 22 wickets at an average of 15.4 and an economy rate of 3.80.

Two overseas players played in the competition. Australian international Alex Blackwell played for the State Otago Sparks and New South Wales opening bowler Sara Hungerford played for the State Auckland Hearts.

Five centuries were scored in the competition by Alex Blackwell, Anna Smith, Sara McGlashan, Rebecca Rolls and Sarah Tsukigawa who also took 5-13 in the same match for Otago against the State Northern Spirit to record the best individual performance in the competition.

Final points were:

	P	*W*	*L*	*T*	*NR*	*Bonus*	*Points*
Wellington	10	7	2	–	1	5	35
Canterbury	10	5	3	–	2	2	26
Central Districts	10	4	5	–	1	3	21
Auckland	10	4	5	–	1	2	20
Northern Districts	10	4	5	–	1	1	19
Otago	10	3	7	–	–	2	14

OTAGO v NORTHERN DISTRICTS — State League

at Carisbrook, Dunedin on 27 December, 2006
Toss : Northern Districts. Umpires : G.C. Holdem & D.G. Paterson
***Northern Districts won by 7 runs (D/L).** Points: Northern Districts 4, Otago 0*

OTAGO

	Runs	Mins	Balls	6s	4s
A.S.M.Kitchin lbw b Browne	1	14	14	-	-
M.J.Kane c & b Milliken	2	30	16	-	-
A.J.Blackwell b Tomlinson	100	122	102	2	9
S.W.Bates c Browne b Hannay	61	79	57	-	6
S.J.Tsukigawa* not out	34	48	45	-	3
K.J.Martin† c Pulford b Tomlinson	0	1	1	-	-
A.L.Kane run out	18	17	15	1	1
C.E.Taylor not out	0	2	0	-	-
T.J.Morrison					
K.M.Spence					
S.M.King					
J.M.Innes					
Extras (lb 10, w 26, nb 4)	40				
TOTAL (41 overs) (6 wkts)	**256**	159			

NORTHERN DISTRICTS

	Runs	Mins	Balls	6s	4s
T.M.Gould not out	27	55	44	-	3
J.M.Fraser c Kitchin b Taylor	55	43	49	3	4
K.L.Pulford lbw b Taylor	1	5	3	-	-
A.J.Wilkins not out	2	5	6	-	-
N.J.Browne*					
M.P.Murphy					
L.E.Milliken					
K.L.Samkin					
M.J.Hannay					
H.R.Huddleston					
J.C.Ullyett†					
K.A.Tomlinson					
Extras (w 7, nb 2)	9				
TOTAL (16.4 overs) (2 wkts)	**94**	55			

Bowling	O	M	R	W
NORTHERN DISTRICTS				
Milliken	8	0	56	1
Browne	8	0	46	1
Murphy	8	1	37	0
Pulford	3	0	23	0
Hannay	9	0	46	1
Huddleston	2	0	25	0
Tomlinson	3	0	13	2
OTAGO				
Bates	2.4	0	22	0
Morrison	6	0	27	0
Tsukigawa	3	0	13	0
Spence	3	0	26	0
Taylor	2	1	6	2

Fall of Wickets	O	ND
1st	9	79
2nd	26	88
3rd	190	-
4th	220	-
5th	220	-
6th	250	-
7th	-	-
8th	-	-
9th	-	-
10th	-	-

AUCKLAND v CENTRAL DISTRICTS — State League

at Melville Park, Auckland on 27 December, 2006
Toss : Auckland. Umpires : B.G. Frost & W.R. Knights
***No result.** Points: Auckland 2, Central DIstricts 2*

CENTRAL DISTRICTS

	Runs	Mins	Balls	6s	4s
S.L.Norman c Mistry b Bullen	44	97	87	-	7
R.H.Priest† lbw b Hungerford	4	12	8	-	1
N.M.Thessman b Hodgson	19	66	46	-	2
S.J.McGlashan b Hodgson	47	74	58	-	5
A.L.Mason* not out	46	79	41	-	6
K.E.Tunnicliffe c Rolls b Bullen	9	16	13	-	2
Z.A.McWilliams c Rolls b Hodgson	2	4	5	-	-
K.M.Cocksedge					
K.E.Broadmore					
K.M.Winkley					
A.K.Burrows					
R.H.Candy					
Extras (b 1, lb 5, w 29, nb 2)	37				
TOTAL (42.5 overs) (6 wkts)	**208**	177			

AUCKLAND

	Runs	Mins	Balls	6s	4s
R.J.Rolls*†					
R.J.Kember					
I.Cronin-Knight					
V.J.Lind					
S.A.P.Hopkins					
S.L.Hungerford					
A.Soma					
S.Coetzee					
A.E.Hodgson					
P.Mistry					
S.M.Bullen					
S.B.Hui					

Bowling	O	M	R	W
AUCKLAND				
Mistry	7	3	28	0
Hungerford	7	0	38	1
Rolls	8	2	42	0
Coetzee	6	0	24	0
Hodgson	8.5	0	39	3
Bullen	6	1	31	2

Fall of Wickets	CD
1st	10
2nd	71
3rd	92
4th	177
5th	205
6th	208
7th	
8th	
9th	
10th	

OTAGO v NORTHERN DISTRICTS — State League

at Carisbrook, Dunedin on 28 December, 2006
Toss : Otago. Umpires : G.C. Holdem & D.G. Paterson
***Otago won by 182 runs.** Points: Otago 5, Northern Districts 0*

OTAGO

	Runs	Mins	Balls	6s	4s
A.S.M.Kitchin lbw b Pulford	25	64	47	-	2
M.J.Kane c Ullyett b Browne	0	5	1	-	-
A.J.Blackwell lbw b Milliken	79	101	74	2	7
S.W.Bates c Gould b Pulford	0	1	1	-	-
S.J.Tsukigawa* b Huddleston	108	115	109	3	11
K.J.Martin† b Pulford	13	23	20	-	2
C.E.Taylor b Browne	2	7	5	-	-
J.M.Innes not out	24	50	44	-	1
A.L.Kane run out	0	2	0	-	-
S.M.King not out	3	4	5	-	-
K.M.Spence					
T.J.Morrison					
Extras (b 5, lb 3, w 28, nb 6)	42				
TOTAL (50 overs) (8 wkts)	**296**	190			

NORTHERN DISTRICTS

	Runs	Mins	Balls	6s	4s
T.M.Gould run out	18	36	43	-	-
J.M.Fraser lbw b Tsukigawa	14	33	24	-	2
K.L.Pulford st Martin b King	13	39	23	-	2
A.J.Wilkins lbw b Tsukigawa	3	18	13	-	-
N.J.Browne* b Tsukigawa	1	12	12	-	-
K.L.Samkin st Martin b Tsukigawa	0	1	1	-	-
M.P.Murphy c Blackwell b King	53	23	12	-	-
L.E.Milliken b Tsukigawa	1	8	11	-	-
M.J.Hannay lbw b Morrison	19	29	37	-	2
H.R.Huddleston not out	8	28	23	-	-
J.C.Ullyett† b Spence	6	10	12	-	1
K.A.Tomlinson					
Extras (lb 3, w 22, nb 1)	26				
TOTAL (35 overs)	**114**	123			

Bowling	O	M	R	W
NORTHERN DISTRICTS				
Milliken	10	1	41	1
Browne	7	0	41	2
Murphy	9	0	61	0
Pulford	10	0	43	3
Tomlinson	3	0	20	0
Hannay	7	0	53	0
Huddleston	4	0	29	1
OTAGO				
Bates	6	1	29	0
Taylor	5	0	19	0
Tsukigawa	9	3	13	5
Innes	2	0	13	0
Morrison	3	0	14	1
King	7	1	12	2
Spence	3	0	11	1

Fall of Wickets

	O	***ND***
1st	7	36
2nd	80	36
3rd	80	59
4th	157	61
5th	193	62
6th	201	62
7th	284	68
8th	287	76
9th	-	102
10th	-	114

AUCKLAND v CENTRAL DISTRICTS — State League

at Melville Park, Auckland on 28 December, 2006
Toss : Auckland. Umpires : B.G. Frost & W.R. Knights
***Central Districts won by 6 wickets.** Points: Central Districts 5, Auckland 0*

AUCKLAND

	Runs	Mins	Balls	6s	4s
R.J.Rolls*† b McWilliams	23	51	38	-	3
R.J.Kember c Broadmore b McWilliams	12	60	51	-	1
I.Cronin-Knight c Broadmore b Mason	31	75	63	-	3
V.J.Lind run out	0	7	5	-	-
A.Soma lbw b Broadmore	0	11	10	-	-
S.A.P.Hopkins run out	3	52	51	-	-
S.L.Hungerford not out	29	46	38	-	1
P.Mistry b Broadmore	0	4	3	-	-
A.E.Hodgson run out	9	27	25	-	-
S.Coetzee run out	1	3	2	-	-
S.M.Bullen b Burrows	0	3	2	-	-
S.B.Hui					
Extras (lb 6, w 18, nb 2)	26				
TOTAL (47.4 overs)	**134**	174			

CENTRAL DISTRICTS

	Runs	Mins	Balls	6s	4s
S.L.Norman c Rolls b Bullen	22	76	64	-	2
R.H.Priest† b Hui	16	20	17	-	3
N.M.Thessman lbw b Bullen	21	77	70	-	-
S.J.McGlashan c Lind b Mistry	17	31	24	-	2
A.L.Mason* not out	31	42	35	-	6
K.E.Tunnicliffe not out	13	32	19	-	2
Z.A.McWilliams					
K.M.Cocksedge					
K.E.Broadmore					
K.M.Winkley					
A.K.Burrows					
R.H.Candy					
Extras (w 14, nb 2)	16				
TOTAL (37.4 overs) (4 wkts)	**136**	141			

Bowling	O	M	R	W
CENTRAL DISTRICTS				
Candy	8	0	20	0
Burrows	8.4	2	40	1
McWilliams	7	2	16	2
Broadmore	10	5	14	2
Winkley	5	1	20	0
Mason	9	2	18	1
AUCKLAND				
Mistry	7	1	30	1
Coetzee	2.4	0	22	0
Hui	8	2	27	1
Hungerford	9	0	28	0
Bullen	6	1	16	2
Hodgson	5	0	13	0

Fall of Wickets

	A	***CD***
1st	42	26
2nd	43	63
3rd	44	79
4th	46	91
5th	86	-
6th	87	-
7th	92	-
8th	125	-
9th	129	-
10th	134	-

CANTERBURY v NORTHERN DISTRICTS — State League

at Queen Elizabeth II Park, Christchurch on 30 December, 2006
Toss : Canterbury. Umpires : E.J. Gray & D.M. Quested
***Canterbury won by 7 wickets.** Points: Canterbury 4, Northern Districts 0*

NORTHERN DISTRICTS

	Runs	Mins	Balls	6s	4s
T.M.Gould b Mitchell	25	45	36	-	1
J.M.Fraser lbw b Watson	0	7	4	-	-
K.L.Pulford not out	52	72	52	-	3
N.J.Browne* c Satterthwaite b Minogue	18	16	15	-	1
A.J.Wilkins c Tiffen b Watson	13	15	13	-	-
M.P.Murphy run out	0	1	1	-	-
K.L.Samkin					
L.E.Milliken					
M.J.Hannay					
H.R.Huddleston					
J.C.Ullyett†					
K.A.Tomlinson					
Extras (lb 7, w 5, nb 1)	13				
TOTAL (20 overs) (5 wkts)	**121**	80			

CANTERBURY

	Runs	Mins	Balls	6s	4s
M.C.Godliman c Ullyett b Huddleston	2	13	14	-	-
M.F.Fahey c & b Tomlinson	21	40	23	-	3
H.M.Tiffen* not out	61	69	51	-	6
R.C.Milburn† b Browne	10	24	12	-	-
A.E.Satterthwaite not out	6	17	11	-	-
H.M.Watson					
S.E.Charteris					
S.K.Burke					
K.E.Minogue					
M.L.Mitchell					
E.M.Bermingham					
E.M.Campbell					
Extras (lb 8, w 12, nb 2)	22				
TOTAL (18.1 overs) (3 wkts)	**122**	83			

Bowling	*O*	*M*	*R*	*W*
CANTERBURY				
Burke	4	0	11	0
Watson	4	0	24	2
Satterthwaite	2	0	16	0
Mitchell	4	0	24	1
Charteris	4	0	25	0
Minogue	2	0	14	1
NORTHERN DISTRICTS				
Milliken	4	1	17	0
Huddleston	4	0	22	1
Pulford	2	0	16	0
Tomlinson	3	0	21	1
Browne	3.1	0	20	1
Murphy	2	0	18	0

Fall of Wickets	***ND***	***C***
1st	4	10
2nd	64	57
3rd	91	99
4th	121	-
5th	121	-
6th	-	-
7th	-	-
8th	-	-
9th	-	-
10th	-	-

CANTERBURY v NORTHERN DISTRICTS — State League

at Queen Elizabeth II Park, Christchurch on 31 December, 2006.
***Abandoned without a ball being bowled.** Points: Canterbury 2, Northern Districts 2*

AUCKLAND v WELLINGTON — State League

at Melville Park, Auckland on 31 December, 2006
Toss : Auckland. Umpires : D.J. Ellwood & W.R. Knights
***Wellington won by 52 runs.** Points: Wellington 4, Auckland 0*

WELLINGTON

	Runs	Mins	Balls	6s	4s
A.M.Smith c Lind b Coetzee	0	6	8	-	-
L.R.Doolan c Coetzee b Mistry	7	8	7	-	1
E.J.Scurr b Hodgson	8	61	42	-	-
M.G.Wakefield c Rolls b Coetzee	3	5	6	-	-
S.J.Hill† b Hui	10	18	11	-	1
L.R.V.S.Harford c Rolls b Hodgson	25	50	38	-	4
A.M.Dodd* c Mistry b Bullen	8	19	22	-	1
A.E.Cooper b Hui	24	34	26	-	3
S.F.M.Devine c Soma b Mistry	29	37	31	-	2
E.C.Perry not out	14	18	14	-	1
M.J.Hodgson not out	8	11	11	-	-
S.E.A.Ruck					
Extras (lb 5, w 9, nb 1)	15				
TOTAL (36 overs) (9 wkts)	**151**	138			

AUCKLAND

	Runs	Mins	Balls	6s	4s
R.J.Rolls*† c Perry b Ruck	28	56	44	-	3
R.J.Kember lbw b Ruck	0	5	1	-	-
I.Cronin-Knight b Devine	0	16	10	-	-
V.J.Lind c Cooper b Doolan	18	49	33	-	3
A.Soma c Dodd b Cooper	4	25	18	-	-
S.A.P.Hopkins b Dodd	5	29	20	-	-
S.L.Hungerford b Doolan	18	16	30	-	2
P.Mistry c Perry b Dodd	13	22	20	-	2
S.Coetzee b Dodd	0	4	2	-	-
A.E.Hodgson b Devine	3	11	10	-	-
S.M.Bullen not out	0	2	1	-	-
S.B.Hui					
Extras (b 1, lb 1, w 8)	10				
TOTAL (31.3 overs)	**99**	122			

Bowling	O	M	R	W
AUCKLAND				
Mistry	6	1	19	2
Coetzee	7	0	34	2
Hui	8	1	34	2
Hungerford	7	0	33	0
Bullen	4	1	11	1
Hodgson	4	1	15	2
WELLINGTON				
Devine	5	1	20	2
Ruck	8	0	18	2
Perry	4	0	16	0
Doolan	7	0	21	2
Cooper	3	0	10	1
Dodd	4.3	1	12	3

Fall of Wickets	***W***	***A***
1st	5	9
2nd	7	15
3rd	10	46
4th	29	55
5th	57	61
6th	68	82
7th	70	82
8th	125	84
9th	128	99
10th	-	99

AUCKLAND v WELLINGTON — State League

at Melville Park, Auckland on 1 January, 2007
Toss : Wellington. Umpires : D.J. Ellwood & W.R. Knights
***Wellington won by 7 wickets.** Points: Wellington 5, Auckland 0*

AUCKLAND

	Runs	Mins	Balls	6s	4s
R.J.Rolls*† c Smith b Cooper	37	94	66	-	3
R.J.Kember c Hill b Devine	11	17	7	-	1
I.Cronin-Knight hit wicket b Devine	4	9	6	-	1
V.J.Lind c Perry b Devine	41	72	65	-	6
A.Soma c Hill b Doolan	4	34	29	-	-
S.A.P.Hopkins lbw b Cooper	4	33	26	-	-
S.L.Hungerford b Cooper	13	11	15	-	2
A.E.Hodgson c Scurr b Cooper	12	43	43	-	-
P.Mistry c Harford b Perry	2	11	14	-	-
S.Coetzee c Perry b Cooper	6	17	9	-	-
S.M.Bullen not out	4	6	6	-	1
S.B.Hui					
Extras (b 1, lb 5, w 16, nb 1)	23				
TOTAL (47.2 overs)	**161**	178			

WELLINGTON

	Runs	Mins	Balls	6s	4s
L.R.Doolan c Rolls b Bullen	53	84	66	-	7
A.M.Smith c Rolls b Hungerford	25	43	40	-	4
E.J.Scurr not out	41	88	72	-	5
M.G.Wakefield c Bullen b Hodgson	3	8	7	-	-
L.R.V.S.Harford not out	17	38	35	-	2
A.M.Dodd*					
S.J.Hill†					
S.F.M.Devine					
A.E.Cooper					
E.C.Perry					
M.J.Hodgson					
S.E.A.Ruck					
Extras (lb 2, w 22, nb 1)	25				
TOTAL (36.3 overs) (3 wkts)	**164**	132			

Bowling	O	M	R	W
WELLINGTON				
Devine	9	1	20	3
Ruck	6	0	29	0
Perry	5	1	14	1
Dodd	9	1	43	0
Doolan	10	1	34	1
Cooper	8.2	0	15	5
AUCKLAND				
Mistry	9	0	49	0
Coetzee	4	0	16	0
Rolls	7.3	3	22	0
Hungerford	4	0	30	1
Hodgson	5	1	18	1
Bullen	7	1	27	1

Fall of Wickets	***A***	***W***
1st	13	63
2nd	20	109
3rd	100	118
4th	104	-
5th	117	-
6th	119	-
7th	130	-
8th	134	-
9th	154	-
10th	161	-

NORTHERN DISTRICTS v WELLINGTON — State League

at Jansen Park, Hamilton on 3 January, 2007
Toss : Wellington. Umpires : R.D. Anderson & D.J. Ellwood
Wellington won by 8 wickets. *Points: Wellington 5, Northern Districts 0*

NORTHERN DISTRICTS

	Runs	Mins	Balls	6s	4s
T.M.Gould c Hill b Devine	2	1	3	-	-
J.M.Fraser c Hill b Devine	1	12	12	-	-
K.L.Pulford c Devine b Hill	8	23	15	-	2
A.J.Wilkins c Hill b Devine	0	15	9	-	-
N.J.Browne* c Hill b Devine	4	29	21	-	-
M.P.Murphy c Hill b Devine	26	37	26	-	4
M.J.Hannay b Dodd	16	64	46	-	1
L.E.Milliken c Hill b Doolan	1	8	4	-	-
K.L.Samkin lbw b Dodd	23	30	37	-	2
H.R.Huddleston not out	14	31	31	-	1
K.A.Tomlinson c Smith b Scurr	4	17	14	-	1
J.C.Ullyett†					
Extras (lb 4, w 11, nb 2)	17				
TOTAL (36 overs)	**116**	138			

WELLINGTON

	Runs	Mins	Balls	6s	4s
L.R.Doolan b Browne	1	7	9	-	-
A.M.Smith c Browne b Hannay	39	75	58	-	6
E.J.Scurr not out	28	102	75	-	1
M.G.Wakefield not out	29	34	32	-	4
A.M.Dodd*					
L.R.V.S.Harford					
S.J.Hill†					
S.F.M.Devine					
A.E.Cooper					
E.C.Perry					
M.J.Hodgson					
S.E.A.Ruck					
Extras (lb 3, w 17)	20				
TOTAL (29 overs) (2 wkts)	**117**	110			

Bowling	*O*	*M*	*R*	*W*
WELLINGTON				
Devine	10	2	23	5
Hill	8	1	37	1
Doolan	6	0	21	1
Cooper	7	1	17	0
Dodd	4.3	1	14	2
Scurr	0.3	0	0	1
NORTHERN DISTRICTS				
Milliken	8	3	17	0
Browne	7	1	18	1
Hannay	7	0	25	1
Pulford	2	0	20	0
Huddleston	3	0	20	0
Wilkins	2	0	14	0

Fall of Wickets

	ND	***W***
1st	2	2
2nd	3	65
3rd	14	-
4th	14	-
5th	43	-
6th	52	-
7th	61	-
8th	94	-
9th	105	-
10th	116	-

OTAGO v AUCKLAND — State League

at Carisbrook, Dunedin on 3 January, 2007
Toss : Auckland. Umpires : M.P. George & C.J. Morris
Otago won by 5 wickets. *Points: Otago 5, Auckland 0*

AUCKLAND

	Runs	Mins	Balls	6s	4s
E.B.Komp b Bates	4	21	22	-	1
R.J.Kember b Tsukigawa	6	18	20	-	1
R.J.Rolls*† c Martin b Tsukigawa	18	40	37	-	2
I.Cronin-Knight c Martin b Spence	12	50	35	-	-
V.J.Lind b Innes	43	88	59	-	5
A.Soma b Spence	4	20	25	-	-
S.L.Hungerford b King	7	17	19	-	-
K.T.Perkins lbw b Innes	11	29	33	-	1
A.E.Hodgson run out	6	27	23	-	-
P.Mistry not out	23	22	25	-	2
S.M.Bullen not out	0	1	0	-	-
S.B.Hui					
Extras (b 2, lb 7, w 15, nb 2)	26				
TOTAL (50 overs) (9 wkts)	**160**	171			

OTAGO

	Runs	Mins	Balls	6s	4s
M.J.Kane lbw b Hui	25	39	47	-	2
A.S.M.Kitchin c Cronin-Knight b Hui	13	55	30	-	3
A.J.Blackwell c Hungerford b Hodgson	27	54	39	1	4
K.J.Martin† b Mistry	38	65	49	-	5
S.J.Tsukigawa* lbw b Hui	19	34	30	-	3
A.L.Kane not out	4	15	6	-	-
C.E.Taylor not out	0	7	12	-	-
S.W.Bates					
J.M.Innes					
S.M.King					
K.M.Spence					
T.J.Morrison					
Extras (lb 2, w 33)	35				
TOTAL (35.3 overs) (5 wkts)	**161**	137			

Bowling	*O*	*M*	*R*	*W*
OTAGO				
Bates	4.3	2	2	1
Tsukigawa	10	2	27	2
Spence	9.3	1	29	2
Morrison	5	1	23	0
King	10	1	30	1
Kane M.J.	1	0	10	0
Innes	9	1	28	2
Taylor	1	0	2	0
AUCKLAND				
Mistry	8	0	26	1
Hodgson	7	1	34	1
Hui	7.3	2	21	3
Hungerford	4	0	28	0
Perkins	2	0	32	0
Bullen	7	1	18	0

Fall of Wickets

	A	***O***
1st	12	36
2nd	12	47
3rd	46	119
4th	52	152
5th	79	158
6th	103	-
7th	128	-
8th	129	-
9th	158	-
10th	-	-

NORTHERN DISTRICTS v WELLINGTON — State League

at Jansen Park, Hamilton on 4 January, 2007
Toss : Wellington. Umpires : R.D. Anderson & D.J. Ellwood
***Northern Districts won by 4 wickets.** Points: Northern Districts 5, Wellington 0*

WELLINGTON

	Runs	Mins	Balls	6s	4s
L.R.Doolan b Pulford	29	78	48	-	4
A.M.Smith b Browne	24	33	30	-	4
E.J.Scurr run out	6	16	9	-	1
M.G.Wakefield c Milliken b Pulford	2	12	12	--	
L.R.V.S.Harford run out	8	38	31	-	-
S.F.M.Devine c Browne b Hannay	3	18	15	-	-
A.E.Cooper c Wilkins b Hannay	13	29	23	-	2
A.M.Dodd* c Ullyett b Milliken	15	36	35	-	2
S.J.Hill† not out	18	45	30	-	2
E.C.Perry c Wilkins b Murphy	14	27	22	-	1
M.J.Hodgson c & b Milliken	0	5	7	-	-
S.E.A.Ruck					
Extras (lb 1, w 24, nb 4)	29				
TOTAL (43 overs)	**161**	173			

NORTHERN DISTRICTS

	Runs	Mins	Balls	6s	4s
J.M.Fraser c Wakefield b Devine	81	126	103	-	10
T.M.Gould c & b Ruck	1	21	11	-	-
K.L.Pulford lbw b Ruck	3	8	5	-	-
A.J.Wilkins lbw b Cooper	23	67	53	-	2
N.J.Browne* not out	10	45	18	-	1
M.P.Murphy b Devine	8	9	12	-	1
M.J.Hannay b Devine	0	2	4	-	-
L.E.Milliken not out	4	4	3	-	1
K.L.Samkin					
H.R.Huddleston					
J.C.Ullyett†					
K.A.Tomlinson					
Extras (lb 6, w 22, nb 4)	32				
TOTAL (34.1 overs) (6 wkts)	**162**	144			

Bowling	O	M	R	W
NORTHERN DISTRICTS				
Milliken	8	0	28	2
Murphy	6	1	22	1
Browne	4	0	34	1
Tomlinson	5	1	17	0
Pulford	10	3	18	2
Hannay	10	0	41	2
WELLINGTON				
Devine	8.1	2	30	3
Ruck	10	0	47	2
Perry	4	0	25	0
Doolan	3	0	17	0
Cooper	5	0	19	1
Dodd	4	0	18	0

Fall of Wickets

	W	ND
1st	41	11
2nd	66	19
3rd	76	113
4th	82	141
5th	93	153
6th	95	153
7th	117	-
8th	127	-
9th	159	-
10th	161	-

OTAGO v AUCKLAND — State League

at Carisbrook, Dunedin on 4 January, 2007
Toss : Otago. Umpires : M.P. George & C.J. Morris
***Auckland won by 8 wickets.** Points: Auckland 5, Otago 0*

OTAGO

	Runs	Mins	Balls	6s	4s
M.J.Kane c Rolls b Hui	25	67	49	-	5
A.S.M.Kitchin c Soma b Mistry	0	1	4	-	-
A.J.Blackwell c Hodgson b Bullen	31	55	54	-	5
K.J.Martin† st Rolls b Hodgson	27	78	46	-	2
S.J.Tsukigawa* c Cronin-Knight b Bullen	5	19	18	-	1
C.E.Taylor c Rolls b Perkins	26	33	34	-	4
A.L.Kane c Kember b Hui	8	31	19	-	-
J.M.Innes b Mistry	0	7	5	-	-
K.M.Spence c Kember b Hui	3	8	10	-	-
S.M.King bHui	0	6	3	-	-
A.M.Te Wake not out	2	4	6	-	-
T.J.Morrison					
Extras (lb 4, w 20, nb 2)	26				
TOTAL (41.1 overs)	**153**	158			

AUCKLAND

	Runs	Mins	Balls	6s	4s
E.B.Komp b Spence	1	12	15	-	-
R.J.Kember run out	1	9	6	-	-
R.J.Rolls*† not out	80	105	79	2	1
I.Cronin-Knight not out	52	102	91	-	5
V.J.Lind					
A.Soma					
K.T.Perkins					
S.L.Hungerford					
P.Mistry					
A.E.Hodgson					
S.M.Bullen					
S.B.Hui					
Extras (lb 1, w 22)	23				
TOTAL (31.5 overs) (2 wkts)	**157**	115			

Bowling	O	M	R	W
AUCKLAND				
Mistry	8	3	14	2
Hodgson	7	1	30	1
Hui	7.1	3	14	4
Bullen	10	1	25	2
Hungerford	4	0	28	0
Kember	2	0	12	0
Perkins	3	0	26	1
OTAGO				
Tsukigawa	6	0	18	0
Spence	7	0	40	1
Taylor	6	1	22	0
King	7	1	28	0
Innes	3	0	19	0
Te Wake	1	0	10	0
Blackwell	1.5	0	19	0

Fall of Wickets

	O	A
1st	2	5
2nd	53	6
3rd	59	-
4th	79	-
5th	131	-
6th	144	-
7th	146	-
8th	151	-
9th	151	-
10th	153	-

CANTERBURY v AUCKLAND — State League

at MainPower Oval, Rangiora on 6 January, 2007
Toss : Auckland. Umpires : G.C. Holdem & I.W. Shine
Canterbury won by 7 wickets. *Points: Canterbury 5, Auckland 0*

AUCKLAND

	Runs	Mins	Balls	6s	4s
E.B.Komp c Charteris b Satterthwaite	22	58	47	-	4
R.J.Kember c & b Watson	9	22	20	-	-
R.J.Rolls*† b McNeill	23	39	31	-	3
I.Cronin-Knight c Milburn b Satterthwaite	1	14	7	-	-
V.J.Lind run out	43	70	56	-	6
A.Soma run out	0	1	1	-	-
S.L.Hungerford b Minogue	20	60	54	-	2
A.E.Hodgson not out	8	42	31	-	2
P.Mistry lbw b Minogue	0	2	3	-	-
S.Coetzee c Godliman b Campbell	9	27	27	-	2
S.B.Hui c & b Campbell	0	8	11	-	-
S.M.Bullen					
Extras (b 2, lb 3, w 24, nb 7)	36				
TOTAL (47 overs)	**171**	176			

CANTERBURY

	Runs	Mins	Balls	6s	4s
M.F.Fahey c Rolls b Bullen	49	97	48	1	6
M.C.Godliman c Cronin-Knight b Hui	22	22	26	-	3
H.M.Tiffen* lbw b Hungerford	8	34	26	-	-
R.C.Milburn† not out	29	67	65	-	4
A.E.Satterthwaite not out	39	47	40	-	6
H.M.Watson					
B.H.McNeill					
S.E.Charteris					
S.K.Burke					
K.E.Minogue					
M.L.Mitchell					
E.M.Campbell					
Extras (lb 3, w 23)	26				
TOTAL (34.1 overs) (3 wkts)	**173**	125			

Bowling

	O	M	R	W
CANTERBURY				
Burke	7	1	34	0
Watson	10	2	27	1
McNeill	9	2	30	1
Satterthwaite	5	0	18	2
Charteris	5	0	26	0
Mitchell	2	0	14	0
Minogue	3	0	12	2
Campbell	6	4	5	2
AUCKLAND				
Mistry	5.1	0	30	0
Hodgson	7	1	35	0
Hui	6	0	39	1
Hungerford	5	0	21	1
Bullen	6	0	35	1
Coetzee	5	0	10	0

Fall of Wickets

	A	*C*
1st	22	37
2nd	67	84
3rd	67	103
4th	73	-
5th	73	-
6th	143	-
7th	143	-
8th	144	-
9th	166	-
10th	171	-

NORTHERN DISTRICTS v CENTRAL DISTRICTS — State League

at Jansen Park, Hamilton on 6 January, 2007
Toss : Central Districts. Umpires : R.D. Anderson & W.R. Knights
Northern Districts won by 20 runs. *Points: Northern Districts 4, Central Districts 0*

NORTHERN DISTRICTS

	Runs	Mins	Balls	6s	4s
T.M.Gould c Priest b Cocksedge	27	72	60	-	3
J.M.Fraser c Priest b Burrows	0	5	4	-	-
K.L.Pulford c Cocksedge b Burrows	25	30	34	-	3
A.J.Wilkins run out	47	102	67	-	6
N.J.Browne* b Winkley	30	43	44	1	4
M.P.Murphy run out	12	16	19	-	3
M.J.Hannay c & b Candy	7	16	20	-	1
L.E.Milliken c Priest b Winkley	2	7	7	-	-
K.L.Samkin lbw b Winkley	4	6	3	-	1
H.R.Huddleston c Broadmore b Burrows	0	6	4	-	-
J.C.Ullyett† not out	4	2	3	-	1
K.A.Tomlinson					
Extras (lb 4, w 6)	10				
TOTAL (44.1 overs)	**168**	157			

CENTRAL DISTRICTS

	Runs	Mins	Balls	6s	4s
S.L.Norman lbw b Pulford	11	42	35	-	2
R.H.Priest† c Browne b Pulford	26	69	52	-	5
N.M.Thessman run out	16	52	45	-	-
S.J.McGlashan b Pulford	6	18	15	-	-
A.L.Mason* c Hannay b Huddleston	1	17	12	-	-
K.E.Tunnicliffe c Milliken b Tomlinson	21	60	45	-	2
Z.A.McWilliams run out	0	8	7	-	-
K.M.Cocksedge run out	26	65	52	-	5
K.E.Broadmore not out	7	21	15	-	-
K.M.Winkley b Murphy	5	11	10	-	1
A.K.Burrows b Tomlinson	0	6	5	-	-
R.H.Candy					
Extras (b 1, lb 1, w 22, nb 5)	29				
TOTAL (47.5 overs)	**148**	176			

Bowling

	O	M	R	W
CENTRAL DISTRICTS				
Candy	8	0	34	1
Burrows	6.1	1	17	3
Broadmore	4	0	19	0
McWilliams	6	2	14	0
Cocksedge	6	2	24	1
Winkley	10	2	27	3
Mason	4	0	29	0
NORTHERN DISTRICTS				
Milliken	10	3	21	0
Murphy	7	2	20	1
Browne	2.3	0	19	0
Pulford	10	0	27	3
Huddleston	9.3	0	27	1
Hannay	5	1	19	0
Tomlinson	3.5	0	13	2

Fall of Wickets

	ND	*CD*
1st	6	39
2nd	41	57
3rd	70	75
4th	134	78
5th	150	80
6th	151	86
7th	156	129
8th	160	135
9th	164	146
10th	168	148

CANTERBURY v AUCKLAND — State League

at MainPower Oval, Rangiora on 7 January, 2007
Toss : Canterbury. Umpires : D.M. Quested & I.W. Shine
Auckland won by 32 runs. *Points: Auckland 4, Canterbury 0*

AUCKLAND

	Runs	Mins	Balls	6s	4s
E.B.Komp lbw b Watson	9	21	23	-	1
R.J.Kember run out	56	106	85	-	6
R.J.Rolls*† c Watson b Campbell	57	94	67	-	5
I.Cronin-Knight b Satterthwaite	12	41	34	-	-
V.J.Lind run out	21	38	27	-	2
S.L.Hungerford c Milburn b Burke	26	28	33	-	3
K.T.Perkins run out	13	34	23	-	-
P.Mistry b Watson	9	10	12	-	-
S.Coetzee not out	1	1	1	-	-
A.E.Hodgson					
S.M.Bullen					
S.B.Hui					
Extras (b 2, w 13, nb 4)	19				
TOTAL (50 overs) (8 wkts)	**223**	190			

CANTERBURY

	Runs	Mins	Balls	6s	4s
M.F.Fahey run out	91	130	97	1	10
M.C.Godliman c Lind b Hui	20	51	50	-	2
H.M.Tiffen* c Rolls b Hungerford	14	37	18	-	2
R.C.Milburn† c Cronin-Knight b Hodgson	21	27	25	-	1
A.E.Satterthwaite not out	11	56	31	-	-
H.M.Watson b Coetzee	6	5	6	-	1
S.K.Burke lbw b Coetzee	2	7	5	-	-
E.M.Bermingham lbw b Hungerford	0	6	8	-	-
S.E.Charteris b Hungerford	0	14	11	-	-
M.L.Mitchell run out	0	1	1	-	-
K.E.Minogue st Rolls b Hungerford	0	5	1	-	-
E.M.Campbell					
Extras (lb 2, w 23, nb 1)	26				
TOTAL (42.1 overs)	**191**	174			

Bowling	O	M	R	W
CANTERBURY				
Burke	10	1	37	1
Watson	10	1	43	2
Satterthwaite	10	1	35	1
Charteris	8	0	45	0
Minogue	4	0	31	0
Campbell	8	0	30	1
AUCKLAND				
Mistry	8	2	30	0
Hodgson	7	2	30	1
Hui	6	0	34	1
Coetzee	9	0	32	2
Hungerford	8.1	1	36	4
Bullen	4	0	27	0

Fall of Wickets

	A	C
1st	16	50
2nd	135	106
3rd	137	152
4th	169	163
5th	173	170
6th	207	177
7th	222	181
8th	223	187
9th	-	187
10th	-	191

NORTHERN DISTRICTS v CENTRAL DISTRICTS — State League

at Jansen Park, Hamilton on 7 January, 2007
Toss : Central Districts. Umpires : R.D. Anderson & W.R. Knights
Northern Districts won by 3 wickets. *Points: Northern Districts 4, Central Districts 0*

CENTRAL DISTRICTS

	Runs	Mins	Balls	6s	4s
S.L.Norman b Pulford	9	43	37	-	-
R.H.Priest† lbw b Browne	6	14	10	-	1
N.M.Thessman lbw b Pulford	10	26	19	-	1
S.J.McGlashan b Murphy	33	85	65	-	4
A.L.Mason* c Ullyett b Pulford	12	15	11	-	3
K.E.Tunnicliffe lbw b Murphy	1	12	11	-	-
Z.A.McWilliams not out	33	118	89	-	1
K.M.Cocksedge c & b Hannay	4	13	19	-	-
K.E.Broadmore lbw b Hannay	0	1	3	-	-
K.M.Winkley c Ullyett b Milliken	21	25	25	-	4
R.H.Candy not out	13	12	14	-	2
A.K.Burrows					
Extras (lb 5, w 28, nb 4)	37				
TOTAL (50 overs) (9 wkts)	**179**	191			

NORTHERN DISTRICTS

	Runs	Mins	Balls	6s	4s
T.M.Gould run out	0	1	2	-	-
J.M.Fraser st Priest b Candy	0	4	1	-	-
K.L.Pulford c Norman b McWilliams	17	46	39	-	2
A.J.Wilkins c Broadmore b Mason	42	102	88	-	6
N.J.Browne* c Priest b Mason	52	109	86	-	5
M.P.Murphy c Thessman b Candy	1	10	1	-	-
H.R.Huddleston not out	48	61	55	-	6
M.J.Hannay b Burrows	4	19	12	-	-
K.L.Samkin not out	0	1	1	-	-
L.E.Milliken					
K.A.Tomlinson					
J.C.Ullyett†					
Extras (lb 6, w 10)	16				
TOTAL (49.1 overs) (7 wkts)	**180**	180			

Bowling	O	M	R	W
NORTHERN DISTRICTS				
Milliken	10	1	26	1
Browne	3	0	14	1
Murphy	10	0	37	2
Pulford	10	0	36	3
Huddleston	4	0	19	0
Hannay	7	0	23	2
Tomlinson	6	2	19	0
CENTRAL DISTRICTS				
Candy	9	4	23	2
Burrows	10	1	33	1
Broadmore	7	0	27	0
McWilliams	9.1	1	32	1
Winkley	6	0	28	0
Mason	8	0	31	2

Fall of Wickets

	CD	ND
1st	15	0
2nd	33	1
3rd	34	35
4th	54	94
5th	60	101
6th	118	149
7th	127	176
8th	127	-
9th	160	-
10th	-	

WELLINGTON v CANTERBURY — State League

at Basin Reserve, Wellington on 10 January, 2007.
Abandoned without a ball being bowled. *Points: Wellington 2, Canterbury 2*

CENTRAL DISTRICTS v OTAGO — State League

at Fitzherbert Park, Palmerston North on 10 January, 2007
Toss : Central Districts. Umpires : K. Cross & M.P. George
Central Districts won by 7 wickets. *Points: Central Districts 5, Otago 0*

OTAGO

	Runs	Mins	Balls	6s	4s
M.J.Kane lbw b Winkley	54	83	67	-	6
A.S.M.Kitchin run out	21	45	48	-	2
S.W.Bates b Mason	19	52	38	-	1
S.J.Tsukigawa* not out	25	59	40	-	2
K.J.Martin† c Mason b Winkley	17	13	18	-	1
C.E.Taylor c Priest b Mason	2	3	7	-	-
J.M.Innes st Priest b Winkley	1	7	11	-	-
A.L.Kane run out	0	1	2	-	-
K.M.Spence b Mason	0	5	5	-	-
S.M.King run out	0	2	3	-	-
T.J.Morrison run out	0	2	5	-	-
A.M.Te Wake					
Extras (b 4, lb 1, w 13)	18				
TOTAL (40.5 overs)	**157**	145			

CENTRAL DISTRICTS

	Runs	Mins	Balls	6s	4s
S.L.Norman c Martin b Spence	0	12	18	-	-
R.H.Priest† c Innes b King	31	60	47	-	5
N.M.Thessman not out	45	135	101	-	4
K.E.Tunnicliffe b Taylor	0	8	13	-	-
A.L.Mason* not out	48	65	5	-	6
S.J.McGlashan					
Z.A.McWilliams					
K.M.Cocksedge					
K.E.Broadmore					
K.M.Winkley					
R.H.Candy					
A.K.Burrows					
Extras (lb 2, w 30, nb 4)	36				
TOTAL (38.3 overs) (3 wkts)	**160**	148			

Bowling	O	M	R	W
CENTRAL DISTRICTS				
Candy	6	1	15	0
Burrows	4.5	2	9	0
McWilliams	6	0	36	0
Broadmore	4	0	24	0
Winkley	10	0	30	3
Cocksedge	2	0	18	0
Mason	8	1	20	3
OTAGO				
Bates	4	2	14	0
Spence	7	0	34	1
Tsukigawa	3	0	17	0
King	10	1	28	1
Taylor	9	1	37	1
Innes	1	0	9	0
Morrison	4.3	1	19	0

Fall of Wickets	O	CD
1st	41	10
2nd	98	71
3rd	119	73
4th	142	-
5th	145	-
6th	150	-
7th	150	-
8th	157	-
9th	157	-
10th	157	-

WELLINGTON v CANTERBURY — State League

at Allied Prime Basin Reserve, Wellington on 11 January, 2007
Toss : Wellington. Umpires : T.J. Parlane & D.M. Quested
***Wellington won by 4 wickets.** Points: Wellington 4, Canterbury 0*

CANTERBURY

	Runs	Mins	Balls	6s	4s
M.F.Fahey run out	5	9	7	-	1
M.C.Godliman lbw b Ruck	0	15	11	-	-
H.M.Tiffen* c & b Cooper	19	42	30	-	2
R.C.Milburn† c Hodgson b Perry	16	61	61	-	-
A.E.Satterthwaite run out	3	9	6	-	-
H.M.Watson c Cooper b Doolan	30	71	62	1	2
B.H.McNeill c Devine b Perry	1	12	14	-	-
S.K.Burke c Dodd b Perry	23	54	46	-	4
S.E.Charteris not out	30	47	35	-	2
M.L.Mitchell b Devine	0	17	12	-	-
K.E.Minogue not out	10	20	18	-	1
E.M.Campbell					
Extras (b 1, lb 1, w 16, nb 3)	21				
TOTAL (50 overs) (9 wkts)	**158**	188			

WELLINGTON

	Runs	Mins	Balls	6s	4s
L.R.Doolan c Tiffen b Watson	18	58	60	-	2
A.M.Smith c Watson b Burke	12	29	27	-	1
E.J.Scurr c Milburn b Satterthwaite	14	34	27	-	2
M.G.Wakefield not out	55	97	73	1	7
L.R.V.S.Harford c Minogue b Charteris	12	25	22	-	2
S.F.M.Devine c Milburn b Charteris	4	6	6	-	1
A.M.Dodd* c Minogue b Satterthwaite	13	29	29	-	2
A.E.Cooper not out	21	30	24		4
S.J.Hill †					
E.C.Perry					
M.J.Hodgson					
S.E.A.Ruck					
Extras (lb 2, w 6, nb 3)	11				
TOTAL (44.2 overs) (6 wkts)	**160**	158			

Bowling	O	M	R	W
WELLINGTON				
Devine	10	0	58	1
Ruck	10	3	31	1
Cooper	10	2	35	1
Dodd	10	3	14	0
Perry	7	5	4	3
Doolan	3	0	14	1
CANTERBURY				
Burke	9	2	38	1
Watson	10	5	12	1
Satterthwaite	10	1	39	2
McNeill	8	0	32	0
Charteris	5	1	18	2
Campbell	2.2	0	19	0

Fall of Wickets	C	W
1st	6	18
2nd	12	41
3rd	38	47
4th	44	67
5th	51	79
6th	52	115
7th	100	-
8th	107	-
9th	123	-
10th	-	-

CENTRAL DISTRICTS v OTAGO — State League

at Fitzherbert Park, Palmerston North on 11 January, 2007
Toss : Otago. Umpires : J.M. Busby & K. Cross
***Central Districts won by 8 wickets.** Points: Central Districts 5, Otago 0*

OTAGO

	Runs	Mins	Balls	6s	4s
M.J.Kane c Candy b Burrows	7	26	13	-	1
A.S.M.Kitchin lbw b Candy	7	15	18	-	1
S.W.Bates c Mason b Candy	0	1	1	-	-
S.J.Tsukigawa* c Priest b Broadmore	5	33	23	-	1
K.J.Martin† c Mason b Broadmore	11	17	18	-	2
C.E.Taylor c Norman b McWilliams	3	21	18	-	-
A.F.Bell not out	8	61	32	-	-
A.L.Kane c & b McWilliams	10	14	21	-	1
K.M.Spence c Mason b Winkley	2	15	13	-	-
S.M.King run out	0	3	5	-	-
A.M.Te Wake run out	5	8	15	-	-
T.J.Morrison					
Extras (lb 3, w 14)	17				
TOTAL (29.3 overs)	**75**	116			

CENTRAL DISTRICTS

	Runs	Mins	Balls	6s	4s
S.L.Norman b Bates	4	8	8	-	1
R.H.Priest† c Martin b Morrison	0	4	1		-
N.M.Thessman not out	32	66	59	-	3
K.E.Tunnicliffe not out	36	62	67	-	5
A.L.Mason*					
S.J.McGlashan					
Z.A.McWilliams					
K.M.Cocksedge					
K.E.Broadmore					
K.M.Winkley					
R.H.Candy					
A.K.Burrows					
Extras (w 4, nb 1)	5				
TOTAL (22.2 overs) (2 wkts)	**77**	71			

Bowling	O	M	R	W
CENTRAL DISTRICTS				
Candy	8	0	29	2
Burrows	4	1	12	1
McWilliams	6	1	12	2
Broadmore	6	2	12	2
Winkley	4.3	3	5	1
Mason	1	0	2	0
OTAGO				
Bates	5	1	20	1
Morrison	10	4	14	1
King	5	0	19	0
Tsukigawa	2	0	16	0
Te Wake	0.2	0	8	0

Fall of Wickets	O	CD
1st	18	5
2nd	18	9
3rd	22	-
4th	40	-
5th	42	-
6th	48	-
7th	63	-
8th	68	-
9th	69	-
10th	75	-

CENTRAL DISTRICTS v CANTERBURY — State League

at Fitzherbert Park, Palmerston North on 13 January, 2007
Toss : Canterbury. Umpires : J.M. Busby & D.J. Walker
***Canterbury won by 5 wickets.** Points: Canterbury 4, Central Districts 0*

CENTRAL DISTRICTS

	Runs	Mins	Balls	6s	4s
S.L.Norman st Milburn b McNeill	17	57	54	-	2
R.H.Priest† b Burke	6	17	14	-	1
N.M.Thessman c Milburn b Campbell	32	93	68	-	2
S.J.McGlashan c Watson b Burke	58	115	90	-	6
A.L.Mason* c Fahey b Burke	28	44	33	-	4
K.M.Cocksedge b Burke	0	6	11	-	-
Z.A.McWilliams not out	18	30	15	-	1
K.E.Tunnicliffe not out	19	19	19	-	1
K.E.Broadmore					
K.M.Winkley					
R.H.Candy					
A.K.Burrows					
Extras (lb 1, w 30, nb 4)	35				
TOTAL (50 overs) (6 wkts)	**213**	193			

CANTERBURY

	Runs	Mins	Balls	6s	4s
M.C.Godliman c & b McWilliams	22	55	45	-	2
M.F.Fahey run out	37	82	64	-	5
H.M.Tiffen* b Mason	20	32	28	-	2
R.C.Milburn† c Broadmore b McWilliams	35	89	66	-	2
A.E.Satterthwaite c Cocksedge b Mason	16	13	15	1	2
H.M.Watson not out	64	85	74	-	7
B.H.McNeill not out	6	13	5	-	-
S.E.Charteris					
S.K.Burke					
K.E.Minogue					
M.L.Mitchell					
E.M.Campbell					
Extras (b 2, lb 3, w 8, nb 1)	14				
TOTAL (49.2 overs) (5 wkts)	**214**	190			

Bowling	O	M	R	W
CANTERBURY				
Burke	10	1	49	4
Watson	10	4	19	0
McNeill	10	3	46	1
Satterthwaite	10	2	40	0
Charteris	1	0	10	0
Minogue	2	0	12	0
Campbell	7	0	36	1
CENTRAL DISTRICTS				
Candy	6	1	18	0
Burrows	10	0	50	0
McWilliams	9.2	0	48	2
Broadmore	9	2	37	0
Mason	5	0	25	2
Winkley	10	2	31	0

Fall of Wickets	CD	C
1st	9	47
2nd	41	85
3rd	93	85
4th	149	111
5th	150	201
6th	172	-
7th	-	-
8th	-	-
9th	-	-
10th	-	-

WELLINGTON v OTAGO — State League

at Allied Prime Basin Reserve, Wellington on 13 January, 2007
Toss : Wellington. Umpires : T.J. Parlane & D.M. Quested
***Otago won by 36 runs (D/L).** Points: Otago 4, Wellington 0*

OTAGO

	Runs	Mins	Balls	6s	4s
M.J.Kane lbw b Bupha-Intr	10	38	30	-	1
A.S.M.Kitchin c & b Devine	1	13	9	-	-
S.W.Bates lbw b Ruck	9	17	10	-	2
S.J.Tsukigawa* b Ruck	6	9	7	-	1
K.J.Martin† c Devine b Doolan	72	133	95	-	3
A.F.Bell c Hodgson b Cooper	16	57	51	-	1
A.L.Kane c Hodgson b Dodd	28	47	54	-	2
C.E.Taylor not out	32	41	27	-	1
A.M.Te Wake run out	6	14	10	-	-
K.M.Spence not out	0	2	0	-	-
S.M.King					
T.J.Morrison					
Extras (b 1, lb 6, w 39, nb 3)	49				
TOTAL (50 overs) (8 wkts)	**229**	190			

WELLINGTON

	Runs	Mins	Balls	6s	4s
L.R.Doolan b Tsukigawa	10	16	20	-	2
A.M.Smith c Spence b Morrison	2	35	27	-	-
E.J.Scurr c & b Tsukigawa	17	40	39	-	3
M.G.Wakefield b Tsukigawa	1	14	14	-	-
L.R.V.S.Harford run out	33	64	46	-	3
A.E.Cooper c Martin b Spence	52	82	66	-	4
A.M.Dodd* c Kane M.J. b King	4	10	12	-	-
S.J.Hill† not out	16	31	25	-	-
S.F.M.Devine not out	9	16	13	-	-
O.R.Bupha-Intr					
M.J.Hodgson					
S.E.A.Ruck					
Extras (lb 1, w 9, nb 4)	14				
TOTAL (43 overs) (7 wkts)	**158**	160			

Bowling	O	M	R	W
WELLINGTON				
Devine	10	0	48	1
Ruck	10	1	30	2
Bupha-Intr	4	0	25	1
Cooper	10	0	58	1
Dodd	10	1	27	1
Doolan	6	0	34	1
OTAGO				
Bates	7	0	30	0
Tsukigawa	10	4	12	3
Morrison	10	3	25	1
Spence	7	0	42	1
Taylor	7	0	34	0
King	2	0	14	1

Fall of Wickets	O	W
1st	15	11
2nd	29	24
3rd	38	32
4th	39	37
5th	98	107
6th	166	115
7th	205	136
8th	226	-
9th	-	-
10th	-	-

CENTRAL DISTRICTS v CANTERBURY — State League

at Fitzherbert Park, Palmerston North on 14 January, 2007
Toss : Central Districts. Umpires : J.M. Busby & D.J. Walker
***Central Districts won by 4 wickets.** Points: Central Districts 4, Canterbury 0*

CANTERBURY

	Runs	Mins	Balls	6s	4s
M.F.Fahey c Thessman b McWilliams	47	78	64	-	7
M.C.Godliman b Burrows	0	5	4	-	-
H.M.Tiffen* b Burrows	78	151	125	-	4
R.C.Milburn† c Priest b Candy	1	10	9	-	-
A.E.Satterthwaite c Thessman b Candy	0	2	3	-	-
H.M.Watson b Burrows	43	67	62	-	4
B.H.McNeill not out	11	23	20	-	-
S.K.Burke lbw b Burrows	0	1	1	-	-
E.M.Bermingham not out	15	18	12	-	1
S.E.Charteris					
K.E.Minogue					
E.M.Campbell					
Extras (lb 1, w 17)	18				
TOTAL (50 overs) (7 wkts)	**213**	**185**			

CENTRAL DISTRICTS

	Runs	Mins	Balls	6s	4s
S.L.Norman lbw b Burke	0	1	1	-	-
K.M.Cocksedge lbw b Campbell	41	94	73	-	6
N.M.Thessman lbw b Burke	2	9	11	-	-
S.J.McGlashan not out	111	167	146	1	7
A.L.Mason* c Charteris b Campbell	14	24	24	1	1
R.H.Priest† b Campbell	2	8	8	-	-
K.E.Tunnicliffe b Watson	15	42	31	-	-
Z.A.McWilliams not out	8	6	5	-	1
K.E.Broadmore					
K.M.Winkley					
R.H.Candy					
A.K.Burrows					
Extras (lb 2, w 18, nb 3)	23				
TOTAL (49.2 overs) (6 wkts)	**216**	182			

Bowling	O	M	R	W
CENTRAL DISTRICTS				
Candy	10	2	24	2
Burrows	9	1	29	4
Broadmore	7	1	44	0
McWilliams	9	2	37	1
Mason	5	0	37	0
Winkley	10	1	41	0
CANTERBURY				
Burke	10	2	34	2
McNeill	10	0	34	0
Watson	9.3	0	51	1
Satterthwaite	5	0	24	0
Charteris	4.5	0	30	0
Campbell	10	1	41	3

Fall of Wickets	***C***	***CD***
1st	0	0
2nd	88	3
3rd	97	106
4th	97	137
5th	183	145
6th	187	206
7th	187	-
8th	-	-
9th	-	-
10th	-	-

WELLINGTON v OTAGO — State League

at Allied Prime Basin Reserve, Wellington on 14 January, 2007
Toss : Wellington. Umpires : T.J. Parlane & D.M. Quested
***Wellington won by 115 runs.** Points: Wellington 5, Otago 0*

WELLINGTON

	Runs	Mins	Balls	6s	4s
L.R.Doolan c Kane A.L. b Tsukigawa	21	49	50	-	2
A.M.Smith c Taylor b Kitchin	101	169	140	-	6
E.J.Scurr c Martin b Morrison	1	4	8	-	-
M.G.Wakefield c Martin b Spence	31	74	54	-	2
A.E.Cooper b Spence	3	14	10	-	-
S.J.Hill† b Spence	10	26	19	-	-
S.F.M.Devine run out	8	10	7	-	1
A.M.Dodd* b Spence	4	10	7	-	-
L.R.V.S.Harford not out	2	8	3	-	-
M.J.Hodgson not out	6	4	6	-	-
O.R.Bupha-Intr					
S.E.A.Ruck					
Extras (lb 5, w 20, nb 4)	29				
TOTAL (50 overs) (8 wkts)	**216**	194			

OTAGO

	Runs	Mins	Balls	6s	4s
A.S.M.Kitchin lbw b Ruck	10	10	14	-	1
M.J.Kane b Devine	0	3	2	-	-
S.W.Bates c Dodd b Ruck	26	23	22	-	5
S.J.Tsukigawa* b Devine	7	13	17	-	1
K.J.Martin† b Devine	14	28	24	-	-
A.F.Bell b Devine	0	6	6	-	-
A.L.Kane lbw b Ruck	10	33	22	-	1
C.E.Taylor lbw b Cooper	2	22	15	-	-
A.M.Te Wake run out	9	30	23	-	-
K.M.Spence c Wakefield b Cooper	7	32	32	-	-
T.J.Morrison not out	0	6	6	-	-
S.M.King					
Extras (lb 1, w 10, nb 5)	16				
TOTAL (30.2 overs)	**101**	118			

Bowling	O	M	R	W
OTAGO				
Bates	8	1	27	0
Tsukigawa	10	1	25	1
Morrison	10	1	30	1
Spence	10	0	51	4
King	6	0	45	0
Kitchin	6	0	33	1
WELLINGTON				
Devine	10	1	39	4
Ruck	10	1	40	3
Dodd	5	2	7	0
Cooper	5.2	2	14	2

Fall of Wickets	***W***	***O***
1st	46	1
2nd	48	28
3rd	142	41
4th	154	54
5th	191	60
6th	192	61
7th	204	77
8th	208	78
9th	-	99
10th	-	101

WELLINGTON v CENTRAL DISTRICTS — State League

at Trentham Memorial Park, Upper Hutt on 20 January, 2007
Toss : Wellington. Umpires : R.D. Anderson & K. Cross
***Wellington won by 54 runs.** Points: Wellington 4, Central Districts 0*

WELLINGTON

	Runs	Mins	Balls	6s	4s
L.R.Doolan c Mason b Candy	2	8	8	-	-
A.M.Smith c Tunnicliffe b Mason	82	154	147	-	8
E.J.Scurr c Winkley b McWilliams	12	38	29	-	2
M.G.Wakefield lbw b Candy	68	81	64	-	10
L.R.V.S.Harford run out	12	31	24	-	-
S.J.Hill† c Norman b McWilliams	16	13	10	-	2
A.E.Cooper not out	17	15	14	-	-
S.F.M.Devine not out	6	8	6	-	-
A.M.Dodd*					
M.J.Hodgson					
O.R.Bupha-Intr					
S.E.A.Ruck					
Extras (lb 5, w 7, nb 1)	13				
TOTAL (50 overs) (6 wkts)	**228**	177			

CENTRAL DISTRICTS

	Runs	Mins	Balls	6s	4s
S.L.Norman lbw b Hill	5	8	10	-	-
R.H.Priest† c Scurr b Devine	0	4	1	-	-
N.M.Thessman b Cooper	7	64	42	-	-
S.J.McGlashan c Harford b Doolan	50	125	91	-	3
A.L.Mason* run out	35	56	51	-	3
K.E.Tunnicliffe c Hodgson b Doolan	4	14	12	-	-
Z.A.McWilliams not out	33	54	45	-	2
K.M.Cocksedge b Doolan	2	5	8	-	-
K.E.Broadmore b Dodd	4	19	22	-	-
K.M.Winkley c Wakefield b Devine	8	7	6	-	2
R.H.Candy not out	9	11	11	-	1
A.K.Burrows					
Extras (lb 5, w 12)	17				
TOTAL (50 overs) (9 wkts)	**174**	193			

Bowling	O	M	R	W
CENTRAL DISTRICTS				
Candy	10	4	26	2
Priest	5	1	15	0
Broadmore	10	1	33	0
McWilliams	10	1	64	2
Winkley	5	0	30	0
Mason	10	0	55	1
WELLINGTON				
Devine	10	3	29	2
Hill	10	2	33	1
Cooper	8	1	35	1
Dodd	10	0	33	1
Doolan	8	0	23	3
Bupha-Intr	4	0	16	0

	W	***CD***
1st	10	6
2nd	34	10
3rd	153	44
4th	187	107
5th	202	114
6th	211	118
7th	-	125
8th	-	149
9th	-	161
10th	-	-

NORTHERN DISTRICTS v AUCKLAND — State League

at Weymouth Oval, Auckland on 20 January, 2007
Toss : Auckland. Umpires : R. Allen & D.G. Paterson
***Auckland won by 48 runs.** Points: Auckland 5, Northern Districts 0*

AUCKLAND

	Runs	Mins	Balls	6s	4s
E.B.Komp c Milliken b Browne	14	45	34	-	2
R.J.Kember b Murphy	14	38	28	-	2
R.J.Rolls*† run out	106	114	88	-	12
I.Cronin-Knight c Ullyett b Browne	4	16	16	-	-
V.J.Lind lbw b Pulford	4	10	6	-	1
K.T.Perkins run out	37	106	65	-	1
M.A.Tremaine run out	3	16	13	-	-
A.E.Hodgson c Ullyett b Tomlinson	11	25	20	-	1
P.Mistry b Murphy	3	8	10	-	-
S.Coetzee not out	2	14	8	-	-
S.M.Bullen lbw b Murphy	2	8	8	-	-
S.B.Hui					
Extras (b 2, lb 7, w 29, nb 2)	40				
TOTAL (49.1 overs)	**240**	205			

NORTHERN DISTRICTS

	Runs	Mins	Balls	6s	4s
T.M.Gould b Coetzee	45	66	66	-	7
J.M.Fraser lbw b Coetzee	17	26	26	-	3
K.L.Pulford b Hui	0	4	4	-	-
A.J.Wilkins c Bullen b Tremaine	14	21	21	-	2
N.J.Browne* c Cronin-Knight b Tremaine	54	108	64	1	3
M.P.Murphy c Coetzee b Bullen	44	71	71	-	5
H.R.Huddleston st Rolls b Mistry	2	9	10	-	-
M.J.Hannay run out	8	14	14	-	-
K.L.Samkin c Cronin-Knight b Tremaine	0	4	2	-	-
L.E.Milliken not out	0	4	0	-	-
J.C.Ullyett† lbw b Tremaine	0	1	1	-	-
K.A.Tomlinson					
Extras (w 5, nb 3)	8				
TOTAL (46 overs)	**192**	167			

Bowling	O	M	R	W
NORTHERN DISTRICTS				
Milliken	10	2	31	0
Murphy	8.1	1	25	3
Browne	10	0	48	2
Tomlinson	7	0	33	1
Pulford	3	0	22	1
Huddleston	7	0	44	0
Hannay	4	0	28	0
AUCKLAND				
Mistry	8	1	28	1
Hodgson	7	0	44	0
Hui	8	2	32	1
Coetzee	5	0	25	2
Tremaine	8	2	22	4
Bullen	10	1	41	1

Fall of Wickets

	A	***ND***
1st	39	42
2nd	42	43
3rd	61	82
4th	71	82
5th	191	164
6th	209	171
7th	219	189
8th	226	192
9th	231	192
10th	240	192

CANTERBURY v OTAGO — State League

at Aorangi Park, Timaru on 20 January, 2007
Toss : Canterbury. Umpires : P.J. Agent & J.M. Busby
Canterbury won by 2 wickets. *Points: Canterbury 4, Otago 0*

OTAGO

	Runs	Mins	Balls	6s	4s
A.J.Blackwell run out	1	3	1	-	-
M.J.Kane c Godliman b Watson	0	14	9	-	-
S.W.Bates b Charteris	45	51	39	-	4
K.J.Martin*† b Campbell	41	54	42	-	3
C.E.Taylor b Campbell	1	4	2	-	-
A.L.Kane st Milburn b Campbell	7	11	7	-	1
A.F.Bell not out	22	30	30	-	1
A.S.M.Kitchin lbw b Watson	0	13	7	-	-
A.M.Te Wake run out	1	3	1	-	-
K.M.Spence not out	4	9	6	-	-
S.M.King					
T.J.Morrison					
Extras (b 1, lb 9, w 2)	12				
TOTAL (24 overs) (8 wkts)	**134**	100			

CANTERBURY

	Runs	Mins	Balls	6s	4s
M.F.Fahey c Martin b Bates	11	17	14	-	1
M.C.Godliman b Spence	1	13	9	-	-
H.M.Tiffen* b Taylor	38	58	52	1	-
R.C.Milburn† c Te Wake b Taylor	21	33	26	-	2
A.E.Satterthwaite st Martin b Taylor	9	33	18	-	-
H.M.Watson c Kitchin b King	0	5	3	-	-
B.H.McNeill st Martin b Taylor	1	10	3	-	-
S.K.Burke b King	9	7	6	-	-
E.M.Bermingham not out	18	16	9	-	2
S.E.Charteris not out	9	12	6	-	-
K.E.Minogue					
E.M.Campbell					
Extras (b 2, lb 3, w 11, nb 2)	18				
TOTAL (24 overs) (8 wkts)	**135**	106			

Bowling	*O*	*M*	*R*	*W*
CANTERBURY				
Burke	4	0	15	0
Watson	5	0	18	2
McNeill	3	0	31	0
Satterthwaite	2	0	9	0
Charteris	5	0	30	1
Campbell	5	0	21	3
OTAGO				
Bates	4	1	7	1
Spence	5	0	29	1
Morrison	5	0	23	0
Taylor	5	0	25	4
Kitchin	1	0	12	0
King	4	0	34	2

Fall of Wickets	***O***	***C***
1st	1	15
2nd	11	17
3rd	69	60
4th	78	90
5th	97	93
6th	98	99
7th	113	104
8th	130	108
9th	-	-
10th	-	-

WELLINGTON v CENTRAL DISTRICTS — State League

at Trentham Memorial Park, Upper Hutt on 21 January, 2007
Toss : Wellington. Umpires : R.D. Anderson & K. Cross
Wellington won by 4 runs. *Points: Wellington 4, Central Districts 0*

WELLINGTON

	Runs	Mins	Balls	6s	4s
L.R.Doolan c Cocksedge b Broadmore	23	39	39	-	3
E.J.Scurr c Mason b McWilliams	28	57	44	-	1
A.E.Cooper c Priest b Burrows	7	48	27	-	-
M.G.Wakefield b McWilliams	4	24	20	-	-
A.M.Dodd* run out	4	34	24	-	-
S.J.Hill† c Burrows b Winkley	22	56	47	-	1
M.J.Hodgson b Winkley	3	14	14	-	-
S.F.M.Devine c sub (C.L.Forsyth) b Candy	30	35	30	-	2
S.J.Bradbury not out	16	32	26	-	2
C.K.Mizzi run out	3	15	15	-	-
S.E.A.Ruck b Burrows	1	8	4	-	-
O.R.Bupha-Intr					
Extras (lb 4, w 15)	19				
TOTAL (48.1 overs)	**160**	190			

CENTRAL DISTRICTS

	Runs	Mins	Balls	6s	4s
S.L.Norman lbw b Devine	7	16	14	-	-
K.M.Cocksedge c Wakefield b Ruck	20	37	27	-	4
N.M.Thessman run out	63	148	104	-	6
S.J.McGlashan b Cooper	2	28	21	-	-
A.L.Mason* c Wakefield b Ruck	12	29	30	-	-
R.H.Priest† b Ruck	0	4	4	-	-
Z.A.McWilliams st Wakefield b Doolan	18	31	32	-	1
K.M.Winkley c Devine b Bupha-Intr	0	2	2	-	-
K.E.Tunnicliffe c Mizzi b Doolan	1	5	2	-	-
K.E.Broadmore run out	2	6	4	-	-
R.H.Candy not out	12	13	12	-	2
A.K.Burrows					
Extras (b 2, lb 1, w 16)	19				
TOTAL (42 overs)	**156**	169			

Bowling	*O*	*M*	*R*	*W*
CENTRAL DISTRICTS				
Candy	10	2	26	1
Burrows	9.1	0	26	2
Broadmore	6	0	24	1
McWilliams	9	2	25	2
Winkley	10	0	39	2
Mason	4	0	16	0
WELLINGTON				
Devine	9	1	37	1
Ruck	10	3	30	3
Cooper	6	1	20	1
Dodd	10	4	24	0
Doolan	4	0	24	2
Bupha-Intr	3	0	18	1

Fall of Wickets	***W***	***CD***
1st	38	14
2nd	60	37
3rd	69	53
4th	69	75
5th	92	77
6th	103	120
7th	114	121
8th	140	129
9th	151	137
10th	160	156

NORTHERN DISTRICTS v AUCKLAND — State League

at Weymouth Oval, Auckland on 21 January, 2007
Toss : Northern Districts. Umpires : R. Allen & D.G Paterson
***Auckland won by 3 wickets.** Points: Auckland 4, Northern Districts 0*

NORTHERN DISTRICTS

	Runs	Mins	Balls	6s	4s
T.M.Gould lbw b Mistry	0	9	9	-	-
J.M.Fraser c Bullen b Hodgson	31	67	49	-	6
K.L.Pulford run out	5	14	13	-	1
A.J.Wilkins c Perkins b Hui	11	27	27	-	2
N.J.Browne* c Perkins b Hui	2	7	6	-	-
M.P.Murphy not out	38	122	86	-	4
H.R.Huddleston c Coetzee b Hodgson	0	1	1	-	-
M.J.Hannay st Rolls b Hodgson	0	5	1	-	-
K.L.Samkin c Cronin-Knight b Coetzee	26	49	52	-	3
L.E.Milliken c Rolls b Mistry	2	10	13	-	-
K.A.Tomlinson not out	19	46	45	-	2
J.C.Ullyett†					
Extras (lb 5, w 12, nb 2)	19				
TOTAL (50 overs) (9 wkts)	**153**	183			

AUCKLAND

	Runs	Mins	Balls	6s	4s
E.B.Komp b Milliken	0	2	4	-	-
R.J.Kember c Huddleston b Murphy	31	94	74	-	3
R.J.Rolls*† c Ullyettb Milliken	0	1	1	-	-
I.Cronin-Knight run out	10	41	29	-	1
V.J.Lind lbw b Browne	0	4	3	-	-
K.T.Perkins c Fraser b Browne	37	128	92	-	3
M.A.Tremaine not out	44	103	72	-	5
P.Mistry c Fraser b Huddleston	6	8	9	-	1
A.E.Hodgson not out	6	8	6	-	1
S.Coetzee					
S.M.Bullen					
S.B.Hui					
Extras (lb 8, w 13)	21				
TOTAL (48.2 overs) (7 wkts)	**155**	198			

Bowling	O	M	R	W
AUCKLAND				
Mistry	10	3	27	2
Coetzee	8	1	22	1
Hui	7	1	23	2
Hodgson	7	0	21	3
Tremaine	10	1	41	0
Bullen	8	2	14	0
NORTHERN DISTRICTS				
Milliken	10	2	27	2
Murphy	10	1	26	1
Browne	9	1	25	2
Hannay	7	2	21	0
Pulford	6	1	14	0
Tomlinson	2	0	13	0
Huddleston	4.2	0	21	1

Fall of Wickets

	ND	A
1st	6	0
2nd	19	0
3rd	46	27
4th	53	30
5th	55	59
6th	55	138
7th	56	146
8th	101	-
9th	105	-
10th	-	-

CANTERBURY v OTAGO — State League

at Aorangi Park, Timaru on 21 January, 2007
Toss : Otago. Umpires : P.J. Agent & J.M. Busby
***Canterbury won by 3 wickets**. Points: Canterbury 5, Otago 0*

OTAGO

	Runs	Mins	Balls	6s	4s
A.J.Blackwell c Burke b Minogue	77	116	88	-	9
M.J.Kane c Godliman b Burke	3	32	17	-	-
S.W.Bates lbw b Watson	5	18	20	-	-
K.J.Martin*† c Charteris b Watson	0	1	2	-	-
A.S.M.Kitchin lbw b McNeill	0	4	3	-	-
A.L.Kane b McNeill	2	15	12	-	-
A.F.Bell c Tiffen b Campbell	20	54	46	-	1
C.E.Taylor lbw b Satterthwaite	23	62	42	-	-
A.M.Te Wake st Milburn b Campbell	6	13	1	-	1
K.M.Spence not out	14	38	36	-	-
T.J.Morrison run out	0	2	0	-	-
E.M.Campbell					
Extras (b 2, lb 4, w 14, nb 6)	26				
TOTAL (45.4 overs)	**176**	182			

CANTERBURY

	Runs	Mins	Balls	6s	4s
M.F.Fahey lbw b King	62	112	82	-	8
M.C.Godliman c Martin b Bates	0	3	1	-	-
H.M.Tiffen* c Martin b Bates	0	6	4	-	-
R.C.Milburn† c Martin b King	34	86	70	-	2
H.M.Watson b Taylor	32	60	42	-	5
A.E.Satterthwaite c Martin b Taylor	3	18	10	-	-
B.H.McNeill not out	22	37	34	-	3
E.M.Bermingham b Taylor	0	1	1	-	-
S.K.Burke not out	6	8	4	-	-
S.E.Charteris					
K.E.Minogue					
S.M.King					
Extras (lb 5, w 5, nb 8)	18				
TOTAL (40 overs) (7 wkts)	**177**	169			

Bowling	O	M	R	W
CANTERBURY				
Burke	9	1	29	1
Watson	10	0	21	2
McNeill	8.4	1	24	2
Charteris	1	0	10	0
Campbell	10	0	42	2
Satterthwaite	3	0	19	1
Minogue	4	0	25	1
OTAGO				
Bates	10	2	43	2
Spence	10	0	40	0
King	9	0	50	2
Morrison	6	1	25	0
Taylor	5	1	14	3

Fall of Wickets

	O	C
1st	24	1
2nd	40	5
3rd	40	102
4th	41	116
5th	49	136
6th	114	163
7th	125	163
8th	145	-
9th	174	-
10th	176	-

CANTERBURY v WELLINGTON — State League Final

at Allied Prime Basin Reserve, Wellington on 27 January, 2007
Toss : Wellington. Umpires : K.C. Manley & I.W. Shine
Canterbury won by 8 wickets.

The match was delayed due to morning drizzle. When play got underway Wellington won the toss and elected to bat. They lost the early wicket of Doolan and the best partnership was 53 for the sixth wicket between Scurr and Hill.

Scurr scored 47 off 88 balls, including two boundaries, and Hill 32 off 41 balls, including theee fours. Wellington were bowled out for 121 in 41.5 overs with Watson, Satterthwaite and Campbell taking three wickets each.

In reply Canterbury cruised to victory in the 39th over. Fahey top scored with 57 off 83 balls, including seven fours, and put on 74 for the second wicket with Tiffen who was 35 not out at the end.

WELLINGTON

	Runs	Mins	Balls	6s	4s
A.M.Smith b Satterthwaite	12	45	44	-	1
L.R.Doolan lbw b Watson	8	17	17	-	1
E.J.Scurr c & b Satterthwaite	47	123	88	-	2
M.G.Wakefield b Satterthwaite	4	3	5	-	1
L.R.V.S.Harford run out	0	7	6	-	-
A.E.Cooper c Charteris b Campbell	10	26	23	-	2
S.J.Hill† c Satterthwaite b Watson	32	51	41	-	3
A.M.Dodd* c Burke b Campbell	1	8	6	-	-
S.F.M.Devine c Milburn b Campbell	0	9	9	-	-
E.C.Perry b Watson	0	10	9	-	-
M.J.Hodgson not out	1	3	3	-	-
S.E.A.Ruck					
Extras (lb 1, w 5)	6				
TOTAL (41.5 overs)	**121**	160			

CANTERBURY

	Runs	Mins	Balls	6s	4s
M.F.Fahey b Perry	57	116	83	-	7
M.C.Godliman lbw b Cooper	10	42	40	-	1
H.M.Tiffen* not out	35	103	82	-	1
R.C.Milburn† not out	10	29	29	-	1
A.E.Satterthwaite					
H.M.Watson					
S.K.Burke					
B.H.McNeill					
S.E.Charteris					
K.E.Minogue					
E.M.Campbell					
E.M.Bermingham					
Extras (lb 1, w 9)	10				
TOTAL (39 overs) (2 wkts)	**122**	146			

Bowling	O	M	R	W
CANTERBURY				
Burke	7	2	14	0
Watson	7.5	1	20	3
McNeill	7	1	21	0
Satterthwaite	8	1	29	3
Campbell	7	2	19	3
Charteris	5	0	17	0
WELLINGTON				
Devine	8	0	35	0
Hill	10	4	33	0
Cooper	9	3	13	1
Dodd	4	0	16	0
Doolan	5	0	18	0
Perry	3	1	6	1

Fall of Wickets	***W***	***C***
1st	12	25
2nd	27	99
3rd	31	-
4th	38	-
5th	82	-
6th	115	-
7th	120	-
8th	120	-
9th	120	-
10th	121	-

REGISTER OF PLAYERS

		Born	At	Type	
Bates Suzannah Wilson	O, NZ	16. 9.87	Dunedin	RHB	RM
Bell Andrea Frances	O	12. 2.86	Otorohanga	RHB	RM
Bermingham Erin Margaret	C	18. 4.88	Greymouth	RHB	RLB
Blackwell Alexandra Joy	O, Aus	31. 8.83	Wagga Wagga, Aust.	RHB	RM
Bradbury Sarah Jane	W	18. 7.85	Wellington	RHB	RLB
Broadmore Kate Ellan	CD	11.11.91	New Plymouth	RHB	RM
Browne Nicola Jane	ND, NZ	14. 9.83	Matamata	RHB	RM
Bullen Saskia Mary	A	20. 7.83	Auckland	RHB	SLA
Bupha-Intr Olivia Raynoo	W	11. 9.86	Wellington	RHB	RM
Burke Sarah Kate	C, NZ	2. 1.82	Christchurch	RHB	RM
Burrows Abby Kirstyn	CD	29. 1.77	Kawerau	RHB	RM
Campbell Emma Maree	C	18. 2.82	Timaru	RHB	RLB
Candy Rachel Helen	CD	23. 7.86	Palmerston North	RHB	RM
Charteris Selena Eloise	C, NZ	5. 6.81	Timaru	RHB	ROB
Cocksedge Kendra Margaret	CD	1. 7.88	New Plymouth	RHB	RM
Coetzee Shanna	A	11. 2.83	Cape Town, S.Africa	RHB	RM
Cooper Amanda Ellen	W	15. 5.83	Wellington	RHB	RM
Cronin-Knight Ingrid	A	6.10.77	Auckland	RHB	RM
Devine Sophie Frances Monique	W, NZ	1. 9.89	Wellington	RHB	RM
Dodd Anna Maree	W, NZ	24.10.80	Foxton	RHB	ROB
Doolan Lucy Rose	W	11.12.87	Lower Hutt	LHB	ROB
Fahey Maria Frances	C, NZ	5. 3.84	Timaru	LHB	ROB
Fraser Janice Mary	ND	3. 2.79	Tokoroa	RHB	RM
Godliman Mandie Claire	C	5. 4.73	Eton, England	RHB	WK
Gould Tamara Michelle	ND	30. 6.86	Timaru	RHB	RLB
Hannay Maree Jennifer	ND	1. 3.84	Whakatane	RHB	ROB
Harford Losalini Ravucake Vuetibau Stephi	W	25. 3.73	Bridgetown, Barbados	RHB	ROB
Hill Sarah Joanne	W	31. 5.79	Feilding	RHB	WK
Hodgson Amy Elizabeth	A	1. 7.84	Auckland	RHB	RM
Hodgson Melinda Jane	W	8. 7.88	Innisfail, Australia	RHB	RM
Hopkins Sarah Anne Phelps	A	7.10.79	Auckland	RHB	WK
Huddleston Holly Rachael	ND	11.10.87	Springs, South Africa	RHB	RM
Hui Sandee Beanne	A	13. 9.88	Manila, Phillipines	RHB	RM
Hungerford Sara Louise	A	13. 2.86	Sydney, Australia	RHB	RM
Innes Jena Maree	O	10. 3.83	Dunedin	RHB	RM
Kane Alana Lois	O	7. 9.83	Tapanui	RHB	RM
Kane Megan Joanna	O	1. 8.82	Tapanui	RHB	ROB
Kember Rosamond Jane	A, NZ	28. 1.85	Auckland	RHB	RLB
King Shannon Meg	O	14.10.87	Mackay, Australia	RHB	RM
Kitchin Abigail Samantha Maria	O	18. 6.81	Palmerston North	RHB	ROB
Komp Elfriede Berta	A	27.10.83	Pretoria, South Africa	RHB	LM
Lind Victoria Jayne	A	15. 5.85	Auckland	RHB	WK
Martin Katey Jane	O	7. 2.85	Dunedin	RHB	WK
Mason Aimee Louise	CD, NZ	11.10.82	New Plymouth	RHB	ROB
McGlashan Sara Jade	CD, NZ	28. 3.82	Napier	RHB	WK
McNeill Beth Hannah	C	10.11.82	Wellington	RHB	RM
McWilliams Zara Ann	CD	29.11.83	Hastings	RHB	RM
Milburn Rowan Claire	C, NZ	18. 6.77	Mosgiel	RHB	WK
Milliken Louise Elizabeth	ND, NZ	19. 9.83	Morrinsville	RHB	RFM
Minogue Kimberley Ellen	C	4. 9.81	Christchurch	RHB	RM
Mistry Prashilla	A	16. 3.87	Auckland	RHB	RM
Mitchell Michelle Leigh	C	8. 5.87	Christchurch	RHB	LM
Mizzi Charlotte Kate	W	17. 9.86	Wellington	RHB	WK
Morrison Tanya Jeanette	O	1. 7.85	Gore	RHB	ROB
Murphy Megan Patricia	ND	22.11.87	Rotorua	RHB	RM
Norman Sarah Luba	CD	17. 5.83	Wellington	RHB	RSM
Perkins Katie Teresa	A	7. 7.88	Auckland	RHB	RM
Perry Elizabeth Cecelia	W	22.11.87	Taumarunui	RHB	RM
Priest Rachel Holly	CD	13. 6.85	New Plymouth	RHB	WK
Pulford Katherine Louise	ND	27. 8.80	Nelson	RHB	RM
Rolls Rebecca Jane	A, NZ	22. 8.75	Napier	RHB	WK
Ruck Sian Elizabeth Ansley	W	8.12.83	Auckland	RHB	LM
Samkin Kirbie-Leigh	ND	8. 7.89	Durban, South Africa	RHB	
Satterthwaite Amy Ella	C	7.10.86	Christchurch	LHB	RM
Scurr Elizabeth Jessica	W	26. 7.83	Dunedin	RHB	ROB

		Born	At	Type	
Smith Anna Michelle	W	12. 5.78	Dunedin	RHB	
Soma Anjana	A	11. 7.79	Auckland	RHB	
Spence Kirsten Mary	O	21. 6.82	Dunedin	RHB	
Taylor Clare Elizabeth	O	22. 5.65	Huddersfield, England	RHB	RM
Te Wake Ariana Michelle	O	30. 9.87	Hamilton	RHB	RM
Thessman Nicole Maree	CD	12.11.76	Palmerston North	RHB	ROB
Tiffen Haidee Maree	C, NZ	4. 9.79	Timaru	RHB	RM
Tomlinson Kerry-Anne	ND	19. 1.90	Gisborne	RHB	RM
Tremaine Megan Anne	A	27. 3.84	Auckland	LHB	RM
Tsukigawa Sarah Jane	O, NZ	16. 6.82	Balclutha	RHB	RM
Tunnicliffe Kelly Elizabeth	CD	25. 6.87	Napier	RHB	ROB
Ullyett Jeanette Christine	ND	2. 8.86	Standerton, S.Africa	RHB	WK
Wakefield Megan Gwenda	W	22. 9.82	Christchurch	RHB	RM
Watson Helen Maree	C, NZ	17. 2.72	Ashburton	RHB	RM
Wilkins Anna Jane	ND	21. 5.80	Hamilton	RHB	WK
Winkley Kelly Marie	CD	16. 6.84	Napier	RHB	ROB

2006/07 STATE LEAGUE AVERAGES

	M	*In*	*NO*	*HS*	*Runs*	*Ave*	*100s*	*50s*	*Ct*	*St*	*O*	*M*	*R*	*W*	*Ave*	*R/O*	*Best*
S.W.Bates	9	8	0	61	165	20.62	-	1	-	-	51.1	10	194	5	38.80	3.79	2-43
A.F.Bell	5	5	2	22*	66	22.00	-	-	-	-							
E.M.Bermingham	6	4	2	18*	33	16.50	-	-	-	-							
A.J.Blackwell	6	6	0	100	315	52.50	1	2	1	-	1.5	0	19	0	-	10.36	-
S.J.Bradbury	1	1	1	16*	16	-	-	-	-	-							
K.E.Broadmore	10	4	1	7*	13	4.33	-	-	5	-	63	11	234	5	46.80	3.71	2-12
N.J.Browne	9	8	1	54	171	24.42	-	2	4	-	53.4	2	265	11	24.09	4.93	2-25
S.M.Bullen	10	5	3	4*	6	3.00	-	-	3	-	68	9	245	10	24.50	3.60	2-16
O.R.Bupha-Intr	4	-	-	-	-	-	-	-	-	-	11	0	59	2	29.50	5.36	1-18
S.K.Burke	9	5	1	23	40	10.00	-	-	2	-	70	10	261	9	29.00	3.73	4-49
A.K.Burrows	10	1	0	0	0	0.00	-	-	1	-	66.5	9	231	12	19.25	3.45	4-29
E.M.Campbell	9	-	-	-	-	-	-	-	1	-	55.2	7	213	15	14.20	3.84	3-19
R.H.Candy	10	3	3	13*	34	-	-	-	2	-	75	14	215	10	21.50	2.86	2-23
S.E.Charteris	9	3	2	30*	39	39.00	-	-	4	-	38.5	1	211	3	70.33	5.43	2-18
K.M.Cocksedge	10	6	0	41	93	15.50	-	-	3	-	8	2	42	1	42.00	5.25	1-24
S.Coetzee	8	6	2	9	19	4.75	-	-	3	-	46.4	1	185	7	26.42	3.96	2-25
A.E.Cooper	10	8	2	52	147	24.50	-	1	3	-	71.4	10	236	14	16.85	3.29	5-15
I.Cronin-Knight	10	9	1	52*	126	15.75	-	1	7	-							
S.F.M.Devine	10	8	2	30	89	14.83	-	-	5	-	89.1	11	339	22	15.40	3.80	5-23
A.M.Dodd	10	7	0	15	49	7.00	-	-	3	-	71	13	208	7	29.71	2.93	3-12
L.R.Doolan	10	10	0	53	172	17.20	-	1	-	-	52	1	206	11	18.72	3.96	3-23
M.F.Fahey	9	9	0	91	380	42.22	-	3	1	-							
J.M.Fraser	9	9	0	81	199	22.11	-	2	2	-							
M.C.Godliman	9	9	0	22	77	8.55	-	-	3	-							
T.M.Gould	9	9	1	45	145	18.12	-	-	1	-							
M.J.Hannay	9	7	0	19	54	7.71	-	-	2	-	56	3	256	6	42.66	4.57	2-23
L.R.V.S.Harford	9	8	2	33	109	18.16	-	-	2	-							
S.J.Hill	10	7	2	32	124	24.80	-	-	8	-							
A.E.Hodgson	10	7	2	12	55	11.00	-	-	1	-	64.5	7	279	12	23.25	4.30	3-21
M.J.Hodgson	10	5	3	8*	18	9.00	-	-	4	-							
S.A.P.Hopkins	4	3	0	5	12	4.00	-	-	-	-							
H.R.Huddleston	9	6	3	48*	72	24.00	-	-	1	-	37.5	0	207	4	51.75	5.47	1-21
S.B.Hui	10	1	0	0	0	0.00	-	-	-	-	73.1	16	288	15	19.20	3.93	4-14
S.L.Hungerford	8	6	1	29*	113	22.60	-	-	1	-	48.1	1	242	7	34.57	5.02	4-36
J.M.Innes	5	3	1	24*	25	12.50	-	-	1	-	15	1	69	2	34.50	4.60	2-28
A.L.Kane	10	10	1	28	87	9.66	-	-	1	-							
M.J.Kane	10	10	0	54	126	12.60	-	1	1	-	1	0	10	0	-	10.00	-
R.J.Kember	10	9	0	56	140	15.55	-	1	2	-	2	0	12	0	-	6.00	-
S.M.King	10	4	1	3*	3	1.00	-	-	-	-	60	4	260	9	28.88	4.33	2-12
A.S.M.Kitchin	10	10	0	25	78	7.80	-	-	2	-	7	0	45	1	45.00	6.43	1-33
E.B.Komp	6	6	0	22	50	8.33	-	-	-	-							
V.J.Lind	10	8	0	43	170	21.25	-	-	3	-							
K.J.Martin	10	10	0	72	233	23.30	-	1	12	4							
A.L.Mason	10	9	3	48*	227	37.83	-	-	6	-	54	3	233	9	25.88	4.31	3-20
S.J.McGlashan	10	8	1	111*	324	46.28	1	2	-	-							
B.H.McNeill	7	5	3	22*	41	20.50	-	-	-	-	55.4	7	218	4	54.50	3.91	2-24
Z.A.McWilliams	10	7	4	33*	112	37.33	-	-	2	-	71.3	11	284	12	23.66	3.97	2-12
R.C.Milburn	9	9	2	35	177	25.28	-	-	6	3							
L.E.Milliken	9	6	2	4*	10	2.50	-	-	5	-	78	13	264	7	37.71	3.38	2-27
K.E.Minogue	9	2	1	10*	10	10.00	-	-	2	-	15	0	94	4	23.50	6.27	2-12
P.Mistry	10	8	1	23*	56	8.00	-	-	2	-	76.1	14	281	9	31.22	3.68	2-14
M.L.Mitchell	5	2	0	0	0	0.00	-	-	-	-	6	0	38	1	38.00	6.33	1-24
C.K.Mizzi	1	1	0	3	3	3.00	-	-	1	-							
T.J.Morrison	10	3	1	0*	0	0.00	-	-	-	-	59.3	11	200	4	50.00	3.36	1-14
M.P.Murphy	9	8	1	44	134	19.14	-	-	-	-	60.1	6	246	8	30.75	4.08	3-25
S.L.Norman	10	10	0	44	119	11.90	-	-	3	-							
K.T.Perkins	5	4	0	37	98	24.50	-	-	2	-	5	0	58	1	58.00	11.60	1-26
E.C.Perry	6	3	1	14*	28	14.00	-	-	4	-	23	7	65	5	13.00	2.83	3-4
R.H.Priest	10	10	0	31	91	9.10	-	-	8	2							
K.L.Pulford	9	9	1	52*	124	15.50	-	1	1	-	56	4	219	12	18.25	3.91	3-27
R.J.Rolls	10	9	1	106	372	46.50	1	2	12	4							
S.E.A.Ruck	10	1	0	1	1	1.00	-	-	1	-	92	15	328	15	21.86	3.56	3-30
K.L.Samkin	9	6	1	26	53	10.60	-	-	-	-							
A.E.Satterthwaite	9	8	3	39*	87	17.40	-	-	3	-	55	5	229	9	25.44	4.16	3-29
E.J.Scurr	10	10	2	47	202	25.25	-	-	2	-	0.3	0	0	1	0.00	0.00	1-0

	M	In	NO	HS	Runs	Ave	100s	50s	Ct	St	O	M	R	W	Ave	R/O	Best
A.M.Smith	9	9	0	101	297	33.00	1	1	2	-							
A.Soma	7	5	0	4	12	2.40	-	-	2	-							
K.M.Spence	10	7	3	14*	30	7.50	-	-	1	-	61.3	1	302	11	27.45	4.91	4-51
C.E.Taylor	10	10	3	32*	91	13.00	-	-	1	-	40	4	159	10	15.90	3.98	4-25
A.M.Te Wake	7	6	1	9	29	5.80	-	-	1	-	1.2	0	18	0	-	13.53	-
N.M.Thessman	10	10	2	63	247	30.87	-	1	3	-							
H.M.Tiffen	9	9	2	78	273	39.00	-	2	3	-							
K.A.Tomlinson	9	2	1	19*	23	23.00	-	-	1	-	32.5	3	149	6	24.83	4.53	2-13
M.A.Tremaine	2	2	1	44*	47	47.00	-	-	-	-	18	3	63	4	15.75	3.50	4-22
S.J.Tsukigawa	8	8	2	108	209	34.83	1	-	1	-	53	10	141	11	12.81	2.66	5-13
K.E.Tunnicliffe	10	10	3	36*	119	17.00	-	-	1	-							
J.C.Ullyett	9	3	1	6	10	5.00	-	-	8								
M.G.Wakefield	10	10	2	68	200	25.00	-	2	5	1							
H.M.Watson	9	6	1	64*	175	35.00	-	1	4	-	76.2	13	235	14	16.78	3.07	3-20
A.J.Wilkins	9	9	1	47	155	19.37	-	-	2	-	2	0	14	0	-	7.00	-
K.M.Winkley	10	4	0	21	34	8.50	-	-	1	-	70.3	9	251	9	27.88	3.56	3-27

HIGHEST STRIKE RATES *(qualification 100 runs)*

		Runs	Balls	S/R
A.J.Blackwell	*O*	315	358	87
S.W.Bates	*O*	165	188	87
R.J.Rolls	*A*	372	451	82
M.F.Fahey	*C*	380	463	82
A.L.Mason	*CD*	227	292	77
K.J.Martin	*O*	233	315	73
J.M.Fraser	*ND*	199	272	73
S.J.Tsukigawa	*O*	209	289	72
H.M.Watson	*C*	175	249	70
M.G.Wakefield	*W*	200	287	69

MOST ECONOMICAL BOWLING *(qualification 30 overs)*

		O	M	R	W	Ave	R/O
S.J.Tsukigawa	*O*	53	10	141	11	12.81	2.66
R.H.Candy	*CD*	75	14	215	10	21.50	2.86
A.M.Dodd	*W*	71	13	208	7	29.71	2.93
H.M.Watson	*C*	76.2	13	235	14	16.78	3.07
A.E.Cooper	*W*	71.4	10	236	14	16.85	3.29
T.J.Morrison	*O*	59.3	11	200	4	50.00	3.36
L.E.Milliken	*ND*	78	13	264	7	37.71	3.38
A.K.Burrows	*CD*	66.5	9	231	12	19.25	3.45
S.E.A.Ruck	*W*	92	15	328	15	21.86	3.56
K.M.Winkley	*CD*	70.3	9	251	9	27.88	3.56

CAREER RECORDS

	M	*In*	*NO*	*HS*	*Runs*	*Ave*	*100s*	*50s*	*Ct*	*St*	*O*	*M*	*R*	*W*	*Ave*	*R/O*	*Best*
S.W.Bates	39	35	2	183*	722	21.87	1	2	10	-	264	35	1096	27	40.59	4.15	3-55
A.F.Bell	5	5	2	22*	66	22.00	-	-	-	-							
E.M.Bermingham	6	4	2	18*	33	16.50	-	-	-	-							
A.J.Blackwell	6	6	0	100	315	52.50	1	2	1	-	1.5	0	19	0	-	10.38	-
S.J.Bradbury	1	1	1	16*	16	-	-	-	-	-							
K.E.Broadmore	10	4	1	7*	13	4.33	-	-	5	-	63	11	234	5	46.80	3.71	2-12
N.J.Browne	69	65	8	94*	1398	24.52	-	10	22	-	511.3	44	2065	74	27.90	4.03	3-16
S.M.Bullen	34	6	4	4*	6	3.00	-	-	9	-	204	26	751	24	31.29	3.68	3-10
O.R.Bupha-Intr	4	-	-	-	-	-	-	-	-	-	11	0	59	2	29.50	5.36	1-18
S.K.Burke	71	43	12	27	271	8.74	-	-	19	-	562.1	80	1953	82	23.81	3.47	4-28
A.K.Burrows	56	22	8	8*	36	2.57	-	-	10	-	404.1	50	1404	54	23.48	3.47	4-29
E.M.Campbell	9	-	-	-	-	-	-	-	1	-	55.2	7	213	15	14.20	3.86	3-19
R.H.Candy	33	9	6	13*	56	18.66	-	-	4	-	179.5	26	633	16	39.56	3.51	3-33
S.E.Charteris	46	11	5	30*	66	11.00	-	-	20	-	301.5	32	1073	53	20.24	3.55	5-31
K.M.Cocksedge	28	20	5	41	203	13.53	-	-	10	-	42	4	172	6	28.66	4.10	2-32
S.Coetzee	22	8	3	9	25	5.00	-	-	3	-	116.4	4	486	13	37.38	4.16	2-25
A.E.Cooper	66	49	10	52	646	16.56	-	1	16	-	370.3	52	1343	70	19.18	3.62	5-15
I.Cronin-Knight	55	48	12	84	691	19.19	-	2	23	-	0.1	0	6	0	-		-
S.F.M.Devine	30	20	5	30	142	9.46	-	-	8	-	218.4	25	791	30	26.36	3.61	5-23
A.M.Dodd	76	51	8	46	515	11.97	-	-	21	-	579	119	1686	71	23.74	2.91	5-7
L.R.Doolan	20	19	0	57	382	20.10	-	3	3	-	95.1	8	347	14	24.78	3.64	3-23
M.F.Fahey	70	65	7	91	1640	28.27	-	13	22	-	112.2	11	429	18	23.83	3.81	4-21
J.M.Fraser	75	74	0	81	1251	16.90	-	3	22	-	74	8	326	6	54.33	4.41	1-12
M.C.Godliman	44	43	2	87	1193	29.09	-	9	3	-							
T.M.Gould	36	35	4	100*	632	20.38	1	-	6	-							
M.J.Hannay	56	49	2	36	386	8.21	-	-	12	-	343.4	21	1516	40	37.90	4.41	4-38
L.R.V.S.Harford	51	47	5	83	969	23.07	-	6	15	-	101.3	7	387	9	43.00	3.81	2-12
S.J.Hill	52	39	6	70*	538	16.30	-	1	36	20							
A.E.Hodgson	13	7	2	12	55	11.00	-	-	1	-	80.5	8	368	13	28.30	4.55	3-21
M.J.Hodgson	10	5	3	8*	18	9.00	-	-	4	-							
S.A.P.Hopkins	4	3	0	5	12	4.00	-	-	-	-							
H.R.Huddleston	15	7	4	48*	83	27.66	-	-	1	-	68.5	3	337	7	48.14	4.89	1-21
S.B.Hui	10	1	0	0	0	0.00	-	-	-	-	73.1	16	288	15	19.20	3.93	4-14
S.L.Hungerford	8	6	1	29*	113	22.60	-	-	1	-	48.1	1	242	7	34.57	5.02	4-36
J.M.Innes	23	18	4	24*	113	8.07	-	-	3	-	77.1	6	350	12	29.16	4.53	2-25
A.L.Kane	36	30	4	37	235	9.03	-	-	3	-	59.4	3	282	4	70.50	4.72	1-10
M.J.Kane	79	71	3	65*	839	12.33	-	3	8	-	238.1	12	990	27	36.66	4.15	4-21
R.J.Kember	56	50	1	94	1059	21.61	-	6	16	-	3.4	0	34	1	34.00	9.28	1-22
S.M.King	17	9	2	10	22	3.14	-	-	4	-	60	4	260	9	28.88	4.33	2-12
A.S.M.Kitchin	24	20	0	25	131	6.55	-	-	3	-	26.1	0	129	3	43.00	4.93	1-7
E.B.Komp	55	39	7	34	336	10.50	-	-	5	-	103.3	10	393	16	24.56	3.79	2-13
V.J.Lind	36	33	2	56	627	20.22	-	2	7	-							
K.J.Martin	58	53	4	74	841	17.16	-	4	33	18							
A.L.Mason	72	65	10	116	1439	26.16	1	3	36	-	614.4	77	2078	89	23.34	3.38	5-25
S.J.McGlashan	62	55	8	111*	1298	27.61	2	6	19	6							
B.H.McNeill	73	54	19	51*	630	18.00	-	1	19	-	573	82	2069	96	21.55	3.61	6-31
Z.A.McWilliams	51	37	13	45	434	18.08	-	-	9	-	316	28	1381	52	26.55	4.37	3-0
R.C.Milburn	86	77	12	82	1128	17.35	-	2	63	32							
L.E.Milliken	62	56	20	60*	487	13.52	-	1	16	-	476.5	41	1802	58	31.06	3.70	4-34
K.E.Minogue	13	2	1	10*	10	10.00	-	-	3	-	20	0	124	4	31.00	6.20	2-12
P.Mistry	20	13	3	23*	78	7.80	-	-	3	-	167.3	30	666	27	24.66	3.97	4-13
M.L.Mitchell	16	6	1	7	19	3.80	-	-	3	-	45.2	5	188	4	47.00	4.14	1-3
C.K.Mizzi	1	1	0	3	3	3.00	-	-	1	-							
T.J.Morrison	38	19	7	9	42	3.50	-	-	-	-	273.3	48	960	25	38.40	3.51	2-17
M.P.Murphy	38	29	7	60*	321	14.59	-	1	6	-	246.1	17	1096	30	36.53	4.45	4-36
S.L.Norman	42	42	3	62	566	14.51	-	1	8	-							
K.T.Perkins	5	4	0	37	98	24.50	-	-	2	-	5	0	58	1	58.00	11.60	1-26
E.C.Perry	35	23	5	27	179	9.94	-	-	12	-	100	9	427	15	28.46	4.27	3-4
R.H.Priest	39	36	3	34	408	12.36	-	-	32	9							
K.L.Pulford	64	62	9	153*	1525	28.77	2	9	16	-	393.1	32	1520	55	27.63	3.86	3-24
R.J.Rolls	90	88	7	118	2591	31.98	4	14	86	48							
S.E.A.Ruck	10	1	0	1	1	1.00	-	-	1	-	92	15	328	15	21.86	3.57	3-30
K.L.Samkin	19	10	3	26	68	9.71	-	-	1	-							
A.E.Satterthwaite	40	24	11	39*	210	16.15	-	-	8	-	229	23	853	34	25.08	3.72	3-28
E.J.Scurr	52	47	8	71	614	15.74	-	2	7	-	85.2	10	317	7	45.28	3.71	3-22

	M	In	NO	HS	Runs	Ave	100s	50s	Ct	St	O	M	R	W	Ave	R/O	Best
A.M.Smith	55	53	5	104	1663	34.64	2	9	13	-							
A.Soma	51	37	7	48	424	14.13	-	-	7	-							
K.M.Spence	72	50	19	25	192	6.19	-	-	5	-	445.4	53	1698	63	26.95	3.81	5-38
C.E.Taylor	56	51	13	65*	966	25.42	-	5	13	-	396.4	60	1446	49	29.51	3.64	4-25
A.M.Te Wake	8	6	1	9	29	5.80	-	-	1	-	3.2	0	43	0	-	12.91	-
N.M.Thessman	71	69	10	85*	1583	26.83	-	8	19	-	2	0	12	0	-	6.00	-
H.M.Tiffen	87	80	21	97	2122	35.96	-	11	45	-	251	29	889	55	16.16	3.54	5-51
K.A.Tomlinson	15	5	1	19*	32	8.00	-	-	1	-	63.5	8	289	8	36.12	4.52	2-13
M.A.Tremaine	11	10	2	44*	66	8.25	-	-	-	-	65	7	240	11	21.81	3.69	4-22
S.J.Tsukigawa	71	64	10	108	911	16.87	1	1	21	-	318.2	37	1248	48	26.00	3.92	5-13
K.E.Tunnicliffe	16	16	3	38	196	15.07	-	-	2	-							
J.C.Ullyett	39	21	6	18	92	6.13	-	-	25	2							
M.G.Wakefield	55	50	9	74*	880	21.46	-	4	16	1	11	0	43	2	21.50	3.91	2-26
H.M.Watson	89	78	30	101	1754	36.54	1	7	26	-	649.5	104	2091	96	21.78	3.21	4-40
A.J.Wilkins	70	69	3	49	1042	15.78	-	-	13	-	31.3	2	200	2	100.00	6.34	1-15
K.M.Winkley	21	9	1	21	54	6.75	-	-	4	-	137.1	17	459	17	27.00	3.34	4-27

PROVINCIAL COMPETITION

The symbol of supremacy in women's provincial cricket has been the Hallyburton Johnstone Shield (1935/36 to 1981/82), Hansells Cup (1982/83 to 1989/90), Pub Charities National Tournament (1990/91 to 1997/98), State Insurance Cup (1998/99 to 2000/01) and State League (2001/02 to date).

WINNERS

1935/36	Wellington	1959/60	Wellington	1983/84	Canterbury
1936/37	Wellington	1960/61	Canterbury	1984/85	Canterbury
1937/38	Wellington	1961/62	Canterbury	1985/86	Canterbury
1938/39	Wellington	1962/63	Otago	1986/87	Canterbury
1939/40	Auckland	1963/64	Canterbury	1987/88	Canterbury
1940/41	Auckland	1964/65	Auckland	1988/89	Canterbury
1941/42	no competition	1965/66	Auckland	1989/90	Wellington
1942/43	Auckland	1966/67	Canterbury	1990/91	Canterbury
1943/44	Canterbury	1967/68	Wellington	1991/92	Canterbury
1944/45	Canterbury	1968/69	North Shore	1992/93	Canterbury
1945/46	Canterbury	1969/70	Wellington	1993/94	Canterbury
1946/47	Auckland	1970/71	North Shore	1994/95	Canterbury
1947/48	Auckland	1971/72	North Shore	1995/96	Canterbury
1948/49	Auckland	1972/73	Canterbury	1996/97	Canterbury
1949/50	Wellington	1973/74	Wellington	1997/98	Canterbury
1950/51	Wellington	1974/75	Wellington	1998/99	Canterbury
1951/52	Auckland	1975/76	Canterbury	1999/00	Auckland
1952/53	Wellington	1976/77	Wellington	2000/01	Auckland
1953/54	Wellington	1977/78	Wellington	2001/02	Auckland
1954/55	Auckland	1978/79	Canterbury	2002/03	Auckland
1955/56	Canterbury	1979/80	Canterbury	2003/04	Canterbury
1956/57	Auckland	1980/81	Canterbury	2004/05	Canterbury/Wellington
1957/58	Auckland	1981/82	Canterbury	2005/06	Central Districts
1958/59	Wellington	1982/83	Canterbury	2006/07	Canterbury

TEAM RECORDS

Highest Totals

302-5	Canterbury v Otago	Christchurch	1998/99
298-4	Canterbury v Wellington	Christchurch	1999/00
296-8	Otago v Northern Districts	Dunedin	2006/07
288-5	Auckland v Central Districts	Auckland	2000/01
285-4	Auckland v Otago	Queenstown	2004/05
275-6	Auckland v Otago	Auckland	2005/06

Lowest Totals

43	Central Districts v Auckland	Wanganui	1999/00
46	Northern Districts v Wellington	Wellington	1999/00
51	Northern Districts v Otago	Dunedin	2004/05
59	Otago v Canterbury	Christchurch	2000/01
61	Otago v Auckland	Auckland	2001/02
61	Wellington v Canterbury	Wellington	2004/05
61	Otago v Auckland	Auckland	2005/06

INDIVIDUAL RECORDS

Centuries

183*	S.W. Bates	Otago v Auckland	Auckland	2005/06
153*	K.L. Pulford	Central Districts v Canterbury	Christchurch	1999/00
141	D.A. Hockley	Canterbury v Auckland	Rangiora	1998/99
141	K.L. Pulford	Central Districts v Otago	Palmerston North	2000/01
128	D.A. Hockley	Canterbury v Wellington	Christchurch	1999/00
120	C.M. Edwards	Northern Districts v Wellington	Hamilton	2002/03
119*	C.M. Edwards	Northern Districts v Canterbury	Christchurch	2000/01
118	E.C. Drumm	Auckland v Central Districts	Auckland	2000/01
118	R.J. Rolls	Auckland v Otago	Queenstown	2004/05
117*	N. Payne	Canterbury v Wellington	Christchurch	1999/00
117	D.A. Hockley	Canterbury v Otago	Christchurch	1998/99
116	E.C. Drumm	Northern Districts v Otago	Hamilton	2005/06
116	A.L. Mason	Central Districts v Wellington	Wanganui	2005/06
115	E.C. Drumm	Northern Districts v Auckland	Auckland	2005/06
114*	E.C. Drumm	Auckland v Central Districts	Wanganui	1999/00
112*	E.C. Drumm	Auckland v Northern Districts	Auckland	2001/02
111*	R.J. Rolls	Auckland v Otago	Auckland	2003/04
111*	S.J. McGlashan	Central Districts v Canterbury	Palmerston North	2006/07
110	P.B. Flannery	Otago v Auckland	Queenstown	2004/05
110	R.J. Rolls	Auckland v Otago	Auckland	2005/06
108	S.J. Tsukigawa	Otago v Northern Districts	Dunedin	2006/07
106	R.J. Rolls	Auckland v Northern Districts	Auckland	2006/07
105*	S.J. McGlashan	Central Districts v Canterbury	Christchurch	2005/06
104*	P.B. Flannery	Canterbury v Otago	Christchurch	2000/01
104	M.K. Tyler	Auckland v Otago	Auckland	1999/00
104	A.M. Smith	Wellington v Northern Districts	Upper Hutt	2005/06
102*	N.A. Pratt	Northern Districts v Otago	Hamilton	1999/00
101	D.A. Hockley	Canterbury v Central Districts	Palmerston North	1998/99
101	H.M. Watson	Auckland v Otago	Dunedin	2000/01
101	A.M. Smith	Wellington v Otago	Wellington	2006/07
100*	M.A.M. Lewis	Wellington v Auckland	Wellington	2003/04
100*	T.M. Gould	Northern Districts v Central Districts	Mt Maunganui	2004/05
100	A.J. Blackwell	Otago v Northern Districts	Dunedin	2006/07

Five Wickets in an Innings

7.1-1-19-7	M.F. Tunupopo	Auckland v Central Districts	Wanganui	1999/00
10-6-8-6	R.J. Steele	Canterbury v Auckland	Auckland	2005/06
10-3-18-6	N. Scripps	Auckland v Northern Districts	Auckland	2003/04
9.2-2-19-6	N. Scripps	Auckland v Wellington	Auckland	2002/03
9-1-20-6	D.M. Trow	Central Districts v Northern Districts	Wanganui	2003/04
9.5-1-31-6	B.H. McNeill	Canterbury v Auckland	Auckland	2001/02
6-1-7-5	A.M. Dodd	Wellington v Otago	Dunedin	2005/06
5.5-1-12-5	C.A. Campbell	Canterbury v Northern Districts	Hamilton	1999/00
9-3-13-5	S.J. Tsukigawa	Otago v Northern Districts	Dunedin	2006/07
8.2-0-15-5	A.E. Cooper	Wellington v Auckland	Auckland	2006/07
10-2-19-5	H.R. Daly	Canterbury v Northern Districts	Rangiora	2002/03
7-1-20-5	C.A. Campbell	Canterbury v Wellington	Wellington	1998/99
8.3-2-21-5	A.E. Cooper	Wellington v Northern Districts	Hamilton	2004/05
10-2-23-5	S.F.M. Devine	Wellington v Northern Districts	Hamilton	2006/07
8-1-24-5	H.J. Rae	Canterbury v Wellington	Lower Hutt	2000/01
10-1-25-5	A.L. Mason	Central Districts v Wellington	Wanganui	1999/00
10-0-27-5	A.M. Little	Wellington v Otago	Wellington	2002/03
10-1-31-5	B.H. McNeill	Canterbury v Otago	Timaru	2002/03
10-0-31-5	S.E. Charteris	Canterbury v Otago	Alexandra	2005/06
10-1-34-5	H.J. Partridge	Northern Districts v Auckland	Auckland	1999/00
8.3-1-37-5	N. Scripps	Auckland v Canterbury	Christchurch	2000/01
9-0-38-5	K.M. Spence	Otago v Northern Districts	Hamilton	2005/06
10-1-51-5	H.M. Tiffen	Canterbury v Auckland	Christchurch	2000/01

Wicketkeeping

DISMISSALS IN AN INNINGS

	(ct/st)				
6	(6/0)	S.J. Hill	Wellington v Northern Districts	Hamilton	2006/07
5	(2/3)	R.J. Rolls	Auckland v Canterbury	Christchurch	2000/01
5	(4/1)	R.C. Milburn	Canterbury v Auckland	Auckland	2003/04
4	(0/4)	R.J. Rolls	Auckland v Wellington	Auckland	1998/99
4	(1/3)	R.C. Milburn	Otago v Wellington	Dunedin	1999/00
4	(0/4)	J.L. Strachan	Canterbury v Northern Districts	Christchurch	2000/01
4	(4/0)	R.C. Milburn	Canterbury v Auckland	Christchurch	2002/03
4	(3/1)	S.J. McGlashan	Central Districts v Canterbury	Palmerston North	2002/03
4	(2/2)	K.J. Martin	Otago v Central Districts	Palmerston North	2002/03
4	(2/2)	S.J. McGlashan	Central Districts v Otago	Palmerston North	2002/03
4	(3/1)	R.J. Rolls	Auckland v Canterbury	Christchurch	2002/03
4	(3/1)	R.C. Milburn	Canterbury v Wellington	Christchurch	2003/04
4	(3/1)	S.J. Hill	Wellington v Otago	Dunedin	2003/04
4	(4/0)	R.H. Priest	Central Districts v Auckland	Napier	2003/04
4	(4/0)	R.C. Milburn	Canterbury v Central Districts	Christchurch	2005/06
4	(3/1)	R.C. Milburn	Canterbury v Central Districts	Christchurch	2005/06
4	(4/0)	J.C. Ullyett	Northern Districts v Central Districts	Palmerston North	2005/06
4	(4/0)	K.J. Martin	Otago v Canterbury	Timaru	2006/07

Fielding

CATCHES IN AN INNINGS

4	M.M. Graham	Central Districts v Northern Districts	Wanganui	1999/00
4	S.J. Tsukigawa	Otago v Canterbury	Dunedin	2003/04
4	E.C. Drumm	Auckland v Central Distyricts	Auckland	2004/05

RECORD PARTNERSHIPS

AUCKLAND

1st	187	R.J. Rolls & R.J. Kember	v Otago	Auckland	2005/06
2nd	136	M.K. Fruin & E.C. Drumm	v Central Districts	Auckland	2000/01
3rd	151*	R.J. Rolls & I. Cronin-Knight	v Otago	Dunedin	2006/07
4th †	157	M.K. Fruin & H.M. Watson	v Otago	Dunedin	2000/01
5th †	120	R.J. Rolls & K. Perkins	v Northern Districts	Auckland	2006/07
6th	79	K. Perkins & M.A. Tremaine	v Northern Districts	Auckland	2006/07
7th	90	K.A. Ramel & A. Soma	v Wellington	Auckland	1998/99
8th	52	C.M. Nicholson & Z.A.A. Plummer	v Central Districts	Auckland	1998/99
9th	35	E.C. Drumm & S.E.M. Cowlrick	v Canterbury	Christchurch	1998/99
10th	22	H.M. Watson & P. Mistry	v Canterbury	Auckland	2005/06

CANTERBURY

1st	163	D.A. Hockley & P.B. Flannery	v Central Districts	Christchurch	1999/00
2nd †	227	D.A. Hockley & N. Payne	v Wellington	Christchurch	1999/00
3rd	98	D.A. Hockley & N. Payne	v Otago	Christchurch	1998/99
4th	144	H.M. Tiffen & J.A. Lawler	v Central Districts	P. North	2000/01
5th	90	R.C. Milburn & H.M. Watson	v Central Districts	P. North	2006/07
6th	87	S.C. Taylor & B.H. McNeill	v Auckland	Christchurch	2004/05
7th	57	S.K. Helmore & M.F. Fahey	v Central Districts	P. North	2000/01
8th	41	L.M. Astle & A.J.M.D. Marsh	v Northern Districts	Hamilton	1999/00
9th	27*	E.M. Bermingham & S.E. Charteris	v Otago	Timaru	2006/07
10th	35*	S.E. Charteris & K.E. Minogue	v Wellington	Wellington	2006/07

CENTRAL DISTRICTS

1st	179*	P.K. Gerrish & C.L. Forsyth	v Wellington	Wellington	2000/01
2nd	94	S.L. Duffill & K.L. Pulford	v Otago	Dunedin	2003/04
3rd	143	N.M. Thessman & A.L. Mason	v Wellington	Wanganui	2005/06
4th	91	K.L. Pulford & E.A. Travers	v Otago	P. North	2000/01
5th	102	S.J. McGlashan & H.J. Lloyd	v Auckland	Napier	2003/04
6th	83	M.M. Graham & S.J. McGlashan	v Otago	Dunedin	1998/99
7th	86	A.L. Mason & E.A. Travers	v Canterbury	P. North	2000/01
8th	42	R.H. Priest & E.C. Perry	v Northern Distrcts	Mt Maunganui	2004/05
9th †	67*	N.M. Thessman & K.M. Sutherland	v Otago	Dunedin	2001/02
10th	36*	D.M. Trow & A.K. Burrows	v Auckland	Auckland	2002/03

NORTHERN DISTRICTS

1st	88	V.J. Brown & N.J. Browne	v Otago	Hamilton	2003/04
2nd	76	T.M. Gould & E.C. Drumm	v Wellington	Upper Hutt	2005/06
3rd	157*	T.M. Gould & M.P. Murphy	v Central Districts	Mt Maunganui	2004/05
4th	137	E.C. Drumm & N.J. Browne	v Canterbury	Hamilton	2005/06
5th	82	N.J.Browne & M.P. Murphy	v Auckland	Auckland	2006/07
6th	138*	N.J. Browne & L.E. Milliken	v Auckland	Auckland	2005/06
7th	66	A.J. Wilkins & K.J. Gibson	v Wellington	Wellington	1999/00
8th	46	M.J. Hannay & J.C. Ullyett	v Canterbury	Christchurch	2004/05
9th	51	K.B. Spence & L.E. Milliken	v Central Districts	Hamilton	2000/01
10th †	48*	M.P. Murphy & K.A. Tomlinson	v Auckland	Auckland	2006/07

OTAGO

1st	† 199	E.J. Scurr & P.B. Flannery	v Auckland	Queenstown	2004/05
2nd	94	R.J. Pullar & S.K Helmore	v Central Districts	Dunedin	2001/02
	94	R.C. Milburn & P.J. te Beest	v Canterbury	Oamaru	2001/02
3rd	† 164	A.J. Blackwell & S.W. Bates	v Northern Districts	Dunedin	2006/07
4th	86	S.W. Bates & K.J. Martin	v Auckland	Auckland	2005/06
5th	109*	S.W. Bates & C.E. Taylor	v Auckland	Auckland	2005/06
6th	68	K.J. Martin & A.L. Kane	v Wellington	Wellington	2006/07
7th	† 106	E.J. Scurr & S.W. Bates	v Auckland	Auckland	2003/04
8th	† 80	C.E. Taylor & K.M. Spence	v Northern Districts	Hamilton	2005/06
9th	56	S.K. Helmore & A.L. Kane	v Auckland	Auckland	2003/04
10th	25	K.J. Martin & T.J. Morrison	v Central Districts	Dunedin	2003/04

WELLINGTON

1st	147	A.M. Smith & L.R. Doolan	v Northern Districts	Upper Hutt	2005/06
2nd	173*	L.R.V.S. Harford & M.A.M. Lewis	v Auckland	Wellington	2003/04
3rd	159	L.R.V.S. Harford & M.A.M. Lewis	v Canterbury	Christchurch	1999/00
4th	98*	M.A.M. Lewis & F.S. King	v Otago	Lower Hutt	2000/01
5th	73	M.A.M. Lewis & A.M. Corbin	v Central Districts	Wellington	2002/03
6th	† 144*	M.A.M. Lewis & M.G. Wakefield	v Auckland	Auckland	2002/03
7th	56	M.A.M. Lewis & A.M. Corbin	v Central Districts	Napier	2001/02
8th	55	A.E. Cooper & S.F.M Devine	v Auckland	Auckland	2006/07
9th	38	S.J. Hill & E.T. McDonald	v Canterbury	Christchurch	2003/04
10th	44	A.M. Corbin & A.J. Green	v Central Districts	Lower Hutt	2000/01

† *record for all teams*

CAREER RECORDS

BATTING	M	In	NO	HS	Runs	Ave	100s	50s
E.C. Drumm	80	78	16	118	2993	48.27	5	17
R.J. Rolls	90	88	7	118	2591	31.98	4	14
H.M. Tiffen	87	80	21	97	2122	35.96	-	11
P.B. Flannery	57	56	7	110	1765	36.02	2	7
M.A.M. Lewis	60	56	11	100*	1755	39.00	1	11
H.M. Watson	89	78	30	101	1754	36.54	1	7
A.M. Smith	55	53	5	104	1663	34.64	2	9
M.F. Fahey	70	65	7	91	1640	28.27	-	13
N. Payne	49	47	7	117*	1614	40.35	1	12
N.M. Thessman	71	69	10	85*	1583	26.83	-	8
K.L. Pulford	64	62	9	153*	1525	28.77	2	9
A.L. Mason	72	65	10	116	1439	26.16	1	3
N.J. Browne	69	65	8	94*	1398	24.52	-	10
S.J. McGlashan	62	55	8	111*	1298	27.61	2	6
J.M. Fraser	75	74	0	81	1251	16.90	-	3
M.C. Godliman	44	43	2	87	1193	29.09	-	9
D.A. Hockley	19	17	1	141	1155	72.18	4	8
R.C. Milburn	86	77	12	82	1128	17.35	-	2
R.J. Kember	56	50	1	94	1059	21.61	-	6
A.J. Wilkins	70	69	3	49	1042	15.78	-	-

BOWLING	M	O	M	R	W	Ave	R/O	Best
N. Scripps	68	583.1	85	1807	124	14.57	3.09	6-18
H.M. Watson	89	649.5	104	2091	96	21.78	3.21	4-40
B.H. McNeill	73	573	82	2069	96	21.55	3.61	6-31
A.L. Mason	72	614.4	77	2078	89	23.34	3.38	5-25
S.K. Burke	71	562.1	80	1953	82	23.81	3.47	4-28
N.J. Browne	69	511.3	44	2065	74	27.90	4.03	3-16
A.M. Dodd	76	579	119	1686	71	23.74	2.91	5-7
A.E. Cooper	66	370.3	52	1343	70	19.18	3.62	5-15
D.M. Trow	63	548.4	93	1525	69	22.10	2.77	6-20
R.J. Steele	48	410.5	103	1029	67	15.35	2.50	4-20
K.M. Spence	72	445.4	53	1698	63	26.95	3.81	5-38
L.E. Milliken	62	476.5	41	1802	58	31.06	3.70	4-34
A.J. Green	54	352	63	1147	55	20.85	3.25	4-17
H.M. Tiffen	87	251	29	889	55	16.16	3.54	5-51
K.L. Pulford	64	393.1	32	1520	55	27.63	3.86	3-24
A.K. Burrows	56	404.1	50	1404	54	23.48	3.47	4-29
S.E. Charteris	46	301.5	32	1073	53	20.24	3.55	5-31
Z.A. McWilliams	51	316	28	1381	52	26.55	4.37	3-0

WICKETKEEPING	ct	st	Total
R.J. Rolls	86	48	134
R.C. Milburn	63	32	95
S.J. Hill	35	21	56
K.J. Martin	33	18	51
E.A. Travers	29	19	48
R.H. Priest	28	9	37
J.C. Ullyett	25	2	27
K.B. Spence	13	10	23

FIELDING	ct
H.M. Tiffen	45
A.L. Mason	36
M.A.M. Lewis	26
H.M. Watson	26
I. Cronin-Knight	23
N.J. Browne	22
J.M. Fraser	22
M.F. Fahey	22

NATIONAL DEVELOPMENT TOURNAMENT

The National Development Tournament was played at Lincoln University for the first time, from 16 to 22 December, 2006. After the fifth round of games was washed out these matches were rescheduled and took the place of the finals day with the tournament winner being the leading points scorer at the end of the round. As it happened, the rescheduled games were also abandoned, leaving Wellington two points clear of defending champion Canterbury.

Auckland's Kelly Sutherland and Lucy Doolan of Wellington shared the Trish McKelvey Trophy for the competition's most outstanding player.

FIRST ROUND

Otago 167-9 lost to **Canterbury** 168-9 by 1 wicket
Auckland 148 lost to **Wellington** 149-0 by 10 wickets
Northern Districts 233-6 defeated **Central Districts** 220 by 13 runs

SECOND ROUND

Auckland 220-4 defeated **Central Districts** 163 by 57 runs
Northern Districts 157 lost to **Canterbury** 158-7 by 3 wickets
Otago 141 lost to **Wellington** 142-4 by 6 wickets

THIRD ROUND

Northern Districts 213-7 lost to **Wellington** 214-7 by 3 wickets
Otago 147-8 lost to **Auckland** 150-5 by 5 wickets
Central Districts 129-8 lost to **Canterbury** 132-0 by 10 wickets

FOURTH ROUND

Otago 67 lost to **Central Districts** 69-3 by 7 wickets
Canterbury 148 met **Wellington** 43-0 (match abandoned)
Northern Districts 189 met **Auckland** 20-2 (match abandoned)

FIFTH ROUND

Wellington v Central Districts
Canterbury v Auckland
Northern Districts v Otago
all matches abandoned

Final placings: Wellington 1, Canterbury 2, Auckland 3, Northern Districts 4, Central Districts 5, Otago 6.

TEST CAREER RECORDS

	M	In	NO	HS	Runs	Ave	100	50	Ct	St	Wkts	Runs	Ave	5WI	10WM	Be
E.P.Allan	4	6	4	29*	87	43.50	-	-	1	-	5	138	27.60	-	-	3-
T.L.Anderson	2	3	0	63	108	36.00	-	1	-	-						
E.A.Badham	3	6	1	42	121	24.20	-	-	7	-	10	275	27.50	-	-	4-
D.Bailey	1	2	0	5	6	3.00	-	-	-	-						
H.R.Bastion	1	-	-	-	-	-	-	-	-	-	0	59	-	-	-	-
K.E.Batty	4	7	1	24	67	11.16	-	-	6	-	2	78	39.00	-	-	1-
L.I.Bayliss	1	-	-	-	-	-	-	-	-	-	5	70	14.00	1	-	5-
B.L.Bevege	5	10	1	100*	400	44.44	1	2	3	-	0	70	-	-	-	-
M.C.Bishop	1	2	0	27	27	13.50	-	-	2	-	0	33	-	-	-	-
E.Blackie	1	2	1	13*	21	21.00	-	-	3	1						
P.Blackler	12	21	0	68	371	17.66	-	1	5	-	18	527	29.27	-	-	4-
B.A.Brentnall	10	16	2	84*	301	21.50	-	1	16	12						
K.D.Brown	3	2	2	50*	52	-	-	1	4	-	7	160	22.85	-	-	3-
S.H.Brown	6	9	3	19	59	9.83	-	-	1	-	9	432	48.00	-	-	3-
N.Browne	1	2	2	5*	5	-	-	-	1	-	0	77	-	-	-	-
N.J.Browne	2	2	0	24	23	12.00	-	-	2	-	1	83	83.00	-	-	1-
D.K.Brownlee	1	2	0	12	17	8.50	-	-	-	-						
H.Buck	1	2	0	16	16	8.00	-	-	-	-						
S.K.Burke	1	1	1	1*	1	-	-	-	-	-	1	57	57.00	-	-	1-
J.A.Burley	6	9	0	46	110	12.22	-	-	3	-	21	553	26.33	1	-	7-
V.E.Burt	3	5	0	15	40	8.00	-	-	-	-	0	28	-	-	-	-
V.L.Burtt	4	8	0	39	101	12.62	-	-	5	-						
C.A.Campbell	9	5	1	29	55	13.75	-	-	2	-	18	720	40.00	-	-	4-
P.F.Carrick	7	11	3	21	63	7.87	-	-	4	-	21	489	23.28	1	-	6-
J.Clark	11	18	0	79	482	26.77	-	2	7	-	0	5	-	-	-	-
A.L.Clough	1	1	0	0	0	0.00	-	-	-	-	1	70	70.00	-	-	1-
W.J.Coe	3	5	1	34	83	20.75	-	-	-	-	6	222	37.00	-	-	2-
M.C.Corby	1	2	0	12	13	6.50	-	-	-	-	0	36	-	-	-	-
D.A.Costello	1	1	0	0	0	0.00	-	-	-	-	2	104	52.00	-	-	2-
J.M.Coulston	5	8	1	24	76	10.85	-	-	3	-	19	341	17.94	-	-	4-
V.R.Coutts	6	11	0	41	136	12.36	-	-	1	-						
S.D.Cowles	7	14	0	46	324	23.14	-	-	6	-	0	13	-	-	-	-
J.Currie	3	5	2	3*	7	2.33	-	-	2	-	3	170	56.66	-	-	3-
E.J.Dickson	2	4	0	65	114	28.50	-	1	-	-						
J.D.Doull	11	22	4	103	779	43.27	1	5	6	-	0	34	-	-	-	-
E.C.Drumm	5	6	3	161*	433	144.33	2	2	-	-	2	175	87.50	-	-	1-
B.M.Duncan	2	3	3	1*	1	-	-	-	1	-	2	115	57.50	-	-	1-
M.H.Dunlop	2	2	0	5	5	2.50	-	-	-	-	3	123	41.00	-	-	1-
J.R.Dunning	6	12	2	71	320	32.00	-	2	5	-	6	170	28.33	-	-	2-
A.E.Ell	1	2	0	1	2	1.00	-	-	-	-	0	55	-	-	-	-
M.F.Fahey	2	4	1	60*	125	41.66	-	1	1	-						
V.H.M.Farrell	3	4	0	5	12	3.00	-	-	5	3						
P.B.Flannery	1	2	0	46	64	32.00	-	-	-	-	0	5	-	-	-	-
K.E.Flavell	6	7	0	204	473	67.57	1	2	2	-						
J.W.Francis	5	7	1	19	46	7.66	-	-	2	-	14	362	25.85	-	-	4-
L.M.Fraser	3	-	-	-	-	-	-	-	-	-	4	210	52.50	-	-	2-
M.K.Fruin	6	8	0	80	188	23.50	-	2	3	1						
J.A.Fryer	3	1	1	7*	7	-	-	-	1	-	5	154	30.80	-	-	4-
J.Fulford	1	2	0	10	12	6.00	-	-	-	-	2	46	23.00	-	-	2-
S.M.Gilchrist	5	3	2	7*	12	12.00	-	-	5	-	14	384	27.42	-	-	3-
G.P.Gooder	1	2	0	11	11	5.50	-	-	-	-	8	73	9.12	1	-	6-
K.V.Gunn	9	12	0	49	194	16.16	-	-	6	1	11	429	39.00	-	-	3-
J.E.Harris	10	7	3	9	26	6.50	-	-	1	-	15	691	46.06	-	-	4-
J.C.Hatcher	4	7	0	23	79	11.28	-	-	-	-						
C.E.Henshilwood	1	2	0	41	48	24.00	-	-	-	-	0	14	-	-	-	-
D.A.Hockley	19	29	4	126*	1301	52.04	4	7	9	-	5	146	29.20	-	-	2-
M.Hollis	1	2	0	24	26	13.00	-	-	-	-	1	81	81.00	-	-	1-
S.L.Illingworth	6	7	3	40*	120	30.00	-	-	5	5						
I.C.P.Jagersma	9	13	5	52	271	33.87	-	1	10	2	4	38	9.50	-	-	4-
Y.Kainuku	1	1	1	23*	23	-	-	-	-	-	1	50	50.00	-	-	1-
K.M.Keenan	5	3	2	26*	32	32.00	-	-	4	-	15	348	23.20	1	-	6-
P.D.Kinsella	6	8	0	53	131	16.37	-	1	3	-						
I.M.Lamason	4	6	2	37*	86	21.50	-	-	-	-	2	136	68.00	-	-	2-
J.G.Lamason	4	8	0	24	87	10.87	-	-	-	-	8	264	33.00	-	-	4-
B.J.Legg	3	4	1	26	30	10.00	-	-	-	-	4	149	37.25	-	-	2-
M.A.M.Lewis	9	12	0	65	252	21.00	-	2	6	-						

	M	In	NO	HS	Runs	Ave	100	50	Ct	St	Wkts	Runs	Ave	5WI	10WM	Best
Lord	15	22	3	39*	258	13.57	-	-	5	-	55	1049	19.07	4	1	6-119
.J.Maker	3	4	0	5	10	2.50	-	-	1	-	5	156	31.20	-	-	3-34
.E.Marett	7	13	4	49	304	33.77	-	-	3	-	9	268	29.77	-	-	2-16
.Marks	2	4	1	23	30	10.00	-	-	-	-						
.J.Martin	1	2	0	46	49	24.50	-	-	-	-						
.L.Mason	2	2	0	14	15	7.50	-	-	2	-	3	105	35.00	-	-	2-68
.McDonald	1	1	0	1	1	1.00	-	-	-	-						
J.McGlashan	2	2	0	14	20	10.00	-	-	-	-						
F.McKelvey	15	26	2	155*	699	29.12	2	1	8	-						
.McKenna	7	14	1	97*	465	35.76	-	3	7	-	0	6	-	-	-	-
.U.McKenzie	7	13	0	61	295	22.69	-	2	3	-	8	214	26.75	-	-	4-18
McLauchlan	4	4	0	4	4	1.00	-	-	1	-	2	83	41.50	-	-	1-7
.L.Miller	3	6	0	32	92	15.33	-	-	1	-						
.Miller	1	2	0	11	11	5.50	-	-	-	-	1	77	77.00	-	-	1-77
.E.Milliken	2	2	0	6	10	5.00	-	-	-	-	2	73	36.50	-	-	2-49
S.Molloy	2	1	1	1*	1	-	-	-	2	-	5	91	18.20	-	-	2-24
Moore	2	3	1	47*	80	40.00	-	-	3	-	0	31	-	-	-	-
.J.Murdoch	6	10	0	72	253	25.30	-	1	1	-						
.J.Musson	1	-	-	-	-	-	-	-	-	-						
.M.Nicholson	4	5	0	46	140	28.00	-	-	1	-	5	170	34.00	-	-	2-25
.M.O'Leary	1	1	0	27	27	27.00	-	-	1	-						
B.Olson	1	1	0	0	0	0.00	-	-	-	-	0	48	-	-	-	-
.M.Oyler	5	8	2	67*	212	35.33	-	1	2	-						
.A.Paton	4	8	1	77*	180	25.71	-	1	4	-	9	160	17.77	-	-	4-35
.V.Plummer	4	6	0	13	28	4.66	-	-	2	-						
J.Powell	7	13	2	63	272	24.72	-	1	9	1						
.Powell	4	7	0	66	145	20.71	-	1	1	-	0	8	-	-	-	-
.M.Prichard	1	2	0	38	43	21.50	-	-	1	-						
.L.Pulford	1	2	0	0	0	0.00	-	-	1	-	2	15	7.50	-	-	2-15
.J.Rattray	9	17	2	59	412	27.46	-	4	1	-	19	461	24.26	1	-	5-76
.Robinson	1	1	1	2*	2	-	-	-	-	-	1	16	16.00	-	-	1-16
.J.Rolls	1	2	1	71	71	71.00	-	1	1	-						
.F.Rouse	1	2	0	35	36	18.00	-	-	-	-						
I.T.Rouse	2	4	2	15*	18	9.00	-	-	-	-						
A.Russell	1	1	0	39	39	39.00	-	-	-	-	1	37	37.00	-	-	1-14
.M.Ryan	5	8	4	10	38	9.50	-	-	3	11						
M.Saulbrey	11	16	4	62	198	16.50	-	1	6	-	35	951	27.17	1	-	5-32
.Savin	1	2	0	15	18	9.00	-	-	-	-						
.Scripps	1	1	1	10*	10	-	-	-	-	-	0	57	-	-	-	-
.A.Signal	6	6	2	55*	82	20.50	-	1	3	-	8	325	40.62	-	-	2-34
.J.Signal	1	2	1	8*	8	8.00	-	-	-	-	0	21	-	-	-	-
.J.Simpson	1	2	0	4	6	3.00	-	-	-	-						
.M.Sinclair	2	4	1	10	26	8.66	-	-	2	-						
.Sinton	1	2	0	10	14	7.00	-	-	-	-						
E.Stead	9	18	2	95	433	27.06	-	3	3	-						
.J.Steele	2	3	0	12	16	5.33	-	-	3	-	8	141	17.62	1	-	5-79
M.Stonell	4	8	0	47	127	15.87	-	-	2	-						
.Sutherland	3	6	0	22	66	11.00	-	-	1	-	2	86	43.00	-	-	1-29
.E.Symons	1	1	0	5	5	5.00	-	-	1	-	2	71	35.50	-	-	2-71
I.J.Taylor	1	2	0	3	3	1.50	-	-	-	-	1	62	62.00	-	-	1-62
.M.Thompson	1	2	1	17*	17	17.00	-	-	1	-	0	18	-	-	-	-
.I.Thorner	3	6	1	37	76	15.20	-	-	-	-	4	78	19.50	-	-	2-33
.M.Tiffen	2	4	3	66*	124	124.00	-	1	1	-						
A.Turner	6	8	1	11*	30	4.28	-	-	2	-	19	469	24.68	-	-	3-42
.J.Turner	6	9	2	65*	208	29.71	-	2	1	-						
.M.Webb	4	8	0	42	110	13.75	-	-	-	-	6	66	11.00	-	-	3-32
.White	3	5	0	17	33	6.60	-	-	-	-	2	85	42.50	-	-	1-5
.Wickham	2	4	0	34	40	10.00	-	-	-	-	3	76	25.33	-	-	2-33
.M.Williams	4	5	1	35*	70	17.50	-	-	1	-	3	158	52.66	-	-	2-19
.Woodbury	2	3	3	7*	7	-	-	-	-	-	4	100	25.00	-	-	2-29

TEAM RECORDS

Highest Totals

517-8	v England	Scarborough	1996
403-8d	v India	Nelson	1994/95
362-5d	v England	Guildford	1996
359	v Australia	Wellington	1974/75
335	v Australia	Melbourne	1971/72

Lowest Totals

44	v England	Christchurch	1934/35
61	v England	Auckland	1948/49
63	v England	Worcester	1954
78	v Australia	Adelaide	1978/79
87	v Australia	Wellington	1947/48

INDIVIDUAL RECORDS

Centuries

204	K.E. Flavell v England at Scarborough	1996
161*	E.C. Drumm v Australia at Christchurch	1994/95
155*	P.F. McKelvey v England at Wellington	1968/69
126*	D.A. Hockley v Australia at Auckland	1989/90
117*	P.F. McKelvey v South Africa at Cape Town	1971/72
115	D.A. Hockley v England at Worcester	1996
112*	E.C. Drumm v England at Guildford	1996
107*	D.A. Hockley v England at Canterbury	1984
107	D.A. Hockley v India at Nelson	1994/95
103	J.D. Doull v England at Christchurch	1968/69
100*	B.L. Bevege v India at Dunedin	1976/77

Five Wickets in an Innings

7-41	J.A. Burley v England at The Oval	1966
6-29	P.F. Carrick v Australia at Melbourne	1971/72
6-42	G.P. Gooder v England at Auckland	1948/49
6-73	K.M. Keenan v England at Worcester	1996
6-119	J. Lord v Australia at Melbourne	1978/79
5-24	J. Lord v South Africa at Durban	1971/72
5-28	L.I. Bayliss v Australia at Dunedin	1960/61
5-32	J.M. Saulbrey v South Africa at Durban	1971/72
5-40	J. Lord v India at Dunedin	1976/77
5-76	S.J. Rattray v India at Cuttack	1984/85
5-78	J. Lord v Australia at Adelaide	1978/79
5-79	R.J. Steele v India at Vapi	2003/04

Ten Wickets in a Match

10-137	J. Lord v Australia at Melbourne	1978/79

Wicketkeeping

DISMISSALS IN AN INNINGS

	(ct/st)				
6	(2/4)	B.A. Brentnall	v South Africa	Johannesburg	1971/72
5	(3/2)	B.A. Brentnall	v England	Auckland	1968/69
4	(1/3)	V.H.M. Farrell	v England	Worcester	1954
4	(4/0)	V.H.M. Farrell	v England	The Oval	1954
4	(1/3)	E.M. Ryan	v Australia	Melbourne	1978/79

DISMISSALS IN A MATCH

	(ct/st)				
7	(3/4)	B.A. Brentnall	v South Africa	Johannesburg	1971/72
7	(2/5)	E.M. Ryan	v Australia	Melbourne	1978/79
6	(4/2)	B.A. Brentnall	v England	Auckland	1968/69
5	(3/2)	B.A. Brentnall	v South Africa	Durban	1971/72
5	(2/3)	S.L. Illingworth	v England	Guildford	1996

Fielding

CATCHES IN AN INNINGS

3	K.E. Batty	v England	Auckland	1948/49
3	P. Moore	v England	The Oval	1966
3	E.A. Badham	v Australia	Sydney	1978/79
3	M.A. M.Lewis	v England	Wanganui	1991/92
3	D.A. Hockley	v England	Scarborough	1996

CATCHES IN A MATCH

4	S.M. Gilchrist	v India	Ahmedabad	1984/85
4	M.A.M. Lewis	v England	Wanganui	1991/92

RECORD PARTNERSHIPS

1st	150	M.K. Fruin & D.A. Hockley	v England	Guildford	1996
2nd	146	M.K. Fruin & K.E. Flavell	v England	Scarborough	1996
3rd	106	K.E. Flavell & E.C. Drumm	v England	Guildford	1996
4th	94	I.J. Powell & R.U. McKenzie	v Australia	Dunedin	1960/61
5th	94*	E.C. Drumm & D.A. Hockley	v England	Guildford	1996
6th	83	D.A. Hockley & K.V. Gunn	v Australia	Christchurch	1989/90
7th	90	B.A. Brentnall & J.A. Burley	v England	Birmingham	1966
8th	87	C.E. Marett & J.M. Saulbrey	v Australia	Wellington	1974/75
9th	60*	K.E. Flavell & K.D. Brown	v England	Scarborough	1996
10th	55*	C.M. Oyler & J. Lord	v England	The Oval	1966

SUMMARY OF TEST CAREER RECORDS

Most Matches

D.A. Hockley	19	P. Blackler	12	J. Clark	11
P.F. McKelvey	15	J.D. Doull	11	J.E. Harris	10
J. Lord	15	J.M. Saulbrey	11	B.A. Brentnall	10

Most Runs

D.A. Hockley	1301	K.E. Flavell	473	J.E. Stead	433
J.D. Doull	779	A. McKenna	465	S.J. Rattray	412
P.F. McKelvey	699	E.C. Drumm	433	B.L. Bevege	400
J. Clark	482				

Most Wickets

J. Lord	55	J.M. Coulston	19	P. Blackler	18
J.M. Saulbrey	35	J.A. Turner	19	K.M. Keenan	15
J.A. Burley	21	S.J. Rattray	19	J.E. Harris	15
P.F. Carrick	21	C.A. Campbell	18		

Most Wicketkeeping Dismissals

	Ct	*St*	*Total*
B.A. Brentnall	15	12	27
E.M. Ryan	3	11	14
I.C.P. Jagersma	10	2	12
S.L. Illingworth	5	5	10

Most Catches

D.A. Hockley	9
P.F. McKelvey	8
E.A. Badham	7
A. McKenna	7
J. Clark	7

ONE-DAY INTERNATIONAL CAREER RECORDS

	M	In	NO	HS	Runs	Ave	100s	50s	Ct	St	O	M	R	W	Ave	R/O	Best
E.P.Allan	7	6	1	17	42	8.40	-	-	2	-	59	8	162	3	54.00	2.75	1-22
T.L.Anderson	26	25	0	85	440	17.60	-	2	9	-							
L.M.Astle	1	-	-	-	-	-	-	-	-	-							
E.A.Badham	13	10	1	30	86	9.55	-	-	5	-	135.3	33	290	12	24.16	2.14	2-14
H.R.Bastion	3	-	-	-	-	-	-	-	1	-	20	2	57	2	28.50	2.85	1-12
S.W.Bates	11	9	0	122	314	34.88	1	1	2	-	40.2	4	192	9	21.33	4.76	2-20
B.L.Bevege	16	16	1	101	488	32.53	1	3	3	-	22.2	7	48	3	16.00	2.16	3-17
B.A.Brentnall	5	3	0	18	40	13.33	-	-	3	3							
K.D.Brown	14	6	3	9*	19	6.33	-	-	4	-	86.4	14	252	10	25.20	2.90	2-8
S.H.Brown	18	9	4	17*	59	11.80	-	-	5	-	170	63	308	19	16.21	1.81	2-3
N.J.Browne	59	42	16	53	667	25.65	-	2	13	-	364.2	37	1335	42	31.78	3.66	4-20
S.K.Burke	26	11	5	10*	51	8.50	-	-	3	-	197.2	24	729	22	33.13	3.69	3-17
J.A.Burley	2	1	0	7	7	7.00	-	-	-	-	13	3	28	0	-	2.15	-
V.L.Burtt	9	8	0	46	168	21.00	-	-	4	-	6	0	31	2	15.50	5.17	2-31
D.Caird	4	4	1	45	72	24.00	-	-	-	-							
C.A.Campbell	85	30	15	12	69	4.60	-	-	15	-	753	150	2018	78	25.87	2.68	3-15
P.F.Carrick	3	2	1	6*	7	7.00	-	-	1	-	29	1	106	6	17.66	3.66	3-43
S.E.Charteris	2	1	1	20*	20	-	-	-	-	-	8	0	52	1	52.00	6.50	1-32
J.Clark	31	31	1	85	875	29.16	-	7	5	-							
D.A.Costello	7	2	1	1	1	1.00	-	-	1	-	56.4	8	139	2	69.50	2.45	2-37
S.D.Cowles	5	5	0	46	93	18.60	-	-	2	-	5	0	24	0	-	4.80	-
S.F.M.Devine	6	4	1	30	47	15.66	-	-	2	-	39.5	1	218	6	36.33	5.47	3-38
A.M.Dodd	31	20	11	20*	155	17.22	-	-	10	-	207.1	24	755	28	26.96	3.64	3-13
J.D.Doull	5	5	0	42	64	12.80	-	-	2	-							
E.C.Drumm	101	94	13	116	2844	35.11	2	19	24	-	257	53	778	37	21.02	3.03	4-31
J.R.Dunning	22	21	4	89	346	20.35	-	1	4	-	157	12	527	13	40.53	3.36	3-29
M.E.Fahey	40	39	2	91	1120	30.27	-	12	9	-							
P.B.Flannery	17	17	2	49*	258	17.20	-	-	3	-							
K.E.Flavell	38	33	9	54	719	29.95	-	2	5	-	70	15	156	7	22.28	2.23	2-5
D.L.Ford	3	2	0	35	46	23.00	-	-	1	-	6	0	32	0	-	5.33	-
F.E.Fraser	5	3	2	54*	94	94.00	-	1	1	-							
L.M.Fraser	13	7	1	8	31	5.16	-	-	2	-	117	20	294	12	24.50	2.51	3-21
M.K.Fruin	23	23	4	51	385	20.26	-	1	4	1							
J.A.Fryer	7	1	1	1*	1	-	-	-	-	-	33	9	115	10	11.50	3.48	3-8
S.M.Gilchrist	8	5	1	12	19	4.75	-	-	4	-	77	21	202	7	28.85	2.62	3-20
A.J.Green	14	8	5	17*	23	7.66	-	-	3	-	108.3	17	392	12	32.66	3.61	5-15
P.A.Gruber	2	1	0	0	0	0.00	-	-	-	-	10	3	35	0	-	3.50	-
K.V.Gunn	45	34	9	52	461	18.44	-	1	14	-	458.5	110	1113	53	21.00	2.42	5-22
K.Hadlee	1	1	0	14	14	14.00	-	-	-	-							
L.R.V.S.Harford	3	3	0	9	20	6.66	-	-	-	-	7	0	30	0	-	4.29	-
J.E.Harris	45	24	12	19*	99	8.25	-	-	9	-	414.2	98	1124	61	18.42	2.71	4-8
S.A.Harris	2	1	1	1*	1	-	-	-	-	-	3	0	19	0	-	6.33	-
C.E.Henshilwood	2	1	1	15*	15	-	-	-	-	-							
D.A.Hockley	118	115	18	117	4064	41.89	4	34	41	-	253.4	41	853	20	42.65	3.36	3-49
S.L.Illingworth	37	29	7	51	342	15.54	-	1	27	21							
I.C.P.Jagersma	34	27	4	58*	453	19.69	-	2	24	9	22	5	48	4	12.00	2.18	2-14
Y.Kainuku	2	2	0	4	4	2.00	-	-	-	-	12	2	49	0	-	4.08	-
K.M.Keenan	55	36	9	57*	348	12.88	-	1	9	-	452	72	1253	70	17.90	2.77	4-5
R.J.Kember	3	3	0	18	42	14.00	-	-	2	-							
F.S.King	15	10	3	31	81	11.57	-	-	2	-	108.1	14	404	21	19.23	3.73	4-24
P.D.Kinsella	20	20	3	57	443	26.05	-	2	-	-							
K.Le Comber	15	14	4	135*	442	44.20	1	2	2	-							
B.J.Legg	18	13	3	17	79	7.90	-	-	2	-	199.4	62	394	20	19.70	1.97	3-4
M.A.M.Lewis	78	73	12	105	1372	22.49	1	4	30	-	5	0	32	0	-	6.40	-
L.Lindsay	2	1	0	27	27	27.00	-	-	-	-	13	0	42	2	21.00	3.23	2-26
J.Lord	15	13	0	25	101	7.76	-	-	2	-	132.3	25	318	25	12.72	2.40	6-10
M.L.Lynch	6	6	0	29	105	17.50	-	-	-	-							
C.E.Marett	14	12	2	24	149	14.90	-	-	-	-	126.5	24	310	16	19.37	2.44	3-14
K.J.Martin	3	3	1	8*	18	9.00	-	-	1	1							
A.L.Mason	56	47	5	71	832	19.80	-	1	23	-	426.1	46	1647	51	32.29	3.87	4-23
E.T.McDonald	3	-	-	-	-	-	-	-	1	-	24	4	50	5	10.00	2.08	2-17
K.McDonald	6	6	0	34	80	13.33	-	-	1	-							
S.J.McGlashan	51	47	10	57	761	20.56	-	2	9	-							

	M	In	NO	HS	Runs	Ave	100s	50s	Ct	St	O	M	R	W	Ave	R/O	Best
P.F.McKelvey	15	14	4	42	214	21.40	-	-	2	-							
A.McKenna	14	13	0	39	214	16.46	-	-	-	-							
S.McLauchlan	29	21	5	34*	137	8.56	-	-	6	-	227.5	47	665	19	35.00	2.91	2-6
B.H.McNeill	10	8	4	88*	157	39.25	-	1	3	-	74.1	9	306	10	30.60	4.12	2-42
R.C.Milburn	2	2	0	25	32	16.00	-	-	2	-							
L.E.Milliken	48	18	8	21	110	11.00	-	-	13	-	370	45	1409	59	23.88	3.81	5-25
K.S.Molloy	5	2	1	0*	0	0.00	-	-	2	-	36	8	99	4	24.75	2.75	2-16
S.R.M.Morris	8	1	0	5	5	5.00	-	-	-	-	69	12	175	7	25.00	2.54	2-13
L.J.Murdoch	25	22	3	69	417	21.94	-	1	4	-							
K.J.Musson	13	10	2	31	86	10.75	-	-	3	-	87.2	12	253	10	25.30	2.89	3-22
C.M.Nicholson	35	22	10	73*	195	16.25	-	1	13	-	272.4	62	707	38	18.60	2.59	4-18
A.M.O'Leary	19	18	3	91*	497	33.13	-	3	3	-							
J.B.Olson	4	4	1	9*	17	5.66	-	-	-	-	27	9	52	4	13.00	1.93	3-16
G.L.Page	2	1	0	5	5	5.00	-	-	-	-	17.2	3	46	6	7.66	2.65	6-20
N.Payne	65	64	7	93	1178	20.66	-	4	17	-	158	48	407	20	20.35	2.57	3-20
M.H.Peters	16	12	5	24	79	11.28	-	-	3	-	155.5	63	291	19	15.31	1.86	2-3
K.V.Plummer	11	10	1	32	100	11.11	-	-	2	-	10	0	36	0	-	3.60	-
L.M.Powell	5	4	0	70	73	18.25	-	1	1	-							
K.L.Pulford	30	25	0	95	527	21.08	-	2	8	-	96.1	6	379	14	27.07	3.94	4-5
R.J.Pullar	51	32	11	27*	253	12.04	-	-	14	-	430.1	80	1215	74	16.41	2.82	5-7
K.A.Ramel	47	37	7	41	519	17.30	-	-	13	-	204.3	26	729	35	20.82	3.56	3-26
S.J.Rattray	15	15	7	60*	305	38.12	-	1	1	-	123.1	16	399	11	36.27	3.23	2-33
R.J.Rolls	104	91	3	114	2201	25.01	2	12	90	43							
E.F.Rouse	3	3	0	48	90	30.00	-	-	-	-							
J.A.Russell	5	4	1	8*	8	2.66	-	-	-	-	26	3	84	1	84.00	3.23	1-20
E.M.Ryan	15	5	1	6*	17	4.25	-	-	13	8							
J.M.Saulbrey	5	5	3	22*	75	37.50	-	-	-	-	43	12	100	4	25.00	2.33	2-32
N.Scripps	7	3	3	9*	12	-	-	-	-	-	50.2	6	206	6	34.33	4.09	2-17
V.S.Sexton	2	2	0	9	12	6.00	-	-	-	-							
E.A.Signal	19	12	5	28*	79	11.28	-	-	5	-	130.3	23	496	7	70.85	3.80	2-26
R.J.Signal	6	3	1	8	12	6.00	-	-	2	-	27	2	89	2	44.50	3.30	1-10
L.J.Simpson	12	11	1	23*	95	9.50	-	-	1	-							
R.J.Steele	32	12	6	8*	41	6.83	-	-	6	-	293	57	831	34	24.44	2.84	3-10
H.M.Tiffen	90	84	12	91	2163	30.04	-	14	25	-	266	43	891	48	18.56	3.35	4-43
E.A.Travers	3	-	-	-	-	-	-	-	-	-							
D.M.Trow	2	1	1	1*	1	-	-	-	1	-	12	3	18	4	4.50	1.50	3-8
S.J.Tsukigawa	12	12	3	78*	248	27.55	-	1	1	-	70.2	3	297	10	29.70	4.22	3-33
M.F.Tunupopo	3	-	-	-	-	-	-	-	2	-	18	4	57	0	-	3.17	-
J.A.Turner	30	14	2	15	54	4.50	-	-	6	-	265.2	42	695	28	24.82	2.61	5-5
N.J.Turner	28	26	2	114	624	26.00	1	2	4	-							
H.M.Watson	51	39	9	115*	504	16.80	1	-	16	-	283.3	38	955	43	22.20	3.36	3-14
N.M.Williams	19	13	2	21*	80	7.27	-	-	1	-	110.5	19	374	15	24.93	3.37	3-37

TEAM RECORDS

Highest Totals

455-5	v Pakistan	Christchurch	1996/97
335-4	v Netherlands	Amstelveen	2002
297-5	v Netherlands	Sydney	1988/89
291-6	v England	Chennai	2006/07
278-3	v Ireland	Dublin	2004

Lowest Totals

58	v Australia	Melbourne	1984/85
61	v Australia	Wellington	1998/99
73	v India	Indore	1984/85
80	v India	Auckland	1981/82
94	v Australia	Melbourne	1990/91

INDIVIDUAL RECORDS

Centuries

135*	K. LeComber v Ireland at Dublin	1996
122	S.W. Bates v India at Chennai	2006/07
117	D.A. Hockley v England at Chester-le-Street	1996
116	E.C. Drumm v England at Oamaru	2000/01
115*	H.M. Watson v Ireland at Dublin	2004
114	N.J. Turner v Netherlands at Sydney	1988/89
114	R.J. Rolls v Australia at Lincoln	2001/02
108*	E.C. Drumm v South Africa at Lincoln	2000/01
105	M.A.M. Lewis v Pakistan at Christchurch	1996/97
104*	R.J. Rolls v Australia at Chennai	2006/07
101	B.L. Bevege v International XI at Auckland	1981/82
100*	D.A. Hockley v Sri Lanka at Chandigarh	1997/98
100	D.A. Hockley v West Indies at Chandigarh	1997/98
100	D.A. Hockley v Australia at Melbourne	1999/00

Five Wickets in an Innings

6-10	J. Lord v India at Auckland	1981/82
6-20	G.L. Page v Trinidad & Tobago at St Albans	1973
5-5	J.A. Turner v Netherlands at Lindfield	1993
5-7	R.J. Pullar v South Africa at Hamilton	1998/99
5-10	R.J. Pullar v India at St Saviour	2002
5-15	A.J Green v Ireland at Dublin	2004
5-22	K.V. Gunn v Australia at Wellington	1989/90
5-25	L.E. Milliken v India, Pretoria	2004/05

Hat-tricks

7.1-1-18-3	J.E. Harris	v West Indies	Chiswick	1993
8-2-22-3	E.C. Drumm	v Australia	Adelaide	1995/96

Most Economical Bowling

10-7-3-0	C.A. Campbell	v Netherlands	Christchurch	2000/01
12-9-4-3	B.J. Legg	v Netherlands	Melbourne	1988/89
12-9-5-3	J.E. Harris	v Netherlands	Lindfield	1993
11.2-7-5-5	J.A. Turner	v Netherlands	Lindfield	1993
10-6-5-4	K.M. Keenan	v West Indies	Chandigarh	1997/98

Most Expensive Bowling

9-1-68-1	L.E. Milliken	v Australia	Auckland	2003/04
8-0-64-0	A.L. Mason	v Australia	Brisbane	2006/07
7-0-63-0	F.S. King	v Australia	Lincoln	2001/02
10-0-60-2	L.E. Milliken	v England	Chennai	2006/07
10-0-59-1	J.E. Harris	v Australia	Auckland	1996/97

Wicketkeeping

DISMISSALS IN AN INNINGS

	(ct/st)				
6	(4/2)	S.L. Illingworth	v Australia	Beckenham	1993
4	(2/2)	E.M. Ryan	v International XI	Auckland	1981/82
4	(2/2)	I.C.P. Jagersma	v Netherlands	Sydney	1988/89
4	(3/1)	S.L. Illingworth	v India	Ealing	1993
4	(3/1)	R.J. Rolls	v England	Oamaru	2000/01
4	(2/2)	R.J. Rolls	v England	Lincoln	2000/01
4	(4/0)	R.J. Rolls	v Australia	Lincoln	2001/02
4	(4/0)	R.J. Rolls	v India	Durham	2002
4	(4/0)	R.J. Rolls	v Sri Lanka	Pretoria	2004/05
4	(3/1)	R.J. Rolls	v Ireland	Pretoria	2004/05
4	(2/2)	R.J. Rolls	v India	Lincoln	2005/06

Fielding

CATCHES IN AN INNINGS

3	S.H. Brown	v England	Hastings	1984
3	S.M. Gilchrist	v India	Indore	1984/85
3	D.A. Hockley	v Australia	Melbourne	1990/91
3	K.A. Ramel	v Netherlands	Ghaziabad	1997/98
3	D.A. Hockley	v Sri Lanka	Chandigarh	1997/98
3	H.M. Watson	v Netherlands	Christchurch	2000/01
3	H.M. Tiffen	v England	Lincoln	2002/03

RECORD PARTNERSHIPS

1st	180	B.L. Bevege & L.J. Murdoch	v International XI	Auckland	1981/82
2nd	170	R.J. Rolls & E.C. Drumm	v Australia	Lincoln	2001/02
3rd	138	D.A. Hockley & M.A.M. Lewis	v Australia	Wellington	1996/97
4th	116	D.A. Hockley & E.C. Drumm	v Australia	Sydney	1997/98
5th	108*	R.J. Rolls & S.J. Tsukigawa	v Australia	Chennai	2006/07
6th	107	E.C. Drumm & N.J. Browne	v India	Lincoln	2005/06
7th	104*	S.J. Tsukigawa & N.J. Browne	v England	Chennai	2006/07
8th	43	N.J. Browne & L.E. Milliken	v England	Chelmsford	2004
9th	58	K.V. Gunn & S. McLauchlan	v Australia	Wellington	1991/92
10th	33	E.C. Drumm & C.A. Campbell	v Australia	Wellington	1996/97

SUMMARY OF ONE-DAY INTERNATIONAL CAREER RECORDS

Most Matches

D.A. Hockley	118	C.A. Campbell	85	K.M. Keenan	55
R.J. Rolls	104	M.A.M. Lewis	78	R.J. Pullar	51
E.C. Drumm	101	N.J. Browne	59	S.J. McGlashan	51
H.M. Tiffen	90	A.L. Mason	56	H.M. Watson	51

Most Runs

D.A. Hockley	4064	M.A.M. Lewis	1372	S.J. McGlashan	761
E.C. Drumm	2844	M.F. Fahey	1120	K.E. Flavell	719
R.J. Rolls	2201	J. Clark	875	N.J. Browne	667
H.M. Tiffen	2163	A.L. Mason	832	N.J. Turner	624

Most Wickets

C.A. Campbell	78	L.E. Milliken	59	N.J. Browne	42
R.J. Pullar	74	K.V. Gunn	53	H.M. Watson	43
K.M. Keenan	70	A.L. Mason	51	C.M. Nicholson	38
J.E. Harris	61	H.M. Tiffen	48	E.C. Drumm	37

Most Wicketkeeping Dismissals

	Ct	*St*	*Total*
R.J. Rolls	90	43	133
S.L. Illingworth	26	21	47
I.C.P. Jagersma	24	9	33
E.M. Ryan	13	8	21

Most Catches

D.A. Hockley	41
M.A.M. Lewis	30
H.M. Tiffen	25
E.C. Drumm	24
A.L. Mason	23
H.M. Watson	16
C.A. Campbell	15

NEW ZEALAND FIRST-CLASS RECORDS

to 1 April, 2007

FIRST-CLASS MATCH DEFINED

The six countries represented at Imperial Cricket Conference on 19 May 1947 reached agreement in regard to definition of a first-class match. This did not have effect retrospectively.

A match of three or more days' duration between two sides of eleven players officially adjudged first-class shall be regarded as a first-class fixture. Matches in which either team has more than eleven players or which are scheduled for less than three days shall not be regarded as first-class. The governing body in each country shall decide the status of teams.

The records have been compiled on the following basis:

(1) Otago and Canterbury from 1863/64 to date
(2) Wellington and Auckland from 1873/74 to date
(3) Nelson from 1873/74 to 1891/92 inclusive
(4) West Coast (North Island) 1879/80
(5) Taranaki from 1882/83 to 1897/98 inclusive
(6) Hawke's Bay from 1883/84 to 1920/21 inclusive
(7) Southland from 1914/15 to 1920/21 inclusive
(8) Central Districts from 1950/51 to date
(9) Northern Districts from 1956/57 to date

Notes:

• Games played by the Melbourne Cricket Club teams of 1899/1900, 1905/1906 and 1926/27, are not treated as first-class in accordance with a decision of the New Zealand Cricket Council.

• Although set down for only two days each, the return matches played by A. Sims' Australian XI in 1913/14 against Canterbury and Wellington are included in these records; so is the match An Australian XI v Minor Associations, 1920/21, and MCC v Wellington, 1932/33.

• From 1933/34 season onwards, only games for which at least three days have been set down are treated as first-class.

• There have now been 2040 first-class matches in New Zealand.

• Unless otherwise stated, the first-class records relate to first-class matches in New Zealand and by New Zealand touring teams overseas. Apart from the games which have taken place in New Zealand, there are a further 561 played by New Zealand overseas as follows:

in Australia	1898/99 to 2004/05	83
in England	1927 to 2004	294
in South Africa	1953/54 to 2005/06	51
in Pakistan	1955/56 to 2001/02	33
in India	1955/56 to 2003/04	44
in West Indies	1971/72 to 2001/02	26
in Sri Lanka	1983/84 to 2002/03	16
in Zimbabwe	1992/93 to 2005/06	12
in Bangladesh	2004/05	2

plus four games by Young New Zealand in Zimbabwe in 1984/85, three games by New Zealand Young Internationals in Zimbabwe 1988/89, one match by Wellington in Australia 1990/91, one match by Canterbury in South Africa 1993/94, three matches by New Zealand Academy in South Africa 1997/98, six games by New Zealand A in England 2000, three matches by New Zealand A in South Africa in 2004/0, three matches by New Zealand A in Sri Lanka in 2005/06 and one match by New Zealand White in Australia 2006/07.

GROUNDS

Ground	No of matches	First and most recent match		Highest and lowest team totals				Highest Innings Best Bowling			
South Dunedin Recreation Ground	9	O v C	1863/64	C	272	v O	1875/76	75	H.W. Moore	C v O	1877/78
		O v C	1877/78	MCC	34	v O	1863/64	8-28	W. Hendley	O v C	1869/70
Hagley Park *(old)* Christchurch	1	C v O	1864/65	C	80	v O	1864/65	22	J. Fulton	O v C	1864/65
		only match		O	61	v C	1864/65	5-17	J.W. Stevens	C v O	1864/65
Hagley Park *(new)* Christchurch	34	C v O	1866/67	SC	554	v Pk A	1998/99	301*	P.G. Fulton	C v A	2002/03
		C v W	2004/05	C	25	v O	1866/67	10-28	A.E. Moss	C v W	1889/90
Basin Reserve * Wellington	383	W v A	1873/74	NZ	671-4	v SL	1990/91	299	M.D. Crowe	NZ v SL	1990/91
		W v ND	2006/07	W	22	v C	1903/04	9-43	T. Eden	N v W	1875/76
Victory Square Nelson	7	N v W	1874/75	N	150	v A	1882/83	31	C.A. Knapp	W v N	1874/75
		N v W	1887/88	W	19	v N	1885/86	8-26	F.H. Cooke	N v W	1887/88
Domain Auckland	33	A v C	1877/78	A	579	v O	1909/10	151*	Harold B. Lusk	C v A	1910/11
		A v C	1912/13	A	13	v C	1877/78	9-75	R. Neill	A v C	1891/92
Caledonian Ground Dunedin	4	O v C	1879/80	O	297	v W	1904/05	88	H.G. Seideberg	O v W	1904/05
		O v W	1904/05	A	48	v O	1889/90	8-36	A.W. Rees	A v O	1889/90
Lancaster Park § Christchurch	334	C v A	1882/83	C	777	v O	1996/97	385	B. Sutcliffe	O v C	1952/53
		NZ v SL	2006/07	O	35	v A	1884/85	9-72	F.H. Cooke	O v C	1884/85
Botanical Gardens Nelson	1	N v W	1883/84	N	56	v W	1883/84	17	L. Fowler	N v W	1883/84
		only match		W	30	v N	1883/84	5-10	G. Fowler	N v W	1883/84
Carisbrook Dunedin	251	O v Tas	1883/84	NSW	752-8d	v O	1923/24	355	B. Sutcliffe	O v A	1949/50
		O v C	2005/06	C	27	v O	1896/97	9-50	A.H. Fisher	O v Q'ld	1896/97
Recreation Ground Napier	20½	HB v W	1884/85	MCC	394	v HB	1906/07	188	C.G. Wilson	O v HB	1908/09
		HB v A	1912/13	HB	42	v C	1897/98	9-47	T.H. Dent	HB v W	1900/01
Farndon Park Napier	4½	HB v T	1891/92	Q'ld	492	v HB	1896/97	135	O.W. Cowley	Q'ld v HB	1896/97
		HB v Q'ld	1896/97	T	39	v HB	1891/92	8-14	S.W Austin	NSW v HB	1893/94
King Edward Park Hawera	2	T v HB	1891/92	T	135	v Fiji	1894/95	62	Hugh B. Lusk	HB v T	1891/92
		T v Fiji	1894/95	T	29	v HB	1891/92	7-?	C.R. Smith	HB v T	1891/92
Bayly Park Hawera	2	T v HB	1896/97	C	260	v T	1897/98	106	W.J. Crawshaw	T v HB	1896/97
		T v C	1897/98	HB	100	v T	1896/97	6-43	D. Reese	C v T	1897/98
Victoria Park Auckland	3	A v C	1908/09	A	470	v HB	1910/11	88	W. Carlton	C v A	1909/10
		A v HB	1910/11	HB	28	v A	1910/11	7-42	A.E. Relf	A v C	1908/09
Nelson Cricket Ground Hastings	3	HB v W	1913/14	C	337	v HB	1914/15	111	V.S. Ransford	Aust v HB	1913/14
		HB v C	1914/15	HB	89	v C	1914/15	8-51	A.A. Mailey	Aust v HB	1913/14
Eden Park Auckland	233	A v Aust	1913/14	A	693-9d	v C	1939/40	336*	W.R. Hammond	E v NZ	1932/33
		NZ v WI	2005/06	NZ	26	v E	1954/55	9-36	A.F. Wensley	A v O	1929/30
Rugby Park Invercargill	5	S v O	1914/15	Aust	195	v S	1920/21	71	A. Galland	O v S	1919/20
		S v Aust	1920/21	C	37	v S	1920/21	8-84	D.J. McBeath	S v C	1920/21
Nelson Park Napier	4	HB v W	1919/20	Aust	405-8d	v HB	1920/21	158	V.S. Ransford	Aust v HB	1920/21
		CD v C	1989/90	CD	153	v W	1985/86	5-51	F.S. Middleton	W v HB	1919/20
Wellington College Ground	1	W v A	1923/24	W	569	v A	1923/24	163	J.S. Hiddleston	W v A	1923/24
		only match		A	280	v W	1923/24	6-172	S.G. Smith	A v W	1923/24
Sportsground † Palmerston North	50	CD v C	1950/51	W	590-8d	v CD	2004/05	236	J.D. Ryder	W v CD	2004/05
		CD v A	2005/06	A	71	v CD	2001/02	7-31	H.B. Cave	CD v A	1952/53
Pukekura Park New Plymouth	51	CD v A	1950/51	O	543-8d	v CD	1978/79	242	M.D. Crowe	CD v O	1989/90
		CD v O	2005/06	CD	59	v A	1958/59	9-100	B.W. Yuile	CD v C	1965/66
McLean Park Napier	59	CD v O	1951/52	O	624	v CD	2006/07	217	L.R.P.L.Taylor	CD v O	2006/07
		CD v C	2006/07	CD	63	v W	2003/04	7-31	Abdul Qadir	P v Shell XI	1988/89
Trafalgar Park Nelson	28	N v W	1891/92	CD	448-3d	v O	1968/69	202*	B.E. Congdon	CD v O	1968/69
		CD v ND	1996/97	CD	65	v W	1995/96	7-23	B.A. Bolton	C v CD	1961/62
Cook's Gardens Wanganui	17	CD v WI	1955/56	MCC	376-7d	v CD	1960/61	138	M.G. Burgess	A v CD	1976/77
		CD v YNZ	1979/80	CD	71	v ND	1962/63	8-37	D.B. Clarke	ND v CD	1962/63
Seddon Park Hamilton	148	ND v A	1956/57	W	608-9d	v ND	1998/99	219	M.D. Bell	W v ND	1998/99
		ND v C	2006/07	ND	32	v A	1996/97	9-48	A.R. Tait	ND v A	1996/97

† now Fitzherbert Park *§ now Jade Stadium* ** now Allied Prime Basin Reserve*

	Ground	No of matches	First and most recent match	Highest and lowest team totals				Highest Innings Best Bowling			
27	Tauranga Domain	1	ND v CD 1965/66	CD	232	v ND	1965/66	64	G.V. Giles	ND v CD	1965
	Tauranga (Inner)		only match	ND	163	v CD	1965/66	5-41	B.W. Yuile	CD v ND	1965
28	Tauranga Domain	6	ND v C 1978/79	ND	370	v O	1982/83	127	J.G. Gibson	ND v C	1978
	Tauranga (Outer)		ND v A 1985/86	O	90	v ND	1982/83	6-75	D.A. Stirling	CD v ND	1981
29	Cobham Oval	11	ND v A 1966/67	ND	363	v CD	1983/84	195	J.M. Parker	ND v C	1972
	Whangarei		ND v C 2000/01	ND	127	v A	1966/67	7-30	R.S. Cunis	A v ND	1966
30	Queen Elizabeth Park	12	CD v A 1966/67	CD	414-7d	v A	1998/99	189	M.S. Sinclair	CD v W	1996
	Masterton		CD v W 2002/03	CD	86	v A	1966/67	6-33	A.J. Penn	W v CD	2002
31	Smallbone Park	17	ND v O 1968/69	CD	456	v ND	1995/96	237*	R.T. Latham	C v ND	1990
	Rotorua		ND v CD 1995/96	A	72	v ND	1991/92	7-74	G.D. Alabaster	O v ND	1968
32	Cornwall Park	3	A v U23 1970/71	A	274-8d	v U23	1970/71	102	R.W. Morgan	A v U23	1970
	Auckland		A v W 2000/01	A	274-9d	v U23	1976/77	8-75	H.J. Howarth	A v U23	1976
				A	75	v W	2000/01				
33	Horton Park	10	CD v ND 1972/73	CD	538	v C	2000/01	212*	D.P. Kelly	CD v C	2000
	Blenheim		CD v A 2002/03	ND	100	v CD	2001/02	7-36	A.M. Schwass	CD v ND	2001
34	Harry Barker Reserve	24	ND v O 1974/75	ND	516	v CD	2006/07	161*	V.R. Brown	C v ND	1986
	Gisborne		ND v CD 2006/07	O	77	v ND	1999/00	6-32	S.B. Styris	ND v O	1999
35	Eden Park No. 2 †	87	A v CD 1975/76	CD	594-8d	v A	1995/96	241	M.J. Horne	O v A	1997
	Auckland		A v CD 2006/07	CD	61	v A	1996/97	7-27	N.A. Mallender	O v A	1984
36	Queen's Park	13	O v CD 1975/76	CD	348	v O	1996/97	162	B.A. Edgar	W v O	1989
	Invercargill		O v CD 2002/03	O	68	v C	1977/78	8-31	D.G. Sewell	O v CD	1996
37	Bledisloe Park	2	ND v A 1976/77	W	297-5d	v ND	1989/90	123	R.H. Vance	W v ND	1989
	Pukekohe		ND v W 1989/90	ND	152	v W	1989/90	5-27	G.R. Larsen	W v ND	1989
38	Hutt Recreation Ground	14	W v ND 1976/77	W	316	v O	1983/84	145*	J.G. Wright	ND v W	1978
	Lower Hutt		W v C 1985/86	W	93	v WI	1979/80	8-24	E.J. Chatfield	W v ND	1979
39	Logan Park	3	O v U23 1977/78	O	313	v U23	1977/78	106	J.M. Parker	ND v O	1978
	Dunedin		O v C 1979/80	O	127	v C	1979/80	6-44	P.J. Petherick	O v U23	1977
40	Temuka Oval	1	YNZ v E 1977/78	E	310	v YNZ	1977/78	104	D.W. Randall	E v YNZ	1977
	Temuka		only match	YNZ	139	v E	1977/78	6-71	G. Miller	E v YNZ	1977
41	Molyneux Park	28	O v CD 1978/79	CD	444-8d	v O	2001/02	179	K.R. Rutherford	O v CD	1988
	Alexandra		O v SL A 2003/04	O	81	v CD	2001/02	8-27	J.T.C. Vaughan	A v O	1996
42	University Oval	14	O v Pak 1978/79	O	404	v ND	2006/07	221*	P.G. Fulton	C v O	2004
	Dunedin		O v A 2006/07	O	46	v Pak	1978/79	6-20	R.J. Webb	O v C	1983
43	Maidstone Park	1	W v CD 1979/80	W	216	v CD	1979/80	63	B.R. Taylor	W v CD	1979
	Upper Hutt		only match	CD	50	v W	1979/80	6-17	J.V. Coney	W v CD	1979
44	Dudley Park	15	C v W 1984/85	C	543-8d	v CD	1996/97	251*	C.Z. Harris	C v CD	1996
	Rangiora		C v W 2002/03	C	62	v A	1998/99	7-17	S.J. Maguiness	W v C	1984
45	Centennial Park	9	O v CD 1984/85	O	430	v CD	1984/85	182	K.R. Rutherford	O v W	1987
	Oamaru		O v W 1998/99	C	94	v O	1994/95	6-36	S.W. Duff	CD v O	1985
46	Levin Domain	3	CD v C 1985/86	W	435-5d	v CD	1987/88	205*	E.B. McSweeney	W v CD	1987
	Levin		CD v W 1987/88	C	68	v CD	1985/86	6-28	P.J. Visser	CD v C	1985
47	Recreational Ground	2	ND v CD 1986/87	CD	368-3d	v ND	1986/87	151	M.D. Crowe	CD v ND	1986
	Morrinsville		ND v W 1988/89	ND	198	v CD	1986/87	5-71	K.W. Martin	CD v ND	1986
48	Albert Park	1	ND v CD 1987/88	ND	259	v CD	1987/88	94	B.A. Young	ND v CD	1987
	Te Awamutu		only match	CD	135	v ND	1987/88	4-41	B.J. Barrett	ND v CD	1987
49	Victoria Park	11	CD v ND 1990/91	W	506-4d	v CD	1993/94	203*	M.S. Sinclair	CD v ND	1998
	Wanganui		CD v O 2002/03	CC	103	v SC	1997/98	6-20	B.C. Strang	Z v NZ XI	1995
50	Burnside Park	1	C v CD 1991/92	C	189-7	v CD	1991/92	63	T.E. Blain	CD v C	1991
	Christchurch		only match	C	124	v CD	1991/92	6-67	D.J. Leonard	CD v C	1991
51	Petone Recreation	2	W v O 1991/92	O	300-8d	v W	1991/92	107	E.B. McSweeney	W v O	1991
	Ground, Lower Hutt		W v A 1998/99	W	142	v O	1991/92	5-37	N.A. Mallender	O v W	1991
52	Sunnyvale	1	O v A 1992/93	O	193	v A	1992/93	51	I.S. Billcliff	O v A	1992
	Dunedin		only match	A	105	v O	1992/93	4-21	N.A. Mallender	O v A	1992
53	Lincoln Green	5	NZA v B 1997/98	NZA	459-8d	v PkA	1998/99	190	M.E. Parlane	NZA v B	1997
	Lincoln		NZA v SA 1998/99	B	130	v NZA	1997/98	6-69	Fazal-e-Akber	Pk A v NZA	1998

† now Eden Park Outer Oval

	Ground	No of matches	First and most recent match		Highest and lowest team totals			Highest Innings Best Bowling			
54	Aorangi Park Timaru	4	C v Z	1997/98	Z	422-8d v C	1997/98	196	A.D.R. Campbell	Z v C	1997/98
			C v O	2003/04	C	100 v Z	1997/98	6-56	M.J. Mason	CD v C	2002/03
55	Owen Delany Park Taupo	6	ND v O	1998/99	WI	450 v NZ A	1999/00	216*	S. Chanderpaul	WI v NZ A	1999/00
			ND v W	2002/03	A	131 v ND	1999/00	7-33	B.P. Martin	ND v A	1999/00
56	Colin Maiden Park Auckland	6	A v ND	1998/99	A	478 v ND	2002/03	175*	G.J. Hopkins	C v A	2002/03
			A v CD	2002/03	A	182 v ND	1999/00	5-64	A.R. Adams	A v ND	1999/00
57	Queen Elizabeth II Park Christchurch	24	C v O	1998/99	W	614-8 v C	2006/07	235	J.A.H. Marshall	ND v C	2001/02
			C v W	2006/07	C	114 v O	1998/99	9-13	P.J. Wiseman	C v CD	2004/05
58	BIL Oval † Lincoln	6	NI v E A	1999/00	A	627-7d v O	2006/07	205	T.G.McIntosh	A v O	2006/07
			CD v ND	2006/07	Pak	100 v NZ A	2000/01	6-70	A. Sheriyar	E A v NZ A	1999/00
59	Queenstown Events Centre	6	O v E	2001/02	NZ A	597-9d v SL A	2003/04	173	M.D. Bell	NZ A v SL A	2003/04
			O v C	2005/06	C	114 v O	2005/06	6-32	J.S. Patel	W v O	2004/05
60	North Harbour Stadium Auckland	1	A v O	2002/03	A	289 v O	2002/03	157	T.G. McIntosh	A v O	2002/03
			only match		O	185 v A	2002/03	4-34	S.B. O'Connor	O v A	2002/03
61	Rangiora Recreation * Ground	2	C v CD	2003/04	C	303 v CD	2003/04	93	B-J.Watling	ND v C	2006/07
			C v ND	2006/07	CD	178 v C	2003/04	5-35	W.A. Wisneski	C v CD	2003/04

† now Bert Sutcliffe Oval ** now MainPower Oval*

PROVINCIAL CAREER RECORDS

Performances for the following teams are not included in the Provincial Career Records:

Team	*Opponent*	
D. Reese's Canterbury XI	Wellington	1913/14
Canterbury/Otago	MCC	1936/37
Auckland/Wellington	MCC	1936/37
Auckland XI	New Zealand	1957/58
ND/CD	MCC	1958/59
Otago Invitation XI	MCC	1962/63
Canterbury XI	New Zealand Touring Team	1967/68

Most Games for One Province

150 players have now represented their province on 50 or more occasions in first-class cricket.

120	Gray E.J.	W
119	Vance R.H.	W
115	Bradburn G.E.	ND
108	Lees W.K.	O
104	Roberts A.D.G.	ND
103	McEwan P.E.	C
102	McSweeney E.B.	W
101	Latham R.T.	C
99	White D.J.	ND
97	Shrimpton M.J.F.	CD
95	Hart M.N.	ND
93	Young B.A.	ND
90	Blair B.R.	O
90*	Dickeson C.W.	ND
90	Morgan R.W.	A
90	McGregor S.N.	O
90	O'Sullivan D.R.	CD
89	Morrison J.F.M.	W
88	Boock S.L.	O
88	Franklin T.J.	A
88	Priest M.W.	C
88	Stead G.R.	C
87	Edgar B.A.	W
85	Duff S.W.	CD
85	Hart R.G.	ND
84	Chatfield E.J.	W
83	Blain T.E.	CD
82	Dunning B.	ND
82	Hadlee B.G.	C
82	Kuggeleijn C.M.	ND
82	Nevin C.J.	W
81	Blair W.L.	O
81	Briasco P.S.	CD
81	Harris C.Z.	C
80	Howarth H.J.	A
80	Hoskin R.N.	O
79	Yovich J.A.F.	ND
79	Larsen G.R.	W
78	Mallender N.A.	O
78	Robertson G.K.	CD
78	Bailey M.D.	ND
77	McIntyre J.M.	A
77	Stead D.W.	C
76	Germon L.K.	C
76	Douglas M.W.	CD
75	Parker J.M.	ND
75*	McCullum S.J.	O
75	Gaffaney C.B.	O
75	Marshall J.A.H.	ND
74	Coney J.V.	W
74	Sulzberger G.P.	CD
73	Sparling J.T.	A
73	Barnes A.C.	A
72	Hastings B.F.	C
72	Troup G.B.	A
72	Wells J.D.	W
72	Bell M.D.	W
69	Alabaster G.D.	O
69	Reid J.F.	A
69*	Boyle D.J.	C
69	Sinclair M.S.	CD
68	Burgess M.G.	A
68	Cameron F.J.	O
68	Sinclair B.W.	W
68	Rutherford K.R.	O
68*	Young R.A.	A
67	Edwards G.N.	CD
67	Harris R.M.	A
67	Patel D.N.	A
66	Puna N.	ND
66	Lawson R.A.	O
65	Alabaster J.C.	O
65	Brown V.R.	C
65	Hunt A.J.	A
65	Webb P.N.	A
65*	Wright M.J.E.	ND
64	Parlane M.E.	ND
64	Murray B.A.G.	W
63	Rutherford I.A.	O
63*	Stott L.W.	A
62	Cunis R.S.	A
62	Hadlee R.J.	C
62*	Smith C.J.P.	CD
62*	Cooper B.G.	ND
62	Papps M.H.W.	C
61	Yuile B.W.	CD
61	Campbell K.O.	O
61	Greatbatch M.J.	CD
61	Walker B.G.K.	A
60	Milburn B.D.	O
60	Newdick G.A.	W
60	Parsons A.E.W.	A
60	Sutcliffe B.	O
60	Roberts S.J.	C
59	Blair R.W.	W
59	Crowe J.J.	A
59	Smith I.D.S.	CD
59	Turner G.M.	O
59	Hartland B.R.	C
59	Smith L.D.	O
58	Dowling G.T.	C
58	Howarth G.P.	ND
58	Patrick W.R.	C
58	Reid J.R.	W
58	Ritchie T.D.	W
58	Thomson K.	C
58	Vivian G.E.	A
58	McIntosh T.G.	A
58	Martin B.P.	ND
57	Bull C.L.	C
57	Burns K.J.	O
57	Petrie E.C.	ND
57	Hamilton L.J.	CD
56	Brice A.W.S.	W
56	Motz R.C.	C
56	Canning T.K.	A
56	Patel J.S.	W
55	Bradburn W.P.	ND
55	Congdon B.E.	CD
55	Jordan A.B.	CD

55	Mills G.H.	O
55	Snedden M.C.	A
55	Sewell D.G.	O
55*	Griggs B.B.J.	CD
55	Marshall H.J.H.	ND
54	Bilby G.P.	W
54*	Crocker L.M.	ND
54	Cromb I.B.	C
54	McGirr H.M.	W
54	Moir A.M.	O
54	Sutton R.E.	A
54	Ward J.T.	C
54	Dobbs P.W.	O
54	Aldridge G.W.	ND
54	Cumming C.D.	O
53	Colquhoun I.A.	CD
53*	Pierce R.A.	CD
53*	Schofield R.M.	CD
53	Toynbee M.H.	CD
53	Watson W.	A
53	Nicol R.J.	A
53	Mason M.J.	CD
52*	Cederwall B.W.	W
51*	Knight A.R.	O
51	Brown S.W.	A
51	Thomson S.A.	ND
51	Jones R.A.	A
50	Boxshall C.	C
50	Butler L.C.	W
50	Horne M.J.	A

** entire first-class career*

Longest Careers for One Province

Seasons			
34	Read R.J.	Canterbury	1904/05-1937/38
31	Reese T.W.	Canterbury	1887/88-1917/18
29	Luckie M.M.F.	Wellington	1891/92-1919/20
27	Fowke J.N.	Canterbury	1880/81-1906/07
27	Downes A.D.	Otago	1887/88-1913/14
27	Dempster C.S.	Wellington	1921/22-1947/48
26	Reese D.	Canterbury	1895/96-1920/21
26	Knight A.R.	Otago	1918/19-1943/44

Most Consecutive Games for One Province

74	White D.J.	Northern Districts	1985/86-1992/93
73	Hart R.G.	Northern Districts	1992/93-2002/03
70	O'Sullivan D.R.	Central Districts	1974/75-1982/83
64	Germon L.K.	Canterbury	1987/88-1993/94
63	Stead D.W.	Canterbury	1975/76-1983/84
60	Smith C.J.P.	Central Districts	1984/85-1990/91
59	Puna N.	Northern Districts	1957/58-1968/69
57	Edwards G.N.	Central Districts	1975/76-1981/82
56	Young B.A.	Northern Districts	1983/84-1989/90
54*	Cromb I.B.	Canterbury	1929/30-1946/47
54	Roberts A.D.G.	Northern Districts	1970/71-1978/79
54	Burns K.J.	Otago	1984/85-1990/91
53	Alabaster G.D.	Otago	1963/64-1972/73
52	Smith L.D.	Otago	1940/41-1955/56
52	Duff S.W.	Central Districts	1989/90-1994/95
51	Morrison J.F.M.	Wellington	1975/76-1982/83
51	Reid J.F.	Auckland	1976/77-1982/83
51	McEwan P.E.	Canterbury	1984/85-1990/91

** his complete career*

Most Centuries for One Province

	Province	100s
Sutcliffe B.	O	17
Edgar B.A.	W	15
Bell M.D.	W	15
Rutherford K.R.	O	14
Greatbatch M.J.	CD	14
Reid J.R.	W	13
Turner G.M.	O	13
Crowe M.D.	CD	13
Sinclair M.S.	CD	13
Franklin T.J.	A	12
Vance R.H.	W	12
Harris C.Z.	C	12
Scott V.J.	A	11
Crowe J.J.	A	11
McEwan P.E.	C	11
Papps M.H.W.	C	11
Hick G.A.	ND	10
Hadlee W.A.	C	10
Burgess M.G.	A	10
Stead G.R.	C	10
McIntosh T.G.	A	10

Most Runs for One Province

	Province	M	In	NO	HS	Runs	Ave	100
Edgar B.A.	W	87	160	3	162	6494	44.17	15
Vance R.H.	W	119	205	18	254*	6440	34.43	12
Sutcliffe B.	O	60	110	8	385*	6028	59.09	17
McEwan P.E.	C	103	185	11	155	5940	34.13	11
Latham R.T.	C	101	176	17	237*	5919	37.22	8
Roberts A.D.G.	ND	104	192	35	128*	5533	35.24	7
Harris C.Z.	C	81	121	31	251*	5293	58.81	12
Blair B.R.	O	90	154	5	143	5057	33.93	7
Franklin T.J.	A	88	157	14	181	5051	35.25	12
Rutherford K.R.	O	68	121	7	226*	5051	44.30	14
Sinclair M.S.	CD	69	118	11	203*	4992	46.65	13
Bell M.D.	W	72	127	11	219	4915	42.37	15
Morrison J.F.M.	W	89	160	22	180*	4694	34.01	6
White D.J.	ND	99	173	15	209	4656	29.46	7
Bradburn G.E.	ND	115	188	23	148*	4614	27.96	4
Parker J.M.	ND	75	139	19	195	4611	38.42	7
Shrimpton M.J.F.	CD	97	171	15	150	4551	29.17	5
Blain T.E.	CD	83	145	15	161	4547	34.97	7
Reid J.R.	W	58	102	8	296	4538	48.27	13
Turner G.M.	O	59	109	14	186*	4439	46.72	13
Hadlee B.G.	C	82	151	11	163*	4429	31.63	6
Stead G.R.	C	88	146	10	190	4410	32.42	10
Greatbatch M.J.	CD	61	107	8	202*	4363	44.07	14
Gaffaney C.B.	O	75	138	11	194	4326	34.06	7
Briasco P.S.	CD	81	146	16	157	4301	33.08	6
McSweeney E.B.	W	102	153	23	205*	4296	33.04	5
McGregor S.N.	O	90	167	13	114*	4259	27.65	3
Crowe J.J.	A	59	95	9	156	4245	49.36	11
Gray E.J.	W	120	181	38	128*	4228	29.56	5
Burgess M.G.	A	68	116	13	146	4228	41.04	10
Papps M.H.W.	C	62	108	6	192	4171	40.89	11
Morgan R.W.	A	90	154	8	166	4162	28.50	7

Highest Averages

2000 RUNS/45.00 AVE	Province	M	In	NO	HS	Runs	Ave	100
Hick G.A.	ND	17	30	4	211*	2055	79.03	10
Crowe M.D.	CD	32	55	7	242	3299	68.72	13
Scott V.J.	A	44	74	15	204	3546	60.10	11
Sutcliffe B.	O	60	110	8	385	6028	59.09	17
Harris C.Z.	C	81	121	31	251*	5293	58.81	12
Jones A.H.	W	39	67	11	181*	2978	53.17	7
Wallace W.M.	A	47	73	5	211	3409	50.13	9
Fulton P.G.	C	38	67	9	301*	2886	49.75	5
Crowe J.J.	A	59	95	9	156	4245	49.36	11
Reid J.R.	W	58	102	8	296	4538	48.27	13
Turner G.M.	O	59	109	14	186*	4439	46.72	13
Sinclair M.S.	CD	69	118	11	203*	4992	46.65	13
Hiddleston J.S.	W	41	75	1	212	3413	46.12	8

Most Wickets for One Province

	Province	M	Wkts	Runs	Ave	5WI	10WM	Best
Chatfield E.J.	W	84	403	7531	18.68	23	7	8-24
Boock S.L.	O	88	399	8235	20.63	28	5	8-57
O'Sullivan D.R.	CD	90	392	9560	24.38	21	3	6-40
Gray E.J.	W	120	357	9778	27.38	13	3	8-37
Howarth H.J.	A	80	332	7361	22.17	18	4	8-75
Blair R.W.	W	59	330	5004	15.16	30	10	9-72
Priest M.W.	C	88	290	8501	29.31	12	3	9-95
Downes A.D.	O	44	287	3902	13.59	33	13	8-35
Hadlee R.J.	C	62	285	4600	16.14	19	2	7-49
Moir A.M.	O	54	282	5926	21.01	20	5	8-37
Dickeson C.W.	ND	90	282	8242	29.22	9	2	7-79
Mallender N.A.	O	78	268	5433	20.27	14	3	7-27
Alabaster J.C.	O	65	264	5738	21.73	14	3	6-39
Cameron F.J.	O	68	258	5204	20.17	9	—	6-21

Most Dismissals for One Province

WICKETKEEPING	Province	M	Caught	Stumped	Total
McSweeney E.B.	W	102	289	39	328
Lees W.K.	O	108	208	36	244
Hart R.G.	ND	85	228	15	243
Germon L.K.	C	76	217	21	238
Nevin C.J.	W	82	223	8	231
Young R.A.	A	68	206	5	211
Young B.A.	ND	93	179	11	190
Milburn B.D.	O	60	148	17	165
Ward J.T.	C	54	136	17	153
Kelly P.J.	A	48	140	12	152
Griggs B.B.J	CD	55	142	5	147
Blain T.E.	CD	83	124	19	143
Croy M.G.	O	42	127	4	131
Colquhoun I.A.	CD	53	102	28	130
Smith I.D.S.	CD	59	119	11	130
Sigley M.A.	CD	44	124	4	128
Schofield R.M.	CD	53	107	15	122
Robinson S.A.	O	45	117	5	122
Wright M.J.E.	ND	65	104	17	121
Petrie E.C.	ND	57	90	22	112
Mills G.H.	O	55	78	29	107
Boxshall C.	C	50	70	36	106
Hopkins G.J.	C	41	91	10	101
Therkleson I.J.	W	39	93	7	100

Represented Most Provinces

5	Guy J.W.	CD, C, O, W, ND
4	Anderson R.W.	C, ND, O, CD
	Congdon B.E.	CD, W, O, C
	Crawshaw W.J.	O, C, W, T
	Hounsell A.R.	C, W, A, ND
	Howell L.G.	C, CD, A, ND
	McGregor P.B.	A, ND, W, CD
	Worker R.V. de R.	A, C, O, W
3	Alabaster G.D.	O, C, ND
	Allcott C.F.W.	HB, A, O
	Alpe S.	A, C, W
	Andrews B.	C, CD, O
	Beard D.D.	W, CD, ND
	Billcliff I.S.	O, W, A
	Bracewell B.P.	CD, O, ND
	Cairns B.L.	CD, O, ND
	Clark L.A.	W, O, A
	Collinge R.O.	CD, W, ND
	Crowe M.D.	A, CD, W
	D'Arcy J.W.	C, O, W
	Frith W.	C, O, W
	Hastings B.F.	W, CD, C
	Holland P.J.	CD, ND, W
	Hopkins G.J.	ND, C, O
3	Hussey J.M.	HB, O, A
	Jones A.H.	CD, O, W
	King R.T.	O, A, CD
	Lane M.E.L.	W, CD, C
	Lusk Harold B.	A, C, W
	McBeath D.J.	O, C, S
	McGlashan P.D.	CD, O, ND
	Macleod D.N.	CD, W, C
	Mills G.	A, HB, O
	Moloney D.A.R.	O, W, C
	Neutze P.S.	O, A, ND
	Paterson J.L.	C, HB, A
	Riley J.D.	C, W, A
	Sampson H.C.	CD, O, C
	Salmon W.J.	W, HB, T
	Stephenson F.C.	O, W, C
	Sutcliffe B.	A, O, ND
	Tracy S.R.	A, C, O
	Twose R.G.	ND, CD, W
	Uttley K.F.M.	O, C, W
	Watson H.C.	O, C, W
	Wiseman P.J.	A, O, C
	Wright E.	A, W, C
	Wright J.G.	ND, C, A

T *Taranaki* S *Southland* HB *Hawke's Bay*

PROVINCIAL RECORDS

MOST WINS IN SUCCESSION

8	Canterbury	1873/74 to 1880/81
7	Canterbury	1912/13 to 1913/14
7	Wellington	1960/61 to 1961/62
6	Canterbury	1910/11 to 1911/12
6	Auckland	1939/40 to 1943/44
6	Wellington	1962/63 to 1963/64
6	Canterbury	1996/97

MOST LOSSES IN SUCCESSION

10	Otago	1961/62 to 1963/64
8	Otago	1929/30 to 1931/32
7	Otago	1874/75 to 1880/81
7	Otago	1920/21 to 1922/23
7	Otago	1926/27 to 1927/28
7	Auckland	1997/98 to 1998/99
7	Otago	2001/02

MOST DRAWS IN SUCCESSION

9	ND	1974/75 to 1975/76
8	Wellington	1974/75 to 1975/76
7	ND	1968/69 to 1969/70
7	CD	1991/92 to 1992/93
7	Wellington	1992/93

MOST GAMES WITHOUT A WIN

38	CD	1973/74 to 1978/79
36	Otago	1960/61 to 1965/66
24	ND	1972/73 to 1975/76
21	ND	1966/67 to 1970/71

MOST GAMES WITHOUT A LOSS

24	Wellington	1984/85 to 1986/87
23	Auckland	1978/79 to 1981/82
22	Auckland	1934/35 to 1943/44
18	Auckland	1961/62 to 1964/65
18	Canterbury	1966/67 to 1969/70

MOST GAMES WITHOUT A DRAW

42	Canterbury	1896/97 to 1909/10
30	Otago	1894/95 to 1907/08
22	Canterbury	1869/70 to 1883/84
20	Canterbury	1919/20 to 1924/25

Highest Individual Innings

for and against the major sides in NZ

	For		Against	
Auckland	290	W.N. Carson v Otago at Dunedin, 1936/37	355	B. Sutcliffe for Otago at Dunedin, 1949/50
Canterbury	301*	P.G. Fulton v Auckland at Christchurch, 2002/03	385	B. Sutcliffe for Otago at Christchurch, 1952/53
Central Dist.	242	M.D. Crowe v Otago at New Plymouth, 1989/90	264	B. Sutcliffe for Otago at Dunedin, 1959/60
Northern Dist.	235	J.A.H. Marshall v Canterbury at Chch, 2001/02	296	J.R. Reid for Wellington at Wellington, 1962/63
Otago	385	B. Sutcliffe v Canterbury at Christchurch, 1952/53	290	W.N. Carson for Auckland at Dunedin, 1936/37
Wellington	296	J.R. Reid v Northern Dist. at Wellington, 1962/63	207	R.T. Hart for Central Dist. at Wellington, 1985/86
MCC/England	336*	W.R. Hammond v NZ at Auckand, 1932/33	222	N.J. Astle for NZ at Christchurch, 2001/02
Australia	293	V.T. Trumper v Canterbury at Christchurch 1913/14	198	W.A. Hadlee for Otago at Dunedin, 1945/46
South Africa	275*	D.J. Cullinan v NZ at Auckland, 1998/99	170	S.B. Styris for NZ at Auckland, 2003/04
West Indies	258	S.M. Nurse v NZ at Christchurch, 1968/69	214	M.S. Sinclair for NZ at Wellington, 1999/00
Pakistan	271	Javed Miandad v NZ at Auckland, 1988/89	204	M.S. Sinclair for NZ at Christchurch, 2000/01
India	192	M. Azharuddin v NZ at Auckand, 1989/90	239	G.T. Dowling for NZ at Christchurch, 1967/68
Sri Lanka	267	P.A. de Silva v NZ at Wellington, 1990/91	299	M.D. Crowe for NZ at Wellington, 1990/91
New Zealand	299	M.D. Crowe v Sri Lanka at Wellington, 1990/91	336*	W.R. Hammond for England at Auckland, 1932/33
Zimbabwe	196	A.D.R. Campbell v Canterbury at Timaru, 1997/98	157	M.J. Horne for NZ at Auckland, 1997/98
Bangladesh	102	Al Sahariar v Southern at Dunedin, 1997/98	190	M.E. Parlane for NZ Academy at Lincoln, 1997/98

Best Bowling

for and against the major sides in NZ

	For		Against	
Auckland	9-36	A.F. Wensley v Otago at Auckland, 1929/30	9-48	A.R. Tait v Auckland at Hamilton, 1996/97
Canterbury	10-28	A.E. Moss v Wellington at Christchurch, 1889/90	9-72	F.H. Cooke for Otago at Christchurch, 1884/85
Central Dist.	9-100	B.W. Yuile v Canterbury at New Plymouth, 1965/66	9-13	P.J. Wiseman for Canterbury at Christchurch, 2004/05
Northern Dist.	9-48	A.R. Tait v Auckland at Hamilton, 1996/97	9-93	P.J. Petherick for Otago at Dunedin, 1975/76
Otago	9-50	A.H. Fisher v Queensland at Dunedin, 1896/97	9-36	A.E. Wensley for Auckland at Auckland, 1929/30
Wellington	9-67	A.W.S. Brice v Auckland at Wellington, 1918/19	10-28	A.E. Moss for Canterbury at Christchurch, 1889/90
MCC/England	8-45	F.S. Trueman v Otago at Dunedin, 1958/59	7-50	H.W. Monaghan for Wellington at Wellington, 1906/07
Australia	8-27	W.J. Whitty v Auckland at Auckland, 1909/10	8-66	G.O. Rabone for Auckland at Auckland, 1956/57
South Africa	6-47	P.M. Pollock v NZ at Wellington, 1963/64	7-75	C.F.W. Allcott for Auckland at Auckland, 1931/32
West Indies	7-37	C.A. Walsh v NZ at Wellington, 1994/95	7-27	C.L. Cairns for at Hamilton, 1999/00
Pakistan	7-16	Farooq Hamid v Wellington at Wellington, 1964/65	7-95	N.A. Huxford for Wellington at Wellington, 1964/65
India	8-76	E.A.S. Prasanna v NZ at Auckland, 1975/76	7-23	R.J. Hadlee for at Wellington, 1975/76
Sri Lanka	6-79	C.P.H. Ramanayake v Wellington at Wellington, 1990/91	6-45	C.H. Thiele for Canterbury at Christchurch, 1982/83
New Zealand	8-100	G.F. Cresswell v Australia B at Dunedin, 1949/50	8-33	H.S.T.L. Hendry for NSW at Wellington, 1923/24
Zimbabwe	6-20	B.C. Strang v NZ XI at Wanganui, 1995/96	5-16	A.R. Tait for NZ A at Dunedin, 1997/98
Bangladesh	6-143	Hasibul Hussain v Northern at Hamilton, 1997/98	7-53	C.L. Cairns for NZ at Hamilton, 2001/02

Highest Totals

for and against the major sides in NZ

	For		Against	
Auckland	693-9 dec	v Canterbury at Auckland, 1939/40	658	by Australians at Auckland, 1913/14
Canterbury	777	v Otago at Christchurch, 1996/97	693-9 dec	by Auckland at Auckland, 1939/40
Central Dist.	594-8 dec	v Auckland at Auckland, 1995/96	624	by Otago at Napier, 2006/07
Northern Dist.	523-7 dec	v Otago at Hamilton, 2006/07	608-9 dec	by Wellington at Hamilton, 1998/99
Otago	624	v Central Districts at Napier, 2006/07	777	by Canterbury at Christchurch, 1996/97
Wellington	614-8	v Canterbury at Christchurch, 2006/07	613-7d	by Canterbury at Christchurch, 2006/07
MCC/England	653-5 dec	v New Zealand at Dunedin, 1935/36	537	by New Zealand at Wellington, 1983/84
Australia	663	v New Zealand at Auckland, 1920/21	484	by New Zealand at Wellington, 1973/74
South Africa	621-5 dec	v New Zealand at Auckland, 1998/99	595	by New Zealand at Auckland, 2003/04
West Indies	660-5 dec	v New Zealand at Wellington, 1994/95	518-9d	by New Zealand at Wellington, 1999/00
Pakistan	616-5 dec	v New Zealand at Auckland, 1988/89	563	by New Zealand at Hamilton, 2003/04
India	512	v President's XI at New Plymouth, 1989/90	502	by New Zealand at Christchurch, 1967/68
Sri Lanka	498	v New Zealand at Napier, 2004/05	671-4	by New Zealand at Wellington, 1990/91
New Zealand	671-4	v Sri Lanka at Wellington, 1990/91	663	by Australia at Auckland, 1920/21
Zimbabwe	422-8 dec	v Canterbury at Timaru, 1997/98	487-7d	by New Zealand at Wellington, 2000/01
Bangladesh	286-9 dec	v Southern at Dunedin, 1997/98	495	by Auckland at Auckland, 2001/02

Lowest Totals

for and against the major sides in NZ

	For		Against	
Auckland	13	v Canterbury at Auckland, 1877/78	28	by Hawke's Bay at Auckland, 1910/11
Canterbury	25	v Otago at Christchurch, 1866/67	13	by Auckland at Auckland, 1877/78
Central Dist.	50	v Wellington at Upper Hutt, 1979/80	68	by Canterbury at Levin, 1985/86
Northern Dist.	32	v Auckland at Hamilton, 1996/97	51	by Central Dist. at Hamilton, 1957/58
Otago	34	v Wellington at Dunedin, 1956/57	25	by Canterbury at Christchurch, 1866/67
Wellington	19	v Nelson at Nelson, 1885/86	32	by Hawke's Bay at Wellington, 1883/84
MCC/England	64	v New Zealand at Wellington, 1977/78	26	by New Zealand at Auckland, 1954/55
Australia	103	v New Zealand at Auckland, 1985/86	42	by New Zealand at Wellington, 1945/46
South Africa	165	v NZ Academy XI at Nelson, 1994/95	73	by Canterbury at Christchurch, 1963/64
West Indies	77	v New Zealand at Auckland, 1955/56	74	by New Zealand at Dunedin, 1955/56
Pakistan	100	v New Zealand A at Lincoln, 2000/01	46	by Otago at Dunedin, 1978/79
India	81	v New Zealand at Wellington, 1975/76	94	by New Zealand at Hamilton, 2002/03
Sri Lanka	93	v New Zealand at Wellington, 1982/83	109	by New Zealand at Napier, 1994/95
New Zealand	26	v England at Auckland, 1954/55	64	by England at Wellington, 1977/78
Zimbabwe	67	v New Zealand A at Dunedin, 1997/98	100	by Canterbury at Timaru, 1997/98
Bangladesh	108	v New Zealand at Hamilton, 2001/02	311	by Central at Wellington, 1997/98

AUCKLAND

Highest Totals

693-9 dec	v Canterbury	Auckland	1939/40
643	v Canterbury	Auckland	1919/20
627-7d	v Otago	Lincoln	2006/07
590	v Canterbury	Auckland	1937/38
579	v Otago	Auckland	1909/10
550-5 dec	v Otago	Auckland	1936/37
547-8 dec	v Northern Districts	Auckland	2000/01
539	v Otago	Dunedin	1926/27
539	v Canterbury	Christchurch	1907/08
537	v Hawke's Bay	Auckland	1920/21
537	v Canterbury	Christchurch	1930/31

Lowest Totals

13	v Canterbury	Auckland	1877/78
48	v Otago	Dunedin	1889/90
48	v Wellington	Wellington	1889/90
53	v Wellington	Wellington	1873/74
55	v Otago	Dunedin	1900/01
56	v Canterbury	Auckland	1931/32
69	v Northern Districts	Auckland	1963/64
71	v Central Districts	Palmerston North	2001/02
72	v Lord Hawke's XI	Auckland	1902/03
72	v Northern Districts	Rotorua	1991/92

Most Appearances

90	Morgan R.W.	67	Harris R.M.	58	McIntosh T.G.
88	Franklin T.J.	67	Patel D.N.	56	Canning T.K.
80	Howarth H.J.	65	Hunt A.J.	55	Snedden M.C.
77	McIntyre J.M.	65	Webb P.N.	54	Sutton R.E.
73	Sparling J.T.	63	Stott L.W.	53	Watson W.
73	Barnes A.C.	62	Cunis R.S.	53	Nicol R.J.
72	Troup G.B.	61	Walker B.G.K.	51	Brown S.W.
69	Reid J.F.	60	Parsons A.E.W.	51	Jones R.A.
68	Burgess M.G.	59	Crowe J.J.	50	Horne M.J.
68	Young R.A.	58	Vivian G.E.		

Longest Careers

Seasons			*Seasons*		
25	Garrard D.R.	1917/18-1941/42	21	Cleverley D.C.	1930/31-1950/51
24	Wallace W.M.	1933/34-1956/57	20	Stemson W.I.	1889/90-1908/09
22	Anthony A.	1909/10-1930/31	20	Horspool E.	1909/10-1928/29
22	McIntyre J.M.	1961/62-1982-83	20	Weir G.L.	1927/28-1946/47
21	Yates R.J.	1873/74-1893/94	20	Morgan R.W.	1957/58-1976/77

Benefits

Troup G.B.	1986/87	Watson W.	1994/95
Snedden M.C.	1989/90	Patel D.N.	1995/96
Crowe J.J.	1990/91	Morrison D.K.	1996/97
Franklin T.J.	1991/92	Pringle C.	1998/99
Hunt A.J.	1992/93	Barnes A.C.	2002/03

Batting

2000 RUNS	Career	M	In	NO	HS	Runs	Ave	100
Franklin T.J.	1980/81-1992/93	88	157	14	181	5051	35.25	12
Crowe J.J.	1982/83-1991/92	59	95	9	156	4245	49.36	11
Burgess M.G.	1966/67-1979/80	68	116	13	146	4228	41.04	10
Morgan R.W.	1957/58-1976/77	90	154	8	166	4162	28.50	7
Reid J.F.	1975/76-1987/88	69	117	17	173	3733	37.33	5
Patel D.N.	1985/86-1994/95	67	102	9	204	3648	39.22	8
Harris R.M.	1955/56-1973/74	67	119	4	157	3598	31.28	3
Scott V.J.	1937/38-1952/53	44	74	15	204	3546	60.10	11
Wallace W.M.	1933/34-1956/57	47	73	5	211	3409	50.13	9
Webb P.N.	1976/77-1986/87	65	114	18	136	3307	34.44	5
Horne M.J.	1992/93-2005/06	50	80	4	209*	3184	41.89	9
McIntosh T.G.	1998/99-2006/07	58	98	9	205	3035	34.10	10
Sparling J.T.	1956/57-1970/71	73	123	17	105	2977	28.08	2
Barnes A.C.	1993/94-2004/05	73	113	10	134*	2893	28.08	4
Jones R.A.	1993/94-2006/07	51	92	6	143	2834	32.95	5
Parsons A.E.W.	1973/74-1982/83	60	113	8	132	2820	26.85	3
Nicol R.J.	2001/02-2006/07	53	82	10	160	2759	38.31	6
Hemus L.G.	1904/05-1921/22	39	71	4	148	2701	40.31	8
Weir G.L.	1927/28-1946/47	42	67	6	191	2625	43.03	7
Whitelaw P.E.	1928/29-1946/47	42	68	4	195	2417	37.76	5
Jarvis T.W.	1964/65-1976/77	46	80	3	118*	2403	31.20	2
Horne P.A.	1979/80-1990/91	40	67	6	209	2380	39.01	4
Vivian G.E.	1966/67-1978/79	58	98	16	111*	2327	28.37	2
Vaughan J.T.C.	1989/90-1996/97	48	81	14	127	2269	33.86	2
Gedye S.G.	1956/57-1964/65	40	73	4	104	2169	31.43	3
Vincent L.	1997/98-2006/07	40	61	5	185*	2132	38.07	4
Mills J.E.	1925/26-1937/38	35	63	1	185	2126	34.29	3
Hunt A.J.	1981/82-1992/93	65	99	15	102*	2069	24.63	1
Canning T.K.	1999/00-2006/07	56	82	10	115	2067	28.70	3
Redmond R.E.	1969/70-1975/76	29	55	4	141*	2004	39.29	4

CENTURY ON DEBUT FOR PROVINCE

† 112*	Brook-Smith W.	v Hawke's Bay	Auckland	1904/05
157	Relf A.E.	v Canterbury	Christchurch	1907/08
† 119	Snedden C.A.	v Hawke's Bay	Auckland	1920/21
† 122	Scott V.J.	v Canterbury	Auckland	1937/38
† 122	Kerr A.C.	v Wellington	Auckland	1941/42
174	Patel D.N.	v Canterbury	Christchurch	1985/86
† 106* & 1	Vaughan J.T.C.	v Wellington	Wellington	1989/90

† indicates player was making his first-class debut

MOST RUNS IN A SEASON

		Runs	Ave
Crowe J.J.	1991/92	1063	62.52
McIntosh T.G.	2002/03	820	58.57
Crowe M.D.	1982/83	736	52.57
Patel D.N.	1986/87	723	55.61
Horne M.J.	2001/02	696	69.60
Horne M.J.	2002/03	671	47.92
Horne P.A.	1986/87	670	67.00
Crowe J.J.	1990/91	667	44.46
Franklin T.J.	1982/83	664	51.07
Nicol R.J.	2002/03	664	47.42
Crowe J.J.	1988/89	644	71.55
Burgess M.G.	1977/78	643	46.00
Jones R.A.	2006/07	630	45.00
Mills K.D.	2000/01	606	101.00
Crowe J.J.	1989/90	600	42.85

HIGHEST INDIVIDUAL INNINGS

290	Carson W.N.	v Otago	Dunedin	1936/37
256	Smith S.G.	v Canterbury	Auckland	1919/20
211	Wallace W.M.	v Canterbury	Auckland	1939/40
209*	Brown S.W.	v Canterbury	Christchurch	1990/91
209*	Horne M.J.	v Northern Districts	Auckland	2003/04
209	Horne P.A.	v Northern Districts	Auckland	1988/89
205	McIntosh T.G.	v Otago	Lincoln	2006/07
204	Scott V.J.	v Otago	Dunedin	1947/48
204	Patel D.N.	v Northern Districts	Auckland	1991/92
198	Scott V.J.	v Canterbury	Auckland	1939/40

MOST CENTURIES IN A SEASON

4	Franklin T.J.	1987/88
4	Crowe J.J.	1991/92

TOTAL NUMBER OF CENTURIES — 273

Most in one season	11	2001/02
1st	Mills G. 106* v Wellington	1895/96
100th	Playle W.R. 102* v Central Districts	1957/58
200th	Crowe J.J. 102 v Otago	1991/92

Bowling

150 WICKETS	*Career*	*M*	*Wkts*	*Runs*	*Ave*	*5WI*	*10WM*	*Best*
Howarth H.J.	1963/64-1978/79	80	332	7361	22.17	18	4	8-75
Sparling J.T.	1956/57-1970/71	73	248	5327	21.47	17	3	7-49
McIntyre J.M.	1961/62-1982/83	77	238	5447	22.88	8	1	6-84
Cunis R.S.	1960/61-1973/74	62	229	4603	20.10	14	2	7-29
Snedden M.C.	1977/78-1989/90	55	217	4631	21.34	10	2	7-49
Stott L.W.	1969/70-1983/84	63	214	5341	24.95	8	—	6-68
Troup G.B.	1974/75-1986/87	72	200	5213	26.06	4	—	6-48
Canning T.K.	1999/00-2006/07	56	196	4822	24.60	6	—	6-44
Adams A.R.	1997/98-2006/07	46	192	4309	22.44	8	1	6-25
Patel D.N.	1985/86-1994/95	67	184	4298	23.35	8	2	7-83
Watson W.	1984/85-1994/95	53	176	4110	23.35	7	—	7-60
Bracewell J.G.	1982/83-1989/90	42	168	4189	24.93	8	2	7-65
Morrison D.K.	1985/86-1996/97	49	168	4034	24.01	7	—	7-82
Cowie J.	1932/33-1949/50	34	154	3379	21.94	6	—	6-44
Sutton R.E.	1958/59-1973/74	54	152	3364	22.13	6	—	7-64

MOST WICKETS IN A SEASON

		Wkts	*Ave*
Canning T.K.	2002/03	46	21.97
Bracewell J.G.	1986/87	43	20.90
Hayes J.A.	1957/58	42	11.38
Lankham W.	1882/83	41	6.31

BEST IN AN INNINGS

9-36	Wensley A.F.	v Otago	Auckland	1929/30
9-75	Neill R.	v Canterbury	Auckland	1891/92
9-86	Neill R.	v Canterbury	Auckland	1897/98
8-27	Vaughan J.T.C.	v Otago	Alexandra	1996/97
8-36	Rees A.W.	v Otago	Dunedin	1889/90
8-51	Neill R.	v Wellington	Auckland	1895/96
8-51	Garrard D.R.	v Canterbury	Auckland	1921/22
8-55	Smith S.G.	v Wellington	Auckland	1919/20
8-65	Smith S.G.	v Otago	Auckland	1923/24

8-66	Rabone G.O.	v Australia	Auckland	1956/57
8-75	Cleverley D.C.	v Wellington	Wellington	1945/46
8-75	Howarth H.J.	v NZ Under 23 XI	Auckland	1976/77

BEST IN A MATCH

14-63	Rees A.W.	v Otago	Dunedin	1889/90
14-65	Hayes J.A.	v Wellington	Auckland	1957/58
14-94	Howarth H.J.	v Otago	Dunedin	1973/74
14-119	Pringle C.	v Otago	Dunedin	1993/94
13-35	Lankham W.	v Taranaki	Auckland	1882/83
13-85	Cunis R.S.	v Canterbury	Christchurch	1963/64
13-104	Oliff C.	v Wellington	Auckland	1912/13
13-107	Smith S.G.	v Wellington	Auckland	1919/20

Wicketkeeping

100 DISMISSALS	*Career*	*M*	*Caught*	*Stumped*	*Total*
Young R.A.	1998/99-2006/07	68	206	5	211
Kelly P.J.	1981/82-1988/89	48	140	12	152

MOST DISMISSALS IN A SEASON

35	(33ct/2st)	Young R.A.	2001/02
35	(35ct)	Young R.A.	2002/03

MOST DISMISSALS IN A MATCH

8	(2ct/6st)	Kent L.A.W. v Wellington	Wellington	1944/45
8	(8ct)	Smith I.D.S. v Central Districts	Nelson	1988/89
8	(8ct)	Vincent L. v Central Districts	Palmerston North	2000/01

MOST DISMISSALS IN AN INNINGS

6	(6ct)	Young R.A.v Wellington	Wellington	2002/03

MOST CATCHES IN A MATCH

8	Smith I.D.S. v Central Districts	Nelson	1988/89
8	Vincent L. v Central Districts	Palmerston North	2000/01

MOST CATCHES IN AN INNINGS

6	Young R.A.v Wellington	Wellington	2002/03

Fielding

MOST CATCHES IN A MATCH

6	Williams N.T. v Hawke's Bay	Napier	1894/95
6	Jarvis T.W. v Northern Districts	Hamilton	1968/69

MOST CATCHES IN AN INNINGS

5	Williams N.T. v Hawkes Bay	Napier	1894/95
5	Crowe J.J. v Canterbury	Auckland	1988/89

Record Partnerships

FOR

Wicket	*Score*	*Batsmen*	*Against*	*At*	*Date*
1st	286	B. Sutcliffe & D.D. Taylor	Canterbury	Auckland	1948/49
2nd	241	T.J. Franklin & J.J. Crowe	Wellington	Wellington	1988/89
3rd	445	P.E. Whitelaw & W.N. Carson	Otago	Dunedin	1936/37
4th	280	J.J. Crowe & D.N. Patel	ND	Auckland	1991/92
5th	347*	M.J. Horne & A.C. Barnes	ND	Auckland	2003/04
6th	209*	A.C. Parore & A.P. O'Dowd	Otago	Dunedin	1991/92
7th	224	V.J. Scott & A.M. Matheson	Canterbury	Auckland	1937/38
8th	189	W.N. Carson & A.M. Matheson	Wellington	Auckland	1938/39
9th	122	R.S. Cunis & H.T. Schuster	Wellington	Wellington	1964/65
10th	119	W.N. Carson & J. Cowie	Otago	Auckland	1937/38

AGAINST

Wicket	*Score*	*Batsmen*	*For*	*At*	*Date*
1st	373	B. Sutcliffe & L. Watt	Otago	Auckland	1950/51
2nd	287	M.D. Bell & J.D. Wells	Wellington	Auckland	1997/98
3rd	261*	M.P. Maynard & S.A. Thomson	ND	Hamilton	1990/91
4th	252	S.A. Thomson & B.A. Young	ND	Auckland	1990/91
5th	266	B. Sutcliffe & W.S. Haig	Otago	Dunedin	1949/50
6th	220	M.H. Toynbee & I.D.S. Smith	CD	Napier	1982/83
7th	165	R.K. Brown & M.E.L. Lane	CD	Palmerston Nth	1993/94
8th	166	R.J. Hadlee & D.R. Hadlee	Canterbury	Christchurch	1983/84
9th	208	W.C. McSkimming & B.E. Scott	Otago	Auckland	2004/05
10th	133	G.A. Bartlett & I.A. Colquhoun	CD	Auckland	1959/60

CANTERBURY

Highest Totals

777	v Otago	Christchurch	1996/97
613-7d	v Wellington	Christchurch	2006/07
559	v Central Districts	Christchurch	1993/94
549	v Northern Districts	Christchurch	1996/97
547-5 dec	v Wellington	Christchurch	1953/54
543-8 dec	v Central Districts	Rangiora	1996/97
537	v Central Districts	Blenheim	1996/97
534	v Central Districts	Palmerston North	1994/95
526-8 dec	v Wellington	Wellington	1931/32
524	v Northern Districts	Rangiora	1997/98

Lowest Totals

25	v Otago	Christchurch	1886/87
27	v Otago	Dunedin	1896/97
32	v Otago	Christchurch	1866/67
34	v Otago	Dunedin	1863/64
37	v Southland	Invercargill	1920/21
37	v Wellington	Wellington	1925/26
38	v Otago	Dunedin	1873/74
42	v Otago	Dunedin	1863/64

42	v Otago	Dunedin	1992/93
44	v Otago	Dunedin	1883/84
46	v Otago	Dunedin	1867/68
46	v Otago	Christchurch	1894/95
46	v Otago	Christchurch	1896/97
49	v Otago	Dunedin	1896/97

Most Appearances

103	McEwan P.E.
101	Latham R.T.
88	Priest M.W.
88	Stead G.R.
82	Hadlee B.G.
81	Harris C.Z.
77	Stead D.W.
76	Germon L.K.
72	Hastings B.F.
69	Boyle D.J.
65	Brown V.R.
62	Hadlee R.J.
62	Papps M.W.H.
60	Roberts S.J.
59	Hartland B.R.
58	Patrick W.R.
58	Dowling G.T.
58	Thomson K.
57	Bull C.L.
56	Motz R.C.
54	Cromb I.B.
54	Ward J.T.
50	Boxshall C.

Longest Careers

Seasons		
34	Read R.J.	1904/05-1937/38
31	Reese T.W.	1887/88-1917/18
27	Fowke J.N.	1880/81-1906/07
26	Reese D.	1895/96-1920/21
25	Moorhouse H.M.	1883/84-1907/08
22	Wheatley J.	1882/83-1903/04
22	Patrick W.R.	1905/06-1926/27
21	Stevens E.C.J.	1863/64-1883/84
21	Wilding F.	1881/82-1901/02
21	Ridley A.E.	1889/90-1909/10
20	Harman T.D.	1882/83-1901/02
20	Hadlee B.G.	1961/62-1980/81

Benefits

McEwan P.E.	1988/89
Hadlee R.J.	1989/90
Latham R.T.	1992/93
Germon L.K./Priest M.W.	1997/98
Harris C.Z.	1998/99
Cairns C.L.	1999/00

Batting

2000 RUNS	*Career*	*M*	*In*	*NO*	*HS*	*Runs*	*Ave*	*100*
McEwan P.E.	1977/78-1990/91	103	185	11	155	5940	34.13	11
Latham R.T.	1980/81-1994/95	101	176	17	237*	5919	37.22	8
Harris C.Z.	1989/90-2006/07	81	121	31	251*	5293	58.81	12
Hadlee B.G.	1961/62-1980/81	82	151	11	163*	4429	31.63	6
Stead G.R.	1993/94-2005/06	88	146	10	190	4410	32.42	10
Papps M.H.W.	1998/99-2006/07	62	108	6	192	4171	40.89	11
Dowling G.T.	1958/59-1971/72	58	100	7	206	3690	39.67	8
Hastings B.F.	1961/62-1976/77	72	122	8	226	3540	31.05	7
Priest M.W.	1984/85-1998/99	88	130	21	119	3457	31.71	4
Boyle D.J.	1980/81-1994/95	69	121	12	149	3216	29.50	3
Hadlee W.A.	1933/34-1951/52	44	80	7	194	3183	43.60	10
Stead D.W.	1969/70-1985/86	77	133	11	193*	3169	25.97	1
Cromb I.B.	1929/30-1946/47	54	96	5	171	2986	32.81	3
Fulton P.G.	2000/01-2006/07	38	67	9	301*	2886	49.75	5
Brown V.R.	1978/79-1986/87	65	111	11	161*	2872	28.72	5
Patrick W.R.	1905/06-1926/27	58	108	7	129*	2803	27.75	2
Hartland B.R.	1986/87-1996/97	59	103	8	150	2771	29.16	5
Coman P.G.	1968/69-1977/78	44	78	4	104	2603	35.17	2
Thomson K.	1959/60-1973/74	58	103	11	136*	2543	27.64	4
Page M.L.	1920/21-1936/37	41	75	2	206	2424	33.20	2
Leggat J.G.	1944/45-1955/56	35	66	6	166	2391	39.85	5
Chapple M.E.	1949/50-1960/61	44	79	9	165	2364	33.77	3

	Career	M	In	NO	HS	Runs	Ave	100
Germon L.K.	1987/88-1997/98	76	101	25	160*	2336	30.73	3
McMillan C.D.	1994/95-2006/07	40	65	9	159	2332	41.64	6
Stewart S.L.	2001/02-2006/07	40	70	2	149	2256	33.17	3
Kerr J.L.	1929/30-1939/40	32	61	3	196	2228	38.41	3
Guillen S.C.	1952/53-1960/61	42	73	5	197	2186	32.14	3
Reese D.	1895/96-1920/21	47	85	4	111	2066	25.50	2
Ryan M.L.	1965/66-1978/79	45	78	8	129	2041	29.15	2
Hadlee R.J.	1971/72-1988/89	62	100	22	93	2012	25.79	–
Roberts A.W.	1927/28-1940/41	35	60	8	181	2004	38.53	2

CENTURY ON DEBUT FOR PROVINCE

† 175	Watson G.	v Otago	Christchurch	1880/81
† 108 & 18	Wood B.B.	v Wellington	Wellington	1907/08
† 105	Talbot R.O.	v Otago	Dunedin	1922/23
5 & 112*	Newman J.A.	v Otago	Christchurch	1927/28
149	Hastings B.F.	v Central Districts	Nelson	1961/62
8 & 135	Parker N.M.	v Wellington	Wellington	1973/74
115	Hopkins G.J.	v Central Districts	Christchurch	1998/99

† indicates player was making his first-class debut

HIGHEST INDIVIDUAL INNINGS

301*	Fulton P.G.	v Auckland	Christchurch	2002/03
251*	Harris C.Z.	v Central Districts	Rangiora	1996/97
237*	Latham R.T.	v Northern Districts	Rotorua	1990/91
226	Hastings B.F.	v NZ Under 23 XI	Christchurch	1964/65
221*	Fulton P.G.	v Otago	Dunedin	2004/05
206	Page M.L.	v Wellington	Wellington	1931/32
206	Dowling G.T.	v Wellington	Christchurch	1962/63
206	Harris C.Z.	v Central Districts	Blenheim	1996/97
204	Cox A.	v Otago	Christchurch	1925/26
198	Harris C.Z.	v Otago	Christchurch	1996/97

MOST RUNS IN A SEASON

		Runs	Ave
Papps M.H.W.	2006/07	1005	91.36
Stead G.R.	2000/01	852	50.11
Fulton P.G.	2004/05	828	69.00
McMillan C.D.	1996/97	809	73.54
Papps M.H.W.	2001/02	793	52.86
Wright J.G.	1986/87	780	60.00
McEwan P.E.	1988/89	758	44.58
Latham R.T.	1988/89	757	58.23
Harris C.Z.	1996/97	748	187.00
Englefield J.I.	2000/01	724	38.10
McEwan P.E.	1983/84	713	59.41
Harris C.Z.	2001/02	656	93.71
Fulton P.G.	2003/04	655	43.66
Papps M.H.W.	2003/04	633	57.54
Hastings B.F.	1964/65	629	62.90
Fulton P.G.	2002/03	628	52.33
Latham R.T.	1987/88	608	50.66
Stewart S.L.	2006/07	606	50.50

MOST CENTURIES IN A SEASON

4 Papps M.H.W. 2006/07

TOTAL NUMBER OF CENTURIES **268**

Most in one season	11	2006/07
1st	Watson G. 175 v Otago	1880/81
100th	Hastings B.F. 136 v Auckland	1964/65
200th	Germon L.K. 114 v Central Districts	1993/94

Bowling

150 WICKETS	Career	M	Wkts	Runs	Ave	5WI	10WM	Best
Priest M.W.	1984/85-1998/99	88	290	8501	29.31	12	3	9-95
Hadlee R.J.	1971/72-1988/89	62	285	4600	16.14	19	2	7-49
Burtt T.B.	1943/44-1954/55	46	241	4991	20.70	16	3	8-35
Motz R.C.	1957/58-1968/69	56	239	4589	19.20	12	3	8-61
Bennett J.H.	1898/99-1919/20	40	205	3367	16.43	17	4	7-35
Hadlee D.R.	1969/70-1983/84	49	195	3918	20.09	10	3	7-55
Roberts S.J.	1985/86-1995/96	60	193	5738	29.73	6	–	5-56
Read R.J.	1904/05-1937/38	44	184	4704	25.56	11	1	7-24
Reese D.	1895/96-1920/21	48	168	3040	18.09	10	1	6-43
Stead D.W.	1969/70-1985/86	77	167	5009	29.99	6	—	7-99
Brown V.R.	1978/79-1986/87	65	159	4393	27.62	4	2	7-28
Merritt W.E.	1926/27-1935/36	24	154	3559	23.11	15	4	8-105
Wisneski W.A.	1996/97-2003/04	44	154	4092	26.57	7	—	7-151

BEST IN AN INNINGS

10-28	Moss A.E.	v Wellington	Christchurch	1889/90
9-13	Wiseman P.J.	v Central Districts	Christchurch	2004/05
9-56	McBeath D.J.	v Auckland	Christchurch	1918/19
9-95	Priest M.W.	v Otago	Dunedin	1989/90
9-98	Robertson W.	v Wellington	Christchurch	1894/95
8-18	Frith W.	v Otago	Christchurch	1880/81
8-33	Callaway S.T.	v Hawkes Bay	Napier	1903/04
8-35	Burtt T.B.	v Otago	Dunedin	1953/54
8-41	Callaway S.T.	v Otago	Dunedin	1900/01
8-59	Robertson W.	v Auckland	Christchurch	1893/94
8-61	Mulcock E.	v Otago	Christchurch	1937/38
8-61	Motz R.C.	v Wellington	Christchurch	1966/67
8-75	Edser H.	v Wellington	Wellington	1883/84
8-96	McBeath D.J.	v Auckland	Auckland	1921/22
8-99	Thomas A.W.	v Auckland	Auckland	1914/15
8-105	Merritt W.E.	v Auckland	Auckland	1931/32

BEST IN A MATCH

15-60	Callaway S.T.	v Hawkes Bay	Napier	1903/04
15-168	McBeath D.J.	v Auckland	Christchurch	1918/19
14-59	Read R.J.	v Southland	Invercargill	1920/21
14-107	Robertson W.	v Auckland	Christchurch	1893/94
13-72	Moss A.E.	v Wellington	Christchurch	1889/90
13-82	Howell W.B.	v Wellington	Christchurch	1902/03
13-90	Frankish F.S.	v Wellington	Wellington	1901/02
13-140	Edser H.	v Wellington	Wellington	1883/84
13-163	Robertson W.	v Wellington	Christchurch	1894/95
13-181	Merritt W.E.	v Otago	Wellington	1935/36

MOST WICKETS IN A SEASON

		Wkts	Ave
Boock S.L.	1977/78	56	15.66
Callaway S.T.	1903/04	47	8.49
Hadlee R.J.	1981/82	45	14.31
Hadlee R.J.	1986/87	45	12.91

Wicketkeeping

100 DISMISSALS	Career	M	Caught	Stumped	Total
Germon L.K.	1987/88-1997/98	76	217	21	238
Ward J.T.	1957/58-1970/71	54	136	17	153
Boxshall C.	1897/98-1914/15	50	70	36	106
Hopkins G.J.	1998/99-2002/03	41	91	10	101

MOST DISMISSALS IN A SEASON

34 (31ct/3st) Germon L.K. 1991/92

MOST DISMISSALS IN A MATCH

9	(9ct)	Germon L.K. v Northern Districts	Christchurch	1992/93

MOST DISMISSALS IN AN INNINGS

6	(6ct)	Germon L.K. v Northern Districts	Christchurch	1992/93
6	(5ct/1st)	Papps M.H.W. v Northern Districts	Gisborne	2004/05

MOST CATCHES IN A MATCH

9	Germon L.K. v Northern Districts	Christchurch	1992/93

MOST CATCHES IN AN INNINGS

6	Germon L.K. v Northern Districts	Christchurch	1992/93

Fielding

MOST CATCHES IN A MATCH

6	Cromb I.B. v Otago	Christchurch	1937/38
6	MacDonald G.K. v Pakistan	Christchurch	1984/85
6	Latham R.T. v Otago	Oamaru	1994/95

MOST CATCHES IN AN INNINGS

5	MacDonald G.K. v Pakistan	Christchurch	1984/85
5	Harris C.Z. v England	Christchurch	2001/02

Record Partnerships

FOR

Wicket	Score	Batsmen	Against	At	Date
1st	306	L.A. Cuff & J.D. Lawrence	Auckland	Christchurch	1893/94
2nd	243	M.H.W. Papps & S.L. Stewart	ND	Hamilton	2006/07
3rd	394*	P.G. Kennedy & R.T. Latham	ND	Rotorua	1990/91
4th	278	M.L. Page & A.W. Roberts	Wellington	Wellington	1931/32
5th	290	G.R. Stead & C.Z. Harris	CD	Blenheim	1996/97
6th	293*	P.G. Fulton & N.T. Broom	Otago	Dunedin	2004/05
7th	265	J.L. Powell & N. Dorreen	Otago	Christchurch	1929/30
8th	220	P.J. Wiseman & B.C. Hiini	ND	Hamilton	2005/06
9th	182*	L.K. Germon & R.M. Ford	Wellington	Christchurch	1989/90
10th	160	L.K. Germon & W.A. Wisneski	ND	Rangiora	1997/98

AGAINST

Wicket	*Score*	*Batsmen*	*For*	*At*	*Date*
1st	286	B. Sutcliffe & D.D. Taylor	Auckland	Auckland	1948/49
2nd	317	R.T. Hart & P.S. Briasco	CD	New Plymouth	1983/84
3rd	278	T.J. Franklin & D.N. Patel	Auckland	Christchurch	1985/86
4th	282	W.A.C. Wilkinson & A.P.F. Chapman	MCC	Christchurch	1922/23
5th	235*	G.P. Sulzberger & J.D. Ryder	CD	Napier	2002/03
6th	184	G.D. Elliott & S.M. Mills	Wellington	Christchurch	2006/07
7th	261	A.D.R. Campbell & P.A. Strang	Zimbabwe	Timaru	1997/98
8th	433	A. Sims & V.T. Trumper	Australia	Christchurch	1913/14
9th	134	J.W. Wilson & N.A. Mallender	Otago	Christchurch	1992/93
10th	184	R.C. Blunt & W. Hawksworth	Otago	Christchurch	1931/32

CENTRAL DISTRICTS

Highest Totals

594-8 dec	v Auckland	Auckland	1995/96
549-8 dec	v Canterbury	Christchurch	1998/99
542-4 dec	v Canterbury	Napier	2002/03
538	v Canterbury	Blenheim	2000/01
526	v Otago	Napier	1995/96
499	v Canterbury	New Plymouth	2004/05
497	v Wellington	Palmerston North	2004/05
485-7 dec	v Wellington	Wellington	1964/65
479	v Northern Districts	Napier	2004/05
475-9 dec	v Canterbury	Christchurch	1995/96

Lowest Totals

50	v Wellington	Upper Hutt	1979/80
51	v Northern Districts	Hamilton	1957/58
59	v Auckland	New Plymouth	1958/59
61	v Auckland	Auckland	1996/97
63	v Wellington	Napier	2003/04
65	v Wellington	Nelson	1995/96
71	v Northern Districts	Wanganui	1962/63
72	v Auckland	Palmerston North	2001/02
74	v Otago	Invercargill	1996/97
78	v Auckland	Auckland	1984/85

Most Appearances

97	Shrimpton M.J.F.
90	O'Sullivan D.R.
85	Duff S.W.
83	Blain T.E.
81	Briasco P.S.
78	Robertson G.K.
76	Douglas M.W
74	Sulzberger G.P.
69	Sinclair M.S.
67	Edwards G.N.
62	Smith C.J.P.
61	Greatbatch M.J.
61	Yuile B.W.
59	Smith I.D.S.
57	Hamilton L.J.
55	Congdon B.E.
55	Jordan A.B.
55	Griggs B.B.J.
53	Colquhoun I.A.
53	Toynbee M.H.
53	Schofield R.M.
53	Pierce R.A.
53	Mason M.J.

Longest Careers

Seasons			Seasons		
19	Shrimpton M.J.F.	1961/62-1979/80	16	Schofield R.M.	1959/60-1974/75
17	Jones A.H.	1979/80-1995/96	16	Snook I.R.	1972/73-1987/88
16	Chapple M.E.	1950/51-1965/66	15	Coutts P.J.C.	1958/59-1972/73

Benefits

O'Sullivan D.R.	1984/85	Duff S.W.	1995/96
Robertson G.K.	1989/90	Greatbatch M.J.	1996/97
Briasco P.S.	1991/92	Douglas M.W.	2000/01
Blain T.E.	1994/95		

Batting

2000 RUNS	*Career*	*M*	*In*	*NO*	*HS*	*Runs*	*Ave*	*100*
Sinclair M.S.	1995/96-2006/07	69	118	11	203*	4992	46.65	13
Shrimpton M.J.F.	1961/62-1979/80	97	171	15	150	4551	29.17	5
Blain T.E.	1982/83-1994/95	83	145	15	161	4547	34.97	7
Greatbatch M.J.	1986/87-1999/00	61	107	8	202*	4363	44.07	14
Briasco P.S.	1982/83-1991/92	81	146	16	157	4301	33.08	6
Douglas M.W.	1987/88-2000/01	76	132	19	144	3838	33.96	7
Edwards G.N.	1973/74-1984/85	67	122	5	177*	3709	31.70	5
Sulzberger G.P.	1995/96-2004/05	74	120	12	159	3505	32.45	8
Smith C.J.P.	1983/84-1990/91	62	118	9	160*	3499	32.10	7
Crowe M.D.	1983/84-1989/90	32	55	7	242	3299	68.72	13
Duff S.W.	1985/86-1995/96	85	129	29	164*	3079	30.79	1
Spearman C.M.	1996/97-2003/04	44	76	3	144	2951	40.42	5
Congdon B.E.	1960/61-1970/71	55	93	8	202*	2807	33.02	3
How J.M.	2000/01-2006/07	43	77	7	169	2523	36.04	8
Payton D.H.	1965/66-1976/77	49	92	4	145	2459	27.94	3
Pierce R.A.	1971/72-1984/85	53	98	5	100*	2296	24.68	1
Smith I.D.S.	1977/78-1986/87	59	95	12	145	2265	27.28	3
Hart R.T.	1982/83-1990/91	37	68	3	207	2222	34.18	5
Yuile B.W.	1959/60-1971/72	61	90	10	146	2190	27.37	1
Griggs B.B.J	2000/01-2006/07	55	86	10	100*	2098	27.60	1

CENTURY ON DEBUT FOR PROVINCE

† 117	MacLeod D.N.	v Wellington	Wanganui	1956/57
† 25 & 119	Sampson H.C.	v Wellington	Wellington	1970/71
119 & 0	Crowe M.D.	v Northern Districts	Whangarei	1983/84
112 & 21	Wilson S.W.J.	v Otago	Blenheim	1990/91
124 & 7*	Smith B.F.	v Otago	Wanganui	2000/01

† indicates player was making his first-class debut

HIGHEST INDIVIDUAL INNINGS

242	Crowe M.D.	v Otago	New Plymouth	1989/90
217	Taylor L.R.P.L.	v Otago	Napier	2006/07
212*	Kelly D.P.	v Canterbury	Blenheim	2000/01
207	Hart R.T.	v Wellington	Wellington	1985/86
203*	Sinclair M.S.	v Northern Districts	Wanganui	1998/99
202*	Congdon B.E.	v Otago	Nelson	1968/69
202*	Greatbatch M.J.	v Otago	Palmerston North	1988/89
202	Greatbatch M.J.	v Northern Districts	Rotorua	1995/96
201*	Smith B.F.	v Canterbury	New Plymouth	2001/02
189	Sinclair M.S.	v Wellington	Masterton	1996/97

MOST RUNS IN A SEASON

		Runs	Ave
Crowe M.D.	1986/87	1348	103.69
Smith B.F.	2000/01	939	58.68
Sinclair M.S.	2005/06	723	51.64
Sinclair M.S.	1996/97	722	48.13
Douglas M.W.	1991/92	714	44.62
Briasco P.S.	1990/91	708	41.64
How J.M.	2002/03	704	44.00
Greatbatch M.J.	1986/87	680	48.57
Edwards G.N.	1980/81	679	56.59
Blain T.E.	1984/85	678	48.42
Smith C.J.P.	1985/86	674	39.64
Hart R.T.	1984/85	665	44.32
Twose R.G.	1991/92	653	36.27
Anderson R.W.	1977/78	646	40.37
Blain T.E.	1990/91	644	46.00
Sulzberger G.P.	1999/00	628	48.30
Greatbatch M.J.	1995/96	623	155.75
Spearman C.M.	2002/03	622	38.87
Kelly D.P.	2000/01	617	38.56
Ingram P.J.	2006/07	617	56.09
Spearman C.M.	2000/01	611	50.91
Smith C.J.P.	1989/90	610	38.12
Briasco P.S.	1988/89	605	46.53

MOST CENTURIES IN A SEASON

6 Crowe M.D. 1986/87

TOTAL NUMBER OF CENTURIES		**184**
Most in one season	10	1986/87 & 2006/07
1st	Hunter A.A. 108 v Otago	1951/52
100th	Blain T.E. 103* v Otago	1990/91

Bowling

150 WICKETS	Career	M	Wkts	Runs	Ave	5WI	10WM	Best
O'Sullivan D.R.	1972/73-1984/85	90	392	9560	24.38	21	3	6-40
Yuile B.W.	1959/60-1971/72	61	233	4485	19.24	11	2	9-100
Robertson G.K.	1979/80-1989/90	78	228	6573	28.78	8	1	6-47
Beard D.D.	1950/51-1960/61	49	213	4531	21.27	8	2	7-56
Duff S.W.	1985/86-1995/96	85	208	6856	32.96	4	2	6-36
Hamilton L.J.	1996/97-2006/07	57	198	5104	25.77	7	—	6-32
Mason M.J.	1997/98-2006/07	53	187	4321	23.10	7	1	6-56
Jordan A.B.	1968/69-1979/80	55	157	4431	28.22	7	—	7-82
Cave H.B.	1950/51-1958/59	37	150	2962	19.74	7	1	7-31

BEST IN AN INNINGS

9-100	Yuile B.W.	v Canterbury	New Plymouth	1965/66
7-28	Yuile B.W.	v Northern Districts	Hamilton	1967/68
7-31	Cave H.B.	v Auckland	Palmerston North	1952/53
7-33	Cave H.B.	v Northern Districts	New Plymouth	1956/57
7-36	Yuile B.W.	v Otago	Nelson	1962/63
7-36	Schwass A.M.	v Northern Districts	Blenheim	2001/02

BEST IN A MATCH

13-64	Cave H.B.	v Auckland	Palmerston North	1952/53
11-99	Beard D.D.	v Otago	Dunedin	1956/57
11-115	Mason M.J.	v Canterbury	Timaru	2002/03
11-134	Robertson G.K.	v Northern Districts	Nelson	1986/87
11-138	Kay D.J.	v Canterbury	Palmerston North	1976/77

MOST WICKETS IN A SEASON

		Wkts	Ave
O'Sullivan D.R.	1978/79	52	19.01
Schwass A.M.	2001/02	45	14.73
O'Sullivan D.R.	1977/78	44	20.22
Blair R.W.	1955/56	42	17.28
Hamilton L.J.	2001/02	42	18.40
O'Sullivan D.R.	1980/81	40	22.00
Mason M.J.	2002/03	40	19.67

Wicketkeeping

100 DISMISSALS	Career	M	Caught	Stumped	Total
Griggs B.B.J	2000/01-2006/07	55	142	5	147
Blain T.E.	1982/83-1994/95	83	124	19	143
Colquhoun I.A.	1953/54-1963/64	53	102	28	130
Smith I.D.S.	1977/78-1986/87	59	119	11	130
Sigley M.A.	1994/95-2002/03	44	124	4	128
Schofield R.M.	1959/60-1974/75	53	107	15	122

MOST DISMISSALS IN A SEASON

36 (35ct/1st)) Griggs B.B.J. 2005/06

MOST DISMISSALS IN A MATCH

9	(9ct)	Schofield R.M. v Wellington	Wellington	1964/65

MOST DISMISSALS IN AN INNINGS

7	(7ct)	Schofield R.M. v Wellington	Wellington	1964/65

MOST CATCHES IN A MATCH

9	Schofield R.M. v Wellington	Wellington	1964/65

MOST CATCHES IN AN INNINGS

7	Schofield R.M. v Wellington	Wellington	1964/65

Fielding

MOST CATCHES IN A MATCH

5	Congdon B.E.v Wellington	Wellington	1964/65
5	Congdon B.E. v Otago	New Plymouth	1970/71
5	Smith I.D.S. v Auckland	New Plymouth	1978/79
5	Edwards G.N. v Otago	Palmerston North	1979/80
5	Briasco P.S. v Canterbury	Christchurch	1984/85
5	Douglas M.W. v Otago	Palmerston North	1988/89
5	How J.M. v Canterbury	Palmerston North	2003/04

MOST CATCHES IN AN INNINGS

4	Congdon B.E. v New Zealand XI	New Plymouth	1962/63
4	Neal D.W. v Auckland	Wanganui	1976/77
4	Unwin P.D. v Wellington	New Plymouth	1988/89

Record Partnerships

FOR

Wicket	Score	Batsmen	Against	At	Date
1st	250	R.T. Hart & C.J.P. Smith	Wellington	Wellington	1985/86
2nd	317	R.T. Hart & P.S. Briasco	Canterbury	New Plymouth	1983/84
3rd	224	M.S. Sinclair & C.M. Spearman	Auckland	Auckland	2003/04
4th	276*	M.D. Crowe & P.S. Briasco	Canterbury	Christchurch	1986/87
5th	301	J.I. Englefield & R.L. Taylor	Wellington	P. North	2004/05
6th	220	M.H. Toynbee & I.D.S. Smith	Auckland	Napier	1982/83
7th	219	B.W. Yuile & B.L. Hampton	Canterbury	Napier	1967/68
8th	173	I.D.S. Smith & G.K. Robertson	ND	Hamilton	1982/83
9th	239	H.B. Cave & I.B. Leggat	Otago	Dunedin	1952/53
10th	133	G.A. Bartlett & I.A. Colquhoun	Auckland	Auckland	1959/60

AGAINST

Wicket	*Score*	*Batsmen*	*For*	*At*	*Date*
1st	316	M.H. Austen & R.T. Hart	Wellington	Wanganui	1993/94
2nd	215	M.D. Bell & M.E. Parlane	Wellington	Napier	2004/05
3rd	227	K.R. Rutherford & B.R. Blair	Otago	Alexandra	1988/89
4th	310	J.D. Ryder & N.R. Parlane	Wellington	P. North	2004/05
5th	341	G.R. Larsen & E.B. McSweeney	Wellington	Levin	1987/88
6th	322	M.G. Orchard & J.A.F. Yovich	CD	Napier	2005/06
7th	192	S.W. Brown & A.C. Parore	Auckland	Auckland	1990/91
8th	143	C.M. Presland & C.W. Dickeson	ND	Whangarei	1983/84
9th	113	G.J. Hopkins & S.J. Cunis	Canterbury	Christchurch	1998/99
10th	89	M.J.E. Wright & S.J. Scott	ND	Wanganui	1978/79

NORTHERN DISTRICTS

Highest Totals

523-7 dec	v Otago	Hamilton	2006/07
520-8 dec	v Otago	Hamilton	1987/88
518-4 dec	v Canterbury	Christchurch	1996/97
516	v CD	Gisborne	2006/07
498-6 dec	v Central Districts	Napier	1992/93
496-8 dec	v Canterbury	Christchurch	2001/02
492	v Auckland	Auckland	1990/91
474	v Wellington	Gisborne	1996/97
472	v Otago	Hamilton	1995/96
460-7 dec	v Otago	Hamilton	2001/02

Lowest Totals

32	v Auckland	Hamilton	1996/97
52	v Canterbury	Hamilton	1966/67
57	v Wellington	Hamilton	1961/62
59	v Canterbury	Hamilton	1960/61
64	v Otago	Dunedin	1971/72
64	v Auckland	Auckland	1987/88
69	v Australia	Hamilton	1973/74
69	v England	Hamilton	1996/97
77	v Auckland	Auckland	2000/01
79	v Auckland	Auckland	1989/90

Most Appearances

115	Bradburn G.E.
104	Roberts A.D.G.
99	White D.J.
95	Hart M.N.
93	Young B.A.
90	Dickeson C.W.
85	Hart R.G.
82	Kuggeleijn C.M.
82	Dunning B.
79	Yovich J.A.F.
78	Bailey M.D.
75	Parker J.M.
75	Marshall J.A.H.
66	Puna N.
65	Wright M.J.E.
64	Parlane M.E.
62	Cooper B.G.
58	Howarth G.P.
58	Martin B.P.
57	Petrie E.C.
55	Bradburn W.P.
55	Marshall H.J.H.
54	Crocker L.M.
54	Aldridge G.W.
51	Thomson S.A.

Longest Careers

Seasons		
17	Dunning B.	1961/62-1977/78
17	Roberts A.D.G.	1967/68-1983/84
17	Bradburn G.E.	1985/86-2001/02
16	Kuggeleijn C.M.	1975/76-1990/91
15	Giles G.V.	1961/62-1975/76
15	Cooper B.G.	1980/81-1994/95
15	Young B.A.	1983/84-1997/98
15	Hart M.N.	1990/91-2004/05
14	Dickeson C.W.	1973/74-1986/87
14	White D.J.	1979/80-1992/93

Benefits

Kuggeleijn C.M.	1990/91
White D.J.	1992/93
Cooper B.G.	1995/96
Young B.A.	1997/98

Batting

2000 RUNS	*Career*	*M*	*In*	*NO*	*HS*	*Runs*	*Ave*	*100*
Roberts A.D.G.	1967/68-1983/84	104	192	35	128*	5533	35.24	7
White D.J.	1979/80-1992/93	99	173	15	209	4656	29.46	7
Bradburn G.E.	1985/86-2001/02	115	188	23	148*	4614	27.96	4
Parker J.M.	1972/73-1983/84	75	139	19	195	4611	38.42	7
Dunning B.	1961/62-1977/78	82	148	10	142	3898	28.24	3
Young B.A.	1983/84-1997/98	93	148	36	138*	3853	34.40	5
Marshall J.A.H.	1997/98-2006/07	75	129	5	235	3548	28.61	5
Bailey M.D.	1989/90-2001/02	78	122	8	180*	3468	30.42	6
Kuggeleijn C.M.	1975/76-1990/91	82	138	12	116	3457	27.43	3
Hart M.N.	1990/91-2004/05	95	140	15	201*	3398	27.18	4
Wright J.G.	1975/76-1983/84	43	84	3	145*	3301	40.75	5
Howarth G.P.	1974/75-1985/86	58	105	6	151	3122	31.53	5
Cooper B.G.	1980/81-1994/95	62	110	4	116*	2982	28.13	4
Parlane M.E.	1992/93-2002/03	64	107	6	146	2958	29.28	6
Yovich J.A.F.	1996/97-2006/07	79	122	23	144	2848	28.76	2
Crocker L.M.	1982/83-1988/89	54	100	3	126	2663	27.45	2
Marshall H.J.H.	1998/99-2006/07	55	96	8	153	2615	29.71	3
Wright M.J.E.	1972/73-1983/84	65	114	10	115	2632	25.30	1
Gibson J.G.	1968/69-1980/81	49	92	5	128	2580	29.65	4
Thomson S.A.	1987/88-1996/97	51	80	20	167	2530	42.16	5
Hart R.G.	1992/93-2003/04	85	119	19	102*	2135	21.35	1
Hick G.A.	1987/88-1988/89	17	30	4	211*	2055	79.03	10
Wealleans K.A.	1988/89-1994/95	43	74	4	112*	2053	29.33	4
Bradburn W.P.	1957/58-1968/69	55	103	5	107	2015	20.56	1

CENTURY ON DEBUT FOR PROVINCE

118	McGregor P.B.	v Auckland	Hamilton	1962/63
† 127*	Mitchell W.J.	v Pakistan	Hamilton	1964/65
14 & 153*	Maynard M.P.	v Auckland	Hamilton	1990/91

† indicates player was making his first-class debut

HIGHEST INDIVIDUAL INNINGS

235	Marshall J.A.H.	v Canterbury	Christchurch	2001/02
212*	Styris S.B.	v Otago	Hamilton	2001/02
211*	Hick G.A.	v Auckland	Auckland	1988/89
209	White D.J.	v Central Districts	Hamilton	1985/86
201*	Hart M.N.	v Auckland	Auckland	2002/03
195	Parker J.M.	v Canterbury	Whangarei	1972/73

195	Maynard M.P.	v Auckland	Auckland	1991/92
194*	White D.J.	v Central Districts	Wanganui	1990/91
180*	Bailey M.D.	v Otago	Hamilton	1997/98
177*	Turner G.M.	v Central Districts	Napier	1976/77

MOST RUNS IN A SEASON

		Runs	*Ave*
Hick G.A.	1988/89	1228	94.46
Maynard M.P.	1991/92	893	68.69
Hick G.A.	1987/88	827	63.61
Marshall H.J.H.	2006/07	766	54.71
Bradburn G.E.	1989/90	726	36.30
Wealleans K.A.	1989/90	721	36.05
Marshall J.A.H.	2001/02	706	39.22
Wright J.G.	1979/80	694	43.43
Turner G.M.	1976/77	672	67.20
Wright J.G.	1981/82	672	51.69
Styris S.B.	2001/02	662	44.13
Parker J.M.	1979/80	640	49.23
Parker J.M.	1981/82	618	103.00
Wealleans K.A.	1990/91	613	40.86
Wright J.G.	1978/79	612	50.91
White D.J.	1990/91	609	40.60
Thomson S.A.	1990/91	602	60.20

MOST CENTURIES IN A SEASON

6 Hick G.A. 1988/89

TOTAL NUMBER OF CENTURIES		**142**
Most in one season	9	1988/89
1st	Everest J.K. 104 v Canterbury	1956/57
100th	Parlane M.E. 132* v Canterbury	1995/96

Bowling

150 WICKETS	*Career*	*M*	*Wkts*	*Runs*	*Ave*	*5WI*	*10WM*	*Best*
Dickeson C.W.	1973/74-1986/87	90	282	8242	29.22	9	2	7-79
Bradburn G.E.	1985/86-2001/02	115	231	7302	31.61	3	—	6-56
Puna N.	1956/57-1968/69	66	224	5314	23.72	11	—	6-25
Yovich J.A.F.	1996/97-2006/07	79	219	7329	33.46	8	1	7-64
Martin B.P.	1999/00-2006/07	58	158	4898	31.00	11	2	7-33
de Groen R.P.	1990/91-1995/96	38	157	3320	21.14	8	2	7-50

BEST IN AN INNINGS

9-48	Tait A.R.	v Auckland	Hamilton	1996/97
8-21	Langdon M.C.	v Auckland	Auckland	1963/64
8-30	Alabaster G.D.	v NZ Under 23 XI	Hamilton	1962/63
8-37	Clarke D.B.	v Central Districts	Wanganui	1962/63
8-49	Kennedy K.D.	v Central Districts	Hamilton	1969/70

BEST IN A MATCH

16-130	Tait A.R.	v Auckland	Hamilton	1996/97
13-99	de Groen R.P.	v Otago	Alexandra	1992/93
12-55	Martin B.P.	v Auckland	Taupo	1999/00
12-109	Lissette A.F.	v Otago	Dunedin	1959/60
11-66	Tuffey D.R.	v Wellington	Hamilton	2000/01

MOST WICKETS IN A SEASON

		Wkts	*Ave*
Tait A.R.	1996/97	53	16.32
de Groen R.P.	1992/93	46	16.84
Yovich J.A.F.	2001/02	40	26.45

Wicketkeeping

100 DISMISSALS	Career	M	Caught	Stumped	Total
Hart R.G.	1992/93-2003/04	85	228	15	243
Young B.A.	1983/84-1997/98	93	179	11	190
Wright M.J.E.	1972/73-1983/84	65	104	17	121
Petrie E.C.	1956/57-1966/67	57	90	22	112

MOST DISMISSALS IN A SEASON

34 (33ct/1st) Hart R.G. 2001/02

MOST DISMISSALS IN A MATCH

9	(9ct)	Young B.A. v Canterbury	Christchurch	1986/87

MOST DISMISSALS IN AN INNINGS

7	(7ct)	Young B.A. v Canterbury	Christchurch	1986/87

MOST CATCHES IN A MATCH

9	Young B.A. v Canterbury	Christchurch	1986/87

MOST CATCHES IN AN INNINGS

7	Young B.A. v Canterbury	Christchurch	1986/87

Fielding

MOST CATCHES IN A MATCH

6	Young B.A. v Wellington	Wellington	1995/96

MOST CATCHES IN AN INNINGS

4	Pairaudeau B.H. v Central Districts	Wanganui	1962/63
4	Harris S.J. (sub) v Otago	Dunedin	1965/66
4	Barton P.H. v Canterbury	Hamilton	1974/75
4	Young B.A. v Wellington	Wellington	1995/96
4	Bailey M.D. v Otago	Alexandra	1996/97

Record Partnerships

FOR

Wicket	Score	Batsmen	Against	At	Date
1st	165	J.G. Wright & G.M. Turner	Wellington	Lower Hutt	1976/77
2nd	237	J.G. Gibson & C.M. Kuggeleijn	Canterbury	Hamilton	1980/81
3rd	261*	M.P. Maynard & S.A. Thomson	Auckland	Hamilton	1990/91
4th	259	G.E. Bradburn & M.E. Parlane	Canterbury	Christchurch	1996/97
5th	155*	J.A.H. Marshall & N.K.W. Horsley	Canterbury	Hamilton	2005/06
6th	322	M.G. Orchard & J.A.F. Yovich	CD	Napier	2005/06
7th	136	D.J. Nash & A.R. Tait	CD	Masterton	1997/98
8th	152	G.E. Bradburn & S.B. Doull	Canterbury	Christchurch	1991/92
	152	J.A.H. Marshall & M.G. Orchard	Wellington	Hamilton	2006/07
9th	188	N.R. Parlane & D.R. Tuffey	Wellington	Wellington	1999/00
10th	113*	P.D. McGlashan & G.W. Aldridge	Wellington	Wellington	2005/06

AGAINST

Wicket	*Score*	*Batsmen*	*For*	*At*	*Date*
1st	310	R.H. Vance & B.A. Edgar	Wellington	Wellington	1988/89
2nd	263	M.J. Greatbatch & M.D. Crowe	CD	Morrinsville	1986/87
3rd	394*	P.G. Kennedy & R.T. Latham	Canterbury	Rotorua	1990/91
4th	280	J.J. Crowe & D.N. Patel	Auckland	Auckland	1991/92
5th	347*	M.J. Horne & A.C. Barnes	Auckland	Auckland	2003/04
6th	175	S.P. Fleming & L.K. Germon	Canterbury	Hamilton	1993/94
7th	205	L.K. Germon & M.W. Priest	Canterbury	Christchurch	1991/92
8th	220	P.J. Wiseman & B.C. Hiini	Canterbury	Hamilton	2005/06
9th	116	V. Pollard & R.O. Collinge	CD	Palmerston North	1964/65
10th	160	L.K. Germon & W.A. Wisneski	Canterbury	Rangiora	1997/98

OTAGO

Highest Totals

624	v Central Districts	Napier	2006/07
602-8 dec	v Canterbury	Dunedin	1928/29
601-9d	v Canterbury	Christchurch	2006/07
589	v Canterbury	Christchurch	1931/32
571-8	v Central Districts	Napier	1995/96
558-8 dec	v Auckland	Dunedin	1949/50
548-7 dec	v Auckland	Dunedin	1996/97
543-8 dec	v Central Districts	New Plymouth	1978/79
521-7 dec	v Auckland	Auckland	1950/51
505	v Central Districts	Palmerston North	1999/00

Lowest Totals

34	v Wellington	Dunedin	1956/57
35	v Auckland	Christchurch	1884/85
36	v New South Wales	Dunedin	1889/90
40	v Canterbury	Dunedin	1869/70
41	v Auckland	Dunedin	1873/74
42	v Canterbury	Dunedin	1871/72
43	v Canterbury	Christchurch	1872/73
44	v Canterbury	Dunedin	1904/05
46	v Pakistan	Dunedin	1978/79
47	v Canterbury	Christchurch	1888/89
49	v Canterbury	Christchurch	1870/71

Most Appearances

108	Lees W.K.	69	Alabaster G.D.	59	Smith L.D.
90	Blair B.R.	68	Cameron F.J.	59	Turner G.M.
90	McGregor S.N.	68	Rutherford K.R.	57	Burns K.J.
88	Boock S.L.	66	Lawson R.A.	55	Mills G.H.
81	Blair W.L.	65	Alabaster J.C.	55	Sewell D.G.
80	Hoskin R.N.	63	Rutherford I.A.	54	Moir A.M.
78	Mallender N.A.	61	Campbell K.O.	54	Dobbs P.W.
75	McCullum S.J.	60	Sutcliffe B.	54	Cumming C.D.
75	Gaffaney C.B.	60	Milburn B.D.	51	Knight A.R.

Longest Careers

Seasons			Seasons		
27	Downes A.D.	1887/88-1913/14	22	McGregor S.N.	1947/48-1968/69
26	Knight A.R.	1918/19-1943/44	21	Groves L.J.	1929/30-1949/50
24	Siedeberg H.G.	1898/99-1921/22	21	Alabaster G.D.	1955/56-1975/76
24	Blair W.L.	1967/68-1990/91	20	Fisher A.H.	1890/91-1909/10
23	Torrance R.C.	1905/06-1927/28	20	Watt L.	1943/44-1962/63
23	Smith L.D.	1934/35-1956/57	20	Milburn B.D.	1963/64-1982/83
23	Mills G.H.	1935/36-1957/58			

Benefits

Lees W.K. 1987/88 Boock S.L. 1989/90 Mallender N.A. 1992/93

Batting

2000 RUNS	Career	M	In	NO	HS	Runs	Ave	100
Sutcliffe B.	1946/47-1961/62	60	110	8	385	6028	59.09	17
Blair B.R.	1977/78-1989/90	90	154	5	143	5057	33.93	7
Rutherford K.R.	1982/83-1994/95	68	121	7	226*	5051	44.30	14
Turner G.M.	1964/65-1982/83	59	109	14	186*	4439	46.72	13
Gaffaney C.B.	1995/96-2004/05	75	138	11	194	4326	34.06	7
McGregor S.N.	1947/48-1968/69	90	167	13	114*	4259	27.65	3
Lees W.K.	1972/73-1987/88	108	179	31	124	3754	25.36	4
Blair W.L.	1967/68-1990/91	81	149	9	140	3654	26.10	2
Hoskin R.N.	1980/81-1992/93	80	138	6	157	3573	27.06	6
Cumming C.D.	2000/01-2006/07	54	99	11	128	3288	37.36	9
McCullum S.J.	1976/77-1990/91	75	131	1	134	3174	24.41	2
Rutherford I.A.	1974/75-1983/84	63	115	3	222	3122	27.87	4
Richardson M.H.	1992/93-2000/01	49	89	10	166	3089	39.10	8
Lawson R.A.	1992/93-2003/04	66	120	5	200	2890	25.13	2
Burns K.J.	1980/81-1991/92	57	98	6	136	2699	29.33	3
Campbell K.O.	1963/64-1978/79	61	108	17	111	2613	28.71	3
Dobbs P.W.	1988/89-1994/95	54	99	6	144*	2606	28.02	3
Alabaster G.D.	1955/56-1975/76	69	108	16	108	2340	25.43	3
Smith L.D.	1934/35-1956/57	59	108	16	109	2277	24.75	1
Knight A.R.	1918/19-1943/44	51	97	3	152	2245	23.88	1

CENTURY ON DEBUT FOR PROVINCE

107 & 38	Patrick W.R.	v Canterbury	Christchurch	1917/18
† 157*	McMullan J.J.M.	v Southland	Dunedin	1917/18
172 & 16	Worker R.V.de R.	v Canterbury	Christchurch	1923/24
35 & 133	Blamires E.O.	v Canterbury	Christchurch	1923/24
† 15 & 105	Watt D.G.	v Canterbury	Christchurch	1943/44
157	Hadlee W.A.	v Auckland	Dunedin	1945/46
197 & 128	Sutcliffe B.	v MCC	Dunedin	1946/47
124 & 90	Horne M.J.	v Central Districts	Wanganui	1996/97

† indicates player was making his first-class debut

HIGHEST INDIVIDUAL INNINGS

385	Sutcliffe B.	v Canterbury	Christchurch	1952/53
355	Sutcliffe B.	v Auckland	Dunedin	1949/50
338*	Blunt R.C.	v Canterbury	Christchurch	1931/32
275	Sutcliffe B.	v Auckland	Auckland	1950/51
264	Sutcliffe B.	v Central Districts	Dunedin	1959/60
241	Horne M.J.	v Auckland	Auckland	1997/98
226*	Rutherford K.R.	v India	Dunedin	1989/90

222	Rutherford I.A.	v Central Districts	New Plymouth	1978/79
221	Blunt R.C.	v Canterbury	Dunedin	1928/29
201	Reid J.R.	v Canterbury	Dunedin	1957/58
201	Sutcliffe B.	v Northern Districts	Hamilton	1960/61
200	Lawson R.A.	v Central Districts	Napier	1995/96

MOST RUNS IN A SEASON

		Runs	*Ave*			*Runs*	*Ave*
Turner G.M.	1975/76	1027	85.58	Broom N.T.	2006/07	644	71.55
Blair B.R.	1989/90	759	47.43	Gaffaney C.B.	1996/97	642	40.12
Cumming C.D.	2002/03	751	46.93	Horne M.J.	2000/01	641	40.06
Rutherford K.R.	1989/90	747	67.90	Rutherford K.R.	1985/86	638	53.16
Sutcliffe B.	1952/53	709	78.77	Cumming C.D.	2000/01	626	44.71
Turner G.M.	1974/75	703	78.11	Rutherford I.A.	1976/77	625	48.67
Blair B.R.	1982/83	680	52.30	Blair B.R.	1986/87	621	47.76
Richardson M.H.	2000/01	675	56.25	Richardson M.H.	1995/96	615	68.33
Rutherford K.R.	1991/92	655	50.38	Gaffaney C.B.	2001/02	609	30.45
Sutcliffe B.	1950/51	651	72.38	Jones A.H.	1984/85	608	55.27
Mohammad Wasim	2002/03	651	40.68	Dobbs P.W.	1990/91	603	50.25

MOST CENTURIES IN A SEASON

4	Turner G.M.	1974/75
4	Turner G.M.	1975/76

TOTAL NUMBER OF CENTURIES		**207**
Most in one season	10	2002/03
1st	Baker J.C. 103 v Hawke's Bay	1901/02
100th	Cairns B.L. 110 v Wellington	1979/80
200th	Hopkins G.J. 139* v Auckland	2006/07

Bowling

150 WICKETS	*Career*	*M*	*Wkts*	*Runs*	*Ave*	*5WI*	*10WM*	*Best*
Boock S.L.	1973/74-1989/90	88	399	8235	20.63	28	5	8-57
Downes A.D.	1887/88-1913/14	44	287	3902	13.59	33	13	8-35
Moir A.M.	1949/50-1961/62	54	282	5926	21.01	20	5	8-37
Mallender N.A.	1983/84-1992/93	78	268	5433	20.27	14	3	7-27
Alabaster J.C.	1956/57-1971/72	65	264	5738	21.73	14	3	6-39
Cameron F.J.	1953/54-1966/67	68	258	5204	20.17	9	—	6-21
Alabaster G.D.	1955/56-1975/76	69	205	4774	23.28	13	1	7-74
Sewell D.G.	1995/96-2005/06	55	178	5198	29.20	7	1	8-31
Fisher A.H.	1890/91-1909/10	40	176	2766	15.71	9	1	9-50
O'Connor S.B.	1994/95-2002/03	35	160	3321	20.75	11	2	6-31
McSkimming W.C.	1999/00-2005/06	41	151	3656	24.21	7	1	6-39

BEST IN AN INNINGS

9-50	Fisher A.H.	v Queensland	Dunedin	1896/97
9-72	Cooke F.H.	v Canterbury	Christchurch	1884/85
9-93	Petherick P.J.	v Northern Districts	Dunedin	1975/76
8-28	Hendley W.	v Canterbury	Dunedin	1869/70
8-31	Sewell D.G.	v Central Districts	Invercargill	1996/97
8-35	Downes A.D.	v Canterbury	Dunedin	1891/92
8-37	Moir A.M.	v Northern Districts	Hamilton	1958/59
8-46	Cairns B.L.	v Wellington	Invercargill	1978/79
8-55	Moir A.M.	v Canterbury	Dunedin	1951/52
8-57	Boock S.L.	v Auckland	Dunedin	1989/90
8-59	Boock S.L.	v Wellington	Invercargill	1978/79

8-61	Cooke F.H.	v Canterbury	Christchurch	1882/83
8-66	Wiseman P.J.	v Wellington	Wellington	1996/97
8-70	Hay W.A.	v Southland	Dunedin	1917/18
8-99	Blunt R.C.	v Auckland	Dunedin	1930/31
8-119	Moir A.M.	v Central Districts	New Plymouth	1953/54
8-136	Shacklock F.J.	v Canterbury	Christchurch	1903/04

BEST IN A MATCH

15-94	Cooke F.H.	v Canterbury	Christchurch	1882/83
15-104	Boock S.L.	v Auckland	Dunedin	1989/90
15-203	Moir A.M.	v Central Districts	New Plymouth	1953/54
14-93	Torrance R.C.	v Hawke's Bay	Napier	1908/09
14-103	Downes A.D.	v Hawke's Bay	Dunedin	1893/94
14-126	Moir A.M.	v Canterbury	Dunedin	1951/52
13-111	Downes A.D.	v Hawke's Bay	Dunedin	1901/02
13-144	Boock S.L.	v Northern Districts	Whangarei	1980/81

MOST WICKETS IN A SEASON

		Wkts	*Ave*
Boock S.L.	1978/79	54	18.51
Mallender N.A.	1991/92	49	12.30
Boock S.L.	1986/87	48	15.48
Petherick P.J.	1977/78	45	17.15
Petherick P.J.	1975/76	42	20.16
O'Connor S.B.	2002/03	42	18.71
Moir A.M.	1953/54	41	17.58
Boock S.L.	1980/81	41	18.46
Boock S.L.	1987/88	41	21.82
Webb M.G.	1973/74	40	14.65
Cairns B.L.	1978/79	40	22.70

Wicketkeeping

100 DISMISSALS	*Career*	*M*	*Caught*	*Stumped*	*Total*
Lees W.K.	1972/73-1987/88	108	208	36	244
Milburn B.D.	1963/64-1982/83	60	148	17	165
Croy M.G.	1994/95-2001/02	42	127	4	131
Robinson S.A.	1984/85-1996/97	45	117	5	122
Hopkins G.J.	2003/04-2006/07	33	111	3	114
Mills G.H.	1935/36-1957/58	55	78	29	107

MOST DISMISSALS IN A SEASON

38 (37ct/1st) Hopkins G.J. 2004/05

MOST DISMISSALS IN A MATCH

10 (10ct) Hopkins G.J. v Canterbury Dunedin 2004/05

MOST DISMISSALS IN AN INNINGS

7 (7ct) Croy M.G. v Auckland Auckland 2001/02

MOST CATCHES IN A MATCH

10 Hopkins G.J. v Canterbury Dunedin 2004/05

MOST CATCHES IN AN INNINGS

7 Croy M.G. v Auckland Auckland 2001/02

Fielding

MOST CATCHES IN A MATCH

6 McCullum N.L. v Central Districts Napier 2006/07

MOST CATCHES IN AN INNINGS

4 Geddes A.E. v Canterbury Christchurch 1903/04

4	Watson E.A. v Canterbury	Dunedin	1953/54
4	Campbell K.O. v Auckland	Dunedin	1969/70
4	Blair W.L. v Canterbury	Invercargill	1977/78
4	Blair W.L. v Northern Districts	Dunedin	1978/79
4	McCullum S.J. v Auckland	Dunedin	1987/88
4	Dobbs P.W. v India	Dunedin	1989/90
4	Burns K.J. v Northern Districts	Dunedin	1990/91
4	Gaffaney C.B. v Wellington	Wellington	1996/97
4	McCullum N.L. v Auckland	Dunedin	2004/05
4	McCullum N.L. v Central Districts	Napier	2006/07

Record Partnerships

FOR

Wicket	*Score*	*Batsmen*	*Against*	*At*	*Date*
1st	373	B. Sutcliffe & L. Watt	Auckland	Auckland	1950/51
2nd	254	K.J. Burns & K.R. Rutherford	Wellington	Oamaru	1987/88
3rd	227	K.R. Rutherford & B.R. Blair	CD	Alexandra	1988/89
4th	235	K.J. Burns & R.N. Hoskin	ND	Hamilton	1987/88
5th	266	B. Sutcliffe & W.S. Haig	Auckland	Dunedin	1949/50
6th	165	G.M. Turner & W.K. Lees	Wellington	Wellington	1975/76
7th	182	B. Sutcliffe & A.W. Gilbertson	Canterbury	Christchurch	1952/53
8th	165*	J.N. Crawford & A.G. Eckhold	Wellington	Wellington	1914/15
9th	208	W.C. McSkimming & B.E. Scott	Auckland	Auckland	2004/05
10th	184	R.C. Blunt & W. Hawksworth	Canterbury	Christchurch	1931/32

AGAINST

Wicket	*Score*	*Batsmen*	*For*	*At*	*Date*
1st	299	M.D. Bell & R.A. Jones	Wellington	Dunedin	2001/02
2nd	279	M.D. Bell & M.E. Parlane	Wellington	Dunedin	2006/07
3rd	445	P.E. Whitelaw & W.N. Carson	Auckland	Dunedin	1936/37
4th	274	R.A. Jones & S.R. Mather	Wellington	Wellington	2000/01
5th	255	B.R. Taylor & J.V. Coney	Wellington	Dunedin	1972/73
6th	293*	P.G. Fulton & N.T. Broom	Canterbury	Dunedin	2004/05
7th	265	J.L. Powell & N. Dorreen	Canterbury	Christchurch	1929/30
8th	215	J.R. Murray & A.C. Cummins	West Indies	Dunedin	1994/95
9th	239	H.B. Cave & I.B. Leggat	CD	Dunedin	1952/53
10th	138	K.C. James & A.W.S. Brice	Wellington	Wellington	1926/27

WELLINGTON

Highest Totals

614-8	v Canterbury	Christchurch	2006/07
608-9 dec	v Northern Districts	Hamilton	1998/99
595	v Auckland	Wellington	1927/28
590-8 dec	v Central Districts	Palmerston North	2004/05
575-7 dec	v Otago	Wellington	1951/52
569	v Auckland	Wellington	1923/24
560	v Otago	Dunedin	1923/24
553	v Canterbury	Wellington	1931/32
547-8d	v Auckland	Wellington	2005/06
544	v Canterbury	Christchurch	1997/98

Lowest Totals

19	v Nelson	Nelson	1885/86
22	v Canterbury	Wellington	1903/04
29	v Nelson	Nelson	1879/80
30	v Nelson	Nelson	1883/84
31	v Nelson	Nelson	1887/88
34	v Canterbury	Wellington	1886/87
35	v Auckland	Wellington	1873/74
36	v Nelson	Nelson	1885/86
37	v Nelson	Nelson	1876/77
42	v New South Wales	Wellington	1895/96
42	v Otago	Wellington	1945/46
45	v Nelson	Wellington	1880/81
48	v Nelson	Nelson	1887/88

Most Appearances

120	Gray E.J.
119	Vance R.H.
102	McSweeney E.B.
89	Morrison J.F.M.
87	Edgar B.A.
84	Chatfield E.J.
82	Nevin C.J.
79	Larsen G.R.
74	Coney J.V.
72	Wells J.D.
72	Bell M.D.
68	Sinclair B.W.
64	Murray B.A.G.
60	Newdick G.A.
59	Blair R.W.
58	Reid J.R.
58	Ritchie T.D.
56	Brice A.W.S.
56	Patel J.S.
54	Bilby G.P.
54	McGirr H.M.
52	Cederwall B.W.
50	Butler L.C.

Longest Careers

Seasons		
29	Luckie M.M.F.	1891/92-1919/20
27	Dempster C.S.	1921/22-1947/48
25	Tucker K.H.	1895/96-1919/20
24	James K.C.	1923/24-1946/47
22	Hutchings J.H.	1903/04-1924/25
22	Collins D.C.	1905/06-1926/27
22	Reaney T.P.L.	1927/28-1948/49
20	McGirr H.M.	1913/14-1932/33
20	Lamason J.R.	1927/28-1946/47

Benefits

Morrison J.F.M.	1983/84
Chatfield E.J.	1985/86
Coney J.V.	1986/87
Edgar B.A.	1987/88
Gray E.J.	1989/90
Vance R.H.	1990/91
McSweeney E.B.	1991/92
Larsen G.R.	1996/97

Batting

2000 RUNS	*Career*	*M*	*In*	*NO*	*HS*	*Runs*	*Ave*	*100*
Edgar B.A.	1975/76-1989/90	87	160	13	162	6494	44.17	15
Vance R.H.	1976/77-1990/91	119	205	18	254*	6440	34.43	12
Bell M.D.	1997/98-2006/07	72	127	11	219	4915	42.37	15
Morrison J.F.M.	1967/68-1983/84	89	160	22	180*	4694	34.01	6
Reid J.R.	1947/48-1964/65	58	102	8	296	4538	48.27	13
McSweeney E.B.	1981/82-1993/94	102	153	23	205*	4296	33.04	5
Gray E.J.	1975/76-1991/92	120	181	38	128*	4228	29.56	5
Murray B.A.G.	1958/59-1972/73	64	116	9	213	3753	35.07	3
Nevin C.J.	1995/96-2006/07	82	125	20	143*	3714	35.37	3
Sinclair B.W.	1955/56-1970/71	68	116	14	148	3583	35.12	2
Hiddleston J.S.	1913/14-1928/29	41	75	1	212	3413	46.12	8
Coney J.V.	1971/72-1986/87	74	126	21	120*	3251	30.96	4
Newdick G.A.	1970/71-1980/81	60	112	6	143	3236	30.52	4

	Career	M	In	NO	HS	Runs	Ave	100
McGirr H.M.	1913/14-1932/33	54	97	4	141	3032	32.60	5
Wells J.D.	1989/90-2000/01	72	113	18	115	3016	31.74	5
Jones A.H.	1985/86-1993/94	39	67	11	181*	2978	53.17	7
Larsen G.R.	1984/85-1998/99	79	118	25	161	2938	31.59	2
Bilby G.P.	1962/63-1976/77	54	95	11	161	2852	33.95	3
Dempster C.S.	1921/22-1947/48	40	76	3	154	2602	35.64	4
Ritchie T.D.	1982/83-1990/91	58	92	14	106	2494	31.97	3
Tindill E.W.T.	1932/33-1949/50	39	73	5	149	2442	35.91	6
Jones R.A.	2000/01-2003/04	36	63	4	188	2343	39.71	7
Burnett G.P.	1987/88-1992/93	44	80	13	203*	2029	30.28	1
Parlane M.E.	2003/04-2006/07	31	53	2	203	2007	39.35	6

CENTURY ON DEBUT FOR PROVINCE

163	Williams A.B.	v Canterbury	Christchurch	1896/97
110 & 5*	Crawford J.N.	v Auckland	Auckland	1917/18
113 & 53	Kortlang H.H.L.	v Auckland	Wellington	1922/23
117 & 6	Bernau E.H.L.	v Auckland	Wellington	1922/23
† 106 & 0	Tindill E.W.T.	v Auckland	Auckland	1932/33
† 110	Ongley J.A.	v Otago	Wellington	1938/39
† 27 &141*	Smith K.F.H.	v Central Districts	Wellington	1953/54
† 132 & 2*	Bilby G.P.	v Central Districts	Wellington	1962/63
† 39 & 156*	Aiken J.M.	v Canterbury	Christchurch	1989/90
115	Fleming S.P.	v Central Districts	Wellington	2001/02

† indicates player was making his first-class debut

HIGHEST INDIVIDUAL INNINGS

296	Reid J.R.	v Northern Districts	Wellington	1962/63
283	Reid J.R.	v Otago	Wellington	1952/53
254*	Vance R.H.	v Northern Districts	Wellington	1988/89
236	Ryder J.D.	v Central Districts	Palmerston North	2004/05
222*	Midlane F.A.	v Otago	Wellington	1914/15
219	Bell M.D.	v Northern Districts	Hamilton	1998/99
216	Bell M.D.	v Auckland	Auckland	1997/98
214*	Kortlang H.H.L.	v Auckland	Wellington	1921/26
213	Murray B.A.G.	v Otago	Dunedin	1968/69
212	Hiddleston J.S.	v Canterbury	Wellington	1925/26
208	Franklin J.E.C.	v Auckland	Wellington	2005/06
205*	McSweeney E.B.	v Central Districts	Levin	1987/88
204	Hiddleston J.S.	v Auckland	Wellington	1925/26
203*	Burnett G.P.	v Northern Districts	Hamilton	1991/92
203	Parlane M.E.	v Auckland	Auckland	2004/05
202	Austen M.H.	v Central Districts	Wanganui	1993/94

MOST RUNS IN A SEASON

		Runs	Ave
Vance R.H.	1988/89	888	80.72
Jones R.A.	2000/01	849	47.16
Bell M.D.	2000/01	844	52.75
Edgar B.A.	1988/89	762	63.50
Edgar B.A.	1978/79	728	45.50
Jones R.A.	2002/03	726	45.37
Edgar B.A.	1989/90	720	40.00
Twose R.G.	1994/95	720	80.00
Jones A.H.	1988/89	701	87.62
Ryder J.D.	2005/06	679	48.50
Edgar B.A.	1987/88	676	52.00
Parlane M.E.	2004/05	646	43.06
Bell M.D.	2005/06	645	46.07
Vance R.H.	1987/88	638	79.65
Jones A.H.	1986/87	627	62.70
Ryder J.D.	2004/05	625	44.64
Parlane M.E.	2005/06	625	44.64
Parlane M.E.	2006/07	613	51.08

MOST CENTURIES IN A SEASON
5 Bell M.D. 2000/01

TOTAL NUMBER OF CENTURIES		**262**
Most in one season	10	1988/89, 1994/95, 2000/01
1st	Heenan G.C. 146* v Hawke's Bay	1886/87
100th	Sinclair B.W. 102* v Northern Districts	1963/64
200th	Chandler P.J.B. 177 v Auckland	1996/97

Bowling

150 WICKETS	*Career*	*M*	*Wkts*	*Runs*	*Ave*	*5WI*	*10WM*	*Best*
Chatfield E.J.	1973/74-1989/90	84	403	7531	18.68	23	7	8-24
Gray E.J.	1975/76-1991/92	120	357	9778	27.38	13	3	8-37
Blair R.W.	1951/52-1964/65	59	330	5004	15.16	30	10	9-72
Brice A.W.S.	1902/03-1927/28	56	229	4684	20.45	17	7	9-67
Upham E.F.	1892/93-1909/10	40	227	3393	14.94	17	2	7-24
Reid J.R.	1947/48-1964/65	58	172	3115	18.11	10	—	7-29
McGirr H.M.	1913/14-1932/33	54	166	4326	26.06	7	1	7-45
O'Brien I.E.	2000/01-2006/07	41	166	3627	21.84	8	1	8-55
Gillespie M.R.	1999/00-2006/07	42	164	4104	25.02	7	—	6-81
Morrison B.D.	1953/54-1964/65	45	163	3858	23.66	7	2	7-42
Franklin J.E.C.	1998/99-2005/06	47	160	3582	22.38	6	1	7-30

BEST IN AN INNINGS

9-67	Brice A.W.S.	v Auckland	Wellington	1918/19
9-72	Blair R.W.	v Auckland	Wellington	1956/57
9-75	Blair R.W.	v Canterbury	Wellington	1956/57
8-13	Firth J.P.	v Hawke's Bay	Wellington	1883/84
8-21	Penn A.J.	v Canterbury	Wellington	2001/02
8-24	Chatfield E.J.	v Northern Districts	Lower Hutt	1979/80
8-34	Fisher F.E.	v Canterbury	Wellington	1952/53
8-36	Blair R.W.	v Otago	Dunedin	1952/53
8-37	Gray E.J.	v Canterbury	Lower Hutt	1985/86
8-50	Butler L.C.	v NZ Under 23 XI	Wellington	1965/66
8-55	O'Brien I.E.	v Auckland	Wellington	2006/07
8-58	Ashbolt F.L.	v Hawke's Bay	Napier	1897/98
8-59	Hiddleston J.S.	v Canterbury	Christchurch	1918/19
8-64	Collinge R.O.	v Auckland	Auckland	1967/68
8-78	Gray E.J.	v Auckland	Wellington	1989/90
8-83	Chatfield E.J.	v Otago	Dunedin	1986/87

BEST IN A MATCH

14-136	Blair R.W.	v Canterbury	Wellington	1956/57
14-151	Gray E.J.	v Canterbury	Lower Hutt	1985/86
13-58	Salmon I.J.	v Nelson	Wellington	1873/74
13-86	Chatfield E.J.	v West Indies	Lower Hutt	1979/80
13-91	Gore A.H.	v Hawke's Bay	Napier	1886/87
13-92	Middleton F.S.	v Hawke's Bay	Wellington	1919/20
13-97	Ashbolt F.L.	v Hawke's Bay	Napier	1897/98
13-117	O'Brien I.E.	v Auckland	Wellington	2006/07
13-157	Tucker K.H.	v Auckland	Wellington	1900/01
13-176	Brice A.W.S.	v Auckland	Wellington	1920/21

MOST WICKETS IN A SEASON

		Wkts	Ave			Wkts	Ave
Chatfield E.J.	1979/80	49	10.51	Gillespie M.R.	2005/06	43	23.16
Gray E.J.	1984/85	48	21.75	Saunders J.V.	1913/14	41	17.58
Chatfield E.J.	1981/82	47	16.87	Chatfield E.J.	1976/77	41	19.48
Blair R.W.	1956/57	46	9.47	O'Brien I.E.	2000/01	41	19.68
Walker M.D.J.	2002/03	45	18.00	Penn A.J.	2001/02	40	18.30

Wicketkeeping

100 DISMISSALS	Career	M	Caught	Stumped	Total
McSweeney E.B.	1981/82-1993/94	102	289	39	328
Nevin C.J.	1995/95-2006/07	82	223	8	231
Therkleson I.J.	1966/67-1973/74	39	93	7	100

MOST DISMISSALS IN A SEASON

46 (46ct) Nevin C.J. 2000/01

MOST DISMISSALS IN A MATCH

10	(10ct)	Nevin C.J. v Otago	Dunedin	1995/96

MOST DISMISSALS IN AN INNINGS

6	(6ct)	Vance R.H. v Otago	Wellington	1977/78
6	(5ct 1st)	Nevin C.J. v Central Districts	Nelson	1995/96

MOST CATCHES IN A MATCH

10	Nevin C.J. v Otago	Dunedin	1995/96

MOST CATCHES IN AN INNINGS

6	Vance R.H. v Otago	Wellington	1977/78

Fielding

MOST CATCHES IN A MATCH

7	Morrison J.F.M. v Northern Districts	Wellington	1980/81

MOST CATCHES IN AN INNINGS

5	Lamason J.R. v Otago	Dunedin	1937/38
5	Morrison J.F.M. v Northern Districts	Wellington	1980/81

Record Partnerships

FOR

Wicket	Score	Batsmen	Against	At	Date
1st	333	B.A. Edgar & A.H. Jones	Auckland	Wellington	1988/89
2nd	287	M.D. Bell & J.D. Wells	Auckland	Auckland	1997/98
3rd	346	G.P. Burnett & R.A. Verry	ND	Hamilton	1991/92
4th	310	J.D. Ryder & N.R. Parlane	CD	P. North	2004/05
5th	341	G.R. Larsen & E.B. McSweeney	CD	Levin	1987/88
6th	226	E.J. Gray & R.W. Ormiston	CD	Wellington	1981/82
7th	250	C.J. Nevin & M.D.J. Walker	Otago	Wellington	2003/04
8th	180	R.G. Twose & M.C. Goodson	Otago	Dunedin	1994/95
9th	127	F.L.H. Mooney & R.A. Buchan	Auckland	Wellington	1943/44
10th	138	K.C. James & A.W.S. Brice	Otago	Wellington	1926/27

AGAINST

Wicket	Score	Batsmen	For	At	Date
1st	287	B.R. Hartland & G.R. Stead	Canterbury	Christchurch	1994/95
2nd	254	K.J. Burns & K.R. Rutherford	Otago	Oamaru	1987/88
3rd	213	G.M. Turner & B.E. Congdon	Otago	Dunedin	1972/73
4th	278	A.W. Roberts & M.L. Page	Canterbury	Wellington	1931/32
5th	301	J.I. Englefield & R.L. Taylor	CD	P. North	2004/05
6th	209	C.Z. Harris & A.J. Redmond	Canterbury	Rangiora	2001/02
7th	241	N.J. Astle & M.W. Priest	Canterbury	Christchurch	1994/95
8th	189	W.N. Carson & A.M. Matheson	Auckland	Auckland	1938/39
9th	188	N.R. Parlane & D.R. Tuffey	ND	Wellington	1999/00
10th	113*	P.D. McGlashan & G.W. Aldridge	Wellington	Wellington	2005/06

INTER-PROVINCIAL RECORDS

AUCKLAND v CANTERBURY

First match	*Played*	*Won by Auckland*	*Won by Canterbury*	*Drawn*
1873/74	123	45	40	38

Highest totals	**A**	693-9 dec		Auckland	1939/40
	C	514-6 dec		Christchurch	2002/03
Lowest totals	**A**	13		Auckland	1877/78
	C	62		Rangiora	1998/99
Highest innings	**A**	256	S.G. Smith	Auckland	1919/20
	C	301*	P.G. Fulton	Christchurch	2002/03
Best bowling *(innings)*	**A**	9-75	R. Neill	Auckland	1891/92
	C	9-56	D.J. McBeath	Christchurch	1918/19
Best bowling *(match)*	**A**	13-85	R.S. Cunis	Christchurch	1963/64
	C	15-168	D.J. McBeath	Christchurch	1918/19

Record Partnerships

AUCKLAND

1st	286	B. Sutcliffe & D.D. Taylor	Auckland	1948/49
2nd	145	A.E.W. Parsons & J.F. Reid	Auckland	1978/79
3rd	278	T.J. Franklin & D.N. Patel	Christchurch	1985/86
4th	206	T.G. McIntosh & L. Vincent	Christchurch	2000/01
5th	161*	B. Sutcliffe & D.D. Taylor	Auckland	1946/47
6th	160	P.N. Webb & P.J. Kelly	Auckland	1985/86
7th	224	V.J. Scott & A.M. Matheson	Auckland	1937/38
8th	153	R.J. Nicol & R.A. Young	Auckland	2001/02
9th	96	C. Pringle & D.K. Morrison	Rangiora	1995/96
10th	83	S.W. Brown & C. Pringle	Christchurch	1990/91

CANTERBURY

1st	306	L.A. Cuff & J.D. Lawrence	Christchurch	1893/94
2nd	179	B.G. Hadlee & N.M. Parker	Auckland	1978/79
3rd	183	G.R. Stead & C.Z. Harris	Christchurch	2000/01
4th	147	M.L. Page & R.O. Talbot	Christchurch	1930/31
5th	158	P.G. Kennedy & M.W. Priest	Christchurch	1991/92
6th	172	L.A. Butterfield & R.C.S.A. Shand	Christchurch	1945/46
7th	142	G.J. Hopkins & P.J. Wiseman	Auckland	2002/03
8th	166	R.J. Hadlee & D.R. Hadlee	Christchurch	1983/84
9th	115	G.J. Hopkins & A.M. Ellis	Auckland	2002/03
10th	83	H.C. Wilson & H.W. Monaghan	Christchurch	1913/14
	83	M. Graham & A.P. Cobden	Auckland	1935/36

AUCKLAND v CENTRAL DISTRICTS

First match	Played	Won by Auckland	Won by Central Districts	Drawn
1950/51	75	28	19	28

Highest totals	**A**	526-4 dec		Auckland	1951/52
	CD	594-8 dec		Auckland	1995/96
Lowest totals	**A**	71		Palmerston North	2001/02
	CD	59		New Plymouth	1958/59
Highest innings	**A**	185*	L. Vincent	Auckland	2004/05
	CD	166	M.S. Sinclair	Masterton	1998/99
Best bowling *(innings)*	**A**	7-29	R.S. Cunis	Auckland	1961/62
	CD	7-31	H.B. Cave	Palmerston North	1952/53
Best bowling *(match)*	**A**	12-146	K.W. Hough	Auckland	1959/60
	CD	13-64	H.B. Cave	Palmerston North	1952/53

Record Partnerships

AUCKLAND

1st	172	R.A. Jones & M.J. Horne	Auckland	2004/05
2nd	167	G.O. Rabone & D.D. Coleman	Auckland	1951/52
3rd	151*	M.J. Horne & A.C. Barnes	Auckland	2001/02
4th	140	R.A. Jones & H.D. Barton	New Plymouth	1997/98
5th	234*	V.J. Scott & J.B. Morris	Auckland	1951/52
6th	165	J.J. Crowe & J.G. Bracewell	Auckland	1987/88
7th	192	S.W. Brown & A.C. Parore	Auckland	1990/91
8th	111	L. Vincent & R.A. Young	Auckland	2004/05
9th	104*	R.A. Young & C.J. Drum	Auckland	2000/01
10th	82	B.G.K. Walker & K.P. Walmsley	Auckland	2003/04

CENTRAL DISTRICTS

1st	172	C.J.P. Smith & P.S. Briasco	New Plymouth	1985/86
2nd	207*	R.G. Twose & M.W. Douglas	Auckland	1991/92
3rd	224	M.S. Sinclair & C.M. Spearman	Auckland	2003/04
4th	155	R.T. Hart & T.E. Blain	Masterton	1989/90
5th	168	B.B.J. Griggs & T.I. Weston	Auckland	2006/07
6th	220	M.H. Toynbee & I.D.S. Smith	Napier	1982/83
7th	165	R.K. Brown & M.E.L. Lane	Palmerston North	1993/94
8th	94	S.W. Duff & D.J. Leonard	Wanganui	1991/92
9th	82	R.J. Schaw & G.J.T. Hegglun	Auckland	2006/07
10th	133	G.A. Bartlett & I.A. Colquhoun	Auckland	1959/60

AUCKLAND v NORTHERN DISTRICTS

First match	*Played*	*Won by Auckland*	*Won by Northern Districts*	*Drawn*
1956/57	69	23	16	30

Highest totals	**A**	547-8 dec		Auckland	2000/01
	ND	492		Auckland	1990/91
Lowest totals	**A**	69		Auckland	1963/64
	ND	32		Hamilton	1996/97
Highest innings	**A**	209	P.A. Horne	Auckland	1988/89
		209*	M.J. Horne	Auckland	2003/04
	ND	211*	G.A. Hick	Auckland	1988/89
Best bowling *(innings)*	**A**	7-28	K.P. Walmsley	Hamilton	2004/05
	ND	9-48	A.R. Tait	Hamilton	1996/97
Best bowling *(match)*	**A**	11-71	J.A. Hayes	Auckland	1957/58
	ND	16-130	A.R. Tait	Hamilton	1996/97

Record Partnerships

AUCKLAND

1st	197	T.J. Franklin & P.A. Horne	Auckland	1985/86
2nd	175	B.A. Pocock & J.M. Aiken	Auckland	2000/01
3rd	152	T.J. Franklin & J.J. Crowe	Rotorua	1983/84
4th	280	J.J. Crowe & D.N. Patel	Auckland	1991/92
5th	347*	M.J. Horne & A.C. Barnes	Auckland	2003/04
6th	157	J.F. Reid & J.R. Wiltshire	Auckland	1977/78
7th	136	T.K. Canning & B.G.K. Walker	Hamilton	2004/05
8th	75*	H.T. Schuster & H.J. Howarth	Hamilton	1964/65
9th	91*	K.D. Mills & C.J. Drum	Auckland	2000/01
10th	103	P.J. Kelly & G.B. Troup	Auckland	1985/86

NORTHERN DISTRICTS

1st	156	J.A.H. Marshall & N.K.W. Horsley	Auckland	2003/04
2nd	167	M.D. Bell & G.E. Bradburn	Hamilton	1994/95
3rd	261*	M.P. Maynard & S.A. Thomson	Hamilton	1990/91
4th	252	S.A. Thomson & B.A. Young	Auckland	1990/91
5th	142	M.P. Maynard & B.A. Young	Auckland	1991/92
6th	146*	G.A. Hick & S.A. Thomson	Auckland	1988/89
7th	127	C.M. Kuggeleijn & S.A. Thomson	Auckland	1988/89
8th	90	R.G. Hart & M.E. Parlane	Hamilton	1994/95
9th	185	M.P. Maynard & S.B. Doull	Auckland	1991/92
10th	82	S.B. Doull & B.P. Martin	Taupo	1999/00

AUCKLAND v OTAGO

First match	*Played*	*Won by Auckland*	*Won by Otago*	*Drawn*
1873/74	113	58	24	31

Highest totals	**A**	627	Lincoln	2006/07
	O	558-8 dec	Dunedin	1949/50
Lowest totals	**A**	48	Dunedin	1889/90
	O	35	Christchurch	1884/85
Highest innings	**A**	290 W.N. Carson	Dunedin	1936/37
	O	355 B. Sutcliffe	Dunedin	1949/50
Best bowling *(innings)*	**A**	9-36 A.F. Wensley	Auckland	1929/30
	O	8-57 S.L. Boock	Dunedin	1989/90
Best bowling *(match)*	**A**	14-63 A.W. Rees	Dunedin	1889/90
	O	15-104 S.L. Boock	Dunedin	1989/90

Record Partnerships

AUCKLAND

1st	240	T.G. McIntosh & M.J. Horne	Dunedin	2001/02
2nd	170	L.G. Hemus & A.E. Relf	Auckland	1909/10
3rd	445	P.E. Whitelaw & W.N. Carson	Dunedin	1936/37
4th	273	T.G. McIntosh & R.J. Nicol	Lincoln	2006/07
5th	197	C.C.R. Dacre & C.F.W. Allcott	Dunedin	1926/27
6th	209*	A.C. Parore & A.P. O'Dowd	Dunedin	1991/92
7th	177*	A.C. Barnes & J.M. Mills	Alexandra	1995/96
8th	140	J.G. Kemp & J.M. McIntyre	Dunedin	1969/70
9th	82	M.Y. Pasupati & P.B. Erasmus	Dunedin	2006/07
10th	119	W.N. Carson & J. Cowie	Auckland	1937/38

OTAGO

1st	373	B. Sutcliffe & L. Watt	Auckland	1950/51
2nd	227	P.W. Dobbs & M.J. Lamont	Dunedin	1990/91
3rd	199	W.S. Haig & B. Sutcliffe	Auckland	1954/55
4th	177	M.J. Lamont & M.H. Richardson	Alexandra	1995/96
5th	266	B. Sutcliffe & W.S. Haig	Dunedin	1949/50
6th	145	M.J. Horne & M.G. Croy	Auckland	1997/98
7th	164	A. Galland & A.R. Knight	Auckland	1925/26
8th	84	L.R. Pearson & J.C. Alabaster	Auckland	1964/65
9th	208	W.C. McSkimming & B.E. Scott	Auckland	2004/05
10th	60	L.D. Smith & G.W.F. Overton	Auckland	1946/47

AUCKLAND v WELLINGTON

First match	Played	Won by Auckland	Won by Wellington	Drawn
1873/74	132	56	32	44

Highest totals	**A**	522		Wellington	1918/19
	W	595		Wellington	1927/28
Lowest totals	**A**	48		Wellington	1889/90
	W	35		Wellington	1873/74
Highest innings	**A**	194	W.N. Carson	Auckland	1936/37
	W	216	M.D. Bell	Auckland	1997/98
Best bowling *(innings)*	**A**	8-51	R. Neill	Auckland	1895/96
	W	9-67	A.W.S. Brice	Wellington	1918/19
Best bowling *(match)*	**A**	14-65	J.A. Hayes	Auckland	1957/58
	W	13-117	I.E. O'Brien	Wellington	2006/07

Record Partnerships

AUCKLAND

1st	201	A. Anthony & E. Horspool	Auckland	1924/25
2nd	241	T.J. Franklin & J.J. Crowe	Wellington	1988/89
3rd	203*	B.A. Pocock & A.C. Parore	Auckland	1997/98
4th	180	A.N.C. Snedden & C.C.R. Dacre	Wellington	1922/23
5th	174	R.W. Morgan & J.G. Kemp	Auckland	1967/68
6th	176	V.J. Scott & O.C. Cleal	Auckland	1940/41
7th	131	G.L. Weir & C.C.R. Dacre	Wellington	1927/28
8th	189	W.N. Carson & A.M. Matheson	Auckland	1938/39
9th	122	H.T. Schuster & R.S. Cunis	Wellington	1964/65
10th	97	A.C. Kerr & H.C. Nottman	Auckland	1941/42

WELLINGTON

1st	333	B.A. Edgar & A.H. Jones	Wellington	1988/89
2nd	287	M.D. Bell & J.D. Wells	Auckland	1997/98
3rd	201	E.G. McLeod & J.R. Lamason	Wellington	1935/36
4th	207	F.T. Badcock & T.C. Lowry	Wellington	1927/28
5th	216	N.R. Parlane & J.E.C. Franklin	Wellington	2005/06
6th	134	K.C. James & H.M. McGirr	Wellington	1926/27
7th	144	J.R. Reid & P.T. Barton	Auckland	1959/60
8th	137	F.L.H. Mooney & F.E. Fisher	Wellington	1952/53
9th	127	F.L.H. Mooney & R.A. Buchan	Wellington	1943/44
10th	113	F.L.H. Mooney & E.C.V. Knapp	Wellington	1943/44

CANTERBURY v CENTRAL DISTRICTS

First match	*Played*	*Won by Canterbury*	*Won by Central Districts*	*Drawn*
1950/51	76	25	19	32

Highest totals	**C**	559		Christchurch	1993/94
	CD	549-8 dec		Christchurch	1998/99
Lowest totals	**C**	68		Levin	1985/86
	CD	91		Christchurch	1954/55
Highest innings	**C**	251*	C.Z. Harris	Rangiora	1996/97
	CD	212*	D.P. Kelly	Blenheim	2000/01
Best bowling *(innings)*	**C**	9-13	P.J. Wiseman	Christchurch	2004/05
	CD	9-100	B.W. Yuile	New Plymouth	1965/66
Best bowling *(match)*	**C**	12-86	P.J. Wiseman	Christchurch	2004/05
	CD	11-115	M.J. Mason	Timaru	2002/03

Record Partnerships

CANTERBURY

1st	185	B.R. Hartland & D.J. Murray	Palmerston North	1994/95
2nd	166	G.T. Dowling & B.F. Hastings	Christchurch	1964/65
3rd	208	M.H.W. Papps & C.D. McMillan	Christchurch	2006/07
4th	204	T.W. Jarvis & K. Thomson	Wanganui	1969/70
5th	290	C.Z. Harris & G.R. Stead	Blenheim	1996/97
6th	149	M.W. Priest & L.K. Germon	Christchurch	1988/89
7th	184*	C.L. Bull & B.P. Isherwood	Nelson	1971/72
8th	136	G.R. Stead & C.J. Anderson	Christchurch	2000/01
9th	113	G.J. Hopkins & S.J. Cunis	Christchurch	1998/99
10th	85	G.T. Dowling & A.F. Rapley	Christchurch	1958/59

CENTRAL DISTRICTGS

1st	178	P.J. Ingram & J.M. How	Napier	2002/03
2nd	317	R.T. Hart & P.S. Briasco	New Plymouth	1983/84
3rd	197	M.J. Greatbatch & M.D. Crowe	New Plymouth	1986/87
4th	276*	M.D. Crowe & P.S. Briasco	Christchurch	1986/87
5th	235*	G.P. Sulzberger & J.D. Ryder	Napier	2002/03
6th	141	B.B.J. Griggs & E.P. Thompson	Christchurch	2004/05
7th	219	B.W. Yuile & B.L. Hampton	Napier	1967/68
8th	133*	B.L. Hampton & R.M. Schofield	Christchurch	1964/65
9th	89	S.W. Duff & D.J. Leonard	Christchurch	1993/94
10th	98	I.A. Rutherford & D.J. Kay	Napier	1977/78

CANTERBURY v NORTHERN DISTRICTS

First match	*Played*	*Won by Canterbury*	*Won by Northern Districts*	*Drawn*
1956/57	69	26	13	30

Highest totals	**C**	549		Christchurch	1996/97
	ND	518-4 dec		Christchurch	1996/97
Lowest totals	**C**	83		Christchurch	1961/62
	ND	52		Hamilton	1966/67
Highest innings	**C**	237*	R.T. Latham	Rotorua	1990/91
	ND	235	J.A.H. Marshall	Christchurch	2001/02
Best bowling *(innings)*	**C**	7-24	J.W. Kiddey	Hamilton	1960/61
	ND	7-58	R.P. de Groen	Hamilton	1995/96
Best bowling *(match)*	**C**	12-81	R.J. Hadlee	Christchurch	1986/87
	ND	11-129	R.P. de Groen	Hamilton	1995/96

Record Partnerships

CANTERBURY

1st	214	B.A. Bolton & G.T. Dowling	Christchurch	1959/60
2nd	243	M.H.W. Papps & S.L. Stewart	Hamilton	2006/07
3rd	394*	P.G. Kennedy & R.T. Latham	Rotorua	1990/91
4th	181	V.R. Brown & R.T. Latham	Gisborne	1986/87
5th	252*	R.T. Latham & M.W. Priest	Christchurch	1988/89
6th	175	S.P. Fleming & L.K. Germon	Hamilton	1993/94
7th	205	L.K. Germon & M.W. Priest	Christchurch	1991/92
8th	220	P.J. Wiseman & B.C. Hiini	Hamilton	2005/06
9th	76	C.R.W. Dickel & K.I. Ferries	Hamilton	1974/75
10th	160	L.K. Germon & W.A. Wisneski	Rangiora	1997/98

NORTHERN DISTRICTS

1st	136	B.A. Pocock & M.D. Bell	Christchurch	1996/97
2nd	237	J.G. Gibson & C.M. Kuggeleijn	Hamilton	1980/81
3rd	150	R.D. Broughton & A.D.G. Roberts	Christchurch	1980/81
4th	259	G.E. Bradburn & M.E. Parlane	Christchurch	1996/97
5th	155*	J.A.H. Marshall & N.K.W. Horsley	Hamilton	2005/06
6th	180	S.A. Thomson & M.N. Hart	Hamilton	1992/93
7th	111	J.A.F. Yovich & R.G. Hart	Gisborne	2003/04
8th	152	G.E. Bradburn & S.B. Doull	Christchurch	1991/92
9th	69	M.N. Hart & S.B. Doull	Rangiora	2000/01
10th	62	M.N. Hart & G.W. Aldridge	Rangiora	2000/01

CANTERBURY v OTAGO

First match	Played	Won by Canterbury	Won by Otago	Drawn
1863/64	166	78	60	28

Highest totals	**C**	777		Christchurch	1996/97
	O	602-8 dec		Dunedin	1928/29
Lowest totals	**C**	25		Christchurch	1866/67
	O	40		Dunedin	1869/70
Highest innings	**C**	221*	P.G. Fulton	Dunedin	2004/05
	O	385	B. Sutcliffe	Christchurch	1952/53
Best bowling *(innings)*	**C**	9-95	M.W. Priest	Dunedin	1989/90
	O	9-72	F.H. Cooke	Christchurch	1884/85
Best bowling *(match)*	**C**	13-181	W.E. Merritt	Christchurch	1935/36
	O	15-94	F.H. Cooke	Christchurch	1882/83

Record Partnerships

CANTERBURY

1st	226*	W.A. Hadlee & J.G. Leggat	Christchurch	1948/49
2nd	210	W.A. Hadlee & F.P. O'Brien	Christchurch	1940/41
3rd	178	R.M. Frew & M.H.W. Papps	Christchurch	2000/01
4th	166	G.T. Dowling & K. Thomson	Dunedin	1966/67
5th	236	C.Z. Harris & N.J. Astle	Christchurch	1996/97
6th	293*	P.G. Fulton & N.T. Broom	Dunedin	2004/05
7th	265	J.L. Powell & N. Dorreen	Christchurch	1929/30
8th	95	R.H. Scott & A.T. Burgess	Christchurch	1946/47
9th	109	J.H. Bennett & A.W. Thomas	Dunedin	1913/14
10th	98	S.A. Orchard & C. Boxshall	Dunedin	1908/09

OTAGO

1st	209	B. Sutcliffe & L. Watt	Dunedin	1947/48
2nd	170	C.C. Hopkins & G.G. Austin	Christchurch	1911/12
3rd	221	R.C. Blunt & J.J.M. McMullan	Dunedin	1928/29
4th	168	K.F.M. Uttley & V.J.T. Chettleburgh	Dunedin	1936/37
5th	147	K.J. Burns & D.J. Walker	Christchurch	1985/86
6th	118	P.C. Semple & G.D. Alabaster	Christchurch	1969/70
7th	182	B. Sutcliffe & A.W. Gilbertson	Christchurch	1952/53
8th	146	M.H. Austen & P.J. Wiseman	Christchurch	1996/97
9th	134	J.W. Wilson & N.A. Mallender	Christchurch	1992/93
10th	184	R.C. Blunt & W. Hawksworth	Christchurch	1931/32

CANTERBURY v WELLINGTON

First match	Played	Won by Canterbury	Won by Wellington	Drawn	Tied
1883/84	138	47	50	40	1

Highest totals	**C**	613-7 dec		Christchurch	2006/07
	W	614-8		Christchurch	2006/07
Lowest totals	**C**	37		Wellington	1925/26
	W	22		Wellington	1903/04
Highest innings	**C**	206	M.L. Page	Wellington	1931/32
		206	G.T. Dowling	Christchurch	1962/63
	W	212	J.S. Hiddleston	Wellington	1925/26
Best bowling *(innings)*	**C**	10-28	A.E. Moss	Christchurch	1889/90
	W	9-75	R.W. Blair	Wellington	1956/57
Best bowling *(match)*	**C**	13-72	A.E. Moss	Christchurch	1889/90
	W	14-136	R.W. Blair	Wellington	1956/57

Record Partnerships

CANTERBURY

1st	287	B.R. Hartland & G.R. Stead	Christchurch	1994/95
2nd	174	G.T. Dowling & J.W. Burtt	Wellington	1967/68
3rd	187*	C.D. McMillan & R.T. Latham	Christchurch	1994/95
4th	278	M.L. Page & A.W. Roberts	Wellington	1931/32
5th	183	C.Z. Harris & C.D. McMillan	Christchurch	1996/97
6th	209	C.Z. Harris & A.J. Redmond	Rangiora	2001/02
7th	241	N.J. Astle & M.W. Priest	Christchurch	1994/95
8th	114	A.W. Thomas & H.B. Whitta	Christchurch	1919/20
9th	182*	L.K. Germon & R.M. Ford	Christchurch	1989/90
10th	85	A.W. Hart & C.H. Thiele	Rangiora	1984/85

WELLINGTON

1st	239	C.S. Dempster & W.H. Dustin	Wellington	1931/32
2nd	209*	A.H. Jones & M.D. Crowe	Christchurch	1992/93
3rd	206	A.H. Preston & J.E.F. Beck	Christchurch	1955/56
4th	187	H.M. McGirr & T.C. Lowry	Christchurch	1930/31
5th	134*	J.F.M. Morrison & R.W. Ormiston	Christchurch	1981/82
6th	184	G.D. Elliott & S.M. Mills	Christchurch	2006/07
7th	176	S.M. Mills & C.J. Nevin	Christchurch	2006/07
8th	154	K.C. James & F.T. Badcock	Christchurch	1926/27
9th	115	E.H.L. Bernau & K.C. James	Wellington	1923/24
10th	87	N.R. Hoar & R. Allen	Christchurch	1944/45

CENTRAL DISTRICTS v NORTHERN DISTRICTS

First match	*Played*	*Won by Central Districts*	*Won by Northern Districts*	*Drawn*
1956/57	68	20	19	29

Highest totals	**CD**	479		Napier	2004/05
	ND	516		Gisborne	2006/07
Lowest totals	**CD**	51		Hamilton	1957/58
	ND	86		New Plymouth	1956/57
Highest innings	**CD**	203*	M.S. Sinclair	Wanganui	1998/99
	ND	209	D.J. White	Hamilton	1985/86
Best bowling *(innings)*	**CD**	7-28	B.W. Yuile	Hamilton	1967/68
	ND	8-37	D.B. Clarke	Wanganui	1962/63
Best bowling *(match)*	**CD**	11-134	G.K. Robertson	Nelson	1986/87
	ND	10-78	D.B. Clarke	Wanganui	1962/63

Record Partnerships

CENTRAL DISTRICTS

1st	215	J.M. How & M.S. Sinclair	Napier	2004/05
2nd	263	M.J. Greatbatch & M.D. Crowe	Morrinsville	1986/87
3rd	210	B.F. Smith & M.W. Douglas	Taupo	2000/01
4th	161	L.G. Howell & M.J. Greatbatch	Rotorua	1995/96
5th	199	M.D. Crowe & M.W. Douglas	Rotorua	1989/90
6th	132*	T.E. Blain & S.W. Duff	Wanganui	1990/91
7th	179	B.B.J. Griggs & C.J.M. Furlong	Hamilton	2001/02
8th	173	I.D.S. Smith & G.K. Robertson	Hamilton	1982/83
9th	116	V. Pollard & R.O. Collinge	Palmerston North	1964/65
10th	48	M.J. Mason & L.J. Hamilton	Blenheim	2001/02

NORTHERN DISTRICTS

1st	167	M.E. Parlane & M.D. Bell	New Plymouth	1994/95
2nd	199	R.E.W. Mawhinney & D.J. White	Hamilton	1985/86
3rd	142	D.J. White & G.W. McKenzie	Hamilton	1985/86
4th	169	D.J. White & B.S. Oxenham	Wanganui	1990/91
5th	128	D.J. White & B.G. Cooper	Nelson	1986/87
6th	322	M.G. Orchard & J.A.F. Yovich	Napier	2005/06
7th	136	D.J. Nash & A.R. Tait	Masterton	1997/98
8th	143	C.M. Presland & C.W. Dickeson	Whangarei	1983/84
9th	107	R.G. Hart & A.R. Tait	Rotorua	1995/96
10th	89	M.J.E. Wright & S.J. Scott	Wanganui	1978/79

CENTRAL DISTRICTS v OTAGO

First match	*Played*	*Won by Central Districts*	*Won by Otago*	*Drawn*
1950/51	75	24	23	28

Highest totals	**CD**	526		Napier	1995/96
	O	624		Napier	2006/07
Lowest totals	**CD**	74		Invercargill	1996/97
	O	73		Dunedin	1986/87
Highest innings	**CD**	242	M.D. Crowe	New Plymouth	1989/90
	O	264	B. Sutcliffe	Dunedin	1959/60
Best bowling *(innings)*	**CD**	7-36	B.W. Yuile	Nelson	1962/63
	O	8-31	D.G. Sewell	Invercargill	1996/97
Best bowling *(match)*	**CD**	11-99	D.D. Beard	Dunedin	1956/57
	O	15-203	A.M. Moir	New Plymouth	1953/54

Record Partnerships

CENTRAL DISTRICTS

1st	137	T.E. Blain & R.T. Hart	Oamaru	1984/85
2nd	242*	J.M. How & M.S. Sinclair	New Plymouth	2005/06
3rd	223	C.J.P. Smith & S.W.J. Wilson	Blenheim	1990/91
4th	207	G.P. Sulzberger & A.J. Penn	Napier	1995/96
5th	168	B.F. Smith & M.W. Douglas	Alexandra	2000/01
6th	144	T.E. Blain & S.W. Duff	Palmerston North	1991/92
7th	123	I.D.S. Smith & S.J. Gill	Napier	1981/82
8th	113	L.R.P.L. Taylor & R.J. Schaw	Napier	2006/07
9th	239	H.B. Cave & I.B. Leggat	Dunedin	1952/53
10th	60*	B.L. Cairns & A.B. Jordan	Wanganui	1975/76

OTAGO

1st	305	R.A. Lawson & M.G. Croy	Napier	1995/96
2nd	169	G.M. Turner & R.W. Anderson	Dunedin	1974/75
3rd	227	K.R. Rutherford & B.R. Blair	Alexandra	1988/89
4th	200	B.R. Blair & G.J. Dawson	Dunedin	1982/83
5th	192	M.H. Richardson & I.S. Billcliff	Napier	1994/95
6th	147	R.N. Hoskin & J.K. Lindsay	Oamaru	1985/86
7th	121*	W.K. Lees & B. Abernethy	Napier	1981/82
8th	102	W.C. McSkimming & B.E. Scott	New Plymouth	2005/06
9th	92	D.E.C. McKechnie & B.L. Cairns	Dunedin	1976/77
10th	78	C.B. Gaffaney & D.G. Sewell	Palmerston North	1999/00

CENTRAL DISTRICTS v WELLINGTON

First match	*Played*	*Won by Central Districts*	*Won by Wellington*	*Drawn*
1950/51	74	15	27	32

Highest totals	**CD**	497		Palmerston North	2004/05
	W	590-8 dec		Palmerston North	2004/05
Lowest totals	**CD**	50		Upper Hutt	1979/80
	W	88		Wellington	1991/92
Highest innings	**CD**	207	R.T. Hart	Wellington	1985/86
	W	236	J.D. Ryder	Palmerston North	2004/05
Best bowling *(innings)*	**CD**	7-55	E.P. Thompson	Napier	2003/04
	W	7-30	J.E.C. Franklin	Wellington	2005/06
Best bowling *(match)*	**CD**	11-149	E.P. Thompson	Napier	2003/04
	W	10-103	B.D. Morrison	Wellington	1955/56

Record Partnerships

CENTRAL DISTRICTS

1st	250	R.T. Hart & C.J.P. Smith	Wellington	1985/86
2nd	157	H.C. Sampson & B.E. Congdon	Wellington	1970/71
3rd	180	C.D. Ingham & M.J. Greatbatch	Napier	1994/95
4th	172*	P.S. Briasco & M.W. Douglas	Palmerston North	1990/91
5th	301	J.I. Englefield & L.R.P.L. Taylor	Palmerston North	2004/05
6th	102	G.R. Hay & B.B.J. Griggs	Wellington	2006/07
7th	134	M.W. Douglas & S.W. Duff	Napier	1991/92
8th	84	P.M. Blackbourn & G.K. Robertson	Palmerston North	1983/84
9th	70	D.W. Neal & J.H. Howell	Wellington	1972/73
10th	52	D.J. Leonard & A.J. Alcock	Wellington	1992/93

WELLINGTON

1st	316	M.H. Austen & R.T. Hart	Wanganui	1993/94
2nd	215	M.D. Bell & M.E. Parlane	Napier	2004/05
3rd	186	J.D. Wells & S.J. Blackmore	New Plymouth	1999/00
4th	310	J.D. Ryder & N.R. Parlane	Palmerston North	2004/05
5th	341	G.R. Larsen & E.B. McSweeney	Levin	1987/88
6th	226	E.J. Gray & R.W. Ormiston	Wellington	1981/82
7th	161	S.P. Fleming & M.D.J. Walker	Wellington	2001/02
8th	135	G.R. Larsen & J.E.C. Franklin	Wellington	1998/99
9th	83	T. Vaikvee & R.O. Collinge	New Plymouth	1973/74
10th	81	L.C. Butler & R.E. Reid	Wanganui	1959/60

NORTHERN DISTRICTS v OTAGO

First match	Played	Won by Northern Districts	Won by Otago	Drawn
1956/57	66	24	19	23

Highest totals	**ND**	523-7 dec		Hamilton	2006/07
	O	457		Hamilton	1987/88
Lowest totals	**ND**	64		Dunedin	1971/72
	O	77		Gisborne	1999/00
Highest innings	**ND**	212*	S.B. Styris	Hamilton	2001/02
	O	201	B. Sutcliffe	Hamilton	1960/61
Best bowling	**ND**	7-42	K. Treiber	Hamilton	1985/86
(innings)	**O**	9-93	P.J. Petherick	Dunedin	1975/76
Best bowling	**ND**	13-99	R.P. de Groen	Alexandra	1992/93
(match)	**O**	13-144	S.L. Boock	Whangarei	1980/81

Record Partnerships

NORTHERN DISTRICTS

1st	151	G.P. Howarth & R.W. Fulton	Gisborne	1974/75
2nd	222	L.M. Crocker & C.M. Kuggeleijn	Hamilton	1983/84
3rd	112	R.W. Fulton & J.M. Parker	Gisborne	1974/75
4th	203	S.A. Thomson & M.P. Maynard	Hamilton	1991/92
5th	117	W.J. Mitchell & P.D. Stone	Hamilton	1966/67
6th	191	S.B. Styris & R.G. Hart	Hamilton	2001/02
7th	131	D.R. Flynn & P.D. McGlashan	Gisborne	2005/06
8th	102	J.A.F. Yovich & B.P. Martin	Dunedin	2005/06
9th	96	R.G. Hart & B.P. Martin	Dunedin	2001/02
	96	A.P. Devcich & G.W. Aldridge	Gisborne	2004/05
10th	97	R.G. Hart & G.L. West	Hamilton	2002/03

OTAGO

1st	260	R.A. Lawson & Mohammad Wasim	Dunedin	2002/03
2nd	220	M.H. Richardson & C.D. Cumming	Hamilton	2000/01
3rd	150	K.B.K. Ibadulla & K.J. Burns	Gisborne	1989/90
4th	235	K.J. Burns & R.N. Hoskin	Hamilton	1987/88
5th	123	R. Hendry & L.R. Pearson	Dunedin	1961/62
6th	146	G.J. Hopkins & N.L. McCullum	Dunedin	2006/07
7th	134	W.K. Lees & R.E.W. Mawhinney	Hamilton	1983/84
8th	129	B. Sutcliffe & T. Flaws	Hamilton	1960/61
9th	39	P.W. Hills & S.L. Boock	Gisborne	1988/89
10th	59	P.W. Hills & V.F. Johnson	Gisborne	1988/89

NORTHERN DISTRICTS v WELLINGTON

First match	Played	Won by Northern Districts	Won by Wellington	Drawn
1956/57	70	12	32	26

Highest totals	**ND**	474	Gisborne	1996/97
	W	608-9 dec	Hamilton	1998/99
Lowest totals	**ND**	57	Hamilton	1961/62
	W	78	Hamilton	2000/01
Highest innings	**ND**	151 G.P. Howarth	Hamilton	1979/80
	W	296 J.R. Reid	Wellington	1962/63
Best bowling *(innings)*	**ND**	7-12 D.R. Tuffey	Hamilton	2000/01
	W	8-24 E.J. Chatfield	Lower Hutt	1979/80
Best bowling *(match)*	**ND**	11-66 D.R. Tuffey	Hamilton	2000/01
	W	12-39 E.J. Chatfield	Lower Hutt	1979/80

Record Partnerships

NORTHERN DISTRICTS

1st	165	G.M. Turner & J.G. Wright	Lower Hutt	1976/77
2nd	162*	J.G. Wright & J.G. Gibson	Lower Hutt	1978/79
3rd	169	J.M. Parker & A.D.G. Roberts	Wellington	1983/84
4th	208	S.A. Thomson & M.P. Maynard	Hamilton	1991/92
5th	149	K.A. Wealleans & B.A. Young	Wellington	1991/92
6th	170	E.C. Petrie & R.J. McPherson	Hamilton	1959/60
7th	94	J.A.F. Yovich & P.D. McGlashan	Hamilton	2005/06
8th	152	J.A.H. Marshall & M.G. Orchard	Hamilton	2006/07
9th	188	N.R. Parlane & D.R. Tuffey	Wellington	1999/00
10th	113*	P.D. McGlashan & G.W. Aldridge	Wellington	2005/06

WELLINGTON

1st	310	B.A. Edgar & R.H. Vance	Wellington	1988/89
2nd	215	M.D. Bell & J.D. Wells	Hamilton	1998/99
3rd	346	G.P. Burnett & R.A. Verry	Hamilton	1991/92
4th	179	P.T. Barton & J.R. Reid	Wellington	1964/65
5th	147*	J.V. Coney & G.P. Bilby	Lower Hutt	1976/77
6th	139	J.F.M. Morrison & R.W. Smith	Wellington	1972/73
7th	137	T.D. Ritchie & G.R. Larsen	Gisborne	1985/86
8th	80	M.D.J. Walker & L.J. Woodcock	Hamilton	2003/04
9th	87	I.J. Therkleson & R.O. Collinge	Whangarei	1973/74
10th	74	M.D.J. Walker & J.S. Patel	Hamilton	2003/04

OTAGO v WELLINGTON

First match	Played	Won by Otago	Won by Wellington	Drawn
1892/93	109	28	53	28

Highest totals	**O**	495	Dunedin	1923/24
	W	575-7 dec	Wellington	1951/52
Lowest totals	**O**	34	Dunedin	1956/57
	W	42	Wellington	1945/46
Highest innings	**O**	182 K.R. Rutherford	Oamaru	1987/88
	W	283 J.R. Reid	Wellington	1951/52
Best bowling *(innings)*	**O**	8-46 B.L. Cairns	Invercargill	1978/79
	W	8-36 R.W. Blair	Dunedin	1952/53
Best bowling *(match)*	**O**	12-277 A.W. Alloo	Dunedin	1923/24
	W	12-87 E.J. Chatfield	Wellington	1973/74

Record Partnerships

OTAGO

1st	193	M.H. Richardson & M.J. Horne	Wellington	2000/01
2nd	254	K.J. Burns & K.R. Rutherford	Oamaru	1987/88
3rd	213	G.M. Turner & B.E. Congdon	Dunedin	1972/73
4th	211*	K.J. Burns & A.H. Jones	Wellington	1984/85
5th	134	C.B. Gaffaney & G.J. Hopkins	Dunedin	2003/04
6th	165	G.M. Turner & W.K. Lees	Wellington	1975/76
7th	143	T.C. Fraser & C.D.G. Toomey	Dunedin	1939/40
8th	165*	J.N. Crawford & A.G. Eckhold	Wellington	1914/15
9th	80	G.H. Mills & L.J. Groves	Dunedin	1937/38
10th	90	B.L. Cairns & G.B. Thomson	Lower Hutt	1979/80

WELLINGTON

1st	299	M.D. Bell & R.A. Jones	Dunedin	2001/02
2nd	279	M.D. Bell & M.E. Parlane	Dunedin	2006/07
3rd	246	B.A.G. Murray & J.F.M. Morrison	Dunedin	1968/69
4th	274	R.A. Jones & S.R. Mather	Wellington	2000/01
5th	255	B.R. Taylor & J.V. Coney	Dunedin	1972/73
6th	184	H.M. McGirr & D.C. Collins	Dunedin	1923/24
7th	250	C.J. Nevin & M.D.J. Walker	Wellington	2003/04
8th	180	R.G. Twose & M.C. Goodson	Dunedin	1994/95
9th	72	F.T. Badcock & K.C. James	Wellington	1926/27
10th	138	K.C. James & A.W.S. Brice	Wellington	1926/27

PROVINCIAL COMPETITION

Plunket Shield

1921/22 – 1974/75

Awarded by the Governor of New Zealand, Lord Plunket, the Shield was given to Canterbury as the association with the best record in the 1906/07 season. From 1907/08 to 1920/21 the trophy was competed for under a challenge system but thereafter on a competition basis.

HOLDERS	*Tenure*	*Challenges resisted*
Canterbury	17 December, 1907	—
Auckland	17 December, 1907 to 1 February, 1911	7
Canterbury	1 February, 1911 to 12 February, 1912	2
Auckland	12 February, 1912 to 31 January, 1913	1
Canterbury	31 January, 1913 to 27 December, 1918	9
Wellington	27 December, 1918 to 24 January, 1919	—
Canterbury	24 January, 1919 to 4 January, 1920	2
Auckland	4 January, 1920 to 10 January, 1921	3
Wellington	10 January, 1921	—

Shell Series

1975/76-2000/01

In 1975/76, a new competition, sponsored by Shell, was established. For the first four seasons this was played under a two-stage system — the first round of 15 games (all teams playing each other) was for the Shell Cup*, while the second round (on a knock-out basis culminating in a final) carried the season's major prize, the Shell Trophy.

From 1979/80, only the Shell Trophy was competed for. The Shell Cup was reallocated to the limited-over competition in 1980/81, while the Plunket Shield was reserved for matches between the North and South Islands.

WINNERS

1921/22	Auckland
1922/23	Canterbury
1923/24	Wellington
1924/25	Otago
1925/26	Wellington
1926/27	Auckland
1927/28	Wellington
1928/29	Auckland
1929/30	Wellington
1930/31	Canterbury
1931/32	Wellington
1932/33	Otago
1933/34	Auckland
1934/35	Canterbury
1935/36	Wellington
1936/37	Auckland
1937/38	Auckland
1938/39	Auckland
1939/40	Auckland
1945/46	Canterbury
1946/47	Auckland
1947/48	Otago
1948/49	Canterbury
1949/50	Wellington
1950/51	Otago
1951/52	Canterbury
1952/53	Otago
1953/54	Central Districts
1954/55	Wellington
1955/56	Canterbury
1956/57	Wellington
1957/58	Otago
1958/59	Auckland
1959/60	Canterbury
1960/61	Wellington
1961/62	Wellington
1962/63	Northern Districts
1963/64	Auckland
1964/65	Canterbury
1965/66	Wellington
1966/67	Central Districts
1967/68	Central Districts
1968/69	Auckland
1969/70	Otago
1970/71	Central Districts
1971/72	Otago
1972/73	Wellington
1973/74	Wellington
1974/75	Otago
1975/76	Canterbury *Canterbury**
1976/77	Otago *Northern Districts**
1977/78	Auckland *Canterbury**
1978/79	Otago *Otago**
1979/80	Northern Districts
1980/81	Auckland
1981/82	Wellington
1982/83	Wellington
1983/84	Canterbury
1984/85	Wellington
1985/86	Otago
1986/87	Central Districts
1987/88	Otago
1988/89	Auckland
1989/90	Wellington
1990/91	Auckland
1991/92	Central Districts & Northern Districts
1992/93	Northern Districts
1993/94	Canterbury
1994/95	Auckland
1995/96	Auckland
1996/97	Canterbury
1997/98	Canterbury
1998/99	Central Districts
1999/00	Northern Districts
2000/01	Wellington

State Championship

from 2001/02

State Insurance took over the sponsorship of the competition in 2001/02. The format remained unchanged.

WINNERS

2001/02	Auckland	2002/03	Auckland	2003/04	Wellington
2004/05	Auckland	2005/06	Central Districts	2006/07	Northern Districts

TEAM RECORDS

Playing Record of the First-class Sides in New Zealand

	P	*W*	*L*	*D*
Canterbury	625	231	210	184*
Wellington	606	219	192	195†
Otago	586	167	267	152
Auckland	568	224	152	192
Central Districts	395	100	130	165*
Northern Districts	362	85	132	145
New Zealand	223	47	74	102
England/MCC	128	61	9	58*
Australia	109	59	7	43
Hawke's Bay	53	9	34	10
Pakistan	51	20	6	25
West Indies	38	11	10	17
India	33	10	8	15
New South Wales	23	16	2	5
South Africa	22	9	1	12
Sri Lanka	22	4	7	11
Nelson	17	9	6	2*
North Island	16	6	5	5
Fiji	15	5	8	2
South Island	15	4	8	3
New Zealand U23 XI	12	—	9	3
New Zealand A	11	7	1	3
Zimbabwe	10	2	3	5
President's XI	9	—	3	6
NZ Academy XI	9	3	3	3
Southland	8	1	5	2
Taranaki	8	1	6	1
Southern	8	4	1	3
Northern	7	2	1	4
Central	7	2	3	2
Bangladesh	7	—	7	—
The Rest	6	1	3	2

	P	*W*	*L*	*D*
Victoria	6	1	1	4
NZ XI	6	—	3	3
Young New Zealand	5	—	2	3
Queensland	5	3	1	1
Pakistan A	5	—	1	4
England A	5	3	—	2
Tasmania	4	—	3	1
Sri Lanka A	4	—	3	1
Shell XI	3	1	1	1
Emerging Players	3	—	1	2
Governor General's XI	2	1	1	—
Commonwealth XI	2	2	—	—
D.H. Robins' XI	2	—	—	2
U-Bix XI	1	—	—	1
West Coast (NI)	1	1	—	—
D. Reese's XI	1	—	1	—
Minor Associations	1	—	1	—
Sir Julien Cahn's XI	1	—	—	1
South Island Army	1	1	—	—
North Island Army	1	—	1	—
New Zealand Army	1	1	—	—
New Zealand Air Force	1	—	1	—
New Zealand Services	1	—	—	1
Canterbury/Otago	1	—	—	1
Auckland/Wellington	1	—	1	—
ND/CD	1	—	—	1
Auckland XI	1	—	—	1
Otago Invitation XI	1	—	1	—
Canterbury XI	1	—	—	1
Board XI	1	—	1	—
Australian Academy XI	1	1	—	—
NZ Major Association XI	1	—	—	1
TOTALS	**4080**	**1334**	**1334**	**1412**

** includes a tie* *† includes two ties*

Highest Match Aggregates

Runs-Wickets			
1945-18	Canterbury v Wellington	Christchurch	1994/95
1905-40	Otago v Wellington	Dunedin	1923/24
1567-37	Auckland v Wellington	Auckland	1936/37
1554-40	Wellington v Auckland	Wellington	1922/23
1531-39	Wellington v Auckland	Wellington	1923/24
1513-34	Central Districts v Otago	Napier	2006/07
1505-25	New Zealand v India	Auckland	1989/90
1501-37	Canterbury v Otago	Christchurch	1931/32

Highest Team Totals

by any first-class team in New Zealand

777	Canterbury v Otago at Christchurch	1996/97
752-8 dec	NSW v Otago at Dunedin	1923/24
693-9 dec	Auckland v Canterbury at Auckland	1939/40
671-4	New Zealand v Sri Lanka at Wellington	1990/91
663	Australia v New Zealand at Auckland	1920/21
660-5 dec	West Indies v New Zealand at Wellington	1994/95
658	Australians v Auckland at Auckland	1913/14
653-5 dec	MCC v New Zealand at Dunedin	1935/36
653	Australians v Canterbury at Christchurch	1913/14
643	Auckland v Canterbury at Auckland	1919/20
627-7d	Auckland v Otago at Lincoln	2006/07
624	Otago v Central Districts at Napier	2006/07
621-5 dec	South Africa v New Zealand at Auckland	1998/99
616-5 dec	Pakistan v New Zealand at Auckland	1988/89
614-8	Wellington v Canterbury at Christchurch	2006/07
613-7d	Canterbury v Wellington at Christchurch	2006/07
610-6 dec	Australia v New Zealand at Auckland	1913/14
608-9 dec	Wellington v Northern Districts at Hamilton	1998/99
602-8 dec	Otago v Canterbury at Dunedin	1928/29
601-9d	Otago v Canterbury at Christchurch	2006/07

Most Runs in a Match by One Side

Runs-Wickets				
1025-20	560 & 465	Wellington v Otago	Dunedin	1923/24
973-6	498-2d & 475-4	Wellington v Canterbury	Christchurch	1994/95
972-12	496 & 476-2d	Canterbury v Wellington	Christchurch	1994/95
971-14	511-6d & 460-8	Australia v New Zealand	Wellington	1973/74
948-20	569 & 379	Wellington v Auckland	Wellington	1923/24
880-20	385 & 495	Otago v Wellington	Dunedin	1923/24
875-18	273 & 602-8d	Otago v Canterbury	Dunedin	1928/29
874-15	391 & 483-5d	New Zealand v India	Auckland	1989/90
855-20	595 & 260	Wellington v Auckland	Wellington	1927/28
851-18	280 & 571-8	Otago v Central Districts	Napier	1995/96
845-14	174 & 671-4d	New Zealand v Sri Lanka	Wellington	1990/91
832-17	401 & 431-7d	Auckland v Wellington	Auckland	1934/35
831-20	435 & 396	Wellington v Auckland	Wellington	1922/23
827-20	448 & 379	Wellington v Otago	Wellington	1926/27
821-20	447 & 374	Wellington v Auckland	Wellington	1925/26
808-13	476 & 332-3	NSW v Wellington	Wellington	1923/24
802-18	276 & 526-8d	Canterbury v Wellington	Wellington	1931/32

Lowest Match Aggregates

completed matches, i.e. not drawn

Runs-Wickets			
151-30	Canterbury v Otago	Christchurch	1866/67
153-31	Otago v Canterbury	Dunedin	1896/97
156-30	Nelson v Wellington	Nelson	1885/86
159-31	Nelson v Wellington	Nelson	1887/88
176-32	Otago v Tasmania	Dunedin	1883/84
183-40	Nelson v Wellington	Nelson	1883/84
192-30	Taranaki v Hawke's Bay	Hawera	1891/92

The lowest aggregates since 1900 are:

Runs-Wickets			
241-30	Otago v Southland	Dunedin	1919/20
278-40	Southland v Otago	Invercargill	1918/19
295-28	New Zealand v Australia	Wellington	1945/46

Lowest Match Aggregates by One Side

55	36 & 19	Wellington v Nelson	Nelson	1885/86
57	25 & 32	Canterbury v Otago	Christchurch	1866/67
64	35 & 29	Taranaki v Hawke's Bay	Hawera	1891/92
72	30 & 42	Wellington v Nelson	Nelson	1883/84
76	34 & 42	Canterbury v Otago	Dunedin	1863/64
76	27 & 49	Canterbury v Otago	Dunedin	1896/97
79	31 & 48	Wellington v Nelson	Nelson	1887/88
80	51 & 29	Wellington v Nelson	Nelson	1879/80
87	40 & 47	Tasmania v Otago	Dunedin	1883/84
95	43 & 52	Otago v Canterbury	Christchurch	1872/73
96	41 & 55	Southland v Otago	Invercargill	1918/19
96	42 & 54	New Zealand v Australia	Wellington	1945/46
97	37 & 60	Wellington v Nelson	Christchurch	1876/77
99	65 & 34	Wellington v Canterbury	Wellington	1886/87

Lowest Team Totals

by any first-class team in New Zealand

13	Auckland v Canterbury at Auckland (included 8 extras)	1877/78
19	Wellington v Nelson at Nelson	1885/86
22	Wellington v Canterbury at Wellington	1903/04
25	Canterbury v Otago at Christchurch	1866/67
26	NZ v England at Auckland	1954/55
27	Canterbury v Otago at Dunedin	1896/97
28	Hawke's Bay v Auckland at Auckland (included 13 extras)	1910/11
29	Wellington v Nelson at Nelson	1879/80
29	Taranaki v Hawke's Bay at Hawera	1891/92

Highest Second Innings Totals

671-4	New Zealand v Sri Lanka	Wellington	1990/91
602-8	Otago v Canterbury	Dunedin	1928/29
589	Otago v Canterbury	Christchurch	1931/32
575-7 dec	Wellington v Otago	Wellington	1951/52
571-8 dec	Otago v Central Districts	Napier	1995/96
539	Auckland v Otago	Dunedin	1926/27
537	Auckland v Canterbury	Christchurch	1930/31
537	New Zealand v England	Wellington	1983/84
526-8 dec	Canterbury v Wellington	Wellington	1931/32
519	Canterbury v Wellington	Christchurch	1930/31

Highest Fourth Innings Totals without Loss for Victory

226-0	Canterbury v Otago	Christchurch	1948/49
175-0	Otago v Central Districts	Masterton	1971/72
174-0	Otago v Northern Districts	Alexandra	1985/86
147-0	Wellington v Otago	Dunedin	2005/06
138-0	Auckland v Otago	Auckland	1937/38
130-0	Wellington v Otago	Wellington	1921/22
130-0	Canterbury v Auckland	Christchurch	1951/52

Highest Fourth Innings Totals

495	lost 145 runs	Otago v Wellington	Dunedin	1923/24
475-4	and won	Wellington v Canterbury	Christchurch	1994/95
473-6	and won	Canterbury v Auckland	Christchurch	1930/31
458	lost 276 runs	Auckland v Wellington	Wellington	1927/28
453-8	and won	Northern Districts v Wellington	Wellington	1995/96
451	lost 98 runs	New Zealand v England	Christchurch	2001/02
429-8	and won	Northern Districts v Central Districts	Lincoln	2006/07
400-9	and won	Northern Districts v Central Districts	Napier	2004/05
388	lost 19 runs	Canterbury v Wellington	Wellington	1929/30
380-8	set 505 runs	Wellington v Auckland	Wellington	1929/30
380-9	set 510 runs	Wellington v Auckland	Auckland	2005/06
375-5	and won	Central Districts v Canterbury	New Plymouth	1986/87
374-8	and won	North Island v South Island	Dunedin	1947/48
372	lost 38 runs	Canterbury v Wellington	Christchurch	2000/01
371-4	and won	Northern Districts v Wellington	Hamilton	1991/92
368-6	and won	Auckland v Central Districts	Auckland	2000/01
362-8	and won	Canterbury v Central Districts	Napier	2002/03
361-6	and won	Auckland v Canterbury	Christchurch	2002/03
357-6	and won	Canterbury v Otago	Christchurch	1927/28
353	lost 148 runs	Otago v Auckland	Alexandra	1995/96
353-2	and won	Wellington v Otago	Dunedin	2001/02
348-5	and won	West Indies v NZ	Auckland	1968/69
347-7	and won	Auckland v Wellington	Auckland	1936/37
345	lost 15 runs	Northern Districts v Central Districts	Nelson	1986/87
344-6	set 418 runs	Sri Lanka v New Zealand	Hamilton	1990/91
344	lost 163 runs	Otago v Wellington	Wellington	1927/28
342-6	and won	Otago v Central Districts	Oamaru	1985/86
341-5	and won	Central Districts v Northern Districts	New Plymouth	1984/85
340-5	and won	Wellington v Auckland	Wellington	1991/92
340	lost 16 runs	Auckland v Northern Districts	Auckland	2002/03
339-5	and won	Central Districts v Otago	Blenheim	1990/91

339	lost 96 runs	Canterbury v Otago	Christchurch	1933/34
339	lost 12 runs	Canterbury v Otago	Dunedin	1947/48
339-2§	and won	Central Districts v Northern Districts	Hamilton	2002/03
337	lost 108 runs	Auckland v Wellington	Wellington	1922/23
336	lost 105 runs	Auckland v Wellington	Wellington	1920/21
335-8	set 385 runs	Northern Districts v Auckland	Auckland	1991/92
335-5	and won	Canterbury v Otago	Christchurch	1995/96
335	lost 32 runs	South Island v North Island	Christchurch	1999/00
334-7	and won	Wellington v Northern Districts	Wellington	1958/59
334	lost 355 runs	Canterbury v Wellington	Christchurch	1926/27
333-8	set 577 runs	Otago v Wellington	Wellington	1951/52
331-6	set 417 runs	England A v New Zealand A	Lincoln	1999/00
328-6	and won	Otago v Canterbury	Christchurch	1974/75
324-5	and won	Canterbury v Auckland	Christchurch	1949/50
324-5	and won	Northern Districts v Auckland	Auckland	1988/89
324-5	and won	New Zealand v Pakistan	Christchurch	1993/94
324	lost 37 runs	Canterbury v Central Districts	Nelson	1982/83
324-7	and won	Wellington v Otago	Oamaru	1998/99
322-6	and won	Northern Districts v Central Districts	Palmerston North	1982/83
322	lost 57 runs	Wellington v Canterbury	Christchurch	1924/25
322-7	and won	Northern Districts v Wellington	Hamilton	1998/99
322	lost 55 runs	Canterbury v Otago	Christchurch	2000/01
320-4	and won	Central Districts v Northern Districts	Hamilton	1996/97
318	lost 36 runs	Fiji v Canterbury	Christchurch	1947/48
318	lost 23 runs	West Indies v Governor General's XI	Auckland	1968/69
318-3†	and won	Wellington v Central Districts	Wellington	1997/98
318	lost 119 runs	Otago v Canterbury	Christchurch	2006/07
317-9	and won	Northern Districts v Central Districts	Gisborne	1979/80
317-7	and won	Otago v Central Districts	Dunedin	1997/98
316-8	and won	England XI v New Zealand XI	Nelson	1991/92
315-4	and won	South Island v North Island	Wellington	1934/35
315	lost 140 runs	Auckland v Central Districts	Palmerston North	2005/06
313	lost 62 runs	Northern Districts v Canterbury	Christchurch	1988/89
313-7	and won	Central Districts v Northern Districts	Hamilton	1999/00
312-5	set 416 runs	Wellington v Canterbury	Christchurch	1917/18
311-7	and won	Otago v Wellington	Wellington	1996/97
310-4	and won	Otago v Central Districts	New Plymouth	1987/88
310-9	and won	Otago v Canterbury	Christchurch	1990/91
308-7	set 410 runs	Wellington v Canterbury	Rangiora	2001/02
307-8	set 341 runs	Australia v Canterbury	Christchurch	1909/10
307-9	set 348 runs	Wellington v Auckland	Wellington	1992/93
307-6	and won	England v New Zealand	Christchurch	1996/97
306-3	and won	Canterbury v Otago	Christchurch	1940/41
303-3	and won	Canterbury v Wellington	Wellington	1918/19
303	lost 365 runs	Auckland v Wellington	Wellington	1923/24
303	lost 197 runs	Wellington v Auckland	Auckland	1953/54
302	lost 69 runs	Canterbury v Wellington	Christchurch	1985/86
302-5	and won	Northern Districts v Wellington	Hamilton	1987/88
301	lost 6 runs	Central Districts v Northern Districts	Hamilton	1977/78
301	lost 99 runs	Otago v Central Districts	New Plymouth	2005/06
300-2	and won	Canterbury v Northern Districts	Christchurch	1984/85
300-8	set 320	Wellington v Northern Districts	Wellington	1991/92
300-9	set 351	Wellington v Otago	Dunedin	1990/91
300-9	set 303	Northern Districts v Central Districts	Nelson	1993/94
300	set 341	Auckland v Wellington	Auckland	1997/98

† after Central Districts had forfeited its second innings *§ after Northern Districts had forfeited its second innings*

Large Victories

BY AN INNINGS AND

364 runs	Sims' Australian XI defeated Canterbury	Christchurch	1913/14
358 runs	Australia defeated New Zealand	Wellington	1904/05
356 runs	Australia defeated Otago	Dunedin	1949/50
354 runs	Auckland defeated Hawke's Bay	Auckland	1920/21
332 runs	Wellington defeated Canterbury	Wellington	1925/26
327 runs	NSW defeated Otago	Dunedin	1923/24
322 runs	Wellington defeated Hawkes Bay	Wellington	1905/06
322 runs	West Indies defeated New Zealand	Wellington	1994/95
277 runs	NSW defeated Canterbury	Christchurch	1923/24
275 runs	Auckland defeated Hawkes Bay	Auckland	1910/11
275 runs	Auckland defeated Northern Districts	Auckland	2000/01
258 runs	New Zealand A defeated Sri Lanka A	Christchurch	2003/04
256 runs	Wellington defeated Otago	Wellington	1899/00

BY A RUNS MARGIN

512 runs	Wellington defeated Auckland	Wellington	1925/26
446 runs	Wellington defeated Otago	Wellington	1926/27
438 runs	Auckland defeated Wellington	Auckland	1934/35
425 runs	Central Districts defeated Otago	Alexandra	2001/02
382 runs	Auckland defeated Canterbury	Christchurch	1920/21
365 runs	Wellington defeated Auckland	Wellington	1923/24
355 runs	Wellington defeated Canterbury	Christchurch	1926/27
343 runs	Auckland defeated Hawke's Bay	Napier	1912/13
343 runs	Canterbury defeated Central Districts	Christchurch	2004/05
342 runs	Canterbury defeated Auckland	Christchurch	1924/25
322 runs	Canterbury defeated Wellington	Christchurch	1910/11
318 runs	Canterbury defeated Auckland	Christchurch	1913/14
318 runs	Northern Districts defeated Auckland	Auckland	2006/07
315 runs	Auckland defeated Otago	Auckland	1907/08
302 runs	Canterbury defeated Central Districts	Christchurch	1951/52
302 runs	Canterbury defeated Northern Districts	Hamilton	1998/99

Tied Matches

Wellington v Nelson	Wellington	1873/74
New Zealand v T.N. Pearce's XI	Scarborough	1958
Central Districts v England XI	New Plymouth	1977/78
Victoria v New Zealand	Melbourne	1982/83
Wellington v Canterbury	Wellington	1988/89

Close Finishes

VICTORY BY 1 WICKET

Canterbury defeated Tasmania	Christchurch	1883/84
Otago defeated Canterbury	Christchurch	1890/91
Wellington defeated Nelson	Nelson	1891/92
Auckland defeated Wellington	Wellington	1893/94
Canterbury defeated Wellington	Wellington	1899/00
Auckland defeated Wellington	Wellington	1911/12
Canterbury defeated Auckland	Auckland	1914/15
Wellington defeated Otago	Wellington	1924/25
Auckland defeated Otago	Auckland	1946/47
Fiji defeated Wellington	Wellington	1947/48
Otago defeated Wellington	Dunedin	1948/49

Auckland defeated Canterbury	Auckland	1950/51
Central Districts defeated Wellington	Wellington	1951/52
Otago defeated Wellington	Dunedin	1952/53
MCC defeated Canterbury	Christchurch	1960/61
Auckland defeated Canterbury	Christchurch	1963/64
Wellington defeated NZ Under-23 XI	Wellington	1965/66
Canterbury defeated Auckland	Auckland	1974/75
Northern Districts defeated Central Districts	Gisborne	1979/80
New Zealand defeated West Indies	Dunedin	1979/80
Otago defeated Wellington	Alexandra	1980/81
Otago defeated Canterbury	Christchurch	1990/91
Otago defeated Wellington	Dunedin	1991/92
Central Districts defeated Auckland	Auckland	1994/95
Canterbury defeated Northern Districts	Christchurch	1994/95
Southern defeated Central	Wanganui	1997/98
Wellington defeated Northern Districts	Hamilton	2001/02
Northern Districts defeated Central Districts	Napier	2004/05

VICTORY BY 10 RUNS OR LESS

1 run	Northern Districts defeated Central Districts	Rotorua	1989/90
2 runs	Auckland defeated Canterbury	Auckland	1903/04
	Wellington defeated Canterbury	Wellington	1935/36
3 runs	Otago defeated Wellington	Wellington	1953/54
	Central Districts defeated Wellington	Wellington	1970/71
	Central Districts defeated Otago	New Plymouth	1970/71
	Canterbury defeated Central Districts	Napier	1979/80
	Auckland defeated Otago	Dunedin	2004/05
4 runs	Auckland defeated Nelson	Nelson	1882/83
	Canterbury defeated Otago	Christchurch	1882/83
	Auckland defeated Wellington	Auckland	1977/78
5 runs	Central Districts defeated Otago	New Plymouth	1953/54
	Northern Districts defeated Central Districts	Napier	1976/77
6 runs	Canterbury defeated Tasmania	Christchurch	1883/84
	Auckland defeated Canterbury	Auckland	1952/53
	South Island XI defeated North Island XI	Wellington	1957/58
	Northern Districts defeated Central Districts	Hamilton	1977/78
	Northern Districts defeated Otago	Dunedin	1978/79
	Central Districts defeated Northern Districts	Napier	1988/89
	Canterbury defeated Auckland	Auckland	2006/07
7 runs	Auckland defeated Canterbury	Christchurch	1873/74
8 runs	Auckland defeated Wellington	Wellington	1945/46
	Auckland defeated Northern Districts	Auckland	1963/64
	Central Districts defeated Auckland	Napier	1982/83
	Auckland defeated Central Districts	Auckland	1999/00
9 runs	Central Districts defeated Auckland	Nelson	1983/84
10 runs	Northern Districts defeated Canterbury	Hamilton	1960/61
	Wellington defeated Central Districts	New Plymouth	1973/74
	Otago defeated Auckland	Dunedin	1975/76

Victory after Follow-on

Auckland (180 & 302)	beat Canterbury (392 & 84)	Auckland	1952/53
Northern Districts (165 & 275)	beat Otago (320-9d & 105)	Dunedin	1961/62
Auckland (69 & 303)	beat Northern Districts (224 & 140)	Auckland	1963/64
Canterbury (166 & 360)	beat Auckland (351-9d & 149)	Christchurch	1973/74
Auckland (101 & 278)	beat Otago (268 & 108)	Dunedin	2004/05

Matches Abandoned without a Ball Being Bowled

these matches are not included in any first-class records

Hawke's Bay v Australia	Napier	1909/10
Central Districts v Northern Districts	Napier	1970/71
†Wellington v Australia	Wellington	1973/74
Central Districts v Australia	Napier	1973/74
†New Zealand v Pakistan	Dunedin	1988/89
†New Zealand President's XI v Australia	Nelson	1992/93
New Zealand A v Sri Lanka	Gisborne	1996/97
Wellington v Canterbury	Wellington	1996/97
†Northern v Pakistan A	Auckland	1998/99
†New Zealand v India	Dunedin	1998/99

† replaced with a limited-overs match

Matches Completed in One Day

Otago v Canterbury	Dunedin	11. 2.1868
Wellington v Auckland	Wellington	29.11.1874
Nelson v Wellington	Nelson	26.12.1887
Otago v Auckland	Dunedin	27.12.1889
Hawke's Bay v Taranaki	Napier	9. 1.1892
Auckland v New South Wales*	Auckland	20. 1.1894
Ireland v New Zealand	Dublin	11. 9.1937
Auckland v Fiji†	Auckland	9. 3.1954

** no play on first day* *† after no play on first two days and three declarations on third*

Most Extras in an Innings

Extras	*B*	*LB*	*NB*	*W*				
† 66	2	9	54	1	NZ Academy XI (459-8d)	v Pakistan A	Lincoln	1998/99
62	25	21	13	3	England (562)	v New Zealand	Leeds	2004
† 60	18	17	20	5	Central Districts (460-4d)	v Wellington	Wellington	1997/98
58	41	14	3	—	Wellington (380-5)	v Auckland	Wellington	1929/30
†58	6	14	30	8	Auckland (322-4d)	v Wellington	Auckland	1993/94
58	4	12	33	9	New Zealand (563)	v Pakistan	Hamilton	2003/04
57	31	16	10	—	New Zealand (387)	v England	Auckland	1929/30
54	35	14	1	4	Auckland (200-8d)	v Wellington	Auckland	1973/74
54	5	16	33	—	New Zealand A (597-9d)	v Sri Lanka A	Queenstown	2003/04
53	26	10	17	—	Canterbury (473-6)	v Auckland	Christchurch	1930/31
†53	4	2	46	1	Wellington (498-2d)	v Canterbury	Christchurch	1994/95
52					Wellington (370)	v Canterbury	Christchurch	1922/23
52	12	7	33	—	New Zealand (468)	v Pakistan	Karachi	1976/77
52	1	27	33	1	Auckland (423-7d)	v Wellington	Wellington	1992/93
† 52	1	15	32	4	Canterbury (537)	v Central Districts	Blenheim	1996/97
52	21	28	3	1	New Zealand (630-6d)	v India	Mohali	2003/04
52	7	9	28	8	Central Districts (499)	v Canterbury	N.Plymouth	2004/05
51	10	11	30	—	Auckland (369)	v West Indies	Auckland	1999/00

50					Otago (602-8d)	v Canterbury	Dunedin	1928/29
50	13	24	11	2	Wellington (356)	v Canterbury	Wellington	1981/82
† 50	3	11	36	—	Southern (554)	v Pakistan A	Christchurch	1998/99

† no balls counted as two extras, regardless of whether runs were scored from the bat

Longest Matches in New Zealand

before 1900

FOUR DAYS

Otago v Canterbury	Dunedin	1875/76
Canterbury v Tasmania	Christchurch	1883/84
Otago v Canterbury	Dunedin	1884/85

Longest Matches in New Zealand

since 1900

SIX DAYS

New Zealand v England	Christchurch	1974/75
New Zealand v India	Christchurch	1975/76
*New Zealand v England	Auckland	1977/78
New Zealand v Pakistan	Napier	1978/79
New Zealand v West Indies	Auckland	1979/80
New Zealand v India	Christchurch	1980/81

** the only match where play took place on all six days.*
The other instances involved the rest day being used after a day's play was lost

FIVE DAYS

Canterbury v Otago	Christchurch	1911/12
Canterbury v Wellington	Christchurch	1922/23
Otago v Wellington	Dunedin	1923/24
Canterbury v Auckland	Christchurch	1924/25
Wellington v Otago	Wellington	1926/27
Northern Districts v Auckland	Taupo	1999/00
Auckland v Wellington	Auckland	2004/05
Wellington v Central Districts	Wellington	2005/06

All other matches of five days duration since 1926/27 have been test matches. A complete list of these up to 1993/94 is on pages 288 and 289 of the 1994 Almanack. *The 1998/99 Shell Trophy final between Central Districts and Otago at Napier was scheduled for five days but completed in three.*

INDIVIDUAL RECORDS

BATTING

Highest Individual Scores

385	Sutcliffe B.	Otago v Canterbury	Christchurch	1952/53
355	Sutcliffe B.	Otago v Auckland	Dunedin	1949/50
338*	Blunt R.C.	Otago v Canterbury	Christchurch	1931/32
336*	Hammond W.R.	England v New Zealand	Auckland	1932/33
317	Rutherford K.R.	New Zealand v D.B. Close's XI	Scarborough	1986
306	Richardson M.H.	New Zealand v Zimbabwe A	Kwekwe	2000/01
301*	Fulton P.G.	Canterbury v Auckland	Christchurch	2002/03
299	Crowe M.D.	New Zealand v Sri Lanka	Wellington	1990/91
296	Reid J.R.	Wellington v Northern Districts	Wellington	1962/63
293	Trumper V.T.	Sims' Australian XI v Canterbury	Christchurch	1913/14
290	Carson W.N.	Auckland v Otago	Dunedin	1936/37
284	Woodfull W.M.	Australia v New Zealand	Auckland	1927/28
283	Reid J.R.	Wellington v Otago	Wellington	1951/52
275*	Cullinan D.J.	South Africa v New Zealand	Auckland	1998/99
275	Sutcliffe B.	Otago v Auckland	Auckland	1950/51
274*	Fleming S.P.	New Zealand v Sri Lanka	Colombo	2002/03
271	Javed Miandad	Pakistan v New Zealand	Auckland	1988/89
268	Sinclair M.S.	New Zealand A v South Africa A	Potchefstroom	2004/05
267*	Young B.A.	New Zealand v Sri Lanka	Dunedin	1996/97
267	de Silva P.A.	Sri Lanka v New Zealand	Wellington	1990/91
264	Sutcliffe B.	Otago v Central Districts	Dunedin	1959/60
262	Fleming S.P.	New Zealand v South Africa	Cape Town	2005/06
259	Turner G.M.	New Zealand v Guyana	Georgetown	1971/72
259	Turner G.M.	New Zealand v West Indies	Georgetown	1971/72
258	Nurse S.M.	West Indies v New Zealand	Christchurch	1968/69
256	Smith S.G.	Auckland v Canterbury	Auckland	1919/20
255*	McGlew D.J.	South Africa v New Zealand	Wellington	1952/53
254*	Vance R.H.	Wellington v Northern Districts	Wellington	1988/89
251*	Harris C.Z.	Canterbury v Central Districts	Rangiora	1996/97
250	Walters K.D.	Australia v New Zealand	Christchurch	1976/77
247*	Chappell G.S.	Australia v New Zealand	Wellington	1973/74
243	Sutcliffe B.	New Zealand v Essex	Southend	1949
242*	Crowe M.D.	New Zealand v South Australia	Adelaide	1985/86
242	Crowe M.D.	Central Districts v Otago	New Plymouth	1989/90
241	Horne M.J.	Otago v Auckland	Auckland	1997/98
239	Dowling G.T.	New Zealand v India	Christchurch	1967/68
237*	Latham R.T.	Canterbury v Northern Districts	Rotorua	1990/91
236	Ryder J.D.	Wellington v Central Districts	Palmerston North	2004/05
235	Marshall J.A.H.	Northern Districts v Canterbury	Christchurch	2001/02
230*	Sutcliffe B.	New Zealand v India	New Delhi	1955/56
227	Hammond W.R.	England v New Zealand	Christchurch	1932/33
226*	Rutherford K.R.	Otago v India	Dunedin	1989/90
226	Hastings B.F.	Canterbury v NZ Under 23 XI	Christchurch	1964/65
225*	Blunt R.C.	New Zealand v Gentlemen	Eastbourne	1931
224	Vincent L.	New Zealand v Sri Lanka	Wellington	2004/05
223*	Turner G.M.	New Zealand v West Indies	Kingston	1971/72
223	Astle N.J.	New Zealand v Queensland	Brisbane	2001/02
222*	Midlane F.A.	Wellington v Otago	Wellington	1914/15
222	Rutherford I.A.	Otago v Central Districts	New Plymouth	1978/79
222	Astle N.J.	New Zealand v England	Christchurch	2001/02

221*	Fulton P.G.	Canterbury v Otago	Dunedin	2004/05
221	Macartney C.G.	NSW v Canterbury	Christchurch	1923/24
221	Blunt R.C.	Otago v Canterbury	Dunedin	1928/29
219	Bell M.D.	Wellington v Northern Districts	Hamilton	1998/99
217	Taylor L.R.P.L.	Central Districts v Otago	Napier	2006/07
216	Fletcher K.W.R.	England v New Zealand	Auckland	1974/75
216	Bell M.D.	Wellington v Auckland	Auckland	1997/98
216*	Chanderpaul S.	West Indies v New Zealand A	Taupo	1999/00
214*	Kortlang H.H.L.	Wellington v Auckland	Wellington	1925/26
214*	Booth B.C.	Australia B v Central Districts	Palmerston North	1966/67
214	Sinclair M.S.	New Zealand v West Indies	Wellington	1999/00
213	Murray B.A.G.	Wellington v Otago	Dunedin	1968/69
213	Trimble S.C.	Australia B v New Zealand	Wellington	1969/70
213	Greenidge C.G.	West Indies v New Zealand	Auckland	1986/87
212*	Woodfull W.M.	Victoria v Canterbury	Christchurch	1924/25
212*	Richardson M.H.	New Zealand A v Sussex	Hove	2000
212*	Kelly D.P.	Central Districts v Canterbury	Blenheim	2000/01
212*	Styris S.B.	Northern Districts v Otago	Hamilton	2001/02
212	Hiddleston J.S.	Wellington v Canterbury	Wellington	1925/26
212	Dempster C.S.	New Zealand v Essex	Leyton	1931
211*	Hick G.A.	Northern Districts v Auckland	Auckland	1988/89
211*	Gibbs H.H.	South Africa v New Zealand	Christchurch	1998/99
211	Warner P.F.	Lord Hawke's XI v Otago	Dunedin	1902/03
211	Wallace W.M.	Auckland v Canterbury	Auckland	1939/40
209*	Brown S.W.	Auckland v Canterbury	Christchurch	1990/91
209*	Horne M.J.	Auckland v Northern Districts	Auckland	2003/04
209	White D.J.	Northern Districts v Central Districts	Hamilton	1985/86
209	Horne P.A.	Auckland v Northern Districts	Auckland	1988/89
208*	Sutcliffe B.	North Island v South Island	Dunedin	1947/48
208	Franklin J.E.C.	Wellington v Auckland	Wellington	2005/06
207	Hart R.T.	Central Districts v Wellington	Wellington	1985/86
206	Page M.L.	Canterbury v Wellington	Wellington	1931/32
206	Donnelly M.P.	New Zealand v England	Lord's	1949
206	Dowling G.T.	Canterbury v Wellington	Christchurch	1962/63
206	Harris C.Z	Canterbury v Central Districts	Blenheim	1996/97
205*	Lloyd C.H.	West Indies v South Island	Dunedin	1968/69
205*	McSweeney E.B.	Wellington v Central Districts	Levin	1987/88
205	McIntosh T.G.	Auckland v Otago	Lincoln	2006/07
204*	Sinclair M.S.	New Zealand v Pakistan	Christchurch	2000/01
204	Cox A.	Canterbury v Otago	Christchurch	1925/26
204	Hiddleston J.S.	Wellington v Auckland	Wellington	1925/26
204	Scott V.J.	Auckland v Otago	Dunedin	1947/48
204	Patel D.N.	Auckland v Northern Districts	Auckland	1991/92
203*	Burnett G.P.	Wellington v Northern Districts	Hamilton	1991/92
203*	Sinclair M.S.	Central Districts v Northern Districts	Wanganui	1998/99
203	Scott V.J.	New Zealand v Combined Services	Gillingham	1949
203	Reid J.R.	New Zealand v Western Province	Cape Town	1961/62
203	Edgar B.A.	Young New Zealand v Zimbabwe	Bulawayo	1984/85
203	Parlane M.E.	Wellington v Auckland	Auckland	2004/05
202*	Congdon B.E.	Central Districts v Otago	Nelson	1968/69
202*	Greatbatch M.J.	Central Districts v Otago	Palmerston North	1988/89
202	Turner G.M.	New Zealand v President's XI	Montego Bay	1971/72
202	Austen M.H.	Wellington v Central Districts	Wanganui	1993/94
202	Greatbatch M.J.	Central Districts v Northern Districts	Rotorua	1995/96
202	Fleming S.P.	New Zealand v Bangladesh	Chittagong	2004/05
201*	Hart M.N.	Northern Districts v Auckland	Auckland	2002/03

201*	Smith B.F.	Central Districts v Canterbury	New Plymouth	2001/02
201	Reid J.R.	Otago v Canterbury	Dunedin	1957/58
201	Sutcliffe B.	Otago v Northern Districts	Hamilton	1960/61
201	Mushtaq Mohammad	Pakistan v New Zealand	Dunedin	1972/73
200*	MacLaren A.C.	MCC v New Zealand	Wellington	1922/23
200*	Bardsley W.	NSW v Auckland	Auckland	1923/24
200*	Thorpe G.P.	England v New Zealand	Christchurch	2001/02
200	Lawson R.A.	Otago v Central Districts	Napier	1995/96

Most Runs in a Season in New Zealand

		M	*I*	*NO*	*HS*	*Runs*	*Ave*	*100*
Crowe M.D.	1986/87	11	21	3	175*	1676	93.11	8
Turner G.M.	1975/76	11	20	4	177*	1244	77.75	5
Hick G.A.	1988/89	8	16	3	211*	1228	94.46	6
Bell M.D.	2000/01	13	21	0	134	1092	52.00	6
Crowe J.J.	1991/92	10	19	2	142*	1063	62.52	4
Vance R.H.	1988/89	10	18	2	254*	1037	64.81	4
Richardson M.H.	2000/01	11	19	2	166	1035	60.88	2
Wright J.G.	1986/87	11	21	2	192	1019	53.63	3
Papps M.H.W.	2006/07	7	11	0	188	1005	91.36	4
Sinclair M.S.	1999/00	14	26	2	214	1004	41.83	3
Vincent L.	2004/05	10	16	2	224	999	71.35	3
Dowling G.T.	1967/68	10	18	1	239	968	56.94	4
Edgar B.A.	1978/79	12	23	0	134	944	41.04	2
Weekes E. de C.	1955/56	8	10	1	156	940	104.44	6
Rutherford K.R.	1989/90	13	19	2	226*	940	55.29	3
Smith B.F.	2000/01	10	17	1	168	939	58.68	2
Edgar B.A.	1981/82	11	19	1	161	934	51.88	3
Sutcliffe B.	1947/48	5	10	1	208*	911	101.22	4
Maynard M.P.	1991/92	10	13	0	195	893	68.69	4
Horne M.J.	1998/99	10	19	2	132	887	52.17	1
Jones A.H.	1988/89	8	15	2	181*	884	68.00	2
Stead G.R.	2000/01	12	20	2	121*	875	48.61	3
Hastings B.F.	1968/69	10	15	4	117*	872	79.27	4
Wright J.G.	1981/82	11	18	0	141	872	48.44	4
Dowling G.T.	1966/67	10	18	2	102*	871	54.43	1
Jones R.A.	2000/01	12	19	0	188	860	45.26	3
Sutcliffe B.	1952/53	7	13	0	385	859	66.07	1
Sinclair M.S.	2003/04	10	16	1	133	851	56.73	2
Fulton P.G.	2004/05	9	14	1	221*	850	65.38	2
Anderson R.W.	1977/78	11	22	0	123	849	38.59	2
Horne M.J.	1996/97	10	17	0	124	843	49.58	3
Bradburn G.E.	1989/90	12	23	1	96	842	38.27	—
Spearman C.M.	1998/99	11	17	1	137	842	52.62	2
Turner G.M.	1974/75	8	15	1	186*	838	59.85	4
Harris C.Z.	1996/97	5	7	1	251*	835	139.16	3
Hick G.A.	1987/88	9	14	1	146	827	63.61	4
Nurse S.M.	1968/69	5	9	0	258	826	91.77	3
Sinclair M.S.	1998/99	11	17	3	203*	823	58.78	2
McIntosh T.G.	2002/03	10	17	3	157	820	58.57	2
Wright J.G.	1989/90	9	12	2	185	818	81.80	3
Reid J.F.	1980/81	10	18	4	173	817	58.35	3
Edwards G.N.	1980/81	11	19	2	177*	812	47.76	2
McMillan C.D.	1996/97	8	12	1	159	809	73.54	3
Crowe M.D.	1992/93	7	14	1	163	803	61.76	3

Most Runs in a Season for New Zealand

		M	I	NO	HS	Runs	Ave	100
Sutcliffe B.	1949	29	49	5	243	2627	59.70	7
Donnelly M.P.	1949	29	45	8	206	2287	61.81	5
Reid J.R.	*1961/62	20	36	2	203	2083	61.26	7

** includes South Africa & Australia*

Most Runs in Season of First-class Debut

			M	I	NO	HS	Runs	Ave
Hay G.R.	CD	2006/07	8	14	1	106	593	45.61
Cooper B.G.	ND	1980/81	7	13	0	105	520	40.00
Briasco P.S.	CD	1982/83	8	15	1	95	519	37.07
Carson W.N.	Auckland	1936/37	3	4	0	290	500	125.00

Highest Average in a Season in New Zealand

		M	I	NO	HS	Runs	Ave	100
Hammond W.R.	1932/33	3	3	1	336*	621	310.50	2
Woodfull W.M.	1924/25	6	9	5	212*	710	177.50	3
Greatbatch M.J.	1995/96	5	6	2	202	623	155.75	4
Javed Miandad	1988/89	4	5	1	271	597	149.25	3
Harris C.Z.	1996/97	5	7	1	251*	835	139.16	3
Woodfull W.M.	1927/28	6	9	3	284	781	130.16	3
Carson W.N.	1936/37	3	4	0	290	500	125.00	2
Bardsley W.	1923/24	6	7	2	200*	623	124.60	1
Cullinan D.J.	1998/99	5	7	2	275*	553	110.60	3
Hiddleston J.S.	1925/26	3	5	0	212	537	107.40	2
Weekes E. de C.	1955/56	8	10	1	156	940	104.44	6
Sutcliffe B.	1946/47	6	8	1	197	722	103.14	3
Parker J.M.	1981/82	7	13	7	117	618	103.00	2
Sutcliffe B.	1947/48	5	10	1	208*	911	101.22	4

minimum 500 runs

Centuries

George Watson registered the first century in New Zealand first-class cricket on 24 February, 1881 when he made 175 for Canterbury v Otago at Hagley Park, Christchurch.

To date, 1865 centuries have been scored in New Zealand with 51 in 1991/92 being the record for one season. A further 363 have been recorded for New Zealand teams overseas.

The following NZ players have made 15 or more centuries during their first-class careers:

Turner G.M.	103
Crowe M.D.	71
Wright J.G.	59
Sutcliffe B.	44
Reid J.R.	39
Dempster C.S.	35
Rutherford K.R.	35
Howarth G.P.	32
Fleming S.P.	31
Spearman C.M.	28
Patel D.N.	26
Dacre C.C.R.	24
Edgar B.A.	24
Greatbatch M.J.	24
Horne M.J.	24
Donnelly M.P.	23
Congdon B.E.	23
Crowe J.J.	22
Sinclair M.S.	22
Parker J.M.	21
Burgess M.G.	20
Richardson M.H.	20
Astle N.J.	19
Lowry T.C.	18
Hadlee W.A.	18
Twose R.G.	18
Bell M.D.	18
Wallace W.M.	17
Scott V.J.	16
Dowling G.T.	16
Jones A.H.	16
McMillan C.D.	16
Hastings B.F.	15
Blunt R.C.	15
Franklin T.J.	15

Most Centuries in a Season in New Zealand

8	Crowe M.D.	1986/87
6	Weekes E. de C.	1955/56
6	Hick G.A.	1988/89
6	Bell M.D.	2000/01
5	Turner G.M.	1975/76
4	Sutcliffe B.	1947/48
4	Hadlee W.A.	1947/48
4	Sutcliffe B.	1950/51
4	Dowling G.T.	1967/68
4	Hastings B.F.	1968/69
4	Turner G.M.	1974/75
4	Wright J.G.	1981/82
4	Franklin T.J.	1987/88
4	Hick G.A.	1987/88
4	Vance R.H.	1988/89
4	Jones A.H.	1990/91
4	Crowe J.J.	1991/92
4	Maynard M.P.	1991/92
4	Greatbatch M.J.	1995/96
4	Ingram P.J.	2006/07
4	Papps M.H.W.	2006/07

Five Centuries in Consecutive Innings

Weekes E. de C.	156	West Indies v Auckland	Auckland	1955/56
	148	West Indies v Canterbury	Auckland	
	123	West Indies v New Zealand	Dunedin	
	119*	West Indies v Wellington	Wellington	
	103	West Indies v New Zealand	Christchurch	

Three Centuries in Consecutive Innings

Macartney C.G.	120	NSW v Wellington	Wellington	1923/24
	120	NSW v Otago	Dunedin	
	221	NSW v Canterbury	Christchurch	
Sutcliffe B.	103	Otago v Auckland	Auckland	1947/48
	118, 125	Otago v Canterbury	Dunedin	
Sutcliffe B.	141, 135	Auckland v Canterbury	Auckland	1948/49
	140	New Zealand XI v The Rest	Christchurch	
Reid J.R.	101, 118*	New Zealand v Orange Free State	Bloemfontein	1961/62
	165	New Zealand v South African Colts XI	East London	
Chappell I.M.	128	Australia v Northern Districts	Hamilton	1973/74
	145, 121	Australia v New Zealand	Wellington	
Crowe M.D.	151	Central Districts v Northern Districts	Morrinsville	1986/87
	144, 151	Central Districts v Canterbury	New Plymouth	
Hick G.A.	211*	Northern Districts v Auckland	Auckland	1988/89
	144, 132	Northern Districts v Wellington	Morrinsville	
Jones A.H.	186	New Zealand v Sri Lanka	Wellington	1990/91
	122, 100*	New Zealand v Sri Lanka	Hamilton	
Maynard M.P.	142	Northern Districts v Otago	Hamilton	1991/92
	195, 110	Northern Districts v Auckland	Auckland	
Greatbatch M.J.	115	Central Districts v Canterbury	Christchurch	1995/96
	202	Central Districts v Northern Districts	Rotorua	
	162*	Central Districts v Auckland	Auckland	
Campbell S.L.	112, 109*	West Indies v Auckland	Auckland	1999/00
	170	West Indies v New Zealand	Hamilton	

Wells J.D.	143	Wellington v Canterbury	Wellington	1999/00
	107 132*	Wellington v Central Districts	New Plymouth	
How J.M.	105 108*	Central Districts v Otago	Queenstown	2004/05
	121	Central Districts v Northern Districts	Napier	
Sinclair M.S.	121 103*	Central Districts v Otago	New Plymouth	2005/06
	101	Central Districts v Auckland	Palmerston North	
Ingram P.J.	119 166*	Central Districts v Canterbury	Christchurch	2006/07
	105	Central Districts v Auckland	Napier	

Century on First-class Debut

† Watson G.	175	Canterbury v Otago	Christchurch	1880/81
Brook-Smith W.	112*	Auckland v Hawke's Bay	Auckland	1904/05
† Wood B.B.	108 & 18	Canterbury v Wellington	Wellington	1907/08
McMullan J.J.M.	157*	Otago v Southland	Dunedin	1917/18
† Snedden C.A.	119	Auckland v Hawke's Bay	Auckland	1920/21
Talbot R.O.	105	Canterbury v Otago	Dunedin	1922/23
Tindill E.W.T.	106 & 0	Wellington v Auckland	Auckland	1932/33
Scott V.J.	122	Auckland v Canterbury	Auckland	1937/38
† Ongley J.A.	110	Wellington v Otago	Wellington	1938/39
† Kerr A.C.	122	Auckland v Wellington	Auckland	1941/42
† Watt D.G.	15 & 105	Otago v Canterbury	Christchurch	1943/44
Smith K.F.H.	27 & 141*	Wellington v Central Districts	Wellington	1953/54
MacLeod D.N.	117	Central Districts v Wellington	Wanganui	1956/57
Bilby G.P.	132 & 2*	Wellington v Central Districts	Wellington	1962/63
† Mitchell W.J.	127*	Northern Districts v Pakistan	Hamilton	1964/65
† Sampson H.C.	25 & 119	Central Districts v Wellington	Wellington	1970/71
Vaughan J.T.C.	106* & 1	Auckland v Wellington	Wellington	1989/90
Aiken J.M.	39 & 156*	Wellington v Canterbury	Christchurch	1989/90

† *only century in first-class cricket*

B.R. Williams scored 103 in his fourth first-class match, not having batted in his first three matches, for Wellington v Central Districts at Wellington, 1989/90.*

Century on First-class Debut in Other Countries

In ENGLAND

Dacre C.C.R.	107	New Zealand v MCC	Lord's	1927
Crowe M.D.	104	D.B. Close's XI v Pakistan	Scarborough	1982
Horne M.J.	133	New Zealand v British Universities	Oxford	1999
Spearman C.M.	111	Gloucestershire v Worcestershire	Worcester	2002
Adams A.R.	124	Essex v Leicestershire	Leicester	2004
Marshall H.J.H.	102	Gloucestershire v Worcestershire	Bristol	2006

J.D.P. Oram scored 103 for New Zealand v Worcestershire at Worcester in 2004 in his first innings in England after not batting in his first game*

In AUSTRALIA

Sutcliffe B.	142	New Zealand v Western Australia	Perth	1953/54
Miller L.S.M.	142	New Zealand v South Australia	Adelaide	1953/54
Patel D.N.	105	New Zealand v Western Australia	Perth	1987/88

In SOUTH AFRICA

Reid J.R.	111	New Zealand v Western Province	Cape Town	1953/54

Kasper R.J.	122*	Natal B v Transvaal B	Pietermaritzburg	1970/71
Harris C.Z.	118*	Canterbury v Eastern Province	Grahamstown	1993/94
Richardson M.H.	173*	New Zealand v Boland	Paarl	2000/01
McCullum B.B.	101	New Zealand v Rest of South Africa	Benoni	2005/06

In WEST INDIES

Hastings B.F.	100*	New Zealand v Jamaica	Kingston	1971/72
Crowe M.D.	118	New Zealand v Shell Award XI	Kingston	1984/85
Styris S.B.	107	New Zealand v West Indies	St George's	2001/02

In INDIA

Taylor B.R.	105	New Zealand v India	Calcutta	1964/65
Burgess M.G.	102	Prime Minister's XI v President's XI	Bombay	1967/68
Parker J.M.	104	New Zealand v India	Bombay	1976/77
Wright J.G.	104	New Zealand v West Zone	Rajkot	1988/89
Crowe M.D.	101*	New Zealand v President's XI	Rajkot	1995/96
Oram J.D.P.	101*	New Zealand v India A	Rajkot	2003/04

M.H. Richardson scored 128 for New Zealand v India at Rajkot in 2003/04 in his first innings in India after not batting in his first game.*

In PAKISTAN

Reid J.R.	105*	NZ v Chief Commissioner's XI	Karachi	1955/56
Anderson R.W.	103*	NZ v NWFP Chief Minister's XI	Peshawar	1976/77

In SRI LANKA

Dempster C.S.	112*	Sir Julien Cahn's XI v Ceylon	Colombo	1936/37
Rutherford K.R.	108	NZ v Board President's XI	Galle	1986/87
Fulton P.G.	101	New Zealand A v Sri Lanka A	Kandy	2005/06

In ZIMBABWE

Franklin T.J.	153*	Young New Zealand v Zimbabwe	Harare	1984/85
Horne M.J.	181	New Zealand v Mashonaland	Harare	1997/98
Sinclair M.S.	100*	New Zealand v President's XI	Mutare	2000/01

In BANGLADESH

McCullum B.B.	143	New Zealand v Bangladesh	Dhaka	2004/05

Century in Last First-class Match

† Phillips J.	110*	Canterbury v Wellington	Christchurch	1898/99
Midlane F.A.	126 & 4	Auckland v Wellington	Wellington	1918/19
† Beechey E.M.	180 & 5	Wellington vAuckland	Wellington	1918/19
† Watt D.G.	15 & 105	Otago v Canterbury	Christchurch	1943/44
Redmond R.E.	103 & 22	Auckland v Otago	Auckland	1975/76
Wadsworth K.J.	117	Canterbury v Otago	Christchurch	1975/76
Parker J.M.	1* & 100	Northern Districts v Wellington	Wellington	1983/84
† Snook I.R.	100*	Central Dists v Northern Dists	Palmerston North	1987/88
Dempsey D.A.	121 & 44	Canterbury v Otago	Dunedin	1987/88
Reid J.F.	112	Auckland v Northern Districts	Hamilton	1987/88
Mawhinney R.E.W.	9* & 108	Otago v Canterbury	Christchurch	1990/91
Twose R.G.	108 & 6	Wellington v Auckland	Wellington	2000/01
Nash D.J.	118 & 11*	Auckland v Otago	Dunedin	2001/02

† only first-class century of career. (D.G. Watt was making his only appearance in first-class cricket. J. Phillips was playing his 124th first-class match and 203rd innings).
J.D. Riley scored 34, 121, 26 and 94 (run out) in his final two first-class matches, for Auckland in 1976/77.*

Century in Each Innings of a Match

Dacre C.C.R.	127* & 101*	Auckland v Victoria	Auckland	1924/25
† Whitelaw P.E.	115 & 155	Auckland v Wellington	Auckland	1934/35
Uttley K.F.M.	132 & 138	Otago v Auckland	Auckland	1937/38
Sutcliffe B.	197 & 128	Otago v MCC	Dunedin	1946/47
Sutcliffe B.	118 & 125	Otago v Canterbury	Dunedin	1947/48
Sutcliffe B.	141 & 135	Auckland v Canterbury	Auckland	1948/49
Sutcliffe B.	243 & 100*	New Zealand v Essex	Southend	1949
Reid J.R.	101 & 118*	New Zealand v Orange Free State	Bloemfontein	1961/62
† Gedye S.G.	104 & 101	Auckland v Central Districts	Auckland	1963/64
† Thomson K.	102 & 102*	Canterbury v Otago	Dunedin	1966/67
Chappell G.S.	247* & 133	Australia v New Zealand	Wellington	1973/74
Chappell I.M.	145 & 121	Australia v New Zealand	Wellington	1973/74
Turner G.M.	101 & 110*	New Zealand v Australia	Christchurch	1973/74
Turner G.M.	135 & 108	Otago v Northern Districts	Gisborne	1974/75
Turner G.M.	105 & 186*	Otago v Central Districts	Dunedin	1974/75
Howarth G.P.	122 & 102	New Zealand v England	Auckland	1977/78
Wright J.G.	113 & 105	Northern Districts v Auckland	Auckland	1981/82
Parker J.M.	117 & 102*	Northern Districts v Central Districts	Tauranga	1981/82
Rutherford K.R.	105 & 104*	Otago v Northern Districts	Alexandra	1985/86
Border A.R.	140 & 114*	Australia v New Zealand	Christchurch	1985/86
Cooper B.G.	105 & 100	Northern Districts v Canterbury	Gisborne	1986/87
Crowe M.D.	144 & 151	Central Districts v Canterbury	New Plymouth	1986/87
Vance R.H.	116* & 123	Wellington v Central Districts	New Plymouth	1988/89
Hick G.A.	144 & 132	Northern Districts v Wellington	Morrinsville	1988/89
Jones A.H.	122 & 100*	New Zealand v Sri Lanka	Hamilton	1990/91
Gurusinha A.P.	119 & 102	Sri Lanka v New Zealand	Hamilton	1990/91
Maynard M.P.	195 & 110	Northern Districts v Auckland	Auckland	1991/92
Crowe M.D.	152 & 137*	Wellington v Canterbury	Christchurch	1992/93
Dravid R.S.	190 & 103*	India v New Zealand	Hamilton	1998/99
Rhodes J.N.	101* & 106*	South Africa v New Zealand A	Lincoln	1998/99
Campbell S.L.	112 & 109*	West Indies v Auckland	Auckland	1999/00
Wells J.D.	107 & 132*	Wellington v Central Districts	New Plymouth	1999/00
Spearman C.M.	100 & 115	New Zealand v North West	Potchefstroom	2000/01
Hopkins G.J.	113 & 175*	Canterbury v Auckland	Auckland	2002/03
Horne M.J.	118 & 209*	Auckland v Northern Districts	Auckland	2003/04
How J.M.	105 & 108*	Central Districts v Otago	Queenstown	2004/05
Sinclair M.S.	121 & 103*	Central Districts v Otago	New Plymouth	2005/06
Ingram P.J.	119 & 166*	Central Districts v Canterbury	Christchurch	2006/07
Jones R.A.	143 & 120	Auckland v Central Districts	Auckland	2006/07

† *maiden first-class century*

Highest Maiden Centuries

301*	Fulton P.G.	Canterbury v Auckland	Christchurch	2002/03
290	Carson W.N.	Auckland v Otago	Dunedin	1936/37
209	White D.J.	Northern Districts v Central Districts	Hamilton	1985/86
204	Cox A.	Canterbury v Otago	Christchurch	1925/26
203*	Burnett G.P.	Wellington v Northern Districts	Hamilton	1991/92
196	Kerr J.L.	Canterbury v Wellington	Christchurch	1932/33
194	Gaffaney C.B.	Otago v Auckland	Dunedin	1996/97
193*	Stead D.W.	Canterbury v Central Districts	Christchurch	1980/81
190	Moloney D.A.R.	Wellington v Auckland	Auckland	1936/37
189	Sinclair M.S.	Central Districts v Wellington	Masterton	1996/97
184	Taylor L.R.P.L.	Central Districts v Wellington	Palmerston North	2004/05
183	Gillespie H.D.	Auckland v Canterbury	Auckland	1929/30

182	McIntosh T.G.	Auckland v Canterbury	Christchurch	2000/01
180	Beechey E.M.	Wellington v Auckland	Wellington	1918/19
180	Dempster C.S.	New Zealand v Warwickshire	Birmingham	1927
180	Mooney F.L.H.	Wellington v Auckland	Wellington	1943/44
179	Ormiston R.W.	Wellington v Central Districts	New Plymouth	1982/83
177	Chandler P.J.B.	Wellington v Auckland	Wellington	1996/97
176	Cuff L.A.	Canterbury v Auckland	Christchurch	1893/94
175	Watson G.	Canterbury v Otago	Christchurch	1880/81
175	Astle N.J.	Canterbury v Northern Districts	Hamilton	1994/95
175	Orchard M.G.	Northern Districts v Central Districts	Napier	2005/06
172	Worker R.V. de R.	Otago v Canterbury	Dunedin	1923/24
172	Englefield J.I.	Canterbury v Central Districts	Blenheim	2000/01
171	Mills S.M.	Wellington v Canterbury	Christchurch	2006/07
167*	Hart R.T.	Central Districts v Canterbury	New Plymouth	1983/84
167	Lawrence J.D.	Canterbury v Auckland	Christchurch	1893/94
165	Redgrave W.P.	Wellington v Hawkes Bay	Wellington	1905/06
165	Chapple M.E.	Canterbury v South Africans	Christchurch	1952/53
165	Truscott P.B.	NZ Under-23 v Auckland	Auckland	1963/64
164*	Duff S.W.	Central Districts v Auckland	Wanganui	1991/92
164	Powell J.L.	Canterbury v Otago	Christchurch	1929/30
163*	How J.M.	Central Districts v Northern Districts	Hamilton	2002/03
163	Menzies R.E.J.	Canterbury v Wellington	Christchurch	1938/39
163	Williams A.B.	Wellington v Canterbury	Christchurch	1896/97
163	Reade L.B.	Central Districts v Northern Districts	Palmerston North	1960/61
161	Larsen G.R.	Wellington v Central Districts	Levin	1987/88
159*	Kennedy P.G.	Canterbury v Northern Districts	Rotorua	1990/91
159	Vincent L.	Auckland v Northern Districts	Auckland	1998/99
158*	Papps M.H.W.	Canterbury v Otago	Christchurch	2001/02
158	Harford N.S.	New Zealand v Oxford University	Oxford	1958
157*	McMullan J.J.M.	Otago v Southland	Dunedin	1917/18
157	Briasco P.S.	Central Districts v Canterbury	New Plymouth	1983/84
156*	Aiken J.M.	Wellington v Canterbury	Christchurch	1989/90
155*	James V.	Canterbury v Otago	Dunedin	1940/41
155*	Parore A.C.	Auckland v Otago	Dunedin	1991/92
155	Badcock F.T.	Wellington v Canterbury	Christchurch	1926/27
155	Oram J.D.P.	Central Districts v Canterbury	Christchurch	1998/99
154	Meuli E.M.	Central Districts v Auckland	Palmerston North	1952/53
153	Watling B-J.	Northern Districts v Otago	Dunedin	2006/07
152	Knight A.R.	Otago v Canterbury	Dunedin	1940/41
152	Kemp R.J.	Wellington v Auckland	Auckland	1947/48
152	Coutts P.J.C.	Central Districts v Canterbury	Christchurch	1966/67
152	Lees W.K.	New Zealand v Pakistan	Karachi	1976/77
152	Brown S.W.	Auckland v Central Districts	Auckland	1990/91
152	Weston T.I.	Central Districts v Auckland	Auckland	2006/07
151	Petrie E.C.	Auckland v Wellington	Auckland	1953/54
150	Crowe M.D.	Auckland v Central Districts	New Plymouth	1981/82

Watson, McMullan and Aiken scored their centuries on their debut in first-class cricket. Beechey was playing in his last first-class game. Carson (aged 20 years 168 days) and Cox (21 years 19 days) were both playing only their second first-class innings and remain the youngest players to score a double-century in New Zealand first-class cricket.

One Hundred Runs before Lunch

Runs	Mins				
* 110	120	Smith S.G.	Auckland v Canterbury	Auckland	1919/20
112	113	Macartney C.G.	NSW v Wellington	Wellington	1923/24
* 116	120	† Punch A.T.E.	NSW v Otago	Dunedin	1923/24
* 101	91	Macartney C.G.	NSW v Otago	Dunedin	1923/24

103	110	Hiddleston J.S.	Wellington v Canterbury	Wellington	1925/26
105	102	Dacre C.C.R.	Auckland v Otago	Dunedin	1926/27
103	103	† Vorrath W.	Otago v Wellington	Dunedin	1927/28
* 106	120	Blunt R.C.	Otago v Canterbury	Christchurch	1928/29
164	130	† Powell J.L.	Canterbury v Otago	Christchurch	1929/30
105	105	Badcock F.T.	Otago v Canterbury	Christchurch	1931/32
* 111	120	Hammond W.R.	England v New Zealand	Auckland	1932/33
102	120	Whitelaw P.E.	Auckland v Wellington	Auckland	1934/35
115	110	Wallace W.M.	New Zealand v Somerset	Taunton	1937
* 110	120	Wallace W.M.	New Zealand v Sussex	Hove	1937
* 103	120	Smith F.B.	Canterbury v Auckland	Auckland	1948/49
100	117	Sutcliffe B.	New Zealand v Essex	Southend	1949
* 100	120	Reid J.R.	Wellington v Otago	Wellington	1951/52
* 122	111	Guillen S.C.	Canterbury v Fiji	Christchurch	1953/54
* 100	126	Smith K.F.H.	Central Districts v Wellington	Wanganui	1959/60
* 108	131	Sutcliffe B.	Otago v Central Districts	Dunedin	1959/60
* 100	140	Sutcliffe B.	Otago v Northern Districts	Wellington	1960/61
* 174	140	Reid J.R.	Wellington v Northern Districts	Wellington	1962/63
120	125	Reid J.R.	Wellington v Northern Districts	Wellington	1964/65
103	120	Murray B.A.G.	New Zealand v President's XI	Rawalpindi	1969/70
* 109	141	Dunning B.	Northern Dist. v Central Dist.	Blenheim	1972/73
111	150	Dempsey D.A.	Canterbury v Otago	Christchurch	1980/81
102	147	† Crowe M.D.	Auckland v Central Districts	New Plymouth	1981/82
* 100	107	Chappell G.S.	Australia v New Zealand	Christchurch	1981/82
* 100	150	Crowe J.J.	Auckland v Northern Districts	Rotorua	1983/84
101	103	Rutherford K.R.	New Zealand v DB Close's XI	Scarborough	1986
* 101	144	Jones A.H.	Wellington v Otago	Wellington	1986/87
* 112	149	McSweeney E.B.	Wellington v Central Districts	Levin	1987/88
* 122	150	Crowe J.J.	Auckland v Wellington	Wellington	1988/89
* 117	160	Greatbatch M.J.	Central Districts v Otago	Palmerston North	1988/89
101	127	Blain T.E.	Central Districts v Wellington	New Plymouth	1988/89
107	136	† Reid R.B.	Auckland v Central Districts	Masterton	1989/90
* 116	136	Thomson S.A.	Northern Districts v Auckland	Auckland	1990/91
141	144	Maynard M.P.	Northern Districts v Auckland	Auckland	1991/92
* 139	92	Patel D.N.	Auckland v Northern Districts	Auckland	1991/92
104	140	Spearman C.M.	Central Districts v Wellington	Wellington	1997/98
101	137	Cairns C.L.	Southern v Central	Wellington	1998/99
103	140	How J.M.	Central Districts v Northern Districts	Napier	2004/05
105	140	Fulton P.G.	Canterbury v Otago	Christchurch	2004/05

** batsman had been not out overnight*

† maiden first-class hundred. Punch, Vorrath, Powell and Reid did not score another century in first-class cricket

Scores of Ninety-nine

	Johnson P.R.	MCC v New Zealand	Christchurch	1906/07
†	Snedden A.N.C.	Auckland v Canterbury	Auckland	1921/22
§	Elmes C.J.	New Zealand v MCC	Auckland	1935/36
*	Whitelaw P.E.	Auckland/Wellington v MCC	Auckland	1936/37
	Sutcliffe B.	Otago v Auckland	Dunedin	1947/48
	Taylor D.D.	Auckland v Canterbury	Auckland	1948/49
†	Leggat J.G.	Canterbury v Auckland	Christchurch	1951/52
	Rae A.F.	West Indies v New Zealand	Auckland	1951/52
	O'Malley P.W.	Canterbury v Wellington	Christchurch	1953/54
†	Beck J.E.F.	New Zealand v South Africa	Cape Town	1953/54
	Hunter A.A.	Central Districts v Auckland	Auckland	1953/54
†	Leggat J.G.	Canterbury v MCC	Christchurch	1954/55

	Sutcliffe B.	Rest v New Zealand XI	Christchurch	1957/58
	Sutcliffe B.	New Zealand v Sussex	Hove	1958
§*	Bartlett G.A.	Central Districts v Auckland	Auckland	1959/60
	McGregor S.N.	Otago v Canterbury	Christchurch	1963/64
†	Cunis R.S.	Auckland v Wellington	Wellington	1966/67
	Surti R.F.	India v New Zealand	Auckland	1967/68
	Turner G.M.	New Zealand v Tasmania	Hobart	1969/70
	Burtt J.W.	Canterbury v Central Districts	Christchurch	1970/71
	Dowling G.T.	Canterbury v Northern Districts	Hamilton	1970/71
	Murray B.A.G.	Wellington v Northern Districts	Wellington	1970/71
	Dowling G.T.	New Zealand v Western Australia	Perth	1970/71
§*	O'Keeffe K.J.	Australia v Auckland	Auckland	1973/74
	Edwards G.N.	Central Districts v Australia	Nelson	1976/77
	Blair W.L.	Otago v Auckland	Auckland	1978/79
	Crowe M.D.	Auckland v Northern Districts	Auckland	1981/82
	Hadlee R.J.	New Zealand v England	Christchurch	1983/84
†	Lees W.K.	Otago v Northern Districts	Hamilton	1983/84
	Vance R.H.	Wellington v Canterbury	Wellington	1984/85
	Coney J.V.	New Zealand v President's XI	St Lucia	1984/85
	Jones A.H.	Wellington v Auckland	Auckland	1985/86
§*	Robertson G.K.	Central Districts v Otago	Oamaru	1985/86
	Wright J.G.	New Zealand v Australia	Melbourne	1987/88
	Crocker L.M.	Northern Districts v Wellington	Hamilton	1987/88
	Moxon M.D.	England v New Zealand	Auckland	1987/88
	McEwan P.E.	Canterbury v Wellington	Christchurch	1988/89
	Hart R.T.	Central Districts v Auckland	Masterton	1989/90
	Wright J.G.	New Zealand v Worcestershire	Worcester	1990
†	Patel D.N.	New Zealand v England	Christchurch	1991/92
+	Wright J.G.	New Zealand v England	Christchurch	1991/92
	Douglas M.W.	Central Districts v Auckland	Wanganui	1991/92
	McSweeney E.B.	Wellington v Canterbury	Wellington	1993/94
	Twose R.G.	Central Districts v Auckland	Palmerston North	1993/94
†	Jones R.A.	Auckland v Otago	Dunedin	1996/97
*	Sinclair M.S.	Central Districts v Northern Districts	Hamilton	1996/97
	Twose R.G.	Wellington v India	Wellington	1998/99
	Yovich J.A.F.	Northern Districts v Auckland	Taupo	1999/00
	Richardson M.H.	New Zealand v Zimbabwe	Harare	2000/01
	Fleming S.P.	New Zealand v South Africa	Bloemfontein	2000/01
	Gaffaney C.B.	Otago v Auckland	Auckland	2000/01
	Nevin C.J.	Wellington v Otago	Wellington	2000/01
	Sinclair M.S.	Central Districts v South Africa	Napier	2003/04
	Gaffaney C.B.	Otago v Wellington	Wellington	2004/05
	McCullum B.B.	New Zealand v Sri Lanka	Napier	2004/05
	Redmond A.J.	Otago v Northern Districts	Gisborne	2005/06
§	Guptill M.J.	Auckland v Wellington	Auckland	2005/06
	Marshall H.J.H.	Northern Districts v Auckland	Auckland	2006/07
	Marshall J.A.H.	Northern Districts v Central Districts	Gisborne	2006/07

** not out* *† batsman was run out* *+ batsman was stumped* *§ highest score in first-class cricket*

Carried Bat Through a Complete Innings

	Score	*Total*			
Harris L.M.	41*	65	Otago v Tasmania	Dunedin	1883/84
Gatehouse G.H.	54*	146	Tasmania v Otago	Dunedin	1883/84
Mills I.	88*	156	Auckland v Otago	Dunedin	1893/94
† Collins J.C.	128*	187	Fiji v Hawke's Bay	Napier	1894/95

Cobcroft L.T.	85*	239	NSW v Wellington	Wellington	1895/96
Mills G.	106*	235	Auckland v Wellington	Auckland	1895/96
Collins D.C.	53*	131	Wellington v Canterbury	Christchurch	1906/07
§ Midlane F.A.	14*	60	Wellington§ v Canterbury	Christchurch	1910/11
Gibbes W.R.L.	75*	193	Wellington v Canterbury	Christchurch	1911/12
† Midlane F.A.	222*	498	Wellington v Otago	Wellington	1914/15
Blunt R.C.	137*	336	Canterbury v Wellington	Wellington	1919/20
† Bardsley W.	200*	352	NSW v Auckland	Auckland	1923/24
Blunt R.C.	131*	204	Otago v Canterbury	Dunedin	1926/27
Dempster C.S.	167*	345	New Zealand v Glamorgan	Cardiff	1927
Kerr J.L.	146*	243	Canterbury v MCC	Christchurch	1935/36
Whitelaw P.E.	99*	183	Auckland/Wellington v MCC	Auckland	1936/37
Tindill E.W.T.	47*	111	Wellington v Otago	Dunedin	1946/47
† Miller L.S.M.	81*	154	Wellington v Otago	Dunedin	1956/57
Playle W.R.	89*	139	Auckland v Northern Districts	Auckland	1959/60
Bradburn W.P.	45*	87	Northern Districts v Wellington	Wellington	1960/61
Bradburn W.P.	37*	57	Northern Districts v Wellington	Hamilton	1961/62
Holloway R.A.	61*	122	Otago v Central Districts	Nelson	1962/63
Turner G.M.	43*	131	New Zealand v England	Lord's	1969
Turner G.M.	223*	386	New Zealand v West Indies	Kingston	1971/72
Redpath I.R.	159*	346	Australia v New Zealand	Auckland	1973/74
Wettimuny S.	63*	144	Sri Lanka v New Zealand	Christchurch	1982/83
† Franklin T.J.	153*	311	Young NZ v Zimbabwe	Harare	1984/85
Rutherford K.R.	89*	241	Otago v Auckland	Dunedin	1984/85
Boon D.C.	58*	103	Australia v New Zealand	Auckland	1985/86
Wright J.G.	149*	307	Canterbury v Auckland	Auckland	1988/89
Smith C.J.P.	90*	154	Central Dists v Northern Dists	Rotorua	1989/90
Murray D.J.	106*	233	Canterbury v Northern Dists	Hamilton	1992/93
Dobbs P.W.	81*	177	Otago v Canterbury	Oamaru	1994/95
Atherton M.A.	94*	228	England v New Zealand	Christchurch	1996/97
Kelly D.P.	212*	538	Central Districts v Canterbury	Blenheim	2000/01
Ingram P.J.	105*	201	Central Districts v Auckland	Auckland	2003/04

† player was on the field for every ball of the match *§ one man absent*

Longest Individual Batting in a Match

Mins	*Runs*				
954	274* & 69*	Fleming S.P.	New Zealand v Sri Lanka	Colombo	2002/03
876	76 & 146*	Greatbatch M.J.	New Zealand v Australia	Perth	1989/90
835	122 & 102	Howarth G.P.	New Zealand v England	Auckland	1977/78
828	75 & 138	Wright J.G.	New Zealand v West Indies	Wellington	1986/87
813	93 & 101	Richardson M.H.	New Zealand v England	Lord's	2004
770	166* & 82	Congdon B.E.	New Zealand v West Indies	Port-of-Spain	1971/72

Longest Individual Innings

Mins	*Runs*				
741	306	Richardson M.H.	New Zealand v Zimbabwe A	Kwekwe	2000/01
720	163	Shoaib Mohammad	Pakistan v New Zealand	Wellington	1988/89
704	259	Turner G.M.	New Zealand v West Indies	Georgetown	1971/72
685	180	Reid J.F.	New Zealand v Sri Lanka	Colombo	1983/84
671	212*	Richardson M.H.	New Zealand A v Sussex	Hove	2000
659	211*	Gibbs H.H.	South Africa v New Zealand	Christchurch	1998/99
658	275*	Cullinan D.J.	South Africa v New Zealand	Auckland	1998/99
655	146*	Greatbatch M.J.	New Zealand v Australia	Perth	1989/90
655	274*	Fleming S.P.	New Zealand v Sri Lanka	Colombo	2002/03

648	158	Radley C.T.	England v New Zealand	Auckland	1977/78
647	251*	Harris C.Z.	Canterbury v Central Districts	Rangiora	1996/97
636	170*	Jones A.H.	New Zealand v India	Auckland	1989/90
625	222	Rutherford I.A.	Otago v Central Districts	New Plymouth	1978/79
610	299	Crowe M.D.	New Zealand v Sri Lanka	Wellington	1990/91
609	120*	Crowe J.J.	New Zealand v Sri Lanka	Colombo	1986/87
605	267*	Young B.A.	New Zealand v Sri Lanka	Dunedin	1996/97
603	259	Turner G.M.	New Zealand v Guyana	Georgetown	1971/72

Fastest Centuries

Mins	*Balls*				
52	45	Cairns B.L.	Otago v Wellington	Lower Hutt	1979/80
52	66	Cooper B.G.	Northern Districts v Canterbury	Gisborne	1986/87
53	63	Motz R.C.	Canterbury v Otago	Christchurch	1967/68

Slowest Centuries

Mins	*Balls*				
516	331	Crowe J.J.	New Zealand v Sri Lanka	Colombo	1986/87
487	397	Radley C.T.	England v New Zealand	Auckland	1977/78
464	390	Austen M.H.	Otago v Canterbury	Christchurch	1996/97
462	341	Greatbatch M.J.	New Zealand v Australia	Perth	1989/90
461	265	Crowe M.D.	New Zealand v Pakistan	Lahore	1990/91
458	341	Astle N.J.	New Zealand v Zimbabwe	Wellington	2000/01
455	307	Howarth G.P.	New Zealand v England	Auckland	1977/78
435	†	Guy J.W.	New Zealand v India	Hyderabad	1955/56
434	380	Reid J.F.	Auckland v Northern Districts	Hamilton	1987/88
434	309	Franklin T.J.	New Zealand v England	Lord's	1990
427	368	Burns K.J.	Otago v Northern Districts	Hamilton	1987/88
426	289	Saqlain Mushtaq	Pakistan v New Zealand	Christchurch	2000/01
422	349	Boyle D.J.	Canterbury v Otago	Rangiora	1993/94
421	291	Woodcock L.J.	Wellington v Auckland	Auckland	2004/05
420	332	Crowe M.D.	New Zealand v West Indies	Georgetown	1984/85
414	399	Wright J.G.	New Zealand v India	Auckland	1980/81
412	325	Wright J.G.	New Zealand v West Indies	Wellington	1986/87
404	311	Reid J.F.	New Zealand v Pakistan	Wellington	1984/85
402	289	Richardson M.H.	New Zealand v England	Lord's	2004

† details not available

Most Boundaries in an Innings

	6s	*4s*		*Runs*			
53	8	45	Rutherford K.R.	317	New Zealand v D.B. Close's XI	Scarborough	1986
50	15	35	Reid J.R.	296	Wellington v Northern Districts	Wellington	1962/63
49	3	46	Sutcliffe B.	385	Otago v Canterbury	Christchurch	1952/53
48	3	45	Fulton P.G.	301*	Canterbury v Auckland	Christchurch	2002/03
47	3	44	Trumper V.T.	293	Sims' Australian XI v Canterbury	Christchurch	1913/14
43	10	33	Hammond W.R.	336*	England v New Zealand	Auckland	1932/33
43	—	43	Richardson M.H.	306	New Zealand v Zimbabwe A	Kwekwe	2000/01
42	1	41	Reid J.R.	283	Wellington v Otago	Wellington	1951/52
42	1	41	Crowe M.D.	242*	New Zealand v South Australia	Adelaide	1985/86
42	3	39	Crowe M.D.	242	Central Districts v Otago	New Plymouth	1989/90
41	—	41	Blunt R.C.	338*	Otago v Canterbury	Christchurch	1931/32
40	—	40	de Silva P.A.	267	Sri Lanka v New Zealand	Wellington	1990/91

Most Sixes in an Innings

Sixes		*Runs*			
15	Reid J.R.	296	Wellington v Northern Districts	Wellington	1962/63
12	Patel D.N.	204	Auckland v Northern Districts	Auckland	1991/92
11	Astle N.J.	222	New Zealand v England	Christchurch	2001/02
11	Spearman C.M.	133	Central Districts v Auckland	Auckland	2003/04
10	Hammond W.R.	336*	England v New Zealand	Auckland	1932/33
10	Robinson R.T.	166	England XI v Northern Districts	Hamilton	1987/88
10	Styris S.B.	212*	Northern Districts v Otago	Hamilton	2001/02
9	Cairns B.L.	110	Otago v Wellington	Lower Hutt	1979/80
9	Botham I.T.	80	England XI v Central Districts	Palmerston North	1983/84
9	Cairns C.L.	120	New Zealand v Zimbabwe	Auckland	1995/96
8	Dacre C.C.R.	176	New Zealand v Derbyshire	Derby	1927
8	Bula I.L.	102	Fiji v Canterbury	Christchurch	1953/54
8	Rutherford K.R.	317	New Zealand v DB Close's XI	Scarborough	1986
8	Germon L.K.	160*	Canterbury v Wellington	Christchurch	1989/90
8	Parore A.C.	111*	Auckland v Wellington	Auckland	1997/98
8	Horne M.J.	209*	Auckland v Northern Districts	Auckland	2003/04
8	Adams A.R.	117*	Auckland v Otago	Lincoln	2006/07
7	Tallon D.	116	Australia v New Zealand	Dunedin	1949/50
7	Sutcliffe B.	80*	New Zealand v South Africa	Johannesburg	1953/54
7	Cairns B.L.	68	New Zealand v New South Wales	Sydney	1980/81
7	Greenidge G.C.	213	West Indies v New Zealand	Auckland	1986/87
7	Hick G.A.	146	Northern Districts v England XI	Hamilton	1987/88
7	Maynard M.P.	195	Northern Districts v Auckland	Auckland	1991/92
7	Hick G.A.	115	England XI v Central Districts	New Plymouth	1991/92
7	Cairns C.L.	158	New Zealand v South Africa	Auckland	2003/04
7	McCullum B.B.	101	New Zealand v Rest of South Africa	Benoni	2005/06

Five Sixes off Consecutive Balls

Germon L.K.	off Vance R.H.	Canterbury v Wellington	Christchurch	1989/90

(Full tosses and deliberate no-balls were provided for him to hit).

Four Sixes off Consecutive Balls

Rutherford K.R.	off Doshi D.R.	New Zealand v DB Close's XI	Scarborough	1986

Three Sixes off Consecutive Balls

Hill C.	off Ollivier K.M.	Australia v New Zealand	Wellington	1904/05
Hammond W.R.	off Newman J.	England v New Zealand	Auckland	1932/33
McRae D.A.N.	off Burke C.	Canterbury v Auckland	Auckland	1937/38
Pritchard T.L.	off Groves L.J.	Wellington v Otago	Dunedin	1937/38
Edwards R.M.	off Carew M.C.	Governor General's XI v West Indies	Auckland	1968/69
Burgess M.G.	off Anderson R.W.	Auckland v Central Districts	Wanganui	1977/78
Stirling D.A.	off Brown V.R.	Central Districts v Canterbury	New Plymouth	1986/87
Thomson S.A.	off Bracewell J.G.	Northern Districts v Auckland	Auckland	1987/88
Hick G.A.	off Duff S.W.	England XI v Central Districts	New Plymouth	1991/92
Astle N.J.	off Wells J.D.	Canterbury v Wellington	Christchurch	1994/95
Vincent L.	off Vettori D.L.	Auckland v Northern Districts	Auckland	1998/99
Astle N.J.	off Caddick A.R.	New Zealand v England	Christchurch	2001/02
Spearman C.M.	off Nicol R.J.	Central Districts v Auckland	Auckland	2003/04
Adams A.R.	off D.J. Bowden	Auckland v Wellington	Wellington	2005/06

Most Ducks in Succession

5	Hayes J.A.	(C, NZ 1954/55)	17,0 / dnb / 0,0 / 0,0
5	Bateman S.N.	(C 1982/83)	5*,0 / 0,0 / 0,0
4	Frith W.	(C 1882/83-1887/88)	0,0 / 0,0
4	Silver R.C.D.	(O 1936/37-1937/38)	12,0 / 0,0 / 0,11
*4	Langdon M.C.	(ND 1957/58)	25,0 / 0,0 / 0,5
4	Hastings B.F.	(C 1963/64)	1,0 / 0,0 / 0,35
4	Steele H.K.C.	(A 1974/75)	0,0 / 0,0
4	Bracewell B.P.	(NZ 1978)	0 / dnb / 0,0 / 0,0*
4	Bradburn G.E.	(ND 1987/88)	0 / 0,0 / 0
4	Morrison D.K.	(NZ 1993/94)	0 / 0,0 / 0,20*
4	Davis H.T.	(NZ, W 1997/98)	7*,0 / 0,0 / 0,21
4	Young R.A.	(A 1999/00)	0,0 / 0,0
4	Martin C.S.	(C NZ 2000/01)	5,0 / 0,0 / 0
4	Gaffaney C.B.	(O 2001/02)	31,0 / 0,0 / 0,56
4	Hamilton L.J.	(CD 2004/05)	11,0/ 0,0/ 0,2

* *first three games in first-class cricket*

Most Scoreless Innings in Succession

10	Visser P.J.	(CD 1984/85-1985/86)	0 / 0,0 / dnb / 0*,0 / dnb / 0*,0* 0,0 / dnb / 0
7	Hamilton L.J.	(CD 1999/00)	0,0* / 0 / 0*,0 / 0 / 0
6	Hayes J.A.	(C, NZ 1954/55-1955/56)	17,0 / dnb / 0,0 / 0,0 / 0*
6	de Groen R.P.	(A 1988/89-1989/90)	1,0* / dnb / 0,0 / 0* / 0*,0*
5	Frith W.	(O, C 1881/82-1887/8)	1,0* / 0,0 / 0,0
*5	Moss A.E.	(C 1889/90)	0,0* / 0,0 / 0*,4*
5	Burrows J.T.	(C 1932/33)	0*,0* / 0* / 0*,0*
5	Hill J.	(O 1961/62-1962/63)	0*,0* / 0* / 0*,0*
5	Unka H.	(ND 1968/69-1971/72)	0* / 0*,0* / dnb / 0*,0
5	Bracewell B.P.	(NZ 1978)	0 / dnb / 0,0 / 0,0*
5	Webb R.J.	(O 1980/81)	1,0 / dnb,0 / 0*,dnb / 0,0*
5	Troup G.B.	(A, NZ 1980/81-1981/82)	0,0* / 0,0 / dnb / 0
5	Bateman S.N.	(C 1982/83)	5*,0 / 0,0 / 0,0

* *first five innings in first-class cricket*

UNUSUAL DISMISSALS

HANDLED THE BALL

Benson E.T.	MCC v Auckland	Auckland	1929/30
Gilbertson A.W.	Otago v Auckland	Auckland	1952/53
Vaughan J.T.C.	NZ Emerging Players v England XI	Hamilton	1991/92

OBSTRUCTING THE FIELD

Hayes J.A.	Canterbury v Central Districts	Christchurch	1954/55

RUN OUT BY THE BOWLER *(while backing up before the ball had been bowled)*

Reese T.W. by Downes A.D.	Canterbury v Otago	Christchurch	1894/95
Smith J. by Allen R.	Canterbury v Wellington	Wellington	1943/44
Randall D.W. by Chatfield E.J.	England v New Zealand	Christchurch	1977/78

STUMPED BY A SUBSTITUTE

Pervez Sajjad by Congdon B.E.	Pakistan v New Zealand	Lahore	1964/65
Congdon B.E. by Burge P.J.P.	Central Districts v Australia	Palmerston North	1966/67

RETIRED (out)

Ransford V.S.	Australia v Hawke's Bay	Napier	1920/21
Chappell G.S.	Australia v Wellington	Wellington	1976/77
Saeed Anwar	Pakistan v New Zealand XI	Napier	1993/94
Basit Ali	Pakistan v New Zealand XI	Napier	1993/94
Inzamam-ul-Haq	Pakistan v New Zealand XI	Napier	1993/94
Spearman C.M.	New Zealand v North West	Potchefstroom	2000/01

REPLACEMENT PLAYERS

Substitute	*Player replaced*			
Lawrence —	Bell A.	Wellington v Nelson	Wellington	1873/74
Cotterill C.N.	White G.	Hawke's Bay v NSW	Napier	1893/94
unknown	Ratu Epeli	Fiji v Auckland	Auckland	1894/95
Kilgour W.A.	*Wilson C.G.	Otago v Auckland	Auckland	1907/08
Bryden J.S.	*Siedeberg H.G.	Otago v Canterbury	Dunedin	1913/14
Graham W.H.	Middleton F.S.	Auckland v Wellington	Wellington	1917/18
Whitta H.B.	*Foster P.S.	Canterbury v Wellington	Christchurch	1919/20
Samuels B.	*Brice A.W.S.	Wellington v Auckland	Auckland	1919/20
Wilson E.S.	Eastman L.C.	Otago v Wellington	Wellington	1927/28
Kubunavanua P.	Logavatu I.T.	Fiji v Canterbury	Christchurch	1947/48
Abernethy B.	Webb R.J.	Otago v Auckland	Dunedin	1982/83
Neutze P.S.	Brown V.R.	Auckland v Wellington	Auckland	1987/88
Brown R.K.	Greatbatch M.J.	CD v Otago	Palmerston North	1991/92
Lee C.D.	Larsen G.R.	Wellington v ND	Hamilton	1991/92
Fleming S.P.	Harris C.Z.	Canterbury v Auckland	Auckland	1991/92
Lee C.D.	*Patel D.N.	Auckland v Otago	Dunedin	1994/95
Garner C.D.	Spearman C.M.	CD v ND	Nelson	1996/97
Cooper D.M.	Howell L.G.	CD v ND	Nelson	1996/97
Lamont M.J.	Horne M.J.	Otago v Auckland	Dunedin	1996/97
Morland N.D.	Wiseman P.J.	Otago v Auckland	Dunedin	1996/97
Sewell D.G.	Kennedy R.J.	Otago v Auckland	Dunedin	1996/97
Irving R.J.R.	Mills J.M.	Auckland v Otago	Dunedin	1996/97
Weenink S.W.	Chandler P.J.B.	Wellington v Canterbury	Christchurch	1996/97
Jonas G.R.	Davis H.T.	Wellington v Canterbury	Christchurch	1996/97
Hartland B.R.	Murray D.J.	Canterbury v Wellington	Christchurch	1996/97
Frew R.M.	Harris C.Z.	Canterbury v Wellington	Christchurch	1996/97
Sharpe M.F.	Allott G.I.	Canterbury v Wellington	Christchurch	1996/97
Hotter S.J.	Davis H.T.	Wellington v CD	Masterton	1996/97
Muir G.A.	Priest M.W.	Canterbury v Zimbabwe	Timaru	1997/98
Pawson S.J.	Priest M.W.	Canterbury v Otago	Dunedin	1997/98
Dry L.R.	Bell M.D.	Wellington v ND	Hamilton	1998/99
Morland N.D.	*Wiseman P.J.	Otago v Auckland	Dunedin	1999/00
Spearman C.M.	Sinclair M.S.	CD v Otago	Palmerston North	1999/00
Todd G.R.	Oram J.D.P.	CD v Wellington	Napier	2000/01
McCullum N.L.	Wiseman P.J.	Otago v Canterbury	Alexandra	2000/01
Robinson G.G.	*Marshall J.A.H.	ND v Canterbury	Gisborne	2004/05
O'Brien I.E.	Rasmussen S.	Wellington v Otago	Dunedin	2006/07

** indicates player did not bat or bowl before being replaced*

REPRESENTED TWO PROVINCES IN ONE SEASON

Sutcliffe B.	Auckland and Otago	1946/47
Sutcliffe B.	Otago and Auckland	1947/48
Clark L.A.	Otago and Auckland	1959/60
Andrews B.	Canterbury and Central Districts	1966/67

On each occasion, the second province was represented in a match against a non-provincial side. No player has played for two provinces in inter-provincial matches in the same season.

BOWLING

Ten Wickets in an Innings

	Overs	Maidens	Runs	Wickets			
* Moss A.E.	21.3	10	28	10	Canterbury v Wellington	Christchurch	1889/90

** on debut – the only instance in first-class cricket*

Nine Wickets in an Innings

	Overs	Maidens	Runs	Wickets			
Wiseman P.J.	16.4	9	13	9	Canterbury v CD	Christchurch	2004/05
Wensley A.F.	24	13	36	9	Auckland v Otago	Auckland	1929/30
Eden T.	15.2	0	43	9	Nelson v Wellington	Wellington	1875/76
Dent T.H.	28	11	47	9	Hawke's Bay v Wellington	Napier	1900/01
Tait A.R.	24.5	8	48	9	ND v Auckland	Hamilton	1996/97
Fisher A.H.	25.2	4	50	9	Otago v Queensland	Dunedin	1896/97
Hadlee R.J.	23.4	4	52	9	New Zealand v Australia	Brisbane	1985/86
Hadlee R.J.	24	5	55	9	New Zealand v West Zone	Rajkot	1988/89
McBeath D.J.	24	7	56	9	Canterbury v Auckland	Christchurch	1918/19
Brice A.W.S.	25.5	5	67	9	Wellington v Auckland	Wellington	1918/19
Cooke F.H.	56	24	73	9	Otago v Canterbury	Christchurch	1884/85
Blair R.W.	35	9	72	9	Wellington v Auckland	Wellington	1956/57
Neill R.	31	7	75	9	Auckland v Canterbury	Auckland	1891/92
Blair R.W.	29.5	9	75	9	Wellington v Canterbury	Wellington	1956/57
Neill R.	24.2	1	86	9	Auckland v Canterbury	Auckland	1897/98
Petherick P.J.	35	10	93	9	Otago v ND	Dunedin	1975/76
Priest M.W.	28.5	5	95	9	Canterbury v Otago	Dunedin	1989/90
Robertson W.	39.3	8	98	9	Canterbury v Wellington	Christchurch	1894/95
Yuile B.W.	45	19	100	9	CD v Canterbury	New Plymouth	1965/66

Sixteen Wickets in a Match

16-130	Tait A.R.	24.5-8-48-9/38.4-13-82-7	Northern Dists v Auckland, Hamilton	1996/97

Fifteen Wickets in a Match

15-60	Callaway S.T.	23.3-10-33-8/17-7-27-7	Canterbury v Hawke's Bay, Napier	1903/04
15-94	Cooke F.H.	40.3-16-61-8/33.3-14-33-7	Otago v Canterbury, Christchurch	1882/83
15-104	Boock S.L.	29.3-13-47-7/34.3-16-57-8	Otago v Auckland, Dunedin	1989/90
15-123	Hadlee R.J.	23.4-4-52-9/28.5-9-71-6	NZ v Australia, Brisbane	1985/86
15-168	McBeath D.J.	24-7-56-9/37-4-112-6	Canterbury v Auckland, Christchurch	1918/19
15-175	Callaway S.T.	35-14-77-7/43.4-11-98-8	NSW v New Zealand, Christchurch	1895/96
15-203	Moir A.M.	24.1-4-84-7/35.1-3-119-8	Otago v Central Dists, New Plymouth	1953/54

Fourteen Wickets in a Match

14-59	Read R.J.	13-3-35-7/14-5-24-7	Canterbury v Southland, Invercargill	1920/21
14-63	Eden T.	15.2-0-43-9/15.5-7-20-5	Nelson v Wellington, Wellington	1875/76
* 14-63	Rees A.W.	13-4-27-6/15.3-3-36-8	Auckland v Otago, Dunedin	1889/90
14-65	Callaway S.T.	36.3-18-47-7/18.2-7-18-7	NSW v Wellington, Wellington	1895/96
14-65	Hayes J.A.	18.2-6-28-7/12.1-3-37-7	Auckland v Wellington, Auckland	1957/58
14-93	Torrance R.C.	23-6-51-7/19-5-42-7	Otago v Hawke's Bay, Napier	1908/09
14-94	Howarth H.J.	22.1-5-42-7/23-6-52-7	Auckland v Otago, Dunedin	1973/74
14-103	Downes A.D.	30-12-32-7/30-8-71-7	Otago v Hawke's Bay, Dunedin	1893/94
* 14-107	Robertson W.	28.2-8-59-8/20.4-7-48-6	Canterbury v Auckland, Christchurch	1893/94
14-119	Pringle C.	27.4-10-63-7/23.5-5-56-7	Auckland v Otago, Dunedin	1993/94
14-126	Moir A.M.	18-1-55-8/25-6-71-6	Otago v Canterbury, Dunedin	1951/52
14-136	Blair R.W.	29.5-9-75-9/26-8-61-5	Wellington v Canterbury, Wellington	1956/57
14-151	Gray E.J.	50-19-114-6/26.1-12-37-8	Wellington v Canterbury, Lower Hutt	1985/86

** on debut*

Four Wickets with Consecutive Balls

Downes A.D.	Otago v Auckland	Dunedin	1893/94

Hat Tricks

Salmon I.J.	Wellington v Nelson	Wellington	1873/74
Lankham W.	Auckland v Taranaki	Auckland	1882/83
Frith C.	Otago v Canterbury	Dunedin	1884/85
Fannin H.A.	Hawkes Bay v Taranaki	Napier	1897/98
Barclay F.	Auckland v Canterbury	Auckland	1903/04
Orchard S.A.	Canterbury v Auckland	Auckland	1909/10
Bennett J.H.	Canterbury v Wellington	Wellington	1911/12
Olliff C.	Auckland v Wellington	Auckland	1912/13
Middleton F.S.	Wellington v Hawke's Bay	Wellington	1919/20
Allom M.J.C.*	England v New Zealand	Christchurch	1929/30
Mulcock E.	Canterbury v Otago	Christchurch	1937/38
Overton G.W.F.	Otago v Canterbury	Christchurch	1946/47
Murray R.M.	Wellington v Otago	Wellington	1949/50
Moir A.M.	Otago v Canterbury	Christchurch	1950/51
Jones J.F.	Wellington v Central Districts	Wellington	1953/54
Reid R.E.	Wellington v Otago	Dunedin	1958/59
Bartlett G.A.	Central Districts v Northern Districts	Hamilton	1959/60
Cameron F.J.	Otago v Northern Districts	Hamilton	1962/63
Blair R.W.	Wellington v Northern Districts	Wellington	1962/63
Alabaster G.D.	Northern Districts v Canterbury	Hamilton	1962/63
Furlong B.D.M.	NZ Under 23 XI v Canterbury	Christchurch	1964/65
Hadlee R.J.	Canterbury v Central Districts	Nelson	1971/72
Petherick P.J.	New Zealand v Pakistan	Lahore	1976/77
Toynbee M.H.	Central Districts v Northern Districts	Gisborne	1979/80
Visser P.J.	Central Districts v Auckland	Nelson	1983/84
Maguiness S.J.	Wellington v Northern Districts	Wellington	1983/84
Beard D.A.	Northern Districts v Central Districts	Nelson	1989/90
Gale A.J.	Otago v Canterbury	Dunedin	1992/93
Harris C.Z.	New Zealand v Orange Free State	Bloemfontein	1994/95
Hayes R.L.	Northern Districts v Central Districts	Rotorua	1995/96
Hotter S.J.	Wellington v Otago	Wellington	1996/97
Anderson T.R.	Central Districts v Auckland	Masterton	1998/99
Canning T.K.	Auckland v Central Districts	Auckland	1999/00
Orchard M.G.	Northern Districts v Canterbury	Gisborne	2003/04
Franklin J.E.C.	New Zealand v Bangladesh	Dhaka	2004/05

** Allom captured 4 wickets with 5 balls in the same over*

Most Wickets in a Single Day's Play in New Zealand

14	Rees A.W.	Auckland v Otago	Dunedin	1889/90
13	Lankham W.	Auckland v Taranaki	Auckland	1882/83
13	Smith C.R.	Hawke's Bay v Taranaki	Hawera	1891/92
13	Cave H.B.	Central Districts v Auckland	Palmerston North	1952/53

Outstanding Analyses

TEN WICKETS IN AN INNINGS

21.3	11	28	10	Moss A.E.	Canterbury v Wellington	Christchurch	1889/90

NINE WICKETS IN AN INNINGS

16.4	9	13	9	Wiseman P.J.	Canterbury v CD	Christchurch	2004/05
24	13	36	9	Wensley A.F.	Auckland v Otago	Auckland	1929/30
15.2	0	43	9	Eden T.	Nelson v Wellington	Wellington	1875/76
28	11	47	9	Dent T.H.	Hawke's Bay v Wellington	Napier	1900/01

EIGHT WICKETS IN AN INNINGS

13	6	13	8	Firth J.P.	Wellington v Hawke's Bay	Wellington	1883/84
19	12	14	8	Austin S.W.	NSW v Hawke's Bay	Napier	1893/94
29	21	18	8	Frith W.	Canterbury v Otago	Christchurch	1880/81
14.5	7	19	8	Fannin H.A.	Hawke's Bay v Auckland	Auckland	1897/98

SEVEN WICKETS IN AN INNINGS

10.1	6	9	7	Bracewell J.G.	Otago v Canterbury	Dunedin	1981/82
13	9	11	7	Fisher A.H.	Otago v Canterbury	Christchurch	1896/97
25.3	16	12	7	Downes A.D.	Otago v Canterbury	Dunedin	1896/97
16	8	12	7	Tuffey D.R.	Northern Districts v Wellington	Hamilton	2000/01
32.1	24	13	7	Lankham W.	Auckland v Taranaki	Auckland	1882/83
10.4	5	16	7	Farooq Hamid	Pakistan v Wellington	Wellington	1964/65
17	10	17	7	Armstrong W.W.	Australia v Wellington	Wellington	1913/14
14.2	7	17	7	Maguiness S.J.	Wellington v Canterbury	Rangiora	1984/85
18.2	7	18	7	Callaway S.T.	NSW v Wellington	Wellington	1895/96

SIX WICKETS IN AN INNINGS

8	5	3	6	Cowie J.	New Zealand v Ireland	Dublin	1937
8	5	4	6	Callaway S.T.	Canterbury v Wellington	Wellington	1903/04
9.2	3	5	6	Bennett A.P.	Nelson v Wellington	Nelson	1885/86
16	11	6	6	Haskell W.J.R.	Wellington v Otago	Wellington	1967/68
14	10	7	6	Dunlop D.	Canterbury v Wellington	Wellington	1886/87
18	14	7	6	Hampton B.L.	Central Districts v Otago	Dunedin	1963/64
15	10	8	6	Downes W.F.	Otago v Canterbury	Christchurch	1866/67
11.2	6	9	6	Fowler G.	Nelson v Wellington	Nelson	1887/88
9.3	6	10	6	Pearson F.A.	Auckland v Hawke's Bay	Auckland	1910/11

FIVE WICKETS IN AN INNINGS

15.2	13	2	5	Ashby D.A.	Canterbury v Auckland	Auckland	1877/78
5	3	3	5	Allcott C.F.W.	New Zealand v Somerset	Taunton	1927
10.3	6	5	5	Bright R.J.	Australia v Central Districts	Nelson	1976/77
9	6	6	5	Parker T.S.	Otago v Canterbury	Christchurch	1866/67
21	18	8	5	Frith C.	Otago v Tasmania	Dunedin	1883/84
4	2	8	5	Burnup C.J.	Lord Hawke's XI v NZ	Wellington	1902/03
8	4	8	5	McBeath D.J.	Southland v Canterbury	Invercargill	1920/21
9	3	9	5	Bennett J.H.	Canterbury v Wellington	Christchurch	1910/11
12	5	9	5	Butterfield L.A.	South Island v North Island	Auckland	1944/45
9.1	5	9	5	Boock S.L.	New Zealand v Middlesex	Lord's	1978

FOUR WICKETS IN AN INNINGS

3.2	2	1	4	Snedden C.A.	Auckland v Hawke's Bay	Auckland	1920/21
6.4	5	2	4	Puna N.	Northern Dists v Central Dists	Hamilton	1957/58
7	6	3	4	Carrington S.M.	Northern Districts v Otago	Tauranga	1982/83
6.5	5	3	4	Woodcock L.J.	Wellington v Otago	Wellington	2001/02

THREE WICKETS IN AN INNINGS

3	3	0	3	Smith K.F.H.	Central Districts v Canterbury	Nelson	1959/60
2.1	2	0	3	Barnes S.G.	Australia v Canterbury	Christchurch	1945/46
5	5	0	3	Gray E.J.	Wellington v Canterbury	Christchurch	1985/86
1.4	0	1	3	Bolton B.A.	Canterbury v Central Districts	Christchurch	1958/59
2	1	1	3	Thomson S.A.	Northern Districts v Canterbury	Christchurch	1992/93
1.4	0	2	3	Anthony A.	Canterbury v Wellington	Christchurch	1908/09
3.3	1	2	3	Thomas A.W.	Canterbury v Otago	Christchurch	1917/18
4	2	2	3	Sparling J.T.	Auckland v Wellington	Auckland	1957/58
5	2	3	3	Cowlishaw W.P.	Canterbury v Otago	Christchurch	1864/65
15	12	3	3	Frith W.	Canterbury v Auckland	Auckland	1877/78
2.3	1	3	3	Richardson G.	Nelson v Wellington	Wellington	1886/87
3	2	3	3	Dowson E.M.	Lord Hawke's XI v Otago	Dunedin	1902/03
5	2	3	3	Pollard V.	New Zealand v England	Auckland	1965/66

Seven Wickets in an Innings on First-class Debut

10-28	Moss A.E.	Canterbury v Wellington	Christchurch	1889/90
8-35	Wilson R.	Queensland v Auckland	Auckland	1896/97
† 8-36	Rees A.W.	Auckland v Otago	Dunedin	1889/90
8-37	Hole H.	Nelson v Wellington	Nelson	1874/75
8-48	O'Connell W.J.	Hawke's Bay v Wellington	Wellington	1919/20
8-59	Robertson W.	Canterbury v Auckland	Christchurch	1893/94
8-70	Hay W.A.	Otago v Southland	Dunedin	1917/18
7-31	Lynch D.	Auckland v Canterbury	Auckland	1877/78
7-36	Mills G.	Auckland v Wellington	Auckland	1886/87
7-39	Lankham W.	Auckland v Canterbury	Christchurch	1882/83
† 7-42	Morrison B.D.	Wellington v Otago	Wellington	1953/54
† 7-46	Stephens W.B.	Auckland v Otago	Auckland	1899/00
7-46	Doig J.A.	Southland v Otago	Invercargill	1914/15
† 7-50	Badcock F.T.	Wellington v Canterbury	Christchurch	1924/25
† 7-54	Turnbull J.A.	Auckland v Central Districts	Auckland	1955/56
7-61	Merrin R.C.	Canterbury XI v NZ Touring Team	Christchurch	1967/68
† 7-95	Noonan D.J.	New South Wales v Canterbury	Christchurch	1895/96
7-95	Huxford N.A.	Wellington v Pakistan	Wellington	1964/65

† 2nd innings

Ten Wickets in a Match on First-class Debut

14-63	Rees A.W.	Auckland v Otago	Dunedin	1889/90
14-107	Robertson W.	Canterbury v Auckland	Christchurch	1893/94
13-72	Moss A.E.	Canterbury v Wellington	Christchurch	1889/90
12-18	Bennett A.P.	Nelson v Wellington	Nelson	1885/86
12-90	Mills W.	Taranaki v Fiji	Hawera	1894/95
12-118	Hay W.A.	Otago v Southland	Dunedin	1917/18
11-43	Fuller E.T.A.	Canterbury v Otago	Christchurch	1872/73
11-97	Wilson R.	Queensland v Auckland	Auckland	1896/97
11-99	Lankham W.	Auckland v Canterbury	Christchurch	1882/83
11-112	Morrison B.D.	Wellington v Otago	Wellington	1953/54
11-126	Noonan D.J.	New South Wales v Canterbury	Christchurch	1895/96
10-30	Lawson H.	Wellington v Nelson	Nelson	1883/84
10-31	MacDonald F.	Otago v Canterbury	Dunedin	1863/64
10-39	Holderness H.V.A.	Otago v Southland	Invercargill	1918/19
10-61	Hole H.	Nelson v Wellington	Nelson	1874/75
10-70	Mills G.	Auckland v Wellington	Auckland	1886/87
10-71	Lawton J.C.	Otago v Canterbury	Christchurch	1890/91
10-90	Brown C.M.	Auckland v Canterbury	Rangiora	1993/94
10-105	Frame W.D.	Otago v Canterbury	Dunedin	1955/56
10-122	Badcock F.T.	Wellington v Canterbury	Christchurch	1924/25
10-133	Leonard D.J.	Central Districts v Northern Districts	Rotorua	1989/90

Ten Wickets in Last First-class Match

† 10-31	MacDonald F.	Otago v Canterbury	Dunedin	1863/64
† 10-61	Hole H.	Nelson v Wellington	Nelson	1874/75
10-91	Downes W.F.	Otago v Canterbury	Dunedin	1875/76
12-114	Lankham W.	Auckland v Canterbury	Auckland	1883/84
13-140	Edser H.	Canterbury v Wellington	Wellington	1883/84
11-25	Fowler G.	Nelson v Wellington	Nelson	1887/88
11-77	Carson W.	Otago v Canterbury	Dunedin	1887/88
† 10-39	Holderness H.V.A.	Otago v Southland	Invercargill	1918/19
10-108	Vivian H.G.	Auckland v Wellington	Auckland	1938/39
11-129	de Groen R.P.	Northern Districts v Canterbury	Hamilton	1995/96

† this was the player's only first-class appearance

Most Wickets in a Season

		Matches	Wkts	Runs	Ave	5WI	10WM	Best
Boock S.L.	1977/78	13	66	1088	16.48	6	–	7-57
Hadlee R.J.	1986/87	11	62	935	15.08	8	1	7-49
Hadlee R.J.	1981/82	10	59	867	14.69	7	–	6-26
Boock S.L.	1978/79	12	58	1238	21.34	4	1	8-59
Thompson G.J.	1902-03	7	57	668	11.71	6	3	8-124
Boock S.L.	1986/87	10	55	920	16.72	6	1	6-62
Callaway S.T.	1903/04	5	54	474	8.77	8	4	8-33
Blair R.W.	1956/57	8	53	784	14.79	6	4	9-72
Tait A.R.	1996/97	9	53	865	16.32	4	1	9-48
Drum C.J.	2001/02	9	53	827	15.60	3	2	6-34
Martin C.S.	2003/04	12	53	1144	21.58	6	1	6-76
Austin S.W.	1893/94	7	52	606	11.65	6	1	8-14
Armstrong W.W.	1913/14	8	52	789	15.17	7	1	7-17
O'Sullivan D.R.	1978/79	9	52	989	19.01	3	–	6-51
Chatfield E.J.	1981/82	10	51	868	17.01	2	–	5-29
Hadlee R.J.	1978/79	10	50	909	18.18	4	–	6-28
Douglas J.W.H.T.	1906/07	9	50	663	13.26	5	1	7-49

Most Wickets in a Season for New Zealand Overseas

		Matches	Wkts	Runs	Ave	5WI	10WM	Best
Burtt T.B.	1949	27	128	2929	22.28	11	2	7-102
Cowie J.	1937	24	114	2275	19.95	6	1	6-3
Merritt W.E.	1927	25	107	2530	23.64	5	1	6-38

Most Wickets in a Season of First-class Debut

			Overs	Mdns	Runs	Wkts	Ave
Robertson W.	Canterbury & NZ	1893/94	*1534	balls	570	47	12.12
Gillespie S.R.	Northern Districts	1979/80	384.5	98	998	45	22.17
Petherick P.J.	Otago	1975/76	286	57	847	42	20.16
Lankham W.	Auckland	1882/83	†1006	balls	259	41	6.31
O'Brien I.E.	Wellington	2000/01	319.1	81	807	41	19.68

** Robertson bowled 222.2 6-ball overs and 40 5-ball overs † Lankham bowled 96.2 5-ball overs and 131 4-ball overs*

Most Balls Bowled in an Innings

444	Howarth H.J.	74-24-138-2	NZ v West Indies	Bridgetown	1971/72
426	Tufnell P.C.R.	71-22-147-2	England v New Zealand	Wellington	1991/92
426	Vettori D.L.	71-24-171-2	New Zealand v India	Mohali	1999/00
420	Howarth H.J.	70-24-144-4	NZ v England	Lord's	1973
420	Boock S.L.	70-10-229-1	NZ v Pakistan	Auckland	1988/89
417	O'Sullivan D.R.	52.1-15-125-4	CD v Otago	New Plymouth	1978/79
414	Doshi D.R.	69-34-79-2	India v New Zealand	Auckland	1980/81
414	Tauseef Ahmed	69-28-106-1	Pakistan v New Zealand	Auckland	1988/89
414	Hick G.A.	69-27-126-4	England v New Zealand	Wellington	1991/92
408	Morgan H.A.	51-16-108-3	Wellington v Otago	Dunedin	1968/69
408	Wiseman P.J.	68-21-123-4	Otago v ND	Hamilton	1995/96
407	Boock S.L.	67.5-31-75-4	Otago v CD	Alexandra	1988/89
399	Cook N.G.B.	66.3-26-153-3	England v NZ	Wellington	1983/84
396	Puna N.	66-23-131-4	ND v Auckland	Hamilton	1964/65
396	Nadkarni R.G.	66-34-114-2	India v NZ	Christchurch	1967/68
390	Chatfield E.J.	65-14-158-1	NZ v Pakistan	Auckland	1988/89

Most Balls Bowled in a Match

629	Badcock F.T.	104.5-44-178-9	Otago v Canterbury	Christchurch	1933/34
624	Dickeson C.W.	104-45-142-11	ND v Wellington	Hamilton	1979/80
618	Gray E.J.	103-39-214-6	Wellington v Otago	Wellington	1984/85
600	Allcott C.F.W.	75-23-161-5	Auckland v Canterbury	Christchurch	1924/25
600	Butler L.C.	100-46-122-4	Wellington v Auckland	Auckland	1965/66

Most Runs Conceded in a Match

304	2-173, 0-131	Dickinson G.R.	Otago v Wellington	Dunedin	1923/24
300	6-172, 4-128	Smith S.G.	Auckland v Wellington	Wellington	1923/24
277	6-136, 6-141	Alloo A.W.	Otago v Wellington	Dunedin	1923/24
266	6-185, 2-81	Merritt W.E.	New Zealand v Kent	Canterbury	1927
243	6-128, 7-115	Grimmett C.V.	Australia v Canterbury	Christchurch	1927/28
241	2-99, 5-142	Brice A.W.S.	Wellington v Otago	Dunedin	1923/24
241	3-123, 1-118	Prabhakar M.	India v New Zealand	Auckland	1989/90
239	6-112, 3-127	McBeath D.J.	Otago v Auckland	Dunedin	1922/23
239	1-60, 4-179	Lambert H.N.	Wellington v Canterbury	Wellington	1931/32
237	0-99, 0-138	Bracewell J.G.	New Zealand v Sussex	Hove	1990
237	4-158, 0-79	Vettori D.L.	New Zealand v South Africa	Hamilton	2003/04
236	2-83, 2-153	Newman J.A.	Canterbury v Otago	Dunedin	1928/29
234	3-86, 4-148	Merritt W.E.	Canterbury v Otago	Dunedin	1928/29
234	4-165, 2-69	Vettori D.L.	New Zealand v Zimbabwe	Bulawayo	1997/98
233	6-117, 4-116	Patel D.N.	Auckland v ND	Auckland	1991/92

Most Runs Conceded in an Innings

70	10	229	1	Boock S.L.	New Zealand v Pakistan	Auckland	1988/89
23.2	0	218	5	Merritt W.E.	New Zealand v NSW	Sydney	1927/28
34	1	206	1	Alloo A.W.	Otago v NSW	Dunedin	1923/24
59	12	204	4	Furlong C.J.M.	CD v Canterbury	Palmerston Nth	1994/95
57	5	200	4	Vettori D.L.	New Zealand v India	Ahmedabad	1999/00
51.2	11	198	5	Pringle C.	Auckland v CD	Auckland	1995/96
41	3	194	3	Callaway S.T.	New Zealand v Australia	Wellington	1904/05
32	1	186	2	Torrance R.C.	Otago v NSW	Dunedin	1923/24
43.1	1	185	6	Merritt W.E.	New Zealand v Kent	Canterbury	1927
46	4	181	0	Hart M.N.	New Zealand v W. Indies	Wellington	1994/95
34	2	180	5	O'Connell W.J.	Hawke's Bay v Auckland	Auckland	1920/21
56	13	179	4	Bennett J.H.	Canterbury v Australia	Christchurch	1913/14
33	0	179	3	McBeath D.J.	Canterbury v NSW	Christchurch	1923/24
31	1	179	4	Lambert H.N.	Wellington v Canterbury	Wellington	1931/32
44	4	179	0	Su'a M.L.	New Zealand v W. Indies	Wellington	1994/95
38	2	178	4	Cunningham W.H.R.	Canterbury v NSW	Christchurch	1923/24
40	4	178	1	Vettori D.L.	New Zealand v Pakistan	Lahore	2001/02
24	1	177	4	Furlong C.J.M.	CD v India	Napier	1998/99

ALL ROUND CRICKET

500 Runs and 25 Wickets in the Same Season

		Runs	Ave	Wkts	Ave
Reid J.R.	1954/55	505	38.84	30	16.53
Sparling J.T.	1959/60	705	37.11	36	19.50
Reid J.R.	1960/61	549	34.31	37	14.78
Pollard V.	1967/68	537	31.58	31	24.74
Taylor B.R.	1968/69	518	39.84	30	28.06
Cairns B.L.	1975/76	538	41.38	27	25.66
Hadlee R.J.	1981/82	500	33.33	59	14.69
Brown V.R.	1984/85	540	38.57	31	31.35
Gray E.J.	1985/86	545	49.54	34	22.00
Priest M.W.	1988/89	603	43.07	28	40.14
Bradburn G.E.	1989/90	842	38.27	30	30.93
Patel D.N.	1990/91	679	52.23	41	28.09
Patel D.N.	1991/92	574	44.15	32	26.78
Duff S.W.	1991/92	559	46.58	28	27.64
Styris S.B.	2001/02	662	44.13	28	17.03
Wiseman P.J.	2003/04	535	38.21	31	31.00

A Century and Five Wickets in Each Innings of the Same Match

rmstrong W.W.	126*	5-27 & 5-25	Australia v New Zealand	Christchurch	1904/05
rawford J.N.	110 & 4*	5-90 & 5-53	Wellington v Auckland	Auckland	1917/18

A Century and Ten Wickets in the Same Match

but not five in each innings

Voolley F.E.	132	6-50 & 4-38	MCC v Otago	Dunedin	1929/30
atel D.N.	6 & 204	6-117 & 4-116	Auckland v ND	Auckland	1991/92

A Century and Five Wickets in One Innings of the Same Match

Vilding F.	104	6-55 & 0-4	Canterbury v Auckland	Christchurch	1884/85
edgrave W.P.	165	5-37	Wellington v Hawke's Bay	Wellington	1905/06
elf A.E.	157	6-64 & 2-48	Auckland v Canterbury	Christchurch	1907/08
rmstrong W.W.	110*	6-47 & 0-25	Australia v New Zealand	Auckland	1913/14
rawford J.N.	6 & 178*	5-149	Otago v Wellington	Wellington	1914/15
nedden A.N.C.	139	5-13 & 2-21	Auckland v Hawke's Bay	Auckland	1920/21
ndrews T.J.E.	111*	5-41	NSW v Canterbury	Christchurch	1923/24
AcGirr H.M.	106	5-17 & 0-22	Wellington v Canterbury	Wellington	1925/26
ellamy F.W.J.	113 & 22*	5-31 & 1-39	Canterbury v Wellington	Christchurch	1934/35
romb I.B.	171	5-66 & 0-56	Canterbury v Wellington	Wellington	1939/40
eid J.R.	0 & 283	5-35 & 1-34	Wellington v Otago	Wellington	1951/52
eid J.R.	150*	7-28 & 1-15	New Zealand v Chief Commissioner's XI	Karachi	1955/56
utcliffe B.	152*	5-102	Otago v ND	Hamilton	1956/57
parling J.T.	105 & 51	7-98 & 2-13	Auckland v Canterbury	Christchurch	1959/60
eid J.R.	165	5-50 & 1-28	Wellington v Auckland	Auckland	1959/60
utler L.C.	101*	5-34	Wellington v CD	New Plymouth	1961/62
labaster G.D.	108 & 35	1-34 & 5-49	Otago v CD	Wanganui	1964/65
aylor B.R.	105 & 0*	5-86	New Zealand v India	Calcutta	1964/65
ollard V.	146 & 16*	3-66 & 6-53	CD v Otago	Dunedin	1967/68
Aotz R.C.	103*	3-41 & 6-57	Canterbury v Otago	Christchurch	1967/68
uile B.W.	146	6-68 & 1-13	CD v Canterbury	Napier	1967/68
nverarity R.J.	108	5-28	Australia B v Otago	Dunedin	1969/70

Morgan R.W.	102 & 52	5-42 & 3-48	Auckland v NZ U 23 XI	Auckland	1970/7
Taylor B.R.	10 & 129*	5-37 & 2-34	Wellington v Canterbury	Wellington	1971/7
Mushtaq Mohammad	201	2-15 & 5-49	Pakistan v New Zealand	Dunedin	1972/7
Morrison J.F.M.	8 & 106	0-4 & 5-69	Wellington v Auckland	Auckland	1977/7
Botham I.T.	103 & 30*	5-73 & 3-38	England v New Zealand	Christchurch	1977/7
Hadlee R.J.	48 & 103	5-61 & 1-76	NZ v Queensland	Brisbane	1980/8
Stead D.W.	2 & 193*	6-79 & 1-67	Canterbury v CD	New Plymouth	1980/8
Crowe M.D.	17 & 151	0-20 & 5-18	CD v Auckland	Auckland	1983/8
Botham I.T.	138	5-59 & 1-137	England v New Zealand	Wellington	1983/8
Crowe M.D.	20 & 143	1-54 & 5-51	CD v ND	New Plymouth	1984/8
Gray E.J.	108	5-54 & 4-52	NZ v Minor Counties	Norwich	1986
Rutherford K.R.	11 & 146	5-72	Otago v Wellington	Wellington	1989/9
Astle N.J.	160	6-22 & 0-45	Canterbury v Otago	Christchurch	1996/9
Nash D.J.	135* & 62	7-39 & 0-22	NZ v Hampshire	Southampton	1999
Bradburn G.E.	35 & 104	5-114	ND v Wellington	Wellington	2000/0
Canning T.K.	115	6-44 & 2-28	Auckland v ND	Hamilton	2004/0

WICKETKEEPING

Most Dismissals in a Season

49	49/0	Nevin C.J.	2000/01
41	31/10	McSweeney E.B.	1984/85
41	35/6	McSweeney E.B.	1989/90
38	37/1	Hopkins G.J.	2004/05
36	32/4	Smith I.D.S.	1990/91
36	35/1	Griggs B.B.J.	2005/06
35	30/5	Smith I.D.S.	1979/80
35	33/2	Young R.A.	2001/02
35	35/0	Young R.A.	2002/03
34	29/5	Lees W.K.	1978/79
34	32/2	Smith I.D.S.	1986/87
34	31/3	Germon L.K.	1991/92
34	33/1	Nevin C.J.	1995/96
34	34/0	Hart R.G.	1997/98
34	33/1	Hart R.G.	2001/02
33	32/1	Wadsworth K.J.	1975/76
33	31/2	McCullum B.B.	2003/04
32	28/4	Smith I.D.S.	1983/84
32	28/4	McSweeney E.B.	1983/84
32	28/4	Robinson S.A.	1990/91
32	31/1	Nevin C.J.	2002/03
32	30/2	Hart R.G.	2003/04
32	31/1	Hopkins G.J.	2005/06
31	30/1	Kelly P.J.	1983/84
31	28/3	Kelly P.J.	1986/87
31	31/0	McSweeney E.B.	1990/91
31	30/1	Young B.A.	1991/92
31	28/3	Blain T.E.	1991/92
31	30/1	Croy M.G.	1998/99
31	31/0	Griggs B.B.J.	2001/02
31	31/0	Young R.A.	2004/05
30	23/7	Murray J.T.	1960/61
30	28/2	Germon L.K.	1992/93
30	29/1	Baker G.R.	1994/95

Most Dismissals in a Match

10	10/0	Nevin C.J., Wellington v Otago	Wellington	1995/96
	10/0	Gilchrist A.C., Australia v New Zealand	Hamilton	1999/00
	10/0	Hopkins G.J., Otago v Canterbury	Dunedin	2004/05
	8/2	Hopkins G.J., New Zealand A v Sri Lanka A	Kandy	2005/06
9	9/0	Schofield R.M., Central Districts v Wellington	Wellington	1964/65
	9/0	Vance R.H., Wellington v Otago	Wellington	1977/78
	8/1	McSweeney E.B., Wellington v Otago	Lower Hutt	1983/84
	9/0	Young B.A., Northern Districts v Canterbury	Christchurch	1986/87
	9/0	Germon L.K., Canterbury v Northern Districts	Christchurch	1992/93
	9/0	Rashid Latif., Pakistan v New Zealand	Auckland	1993/94
	9/0	Hopkins G.J., Otago v Wellington	Queenstown	2004/05
	9/0	Hopkins G.J., Otago v Northern Districts	Dunedin	2005/06
8	3/5	James K.C., NZ v Derbyshire	Derby	1927
	1/7	Jackman C.K.Q., Canterbury v Wellington	Wellington	1935/36
	2/6	Kent L.A.W., Auckland v Wellington	Wellington	1944/45

	8/0	Curtis W.M., North Island XI v South Island XI	Wellington	1957/58
	8/0	Petrie E.C., NZ v Sussex	Hove	1958
	5/3	Dick A.E., NZ v Griqualand West	Kimberley	1961/62
	8/0	Parks J.M., England v NZ	Christchurch	1965/66
	7/1	Therkleson, I.J., Wellington v Northern Districts	Whangarei	1973/74
	8/0	Marsh R.W., Australia v NZ	Christchurch	1976/77
	8/0	Lees W.K., NZ v Sri Lanka	Wellington	1982/83
	4/4	McSweeney E.B., Wellington v Northern Districts	Wellington	1984/85
	8/0	Smith I.D.S., Auckland v Central Districts	Nelson	1988/89
	8/0	Smith I.D.S., NZ v Sri Lanka	Hamilton	1990/91
	7/1	Hart R.G., Northern Districts v Canterbury	Hamilton	1994/95
	7/1	Germon L.K., Canterbury v Central Districts	Palmerston North	1994/95
	7/1	Nevin C.J., Wellington v Central Districts	Nelson	1995/96
	8/0	Vincent L., Auckland v Central Districts	Palmerston North	2000/01
	8/0	Howell G.A., Wellington v Northern Districts	Hamilton	2001/02
	7/1	McCullum B.B., Canterbury v Northern Districts	Christchurch	2003/04
	7/1	Papps M.W.H., Canterbury v Northern Districts	Gisborne	2004/05
	8/0	van Wyk C.F.K., Canterbury v Auckland	Auckland	2006/07
	8/0	McGlashan P.D., Northern Districts v Auckland	Auckland	2006/07

Most Dismissals in an Innings

7	7/0	Schofield R.M., Central Districts v Wellington	Wellington	1964/65
	7/0	Wasim Bari, Pakistan v NZ	Auckland	1978/79
	7/0	Young B.A., Northern Districts v Canterbury	Christchurch	1986/87
	7/0	Smith I.D.S., NZ v Sri Lanka	Hamilton	1990/91
	7/0	Croy M.G., Otago v Auckland	Auckland	2001/02
	7/0	Hopkins G.J., New Zealand A v South Africa A	Centurion	2004/05
	5/2	Hopkins G.J., New Zealand A v Sri Lanka A	Kandy	2005/06
6	4/2	Mooney F.L.H., NZ v Warwickshire	Birmingham	1949
	5/1	Wadsworth K.J., NZ v Surrey	The Oval	1973
	6/0	Downes L.W., Central Districts v Canterbury	Nelson	1975/76
	5/1	Kirmani S.M.H., India v NZ	Christchurch	1975/76
	6/0	Vance R.H., Wellington v Otago	Wellington	1977/78
	6/0	Downton P.R., England XI v Otago	Dunedin	1977/78
	6/0	Germon L.K., Canterbury v Northern Districts	Christchurch	1992/93
	5/1	Hart R.G., Northern Districts v Canterbury	Hamilton	1994/95
	5/1	Nevin C.J., Wellington v Central Districts	Nelson	1995/96
	6/0	Parore A.C., New Zealand A v Pakistan A	Hamilton	1998/99
	6/0	Young R.A., Auckland v Wellington	Wellington	2002/03
	6/0	Hopkins G.J., Otago v Canterbury	Dunedin	2004/05
	5/1	Papps M.H.W., Canterbury v Northern Districts	Gisborne	2004/05
	6/0	McGlashan P.D., Northern Districts v Auckland	Auckland	2006/07
	6/0	Watling B-J., Northern Districts v Central Districts	Gisborne	2006/07

Most Catches in a Season

49	Nevin C.J.	2000/01	31	McSweeney E.B.	1990/91
37	Hopkins G.J.	2004/05	31	Germon L.K.	1991/92
35	McSweeney E.B.	1989/90	31	Griggs B.B.J.	2001/02
35	Young R.A.	2002/03	31	Nevin C.J.	2002/03
35	Griggs B.B.J.	2005/06	31	McCullum B.B.	2003/04
34	Hart R.G.	1997/98	31	Young R.A.	2004/05
33	Nevin C.J.	1995/96	31	Hopkins G.J.	2005/06
33	Hart R.G.	2001/02	30	Smith I.D.S.	1979/80
33	Young R.A.	2001/02	30	Kelly P.J.	1983/84
32	Wadsworth K.J.	1975/76	30	Young B.A.	1991/92
32	Smith I.D.S.	1986/87	30	Croy M.G.	1998/99
32	Smith I.D.S.	1990/91	30	Hart R.G.	2003/04
31	McSweeney E.B.	1984/85			

Most Catches in a Match

10	Nevin C.J., Wellington v Otago	Wellington	1995/96
	Gilchrist A.C., Australia v New Zealand	Hamilton	1999/00
	Hopkins G.J., Otago v Canterbury	Dunedin	2004/05
9	Schofield R.M., Central Districts v Wellington	Wellington	1964/65
	Vance R.H., Wellington v Otago	Wellington	1977/78
	Young B.A., Northern Districts v Canterbury	Christchurch	1986/87
	Germon L.K., Canterbury v Northern Districts	Christchurch	1992/93
	Rashid Latif., Pakistan v New Zealand	Auckland	1993/94
	Hopkins G.J., Otago v Wellington	Queenstown	2004/05
	Hopkins G.J., Otago v Northern Districts	Dunedin	2005/06
8	Curtis W.M., North Island XI v South Island XI	Wellington	1957/58
	Petrie E.C., NZ v Sussex	Hove	1958
	Parks J.M., England v NZ	Christchurch	1965/66
	Marsh R.W., Australia v NZ	Christchurch	1976/77
	Lees W.K., NZ v Sri Lanka	Wellington	1982/83
	McSweeney E.B., Wellington v Otago	Lower Hutt	1983/84
	Smith I.D.S., Auckland v Central Districts	Nelson	1988/89
	Smith I.D.S., NZ v Sri Lanka	Hamilton	1990/91
	Vincent L., Auckland v Central Districts	Palmerston North	2000/01
	Howell G.A., Wellington v Northern Districts	Hamilton	2001/02
	van Wyk C.F.K., Canterbury v Auckland	Auckland	2006/07
	McGlashan P.D., Northern Districts v Auckland	Auckland	2006/07
	Hopkins G.J., New Zealand A v Sri Lanka A	Kandy	2005/06

Most Catches in an Innings

7	Schofield R.M., Central Districts v Wellington	Wellington	1964/65
	Wasim Bari, Pakistan v NZ	Auckland	1978/79
	Young B.A., Northern Districts v Canterbury	Christchurch	1986/87
	Smith I.D.S., NZ v Sri Lanka	Hamilton	1990/91
	Croy M.G., Otago v Auckland	Auckland	2001/02
	Hopkins G.J., New Zealand A v South Africa A	Centurion	2004/05
6	Downes L.W., Central Districts v Canterbury	Nelson	1975/76
	Vance R.H., Wellington v Otago	Wellington	1977/78
	Downton P.R., England XI v Otago	Dunedin	1977/78
	Germon L.K., Canterbury v Northern Districts	Christchurch	1992/93
	Parore A.C., New Zealand A v Pakistan A	Hamilton	1998/99
	Young R.A., Auckland v Wellington	Wellington	2002/03
	Hopkins G.J., Otago v Canterbury	Dunedin	2004/05
	McGlashan P.D., Northern Districts v Auckland	Auckland	2006/07
	Watling B-J., Northern Districts v Central Districts	Gisborne	2006/07

Most Stumpings in a Season

13	Jackman C.K.Q.	1935/36	13	Kent L.A.W.	1944/45

Most Stumpings in a Match

7	Jackman C.K.Q., Canterbury v Wellington	Wellington	1935/36
6	Kent L.A.W., Auckand v Wellington	Wellington	1944/45
5	James K.C., NZ v Surrey	The Oval	1927
	James K.C., NZ v Derbyshire	Derby	1927
	Burns R.C., Canterbury v Otago	Dunedin	1928/29
	Mills A.S., Otago v Fiji	Dunedin	1947/48

Most Stumpings in an Innings

4	Jackman C.K.Q., Canterbury v Wellington	Wellington	1935/36
	Tindill E.W.T., NZ v Glamorgan	Cardiff	1937
	Kent L.A.W., Auckland v Wellington	Wellington	1944/45
	Mills A.S., Otago v Fiji	Dunedin	1947/48
	McSweeney E.B., Wellington v Northern Districts	Wellington	1984/85

FIELDING

Most Catches in a Season

23	Murray B.A.G.	1967/68	16	Harris C.Z.	2006/07
22	Coney J.V.	1977/78	15	Playle W.R.	1958/59
20	Howarth H.J.	1973/74	15	Bradburn W.P.	1963/64
18	Sinclair M.S.	2001/02	15	Turner G.M.	1975/76
17	Crowe M.D.	1986/87	15	Blair W.L.	1978/79
17	Boyle D.J.	1990/91	15	Crowe J.J.	1990/91
17	Parlane N.R.	2002/03	15	Knight N.V.	1996/97
16	Burgess M.G.	1977/78	15	Vincent L.	1999/00
16	Edgar B.A.	1978/79	15	Bradburn G.E.	2000/01
16	Crowe M.D.	1981/82	15	How J.M.	2003/04
16	Crowe M.D.	1983/84	15	Bell M.D.	2004/05
16	Fleming S.P.	1993/94			

Most Catches in a Match

7	Morrison J.F.M., Wellington v Northern Districts	Wellington	1980/81
	Fleming S.P., New Zealand v Zimbabwe	Harare	1997/98
6	Marchant J.W.A., Wellington v Nelson	Wellington	1873/74
	Williams N.T., Auckland v Hawke's Bay	Napier	1894/95
	Cromb I.B., Canterbury v Otago	Christchurch	1937/38
	Ikin J.T., MCC v Auckland	Auckland	1946/47
	Reid J.R., NZ v South Zone	Bangalore	1955/56
	Jarvis T.W., Auckland v Northern Districts	Hamilton	1968/69
	Anderson R.W., Rest v NZ	New Plymouth	1974/75
	MacDonald G.K., Canterbury v Pakistan	Christchurch	1984/85
	Young B.A., New Zealand v Pakistan	Auckland	1993/94
	Latham R.T., Canterbury v Otago	Oamaru	1994/95
	Young B.A., Northern Districts v Wellington	Wellington	1995/96
	Chandler P.J.B., New Zealand A v England	Wanganui	1996/97
	McHardy D.S., Wellington v Northern Districts	Hamilton	1996/97

	Fleming S.P., New Zealand v Australia	Brisbane	1997/98
	Bell M.D., Wellington v Canterbury	Wellington	2003/04
	Fleming S.P., New Zealand v West Indies	Wellington	2005/06
	McCullum N.L., Otago v Central Districts	Napier	2006/07

Most Catches in an Innings

5	Williams N.T., Auckand v Hawke's Bay	Napier	1894/95
	Lamason J.R., Wellington v Otago	Dunedin	1937/38
	Lamason J.R., NI Army v SI Army	Wellington	1942/43
	Ikin J.T., MCC v Auckland	Auckland	1946/47
	Rabone G.O., NZ v Oxford University	Oxford	1949
	Reid J.R., NZ v South Zone	Bangalore	1955/56
	Morrison J.F.M., Wellington v Northern Districts	Wellington	1980/81
	MacDonald G.K., Canterbury v Pakistan	Christchurch	1984/85
	Crowe J.J., Auckland v Canterbury	Auckland	1988/89
	Fleming S.P., New Zealand v Zimbabwe	Harare	1997/98
	Harris C.Z., Canterbury v England	Christchurch	2001/02

OLDEST PLAYERS

AGE Years/days			
52/189	Boxshall C.	Canterbury v Wellington	1914/15
51/216	Read R.J.	Canterbury v Auckland	1937/38
51/203	Lyttelton C.J. †	Governor-General's XI v MCC	1960/61
51/87	Wilson C.G.	Wellington v Hawke's Bay	1919/20
51/32	MacLaren A.C.	MCC v New Zealand	1922/23
50/284	Wilson E.S.	Otago v Wellington	1927/28
50/269	Hay T.D.B.	New Zealand v Royal Navy	1927
50/184	Reese T.W.	Canterbury v Otago	1917/18
50/86	Dufaur F.E.	Auckland v Wellington	1882/83
49/88	Allcott C.F.W.	Otago v Auckland	1945/46
49/48	Wilding F.	Canterbury v Hawke's Bay	1901/02
48/96	Hartley J.C.	MCC v Auckland	1922/23
48/40	Hallamore R.G.	Southland v Otago	1918/19
48/26	Badcock F.T.	New Zealanders v H.D.G. Leveson-Gower's XI	1945
47/357	Board J.H.	Hawke's Bay v Wellington	1914/15
47/325	Rowntree R.W.	Auckland v South Africa	1931/32
47/177	Fox R.H.	New Zealand v Civil Service	1927
47/151	Jones S.P.	Auckland v Otago	1908/09
47/114	Hughes W.J.	Hawke's Bay v Wellington	1905/06
47/98	Brice A.W.S.	Wellington v Australia	1927/28
47/70	Fowke J.N.	Canterbury v MCC	1906/07
46/319	Kortlang H.H.L.	Wellington v Auckland	1926/27
46/149	Stevens E.C.J.	Canterbury v Otago	1883/84
46/125	Allen R.	Wellington v Fiji	1953/54
46/14	Downes A.D.	Otago v Canterbury	1913/14
45/364	Blackie D.D.	Australia v New Zealand	1927/28
45/292	Handford A.	Southland v Otago	1914/15
45/270	Wynyard E.G.	MCC v Wellington	1906/07
45/241	Blamires E.O.	Otago v Canterbury	1926/27
45/39	Smith S.G.	Auckland v Wellington	1925/26
45/6	Beard D.D.	Northern Districts v Wellington	1964/65
44/349	Levers W.C.S.	Hawke's Bay v Wellington	1908/09
44/338	Knight A.R.	Otago v Canterbury	1943/44
44/308	Chadwick C.S.	Otago v Auckland	1924/25
44/226	Tucker K.H.	Wellington v Hawke's Bay	1919/20
44/182	Anthony A.	Auckland v Wellington	1930/31
44/178	Siedeberg H.G.	Otago v Wellington	1921/22
44/126	Garrard D.R.	Auckland v Wellington	1941/42
44/105	Newman J.A.	Canterbury v Otago	1928/29
44/75	Cate W.A.	New Zealand v MCC	1922/23
44/70	Wallace W.M.	Governor General's XI v MCC	1960/61
44/59	Dempster C.S.	Wellington v Auckland	1947/48
44/7	Wheatley J.	Canterbury v Hawke's Bay	1903/04

† Lord Cobham

YOUNGEST PLAYERS

AGE Years/days			
15/224	Dacre C.C.R.	Auckland v Wellington	1914/15
15/272	Midlane F.A.	Wellington v Hawke's Bay	1898/99
15/319	Ollivier A.M.	Canterbury v Otago	1866/67
16/36	Hartland J.F.	Canterbury v Otago	1877/78

AGE Years/days			
16/84	Broad C.H.	Nelson v Wellington	1888/89
16/86	McGregor S.N.	Otago v Fiji	1947/48
16/87	Dacre L.M.	Auckland v Wellington	1912/13
16/89	Anderson C.J.	Canterbury v Central Districts	2006/07
16/130	Coutts H.D.	Taranaki v Auckland	1882/83
16/147	Puna K.N.	New Zealand Under 23 XI v Otago	1971/72
16/173	Aaqib Javed	Pakistan v President's XI	1988/89
16/242	Collins J.U.	Nelson v Wellington	1884/85
16/250	Taylor L.G.	Auckland v Hawke's Bay	1910/11
16/273	Tendulkar S.R.	India v President's XI	1989/90
16/285	Reese D.	Canterbury v Wellington	1895/96
16/311	Hale H.	Tasmania v Otago	1883/84
16/325	Morgan R.W.	Auckland v Northern Districts	1957/58
16/330	Maunder P.A.	Central Districts v Auckland	1961/62
17/4	Wallace W.M.	Auckland v Wellington	1933/34
17/5	Frater R.E.	Auckland v Wellington	1918/19
17/12	Bell M.D.	Northern Districts v New Zealand Academy XI	1993/94
17/49	Williams A.B.	Otago v Canterbury	1886/87
17/52	Blunt R.C.	Canterbury v Otago	1917/18
17/65	Mitchell W.J.	Northern Districts v Pakistan	1964/65
17/66	Wilding A.F.	Canterbury v Auckland	1900/01
17/77	Clarke D.B.	Auckland v Central Districts	1950/51
17/93	Hay T.D.B.	Auckland v Wellington	1893/94
17/107	Rutherford K.R.	Otago v Auckland	1982/83
17/110	Cooke F.H.	Otago v Canterbury	1879/80
17/112	Barron J.R.	Otago v Canterbury	1917/18
17/119	Crowe M.D.	Auckland v Canterbury	1979/80
17/124	MacNeil H.	Otago v Canterbury	1877/78
17/152	Butler L.C.	Wellington v Auckland	1951/52
17/174	McIntyre J.M.	Auckland v Canterbury	1961/62
17/179	Rutherford I.A.	Otago v Canterbury	1974/75
17/182	Robin T.P.	Central Districts v Canterbury	1999/00
17/185	Robinson S.A.	Otago v Northern Districts	1984/85
17/213	Turner G.M.	Otago v Canterbury	1964/65
17/222	Hemi R.C.	Auckland v Wellington	1950/51
17/244	Ghulam Abbas	Pakistan v Auckland	1964/65
17/258	Rose G.A.	Central Districts v Northern Districts	1958/59
17/268	Snedden A.N.C.	Auckland v Wellington	1909/10
17/268	Beuth J.A.	Northern Districts v New Zealand Under 23 XI	1962/63
17/274	Ashbolt F.L.	Wellington v Auckland	1893/94
17/276	Collinge R.O.	Central Districts v Auckland	1963/64
17/278	Nicholls J.G.	Otago v Canterbury	1876/77
17/286	Hickmott R.G.	Canterbury v Wellington	1911/12
17/291	Bennett J.H.	Canterbury v Otago	1898/99
17/294	Cairns A.E.	Otago v Canterbury	1867/68
17/305	Gill M.F.	Central Districts v Wellington	1974/75
17/307	Currie E.W.	Otago v New South Wales	1893/94
17/307	Hastings B.F.	Wellington v Canterbury	1957/58
17/325	Bartlett G.A.	Central Districts v Northern Districts	1958/59
17/328	Cushen J.A.J.	Otago v Canterbury	1967/68
17/329	West R.M.	Central Districts v Northern Districts	1996/97
17/336	Lambert H.N.	Wellington v Canterbury	1917/18
17/352	Motz R.C.	Canterbury v Northern Districts	1957/58
17/355	Tarrant D.R.	Central Districts v Auckland	1954/55
17/362	Vettori D.L.	Northern Districts v England	1996/97

CAREER RECORDS

The following career records cover the complete first-class careers of New Zealand players. Matches for other than New Zealand teams e.g. county sides, are included.
To qualify for inclusion a player must have appeared in first-class cricket in New Zealand while a bona fide resident of the country — professional coaches and the like thus being excluded.

Batting

3000 RUNS	*Career*	*M*	*In*	*NO*	*HS*	*Runs*	*Ave*	*100*
Turner G.M.	1964/65-1982/83	455	792	101	311*	34,346	49.70	103
Wright J.G.	1975/76-1992/93	366	636	44	192	25,073	42.35	59
Crowe M.D.	1979/80-1995/96	247	412	62	299	19,608	56.02	71
Sutcliffe B.	1941/42-1965/66	233	407	39	385	17,447	47.41	44
Howarth G.P.	1968/69-1985/86	338	584	42	183	17,294	31.90	32
Reid J.R.	1947/48-1965	246	418	28	296	16,128	41.35	39
Patel D.N.	1976-1996/97	358	558	51	204	15,188	29.95	26
Fleming S.P.	1991/92-2006/07	228	375	31	274*	14,889	43.28	31
Rutherford K.R.	1982/83-1999/00	220	383	33	317	13,974	39.92	35
Congdon B.E.	1960/61-1978	241	416	40	202*	13,101	34.84	23
Hitchcock R.E.	1947/48-1964	323	519	71	153*	12,473	27.84	13
Dacre C.C.R.	1914/15-1936	269	439	20	223	12,230	29.18	24
Dempster C.S.	1921/22-1947/48	184	306	36	212	12,145	44.98	35
Hadlee R.J.	1971/72-1990	342	473	93	210*	12,052	31.71	14
Edgar B.A.	1975/76-1989/90	175	307	26	203	11,304	40.22	24
Parker J.M.	1971-1983/84	207	362	39	195	11,254	34.84	21
Smith S.G.	1899/00-1925/26	211	379	30	256	10,920	31.28	14
Cairns C.L.	1988-2005/06	217	341	38	158	10,702	35.32	13
Spearman C.M.	1993/94-2006	179	325	15	341	11,954	38.56	28
Burgess M.G.	1963/64-1980/81	192	322	35	146	10,281	35.82	20
Crowe J.J.	1977/78-1991/92	180	304	34	159	10,233	37.90	22
Richardson M.H.	1989/90-2004/05	157	264	31	306	9994	42.89	20
Greatbatch M.J.	1982/83-1999/00	170	292	31	202*	9890	37.89	24
Twose R.G.	1989-2000/01	178	300	35	277*	9802	36.98	18
Lowry T.C.	1917/18-1937/38	198	322	20	181	9421	31.19	18
Dowling G.T.	1958/59-1971/72	158	282	13	239	9399	34.94	16
Sinclair M.S.	1995/96-2006/07	131	223	22	268	9327	46.40	22
Astle N.J.	1991/92-2006/07	171	272	24	223	9321	37.58	19
Donnelly M.P.	1936/37-1960/61	131	221	26	208*	9250	47.43	23
Jones A.H.	1979/80-1995/96	145	254	33	186	9180	41.53	16
Horne M.J.	1992/93-2005/06	128	219	11	241	8501	40.87	24
Arnold P.A.	1953/54-1960	174	306	15	122	8013	27.53	7
Blunt R.C.	1917/18-1935	123	209	15	338*	7953	40.99	15
Bell M.D.	1993/94-2006/07	141	241	16	219	7939	35.28	18
Coney J.V.	1970/71-1986/87	165	272	48	174*	7872	35.14	8
McMillan C.D.	1994/95-2006/07	1137	224	27	168*	7815	39.67	16
Franklin T.J.	1980/81-1992/93	148	254	20	181	7794	33.30	15
Wallace W.M.	1933/34-1960/61	121	192	17	211	7757	44.32	17
Hastings B.F.	1957/58-1976/77	163	273	32	226	7685	31.89	15
Hadlee W.A.	1933/34-1951/52	117	203	17	198	7523	40.44	18
Young B.A.	1983/84-1998/99	163	276	43	267*	7489	32.14	10
Harris C.Z.	1989/90-2006/07	128	200	42	251*	7228	45.75	14
Vance R.H.	1976/77-1990/91	135	230	18	254*	6955	32.80	12
Parore A.C.	1988/89-2001/02	163	252	43	155*	6826	32.66	10
McEwan P.E.	1976/77-1990/91	115	206	15	155	6677	34.95	12

	Career	M	In	NO	HS	Runs	Ave	100
McGregor S.N.	1947/48-1968/69	148	274	16	114*	6573	25.47	5
James K.C.	1923/24-1946/47	204	330	41	109*	6413	22.19	7
Latham R.T.	1980/81-1994/95	108	189	19	237*	6298	37.05	9
Murray B.A.G.	1958/59-1972/73	102	187	11	213	6257	35.55	6
Morrison J.F.M.	1965/66-1983/84	126	225	25	180*	6142	30.71	7
Sinclair B.W.	1955/56-1970/71	118	204	18	148	6114	32.87	6
Blair B.R.	1977/78-1989/90	110	190	6	143	5995	32.58	7
Morgan R.W.	1957/58-1976/77	136	229	13	166	5940	27.50	8
Roberts A.D.G.	1967/68-1983/84	112	206	37	128*	5865	34.70	7
Page M.L.	1920/21-1942/43	132	213	17	206	5857	29.88	9
Shrimpton M.J.F.	1961/62-1979/80	122	218	23	150	5812	29.80	7
Blain T.E.	1982/83-1994/95	118	199	30	161	5749	34.02	8
Parlane M.E.	1992/93-2006/07	109	183	8	203	5664	32.36	13
Reid J.F.	1975/76-1987/88	101	170	22	180	5650	38.17	11
Scott V.J.	1937/38-1952/53	80	130	17	204	5620	49.73	16
Cumming C.D.	1995/96-2006/07	99	180	16	187	5615	34.23	11
Anderson R.W.	1967/68-1981/82	111	197	14	155	5609	30.65	8
Smith I.D.S.	1977/78-1991/92	178	250	42	173	5570	26.77	6
Gray E.J.	1975/76-1991/92	162	241	51	128*	5472	28.80	6
Jones R.A.	1993/94-2006/07	96	170	10	188	5367	33.54	12
Chapple M.E.	1949/50-1971/72	119	201	16	165	5344	28.88	4
Pollard V.	1964/65-1974/75	130	207	33	146	5314	30.54	6
Styris S.B.	1994/95-2006/07	109	179	18	212*	5181	32.18	9
Mills J.E.	1925/26-1937/38	97	161	8	185	5025	32.84	11
Graham H.	1892/93-1906/07	113	200	9	124	5023	26.29	7
Weir G.L.	1927/28-1946/47	107	172	16	191	5022	32.19	10
Stead G.R.	1991/92-2005/06	101	165	10	190	4984	32.15	10
Bradburn G.E.	1985/86-2001/02	127	206	27	148*	4978	27.81	4
McSweeney E.B.	1979/80-1993/94	121	177	30	205*	4947	33.65	6
Lees W.K.	1970/71-1987/88	146	243	43	152	4932	24.66	5
Pairaudeau B.H.	1946/47-1966/67	89	159	5	163	4930	32.01	11
White D.J.	1979/80-1993/94	106	187	17	209	4926	28.98	7
Papps M.H.W.	1998/99-2006/07	82	144	9	192	4919	36.43	12
Kerr J.L.	1929/30-1942/43	89	157	7	196	4829	32.19	8
Douglas M.W.	1987/88-2000/01	94	160	23	144	4808	35.09	9
Miller L.S.M.	1950/51-1959/60	82	142	15	144	4777	37.61	5
Grimmett C.V.	1911/12-1940/41	248	321	54	71*	4720	17.67	—
Gaffaney C.B.	1995/96-2004/05	83	152	11	194	4711	33.41	8
Pocock B.A.	1990/91-2000/01	100	176	16	167	4699	29.36	10
Marshall H.J.H.	1998/99-2006/07	84	142	11	168	4679	35.71	10
Jarvis T.W.	1964/65-1976/77	97	167	8	182	4666	29.34	6
Sparling J.T.	1956/57-1970/71	127	215	26	105	4606	24.11	2
Edwards G.N.	1973/74-1984/85	92	164	8	177*	4589	29.41	5
Vincent L.	1997/98-2006/07	84	135	10	224	4584	36.67	10
Taylor B.R.	1963/64-1979/80	141	210	25	173	4579	24.75	4
Hadlee B.G.	1961/62-1980/81	84	155	11	163*	4539	31.52	6
Vivian H.G.	1930/31-1938/39	85	143	15	165	4443	34.71	6
Hart M.N.	1990/91-2004/05	135	198	26	201*	4418	25.68	4
Briasco P.S.	1982/83-1991/92	83	148	16	157	4390	33.25	6
Bracewell J.G.	1978/79-1990	149	208	40	110*	4354	25.91	4
Thomson S.A.	1987/88-1996/97	90	148	38	167	4209	38.26	6
Cairns B.L.	1971/72-1988	148	226	25	110	4165	20.72	1
Marshall J.A.H.	1997/98-2006/07	88	150	5	235	4130	28.48	6

	Career	M	In	NO	HS	Runs	Ave	100
McGirr H.M.	1913/14-1932/33	88	146	7	141	3992	28.71	5
Cromb I.B.	1929/30-1946/47	88	148	12	171	3950	29.04	3
Priest M.W.	1984/85-1998/99	109	154	25	119	3945	30.58	4
Dunning B.	1961/62-1977/78	83	150	10	142	3929	28.06	3
Guy J.W.	1953/54-1972/73	90	165	13	115	3923	25.80	3
Nevin C.J.	1995/96-2006/07	88	134	20	143*	3890	34.12	3
Bailey M.D.	1989/90-2001/02	89	138	9	180*	3882	30.09	8
Hopkins G.J.	1997/98-2006/07	94	150	24	175*	3866	30.68	7
Harris R.M.	1955/56-1973/74	73	130	5	157	3863	30.90	3
Yuile B.W.	1959/60-1971/72	123	187	31	146	3850	24.67	1
Parsons A.E.W.	1971/72-1982/83	82	156	10	141	3847	26.34	4
Sulzberger G.P.	1995/96-2004/05	83	135	12	159	3836	31.18	8
Hiddleston J.S.	1909/10-1928/29	52	97	1	212	3818	39.77	8
Rutherford I.A.	1974/75-1983/84	79	144	4	222	3794	27.10	5
Taylor D.D.	1946/47-1960/61	95	168	6	143	3772	23.28	1
Hartland B.R.	1986/87-1996/97	83	150	8	150	3753	26.42	5
Kuggeleijn C.M.	1975/76-1990/91	89	151	15	116	3747	27.55	4
MacGibbon A.R.	1947/48-1961/62	124	206	20	94	3699	19.88	—
Blair W.L.	1967/68-1990/91	82	151	9	140	3698	26.04	2
Webb P.N.	1976/77-1986/87	75	130	19	136	3671	33.07	5
Wadsworth K.J.	1968/69-1975/76	118	164	23	117	3664	25.98	2
Fulton P.G.	2000/01-2006/07	53	87	9	301*	3659	46.91	6
Vettori D.L.	1996/97-2006/07	119	163	23	137*	3649	26.06	4
Roberts A.W.	1927/28-1950/51	84	135	17	181	3645	30.88	3
Leggat J.G.	1944/45-1955/56	57	106	9	166	3634	37.46	7
Austen M.H.	1982/83-1996/97	66	120	8	202*	3619	32.31	6
Howell L.G.	1990/91-2004/05	83	143	16	181	3586	28.23	3
Hoskin R.N.	1980/81-1992/93	81	140	7	157	3580	26.91	6
Nash D.J.	1990/91-2001/02	120	168	37	135*	3555	27.13	5
Patrick W.R.	1905/06-1926/27	74	138	8	143	3536	27.20	4
Smith C.J.P.	1983/84-1990/91	62	118	9	160*	3499	32.10	7
Motz R.C.	1957/58-1969	142	225	21	103*	3494	17.12	1
Larsen G.R.	1984/85-1998/99	103	157	35	161	3491	28.61	2
Wiseman P.J.	1991/92-2006	157	213	44	130	3487	20.63	2
Brown V.R.	1978/79-1989/90	83	136	17	161*	3485	29.28	6
Rabone G.O.	1940/41-1960/61	82	135	14	125	3425	28.30	3
Pritchard T.L.	1937/38-1956	200	293	41	81	3363	13.34	—
Newdick G.A.	1970/71-1980/81	61	114	6	143	3292	30.48	4
Lawson R.A.	1992/93-2003/04	73	133	6	200	3278	25.81	3
Vivian G.E.	1964/65-1978/79	88	140	25	137*	3259	28.33	3
Moloney D.A.R.	1929/30-1940/41	64	119	7	190	3219	28.74	2
Boyle D.J.	1980/81-1994/95	69	121	12	149	3216	29.50	3
Stead D.W.	1968/69-1985/86	80	139	11	193*	3205	25.03	1
Alabaster G.D.	1955/56-1975/76	96	154	20	108	3200	23.88	3
Reese D.	1895/96-1920/21	72	134	8	148	3186	25.28	4
McCullum S.J.	1976/77-1990/91	75	131	1	134	3174	24.41	2
Duff S.W.	1985/86-1995/96	88	134	29	164*	3167	30.16	1
Vaughan J.T.C.	1989/90-1996/97	70	120	20	127	3159	31.59	2
Harford N.S.	1953/54-1966/67	74	122	8	158	3149	27.62	3
Merritt W.E.	1926/27-1946	125	191	33	87	3147	19.91	—
Oram J.D.P.	1997/98-2006/07	64	101	15	155	3147	36.59	6
Mooney F.L.H.	1941/42-1954/55	91	150	14	180	3143	23.11	2
Redmond R.E.	1963/64-1975/76	53	100	7	141*	3134	33.69	5

	Career	M	In	NO	HS	Runs	Ave	100
Thomson K.	1959/60-1973/74	71	125	14	136*	3134	28.23	5
Tindill E.W.T.	1932/33-1949/50	69	116	13	149	3127	30.35	6
Harris P.G.Z.	1949/50-1964/65	69	120	9	118	3126	28.16	5
Germon L.K.	1987/88-2001/02	103	142	35	160*	3123	29.18	4
Englefield J.I.	1998/99-2005/06	55	97	7	172	3113	34.58	3
Franklin J.E.C.	1998/99-2006/07	89	131	19	208	3106	27.73	3
McIntosh T.G.	1998/99-2006/07	64	108	9	205	3084	31.15	10
McCullum B.B.	1999/00-2006/07	59	98	6	160	3071	33.38	6
Wells J.D.	1989/90-2000/01	73	115	18	143	3058	31.52	5
Ryan M.L.	1965/66-1978/79	66	113	9	129	3023	29.06	3
How J.M.	2000/01-2006/07	59	100	8	169	3018	32.80	8
Barnes A.C.	1993/94-2004/05	78	121	10	134*	3006	27.08	4

Bowling

200 WICKETS	Career	M	Wkts	Runs	Ave
Hadlee R.J.	1971/72-1990	342	1490	26,998	18.11
Grimmett C.V.	1911/12-1940/41	248	1424	31,740	22.28
Smith S.G.	1899/00-1925/26	211	955	17,272	18.08
Pritchard T.L.	1937/38-1956	200	818	19,062	23.30
Patel D.N.	1976-1996/97	358	654	21,737	33.23
Cairns C.L.	1988-2005/06	217	647	18,322	28.31
Boock S.L.	1973/74-1989/90	164	640	14,314	22.36
Chatfield E.J.	1973/74-1989/90	157	587	13,429	22.87
Saunders J.V.	1899/00-1913/14	107	553	12,065	21.81
Howarth H.J.	1962/63-1978/79	145	541	13,674	25.27
Blair R.W.	1951/52-1964/65	119	537	9961	18.54
Merritt W.E.	1926/27-1946	125	536	13,669	25.50
Collinge R.O.	1963/64-1978	163	524	12,793	24.41
O'Sullivan D.R.	1971-1984/85	136	523	13,554	25.91
Bracewell J.G.	1978/79-1990	149	522	13,919	26.66
Motz R.C.	1957/58-1969	142	518	11,769	22.72
Alabaster J.C.	1955/56-1971/72	143	500	12,688	25.37
Cairns B.L.	1971/72-1988	148	473	12,544	26.52
Reid J.R.	1947/48-1965	246	466	10,535	22.60
Cameron F.J.	1952/53-1966/67	119	447	9658	21.60
Gray E.J.	1975/76-1991/92	162	444	12,522	28.20
Morrison D.K.	1985/86-1996/97	142	440	13,298	30.22
Taylor B.R.	1963/64-1979/80	141	422	10,605	25.13
Wiseman P.J.	1991/92-2006	159	417	14,158	33.95
Burtt T.B.	1943/44-1954/55	84	408	9054	22.19
Snedden M.C.	1977/78-1990	118	387	9918	25.62
Cunis R.S.	1960/61-1976/77	132	386	10,287	26.65
Vettori D.L.	1996/97-2006/07	119	381	12,288	32.25
Yuile B.W.	1959/60-1971/72	123	375	8209	21.89
Moir A.M.	1949/50-1961/62	97	368	9040	24.56
Cave H.B.	1945/46-1958/59	117	362	8663	23.93
Cowie J.	1932/33-1949/50	86	359	8002	22.28
MacGibbon A.R.	1947/48-1961/62	124	356	9301	26.12
Hadlee D.R.	1966/67-1983/84	111	351	8853	25.22
Martin C.S.	1997/98-2006/07	110	343	10,598	30.89
McIntyre J.M.	1961/62-1982/83	113	336	7917	23.56
Priest M.W.	1984/85-1998/99	109	329	10,478	31.84

	Career	M	Wkts	Runs	Ave
Callaway S.T.	1888/89-1906/07	62	320	5460	17.06
Sparling J.T.	1956/57-1970/71	127	318	7226	22.72
Downes A.D.	1888/89-1913/14	51	311	4564	14.67
Franklin J.E.C.	1998/99-2006/07	89	310	7690	24.80
Hayes J.A.	1946/47-1960/61	78	292	6759	23.14
Dickeson C.W.	1973/74-1986/87	90	282	8242	29.22
Beard D.D.	1945/46-1964/65	66	278	6000	21.58
O'Connor S.B.	1994/95-2002/03	73	278	6582	23.67
Adams A.R.	1997/98-2006/07	74	278	7023	25.26
Alabaster G.D.	1955/56-1975/76	96	275	6388	23.22
Troup G.B.	1974/75-1986/87	100	272	7541	27.72
Watson W.	1984/85-1994/95	93	272	7485	27.52
Upham E.F.	1892/93-1909/10	49	265	4414	16.65
Nash D.J.	1990/91-2001/02	120	255	7165	28.09
Walmsley K.P	1994/95-2005/06	67	253	6302	24.90
Robertson G.K.	1979/80-1989/90	88	252	7469	29.59
Penn A.J.	1994/95-2003/04	66	252	5806	23.03
Bradburn G.E.	1985/86-2001/02	127	250	8174	32.69
Doull S.B.	1989/90-2001/02	99	250	7233	28.93
Wisneski W.A.	1992/93-2003/04	71	248	6467	26.07
Brice A.W.S.	1902/03-1927/28	61	247	5260	21.29
Bennett J.H.	1898/99-1919/20	52	241	4476	18.58
McGirr H.M.	1913/14-1932/33	88	239	6571	27.49
Tuffey D.R.	1996/97-2006/07	70	237	6146	25.93
Puna N.	1956/57-1968/69	70	229	5597	24.44
Dunning J.A.	1923/24-1937/38	60	228	6290	27.58
Pollard V.	1964/65-1974/75	130	224	6931	30.94
Vivian H.G.	1930/31-1938/39	85	223	6160	27.62
Cromb I.B.	1929/30-1946/47	88	222	6152	27.71
Badcock F.T.	1924/25-1945	53	221	5211	23.57
Allcott C.F.W.	1920/21-1945/46	82	220	5882	26.73
Yovich J.A.F.	1996/97-2006/07	80	219	7129	32.55
Sewell D.G.	1995/96-2005/06	67	218	6260	28.71
Duff S.W.	1985/86-1995/96	88	217	7051	32.49
Davis H.T.	1991/92-2003/04	71	215	6693	31.13
Blunt R.C.	1917/18-1935	123	214	6638	31.01
Stott L.W.	1969/70-1983/84	63	214	5341	24.95
Hart M.N.	1990/91-2004/05	135	212	7424	35.01
Hamilton L.J.	1996/97-2006/07	60	212	5391	25.42
de Groen R.P.	1987/88-1995/96	60	210	5266	25.07
Stirling D.A.	1981/82-1991/92	84	206	6948	33.72
Canning T.K.	1998/99-2006/07	61	206	5042	24.47
Congdon B.E.	1960/61-1978	241	204	6125	30.02
Roberts S.J.	1985/86-1995/96	63	203	6001	29.56
Mason M.J.	1997/98-2006/07	61	202	4911	24.31
Burke C.	1937/38-1953/54	60	200	5199	25.99

Wicketkeeping

100 DISMISSALS	*Career*	*M*	*Caught*	*Stumped*	*Total*
Smith I.D.S.	1977/78-1991/92	178	390	36	426
James K.C.	1923/24-1946/47	204	310	112	422
McSweeney E.B.	1979/80-1993/94	121	340	45	385
Parore A.C.	1988/89-2001/02	163	358	24	382
Lees W.K.	1970/71-1987/88	146	292	44	336
Hart R.G.	1992/93-2003/04	110	298	17	315
Wadsworth K.J.	1968/69-1975/76	118	256	26	282
Germon L.K.	1987/88-2001/02	103	256	26	282
Hopkins G.J.	1997/98-2006/07	94	247	18	265
Ward J.T.	1957/58-1970/71	95	227	27	254
Nevin C.J.	1995/96-2006/07	88	233	8	241
Petrie E.C.	1950/51-1966/67	115	194	37	231
Mooney F.L.H.	1941/42-1954/55	91	164	54	218
Blain T.E.	1982/83-1994/95	118	190	26	216
Young R.A.	1998/99-2006/07	68	206	5	211
Croy M.G.	1994/95-2001/02	65	183	14	197
Young B.A.	1983/84-1997/98	163	185	11	196
Milburn B.D.	1963/64-1982/83	75	176	19	195
van Wyk C.F.K.	2000/01-2006/07	56	168	9	177
Dick A.E.	1956/57-1968/69	78	133	21	154
Kelly P.J.	1980/81-1988/89	49	140	13	153
Griggs B.B.J.	2000/01/2006/07	55	142	5	147
McCullum B.B.	1999/00/2006/07	59	128	12	140
Colquhoun I.A.	1953/54-1963/64	57	108	28	136
Guillen S.C.	1947/48-1960/61	66	100	34	134
Sigley M.A.	1994/95-2002/03	44	124	4	128
Boxshall C.	1897/98-1914/15	65	81	43	124
Schofield R.M.	1964/65-1974/75	53	107	15	122
Robinson S.A.	1984/85-1996/97	45	117	5	122
Wright M.J.E.	1972/73-1983/84	65	104	17	121
Mills G.H.	1935/36-1957/58	59	85	34	119
Tindill E.W.T.	1932/33-1949/50	69	85	33	118
Edwards G.N.	1973/74-1984/85	92	88	16	104
Therkleson I.J.	1966/67-1973/74	39	93	7	100

Leading Career Averages

BATTING *(qualification 3000 runs)*	*M*	*In*	*NO*	*HS*	*Runs*	*Ave*
Crowe M.D.	247	412	62	299	19,608	56.02
Scott V.J.	80	130	17	204	5620	49.73
Turner G.M.	455	792	101	311*	34,346	49.70
Donnelly M.P.	131	221	26	208*	9250	47.43
Sutcliffe B.	233	407	39	385	17,447	47.41
Fulton P.G.	53	87	9	301*	3659	46.91
Sinclair M.S.	131	223	22	268	9327	46.40
Harris C.Z.	128	200	42	251*	7228	45.75
Dempster C.S.	184	306	36	212	12,145	44.98
Wallace W.M.	121	192	17	211	7757	44.32
Fleming S.P.	228	375	31	274*	14,889	43.28
Richardson M.H.	157	264	31	306	9994	42.89
Wright J.G.	366	636	44	192	25,073	42.35
Jones A.H.	145	254	33	186	9180	41.53
Reid J.R.	246	418	28	296	16,128	41.35
Blunt R.C.	123	209	15	338*	7953	40.99
Horne M.J.	128	219	11	241	8501	40.87
Hadlee W.A.	117	203	17	198	7523	40.44
Edgar B.A.	175	307	26	203	11,304	40.22

BOWLING *(qualification 200 wickets)*	*M*	*Wkts*	*Runs*	*Ave*
Downes A.D.	51	311	4564	14.67
Upham E.F.	49	265	4414	16.65
Callaway S.T.	62	320	5460	17.06
Smith S.G.	211	955	17,272	18.08
Hadlee R.J.	342	1490	26,998	18.11
Blair R.W.	119	537	9961	18.54
Bennett J.H.	52	241	4476	18.58

(C.J. Drum took 199 wickets at 19.46)

HIGHEST PARTNERSHIPS

FIRST WICKET

387	Turner G.M.	Jarvis T.W.	NZ v West Indies	Georgetown	1971/72
373	Sutcliffe B.	Watt L.	Otago v Auckland	Auckland	1950/51
333	Edgar B.A.	Jones A.H.	Wellington v Auckland	Wellington	1988/89
316	Austen M.H.	Hart R.T.	Wellington v Central Districts	Wanganui	1993/94
310	Edgar B.A.	Vance R.H.	Wellington v Northern Districts	Wellington	1988/89
306	Cuff L.A.	Lawrence J.D.	Canterbury v Auckland	Christchurch	1893/94
305	Lawson R.A.	Croy M.G.	Otago v Central Districts	Napier	1995/96
299	Bell M.D.	Jones R.A.	Wellington v Otago	Dunedin	2001/02
287	Hartland B.R.	Stead G.R.	Canterbury v Wellington	Christchurch	1994/95
286	Sutcliffe B.	Taylor D.D.	Auckland v Canterbury	Auckland	1948/49
276	Dempster C.S.	Mills J.E.	NZ v England	Wellington	1929/30
276	Griffith A.F.G.	Campbell S.L.	West Indies v NZ	Hamilton	1999/00
268	Turner G.M.	Dowling G.T.	NZ v President's XI	Montego Bay	1971/72
260	Lawson R.A.	Mohammad Wasim	Otago v Northern Districts	Dunedin	2002/03
259	Austen M.H.	Aiken J.M.	Wellington v Otago	Wellington	1994/95
252	Sutcliffe B.	Scott V.J.	NZ v Rest	Christchurch	1948/49
250	Hart R.T.	Smith C.J.P.	Central Districts v Wellington	Wellington	1985/86
247	Sutcliffe B.	Scott V.J.	NZ v Combined Services	Gillingham	1949
244	Richardson M.H.	Papps M.H.W.	NZ v Kent	Canterbury	2004
240	McIntosh T.G.	Horne M.J.	Auckland v Otago	Dunedin	2001/02
239	Dempster C.S.	Dustin W.H.	Wellington v Canterbury	Wellington	1931/32
239	Smith D.	Parks J.H.	MCC v Otago	Dunedin	1935/36
235	Hadlee W.A.	Page M.L.	Canterbury v Wellington	Christchurch	1936/37
231	Richardson M.H.	Vincent L.	NZ v India	Mohali	2003/04
230	Murray B.A.G.	Turner G.M.	NZ v President's XI	Rawalpindi	1969/70
229	Sutcliffe B.	Scott V.J.	NZ v Surrey	Oval	1949
226*	Hadlee W.A.	Leggat J.G.	Canterbury v Otago	Christchurch	1948/49
225	Richardson P.E.	Watson W.	MCC v Wellington	Wellington	1958/59
225	Greenidge C.G.	Haynes D.L.	West Indies v NZ	Christchurch	1979/80
220	Sutcliffe B.	Taylor D.D.	Auckland v Canterbury	Auckland	1948/49
220	Bell M.D.	Jones R.A.	Wellington v Canterbury	Christchurch	2000/01
219*	Edgar B.A.	Vance R.H.	Wellington v Central Districts	Wellington	1987/88
218	Hadlee W.A.	Leggat J.G.	Canterbury v Wellington	Christchurch	1947/48
218	Dempsey D.A.	Hadlee B.G.	Canterbury v Otago	Christchurch	1980/81
215	Sinclair M.S.	How J.M.	Central Districts v Northern Districts	Napier	2004/05
214	Woodfull W.M.	Ponsford W.H.	Australia v Otago	Dunedin	1927/28
214	Bolton B.A.	Dowling G.T.	Canterbury v Northern Districts	Christchurch	1959/60
214	Spearman C.M.	Twose R.G.	NZ v Zimbabwe	Auckland	1995/96
213	Lawson R.A.	Bell M.D.	NZ Academy XI v Zimbabwe	Whangarei	1995/96
213	Gaffaney C.B.	Parlane M.E.	NZ Academy XI v Bangladesh	Christchurch	1997/98
211	Turner G.M.	Parker J.M.	NZ v MCC	Lord's	1973
211	Bell M.D.	Donaldson G.T.	Wellington v Central Districts	Wellington	2003/04
209	Sutcliffe B.	Watt L.	Otago v Canterbury	Dunedin	1947/48
209	Harris B.Z.	Boyle D.J.	Canterbury v Otago	Christchurch	1991/92
208	Blunt R.C.	Worker R.V. de R.	Canterbury v MCC	Christchurch	1922/23
208	Athey C.W.J.	Robinson R.T.	England XI v Northern Districts	Hamilton	1987/88
207	Sadiq Mohammad	Zaheer Abbas	Pakistan v Wellington	Wellington	1972/73
201	Anthony A.	Horspool E.	Auckland v Wellington	Auckland	1924/25
201	Astle T.D.	Papps M.H.W.	Canterbury v Wellington	Christchurch	2006/07

SECOND WICKET

317	Hart R.T.	Briasco P.S.	Central Districts v Canterbury	New Plymouth	1983/84
315*	Gibbs H.H.	Kallis J.H.	South Africa v NZ	Christchurch	1998/99
303	Dempster C.S.	Allcott C.F.W.	NZ v Warwickshire	Birmingham	1927
287	Bell M.D.	Wells J.D.	Wellington v Auckland	Auckland	1997/98
279	Bell M.D.	Parlane M.E.	Wellington v Otago	Dunedin	2006/07
263	Greatbatch M.J.	Crowe M.D.	Central Districts v Northern Districts	Morrinsville	1986/87
256	Anderson R.W.	Edgar B.A.	NZ v Scotland	Dundee	1978

254	Burns K.J.	Rutherford K.R.	Otago v Wellington	Oamaru	1987/88
252	Baker W.A.	Beechey E.M.	Wellington v Auckland	Wellington	1918/19
250	Bell M.D.	Sinclair M.S.	New Zealand A v Sri Lanka A	Queenstown	2003/04
248	Horne M.J.	Fleming S.P.	Southern v Pakistan A	Christchurch	1998/99
245	Horne M.J.	Fleming S.P.	NZ v British Universities	Oxford	1999
244	Spearman C.M.	Sinclair M.S.	Central Districts v Northern Districts	Wanganui	1998/99
243	Papps M.H.W.	Stewart S.L.	Canterbury v Northern Districts	Hamilton	2006/07
242*	How J.M.	Sinclair M.S.	Central Districts v Otago	New Plymouth	2005/06
241	Franklin T.J.	Crowe J.J.	Auckland v Wellington	Wellington	1988/89
241	Wright J.G.	Jones A.H.	NZ v England	Wellington	1991/92
237	Gibson J.G.	Kuggeleijn C.M.	Northern Districts v Canterbury	Hamilton	1980/81
231	Carew M.C.	Nurse S.M.	West Indies v NZ	Christchurch	1968/69
229	Hemus L.G.	Midlane F.A.	Auckland v Wellington	Wellington	1918/19
227	Baker W.A.	Kortlang H.H.L.	Wellington v Otago	Dunedin	1923/24
227	Dobbs P.W.	Lamont M.J.	Otago v Auckland	Dunedin	1990/91
222	Warner P.F.	Fane F.L.	Lord Hawke's XI v Otago	Dunedin	1902/03
222	Crocker L.M.	Kuggeleijn C.M.	Northern Districts v Otago	Hamilton	1983/84
222	McCullum B.B.	Cumming C.D.	Otago v Auckland	Dunedin	2001/02
220	Macartney C.G.	Punch A.T.E.	NSW v Otago	Dunedin	1923/24
220	Richardson M.H.	Cumming C.D.	Otago v Northern Districts	Hamilton	2000/01
215	Bell M.D.	Wells J.D.	Wellington v Northern Districts	Hamilton	1998/99
215	Bell M.D.	Parlane M.E.	Wellington v Central Districts	Napier	2004/05
213	Barnett G.E.F.	Sinclair M.S.	Central Districts v Otago	New Plymouth	2005/06
212	Horspool E.	Snedden A.N.C.	Auckland v Victoria	Auckland	1924/25
210	Hadlee W.A.	O'Brien F.P.	Canterbury v Otago	Christchurch	1940/41
210	Howarth G.P.	Crowe J.J.	NZ v West Indies	Kingston	1984/85
209*	Jones A.H.	Crowe M.D.	Wellington v Canterbury	Christchurch	1992/93
207*	Twose R.G.	Douglas M.W.	Central Districts v Auckland	Auckland	1991/92
207	Mills J.E.	Blunt R.C.	NZ v H.D.G. Leveson-Gower's XI	Scarborough	1927
207	Vaughan M.P.	Hussain N.	England v Canterbury	Christchurch	2001/02
206	Raman W.V.	Gursharan Singh	India v Otago	Dunedin	1989/90
204	Gavaskar S.M.	Amarnath S.	India v NZ	Auckland	1975/76
202	Naushad Ali	Saeed Ahmed	Pakistan v Canterbury	Christchurch	1964/65
200	Smith R.W.	Bilby G.P.	Wellington v Northern Districts	Whangarei	1973/74

THIRD WICKET

467†	Jones A.H.	Crowe M.D.	New Zealand v Sri Lanka	Wellington	1990/91
445	Whitelaw P.E.	Carson W.N.	Auckland v Otago	Dunedin	1936/37
394*	Kennedy P.G.	Latham R.T.	Canterbury v Northern Districts	Rotorua	1990/91
346	Burnett G.P.	Verry R.A.	Wellington v Northern Districts	Hamilton	1991/92
278	Franklin T.J.	Patel D.N.	Auckland v Canterbury	Christchurch	1985/86
265	Horne M.J.	Barnes A.C.	Auckland v Bangladesh	Auckland	2001/02
264	Chappell I.M.	Chappell G.S.	Australia v NZ	Wellington	1973/74
261*	Maynard M.P.	Thomson S.A.	Northern Districts v Auckland	Hamilton	1990/91
255	Lloyd C.H.	Davis C.A.	West Indies v South Island	Dunedin	1968/69
252*	Howarth G.P.	Roberts A.D.G.	Northern Districts v Pakistan	Gisborne	1978/79
248	Shoaib Mohammad	Javed Miandad	Pakistan v New Zealand	Auckland	1988/89
246	Rabone G.O.	Reid J.R.	NZ v Nottinghamshire	Nottingham	1949
246	Murray B.A.G.	Morrison J.F.M.	Wellington v Otago	Dunedin	1968/69
245	Crowe M.D.	Coney J.V.	NZ v South Australia	Adelaide	1985/86
244	Nicol R.J.	Vincent L.	Auckland v Otago	Auckland	2004/05
241	Wright J.G.	Crowe M.D.	New Zealand v West Indies	Wellington	1986/87
229	Miller L.S.M.	Sutcliffe B.	NZ v South Australia	Adelaide	1953/54
227	Rutherford K.R.	Blair B.R.	Otago v Central Districts	Alexandra	1988/89
226	Haynes D.L.	Richardson R.B.	West Indies v Shell XI	Napier	1986/87
224	Reid J.F.	Crowe M.D.	NZ v Australia	Brisbane	1985/86
224	Sinclair M.S.	Spearman C.M.	Central Districts v Auckland	Auckland	2003/04
223	Smith C.J.P.	Wilson S.W.J.	Central Districts v Otago	Blenheim	1990/91
222*	Sutcliffe B.	Reid J.R.	NZ v India	New Delhi	1955/56
222	Snedden A.N.C.	Smith S.G.	Auckland v Hawke's Bay	Auckland	1920/21
221	Blunt R.C.	McMullan J.J.M.	Otago v Canterbury	Dunedin	1928/29
221	Lara B.C.	Adams J.C.	West Indies v New Zealand	Wellington	1994/95

220	Shoaib Mohammad	Javed Miandad	Pakistan v New Zealand	Wellington	1988/89
218	Woodfull W.M.	Schneider K.J.	Australia v NZ	Auckland	1927/28
217	Dobbs P.W.	Rutherford K.R.	Otago v Central Districts	Blenheim	1990/91
216	Hemus L.G.	Smith S.G.	Auckland v Canterbury	Auckland	1919/20
214	Anthony A.	Gillespie H.D.	Auckland v Canterbury	Auckland	1929/30
213	Turner G.M.	Congdon B.E.	Otago v Wellington	Dunedin	1972/73
213	Jones A.H.	Crowe M.D.	NZ v Australia	Adelaide	1987/88
212	Booth B.C.	Burge P.J.P.	Australia B v NZ	Auckland	1966/67
210	Howarth G.P.	Crowe M.D.	NZ v Essex	Chelmsford	1983
210	Edgar G.A.	Crowe M.D.	NZ v England	Lord's	1986
210	Smith B.F.	Douglas M.W.	Central Districts v Northern Districts	Taupo	2000/01
209	McCosker R.G.	Chappell G.S.	Australia v Wellington	Wellington	1976/77
208	Papps M.H.W.	McMillan C.D.	Canterbury v Central Districts	Christchurch	2006/07
206	Preston A.H.	Beck J.E.F.	Wellington v Canterbury	Christchurch	1955/56
204	Harford N.S.	Reid J.R.	NZ v Oxford University	Oxford	1958
204	Twose R.G.	Crowe M.D.	NZ v Indian Colts XI	Hyderabad	1995/96
204	Fleming S.P.	Styris S.B.	NZ v Bangladesh	Chittagong	2004/05
203*	Pocock B.A.	Parore A.C.	Auckland v Wellington	Auckland	1997/98
201	McLeod E.G.	Lamason J.R.	Wellington v Auckland	Wellington	1935/36

† *world record*

FOURTH WICKET

350	Mushtaq Mohammad	Asif Iqbal	Pakistan v NZ	Dunedin	1972/73
324	Reid J.R.	Wallace W.M.	NZ v Cambridge University	Cambridge	1949
310	Ryder J.D.	Parlane N.R.	Wellington v Central Districts	Palmerston North	2004/05
299	Wallace W.M.	Donnelly M.P.	NZ v Leicestershire	Leicester	1949
282	Wilkinson W.A.C.	Champman A.P.F.	MCC v Canterbury	Christchurch	1922/23
280	Crowe J.J.	Patel D.N.	Auckland v Northern Districts	Auckland	1991/92
278	Roberts A.W.	Page M.L.	Canterbury v Wellington	Wellington	1931/32
276*	Crowe M.D.	Briasco P.S.	Central Districts v Canterbury	Christchurch	1986/87
274	Jones R.A.	Mather S.R.	Wellington v Otago	Wellington	2000/01
273	McIntosh T.G.	Nicol R.J.	Auckland v Otago	Lincoln	2006/07
266	Denness M.H.	Fletcher K.W.R.	England v NZ	Auckland	1974/75
259	Bradburn G.E.	Parlane M.E.	Northern Districts v Canterbury	Christchurch	1996/97
254	Reid J.R.	Miller L.S.M.	NZ v Natal	Durban	1953/54
252	Thomson S.A.	Young B.A.	Northern Districts v Auckland	Auckland	1990/91
243	Horne M.J.	Astle N.J.	New Zealand v Zimbabwe	Auckland	1997/98
240	Fleming S.P.	McMillan C.D.	New Zealand v Sri Lanka	Colombo	1997/98
235	Burns K.J.	Hoskin R.N.	Otago v Northern Districts	Hamilton	1987/88
229	Congdon B.E.	Hastings B.F.	NZ v Australia	Wellington	1973/74
219	Vivian H.G.	Page M.L.	NZ v Oxford University	Oxford	1931
218	Crowe J.J.	Coney J.V.	NZ v Glamorgan	Swansea	1986
214	Ransford V.S.	Lampard A.W.	Australia v NZ	Auckland	1920/21
211*	Jones A.H.	Burns K.J.	Otago v Wellington	Wellington	1984/85
211	White D.J.	Young B.A.	Northern Districts v Auckland	Auckland	1992/93
208	Thomson S.A.	Maynard M.P.	Northern Districts v Wellington	Hamilton	1991/92
207	Midlane F.A.	Richardson C.A.	Wellington v Otago	Wellington	1899/00
207	Badcock F.T.	Lowry T.C.	Wellington v Auckland	Wellington	1927/28
207	Sulzberger G.P.	Penn A.J.	Central Districts v Otago	Napier	1995/96
206	McCullum S.J.	Dawson G.J.	Otago v Northern Districts	Dunedin	1983/84
206	Stewart A.J.	Hussain N.	England v New Zealand XI	Palmerston North	1996/97
206	McIntosh T.G.	Vincent L.	Auckland v Canterbury	Christchurch	2000/01
204	Harvey R.N.	Simpson R.B.	Australia B v Otago	Dunedin	1956/57
204	Jarvis T.W.	Thomson K.	Canterbury v Central Districts	Wanganui	1969/70
204	Redmond A.J.	Broom N.T.	Otago v Northern Districts	Hamilton	2006/07
203	Thomson S.A.	Maynard M.P.	Northern Districts v Otago	Hamilton	1991/92
200	Blair B.R.	Dawson G.J.	Otago v Central Districts	Dunedin	1982/83

FIFTH WICKET

347*	Horne M.J.	Barnes A.C.	Auckland v Northern Districts	Auckland	2003/04
341	Larsen G.R.	McSweeney E.B.	Wellington v Central Districts	Levin	1987/88
319	Rutherford K.R.	Gray E.J.	NZ v DB Close's XI	Scarborough	1986

301	Englefield J.I.	Taylor L.R.P.L.	Central Districts v Wellington	Palmerston North	2004/05
290	Harris C.Z.	Stead G.R.	Canterbury v Central Districts	Blenheim	1996/97
266	Sutcliffe B.	Haig W.S.	Otago v Auckland	Dunedin	1949/50
258	Salim Malik	Inzamam-ul-Haq	Pakistan v New Zealand	Wellington	1993/94
255	Taylor B.R.	Coney J.V.	Wellington v Otago	Dunedin	1972/73
252*	Latham R.T.	Priest M.W.	Canterbury v Northern Districts	Christchurch	1988/89
244	Reid J.R.	Chapple M.E.	NZ v Western Province	Cape Town	1962/63
242	Hammond W.R.	Ames L.E.G.	England v NZ	Christchurch	1932/33
236	Harris C.Z.	Astle N.J.	Canterbury v Otago	Christchurch	1996/97
235*	Woodfull W.M.	Ransford V.S.	Victoria v NZ	Christchurch	1924/25
235*	Sulzberger G.P.	Ryder J.D.	Central Districts v Canterbury	Napier	2002/03
234*	Scott V.J.	Morris J.B.	Auckland v Central Districts	Auckland	1951/52
233	Moloney D.A.R.	Kerr J.L.	NZ v England XI	Folkestone	1937
222	Astle N.J.	McMillan C.D.	New Zealand v Zimbabwe	Wellington	2000/01
219	Broom N.T.	Hopkins G.J.	Otago v Auckland	Lincoln	2006/07
216	Parlane N.R.	Franklin J.E.C.	Wellington v Auckland	Wellington	2005/06
213	Ritchie G.M.	Matthews G.R.J.	Australia v NZ	Wellington	1985/86
203	Booth B.C.	Davies G.R.	Australia B v Central Districts	Palmerston North	1966/67
201	Alexander W.C.	Richardson V.Y.	Australia v Auckland	Auckland	1927/28
201	Burgess M.G.	Jarvis T.W.	Auckland v Central Districts	Auckland	1971/72

SIXTH WICKET

322	Orchard M.G.	Yovich J.A.F.	Northern Districts v Central Districts	Napier	2005/06
293*	Fulton P.G.	Broom N.T.	Canterbury v Otago	Dunedin	2004/05
281	Thorpe G.P.	Flintoff A.	England v New Zealand	Christchurch	2001/02
269	Trumper V.T.	Hill C.	Australia v NZ	Wellington	1904/05
256	Martyn D.R.	Gilchrist A.C.	Australia v New Zealand	Wellington	2004/05
246*	Crowe J.J.	Hadlee R.J.	NZ v Sri Lanka	Colombo	1986/87
240	Parfitt P.H.	Knight B.R.	England v NZ	Auckland	1962/63
238	McDonald R.	Cowley O.W.	Queensland v Hawke's Bay	Napier	1896/97
233	Crawford J.N.	Armstrong W.W.	Australia v NZ	Auckland	1913/14
232	Botham I.T.	Randall D.W.	England v New Zealand	Wellington	1983/84
226	Gray E.J.	Ormiston R.W.	Wellington v Central Districts	Wellington	1981/82
220	Turner G.M.	Wadsworth K.J.	NZ v West Indies	Kingston	1971/72
220	Toynbee M.H.	Smith I.D.S.	Central Districts v Auckland	Napier	1982/83
216	Hart M.N.	Marshall H.J.H.	Northern Districts v Central Districts	Napier	2004/05
212*	McMillan C.D.	Parore A.C.	New Zealand v President's XI	Jodhpur	1999/00
209*	Parore A.C.	O'Dowd A.P.	Auckland v Otago	Dunedin	1991/92
209	Harris C.Z.	Redmond A.J.	Canterbury v Wellington	Rangiora	2001/02
203	Ormiston R.W.	Coney J.V.	Wellington v Central Districts	New Plymouth	1982/83
201	Harris C.Z.	Parore A.C	New Zealand v Orange Free State	Bloemfontein	1994/95
201	Tendulkar S.R.	Mongia N.R.	India v Central Districts	Napier	1998/99

SEVENTH WICKET

265	Powell J.L.	Dorreen N.	Canterbury v Otago	Christchurch	1929/30
261	Campbell A.D.R.	Strang P.A.	Zimbabwe v Canterbury	Timaru	1997/98
250	Nevin C.J.	Walker M.D.J.	Wellington v Otago	Wellington	2003/04
248	Yousuf Youhana	Saqlain Mushtaq	Pakistan v New Zealand	Christchurch	2000/01
246	McGlew D.J.	Murray A.R.A.	South Africa v NZ	Wellington	1952/53
244	Patrick W.R.	Allcott C.F.W.	NZ v NSW	Sydney	1925/26
241	Astle N.J.	Priest M.W.	Canterbury v Wellington	Christchurch	1994/95
229	Schneider K.J.	Oldfield W.A.S.	Australia v Canterbury	Christchurch	1927/28
225	Cairns C.L.	Oram J.D.P.	NZ v South Africa	Auckland	2003/04
224	Scott V.J.	Matheson A.M.	Auckland v Canterbury	Auckland	1937/38
219	Yuile B.W.	Hampton B.L.	Central Districts v Canterbury	Napier	1967/68
217	Walters K.D.	Gilmour G.J.	Australia v NZ	Christchurch	1976/77
212	Katich S.M.	Gilchrist A.C.	Australia v New Zealand	Christchurch	2004/05
205	Germon L.K.	Priest M.W.	Canterbury v Northern Districts	Christchurch	1991/92
192	Brown S.W.	Parore A.C.	Auckland v Central Districts	Auckland	1990/91
191	Wright J.G.	Smith I.D.S.	NZ v Western Australia	Perth	1989/90
186	Lees W.K.	Hadlee R.J.	NZ v Pakistan	Karachi	1976/77
186	Leggat R.I.	Hadlee D.R.	Canterbury v Sri Lanka	Christchurch	1982/83

184*	Bull C.L.	Isherwood B.P.	Canterbury v Central Districts	Nelson	1971/72
183	Oram J.D.P.	Vettori D.L.	New Zealand v South Africa	Centurion	2005/06
182	Sutcliffe B.	Gilbertson A.W.	Otago v Canterbury	Christchurch	1952/53
182	Weston T.I.	Thompson E.P.	Central Districts v Canterbury	Christchurch	2005/06
179	Griggs B.B.J.	Furlong C.J.M.	Central Districts v Northern Districts	Hamilton	2001/02
177*	Barnes A.C.	Mills J.M.	Auckland v Otago	Alexandra	1995/96
176	Rabone G.O.	Mooney F.L.H.	NZ v MCC	Lord's	1949
176	Mills S.M.	Nevin C.J.	Wellington v Canterbury	Christchurch	2006/07

EIGHTH WICKET

433†	Trumper V.T.	Sims A.	Sims' Australian XI v Canterbury	Christchurch	1913/14
256	Fleming S.P.	Franklin J.E.C.	New Zealand v South Africa	Cape Town	2005/06
253	Astle N.J.	Parore A.C.	New Zealand v Australia	Perth	2001/02
220	Wiseman P.J.	Hiini B.C.	Canterbury v Northern Districts	Hamilton	2005/06
215	Murray J.R.	Cummins A.C.	West Indies v Otago	Dunedin	1994/95
210	Stead G.R.	Bond S.E.	Canterbury v Northern Districts	Christchurch	2004/05
190*	Mills J.E.	Allcott C.F.W.	NZ v Civil Service	Chiswick	1927
189	Carson W.N.	Matheson A.M.	Auckland v Wellington	Auckland	1938/39
185	Nash D.J.	Mills K.D.	Auckland v Wellington	Wellington	2000/01
180	Twose R.G.	Goodson M.C.	Wellington v Otago	Dunedin	1994/95
173	Smith I.D.S.	Robertson G.K.	Central Districts v Northern Districts	Hamilton	1982/83
172*	Walker B.G.K.	Mills K.D.	Auckland v Wellington	Auckland	1999/00
166	Hadlee R.J.	Hadlee D.R.	Canterbury v Auckland	Christchurch	1983/84
165*	Eckhold A.G.	Crawford J.N.	Otago v Wellington	Wellington	1914/15
161	McSweeney E.B.	Snedden M.C.	Shell XI v West Indies	Napier	1986/87
157	McLaren A.C.	McLean J.F.	MCC v NZ	Wellington	1922/23
154	James K.C.	Badcock F.T.	Wellington v Canterbury	Christchurch	1926/27
153	Nicol R.J.	Young R.A.	Auckland v Canterbury	Auckland	2001/02
152	Bradburn G.E.	Doull S.B.	Northern Districts v Canterbury	Christchurch	1991/92
152	Marshall J.A.H.	Orchard M.G.	Northern Districts v Wellington	Hamilton	2006/07

† *world record*

NINTH WICKET

239	Cave H.B.	Leggat I.B.	Central Districts v Otago	Dunedin	1952/53
209	Wiseman P.J.	Martin B.P.	New Zealand A v Sri Lanka A	Christchurch	2003/04
208	McSkimming W.C.	Scott B.E.	Otago v Auckland	Auckland	2004/05
188	Parlane N.R.	Tuffey D.R.	Northern Districts v Wellington	Wellington	1999/00
185	Maynard M.P.	Doull S.B.	Northern Districts v Auckland	Auckland	1991/92
182*	Germon L.K.	Ford R.M.	Canterbury v Wellington	Christchurch	1989/90
170*	Hart M.N.	Yovich J.A.F.	Northern Districts v South Africa	Hamilton	1998/99
163*	Cowdrey M.C.	Smith A.C.	England v NZ	Wellington	1962/63
139	Hart R.G.	Tait A.R.	Northern Districts v Wellington	Gisborne	1996/97
136	Smith I.D.S.	Snedden M.C.	NZ v India	Auckland	1989/90
135	Hart R.G.	Penn A.J.	Central v Northern	Rangiora	1998/99
134	Wilson J.W.	Mallender N.A.	Otago v Canterbury	Christchurch	1992/93
127	Mooney F.L.H.	Buchan R.A.	Wellington v Auckland	Wellington	1943/44
122	Schuster H.T.	Cunis R.S.	Auckland v Wellington	Wellington	1964/65
121	Cheetham J.E.	Murray A.R.A.	South Africa v Canterbury	Christchurch	1952/53
118	Coney J.V.	Cairns B.L.	NZ v England	Wellington	1983/84
116	Nevin C.J.	Davis H.T.	Wellington v Auckland	Auckland	1995/96
115	Robertson G.K.	Hart R.T.	Central Districts v Otago	Oamaru	1985/86
115	Hopkins G.J.	Ellis A.M.	Canterbury v Auckland	Auckland	2002/03

TENTH WICKET

184	Blunt R.C.	Hawksworth W.	Otago v Canterbury	Christchurch	1931/32
160	Germon L.K.	Wisneski W.A.	Canterbury v Northern Districts	Rangiora	1997/98
151	Hastings B.F.	Collinge R.O.	NZ v Pakistan	Auckland	1972/73
138	James K.C.	Brice A.W.S.	Wellington v Otago	Wellington	1926/27
133	Bartlett G.A.	Colquhoun I.A.	Central Districts v Auckland	Auckland	1959/60
124	Bracewell J.G.	Boock S.L.	NZ v Australia	Sydney	1985/86
123	Brice A.W.S.	Beard T.	Wellington v Otago	Wellington	1927/28

119	Carson W.N.	Cowie J.	Auckland v Otago	Auckland	1937/38
118	Astle N.J.	Cairns C.L.	New Zealand v England	Christchurch	2001/02
113	Mooney F.L.H.	Knapp E.C.V.	Wellington v Auckland	Wellington	1943/44
113*	McGlashan P.D.	Aldridge G.W.	Northern Districts v Wellington	Wellington	2005/06
107	Motz R.C.	Cameron F.J.	NZ v Worcestershire	Worcester	1965
106*	Astle N.J.	Morrison D.K.	New Zealand v England	Auckland	1996/97
105	Cherry R.W.	Torrance R.C.	Otago v Canterbury	Christchurch	1925/26
104	James K.C.	Massey H.B.	Wellington v Australia	Wellington	1927/28
103	Kelly P.J.	Troup G.B.	Auckland v Northern Districts	Auckland	1985/86
101	Astle N.J.	Owens M.B.	Canterbury v Northern Districts	Hamilton	1994/95
100	Lee C.D.	Brown C.M.	Auckland v Otago	Dunedin	1994/95

Hundred Partnership for the First Wicket in Both Innings

154 & 155	Shepherd J.S.F.	Worker R.V. de.R.	Otago v Wellington	Dunedin	1923/24
220 & 286	Taylor D.D.	Sutcliffe B.	Auckland v Canterbury	Auckland	1948/49
102 & 155	Blair W.L.	Turner G.M.	Otago v Auckland	Auckland	1972/73
172 & 148	Briasco P.S.	Smith C.J.P.	Central Districts v Auckland	New Plymouth	1985/86
107	Broad B.C.	Moxon M.D.	England XI v Northern Districts	Hamilton	1987/88
208	Athey C.W.J.	Robinson R.T.			
109 & 111	Wealleans K.A.	White D.J.	Northern Districts v India	Hamilton	1989/90
116 & 102	Greatbatch M.J.	Latham R.T.	New Zealand v Zimbabwe	Bulawayo	1992/93
145 & 131	Lawson R.A.	Gaffaney C.B.	Otago v Wellington	Wellington	1996/97
118* & 179	Twose R.G.	Bell M.D.	Wellington v Central Districts	Wellington	1997/98
102 & 112	Spearman C.M.	Kelly D.P.	Central Districts v Wellington	New Plymouth	1999/00
220	Bell M.D.	Jones R.A.	Wellington v Canterbury	Christchurch	2000/01
127	Nevin C.J.	Jones R.A.			
141	Cumming C.D.	Mohammad Wasim	Otago v Wellington	Wellington	2002/03
147	Gaffaney C.B.	Cumming C.D.			
104 & 118	Richardson M.H.	McIntosh T.G.	Auckland v Northern Districts	Auckland	2002/03

FAMILIES IN FIRST-CLASS CRICKET

Great-grandfather and Great-grandson

Orchard S.A.	(C)	Orchard M.G.	(ND)

Three Generations

Anderson W.M.	(C)	Anderson R.W.	(C, ND, O, CD)	Anderson T.R.	(CD)
*Blair J.R.	(O)	Blair R.A.J.	(O)	Blair W.L.	(O)
				Blair B.R.	(O, ND)
Burton H.G.E.L.	(W)	Burton H.E.L.	(W, A)	Burton J.E.L.	(W)
*Burtt N.V.	(C)	Burtt J.W.	(C, CD)	Burtt L.M.	(C)
Smith F.A.	(C)	Smith F.B.	(C)	Smith G.B.	(C)
*Carson W.	(O)	Carson W.N.	(A)	Carson J.R.	(A, ND)
Snedden A.N.C.	(A)	Snedden W.N.	(A)	Snedden M.C.	(A)

** J.R. Blair is the uncle of R.A.J. Blair. The Carsons are uncles and nephews. J.W. Burtt is the uncle of L.M. Burtt.*

Grandfather and Grandson

Milnes L.A.	(O)	Milnes G.S.	(CD)
Roberts H.	(W)	du Chateau V.H.	(W)

Father and Three Sons

Cotterill A.J.	(C)	Cotterill A.K.	(HB)	Cotterill B.W.	(HB)	Cotterill G.R.	(HB)
Hadlee W.A.	(C, O)	Hadlee B.G.	(C)	Hadlee D.R.	(C)	Hadlee R.J.	(C)

Father and Two Sons

Blacklock J.W.	(W)	Blacklock C.P.	(W)	Blacklock J.P.	(W)
Blair R.A.J.	(O)	Blair W.L.	(O)	Blair B.R.	(O, ND)
Crowe D.W.	(W,C)	Crowe M.D.	(A, CD, W)	Crowe J.J.	(A, SA)
Garrard C.W.	(C)	Garrard W.R.	(A)	Garrard D.R.	(A)
Furlong B.D.M.	(CD)	Furlong J.B.M.	(CD)	Furlong C.J.M.	(CD)
Harris P.G.Z.	(C)	Harris B.Z.	(C, O)	Harris C.Z.	(C)
Howell J.H.	(CD)	Howell L.G.	(C, CD, A, ND)	Howell G.A.	(C, W)
McCullum S.J.	(O)	McCullum B.B.	(O, C)	McCullum N.L.	(O)
McVicar A.C.	(Minor Assocs)	McVicar S.A.	(W)	McVicar C.C.	(CD)
Puna N.	(ND)	Puna K.N.	(ND)	Puna A.	(ND)
Reaney P.S.	(HB)	Reaney H.E.I.	(W)	Reaney T.P.L.	(W, CD)

Father and One Son

Airey W.F.	(W)	Airey D.M.L.	(W)
Aldridge C.W.	(C)	Aldridge G.W.	(ND)
Allen R.	(W)	Allen G.S.	(W)
Andrews S.	(C)	Andrews B.	(C, CD, O)
Astle A.M.	(CD)	Astle T.D.	(C)
Baker J.C.	(O)	Clark J.B.	(O)
Barclay W.S.	(W)	Barclay C.W.	(CD)
Barton P.H.	(ND, O)	Barton H.D.	(A, C)
Barry R.W.	(C)	Barry R.	(C)
Beard D.D.	(W, CD, ND)	Beard D.A.	(ND)
Blackmore J.H.	(ND)	Blackmore S.J.	(W)
Bradburn W.P.	(ND)	Bradburn G.E.	(ND)
Burgess G.C.	(A)	Burgess M.G.	(A)
Burtt N.V.	(C)	Burtt J.W.	(C, CD)
Cairns B.L.	(CD, O, ND)	Cairns C.L.	(ND, C)

Campbell K.O.	(O)	Campbell P.A.	(O)
Child E.L.	(A, ND)	Child M.J.	(ND)
Clark L.G.	(O)	Clark L.A.	(W, O, A)
Collins W.E.	(W)	Collins D.C.	(W)
Cuff L.A.	(C, A)	Cuff A.G.	(Tasmania)
Cunis R.S.	(A, ND)	Cunis S.J.	(C)
Douglas G.W.	(CD)	Douglas M.W.	(CD, W)
Edgar A.J.	(W)	Edgar B.A.	(W)
Freeman T.A.	(O)	Freeman B.T.	(O)
Fulton F.	(O, HB)	Fulton P.R.	(HB)
Gasson E.A. snr	(C)	Gasson E.A. jnr	(C)
Gearry G.N.	(C)	Gearry R.M.	(C, CD)
Gedye A.E.	(W)	Gedye S.G.	(A)
Gilbertson J.	(S)	Gilbertson A.W.	(O)
Hartland I.R.	(C)	Hartland B.R.	(C)
Hastings B.F.	(W, CD, C)	Hastings M.A.	(C)
Hay W.P.C.	(A)	Hay S.C.	(A)
Hill A.J.	(CD)	Hill J.V.	(CD)
Hill J.	(O)	Hill R.J.	(O)
Holden W.J.	(O)	Holden A.C.	(O)
Howden C.E.	(O)	Howden C.P.	(O)
Ibadulla K.	(O)	Ibadulla K.B.K.	(O)
Jefferson R.G.	(O, W)	Jefferson M.R.	(W)
Kelly J.W.H.	(W)	Kelly P.J.	(A)
Kerr A.	(A)	Kerr A.C.	(A)
Lankham G.	(A)	Lankham W.	(A)
Lowry T.H.	(HB)	Lowry T.C.	(A, W)
McGirr W.P.	(W)	McGirr H.M.	(W)
McKnight S.G.	(O)	McKnight K.J.	(O)
McKenzie N.M.	(O)	McKenzie M.N.	(C, O)
Mills G.	(A, HB, O)	Mills J.E.	(A)
Morgan H.A.	(W)	Morgan R.G.	(ND, A)
Murdoch D.H.	(O)	Murdoch G.H.	(O)
Newman A.	(W)	Newman P.A.	(CD)
O'Brien J.J.	(HB)	O'Brien M.A.	(W)
Oakley J.H.	(W)	Oakley D.F.	(W)
Ollivier A.M.	(C)	Ollivier K.M.	(C)
Ongley A.M.	(HB)	Ongley J.A.	(W, CD)
Parker N.M.	(O, C)	Parker M.M.	(O)
Postles A.J.	(A)	Postles B.J.	(A)
Redmond R.E.	(W, A)	Redmond A.J.	(C, O)
Rees W.L.	(A)	Rees A.W.	(A, HB)
Reese T.W.	(C)	Reese D.W.	(C)
Reid J.R.	(W, O)	Reid R.B.	(W, A)
Roberts A.	(W)	Roberts S.A.	(A)
Roberts H.	(W)	Roberts E.J.	(W)
Sale E.V.	(A)	Sale V.S.	(A)
Standidge J.A.	(W)	Standidge P.H.	(W)
Stead D.W.	(C)	Stead G.R.	(C)
Tindill E.W.T.	(W)	Tindill P.	(W)
Vance R.A.	(W)	Vance R.H.	(W)
Vivian H.G.	(A)	Vivian G.E.	(A)
Wallace W.M.	(A)	Wallace G.M.	(A)
Ward J.T.	(C)	Ward B.J.	(C)
Wilding F.	(C)	Wilding A.F.	(C)
Wright G.T.	(C)	Wright J.G.	(ND, C, A)

Father and Son in Same First-class Match

Reese T.W. & Reese D.W.	Canterbury v Otago	Dunedin	1917/18

Five Brothers

Cotterill A.J. (C) Cotterill C.N. (HB) Cotterill E.J. (C, A) Cotterill H. (C) Cotterill W.J. (C)

Four Brothers

Bayly A.	(T)	Bayly F.	(T)	Bayly G.T.	(T)	Bayly H.	(T)
Bracewell B.P.	(CD, O, ND)	Bracewell D.W.	(CD, C)	Bracewell J.G.	(O, A)	Bracewell M.A.	(O)
Mills E.	(A)	Mills G.	(A, HB, O)	Mills I.	(A)	Mills W.	(T, A)

Three Brothers

Alloo A.P.	(O)	Alloo A.W.	(O)	Alloo H.C.	(O)
Blacklock A.	(W)	Blacklock J.W.	(W)	Blacklock R.V.	(W)
Carlton W.	(A, C)	Carlton A.R.	(Vic)	Carlton J.	(Vic)
Cotterill A.K.	(HB)	Cotterill B.W.	(HB)	Cotterill G.R.	(HB)
Eden J.	(N)	Eden T.	(N)	Eden W.	(N)
Fowler G.	(N)	Fowler L.	(N)	Fowler S.	(N)
Gore A.H.	(W, HB)	Gore C.S.	(W)	Gore R.	(W)
Hadlee B.G.	(C)	Hadlee D.R.	(C)	Hadlee R.J.	(C)
Harman A.F.G.	(C)	Harman R.D.	(C)	Harman T.D.	(C)
Knapp C.	(N)	Knapp H.	(N)	Knapp K.	(N)
Lusk Hugh B.	(A, HB)	Lusk R.B.	(T)	Lusk W.N.B.	(A)
Mace C.	(O)	Mace H.	(W)	Mace J.	(O)
Meldrum A.L.	(A)	Meldrum D.	(A)	Meldrum W.	(A)
Newman A.	(W)	Newman J.	(C, W)	Newman S.	(W)
Parker K.J.	(A)	Parker J.M.	(ND)	Parker N.M.	(O, C)
Reese D.	(C)	Reese J.B.	(C)	Reese T.W.	(C)
Ridley A.E.	(C)	Ridley H.C.	(C)	Ridley R.	(C)
Salmon I.J.	(W)	Salmon J.A.N.	(W)	Salmon W.J.	(W, HB, T)

Two Brothers

Aberhart D.C.	(CD, C)	Aberhart W.M.	(W)
Alabaster G.D.	(O, C, ND)	Alabaster J.C.	(O)
Austin G.G.	(O)	Austin T.T.L.	(O)
Baker G.H.	(W)	Baker W.A.	(W)
Bannerman J.W.H.	(S)	Bannerman W.E.	(O)
Barton P.H.	(ND, O)	Barton R.H.	(ND)
Beal C.E.	(O, C)	Beal W.M.	(O)
Beuth D.	(CD)	Beuth A.J.	(ND)
Billcliff I.S.	(O, W, A)	Billcliff M.R.	(O)
Bishop H.A.	(HB, C)	Bishop R.E.	(HB)
Blacklock C.P.	(W)	Blacklock J.P.	(W)
Blair B.R.	(O, ND)	Blair W.L.	(O)
Blakely D.J.	(O)	Blakely J.W.	(O)
Blamires E.O.	(W, O)	Blamires H.L.	(HB)
Boddington E.R.	(N, W)	Boddington H.A.	(N, O)
Boyle D.J.	(C)	Boyle J.G.	(W, C)
Burtt N.V.	(C)	Burtt T.B.	(C)
Cairns A.E.	(O)	Cairns H.W.	(O)
Cameron D.S.	(O)	Cameron H.R.	(O)
Cederwall B.W.	(W)	Cederwall G.N.	(W)

Chadwick C.S.	(O)	Chadwick L.N.	(O)
Clarke D.B.	(A, ND)	Clarke D.S.	(ND)
Collins J.U.	(N, C)	Collins W.E.	(W)
Coney C.J.	(W)	Coney J.V.	(W)
Cornelius C.J.	(C)	Cornelius W.A.	(C)
Cresswell A.E.	(W, CD)	Cresswell G.F.	(W, CD)
Cross C.S.	(N, W)	Cross H.	(N)
Crowe J.J.	(A)	Crowe M.D.	(A, CD, W)
Dacre C.C.R.	(A)	Dacre L.M.	(A)
Doull L.J.	(W)	Doull S.B.	(ND)
Dryden C.H.	(W)	Dryden W.E.	(W)
Farrant A.J.	(C)	Farrant D.G.	(C)
Fisher A.H.	(O)	Fisher R.L.	(C)
Frankish E.H.	(C)	Frankish F.S.	(C)
Frith C.	(C, O)	Frith W.	(C, O, W)
Fulton F.	(O, HB)	Fulton J.C.	(O)
Furlong C.J.M.	(CD)	Furlong J.B.M.	(CD)
Garrard D.R.	(A)	Garrard W.R.	(A)
Gatenby D.J.	(C)	Gatenby P.R.	(Tasmania)
Gilbertson J.	(S)	Gilbertson J.H.	(S)
Graham A.C.	(O)	Graham C.G.	(O)
Hamilton A.J.	(S)	Hamilton D.C.	(S)
Hampton B.L.	(CD)	Hampton I.R.	(CD)
Harris B.Z.	(C, O)	Harris C.Z.	(C)
Hart M.N.	(ND)	Hart R.G.	(ND)
Hatch K.	(W)	Hatch R.J.	(W)
Hay T.D.B.	(A)	Hay W.P.C.	(A)
Hickson H.C.	(W)	Hickson W.R.S.	(W)
Holdship A.R.	(W)	Holdship W.E.	(Middlesex)
Horne M.J.	(A, O)	Horne P.A.	(A)
Howarth G.P.	(A, ND)	Howarth H.J.	(A)
Howell L.G.	(C, CD, A, ND)	Howell G.A.	(C, W)
Howden A.M.	(A)	Howden C.E.	(O)
Lynch D.	(A)	Lynch R.F.	(W)
Lynch R.K.	(A)	Lynch S.M.	(A)
McCullum B.B.	(O, C)	McCullum N.L.	(O)
McVicar S.A.	(W)	McVicar C.C.	(CD)
Marshall J.A.H.	(ND)	Marshall H.J.H.	(ND)
Martin J.H.	(HB)	Martin H.	(HB)
Matthias H.R.	(C)	Matthias R.B.	(C)
Morris J.B.	(A)	Morris P.P.W.	(A)
Naughton D.	(W)	Naughton M.P.	(W)
Neill R.	(A)	Neill T.	(A)
Nicholson C.R.	(C, O)	Nicholson K.A.	(O)
O'Rourke M.H.	(A)	O'Rourke P.W.	(W)
Ollivier A.M.	(C)	Ollivier F.M.	(C)
Ormiston I.W.	(W)	Ormiston R.W.	(CD, W)
Papps M.H.W.	(C)	Papps T.J.T.	(C)
Parlane M.E.	(ND, W)	Parlane N.R.	(ND, W)
Powell J.L.	(C)	Powell R.F.J.	(C)
Powys A.L.	(C)	Powys R.A.N.	(C)
Puna A.	(ND)	Puna K.N.	(ND)
Reaney H.E.I.	(W)	Reaney T.P.L.	(W, CD)
Richardson C.A.	(W)	Richardson W.A.	(NSW)
Ritchie A.W.	(A)	Ritchie D.C.	(A)
Robertson G.K.	(CD)	Robertson S.P.	(CD)
Rutherford I.A.	(O, CD)	Rutherford K.R.	(O)

Schofer J.W.J.	(W)	Schofer P.J.	(W)
Scott A.H.	(A)	Scott V.J.	(A)
Shaw G.S.	(A, O)	Shaw L.J.	(A)
Snedden A.N.C.	(A)	Snedden Cyril A.	(A)
Snedden Colin A.	(A)	Snedden W.N.	(A)
Sorenson B.J.	(A)	Sorenson R.G.	(A)
Toomey C.D.G.	(O)	Toomey F.J.	(O)
Thomson K.	(C)	Thomson W.A.	(C)
Tucker K.H.	(W)	Tucker S.G.	(W)
Turnbull A.J.	(O)	Turnbull P.J.	(O)
Wallace G.F.	(A)	Wallace W.M.	(A)
Watson E.A.	(O)	Watson L.F.	(O)
Watson H.C.	(O)	Watson L.C.	(O)
Webb M.G.	(O, C)	Webb R.J.	(O)
Weir A.F.	(A)	Weir G.L.	(A)
West G.L.	(CD, ND)	West R.M.	(CD, W)
Westbrook K.R.	(Tasmania)	Westbrook R.A.	(O)
White N.M.	(HB)	White P.C.	(HB)
Williams P.F.C.	(Gloucestershire)	Williams J.N.	(HB)
Wilson A.C.	(C)	Wilson W.C.	(C)
Wyatt I.E.	(A)	Wyatt J.L.	(ND)

Uncle and Nephew

instances not included in previous lists

Bailey J.F.	(ND)	Bailey M.D.	(ND)
Burtt J.W.	(C, CD)	Burtt L.M.	(C)
CarltonW.	(A, C)	Carlton T.A.	(C, O)
Carson W.	(O)	Carson W.N.	(A)
Carson W.N.	(A)	Carson J.R.	(A, ND)
Crawford C.G.	(C)	Playle W.R.	(A)
Cunningham W.H.R.	(C)	Anderson G.F.	(C)
Dacre C.C.R. (A) & Dacre L.M.	(A)	Coleman D.D.	(A)
Fulton J.	(O)	{ Fulton F.	(O, HB)
		Fulton J.C.	(O)
Fulton R.W.	(C, ND)	Fulton P.G.	(C)
Griffiths B.G.	(W)	Maguiness S.J.	(W)
Pocock M.G.	(ND)	Pocock B.A.	(A, ND)
Roberts B.L.	(ND)	Cairns C.L.	(ND, C)
Westbrook N.R.	(Tasmania)	Westbrook R.A.	(O)
Wilson R.S.	(O)	Paul J.M.	(O)
Wilson T.J.	(O)	Wilson J.W.	(O)

Cousins

Bateman G.C.	(C)	Bateman S.N.	(C)
Hoskin R.N.	(O)	Lamont M.J.	(O)
Hotter S.J.	(W)	Verry R.A.	(W)
Leggat I.B.	(CD)	Leggat J.G.	(C)
Lusk Harold B.	(A, C, W)	{ Lusk Hugh B.	(A, HB)
		Lusk R.B.	(T)
		Lusk W.N.B.	(A)
McMillan C.D.	(C)	McMillan J.M.	(O)
Pringle M.R.	(A)	Webb P.N.	(A)
Reid B.A.	(WA)	Reid J.F.	(A)
Talbot G.L.	(C)	Talbot R.O.	(C, O)
Vettori D.L.	(ND)	Hill J.V.	(CD)

REDPATH CUP

Presented by Mr David Redpath

Awarded to the New Zealand batsman whose performances in first-class cricket have been, in the opinion of the Board of Control, the most meritorious since the award was last made.

HOLDERS

Season's first-class figures

		Team	In	NO	HS	Runs	Ave
1920/21	Anthony A.	Auckland	5	1	113	251	62.75
1921/22	Hiddleston J.S.	Wellington	8	1	118	396	56.57
1922/23	Blunt R.C.	Canterbury	12	1	174	583	53.00
1923/24	Hiddleston J.S.	Wellington	12	—	163	619	51.58
1924/25	Worker R.V. de R.	Otago	12	2	121*	491	49.10
1925/26	Allcott C.F.W.	Auckland	9 †	2	116	359	51.28
1926/27	Blunt R.C.	Otago	12 §	1	187	758	69.80
1927/28	Dempster C.S.	Wellington	12	1	145	616	56.00
1928/29	Weir G.L.	Auckland	4	2	106*	262	131.00
1929/30	Dempster C.S.	Wellington	10	4	141*	559	93.16
1930/31	Dempster C.S.	Wellington	42 †	6	212	1901	52.80
1931/32	Roberts A.W.	Canterbury	10	1	181	476	52.88
1932/33	Dempster C.S.	Wellington	9	2	83*	336	48.00
1933/34	Vivian H.G.	Auckland	5	—	64	263	52.60
1934/35	Whitelaw P.E.	Auckland	7	—	155	472	67.42
1935/36	Kerr J.L.	Canterbury	13 †	2	146	655	59.54
1936/37	Whitelaw P.E.	Auckland	6	1	195	410	82.00
1937/38	Uttley K.F.M.	Otago	6	—	138	420	70.00
1938/39	Wallace W.M.	Auckland	6	1	105	270	54.00
1939/40	Donnelly M.P.	Canterbury	5	1	104	302	75.50
1940-45	no award						
1945/46	Hadlee W.A.	Otago	7	—	198	449	66.14
1946/47	Sutcliffe B.	Auckland & Otago	8	1	197	722	103.14
1947/48	Sutcliffe B.	Otago	10	1	208*	911	101.22
1948/49	Sutcliffe B.	Auckland	6	—	141	511	85.16
1949/50	Sutcliffe B.	Otago	9	—	355	695	77.55
1950/51	Sutcliffe B.	Otago	12	—	275	798	66.50
1951/52	Scott V.J.	Auckland	10	2	151*	459	57.37
1952/53	Miller L.S.M.	Central Districts	9	3	128*	545	90.83
1953/54	Sutcliffe B.	Otago	34 †	2	196	1691	52.84
1954/55	Reid J.R.	Wellington	15	2	106	505	38.84
1955/56	Reid J.R.	New Zealand	33 †	6	150*	1227	45.44
1956/57	Miller L.S.M.	Wellington	13	3	83	559	55.90
1957/58	Miller L.S.M.	Wellington	14	1	95	549	42.23
1958/59	Pairaudeau B.H.	Northern Districts	11	1	80	456	45.60
1959/60	Reid J.R.	Wellington	16	1	165	724	48.26
1960/61	Harris P.G.Z.	Canterbury	14	2	108	597	49.75
1961/62	Reid J.R.	Wellington	40 †	2	203	2188	57.57
1962/63	Reid J.R.	Wellington	14	1	296	681	52.38
1963/64	Sinclair B.W.	Wellington	15	1	138	641	45.78
1964/65	Pollard V.	Central Districts	43 †	6	85	1081	29.21
1965/66	Sinclair B.W.	Wellington	17	2	114	700	56.66
1966/67	Dowling G.T.	Canterbury	18	2	102*	871	46.66
1967/68	Dowling G.T.	Canterbury	18	1	239	968	56.94
1968/69	Hastings B.F.	Canterbury	15	4	117*	872	79.27
1969/70	Murray B.A.G.	Wellington	51 †	3	157	2079	43.31

		Team	In	NO	HS	Runs	Ave
1970/71	Dowling G.T.	Canterbury	16	1	102	667	44.66
1971/72	Turner G.M.	Otago	27†	5	259	1708	77.63
1972/73	Congdon B.E.	Otago	38†	6	126	1728	54.00
1973/74	Turner G.M.	Otago	17†	2	110*	714	47.60
1974/75	Turner G.M.	Otago	15	1	186*	838	59.85
1975/76	Turner G.M.	Otago	20	4	177*	1244	77.75
1976/77	Burgess M.G.	Auckland	28†	1	138	1064	39.40
1977/78	Howarth G.P.	Northern Districts	22	1	122	685	32.61
1978/79	Howarth G.P.	Northern Districts	11	1	147*	505	50.50
1979/80	Howarth G.P.	Northern Districts	22	2	151	767	38.35
1980/81	Reid J.F.	Auckland	18	4	173	817	58.35
1981/82	Edgar B.A.	Wellington	19	1	161	934	51.88
1982/83	Edgar B.A.	Wellington	30†	5	146	1116	44.64
1983/84	Coney J.V.	Wellington	19†	4	174*	736	49.06
1984/85	Coney J.V.	Wellington	26†	4	111*	877	39.86
1985/86	Crowe M.D.	Central Districts	31†	9	242*	1667	75.77
1986/87	Crowe M.D.	Central Districts	22†	3	175*	1703	89.63
1987/88	Crowe M.D.	Central Districts	16†	2	144	1064	76.00
1988/89	Jones A.H.	Wellington	25†	2	181*	1079	46.91
1989/90	Wright J.G.	Auckland	32†	5	185	1641	60.77
1990/91	Crowe M.D.	Wellington	15†	3	299	847	70.58
1991/92	Wright J.G.	Auckland	14	0	116	518	37.00
1992/93	Rutherford K.R.	Otago	26†	3	105	907	39.43
1993/94	Jones A.H.	Wellington	20†	0	143	934	46.70
1994/95	Parore A.C.	New Zealand	36†	7	127*	1050	36.20
1995/96	Twose R.G.	New Zealand	10†	2	119*	452	56.50
1996/97	Fleming S.P.	Canterbury	16†	1	129	629	41.93
1997/98	Horne M.J.	Otago	22†	1	241	1114	53.04
1998/99	Horne M.J.	Otago	19	2	132	887	52.17
1999/00	Cairns C.L.	New Zealand	26†	3	109	903	39.26
2000/01	Richardson M.H.	Otago	45†	5	306	2672	66.80
2001/02	Astle N.J.	Canterbury	15†	3	223	899	74.91
2002/03	Richardson M.H.	Auckland	25†	2	113	885	38.47
2003/04	Styris S.B.	Northern Districts	17†	1	170	663	41.43
2004/05	Marshall H.J.H.	Northern Districts	16†	0	160	730	45.62
2005/06	Sinclair M.S.	Central Districts	18†	2	121	848	53.00
2006/07	Papps M.H.W.	Canterbury	18†	0	188	1141	63.38

† *including matches for New Zealand teams overseas*

§ *these figures include Blunt's scores for Otago and New Zealand against the Melbourne Cricket Club*

WINSOR CUP

Presented by Sir Arthur Donnelly to perpetuate the memory of Mr W.H. Winsor

Presented to the New Zealand bowler whose performances in first-class cricket have been, in the opinion of the Board of Control, the most meritorious since the award was last made.

HOLDERS

Season's first-class figures

		Team	Matches	O	M	R	W	Ave
1938/39	Cowie J.	Auckland	4	150	20	444	21	21.14
1939/40	Pritchard T.L.	Wellington	3	113.3	9	404	23	17.56
1940-45	no award							
1945/46	Cowie J.	Auckland	5	209	69	433	24	18.04
1946/47	Cowie J.	Auckland	5	257.4	61	578	26	22.23
1947/48	Burtt T.B.	Canterbury	4	256	57	666	26	25.61
1948/49	Cresswell A.E.	Wellington	4	152	27	343	22	15.59
1949/50	Cresswell G.F.	Wellington	4	235	111	304	20	15.20
1950/51	Burtt T.B.	Canterbury	6	363.2	151	673	44	15.29
1951/52	Burtt T.B.	Canterbury	6	317	120	643	37	17.37
1952/53	Rabone G.O.	Auckland	5	174	44	405	23	17.60
1953/54	MacGibbon A.R.	Canterbury†	17	463.7	98	1271	63	20.17
1954/55	Reid J.R.	Wellington	8	279.1	121	496	30	16.53
1955/56	Cave H.B.	Central Districts*	18	673.4	271	1259	50	25.18
1956/57	Cave H.B.	Central Districts	9	358.3	138	685	41	16.70
1957/58	Hayes J.A.	Auckland	6	244.3	49	568	48	11.83
1958/59	Hough K.W.	Auckland	8	411.3	151	701	46	15.23
1959/60	Alabaster J.C.	Otago	9	313	78	824	47	17.53
1960/61	Alabaster J.C.	Otago	10	426.3	125	964	49	19.61
1961/62	Blair R.W.	Wellington	6	252	96	535	44	12,15
1962/63	Blair R.W.	Wellington	7	244.2	77	562	32	17.56
1963/64	Blair R.W.	Wellington	9	408.1	135	856	49	17.46
1964/65	Motz R.C.	Canterbury*	26	890	272	2179	93	23.43
1965/66	Puna N.	Northern Districts	8	338	126	706	38	18.57
1966/67	Pollard V.	Central Districts	11	345.4	141	672	41	16.39
1967/68	Motz R.C.	Canterbury	10	369.2	115	907	47	19.29
1968/69	Motz R.C.	Canterbury	9	265.2	54	880	40	22.00
1969/70	Howarth H.J.	Auckland*	24	991.4	355	2173	100	21.73
1970/71	Collinge R.O.	Wellington	9	230.6	46	677	37	18.29
1971/72	Taylor B.R.	Wellington*	15	560.5	118	1474	69	21.36
1972/73	Collinge R.O.	Wellington*	23	659.2	149	1806	83	21.75
1973/74	Hadlee D.R.	Canterbury*	13	336.3	35	1451	38	38.18
1974/75	Alabaster G.D.	Otago	6	182.2	26	684	34	20.11
1975/76	Collinge R.O.	Northern Districts	9	215.3	39	623	43	14.48
1976/77	Hadlee R.J.	Canterbury	15	418.2	41	1768	49	36.08
1977/78	Hadlee R.J.	Canterbury	10	266.1	56	860	42	20.47
1978/79	Hadlee R.J.	Canterbury	10	299.1	56	909	50	18.18
1979/80	Hadlee R.J.	New Zealand	3	161.3	50	361	19	19.00
1980/81	Hadlee R.J.	New Zealand*	8	349	89	855	37	23.10
1981/82	Hadlee R.J.	Canterbury	10	424.2	135	868	59	14.74
1982/83	Hadlee R.J.	Canterbury*	12	498	147	1132	59	19.18
1983/84	Hadlee R.J.	Canterbury*	10	310.4	111	587	48	12.22
1984/85	Hadlee R.J.	Canterbury*	12	429.5	119	1061	53	20.01
1985/86	Hadlee R.J.	Canterbury*	11	553.1	129	1314	72	18.25
1986/87	Hadlee R.J.	Canterbury*	12	446.1	116	1047	66	15.86
1987/88	Chatfield E.J.	Wellington*	9	355.1	114	672	24	28.00

		Team	Matches	O	M	R	W	Ave
1988/89	Hadlee R.J.	Canterbury*	7	247.5	59	541	34	15.91
1989/90	Hadlee R.J.	New Zealand*	9	349	71	1014	43	23.58
1990/91	Watson W.	New Zealand	8	333.3	92	807	26	31.03
1991/92	Cairns C.L.	Canterbury	8	294	67	872	42	20.76
1992/93	Morrison D.K.	Auckland	8	263.2	66	598	38	15.73
1993/94	Morrison D.K.	Auckland*	9	327.3	59	1021	28	36.46
1994/95	Morrison D.K.	Auckland*	11	368.5	82	1016	40	25.40
1995/96	Cairns C.L.	New Zealand*	8	232.4	62	631	26	24.26
1996/97	Doull S.B.	New Zealand*	8	255.3	67	715	33	21.66
1997/98	Cairns C.L.	Canterbury*	12	399	113	1124	51	22.03
1998/99	Penn A.J.	Central Districts	9	288	76	763	40	19.07
1999/00	Cairns C.L.	New Zealand*	17	508.5	124	1541	67	23.00
2000/01	Tuffey D.R.	Northern Districts*	12	396.5	118	1104	54	20.44
2001/02	Drum C.J.	Auckland	9	317.3	96	827	53	15.60
2002/03	Bond S.E.	Canterbury*	6	183.5	44	600	30	20.00
2003/04	Martin C.S.	Canterbury	12	448	141	1144	53	21.68
2004/05	Vettori D.L.	Northern Districts*	8	395.5	102	1052	40	26.30
2005/06	Martin C.S.	Auckland*	13	386.3	90	1199	50	23.98
2006/07	Martin C.S.	Auckland*	13	452	94	1424	52	27.38

† including 16 matches for New Zealand overseas   ** includes matches for New Zealand teams overseas*

TOURING TEAMS IN NEW ZEALAND

		FIRST-CLASS MATCHES				ALL MATCHES			
		P	W	L	D	P	W	L	D
1863/64	G. Parr's England Team	—	—	—	—	4	3	—	1
1876/77	J. Lillywhite's England Team	—	—	—	—	8	6	—	2
1877/78	Australia	—	—	—	—	7	5	1	1
1880/81	Australia	—	—	—	—	10	6	1	3
1881/82	A. Shaw's England Team	—	—	—	—	7	5	—	2
1883/84	Tasmania	4	—	3	1	7	2	3	2
1886/87	Australia	—	—	—	—	5	2	—	3
1887/88	C.A. Smith's England Team	—	—	—	—	3	—	—	3
1888/89	English Footballers	—	—	—	—	1	—	—	1
1889/90	New South Wales	5	4	—	1	7	6	—	1
1893/94	New South Wales	7	4	1	2	8	4	1	3
1894/95	Fiji	6	2	2	2	8	4	2	2
1895/96	New South Wales	5	3	1	1	5	3	1	1
1896/97	Australia	—	—	—	—	5	3	—	2
1896/97	Queensland	5	3	1	1	8	4	1	3
1899/00	Melbourne Cricket Club	—	—	—	—	7	6	—	1
1902/03	Lord Hawke's England Team	7	7	—	—	18	18	—	—
1904/05	Australia	4	3	—	1	6	4	—	2
1905/06	Melbourne Cricket Club	—	—	—	—	10	8	—	2
1906/07	MCC	11	6	2	3	16	10	2	4
1909/10	Australia	6	5	—	1	9	7	—	2
1913/14	A. Sims' Australian Team	8	6	—	2	16	8	—	8
1920/21	Australia	9	6	—	3	15	12	—	3
1922/23	MCC	8	6	—	2	14	11	—	3
1923/24	New South Wales	6	5	—	1	12	8	—	4
1924/25	Victoria	6	1	1	4	12	4	1	7
1926/27	Melbourne Cricket Club	—	—	—	—	13	5	—	8
1927/28	Australia	6	4	—	2	13	6	—	7
1929/30	MCC	8	2	—	6	17	9	—	8
1930/31	West Indies	—	—	—	—	1	—	—	1
1931/32	South Africa	3	3	—	—	3	3	—	—
1932/33	MCC	3	—	—	3	3	—	—	3
1935/36	MCC	8	2	1	5	18	5	1	12
1936/37	MCC	3	1	—	2	3	1	—	2
1938/39	Sir Julien Cahn's XI	1	—	—	1	10	2	—	8
1945/46	Australia	5	5	—	—	5	5	—	—
1946/47	MCC	4	2	—	2	4	2	—	2
1947/48	Fiji	5	2	3	—	17	6	3	8
1949/50	Australia B	5	3	—	2	14	9	—	5
1950/51	MCC	4	3	—	1	4	3	—	1
1951/52	West Indies	4	2	—	2	5	3	—	2
1952/53	South Africa	4	1	—	3	5	1	—	4
1953/54	Fiji	4	1	3	—	17	8	6	3
1954/55	MCC	4	4	—	—	4	4	—	—
1955/56	West Indies	8	6	1	1	15	11	1	3
1956/57	Australia B	7	5	—	2	12	7	—	5
1958/59	MCC	5	3	—	2	5	3	—	2
1959/60	Australia B	6	2	—	4	9	4	—	5

		FIRST-CLASS MATCHES				ALL MATCHES			
		P	*W*	*L*	*D*	*P*	*W*	*L*	*D*
1960/61	MCC	10	4	1	5	21	11	1	9
1961/62	Fiji	—	—	—	—	22	9	9	4
1961/62	R.A. Roberts' Commonwealth XI	2	2	—	—	3	2	—	1
1962/63	MCC	4	4	—	—	4	4	—	—
1963/64	South Africa	4	1	—	3	7	1	—	6
1964/65	Pakistan	10	2	—	8	12	4	—	8
1965/66	MCC	4	—	—	4	4	—	—	4
1966/67	Australia B	9	1	2	6	10	2	2	6
1967/68	Fiji	—	—	—	—	25	12	7	6
1967/68	India	6	4	1	1	6	4	1	1
1968/69	West Indies	6	1	2	3	7	1	2	4
1969/70	Australia B	8	2	—	6	8	2	—	6
1970/71	MCC	2	1	—	1	5	3	1	1
1972/73	Pakistan	8	5	1	2	11	6	3	2
1973/74	Australia	7	2	1	4	11	6	1	4
1974/75	MCC	3	1	—	2	5	1	—	4
1975/76	India	6	3	1	2	9	3	4	2
1976/77	Australia	6	5	—	1	8	5	2	1
1977/78	Fiji	—	—	—	—	15	5	4	6
1977/78	England	8	3	1	4 †	9	4	1	4 †
1978/79	Pakistan	8	5	—	3	10	6	1	3
1979/80	West Indies	5	—	2	3	8	2	3	3
1979/80	D.H. Robins' XI	2	—	—	2	8	5	1	2
1980/81	India	5	1	1	3	7	1	3	3
1981/82	Australia	5	1	1	3	11	4	4	3
1982/83	England	—	—	—	—	3	—	3	—
1982/83	Sri Lanka	4	—	3	1	9	1	7	1
1983/84	England	7	1	1	5	11	4	2	5
1984/85	Pakistan	5	1	2	2	9	1	5	3
1985/86	Australia	5	1	1	3	11	5	3	3
1986/87	West Indies	5	1	1	3	9	5	1	3
1987/88	England	7	2	1	4	12	5	3	4
1988/89	Pakistan	5	1	—	4	12	2	5	5
1989/90	India	6	1	1	4	10	2	4	4
1989/90	Australia	1	—	1	—	6	5	1	—
1990/91	Sri Lanka	7	1	—	6	10	1	3	6
1990/91	England	—	—	—	—	3	1	2	—
1991/92	England	7	4	—	3	11	8	—	3
1991/92	Zimbabwe	—	—	—	—	3	1	2	—
1991/92	Australia	—	—	—	—	1	1	—	—
1991/92	Sri Lanka	—	—	—	—	1	1	—	—
1992/93	Pakistan	1	1	—	—	4	2	2	—
1992/93	Australia	4	2	1	1	10	5	4	1
1993/94	Pakistan	5	2	1	2	11	6	2	3 †
1993/94	India	3	—	—	3	7	2	2	3
1994/95	West Indies	3	1	—	2	8	6	—	2
1994/95	Australia	—	—	—	—	4	3	1	—
1994/95	South Africa	2	2	—	—	6	3	2	1 †
1994/95	India	—	—	—	—	4	2	2	—
1994/95	Sri Lanka	4	2	—	2	9	4	2	3
1994/95	Australian Academy	1	1	—	—	5	5	—	—

		FIRST-CLASS MATCHES				ALL MATCHES			
		P	W	L	D	P	W	L	D
1995/96	Pakistan	1	1	—	—	5	3	2	—
1995/96	Zimbabwe	4	1	—	3	8	3	2	3
1996/97	England	6	4	1	1	12	6	3	3†
1996/97	Sri Lanka	2	—	2	—	6	2	3	1
1997/98	Bangladesh	4	—	4	—	7	—	6	1
1997/98	Zimbabwe	4	1	3	—	10	3	7	—
1998/99	Pakistan A	5	—	1	4	10	1	4	5
1998/99	India	4	1	2	1	10	3	5	2
1998/99	South Africa	5	1	—	4	13	5	2	6
1999/00	England A	5	3	—	2	10	7	—	3
1999/00	West Indies	4	—	2	2	10	—	8	2
1999/00	Australia	5	4	—	1	11	8	1	2
2000/01	Zimbabwe	2	—	—	2	6	3	1	2
2000/01	Sri Lanka	—	—	—	—	6	4	2	—
2000/01	Pakistan	5	1	2	2	10	3	5	2
2001/02	Bangladesh	3	—	3	—	4	—	3	1
2001/02	England	5	1	1	3	12	4	5	3
2002/03	India	3	—	2	1	11	2	8	1
2003/04	Pakistan	3	1	—	2	9	3	4	2
2003/04	South Africa	4	1	1	2	11	3	6	2
2003/04	Sri Lanka A	4	—	3	1	6	—	5	1
2004/05	Sri Lanka	3	—	1	2	5	—	2	3
2004/05	FICA World XI	—	—	—	—	3	1	2	—
2004/05	Australia	3	2	—	1	9	8	—	1
2005/06	Australia	—	—	—	—	3	2	1	—
2005/06	Sri Lanka	—	—	—	—	4	1	3	—
2005/06	West Indies	3	—	2	1	9	1	7	1
2006/07	Sri Lanka	2	1	1	—	10	4	4	2
2006/07	Australia	—	—	—	—	3	—	3	—

† *includes a tie*

NB: From 1900 the basis for the inclusion is any of the following:

a) First-class matches were played.
b) The touring side was its country's official team.
c) The touring side played an official New Zealand team.
d) Matches in the 1992 World Cup are not included, although preliminary games played by Zimbabwe, Australia and Sri Lanka are.

NEW ZEALAND TOURING TEAMS

		FIRST-CLASS MATCHES				ALL MATCHES			
		P	W	L	D	P	W	L	D
1898/99	Australia	2	—	2	—	4	1	2	1
1913/14	Australia	4	1	2	1	9	5	2	2
1925/26	Australia	4	—	1	3	9	3	1	5
1927	Great Britain	26	7	5	14	38	12	5	21
	Ceylon	—	—	—	—	1	—	—	1
1927/28	Australia	1	—	1	—	1	—	1	—
1931	Great Britain	32	6	3	23	36	7	3	26
1937	Great Britain	32	9	9	14	38	14	9	15
	Ceylon	—	—	—	—	1	—	—	1
1937/38	Australia	3	—	3	—	3	—	3	—
1949	Great Britain	32	13	1	18	35	14	1	20
	West Germany	—	—	—	—	1	1	—	—
1953/54	South Africa	16	3	4	9	17	3	4	10
	Australia	3	2	—	1	3	2	—	1
1955/56	Pakistan	6	1	3	2	6	1	3	2
	India	10	2	3	5	10	2	3	5
1958	Great Britain	31	7	6	18 †	35	7	6	22
1961/62	South Africa	18	5	2	11	24	7	2	15
	Australia	3	—	2	1	3	—	2	1
1964/65	India	4	—	1	3	4	—	1	3
	Pakistan	3	—	2	1	3	—	2	1
1965	Great Britain	19	3	6	10	21	4	6	11
	Holland	—	—	—	—	1	—	—	1
	Bermuda	—	—	—	—	2	—	—	2
	USA	—	—	—	—	1	1	—	—
1967/68	Australia	4	—	2	2	7	2	2	3
1969	Great Britain	18	4	3	11	22	5	4	13
1969/70	India	5	1	1	3	5	1	1	3
1969/70	Pakistan	4	1	—	3	4	1	—	3
1969/70	Australia	3	—	—	3	8	3	—	5
1970/71	Australia	1	—	—	1	2	—	1	1
1971/72*	Australia	—	—	—	—	2	1	—	1
1971/72	West Indies	13	1	—	12	16	4	—	12
1972/73	Australia	1	—	—	1	3	2	—	1
1973	Great Britain	19	3	2	14	23	4	3	16
1973/74	Australia	9	2	5	2	13	5	6	2
1974/75	Australia	—	—	—	—	3	3	—	—
1975	England *(Prudential Cup)*	—	—	—	—	4	2	2	—
1976/77	Pakistan	6	1	3	2	7	2	3	2
	India	3	—	2	1	3	—	2	1
1978	Great Britain	16	5	4	7	20	5	8	7
1979	Great Britain *(Prudential Cup)*	—	—	—	—	4	2	2	—
1980/81	Australia	7	1	2	4	29	14	9	6
1982/83	Australia	2	—	—	2 †	4	1	1	2 †
1982/83	Australia	—	—	—	—	18	12	6	—
1983	England	13	7	3	3	21	11	6	4
1983/84	Sri Lanka	5	2	—	3	8	4	1	3
1984/85	Sri Lanka	—	—	—	—	2	1	1	—
	Pakistan	5	—	2	3	9	1	5	3
1984/85	Australia *(WCC)*	—	—	—	—	4	1	2	1
1984/85	West Indies	7	—	2	5	12	—	7	5
1985/86	Australia	6	2	1	3	8	2	1	5

		FIRST-CLASS MATCHES				ALL MATCHES			
		P	W	L	D	P	W	L	D
1985/86	Australia	—	—	—	—	11	3	6	2
1985/86	Sri Lanka	—	—	—	—	2	1	1	—
	Sharjah	—	—	—	—	2	—	2	—
	Hong Kong	—	—	—	—	2	2	—	—
1986	England	15	4	—	11	18	5	1	12
	Holland	—	—	—	—	2	1	1	—
1986/87	Sri Lanka	2	—	—	2	2	—	—	2
1987/88	India *(Reliance World Cup)*	—	—	—	—	6	2	4	—
1987/88	Australia	6	1	2	3	19	8	8	3
1987/88	Sharjah	—	—	—	—	4	2	2	—
1988/89	India	6	1	2	3	10	1	6	3
1988/89	Australia	—	—	—	—	1	—	1	—
1989/90	Australia	3	—	—	3	4	—	1	3
1990	Sharjah	—	—	—	—	3	1	2	—
	England	12	4	2	6	19	8	5	6
1990/91	Pakistan	5	—	3	2	8	—	6	2
1990/91	Australia	—	—	—	—	10	3	7	—
1991/92	Australia	—	—	—	—	6	4	2	—
1992/93	Zimbabwe	3	2	—	1	6	5	—	1
	Sri Lanka	2	—	1	1	7	—	5	2
1993/94	Australia	7	2	3	2	16	5	9	2
1994	Sharjah	—	—	—	—	3	1	2	—
	Great Britain	12	1	3	8	21	8	5	8
1994/95	India	—	—	—	—	4	—	3	1
	South Africa	7	2	3	2	16	3	9	4
1995/96	India	6	—	1	5	11	2	4	5
1995/96	India & Pakistan *(Wills World Cup)*	—	—	—	—	6	3	3	—
1995/96	West Indies	4	1	2	1	13	7	5	1
1996/97	Sharjah	—	—	—	—	5	1	3	1 †
1996/97	Pakistan	3	1	1	1	6	2	3	1
1996/97	India *(Independence Cup)*	—	—	—	—	3	1	2	—
1997/98	Kenya	—	—	—	—	3	2	—	1
	Zimbabwe	3	—	—	3	7	2	1	4 †
1997/98	Australia	6	—	5	1	21	5	13	3 †
1997/98	Sharjah	—	—	—	—	4	1	3	—
1997/98	Sri Lanka	5	1	2	2	11	3	4	4
1998	Malaysia *(Commonwealth Games)*	—	—	—	—	5	4	1	—
1998/99	Bangladesh *(Wills International Cup)*	—	—	—	—	2	1	1	—
1999	England	10	5	2	3	26	14	8	4
1999/00	India	6	—	2	4	11	2	5	4
2000/01	Singapore	—	—	—	—	2	—	2	—
2000/01	Zimbabwe	4	2	—	2	8	4	2	2
2000/01	Kenya	—	—	—	—	3	3	—	—
2000/01	South Africa	6	2	2	2	14	4	7	3
2000/01	Sharjah	—	—	—	—	4	1	3	—
2001/02	Sri Lanka	—	—	—	—	7	3	4	—
2001/02	Australia	5	—	1	4	21	6	8	7
2001/02	Sharjah	—	—	—	—	4	1	3	—
2001/02	Pakistan	1	—	1	—	4	—	4	—
2001/02	West Indies	2	1	—	1	8	3	3	2
2002/03	Australia	—	—	—	—	4	4	—	—
2002/03	Sri Lanka *(ICC Champions Trophy)*	—	—	—	—	4	2	2	—
2002/03	South Africa *(World Cup)*	—	—	—	—	11	7	4	—
2002/03	Sri Lanka	2	—	—	2	9	3	2	4

		FIRST-CLASS MATCHES				ALL MATCHES			
		P	W	L	D	P	W	L	D
2003/04	India	4	—	—	4	10	1	4	5
2003/04	Pakistan	—	—	—	—	5	—	5	—
2003/04	England	7	1	4	2	16	7	5	4
2004	England *(ICC Champions Trophy)*	—	—	—	—	2	1	1	—
2004/05	Bangladesh	2	2	—	—	6	5	—	1
2004/05	Australia	3	—	3	—	6	2	4	—
2005/06 {	Namibia	—	—	—	—	2	2	—	—
2005/06 {	Zimbabwe	2	2	—	—	8	7	1	—
2005/06	South Africa	—	—	—	—	8	3	4	1
2005/06	South Africa	4	—	2	2	4	—	2	2
2006/07	India *(ICC Champions Trophy)*	—	—	—	—	6	4	2	—
2006/07	Australia	—	—	—	—	8	2	6	—
2006/07	West Indies *(World Cup)*	—	—	—	—	12	8	4	—

NB: 1) All tours refer to those undertaken by official New Zealand sides. Unofficial practice matches have not been included in the totals.

2) The first team from New Zealand to tour overseas was Canterbury who visited Victoria and Tasmania in 1878/79. This was the first tour ever undertaken by a domestic association from any country. (None of the games are ranked as first-class.)

3) Where countries are bracketed it indicates this represented a single tour. Where there is more than one entry for the same season but countries are not bracketed, the tours were not connected.

4) The 1974/75, second 1982/83, 1990/91, 1993/94 and 1997/98 tours to Australia included a return trip after the teams had come back to New Zealand. They are all listed as single tours for the purposes of this article.

5) The 1986/87 tour to Sri Lanka was scheduled for 8 matches. The team returned home after 2 matches due to unrest in Sri Lanka.

Eighty-seven official New Zealand sides have toured overseas since the first in February, 1899. The teams were as follows:

1) **1898/99 to Australia**
L.T. Cobcroft *(captain)*, F.L. Ashbolt, J.C. Baker, C. Boxshall, A.D. Downes, A.H. Fisher, F.S. Frankish, Hugh B. Lusk, G. Mills, I. Mills, D. Reese, A. Sims, E.F. Upham.

2) **1913/14 to Australia**
D. Reese *(captain)*, J.H. Bennett, C. Boxshall, T.A. Carlton, L.G. Hemus, R.G. Hickmott, W.R. Patrick, C.W. Robinson, D.M. Sandman, R.C. Somervell, A.N.C. Snedden, L.G. Taylor, B.J. Tuckwell, H.J. Tattersall.

3) **1925/26 to Australia**
W.R. Patrick *(captain)*, C.F.W. Allcott, A.W. Alloo, R.C. Blunt, C.G. Crawford, W.H.R. Cunningham, C.C.R. Dacre, H.D. Gillespie, R.W. Hope, K.C. James, T.C. Lowry, D.J. McBeath, C.J. Oliver, R.V. de R. Worker.

4) **1927 to Great Britain, Ceylon and Australia**
T.C. Lowry *(captain)*, C.F.W. Allcott, E.H.L. Bernau, E.D. Blundell*, R.C. Blunt, W.H.R. Cunningham, C.C.R. Dacre, C.S. Dempster, R.H. Fox*, T.D.B. Hay*, M. Henderson, K.C. James, H.M. McGirr, W.E. Merritt, J.E. Mills, C.J. Oliver, M.L. Page.

5) **1931 to Great Britain**
T.C. Lowry *(captain)*, C.F.W. Allcott, R.C. Blunt, I.B. Cromb, C.S. Dempster, K.C. James, J.L. Kerr, A.M. Matheson, W.E. Merritt, J.E. Mills, M.L. Page, R.O. Talbot, H.G. Vivian, G.L. Weir.

6) **1937 to Great Britain, Ceylon and Australia**
M.L. Page *(captain)*, W.N. Carson, J. Cowie, M.P. Donnelly, J.A. Dunning, N. Gallichan, W.A. Hadlee, J.L. Kerr, J.R. Lamason, T.C. Lowry, D.A.R. Moloney, C.K. Parsloe*, A.W. Roberts, E.W.T. Tindill, H.G. Vivian, W.M. Wallace, G.L. Weir.

7) **1949 to Great Britain and West Germany**
W.A. Hadlee *(captain)*, C. Burke, T.B. Burtt, H.B. Cave, J. Cowie, G.F. Cresswell, M.P. Donnelly, J.A. Hayes, F.L.H. Mooney, G.O. Rabone, J.R. Reid, V.J. Scott, F.B. Smith, B. Sutcliffe, W.M. Wallace.

8) **1953/54 to South Africa and Australia**
G.O. Rabone *(captain)*, J.E.F. Beck, W. Bell, R.W. Blair, M.E. Chapple, E.W. Dempster, J.G. Leggat*, I.B. Leggat, A.R. MacGibbon, L.S.M. Miller, F.L.H. Mooney, G.W.F. Overton, M.B. Poore, J.R. Reid, B. Sutcliffe.

9) **1955/1956 to Pakistan and India**
H.B. Cave *(captain)*, J.C. Alabaster, J.W. Guy, J.A. Hayes, N.S. Harford, P.G.Z. Harris, J.G. Leggat, A.R. MacGibbon, S.N. McGregor, T.G. McMahon, A.M. Moir, E.C. Petrie, M.B. Poore, J.R. Reid, B. Sutcliffe.

10) **1958 to Great Britain**
J.R. Reid *(captain)*, J.C. Alabaster, R.W. Blair, H.B. Cave, J.W. D'Arcy, N.S. Harford, J.A. Hayes, T. Meale, A.R. MacGibbon, L.S.M. Miller, A.M. Moir, E.C. Petrie, W.R. Playle, J.T. Sparling, B. Sutcliffe, J.T. Ward.

11) **1961/62 to South Africa and Australia**
J.R. Reid *(captain)*, J.C. Alabaster, G.A. Bartlett, P.T. Barton, F.J. Cameron, M.E. Chapple, A.E. Dick, G.T. Dowling, J.W. Guy, P.G.Z. Harris, S.N. McGregor, R.C. Motz, J.T. Sparling, J.T. Ward, B.W. Yuile.

12) **1964/65 to India, Pakistan, Great Britain, Holland, Bermuda and USA**
J.R. Reid *(captain)*, F.J. Cameron, R.O. Collinge, B.E. Congdon, A.E. Dick*, G.T. Dowling, T.W. Jarvis, R.C. Motz, R.W. Morgan, V. Pollard, B.W. Sinclair, B. Sutcliffe, B.R. Taylor, G.E. Vivian, J.T. Ward, B.W. Yuile.

13) **1967/68 to Australia**
B.W. Sinclair *(captain)*, J.C. Alabaster, M.G. Burgess, R.O. Collinge, B.E. Congdon, R.I. Harford, T.W. Jarvis, R.C. Motz, B.A.G. Murray, V. Pollard, B.R. Taylor, K. Thomson, B.W. Yuile.

14) **1969 to Great Britain, India and Pakistan**
G.T. Dowling *(captain)*, M.G. Burgess, R.O. Collinge, B.E. Congdon, R.S. Cunis, D.R. Hadlee, B.F. Hastings, H.J. Howarth, B.A.G. Murray, B.D. Milburn, V. Pollard, B.R. Taylor, D.G. Trist*, G.M. Turner, K.J. Wadsworth, B.W. Yuile.

15) **1969/70 to Australia**
G.T. Dowling *(captain)*, M.G. Burgess, R.O. Collinge, B.E. Congdon, R.S. Cunis, D.R. Hadlee, B.F. Hastings, H.J. Howarth, R.W. Morgan*, B.W. Sinclair, G.M. Turner, G.E. Vivian, K.J. Wadsworth.

16) **1970/1971 to Australia**
G.T. Dowling *(captain)*, M.G. Burgess, B.E. Congdon, R.O. Collinge, R.S. Cunis, H.J. Howarth, T.W. Jarvis, R.W. Morgan, B.R. Taylor, G.M. Turner, G.E. Vivian, K.J. Wadsworth.

17) **1971/72 to Australia**
R.W. Morgan *(captain)*, B. Andrews, R.W. Anderson, B. Dunning, B.G. Hadlee, R.J. Hadlee, W.A. Greenstreet, G.A. Newdick, R.E. Redmond, M.L. Ryan, M.J.F. Shrimpton, D.G. Trist.

18) **1971/72 to West Indies**
G.T. Dowling *(captain)*, J.C. Alabaster, M.G. Burgess, K.O. Campbell, M.E. Chapple*, R.O. Collinge, B.E. Congdon, R.S. Cunis, B.F. Hastings, H.J. Howarth, T.W. Jarvis, R.W. Morgan*, B.R. Taylor, G.M. Turner, G.E. Vivian, K.J. Wadsworth, M.G. Webb.

19) **1972/73 to Australia**
B.E. Congdon *(captain)*, B. Andrews, R.S. Cunis, B. Dunning, R.J. Hadlee, B.F. Hastings, A.B. Jordan, D.R. O'Sullivan, R.E. Redmond, G.M. Turner, G.E. Vivian, K.J. Wadsworth.

20) **1973 to Great Britain**
B.E. Congdon *(captain)*, R.W. Anderson, M.G. Burgess, R.O. Collinge, E.K. Gillott, D.R. Hadlee, R.J. Hadlee, B.F. Hastings, H.J. Howarth, J.M. Parker, V. Pollard, R.E. Redmond, B.R. Taylor, G.M. Turner, K.J. Wadsworth.

21) **1973/74 to Australia**
B.E. Congdon *(captain)*, G.D. Alabaster, B. Andrews, K.O. Campbell, B.L. Cairns, J.V. Coney*, D.R. Hadlee, R.J. Hadlee, B.F. Hastings, J.F.M. Morrison, D.R. O'Sullivan, J.M. Parker, M.J.F. Shrimpton, G.M. Turner, K.J. Wadsworth.

22) **1974/75 to Australia**
B.E. Congdon *(captain)*, B.L. Cairns, E.J. Chatfield, R.O. Collinge, G.N. Edwards, D.R. Hadlee, B.F. Hastings, G.P. Howarth, H.J. Howarth, J.F.M. Morrison, J.M. Parker, G.M. Turner, K.J. Wadsworth.

23) **1975 to England** *(World Cup)*
G.M. Turner *(captain)*, B.L. Cairns, R.O. Collinge, B.G. Hadlee, D.R. Hadlee, R.J. Hadlee, B.F. Hastings, G.P. Howarth, H.J. Howarth, B.J. McKechnie, J.F.M. Morrison, D.R. O'Sullivan, J.M. Parker, K.J. Wadsworth.

24) **1976/77 to Pakistan and India**
G.M. Turner *(captain)*, R.W. Anderson, M.G. Burgess, B.L. Cairns, R.O. Collinge, R.J. Hadlee, G.P. Howarth, W.K. Lees, J.F.M. Morrison, D.R. O'Sullivan, J.M. Parker, N.M. Parker, P.J. Petherick, A.D.G. Roberts, G.B. Troup.

25) **1978 to Great Britain**
M.G. Burgess *(captain)*, R.W. Anderson, S.L. Boock, B.P. Bracewell, B.L. Cairns, R.O. Collinge*, B.E. Congdon, B.A. Edgar, G.N. Edwards, D.R. Hadlee, R.J. Hadlee, G.P. Howarth, J.M. McIntyre, J.M. Parker, G.B. Thomson, G.B. Troup*, J.G. Wright.

26) **1979 to England** *(World Cup)*
M.G. Burgess *(captain)*, B.L. Cairns, E.J. Chatfield, J.V. Coney, B.A. Edgar, R.J. Hadlee, G.P. Howarth, W.K. Lees, B.J. McKechnie, J.F.M. Morrison, L.W. Stott, G.B. Troup, G.M. Turner, J.G. Wright.

27) **1980/81 to Australia**
G.P. Howarth *(captain)*, B.P. Bracewell*, J.G. Bracewell, S.L. Boock, M.G. Burgess, B.L. Cairns, E.J. Chatfield, J.V. Coney, B.A. Edgar, R.J. Hadlee, W.K. Lees, P.E. McEwan, B.J. McKechnie*, J.M. Parker, I.D.S. Smith, M.C. Snedden, G.B. Troup, J.G. Wright.

28) **1982/83 to Australia**
G.P. Howarth *(captain)*, B.R. Blair, S.M. Carrington, E.J. Chatfield, J.V. Coney, M.D. Crowe, B.A. Edgar, W.K. Lees, J.F.M. Morrison, J.F. Reid, G.K. Robertson, M.C. Snedden, G.B. Troup.

29) **1982/83 to Australia**
G.P. Howarth *(captain)*, B.L. Cairns, E.J. Chatfield, J.V. Coney, J.J. Crowe, M.D. Crowe*, B.A. Edgar, T.J. Franklin*, R.J. Hadlee, W.K. Lees, J.F.M. Morrison, M.C. Snedden, G.B. Troup, G.M. Turner, P.N. Webb, R.J. Webb*, J.G. Wright.

30) **1983 to England**
G.P. Howarth *(captain)*, J.G. Bracewell, B.L. Cairns, E.J. Chatfield, J.V. Coney, J.J. Crowe, M.D. Crowe, B.A. Edgar, T.J. Franklin, E.J. Gray, R.J. Hadlee, W.K. Lees, I.D.S. Smith, M.C. Snedden, S.R. Tracy*, G.M. Turner, J.G. Wright.

31) **1983/84 to Sri Lanka**
G.P. Howarth *(captain)*, S.L. Boock, J.G. Bracewell, B.L. Cairns, E.J. Chatfield, J.V. Coney, J.J. Crowe, M.D. Crowe, B.A. Edgar, R.J. Hadlee, J.F. Reid, I.D.S. Smith, D.A. Stirling, J.G. Wright.

32) **1984/85 to Pakistan and Sri Lanka**
J.V. Coney *(captain)*, S.L. Boock, J.G. Bracewell, B.L. Cairns, E.J. Chatfield, J.J. Crowe, M.D. Crowe, B.A. Edgar, E.J. Gray, P.E. McEwan, J.F. Reid, I.D.S. Smith, M.C. Snedden, D.A. Stirling, J.G. Wright.

33) **1984/85 to Australia** *(World Championship of Cricket)*
G.P. Howarth *(captain)*, B.P. Bracewell, J.G. Bracewell, B.L. Cairns, E.J. Chatfield, J.V. Coney, J.J. Crowe, M.D. Crowe, R.J. Hadlee, P.E. McEwan, J.F. Reid, I.D.S. Smith, M.C. Snedden, J.G. Wright.

34) **1984/85 to West Indies**
G.P. Howarth *(captain)*, S.L. Boock, J.G. Bracewell, B.L. Cairns, E.J. Chatfield, J.V. Coney, J.J. Crowe, M.D. Crowe, R.J. Hadlee, R.T. Hart, K.R. Rutherford, I.D.S. Smith, D.A. Stirling, G.B. Troup, J.G. Wright.

35) **1985/86 to Australia**
J.V. Coney *(captain)*, S.L. Boock, J.G. Bracewell*, V.R. Brown, B.L. Cairns, E.J. Chatfield, J.J. Crowe, M.D. Crowe, B.A. Edgar, T.J. Franklin, R.J. Hadlee, E.B. McSweeney*, J.F. Reid, I.D.S. Smith, M.C. Snedden, J.G. Wright.

36) **1985/86 to Australia**
J.V. Coney *(captain)*, B.R. Blair, S.L. Boock, J.G. Bracewell, E.J. Chatfield, J.J. Crowe, M.D. Crowe, B.A. Edgar, S.R. Gillespie, R.J. Hadlee, E.B. McSweeney, J.F. Reid, M.C. Snedden, J.G. Wright.

37) **1985/86 to Sri Lanka, Sharjah and Hong Kong**
J.G. Wright *(captain)*, T.E. Blain, B.R. Blair, J.G. Bracewell, E.J. Chatfield, J.J. Crowe, M.D. Crowe, E.J. Gray, E.B. McSweeney, G.K. Robertson, K.R. Rutherford, M.C. Snedden, W. Watson.

38) **1986 to England and Holland**
J.V. Coney *(captain)*, B.J. Barrett, T.E. Blain, J.G. Bracewell, E.J. Chatfield, J.J. Crowe, M.D. Crowe, B.A. Edgar, T.J. Franklin, E.J. Gray, R.J. Hadlee, K.R. Rutherford, I.D.S. Smith, D.A. Stirling, W. Watson, J.G. Wright.

39) **1986/87 to Sri Lanka**
J.J. Crowe *(captain)*, J.G. Bracewell, E.J. Chatfield, M.D. Crowe, E.J. Gray, R.J. Hadlee, P.A. Horne, A.H. Jones, E.B. McSweeney, D.K. Morrison, D.N. Patel, K.R. Rutherford, I.D.S. Smith, M.C. Snedden.

40) **1987/88 to India** *(World Cup)*
J.J. Crowe *(captain)*, S.L. Boock, J.G. Bracewell, E.J. Chatfield, M.D. Crowe, P.A. Horne, A.H. Jones, D.K. Morrison, D.N. Patel, K.R. Rutherford, I.D.S. Smith, M.C. Snedden, W. Watson, J.G. Wright.

41) **1987/88 to Australia**
J.J. Crowe *(captain)*, T.E. Blain*, J.G. Bracewell, V.R. Brown*, E.J. Chatfield, M.D. Crowe, S.R. Gillespie*, E.J. Gray, R.J. Hadlee, P.A. Horne, A.H. Jones, D.K. Morrison, D.N. Patel, K.R. Rutherford, I.D.S. Smith, M.C. Snedden, W. Watson, J.G. Wright.

42) **1987/88 to Sharjah**
J.G. Wright *(captain)*, T.E. Blain, E.J. Chatfield, M.J. Greatbatch, R.J. Hadlee, A.H. Jones, C.M. Kuggeleijn, D.K. Morrison, D.N. Patel, K.R. Rutherford, I.D.S. Smith, R.H. Vance, W. Watson.

43) **1988/89 to India**
J.G. Wright *(captain)*, T.E. Blain, J.G. Bracewell, E.J. Chatfield, T.J. Franklin, E.J. Gray, M.J. Greatbatch, R.J. Hadlee, A.H. Jones, C.M. Kuggeleijn, D.K. Morrison, K.R. Rutherford, I.D.S. Smith, M.C. Snedden, R.H. Vance, W. Watson*.

44) **1988/89 to Australia**
J.G. Wright *(captain)*, E.J. Chatfield, J.J. Crowe, M.D. Crowe, M.J. Greatbatch, A.H. Jones, C.M. Kuggeleijn, D.K. Morrison, I.D.S. Smith, M.C. Snedden, R.H. Vance, W. Watson.

45) **1989/90 to Australia**
J.G. Wright *(captain)*, B.P. Bracewell, J.G. Bracewell, C.L. Cairns*, J.J. Crowe, M.D. Crowe, M.J. Greatbatch, A.H. Jones, D.K. Morrison, D.N. Patel*, G.K. Robertson, I.D.S. Smith, M.C. Snedden, R.H. Vance, W. Watson.

46) **1990 to Sharjah and England**
J.G. Wright *(captain)*, J.G. Bracewell, J.J. Crowe, M.D. Crowe, T.J. Franklin, M.J. Greatbatch, Sir R.J. Hadlee, A.H. Jones, J.P. Millmow, D.K. Morrison, A.C. Parore, M.W. Priest, C. Pringle*, K.R. Rutherford, I.D.S. Smith, M.C. Snedden, S.A. Thomson, W. Watson*.

47) **1990/91 to Pakistan**
M.D. Crowe *(captain)*, G.E. Bradburn, T.J. Franklin, M.J. Greatbatch, P.A. Horne, D.K. Morrison, A.C. Parore, D.N. Patel, M.W. Priest, C. Pringle, S.J. Roberts, K.R. Rutherford, I.D.S. Smith, W. Watson, D.J. White.

48) **1990/91 to Australia**
M.D. Crowe *(captain)*, G.E. Bradburn, M.J. Greatbatch, C.Z. Harris, A.H. Jones, G.R. Larsen*, R.T. Latham, D.K. Morrison, R.G. Petrie, C. Pringle, R.B. Reid*, K.R. Rutherford, I.D.S. Smith, W. Watson, J.G. Wright, B.A. Young.

49) **1991/92 to Australia**
M.D. Crowe *(captain)*, G.E. Bradburn, C.L. Cairns, M.J. Greatbatch, C.Z. Harris, T.J. Franklin, A.H. Jones, D.K. Morrison, D.N. Patel, A.C. Parore, C. Pringle, I.D.S. Smith, S.A. Thomson, W. Watson, K.A. Wealleans.

50) **1992/93 to Zimbabwe and Sri Lanka**
M.D. Crowe *(captain)*, G.E. Bradburn*, S.B. Doull, M.J. Greatbatch, M.J. Haslam, C.Z. Harris, B.R. Hartland, A.H. Jones, G.R. Larsen, R.T. Latham, D.J. Nash, M.B. Owens*, D.N. Patel, A.C. Parore, C. Pringle*, K.R. Rutherford, M.L. Su'a, J.T.C. Vaughan*, W. Watson, J.G. Wright*.

51) **1993/94 to Australia**
M.D. Crowe *(captain)*, T.E. Blain, C.L. Cairns, S.B. Doull, R.P. de Groen*, M.J. Greatbatch, C.Z. Harris*, M.J. Haslam, A.H. Jones, R.T. Latham*, G.R. Larsen*, D.K. Morrison, D.N. Patel, B.A. Pocock, C. Pringle*, K.R. Rutherford, M.L. Su'a, S.A. Thomson*, W. Watson, D.J. White*, B.A. Young.

52) **1994 to Sharjah and England**
K.R. Rutherford *(captain)*, M.D. Crowe, H.T. Davis, M.W. Douglas, S.B. Doull, S.P. Fleming, M.J. Greatbatch, M.N. Hart, B.R. Hartland, C.Z. Harris, G.R. Larsen, D.K. Morrison, D.J. Nash, M.B. Owens*, A.C. Parore, B.A. Pocock, C. Pringle, S.A. Thomson, S.J. Roberts*, B.A. Young. (Harris and Douglas were selected only for Sharjah but Douglas re-appeared as an additional player during the England tour. Larsen captained the team in Sharjah as Rutherford was not available for that part of the tour).

53) **1994/95 to India and South Africa**
K.R. Rutherford *(captain)*, M.D. Crowe, R.P. de Groen, S.B. Doull, S.P. Fleming, L.K. Germon, C.Z. Harris, M.N. Hart, B.R. Hartland, D.K. Morrison*, D.J. Murray, D.J. Nash, A.C. Parore, M.W. Priest*, C. Pringle, M.L. Su'a, S.A. Thomson, B.A. Young.

54) **1995/96 to India**
L.K. Germon *(captain)*, N.J. Astle*, C.L. Cairns, M.D. Crowe, S.B. Doull, S.P. Fleming, A.J. Gale, M.J. Greatbatch, M.N. Hart, M.J. Haslam, G.R. Larsen*, D.K. Morrison, D.J. Nash, A.C. Parore, S.A. Thomson, R.G. Twose, B.A. Young.

55) **1995/96 to India and Pakistan** *(World Cup)*
L.K. Germon *(captain)*, N.J. Astle, C.L. Cairns, S.P. Fleming, C.Z. Harris, R.J. Kennedy, G.R. Larsen, D.K. Morrison, D.J. Nash, A.C. Parore, D.N. Patel, C.M. Spearman, S.A. Thomson, R.G. Twose.

56) **1995/96 to West Indies**
L.K. Germon *(captain)*, N.J. Astle, M.D. Bailey*, C.L. Cairns, S.P. Fleming, C.Z. Harris, M.J. Haslam*, R.J. Kennedy, G.R. Larsen, D.K. Morrison, D.J. Nash, A.C. Parore, D.N. Patel, C.M. Spearman, S.A. Thomson, R.G. Twose, J.T.C. Vaughan*.

57) **1996/97 to Sharjah and Pakistan**
L.K. Germon *(captain)*, N.J. Astle, C.L. Cairns, S.B. Doull, S.P. Fleming, M.J. Greatbatch, C.Z. Harris, M.N. Hart*, M.J. Haslam, G.R. Jonas*, R.J. Kennedy*, G.R. Larsen, D.K. Morrison, A.C. Parore, D.N. Patel, C.M. Spearman, J.T.C. Vaughan, P.J. Wiseman*, B.A. Young.

58) **1996/97 to India** *(Independence Cup)*
S.P. Fleming *(captain)*, N.J. Astle, C.L. Cairns, H.T. Davis, C.Z. Harris, M.J. Horne, G.R. Larsen, C.D. McMillan, S.B. O'Connor, A.C. Parore, D.N. Patel, A.J. Penn, D.L. Vettori, B.A. Young.

59) **1997/98 to Kenya & Zimbabwe**
S.P. Fleming *(captain)*, N.J. Astle, C.L. Cairns, H.T. Davis, C.Z. Harris, M.J. Horne, G.R. Larsen, C.D. McMillan, S.B. O'Connor, A.C. Parore, B.A. Pocock, D.G. Sewell, C.M. Spearman, D.L. Vettori, P.J. Wiseman.

60) **1997/98 to Australia**
S.P. Fleming *(captain)*, G.I. Allott, N.J. Astle, C.L. Cairns, H.T. Davis, S.B. Doull, C.J. Drum*, C.Z. Harris*, M.J. Horne, G.R. Larsen*, C.D. McMillan, D.J. Nash*, S.B. O'Connor, A.C. Parore, B.A. Pocock, C.M. Spearman*, R.G. Twose*, D.L. Vettori, B.A. Young.

61) **1997/98 to Sharjah**
S.P. Fleming *(captain)*, N.J. Astle, C.L. Cairns, S.B. Doull, C.Z. Harris, M.J. Horne, L.G. Howell, C.D. McMillan, D.J. Nash, S.B. O'Connor, A.C. Parore, M.W. Priest, P.J. Wiseman.

62) **1997/98 to Sri Lanka**
S.P. Fleming *(captain)*, N.J. Astle, C.L. Cairns, S.B. Doull, C.Z. Harris, M.J. Horne, C.D. McMillan, D.J. Nash, S.B. O'Connor, A.C. Parore, M.W. Priest, C.M. Spearman, A.R. Tait*, D.L. Vettori, P.J. Wiseman, B.A. Young.

63) **1998 to Malaysia** *(Commonwealth Games)*
S.P. Fleming *(captain)*, G.I. Allott, N.J. Astle, M.D. Bailey, M.D. Bell, C.J. Drum, C.Z. Harris, M.J. Horne, C.D. McMillan, S.B. O'Connor, A.C. Parore, A.R. Tait, D.L. Vettori, P.J. Wiseman.

64) **1998/99 to Bangladesh** *(Wills International Cup)*
S.P. Fleming *(captain)*, G.I. Allott, N.J. Astle, M.D. Bailey, M.D. Bell, S.B. Doull, C.Z. Harris, M.J. Horne, C.D. McMillan, S.B. O'Connor, A.C. Parore, A.R. Tait, D.L. Vettori, P.J. Wiseman.

65) **1999 to England**
S.P. Fleming *(captain)*, G.I. Allott, N.J. Astle, M.D. Bell*, C.E. Bulfin, C.L. Cairns, M.G. Croy*, S.B. Doull, C.Z. Harris, M.N. Hart, M.J. Horne, G.R. Larsen, C.D. McMillan, D.J. Nash, S.B. O'Connor*, A.C. Parore, A.J. Penn*, R.G. Twose, D.L. Vettori, B.G.K. Walker*.

66) **1999/00 to India**
S.P. Fleming *(captain)*, N.J. Astle, M.D. Bell, C.L. Cairns, C.J. Drum, C.Z. Harris, M.J. Horne, C.D. McMillan, D.J. Nash, S.B. O'Connor, A.C. Parore, A.J. Penn, C.M. Spearman, G.R. Stead*, S.B. Styris*, A.R. Tait*, R.G. Twose*, D.L. Vettori, P.J. Wiseman.

67) **2000/01 to Singapore, Zimbabwe, Kenya & South Africa**
S.P. Fleming *(captain)*, G.I. Allott, N.J. Astle, C.L. Cairns, C.Z. Harris, M.J. Horne, C.D. McMillan, H.J.H. Marshall, C.S. Martin, D.J. Nash, C.J. Nevin, S.B. O'Connor, A.C. Parore, A.J. Penn, M.H. Richardson, M.S. Sinclair, C.M. Spearman, S.B. Styris, G.P. Sulzberger, D.R. Tuffey, R.G. Twose, D.L. Vettori, B.G.K. Walker, K.P. Walmsley, P.J. Wiseman. (Apart from a number of players being replaced because of injury, this party was reselected and changed several times depending on the nature of the matches being played).

68) 2000/01 to Sharjah
C.D. McMillan *(captain),* A.R. Adams, M.D. Bell, G.E. Bradburn, J.E.C. Franklin, C.Z. Harris, K.D. Mills, C.J. Nevin, J.D.P. Oram, M.S. Sinclair, D.R.Tuffey, L. Vincent, B.G.K. Walker.

69) 2001/02 to Sri Lanka
S.P. Fleming *(captain),* N.J. Astle, G.E. Bradburn, J.E.C. Franklin, C.Z. Harris, K.D. Mills, C.D. McMillan, D.J. Nash, J.D.P. Oram, A.C. Parore, M.S. Sinclair, D.R.Tuffey, D.L. Vettori, L. Vincent.

70) 2001/02 to Australia
S.P. Fleming *(captain),* A.R. Adams, N.J. Astle, M.D. Bell, S.E. Bond*, C.L. Cairns, C.J. Drum*, J.E.C. Franklin, C.Z. Harris, B.B. McCullum, C.D. McMillan, C.S. Martin, D.J. Nash, S.B. O'Çonnor, A.C. Parore, M.H. Richardson, M.S. Sinclair, S.B. Styris, G.P. Sulzberger, D.R. Tuffey, D.L. Vettori, L. Vincent, P.J. Wiseman*.

71) 2001/02 to Sharjah & Pakistan
S.P. Fleming *(captain),* A.R. Adams, N.J. Astle, I.G. Butler, J.E.C. Franklin, C.Z. Harris, R.G. Hart, M.J. Horne, C.D. McMillan, C.S. Martin, C.J. Nevin, J.D.P. Oram, M.H. Richardson, M.S. Sinclair, S.B. Styris, D.R. Tuffey, D.L. Vettori, L. Vincent, B.G.K. Walker.

72) 2001/02 to West Indies
S.P. Fleming *(captain),* N.J. Astle, S.E. Bond, I.G. Butler, C.Z. Harris, M.N. Hart, R.G. Hart, P.A. Hitchcock, M.J. Horne, C.D. McMillan, C.S. Martin, C.J. Nevin, J.D.P. Oram, M.H. Richardson, S.B. Styris, D.R. Tuffey, D.L. Vettori, L. Vincent.

73) 2002/03 to Australia & Sri Lanka *(ICC Champions Trophy)*
S.P. Fleming *(captain),* N.J. Astle, S.E. Bond, I.G. Butler*, C.Z. Harris, M.N. Hart*, P.A. Hitchcock, M.J. Horne*, C.D. McMillan*, K.D. Mills, C.J. Nevin, J.D.P. Oram, M.S. Sinclair, S.B. Styris, G.P. Sulzberger, D.R. Tuffey, D.L. Vettori, L. Vincent, B.G.K. Walker*, J.A.F. Yovich*.

74) 2002/03 to South Africa *(World Cup)*
S.P. Fleming *(captain),* C.L. Cairns, A.R. Adams, N.J. Astle, S.E. Bond, C.Z. Harris, B.B. McCullum, C.D. McMillan, K.D. Mills, J.D.P. Oram, M.S. Sinclair, S.B. Styris, D.R. Tuffey, D.L. Vettori, L. Vincent.

75) 2002/03 to Sri Lanka
S.P. Fleming *(captain),* A.R. Adams, S.E. Bond, I.G. Butler, C.L. Cairns, C.Z. Harris, R.G. Hart, M.J. Horne, R.A. Jones, B.B. McCullum, K.D. Mills, C.J. Nevin, J.D.P. Oram, M.H. Richardson, M.S. Sinclair, S.B. Styris, D.R. Tuffey, D.L. Vettori, L. Vincent, P.J. Wiseman.

76) 2003/04 to India
S.P. Fleming *(captain),* N.J. Astle, I.G. Butler, C.L. Cairns*, C.Z. Harris*, R.G. Hart, P.A. Hitchcock*, R.A. Jones, B.B. McCullum*. C.D. McMillan, M.J. Mason, K.D. Mills*, C.J. Nevin*, J.D.P. Oram, M.H. Richardson, S.B. Styris, D.R. Tuffey, D.L. Vettori, L. Vincent, P.J. Wiseman.

77) 2003/04 to Pakistan
C.L. Cairns *(captain),* D.L. Vettori, T.K. Canning, C.D. Cumming, C.Z. Harris, P.A. Hitchcock, R.A. Jones, B.B. McCullum, H.J.H. Marshall, M.J. Mason, J.D.P. Oram, M.S. Sinclair, D.R. Tuffey, M.D.J. Walker, K.P. Walmsley.

78) 2004 to England
S.P. Fleming *(captain),* A.R. Adams*, N.J. Astle, S.E. Bond, I.G. Butler*, C.L. Cairns, J.E.C. Franklin*, C.Z. Harris*, G.J. Hopkins*, B.B. McCullum, C.D. McMillan, H.J.H Marshall*, C.S. Martin, K.D. Mills, J.D.P. Oram, M.H.W Papps, M.H. Richardson, S.B. Styris, D.R. Tuffey, D.L. Vettori.

79) 2004 to England *(Champions Trophy)*
S.P. Fleming *(captain),* N.J. Astle, I.G. Butler, C.L. Cairns, C.Z. Harris, B.B. McCullum, C.D. McMillan, H.J.H. Marshall, K.D. Mills, J.D.P Oram, M.H.W. Papps, S.B. Styris, D.R. Tuffey, D.L. Vettori.

80) 2004/05 to Bangladesh
S.P. Fleming *(captain),* A.R. Adams*, N.J. Astle, I.G. Butler, C.L. Cairns*, J.E.C. Franklin, P.G.Fulton*, C.Z. Harris*, B.B. McCullum, C.D. McMillan*, H.J.H. Marshall, C.S. Martin, K.D. Mills, J.D.P. Oram, M.H. Richardson, M.S. Sinclair, S.B. Styris, D.L. Vettori, P.J. Wiseman.

81) 2004/05 to Australia
S.P. Fleming *(captain)*, A.R. Adams*, N.J. Astle, I.G. Butler, C.L. Cairns*, T.K. Canning*, J.E.C. Franklin, C.Z. Harris*, G.J.Hopkins*, B.B. McCullum, C.D. McMillan*, H.J.H. Marshall, C.S. Martin, K.D. Mills, J.D.P.Oram, M.H. Richardson, M.S. Sinclair, S.B. Styris, D.L. Vettori, P.J. Wiseman.

82) 2005/06 to Namibia and Zimbabwe

S.P. Fleming *(captain)*, A.R. Adams*, N.J. Astle, S.E. Bond, C.L. Cairns*, C.D. Cumming, J.E.C. Franklin, B.B. McCullum, C.D. McMillan*, H.J.H. Marshall, J.A.H. Marshall, C.S. Martin, K.D. Mills, J.D.P. Oram, J.S. Patel*, S.B. Styris, D.L. Vettori, L. Vincent, P.J. Wiseman.

83) 2005/06 to South Africa

S.P. Fleming *(captain)*, A.R. Adams, N.J. Astle, S.E. Bond, J.E.C. Franklin, H.J.H. Marshall, J.A.H. Marshall, B.B. McCullum, C.D. McMillan, K.D. Mills, J.D.P. Oram, J.S. Patel, S.B. Styris, D.L. Vettori, L. Vincent.

84) 2005/06 to South Africa

S.P. Fleming *(captain)*, N.J. Astle, S.E. Bond, P.G. Fulton, J.E.C. Franklin, J.M. How, B.B. McCullum, H.J.H Marshall, C.S. Martin, M.J. Mason*, K.D. Mills, J.D.P. Oram, M.H.W. Papps, J.S. Patel, S.B. Styris, D.L. Vettori

85) 2006/07 to India *(ICC Champions Trophy)*

S.P. Fleming *(captain)*, N.J. Astle, S.E. Bond, J.E.C. Franklin, P.G. Fulton, M.R. Gillespie, B.B. McCullum, H.J.H. Marshall, K.D. Mills, J.D.P. Oram, J.S. Patel, S.B. Styris, L.R.P.L. Taylor*, D.L. Vettori, L. Vincent.

86) 2006/07 to Australia

S.P. Fleming *(captain)*, A.R. Adams, N.J. Astle, S.E. Bond, J.E.C. Franklin, P.G. Fulton, M.R. Gillespie, B.B. McCullum, C.D. McMillan, H.J.H. Marshall, M.J. Mason, K.D. Mills*, J.D.P. Oram*, J.S. Patel, S.B. Styris*, L.R.P.L. Taylor, D.L. Vettori, L. Vincent*.

87) 2006/07 to West Indies *(World Cup)*

S.P. Fleming *(captain)*, S.E. Bond, J.E.C. Franklin, P.G. Fulton, M.R. Gillespie, B.B. McCullum, C.D. McMillan, H.J.H. Marshall*, C.S. Martin*, M.J. Mason, J.D.P. Oram, J.S. Patel, S.B. Styris, L.R.P.L. Taylor, D.R. Tuffey, D.L. Vettori, L. Vincent.

** replacement or temporary addition to the touring party*

NEW ZEALAND TEST RECORDS

REGISTER OF PLAYERS

	Born	*Died*	*Type*		*Test Career*
Adams Andre Ryan	17/7/1975 Auckland		RHB	RFM	2001/02
Alabaster John Chaloner	11/7/1930 Invercargill		RHB	RLB	1955/56-1971/72
Allcott Cyril Francis Walter	7/10/1896 Lower Moutere	19/11/1973 Auckland	LHB	LM	1929/30-1931/32
Allott Geoffrey Ian	24/12/1971 Christchurch		RHB	LFM	1995/96-1999
Anderson Robert Wickham	2/10/1948 Christchurch		RHB	RLB	1976/77-1978
Anderson William McDougall	8/10/1919 Westport	21/12/1979 Christchurch	LHB	RLBG	1945/46
Andrews Bryan	4/4/1945 Christchurch		RHB	RFM	1973/74
Astle Nathan John	15/9/1971 Christchurch		RHB	RM	1995/96-2006/07
Badcock Frederick Theodore	9/8/1897 Abbottabad, India	19/9/1982 Perth	RHB	RM	1929/30-1932/33
Barber Richard Trevor	3/6/1925 Otaki		RHB	WK	1955/56
Bartlett Gary Alex	3/2/1941 Blenheim		RHB	RF	1961/62-1967/68
Barton Paul Thomas	9/10/1935 Wellington		RHB	SLA	1961/62-1962/63
Beard Donald Derek	14/1/1920 Palmerston North	15/7/1982 Lancaster	RHB	RM	1951/52-1955/56
Beck John Edward Francis	1/8/1934 Wellington	23/4/2000 Waikanae	LHB		1953/54-1955/56
Bell Matthew David	25/2/1977 Dunedin		RHB		1998/99-2001/02
Bell William	5/9/1931 Dunedin	23/7/2002 Auckland	RHB	RLB	1953/54
Bilby Grahame Paul	7/5/1941 Wellington		RHB		1965/66
Blain Tony Elston	17/2/1962 Nelson		RHB	WK	1986-1993/94
Blair Robert William	23/6/1932 Petone		RHB	RFM	1952/53-1963/64
Blunt Roger Charles	3/11/1900 Durham, England	22/6/1966 London	RHB	RLBG	1929/30-1931/32
Bolton Bruce Alfred	31/5/1935 Christchurch		RHB	RLB	1958/59
Bond Shane Edward	7/6/1975 Christchurch		RHB	RF	2001/02-2006/07
Boock Stephen Lewis	20/9/1951 Dunedin		RHB	SLA	1977/78-1988/89
Bracewell Brendon Paul	14/9/1959 Auckland		RHB	RFM	1978-1984/85
Bracewell John Garry	15/4/1958 Auckland		RHB	ROB	1980/81-1990
Bradburn Grant Eric	26/5/1966 Hamilton		RHB	ROB	1990/91-2000/01
Bradburn Wynne Pennell	24/11/1938 Thames		RHB	RSM	1963/64
Brown Vaughan Raymond	3/11/1959 Christchurch		LHB	ROB	1985/86
Burgess Mark Gordon	17/7/1944 Auckland		RHB	ROB	1967/68-1980/81

	Born	Died	Type		Test Career
Burke Cecil	22/3/1914 Auckland	4/8/1997 Auckland	RHB	RLB	1945/46
Burtt Thomas Browning	22/1/1915 Christchurch	24/5/1988 Christchurch	RHB	SLA	1946/47-1952/53
Butler Ian Gareth	24/11/1981 Auckland		RHB	RF	2001/02-2004/05
Butterfield Leonard Arthur	29/8/1913 Christchurch	5/7/1999 Christchurch	RHB	RM	1945/46
Cairns Bernard Lance	10/10/1949 Picton		RHB	RM	1973/74-1985/86
Cairns Christopher Lance	13/6/1970 Picton		RHB	RFM	1989/90-2004
Cameron Francis James	1/6/1932 Dunedin		RHB	RFM	1961/62-1965
Cave Henry Butler	10/10/1922 Wanganui	15/9/1989 Wanganui	RHB	RM	1949-1958
Chapple Murray Ernest	25/7/1930 Christchurch	31/7/1985 Hamilton	RHB	SLA	1952/53-1965/66
Chatfield Ewen John	3/7/1950 Dannevirke		RHB	RM	1974/75-1988/89
Cleverley Donald Charles	23/12/1909 Oamaru	16/2/2004 Southport, Aust.	LHB	RFM	1931/32-1945/46
Collinge Richard Owen	2/4/1946 Wellington		RHB	LFM	1964/65-1978
Colquhoun Ian Alexander	8/6/1924 Wellington	26/2/2005 Paraparaumu Beach	RHB	WK	1954/55
Coney Jeremy Vernon	21/6/1952 Wellington		RHB	RSM	1973/74-1986/87
Congdon Bevan Ernest	11/2/1938 Motueka		RHB	RM	1964/65-1978
Cowie John	30/3/1912 Auckland	3/6/1994 Lower Hutt	RHB	RFM	1937-1949
Cresswell George Fenwick	22/3/1915 Wanganui	10/1/1966 Blenheim	LHB	RM	1949-1950/51
Cromb Ian Burns	25/6/1905 Christchurch	6/3/1984 Christchurch	RHB	RM	1931-1931/32
Crowe Jeffrey John	14/9/1958 Auckland		RHB		1982/83-1989/90
Crowe Martin David	22/9/1962 Auckland		RHB	RM	1981/82-1995/96
Cumming Craig Derek	31/8/1975 Timaru		RHB	RM	2004/05-2006/07
Cunis Robert Smith	5/1/1941 Whangarei		RHB	RFM	1963/64-1971/72
D'Arcy John William	23/4/1936 Christchurch		RHB		1958
de Groen Richard Paul	5/8/1962 Otorohanga		RHB	RM	1993/94-1994/95
Davis Heath Te-Ihi-O-Te-Rangi	30/11/1971 Lower Hutt		RHB	RF	1994-1997/98
Dempster Charles Stewart	15/11/1903 Wellington	12/2/1974 Wellington	RHB		1929/30-1932/33
Dempster Eric William	25/1/1925 Wellington		LHB	SLA	1952/53-1953/54
Dick Arthur Edward	10/10/1936 Middlemarch		RHB	WK	1961/62-1965
Dickinson George Ritchie	11/3/1903 Dunedin	17/3/1978 Lower Hutt	RHB	RF	1929/30-1931/32
Donnelly Martin Paterson	17/10/1917 Ngaruawahia	22/10/1999 Sydney	LHB	SLA	1937-1949
Doull Simon Blair	6/8/1969 Pukekohe		RHB	RM	1992/93-1999/00
Dowling Graham Thorne	4/3/1937 Christchurch		RHB		1961/62-1971/72
Drum Christopher James	10/7/1974 Auckland		RHB	RFM	2000/01-2001/02

	Born	Died	Type		Test Career
Dunning John Angus	6/2/1903 Omaha	24/6/1971 Adelaide	RHB	RM	1932/33-1937
Edgar Bruce Adrian	23/11/1956 Wellington		LHB	WK	1978-1986
Edwards Graham Neil	27/5/1955 Nelson		RHB	WK	1976/77-1980/81
Emery Raymond William George	28/3/1915 Auckland	18/12/1982 Auckland	RHB	RM	1951/52
Fisher Frederick Eric	28/7/1924 Johnsonville	19/6/1996 Palmerston North	RHB	LM	1952/53
Fleming Stephen Paul	1/4/1973 Christchurch		LHB		1993/94-2006/07
Foley Henry	28/1/1906 Wellington	16/10/1948 Brisbane	LHB		1929/30
Franklin James Edward Charles	7/11/1980 Wellington		LHB	LFM	2000/01-2006/07
Franklin Trevor John	18/3/1962 Auckland		RHB	RM	1983-1990/91
Freeman Douglas Linford	8/9/1914 Sydney	31/5/1994 Sydney	RHB	RLBG	1932/33
Fulton Peter Gordon	1/2/1979 Christchurch		RHB	RM	2005/06
Gallichan Norman	3/6/1906 Palmerston North	25/3/1969 Taupo	RHB	SLA	1937
Gedye Sidney Graham	2/5/1929 Otahuhu		RHB		1963/64-1964/65
Germon Lee Kenneth	4/11/1968 Christchurch		RHB	WK	1995/96-1996/97
Gillespie Stuart Ross	2/3/1957 Wanganui		RHB	RFM	1985/86
Gray Evan John	18/11/1954 Wellington		RHB	SLA	1983-1988/89
Greatbatch Mark John	11/12/1963 Auckland		LHB		1987/88-1996/97
Guillen Simpson Clairmonte	24/9/1924 Port of Spain, Trinidad		RHB	WK	1955/56
Guy John William	29/8/1934 Nelson		LHB		1955/56-1961/62
Hadlee Dayle Robert	6/1/1948 Christchurch		RHB	RM	1969-1977/78
Hadlee Richard John	3/7/1951 Christchurch		LHB	RFM	1972/73-1990
Hadlee Walter Arnold	4/6/1915 Lincoln	29/9/2006 Christchurch	RHB		1937-1950/51
Harford Noel Sherwin	30/8/1930 Winton	30/3/1981 Auckland	RHB	RM	1955/56-1958
Harford Roy Ivan	30/5/1936 London, England		LHB	WK	1967/68
Harris Chris Zinzan	20/11/1969 Christchurch		LHB	RM	1992/93-2001/02
Harris Parke Gerald Zinzan	18/7/1927 Christchurch	1/12/1991 Christchurch	RHB	ROB	1955/56-1964/65
Harris Roger Meredith	27/7/1933 Otahuhu		RHB	RM	1958/59
Hart Matthew Norman	16/5/1972 Hamilton		LHB	SLA	1993/94-1995/96
Hart Robert Garry	2/12/1974 Hamilton		RHB	WK	2001/02-2003/04
Hartland Blair Robert	22/10/1966 Christchurch		RHB		1991/92-1994
Haslam Mark James	26/9/1972 Bury, England		LHB	SLA	1992/93-1995/96
Hastings Brian Frederick	23/3/1940 Wellington		RHB		1968/69-1975/76
Hayes John Arthur	11/1/1927 Auckland		RHB	RF	1950/51-1958

	Born	*Died*	*Type*			*Test Career*
Henderson Matthew	2/8/1895 Auckland	17/6/1970 Wellington	LHB	LFM		1929/30
Horne Matthew Jeffery	5/12/1970 Auckland		RHB	RM		1996/97-2002/03
Horne Philip Andrew	21/1/1960 Upper Hutt		LHB			1986/87-1990/91
Hough Kenneth William	24/10/1928 Sydney		RHB	RM		1958/59
How Jamie Michael	19/5/1981 New Plymouth		RHB	ROB		2005/06-2006/07
Howarth Geoffrey Philip	29/3/1951 Auckland		RHB	ROB		1974/75-1984/85
Howarth Hedley John	25/12/1943 Auckland		LHB	SLA		1969-1976/77
James Kenneth Cecil	12/3/1904 Wellington	21/8/1976 Palmerston North	RHB	WK		1929/30-1932/33
Jarvis Terrence Wayne	29/7/1944 Auckland		RHB			1964/65-1972/73
Jones Andrew Howard	9/5/1959 Wellington		RHB	ROB		1986/87-1994/95
Jones Richard Andrew	22/10/1973 Auckland		RHB			2003/04
Kennedy Robert John	3/6/1972 Dunedin		RHB	RFM		1995/96
Kerr John Lambert	28/12/1910 Dannevirke	27/5/2007 Christchurch	RHB			1931-1937
Kuggeleijn Christopher Mary	10/5/1956 Auckland		RHB	ROB		1988/89
Larsen Gavin Rolf	27/9/1962 Wellington		RHB	RM		1994-1995/96
Latham Rodney Terry	12/6/1961 Christchurch		RHB			1991/92-1992/93
Lees Warren Kenneth	19/3/1952 Dunedin		RHB	WK		1976/77-1983
Leggat Ian Bruce	7/6/1930 Invercargill		RHB	RM		1953/54
Leggat John Gordon	27/5/1926 Wellington	9/3/1973 Christchurch	RHB			1951/52-1955/56
Lissette Allen Fisher	6/11/1919 Morrinsville	24/1/1973 Hamilton	RHB	SLA		1955/56
Loveridge Greg Riaka	15/1/1975 Palmerston North		RHB	RLB		1995/96
Lowry Thomas Coleman	17/2/1898 Fernhill	20/7/1976 Hastings	RHB	ROB	WK	1929/30-1931
McCullum Brendon Barrie	27/9/1981 Dunedin		RHB		WK	2003/04-2006/07
McEwan Paul Ernest	19/12/1953 Christchurch		RHB	RM		1979/80-1984/85
MacGibbon Anthony Roy	28/8/1924 Christchurch		RHB	RFM		1950/51-1958
McGirr Herbert Mendelson	5/11/1891 Wellington	14/4/1964 Nelson	RHB	RFM		1929/30
McGregor Spencer Noel	18/12/1931 Dunedin		RHB			1954/55-1964/65
McLeod Edwin George	14/10/1900 Auckland	14/9/1989 Wellington	LHB	RLB		1929/30
McMahon Trevor George	8/11/1929 Wellington		RHB	WK		1955/56
McMillan Craig Douglas	13/9/1976 Christchurch		RHB	RM		1997/98-2004/05
McRae Donald Alexander Noel	25/12/1912 Christchurch	10/8/1986 Christchurch	LHB	LM		1945/46
Marshall Hamish John Hamilton	15/2/1979 Warkworth		RHB	RM		2000/01-2005/06

	Born	Died	Type		Test Career
Marshall James Andrew Hamilton	15/2/1979 Warkworth		RHB	RM	2004/05-2005/06
Martin Christopher Stewart	10/12/1974 Christchurch		RHB	RFM	2000/01-2006/07
Mason Michael James	27/8/1974 Carterton		RHB	RFM	2003/04
Matheson Alexander Malcolm	27/2/1906 Omaha	31/12/1985 Auckland	RHB	RFM	1929/30-1931
Meale Trevor	11/11/1928 Auckland		LHB		1958
Merritt William Edward	18/8/1908 Sumner	9/6/1977 Christchurch	RHB	RLBG	1929/30-1931
Meuli Edgar Milton	20/2/1926 Hawera	15/4/2007 Auckland	RHB	RLB	1952/53
Milburn Barry Douglas	24/11/1943 Dunedin		RHB	WK	1968/69
Miller Lawrence Somerville Martin	31/3/1923 New Plymouth	17/12/1996 Kapiti	LHB	LSM	1952/53-1958
Mills John Ernest	3/9/1905 Dunedin	11/12/1972 Hamilton	LHB		1929/30-1932/33
Mills Kyle David	15/3/1979 Auckland		RHB	RFM	2004-2005/06
Moir Alexander McKenzie	17/7/1919 Dunedin	17/6/2000 Dunedin	RHB	RLB	1950/51-1958/59
Moloney Denis Andrew Robert	11/8/1910 Dunedin	15/7/1942 El Alamein	RHB	RLB	1937
Mooney Francis Leonard Hugh	26/5/1921 Wellington	8/3/2004 Wellington	RHB	WK	1949-1953/54
Morgan Ross Winston	12/2/1941 Auckland		RHB	ROB	1964/65-1971/72
Morrison Bruce Donald	17/12/1933 Lower Hutt		LHB	RM	1962/63
Morrison Daniel Kyle	3/2/1966 Auckland		RHB	RFM	1987/88-1996/97
Morrison John Francis MacLean	27/8/1947 Wellington		RHB	SLA	1973/74-1981/82
Motz Richard Charles	12/1/1940 Christchurch	29/4/2007 Christchurch	RHB	RFM	1961/62-1969
Murray Bruce Alexander Grenfell	18/9/1940 Wellington		RHB	RLB	1967/68-1970/71
Murray Darrin James	4/9/1967 Christchurch		RHB		1994/95
Nash Dion Joseph	20/11/1971 Auckland		RHB	RFM	1992/93-2001/02
Newman Jack	3/7/1902 Brightwater	23/9/1996 Nelson	RHB	LM	1931/32-1932/33
O'Brien Iain Edward	10/7/1976 Lower Hutt		RHB	RM	2004/05
O'Connor Shayne Barry	15/11/1973 Hastings		LHB	LFM	1997/98-2001/02
Oram Jacob David Philip	28/7/1978 Palmerston North		LHB	RM	2002/03-2006/07
O'Sullivan David Robert	16/11/1944 Palmerston North		RHB	SLA	1972/73-1976/77
Overton Guy William Fitzroy	8/6/1919 Dunedin	7/9/1993 Winton	LHB	RFM	1953/54
Owens Michael Barry	11/11/1969 Christchurch		RHB	RFM	1992/93-1994
Page Milford Laurenson	8/5/1902 Lyttelton	13/2/1987 Christchurch	RHB	ROB	1929/30-1937
Papps Michael Hugh William	2/7/1979 Christchurch		RHB		2003/04-2005/06
Parker John Morton	21/2/1951 Dannevirke		RHB	WK	1972/73-1980/81

	Born	*Died*	*Type*			*Test Career*
Parker Norman Murray	28/8/1948 Dannevirke		RHB	RLB		1976/77
Parore Adam Craig	23/1/1971 Auckland		RHB	WK		1990-2001/02
Patel Dipak Narshibhai	25/10/1958 Nairobi, Kenya		RHB	ROB		1986/87-1996/97
Patel Jeetan Shashi	7/5/1980 Wellington		RHB	ROB		2005/06
Petherick Peter James	25/9/1942 Ranfurly		RHB	ROB		1976/77
Petrie Eric Charlton	22/5/1927 Ngaruawahia	14/8/2004 Omokoroa	RHB	WK		1955/56-1965/66
Playle William Rodger	1/12/1938 Palmerston North		RHB			1958-1962/63
Pocock Blair Andrew	18/6/1971 Papakura		RHB			1993/94-1997/98
Pollard Victor	7/9/1945 Burnley, England		RHB	ROB		1964/65-1973
Poore Matt Beresford	1/6/1930 Christchurch		RHB	ROB		1952/53-1955/56
Priest Mark Wellings	12/8/1961 Greymouth		LHB	SLA		1990-1997/98
Pringle Christopher	26/1/1968 Auckland		RHB	RFM		1990/91-1994/95
Puna Narotam	28/10/1929 Surat, India	7/6/1996 Hamilton	RHB	ROB		1965/66
Rabone Geoffrey Osborne	6/11/1921 Gore	19/1/2006 Auckland	RHB	ROB		1949-1954/55
Redmond Rodney Ernest	29/12/1944 Whangarei		LHB	SLA		1972/73
Reid John Fulton	3/3/1956 Auckland		LHB	RLB	WK	1978/79-1985/86
Reid John Richard	3/6/1928 Auckland		RHB	RFM	WK	1949-1965
Richardson Mark Hunter	11/6/1971 Hastings		LHB	SLA		2000/01-2004/05
Roberts Andrew Duncan Glenn	6/5/1947 Te Aroha	26/10/1989 Wellington	RHB	RM		1975/76-1976/77
Roberts Albert William	20/8/1909 Christchurch	13/5/1978 Christchurch	RHB	RM		1929/30-1937
Robertson Gary Keith	15/7/1960 New Plymouth		RHB	RFM		1985/86
Rowe Charles Gordon	30/6/1915 Glasgow, Scotland	9/6/1995 Palmerston North	RHB			1945/46
Rutherford Kenneth Robert	26/10/1965 Dunedin		RHB	RM		1984/85-1994/95
Scott Roy Hamilton	6/3/1917 Clyde	5/8/2005 Christchurch	RHB	RM		1946/47
Scott Verdun John	31/7/1916 Devonport	2/8/1980 Devonport	RHB	RM		1945/46-1951/52
Sewell David Graham	20/10/1977 Christchurch		RHB	LFM		1997/98
Shrimpton Michael John Froud	23/6/1940 Feilding		RHB	RLBG		1962/63-1973/74
Sinclair Barry Whitley	23/10/1936 Wellington		RHB			1962/63-1967/68
Sinclair Ian McKay	1/6/1933 Rangiora		LHB	ROB		1955/56
Sinclair Mathew Stuart	9/11/1975 Katherine, Australia		RHB			1999/00-2006/07
Smith Frank Brunton	13/3/1922 Rangiora	6/7/1997 Christchurch		RHB		1946/47-1951/52
Smith Horace Dennis	8/1/1913 Toowoomba, Aust	25/1/1986 Christchurch	RHB	RFM		1932/33
Smith Ian David Stockley	28/2/1957 Nelson		RHB	WK		1980/81-1991/92

	Born	Died	Type		Test Career
Snedden Colin Alexander	7/1/1918 Auckland		RHB	ROB	1946/47
Snedden Martin Colin	23/11/1958 Auckland		LHB	RFM	1980/81-1990
Sparling John Trevor	24/7/1938 Auckland		RHB	ROB	1958-1963/64
Spearman Craig Murray	4/7/1972 Auckland		RHB		1995/96-2000/01
Stead Gary Raymond	9/1/1972 Christchurch		RHB	RLB	1998/99-1999/00
Stirling Derek Alexander	5/10/1961 Upper Hutt		RHB	RFM	1984/85-1986
Styris Scott Bernard	10/7/1975 Brisbane, Aust		RHB	RM	2001/02-2005/06
Su'a Murphy Logo	7/11/1966 Wanganui		LHB	LFM	1991/92-1994/95
Sutcliffe Bert	17/11/1923 Auckland	20/4/2001 Auckland	LHB	SLA	1946/47-1965
Taylor Bruce Richard	12/7/1943 Timaru		LHB	RFM	1964/65-1973
Taylor Donald Dougald	2/3/1923 Auckland	5/12/1980 Auckland	RHB	RLBG	1946/47-1955/56
Thomson Keith	26/2/1941 Methven		RHB		1967/68
Thomson Shane Alexander	27/1/1969 Hamilton		RH1B	ROB	1989/90-1995/96
Tindill Eric William Thomas	18/12/1910 Nelson		LHB	WK	1937-1946/47
Troup Gary Bertram	3/10/1952 Taumarunui		RHB	LFM	1976/77-1985/86
Truscott Peter Bennetts	14/8/1941 Pahiatua		RHB		1964/65
Tuffey Daryl Raymond	11/6/1978 Milton		RHB	RFM	1999/00-2004
Turner Glenn Maitland	26/5/1947 Dunedin		RHB		1968/69-1982/83
Twose Roger Graham	17/4/1968 Torquay, England		LHB	RM	1995/96-1999
Vance Robert Howard	31/3/1955 Wellington		RHB		1987/88-1989/90
Vaughan Justin Thomas Caldwell	30//8/1967 Hereford, England		LHB	RM	1992/93-1996/97
Vettori Daniel Luca	27/1/1979 Auckland		LHB	SLA	1996/97-2006/07
Vincent Lou	11/11/1978 Warkworth		RHB	WK	2001/02-2005/06
Vivian Graham Ellery	28/2/1946 Auckland		LHB	RLB	1964/65-1971/72
Vivian Henry Gifford	4/11/1912 Auckland	12/8/1983 Auckland	LHB	SLA	1931-1937
Wadsworth Kenneth John	30/11/1946 Nelson	19/8/1976 Nelson	RHB	WK	1969-1975/76
Walker Brooke Graeme Keith	25/3/1977 Auckland		RHB	RLB	2000/01-2001/02
Wallace Walter Mervyn	19/12/1916 Auckland		RHB		1936-1952/53
Walmsley Kerry Peter	23/8/1973 Dunedin		RHB	RFM	1994/95-2000/01
Ward John Thomas	11/3/1937 Timaru		RHB	WK	1963/64-1967/68
Watson William	31/8/1965 Auckland		RHB	RFM	1986-1993/94
Watt Leslie	17/9/1924 Waitati	15/11/1996 Dunedin	RHB		1954/55

	Born	Died	Type		Test Career
Webb Murray George	22/6/1947 Invercargill		RHB	RFM	1970/71-1973/74
Webb Peter Neil	14/7/1957 Auckland		RHB	WK	1979/80
Weir Gordon Lindsay	2/6/1908 Auckland	31/10/2003 Auckland	RHB	RM	1929/30-1937
White David John	26/6/1961 Gisborne		RHB	ROB	1990/91
Whitelaw Paul Erskine	10/2/1910 Auckland	28/8/1988 Auckland	RHB		1932/33
Wiseman Paul John	4/5/1970 Auckland		RHB	ROB	1997/98-2004/05
Wright John Geoffrey	5/7/1954 Darfield		LHB	RM	1977/78-1992/93
Young Bryan Andrew	3/11/1964 Whangarei		RHB	WK	1993/94-1998/99
Yuile Bryan William	29/10/1941 Palmerston North		RHB	SLA	1962/63-1969/70

TEST UMPIRES

The following is the complete list of New Zealand test umpires:

Umpire	Tests
Bowden B.F.	41 *
Dunne R.S.	39 *
Aldridge B.L.	26 *
Goodall F.R.	24
Woodward S.J.	24
Cowie D.B.	22 *
Martin W.T.	15
Copps D.E.A.	13
Gardiner W.R.C.	9
Shortt R.W.R.	9
MacKintosh E.C.A.	8
Hastie J.B.R.	7
Cave K.	6
Monteith R.L.	6
Quested D.M.	5
Pengelly M.F.	4
Harris J.C.	4
Morris G.C.	4
Hill A.L.	4 *
Cobcroft L.T.	3
McLellan J.	3
Pearce T.M.	3
Cowie J.	3
Gwynne W.J.C.	3
Kinsella D.A.	3
McHarg R.L.	3
King C.E.	3
Butler W.	2
Forrester J.T.	2
Brown J.M.A.	2
Tonkinson S.B.	2
Currie R.G.	2
Clark L.G.	2
Dumbleton D.P.	2
Watkin E.A.	2
Page W.P.	1
Burgess T.	1
Torrance R.C.	1
Gourlay H.W.	1
Montgomery O.R.	1
Brook E.G.	1
Vine B.	1
Jelley A.E.	1
Tindill E.W.T.	1
Johnston L.C.	1
Burns D.C.	1
Cassie H.B.	1
Bricknell B.A.	1
Higginson I.C.	1

* *includes test matches overseas*

The following overseas umpires have stood in test matches in New Zealand:

Umpire	Tests
Harper D.J. *(Aus)*	8
de Silva E.A.R. *(SL)*	6
Hair D.B. *(Aus)*	5
Bucknor S.A. *(WI)*	4
Koertzen R.E. *(SA)*	4
Randell S.G. *(Aus)*	3
Orchard D.L. *(SA)*	3
Tiffin R.B. *(Zim)*	3
Shepherd D.R. *(Eng)*	3
Aleem Dar *(Pak)*	3
Venkataraghavan S. *(Ind)*	3
Ramaswamy V.K. *(Ind)*	2
Cooray B.C. *(SL)*	2
Francis K.T. *(SL)*	2
Mahboob Shah *(Pak)*	2
Davis S.J. *(Aus)*	2
Bird H.D. *(Eng)*	2
Benson M.R. *(Eng)*	2
Jerling B.G. *(SA)*	2
Taufel S.J.A. *(Aus)*	2
Robinson I.D. *(Zim)*	1
Nichols E.A. *(WI)*	1
Plews N.T. *(Eng)*	1
Riazuddin *(Pak)*	1
Jayaprakash A.V. *(Ind)*	1
Khizar Hayat *(Pak)*	1
Elliott C.S. *(Eng)*	1
Barker L.H. *(WI)*	1
Lloyds J.W. *(Eng)*	1
Howell I.L *(SA)*	1

The following pairs of umpires have stood together in the most tests:

Pair	Tests
Goodall F.R. & Woodward S.J.	10
Aldridge B.L. & Dunne R.S.	7
Aldridge B.L. & Woodward S.J.	6
Copps D.E.A. & Gardiner W.R.C.	5
Copps D.E.A. & Martin W.T.	4
MacKintosh E.C.A. & Shortt R.W.R.	4
Harris J.C. & Pearce T.M.	3
MacKintosh E.C.A. & Martin W.T.	3
Cobcroft L.T. & Cave K.	3
Dunne R.S. & Woodward S.J.	3

These umpires have stood in every test of a series *(minimum 3 matches)*:

Cave K. (4)	v England	1929/30
Martin W.T. (3)	v England	1965/66
MacKintosh E.C.A. (3)	v West Indies	1968/69
Goodall F.R. (3)	v England	1983/84
Woodward S.J. (3)	v England	1983/84
Aldridge B.L. (3)	v Sri Lanka	1990/91
Aldridge B.L. (3)	v England	1991/92
Dunne R.S. (3)	v England	1991/92
Aldridge B.L. (3)	v Australia	1992/93

TEAM RECORDS

New Zealand's Test Victories

1) **v West Indies** at Auckland 1955/56
NZ 255 & 157-9d WI 145 & 77
NZ won by 190 runs

2) **v South Africa** at Cape Town 1961/62
NZ 385 & 212-9d SA 190 & 335
NZ won by 72 runs

3) **v South Africa** at Port Elizabeth 1961/62
NZ 275 & 228 SA 190 & 273
NZ won by 40 runs

4) **v India** at Christchurch 1967/68
NZ 502 & 88-4 I 288 & 301
NZ won by 6 wickets

5) **v West Indies** at Wellington 1968/69
WI 297 & 148 NZ 282 & 166-4
NZ won by 6 wickets

6) **v India** at Nagpur 1969/70
NZ 319 & 214 I 257 & 109
NZ won by 167 runs

7) **v Pakistan** at Lahore 1969/70
P114 & 208 NZ 241 & 82-5
NZ won by 5 wickets

8) **v Australia** at Christchurch 1973/74
A 223 & 259 NZ 255 & 230-5
NZ won by 5 wickets

9) **v India** at Wellington 1975/76
I 220 & 81 NZ 334
NZ won by an innings and 33 runs

10) **v England** at Wellington 1977/78
NZ 228 & 123 E 215 & 64
NZ won by 72 runs

11) **v West Indies** at Dunedin 1979/80
WI 140 & 212 NZ 249 & 104-9
NZ won by 1 wicket

12) **v India** at Wellington 1980/81
NZ 375 & 100 I 233 & 190
NZ won by 62 runs

13) **v Australia** at Auckland 1981/82
A 210 & 280 NZ 387 & 109-5
NZ won by 5 wickets

14) **v Sri Lanka** at Christchurch 1982/83
NZ 344 SL 144 & 175
NZ won by an innings and 25 runs

15) **v Sri Lanka** at Wellington 1982/83
SL 240 & 93 NZ 201 & 134-4
NZ won by 6 wickets

16) **v England** at Leeds 1983
E 225 & 252 NZ 377 & 103-5
NZ won by 5 wickets

17) **v England** at Christchurch 1983/84
NZ 307 E 82 & 93
NZ won by an innings and 132 runs

18) **v Sri Lanka** at Kandy 1983/84
NZ 276 & 201-8d SL 215 & 97
NZ won by 165 runs

19) **v Sri Lanka** at Colombo 1983/84
SL 225 & 142 NZ 459
NZ won by an innings and 61 runs

20) **v Pakistan** at Auckland 1984/85
P 169 & 183 NZ 451-9d
NZ won by an innings and 99 runs

21) **v Pakistan** at Dunedin 1984/85
P274 & 223 NZ 220 & 278-8
NZ won by 2 wickets

22) **v Australia** at Brisbane 1985/86
A 179 & 333 NZ 553-7d
NZ won by an innings and 41 runs

23) **v Australia** at Perth 1985/86
A 203 & 259 NZ 299 & 164-4
NZ won by 6 wickets

24) **v Australia** at Auckland 1985/86
A 314 & 103 NZ 258 & 160-2
NZ won by 8 wickets

25) **v England** at Nottingham 1986
E 256 & 230 NZ 413 & 77-2
NZ won by 8 wickets

26) **v West Indies** at Christchurch 1986/87
WI 100 & 264 NZ 332-9d & 33-5
NZ won by 5 wickets

27) **v India** at Bombay 1988/89
NZ 236 & 279 I 234 & 145
NZ wonby 136 runs

28) **v India** at Christchurch 1989/90
NZ 459 & 2-0 I 164 & 296
NZ won by 10 wickets

29) **v Australia** at Wellington 1989/90
A 110 & 269 NZ 202 & 181-1
NZ won by 9 wickets

30) **v Zimbabwe** at Harare 1992/93
NZ 335 & 262-5d Z 283-9d & 137
NZ won by 177 runs

31) **v Australia** at Auckland 1992/93
A 139 & 285 NZ 224 & 201-5
NZ won by 5 wickets

32) **v Pakistan** at Christchurch 1993/94
P 344 & 179 NZ 200 & 324-5
NZ won by 5 wickets

33) v **South Africa** at Johannesburg 1994/95
NZ 411 & 194 SA 179 & 289
NZ won by 137 runs

34) v **Pakistan** at Lahore 1996/97
NZ 155 & 311 P 191 & 231
NZ won by 44 runs

35) v **Sri Lanka** at Dunedin 1996/97
NZ 586-7d SL 222 & 328
NZ won by an innings & 36 runs

36) v **Sri Lanka** at Hamilton 1996/97
NZ 222 & 273 SL 170 & 205
NZ won by 120 runs

37) v **Zimbabwe** at Wellington 1997/98
Z 180 & 250 NZ 411 & 20-0
NZ won by 10 wickets

38) v **Zimbabwe** at Auckland 1997/98
Z 170 & 277 NZ 460
NZ won by an innings and 13 runs

39) v **Sri Lanka** at Colombo 1997/98
NZ 305 & 444-6d SL 285 & 297
NZ won by 167 runs

40) v **India** at Wellington 1998/99
I 208 & 356 NZ 352 & 215-6
NZ won by 4 wickets

41) v **England** at Lord's 1999
E 186 & 229 NZ 358 & 60-1
NZ won by 9 wickets

42) v **England** at The Oval 1999
NZ 236 & 162 E 153 & 162
NZ won by 83 runs

43) v **West Indies** at Hamilton 1999/00
WI 365 & 97 NZ 393 & 70-1
NZ won by 9 wickets

44) v **West Indies** at Wellington 1999/00
NZ 518-9d WI 179 & 234
NZ won by an innings and 105 runs

45) v **Zimbabwe** at Bulawayo 2000/01
Z 350 & 119 NZ 338 & 132-3
NZ won by 7 wickets

46) v **Zimbabwe** at Harare 2000/01
NZ 465 & 74-2 Z 166 & 370
NZ won by 8 wickets

47) v **Pakistan** at Hamilton 2000/01
P 104 & 118 NZ 407-4d
NZ won by an innings & 185 runs

48) v **Bangladesh** at Hamilton 2001/02
NZ 365-9d B 205 & 108
NZ won by an innings and 52 runs

49) v **Bangladesh** at Wellington 2001/02
B 132 & 135 NZ 341-6d
NZ won by an innings and 74 runs

50) v **England** at Auckland 2001/02
NZ 202 & 269-9d E 160 & 233
NZ won by 78 runs

51) v **West Indies** at Bridgetown 2001/02
NZ 337 & 243 WI 107 & 269
NZ won by 204 runs

52) v **India** at Wellington 2002/03
I 161 & 121 NZ 247 & 36-0
NZ won by 10 wickets

53) v **India** at Hamilton 2002/03
I 99 & 154 NZ 94 & 160-6
NZ won by 4 wickets

54) v **South Africa** at Auckland 2003/04
SA 296 & 349 NZ 595 & 53-1
NZ won by 9 wickets

55) v **Bangladesh** at Dhaka 2004/05
B 177 & 126 NZ 402
NZ won by an innings and 99 runs

56) v **Bangladesh** at Chittagong 2004/05
NZ 545-6d B 182 & 262
NZ won by an innings and 101 runs

57) v **Sri Lanka** at Wellington 2004/05
SL 211 & 273 NZ 522-9d
NZ won by an innings and 38 runs

58) v **Zimbabwe** at Harare 2005/06
NZ 452-9d Z 59 & 99
NZ won by an innings and 294 runs

59) v **Zimbabwe** at Bulawayo 2005/06
Z 231 & 207 NZ 484
NZ won by an innings and 46 runs

60) v **West Indies** at Auckland 2005/06
NZ 275 & 272 WI 257 & 263
NZ won by 27 runs

61) v **West Indies** at Wellington 2005/06
WI 192 & 215 NZ 372 & 37-0
NZ won by 10 wickets

62) v **Sri Lanka** at Christchurch 2006/07
SL 154 & 179 NZ 206 & 119-5
NZ won by 5 wickets

Test Record by Series

					Cumulative					
		TOTAL						***BY OPPONENT***		
Season	***Opponent***	***Won***	***Lost***	***Drawn***	***Won***	***Lost***	***Drawn***	***Won***	***Lost***	***Drawn***
1929/30	England*	—	1	3	—	1	3	—	1	3
1931	England	—	1	2	—	2	5	—	2	5
1931/32	South Africa*	—	2	—	—	4	5	—	2	—
1932/33	England*	—	—	2	—	4	7	—	2	7
1937	England	—	1	2	—	5	9	—	3	9
1945/46	Australia*	—	1	—	—	6	9	—	1	—
1946/47	England*	—	—	1	—	6	10	—	3	10
1949	England	—	—	4	—	6	14	—	3	14
1950/51	England*	—	1	1	—	7	15	—	4	15
1951/52	West Indies*	—	1	1	—	8	16	—	1	1
1952/53	South Africa*	—	1	1	—	9	17	—	3	1
1953/54	South Africa	—	4	1	—	13	18	—	7	2
1954/55	England*	—	2	—	—	15	18	—	6	15
1955/56	Pakistan	—	2	1	—	17	19	—	2	1
1955/56	India	—	2	3	—	19	22	—	2	3
1955/56	West Indies*	1	3	—	1	22	22	1	4	1
1958	England	—	4	1	1	26	23	—	10	16
1958/59	England*	—	1	1	1	27	24	—	11	17
1961/62	South Africa	2	2	1	3	29	25	2	9	3
1962/63	England*	—	3	—	3	32	25	—	14	17
1963/64	South Africa*	—	—	3	3	32	28	2	9	6
1964/65	Pakistan*	—	—	3	3	32	31	—	2	4
1964/65	India	—	1	3	3	33	34	—	3	6
1964/65	Pakistan	—	2	1	3	35	35	—	4	5
1965	England	—	3	—	3	38	35	—	17	17
1965/66	England*	—	—	3	3	38	38	—	17	20
1967/68	India*	1	3	—	4	41	38	1	6	6
1968/69	West Indies*	1	1	1	5	42	39	2	5	2
1969	England	—	2	1	5	44	40	—	19	21
1969/70	India	1	1	1	6	45	41	2	7	7
1969/70	Pakistan	1	—	2	7	45	43	1	4	7
1970/71	England*	—	1	1	7	46	44	—	20	22
1971/72	West Indies	—	—	5	7	46	49	2	5	7
1972/73	Pakistan*	—	1	2	7	47	51	1	5	9
1973	England	—	2	1	7	49	52	—	22	23
1973/74	Australia	—	2	1	7	51	53	—	3	1
1973/74	Australia*	1	1	1	8	52	54	1	4	2
1974/75	England*	—	1	1	8	53	55	—	23	24
1975/76	India*	1	1	1	9	54	56	3	8	8
1976/77	Pakistan	—	2	1	9	56	57	1	7	10
1976/77	India	—	2	1	9	58	58	3	10	9
1976/77	Australia*	—	1	1	9	59	59	1	5	3
1977/78	England*	1	1	1	10	60	60	1	24	25
1978	England	—	3	—	10	63	60	1	27	25
1978/79	Pakistan*	—	1	2	10	64	62	1	8	12
1979/80	West Indies*	1	—	2	11	64	64	3	5	9
1980/81	Australia	—	2	1	11	66	65	1	7	4
1980/81	India*	1	—	2	12	66	67	4	10	11
1981/82	Australia*	1	1	1	13	67	68	2	8	5
1982/83	Sri Lanka*	2	—	—	15	67	68	2	—	—

					Cumulative					
		TOTAL						BY OPPONENT		
Season	*Opponent*	*Won*	*Lost*	*Drawn*	*Won*	*Lost*	*Drawn*	*Won*	*Lost*	*Drawn*
1983	England	1	3	—	16	70	68	2	30	25
1983/84	England*	1	—	2	17	70	70	3	30	27
1983/84	Sri Lanka	2	—	1	19	70	71	4	—	1
1984/85	Pakistan	—	2	1	19	72	72	1	10	13
1984/85	Pakistan*	2	—	1	21	72	73	3	10	14
1984/85	West Indies	—	2	2	21	74	75	3	7	11
1985/86	Australia	2	1	—	23	75	75	4	9	5
1985/86	Australia*	1	—	2	24	75	77	5	9	7
1986	England	1	—	2	25	75	79	4	30	29
1986/87	West Indies*	1	1	1	26	76	80	4	8	12
1986/87	Sri Lanka	—	—	1	26	76	81	4	—	2
1987/88	Australia	—	1	2	26	77	83	5	10	9
1987/88	England*	—	—	3	26	77	86	4	30	32
1988/89	India	1	2	—	27	79	86	5	12	11
1988/89	Pakistan*	—	—	2	27	79	88	3	10	16
1989/90	Australia	—	—	1	27	79	89	5	10	10
1989/90	India*	1	—	2	28	79	91	6	12	13
1989/90	Australia*	1	—	—	29	79	91	6	10	10
1990	England	—	1	2	29	80	93	4	41	34
1990/91	Pakistan	—	3	—	29	83	93	3	13	16
1990/91	Sri Lanka*	—	—	3	29	83	96	4	—	5
1991/92	England*	—	2	1	29	85	97	4	33	35
1992/93	Zimbabwe	1	—	1	30	85	98	1	—	1
1992/93	Sri Lanka	—	1	1	30	86	99	4	1	6
1992/93	Pakistan*	—	1	—	30	87	99	3	14	16
1992/93	Australia*	1	1	1	31	88	100	7	11	11
1993/94	Australia	—	2	1	31	90	101	7	13	12
1993/94	Pakistan*	1	2	—	32	92	101	4	16	16
1993/94	India*	—	—	1	32	92	102	6	12	14
1994	England	—	1	2	32	93	104	4	34	37
1994/95	South Africa	1	2	—	33	95	104	3	11	6
1994/95	West Indies*	—	1	1	33	96	105	4	9	13
1994/95	South Africa*	—	1	—	33	97	105	3	12	6
1994/95	Sri Lanka*	—	1	1	33	98	106	4	2	7
1995/96	India	—	1	2	33	99	108	6	13	16
1995/96	Pakistan*	—	1	—	33	100	108	4	17	16
1995/96	Zimbabwe*	—	—	2	33	100	110	1	—	3
1995/96	West Indies	—	1	1	33	101	111	4	10	14
1996/97	Pakistan	1	1	—	34	102	111	5	18	16
1996/97	England*	—	2	1	34	104	112	4	36	38
1996/97	Sri Lanka*	2	—	—	36	104	112	6	2	7
1997/98	Zimbabwe	—	—	2	36	104	114	1	—	5
1997/98	Australia	—	2	1	36	106	115	7	15	13
1997/98	Zimbabwe*	2	—	—	38	106	115	3	—	5
1997/98	Sri Lanka	1	2	—	39	108	115	7	4	7
1998/99	India*	1	—	1	40	108	116	7	13	17
1998/99	South Africa*	—	1	2	40	109	118	3	13	8
1999	England	2	1	1	42	110	119	6	37	39
1999/00	India	—	1	2	42	111	121	7	14	19
1999/00	West Indies*	2	—	—	44	111	121	6	10	14
1999/00	Australia*	—	3	—	44	114	121	7	18	13
2000/01	Zimbabwe	2	—	—	46	114	121	5	—	5

Season	Opponent	TOTAL Won	Lost	Drawn	Cumulative Won	Lost	Drawn	BY OPPONENT Won	Lost	Drawn
2000/01	South Africa	—	2	1	46	116	122	3	15	9
2000/01	Zimbabwe*	—	—	1	46	116	123	5	—	6
2000/01	Pakistan*	1	1	1	47	117	124	6	19	17
2001/02	Australia	—	—	3	47	117	127	7	18	16
2001/02	Bangladesh*	2	—	—	49	117	127	2	—	—
2001/02	England*	1	1	1	50	118	128	7	38	40
2001/02	Pakistan	—	1	—	50	119	128	6	20	17
2001/02	West Indies	1	—	1	51	119	129	7	10	15
2002/03	India*	2	—	—	53	119	129	9	14	19
2002/03	Sri Lanka	—	—	2	53	119	131	7	4	9
2003/04	India	—	—	2	53	119	133	9	14	21
2003/04	Pakistan*	—	1	1	53	120	134	6	21	18
2003/04	South Africa*	1	1	1	54	121	135	4	16	10
2004	England	—	3	—	54	124	135	7	41	40
2004/05	Bangladesh	2	—	—	56	124	135	4	—	—
2004/05	Australia	—	2	—	56	126	135	7	20	16
2004/05	Australia*	—	2	1	56	128	136	7	22	17
2004/05	Sri Lanka*	1	—	1	57	128	137	8	4	10
2005/06	Zimbabwe	2	—	—	59	128	137	7	—	6
2005/06	West Indies*	2	—	1	61	128	138	9	10	16
2005/06	South Africa	—	2	1	61	130	139	4	18	11
2006/07	Sri Lanka*	1	1	—	62	131	139	9	5	10

** home series*

Summary of Results

	Played	Won	Lost	Drawn
v England	88	7	41	40
v Australia	46	7	22	17
v South Africa	33	4	18	11
v West Indies	35	9	10	16
v India	44	9	14	21
v Pakistan	45	6	21	18
v Sri Lanka	24	9	5	10
v Zimbabwe	13	7	—	6
v Bangladesh	4	4	—	—
Total	**332**	**62**	**131**	**139**

Decade by Decade

	Played	Won	Lost	Drawn
1929/30 to 1937	14	—	5	9
1945/46 to 1954/55	19	—	10	9
1955/56 to 1964/65	43	3	23	17
1965/66 to 1974/75	40	5	15	20
1975/76 to 1984/85	54	13	21	20
1985/86 to 1994/95	67	12	24	31
1995/96 to 2004/05	85	24	30	31
2005/06 to 2006/07	10	5	3	2
Total	**332**	**62**	**131**	**139**

Highest Totals

For

671-4	v Sri Lanka	Wellington	1990/91
630-6d	v India	Mohali	2003/04
595	v South Africa	Auckland	2003/04
593-8d	v South Africa	Cape Town	2005/06
586-7d	v Sri Lanka	Dunedin	1996/97
563	v Pakistan	Hamilton	2003/04
561	v Sri Lanka	Napier	2004/05
553-7d	v Australia	Brisbane	1985/86
551-9d	v England	Lord's	1973
545-6d	v Bangladesh	Chittagong	2004/05
543-3d	v West Indies	Georgetown	1971/72
537	v England	Wellington	1983/84
534-9d	v Australia	Perth	2001/02
522-9d	v Sri Lanka	Wellington	2004/05
518-9d	v West Indies	Wellington	1999/00
515-7d	v Sri Lanka	Colombo	2002/03
512-6d	v England	Wellington	1987/88
509	v South Africa	Hamilton	2003/04
505	v South Africa	Cape Town	1953/54
502	v India	Christchurch	1967/68

Against

660-5d	by West Indies	Wellington	1994/95
643	by Pakistan	Lahore	2001/02
621-5d	by South Africa	Auckland	1998/99
616-5d	by Pakistan	Auckland	1988/89
607-6d	by Australia	Brisbane	1993/94
593-6d	by England	Auckland	1974/75
585	by Australia	Brisbane	2004/05
583-7d	by India	Ahmedabad	1999/00
580-9d	by England	Christchurch	1991/92
575-8d	by Australia	Adelaide	2004/05
571-8d	by Pakistan	Christchurch	2000/01
570-8d	by Australia	Wellington	2004/05
567-8d	by England	Nottingham	1994
565-9d	by Pakistan	Karachi	1976/77
564-8	by West Indies	Bridgetown	1971/72
562-7d	by England	Auckland	1962/63
561	by Pakistan	Lahore	1955/56
560-8d	by England	Christchurch	1932/33
558-8d	by Australia	Hobart	2001/02
552	by Australia	Christchurch	1976/77
550	by England	Christchurch	1950/51

Lowest Totals

For

26	v England	Auckland	1954/55
42	v Australia	Wellington	1945/46
47	v England	Lord's	1958
54	v Australia	Wellington	1945/46
65	v England	Christchurch	1970/71
67	v England	Leeds	1958
67	v England	Lord's	1978

70	v Pakistan	Dacca	1955/56
73	v Pakistan	Lahore	2001/02
74	v West Indies	Dunedin	1955/56
74	v England	Lord's	1958
76	v Australia	Brisbane	2004/05
79	v South Africa	Johannesburg	1953/54
79	v Pakistan	Rawalpindi	1964/65
85	v England	Manchester	1958
89	v England	Auckland	1962/63
93	v Pakistan	Hamilton	1992/93
94	v England	Birmingham	1958
94	v West Indies	Bridgetown	1984/85
94	v India	Hamilton	2002/03
97	v England	Nottingham	1973

Against

59	by Zimbabwe	Harare	2005/06
64	by England	Wellington	1977/78
77	by West Indies	Auckland	1955/56
81	by India	Wellington	1975/76
82	by England	Christchurch	1983/84
83	by India	Mohali	1999/00
88	by India	Bombay	1964/65
89	by India	Hyderabad	1969/70
93	by Sri Lanka	Wellington	1982/83
93	by England	Christchurch	1983/84
97	by Sri Lanka	Kandy	1983/84
97	by West Indies	Hamilton	1999/00
99	by India	Hamilton	2002/03
99	by Zimbabwe	Harare	2005/06

Longest Innings

Mins	*Runs*			
851	671-4	v Sri Lanka	Wellington	1990/91
815	459	v Sri Lanka	Colombo	1983/84
802	630-6 dec	v India	Mohali	2003/04
790	406-5	v Sri Lanka	Colombo	1986/87
784	512-6 dec	v England	Wellington	1987/88
780	543-3 dec	v West Indies	Georgetown	1971/72
768	551-9 dec	v England	Lord's	1973
760	482-6 dec	v Pakistan	Lahore	1964/65
753	487-7 dec	v Zimbabwe	Wellington	2000/01
738	492	v Pakistan	Wellington	1984/85
732	447	v Pakistan	Wellington	1988/89
724	537	v England	Wellington	1983/84
713	403	v Pakistan	Auckland	1988/89
710	484	v Australia	Wellington	1973/74
709	440	v England	Nottingham	1973
705	593-8d	v South Africa	Cape Town	2005/06

Largest First Innings Leads

*393	v Zimbabwe	Harare	2005/06
*374	v Australia	Brisbane	1985/86
*364	v Sri Lanka	Dunedin	1996/97
*363	v Bangladesh	Chittagong	2004/05
*339	v West Indies	Wellington	1999/00
*311	v Sri Lanka	Wellington	2004/05
*303	v Pakistan	Hamilton	2000/01
*299	v Zimbabwe	Harare	2000/01
*299	v South Africa	Auckland	2003/04
298	v England	Lord's	1973
297	v England	Manchester	1999
*295	v India	Christchurch	1989/90
*290	v Zimbabwe	Auckland	1997/98
289	v West Indies	Bridgetown	1971/72
*282	v Pakistan	Auckland	1984/85
*253	v Zimbabwe	Bulawayo	2005/06
232	v West Indies	Christchurch	1979/80
*232	v West Indies	Christchurch	1986/87
*231	v Zimbabwe	Wellington	1997/98
*225	v England	Christchurch	1983/84
*225	v Bangladesh	Dhaka	2004/05
*214	v India	Christchurch	1967/68
209	v India	Bombay	1964/65
*209	v Bangladesh	Wellington	2001/02
204	v India	Calcutta	1955/56
*203	v Sri Lanka	Colombo	1983/84
*200	v Sri Lanka	Christchurch	1982/83

** New Zealand won the match*

Opposition Following-on

South Africa	Cape Town	1953/54
India	Bombay	1964/65
*India	Christchurch	1967/68
*Sri Lanka	Christchurch	1982/83
*England	Christchurch	1983/84
*India	Christchurch	1989/90
*Sri Lanka	Dunedin	1996/97
*West Indies	Wellington	1999/00
*Zimbabwe	Harare	2000/01
*Bangladesh	Hamilton	2001/02
India	Mohali	2003/04
*Bangladesh	Chittagong	2004/05
*Zimbabwe	Harare	2005/06

** New Zealand won the match*

NB: *New Zealand did not enforce the follow-on v South Africa at Cape Town, 1961/62 and v West Indies at Bridgetown in 2001/02 although they could have done so. They eventually won both games.*

GROUNDS

Results by Grounds

In New Zealand	P	W	L	D
Eden Park, Auckland	47	9	15	23
Jade Stadium, Christchurch	40	8	16	16
Basin Reserve, Wellington	46	13	15	18
Carisbrook, Dunedin	10	3	4	3
McLean Park, Napier	5	—	1	4
Westpac Park, Hamilton	13	5	2	6
Total	**161**	**38**	**53**	**70**

In Australia	P	W	L	D
Melbourne Cricket Ground	3	—	1	2
Sydney Cricket Ground	2	—	1	1
Adelaide Oval	3	—	2	1
WACA Ground, Perth	6	1	2	3
Woolloongabba, Brisbane	7	1	5	1
Bellerive Oval, Hobart	3	—	1	2
Total	**24**	**2**	**12**	**10**

In Sri Lanka	P	W	L	D
Kandy, Asgiriya Stadium	2	1	—	1
Sinhalese Sports Club Ground, Colombo	3	—	2	1
Colombo C.C. Ground, Colombo	2	1	—	1
Tyrone Fernando Stadium, Moratuwa	1	—	—	1
R. Premadasa Stadium, Colombo	1	1	—	—
Galle International Stadium	1	—	1	—
P. Saravanamuttu Stadium	1	—	—	1
Total	**11**	**3**	**3**	**5**

In West Indies	P	W	L	D
Queen's Park Oval, Port of Spain	3	—	—	3
Sabina Park, Kingston	2	—	1	1
Kensington Park, Bridgetown	4	1	2	1
Bourda, Georgetown	2	—	—	2
St Johns Recreation Ground, Antigua	1	—	—	1
Queen's Park, Grenada	1	—	—	1
Total	**13**	**1**	**3**	**9**

In Zimbabwe	P	W	L	D
Bulawayo Athletic Club	1	—	—	1
Harare Sports Club, Harare	4	3	—	1
Queens Sports Club, Bulawayo	3	2	—	1
Total	**8**	**5**	**—**	**3**

In Bangladesh	P	W	L	D
National Stadium, Dhaka	1	1	—	—
Chittagong Stadium	1	1	—	—
Total	**2**	**2**	**—**	**—**

In Pakistan	P	W	L	D
National Stadium, Karachi	6	—	3	3
Bagh-e-Jinnah, Lahore	1	—	1	—
Dacca Stadium, Dacca	2	—	—	2
Niaz Stadium, Hyderabad	2	—	2	—
Rawalpindi Club Ground	1	—	1	—
Lahore (Gaddafi) Stadium	7	2	4	1
Iqbal Stadium, Faisalabad	1	—	1	—
Rawalpindi Cricket Stadium	1	—	1	—
Total	**21**	**2**	**13**	**6**

In South Africa	P	W	L	D
Kingsmead, Durban	3	—	3	—
Ellis Park, Johannesburg	2	—	2	—
New Wanderers, Johannesburg	5	1	2	2
Newlands, Cape Town	4	1	1	2
St George's Park, Port Elizabeth	3	1	2	—
Goodyear Park, Bloemfontein	1	—	1	—
SuperSport Park, Centurion	1	—	1	—
Total	**19**	**3**	**12**	**4**

In England	P	W	L	D
Lord's, London	14	1	6	7
Oval, London	9	1	4	4
Headingley, Leeds	6	1	4	1
Trent Bridge, Nottingham	8	1	5	2
Old Trafford, Manchester	6	—	2	4
Egbaston, Birmingham	4	—	4	—
Total	**47**	**4**	**25**	**18**

In India	P	W	L	D
Brabourne Stadium, Bombay	3	—	2	1
Wankhede Stadium, Bombay	2	1	1	—
Fateh Maidan, (Lal Bahadur Stadium) Hyderbad	3	—	1	2
Feroz Shah Kotla, Delhi	2	—	1	1
Eden Gardens, Calcutta	2	—	—	2
Corporation Stadium, Madras	2	—	1	1
Chepauk, (Chidambaram Stadium) Madras	2	—	1	1
VCA Ground, Nagpur	1	1	—	—
Green Park, Kanpur	2	—	1	1
Chinnaswamy Stadium, Bangalore	2	—	2	—
Barabati Stadium, Cuttack	1	—	—	1
Punjab C.A. Stadium, Mohali	2	—	—	2
Sardar Patel Stadium, Ahmedabad	2	—	—	2
Total	**26**	**2**	**10**	**14**

Record Performances in Tests on Each NZ Ground v All Countries

Venue	***Highest Total*** *by NZ* *v NZ*	***Lowest Total*** *by NZ* *v NZ*	***Highest Individual Innings*** *by NZ* *v NZ*	***Best Bowling*** *by NZ* *v NZ*
Auckland 47 Tests	595 2003/04 v South Africa 621-5d 1998/99 by South Africa	26 1954/55 v England 77 1955/56 by West Indies	173 Smith I.D.S. 1989/90 v India 336* Hammond W.R. 1932/33 for England	7-87 Vettori D.L. 1999/00 v Australia 8-76 Prasanna E.A.S. 1975/76 for India
Christchurch 40 Tests	502 1967/68 v India 580-9d 1991/92 by England	65 1970/71 v England 82 1983/84 by England	239 Dowling G.T. 1967/68 v India 258 Nurse S.M. 1968/69 for West Indies	7-116 Hadlee R.J. 1985/86 v Australia 7-47 Tufnell P.C.R. 1991/92 for England
Dunedin 10 Tests	586-7d 1996/97 v Sri Lanka 507-6d 1972/73 by Pakistan	74 1955/56 v West Indies 140 1979/80 by West Indies	267* Young B.A. 1996/97 v Sri Lanka 201 Mushtaq Mohammad 1972/73 for Pakistan	6-51 Hadlee R.J. 1984/85 v Pakistan 7-52 Intikhab Alam 1972/73 for Pakistan
Wellington 46 Tests	671-4 1990/91 v Sri Lanka 660-5d 1994/95 by West Indies	42 1945/46 v Australia 64 1977/78 by England	299 Crowe M.D. 1990/91 v Sri Lanka 267 de Silva P.A. 1990/91 for Sri Lanka	7-23 Hadlee R.J. 1975/76 v India 7-37 Walsh C.A. 1994/95 for West Indies
Napier 5 Tests	561 2004/05 v Sri Lanka 498 2004/05 by Sri Lanka	109 1994/95 v Sri Lanka 183 1994/95 by Sri Lanka	160 Marshall H.J.H. 2004/05 v Sri Lanka 141 Jayawardene D.P.M.D. for Sri Lanka 2004/05	5-98 Morrison D.K. 1989/90 v India 5-43 Vaas W.P.J.U.C. 1994/95 for Sri Lanka
Hamilton 13 Tests	563 2003/04 v Pakistan 463 2003/04 by Pakistan	93 1992/93 v Pakistan 97 1999/00 by West Indies	192 Fleming S.P. 2003/04 v Pakistan 190 Dravid R.S. 1998/99 for India	7-27 Cairns C.L. 1999/00 v West Indies 5-22 Waqar Younis 1992/93 for Pakistan
ALL TESTS IN NZ 161 Tests	671-4 1990/91 v Sri Lanka Wellington 660-5d 1994/95 by West Indies Wellington	26 1954/55 v England Auckland 64 1977/78 by England Wellington	299 Crowe M.D. 1990/91 v Sri Lanka Wellington 336* Hammond W.R. 1932/33 for England Auckland	7-23 Hadlee R.J. 1975/76 v India Wellington 8-76 Prasanna E.A.S. 1975/76 for India Auckland

Record Performances in Tests v All Opponents

Opponent	*Highest Total* *by NZ* *v NZ*	*Lowest Total* *by NZ* *v NZ*	*Highest Individual Innings* *by NZ* *v NZ*	*Best Bowling* *by NZ* *v NZ*
England	551-9d Lord's 1973 593-6 Auckland 1974/75	26 Auckland 1954/55 64 Wellington 1977/78	222 Astle N.J. Christchurch, 2001/02 336* Hammond W.R. Auckland, 1932/33	7-74 Cairns B.L. Leeds, 1983 7-32 Underwood D.L. Lord's, 1969
Australia	553-7d Brisbane 1985/1986 607-6d Brisbane 1993/94	42 Wellington 1945/46 103 Auckland 1985/86	188 Crowe M.D. Brisbane, 1985/86 250 Walters K.D. Christchurch, 1977/78	9-52 Hadlee R.J. Brisbane, 1985/86 6-31 Warne S.K. Hobart 1993/94
South Africa	595 Auckland 2003/04 621-5d Auckland 1998/99	79 Johannesburg 1953/54 148 Johannesburg 1953/54	262 Fleming S.P. Cape Town, 2005/06 275* Cullinan D.J. Auckland, 1998/99	6-60 Reid J.R. Dunedin, 1963/64 8-53 Lawrence G.B. Johannesburg, 1961/62
West Indies	543-3d Georgetown 1971/72 660-5d Wellington 1994/95	74 Dunedin 1955/56 77 Auckland 1955/56	259 Turner G.M. Georgetown, 1971/72 258 Nurse S.M. Christchurch, 1968/69	7-27 Cairns C.L. Hamilton, 1999/00 7-37 Walsh C.A. Wellington, 1994/95
India	630-6d Mohali 2003/04 583-7d Ahmedabad 1999/00	94 Hamilton 2002/03 81 Wellington 1975/76	239 Dowling G.T. Christchurch, 1967/68 231 Mankad M.H. Madras, 1955/56	7-23 Hadlee R.J. Wellington, 1975/76 8-72 Venkataraghavan S. Delhi, 1964/65
Pakistan	563 Hamilton 2003/04 643 Lahore 2001/02	70 Dacca 1955/56 102 Faisalabad 1990/91	204* Sinclair M.S. Christchurch, 2000/01 329 Inzamam-ul-Haq Lahore, 2001/02	7-52 Pringle C. Faisalabad 1990/91 7-52 Intikhab Alam. Dunedin, 1972/73
Sri Lanka	671-4 Wellington 1990/91 498 Napier 2004/05	102 Colombo 1992/93 93 Wellington 1982/83	299 Crowe M.D. Wellington, 1990/91 267 de Silva P.A. Wellington, 1990/91	7-130 Vettori D.L. Wellington 2006/07 6-72 Dharmasena H.D.P.K. Galle, 1997/98
Zimbabwe	487-7d Wellington 2000/01 461 Bulawayo 1997/98	207 Harare 1997/98 59 Harare 2005/06	157 Horne M.J. Auckland, 1997/98 203* Whittall G.J. Bulawayo, 1997/98	6-50 Patel D.N. Harare, 1992/93 8-109 Strang P.A. Bulawayo, 2000/0
Bangladesh	545-6d Chittagong 2004/05 262 Chittagong 2004/05	341-6d Wellington 2001/02 108 Hamilton 2001/02	202 Fleming S.P. Chittagong, 2004/05 67 Mohamad Ashraful Dhaka, 2004/05	7-53 Cairns C.L. Hamilton, 2001/02 6-122 Mohammad Rafique Dhaka, 2004/05

INDIVIDUAL RECORDS

BATTING

Test Centuries

(200 instances)

299	Crowe M.D. v Sri Lanka at Wellington	1990/91
274*	Fleming S.P. v Sri Lanka at Colombo	2002/03
267*	Young B.A. v Sri Lanka at Dunedin	1996/97
262	Fleming S.P. v South Africa at Cape Town	2005/06
259	Turner G.M. v West Indies at Georgetown	1971/72
239	Dowling G.T. v India at Christchurch	1967/68
230*	Sutcliffe B. v India at New Delhi	1955/56
224	Vincent L. v Sri Lanka at Wellington	2004/05
223*	Turner G.M. v West Indies at Kingston	1971/72
222	Astle N.J. v England at Christchurch	2001/02
214	Sinclair M.S. v West Indies at Wellington	1999/00
206	Donnelly M.P. v England at Lord's	1949
204*	Sinclair M.S. v Pakistan at Christchurch	2000/01
202	Fleming S.P. v Bangladesh at Chittagong	2004/05
192	Fleming S.P. v Pakistan at Hamilton	2003/04
188	Crowe M.D. v West Indies at Georgetown	1984/85
188	Crowe M.D. v Australia at Brisbane	1985/86
186	Jones A.H. v Sri Lanka at Wellington	1990/91
185	Wright J.G. v India at Christchurch	1989/90
182	Jarvis T.W. v West Indies at Georgetown	1971/72
180	Reid J.F. v Sri Lanka at Colombo	1983/84
176	Congdon B.E. v England at Nottingham	1973
175	Congdon B.E. v England at Lord's	1973
174*	Coney J.V. v England at Wellington	1983/84
174*	Fleming S.P. v Sri Lanka at Colombo	1997/98
174	Crowe M.D. v Pakistan at Wellington	1988/89
173	Smith I.D.S. v India at Auckland	1989/90
170*	Jones A.H. v India at Auckland	1989/90
170	Styris S.B. v South Africa at Auckland	2003/04
166*	Congdon B.E. v West Indies at Port of Spain	1971/72
161	Edgar B.A. v Australia at Auckland	1981/82
160	Marshall H.J.H. v Sri Lanka at Napier	2004/05
158*	Reid J.F. v Pakistan at Auckland	1984/85
158	Cairns C.L. v South Africa at Auckland	2003/04
157	Horne M.J. v Zimbabwe at Auckland	1997/98
156*	Astle N.J. v Australia at Perth	2001/02
152	Lees W.K. v Pakistan at Karachi	1976/77
151*	Sutcliffe B. v India at Calcutta	1964/65
151*	Hadlee R.J. v Sri Lanka at Colombo	1986/87
150	Jones A.H. v Australia at Adelaide	1987/88
150	Sinclair M.S. v South Africa at Port Elizabeth	2000/01
148	Reid J.F. v Pakistan at Wellington	1984/85
147	Howarth G.P. v West Indies at Christchurch	1979/80
146*	Greatbatch M.J. v Australia at Perth	1989/90
146	Marshall H.J.H. v Australia at Christchurch	2004/05
145	Richardson M.H. v India at Mohali	2003/04
143	Dowling G.T. v India at Dunedin	1967/68

143	Crowe M.D. v England at Wellington	1987/88
143	Jones A.H. v England at Wellington	1991/92
143	Jones A.H. v Australia at Perth	1993/94
143	Richardson M.H. v Bangladesh at Hamilton	2001/02
143	McCullum B.B. v Bangladesh at Dhaka	2004/05
142	Reid J.R. v South Africa at Johannesburg	1961/62
142	Crowe M.D. v England at Lord's	1994
142	McMillan C.D. v Sri Lanka at Colombo	1997/98
142	McMillan C.D. v Zimbabwe at Wellington	2000/01
141	Wright J.G. v Australia at Christchurch	1981/82
141	Astle N.J. v Zimbabwe at Wellington	2000/01
140	Crowe M.D. v Zimbabwe at Harare	1992/93
139	McMillan C.D. v Zimbabwe at Wellington	1997/98
138	Sinclair B.W. v South Africa at Auckland	1963/64
138	Wright J.G. v West Indies at Wellington	1986/87
137*	Sutcliffe B. v India at Hyderabad	1955/56
137*	Howarth G.P. v India at Wellington	1980/81
137*	Vettori D.L. v Pakistan at Hamilton	2003/04
137	Crowe M.D. v Australia at Christchurch	1985/86
137	Crowe M.D. v Australia at Adelaide	1987/88
136	Dempster C.S. v England at Wellington	1929/30
135	Reid J.R. v South Africa at Cape Town	1953/54
133	Greatbatch M.J. v Pakistan at Hamilton	1992/93
133	Horne M.J. v Australia at Hobart	1997/98
133	Oram J.D.P. v South Africa at Centurion	2005/06
132	Congdon B.E. v Australia at Wellington	1973/74
130	Sinclair B.W. v Pakistan at Lahore	1964/65
130	Wright J.G. v England at Auckland	1983/84
130	Fleming S.P. v West Indies at Bridgetown	2001/02
129	Dowling G.T. v India at Bombay	1964/65
129	Edgar B.A. v Pakistan at Christchurch	1978/79
129	Fleming S.P. v England at Auckland	1996/97
128	Reid J.R. v Pakistan at Karachi	1964/65
128	Crowe J.J. v England at Auckland	1983/84
128	Astle N.J. v Zimbabwe at Bulawayo	2005/06
127	Edgar B.A. v West Indies at Auckland	1979/80
127	Vettori D.L. v Zimbabwe at Harare	2005/06
126*	Oram J.D.P. v Australia at Brisbane	2004/05
126	Congdon B.E. v West Indies at Bridgetown	1971/72
126	Cairns C.L. v India at Hamilton	1998/99
125	Astle N.J. v West Indies at Bridgetown	1995/96
124	Taylor B.R. v West Indies at Auckland	1967/68
124	Cairns C.L. v Zimbabwe at Harare	2000/01
123*	Reid J.F. v India at Christchurch	1980/81
123	Howarth G.P. v England at Lord's	1978
122*	Franklin J.E.C. v South Africa at Cape Town	2005/06
122	Howarth G.P. v England at Auckland	1977/78
122	Jones A.H. v Sri Lanka at Hamilton	1990/91
121	Parker J.M. v England at Auckland	1974/75
120*	Crowe J.J. v Sri Lanka at Colombo	1986/87
120*	Thomson S.A. v Pakistan at Christchurch	1993/94
120	Dempster C.S. v England at Lord's	1931
120	Reid J.R. v India at Calcutta	1955/56
120	Young B.A. v Pakistan at Christchurch	1993/94
120	Cairns C.L. v Zimbabwe at Auckland	1995/96
119*	Reid J.R. v India at Delhi	1955/56

119*	Burgess M.G. v Pakistan at Dacca	1969/70
119*	Oram J.D.P. v South Africa at Hamilton	2003/04
119	Wright J.G. v England at The Oval	1986
119	Crowe M.D. v West Indies at Wellington	1986/87
119	Latham R.T. v Zimbabwe at Bulawayo	1992/93
119	Styris S.B. v India at Mohali	2003/04
117*	Hastings B.F. v West Indies at Christchurch	1968/69
117*	Wright J.G. v Australia at Wellington	1989/90
117	Mills J.E. v England at Wellington	1929/30
117	Morrison J.F.M. v Australia at Sydney	1973/74
117	Turner G.M. v India at Christchurch	1975/76
117	Fleming S.P. v England at Nottingham	2004
116	Hadlee W.A. v England at Christchurch	1946/47
116	Sutcliffe B. v England at Christchurch	1950/51
116	Pollard V. v England at Nottingham	1973
116	Wright J.G. v England at Wellington	1991/92
115	Crowe M.D. v England at Manchester	1994
114	Sinclair B.W. v England at Auckland	1965/66
114	Howarth G.P. v Pakistan at Napier	1978/79
114	Astle N.J. v Zimbabwe at Auckland	1997/98
114	Astle N.J. v Sri Lanka at Napier	2004/05
113*	Smith I.D.S. v England at Auckland	1983/84
113*	Wright J.G. v India at Napier	1989/90
113	Turner G.M. v India at Kanpur	1976/77
113	Crowe M.D. v India at Auckland	1989/90
112	Crowe J.J. v West Indies at Kingston	1984/85
112	Spearman C.M. v Zimbabwe at Auckland	1995/96
111*	Coney J.V. v Pakistan at Dunedin	1984/85
111	McGregor S.N. v Pakistan at Lahore	1955/56
111	Burgess M.G. v Pakistan at Lahore	1976/77
111	McCullum B.B. v Zimbabwe at Harare	2005/06
110*	Turner G.M. v Australia at Christchurch	1973/74
110	Turner G.M. v Pakistan at Dacca	1969/70
110	Hastings B.F. v Pakistan at Auckland	1972/73
110	Wright J.G. v India at Auckland	1980/81
110	Bracewell J.G. v England at Nottingham	1986
110	Horne M.J. v Zimbabwe at Bulawayo	2000/01
110	Parore A.C. v Australia at Perth	2001/02
109	Barton P.T. v South Africa at Port Elizabeth	1961/62
109	Cairns C.L. v Australia at Wellington	1999/00
108*	Crowe M.D. v Pakistan at Lahore	1990/91
108	Parker J.M. v Australia at Sydney	1973/74
108	Reid J.F. v Australia at Brisbane	1985/86
108	Styris S.B. v England at Nottingham	2004
107*	Congdon B.E. v Australia at Christchurch	1976/77
107*	Greatbatch M.J. v England at Auckland	1987/88
107*	Rutherford K.R. v England at Wellington	1987/88
107*	McMillan C.D. v England at Manchester	1999
107	Rabone G.O. v South Africa at Durban	1953/54
107	Redmond R.E. v Pakistan at Auckland	1972/73
107	Wright J.G. v Pakistan at Karachi	1984/85
107	Crowe M.D. v Sri Lanka at Colombo	1992/93
107	Styris S.B. v West Indies at St George's	2001/02
106	Reid J.F. v Pakistan at Hyderabad	1984/85
106	Crowe M.D. v England at Lord's	1986
106	Richardson M.H. v Pakistan at Hamilton	2000/01

106	McMillan C.D. v Bangladesh at Hamilton	2001/02
106	Vincent L. v India at Mohali	2003/04
105*	Pollard V. v England at Lord's	1973
105	Taylor B.R. v India at Calcutta	1964/65
105	Hastings B.F. v West Indies at Bridgetown	1971/72
105	Burgess M.G. v England at Lord's	1973
105	Rutherford K.R. v Sri Lanka at Moratuwa	1992/93
105	Bell M.D. v Pakistan at Hamilton	2000/01
105	Fleming S.P. v Australia at Perth	2001/02
104	Page M.L. v England at Lord's	1931
104	Congdon B.E. v England at Christchurch	1965/66
104	Burgess M.G. v England at Auckland	1970/71
104	Parker J.M. v India at Bombay	1976/77
104	Crowe M.D. v West Indies at Auckland	1986/87
104	Vincent L. v Australia at Perth	2001/02]
103*	Styris S.B. v West Indies at Auckland	2005/06
103	Hadlee R.J. v West Indies at Christchurch	1979/80
103	Wright J.G. v England at Auckland	1987/88
103	Astle N.J. v West Indies at St John's	1995/96
103	Astle N.J. v India at Ahmedabad	2003/04
102*	Astle N.J. v England at Auckland	1996/97
102	Guy J.W. v India at Hyderabad	1955/56
102	Howarth G.P. v England at Auckland	1977/78
102	Rutherford K.R. v Australia at Christchurch	1992/93
101*	Coney J.V. v Australia at Wellington	1985/86
101	Sutcliffe B. v England at Manchester	1949
101	Harris P.G.Z. v South Africa at Cape Town	1961/62
101	Burgess M.G. v West Indies at Kingston	1971/72
101	Hastings B.F. v Australia at Wellington	1973/74
101	Turner G.M. v Australia at Christchurch	1973/74
101	Franklin T.J. v England at Lord's	1990
101	Wright J.G. v Sri Lanka at Hamilton	1990/91
101	Astle N.J. v England at Manchester	1999
101	Richardson M.H. v England at Lord's	2004
100*	Jones A.H. v Sri Lanka at Hamilton	1990/91
100*	Parore A.C. v West Indies at Christchurch	1994/95
100*	McMillan C.D. v India at Mohali	2003/04
100	Vivian H.G. v South Africa at Wellington	1931/32
100	Reid J.R. v England at Christchurch	1962/63
100	Crowe M.D. v England at Wellington	1983/84
100	Horne M.J. v England at Lord's	1999

Century on Test Debut

117 & 7	Mills J.E. v England at Wellington	1929/30
105 & 0*	Taylor B.R. v India at Calcutta	1964/65
107 & 56	Redmond R.E. v Pakistan at Auckland	1972/73
11 & 107*	Greatbatch M.J. v England at Auckland	1987/88
214	Sinclair M.S. v West Indies at Wellington	1999/00
104 & 54	Vincent L. v Australia at Perth	2001/02
107 & 69*	Styris S.B. v West Indies at St George's	2001/02

Centuries in Both Innings of a Test

101 & 110*	Turner G.M. v Australia at Christchurch	1973/74
122 & 102	Howarth G.P. v England at Auckland	1977/78
122 & 100*	Jones A.H. v Sri Lanka at Hamilton	1990/91

NB: *In the same match that Jones achieved this feat A.P. Gurusinha (119 & 102) also scored a century in each innings. This is only the second occasion that a player from each side has scored centuries in each innings of a test (A.R. Morris and D.C.S. Compton, Australia v England, Adelaide, 1946/47).*

200 Runs in a Test

343	Fleming S.P. (274* & 69*) v Sri Lanka at Colombo	2002/03
329	Crowe M.D. (30 & 299) v Sri Lanka at Wellington	1990/91
267	Young B.A. (267*) v Sri Lanka at Dunedin	1996/97
262	Fleming S.P. (262) v South Africa at Cape Town	2005/06
259	Turner G.M. (259) v West Indies at Georgetown	1971/72
254	Sinclair M.S. (204* & 50*) v Pakistan at Christchurch	2000/01
252	Fleming S.P. (78 & 174*) v Sri Lanka at Colombo	1997/98
248	Congdon B.E. (166* & 82) v West Indies at Port of Spain	1971/72
244	Dowling G.T. (239 & 5) v India at Christchurch	1967/68
244	Turner G.M. (223* & 21) v West Indies at Kingston	1971/72
232	Astle N.J. (10 & 222) v England at Christchurch	2001/02
230	Sutcliffe B. (230*) v India at Delhi	1955/56
224	Howarth G.P. (122 & 102) v England at Auckland	1977/78
224	Vincent L. (224) v Sri Lanka at Wellington	2004/05
222	Greatbatch M.J. (76 & 146*) v Australia at Perth	1989/90
222	Jones A.H. (122 & 100*) v Sri Lanka at Hamilton	1990/91
216	Dempster C.S. (136 & 80*) v England at Wellington	1929/30
214	Jones A.H. (150 & 64) v Australia at Adelaide	1987/88
214	Sinclair M.S. (214) v West Indies at Wellington	1999/00
213	Wright J.G. (75 & 138) v West Indies at Wellington	1986/87
211	Turner G.M. (101 & 110*) v Australia at Christchurch	1973/74
206	Donnelly M.P. (206) v England at Lord's	1949
204	Reid J.R. (128 & 76) v Pakistan at Karachi	1964/65
202	Reid J.R. (60 & 142) v South Africa at Johannesburg	1961/62
202	Fleming S.P. (202) v Bangladesh at Chittagong	2004/05
201	Coney J.V. (27 & 174*) v England at Wellington	1983/84
201	Crowe M.D. (140 & 61) v Zimbabwe at Harare	1992/93

A Century and a Fifty in a Test

136 & 80*	Dempster C.S. v England at Wellington	1929/30
52 & 120	Dempster C.S. v England at Lord's	1931
100 & 73	Vivian H.G. v South Africa at Wellington *(aged 19)*	1931/32
107 & 68	Rabone G.O. v South Africa at Durban	1953/54
60 & 142	Reid J.R. v South Africa at Johannesburg	1961/62
74 & 100	Reid J.R. v England at Christchurch	1962/63
128 & 76	Reid J.R. v Pakistan at Karachi	1964/65
59 & 119*	Burgess M.G. v Pakistan at Dacca	1969/70
166* & 82	Congdon B.E. v West Indies at Port of Spain	1971/72
107 & 56	Redmond R.E. v Pakistan at Auckland	1972/73
75 & 138	Wright J.G. v West Indies at Wellington	1986/87
150 & 64	Jones A.H. v Australia at Adelaide	1987/88
76 & 146*	Greatbatch M.J. v Australia at Perth	1989/90
140 & 61	Crowe M.D. v Zimbabwe at Harare	1992/93

105 & 53	Rutherford K.R. v Sri Lanka at Moratuwa	1992/93
57 & 102	Rutherford K.R. v Australia at Christchurch	1992/93
70 & 115	Crowe M.D. v England at Manchester	1994
57 & 120	Cairns C.L. v Zimbabwe at Auckland	1995/96
54 & 125	Astle N.J. v West Indies at Bridgetown	1995/96
78 & 174*	Fleming S.P. v Sri Lanka at Colombo	1997/98
109 & 69	Cairns C.L. v Australia at Wellington	1999/00
141 & 51*	Astle N.J. v Zimbabwe at Wellington	2000/01
204 & 50*	Sinclair M.S. v Pakistan at Christchurch	2000/01
104 & 54	Vincent L. v Australia at Perth	2001/02
107 & 69*	Styris S.B. v West Indies at St George's	2001/02
274* & 69*	Fleming S.P. v Sri Lanka at Colombo	2002/03
103 & 51	Astle N.J. v India at Ahmedabad	2003/04
93 & 101	Richardson M.H. v England at Lord's	2004

NB: *Redmond's feat of scoring a century and a fifty in his only test is unique. Only he and A.G. Ganteaume (112 WI v England, Port of Spain 1947/48) have made a century in their only test.*

Centuries in Three Successive Test Innings

Jones A.H. 186, Wellington, 122 and 100* Hamilton v Sri Lanka 1990/91

Centuries in Two Successive Test Innings

Reid J.R. 119*, Delhi and 120, Calcutta v India 1955/56
Burgess M.G. 119*, Dacca v Pakistan 1969/70 and 104, Auckland v England 1970/71
Congdon B.E. 176, Nottingham and 175, Lord's v England 1973
Pollard V. 116, Nottingham and 105*, Lord's v England 1973
Turner G.M. 101 and 110*, Christchurch v Australia 1973/74
Howarth G.P. 122 and 102, Auckland v England 1977/78 – 94 v England, Oval 1978
Crowe M.D. 143, Wellington v England 1987/88 and 174, Wellington v Pakistan 1988/89
Wright J.G. 185, Christchurch and 113* Napier v India 1989/90
Astle N.J. 125, Bridgetown and 103, St Johns v West Indies 1995/96

NB: *M.G. Burgess scored centuries in three successive tests — all played in different countries! He followed the two centuries above with 15 & 101 v West Indies at Kingston, 1971/72.*

B.E .Congdon scored centuries in successive tests v West Indies 1971/72 — 166 & 82 at Port of Spain and 126 at Bridgetown.*

G.T. Dowling did likewise with 143 & 10 at Dunedin and 239 & 5 at Christchurch v India 1967/68.

In successive tests v Pakistan 1984/85 J.F. Reid scored 106 & 21 at Hyderabad, 97 at Karachi, 148 & 3 at Wellington and 158 at Auckland.*

Fifty on Test Debut

3 & 51	Vivian H.G. v England at The Oval *(aged 18)*	1931
52 & 56	Wallace W.M. v England at Lord's	1937
64 & 0	Moloney D.A.R. v England at Lord's	1937
58	Sutcliffe B. v England at Christchurch	1946/47
50 & 25	Reid J.R. v England at Manchester	1949
93 & 64	Harford N.S. v Pakistan at Lahore	1955/56
54 & 23	Barton P.T. v South Africa at Durban	1961/62
74 & 58	Dowling G.T. v South Africa at Johannesburg	1961/62
64 & 1	Yuile B.W. v England at Auckland	1962/63
10 & 52	Gedye S.G. v South Africa at Wellington	1963/64
66 & 5	Morgan R.W. v Pakistan at Auckland	1964/65
17 & 54	Murray B.A.G. v India at Dunedin	1967/68
50 & 39	Burgess M.G. v India at Dunedin	1967/68
69 & 0*	Thomson K. v India at Christchurch	1967/68
6 & 51*	Howarth G.P. v England at Auckland	1974/75
14 & 92	Anderson R.W. v Pakistan at Lahore	1976/77
55 & 19	Wright J.G. v England at Wellington	1977/78
56 & 0*	Harris C.Z. v Sri Lanka at Moratuwa	1992/93

38 & 53	Young B.A. v Australia at Brisbane	1993/94
16 & 92	Fleming S.P. v India at Hamilton	1993/94
54 & 0	McMillan C.D. v Australia at Brisbane	1997/98
59 & 12	Papps M.H.W. v South Africa at Hamilton	2003/04
57 & 19*	McCullum B.B. v South Africa at Hamilton	2003/04
74 & 7	Cumming C.D. v Australia at Christchurch	2004/05

NB: *H.M. McGirr scored 51 in his first (and only) test innings but it was his second test appearance.*

Two Fifties in a Test

52 & 56	†Wallace W.M. v England at Lord's	1937
58 & 50	Vivian H.G. v England at Old Trafford	1937
96 & 54*	Smith F.B. v England at Headingley	1949
75 & 80	Donnelly M.P. v England at Old Trafford	1949
88 & 54	Sutcliffe B. v England at The Oval	1949
55 & 58	Wallace W.M. v England at The Oval	1949
93 & 64	†Harford N.S. v Pakistan at Lahore	1955/56
74 & 58	†Dowling G.T. v South Africa at Johannesburg	1961/62
55 & 55	Pollard V. v England at Lord's *(aged 19)*	1965
66 & 60	Burgess M.G. v India at Wellington	1967/68
58 & 58	Morrison J.F.M. v England at Auckland	1974/75
54 & 54	Congdon B.E. v India at Auckland	1975/76
55 & 54	Edwards G.N. v England at Auckland	1977/78
62 & 76	Edgar B.A. v England at Nottingham	1983
62 & 60	Howarth G.P. v Sri Lanka at Kandy	1983/84
57 & 84	Crowe M.D. v Pakistan at Dunedin	1984/85
50 & 52	Edgar B.A. v Australia at Sydney	1985/86
56 & 59	Wright J.G. v Australia at Auckland	1985/86
82 & 79	Crowe M.D. v Australia at Melbourne	1987/88
87 & 88	Greatbatch M.J. v Zimbabwe at Bulawayo	1992/93
74 & 89	Rutherford K.R. v Zimbabwe at Harare	1992/93
63 & 59	Rutherford K.R. v India at Hamilton	1993/94
79 & 53	Fleming S.P. v South Africa at Cape Town	1994/95
59 & 51*	Twose R.G. v Pakistan at Christchurch	1995/96
57 & 52	Cairns C.L. v England at Christchurch	1996/97
92 & 84	McMillan C.D. v India at Hamilton	1998/99
93 & 60	Horne M.J. v South Africa at Auckland	1998/99
57 & 99	Fleming S.P. v South Africa at Bloemfontein	2000/01
57 & 71	Vincent L. v England at Wellington	2001/02
95 & 71	Richardson M.H. v West Indies at St George's	2001/02
55 & 55	Richardson M.H. v Sri Lanka at Kandy	2002/03
54 & 83*	McMillan C.D. v India at Ahmedabad	2003/04

† on debut

Fifties in Successive Test Innings

The following reached 50 in four successive test innings:

Donnelly M.P. 62, 206, 75 & 80 v England, 1949
Sutcliffe B. 101, 88, 54 v England 1949 and 116 v England 1950/51
Congdon B.E. 166*, 82, 126 and 61* v West Indies 1971/72
54, 54, 58 & 52 v India 1975/76
Coney J.V. 101*, 98, 93 v Australia 1985/86 and 51 v England 1986
Rutherford K.R. 74, 89 v Zimbabwe and 105, 53 v Sri Lanka 1992/93

Highest Score in Each Batting Position

Position in batting order					
1 or 2	267*	Young B.A.	v Sri Lanka	Dunedin	1996/97
3	274*	Fleming S.P.	v Sri Lanka	Colombo	2002/03
4	299	Crowe M.D.	v Sri Lanka	Wellington	1990/91
5	222	Astle N.J.	v England	Christchurch	2001/02
6	174*	Coney J.V.	v England	Wellington	1983/84
7	158	Cairns C.L.	v South Africa	Auckland	2003/04
8	127	Vettori D.L.	v Zimbabwe	Harare	2005/06
9	173	Smith I.D.S.	v India	Auckland	1989/90
10	83*	Bracewell J.G.	v Australia	Sydney	1985/86
11	68*	Collinge R.O.	v Pakistan	Auckland	1972/73

Century Partnership for The First Wicket

					Final innings total
276	Dempster C.S. Mills J.E.	v England	Wellington	1929/30	440
133	Sutcliffe B. Hadlee W.A.	v England	Christchurch	1946/47	345-9d
112	Sutcliffe B. Scott V.J	v England	Leeds	1949	195-2
121	Sutcliffe B. Scott V.J.	v England	The Oval	1949	345
126	Rabone G.O. Chapple M.E.	v South Africa	Cape Town	1953/54	505
101	McGregor S.N. Leggat J.G.	v India	Delhi	1955/56	112-1
136	Dowling G.T. Jarvis T.W.	v Pakistan	Lahore	1964/65	482-6d
126	Dowling G.T. Murray B.A.G.	v India	Christchurch	1967/68	502
112	Dowling G.T. Turner G.M.	v West Indies	Auckland	1968/69	297-8d
115	Dowling G.T. Turner G.M.	v West Indies	Christchurch	1968/69	367-6
106	Dowling G.T. Murray B.A.G.	v India	Hyderabad	1969/70	181
387	Turner G.M. Jarvis T.W.	v West Indies	Georgetown	1971/72	543-3d
159	Redmond R.E. Turner G.M.	v Pakistan	Auckland	1972/73	402
107	Parker J.M. Turner G.M.	v Australia	Auckland	1973/74	158
100	Wright J.G. Edgar B.A.	v Australia	Sydney	1985/86	193

117	Wright J.G. Franklin T.J.	v England	Auckland	1987/88	350-7d
149	Wright J.G. Franklin T.J.	v India	Napier	1989/90	178-1
185	Wright J.G. Franklin T.J.	v England	Lord's	1990	462-9d
134	Franklin T.J. Wright J.G.	v Sri Lanka	Wellington	1990/91	671-4
161	Franklin T.J. Wright J.G.	v Sri Lanka	Hamilton	1990/91	374-6d
116	Greatbatch M.J. Latham R.T.	v Zimbabwe	Bulawayo	1992/93	325-3d
102	Greatbatch M.J. Latham R.T.	v Zimbabwe	Bulawayo	1992/93	222-5d
110	Hartland B.R. Wright J.G.	v Sri Lanka	Moratuwa	1992/93	195-5
110	Greatbatch M.J. Hartland B.R.	v Pakistan	Hamilton	1992/93	264
111	Greatbatch M.J. Wright J.G.	v Australia	Wellington	1992/93	329
214	Spearman C.M. Twose R.G.	v Zimbabwe	Auckland	1995/96	441-5d
107	Young B.A. Horne M.J.	v South Africa	Christchurch	1998/99	127-1
131	Horne M.J. Stead G.R.	v India	Ahmedabad	1999/00	252-2
102	Richardson M.H. Bell M.D.	v Pakistan	Christchurch	2000/01	476
181	Richardson M.H. Bell M.D.	v Pakistan	Hamilton	2000/01	407-4d
104	Richardson M.H. Horne M.J.	v Bangladesh	Wellington	2001/02	341-6d
117	Richardson M.H. Vincent L.	v West Indies	St George's	2001/02	256-5
231	Richardson M.H. Vincent L.	v India	Mohali	2003/04	630-6d
163	Richardson M.H. Fleming S.P.	v England	Nottingham	2004	384

Pairs in Test Matches Involving New Zealand

By New Zealand *(53)*

*James K.C. v England at Christchurch	1929/30
*Badcock F.T. v England at Christchurch	1929/30
Cowie J. v England at Manchester	1937
*Rowe C.G. v Australia at Wellington	1945/46
*Butterfield L.A. v Australia at Wellington	1945/46
Miller L.S.M. v South Africa at Johannesburg	1953/54
Poore M.B. v England at Auckland	1954/55
Colquhoun I.A. v England at Auckland	1954/55
Hayes J.A. v England at Auckland	1954/55
Blair R.W. v West Indies at Dunedin	1955/56
Cave H.B. v West Indies at Dunedin	1955/56
MacGibbon A.R. v India at Madras	1955/56
Harford N.S. v England at Leeds	1958
Motz R.C. v South Africa at Cape Town	1961/62
Blair R.W. v England at Christchurch	1962/63
Blair R.W. v South Africa at Auckland	1963/64
Shrimpton M.J.F. v South Africa at Auckland	1963/64
Dick A.E. v Pakistan at Rawalpindi	1964/65
Bartlett G.A. v England at Christchurch	1965/66
Jarvis T.W. v Pakistan at Wellington	1972/73
Lees W.K. v England at Christchurch	1977/78
*Bracewell B.P. v England at The Oval	1978
Cairns B.L. v Australia at Brisbane	1980/81
Edgar B.A. v Australia at Perth	1980/81
Troup G.B. v India at Wellington	1980/81
Coney J.V. v Australia at Christchurch	1981/82
Smith I.D.S. v Australia at Christchurch	1981/82
Bracewell J.G. v Pakistan at Hyderabad	1984/85
*Rutherford K.R. v West Indies at Port of Spain	1984/85
Wright J.G. v England at Lord's	1986
Morrison D.K. v Australia at Melbourne	1987/88
*Kuggeleijn C.M. v India at Bangalore	1988/89
Snedden M.C. v India at Hyderabad	1988/89
Morrison D.K. v Sri Lanka at Hamilton	1990/91
Hartland B.R. v England at Auckland	1991/92
Su'a M.L. v Pakistan at Hamilton	1992/93
Morrison D.K. v Australia at Hobart	1993/94
Doull S.B. v West Indies at Wellington	1994/95
Nash D.J. v Sri Lanka at Napier	1994/95
Harris C.Z. v West Indies at Bridgetown	1995/96
Patel D.N. v England at Auckland	1996/97
Doull S.B. v England at Wellington	1996/97
Fleming S.P. v Australia at Hobart	1997/98
Vettori D.L. v Sri Lanka at Galle	1997/98
Wiseman P.J. v India at Wellington	1998/99
Twose R.G. v England at Edgbaston	1999
Wiseman P.J. v India at Kanpur	1999/00
O'Connor S.B. v Australia at Hamilton	1999/00
*Franklin J.E.C. v Pakistan at Auckland	2000/01
Martin C.S. v Pakistan at Auckland	2000/01
Martin C.S. v Pakistan at Lahore	2001/02
Martin C.S. v Australia at Brisbane	2004/05
Martin C.S. v West Indies at Auckland	2005/06

Against New Zealand *(28)*

Javed Burki for Pakistan at Wellington	1964/65
Jaisimha M.L. for India at Hyderabad	1969/70
Knott A.P.E. for England at Lord's	1973
Stackpole K.R. for Australia at Auckland	1973/74
Chandrasekhar B.S. for India at Wellington	1975/76
Hendrick M. for England at Wellington	1977/78
Kallicharran A.I. for West Indies at Dunedin	1979/80
Wood G.M. for Australia at Perth	1980/81
Holland R.G. for Australia at Brisbane	1985/86
*Patel R.G. for India at Bombay	1988/89
Malcolm D.E. for England at Birmingham	1990
Waqar Younis for Pakistan at Faisalabad	1990/91
Aamer Sohail for Pakistan at Hamilton	1992/93
Langer J.L. for Australia at Auckland	1992/93
Streak H.H. for Zimbabwe at Harare	1997/98
Rennie G.J. for Zimbabwe at Auckland	1997/98
Mbangwa M. for Zimbabwe at Auckland	1997/98
Walsh C.A. for West Indies at Wellington	1999/00
Nkala M.L. for Zimbabwe at Harare	2000/01
Monjurul Islam for Bangladesh at Wellington	2001/02
Laxman V.V.S. for India at Wellington	2002/03
Khan Z. for India at Hamilton	2002/03
Tareq Aziz for Bangladesh at Dhaka	2004/05
Mohammad Ashraful for Bangladesh at Chittagong	2004/05
Mpofu C.B. for Zimbabwe at Harare	2005/06
*Silva L.P.C. for Sri Lanka at Christchurch	2006/07
Malinga S.L. for Sri Lanka at Wellington	2006/07
Muralitharan M. for Sri Lanka at Wellington	2006/07

** on debut*

BOWLING

Ten Wickets in a Match

(22 instances)

15-123	Hadlee R.J. v Australia at Brisbane	1985/86
12-149	Vettori D.L. v Australia at Auckland	1999/00
12-170	Vettori D.L. v Bangladesh at Chittagong	2004/05
11-58	Hadlee R.J. v India at Wellington	1975/76
11-102	Hadlee R.J. v West Indies at Dunedin	1979/80
11-152	Pringle C. v Pakistan at Faisalabad	1990/91
11-155	Hadlee R.J. v Australia at Perth	1985/86
11-169	Nash D.J. v England at Lord's	1994
11-180	Martin C.S. v South Africa at Auckland	2003/04
10-88	Hadlee R.J. v India at Bombay	1988/89
10-99	Bond S.E. v Zimbabwe at Bulawayo	2005/06
10-100	Hadlee R.J. v England at Wellington	1977/78
10-100	Cairns C.L. v West Indies at Hamilton	1999/00
10-102	Hadlee R.J. v Sri Lanka at Colombo	1983/84
10-106	Bracewell J.G. v Australia at Auckland	1985/86
10-124	Chatfield E.J. v West Indies at Port of Spain	1984/85
10-140	Cowie J. v England at Manchester	1937
10-140	Hadlee R.J. v England at Nottingham	1986
10-144	Cairns B.L. v England at Leeds	1983
10-166	Troup G.B. v West Indies at Auckland	1979/80
10-176	Hadlee R.J. v Australia at Melbourne	1987/88
10-183	Vettori D.L. v Sri Lanka at Wellington	2006/07

Five Wickets in an Innings

(163 instances)

9-52	Hadlee R.J. v Australia at Brisbane	1985/86
7-23	Hadlee R.J. v India at Wellington	1975/76
7-27	Cairns C.L. v West Indies at Hamilton	1999/00
7-52	Pringle C. v Pakistan at Faisalabad	1990/91
7-53	Cairns C.L. v Bangladesh at Hamilton	2001/02
7-65	Doull S.B. v India at Wellington	1998/99
7-74	Taylor B.R. v West Indies at Bridgetown	1971/72
7-74	Cairns B.L. v England at Leeds	1983
7-87	Boock S.L. v Pakistan at Hyderabad	1984/85
7-87	Vettori D.L. v Australia at Auckland	1999/00
7-89	Morrison D.K. v Australia at Wellington	1992/93
7-116	Hadlee R.J. v Australia at Christchurch	1985/86
7-130	Vettori D.L. v Sri Lanka at Wellington	2006/07
7-143	Cairns B.L. v England at Wellington	1983/84
6-26	Hadlee R.J. v England at Wellington	1977/78
6-27	Nash D.J. v India at Mohali	1999/00
6-28	Vettori D.L. v Bangladesh at Dhaka	2004/05
6-32	Bracewell J.G. v Australia at Auckland	1985/86
6-37	Morrison D.K. v Australia at Auckland	1992/93
6-38	Bartlett G.A. v India at Christchurch	1967/68
6-40	Cowie J. v Australia at Wellington	1945/46
6-46	Butler I.G. v Pakistan at Wellington	2003/04
6-49	Hadlee R.J. v India at Bombay	1988/89
6-50	Hadlee R.J. v West Indies at Christchurch	1986/87
6-50	Patel D.N. v Zimbabwe at Harare	1992/93

6-51	Hadlee R.J. v Pakistan at Dunedin	1984/85
6-51	Bracewell J.G. v India at Bombay	1988/89
6-51	Bond S.E. v Zimbabwe at Bulawayo	2005/06
6-52	Cairns C.L. v England at Auckland	1991/92
6-53	Hadlee R.J. v England at The Oval	1983
6-54	Tuffey D.R. v England at Auckland	2001/02
6-54	Martin C.S. v Sri Lanka at Wellington	2004/05
6-57	Hadlee R.J. v Australia at Melbourne	1980/81
6-60	Reid J.R. v South Africa at Dunedin	1963/64
6-63	Motz R.C. v India at Christchurch	1967/68
6-63	Collinge R.O. v India at Christchurch	1975/76
6-64	Vettori D.L. v Sri Lanka at Colombo	1997/98
6-67	Cowie J. v England at Manchester	1937
6-68	Rabone G.O. v South Africa at Cape Town	1953/54
6-68	Hadlee R.J. v West Indies at Dunedin	1979/80
6-69	Motz R.C. v West Indies at Wellington	1968/69
6-69	Morrison D.K. v West Indies at Christchurch	1994/95
6-70	Vettori D.L. v Bangladesh at Chittagong	2004/05
6-71	Hadlee R.J. v Australia at Brisbane	1985/86
6-73	Chatfield E.J. v West Indies at Port of Spain	1984/85
6-76	Cunis R.S. v England at Auckland	1970/71
6-76	Nash D.J. v England at Lord's	1994
6-76	Martin C.S. v South Africa at Auckland	2003/04
6-77	Cairns C.L. v England at Lord's	1999
6-78	Watson W. v Pakistan at Lahore	1990/91
6-80	Hadlee R.J. v England at Lord's	1986
6-80	Hadlee R.J. v England at Nottingham	1986
6-83	Cowie J. v England at Christchurch	1946/47
6-85	Cairns B.L. v West Indies at Christchurch	1979/80
6-85	Bracewell J.G. v Australia at Wellington	1989/90
6-87	Vettori D.L. v Australia at Perth	2001/02
6-90	Hadlee R.J. v Australia at Perth	1985/86
6-95	Troup G.B. v West Indies at Auckland	1979/80
6-100	Hadlee R.J. v Australia at Christchurch	1981/82
6-100	Vettori D.L. v Bangladesh at Chittagong	2004/05
6-105	Hadlee R.J. v West Indies at Auckland	1986/87
6-113	Patel D.N. v Zimbabwe at Bulawayo	1992/93
6-119	Franklin J.E.C v Australia at Auckland	2004/05
6-127	Vettori D.L. v India at Kanpur	1999/00
*6-155	Moir A.M. v England at Christchurch	1950/51
6-162	Burtt T.B. v England at Manchester	1949
*6-168	Cresswell G.F. v England at The Oval	1949
5-26	Taylor B.R. v India at Bombay	1964/65
5-28	Hadlee R.J. v England at Christchurch	1983/84
5-28	Boock S.L. v Sri Lanka at Kandy	1983/84
5-28	Franklin J.E.C v Bangladesh at Dhaka	2004/05
5-29	Hadlee R.J. v Sri Lanka at Colombo	1983/84
5-31	Cairns C.L. v England at The Oval	1999
5-31	Cairns C.L. v Zimbabwe at Bulawayo	2000/01
5-33	Cairns B.L. v India at Wellington	1980/81
5-34	Cameron F.J. v Pakistan at Auckland	1964/65
5-34	Howarth H.J. v India at Nagpur	1969/70
5-34	Hadlee R.J. v West Indies at Dunedin	1979/80
5-37	Martin C.S. v South Africa at Johannesburg	2005/06
5-39	Hadlee R.J. v Australia at Wellington	1989/90

5-41	Taylor B.R. v West Indies at Port of Spain	1971/72
5-41	Morrison D.K. v Pakistan at Hamilton	1992/93
5-44	Cairns C.L. v West Indies at Wellington	1999/00
5-46	Doull S.B. v Pakistan at Lahore	1996/97
5-47	Hadlee R.J. v India at Christchurch	1980/81
5-48	Cameron F.J. v South Africa at Cape Town	1961/62
5-50	Cairns C.L. v Zimbabwe at Harare	1997/98
5-51	O'Connor S.B. v Australia at Hamilton	1999/00
5-53	Hadlee R.J. v England at Birmingham	1990
5-53	Franklin J.E.C. v West Indies at Wellington	2005/06
5-55	Cairns B.L. v India at Madras	1976/77
5-55	Martin C.S. v South Africa at Wellington	2003/04
5-58	Doull S.B. v Sri Lanka at Dunedin	1996/97
5-61	Morrison D.K. v West Indies at St Johns	1995/96
5-62	Moir A.M. v England at Auckland	1954/55
5-62	Hadlee R.J. v Pakistan at Christchurch	1978/79
5-62	Cairns C.L. v Sri Lanka at Colombo	1997/98
5-62	Vettori D.L. v Australia at Auckland	1999/00
5-63	Hadlee R.J. v Australia at Auckland	1981/82
5-63	Chatfield E.J. v Sri Lanka at Colombo	1983/84
5-63	Davis H.T. v Sri Lanka at Hamilton	1996/97
5-64	MacGibbon A.R. v England at Birmingham	1958
5-65	Congdon B.E. v India at Auckland	1975/76
5-65	Hadlee R.J. v Australia at Sydney	1985/86
5-65	Hadlee R.J. v Australia at Perth	1985/86
5-65	Hadlee R.J. v India at Bangalore	1988/89
5-66	Doull S.B. v Pakistan at Auckland	1993/94
5-67	Boock S.L. v England at Auckland	1977/78
5-67	Hadlee R.J. v Australia at Melbourne	1987/88
5-68	Snedden M.C. v West Indies at Christchurch	1986/87
5-68	Hadlee R.J. v Australia at Adelaide	1987/88
5-69	Burtt T.B. v West Indies at Christchurch	1951/52
5-69	Morrison D.K. v England at Christchurch	1987/88
5-69	Bond S.E. v West Indies at Auckland	2005/06
5-71	Martin C.S. v Zimbabwe at Wellington	2000/01
5-73	Hadlee R.J. v Sri Lanka at Colombo	1983/84
5-73	Su'a M.L. v Pakistan at Hamilton	1992/93
5-73	Doull S.B. v South Africa at Durban	1994/95
5-74	Collinge R.O. v England at Leeds	1973
5-75	Bracewell J.G. v India at Auckland	1980/81
5-75	Morrison D.K. v India at Christchurch	1989/90
5-75	Cairns C.L. v Sri Lanka at Auckland	1990/91
5-75	Doull S.B. v England at Wellington	1996/97
5-77	Hart M.N. v South Africa at Johannesburg	1994/95
5-78	Bond S.E. v West Indies at Bridgetown	2001/02
5-79	Cairns C.L. v England at Nottingham	2004
5-80	Howarth H.J. v Pakistan at Karachi	1969/70
5-82	Collinge R.O. v Australia at Auckland	1973/74
*5-82	Wiseman P.J. v Sri Lanka at Colombo	1997/98
5-83	Cameron F.J. v South Africa at Johannesburg	1961/62
5-84	Hadlee R.J. v England at Lord's	1978
5-84	Vettori D.L. v Sri Lanka at Hamilton	1996/97
5-85	Su'a M.L. v Zimbabwe at Harare	1992/93
*5-86	Taylor B.R. v India at Calcutta	1964/65
5-86	Motz R.C. v India at Dunedin	1967/68

5-87	Cairns B.L. v Australia at Brisbane	1980/81
5-87	Hadlee R.J. v Australia at Perth	1980/81
5-87	Tuffey D.R. v Pakistan at Hamilton	2003/04
5-90	Wiseman P.J. v Zimabwe at Bulawayo	2000/01
5-93	Hadlee R.J. v England at Lord's	1983
5-93	Patel D.N. v Australia at Auckland	1992/93
5-93	Nash D.J. v England at Lord's	1994
5-95	Chatfield E.J. v England at Leeds	1983
5-97	Burtt T.B. v England at Leeds	1949
5-98	Morrison D.K. v India at Napier	1989/90
5-104	Hadlee R.J. v Pakistan at Auckland	1978/79
5-104	Bond S.E. v West Indies at St George's	2001/02
5-104	Martin C.S. v South Africa at Auckland	2003/04
5-106	Vettori D.L. v Australia at Christchurch	2004/05
5-108	Motz R.C. v England at Birmingham	1965
5-109	Hadlee R.J. v Australia at Melbourne	1987/88
5-113	Motz R.C. v West Indies at Christchurch	1968/69
5-117	Boock S.L. v Pakistan at Wellington	1984/85
5-121	Hadlee R.J. v Pakistan at Lahore	1976/77
5-127	Cowie J. v England at Leeds	1949
5-137	Cairns C.L. v Pakistan at Rawalpindi	1996/97
5-138	Vettori D.L. v Australia at Hobart	2001/02
5-145	Morrison D.K. v India at Auckland	1989/90
5-146	Cairns C.L. v Australia at Brisbane	2001/02
5-148	O'Sullivan D.R. v Australia at Adelaide	1973/74
5-152	Martin C.S. v Australia at Brisbane	2004/05
5-152	Vettori D.L. v Australia at Adelaide	2004/05
5-153	Morrison D.K. v Sri Lanka at Wellington	1990/91

** on debut*

Hat-tricks

Petherick P.J. v Pakistan at Lahore	1976/77
Franklin J.E.C. v Bangladesh at Dhaka	2004/05

All Round Cricket

Rabone G.O. 56 and 6-68 & 1-16 v South Africa at Cape Town	1953/54
Taylor B.R. 105 & 0 and 5-86 v India at Calcutta	1964/65
Congdon B.E. 54 & 54 and 5-65 v India at Auckland	1975/76
Hadlee R.J. 54* & 5 and 5-104 & 0-8 v Pakistan at Auckland	1978/79
Hadlee R.J. 51 & 17 and 5-34 & 6-68 v West Indies at Dunedin	1979/80
Hadlee R.J. 84 & 11 and 6-53 & 2-99 v England at The Oval	1983
Cairns B.L. 3 & 64 and 7-143 v England at Wellington	1983/84
Hadlee R.J. 99 and 3-16 & 5-28 v England at Christchurch	1983/84
Hadlee R.J. 54 and 9-52 & 6-71 v Australia at Brisbane	1985/86
Hadlee R.J. 68 and 6-80 & 4-60 v England at Nottingham	1986
Bracewell J.G. 52 & 32 and 2-81 & 6-51 v India at Bombay	1988/89
Patel D.N. 6 & 58* and 2-81 & 6-50 v Zimbabwe at Harare	1992/93
Nash D.J. 56 and 6-76 & 5-93 v England at Lord's	1994
Cairns C.L. 12 & 71* and 5-50 & 0-44 v Zimbabwe at Harare	1997/98
Cairns C.L. 11 & 80 and 5-31 & 1-50 v England at The Oval	1999
Cairns C.L. 72 and 3-73 & 7-27 v West Indies at Hamilton	1999/00
Cairns C.L. 61 & 43 and 5-146 & 1-29 v Australia at Brisbane	2001/02
Vettori D.L. 20 & 59 and 5-152 & 1-35 v Australia at Adelaide	2004/05
Vettori D.L. 0 & 51 and 3-53 & 7-130 v Sri Lanka at Wellington	2006/07

** Taylor is the only player from any country to score a century and take five wickets in an innings on debut.*

WICKETKEEPING AND FIELDING

MOST DISMISSALS IN AN INNINGS BY A WICKETKEEPER

7*	Smith I.D.S. v Sri Lanka at Hamilton *(all caught)*	1990/91
5	Harford R.I. v India at Wellington *(all caught)*	1967/68
5	Wadsworth K.J. v Pakistan at Auckland *(all caught)*	1972/73
5	Lees W.K. v Sri Lanka at Wellington *(all caught)*	1982/83
5	Smith I.D.S. v England at Auckland *(4ct 1st)*	1983/84
5	Smith I.D.S. v Sri Lanka at Auckland *(all caught)*	1990/91
5	Parore A.C. v England at Auckland *(all caught)*	1991/92
5	Parore A.C. v Sri Lanka at Colombo *(4ct 1st)*	1992/93
5	Parore A.C. v Zimbabwe at Harare *(all caught)*	2000/01
5	Parore A.C. v Pakistan at Auckland *(all caught)*	2000/01

** equals world test record*

MOST DISMISSALS IN A MATCH

8	Lees W.K. v Sri Lanka at Wellington *(all caught)*	1982/83
8	Smith I.D.S. v Sri Lanka at Hamilton *(all caught)*	1990/91
7	Dick A.E. v South Africa at Durban *(6ct 1st)*	1961/62
7	Harford R.I. v India at Wellington *(all caught)*	1967/68
7	Smith I.D.S. v India at Wellington *(all caught)*	1980/81
7	Smith I.D.S. v England at Leeds *(all caught)*	1983
7	Parore A.C. v Pakistan at Auckland *(all caught)*	2000/01
7	Parore A.C. v Pakistan at Hamilton *(all caught)*	2000/01

MOST STUMPINGS IN AN INNINGS

2	Mooney F.L.H. v England at Leeds	1949
2	Milburn B.D. v West Indies at Christchurch	1968/69
2	Lees W.K. v Pakistan at Hyderabad	1976/77
2	Lees W.K. v Pakistan at Karachi	1976/77
2	Lees W.K. v India at Madras	1976/77

MOST STUMPINGS IN A MATCH

2	5 instances as above plus	
	Smith I.D.S. v Australia at Sydney	1985/86
	Parore A.C. v Australia at Auckland	1999/00
	McCullum B.B. v Zimbabwe at Harare	2005/06

REPLACEMENT WICKETKEEPERS IN TEST MATCHES

Wicketkeeper	*Replacement*	*Dismissal*			
Mooney F.L.H.	Sutcliffe B.	—	v South Africa	Port Elizabeth	1953/54
Petrie E.C.	Reid J.R.	Richardson P.E. *(st)*	v England	Manchester	1958
Petrie E.C.	Reid J.R.	—	v England	Christchurch	1958/59
Ward J.T.	Morgan R.W.	Jaisimha M.L. *(c)*	v India	Calcutta	1964/65
Ward J.T.	Congdon B.E.	Hanumant Singh *(c)*	v India	Delhi	1964/65
Dick A.E.	Reid J.R.	—	v Pakistan	Lahore	1964/65
Dick A.E.	Congdon B.E. (sub)	Pervez Sajjad *(st)*	v Pakistan	Lahore	1964/65
Lees W.K.	Anderson R.W.	—	v Pakistan	Hyderabad	1976/77
Smith I.D.S.	Edgar B.A.	Laird B.M. *(c)*	v Australia	Christchurch	1981/82
Smith I.D.S.	Crowe M.D.	—	v West Indies	Kingston	1984/85
Smith I.D.S.	Horne P.A.	—	v Australia	Melbourne	1987/88
Smith I.D.S.	Blain T.E.	—	v India	Hyderabad	1988/89
Smith I.D.S.	Horne P.A.	—	v Pakistan	Faisalabad	1990/91
Smith I.D.S.	Parore A.C. (sub)	Shoaib Mohammad *(c)* Aaqib Javed *(c)*	v Pakistan	Faisalabad	1990/91
McCullum B.B.	Sinclair M.S.	Jayawardene D.P.M.D.	v Sri Lanka	Wellington	2006/07

MOST CATCHES IN AN INNINGS

5	Fleming S.P. v Zimbabwe at Harare	1997/98
4	Crowe J.J. v West Indies at Bridgetown	1984/85
4	Crowe M.D. v West Indies at Kingston	1984/85
4	Fleming S.P. v Australia at Brisbane	1997/98
4	Fleming S.P. v Zimbawe at Harare	2005/06
4	Fleming S.P. v West Indies at Wellington	2005/06

MOST CATCHES IN A MATCH

7	Fleming S.P. v Zimbabwe at Harare	1997/98
6	Young B.A. v Pakistan at Auckland	1993/94
6	Fleming S.P. v Australia at Brisbane	1997/98
6	Fleming S.P. v West Indies at Wellington	2005/06
5	Harris C.Z. v Zimbabwe at Bulawayo	1997/98
5	Fleming S.P. v India at Wellington	1998/99
5	Sinclair M.S. v Bangladesh at Chittagong	2004/05

RECORD PARTNERSHIPS

NEW ZEALAND v ENGLAND

New Zealand

1st	276	Dempster C.S. & Mills J.E.	Wellington	1929/30
2nd	241	Wright J.G. & Jones A.H.	Wellington	1991/92
3rd	210	Edgar B.A. & Crowe M.D.	Lord's	1986
4th	155	Crowe M.D. & Greatbatch M.J.	Wellington	1987/88
5th	180	Crowe M.D. & Thomson S.A.	Lord's	1994
6th	141	Crowe M.D. & Parore A.C.	Manchester	1994
7th	117	Patel D.N. & Cairns C.L.	Christchurch	1991/92
8th	104	Roberts A.W. & Moloney D.A.R.	Lord's	1937
9th	118	Coney J.V. & Cairns B.L.	Wellington	1983/84
10th	118	Astle N.J. & Cairns C.L.	Christchurch	2001/02

England

1st	223	Fowler G. & Tavare C.J.	The Oval	1983
2nd	369	Edrich J.H. & Barrington K.F.	Leeds	1965
3rd	245	Hammond W.R. & Hardstaff J.	Lord's	1937
4th	266	Denness M.H. & Fletcher K.W.R.	Auckland	1974/75
5th	242	Hammond W.R. & Ames L.E.G.	Christchurch	1932/33
6th	281	Thorpe G.P. & Flintoff A.	Christchurch	2001/02
7th	149	Knott A.P.E. & Lever P.	Auckland	1970/71
8th	246	Ames L.E.G. & Allen G.O.B.	Lord's	1931
9th	163*	Cowdrey M.C. & Smith A.C.	Wellington	1962/63
10th	59	Knott A.P.E. & Gifford N.	Nottingham	1973

NEW ZEALAND v AUSTRALIA

New Zealand

1st	111	Greatbatch M.J. & Wright J.G.	Wellington	1992/93
2nd	132	Horne M.J. & Parore A.C.	Hobart	1997/98
3rd	224	Reid J.F. & Crowe M.D.	Brisbane	1985/86
4th	229	Congdon B.E. & Hastings B.F.	Wellington	1973/74
5th	97	Fleming S.P. & McMillan C.D.	Hobart	2001/02
6th	110	Fleming S.P. & Cairns C.L.	Wellington	1999/00
7th	132*	Coney J.V. & Hadlee R.J.	Wellington	1985/86
8th	253	Astle N.J. & Parore A.C.	Perth	2001/02
9th	73	Howarth H.J. & Hadlee D.R.	Christchurch	1976/77
10th	124	Bracewell J.G. & Boock S.L.	Sydney	1985/86

Australia

1st	224	Langer J.L. & Hayden M.L.	Brisbane	2001/02
2nd	235	Slater M.J. & Boon D.C.	Hobart	1993/94
3rd	264	Chappell I.M. & Chappell G.S.	Wellington	1973/74
4th	184	Langer J.L. & Lehmann D.S.	Adelaide	2004/05
5th	213	Ritchie G.M. & Matthews G.R.J.	Wellington	1985/86
6th	256	Martyn D.R. & Gilchrist A.C.	Wellington	2004/05
7th	217	Walters K.D. & Gilmour G.J.	Christchurch	1976/77
8th	135	Gilchrist A.C. & Lee B.	Brisbane	2001/02
9th	74	Gilchrist A.C. & Kasprowicz M.S.	Auckland	2004/05
10th	114	Gillespie J.N. & McGrath G.D.	Brisbane	2004/05

NEW ZEALAND v SOUTH AFRICA

New Zealand

1st	126	Rabone G.O. & Chapple M.E.	Cape Town	1953/54
2nd	90	Horne M.J. & Astle N.J.	Auckland	1998/99
3rd	125	Richardson M.H. & Styris S.B.	Auckland	2003/04
4th	171	Sinclair B.W. & McGregor S.N.	Auckland	1963/64
5th	176	Reid J.R. & Beck J.E.F.	Cape Town	1953/54
6th	100	Vivian H.G. & Badcock F.T.	Wellington	1931/32
7th	225	Cairns C.L. & Oram J.D.P.	Auckland	2003/04
8th	256	Fleming S.P. & Franklin J.E.C.	Cape Town	2005/06
9th	87	Oram J.D.P. & Wiseman P.J.	Hamilton	2003/04
10th	57	Doull S.B. & de Groen R.P.	Johannesburg	1994/95

South Africa

1st	196	Mitchell B. & Christy J.A.H.	Christchurch	1931/32
2nd	315*	Gibbs H.H. & Kallis J.H.	Christchurch	1998/99
3rd	183	Kirsten G. & Cullinan D.J.	Auckland	1998/99
4th	171	Smith G.C. & Kirsten G.	Wellington	2003/04
5th	141	Cullinan D.J. & Rhodes J.N.	Auckland	1998/99
6th	126*	Cullinan D.J. & Pollock S.M.	Auckland	1998/99
7th	246	McGlew D.J. & Murray A.R.A.	Wellington	1952/53
8th	136	McKenzie N.D. & Boje N.	Port Elizabeth	2000/01
9th	60	Pollock P.M. & Adcock N.A.T.	Port Elizabeth	1961/62
10th	47	McGlew D.J. & Bromfield H.D.	Port Elizabeth	1961/62

NEW ZEALAND v WEST INDIES

New Zealand

1st	387	Turner G.M. & Jarvis T.W.	Georgetown	1971/72
2nd	210	Howarth G.P. & Crowe J.J.	Kingston	1984/85
3rd	241	Wright J.G. & Crowe M.D.	Wellington	1986/87
4th	189	Sinclair M.S. & Astle N.J.	Wellington	1999/00
5th	144	Astle N.J. & Vaughan J.T.C.	Bridgetown	1995/96
6th	220	Turner G.M. & Wadsworth K.J.	Kingston	1971/72
7th	143	Crowe M.D. & Smith I.D.S.	Georgetown	1984/85
8th	136	Congdon B.E. & Cunis R.S.	Port of Spain	1971/72
9th	62*	Pollard V. & Cunis R.S.	Auckland	1968/69
	62	McCullum B.B. & Bond S.E.	Auckland	2005/06
10th	45	Morrison D.K. & Kennedy R.J.	Bridgetown	1995/96

West Indies

1st	276	Griffith A.F.G. & Campbell S.L.	Hamilton	1999/00
2nd	269	Fredericks R.C. & Rowe L.G.	Kingston	1971/72
3rd	221	Lara B.C. & Adams J.C.	Wellington	1994/95
4th	162	Weekes E.D. & Smith O.G.	Dunedin	1955/56
	162	Greenidge C.G. & Kallicharan A.I.	Christchurch	1979/80
5th	189	Worrell F.M.M. & Walcott C.L.	Auckland	1951/52
6th	254	Sobers G.S. & Davis C.A.	Bridgetown	1971/72
7th	143	Atkinson D.S. & Goddard J.D.C.	Christchurch	1955/56
8th	83	Richards I.V.A. & Marshall M.D.	Bridgetown	1984/85
9th	70	Marshall M.D. & Garner J.	Bridgetown	1984/85
10th	31	Findlay T.M. & Shillingford G.C.	Bridgetown	1971/72

NEW ZEALAND v INDIA

New Zealand

1st	231	Richardson M.H. & Vincent L.	Mohali	2003/04
2nd	155	Dowling G.T. & Congdon B.E.	Dunedin	1967/68
3rd	222*	Sutcliffe B. & Reid J.R.	New Delhi	1955/56
4th	160	Twose R.G. & McMillan C.D.	Hamilton	1998/99
5th	140	McMillan C.D. & Parore A.C.	Hamilton	1998/99
6th	137	McMillan C.D. & Cairns C.L.	Wellington	1998/99
7th	163	Sutcliffe B. & Taylor B.R.	Calcutta	1964/65
8th	137	Nash D.J. & Vettori D.L.	Wellington	1998/99
9th	136	Smith I.D.S. & Snedden M.C.	Auckland	1989/90
10th	61	Ward J.T. & Collinge R.O.	Madras	1964/65

India

1st	413	Mankad M.H. & Roy P.	Madras	1955/56
2nd	204	Gavaskar S.M. & Amarnath S.	Auckland	1975/76
3rd	238	Umrigar P.R. & Manjrekar V.L.	Hyderabad	1955/56
4th	281	Tendulkar S.R. & Ganguly S.C.	Ahmedabad	1999/00
5th	182	Dravid R.S. & Ganguly S.C.	Ahmedabad	2003/04
6th	193*	Sardesai D.N. & Hanumant Singh	Bombay	1964/65
7th	128	Tendulkar S.R. & More K.S.	Napier	1989/90
8th	144	Dravid R.S. & Srinath J.	Hamilton	1998/99
9th	105	Kirmani S.M.H. & Bedi B.S.	Bombay	1976/77
	105	Kirmani S.M.H. & Yadav N.S.	Auckland	1980/81
10th	57	Desai R.B. & Bedi B.S.	Dunedin	1967/68

NEW ZEALAND v PAKISTAN

New Zealand

1st	181	Richardson M.H. & Bell M.D.	Hamilton	2000/01
2nd	195	Wright J.G. & Howarth G.P.	Napier	1978/79
3rd	178	Sinclair B.W. & Reid J.R.	Lahore	1964/65
4th	147	McMillan C.D. & Fleming S.P.	Hamilton	2000/01
5th	183	Burgess M.G. & Anderson R.W.	Lahore	1976/77
6th	145	Reid J.F. & Hadlee R.J.	Wellington	1984/85
7th	186	Lees W.K. & Hadlee R.J.	Karachi	1976/77
8th	125	Fleming S.P. & Vettori D.L.	Hamilton	2003/04
9th	99	Vettori D.L. & Tuffey D.R.	Hamilton	2003/04
10th	151	Hastings B.F. & Collinge R.O.	Auckland	1972/73

Pakistan

1st	172	Rameez Raja & Shoaib Mohammad	Karachi	1990/91
2nd	262	Saeed Anwar & Ijaz Ahmed	Rawalpindi	1996/97
3rd	248	Shoaib Mohammad & Javed Miandad	Auckland	1988/89
4th	350	Mushtaq Mohammad & Asif Iqbal	Dunedin	1972/73
5th	281	Javed Miandad & Asif Iqbal	Lahore	1976/77
6th	217	Hanif Mohammad & Majid Khan	Lahore	1964/65
7th	308	Waqar Hassan & Imtiaz Ahmed	Lahore	1955/56
8th	89	Anil Dalpat & Iqbal Qasim	Karachi	1984/85
9th	78	Inzamam-ul-Haq & Shoaib Akhtar	Lahore	2001/02
10th	65	Salah-ud-din & Mohammad Farooq	Rawalpindi	1964/65

NEW ZEALAND v SRI LANKA

New Zealand

1st	161	Franklin T.J. & Wright J.G.	Hamilton	1990/91
2nd	172	Richardson M.H. & Fleming S.P.	Colombo	2002/03
3rd	467	Jones A.H. & Crowe M.D.	Wellington	1990/91
4th	240	Fleming S.P. & McMillan C.D.	Colombo	1997/98
5th	151	Rutherford K.R. & Harris C.Z.	Moratuwa	1992/93
6th	246*	Crowe J.J. & Hadlee R.J.	Colombo	1986/87
7th	75	Fleming S.P. & Vettori D.L.	Christchurch	2006/07
8th	98	Vincent L. & Mills K.D.	Wellington	2004/05
9th	59	Vincent L. & Wiseman P.J.	Wellington	2004/05
10th	52	Lees W.K. & Chatfield E.J.	Christchurch	1982/83

Sri Lanka

1st	102	Mahanama R.S. & Hathurusinghe U.C.	Colombo	1992/93
2nd	138	Mahanama R.S. & Gurusinha A.P.	Moratuwa	1992/93
3rd	184	Atapattu M.S. & Jayawardene D.P.M.D.	Napier	2004/05
4th	192	Gurusinha A.P. & Tillakaratne H.P.	Dunedin	1994/95
5th	133	Jayawardene D.P.M.D. & Tillakaratne H.P.	Colombo	2002/03
6th	109	Madugalle R.S. & Ranatunga A.	Colombo	1983/84
	109	Kuruppu D.S.B.P. & Madugalle R.S.	Colombo	1986/87
7th	137	Kaluwitharana R.S. & Vaas W.P.J.U.C.	Dunedin	1996/97
8th	89	Samaraweera T.T. & Chandana U.D.U.	Wellington	2004/05
9th	44	Sangakkara K.C. & Malinga S.L.	Christchurch	2006/07
10th	71	Kaluwitharana R.S. & Muralitharan M.	Colombo	1997/98

NEW ZEALAND v ZIMBABWE

New Zealand

1st	214	Spearman C.M. & Twose R.G.	Auckland	1995/96
2nd	127	Latham R.T. & Jones A.H.	Bulawayo	1992/93
3rd	137	Vincent L. & Fleming S.P.	Bulawayo	2005/06
4th	243	Horne M.J. & Astle N.J.	Auckland	1997/98
5th	222	Astle N.J. & McMillan C.D.	Wellington	2000/01
6th	120	Fleming S.P. & McCullum B.B.	Harare	2005/06
7th	108	McMillan C.D. & Nash D.J.	Wellington	1997/98
8th	144	Cairns C.L. & Nash D.J.	Harare	2000/01
9th	78	Parore A.C. & Vettori D.L.	Bulawayo	2000/01
10th	27	McMillan C.D. & Doull S.B.	Auckland	1997/98

Zimbabwe

1st	156	Rennie G.J. & Flower G.W.	Harare	1997/98
2nd	107	Arnott K.J. & Campbell A.D.R.	Harare	1992/93
3rd	70	Flower A. & Whittall G.J.	Bulawayo	1997/98
4th	130	Rennie G.J. & Flower A.	Wellington	2000/01
5th	131	Flower A. & Whittall G.J.	Harare	2000/01
6th	151	Whittall G.J. & Streak H.H.	Harare	2000/01
7th	91	Whittall G.J. & Strang P.A.	Hamilton	1995/96
8th	94	Campbell A.D.R. & Streak H.H.	Wellington	1997/98
9th	46	Crocker G.J. & Burmester M.G.	Harare	1992/93
10th	40	Whittall G.J. & Matambanadzo E.	Bulawayo	1997/98

NEW ZEALAND v BANGLADESH

New Zealand

1st	104	Richardson M.H. & Horne M.J.	Wellington	2001/02
2nd	63	Sinclair M.S. & Fleming S.P.	Dhaka	2004/05
3rd	204	Fleming S P & Styris S B	Chittagong	2004/05
4th	130	Fleming S.P. & McMillan C.D.	Wellington	2001/02
5th	190	Richardson M.H. & McMillan C.D.	Hamilton	2001/02
6th	89	McMillan C.D. & Cairns C.L.	Hamilton	2001/02
7th	71	McCullum B.B. & Vettori D.L.	Dhaka	2004/05
8th	57	McCullum B.B. & Franklin J.E.C.	Dhaka	2004/05
9th	20	McCullum B.B. & Wiseman P.J.	Dhaka	2004/05
10th	31	Wiseman P.J. & Butler I.G.	Dhaka	2004/05

Bangladesh

1st	39	Javed Omer & Al Sahariar	Hamilton	2001/02
2nd	32	Javed Omer & Aftab Ahmed	Chittagong	2004/05
3rd	60	Habibul Bashar & Aminul Islam	Hamilton	2001/02
4th	115	Rajin Saleh & Mohammad Ashraful	Dhaka	2004/05
5th	26	Javed Omer & Alok Kapali	Chittagong	2004/05
6th	49	Rajin Saleh & Khalid Masud	Chittagong	2004/05
7th	38	Khalid Masud & Mushfiqur Rahman	Chittagong	2004/05
8th	39	Mushfiqur Rahman & Mohammad Rafique	Chittagong	2004/05
9th	49	Khaled Masud & Masrafe bin Mortaza	Wellington	2001/02
10th	45	Tapash Baisya & Enamul Haque	Chittagong	2004/05

CAREER RECORDS

Averages

	M	*I*	*NO*	*HS*	*Runs*	*Ave*	*100*	*50*	*Ct*	*St*	*Wkts*	*Runs*	*Ave*	*Best*	*5WI*	*10WM*
Adams A.R.	1	2	0	11	18	9.00	—	—	1	—	6	105	17.50	3-44	—	—
Alabaster J.C.	21	34	6	34	272	9.71	—	—	7	—	49	1863	38.02	4-46	—	—
Allcott C.F.W.	6	7	2	33	113	22.60	—	—	3	—	6	541	90.17	2-102	—	—
Allott G.I.	10	15	7	8*	27	3.37	—	—	2	—	19	1111	58.47	4-74	—	—
Anderson R.W.	9	18	0	92	423	23.50	—	3	1	—	—	—	—	—	—	—
Anderson W.M.	1	2	0	4	5	2.50	—	—	1	—	—	—	—	—	—	—
Andrews B.	2	3	2	17	22	22.00	—	—	1	—	2	154	77.00	2-40	—	—
Astle N.J.	81	137	10	222	4702	37.02	11	24	70	—	51	2143	42.01	3-27	—	—
Badcock F.T.	7	9	2	64	137	19.57	—	2	1	—	16	610	38.13	4-80	—	—
Barber R.T.	1	2	0	12	17	8.50	—	—	1	—	—	—	—	—	—	—
Bartlett G.A.	10	18	1	40	263	15.47	—	—	8	—	24	792	33.00	6-38	1	—
Barton P.T.	7	14	0	109	285	20.36	1	1	4	—	—	—	—	—	—	—
Beard D.D.	4	7	2	31	101	20.20	—	—	2	—	9	302	33.56	3-22	—	—
Beck J.E.F.	8	15	0	99	394	26.27	—	3	—	—	—	—	—	—	—	—
Bell M.D.	13	23	1	105	484	22.00	1	2	10	—	—	—	—	—	—	—
Bell W.	2	3	3	21*	21	—	—	—	1	—	2	235	117.50	1-54	—	—
Bilby G.P.	2	4	0	28	55	13.75	—	—	3	—	—	—	—	—	—	—
***Blain** T.E.	11	20	3	78	456	26.82	—	2	19	2	—	—	—	—	—	—
Blair R.W.	19	34	6	64*	189	6.75	—	1	5	—	43	1515	35.23	4-85	—	—
Blunt R.C.	9	13	1	96	330	27.50	—	1	5	—	12	472	39.33	3-17	—	—
Bolton B.A.	2	3	0	33	59	19.67	—	—	1	—	—	—	—	—	—	—
Bond S.E.	16	17	7	41*	138	13.80	—	—	6	—	74	1636	22.10	6-51	4	1
Boock S.L.	30	41	8	37	207	6.27	—	—	14	—	74	2564	34.64	7-87	4	—
Bracewell B.P.	6	12	2	8	24	2.40	—	—	1	—	14	585	41.78	3-110	—	—
Bracewell J.G.	41	60	11	110	1001	20.42	1	4	31	—	102	3653	35.81	6-32	4	1
Bradburn G.E.	7	10	2	30*	105	13.12	—	—	6	—	6	460	76.66	3-134	—	—
Bradburn W.P.	2	4	0	32	62	15.50	—	—	2	—	—	—	—	—	—	—
Brown V.R.	2	3	1	36*	51	25.50	—	—	3	—	1	176	176.00	1-17	—	—
Burgess M.G.	50	92	6	119*	2684	31.21	5	14	34	—	6	212	35.33	3-23	—	—
Burke C.	1	2	0	3	4	2.00	—	—	—	—	2	30	15.00	2-30	—	—
Burtt T.B.	10	15	3	42	252	21.00	—	—	2	—	33	1170	35.45	6-162	3	—
Butler I.G.	8	10	2	26	76	9.50	—	—	4	—	24	884	36.83	6-46	1	—
Butterfield L.A.	1	2	0	0	0	0.00	—	—	—	—	0	24	—	—	—	—
Cairns B.L.	43	65	8	64	928	16.28	—	2	30	—	130	4279	32.91	7-74	6	1
Cairns C.L.	62	104	5	158	3320	33.53	5	22	14	—	218	6410	29.40	7-27	13	1
Cameron F.J.	19	30	20	27*	116	11.60	—	—	2	—	62	1849	29.82	5-34	3	—
Cave H.B.	19	31	5	22*	229	8.81	—	—	8	—	34	1467	43.15	4-21	—	—
Chapple M.E.	14	27	1	76	497	19.12	—	3	10	—	1	84	84.00	1-24	—	—
Chatfield E.J.	43	54	33	21*	180	8.57	—	—	7	—	123	3958	32.17	6-73	3	1
Cleverley D.C.	2	4	3	10*	19	19.00	—	—	—	—	0	130	—	—	—	—
Collinge R.O.	35	50	13	68*	533	14.41	—	2	10	—	116	3393	29.25	6-63	3	—
†**Colquhoun** I.A.	2	4	2	1*	1	0.50	—	—	4	—	—	—	—	—	—	—
Coney J.V.	52	85	14	174*	2668	37.57	3	16	64	—	27	966	35.77	3-28	—	—
***Congdon** B.E.	61	114	7	176	3448	32.22	7	19	44*	—	59	2154	36.51	5-65	1	—
Cowie J.	9	13	4	45	90	10.00	—	—	3	—	45	969	21.53	6-40	4	1
Cresswell G.F.	3	5	3	12*	14	7.00	—	—	—	—	13	292	22.46	6-168	1	—
Cromb I.B.	5	8	2	51*	123	20.50	—	1	1	—	8	442	55.25	3-113	—	—
Crowe J.J.	39	65	4	128	1601	26.24	3	6	41	—	0	9	—	—	—	—
Crowe M.D.	77	131	11	299	5444	45.36	17	18	71	—	14	676	48.28	2-25	—	—

	M	I	NO	HS	Runs	Ave	100	50	Ct	St	Wkts	Runs	Ave	Best	5WI	10W
Cumming C.D.	7	13	1	74	327	27.25	—	1	2	—	—	—	—	—	—	—
Cunis R.S.	20	31	8	51	295	12.83	—	1	1	—	51	1887	37.00	6-76	1	—
D'Arcy J.W.	5	10	0	33	136	13.60	—	—	—	—	—	—	—	—	—	—
de Groen R.P.	5	10	4	26	45	7.50	—	—	—	—	11	505	45.90	3-40	—	—
Davis H.T.	5	7	4	8*	20	6.66	—	—	4	—	17	499	29.35	5-63	1	—
Dempster C.S.	10	15	4	136	723	65.73	2	5	2	—	0	10	—	—	—	—
Dempster E.W.	5	8	2	47	106	17.67	—	—	1	—	2	219	109.50	1-24	—	—
†**Dick** A.E.	17	30	4	50*	370	14.73	—	1	47	4	—	—	—	—	—	—
Dickinson G.R.	3	5	0	11	31	6.20	—	—	3	—	8	245	30.63	3-66	—	—
Donnelly M.P.	7	12	1	206	582	52.91	1	4	7	—	0	20	—	—	—	—
Doull S.B.	32	50	11	46	570	14.61	—	—	16	—	98	2872	29.30	7-65	6	—
Dowling G.T.	39	77	3	239	2306	31.16	3	11	23	—	1	19	19.00	1-19	—	—
Drum C.J.	5	5	2	4	10	3.33	—	—	4	—	16	482	30.12	3-36	—	—
Dunning J.A.	4	6	1	19	38	7.60	—	—	2	—	5	493	98.60	2-35	—	—
***Edgar** B.A.	39	68	4	161	1958	30.59	3	12	14*	—	0	3	—	—	—	—
***Edwards** G.N.	8	15	0	55	377	25.13	—	3	7*	—	—	—	—	—	—	—
Emery R.W.G.	2	4	0	28	46	11.50	—	—	—	—	2	52	26.00	2-52	—	—
Fisher F.E.	1	2	0	14	23	11.50	—	—	—	—	1	78	78.00	1-78	—	—
Fleming S.P.	104	177	10	274*	6620	39.64	9	41	159	—	—	—	—	—	—	—
Foley H.	1	2	0	2	4	2.00	—	—	—	—	—	—	—	—	—	—
Franklin J.E.C.	21	28	5	122*	505	21.95	1	1	9	—	76	2143	28.19	6-119	3	—
Franklin T.J.	21	37	1	101	828	23.00	1	4	8	—	—	—	—	—	—	—
Freeman D.L.	2	2	0	1	2	1.00	—	—	—	—	1	169	169.00	1-91	—	—
Fulton P.G.	5	7	0	75	185	26.42	—	1	3	—						
Gallichan N.	1	2	0	30	32	16.00	—	—	—	—	3	113	37.67	3-99	—	—
Gedye S.G.	4	8	0	55	193	24.13	—	2	—	—	—	—	—	—	—	—
†**Germon** L.K.	12	21	3	55	382	21.22	—	1	27	2	—	—	—	—	—	—
Gillespie S.R.	1	1	0	28	28	28.00	—	—	—	—	1	79	79.00	1-79	—	—
Gray E.J.	10	16	0	50	248	15.50	—	1	6	—	17	886	52.11	3-73	—	—
Greatbatch M.J.	41	71	5	146*	2021	30.62	3	10	27	—	0	0	—	—	—	—
†**Guillen** S.C.	3	6	0	41	98	16.33	—	—	4	1	—	—	—	—	—	—
Guy J.W.	12	23	2	102	440	20.95	1	3	2	—	—	—	—	—	—	—
Hadlee D.R.	26	42	5	56	530	14.32	—	1	8	—	71	2389	33.65	4-30	—	—
Hadlee R.J.	86	134	19	151*	3124	27.16	2	15	39	—	431	9611	22.29	9-52	36	9
Hadlee W.A.	11	19	1	116	543	30.17	1	2	6	—	—	—	—	—	—	—
Harford N.S.	8	15	0	93	229	15.27	—	2	—	—	—	—	—	—	—	—
†**Harford** R.I.	3	5	2	6	7	2.33	—	—	11	—	—	—	—	—	—	—
Harris C.Z.	23	42	4	71	777	20.44	—	5	14	—	16	1170	73.12	2-16	—	—
Harris P.G.Z.	9	18	1	101	378	22.24	1	1	6	—	0	14	—	—	—	—
Harris R.M.	2	3	0	13	31	10.33	—	—	—	—	—	—	—	—	—	—
Hart M.N.	14	24	4	45	353	17.65	—	—	9	—	29	1438	49.58	5-77	1	—
†**Hart** R.G.	11	19	3	57*	260	16.25	—	1	29	1	—	—	—	—	—	—
Hartland B.R.	9	18	0	52	303	16.83	—	1	5	—	—	—	—	—	—	—
Haslam M.J.	4	2	1	3	4	4.00	—	—	2	—	2	245	122.50	1-33	—	—
Hastings B.F.	31	56	6	117*	1510	30.20	4	7	23	—	0	9	—	—	—	—
Hayes J.A.	15	22	7	19	73	4.87	—	—	3	—	30	1217	40.57	4-36	—	—
Henderson M.	1	2	1	6	8	8.00	—	—	1	—	2	64	32.00	2-38	—	—
Horne M.J.	35	65	2	157	1788	28.38	4	5	17	—	0	26	—	—	—	—
Horne P.A.	4	7	0	27	71	10.14	—	—	3	—	—	—	—	—	—	—
Hough K.W.	2	3	2	31*	62	62.00	—	—	1	—	6	175	29.17	3-79	—	—
How J.M.	6	10	1	37	131	14.55	—	—	8	—						
Howarth G.P.	47	83	5	147	2531	32.44	6	11	29	—	3	271	90.33	1-13	—	—
Howarth H.J.	30	42	18	61	291	12.13	—	1	33	—	86	3178	36.95	5-34	2	—
†**James** K.C.	11	13	2	14	52	4.73	—	—	11	5	—	—	—	—	—	—

	M	*I*	*NO*	*HS*	*Runs*	*Ave*	*100*	*50*	*Ct*	*St*	*Wkts*	*Runs*	*Ave*	*Best*	*5WI*	*10WM*
Jarvis T.W.	13	22	1	182	625	29.76	1	2	3	—	0	3	—	—	—	—
Jones A.H.	39	74	8	186	2922	44.27	7	11	25	—	1	194	194.00	1-40	—	—
Jones R.A.	1	2	0	16	23	11.50	—	—	—	—	—	—	—	—	—	—
Kennedy R.J.	4	5	1	22	28	7.00	—	—	2	—	6	380	63.33	3-28	—	—
Kerr J.L.	7	12	1	59	212	19.27	—	1	4	—	—	—	—	—	—	—
Kuggeleijn C.M.	2	4	0	7	7	1.75	—	—	1	—	1	67	67.00	1-50	—	—
Larsen G.R.	8	13	4	26*	127	14.11	—	—	5	—	24	689	28.70	3-57	—	—
Latham R.T.	4	7	0	119	219	31.28	1	—	5	—	0	6	—	—	—	—
†**Lees** W.K.	21	37	4	152	778	23.57	1	1	52	7	0	4	—	—	—	—
Leggat I.B.	1	1	0	0	0	0.00	—	—	2	—	0	6	—	—	—	—
Leggat J.G.	9	18	2	61	351	21.94	—	2	—	—	—	—	—	—	—	—
Lissette A.F.	2	4	2	1*	2	1.00	—	—	1	—	3	124	41.33	2-73	—	—
Loveridge G.R.	1	1	1	4*	4	—	—	—	—	—	—	—	—	—	—	—
Lowry T.C.	7	8	0	80	223	27.88	—	2	8	—	0	5	—	—	—	—
†**McCullum** B.B.	25	39	3	143	1157	32.13	2	6	64	6	—	—	—	—	—	—
McEwan P.E.	4	7	1	40*	96	16.00	—	—	5	—	0	13	—	—	—	—
MacGibbon A.R.	26	46	5	66	814	19.85	—	3	13	—	70	2160	30.86	5-64	1	—
McGirr H.M.	2	1	0	51	51	51.00	—	1	—	—	1	115	115.00	1-65	—	—
McGregor S.N.	25	47	2	111	892	19.82	1	3	9	—	—	—	—	—	—	—
McLeod E.G.	1	2	1	16	18	18.00	—	—	—	—	0	5	—	—	—	—
†**McMahon** T.G.	5	7	4	4*	7	2.33	—	—	7	1	—	—	—	—	—	—
McMillan C.D.	55	91	10	142	3116	38.46	6	19	22	—	28	1257	44.89	3-48	—	—
McRae D.A.N.	1	2	0	8	8	4.00	—	—	—	—	0	44	—	—	—	—
Marshall H.J.H.	13	19	2	160	652	38.35	2	2	1	—	0	4	—	—	—	—
Marshall J.A.H.	5	7	0	52	166	23.71	—	1	3	—	—	—	—	—	—	—
Martin C.S.	33	44	21	7	52	2.26	—	—	9	—	106	3636	34.30	6-54	7	1
Mason M.J.	1	2	0	3	3	1.50	—	—	—	—	0	105	—	—	—	—
Matheson A.M.	2	1	0	7	7	7.00	—	—	2	—	2	136	68.00	2-7	—	—
Meale T.	2	4	0	10	21	5.25	—	—	—	—	—	—	—	—	—	—
Merritt W.E.	6	8	1	19	73	10.43	—	—	2	—	12	617	51.42	4-104	—	—
Meuli E.M.	1	2	0	23	38	19.00	—	—	—	—	—	—	—	—	—	—
†**Milburn** B.D.	3	3	2	4*	8	8.00	—	—	6	2	—	—	—	—	—	—
Miller L.S.M.	13	25	0	47	346	13.84	—	—	1	—	0	1	—	—	—	—
Mills J.E.	7	10	1	117	241	26.78	1	—	1	—	—	—	—	—	—	—
Mills K.D.	7	12	3	31	120	13.33	—	—	2	—	17	534	31.41	4-43	—	—
Moir A.M.	17	30	8	41*	327	14.86	—	—	2	—	28	1418	50.64	6-155	2	—
Moloney D.A.R.	3	6	0	64	156	26.00	—	1	3	—	0	9	—	—	—	—
†**Mooney** F.L.H.	14	22	2	46	343	17.15	—	—	22	8	0	0	—	—	—	—
***Morgan** R.W.	20	34	1	97	734	22.24	—	5	12*	—	5	609	121.80	1-16	—	—
Morrison B.D.	1	2	0	10	10	5.00	—	—	1	—	2	129	64.50	2-129	—	—
Morrison D.K.	48	71	26	42	379	8.42	—	—	14	—	160	5549	34.68	7-89	10	—
Morrison J.F.M.	17	29	0	117	656	22.62	1	3	9	—	2	71	35.50	2-52	—	—
Motz R.C.	32	56	3	60	612	11.55	—	3	9	—	100	3148	31.48	6-63	5	—
Murray B.A.G.	13	26	1	90	598	23.92	—	5	21	—	1	0	0.00	1-0	—	—
Murray D.J.	8	16	1	52	303	20.20	—	1	6	—	—	—	—	—	—	—
Nash D.J.	32	45	14	89*	729	23.51	—	4	13	—	93	2649	28.48	6-27	3	1
Newman J.	3	4	0	19	33	8.25	—	—	—	—	2	254	127.00	2-76	—	—
O'Brien I.E.	2	3	0	5	10	3.33	—	—	1	—	2	197	98.50	1-73	—	—
O'Connor S.B.	19	27	9	20	105	5.83	—	—	6	—	53	1724	32.52	5-51	1	—
O'Sullivan D.R.	11	21	4	23*	158	9.29	—	—	2	—	18	1221	67.83	5-148	1	—
Oram J.D.P.	22	39	8	133	1221	39.38	3	4	13	—	42	1451	34.54	4-41	—	—
Overton G.W.F.	3	6	1	3*	8	1.60	—	—	1	—	9	258	28.67	3-65	—	—
Owens M.B.	8	12	6	8*	16	2.66	—	—	3	—	17	585	34.44	4-99	—	—
Page M.L.	14	20	0	104	492	24.60	1	2	6	—	5	231	46.20	2-21	—	—

	M	I	NO	HS	Runs	Ave	100	50	Ct	St	Wkts	Runs	Ave	Best	5WI	10W
Papps M.H.W.	6	12	1	86	229	20.81	—	2	7	—	—	—	—	—	—	—
Parker J.M.	36	63	2	121	1498	24.56	3	5	30	—	1	24	24.00	1-24	—	—
Parker N.M.	3	6	0	40	89	14.83	—	—	2	—	—	—	—	—	—	—
***Parore** A.C.	78	128	19	110	2865	26.28	2	14	197	7	—	—	—	—	—	—
Patel D.N.	37	66	8	99	1200	20.68	—	5	15	—	75	3154	42.05	6-50	3	—
Patel J.S.	1	1	1	27*	27	—	—	—	1	—	3	117	39.00	3-117	—	—
Petherick P.J.	6	11	4	13	34	4.86	—	—	4	—	16	685	42.81	3-90	—	—
†**Petrie** E.C.	14	25	5	55	258	12.90	—	1	25	—	—	—	—	—	—	—
Playle W.R.	8	15	0	65	151	10.07	—	1	4	—	—	—	—	—	—	—
Pocock B.A.	15	29	0	85	665	22.93	—	6	5	—	0	20	—	—	—	—
Pollard V.	32	59	7	116	1266	24.35	2	7	19	—	40	1853	46.33	3-3	—	—
Poore M.B.	14	24	1	45	355	15.43	—	—	1	—	9	367	40.78	2-28	—	—
Priest M.W.	3	4	0	26	56	14.00	—	—	—	—	3	158	52.66	2-42	—	—
Pringle C.	14	21	4	30	175	10.29	—	—	3	—	30	1389	46.30	7-52	1	1
Puna N.	3	5	3	18*	31	15.50	—	—	1	—	4	240	60.00	2-40	—	—
Rabone G.O.	12	20	2	107	562	31.22	1	2	5	—	16	635	36.69	6-68	1	—
Redmond R.E.	1	2	0	107	163	81.50	1	1	—	—	—	—	—	—	—	—
Reid J.F.	19	31	3	180	1296	46.28	6	2	9	—	0	7	—	—	—	—
***Reid** J.R.	58	108	5	142	3428	33.28	6	22	43*	1	85	2835	33.35	6-60	1	—
Richardson M.H.	38	65	3	145	2776	44.77	4	19	26	—	1	21	21.00	1-16	—	—
Roberts A.D.G.	7	12	1	84*	254	23.09	—	1	4	—	4	182	45.50	1-12	—	—
Roberts A.W.	5	10	1	66*	248	27.56	—	3	4	—	7	209	29.86	4-101	—	—
Robertson G.K.	1	1	0	12	12	12.00	—	—	—	—	1	91	91.00	1-91	—	—
Rowe C.G.	1	2	0	0	0	0.00	—	—	1	—	—	—	—	—	—	—
Rutherford K.R.	56	99	8	107*	2465	27.08	3	18	32	—	1	161	161.00	1-38	—	—
Scott R.H.	1	1	0	18	18	18.00	—	—	—	—	1	74	74.00	1-74	—	—
Scott V.J.	10	17	1	84	458	28.63	—	3	7	—	0	14	—	—	—	—
Sewell D.G.	1	1	1	1*	1	—	—	—	—	—	0	90	—	—	—	—
Shrimpton M.J.F.	10	19	0	46	265	13.95	—	—	2	—	5	158	31.60	3-35	—	—
Sinclair B.W.	21	40	1	138	1148	29.44	3	3	8	—	2	32	16.00	2-32	—	—
Sinclair I.M.	2	4	1	18*	25	8.33	—	—	1	—	1	120	120.00	1-79	—	—
***Sinclair** M.S.	27	46	5	214	1448	35.31	3	4	26	—	0	13	—	—	—	—
Smith F.B.	4	6	1	96	237	47.40	—	2	1	—	—	—	—	—	—	—
Smith H.D.	1	1	0	4	4	4.00	—	—	—	—	1	113	113.00	1-113	—	—
†**Smith** I.D.S.	63	88	17	173	1815	25.56	2	6	168	8	0	5	—	—	—	—
Snedden C.A.	1	—	—	—	—	—	—	—	—	—	0	46	—	—	—	—
Snedden M.C.	25	30	8	33*	327	14.86	—	—	7	—	58	2199	37.91	5-68	1	—
Sparling J.T.	11	20	2	50	229	12.72	—	1	3	—	5	327	65.40	1-9	—	—
Spearman C.M.	19	37	2	112	922	26.34	1	3	20	—	—	—	—	—	—	—
Stead G.R.	5	8	0	78	278	34.75	—	2	2	—	0	1	—	—	—	—
Stirling D.A.	6	9	2	26	108	15.42	—	—	1	—	13	601	46.23	4-88	—	—
Styris S.B.	27	44	4	170	1527	38.17	5	6	23	—	20	973	48.65	3-28	—	—
Su'a M.L.	13	18	5	44	165	12.69	—	—	8	—	36	1377	38.25	5-73	2	—
Sutcliffe B.	42	76	8	230*	2727	40.10	5	15	20	—	4	344	86.00	2-38	—	—
Taylor B.R.	30	50	6	124	898	20.41	2	2	10	—	111	2953	26.60	7-74	4	—
Taylor D.D.	3	5	0	77	159	31.80	—	1	2	—	—	—	—	—	—	—
Thomson K.	2	4	1	69	94	31.33	—	1	—	—	1	9	9.00	1-9	—	—
Thomson S.A.	19	35	4	120*	958	30.90	1	5	7	—	19	953	50.15	3-63	—	—
†**Tindill** E.W.T.	5	9	1	37*	73	9.13	—	—	6	1	—	—	—	—	—	—
Troup G.B.	15	18	6	13*	55	4.58	—	—	2	—	39	1454	37.28	6-95	1	1
Truscott P.B.	1	2	0	26	29	14.50	—	—	1	—	—	—	—	—	—	—
Tuffey D.R.	22	30	7	35	263	11.43	—	—	12	—	66	2057	31.16	6-54	2	—
Turner G.M.	41	73	6	259	2991	44.64	7	14	42	—	0	5	—	—	—	—
Twose R.G.	16	27	2	94	628	25.12	—	6	5	—	3	130	43.33	2-36	—	—

	M	I	NO	HS	Runs	Ave	100	50	Ct	St	Wkts	Runs	Ave	Best	5WI	10WM
Vance R.H.	4	7	0	68	207	29.57	—	1	—	—	—	—	—	—	—	—
Vaughan J.T.C.	6	12	1	44	201	18.27	—	—	4	—	11	450	40.90	4-27	—	—
Vettori D.L.	73	105	16	137*	2250	25.28	2	13	36	—	229	7848	34.27	7-87	13	3
Vincent L.	22	38	1	224	1295	35.00	3	9	19	—	0	2	—	—	—	—
Vivian G.E.	5	6	0	43	110	18.33	—	—	3	—	1	107	107.00	1-14	—	—
Vivian H.G.	7	10	0	100	421	42.10	1	5	4	—	17	633	37.24	4-58	—	—
†**Wadsworth** K.J.	33	51	4	80	1010	21.49	—	5	92	4	—	—	—	—	—	—
Walker B.G.K.	5	8	2	27*	118	19.66	—	—	—	—	5	399	79.80	2-92	—	—
Wallace W.M.	13	21	0	66	439	20.90	—	5	5	—	0	5	—	—	—	—
Walmsley K.P.	3	5	0	5	13	2.60	—	—	—	—	9	391	43.44	3-70	—	—
†**Ward** J.T.	8	12	6	35*	75	12.50	—	—	16	1	—	—	—	—	—	—
Watson W.	15	18	6	11	60	5.00	—	—	4	—	40	1387	34.67	6-78	1	—
Watt L.	1	2	0	2	2	1.00	—	—	—	—	—	—	—	—	—	—
Webb M.G.	3	2	0	12	12	6.00	—	—	—	—	4	471	117.75	2-114	—	—
Webb P.N.	2	3	0	5	11	3.67	—	—	2	—	—	—	—	—	—	—
Weir G.L.	11	16	2	74*	416	29.71	—	3	3	—	7	209	29.86	3-38	—	—
White D.J.	2	4	0	18	31	7.75	—	—	—	—	0	5	—	—	—	—
Whitelaw P.E.	2	4	2	30	64	32.00	—	—	—	—	—	—	—	—	—	—
Wiseman P.J.	25	34	8	36	366	14.07	—	—	11	—	61	2903	47.59	5-82	2	—
Wright J.G.	82	148	7	185	5334	37.82	12	23	38	—	0	5	—	—	—	—
Young B.A.	35	68	4	267*	2034	31.78	2	12	54	—	—	—	—	—	—	—
Yuile B.W.	17	33	6	64	481	17.81	—	1	12	—	34	1213	35.68	4-43	—	—

Note: There have now been 65 dismissals made by substitutes: M.J. Greatbatch (5), J.G. Bracewell, J.J. Crowe, T.W. Jarvis (4), C.Z. Harris (3), J.A.H. Marshall, D.R. O'Sullivan, A.C. Parore, K.R. Rutherford, G.E. Vivian (2), J.C. Alabaster, R.W. Anderson, S.E. Bond, S.L. Boock, G.E. Bradburn, C. Burke, C. Cachopa, R.O. Collinge, B.E. Congdon, M.D. Crowe, H.T. Davis, C.J. Drum, E.W. Dempster, G.T. Dowling, B.A. Edgar, G.N. Edwards, S.G. Gedye, M.N. Hart, M.A. Hastings, J.M. How, I.B. Leggat, T.G. McMahon, P.E. McEwan, M.N. McKenzie, H.J.H. Marshall, M.J. Mason, S.M. Mills, R.C. Motz, S.B. O'Connor, N.M. Parker, M.W. Priest, T.D. Ritchie, L. Vincent, B.G.K. Walker catches and B.E. Congdon a stumping. The latter is one of only two instances in tests of a substitute making a stumping.

† all test appearances were as wicketkeeper.
A.C. Parore had 67 tests as wicketkeeper, T.E. Blain (9), G.N. Edwards (4), B.A. Edgar and J.R. Reid one each.

** record includes catches taken while keeping wicket as follows: A.C. Parore (194), T.E. Blain (18), B.A. Edgar (4), J.R. Reid (2), B.E. Congdon, R.W. Morgan and M.S. Sinclair one each. Edwards' catches were all made while keeping wicket.*

Vettori's record includes one match for ICC World XI.

SUMMARY OF TEST CAREER RECORDS

Most Matches

Fleming S.P.	104	Morrison D.K.	48	Parker J.M.	36
Hadlee R.J.	86	Howarth G.P.	47	Collinge R.O.	35
Wright J.G.	82	Cairns B.L.	43	Young B.A.	35
Astle N.J.	81	Chatfield E.J.	43	Horne M.J.	35
Parore A.C.	78	Sutcliffe B.	42	Wadsworth K.J.	33
Crowe M.D.	77	Turner G.M.	41	Martin C.S.	33
Vettori D.L.	73	Bracewell J.G.	41	Motz R.C.	32
Smith I.D.S.	63	Greatbatch M.J.	41	Pollard V.	32
Cairns C.L.	62	Dowling G.T.	39	Doull S.B.	32
Congdon B.E.	61	Edgar B.A.	39	Nash D.J.	32
Reid J.R.	58	Crowe J.J.	39	Hastings B.F.	31
Rutherford K.R.	56	Jones A.H.	39	Howarth H.J.	30
McMillan C.D	55	Richardson M.H.	38	Taylor B.R.	30
Coney J.V.	52	Patel D.N.	37	Boock S.L.	30
Burgess M.G.	50				

Most Runs

Fleming S.P.	6620	Sutcliffe B.	2727	Styris S.B.	1527
Crowe M.D.	5444	Burgess M.G.	2684	Hastings B.F.	1510
Wright J.G.	5334	Coney J.V.	2668	Parker J.M.	1498
Astle N.J.	4702	Howarth G.P.	2531	Sinclair M.S.	1448
Congdon B.E.	3448	Rutherford K.R.	2465	Reid J.F.	1296
Reid J.R.	3428	Dowling G.T.	2306	Vincent L.	1295
Cairns C.L.	3320	Vettori D.L.	2250	Pollard V.	1266
Hadlee R.J.	3124	Young B.A.	2034	Oram J.D.P.	1221
McMillan C.D.	3116	Greatbatch M.J.	2021	Patel D.N.	1200
Turner G.M.	2991	Edgar B.A.	1958	McCullum B.B.	1157
Jones A.H.	2922	Smith I.D.S.	1815	Sinclair B.W.	1148
Parore A.C.	2865	Horne M.J.	1788	Wadsworth K.J.	1010
Richardson M.H.	2776	Crowe J.J.	1601	Bracewell J.G.	1001

Most Wickets

Hadlee R.J.	431	Motz R.C.	100	MacGibbon A.R.	70
Vettori D.L.	229	Doull S.B.	98	Tuffey D.R.	66
Cairns C.L.	218	Nash D.J.	93	Cameron F.J.	62
Morrison D.K.	160	Howarth H.J.	86	Wiseman P.J.	61
Cairns B.L.	130	Reid J.R.	85	Congdon B.E.	59
Chatfield E.J.	123	Franklin J.E.C.	76	Snedden M.C.	58
Collinge R.O.	116	Patel D.N.	75	O'Connor S.B.	53
Taylor B.R.	111	Boock S.L.	74	Cunis R.S.	51
Martin C.S.	106	Bond S.E.	74	Astle N.J.	51
Bracewell J.G.	102	Hadlee D.R.	71		

Most Catches

Fleming S.P.	159	Turner G.M.	42	Burgess M.G.	34
Crowe M.D.	71	Reid J.R.	41	Howarth H.J.	33
Astle N.J.	70	Crowe J.J.	41	Rutherford K.R.	32
Coney J.V.	64	Hadlee R.J.	39	Bracewell J.G.	31
Young B.A.	54	Wright J.G.	38	Parker J.M.	30
Congdon B.E.	43	Vettori D.L.	36	Cairns B.L.	30

Most Wicketkeeping Dismissals

	Ct	St	Total
Parore A.C.	194	7	201
Smith I.D.S.	168	8	176
Wadsworth K.J.	92	4	96
McCullum B.B.	64	6	70
Lees W.K.	52	7	59
Dick A.E.	47	4	51

Test Captains

		RESULTS				TOSS	
		P	W	L	D	W	L
Fleming S.P.	1996/97 to 2006/07	80	28	27	25	37	43
Reid J.R.	1955/56 to 1965	34	3	18	13	17	17
Howarth G.P.	1979/80 to 1984/85	30	11	7	12	17	13
Dowling G.T.	1967/68 to 1971/72	19	4	7	8	10	9
Rutherford K.R.	1992/93 to 1994/95	18	2	11	5	12	6
Congdon B.E.	1971/72 to 1974/75	17	1	7	9	4	13
Crowe M.D.	1990/91 to 1993/94	16	2	7	7	8	8
Coney J.V.	1984/85 to 1986/87	15	5	4	6	8	7
Wright J.G.	1987/88 to 1990	14	3	3	8	8	6
Germon L.K.	1995/96 to 1996/97	12	1	5	6	6	6
Turner G.M.	1975/76 to 1976/77	10	1	6	3	2	8
Burgess M.G.	1977/78 to 1980/81	10	1	6	3	4	6
Cave H.B.	1955/56	9	0	5	4	5	4
Hadlee W.A.	1945/46 to 1950/51	8	0	2	6	4	4
Lowry T.C.	1929/30 to 1931	7	0	2	5	5	2
Page M.L.	1931/32 to 1937	7	0	3	4	4	3
Crowe J.J.	1986/87 to 1987/88	6	0	1	5	3	3
Rabone G.O.	1953/54 to 1954/55	5	0	4	1	2	3
Sutcliffe B.	1951/52 to 1953/54	4	0	3	1	4	0
Sinclair B.W.	1965/66 to 1967/68	3	0	1	2	3	0
Nash D.J.	1998/99	3	0	1	2	3	0
Wallace W.M.	1952/53	2	0	1	1	0	2
Chapple M.E.	1965/66	1	0	0	1	0	1
Parker J.M.	1976/77	1	0	0	1	0	1
Smith I.D.S.	1990/91	1	0	0	1	1	0
Totals		**332**	**62**	**131**	**139**	**167**	**165**

Test Debuts

New Zealand has now played 332 test matches. In 189 there have been no new test caps. In the other 143 the records are:

11 players making debut 1929/30 v England at Christchurch (NZ's first test match)
6 players making debut 1937 v England at Lord's (NZ's first test since 1932/33)
6 players making debut 1945/46 v Australia at Wellington (NZ's first test after Second World War)
6 players making debut 1946/47 v England at Christchurch (test after one above)
5 players making debut 1961/62 v South Africa at Durban

Of the 12 players who made their debuts in the 1945/46 and 1946/47 tests above, seven did not appear again. In eight successive tests at least one player made his test debut — South Africa 1963/64 (3), Pakistan 1964/65 (3), India 1964/65 (2). In nine successive tests there were no new caps — England 1969 (2), India 1969/70 (3), Pakistan 1969/70 (3), England 1970/71 (1) and South Africa 1998/99 (1), England 1999 (4), India 1999/00 (3), West Indies 1999/00 (1).

Youngest/Oldest Test Players

YOUNGEST PLAYERS

			Bat	Bowl
18 years 10 days	Vettori D.L. v England at Wellington	1996/97	3* & 2*	2-98
18 years 197 days	Freeman D.L. v England at Christchurch	1932/33	1	0-78
18 years 267 days	Vivian H.G. v England at The Oval	1931	3 & 51	2-96
18 years 295 days	Collinge R.O. v Pakistan at Wellington	1964/65	0*	2-51 & 3-43
18 years 316 days	Bracewell B.P. v England at The Oval	1978	0 & 0	2-46 & 1-26
19 years 5 days	Vivian G.E. v India at Calcutta	1964/65	1 & 43	0-37 & 1-14
19 years 145 days	Beck J.E.F. v South Africa at Johannesburg	1953/54	16 & 7	
19 years 154 days	Rutherford K.R. v West Indies at Port of Spain	1984/85	0 & 0	
19 years 157 days	Crowe M.D. v Australia at Wellington	1981/82	9	0-14
19 years 163 days	Parore A.C. v England at Birmingham	1990	12* & 20	4ct/1st
19 years 164 days	Cairns C.L. v Australia at Perth	1989/90	1 & 28	0-60
19 years 173 days	Pollard V. India at Madras	1964/65	3	3-90 & 1-32
19 years 186 days	Playle W.R. v England at Birmingham	1958	4 & 8	
19 years 252 days	Donnelly M.P. v England at Lord's	1937	0 & 21	
19 years 340 days	Sewell D.G. v Zimbabwe at Bulawayo	1997/98	1*	0-81 & 0-9
19 years 344 days	Sparling J.T. v England at Leeds	1958	9* & 18	1-78

OLDEST PLAYERS *(age on last day of final test)*

41 years 294 days	Alabaster J.C. v West Indies at Port of Spain	1971/72	18	0-49 & 1-5
41 years 196 days	Sutcliffe B. v England at Birmingham	1965	4* & 53	
40 years 198 days	Congdon B.E. v England at Lord's	1978	2 & 3	0-12

OLDEST PLAYER ON DEBUT

38 years 101 days	McGirr H.M.† v England at Auckland	1929/30		0-46

† he made 51 in his first test innings in his second test

YOUNGEST CENTURY MAKER

19 years 121 days†	Vivian H.G. 100 v South Africa at Wellington	1931/32

† world record at that time

OLDEST CENTURY MAKERS

41 years 109 days	Sutcliffe B. 151* v India at Calcutta	1964/65
39 years 12 days	Congdon B.E. 107* v Australia at Christchurch	1976/77

YOUNGEST CAPTAIN

23 years 319 days	Fleming S.P. v England at Christchurch	1996/97	62 & 11
25 years 252 days	Parker J.M. v Pakistan at Karachi	1976/77	24 & 16

OLDEST CAPTAIN *(age on last day of final test)*

37 years 40 days	Reid J.R. v England at Leeds	1965	54 & 5	
36 years 359 days	Congdon B.E. v England at Christchurch	1974/75	38	0-27
36 years 88 days	Wallace W.M. v South Africa at Auckland	1952/53	23	
36 years 5 days	Wright J.G. v England at Birmingham	1990	24 & 46	

LONGEST INTERVAL BETWEEN TEST APPEARANCES

14 years 28 days Cleverley D.C. — v South Africa at Christchurch 1/3/32
v Australia at Wellington 29/3/46

Only A.J. Traicos (22 years 222 days), G. Gunn (17 years 316 days), Younis Ahmed (17 years 111 days) and J.M.M. Commaille (14 years 95 days) have a longer interval between tests but Cleverley is unique in that the above matches were his only two tests.

NEW ZEALAND LIMITED-OVERS RECORDS

This section of the *Almanack* is devoted to limited-overs matches in New Zealand (other than one-day internationals) and has been compiled from the following games:

1. 705 matches in national competitions (Shell Cup, State Shield etc) from 1971/72 to 2006/07.

2. 50 matches between provincial sides and overseas teams from 1970/71 to 2004/05.

1970/71	Wellington v MCC
	Otago v MCC
	Central Districts v MCC
1972/73	Central Districts v Pakistan
1973/74	Wellington v Australia
	Central Districts v Australia
1975/76	Wellington v India
1977/78	Northern Districts v England XI
1978/79	Auckland v Pakistan
	Canterbury v Pakistan
1979/80	Auckland XI v West Indies
	Central Districts v West Indies
1981/82	Northern Districts v Australia
	Central Districts v Australia
1983/84	Otago v England XI
1984/85	Wellington v New South Wales
1985/86	Auckland v Australia
1986/87	Auckland v West Indies
	Central Districts v South Australia *(4 matches)*
1987/88	Wellington v England
	Auckland v Victoria *(2 matches)*
	Wellington v Queensland
	Canterbury v Queensland
	Otago v Queensland
1988/89	Auckland v Pakistan
1991/92	Auckland v England
	Auckland v Australia
	Northern Districts v Zimbabwe *(2 matches)*
1993/94	Canterbury v New South Wales
1994/95	Auckland v West Indies
	Central Districts v India
	Wellington v South Africa
	Canterbury v Sri Lanka
1996/97	Central Districts v Sri Lanka
1997/98	Canterbury v Bangladesh
1998/99	Northern v Pakistan A
2000/01	Wellington v New South Wales
	Canterbury v Zimbabwe
2001/02	Northern Districts v England *(2 matches)*
2003/04	Wellington v Pakistan
	Northern Districts v South Africa
2004/05	Central Districts v Sri Lanka

3. Three matches in the Data General competition in 1986/87.

4. Six matches in the Shell Shield competition in 1997/98.

5. 30 other matches not involving provincial sides.

1972/73	New Zealand Under 23 XI v Pakistan
1976/77	Australia v Invitation XIs *(2 matches)*
1981/82	North Island v South Island
1982/83	Sri Lanka v NZ Minor Associations *(2 matches)*

1992/93	New Zealand President's XI v Australia
1993/94	North Island v South Island
	Sir Ron Brierley XI v Pakistan
1994/95	North Island v South Island
	Sir Ron Brierley XI v West Indies
	New Zealand Academy XI v Sri Lanka
	New Zealand Academy XI v Australian Academy XI
1996/97	New Zealand Academy XI v England
1997/98	New Zealand Academy XI v Zimbabwe
1998/99	New Zealand A v Pakistan A *(3 matches)*
	New Zealand Academy XI v South Africa
1999/00	New Zealand Academy XI v England A *(2 matches)*
	New Zealand A v England A *(3 matches)*
2000/01	North Island Selection XI v Sri Lanka
2003/04	South Island v North Island
	New Zealand A v Sri Lanka A *(2 matches)*
2004/05	New Zealand v FICA World XI *(3 matches)*
	North Island v South Island

TEAM RECORDS

Highest Totals

376-3	Central Districts v Otago	New Plymouth	1996/97
354-5	Central Districts v Canterbury	Christchurch	2003/04
339-5	Central Districts v Otago	Hastings	1998/99
332-5	Northern Districts v Canterbury	Christchurch	2006/07
329-5	Canterbury v Northern Districts	Christchurch	1995/96
328-4	New Zealand A v Sri Lanka A	Lincoln	2003/04
318-5	Auckland v Northern Districts	Auckland	2000/01
315-5	Northern Districts v Otago	Dunedin	2005/06
313-7	Canterbury v Northern Districts	Timaru	1993/94
309-8	Auckland v Northern Districts	Gisborne	1982/83
309-8	Canterbury v Wellington	Christchurch	2003/04
309-6	Canterbury v Central Districts	Christchurch	1994/95
308-9	Wellington v Canterbury	Christchurch	2003/04
307-3	Canterbury v Wellington	Timaru	2004/05
306-2	Northern Districts v Auckland	Gisborne	1982/83
305-6	Central Districts v Otago	Oamaru	1999/00
303-6	Auckland v Canterbury	Christchurch	2006/07
300-5	Wellington v Auckland	Wellington	2001/02
300-3	Canterbury v Otago	Timaru	2003/04

Lowest Totals

48	Pakistan v Auckland	Auckland	1988/89
58	Central Districts v Wellington	Wellington	2001/02
64	Otago v Wellington	Alexandra	1984/85
64	Otago v Central Districts	Invercargill	2004/05
66	Wellington v Canterbury	Wellington	1996/97
67	Otago v Central Districts	Invercargill	2000/01
67	Central Districts v Canterbury	Christchurch	2002/03
70	Auckland v Northern Districts	Pukekohe	1977/78
72	New Zealand Academy XI v South Africa	Alexandra	1998/99
73	Auckland v Central Districts	Auckland	2000/01
75	Canterbury v Otago	Christchurch	1973/74
76	Northern Districts v Central Districts	Mt Maunganui	1987/88
76	Otago v Queensland	Dunedin	1987/88
78	Central Districts v Auckland	New Plymouth	1988/89
79	Wellington v Otago	Wellington	1999/00
80	Northern Districts v Wellington	Wellington	1982/83
81	Northern Districts v Zimbabwe	Cambridge	1991/92
81	Central Districts v Northern Districts	Levin	1995/96
81	Wellington v Canterbury	Wellington	1996/97
81	FICA World XI v New Zealand	Hamilton	2004/05
81	Wellington v Otago	Dunedin	2005/06
85	Northern Districts v Wellington	Mt Maunganui	1997/98
88	Northern Districts v Canterbury	Christchurch	1994/95
89	Central Districts v Wellington	Wellington	1985/86

Most Extras in an Innings

55	Northern Districts (271-8)	v Wellington (228)	Hamilton	2002/03
51	NZ Academy XI (183)	v England A (184-4)	Lincoln	1999/00
48	Wellington (211-7)	v Otago (208-8)	Wellington	1996/97
45	Wellington (251-8)	v Otago (250-6)	Alexandra	1997/98
45	England A (219-7)	v New Zealand A (216)	Auckland	1999/00
43	Otago (250-6)	v Wellington (251-8)	Alexandra	1997/98
42	Canterbury (286-8)	v Otago (149)	Christchurch	1996/97
42	Otago (233-9)	v Wellington (200)	Alexandra	1999/00
42	Northern Districts (202-9)	v Auckland (157-6)	Hamilton	2002/03
41	Northern Districts (215)	v Auckland (217-6)	Whangarei	1995/96

Fewest Extras in an Innings

1	Canterbury (205-6)	v Wellington (203)	Timaru	1986/87
2	Pakistan (216-4)	v NZ Under 23 XI	Rotorua	1972/73
2	Otago (114)	v Canterbury (113)	Christchurch	1979/80
2	Auckland (163-4)	v Otago (162)	Oamaru	1981/82
2	Auckland (105)	v Otago (214-9)	Dunedin	1993/94
2	Otago (279-5)	v Central Districts (275-7)	Palmerston North	2006/07

Tied Match

Wellington v South Africa	Wellington	1994/95
Northern Districts v Auckland	Hamilton	2005/06

Close Finishes

RUNS *(winning team listed first)*

1	Northern Districts v Canterbury	Hamilton	1982/83
1	Northern Districts v Zimbabwe	Pukekohe	1991/92
1	Auckland v Central Districts	Auckland	1994/95
1	Otago v Auckland	Alexandra	1995/96
1	Central Districts v Wellington	Wellington	1996/97
1	Northern Districts v Wellington *(D/L)*	Taupo	2004/05
1	Otago v Northern Districts	Taupo	2005/06
2	Central Districts v Northern Districts	Tauranga	1989/90
2	Canterbury v Wellington	Christchurch	1995/96
2	Canterbury v Auckland	Auckland	1999/00
2	Wellington v Otago	Alexandra	2002/03
3	Auckland v Northern Districts	Hamilton	1972/73
3	Auckland v Northern Districts	Auckland	1981/82
3	Canterbury v Wellington	Christchurch	1991/92
3	Northern Districts v Auckland	Mt Maunganui	1993/94
3	Canterbury v Otago	Christchurch	1998/99
3	Wellington v Otago	Queenstown	2001/02
4	Otago v Wellington	Wellington	1987/88
4	Canterbury v Northern Districts	Rotorua	1993/94
4	Wellington v Central Districts	Wellington	1994/95
4	Otago v Central Districts	Alexandra	2006/07
5	Northern Districts v Otago	Taupo	1995/96
5	Auckland v Otago	Auckland	1999/00
5	Wellington v Auckland	Auckland	2000/01

ONE WICKET *(winning team listed first)*

Wellington v Auckland	Wellington	1973/74
Otago v Canterbury	Christchurch	1979/80
Central Districts v Australia	New Plymouth	1981/82
Canterbury v Central Districts	Christchurch	1986/87
Otago v Northern Districts	Gisborne	1986/87
Auckland v Northern Districts	Hamilton	1989/90
Otago v Auckland	Auckland	1990/91
Wellington v Otago	Alexandra	1992/93
Central Districts v Wellington	Masterton	1993/94
Wellington v Northern Districts	Wellington	1996/97
Central Districts v Canterbury	Napier	1996/97
Wellington v Northern Districts	Whangarei	1999/00
Auckland v Northern Districts	Auckland	1999/00
Otago v Wellington	Dunedin	2000/01
Central Districts v Wellington	Waikanae	2000/01
Canterbury v Auckland	Auckland	2001/02
Otago v Northern Districts	Invercargill	2003/04

SCORES LEVEL *(won by team listed first, having lost fewer wickets)*

Otago (223-5) v Wellington (223-9)	Dunedin	1979/80
Canterbury (182-7) v Auckland (182-9)	Christchurch	1983/84
Canterbury (136-9) v Auckland (136)	Ashburton	1985/86
Queensland (174-8) v Wellington (174)	Wellington	1987/88
Wellington (227-8) v Auckland (227)	Wellington	1995/96
Canterbury (238-6) v Auckland (238-7)	Auckland	1995/96

Large Victories

RUNS *(winning team listed first)*

200	Central Districts v Otago	Hastings	1998/99
200	Central Districts v Otago	Invercargill	2004/05
197	South Africa v New Zealand Academy XI	Alexandra	1998/99
189	New Zealand A v Pakistan A	Mt Maunganui	1998/99
186	Wellington v Auckland	Wellington	1971/72
153	Otago v Wellington	Alexandra	1982/83
152	Canterbury v Central Districts	Napier	1995/96
152	Otago v Auckland	Auckland	2004/05
151	Wellington v Northern Districts	Mt Maunganui	1997/98

TEN WICKETS *(winning team listed first)*

Northern Districts (71-0) v Auckland (70)	Pukekohe	1977/78
West Indies (132-0) v Central Districts (130)	New Plymouth	1979/80
Canterbury (120-0) v Auckland (119)	Christchurch	1987/88
Auckland (81-0) v Central Districts (78)	New Plymouth	1988/89
Wellington (205-0) v Canterbury (202-7)	Wellington	1994/95
Auckland (164-0) v Central Districts (163)	Auckland	1998/99

Most Run Outs

INNINGS

5	Wellington v Auckland	Wellington	1974/75
5	Northern Districts v Wellington	Hamilton	1992/93
5	Central Districts v Northern Districts	Hamilton	2000/01
5	Otago v Canterbury	Alexandra	2004/05

MATCH

7	Wellington v Auckland	Wellington	1974/75
7	Auckland v Canterbury	Auckland	1999/00

INDIVIDUAL RECORDS

Centuries

177	Pyke J.K.	South Australia v Central Districts	Palmerston North	1986/87
161	Hartland B.R.	Canterbury v Northern Districts	Timaru	1993/94
152*	Marshall J.A.H.	Northern Districts v Canterbury	Christchurch	2006/07
149	Nevin C.J.	Wellington v Central Districts	Wellington	1997/98
147*	Edgar B.A.	Wellington v Northern Districts	Gisborne	1981/82
145	Vincent L.	Auckland v Central Districts	Napier	1999/00
143	Cairns C.L.	Canterbury v Auckland	Christchurch	1994/95
140	Scott D.G.	Auckland v Northern Districts	Hamilton	1986/87
140	Kelly D.P.	Central Districts v Wellington	Waikanae	1999/00
139*	Tendulkar S.R.	India v Central Districts	Napier	1994/95
138	Vettori D.L.	Northern Districts v Canterbury	Auckland	2004/05
137*	Papps M.H.W.	Canterbury v Northern Districts	Taupo	2005/06
134*	Howell L.G.	Canterbury v Otago	Oamaru	1997/98
133*	Vincent L.	Auckland v Northern Districts	Auckland	2000/01
133	Nevin C.J.	Wellington v Northern Districts	Wellington	2005/06
132*	Taylor L.R.P.L.	Central Districts v Otago	Dunedin	2003/04
132	Papps M.H.W.	Canterbury v Otago	Alexandra	2003/04
132	Parlane M.E.	Wellington v Central Districts	Wellington	2006/07
131	Astle N.J.	Canterbury v Wellington	Wellington	1995/96
131	Fleming S.P.	Wellington v Canterbury	Christchurch	2003/04
130*	Crowe J.J.	Auckland v Northern Districts	Auckland	1991/92
129*	Papps M.H.W.	Canterbury v Wellington	Timaru	2004/05
129	Astle N.J.	Canterbury v Northern Districts	Christchurch	1995/96
129	Vincent L.	Auckland v Canterbury	Christchurch	2006/07
128*	Edgar B.A.	Wellington v Central Districts	Wanganui	1982/83
128*	Richardson M.H.	Otago v Central Districts	New Plymouth	1996/97
127	Oram J.D.P.	Central Districts v Auckland	Auckland	1997/98
126	Vivian G.E.	Auckland v Wellington	Auckland	1977/78
126	Tavare C.J.	England XI v Otago	Alexandra	1983/84
126	Spearman C.M.	Central Districts v Canterbury	Nelson	1997/98
126	Knight N.V.	England v Northern Districts	Hamilton	2001/02
125	Crowe M.D.	Central Districts v Otago	Alexandra	1988/89
125	McMillan C.D.	Canterbury v Northern Districts	Hamilton	1998/99
125	Oram J.D.P.	Central Districts v Auckland	Auckland	2003/04
124*	Twose R.G.	Wellington v Otago	Wellington	2000/01
124	McMillan C.D.	Canterbury v Northern Districts	Auckland	2004/05
123	Styris S.B.	Northern Districts v Otago	Hamilton	1999/00
123	Astle N.J.	Canterbury v Northern Districts	Gisborne	2004/05
122*	McMillan C.D.	Canterbury v Wellington	Wellington	2002/03
122	Astle N.J.	Canterbury v Wellington	Christchurch	1999/00
122	Parlane M.E.	Northern Districts v Canterbury	Timaru	2002/03
121*	Twose R.G.	Wellington v Northern Districts	Wellington	1996/97
121*	Bell M.D.	Wellington v Central Districts	New Plymouth	1997/98
121	Williams S.C.	West Indies v Sir Ron Brierley XI	Hamilton	1994/95
121	Douglas M.W.	Central Districts v Canterbury	Christchurch	1997/98
121	Astle N.J.	Canterbury v Otago	Christchurch	2000/01
121	Taylor L.R.P.L.	Central Districts v Wellington	Palmerston North	2005/06
120*	Fleming S.P.	Wellington v Otago	Wellington	2000/01
120*	Fleming S.P.	Wellington v Northern Districts	Wellington	2003/04
118	Reid J.F.	Auckland v Central Districts	Auckland	1985/86
117	Pocock B.A.	Northern Districts v Wellington	Hamilton	1995/96
116*	Watling B-J.	Northern Districts v Otago	Dunedin	2005/06

116	Murray D.J.	Canterbury v Central Districts	Napier	1996/97
116	Barnes A.C.	Auckland v Otago	Alexandra	2003/04
116	Nevin C.J.	Wellington v Auckland	Auckland	2003/04
115*	Rutherford K.R.	Otago v Northern Districts	Alexandra	1991/92
115*	Howell L.G.	Central Districts v Northern Districts	Whangarei	1994/95
115*	Fulton P.G.	Canterbury v Otago	Timaru	2003/04
115	Cairns C.L.	Canterbury v Wellington	Christchurch	1992/93
114	McMillan C.D.	Canterbury v Wellington	Christchurch	1995/96
114	Astle N.J.	Canterbury v Otago	Alexandra	1996/97
114	Taylor L.R.P.L.	Central Districts v Otago	Napier	2005/06
113*	Richardson M.H.	Otago v Northern Districts	Mt Maunganui	1996/97
113*	McMillan C D	Canterbury v Otago	Alexandra	2004/05
113	Ingham C.D.	Central Districts v Otago	Napier	1994/95
113	Cairns C.L.	Canterbury v Otago	Christchurch	1996/97
113	Weenink S.W.	Wellington v Central Districts	Wellington	1996/97
112*	Trott I.J.L.	Otago v Northern Districts	Hamilton	2005/06
112	Cumming C.D.	Otago v Northern Districts	Dunedin	2006/07
111*	Howell L.G.	Central Districts v Otago	New Plymouth	1996/97
111	Parlane M.E.	Northern Districts v Wellington	Whangarei	1999/00
111	Nevin C.J.	Wellington v Auckland	Wellington	2001/02
110	Crowe M.D.	Wellington v Canterbury	Christchurch	1992/93
110	Sinclair M.S.	Central Districts v Otago	Oamaru	1999/00
109*	McMillan C.D.	Canterbury v Central Districts	New Plymouth	2001/02
109	Sleep P.R.	South Australia v Central Districts	New Plymouth	1986/87
109	Crowe M.D.	Wellington v Auckland	Wellington	1990/91
109	Doody B.J.K.	Canterbury v Auckland	Christchurch	1997/98
109	Astle N.J.	Canterbury v Otago	Invercargill	1999/00
109	Astle N.J.	New Zealand v FICA World XI	Wellington	2004/05
109	Vettori D.L.	Northern Districts v Auckland	Auckland	2004/05
108	Blair W.L.	Otago v Auckland	Auckland	1982/83
108	Latham R.T.	Canterbury v Otago	Oamaru	1994/95
108	Campbell S.C.	West Indies v Sir Ron Brierley XI	Hamilton	1994/95
108	Howell L.G.	Central Districts v Wellington	New Plymouth	1995/96
108	Hitchcock P.A.	Auckland v Northern Districts	Auckland	2005/06
107*	Douglas M.W.	Central Districts v Wellington	New Plymouth	1997/98
107*	Barnes A.C.	Auckland v Northern Districts	Hamilton	1999/00
107*	Elliott G.D.	Wellington v Canterbury	Christchurch	2006/07
107	Hick G.A.	Auckland v Otago	Alexandra	1997/98
107	Harris C.Z.	Canterbury v Central Districts	Napier	1998/99
107	Sinclair M.S.	New Zealand A v Sri Lanka A	Lincoln	2003/04
107	Taylor L.R.P.L.	Central Districts v Otago	New Plymouth	2005/06
107	Hitchcock P.A.	Auckland v Northern Districts	Hamilton	2005/06
106*	Edgar B.A.	Wellington v Otago	Wellington	1981/82
106*	Lamb A.J.	England XI v Otago	Alexandra	1983/84
106*	de Silva P.A.	Auckland v Canterbury	Auckland	1996/97
106*	Howell L.G.	Auckland v Central Districts	New Plymouth	2001/02
106	Vance R.H.	Wellington v Auckland	Auckland	1981/82
106	McEwan P.E.	Canterbury v Wellington	Wellington	1987/88
106	Chandler P.J.B.	Wellington v Canterbury	Christchurch	1996/97
106	Richardson M.H.	Otago v Central Districts	New Plymouth	1997/98
106	Fleming S.P.	New Zealand v FICA World XI	Christchurch	2004/05
105*	Pamment J.I.	Auckland v Wellington	Wellington	1993/94
105*	Twose R.G.	Wellington v Northern Districts	Wellington	1994/95
105*	Fleming S.P.	Canterbury v Central Districts	Napier	1996/97
105*	Twose R.G.	Central v Bangladesh	Wellington	1997/98

105*	Sinclair M.S.	North Island v South Island	Christchurch	2003/04
105	Inzamam-ul-Haq	Pakistan v Sir Ron Brierley XI	Hamilton	1993/94
105	Twose R.G.	Central v Bangladesh	Wellington	1997/98
104*	Crowe M.D.	Central Districts v Auckland	Auckland	1989/90
104*	Bell M.D.	Wellington v Northern Districts	Mt Maunganui	1997/98
104	Dempsey D.A.	Canterbury v Northern Districts	Hamilton	1980/81
104	Fleming S.P.	Wellington v Auckland	Wellington	2005/06
104	Ingram P.J.	Central Districts v Northern Districts	Hamilton	2006/07
103*	Hartland B.R.	Canterbury v Northern Districts	Christchurch	1991/92
103	McRae G.P.	Central Districts v Auckland	Wanganui	1994/95
103	Twose R.G.	Wellington v Canterbury	Christchurch	1995/96
102*	Burnett G.P.	Wellington v Northern Districts	Hamilton	1992/93
102*	Cumming C.D.	Otago v Northern Districts	Taupo	2006/07
102	Blair W.L.	Otago v Wellington	Dunedin	1979/80
102	Franklin T.J.	Auckland v Northern Districts	Auckland	1981/82
102	Wright J.G.	Canterbury v Wellington	Wellington	1985/86
102	Rutherford K.R.	Otago v Wellington	Alexandra	1993/94
102	Cooper B.G.	Northern Districts v Otago	Alexandra	1994/95
102	Fleming S.P.	Canterbury v Northern Districts	Christchurch	1995/96
102	Twose R.G.	Wellington v Northern Districts	Hamilton	1998/99
102	Hore A.J.	Otago v Wellington	Wellington	2001/02
102	Stewart S.L.	Canterbury v Wellington	Wellington	2003/04
102	Papps M.H.W.	Canterbury v Wellington	Wellington	2004/05
101*	Crowe M.D.	Central Districts v Northern Districts	Whangarei	1983/84
101*	Maynard M.P.	Northern Districts v Auckland	Hamilton	1990/91
101*	Aiken J.M.	Wellington v Canterbury	Wellington	1994/95
101*	Young B.A.	Northern Districts v Central Districts	Mt Maunganui	1995/96
101*	Stead G.R.	Canterbury v Auckland	Auckland	2001/02
101*	Astle N.J.	Canterbury v Central Districts	Christchurch	2001/02
101*	Gaffaney C.B.	Otago v Auckland	Auckland	2004/05
101	White D.J.	Northern Districts v Central Districts	Tauranga	1989/90
101	Burnett G.P.	Northern Districts v Central Districts	Whangarei	1994/95
101	Parlane M.E.	Northern Districts v Canterbury	Taupo	1994/95
101	McMillan C.D.	Canterbury v Central Districts	Christchurch	1994/95
101	Stewart S.L.	Canterbury v Otago	Dunedin	2005/06
101	Houpapa D.W.	Auckland v Wellington	Wellington	2006/07
100*	Bell M.D.	Wellington v Canterbury	Wellington	1999/00
100*	Marshall J.A.H.	Northern Districts v Canterbury	Christchurch	2000/01
100	Rutherford I.A.	Otago v Auckland	Auckland	1980/81
100	Hick G.A.	Northern Districts v Canterbury	Rangiora	1987/88
100	Brown S.W.	Auckland v Northern Districts	Hamilton	1990/91
100	Douglas M.W.	Wellington v South Africa	Wellington	1994/95
100	Hart M.N.	Northern Districts v Central Districts	Napier	1996/97
100	Twose R.G.	Wellington v Canterbury	Christchurch	1996/97
100	Wells J.D.	Wellington v Auckland	Wellington	1997/98
100	Stead G.R.	Canterbury v Otago	Oamaru	1997/98
100	Ingram P.J.	Central Districts v Otago	Invercargill	2001/02
100	Nevin C.J.	Wellington v Canterbury	Wellington	2002/03

Fastest Centuries

Balls				
54	Fleming S.P.	New Zealand v FICA World XI	Christchurch	2004/05
65	de Silva P.A.	Auckland v Canterbury	Auckland	1996/97
72	Howell L.G.	Central Districts v Otago	New Plymouth	1996/97
77	McMillan C.D.	Canterbury v Central Districts	New Plymouth	2001/02
78	Astle N.J.	Canterbury v Central Districts	Christchurch	2001/02
79	Hick G.A.	Northern Districts v Canterbury	Rangiora	1987/88
83	Fleming S.P.	Canterbury v Central Districts	Napier	1996/97
83	Nevin C.J.	Wellington v Central Districts	Wellington	1997/98
86	Vettori D.L.	Northern Districts v Canterbury	Auckland	2004/05
86	Hitchcock P.A.	Auckland v Northern Districts	Hamilton	2005/06
87	Marshall J.A.H.	Northern Districts v Canterbury	Christchurch	2000/01
87	Houpapa D.W.	Auckland v Wellington	Wellington	2006/07
88	Dempsey D.A.	Canterbury v Northern Districts	Hamilton	1980/81
88	Cairns C.L.	Canterbury v Auckland	Christchurch	1994/95
88	Twose R.G.	Wellington v Canterbury	Christchurch	1995/96
89	McMillan C.D.	Canterbury v Wellington	Wellington	2002/03
89	Parlane M.E.	Wellington v Central Districts	Wellington	2006/07
91	Ingram P.J.	Central Districts v Northern Districts	Hamilton	2006/07
92	McMillan C.D.	Canterbury v Northern Districts	Hamilton	1998/99
92	McMillan C.D.	Canterbury v Otago	Alexandra	2004/05
94	Fleming S.P.	Canterbury v Northern Districts	Christchurch	1995/96
94	Hore A.J.	Otago v Wellington	Wellington	2001/02
94	McMillan C.D.	Canterbury v Northern Districts	Auckland	2004/05
94	Taylor L.R.P.L.	Central Districts v Otago	New Plymouth	2005/06
99	Rutherford K.R.	Otago v Wellington	Alexandra	1993/94
99	Astle N.J.	Canterbury v Northern Districts	Christchurch	1995/96
99	Twose R.G.	Wellington v Canterbury	Christchurch	1996/97
99	Hitchcock P.A.	Auckland v Northern Districts	Auckland	2005/06

Fastest Fifties

Balls				
20	Cairns C.L.	Canterbury v Northern Districts	Timaru	2002/03
22	Maynard M.P.	Otago v Auckland	Alexandra	1997/98
23	Greatbatch M.J.	Central Districts v Otago	New Plymouth	1996/97
26	Cairns B.L.	Northern Districts v Canterbury	Rangiora	1987/88
26	Bulfin C.E.	Central Districts v Wellington	New Plymouth	1997/98
26	McSkimming W.C.	Otago v Northern Districts	Oamaru	2000/01
27	Loveridge G.R.	Central Districts v Wellington	Wellington	1995/96
27	de Silva P.A.	Auckland v Canterbury	Auckland	1996/97
27	Vettori D.L.	Northern Districts v Auckland	Auckland	1999/00
28	Cooper B.G.	Northern Districts v Otago	Mt Maunganui	1994/95
28	Parlane M.E.	Northern Districts v Wellington	Mt Maunganui	1994/95
28	Spearman C.M.	Central Districts v Otago	New Plymouth	2002/03
28	Mills K.D.	Auckland v Canterbury	Christchurch	2006/07
29	Fleming S.P.	Wellington v Northern Districts	Taupo	2004/05
30	Spearman C.M.	Auckland v Wellington	Wellington	1995/96
30	Doull S.B.	Northern Districts v England	Hamilton	2001/02
31	Spearman C.M.	Central Districts v Canterbury	Christchurch	2003/04
32	Petrie R.G.	Wellington v Northern Districts	Mt Maunganui	1994/95
32	Howell L.G.	Canterbury v Wellington	Christchurch	1998/99
32	McMillan C.D.	Canterbury v Northern Districts	Hamilton	1998/99
32	Nevin C.J.	Wellington v Canterbury	Wellington	1999/00
32	Horne M.J.	Auckland v Wellington	Wellington	2001/02

32	Hore A.J.	Otago v Wellington	Wellington	2001/02
32	Wilson J.W.	Otago v Auckland	Auckland	2004/05
32	Styris S.B.	Northern Districts v Wellington	Taupo	2004/05
32	Diamanti B.J.	Central Districts v Otago	Palmerston North	2006/07
33	Blain T.E.	Central Districts v Wellington	Wellington	1991/92
33	Finch C.W.J.	Otago v Central Districts	New Plymouth	1993/94
33	Brown R.K.	Central Districts v Otago	Hastings	1998/99
33	Horne M.J.	Auckland v Central Districts	Auckland	2001/02
33	Thompson E.P.	Central Districts v Wellington	Nelson	2006/07
34	Dempsey D.A.	Canterbury v Northern Districts	Hamilton	1980/81
34	Gill S.J.	Central Districts v Wellington	Wanganui	1982/83
34	McEwan P.E.	Canterbury v Central Districts	Ashburton	1988/89
34	Cairns C.L.	Canterbury v Otago	Dunedin	1991/92
34	Howell L.G.	Central Districts v Northern Districts	Taupo	1996/97
34	Hart R.G.	Northern Districts v Wellington	Wellington	1996/97
34	Parlane M.E.	Northern Districts v Central Districts	Hamilton	1997/98
34	Walker M.D.J.	Wellington v Auckland	Wellington	2001/02
34	Vettori D.L.	Northern Districts v Canterbury	Auckland	2004/05

Note: I.D.S. Smith reached fifty from 24 balls for Auckland v Central Districts at Auckland, 1989/90 but the game was abandoned and restarted the following day and none of the performances in the game are included in any records).

Five Wickets in an Innings

7-0-23-7	Watson W.	Auckland v Otago	Auckland	1984/85
8-1-28-7	Penn A.J.	Wellington v Northern Districts	Mt Maunganui	2000/01
7.1-0-49-7	Marshall E.J.	Otago v Auckland	Dunedin	1993/94
10-5-12-6	Barrett B.J.	Northern Districts v Otago	Gisborne	1986/87
5.5-0-12-6	Cairns C.L.	New Zealand v FICA World XI	Hamilton	2004/05
9.3-1-25-6	Mason M.J.	Central Districts v Auckland	Auckland	2003/04
9.5-3-26-6	Vaughan J.T.C.	Auckland v Otago	Auckland	1995/96
10-2-26-6	Su'a M.L.	Auckland v Central Districts	New Plymouth	1995/96
7.7-2-31-6	Intikhab Alam	Pakistan v NZ Under 23 XI	Rotorua	1972/73
10-1-37-6	Cairns C.L.	Canterbury v Wellington	Christchurch	1996/97
9.3-0-43-6	Wisneski W.A.	Canterbury v Auckland	Christchurch	1996/97
10-1-49-6	Penn A.J.	Central Districts v Northern Districts	Napier	1996/97
6-1-7-5	Adams A.R.	Auckland v Northern Districts	Auckland	1999/00
7.3-3-9-5	McSkimming W.C.	Otago v Wellington	Dunedin	2005/06
5.3-2-10-5	Hitchcock P.A.	Wellington v Central Districts	Wellington	2001/02
3-0-11-5	Thompson S.	New South Wales v Canterbury	Christchurch	1993/94
8.3-2-12-5	Turner A.D.	Wellington v Otago	Wellington	2002/03
8.1-3-14-5	Shaw H.J.	Canterbury v Central Districts	Christchurch	2002/03
10-4-16-5	Brown C.M.	Auckland v Otago	Auckland	1996/97
8.3-2-17-5	Cederwall G.N.	Wellington v Canterbury	Rangiora	1984/85
8.4-1-19-5	Snedden M.C.	Auckland v Canterbury	Auckland	1982/83
9-2-19-5	Barnes A.C.	Auckland v Central Districts	Auckland	1998/99
10-2-19-5	Penn A.J.	Wellington v Auckland	Auckland	2001/02
10-4-19-5	Hamilton L.J.	Central Districts v Otago	Invercargill	2004/05
10-4-20-5	Visser P.J.	Central Districts v Otago	New Plymouth	1985/86
10-1-20-5	Adams A.R.	Auckland v Central Districts	Auckland	1999/00
10-1-21-5	McNally S.R.	Canterbury v Auckland	Auckland	1984/85
10-4-22-5	Walker M.D.J.	Wellington v Central Districts	New Plymouth	2002/03
5.4-0-22-5	Schwass A.M.	Central Districts v Northern Districts	Taupo	2004/05
7-0-23-5	Collinge R.O.	Wellington v Otago	Wellington	1974/75
10-2-23-5	Brown S.W.	Auckland v Northern Districts	Auckland	1991/92
6.4-0-23-5	Cairns C.L.	Canterbury v Central Districts	Timaru	1995/96
8.5-1-24-5	Wundke S.C.	South Australia v Central Districts	Palmerston North	1986/87

10-4-24-5	Petrie R.G.	Canterbury v Auckland	Christchurch	1989/90
9.3-1-25-5	Maxwell N.D.	Canterbury v Auckland	Christchurch	1997/98
10-2-26-5	Priest M.W.	Canterbury v Auckland	Auckland	1988/89
7.1-1-26-5	Burtt L.M.	Canterbury v Auckland	Auckland	2005/06
9-0-27-5	Hunt A.J.	Auckland v Canterbury	Ashburton	1985/86
10-1-28-5	Holland R.G.	NSW v Wellington	Wellington	1984/85
10-2-30-5	Twose R.G.	Wellington v Otago	Alexandra	1995/96
10-3-30-5	Larsen G.R.	Wellington v Auckland	Wellington	1995/96
9.5-0-32-5	Cederwall G.N.	Wellington v Central Districts	Nelson	1984/85
10-2-34-5	Parry D.R.	West Indies v Auckland	Auckland	1979/80
10-1-34-5	Beard D.A.	Northern Districts v Central Districts	New Plymouth	1990/91
10-2-34-5	Anderson C.J.	Canterbury v Wellington	Wellington	2001/02
9-0-34-5	Aldridge G.W.	Northern Districts v Canterbury	Timaru	2004/05
10-1-35-5	Jamieson M.D.	Central Districts v Wellington	Masterton	1980/81
9-0-35-5	O'Brien I.E.	Wellington v Central Districts	Wellington	2004/05
8.5-1-36-5	Robertson G.K.	Central Districts v Northern Districts	Wanganui	1984/85
10-2-38-5	Hellaby A.T.R.	Auckland v Central Districts	Auckland	1987/88
9-0-38-5	McMillan C.D.	Canterbury v Northern Districts	Whangarei	1996/97
9.5-0-39-5	Roberts S.J.	Canterbury v Central Districts	Nelson	1994/95
10-0-39-5	Brown C.M.	Auckland v Northern Districts	Mt Maunganui	1996/97
10-2-40-5	Harvie M.J.	Otago v Northern Districts	Dunedin	2006/07
10-1-41-5	Drum C.J.	Auckland v Canterbury	Christchurch	1998/99
9.5-0-42-5	Su'a M.L.	Auckland v Northern Districts	Auckland	1993/94
10-2-42-5	Blake D.C.	Central Districts v Northern Districts	New Plymouth	1997/98
10-1-43-5	Gale A.J.	Otago v Northern Districts	Alexandra	1991/92
10-0-43-5	Martin C.S.	Canterbury v Northern Districts	Mt Maunganui	1999/00
10-0-43-5	O'Brien I.E.	Wellington v Central Districts	Wellington	2005/06
9.3-3-44-5	Stott L.W.	Auckland v Otago	Oamaru	1981/82
10-0-44-5	Nash D.J.	Northern Districts v Otago	Taupo	1995/96
10-0-45-5	McNally S.R.	Canterbury v Otago	Christchurch	1984/85
10-0-48-5	Leonard D.J.	Central Districts v Canterbury	Levin	1989/90
10-2-58-5	Yardley B.	Australia v Northern Districts	Hamilton	1981/82
8.5-0-58-5	Diamanti B.J.	Central Districts v Northern Districts	Hamilton	2006/07

(Note: A.J. Alcock had figures of 10-3-31-5 for Central Districts v Canterbury at Christchurch, 1993/94, but the game was abandoned and none of the performances in the game are included in any records).

Most Expensive Bowling

10-0-93-2	Presland C.M.	Northern Districts v Auckland	Gisborne	1982/83
9-0-85-1	Kennedy R.J.	Otago v Canterbury	Christchurch	1996/97
10-1-85-0	Kennedy R.J.	Otago v Central Districts	New Plymouth	1996/97
9-1-84-0	Styris S.B.	Northern Districts v Auckland	Auckland	2000/01
10-0-83-2	Welch G.	Wellington v Central Districts	New Plymouth	1997/98
10-0-80-3	Blair B.R.	Otago v Central Districts	Oamaru	1982/83
9-0-80-0	Rushton N.W.	Otago v Canterbury	Timaru	2003/04
10-0-78-0	Pryor C.R.	Otago v Wellington	Wellington	2000/01
10-2-77-0	Stott L.W.	Auckland v Northern Districts	Gisborne	1982/83
10-0-77-0	Kennedy R.J.	Otago v Canterbury	Oamaru	1997/98
10-0-77-3	Martin B.P.	New Zealand A v Sri Lanka A	lincoln	2003/04
10-0-76-1	Thomson G.B.	Otago v Wellington	Alexandra	1980/81
10-0-76-3	McNally S.R.	Canterbury v Northern Districts	Rangiora	1981/82
10-0-76-2	Findlay C.O.	Central Districts v Canterbury	Christchurch	1998/99
10-0-75-1	Marshall E.J.	Otago v Central Districts	Dannevirke	1992/93
10-0-75-1	Hastings M.A.	Canterbury v Central Districts	New Plymouth	1997/98
10-0-75-1	Martin C.S.	Canterbury v Central Districts	Christchurch	2003/04
9-0-75-2	Burtt L.M.	Canterbury v Northern Districts	Christchurch	2006/07

ALSO NOTE *(8-ball overs)*

1-0-18-0	Payton D.H.	Central Districts v Wellington	Wellington	1973/74
1-0-18-1	Redpath I.R.	Australia v Central Districts	New Plymouth	1973/74
2-0-29-0	Child M.J.	Northern Districts v Central Districts	Palmerston North	1975/76
3-0-37-0	Dunning B.	Northern Districts v Canterbury	Christchurch	1977/78
4-0-42-1	Maingay C.T.	Auckland v Wellington	Wellington	1971/72
5-0-48-0	Coles M.J.	Wellington v Canterbury	Christchurch	1975/76
6-0-56-0	Cater S.B.	Wellington v Auckland	Auckland	1977/78
6-0-56-0	Gilmour G.J.	Australia v Invitation XI	Christchurch	1976/77
7-0-68-1	Aldridge C.W.	Northern Districts v Auckland	Auckland	1978/79

ALSO NOTE *(6-ball overs)*

1-0-22-0	Pryor C.R.	Auckland v Wellington	Wellington	1998/99
2-0-26-0	Roberts S.J.	Canterbury v Wellington	Ohoka	1990/91
2.2-0-29-0	Harvie M.J.	Otago v Wellington	Wellington	2006/07
3-0-42-1	McMillan C.D.	Canterbury v Central Districts	Napier	1996/97
3.1-0-57-0	Muralitharan M.	FICA World XI v New Zealand	Christchurch	2004/05
4-0-46-0	Trott I.J.L.	Otago v Canterbury	Dunedin	2005/06
5-0-47-0	Kuggeleijn C.M.	Northern Districts v Wellington	Wellington	1990/91
5.3-0-50-0	Abernethy B.	Otago v Auckland	Oamaru	1981/82
6-0-65-0	de Silva D.S.	Sri Lanka v Minor Associations	Wanganui	1982/83
7-0-71-2	Aldridge G.W.	Northern Districts v Wellington	Taupo	2004/05

Most Economical Bowling

10-7-5-2	Boock S.L.	Otago v Central Districts	Alexandra	1986/87
10-5-6-2	Larsen G.R.	Wellington v Otago	Alexandra	1992/93
*8-3-7-2	Williams J.C.	Auckland v Northern Districts	Auckland	1971/72
10-6-8-1	Hills P.W.	Otago v Auckland	Oamaru	1981/82
10-6-8-2	Nuttall A.J.	Canterbury v Wellington	Christchurch	1988/89
10-4-8-0	Duff S.W.	Central Districts v Wellington	New Plymouth	1989/90
10-5-8-3	Vaughan J.T.C.	Auckland v Central Districts	Waikanae	1993/94
10-5-8-1	Harris C.Z.	Canterbury v Auckland	Christchurch	1995/96
*7-0-9-0	Dunning B.	Northern Districts v Canterbury	Christchurch	1976/77
10-6-9-1	Boock S.L.	Otago v Canterbury	Christchurch	1979/80
10-4-9-1	de Mel A.L.F.	Sri Lanka v Minor Associations	Wanganui	1982/83
10-5-9-2	Astle N.J.	Canterbury v Northern Districts	Christchurch	1991/92
10-4-9-2	Astle N.J.	Canterbury v Wellington	Christchurch	1993/94
10-3-9-1	de Groen R.P.	Northern Districts v Central Districts	Levin	1995/96
10-6-9-2	McCullum N.J.	Otago v Auckland	Auckland	2000/01
*7-1-10-2	Kirk C.M.	Canterbury v Otago	Christchurch	1973/74
10-5-10-3	McIntyre J.M.	Auckland v Canterbury	Auckland	1980/81
10-4-10-2	Pigott A.C.S.	Wellington v Northern Districts	Tauranga	1983/84
10-6-10-0	Bracewell J.G.	Auckland v Canterbury	Auckland	1986/87
10-7-10-4	Duers K.G.	Zimbabwe v Northern Districts	Cambridge	1991/92
10-3-10-2	Williams B.R.	Wellington v Northern Districts	Gisborne	1993/94
10-3-10-3	Larsen G.R.	Wellington v Canterbury	Rangiora	1994/95

* *8-ball overs*

(Note: C.M. Brown had figures of 10-5-6-2 for Auckland v Otago at Dunedin, 1993/94 but the game was abandoned and none of the performances in the game are included in any records).

Hat-tricks

7-0-23-7	Watson W.	Auckland v Otago	Auckland	1984/85
10-0-48-4	Briasco P.S.	Central Districts v Auckland	Napier	1989/90
10-1-40-3	Walker M.D.J.	Wellington v Otago	Dunedin	2000/01

Wicketkeeping

DISMISSALS

	(ct/st)				
6	(5/1)	Murray D.A.	West Indies v Central Districts	New Plymouth	1979/80
6	(6/0)	McSweeney E.B.	Wellington v Auckland	Wellington	1982/83
6	(6/0)	McSweeney E.B.	Wellington v Northern Districts	Wellington	1988/89
6	(6/0)	McRae G.P.	Central Districts v Wellington	Masterton	1994/95
5	(5/0)	Dykes R.A.	Auckland v Wellington	Wellington	1973/74
5	(4/1)	Smith I.D.S.	Central Districts v Northern Districts	Hamilton	1981/82
5	(5/0)	Milburn B.D.	Otago v Central Districts	Oamaru	1982/83
5	(5/0)	Wright M.J.E.	Northern Districts v Auckland	Gisborne	1982/83
5	(5/0)	Germon L.K.	Canterbury v Otago	Christchurch	1988/89
5	(3/2)	Blain T.E.	Central Districts v Auckland	New Plymouth	1992/93
5	(4/1)	Adams J.C.	West Indies v Auckland	Auckland	1994/95
5	(4/1)	Nevin C.J.	Wellington v Otago	Wellington	1997/98
5	(4/1)	Nevin C.J.	Wellington v Otago	Wellington	2000/01
5	(5/0)	Griggs B.B.J.	Central Districts v Auckland	Auckland	2000/01
5	(5/0	Vincent L.	Auckland v Otago	Auckland	2002/03
5	(4/1)	Nevin C.J.	North Island v South Island	Christchurch	2003/04
5	(5/0)	McCullum B.B.	New Zealand v FICA World XI	Hamilton	2004/05
5	(4/1)	Mills S.M.	Wellington v Northern Districts	Wellington	2006/07

THREE STUMPINGS IN AN INNINGS

Rixon S.J.	NSW v Wellington	Wellington	1984/85
Dyer G.C.	NSW v Wellington	Wellington	1986/87

Fielding

CATCHES

5	Wilson J.W.	Otago v Auckland	Dunedin	1993/94
4	Redmond R.E.	Auckland v Otago	Auckland	1972/73
4	Sampson H.C.	Otago v Canterbury	Christchurch	1974/75
4	Howarth G.P.	Invitation XI v Australia	Auckland	1976/77
4	Wiltshire J.R.	Auckland v Northern Districts	Auckland	1978/79
4	Dickeson C.W.	Northern Districts v Canterbury	Hamilton	1980/81
4	Cooper B.G.	Northern Districts v Central Districts	Palmerston North	1982/83
4	Hore A.J.	Otago v Canterbury	Christchurch	1998/99

HISTORY OF THE LIMITED-OVER COMPETITION IN NEW ZEALAND

2006/07 was the 36th season of limited over competition between the six New Zealand first-class sides. In that time there have been several changes both in sponsorship and format.

For the first six seasons a knock-out competition was sponsored by the New Zealand Motor Corporation. Each innings was limited to 40 eight-ball overs during the initial two seasons, reduced to 35 thereafter. In 1977/78 and 1978/79 the sponsors changed and the teams competed for the Gillette Cup. In the first season 30 eight-ball overs were used but the limit reverted to 35 the following year. There was no sponsorship for the competition in 1979/80, known simply as the National Knock-out, where 50 six-ball overs was the limit for each innings.

In 1980/81. the Shell Cup, previously contested for as part of the first-class season, became the limited-over prize and the contest was run on a league basis for the first time with each side playing the other once.

In keeping with the previous limited-over competitions, a final was arranged, this time between the top two teams of the league table, points gained being disregarded at this stage. Fifty six-ball overs was the limit on each innings.

From 1985/86 the competition was held in its entirety, prior to the Shell Trophy series with no final. From 1989/90 the top four teams in the league table went on to semi-final play-offs, previous points being disregarded. The top two teams gained home ground advantage, the venue for the final being decided in a similar manner.

From 1993/94 to 1998/99 the top two sides played each other, with the winner going into the grand final. The loser then played the winner of the game between third and fourth to find the other finalist. From 1999/00, the leading team after the round robin went straight to the final with the second and third-placed sides meeting in a semi-final to find the other finalist. The finals became a best-of-three series.

In 2001/02, with a change of sponsor, the competition was renamed the State Shield. The format remained unaltered except the final reverted to a single game.

Winners of Limited-over Competitions

NEW ZEALAND MOTOR CORPORATION KNOCK-OUT

1971/72	Canterbury
1972/73	Auckland
1973/74	Wellington
1974/75	Wellington
1975/76	Canterbury
1976/77	Canterbury

GILLETTE CUP

1977/78	Canterbury
1978/79	Auckland

NATIONAL KNOCK-OUT

1979/80	Northern Districts

SHELL CUP

1980/81	Auckland
1981/82	Wellington
1982/83	Auckland
1983/84	Auckland
1984/85	Central Districts
1985/86	Canterbury
1986/87	Auckland
1987/88	Otago
1988/89	Wellington
1989/90	Auckland
1990/91	Wellington
1991/92	Canterbury
1992/93	Canterbury
1993/94	Canterbury
1994/95	Northern Districts
1995/96	Canterbury
1996/97	Canterbury
1997/98	Northern Districts
1998/99	Canterbury
1999/00	Canterbury
2000/01	Central Districts

STATE SHIELD

2001/02	Wellington
2002/03	Northern Districts
2003/04	Central Districts
2004/05	Northern Districts
2005/06	Canterbury
2006/07	Auckland

Table of Results

1971/72 – 2006/07

	P	*W*	*L*	*T*	*NR*
Auckland	239*	109	111	1	18
Canterbury	249	142	94	–	13
Central Districts	232	97	116	–	19
Northern Districts	240	112	121	1	6
Otago	225	78	136	–	11
Wellington	243	136	96	–	11

** The Auckland and Central Districts totals include a match won by the toss of a coin against Central Districts and Northern Districts respectively.*

Northern Districts v Otago in 1980/81, Auckland v Wellington in 1985/86, Canterbury v Auckland, Auckland v Central Districts and Wellington v Otago in 1991/92, Central Districts v Auckland and Auckland v Wellington in 1996/97, Canterbury v Northern Districts in 1997/98, Central Districts v Canterbury in 1999/00 and Central Districts v Otago, Northern Districts, Canterbury and Auckland and Auckland v Canterbury in 2000/01 were abandoned without a ball being bowled. Wellington v Auckland in 1984/85 and Northern Districts v Canterbury 1988/89 were abandoned after one innings had been completed. The semi-final between Canterbury and Central Districts 1993/94 was due to be replayed after a match had been started and abandoned. However, no play at all was possible in the scheduled replay.

INTER-PROVINCIAL RECORDS

	Highest Score	*Lowest Score*	*Highest Individual Score*	*Best Bowling*
Auckland	318-5 v N.D. 2000/01	70 v N.D. 1977/78	L. Vincent 145 v C.D. 1999/00	W. Watson 7-0-23-7 v Otago 1984/85
Canterbury	329-5 v N.D. 1995/96	75 v Otago 1973/74	B.R. Hartland 161 v N.D. 1993/94	C.L. Cairns 10-1-37-6 v Wellington 1996/97
Central Districts	376-3 v Otago 1996/97	58 v Wellington 2001/02	D.P. Kelly 140 v Wellington 1999/00	M.J. Mason 9.3-1-25-6 v Auckland 2003/04
Northern Districts	332-5 v Canterbury 2006/07	76 v C.D. 1987/88	J.A.H. Marshall 152* v Canterbury 2006/07	B.J. Barrett 10-5-12-6 v Otago 1986/87
Otago	299-9 v CD 2004/05	64 v Wellington/CD 1984/85 2004/05	M.H. Richardson 128* v C.D. 1996/97	E.J. Marshall 7.1-0-49-7 v Auckland 1993/94
Wellington	308-9 v Canterbury 2003/04	66 v Canterbury 1996/97	C.J. Nevin 149 v CD 1997/98	A.J. Penn 8-1-28-7 v ND 2000/01

	Most Economical Bowling	Most Expensive Bowling	Most Catches/ Stumpings in an innings
Auckland	J.T.C. Vaughan 10-5-8-3 v C.D. 1993/94 J.C. Williams 8-3-7-2 (8 ball overs) v N.D. 1971/72	L.W. Stott 10-2-77-0 v N.D. 1982/83	R.A. Dykes 5c v Wellington 1973/74 L. Vincent 5c v Otago 2002/03
Canterbury	A.J. Nuttall 10-6-8-2 v Wellington 1988/89 C.Z. Harris 10-5-8-1 v Auckland 1995/96	S.R. McNally 10-0-76-3 v N.D. 1981/82	L.K. Germon 5c v Otago 1988/89
Central Districts	S.W. Duff 10-4-8-0 v Wellington 1989/90	C.O. Findlay 10-0-76-2 v Canterbury 1998/99	G.P. McRae 6c v Wellington 1994/95
Northern Districts	R.P. de Groen 10-3-9-1 v C.D. 1995/96	C.M. Presland 10-0-93-2 v Auckland 1982/83	M.J.E. Wright 5c v Auckland 1982/83
Otago	S.L. Boock 10-7-5-2 v C.D. 1986/87	R.J. Kennedy 9-0-85-1 v Canterbury 1996/97 R.J. Kennedy 10-1-85-0 v C.D. 1996/97	B.D. Milburn 5c v C.D. 1982/83 J.W. Wilson 5c v Auckland 1993/94
Wellington	G.R. Larsen 10-5-6-2 v Otago 1992/93	G. Welch 10-0-83-2 v CD 1997/98	E.B. McSweeney 6c v Auckland 1982/83 E.B. McSweeney 6c v N.D. 1988/89

RECORD PARTNERSHIPS

AUCKLAND

1st	166*	Young B.A. & Pocock B.A.	v Central Districts	Auckland	1998/99
2nd	156	Hitchcock P.A. & Jones R.A.	v Canterbury	Auckland	2006/07
3rd	129	Crowe J.J. & Vaughan J.T.C.	v Otago	Alexandra	1991/92
4th	157	Nicol R.J. & Barnes A.C.	v Otago	Auckland	2003/04
5th	171	Vivian G.E. & Reid J.F.	v Wellington	Auckland	1977/78
6th	109	Lynch S.M. & Vaughan J.T.C.	v Otago	Auckland	1996/97
7th	87	Mills K.D. & Hitchcock P.A.	v Central Districts	Auckland	2004/05
8th	† 121	Canning T.K. & Morgan R.G.	v Otago	Alexandra	2000/01
9th	59	Mills J.M. & Haslam M.J.	v Wellington	Wellington	1998/99
10th	47	Lyon B.J. & Walmsley K.P.	v Central Districts	Auckland	1997/98
	47*	Parore A.C. & Haslam M.J.	v Canterbury	Auckland	2001/02

CANTERBURY

1st	168	Papps M.H.W. & Astle N.J.	v Wellington	Timaru	2004/05
2nd	† 189	Hartland B.R. & Howell L.G.	v Northern Districts	Timaru	1993/94
3rd	174	McMillan C.D. & Latham R.T.	v Central Districts	Christchurch	1994/95
4th	† 221	Howell L.G. & Stead G.R.	v Otago	Oamaru	1997/98
5th	† 198	Cairns C.L. & Germon L.K.	v Wellington	Christchurch	1992/93
6th	† 142	Cairns C.L. & Fleming S.P.	v Central Districts	Napier	1993/94
7th	74	Redmond A.J. & Wisneski W.A.	v Wellington	Wellington	2001/02
8th	91	Harris C.Z. & Wiseman P.J.	v Central Districts	Christchurch	2003/04
9th	53	Howell L.G. & Petrie R.G.	v Wellington	Wellington	1991/92
10th	34*	Anderson C.J. & Burson R.D.	v Otago	Oamaru	2001/02

CENTRAL DISTRICTS

1st	155	Spearman C.M. & How J.M.	v Canterbury	Christchurch	2003/04
2nd	172	How J.M. & Taylor L.R.P.L.	v Northern Districts	Masterton	2004/05
3rd	156	Oram J.D.P. & Douglas M.W.	v Otago	Hastings	1998/99
4th	132	Sinclair M.S. & Oram J.D.P.	v Auckland	Auckland	2003/04
5th	153*	Harden R.J. & Blain T.E.	v Canterbury	Christchurch	1990/91
6th	103	Sandbrook I.P. & Griggs B.B.J.	v Canterbury	Nelson	2002/03
7th	109	Sulzberger G.P. & Furlong C.J.M.	v Otago	Palmerston Nth	1997/98
8th	79	Findlay C.O. & Furlong C.J.M.	v Northern Districts	Nelson	1998/99
9th	92	Loveridge G.R. & Penn A.J.	v Canterbury	Napier	1996/97
10th	50	Garner C.D. & Alcock A.J.	v Otago	Oamaru	1993/94

NORTHERN DISTRICTS

1st	168	Marshall J.A.H. & Vettori D.L.	v Wellington	Hamilton	2002/03
2nd	126*	Parlane M.E. & Parlane N.R.	v Otago	Alexandra	1999/00
3rd	199*	Parker J.M. & Cooper B.G.	v Auckland	Gisborne	1982/83
4th	123	Parore A.C. & Thomson S.A.	v Canterbury	Mt Maunganui	1995/96
5th	137	Nash D.J. & Bradburn G.E.	v Otago	Taupo	1997/98
6th	115	Bell M.D. & Hart M.N.	v Central Districts	Napier	1996/97
7th	96	Styris S.B. & McGlashan P.D.	v Central Districts	Masterton	2004/05
8th	75	Dickeson C.W. & Child M.J.	v Auckland	Pukekohe	1980/81
9th	68*	Hart R.G. & Styris S.B.	v Wellington	Wellington	1996/97
10th	† 62	Aldridge G.W. & Butler I.G.	v Canterbury	Hamilton	2003/04

OTAGO

1st	154	Hore A.J. & Lawson R.A.	v Wellington	Wellington	2001/02
2nd	134*	Richardson M.H. & Lamont M.J.	v Auckland	Auckland	1998/99
3rd	138	Gaffaney C.B. & Lawson R.A.	v Wellington	Dunedin	2003/04
4th	190	Trott I.J.L. & Broom N.T.	v Northern Districts	Hamilton	2005/06
5th	130	McKenzie M.N. & McGlashan P.D.	v Northern Districts	Rotorua	2002/03
6th	129	Trott I.J.L. & McCullum N.L.	v Auckland	Alexandra	2005/06
7th	103*	Richardson M.H. & Campbell P.A.	v Central Districts	New Plymouth	1996/97
8th	93	McSkimming W.C. & Morland N.D.	v Central Districts	New Plymouth	2002/03
9th	51	Scott B.E. & Shaw G.S.	v Northern Districts	Dunedin	2005/06
10th	56*	McSkimming W.C. & Sewell D.G.	v Northern Districts	Oamaru	2000/01

WELLINGTON

1st	† 205*	Aiken J.M. & Douglas M.W.	v Canterbury	Wellington	1994/95
2nd	173	Weenink S.W. & Wells J.D.	v Central Districts	Wellington	1996/97
3rd	† 244*	Fleming S.P. & Twose R.G.	v Otago	Wellington	2000/01
4th	143	Jones A.H. & Coney J.V.	v Canterbury	Timaru	1986/87
5th	127	Twose R.G. & Kerr R.J.	v Northern Districts	Wellington	1996/97
6th	109	Nevin C.J. & Franklin J.E.C.	v Northern Districts	Wellington	2005/06
7th	† 130*	Bell M.D. & Mather S.R.	v Northern Districts	Mt Maunganui	1997/98
8th	98*	Taylor B.R. & Collinge R.O.	v Central Districts	Lower Hutt	1971/72
9th	† 98	Doull L.J. & Williams B.R.	v Otago	Alexandra	1993/94
10th	36*	Jefferson M.R. & R.J. Kennedy	v Canterbury	Christchurch	1999/00

† *record for all teams*

DOMESTIC ONE-DAY CAREER RECORDS

BATTING		*M*	*In*	*NO*	*HS*	*Runs*	*Ave*	*100s*	*50s*
Harris C.Z.	*C*	122	111	37	107	3385	45.74	1	20
Parlane M.E.	*ND, W*	119	119	7	132	3351	29.91	4	20
Astle N.J.	*C*	99	90	12	131	3285	42.11	8	16
Howell L.G.	*C. CD, A, ND*	105	105	14	134*	3022	33.20	5	22
Barnes A.C.	*A*	114	112	11	116	2866	28.37	2	20
Nevin C.J.	*W*	112	106	6	149	2823	28.23	5	13
Twose R.G.	*ND, CD, W*	95	93	9	124*	2769	32.96	6	16
Sinclair M.S.	*CD*	98	95	12	110	2670	32.16	1	21
Fleming S.P.	*C, W*	75	70	11	131	2590	43.89	6	17
McMillan C.D.	*C*	88	84	12	125	2550	35.41	7	9
Bell M.D.	*ND, W*	109	104	8	121*	2462	25.64	3	12
Spearman C.M.	*A, CD*	90	90	1	126	2421	27.20	1	17
Gaffaney C.B.	*O*	107	104	7	101*	2357	24.29	1	11
Douglas M.W.	*CD, W*	101	98	8	121	2326	25.84	2	10
Cairns C.L.	*ND, C*	91	82	13	143	2300	33.33	3	10
Young B.A.	*ND, A*	85	83	8	101*	2284	30.45	1	15
Richardson M.H.	*A, O*	76	74	7	128*	2283	34.07	3	14
Lawson R.A.	*O*	90	87	7	83*	2241	28.01	—	16
Jones R.A.	*A, W*	98	97	6	92	2216	24.35	—	10
Latham R.T.	*C*	84	80	4	108	2206	29.02	1	9
Marshall J.A.H.	*ND*	71	69	7	152*	2184	35.22	2	14
Crowe M.D.	*A, CD, W*	57	56	5	125	2171	42.56	5	12
Bailey M.D.	*ND*	103	101	14	76*	2159	24.81	—	11
Stead G.R.	*C*	99	87	12	101*	2081	27.74	2	9
Bradburn G.E.	*ND*	121	110	15	80*	2048	21.55	—	5

BOWLING		M	O	M	R	W	Ave	R/O	Best
Tait A.R.	*ND*	90	757.4	75	3138	128	24.51	4.14	4-29
Harris C.Z.	*C*	122	957.3	65	3473	125	27.78	3.62	4-28
Petrie R.G.	*C, W*	100	736	58	3146	119	26.43	4.27	5-24
Hitchcock P.A.	*A, W*	73	598.3	37	2779	113	24.59	4.64	5-10
Priest M.W.	*C*	89	724.5	69	2668	106	25.16	3.68	5-26
Cairns C.L.	*ND, C*	91	587.2	39	2412	103	23.41	4.10	6-37
Martin C.S.	*C, A*	71	593.3	55	2688	103	26.09	4.52	5-43
Astle N.J.	*C*	99	728.2	86	2479	102	24.30	3.40	4-14
Styris S.B.	*ND, A*	80	557	46	2389	98	24.37	4.29	4-19
Aldridge G.W.	*ND*	67	501	36	2299	98	23.45	4.59	5-34
Vaughan J.T.C.	*A*	56	500	50	1760	97	18.14	3.52	6-26
Mason M.J.	*CD*	66	514	60	2101	95	22.11	4.09	6-25
Larsen G.R.	*W*	87	765.4	103	2334	94	24.82	3.04	5-30
Gale A.J.	*O*	75	673	69	2583	93	27.77	3.83	5-43
Wisneski W.A.	*CD, C*	70	571.3	40	2538	92	27.58	4.44	6-43
Bradburn G.E.	*ND*	121	895.4	59	3264	89	36.67	3.65	4-28
Hart M.N.	*ND*	102	628.1	55	2442	89	27.43	3.88	4-7
Yovich J.A.F.	*ND*	79	422.5	21	2258	89	25.37	5.34	4-44
Twose R.G.	*ND, CD, W*	95	480.3	28	1896	87	21.79	3.94	5-30
Jonas G.R.	*W, O*	56	492	36	2147	86	24.96	4.36	4-18

MOST ECONOMICAL BOWLING *(qualification 100 overs)*

		O	M	R	W	Ave	R/O
Hadlee R.J.	*C*	174.4	33	440	29	15.17	2.51
Boock S.L.	*O*	338.2	74	947	47	20.12	2.79
McIntyre J.M.	*A*	118	25	335	15	22.33	2.83
Webb R.J.	*O*	117.4	16	344	20	17.20	2.92
Mallender N.A.	*O*	458.4	83	1356	72	18.83	2.95
Chatfield E.J.	*W*	305	68	902	50	18.04	2.95

FIELDING		Ct	St	Total
Nevin C.J.	*W*	144	12	156
Hart R.G.	*ND*	117	30	147
McSweeney E.B.	*CD, W*	97	26	123
Germon L.K.	*C, O*	88	18	106
Hopkins G.J.	*ND, C, O*	87	16	103
Blain T.E.	*CD, C*	62	15	77
Griggs B.B.J.	*CD*	74	3	77
Croy M.G.	*O*	64	9	73
Young R.A.	*A*	61	12	73
Harris C.Z.	*C*	69	—	69
Young B.A.	*ND, A*	46	12	58
Vincent L.	*A*	55	3	58
Bradburn G.E.	*ND*	57	—	57
Bell M.D.	*ND, W*	56	—	56
Hart M.N.	*ND*	55	—	55
McGlashan P.D.	*CD, O, ND*	46	7	53
Douglas M.W.	*CD, W*	47	5	52

NEW ZEALAND ONE-DAY INTERNATIONAL RECORDS

TEAM RECORDS

Results

1972/73	Pakistan	Christchurch	NZ 187	P 165	*NZ won by 22 runs*
1973	England	Swansea	NZ 158	E 159-3	*England won by 7 wickets*
	England	Manchester	E 167-8		*abandoned*
1973/74	Australia	Dunedin	NZ 194-9	A 195-3	*Australia won by 7 wickets*
	Australia	Christchurch	A 265-5	NZ 234-6	*Australia won by 31 runs*
1974/75	England	Melbourne	NZ 262-8	E 196	*NZ won by 66 runs*
	England	Dunedin	E 136	NZ 15-0	*abandoned*
	England	Wellington	NZ 227	E 35-1	*abandoned*
1975	East Africa	Birmingham	NZ 309-5	EA 128-8	*NZ won by 181 runs*
World Cup	England	Nottingham	E 266-6	NZ 186	*England won by 80 runs*
	India	Manchester	I 230-9	NZ 233-6	*NZ won by 4 wickets*
	West Indies	The Oval	NZ 158	WI 159-5	*West Indies won by 5 wickets*
1975/76	India	Christchurch	I 154	NZ 155-1	*NZ won by 9 wickets*
	India	Auckland	NZ 236-8	I 156	*NZ won by 80 runs*
1976/77	Pakistan	Sialkot	NZ 198-8	P 197-9	*NZ won by 1 run*
1978	England	Scarborough	E 206-8	NZ 187-8	*England won by 19 runs*
	England	Manchester	E 278-5	NZ 152	*England won by 126 runs*
1979	Sri Lanka	Nottingham	SL 189	NZ 190-1	*NZ won by 9 wickets*
World Cup	India	Leeds	I 182	NZ 183-2	*NZ won by 8 wickets*
	West Indies	Nottingham	WI 244-7	NZ 212-9	*West Indies won by 32 runs*
	England	Manchester	E 221-8	NZ 212-9	*England won by 9 runs*
1979/80	West Indies	Christchurch	WI 203-7	NZ 207-9	*NZ won by 1 wicket*
1980/81	Australia	Adelaide	A 217-9	NZ 219-7	*NZ won by 3 wickets*
	Australia	Sydney	A 289-3	NZ 195	*Australia won by 94 runs*
	Australia	Melbourne	NZ 156	A 159-6	*Australia won by 4 wickets*
	India	Perth	I 162	NZ 157	*India won by 5 runs*
	India	Brisbane	I 204	NZ 205-7	*NZ won by 3 wickets*
	India	Adelaide	I 230-7	NZ 224	*India won by 6 runs*
	India	Melbourne	I 112-9	NZ 113-0	*NZ won by 10 wickets*
	Australia	Sydney	NZ 220-8	A 219-7	*NZ won by 1 run*
	India	Brisbane	NZ 242-9	I 220	*NZ won by 22 runs*
	Australia	Sydney	A 180	NZ 23-1	*abandoned*
	Australia	Sydney	NZ 233-6	A 155	*NZ won by 78 runs*
	Australia	Melbourne	NZ 126	A 130-3	*Australia won by 7 wickets*
	Australia	Melbourne	A 235-4	NZ 229-8	*Australia won by 6 runs*
	Australia	Sydney	NZ 215-8	A 218-4	*Australia won by 6 wickets*
1980/81	India	Auckland	NZ 218-6	I 140-9	*NZ won by 78 runs*
	India	Hamilton	NZ 210-8	I 153	*NZ won by 57 runs*

Season	Opponent	Venue	First innings	Second innings	Result
1981/82	Australia	Auckland	NZ 240-6	A 194	*NZ won by 46 runs*
	Australia	Dunedin	NZ 159-9	A 160-4	*Australia won by 6 wickets*
	Australia	Wellington	NZ 74	A 75-2	*Australia won by 8 wickets*
1982/83	Australia	Melbourne	NZ 181	A 182-2	*Australia won by 8 wickets*
	England	Melbourne	NZ 239-8	E 237-8	*NZ won by 2 runs*
	England	Brisbane	E 267-6	NZ 213	*England won by 54 runs*
	Australia	Sydney	NZ 226-8	A 179	*NZ won by 47 runs*
	England	Sydney	NZ 199	E 200-2	*England won by 8 wickets*
	Australia	Melbourne	NZ 246-6	A 188	*NZ won by 58 runs*
	England	Adelaide	E 296-5	NZ 297-6	*NZ won by 4 wickets*
	Australia	Adelaide	NZ 200-9	A 153	*NZ won by 47 runs*
	England	Perth	E 88-7	NZ 89-3	*NZ won by 7 wickets*
	Australia	Perth	A 191-9	NZ 164	*Australia won by 27 runs*
	Australia	Sydney	NZ 193-7	A 155-4	*Australia won on faster scoring rate*
	Australia	Melbourne	A 302-8	NZ 153	*Australia won by 149 runs*
1982/83	England	Auckland	E 184	NZ 187-4	*NZ won by 6 wickets*
	England	Wellington	NZ 295-6	E 192	*NZ won by 103 runs*
	England	Christchurch	NZ 211-8	E 127	*NZ won by 84 runs*
	Sri Lanka	Dunedin	NZ 183-8	SL 118-9	*NZ won by 65 runs*
	Australia	Sydney	NZ 138-8	A 124	*NZ won by 14 runs*
	Sri Lanka	Napier	SL 167-8	NZ 168-3	*NZ won by 7 wickets*
	Sri Lanka	Auckland	NZ 304-5	SL 188-6	*NZ won by 116 runs*
1983 *World Cup*	England	The Oval	E 322-6	NZ 216	*England won by 106 runs*
	Pakistan	Birmingham	NZ 238-9	P 186	*NZ won by 52 runs*
	Sri Lanka	Bristol	SL 206	NZ 209-5	*NZ won by 5 wickets*
	England	Birmingham	E 234	NZ 238-8	*NZ won by 2 wickets*
	Sri Lanka	Derby	NZ 181	SL 184-7	*Sri Lanka won by 3 wickets*
	Pakistan	Nottingham	P 261-3	NZ 250	*Pakistan won by 11 runs*
1983/84	England	Christchurch	E 188-9	NZ 134	*England won by 54 runs*
	England	Wellington	NZ 135	E 139-4	*England won by 6 wickets*
	England	Auckland	E 209-9	NZ 210-3	*NZ won by 7 wickets*
1983/84	Sri Lanka	Colombo	NZ 234-6	SL 130	*NZ won by 104 runs*
	Sri Lanka	Moratuwa	SL 157-8	NZ 116	*Sri Lanka won by 41 runs*
	Sri Lanka	Colombo	NZ 201-8	SL 115	*NZ won by 86 runs*
1984/85	Sri Lanka	Colombo	NZ 171-6	SL 174-6	*Sri Lanka won by 4 wickets*
	Sri Lanka	Moratuwa	SL 114-9	NZ 118-3	*NZ won by 7 wickets*
	Pakistan	Peshawar	P 191-5	NZ 145	*Pakistan won by 46 runs*
	Pakistan	Faisalabad	P 157-5	NZ 152-7	*Pakistan won by 5 runs*
	Pakistan	Sialkot	NZ 187-9	P 153-8	*NZ won by 34 runs*
	Pakistan	Multan	NZ 213-8	P 214-9	*Pakistan won by 1 wicket*
1984/85	Pakistan	Napier	NZ 277-6	P 167-9	*NZ won by 110 runs*
	Pakistan	Hamilton	P 221-4	NZ 222-6	*NZ won by 4 wickets*
	Pakistan	Christchurch	NZ 264-8	P 251	*NZ won by 13 runs*
	Pakistan	Auckland	P 189		*abandoned*
1984/85 *World Championship of Cricket*	West Indies	Sydney	NZ 57-2		*abandoned*
	Sri Lanka	Melbourne	NZ 223	SL 172	*NZ won by 51 runs*
	India	Sydney	NZ 206	I 207-3	*India won by 7 wickets*
	West Indies	Sydney	NZ 138-9	WI 139-4	*West Indies won by 6 wickets*

1984/85	West Indies	Antigua	WI 231-8	NZ 208-8	*West Indies won by 23 runs*
	West Indies	Port of Spain	NZ 51-3	WI 55-4	*West Indies won by 6 wickets*
	West Indies	Berbice	WI 259-5	NZ 129	*West Indies won by 130 runs*
	West Indies	Port of Spain	NZ 116	WI 117-0	*West Indies won by 10 wickets*
	West Indies	Bridgetown	WI 265-3	NZ 153-8	*West Indies won by 112 runs*
1985/86	Australia	Melbourne	NZ 161-7		*abandoned*
	India	Brisbane	NZ 259-9	I 263-5	*India won by 5 wickets*
	Australia	Sydney	NZ 152	A 153-6	*Australia won by 4 wickets*
	India	Perth	I 113	NZ 115-7	*NZ won by 3 wickets*
	Australia	Perth	NZ 159-6	A 161-6	*Australia won by 4 wickets*
	India	Melbourne	I 238-8	NZ 239-5	*NZ won by 5 wickets*
	India	Adelaide	NZ 172	I 174-5	*India won by 5 wickets*
	Australia	Adelaide	NZ 276-7	A 70	*NZ won by 206 runs*
	Australia	Sydney	A 239-7	NZ 140	*Australia won by 99 runs*
	India	Launceston	I 202-9	NZ 168-9	*India won by 21 runs (target adjusted)*
1985/86	Australia	Dunedin	NZ 186-6	A 156	*NZ won by 30 runs*
	Australia	Christchurch	NZ 258-7	A 205	*NZ won by 53 runs*
	Australia	Wellington	NZ 229-9	A 232-7	*Australia won by 3 wickets*
	Australia	Auckland	A 231	NZ 187-9	*Australia won by 44 runs*
1985/86	Sri Lanka	Colombo	SL 137-9	NZ 140-4	*NZ won by 6 wickets*
	Pakistan	Colombo	NZ 214-8	P 217-6	*Pakistan won by 4 wickets*
	India	Sharjah	NZ 132-8	I 134-7	*India won by 3 wickets*
	Pakistan	Sharjah	NZ 64	P 66-0	*Pakistan won by 10 wickets*
1986	England	Leeds	NZ 217-8	E 170	*NZ won by 47 runs*
	England	Manchester	NZ 284-5	E 286-4	*England won by 6 wickets*
1986/87	West Indies	Dunedin	WI 237-9	NZ 142	*West Indies won by 95 runs*
	West Indies	Auckland	NZ 213	WI 217-4	*West Indies won by 6 wickets*
	West Indies	Wellington	*abandoned without a ball being bowled*		
	West Indies	Christchurch	NZ 191-9	WI 192-0	*West Indies won by 10 wickets*
1987/88	Zimbabwe	Hyderabad	NZ 242-7	Z 239	*NZ won by 3 runs*
World Cup	India	Bangalore	I 252-7	NZ 236-8	*India won by 16 runs*
	Australia	Indore	A 199-4	NZ 196-9	*Australia won by 3 runs*
	Zimbabwe	Calcutta	Z 227-5	NZ 228-6	*NZ won by 4 wickets*
	Australia	Chandigarh	A 251-8	NZ 234	*Australia won by 17 runs*
	India	Nagpur	NZ 221-9	I 224-1	*India won by 9 wickets*
1987/88	Australia	Perth	NZ 232-9	A 231	*NZ won by 1 run*
	Sri Lanka	Sydney	SL 174	NZ 178-4	*NZ won by 6 wickets*
	Australia	Melbourne	A 216	NZ 210-9	*Australia won by 6 runs*
	Sri Lanka	Adelaide	SL 241	NZ 242-6	*NZ won by 4 wickets*
	Sri Lanka	Hobart	NZ 199-7	SL 200-6	*Sri Lanka won by 4 wickets*
	Sri Lanka	Brisbane	SL 164-8	NZ 167-6	*NZ won by 4 wickets*
	Australia	Brisbane	NZ 176-5	A 177-5	*Australia won by 5 wickets*
	Australia	Sydney	A 221-8	NZ 143	*Australia won by 78 runs*
	Australia	Melbourne	NZ 177	A 180-2	*Australia won by 8 wickets*
	Australia	Sydney	NZ 168-5	A 169-4	*Australia won by 6 wickets*

1987/88	England	Dunedin	NZ 204	E 207-5	*England won by 5 wickets*
	England	Christchurch	NZ 186-8	E 188-4	*England won by 6 wickets*
	England	Napier	E 219	NZ 223-3	*NZ won by 7 wickets*
	England	Auckland	E 208	NZ 211-6	*NZ won by 4 wickets*
1987/88	India	Sharjah	I 267-6	NZ 194-8	*India won by 73 runs*
	Sri Lanka	Sharjah	NZ 258-8	SL 159	*NZ won by 99 runs*
	Sri Lanka	Sharjah	NZ 249-7	SL 206-9	*NZ won by 43 runs*
	India	Sharjah	I 250-7	NZ 198	*India won by 52 runs*
1988/89	India	Visakhapatnam	NZ 196-9	I 197-6	*India won by 4 wickets*
	India	Cuttack	NZ 160-7	I 161-5	*India won by 5 wickets*
	India	Indore	I 222-6	NZ 169-9	*India won by 53 runs*
	India	Baroda	NZ 278-3	I 282-8	*India won by 2 wickets*
	India	Jammu	*abandoned without a ball being bowled*		
1988/89	Pakistan	Dunedin	P 170-9	NZ 174-2	*NZ won by 8 wickets*
	Pakistan	Christchurch	P 170-7	NZ 171-3	*NZ won by 7 wickets*
	Pakistan	Wellington	P 253-6	NZ 254-4	*NZ won by 6 wickets*
	Pakistan	Auckland	NZ 249	P 251-3	*Pakistan won by 7 wickets*
	Pakistan	Hamilton	P 138-9	NZ 139-3	*NZ won by 7 wickets*
1989/90	India	Dunedin	NZ 246-6	I 138	*NZ won by 108 runs*
	Australia	Christchurch	A 244-8	NZ 94	*Australia won by 150 runs*
	India	Wellington	I 221	NZ 220	*India won by 1 run*
	Australia	Auckland	A 239-6	NZ 167-2	*Australia won on faster scoring rate*
	Australia	Auckland	NZ 162	A 164-2	*Australia won by 8 wickets*
1989/90	Australia	Sharjah	A 258-5	NZ 195-7	*Australia won by 63 runs*
	Bangladesh	Sharjah	NZ 338-4	B 177-5	*NZ won by 161 runs*
	Pakistan	Sharjah	NZ 74	P 75-2	*Pakistan won by 8 wickets*
1990	England	Leeds	E 295-6	NZ 298-6	*NZ won by 4 wickets*
	England	The Oval	NZ 212-6	E 213-4	*England won by 6 wickets*
1990/91	Pakistan	Lahore	P 196-8	NZ 177	*Pakistan won by 19 runs*
	Pakistan	Peshawar	NZ 127	P 128-2	*Pakistan won by 8 wickets*
	Pakistan	Sialkot	P 223-2	NZ 118	*Pakistan won by 105 runs*
1990/91	Australia	Sydney	A 236-9	NZ 174-7	*Australia won by 61 runs target reduced*
	England	Adelaide	NZ 199-6	E 192-9	*NZ won by 7 runs*
	Australia	Adelaide	NZ 208-7	A 210-4	*Australia won by 6 wickets*
	England	Perth	NZ 158	E 161-6	*England won by 4 wickets*
	Australia	Melbourne	A 263-7	NZ 224-8	*Australia won by 39 runs*
	England	Sydney	E 194	NZ 161	*England won by 33 runs*
	England	Brisbane	E 203-6	NZ 204-2	*NZ won by 8 wickets*
	Australia	Hobart	NZ 194-6	A 193	*NZ won by 1 run*
	Australia	Sydney	NZ 199-7	A 202-4	*Australia won by 6 wickets*
	Australia	Melbourne	NZ 208-6	A 209-3	*Australia won by 7 wickets*
1990/91	Sri Lanka	Napier	SL 177-8	NZ 178-5	*NZ won by 5 wickets*
	Sri Lanka	Auckland	NZ 242-5	SL 201	*NZ won by 41 runs*
	Sri Lanka	Dunedin	NZ 272-6	SL 165	*NZ won by 107 runs*
	England	Christchurch	E 230-7	NZ 216-8	*England won by 14 runs*
	England	Wellington	NZ 196-8	E 187	*NZ won by 9 runs*
	England	Auckland	NZ 224-7	E 217	*NZ won by 7 runs*

1991/92	England	Auckland	NZ 178-7	E 179-3	*England won by 7 wickets*
	England	Dunedin	NZ 186-7	E 188-7	*England won by 3 wickets*
	England	Christchurch	E 255-7	NZ 184-8	*England won by 71 runs*
1991/92	Australia	Auckland	NZ 248-6	A 211	*NZ won by 37 runs*
World Cup	Sri Lanka	Hamilton	SL 206-9	NZ 210-4	*NZ won by 6 wickets*
	South Africa	Auckland	SA 190-7	NZ 191-3	*NZ won by 7 wickets*
	Zimbabwe	Napier	NZ 163-3	Z 105-7	*NZ won by 49 runs target reduced*
	West Indies	Auckland	WI 203-7	NZ 206-5	*NZ won by 5 wickets*
	India	Dunedin	I 230-6	NZ 231-6	*NZ won by 4 wickets*
	England	Wellington	E 200-8	NZ 201-3	*NZ won by 7 wickets*
	Pakistan	Christchurch	NZ 166	P 167-3	*Pakistan won by 7 wickets*
	Pakistan	Auckland	NZ 262-7	P 264-6	*Pakistan won by 4 wickets*
1992/93	Zimbabwe	Bulawayo	NZ 244-7	Z 222-9	*NZ won by 22 runs*
	Zimbabwe	Harare	Z 271-6	NZ 272-6	*NZ won by 4 wickets*
1992/93	Sri Lanka	Colombo	NZ 166-9	SL 41-2	*abandoned*
	Sri Lanka	Colombo	NZ 190-7	SL 192-2	*SL won by 8 wickets*
	Sri Lanka	Colombo	SL 262-6	NZ 231	*SL won by 31 runs*
1992/93	Pakistan	Wellington	P 158-8	NZ 108	*Pakistan won by 50 runs*
	Pakistan	Napier	P 136-8	NZ 137-4	*NZ won by 6 wickets*
	Pakistan	Auckland	P 139	NZ 140-4	*NZ won by 6 wickets*
1992/93	Australia	Dunedin	A 258-4	NZ 129	*Australia won by 129 runs*
	Australia	Christchurch	NZ 196-8	A 197-9	*Australia won by 1 wicket*
	Australia	Wellington	NZ 214	A 126	*NZ won by 88 runs*
	Australia	Hamilton	A 247-7	NZ 250-7	*NZ won by 3 wickets*
	Australia	Auckland	A 232-8	NZ 229-8	*Australia won by 3 runs*
1993/94	South Africa	Adelaide	*abandoned without a ball being bowled*		
	Australia	Adelaide	NZ 135	A 136-2	*Australia won by 8 wickets*
	Australia	Melbourne	A 202-5	NZ 199-9	*Australia won by 3 runs*
	South Africa	Hobart	SA 147-7	NZ 148-6	*NZ won by 4 wickets*
	South Africa	Brisbane	NZ 256-7	SA 219-8	*NZ won by 9 runs target reduced*
	Australia	Sydney	NZ 198-9	A 185	*NZ won by 13 runs*
	South Africa	Perth	NZ 150	SA 151-5	*SA won by 5 wickets*
	Australia	Melbourne	A 217-3	NZ 166	*Australia won by 51 runs*
1993/94	Pakistan	Dunedin	NZ 122-9	P 123-5	*Pakistan won by 5 wickets*
	Pakistan	Auckland	P 146	NZ 110	*Pakistan won by 36 runs*
	Pakistan	Wellington	P 213-6	NZ 202-8	*Pakistan won by 11 runs*
	Pakistan	Auckland	P 161-9	NZ 161	*Tie*
	Pakistan	Christchurch	P 145-9	NZ 146-3	*NZ won by 7 wickets*
	India	Napier	NZ 240-5	I 212-9	*NZ won by 28 runs*
	India	Auckland	NZ 142	I 143-3	*India won by 7 wickets*
	India	Wellington	I 255-5	NZ 243-9	*India won by 12 runs*
	India	Christchurch	I 222-6	NZ 223-4	*NZ won by 6 wickets*
1993/94	Australia	Sharjah	NZ 207-9	A 208-3	*Australia won by 7 wickets*
	Sri Lanka	Sharjah	NZ 217-8	SL 215-9	*NZ won by 2 runs*
	Pakistan	Sharjah	P 328-2	NZ 266-7	*Pakistan won by 62 runs*
1994	England	Birmingham	E 224-8	NZ 182	*England won by 42 runs*
	England	Lord's	*abandoned without a ball being bowled*		

1994/95	West Indies	Goa	WI 123	NZ 25-1	*abandoned*
	India	Baroda	NZ 269-4	I 271-3	*India won by 7 wickets*
	West Indies	Guwahati	WI 306-6	NZ 171-9	*West Indies won by 135 runs*
	India	Delhi	I 289-3	NZ 182	*India won by 107 runs*
1994/95	South Africa	Cape Town	SA 203-8	NZ 134	*South Africa won by 69 runs*
	Sri Lanka	Bloemfontein	SL 288-4	NZ 66-1	*abandoned*
	South Africa	Verwoerdburg	SA 314-7	NZ 233	*South Africa won by 81 runs*
	Pakistan	Port Elizabeth	NZ 201	P 206-5	*Pakistan won by 5 wickets*
	Sri Lanka	East London	NZ 255-4	SL 257-5	*Sri Lanka won by 5 wickets*
	Pakistan	East London	NZ 172	P 175-5	*Pakistan won by 5 wickets*
1994/95	West Indies	Auckland	NZ 167-6	WI 149-1	*West Indies won by 9 wickets target reduced*
	West Indies	Wellington	WI 246-7	NZ 205	*West Indies won by 41 runs*
	West Indies	Christchurch	NZ 146	WI 149-1	*West Indies won by 9 wickets*
1994/95	India	Napier	I 160	NZ 162-6	*NZ won by 4 wickets*
	Australia	Auckland	A 254-5	NZ 227-9	*Australia won by 27 runs*
	South Africa	Christchurch	NZ 249-7	SA 203	*NZ won by 46 runs*
	Australia	Auckland	NZ 137-9	A 138-4	*Australia won by 6 wickets*
1994/95	Sri Lanka	Christchurch	NZ 271-6	SL 238	*NZ won by 33 runs*
	Sri Lanka	Hamilton	NZ 280-6	SL 117-6	*NZ won by 57 runs target reduced*
	Sri Lanka	Auckland	SL 250-6	NZ 199	*Sri Lanka won by 51 runs*
1995/96	India	Jamshedpur	I 236	NZ 237-2	*NZ won by 8 wickets*
	India	Amritsar	NZ 145	I 146-4	*India won by 6 wickets*
	India	Goa	*abandoned without a ball being bowled*		
	India	Pune	NZ 235-6	I 236-5	*India won by 5 wickets*
	India	Nagpur	NZ 348-8	I 249	*NZ won by 99 runs*
	India	Bombay	NZ 126	I 128-4	*India won by 6 wickets*
1995/96	Pakistan	Dunedin	P 189-9	NZ 169	*Pakistan won by 20 runs*
	Pakistan	Christchurch	P 232-9	NZ 236-9	*NZ won by 1 wicket*
	Pakistan	Wellington	P 261-4	NZ 207	*Pakistan won by 54 runs*
	Pakistan	Auckland	NZ 244-8	P 212	*NZ won by 32 runs*
1995/96	Zimbabwe	Auckland	NZ 278-5	Z 204	*NZ won by 74 runs*
	Zimbabwe	Wellington	Z 181-9	NZ 184-4	*NZ won by 6 wickets*
	Zimbabwe	Napier	Z 267-7	NZ 246	*Zimbabwe won by 21 runs*
1995/96	England	Ahmedabad	NZ 239-6	E 228-9	*NZ won by 11 runs*
World Cup	Holland	Baroda	NZ 307-8	H 188-7	*NZ won by 119 runs*
	South Africa	Faisalabad	NZ 177-9	SA 178-5	*Sth Africa won by 5 wickets*
	UAE	Faisalabad	NZ 276-8	UAE 167-9	*NZ won by 109 runs*
	Pakistan	Lahore	P 281-5	NZ 235	*Pakistan won by 46 runs*
	Australia	Madras	NZ 286-9	A 289-4	*Australia won by 6 wickets*
1995/96	West Indies	Kingston	NZ 243	WI 247-9	*West Indies won by 1 wicket*
	West Indies	Port of Spain	WI 238-7	NZ 239-6	*NZ won by 4 wickets*
	West Indies	Port of Spain	NZ 219-8	WI 225-3	*West Indies won by 7 wickets*
	West Indies	Georgetown	NZ 158	WI 154	*NZ won by 4 runs*
	West Indies	Arnos Vale	NZ 241-8	WI 242-3	*West Indies won by 7 wickets*

Season	Opponent	Venue			Result
1996/97	Sri Lanka	Sharjah	NZ 206-8	SL 177	*NZ won by 29 runs*
	Pakistan	Sharjah	NZ 197	P 198-6	*Pakistan won by 4 wickets*
	Sri Lanka	Sharjah	NZ 169-8	SL 169	*Tie*
	Pakistan	Sharjah	NZ 192	P 196-6	*Pakistan won by 4 wickets*
	Pakistan	Sharjah	P 160	NZ 119	*Pakistan won by 41 runs*
1996/97	Pakistan	Gujranwala	P 228-8	NZ 217	*Pakistan won by 11 runs*
	Pakistan	Sialkot	P 277-9	NZ 231	*Pakistan won by 46 runs*
	Pakistan	Karachi	P 234-4	NZ 235-3	*NZ won by 7 wickets*
1996/97	England	Christchurch	NZ 222-6	E 226-6	*England won by 4 wickets*
	England	Auckland	NZ 253-8	E 134-4	*England won by 6 wickets target reduced*
	England	Napier	NZ 237	E 237-8	*Tie*
	England	Auckland	NZ 153	E 144	*NZ won by 9 runs*
	England	Wellington	NZ 228-8	E 200	*NZ won by 28 runs*
1996/97	Sri Lanka	Auckland	*abandoned without a ball being bowled*		
	Sri Lanka	Christchurch	NZ 201-9	SL 202-4	*Sri Lanka won by 6 wickets*
	Sri Lanka	Wellington	NZ 201	SL 132	*NZ won by 69 runs*
1996/97	Pakistan	Mohali	NZ 285-7	P 263-9	*NZ won by 22 runs*
	India	Bangalore	NZ 220-9	I 221-2	*India won by 8 wickets*
	Sri Lanka	Hyderabad	SL 214	NZ 162	*Sri Lanka won by 52 runs*
1997/98	Zimbabwe	Bulawayo	Z 233-8	NZ 233-9	*Tie*
	Zimbabwe	Harare	NZ 185-7	Z 188-7	*Zimbabwe won by 3 wickets*
	Zimbabwe	Harare	NZ 294-7	Z 211	*NZ won by 83 runs*
1997/98	South Africa	Adelaide	NZ 224-6	SA 177	*NZ won by 47 runs*
	Australia	Adelaide	NZ 260-7	A 263-7	*Australia won by 3 wickets*
	South Africa	Hobart	SA 174-9	NZ 173-7	*South Africa won by 1 run*
	Australia	Melbourne	NZ 141	A 142-4	*Australia won by 6 wickets*
	South Africa	Brisbane	SA 300-6	NZ 298-9	*South Africa won by 2 runs*
	Australia	Sydney	A 250	NZ 119	*Australia won by 131 runs*
	South Africa	Perth	SA 233-7	NZ 166	*South Africa won by 67 runs*
	Australia	Melbourne	A 251-4	NZ 253-6	*NZ won by 4 wickets*
1997/98	Zimbabwe	Hamilton	NZ 248-7	Z 208	*NZ won by 40 runs*
	Zimbabwe	Wellington	Z 138	NZ 139-2	*NZ won by 8 wickets*
	Australia	Christchurch	NZ 212-7	A 215-3	*Australia won by 7 wickets*
	Australia	Wellington	A 297-6	NZ 231	*Australia won by 66 runs*
	Australia	Napier	A 236	NZ 240-3	*NZ won by 7 wickets*
	Australia	Auckland	NZ 223-7	A 193	*NZ won by 30 runs*
	Zimbabwe	Christchurch	Z 228-7	NZ 227-9	*Zimbabwe won by 1 run*
	Zimbabwe	Napier	Z 207-8	NZ 211-1	*NZ won by 9 wickets*
	Zimbabwe	Auckland	NZ 231-9	Z 229-9	*NZ won by 2 runs*
1997/98	India	Sharjah	I 220-9	NZ 205	*India won by 15 runs*
	Australia	Sharjah	NZ 159	A 160-4	*Australia won by 6 wickets*
	India	Sharjah	I 181	NZ 183-6	*NZ won by 4 wickets*
	Australia	Sharjah	NZ 259-5	A 261-5	*Australia won by 5 wickets*
1997/98	Sri Lanka	Colombo	NZ 200-9	SL 201-3	*Sri Lanka won by 7 wickets*
	India	Colombo	NZ 219-8	I 131-3	*abandoned*
	Sri Lanka	Galle	*abandoned without a ball being bowled*		
	India	Galle	*abandoned without a ball being bowled*		
	India	Colombo	NZ 128-5		*abandoned*
	Sri Lanka	Colombo	SL 293-4	NZ 206	*Sri Lanka won by 87 runs*

1998/99	Zimbabwe	Dhaka	Z 258-7	NZ 260-5	*NZ won by 5 wickets*
ICC Knockout	Sri Lanka	Dhaka	NZ 188	SL 191-5	*Sri Lanka won by 5 wickets*
1998/99	India	Taupo	I 257-5	NZ 200-5	*NZ won by 5 wickets (D/L)*
	India	Napier	NZ 213	I 214-8	*India won by 2 wickets*
	India	Wellington	I 208-4	NZ 89-2	*abandoned*
	India	Auckland	NZ 207-7	I 208-5	*India won by 5 wickets*
	India	Christchurch	NZ 300-8	I 230	*NZ won by 70 runs*
1998/99	South Africa	Dunedin	SA 211	NZ 215-7	*NZ won by 3 wickets*
	South Africa	Christchurch	NZ 220-9	SA 224-3	*SA won by 7 wickets*
	South Africa	Auckland	SA 212-7	NZ 215-3	*NZ won by 7 wickets*
	South Africa	Napier	NZ 257-8	SA 10-0	*abandoned*
	South Africa	Napier	NZ 191	SA 194-8	*SA won by 2 wickets*
	South Africa	Auckland	SA 290-5	NZ 147	*SA won by 143 runs*
	South Africa	Wellington	SA 249-4		*abandoned*
1999	Bangladesh	Chelmsford	B 116	NZ 117-4	*NZ won by 6 wickets*
World Cup	Australia	Cardiff	A 213-8	NZ 214-5	*NZ won by 5 wickets*
	West Indies	Southampton	NZ 156	WI 158-3	*WI won by 7 wickets*
	Pakistan	Derby	P 269-8	NZ 207-8	*Pakistan won by 62 runs*
	Scotland	Edinburgh	S 121	NZ 123-4	*NZ won by 6 wickets*
	Zimbabwe	Leeds	Z 175	NZ 70-3	*abandoned*
	South Africa	Birmingham	SA 287-5	NZ 213-8	*SA won by 74 runs*
	India	Nottingham	I 251-6	NZ 253-5	*NZ won by 5 wickets*
	Pakistan	Manchester	NZ 241-7	P 242-1	*Pakistan won by 9 wickets*
1999/00	India	Rajkot	NZ 349-9	I 306	*NZ won by 43 runs*
	India	Hyderabad	I 376-2	NZ 202	*India won by 174 runs*
	India	Gwalior	I 261-5	NZ 247-8	*India won by 14 runs*
	India	Guwahati	NZ 236-9	I 188	*NZ won by 48 runs*
	India	Delhi	NZ 179-9	I 181-3	*India won by 7 wickets*
1999/00	West Indies	Auckland	WI 268-7	NZ 250-7	*NZ won by 3 wickets (D/L)*
	West Indies	Taupo	WI 192	NZ 194-3	*NZ won by 7 wickets*
	West Indies	Napier	WI 159	NZ 160-6	*NZ won by 4 wickets*
	West Indies	Wellington	WI 171-9	NZ 172-2	*NZ won by 8 wickets*
	West Indies	Christchurch	NZ 302-6	WI 282	*NZ won by 20 runs*
1999/00	Australia	Wellington	A 119-1	NZ	*Abandoned*
	Australia	Auckland	NZ 122	A 123-5	*Australia won by 5 wickets*
	Australia	Dunedin	A 310-4	NZ 260	*Australia won by 50 runs*
	Australia	Christchurch	A 349-6	NZ 301-9	*Australia won by 48 runs*
	Australia	Napier	NZ 243-9	A 245-5	*Australia won by 5 wickets*
	Australia	Auckland	A 191	NZ 194-3	*NZ won by 7 wickets*
2000/01	Pakistan	Singapore	P 191-6	NZ 179	*Pakistan won by 12 runs*
	South Africa	Singapore	NZ 158	SA 159-2	*SA won by 8 wickets*
2000/01	Zimbabwe	Harare	Z 183-8	NZ 184-3	*NZ won by 7 wickets*
	Zimbabwe	Bulawayo	Z 273-5	NZ 252	*Zimbabwe won by 21 runs*
	Zimbabwe	Bulawayo	NZ 264-8	Z 268-4	*Zimbabwe won by 6 wkts*
2000/01	Zimbabwe	Nairobi	NZ 265-7	Z 201	*NZ won by 64 runs*
ICC Knockout	Pakistan	Nairobi	P 252	NZ 255-6	*NZ won by 4 wickets*
	India	Nairobi	I 264-6	NZ 265-6	*NZ won by 4 wickets*

2000/01	South Africa	Potchefstroom	SA 191-2	NZ	*abandoned*
	South Africa	Benoni	NZ 194-8	SA 197-4	*SA won by 6 wkts*
	South Africa	Centurion	SA 324-4	NZ 189	*SA won by 115 runs (D/L)*
	South Africa	Kimberley	NZ 287-6	SA 289-5	*SA won by 5 wickets*
	South Africa	Durban	NZ 114-5	SA 158-4	*SA won by 6 wickets(D/L)*
	South Africa	Cape Town	NZ 256-9	SA 258-7	*SA won by 3 wickets*
2000/01	Zimbabwe	Taupo	Z 300-7	NZ 210	*Zimbabwe won by 70 runs (D/L)*
	Zimbabwe	Wellington	Z 236-7	NZ 237-2	*NZ won by 8 wickets*
	Zimbabwe	Auckland	NZ 273-9	Z 274-9	*Zimbabwe won by 1 wicket*
2000/01	Sri Lanka	Napier	SL 213-8	NZ 152	*Sri Lanka won by 61 runs*
	Sri Lanka	Wellington	NZ 205-8	SL 209-7	*Sri Lanka won by 3 wickets*
	Sri Lanka	Auckland	NZ 181	SL 182-1	*Sri Lanka won by 9 wickets*
	Sri Lanka	Hamilton	NZ 182-9	SL 155-5	*Sri Lanka won by 3 runs (D/L)*
	Sri Lanka	Christchurch	NZ 282-6	SL 269	*NZ won by 13 runs*
2000/01	Pakistan	Auckland	NZ 149	P 150-4	*Pakistan won by 6 wickets*
	Pakistan	Napier	P 135	NZ 136-4	*NZ won by 6 wickets*
	Pakistan	Wellington	P 243-9	NZ 215	*Pakistan won by 28 runs*
	Pakistan	Christchurch	NZ 284-5	P 146	*NZ won by 138 runs*
	Pakistan	Dunedin	P 285	NZ 290-6	*NZ won by 4 wickets*
2000/01	Sri Lanka	Sharjah	SL 269-9	NZ 163	*Sri Lanka won by 106 runs*
	Pakistan	Sharjah	NZ 266-7	P 270-2	*Pakistan won by 8 wickets*
	Pakistan	Sharjah	NZ 127	P 131-3	*Pakistan won by 7 wickets*
	Sri Lanka	Sharjah	NZ 248-6	SL 169-8	*NZ won by 79 runs*
2001/02	Sri Lanka	Colombo	SL 220	NZ 204-9	*Sri Lanka won by 16 runs*
	India	Colombo	NZ 211-8	I 127	*NZ won by 84 runs*
	Sri Lanka	Colombo	NZ 236-8	SL 240-5	*Sri Lanka won by 5 wickets*
	India	Colombo	NZ 200	I 133	*NZ won by 67 runs*
	Sri Lanka	Colombo	SL 221-6	NZ 115-9	*Sri Lanka won by 106 runs*
	India	Colombo	NZ 264-7	I 267-3	*India won by 7 wickets*
2001/02	Australia	Melbourne	NZ 199-8	A 176	*NZ won by 23 runs*
	South Africa	Hobart	SA 257-7	NZ 231-9	*SA won by 26 runs*
	Australia	Sydney	NZ 235-9	A 212	*NZ won by 23 runs*
	South Africa	Brisbane	SA 241	NZ 244-6	*NZ won by 4 wickets*
	Australia	Adelaide	NZ 242-5	A 165	*NZ won by 77 runs*
	South Africa	Adelaide	SA 253-5	NZ 160	*SA won by 93 runs*
	Australia	Melbourne	NZ 245-8	A 248-8	*Australia won by 2 wickets*
	South Africa	Perth	SA 270-5	NZ 203-8	*SA won by 67 runs*
	South Africa	Melbourne	NZ 190	SA 191-2	*SA won by 8 wickets*
	South Africa	Sydney	NZ 175	SA 173-4	*SA won by 6 wickets (D/L)*
2001/02	England	Christchurch	E 196	NZ 198-6	*NZ won by 4 wickets*
	England	Wellington	NZ 244-8	E 89	*NZ won by 155 runs*
	England	Napier	E 244-5	NZ 201	*England won by 43 runs*
	England	Auckland	E 193-6	NZ 189	*England won by 33 runs (D/L)*
	England	Dunedin	E 218-8	NZ 223-5	*NZ won by 5 wickets*
2001/02	Sri Lanka	Sharjah	NZ 218-8	SL 207	*NZ won by 11 runs*
	Pakistan	Sharjah	P 288-6	NZ 237-8	*Pakistan won by 51 runs*
	Sri Lanka	Sharjah	SL 243-9	NZ 197-9	*Sri Lanka won by 46 runs*
	Pakistan	Sharjah	NZ 213-9	P 217-2	*Pakistan won by 8 wickets*
2001/02	Pakistan	Karachi	P 275-6	NZ 122	*Pakistan won by 153 runs*
	Pakistan	Rawalpindi	NZ 277-5	P 278-7	*Pakistan won by 3 wickets*
	Pakistan	Lahore	P 278-5	NZ 212	*Pakistan won by 66 runs*

Season	Opponent	Venue	First innings	Second innings	Result
2001/02	West Indies	Kingston	NZ 176	WI	*abandoned*
	West Indies	Gros Islet	NZ 248-7	WI 250-4	*West Indies won by 6 wickets*
	West Indies	Gros Islet	NZ 210-7	WI 211-3	*West Indies won by 7 wickets*
	West Indies	Port of Spain	NZ 212-5	WI 202-9	*NZ won by 9 runs (D/L)*
	West Indies	Arnos Vale	NZ 291-8	WI 292-6	*West Indies won by 4 wickets*
2002/03	Australia	Colombo	A 296-7	NZ 132	*Australia won by 164 runs*
Champions Trophy	Bangladesh	Colombo	NZ 244-9	B 77	*NZ won by 167 runs*
2002/03	India	Auckland	I 108	NZ 109-7	*NZ won by 3 wickets*
	India	Napier	NZ 254-9	I 219	*NZ won by 35 runs*
	India	Christchurch	I 108	NZ 109-5	*NZ won by 5 wickets*
	India	Queenstown	I 122	NZ 123-3	*NZ won by 7 wickets*
	India	Wellington	NZ 168	I 169-8	*India won by 2 wickets*
	India	Auckland	NZ 199-9	I 200-9	*India won by 1 wicket*
	India	Hamilton	I 122	NZ 125-4	*NZ won by 6 wickets*
2002/03	Sri Lanka	Bloemfontein	SL 272-7	NZ 225	*Sri Lanka won by 47 runs*
World	West Indies	Port Elizabeth	NZ 241-7	WI 221	*NZ won by 20 runs*
Cup	South Africa	Johannesburg	SL 306-6	NZ 229-1	*NZ won by 9 wickets (D/L)*
	Kenya	Nairobi			*NZ forfeited the match*
	Bangladesh	Kimberley	B 198-7	NZ 199-3	*NZ won by 7 wickets*
	Canada	Benoni	C 196	NZ 197-5	*NZ won by 5 wickets*
	Zimbabwe	Bloemfontein	Z 252-7	NZ 253-4	*NZ won by 6 wickets*
	Australia	Port Elizabeth	A 208-9	NZ 112	*Australia won by 96 runs*
	India	Centurion	NZ 146	I 150-3	*India won by 7 wickets*
2002/03	Pakistan	Dambulla	P 116	NZ 117-3	*NZ won by 7 wickets*
	Sri Lanka	Dambulla	NZ 139	SL 143-5	*Sri Lanka won by 5 wickets*
	Sri Lanka	Dambulla	NZ 156-8	SL 147	*NZ won by 9 runs*
	Pakistan	Dambulla	P 203-9	NZ 181	*Pakistan won by 22 runs*
	Pakistan	Dambulla	P 198	NZ 200-6	*NZ won by 4 wickets*
2003/04	India	Chennai	I 141-3	NZ	*abandoned*
	Australia	Faridabad	NZ 97	A 101-2	*Australia won by 8 wickets*
	Australia	Pune	NZ 258-9	A 259-8	*Australia won by 2 wickets*
	India	Cuttack	I 246-6	NZ 249-6	*NZ won by 4 wickets*
	Australia	Guwahati	A 225-7	NZ 181	*Australia won by 44 runs*
	India	Hyderabad	I 353-5	NZ 208	*India won by 145 runs*
2003/04	Pakistan	Lahore	NZ 291-5	P 292-7	*Pakistan won by 3 wickets*
	Pakistan	Lahore	P 281-6	NZ 157	*Pakistan won by 124 runs*
	Pakistan	Faisalabad	P 314-7	NZ 263-7	*Pakistan won by 51 runs*
	Pakistan	Rawalpindi	NZ 183	P 184-3	*Pakistan won by 7 wickets*
	Pakistan	Rawalpindi	P 277-4	NZ 228-6	*Pakistan won by 49 runs*
2003/04	Pakistan	Auckland	P 229-7	NZ 230-6	*NZ won by 4 wickets*
	Pakistan	Queenstown	NZ 235-8	P 236-4	*Pakistan won by 6 wickets*
	Pakistan	Christchurch	P 255-9	NZ 259-3	*NZ won by 7 wickets*
	Pakistan	Napier	P 126	NZ 127-2	*NZ won by 8 wickets*
	Pakistan	Wellington	NZ 307-8	P 303	*NZ won by 4 runs*
2003/04	South Africa	Auckland	NZ 225-8	SA 226-5	*SA won by 5 wickets*
	South Africa	Christchurch	SA 253-8	NZ 255-5	*NZ won by 5 wickets*
	South Africa	Wellington	NZ 254-5	SA 249-7	*NZ won by 5 runs*
	South Africa	Dunedin	SA 259-7	NZ 264-4	*NZ won by 6 wickets*
	South Africa	Auckland	NZ 193-8	SA 175-5	*NZ won by 2 runs (D/L)*
	South Africa	Napier	SA 186-9	NZ 190-5	*NZ won by 5 wickets*

2004	England	Manchester	*abandoned without a ball being bowled*		
	West Indies	Birmingham	WI 122-4	NZ 97-2	*abandoned*
	England	Chester-le-Street	E 101	NZ 103-3	*NZ won by 7 wickets*
	West Indies	Cardiff	WI 216	NZ 220-5	*NZ won by 5 wickets*
	England	Bristol	E 237-7	NZ 241-4	*NZ won by 6 wickets*
	West Indies	Southampton	*abandoned without a ball being bowled*		
	West Indies	Lord's	NZ 266	WI 159	*NZ won by 107 runs*
2004	USA	The Oval	NZ 347-4	USA 137	*NZ won by 210 runs*
Champions Trophy	Australia	The Oval	NZ 198	A 199-3	*Australia won by 7 wickets*
2004/05	Bangladesh	Chittagong	NZ 224	B 86	*NZ won by 138 runs*
	Bangladesh	Dhaka	B 146	NZ 148-7	*NZ won by 3 wickets*
	Bangladesh	Dhaka	NZ 250-7	B 167-7	*NZ won by 83 runs*
2004/05	Australia	Melbourne	A 246-9	NZ 247-6	*NZ won by 4 wickets*
	Australia	Sydney	A 261-7	NZ 244	*Australia won by 17 runs*
	Australia	Brisbane	*abandoned without a ball being bowled*		
2004/05	Sri Lanka	Auckland	SL 141	NZ 144-3	*NZ won by 7 wickets*
2004/05	Australia	Wellington	A 236-7	NZ 226	*Australia won by 10 runs*
	Australia	Christchurch	A 314-6	NZ 208	*Australia won by 106 runs*
	Australia	Auckland	A 264-5	NZ 178	*Australia won by 86 runs*
	Australia	Welllington	NZ 233	A 236-3	*Australia won by 7 wickets*
	Australia	Napier	A 347-5	NZ 225-8	*Australia won by 122 runs*
2005/06	Zimbabwe	Bulawayo	NZ 397-5	Z 205	*NZ won by 192 runs*
	India	Bulawayo	NZ 215	I 164	*NZ won by 51 runs*
	Zimbabwe	Harare	NZ 238	Z 211	*NZ won by 27 runs*
	India	Harare	NZ 278-9	I 279-4	*India won by 6 wickets*
	India	Harare	I 276	NZ 278-4	*NZ won by 6 wickets*
2005/06	South Africa	Bloemfontein	NZ 249-8	SA 250-8	*SA won by 2 wickets*
	South Africa	Cape Town	SA 201-9	NZ 182	*SA won by 19 runs*
	South Africa	Port Elizabeth	NZ 243-9	SA 245-6	*SA won by 4 wickets*
	South Africa	Durban	SA 79-2	NZ	*Abandoned*
	South Africa	Centurion	NZ 215	SA 140-5	*SA won by 5 wickets (D/L)*
2005/06	Australia	Auckland	A 252-8	NZ 105	*Australia won by 147 runs*
	Australia	Wellington	A 322-5	NZ 320	*Australia won by 2 runs*
	Australia	Christchurch	A 331-7	NZ 332-8	*NZ won by 2 wickets*
2005/06	Sri Lanka	Queenstown	SL 164	NZ 166-3	*NZ won by 7 wickets*
	Sri Lanka	Christchurch	SL 255-7	NZ 256-5	*NZ won by 5 wickets*
	Sri Lanka	Wellington	NZ 224-9	SL 203	*NZ won by 21 runs*
	Sri Lanka	Napier	SL 273-6	NZ 253	*Sri Lanka won by 20 runs*
2005/06	West Indies	Wellington	NZ 288-9	WI 207	*NZ won by 81 runs*
	West Indies	Queenstown	WI 200-9	NZ 204-7	*NZ won by 3 wickets*
	West Indies	Christchurch	NZ 276-6	WI 255	*NZ won by 21 runs*
	West Indies	Napier	NZ 324-6	WI 233-8	*NZ won by 91 runs*
	West Indies	Auckland	NZ 233	WI 234-7	*West Indies won by 3 wicket*
2006/07	South Africa	Mumbai	NZ 195	SA 108	*NZ won by 87 runs*
Champions Trophy	Sri Lanka	Mumbai	NZ 165	SL 166-3	*Sri Lanka won by 7 wkts*
	Pakistan	Mohali	NZ 274-3	P 223	*NZ won by 51 runs*
	Australia	Mohali	A 240-9	NZ 206	*Australia won by 34 runs*
2006/07	Sri Lanka	Napier	NZ 285-8	SL 289-3	*Sri Lanka won by 7 wickets*
	Sri Lanka	Queenstown	SL 224-7	NZ 228-9	*NZ won by 1 wicket*
	Sri Lanka	Christchurch	SL 112	NZ 110-6	*NZ won by 4 wickets (D/L)*

	Sri Lanka	Auckland	SL 262-3	NZ 73	*Sri Lanka won by 189 runs*
	Sri Lanka	Hamilton	*abandoned without a ball being bowled*		
2006/07	Australia	Hobart	A 289-8	NZ 184	*Australia won by 105 runs*
	England	Hobart	NZ 205-9	E 206-7	*England won by 3 wickets*
	Australia	Sydney	NZ 218	A 224-8	*Australia won by 2 wickets*
	England	Adelaide	NZ 210	E 120	*NZ won by 90 runs*
	Australia	Perth	A 343-5	NZ 335-5	*Australia won by 8 runs*
	England	Perth	NZ 318-7	E 260-8	*NZ won by 58 runs*
	Australia	Melbourne	NZ 290-7	A 291-5	*Australia won by 5 wickets*
	England	Brisbane	E 270-7	NZ 256-8	*England won by 14 runs*
2006/07	Australia	Wellington	A 148	NZ 149-0	*NZ won by 10 wickets*
	Australia	Auckland	A 336-4	NZ 340-5	*NZ won by 5 wickets*
	Australia	Hamilton	A 346-5	NZ 350-9	*NZ won by 1 wicket*
2006/07	England	Gros Islet	E 209-7	NZ 210-4	*NZ won by 6 wickets*
World Cup	Kenya	Gros Islet	NZ 331-7	K 183	*NZ won by 148 runs*
	Canada	Gros Islet	NZ 363-5	C 249	*NZ won by 114 runs*
	West Indies	Antigua	WI 177	NZ 179-3	*NZ won by 7 wickets*
	Bangladesh	Antigua	B 174	NZ 178-1	*NZ won by 9 wickets*
	Ireland	Guyana	NZ 263-8	I 134	*NZ won by 129 runs*
	Sri Lanka	Grenada	NZ 219-7	SL 222-4	*Sri Lanka won by 6 wickets*
	South Africa	Grenada	SA 193-7	NZ 196-5	*NZ won by 5 wickets*
	Australia	Grenada	A 348-6	NZ 133	*Australia won by 215 runs*
	Sri Lanka	Kingston	SL 289-5	NZ 208	*Sri Lanka won by 81runs*

Summary of Results

	Played	Won	Lost	Tie	Abandoned
v Australia	109	30	76	—	3
v Pakistan	78	29	47	1	1
v India	75	35	36	—	4
v Sri Lanka	68	34	30	1	3
v England	60	29	27	1	3
v South Africa	47	16	27	—	4
v West Indies	46	18	23	—	5
v Zimbabwe	28	19	7	1	1
v Bangladesh	8	8	—	—	—
v Canada	2	2	—	—	—
v East Africa	1	1	—	—	—
v Holland	1	1	—	—	—
v UAE	1	1	—	—	—
v Scotland	1	1	—	—	—
v USA	1	1	—	—	—
v Kenya	1	1	—	—	—
v Ireland	1	1	—	—	—
TOTALS	**528**	**227**	**273**	**4**	**24**

In addition, New Zealand forfeited their match against Kenya, at Nairobi, 2002/03

One-day International Captains

		Results					Toss	
		P	W	L	Tie	NR	W	L
Fleming S.P.	1996/97 to 2006/07	218	98	106	1	13	106	112
Howarth G.P.	1979/80 to 1984/85	60	31	26	—	3	23	37
Crowe M.D.	1989/90 to 1992/93	44	21	22	—	1	26	18
Rutherford K.R.	1993/94 to 1994/95	37	10	24	1	2	19	18
Germon L.K.	1995/96 to 1996/97	36	15	19	2	—	19	17
Wright J.G.	1982/83 to 1990	31	16	15	—	—	20	11
Coney J.V.	1984/85 to 1986/87	25	8	16	—	1	12	13
Crowe J.J.	1985/86 to 1987/88	16	4	12	—	—	7	9
Vettori D.L.	2004/05 to 2006/07	11	8	3	—	—	9	2
Turner G.M.	1974/75 to 1976/77	8	5	2	—	1	5	3
Burgess M.G.	1978 to 1980/81	8	2	6	—	—	6	2
McMillan C.D.	2000/01 to 2001/02	8	2	6	—	—	3	5
Congdon B.E.	1972/73 to 1974/75	7	2	3	—	2	4	3
Nash D.J.	1998/99	7	3	3	—	1	4	3
Cairns C.L.	2001/02 to 2003/04	7	1	6	—	—	4	3
Larsen G.R.	1993/94	3	1	2	—	—	2	1
Jones A.H.	1992/93	2	—	2	—	—	1	1
TOTALS		**528**	**227**	**273**	**4**	**24**	**270**	**258**

Other One-day Internationals Played in New Zealand

Season	Venue					Result
1989/90	Christchurch	A	187-9	I	169	*Australia won by 18 runs*
	Hamilton	I	211-8	A	212-3	*Australia won by 7 wickets*
1991/92	New Plymouth	Z	312-4	SL	313-7	*Sri Lanka won by 3 wickets*
World Cup	Wellington	SA	195	SL	198-7	*Sri Lanka won by 3 wickets*
	Christchurch	SA	200-8	WI	136	*South Africa won by 64 runs*
	Hamilton	I	203-7	Z	104-1	*India won by 55 runs**
	Wellington	I	197	WI	195-5	*West Indies won by 5 wickets**
1994/95	Wellington	SA	123	A	124-7	*Australia won by 3 wickets*
	Hamilton	SA	223-6	I	209-9	*South Africa won by 14 runs*
	Dunedin	A	250-6	I	252-5	*India won by 5 wickets*

** target reduced*

Highest Totals

For

397-5	v Zimbabwe	Bulawayo	2005/06
363-5	v Canada	Gros Islet	2006/07
350-9	v Australia	Hamilton	2006/07
349-9	v India	Rajkot	1999/00
348-8	v India	Nagpur	1995/96
347-4	v USA	The Oval	2004
340-5	v Australia	Auckland	2006/07
338-4	v Bangladesh	Sharjah	1989/90
335-5	v Australia	Perth	2006/07
332-8	v Australia	Christchurch	2005/06
331-7	v Kenya	Gros Islet	2006/07
324-6	v West Indies	Napier	2005/06
320	v Australia	Wellington	2005/06
318-7	v England	Perth	2006/07
309-5	v East Africa	Birmingham	1975
307-5	v Holland	Baroda	1995/96
307-8	v Pakistan	Wellington	2003/04
304-5	v Sri Lanka	Auckland	1982/83
302-6	v West Indies	Christchurch	1999/00
301-9	v Australia	Christchurch	1999/00
300-8	v India	Christchurch	1998/99

Against

376-2	by India	Hyderabad	1999/00
353-5	by India	Hyderabad	2003/04
349-6	by Australia	Christchurch	1999/00
348-6	by Australia	Grenada	2006/07
347-5	by Australia	Napier	2004/05
346-5	by Australia	Hamilton	2006/07
343-5	by Australia	Perth	2006/07
336-4	by Australia	Auckland	2006/07
331-7	by Australia	Christchurch	2005/06
328-2	by Pakistan	Sharjah	1993/94
324-4	by South Africa	Centurion	2000/01
322-6	by England	The Oval	1983
322-5	by Australia	Wellington	2005/06
314-7	by South Africa	Verwoerdburg	1994/95
314-7	by Pakistan	Faisalabad	2003/04

314-6	by Australia	Christchurch	2004/05
310-4	by Australia	Dunedin	1999/00
306-6	by West Indies	Guwahati	1994/85
306-6	by South Africa	Johannesburg	2002/03
306	by India	Rajkot	1999/00
303	by Pakistan	Wellington	2003/04
302-8	by Australia	Melbourne	1982/83
300-6	by South Africa	Brisbane	1997/98
300-7	by Zimbabwe	Taupo	2000/01

Zimbabwe scored 312-4 against Sri Lanka 313-7 at New Plymouth, 1991/92

Lowest Totals

For

64	v Pakistan	Sharjah	1985/86
73	v Sri Lanka	Auckland	2006/07
74	v Australia	Wellington	1981/82
74	v Pakistan	Sharjah	1989/90
94	v Australia	Christchurch	1989/90
97	v Australia	Faridabad	2003/04

Against

70	by Australia	Adelaide	1985/86
77	by Bangladesh	Colombo	2002/03
86	by Bangladesh	Chittagong	2004/05
89	by England	Wellington	2001/02

Highest Match Aggregates

696	New Zealand v Australia	Hamilton	2006/07
678	Australia v New Zealand	Perth	2006/07
676	New Zealand v Australia	Auckland	2006/07
663	New Zealand v Australia	Christchurch	2005/06
655	India v New Zealand	Rajkot	1999/00
650	New Zealand v Australia	Christchurch	1999/00
642	New Zealand v Australia	Wellington	2005/06
625	Zimbabwe v Sri Lanka	New Plymouth	1991/92
612	New Zealand v Canada	Gros Islet	2006/07
610	New Zealand v Pakistan	Wellington	2003/04
602	Zimbabwe v New Zealand	Bulawayo	2005/06

Lowest Match Aggregates

130	New Zealand v Pakistan	Sharjah	1985/86
149	New Zealand v Australia	Wellington	1981/82
149	New Zealand v Pakistan	Sharjah	1989/90
198	New Zealand v Australia	Faridabad	2003/04

INDIVIDUAL RECORDS

Centuries

172	Vincent L.	v Zimbabwe	Bulawayo	2005/06
171*	Turner G.M.	v East Africa	Birmingham	1975
145*	Astle N.J.	v USA	The Oval	2004
141	Styris S.B.	v Sri Lanka	Bloemfontein	2002/03
140	Turner G.M.	v Sri Lanka	Auckland	1982/83
134*	Fleming S.P.	v South Africa	Johannesburg	2002/03
130	Harris C.Z.	v Australia	Madras	1995/96
128*	Taylor L.R.P.L.	v Sri Lanka	Napier	2006/07
122*	Astle N.J.	v England	Dunedin	2001/02
120	Astle N.J.	v Zimbabwe	Auckland	1995/96
120	Astle N.J.	v India	Rajkot	1999/00
119	Astle N.J.	v Pakistan	Dunedin	2000/01
118*	Sinclair M.S.	v Sri Lanka	Sharjah	2000/01
118*	Astle N.J.	v West Indies	Christchurch	2005/06
117	Astle N.J.	v Pakistan	Mohali	1996/97
117	Sinclair M.S.	v Pakistan	Sharjah	2000/01
117	Astle N.J.	v India	Colombo	2001/02
117	Taylor L.R.P.L.	v Australia	Auckland	2006/07
117	McMillan C.D.	v Australia	Hamilton	2006/07
116*	Fleming S.P.	v Australia	Melbourne	1997/98
115*	Fleming S.P.	v Pakistan	Christchurch	2003/04
115*	Astle N.J.	v India	Harare	2005/06
115	Cairns C.L.	v India	Christchurch	1998/99
114*	Turner G.M.	v India	Manchester	1975
114	Astle N.J.	v India	Nagpur	1995/96
112	Fulton P.G.	v Sri Lanka	Napier	2005/06
111*	Fleming S.P.	v Australia	Napier	1997/98
111*	Styris S.B.	v Sri Lanka	Grenada	2006/07
111	Greatbatch M.J.	v England	The Oval	1990
108	Rutherford K.R.	v India	Baroda	1994/95
108	Parore A.C.	v South Africa	Verwoerdburg	1994/95
108	Astle N.J.	v India	Colombo	2001/02
108	Fleming S.P.	v South Africa	Christchurch	2003/04
107*	Crowe M.D.	v India	Jamshedpur	1995/96
106*	Fleming S.P.	v West Indies	PortofSpain	1995/96
106	Fleming S.P.	v England	Brisbane	2006/07
105*	Crowe M.D.	v England	Auckland	1983/84
105	McMillan C.D.	v Pakistan	Rawalpindi	2001/02
104*	Astle N.J.	v Zimbabwe	Napier	1997/98
104*	McMillan C.D.	v Pakistan	Christchurch	2000/01
104	Wadsworth K.J.	v Australia	Christchurch	1973/74
104	Crowe M.D.	v India	Dunedin	1989/90
104	Astle N.J.	v Australia	Napier	1999/00
103	Cairns C.L.	v India	Pune	1995/96
103	Twose R.G.	v South Africa	Cape Town	2000/01
102*	Edgar B.A.	v Australia	Melbourne	1980/81
102*	Greatbatch M.J.	v England	Leeds	1990
102*	Rutherford K.R.	v Sri Lanka	East London	1994/95
102*	Cairns C.L.	v India	Nairobi	2000/01
102*	Cairns C.L.	v South Africa	Brisbane	2001/02

102*	Astle N.J.	v Zimbabwe	Bloemfontein	2002/03
102*	Fleming S.P.	v Bangladesh	Antigua	2006/07
102	Vincent L.	v West Indies	Napier	2005/06
101*	Marshall H.J.H.	v Pakistan	Faisalabad	2003/04
101*	Styris S.B.	v Pakistan	Auckland	2003/04
101*	Oram J.D.P.	v Australia	Perth	2006/07
101	Congdon B.E.	v England	Wellington	1974/75
101	Wright J.G.	v England	Napier	1987/88
101	Astle N.J.	v England	Ahmedabad	1995/96
101	Styris S.B.	v Australia	Christchurch	2005/06
101	Vincent L.	v Canada	Gros Islet	2006/07
100*	Crowe M.D.	v Australia	Auckland	1991/92
100*	Astle N.J.	v South Africa	Auckland	1998/99

Successive Centuries

Greatbatch M.J. (2) 102* and 111 v England 1990

Most Successive Fifties

Jones A.H. (6) 57 v India and 55*, 62*, 67, 82, 63* v Pakistan 1988/89

Five Wickets in an Innings

9-3-19-6	Bond S.E.	v India	Bulawayo	2005/06
10-2-23-6	Bond S.E.	v Australia	Port Elizabeth	2002/03
7-0-25-6	Styris S.B.	v West Indies	Port of Spain	2001/02
10-2-22-5	Hart M.N.	v West Indies	Goa	1994/95
8.4-1-22-5	Adams A.R.	v India	Queenstown	2002/03
7-1-23-5	Collinge R.O.	v India	Christchurch	1975/76
9.3-2-23-5	Bond S.E.	v Australia	Wellington	2006/07
10.1-4-25-5	Hadlee R.J.	v Sri Lanka	Bristol	1983
9.2-2-25-5	Bond S.E.	v Australia	Adelaide	2001/02
8.3-4-26-5	Hadlee R.J.	v Australia	Sydney	1980/81
10-3-26-5	Oram J.D.P.	v India	Auckland	2002/03
11-3-28-5	Cairns B.L.	v England	Scarborough	1978
9.2-1-30-5	Vettori D.L.	v West Indies	Lord's	2004
9-1-32-5	Hadlee R.J.	v India	Perth	1980/81
10-2-32-5	Hadlee R.J.	v England	Christchurch	1983/84
10-1-32-5	Latham R.T.	v Australia	Auckland	1992/93
10-1-34-5	Chatfield E.J.	v Australia	Adelaide	1980/81
10-0-34-5	Morrison D.K.	v Sri Lanka	Sharjah	1996/97
9.4-1-36-5	Oram J.D.P.	v USA	The Oval	2004
10-0-38-5	Hadlee R.J.	v Pakistan	Dunedin	1988/89
10-0-39-5	O'Connor S.B.	v Zimbabwe	Wellington	1997/98
10-0-42-5	Harris C.Z.	v Pakistan	Sialkot	1996/97
7.4-0-4-25	Cairns C.L.	v Australia	Napier	1997/98
10-1-42-5	Franklin J.E.C.	v England	ChesterleStreet	2004
11-1-45-5	Pringle C.	v England	Birmingham	1994
10-0-46-5	Morrison D.K.	v Pakistan	Christchurch	1995/96
9.2-0-46-5	O'Connor S.B.	v Pakistan	Nairobi	2000/01

Most Economical Bowling

10-4-8-1	Chatfield E.J.	v Sri Lanka	Dunedin	1982/83
12-6-10-0	Hadlee R.J.	v East Africa	Birmingham	1975
10-6-10-0	Cairns B.L.	v Sri Lanka	Dunedin	1982/83
10-2-11-2	Tuffey D.R.	v India	Christchurch	2002/03
10-5-12-2	Larsen G.R.	v South Africa	Hobart	1993/94
10-2-12-1	Harris C.Z.	v Pakistan	Napier	2000/01
10-5-13-0	Chatfield E.J.	v India	Adelaide	1985/86
10-3-14-2	Snedden M.C.	v Pakistan	Hamilton	1988/89
10-5-14-1	Larsen G.R.	v Zimbabwe	Wellington	1995/96
10-4-14-4	Vettori D.L.	v Sri Lanka	Dambulla	2002/03
10-3-14-3	Vettori D.L.	v USA	The Oval	2004
10-2-15-2	Chatfield E.J.	v England	Dunedin	1987/88
10-2-15-1	Watson W.	v England	Christchurch	1990/91
10-3-15-3	Allott G.I.	v Scotland	Edinburgh	1999
10-3-15-1	Harris C.Z.	v West Indies	Wellington	1999/00
10-4-15-2	Bond S.E.	v Bangladesh	Antigua	2006/07

Most Expensive Bowling

12-1-105-2	Snedden M.C.	v England	The Oval	1983
9-0-85-0	Drum C.J.	v India	Hyderabad	1999/00
11-0-84-0	Cairns B.L.	v England	Manchester	1978
10-0-83-2	Gillespie M.R.	v Australia	Hamilton	2006/07
10-0-80-1	Canning T.K.	v Australia	Napier	2004/05
10-0-80-0	Tuffey D.R.	v Australia	Auckland	2006/07
†7-0-77-1	Congdon B.E.	v Australia	Christchurch	1973/74
10-0-77-0	Oram J.D.P.	v Australia	Sydney	2004/05
10-0-76-1	Snedden M.C.	v England	Brisbane	1982/83
10-0-76-1	Troup G.B.	v England	Adelaide	1982/83
10-0-76-0	Cairns C.L.	v Australia	Christchurch	1999/00
10-0-76-1	Hamilton L.J.	v Australia	Napier	2004/05
10-1-76-1	Gillespie M.R.	v Australia	Perth	2006/07
10-0-75-1	Chatfield E.J.	v Pakistan	Christchurch	1984/85
10-0-75-0	de Groen R.P.	v Sri Lanka	Bloemfontein	1994/95

† *8-ball overs*

Hat-tricks

9-1-35-3	Morrison D.K.	v India	Napier	1993/94
10-0-61-4	Bond S.E.	v Australia	Hobart	2006/07

Most Wicketkeeping Dismissals in an Innings

*5	Parore A.C.	v West Indies	Goa	1994/95
†5	McCullum B.B.	v India	Napier	2002/03
5	McCullum B.B	v India	Christchurch	2002/03
5	McCullum B.B.	v South Africa	Napier	2003/04
4	Lees W.K.	v India	Leeds	1979
4	Lees W.K.	v Australia	Sydney	1982/83
4	Parore A.C.	v Pakistan	Napier	1992/93
4	Blain T.E.	v South Africa	Hobart	1993/94
4	Germon L.K.	v Sri Lanka	Sharjah	1996/97
*4	Germon L.K.	v England	Wellington	1996/97
†4	Parore A.C.	v West Indies	Wellington	1999/00
4	McCullum B.B.	v Sri Lanka	Dambulla	2002/03
4	McCullum B.B.	v Pakistan	Dambulla	2002/03
†4	McCullum B.B.	v Zimbabwe	Harare	2005/06
4	McCullum B.B.	v England	Gros Islet	2006/07
4	McCullum B.B.	v West Indies	Antigua	2006/07

*† includes one stumping * includes two stumpings*

Most Catches in an Innings by a Fielder

4	Bracewell J.G. *(sub)*	v Australia	Adelaide	1980/81
4	Rutherford K.R.	v India	Napier	1994/95
4	Harris C.Z.	v India	Colombo	2001/02
4	Fleming S.P.	v England	Adelaide	2006/07

WALTER HADLEE TROPHIES

Awarded for the most meritorious batting and bowling performances by a New Zealand player in one-day internationals under the board's jurisdiction and other one-day matches as designated from time to time by the Board of Control.

BATTING		BOWLING	
1988/89	Jones A.H.	1988/89	Snedden M.C.
1989/90	Crowe M.D.	1989/90	Snedden M.C.
1990/91	Crowe M.D.	1990/91	Pringle C.
1991/92	Crowe M.D.	1991/92	Patel D.N.
1992/93	Crowe M.D.	1992/93	Larsen G.R.
1993/94	Thomson S.A.	1993/94	Pringle C.
1994/95	Parore A.C.	1994/95	Pringle C.
1995/96	Astle N.J.	1995/96	Larsen G.R.
1996/97	Fleming S.P.	1996/97	Harris C.Z.
1997/98	Harris C.Z.	1997/98	Cairns C.L.
1998/99	Astle N.J.	1998/99	Allott G.I.
1999/00	Astle N.J.	1999/00	Allott G.I.
2000/01	Twose R.G.	2000/01	Tuffey D.R.
2001/02	Astle N.J.	2001/02	Bond S.E.
2002/03	Fleming S.P.	2002/03	Bond S.E.
2003/04	Fleming S.P.	2003/04	Tuffey D.R.
2004/05	Marshall H.J.H.	2004/05	Vettori D.L.
2005/06	Astle N.J.	2005/06	Bond S.E.
2006/07	Styris S.B.	2006/07	Bond S.E.

RECORD PARTNERSHIPS

New Zealand v England

New Zealand				
1st	152	Turner G.M. & Edgar B.A.	Wellington	1982/83
2nd	104	Fleming S.P. & Marshall H.J.H.	Bristol	2004
3rd	160	Howarth G.P. & Crowe M.D.	Auckland	1983/84
4th	100	Astle N.J. & McMillan C.D.	Dunedin	2001/02
5th	138*	Styris S.B. & Oram J.D.P.	Gros Islet	2006/07
6th	122	Rutherford K.R. & Harris C.Z.	Christchurch	1990/91
7th	70	Coney J.V. & Hadlee R.J.	Birmingham	1983
8th	68	Congdon B.E. & Cairns B.L.	Scarborough	1978
9th	63	Hadlee R.J. & Troup G.B.	Brisbane	1982/83
10th	30	Hart M.N. & Morrison D.K.	Birmingham	1994
England				
1st	193	Gooch G.A. & Athey C.W.J.	Manchester	1986
2nd	113	Gooch G.A. & Smith R.A.	Leeds	1990
3rd	190*	Tavare C.J. & Lamb A.J.	Sydney	1982/83
4th	122	Strauss A.J. & Flintoff A.	Bristol	2004
5th	113	Gower D.I. & Randall D.W.	Brisbane	1982/83
6th	68	Randall D.W. & Marks V.J.	Christchurch	1983/84
7th	58	White C. & Cork D.G.	Napier	1996/97
8th	76	Nixon P.A. & Plunkett L.E.	Perth	2006/07
9th	15	Thorpe G.P. & Gough D.	Wellington	1996/97
10th	27	Gough D. & Caddick A.R.	Wellington	1996/97

New Zealand v Australia

New Zealand				
1st	149*	Vincent L. & Fleming S.P.	Wellington	2006/07
2nd	151	Vincent L. & Fulton P.G.	Melbourne	2006/07
3rd	121	Astle N.J. & Twose R.G.	Dunedin	1999/00
4th	168	Germon L.K. & Harris C.Z.	Madras	1995/96
5th	148	Twose R.G. & Cairns C.L.	Cardiff	1999
6th	165	McMillan C.D.& McCullum B.B.	Hamilton	2006/07
7th	103	Oram J.D.P. & Vettori D.L.	Mohali	2006/07
8th	72	Harris C.Z. & Vettori D.L.	Melbourne	2001/02
9th	74*	McCullum B.B. & Vettori D.L.	Christchurch	2005/06
10th	50	Mills K.D. & Bond S.E.	Colombo	2002/03
Australia				
1st	189	Waugh M.E. & Gilchrist A.C.	Christchurch	1999/00
2nd	200	Hayden M.L. & Ponting R.T.	Perth	2006/07
3rd	133	Hayden M.L. & Martyn D.R.	Christchurch	2004/05
4th	154	Ponting R.T. & Hodge B.J.	Melbourne	2006/07
5th	220	Symonds A. & Clarke M.J.	Wellington	2005/06
6th	136*	Clarke M.J. & Hussey M.E.K.	Auckland	2004/05
7th	74	Lehmann D.S. & Hogg G.B.	Sydney	2004/05
8th	97	Bevan M.G. & Bichel A.J.	Port Elizabeth	2002/03
9th	46	Marsh R.W. & Lawson G.F.	Adelaide	1980/81
10th	31	Martyn D.R. & McGrath G.D.	Auckland	1999/00

New Zealand v India

New Zealand				
1st	140	Wright J.G. & Jones A.H.	Baroda	1988/89
2nd	138	Astle N.J. & Fleming S.P.	Colombo	2001/02
3rd	180	Parore A.C. & Rutherford K.R.	Baroda	1994/95
4th	152	Crowe M.D. & Rutherford K.R.	Dunedin	1989/90
5th	147	Twose R.G. & Cairns C.L.	Pune	1995/96
6th	122	Cairns C.L. & Harris C.Z.	Nairobi	2000/01
7th	79	Burgess M.G. & Cairns B.L.	Adelaide	1980/81
8th	43	Nash D.J. & Vettori D.L.	Colombo	2001/02
9th	39	Snedden M.C. & Watson W.	Nagpur	1987/88
10th	52*	Tuffey D.R. & Bond S.E.	Auckland	2002/03
India				
1st	182	Sehwag V. & Tendulkar S.R.	Hyderabad	2003/04
2nd	331	Tendulkar S.R. & Dravid R.S.	Hyderabad	1999/00
3rd	158	Sidhu N.S. & Amarnath M.	Sharjah	1987/88
4th	129*	Kaif M. & Dravid R.S.	Centurion	2002/03
5th	92	Vengsarkar D.B. & Patil S.M.	Brisbane	1980/81
6th	127	Azharuddin M. & Sharma A.K.	Baroda	1988/89
7th	55	Abid Ali S. & Madan Lal S.	Manchester	1975
8th	82*	Kapil Dev & More K.S.	Bangalore	1987/88
9th	118	Yadav Jai P. & Pathan I.K.	Bulawayo	2005/06
10th	24	Kumble A.R. & Prasad B.K.V.	Rajkot	1999/00

New Zealand v Pakistan

New Zealand

1st	193	Fleming S.P. & Astle N.J.	Dunedin	2000/01
2nd	148	Fleming S.P. & Marshall H.J.H.	Christchurch	2003/04
3rd	135	Astle N.J. & Twose R.G.	Nairobi	2000/01
4th	157	Marshall H.J.H. & McMillan C.D.	Wellington	2003/04
5th	108*	Crowe M.D. & Smith I.D.S.	Wellington	1988/89
6th	112*	McMillan C.D. & Harris C.Z.	Christchurch	2000/01
7th	115	Parore A.C. & Germon L.K.	Sharjah	1996/97
8th	48*	Harris C.Z. & Larsen G.R.	Sharjah	1993/94
9th	59	Lees W.K. & Bracewell J.G.	Nottingham	1983
10th	33	Germon L.K. & Morrison D.K.	Wellington	1995/96

Pakistan

1st	199	Yasir Hameed & Imran Farhat	Rawalpindi	2003/04
2nd	263	Aamer Sohail & InzamamulHaq	Sharjah	1993/94
3rd	157*	Saeed Anwar & InzamamulHaq	Sharjah	2000/01
4th	161	Yousuf Youhana & Younis Khan	Karachi	2001/02
5th	108*	Ijaz Ahmed & Wasim Akram	Karachi	1996/97
6th	94	InzamamulHaq & Abdul Razzaq	Wellington	2003/04
7th	108	Rameez Raja & Anil Dalpat	Christchurch	1984/85
8th	65*	Abdul Razzaq & Mohammad Sami	Lahore	2003/04
9th	31*	Salim Malik & Mushtaq Ahmed	Gujranwala	1996/97
10th	39	Shoaib Akhtar & Mohammad Sami	Napier	2003/04

New Zealand v West Indies

New Zealand

1st	136	How J.M. & Astle N.J.	Wellington	2005/06
2nd	156	Vincent L. & Astle N.J.	Napier	2005/06
3rd	170	Astle N.J. & Twose R.G.	Christchurch	1999/00
4th	139	McMillan C.D. & Vincent L.	Arnos Vale	2001/02
5th	99	Astle N.J. & Marshall H.J.H.	Christchurch	2005/06
6th	122*	Astle N.J. & Styris S.B.	Port of Spain	2001/02
7th	111	Parore A.C. & Patel D.N.	Kingston	1995/96
8th	63*	Vettori D.L. & Franklin J.E.C.	Queenstown	2005/06
9th	44*	Harris C.Z. & Vaughan J.T.C.	Arnos Vale	1995/96
10th	48*	Nash D.J. & Pringle C.	Guwahati	1994/95

West Indies

1st	192*	Greenidge C.G. & Haynes D.L.	Christchurch	1986/87
2nd	184	Haynes D.L. & Gomes H.A.	Bridgetown	1984/85
3rd	186	Lara B.C. & Simmons P.V.	Arnos Vale	1995/96
4th	120	Hooper C.L. & Richards I.V.A.	Dunedin	1986/87
5th	91	Adams J.C. & Holder R.I.C.	Port of Spain	1995/96
6th	50	Chanderpaul S. & Hinds W.W.	Auckland	2005/06
7th	98	Sarwan R.R. & Jacobs R.D.	Port Elizabeth	2002/03
8th	48	Perry N.O. & Dillon M.	Napier	1999/00
9th	77	Sarwan R.R. & Bradshaw I.D.R.	Christchurch	2005/06
10th	26*	Harper R.A. & Walsh C.A.	Kingston	1995/96

New Zealand v Sri Lanka

New Zealand

1st	132	Turner G.M. & Edgar B.A.	Auckland	1982/83
2nd	151	Astle N.J. & Taylor L.R.P.L.	Napier	2006/07
3rd	136	Parore A.C. & Rutherford K.R.	East London	1994/95
4th	97	Reid J.F. & Crowe J.J.	Colombo	1983/84
5th	75	Astle N.J. & Greatbatch M.J.	Sharjah	1996/97
6th	95	Blain T.E. & Hadlee R.J.	Hobart	1987/88
7th	85*	Harris C.Z. & Vincent L.	Christchurch	2000/01
8th	64*	Styris S.B. & Franklin J.E.C.	Grenada	2006/07
9th	47*	Cairns B.L. & Boock S.L.	Colombo	1983/84
10th	65	Snedden M.C. & Chatfield E.J.	Derby	1983

Sri Lanka

1st	201	Tharanga W.U. & Jayasuriya S.	Napier	2006/07
2nd	170	Jayasuriya S.T. & Tillakaratne H.P.	Bloemfontein	2002/03
3rd	184	Jayasuriya S.T. & Jayawardene D.P.M.D.	Sharjah	2000/01
4th	127	Kaluwitharana R.S. & Ranatunga A.	Dhaka	1998/99
5th	110	Atapattu M.S. & Arnold R.P.	Colombo	2001/02
6th	103*	Arnold R.P. & Perera A.S.A.	Colombo	2001/02
7th	52	de Alwis R.G. & Ratnayeke J.R.	Sydney	1987/88
8th	56	de Silva D.S. & Ratnayeke J.R.	Napier	1982/83
9th	45*	Ranatunga A. & de Silva D.S.	Moratuwa	1983/84
10th	29	de Silva D.S. & John V.	Melbourne	1984/85

New Zealand v Zimbabwe

New Zealand

1st	204	Vincent L. & Fleming S.P.	Bulawayo	2005/06
2nd	121	Vincent L. & McMillan C.D.	Bulawayo	2005/06
3rd	152	Spearman C.M. & Twose R.G.	Harare	2000/01
4th	130	Crowe M.D. & Rutherford K.R.	Harare	1992/93
5th	95	Twose R.G. & McMillan C.D.	Nairobi	2000/01
6th	75	Cairns C.L. & Harris C.Z.	Hamilton	1997/98
7th	50	Harris C.Z. & Parore A.C.	Christchurch	1997/98
8th	79	Styris S.B. & Vettori D.L.	Harare	2005/06
9th	55	Harris C.Z. & Larsen G.R.	Bulawayo	1997/98
10th	28	Franklin J.E.C. & Martin C.S.	Taupo	2000/01

Zimbabwe

1st	124	Flower A. & Flower G.W.	Harare	1992/93
2nd	91	Campbell A.D.R. & Carlisle S.V.	Wellington	2000/01
3rd	154	Carlisle S.V. & Flower A.	Taupo	2000/01
4th	123	Rennie G.J. & Campbell A.D.R.	Harare	1997/98
5th	70	Flower A. & Whittall G.J.	Christchurch	1997/98
6th	82	Flower A. & Viljoen D.P.	Auckland	2000/01
7th	68	Taibu T. & Streak H.H.	Bloemfontein	2002/03
8th	117	Houghton D.L. & Butchart I.P.	Hyderabad	1987/88
9th	54*	Strang P.A. & Rennie J.A.	Napier	1997/98
10th	23	Strang B.C. & Whittall A.R.	Harare	1997/98

New Zealand v South Africa

New Zealand				
1st	114	Greatbatch M.J. & Latham R.T.	Auckland	1991/92
2nd	140*	Fleming S.P. & Astle N.J.	Johannesburg	2002/03
3rd	126	Marshall H.J.H. & Styris S.B.	Dunedin	2003/04
4th	150	Twose R.G. & Cairns C.L.	Cape Town	2000/01
5th	106	Parore A.C. & Thomson S.A.	Centurion	1994/95
6th	124	McMillan C.D. & Harris C.Z.	Adelaide	1997/98
7th	84*	Cairns C.L. & Parore A.C.	Brisbane	2001/02
8th	69	Parore A.C. & Nash D.J.	Brisbane	1997/98
9th	47*	Parore A.C. & Vettori D.L.	Perth	2001/02
10th	29*	Parore A.C. & Bond S.E.	Hobart	2001/02
South Africa				
1st	176	Kirsten G. & Gibbs H.H.	Birmingham	1999
2nd	172	Kirsten G. & Kallis J.H.	Kimberley	2000/01
3rd	139*	Kallis J.H. & Dippenaar H.H.	Melbourne	2001/02
4th	145	Kallis J.H. & Cullinan D.J.	Auckland	1998/99
5th	138	Rhodes J.N. & Boucher M.V.	Perth	2001/02
6th	97*	Rhodes J.N. & Pollock S.M.	Perth	2001/02
7th	65	Kemp J.M. & Pollock S.M.	Bloemfontein	2005/06
8th	69*	Klusener L. & Abrahams S.	Cape Town	2000/01
9th	22*	Pollock S.M. & Ntini M.	Christchurch	2003/04
10th	67*	Morkel J.A. & Ntini M.	Napier	2003/04

New Zealand v Bangladesh

New Zealand				
1st	158	Crowe M.D. & Wright J.G.	Sharjah	1989/90
2nd	134*	Fleming S.P. & Marshall H.J.H.	Antigua	2006/07
3rd	91	Jones A.H. & Greatbatch M.J.	Sharjah	1989/90
4th	61*	Styris S.B. & Cairns C.L.	Kimberley	2002/03
5th	86	Styris S.B. & McMillan C.D.	Dhaka	2004/05
6th	49	Styris S.B. & Cairns C.L.	Chittagong	2004/05
7th	43	Cairns C.L. & Vettori D.L.	Dhaka	2004/05
8th	23	Cairns C.L. & Vettori D.L.	Chittagong	2004/05
9th	33	Cairns C.L. & Adams A.R.	Chittagong	2004/05
10th	2*	Mills K.D. & Hitchcock P.A.	Colombo	2002/03
Bangladesh				
1st	55	Javed Omer & Tamim Iqbal	Antigua	2006/07
2nd	27	Mohammad Rafique & Nafees Iqbal	Dhaka	2004/05
3rd	43	Aftab Ahmed & Saqibul Hasan	Antigua	2006/07
4th	38	Nafees Iqbal & Mohammad Ashraful	Dhaka	2004/05
5th	34	Mohammad Ashraful & Akram Khan	Kimberley	2002/03
6th	56	Rajin Saleh & Khalid Masud	Dhaka	2004/05
7th	29	Khalid Masud & Alok Kapali	Dhaka	2004/05
8th	70*	Khalid Masud & Mohammad Rafique	Kimberley	2002/03
9th	14	Mohammad Rafique & Monjurul Islam	Colombo	2002/03
10th	34	Mohammad Rafique & Syed Rasel	Antigua	2006/07

CAREER RECORDS

Averages

	M	In	NO	HS	Runs	Ave	100	50	Ct	St	Balls	Runs	Wkts	Ave	5WI	Best	R/100B	B/W
Adams A.R.	42	34	10	45	419	17.45	—	—	8	—	1885	1643	53	31.00	1	5-22	87	35
Allott G.I.	31	11	6	7*	17	3.40	—	—	5	—	1528	1207	52	23.21	—	4-35	78	29
Anderson R.W.	2	2	1	12	16	16.00	—	—	1	—	—	—	—	—	—	—	—	—
Astle N.J.	223	217	14	145*	7090	34.92	16	41	83	—	4850	3809	99	38.47	—	4-43	78	48
Bailey M.D.	1	—	—	—	—	—	—	—	—	—	—	—	—	—	—	—	—	—
Bell M.D.	7	7	0	66	133	19.00	—	1	1	—	—	—	—	—	—	—	—	—
Blain T.E.	38	38	11	49*	442	16.37	—	—	37	1	—	—	—	—	—	—	—	—
Blair B.R.	14	14	2	29*	174	12.50	—	—	4	—	30	34	1	34.00	—	1-7	113	30
Bond S.E.	67	28	14	31*	200	14.28	—	—	15	—	3446	2416	125	19.32	4	6-19	70	27
Boock S.L.	14	7	4	12	30	10.00	—	—	5	—	700	513	15	34.20	—	3-28	73	46
Bracewell B.P.	1	1	1	0*	0	—	—	—	—	—	66	41	1	41.00	—	1-41	62	66
Bracewell J.G.	53	43	12	43	512	16.51	—	—	19	—	2447	1884	33	57.09	—	2-3	76	74
Bradburn G.E.	11	10	3	30	60	8.57	—	—	2	—	385	318	6	53.00	—	2-18	82	64
Brown V.R.	3	3	0	32	44	14.66	—	—	2	—	66	75	1	75.00	—	1-24	113	66
Bulfin C.E.	4	2	1	7*	9	9.00	—	—	1	—	102	109	0	—	—	—	106	—
Burgess M.G.	26	20	0	47	336	16.80	—	—	8	—	74	69	1	69.00	—	1-10	93	74
Butler I.G.	15	6	4	3	6	3.00	—	—	6	—	593	558	14	39.85	—	3-41	94	42
Cairns B.L.	78	65	6	60	987	16.73	—	2	19	—	4015	2717	89	30.47	1	5-28	67	45
Cairns C.L.	*215	193	25	115	4950	29.46	4	26	66	—	8168	6594	201	32.80	1	5-42	80	40
Canning T.K.	4	4	1	23*	52	17.33	—	—	1	—	204	203	5	40.60		2-30	100	41
Chatfield E.J.	115	48	37	19*	118	10.72	—	—	19	—	6129	3666	142	25.81	1	5-34	59	43
Collinge R.O.	16	10	4	19	53	8.83	—	—	1	—	915	517	19	27.21	1	5-23	56	48
Coman P.G.	3	3	0	38	62	20.66	—	—	2	—	—	—	—	—	—	—	—	—
Coney J.V.	88	80	19	66*	1874	30.72	—	8	40	—	2931	2039	54	37.75	—	4-46	69	54
Congdon B.E.	12	10	3	101	373	54.71	1	2	1	—	501	322	8	40.25	—	2-17	64	62
Crowe J.J.	75	71	12	88*	1518	25.72	—	7	28	—	6	1	0	—	—	—	16	—
Crowe M.D.	143	140	18	107*	4704	38.55	4	34	66	—	1296	954	29	32.89	—	2-9	73	44
Cumming C.D.	12	12	1	45*	161	14.63	—	—	6	—	18	17	0	—	—	—	94	—
Davis H.T.	11	6	4	7*	13	6.50	—	—	2	—	432	436	11	39.63	—	4-35	100	39
de Groen R.P.	12	8	3	7*	12	2.40	—	—	2	—	549	478	8	59.75	—	2-34	87	68
Douglas M.W.	6	6	0	30	55	9.16	—	—	2	—	—	—	—	—	—	—	—	—
Doull S.B.	42	27	13	22	172	12.28	—	—	10	—	1745	1459	36	40.52	—	4-25	83	48
Drum C.J.	5	2	2	7*	9	—	—	—	1	—	216	261	4	65.25	—	2-31	120	54
Edgar B.A.	64	64	5	102*	1814	30.74	1	10	12	—	12	5	0	—	—	—	41	—
Edwards G.N.	7	7	0	41	164	23.42	—	—	7	—	6	5	1	5.00	—	1-5	83	6
Fleming S.P.	*280	269	21	134*	8037	32.40	8	49	133	—	29	28	1	28.00	—	1-8	96	29
Franklin J.E.C.	65	44	15	45*	508	17.51	—	—	19	—	2804	2392	64	27.37	1	5-42	85	43
Franklin T.J.	3	3	0	21	27	9.00	—	—	—	—	—	—	—	—	—	—	—	—
Fulton P.G.	36	35	4	112	1112	35.87	1	7	10	—	—	—	—	—	—	—	—	—
Germon L.K.	37	31	5	89	519	19.96	—	3	21	9	—	—	—	—	—	—	—	—
Gillespie M.R.	17	9	4	28	63	12.60	—	—	2	—	813	759	18	42.16	—	3-39	93	45
Gillespie S.R.	19	11	5	18*	70	11.66	—	—	7	—	963	736	23	32.00	—	4-30	76	41
Gray E.J.	10	7	1	38	98	16.33	—	—	3	—	386	286	8	35.75	—	2-26	74	48
Greatbatch M.J.	84	83	5	111	2206	28.28	2	13	35	—	6	5	0	—	—	—	83	—
Hadlee B.G.	2	2	1	19	26	26.00	—	—	—	—	—	—	—	—	—	—	—	—
Hadlee D.R.	12	8	2	20	56	9.33	—	—	3	—	683	410	23	17.82	—	4-34	60	29
Hadlee R.J.	115	98	17	79	1751	21.61	—	4	27	—	6182	3407	158	21.56	5	5-25	55	39
Hamilton L.J.	2	2	2	2*	3	—	—	—	—	—	108	143	1	143.00	—	1-76	132	108
Harris C.Z.	250	213	62	130	4379	29.00	1	16	96		10667	7613	203	37.50	1	5-42	71	53
Hart M.N.	13	8	0	16	61	7.62	—	—	7	—	572	373	13	28.69	1	5-22	65	44
Hart R.G.	2	1	0	0	0	0.00	—	—	1	—	—	—	—	—	—	—	—	—
Hart R.T.	1	1	0	3	3	3.00	—	—	—	—	—	—	—	—	—	—	—	—
Hartland B.R.	16	16	1	68*	311	20.73	—	2	5	—	—	—	—	—	—	—	—	—
Haslam M.J.	1	1	0	9	9	—	—	—	—	—	30	28	1	28.00	—	1-28	93	30
Hastings B.F.	12	10	1	37	176	19.55	—	—	4	—	—	—	—	—	—	—	—	—
Hayes R.L.	1	1	0	13	13	13.00	—	—	—	—	42	31	0	—	—	—	73	—
Hitchcock P.A.	13	6	2	10	30	7.50	—	—	4	—	516	412	12	34.33	—	3-30	79	43
Hopkins G.J.	5	1	0	0	0	0.00	—	—	8	—	—	—	—	—	—	—	—	—
Horne M.J.	50	48	0	74	980	20.41	—	5	12	—	—	—	—	—	—	—	—	—
Horne P.A.	4	4	0	18	50	12.50	—	—	—	—	—	—	—	—	—	—	—	—

	M	In	NO	HS	Runs	Ave	100	50	Ct	St	Balls	Runs	Wkts	Ave	5WI	Best	R/100B	B/W
How J.M.	6	5	0	66	141	28.20	—	2	2	—	—	—	—	—	—	—	—	—
Howarth G.P.	71	66	5	76	1384	22.72	—	6	16	—	90	68	3	22.67	—	1-4	75	30
Howarth H.J.	10	6	3	11	21	7.00	—	—	3	—	556	304	14	27.71	—	3-24	54	39
Howell L.G.	12	12	0	68	287	23.92	—	4	2	—	—	—	—	—	—	—	—	—
Jones A.H.	87	87	9	93	2784	35.69	—	25	23	—	306	216	4	54.00	—	2-42	70	76
Jones R.A.	5	5	0	63	168	33.60	—	1	—	—	—	—	—	—	—	—	—	—
Kennedy R.J.	7	4	3	8*	17	17.00	—	—	1	—	312	283	5	56.60	—	2-36	90	62
Kuggeleijn C.M.	16	11	2	40	142	15.77	—	—	9	—	817	604	12	50.33	—	2-31	74	68
Larsen G.R.	121	70	27	37	629	14.62	—	—	23	—	6368	4000	113	35.39	—	4-24	62	56
Latham R.T.	33	33	4	60	583	20.10	—	1	11	—	450	386	11	35.09	1	5-32	85	40
Lees W.K.	31	24	5	26	215	11.31	—	—	28	2	—	—	—	—	—	—	—	—
McCullum B.B.	114	90	19	86*	1636	23.04	—	6	168	12	—	—	—	—	—	—	—	—
McEwan P.E.	17	15	0	41	204	13.60	—	—	1	—	420	353	6	58.83	—	2-29	84	70
McKechnie B.J.	14	8	4	27	54	13.50	—	—	2	—	818	495	19	26.05	—	3-23	60	43
McMillan C.D.	197	183	16	117	4707	28.18	3	28	44	—	1879	1717	49	35.04	—	3-20	91	38
McSweeney E.B.	16	14	5	18*	73	8.11	—	—	14	3	—	—	—	—	—	—	—	—
Marshall H.J.H.	66	62	9	101*	1454	27.43	1	12	18	—	—	—	—	—	—	—	—	—
Marshall J.A.H.	8	8	0	50	85	10.62	—	1	—	—	—	—	—	—	—	—	—	—
Martin C.S.	9	6	1	3	6	1.20	—	—	3	—	438	397	11	36.09	—	3-62	90	39
Mason M.J.	19	5	2	13*	22	7.33	—	—	4	—	891	767	21	36.52	—	4-24	86	42
Millmow J.P.	5	1	1	0*	0	—	—	—	1	—	270	232	4	58.00	—	2-22	85	67
Mills K.D.	65	37	18	44*	261	13.73	—	—	21	—	3227	2511	89	28.21	—	4-14	77	36
Morrison D.K.	96	43	24	20*	171	9.00	—	—	19	—	4586	3470	126	27.53	2	5-34	75	36
Morrison J.F.M.	19	16	3	55	301	23.15	—	1	6	—	283	199	8	24.87	—	3-24	70	35
Murray D.J.	1	1	0	3	3	3.00	—	—	—	—	—	—	—	—	—	—	—	—
Nash D.J.	81	53	13	42	624	15.60	—	—	25	—	3416	2622	64	40.96	—	4-38	76	53
Nevin C.J.	37	36	0	74	732	20.33	—	4	16	3	—	—	—	—	—	—	—	—
O'Connor S.B.	38	13	6	8	24	3.42	—	—	11	—	1487	1397	46	30.36	2	5-39	93	32
O'Sullivan D.R.	3	2	1	1*	2	2.00	—	—	—	—	168	123	2	61.50	—	1-38	73	84
Oram J.D.P.	102	78	10	101*	1547	22.75	1	6	29	—	4465	3364	110	30.58	2	5-26	75	40
Owens M.B.	1	1	0	0	0	0.00	—	—	—	—	48	37	0	—	—	—	77	—
Papps M.H.W.	6	6	2	92*	207	51.75	—	2	1	—	—	—	—	—	—	—	—	—
Parker J.M.	25	21	0	66	280	13.33	—	1	11	1	16	10	1	10.00	—	1-10	62	16
Parker N.M.	1	1	0	0	0	0.00	—	—	1	—	—	—	—	—	—	—	—	—
Parore A.C.	179	161	32	108	3314	25.68	1	14	116	25	—	—	—	—	—	—	—	—
Patel D.N.	75	63	10	71	623	11.75	—	1	23	—	3251	2260	45	50.22	—	3-22	69	72
Patel J.S.	23	7	2	34	56	11.20	—	—	8	—	1206	1009	32	31.53	—	3-11	83	37
Penn A.J.	5	3	1	15	23	11.50	—	—	1	—	159	201	1	201.00	—	1-50	126	159
Petrie R.G.	12	8	3	21	65	13.00	—	—	2	—	660	449	12	37.41	—	2-25	68	55
Pollard V.	3	2	0	55	67	33.50	—	1	1	—	—	—	—	—	—	—	—	—
Priest M.W.	18	14	4	24	103	10.30	—	—	2	—	752	590	8	73.75	—	2-27	78	94
Pringle C.	64	41	19	34*	193	8.77	—	—	7	—	3314	2459	103	23.87	1	5-45	74	32
Redmond R.E.	2	1	0	3	3	3.00	—	—	—	—	—	—	—	—	—	—	—	—
Reid J.F.	25	24	1	88	633	27.16	—	4	5	—	—	—	—	—	—	—	—	—
Reid R.B.	9	9	0	64	248	27.55	—	2	3	—	7	13	1	13.00	—	1-13	185	7
Richardson M.H.	4	4	0	26	42	10.50	—	—	1	—	—	—	—	—	—	—	—	—
Roberts A.D.G.	1	1	0	16	16	16.00	—	—	1	—	56	30	1	30.00	—	1-30	53	56
Roberts S.J.	2	1	1	1*	1	—	—	—	—	—	42	47	0	—	—	—	111	—
Robertson G.K.	10	6	0	17	49	8.16	—	—	2	—	498	321	6	53.50	—	2-29	64	83
Rutherford K.R.	121	115	9	108	3143	29.65	2	18	41	—	389	323	10	32.30	—	2-39	83	38
Sinclair M.S.	45	44	2	118*	1180	28.09	2	7	15		—	—	—	—	—	—	—	—
Smith I.D.S.	98	77	16	62*	1055	17.29	—	3	81	5	—	—	—	—	—	—	—	—
Snedden M.C.	93	54	19	64	535	15.28	—	1	19	—	4525	3237	114	28.39	—	4-34	71	39
Spearman C.M.	51	50	0	86	936	18.72	—	5	15	—	3	6	0	—	—	—	—	—
Stirling D.A.	6	5	2	13*	21	7.00	—	—	3	—	246	207	6	34.33	—	2-29	84	41
Stott L.W.	1	—	—	—	—	—	—	—	1	—	72	48	3	16.00	—	3-48	66	24
Styris S.B.	133	114	15	141	3158	31.89	4	19	52	—	4803	3784	116	32.42	1	6-25	78	41
Su'a M.L.	12	7	2	12*	24	4.80	—	—	1	—	463	367	9	40.77	—	4-59	79	51
Sulzberger G.P.	3	2	1	6*	9	9.00	—	—	—	—	132	102	3	34.00	—	1-28	77	44
Tait A.R.	5	5	2	13*	35	11.66	—	—	—	—	120	88	3	29.33	—	2-37	73	40
Taylor B.R.	2	1	0	22	22	22.00	—	—	1	—	114	62	4	15.50	—	3-25	54	28
Taylor L.R.P.L.	24	22	1	128*	706	33.61	2	3	15	—	12	16	0	—	—	—	—	133
Thomson S.A.	56	52	10	83	964	22.95	—	5	18	—	2121	1602	42	38.14	—	3-14	75	50
Troup G.B.	22	12	8	39	101	25.25	—	—	2	—	1180	791	32	23.97	—	4-19	67	36

	M	In	NO	HS	Runs	Ave	100	50	Ct	St	Balls	Runs	Wkts	Ave	5WI	Best	R/100B	B/W
Tuffey D.R.	80	41	20	20*	154	7.33	—	—	19	—	3674	2910	91	31.97	—	4-24	79	40
Turner G.M.	41	40	6	171*	1598	47.00	3	9	13	—	6	0	0	—	—	—	—	—
Twose R.G.	87	81	11	103	2717	38.81	1	20	37	—	272	237	4	59.25	—	2-31	87	68
Vance R.H.	8	8	0	96	248	31.00	—	1	4	—	—	—	—	—	—	—	—	—
Vaughan J.T.C.	18	16	7	33	162	18.00	—	—	4	—	696	524	15	34.93	—	4-33	75	46
Vettori D.L.	†201	127	39	83	1284	14.59	—	3	53	—	9491	6689	203	32.95	1	5-30	70	46
Vincent L.	97	94	10	172	2376	28.28	3	11	37	—	14	25	0	—	—	—	—	178
Vivian G.E.	1	1	0	14	14	14.00	—	—	—	—	—	—	—	—	—	—	—	—
Wadsworth K.J.	14	11	1	104	302	30.20	1	—	15	3	—	—	—	—	—	—	—	—
Walker B.G.K.	11	7	4	16*	47	15.66	—	—	5	—	438	417	8	52.12	—	2-43	95	54
Walker M.D.J.	3	1	0	10	10	10.00	—	—	2	—	132	119	4	29.75	—	4-49	90	33
Walmsley K.P.	2	—	—	—	—	—	—	—	—	—	120	117	2	58.60	—	1-53	97	60
Watson W.	61	24	13	21	86	7.81	—	—	9	—	3251	2247	74	30.36	—	4-27	69	43
Webb P.N.	5	5	1	10*	38	9.50	—	—	3	—	—	—	—	—	—	—	—	—
Webb R.J.	3	1	1	6*	6	—	—	—	—	—	161	105	4	26.25	—	2-28	65	40
White D.J.	3	3	0	15	37	12.33	—	—	1	—	—	—	—	—	—	—	—	—
Wilson J.W.	6	6	1	44*	103	20.60	—	—	4	—	242	260	4	65.00	—	2-21	107	61
Wiseman P.J.	15	7	5	16	45	22.50	—	—	2	—	450	368	12	30.66	—	4-45	81	37
Wisneski W.A.	3	2	1	6	10	10.00	—	—	1	—	114	123	0	—	—	—	107	—
Wright J.G.	149	148	1	101	3891	26.46	1	24	51	—	24	8	0	—	—	—	33	—
Young B.A.	74	73	5	74	1668	24.52	—	9	28	—	—	—	—	—	—	—	—	—

** includes one match for ICC World XI*
† includes four matches for ICC World XI

AMENDMENTS

To previous editions

2006
Page 20
New Zealand played eight tests

Page 124
New Zealand won by 21 runs

Page 134
Canterbury finished in fourth place

SUMMARY OF ONE-DAY INTERNATIONAL CAREER RECORDS

Most Matches

Fleming S.P.	280	Parore A.C.	179	Larsen G.R.	121
Harris C.Z.	250	Wright J.G.	149	Chatfield E.J.	115
Astle N.J.	223	Crowe M.D.	143	Hadlee R.J.	115
Cairns C.L.	215	Styris S.B.	133	McCullum B.B.	114
Vettori D.L.	201	Rutherford K.R.	121	Oram J.D.P.	102
McMillan C.D.	197				

Most Runs

		Ave			*Ave*
Fleming S.P.	8037	32.40	Coney J.V.	1874	30.72
Astle N.J.	7090	34.92	Edgar B.A.	1814	30.74
Cairns C.L.	4950	29.46	Hadlee R.J.	1751	21.61
McMillan C.D.	4707	28.18	Young B.A.	1668	24.52
Crowe M.D.	4704	38.55	McCullum B.B.	1636	23.04
Harris C.Z.	4379	29.00	Turner G.M.	1598	47.00
Wright J.G.	3891	26.46	Oram J.D.P.	1547	22.75
Parore A.C.	3314	25.68	Crowe J.J.	1518	25.72
Styris S.B.	3158	31.89	Marshall H.J.H.	1454	27.43
Rutherford K.R.	3143	29.65	Howarth G.P.	1384	22.72
Jones A.H.	2784	35.69	Vettori D.L.	1284	14.39
Twose R.G.	2717	38.81	Sinclair M.S.	1180	28.09
Vincent L.	2376	28.28	Fulton P.G.	1112	35.87
Greatbatch M.J.	2206	28.28	Smith I.D.S.	1055	17.29

Most Wickets

		Ave			*Ave*
Harris C.Z.	203	37.50	Bond S.E.	125	19.32
Vettori D.L.	203	32.95	Styris S.B.	116	32.42
Cairns C.L.	201	32.80	Snedden M.C.	114	28.39
Hadlee R.J.	158	21.56	Larsen G.R.	113	35.39
Chatfield E.J.	142	25.81	Oram J.D.P.	110	30.58
Morrison D.K.	126	27.53	Pringle C.	103	23.87

Most Economical Bowling

(qualification 600 balls)

	Balls bowled	***Runs conceded***	***Runs conceded per 100 balls***		***Balls bowled***	***Runs conceded***	***Runs conceded per 100 balls***
Hadlee R.J.	6182	3407	55.11	Larsen G.R.	6368	4000	62.81
Collinge R.O.	915	517	56.50	Troup G.B.	1180	791	67.03
Chatfield E.J.	6129	3666	59.81	Cairns B.L.	4015	2717	67.67
Hadlee D.R.	683	410	60.02	Petrie R.G.	660	449	68.03
McKechnie B.J.	818	495	60.51	Watson W.	3251	2247	69.11

Best Strike Rates

(qualification 600 balls)

	Balls bowled	Wickets	Balls per wicket
Bond S.E.	3446	125	27.56
Allott G.I.	1528	52	29.38
Hadlee D.R.	683	23	29.69
Pringle C.	3314	103	32.17
O'Connor S.B.	1487	46	32.33
Adams A.R.	1885	53	35.56
Morrison D.K.	4586	126	36.39
Troup G.B.	1180	32	36.87
Mills K.D.	3227	89	36.25
Patel J.S.	1208	32	37.68

Register of New Zealand One-day Cricketers Who Have Not Played Test Cricket

	Born	Type	
Bailey Mark David	26/11/1970 Hamilton	RHB	RM
Blair Bruce Robert	27/12/1957 Dunedin	LHB	RM
Bulfin Carl Edwin	19/8/1973 Blenheim	RHB	RFM
Canning Tamahau Karangatukituki	7/4/1977 Adelaide, Australia	RHB	RFM
Coman Peter George	13/4/1943 Christchurch	RHB	
Douglas Mark William	20/10/1968 Nelson	LHB	
Gillespie Mark Raymond	17/10/1979 Wanganui	RHB	RFM
Hadlee Barry George	14/12/1941 Christchurch	RHB	
Hamilton Lance John	5/4/1973 Papakura	RHB	LFM
Hart Ronald Terence	7/11/1961 Lower Hutt	RHB	
Hayes Roydon Leslie	9/5/1971 Paeroa	RHB	RFM
Hitchcock Paul Anthony	23/1/1975 Whangarei	RHB	RM
Hopkins Gareth James	24/11/1976 Lower Hutt	RHB	WK
Howell Llorne Gregory	8/7/1972 Napier	RHB	
McKechnie Brian John	6/11/1953 Gore	RHB	RM
McSweeney Ervin Bruce	8/3/1957 Wellington	RHB	WK
Millmow Jonathan Paul	22/9/1967 Wellington	RHB	RFM
Nevin Christopher John	3/8/1975 Dunedin	RHB	WK
Penn Andrew Jonathan	27/7/1974 Wanganui	RHB	RFM
Petrie Richard George	23/8/1967 Christchurch	RHB	RFM
Reid Richard Bruce	3/12/1958 Lower Hutt	RHB	
Roberts Stuart James	22/3/1965 Christchurch	RHB	RFM
Stott Leslie Warren	8/12/1946 Rochdale, England	RHB	RM
Sulzberger Glen Paul	14/3/1973 Kaponga	LHB	ROB
Tait Alex Ross	13/6/1972 Paparoa	RHB	RM
Taylor Ross Luteru	8/3/1984 Lower Hutt	RHB	ROB
Webb Richard John	15/9/1952 Invercargill	RHB	RFM
Walker Matthew David John	17/1/1977 Opunake	RHB	RM
Wilson Jeffrey William	24/10/1973 Invercargill	RHB	RFM
Wisneski Warren Anthony	19/2/1969 New Plymouth	RHB	RM

MINOR CRICKET

HIGHEST TEAM TOTALS

922-9	Australians v South Canterbury	Temuka	1913/14
741	Murphy's Pipe Works v Petone	Wellington	1919/20
709	Australians v Southland	Invercargill	1913/14
701-6 dec	Murphy's Pipe Works v Seatoun	Wellington	1919/20
686	Nelson City v Buller	Nelson	1954/55
681	New Zealand v Northern Districts (NSW)	West Maitland	1925/26
653-9 dec	Hawkes Bay v Wairarapa	Napier	1946/47
† 650-9 dec	Manawatu v South Canterbury	Palmerston North	1993/94
† 649	Nelson v Wairarapa	Nelson	1984/85
† 643	Nelson v North Canterbury	Nelson	1984/85
† 641-7	Nelson v Taranaki	Nelson	1983/84
633-7 dec	North v Returned Soldiers	Wellington	1917/18
† 633-9	Wellington City v Bay of Plenty	Mt Maunganui	1997/98
† 632	Nelson v Waikato	Nelson	1963/64
629-7 dec	Midland II v Railways	Wellington	1921/22
623	North Canterbury v South Canterbury	Christchurch	1907/08
619-3	Cornwall U19 v Sri Lanka CC U19	Auckland	1997/98
611	Australian Academy XI v NZ Academy XI	Lincoln	1999/00
609	Napier United A v Napier United B	Napier	1898/99
603-7 dec	Tinwald v Ashburton A	Ashburton	1927/28
603-7 dec	Australians v Wairarapa	Masteron	1949/50
603-8 dec	New South Wales v South Canterbury	Timaru	1923/24
602-9 dec	New Zealand v Melbourne CC	Christchurch	1926/27
† 602	Nelson v Hawkes Bay	Nelson	1959/60

† *denotes Hawke Cup/U-Bix Cup/Fuji Xerox Cup Challenge match*

HIGHEST INDIVIDUAL SCORES

400	C.D. Knight	Cornwall U19 v Sri Lanka CC U19	Auckland	1997/98
358	S. Goulding	St Bedes v Sydenham	Christchurch	2006/07
354	J.N. Crawford	Australians v South Canterbury	Temuka	1913/14
343*	J. Gray	Sydenham v Christ's College	Christchurch	1917/18
335	W.W. Armstrong	Melbourne CC v Southland	Invercargill	1905/06
334*	Harold B. Lusk	West Christchurch v St Albans	Christchurch	1915/16
324*	D.N. Hakaraia	Waitakere U17 v Howick Pakuranga U17	Auckland	1999/00
311	H.M. Butterworth	School B v Wanganui	Wanganui	1914/15
303*	M.D. Bell	ND U20 v Wellington U20	Wanganui	1994/95
300*	W.J. Hendy	Auckland Suburban Association v Christchurch HSOB	Christchurch	1925/26

HIGHEST PARTNERSHIPS

	Wkt				
518	2nd	A. Young & F.L. McMahon	Wanderers v Taruheru	Gisborne	1910/11
441	1st	J.E. Mills & H.D. Gillespie	Eden v University	Auckland	1924/25
437*	2nd	R. Eden & M.R. Eden	Wanderers v Wakefield	Nelson	1922/23
394	1st	R.S. Scragg & J.V. Hill	Central Districts A v Otago A	P. North	2001/02
393	1st	M.E.L. Lane & J. Lane	Marlborough v Buller	Blenheim	1992/93
391	4th	T.P.L. Reaney & H. Hawthorne	Hawkes Bay v Wairarapa	Napier	1946/47
375	2nd	A.C. Barnes & S.M. Lynch	Cornwall v Waitakere	Auckland	1996/97
374*	1st	T.D. Astle & K.R. Ambler	Canterbury U19 v Auckland U19	Lincoln	2004/05
360	1st	G. Marshall & H.C. Wilson	Napier United A v Napier United B	Napier	1898/99
360	1st	B. Sutcliffe & F.J. Craig	Takapuna Grammar v Mt Albert Grammar	Devonport	1942/43